THE DYNAMICS OF WORLD POWER

The Far East

THE DYNAMICS OF WORLD POWER

A DOCUMENTARY HISTORY OF UNITED STATES FOREIGN POLICY 1945–1973

General Editor
ARTHUR M. SCHLESINGER, JR.
Albert Schweitzer Professor
in the Humanities
City University of New York

Volume IV
The Far East

RUSSELL BUHITE
Professor of History
University of Oklahoma

New York

CHELSEA HOUSE PUBLISHERS
IN ASSOCIATION WITH
McGRAW-HILL BOOK COMPANY
New York   Toronto   London   Sydney

1973

Managing Editor: *KARYN GULLEN BROWNE*

Consulting Editor: *LEON FRIEDMAN*
Editorial Staff: *BETSY NICOLAUS, ALICE SHERMAN, GRACE CORSO, ELLEN TABAK, IRVING RUDERMAN*

Library of Congress Cataloging in Publication Data
Schlesinger, Arthur Meier, 1917-   comp.
The dynamics of world power.
CONTENTS: v. 1. Western Europe, edited by R. Dallek.
— v. 2. Eastern Europe and the Soviet Union, edited
by W. LaFeber. — v. 3. Latin America, edited by
R. Burr. — v. 4. The Far East, edited by R. Buhite.
— v. 5. The United Nations, edited by R. C. Hottelet.
Subsaharan Africa, edited by J. Herskovits.
1. United States—Foreign relations—1945—
— Sources. I. Dallek, Robert. II. LaFeber, Walter.
III. Burr, Robert N. IV. Title.
E744.S395   327.73   78-150208
ISBN 0-07-079729-3
1234567890 HDBP 76543

CONTENTS

Volume IV
The Far East

The General Introduction to this Series
By Professor Arthur M. Schlesinger, jr. appears
in Volume I.

The United States and the Far East.... *Russell Buhite*   xxvii

THE UNITED STATES AND JAPAN

Commentary   3

WARTIME DECLARATIONS

A.   The Cairo Declaration, December 1, 1943   7
B.   The Potsdam Proclamation, July 26, 1945   7
C.   Statement by President Harry S. Truman on Japanese Acceptance of
Surrender Terms, August 14, 1945   9

UNITED STATES OCCUPATION OF JAPAN, 1945-1951

A.   United States Initial Post-Surrender Policy for Japan, August 29, 1945   10
B.   United States Demobilization Directive for Japan, September 2, 1945   16
C.   Message Outlining Authority of General Douglas MacArthur as U.S.
Supreme Commander, September 6, 1945   17
D.   Agreement Establishing Far Eastern Commission and Allied Council
for Japan, Moscow, December 27, 1945   18
E.   Constitution of Japan, May 3, 1947   21

UNITED STATES CONTROL OVER
JAPANESE FOREIGN RELATIONS

F.   Relaxation of Control over Foreign Policy and Trade, May 6, 1949   41
G.   United States Encouragement of Japanese Participation in International
Relations, August 18, 1949   41

H.   Statement by General Frank R. McCoy, U.S. Member of the Far
Eastern Commission, on United States Reparation Policy, May 12, 1949   42

UNITED STATES LABOR POLICY
IN JAPAN

I.   Letter from General Kuzma Derevyanko, Soviet Member of the Allied
Council for Japan, to General Douglas A. MacArthur, Supreme Commander
for the Allied Powers, June 11, 1949   47
J.   Comment by General MacArthur on Derevyanko's Letter, June 13, 1949   48

THE JAPANESE PEACE TREATY

K.   United States Memorandum, November 24, 1950   49
L.   Note from the Soviet Union to the United States, November 20, 1950   50
M.   Note from the United States to the Soviet Union, December 28, 1950   52

UNITED STATES AGREEMENT WITH SOVEREIGN JAPAN

A.   United States-Japanese Security Treaty, Signed, September 8, 1951,
Effective, April 28, 1952   67
B.   United States-Japanese Mutual Defense Assistance Agreement, March
8, 1954   68

EXCHANGE OF VIEWS ON NUCLEAR
WEAPONS TEST

C.   Prime Minister of Japan, Nobusuke Kishi, to President Dwight D.
Eisenhower, September 24, 1957   73
D.   President Eisenhower to Prime Minister Kishi, October 3, 1957   74
E.   Treaty of Mutual Cooperation and Security Between the United
States and Japan, January 19, 1960   75

UNITED STATES POLICY TOWARD JAPAN, 1960-1970

A.   Statement Issued on Postponement of President Eisenhower's Visit
to Japan, June 16, 1960   78
B.   Joint Communiqué by President John F. Kennedy and Prime Minister
Hayato Ikeda of Japan on United States-Japanese Relations, June 22, 1961   78

OKINAWA PROBLEM

C.   Statement by President Kennedy on Measures to Strengthen Civil and
Local Government in the Ryukyu Islands, March 19, 1962   79
D.   Statement by Secretary of State Dean Rusk on a Joint Program of
Economic Assistance to the Ryukyu Islands, November 1, 1962   81

*   *   *

E.   Address by U. Alexis Johnson, Deputy Under Secretary of State for
Political Affairs, on Japan's Role as a World Power, March 28, 1963   82
F.   Joint Communiqué Issued by President Lyndon B. Johnson and Prime
Minister Eisaku Sato of Japan on Matters of Mutual Interest, January 13, 1965   85

G. Statement by President Johnson on the Election of the Ryukyuan
Chief Executive, December 20, 1965   87
H. Statements by Secretary of Defense Robert McNamara on Japan's Future
Role in Asia, July 15, 1966   88
I. Joint Communiqué Issued by President Johnson and Prime Minister
Sato on Matters of Mutual Interest, November 15, 1967   90
J. Joint United States-Japanese Statement on Return of the Bonin Islands
to Japanese Administration, April 5, 1968   93
K. Comments by Secretary of State Rusk on the Ryukyu Islands, May 17, 1968   94
L. Joint Communiqué Issued by President Richard M. Nixon and Prime
Minister Sato on Restoration of Okinawa to Normal Status, November 21, 1969   94
M. Comments by Under Secretary Johnson on the Future of United States
Relations with the Far East, April 10, 1970   96
N. United States Statement on U.S.-Japanese Treaty of Mutual Cooperation
and Security, June 22, 1970   100

THE UNITED STATES AND CHINA

Commentary   103

WORLD WAR II POLICY TOWARD
CHINESE NATIONALISTS AND CHINESE COMMUNISTS

A. Recommendation of U.S. Ambassador Patrick Hurley Against American
Aid to the Chinese Communists, January-February, 1945   105
B. Recommendations of George Atcheson, American Chargé d'Affaires, on
Supplying Arms and Military Equipment to Chinese Communists, February
28, 1945   106
C. Interview Between Ambassador Hurley and Marshal Joseph Stalin on
Chinese Communists and Nationalists, April 15, 1945   110
D. Instructions Given by Secretary of State E. R. Stettinus to Ambassador
Hurley on Russian Intervention in China, April 23, 1945   111
E. Yalta Far Eastern Agreement, February 11, 1945   112
F. Treaty of Friendship and Alliance Between the Republic of China and
the U.S.S.R., August 14, 1945   113
G. Comment by President Harry S. Truman on Ambassador Hurley's
Resignation, 1956   115

THE MISSION OF GENERAL GEORGE C. MARSHALL
IN CHINA, 1945-1947

A. President Truman to General Marshall, Special Representative of the
President to China, December 15, 1945   118
B. Statement by President Truman on United States Policy Toward China,
December 15, 1945   119
C. President Truman to President Chiang Kai-shek, August 10, 1946   121
D. Chinese Ambassador V. K. Wellington Koo to President Truman, August
28, 1946   122
E. General Marshall to President Chiang Kai-shek, October 1, 1946   123
F. President Chiang Kai-shek to General Marshall, October 2, 1946   123

G. Statement by General Marshall, January 7, 1947   124
H. Statement by President Truman on United States Policy Toward China,
December 18, 1946   128
I. Views of U.S. Ambassador to China, John Leighton Stuart, on the
Chinese Communists, July 1, 1947   133

THE MISSION OF U.S. GENERAL ALBERT C. WEDEMEYER IN CHINA

A. Remarks by General Wedemeyer on China, August 22, 1947   136
B. Statements by General Wedemeyer on the Conclusion of His Mission
in China, August 24, 1947   140
C. Report by General Wedemeyer to President Truman on His Mission
in China, September 19, 1947   142
D. Secretary of State George C. Marshall to President Truman,
September 25, 1947   150

UNITED STATES POLICY IN CHINA, 1948-1949

A. Ambassador Stuart to Secretary Marshall, August 10, 1948   151
B. Secretary Marshall's Policy Directives, August 12 and 13, 1948   153
C. Policy Review, October, 1948   153
D. President Chiang Kai-shek to President Truman, November 9, 1948   155
E. President Truman to President Chiang Kai-shek, November 11, 1948   155
F. Ambassador Stuart to Secretary Marshall, December 21, 1948   157
G. Secretary of State Dean Acheson to Senator Tom Connally, Chairman
of the Senate Committee on Foreign Relations, March 15, 1949   158
H. Statement by Secretary Acheson on Basic Principles of United States
Policy Toward the Far East, August 5, 1949   160

Treaty of Friendship, Alliance and Mutual Assistance Between the U.S.S.R.
and the People's Republic of China, February 14, 1950   161

DOCUMENTS RELATED TO LOYALTY OF STATE DEPARTMENT PERSONNEL INVOLVED WITH THE UNITED STATES CHINA POLICY

A. Investigation of Charges Against John Carter Vincent, April 18, 1947   165
B. Investigation of Charges Against Owen Lattimore, July 20, 1950   173
C. Investigation of Charges Against John Stewart Service, July 20, 1950   180
D. Report on Basis of Allegations Against State Department Personnel,
July 20, 1950   186

THE CHINA LOBBY

A. Comments by Secretary Acheson and Senator Wayne Morse on the Existence
of a China Lobby in the United States, June 7, 1951   191
B. Attempts to Influence Public Opinion on Behalf of Nationalist China,
March 25, 1963   199

UNITED STATES POLICY IN CHINA, 1952-1960

A. United States-China Mutual Defense Treaty, December 2, 1954   208

THE FORMOSA CRISIS

B. President Dwight D. Eisenhower to Congress on Defense of Formosa,
January 24, 1955   210
C. Joint Congressional Resolution on Defense of Formosa, January 25 and
28, 1955   213

TALKS BETWEEN THE UNITED STATES
AND COMMUNIST CHINA, 1955

D. Statement by Secretary of State John Foster Dulles, July 26, 1955   214
E. Announcement of Mutual Return of Civilians to Their Respective
Countries, September 10, 1955   216
F. State Department Announcement on Return of Civilians, January 21, 1956 217

EISENHOWER ADMINISTRATION POLICY
TOWARD COMMUNIST CHINA

G. Statement by Secretary Dulles on United States Policy Toward Communist
China, March 13, 1957   220
H. Address by Secretary Dulles on United States Policy Toward Communist
China, June 28, 1957   221
I. State Department Announcement on Trade with Communist China, April
20, 1957   227
J. Comment by Acting Secretary of State Christian A. Herter on Travel by
American Citizens in Communist China, August 13, 1957   229
K. Department of State Memorandum on United States Policy Toward
Communist China, August 11, 1958   230

AMBASSADORIAL TALKS BETWEEN THE
UNITED STATES AND COMMUNIST CHINA

L. Letter from U.S. Representative at the Geneva Talks to the Representative
of the People's Republic of China, March 12, 1958   236
M. Nationalist Chinese Statement on Resumption of Talks, June 30, 1958 237

THE TAIWAN STRAITS CRISIS

N. Comment by Secretary Dulles, September 4, 1958   239
O. Chinese Communist Comment, September 6, 1958   241
P. Nikita Khrushchev, Chairman of the Council of Ministers of the U.S.S.R.,
to President Eisenhower, September 7, 1958   241
Q. Address by President Eisenhower, September 11, 1958   245
R. President Eisenhower to Chairman Khrushchev, September 12, 1958   250
S. Theodore F. Green, Chairman of the Senate Foreign Relations Committee,
to President Eisenhower, September 28, 1958   251
T. President Eisenhower to Senator Green, October 2, 1958   252
U. Comments by Secretary Dulles at a News Conference, October 28, 1958 254

UNITED STATES REACTION TO CHINESE COMMUNIST ACTIONS IN TIBET

V.   Statement of Concern by Acting Secretary of State Herter, March 26, 1959   255
W.   State Department Statement, March 28, 1959   256
X.   Speech by Senator Clair Engle on Revision of United States China
Policy, May 21, 1959   256
Y.   Address by Under Secretary of State Douglas Dillon on United States
China Policy, October 7, 1959   261

COMMUNIST CHINA AND THE UNITED NATIONS

Z.   Statement by U.N. Ambassador James J. Wadsworth on the Admission
of China to the United Nations, October 1, 1960   264

UNITED STATES POLICY IN CHINA, 1960-1968

A.   Address by Roger Hilsman, Assistant Secretary of State for Far Eastern
Affairs, on Redefinition of United States China Policy, December 13, 1963   267
B.   Speech by J. William Fulbright, Chairman of the Senate Foreign Relations
Committee, on United States China Policy, March 25, 1964   275
C.   Address by William P. Bundy, Assistant Secretary of State for Far
Eastern Affairs, on United States Asian Policy, September 29, 1964   276
D.   Comment by Secretary of State Dean Rusk, September 29, 1964   279
E.   Chinese Communist Announcement, October 16, 1964   280
F.   Statement by President Lyndon B. Johnson, October 16, 1964   282

STATE DEPARTMENT POLICY STATEMENTS

G.   Address by Marshall Green, Deputy Assistant Secretary of State for
Far Eastern Affairs, on United States Policy Toward Communist
China, February 26, 1965   283
H.   Address by U.S. Ambassador-at-Large Averell Harriman on Chinese
Communist Membership in the United Nations, October 31, 1965   286

THE SINO-SOVIET DISPUTE AND IMPLICATIONS FOR UNITED STATES CHINA POLICY

I.   Statement of Roger Hilsman, Department of Law and Government,
Columbia University, New York, March 10, 1965   289
J.   Statement of Dr. Harold C. Hinton, Institute for Sino-Soviet Studies,
George Washington University, Washington D. C., March 10, 1965   294
K.   Statement of Dr. George E. Taylor, Director, Far Eastern and Russian
Institute, The University of Washington, March 16, 1965   298
L.   Statement of Marshall Green, Deputy Assistant Secretary of State for
Far Eastern Affairs, March 23, 1965   301

TESTIMONY OF UNITED STATES SCHOLARS BEFORE THE SENATE FOREIGN RELATIONS COMMITTEE ON UNITED STATES POLICY TOWARD CHINA

M. Statement of A. Doak Barnett, March 8, 1966   305
N. Statement of John K. Fairbank, March 10, 1966   308
O. Statement of Hans Morgenthau, March 30, 1966   309

JOHNSON ADMINISTRATION POLICY
TOWARD CHINA

P. Statement by Secretary Rusk on United States Policy Toward China,
March 16, 1966   315
Q. Statement by Secretary Rusk on the Situation in Communist China,
September 16, 1966   327
R. Statement by Secretary Rusk on the Free Nations of Asia, October
12, 1967   327
S. Address by Under Secretary Nicolas Katzenbach on a Realistic View of
Communist China, May 21, 1968   329

UNITED STATES POLICY IN CHINA, 1969-1970

A. Address by Under Secretary Elliot Richardson on Foreign Policy Aims
and Strategy of the Nixon Administration, September 5, 1969   334
B. State Department Statement on the Relaxing of Trade Restrictions with
Communist China, December 19, 1969   334
C. State Department Statement on the Resumption of United States-Communist
China Warsaw Meetings, January 8, 1970   336

THE UNITED STATES AND KOREA

Commentary   339

THE PARTITION OF KOREA

A. Report of the Meeting of Foreign Affairs Ministers of the U.S.S.R., the
United States and the United Kingdom, December 27, 1945   343
B. Communiqué No. 5 of the United States-Soviet Joint Commission,
April 18, 1946   344
C. Secretary Marshall to Soviet Foreign Minister V. Molotov on Reconvening
of the Joint Commission on Korea, April 8, 1947   345
D. Secretary Marshall to Foreign Minister Molotov on the Moscow Agreement,
May 2, 1947   346
E. Acting Secretary of State Robert Lovett to Foreign Minister Molotov on
the United States' Intention to Refer the Korean Question to the United
Nations, September 17, 1947   347
F. General Assembly Resolution on the Independence of Korea, November
14, 1947   348
G. Proclamation by U.S. Commander Hodge, Calling for General Elections
in Korea, March 1, 1948   350
H. Letter from Commander Hodge Congratulating Members of the Korean
National Assembly, May 27, 1948   350
I. State Department Announcement on the Withdrawal of Forces from
Korea, September 20, 1948   352
J. United States Statement on Korean Independence, December 7, 1948   352

K. State Department Statement on United States Policy in Korea, June
8, 1949   355

MILITARY ASSISTANCE TO KOREA

A. John J. Muccio, U.S. Ambassador to Korea, to Syngman Rhee, President of
the Republic of Korea, on U.S. Military Advisors for Korea, May 2, 1949   357
B. Speech by Secretary Acheson on a Review of United States Policy to 1950,
January 12, 1950   357

NORTH KOREAN INVASION OF SOUTH KOREA

A. Security Council Resolution, June 25, 1950   365
B. Statement by President Truman, June 27, 1950   366
C. Statement by Warren Austin, U.S. Representative to the United Nations,
June 27, 1950   367
D. The Second Security Council Resolution, June 27, 1950   368
E. Statement by President Truman on Further Military Action in Korea,
June 30, 1950   369
F. The Third Security Council Resolution, July 7, 1950   369
G. Account by President Truman on His Response to the North Korean
Attack, 1956   370
H. Speech by Senator Robert Taft Criticizing Administration Policy, June
28, 1950   373
I. Speech by Ambassador Austin on the Future of Korea, September
30, 1950   377
J. General Assembly Resolution Declaring Communist China an Aggressor,
February 1, 1951   381

THE TRUMAN-MACARTHUR CONTROVERSY

A. President Truman to Ambassador Austin on United States Action Relative
to Formosa, August 28, 1950   382
B. Message from General MacArthur to Veterans of Foreign Wars,
August, 1950   383
C. Message from Secretary of Defense Louis A. Johnson to General
MacArthur, August 26, 1950   386
D. Message from President Truman to General MacArthur, August 29, 1950   386
E. Comment by President Truman on Differences over Formosa, 1956   387
F. General MacArthur's Surrender Demand to North Korean Forces,
October 9, 1950   388
G. Announcement by President Truman Relative to His Meeting with
General MacArthur at Wake Island, October 15, 1950   389
H. Comment by President Truman on his Meeting at Wake Island with
General MacArthur, 1956   390
I. Comment by General MacArthur on the Meeting with President Truman
at Wake Island, 1964   392
J. General MacArthur's Report to the Security Council on Entry of the
Chinese Communists into the Korean War, November 5, 1950   394
K. Statement of President Truman, November 16, 1950   395
L. Special Communiqué Issued by General MacArthur, November 28, 1950   396
M. Statement of President Truman, November 30, 1950   397
N. Message from Joint Chiefs of Staff to General MacArthur, December
6, 1950   397

O. Message from Joint Chiefs of Staff to General MacArthur, March 20, 1951   398
P. Statement by General MacArthur, March 24, 1951   399
Q. Message from Joint Chiefs of Staff to General MacArthur, March 24, 1951   400
R. Letters Exchanged by Hon. Joseph W. Martin, Jr. and General MacArthur, March, 1951   400
S. President Truman's Recall of General MacArthur, April 10, 1951   401
T. Comment by President Truman on His Dismissal of MacArthur, 1956   402

TRUCE ARRANGEMENTS

A. Special United Nations Report on Korea, October 18, 1952   405

CORRESPONDENCE BETWEEN PRESIDENT EISENHOWER AND PRESIDENT RHEE ON THE KOREAN ARMISTICE

B. President Eisenhower to President Rhee, June 6, 1953   414
C. President Rhee to President Eisenhower, June 19, 1953   416

*   *   *

D. Summary of the Major Provisions of the Korean Armistice, July 27, 1953   418
E. Treaty of Mutual Defense Between the United States and South Korea, October 1, 1953   425
F. Declaration by the Sixteen Nations Participating in the United Nations Action in Korea Regarding a Korean Settlement, June 15, 1954   426

UNITED STATES POLICY TOWARD KOREA, 1960-1970

A. Communiqué Issued Subsequent to Talks Between Chairman Chung Hee Park of South Korea and President John F. Kennedy, November 14, 1961   428

NORTH KOREAN SEIZURE OF THE U.S.S. PUEBLO

B. Defense Department Statement, January 23, 1968   429
C. State Department Statement, January 23, 1968   430
D. Statement by Arthur Goldberg, U.S. Ambassador to the United Nations, January 26, 1968   431
E. Address by Secretary of State Dean Rusk, February 10, 1968   435
F. State Department Statement on the Release of the U.S.S. *Pueblo* Crew, December 22, 1968   436
G. Statement by President Lyndon B. Johnson, December 22, 1968   437
H. Statement by Secretary Rusk, December 22, 1968   438
I. North Korean Document Signed by the United States, December 22, 1968   439
J. United States Statement on the American Reconnaissance Plane Shot Down by North Korea, April 17, 1969   439

THE UNITED STATES AND VIETNAM

Commentary   445

AMERICAN POLICY TOWARD FRENCH PRESENCE IN VIETNAM

A. Communiqué Issued on United States-French Discussions on Indochina, June 18, 1952 — 450

B. Replies by Ho Chi Minh, President of the Democratic Republic of Vietnam, to Questions Submitted by the Swedish Newspaper *Expressen*, November 29, 1953 — 451

C. French Declaration on Indochina, July 3, 1953 — 452

D. Communiqué Issued by France and the United States Relative to French Aims and American Aid in Indochina, September 30, 1953 — 453

THE GENEVA CONFERENCE

E. Communiqué Issued Subsequent to Talks Between Secretary of State John Foster Dulles and French Foreign Minister M. Bidault, April 14, 1954 — 454

F. The Indochina Armistice Agreements, July 20, 1954 — 455

G. Protest by the South Vietnamese Delegation Against the Geneva Agreements, July 21, 1954 — 471

H. Statement by Under Secretary of State Walter B. Smith on the Final Declaration of the Geneva Conference, July 21, 1954 — 472

SEATO TREATY AND DEFENSE OF VIETNAM, 1954-1961

A. The Southeast Asia Collective Defense Treaty, February 19, 1955 — 473

B. Communiqué Issued on United States-French Talks on Indochina, September 29, 1954 — 477

C. Letter from President Eisenhower to Ngo Dinh Diem, President of the Council of Ministers of Vietnam, on United States Aid, October 23, 1954 — 477

D. Letters of Congratulations from President Eisenhower to President Diem on Progress Made in South Vietnam, July 6, 1956 — 478

E. Statement Issued Following Talks Between President Eisenhower and President Diem, May 11, 1957 — 479

KENNEDY ADMINISTRATION POLICY IN VIETNAM

A. Statement by Secretary Rusk on the Communist Threat to South Vietnam, May 4, 1961 — 481

B. Letter from President Kennedy to President Diem on the Communist Threat, December 14, 1961 — 482

C. Interview Between President Kennedy and Walter Cronkite of CBS-TV News on Vietnam, September 2, 1963 — 483

D. Interview Between President Kennedy and NBC-TV Newsmen Chet Huntley and David Brinkley on Vietnam, September 9, 1963 — 484

E. White House Statement on the Vietnamese Situation, October 2, 1963 — 485

JOHNSON ADMINISTRATION POLICY TOWARD VIETNAM

INCREASED MILITARY AID

A. Letter from President Johnson to General Duong Van Minh, Chairman of the Military Revolutionary Council in Vietnam, Assuring U.S. Support to South Vietnam, December 31, 1963 — 486

B. Appeal by President Johnson for More Aid to South Vietnam, May 18, 1964 — 487

C. Message by President Johnson to the American People, August 4, 1964   488
D. Message from President Johnson to Congress, August 5, 1964   489
E. Joint Resolution of Congress: Public Law 88–408, August 10, 1964   490

AIR ATTACKS ON NORTH VIETNAM

F. White House Statement, February 7, 1965   491
G. White House Statement, February 11, 1965   492

ESCALATION OF THE WAR

H. Statement by President Johnson on U.S. Policy Toward Vietnam, March 25, 1965   493
I. Speech by President Johnson on "Pattern for Peace in Southeast Asia," April 7, 1965   494
J. Address by Secretary Rusk on "Steps to Peace," June 23, 1965   498
K. Statement by President Johnson: "We Will Stand in Vietnam," July 28, 1965   500

PEACE EFFORTS

L. Statement by North Vietnamese Prime Minister Pham Van Dong on Terms for Negotiations, April 8, 1965   501
M. Restatement of U.S. Position on Vietnam in "Fourteen Points," December, 1965   502
N. U.S. Ambassador Arthur J. Goldberg to U.N. Secretary General U Thant on Peace Efforts, January 4, 1966   503
O. Letter to Certain Heads of State From North Vietnamese President Ho Chi Minh, Restating Conditions for Negotiations, January 24, 1966   504
P. Statement by President Johnson on Resumption of Bombing North Vietnam, January 31, 1966   505
Q. Address by French President Charles de Gaulle on Vietnam, September 1, 1966   507
R. Joint Statement Issued on the Manila Conference, October 25, 1966   508

CORRESPONDENCE BETWEEN AMBASSADOR GOLDBERG AND SECRETARY GENERAL U THANT ON UNITED STATES POLICY IN VIETNAM

S. Goldberg to U Thant, December 19, 1966   509
T. U Thant to Goldberg, December 30, 1966   510
U. Goldberg to U Thant, December 31, 1966   511

*   *   *

V. Speech by President Johnson on U.S. Policy in Asia, July 12, 1966   512

PROPOSALS FOR PEACE NEGOTIATIONS

A. Pope Paul VI to President Johnson, February 7, 1967   515
B. President Johnson to Pope Paul, February 8, 1967   515
C. Pope Paul to President Ho Chi Minh, February 8, 1967   516

D. President Ho Chi Minh to Pope Paul, February 13, 1967   516
E. President Johnson to President Ho Chi Minh, February 8, 1967   517
F. President Ho Chi Minh to President Johnson, February 15, 1967   518
G. Speech by President Johnson Reaffirming U.S. Policy in Vietnam,
September 29, 1967   519
H. Statement by President Johnson, December 23, 1967   522
I. Statement by Foreign Minister Trinh of the Democratic Republic of
Vietnam, December 29, 1967   522

COMMENTS REGARDING VIETNAM BY MEMBERS OF THE SENATE

A. Testimony of Senator J. William Fulbright (Ark.), Chairman of Committee,
March 11, 1968   524
B. Testimony of Senator Wayne Morse (Ore.), March 11, 1968   526
C. Testimony of Senator Karl Mundt (S. Dak.), March 11, 1968   528
D. Testimony of Senator Frank Church (Idaho), March 11, 1968   529
E. Testimony of Senator Clifford Case (N.J.), March 11, 1968   531
F. Testimony of Senator Stuart Symington (Mo.), March 11, 1968   532
G. Testimony of Senator Claiborne Pell (R.I.), March 11, 1968   533
H. Testimony of Senator Albert Gore (Tenn.), March 12, 1968   533
I. Testimony of Senator Joseph Clark (Pa.), March 12, 1968   534

PEACE TALKS

A. Address by President Johnson on New Steps Toward Peace in Vietnam,
March 31, 1968   536
B. Address by President Johnson on the Bombing Halt of North Vietnam,
October 31, 1968   538
C. Vietnam Reappraisal by Clark M. Clifford, Former Secretary of
Defense, July, 1969   540

NIXON ADMINISTRATION POLICY TOWARD VIETNAM

A. Statement by Ambassador Henry Cabot Lodge, Head of U.S. Delegation
at First Plenary Session of Vietnam Meetings, on the Task of Peace, January
25, 1969   549
B. Speech by President Richard M. Nixon on Vietnam, May 14, 1969   551
C. Address by President Nixon on the Pursuit of Peace in Vietnam,
November 3, 1969   557

THE UNITED STATES AND LAOS

Commentary   571

INDEPENDENCE OF LAOS

A. Treaty of Amity and Association Between the French Republic and the
Kingdom of Laos, October 22, 1953   573
B. Geneva Agreement on the Cessation of Hostilities in Laos, July 20, 1954   575

AMERICAN SUPPORT OF ROYAL GOVERNMENT

A. United States Statement on the Communist Military Threat to Laos,
August 1, 1959   580
B. United States Response to Soviet Charges of American Aggression in
Laos, August 19, 1959   580
C. State Department Statement on the United States Agreement to Increase
Military Aid to Laos, August 26, 1959   581
D. United States Pledge to Support Laos, September 5, 1959   582

EXCHANGE OF NOTES BETWEEN THE UNITED STATES AND THE SOVIET UNION ON LAOS

E. Soviet Note to the United States, December 13, 1960   583
F. United States Note to the Soviet Union, December 17, 1960   585

*   *   *

G. Statement by President Kennedy on Laos, March 23, 1961   586
H. British Aide Memoire to the Soviet Union on Laos, March 23, 1961   588

GENEVA CONFERENCE ON LAOS AND AGREEMENT ON NEUTRALITY

A. British-Soviet Message for a Ceasefire in Laos, April 24, 1961   590
B. Statement by Secretary Rusk on the Opening of the Geneva Conference
on Laos, May 17, 1961   590

EXCHANGE OF CORRESPONDENCE BETWEEN CHAIRMAN KHRUSHCHEV AND PRESIDENT KENNEDY ON A COALITION AGREEMENT IN LAOS

C. Chairman Khrushchev to President Kennedy, June 12, 1962   596
D. President Kennedy to Chairman Khrushchev, June 12, 1962   596

*   *   *

E. Declaration on The Neutrality of Laos, July 23, 1962   597
F. Protocol to Declaration on Neutrality of Laos, July 23, 1962   599

CONTINUED THREAT TO LAOS

A. Address by Secretary Rusk on the Importance of Laos, June 14, 1964   606

STATEMENTS BY THE UNITED STATES AND THE SOVIET UNION ON THE SITUATION IN LAOS

B. Statement by the Soviet Union, July 26, 1964   608
C. United States Statement, July 30, 1964   610
D. State Department Statement Reaffirming Support of Geneva Agreements
on Laos, January 18, 1965   612

E.   Address by Prince Souvanna Phouma, Prime Minister of Laos, on "The North Vietnamese Have Carried the War to Laos," October 18, 1966   612
F.   Statement by U.S. Ambassador W. Averell Harriman Reviewing North Vietnamese Violations of Agreement on Laos, June 5, 1968   613
G.   Statement by President Nixon on the Scope of United States Involvement in Laos, March 6, 1970   616

THE UNITED STATES AND CAMBODIA

Commentary   625

INDEPENDENCE OF CAMBODIA

A.   Geneva Agreement on the Cessation of Hostilities in Cambodia, July 20, 1954   627
B.   Letter from Secretary Dulles to Cambodian Foreign Minister Nong Kimny on United States Policy Toward Cambodia, April 19, 1956   630

VIOLATION OF NEUTRALITY

A.   Letter from Prince Norodom Sihanouk, Cambodian Chief of State, to President Kennedy on Recognition and Guarantee of Neutrality and Territorial Integrity, August 20, 1962   631
B.   Letter from President Kennedy to Prince Sihanouk on Cambodian Border Areas, August 31, 1962   632
C.   Note from Cambodia to the United States on Discontinuing American Aid, November 30, 1963   633
D.   State Department Statement Rejecting Allegations of United States Plotting Against Cambodia, November 21, 1963   634
E.   Statement by Adlai E. Stevenson, U.S. Ambassador to the U.N., on United States and South Vietnamese Relations with Cambodia, May 21, 1964   635
F.   Letter from Ambassador Stevenson to Sivert A. Nielsen, President of U.N. Security Council, Denying Cambodian Charges of Spreading Poisonous Chemicals in Cambodia, August 14, 1964   638
G.   Statement by Secretary Rusk on the Neutrality and Territorial Integrity of Cambodia, April 25, 1965   639
H.   Letter from Secretary Rusk to Cambodian Foreign Minister Koun Wick Severing Diplomatic Relations with Cambodia, May 6, 1965   639
I.   Letter from Ambassador Goldberg to Secretary General U Thant on the United States Desire to See Cambodia "Pursue Its Chosen Path in Peace," January 3, 1966   640
J.   United States Note to Cambodia on Violation of Territory, December 4, 1967   641
K.   White House Announcement on the Appointment of Ambassador Chester Bowles to Cambodia, January 4, 1968   642
L.   Joint Communiqué on Talks Between Ambassador Bowles and Cambodian Officials, January 12, 1968   643
M.   Statement by Secretary of State William Rogers on the Resumption of Diplomatic Relations Between the United States and Cambodia, July 2, 1969   644

INVASION OF CAMBODIAN TERRITORY

A. Initial United States Response to the Cambodian Coup, March 19, 1970   645
B. Press Conference Comments by President Nixon on the Cambodian Situation, March 23, 1970   645
C. Address by President Nixon on the American Military Strike into Cambodia, April 30, 1970   646
D. Report by President Nixon on the Conclusion of the Cambodian Operation, June 30, 1970   651

THE UNITED STATES AND THAILAND

Commentary   659

POSTWAR SETTLEMENTS

A. Proclamation by Thailand Nullifying the 1942 Declaration of War Against the United States, August 17, 1945   661
B. Statement by Secretary of State James F. Byrnes on United States Relations with Thailand, August 20, 1945   662

AMERICAN AID TO THAILAND

A. Statement by Secretary of State John Foster Dulles on United States Military Aid to Laos and Thailand in Face of Viet Minh Aggression, May 9, 1953   663
B. Department of Defense Statement on Increased Military Aid to Thailand, July 13, 1954   663
C. Joint Communiqué Issued by the United States and Thailand on Peace in Southeast Asia, May 18, 1961   664
D. Joint Statement by Secretary Rusk and Foreign Minister Thanat Khoman on United States Policy Toward Thailand, March 6, 1962   665
E. Statement by President Kennedy on the Dispatch of Troops to Thailand, May 15, 1962   667
F. Address by Marshall Green, Deputy Assistant Secretary of State for Far Eastern Affairs, on Thai Countermeasures to the Threat of Communist Subversion, March 14, 1965   668
G. Joint Communiqué Issued on Thai-United States Discussions on Southeast Asia, February 15, 1966   668
H. Comments by William P. Bundy, Assistant Secretary of State for Far Eastern Affairs, on United States Assistance to the Thai Counter-Insurgency Program, September 4, 1966   669
I. White House Statement on Thai-United States Discussions on Economic Development and International Security, October 7, 1966   670
J. State Department Comment on a Secret Defense Paper Signed with Thailand in 1965, July 10, 1969   671
K. Comment by Premier Thanom Kittikachorn of Thailand on the Existence of a Secret Agreement Between the United States and Thailand, July 11, 1969   672

L.   Statement by President Nixon on United States Relations with
Thailand, July 28, 1969   672
M.   Joint Statement Issued by the United States and Thailand on Reduction
of U.S. Forces, August 26, 1969   673

THE UNITED STATES AND INDONESIA

Commentary   677

POLICY TOWARD INDONESIAN INDEPENDENCE

A.   United Nations Security Council Resolution on the Indonesian Question,
January 28, 1949   679
B.   Statement by Warren Austin, U.S. Representative to the U.N. Security
Council, on Implementation of the January 28 Resolution on Indonesia,
March 10, 1949   682

ECONOMIC AND MILITARY ASSISTANCE

NEW GUINEA PROBLEM

A.   Comment by Secretary Dulles on United States Policy and Indonesia,
April 3, 1956   686
B.   Comment by Secretary Dulles Concerning the United States Position on
the Status of New Guinea, November 19, 1957   686
C.   Comment by Secretary Dulles on Recent Political Developments in
Indonesia, February 11, 1958   687
D.   Comment by Secretary Dulles on United States Policy Regarding Arms
Shipments to Indonesia, April 8, 1958   687
E.   Comment by Secretary Dulles on United States Policy of Nonintervention
in the Indonesian Rebellion, May 20, 1958   689

AGREEMENT BETWEEN THE UNITED STATES AND INDONESIA ON THE SALE OF MILITARY EQUIPMENT AND SERVICES TO INDONESIA

F.   Howard P. Jones, U.S. Ambassador to Indonesia, to Dr. Raden Soebandrio,
Indonesian Minister of Foreign Affairs, August 13, 1958   689
G.   Dr. Soebandrio to Ambassador Jones, August 13, 1958   690

INDONESIAN DISPUTES WITH NEIGHBORING COUNTRIES

H.   Statement by Jonathan B. Bingham, U.S. Representative to the U.N.
General Assembly, on the West New Guinea Question, November 22, 1961   690
I.   United States Proposals for the Settlement of the West New Guinea
Dispute, May 26, 1962   692
J.   Statement by Attorney General Robert F. Kennedy on His Mission to
the Far East Concerning the Malaysia Dispute, January 28, 1964   693
K.   Comment by Secretary Rusk on Continuation of the United States
Aid Program to Indonesia, April 3, 1964   693

L. Department of State Comment Opposing Legislation to Terminate
United States Aid to Indonesia, August 14, 1964 — 694
M. Statement by Ambassador Stevenson on the United States Position in
the Malaysian-Indonesian Dispute, September 10, 1964 — 694

COOLING OF RELATIONS

N. United States Information Agency Statement on Closing of Their
Libraries and Reading Rooms in Indonesia, March 4, 1965 — 697
O. Comment by Secretary Rusk on Improving United States Relations with
Indonesia, March 7, 1965 — 698
P. Statement by Secretary Rusk, Made Before Senate Foreign Relations
Committee, on the Status of United States Assistance to Indonesia,
March 9, 1965 — 698
Q. Joint Communiqué Issued at Meetings Between Ambassador Ellsworth
Bunker, And Indonesian Officials on United States-Indonesian Relations,
April 15, 1965 — 699

OUSTER OF SUKARNO

R. Report by the Hsinhua News Agency (of the People's Republic of China)
on Political Changes in Indonesia, October 19, 1965 — 700
S. Comment by Secretary Rusk on Noninvolvement in the Indonesia
Situation, November 5, 1965 — 700
T. Joint Statement Issued on United States-Indonesian Matters of Mutual
Interest, September 27, 1966 — 700

THE UNITED STATES AND THE PHILIPPINES

Commentary — 705

PHILIPPINE INDEPENDENCE

A. Act to Provide American Military Assistance to the Philippines, June
26, 1946 — 707
B. Proclamation by President Truman on Philippine Independence, July
4, 1946 — 709
C. Treaty Defining Relations Between the United States and the Philippines,
July 4, 1946, Effective October 22, 1946 — 710

ECONOMIC AND MILITARY ASSISTANCE

A. Report of the Bell Commission on an Economic Survey of the Philippines,
October 9, 1950 — 713
B. Report by Myron M. Cowan, U.S. Ambassador to the Philippines, on
Progress and Developments in the Philippines, June 15, 1951 — 715
C. Mutual Defense Treaty Between the United States and the Republic of
the Philippines, August 30, 1951 — 717
D. Note from Secretary Dulles to the Philippine Chargé d'Affaires on
Establishment of a Council Under the United States-Philippine Mutual
Defense Treaty, June 23, 1954 — 719

E.   State Department Statement on the Revised United States-Philippine
Trade Agreement, September 4, 1955   719
F.   Statement Issued Subsequent to Talks Between Vice President Richard
M. Nixon and Philippine President Ramon Magsaysay on Military Bases,
July 3, 1956   720
G.   Joint United States-Philippine Announcement of a Mutual Defense
Board, May 15, 1958   721
H.   Note from George M. Abbott, U.S. Chargé d'Affaires, to Felixberto M.
Serrano, Philippine Secretary of Foreign Affairs, on Transfer of Portions of
Subic Bay, a U.S. Naval Base, to Philippine Authority, December 7, 1959   722
I.   Joint Statement Issued by President Eisenhower and Philippine President
Carlos Garcia on Matters of Mutual Interest, June 16, 1960   723
J.   Statement by President Kennedy on the Postponement of Philippine
President Diosdado Macapagal's Visit to the United States, May 15, 1962   724
K.   United States Authorization for the Appropriation of $73 Million for
Philippine War Damage Claims, August 30, 1962   725
L.   Joint Communiqué Issued by President Johnson and President Macapagal
on Matters of International and Mutual Significance, October 6, 1964   726
M.   Department of State Announcement on an Amendment to the United
States-Philippine Military Bases Agreement, August 10, 1965   728
N.   Joint Communiqué Issued by President Johnson and Philippine President
Ferdinand Marcos on International Developments of Common Significance,
September 15, 1966   728
O.   Joint Announcement by the United States and the Philippines on
Reduction of the Duration of the Military Bases Agreement, September
16, 1966   730

THE UNITED STATES AND
INDIA AND PAKISTAN

Commentary   733

INDEPENDENCE

A.   Message from President Truman to Governor General Mountbatten of
India on the Creation of the Dominion, August 15, 1947   735
B.   Message from President Truman to Governor General Jinnah of Pakistan
on the Creation of the Dominion, August 15, 1947   735

MILITARY AID TO PAKISTAN

A.   Message from President Eisenhower to Indian Prime Minister Jawaharlal
Nehru on the Defensive Purpose of United States Military Aid to Pakistan,
February 24, 1954   736
B.   Mutual Defense Assistance Agreement Between the United States and
Pakistan, May 19, 1954   736
C.   Joint Communiqué Issued by President Eisenhower and Prime Minister
Hussein Shahud Sahrawardy of Pakistan on United States-Pakistan Relations,
July 13, 1957   740

D. Statement by Secretary Dulles on United States Financial Aid to India, March 4, 1958   741

ECONOMIC AID TO INDIA

A. Comment by Secretary Dulles on United States Policy with India, October 17, 1958   743
B. Statement by U.N. Representative Stevenson on the United States View of the Indian Invasion of Goa, December 18, 1961   743

THE SINO-INDIAN BORDER WAR OF 1962

C. Address by Prime Minister Nehru to the Indian Nation on the Chinese Invasion, October 22, 1962   745
D. Letter from Prime Minister Nehru to Premier Chou En-Lai of the People's Republic of China, Preconditioning Negotiations, October 27, 1962   746
E. Note from Secretary Rusk to Prime Minister Nehru on Military Aid to India, November 14, 1962   746
F. State Department Statement on Military Aid to India and Pakistan, November 17, 1962   747
G. Statement by President Kennedy on the Harriman-Nitze Mission to India, November 20, 1962   747
H. Comment by Secretary Rusk on the Significance of a Chinese Attack, November 28, 1962   748
I. Comment by President Kennedy on Aid to India, February 21, 1963   749
J. Remarks by W. Averell Harriman, Under Secretary of State for Political Affairs, on Soviet Aid to India, April 18, 1963   749

KASHMIR AND THE CONFLICT BETWEEN INDIA AND PAKISTAN

A. Statement by U.N. Representative Stevenson: "The Problem of Kashmir Cannot be Settled Unilaterally by Either Pakistan or India," February 14, 1964   751
B. Statement by U.N. Ambassador Goldberg on a Ceasefire, September 4, 1965   752
C. Statement by U.N. Ambassador Goldberg on Arms Shipments to India and Pakistan, September 17, 1965   753
D. Statement by President Johnson on Acceptance of the Ceasefire, September 22, 1965   753
E. The Declaration of Tashkent, January 10, 1966   754
F. Resolution on United States Participation in Relieving Victims of Hunger in India, April 19, 1966   756

APPENDIX A
Commentary   761

JAPAN

Report by Secretary of State William Rogers Concerning the Agreement with Japan on the Ryukyu and Daito Islands, September 5, 1971   762

Address by U. Alexis Johnson, Under Secretary for Political Affairs on Trends in United States-Japanese Relations, October 18, 1971   766

CHINA

Announcement by Department of State Press Officer Charles W. Bray on Steps
Taken on Contacts with Mainland China, March 15, 1971   769

Comments by President Nixon on China, April 29, 1971   770

Statement by President Nixon Announcing Acceptance of the Invitation
to Visit People's Republic of China, July 15, 1971   772

Statement by Secretary Rogers on the U.N. Decision on Chinese
Representation, October 26, 1971   773

Communiqué Issued by President Nixon and Premier Chou En-Lai at the
Conclusion of Their Meetings in China, February 27, 1972   774

VIETNAM

Address by President Nixon on a New Peace Initiative for All Indochina,
October 7, 1970   778

Remarks by Ambassador David K. E. Bruce, Head of U.S. Delegation at the
95th Plenary Session of the Meetings on Vietnam, December 17, 1970   781

State Department Statement on United States Assistance for the South
Vietnamese Operation in Laos, February 8, 1971   782

KOREA

Joint Statement by the United States and Korea on U.S. Troop Reduction and
Korean Modernization, February 6, 1971   784

PAKISTAN AND INDIA

State Department Statement on the Situation in East Pakistan, April 7, 1971   785
United States Position on the India-Pakistan War, December 3, 4, 6, 1971   785

GENERAL

Address by Marshall Green, Assistant Secretary for East Asian and Pacific
Affairs, on the Nixon Doctrine, January 19, 1971   789

APPENDIX B

Commentary   793

VIETNAM

News Conference Statement by Henry A. Kissinger, U.S. Representative at
the Paris Peace Talks, on the Status of the Vietnam Ceasefire, October 26,
1972   795

News Conference Statement by Henry Kissinger on the Status of the Vietnam
Ceasefire, December 16, 1972   800

Address by President Nixon Announcing the End of the Vietnam War, January
23, 1973   806

The Vietnam Agreement and Protocols, January 27, 1973   808

INDEX   845

Volume I
Western Europe

Volume II
Eastern Europe
and the Soviet Union

Volume III
Latin America

Volume V
The United Nations
Subsaharan Africa

THE UNITED STATES
AND THE FAR EAST

For much of their history Americans have manifested a predominant interest in Europe, giving relatively little attention to Asia. This Europe-first attitude was, of course, a natural development because it was to Europe that America owed its social, cultural, and political heritage—its language, religion, ethics, artistic taste, and political philosophy. It was also with Europe that the United States had its closest economic ties. Moreover, until most recently, Europe was the center of world politics—where alliances were made, wars fought, and, important to the history of Asia, where imperialistic policies were conceived. Asia was more remote in many ways: its languages were extremely difficult for Westerners; religious practices were widely divergent from the Western experience; economic life was frequently primitive by comparison; and significantly, Asia was geographically distant. Accordingly, prior to the Second World War there was relatively little scholarly study of Asia in the United States and few courses in Asian history or politics taught at American universities; only a handful of American historians dealt with China and Japan and almost none with Southeast Asia.

While American foreign policy did not totally reflect this attitude, neither could it be said that United States Far Eastern policy was highly developed or considered terribly vital until the 1890's. Then for a variety of reasons including commercial rivalry with other powers, the United States asserted itself more vigorously and, by virtue of the Spanish-American War, acquired the Philippines. Twentieth century policy makers devoted considerably more time and energy to Far Eastern questions, at times out of proportion to tangible American interests, but until the Second World War they seldom demonstrated a willingness to back diplomatic pronouncements with American power.

Since the outbreak of the Japanese-American War in the Pacific, however, there has been a dramatic increase in American interest and the American presence. The United States has fought three major wars in Asia, sacrificing in each the lives of thousands of its young men. It undertook the task of rebuilding a defeated and devastated Japan, oversaw the independence of the Philippine Islands, and committed itself to securing a degree of economic and political stability in the area. In some measure, it made these commitments because of a realization of the postwar economic and strategic importance of Asia, which contained huge quantities of the world's raw materials—tin, rubber, bauxite, tungsten, iron ore, and petroleum. Containing also a majority of the world's population, Asia represents an almost unlimited market potential. More than this, the United States has been motivated by a sense of idealism, often perhaps misguided, to assist underdeveloped nations and to promote self-determination of peoples.

The United States has thus focused more attention on Asia since the Second World War partially because of the great social ferment there. The diminution of European imperial control brought about by the war hastened the explosion of nationalistic forces in the region and led ultimately to the expulsion of the colonial powers. This made much of Asia a vacuum area. Indigenous politicians, thrust into important positions of power and responsibility, were called upon to reach new social and economic levels beyond their ability to achieve without external assistance. Recognition of the living standards and individual opportunities of Western people created pressures to accomplish in decades what had taken centuries in the West. The result was that much of the region, either directly or indirectly, was to get entangled in the diplomacy of the Cold War.

The central country in United States-Asian policy in both the pre-World War II period and during the Cold War has been China. Prior to the Second World War China dominated American policy makers' thinking because of its size and because China was the country exploited or dominated by the Western powers and by Japan. The most vital Far Eastern interests of the United States in the twentieth century were the right to commercial access to China and Japan, the ability to sail American ships along the China coast and through the sea lanes of Southeast Asia, and access to Southeast Asian raw materials and commerce. Also, in the public mind and of some concern to policy makers, was the ideal of an independent, democratic Chinese nation. When the actions of Japan infringed upon the former, the United States protested and essentially compromised its relatively small economic interest in China rather than risk a war with Japan; though expressing concern for China's territorial integrity, she never seriously contemplated intervention for this ideal. But the historic American interest in China and frequent protests regarding Japan's violation of the post First World War treaty structure combined with the generous Sino-American loan arrangements, did contribute to the deterioration of United States-Japanese relations. Then, when Japan moved southward, the United States retaliated with actions that ultimately led to a lengthy Japanese-American war.

After 1949, China retained its predominant position in American policy because, with the culmination of nearly three decades of revolution in the Communist takeover, it suddenly became the leading Asian spokesman of the anti-imperialist, anti-western position. Now China itself was a growing power in a position to act; in attempting to spread its influence and ideology to the South, China, in the view of American officials, took the place of Japan. That is, the United States saw China threatening to achieve hegemony in Eastern Asia just as Japan had done. Backed by Soviet power, China seemed an aggressive, violently anti-American colossus, which, it was believed, threatened American interests and goals in Asia. Consequently, the United States sought to "contain" her power in the region; it supported Chiang Kai-shek's nationalist regime on Formosa, beefed up its military and naval power in East Asia and committed itself to the defense of numerous adjacent states.

Because of Chinese and Soviet power and American opposition to it, most of the smaller countries of Asia were tugged one way and another in their international relations. They were in most cases forced to take sides even though to do so presented them with disagreeable alternatives: alliance or cooperation with the United States which could provide the military and material assistance requisite for security and internal progress but which represented the imperialism and racism which they intensely disliked; and, association with Communist China whose growing power they distrusted and whose ideology they feared.

South Korea, direct victim of Soviet-supported North Korean and Chinese aggression in 1950 became an enthusiastic ally of the United States in the area. The United States intervened in Korea to preserve the sanctity of the United Nations, to thwart Communist power in the region, and to block any threat to Japan; in succeeding years it also wrote defense agreements to strengthen South Korea. The Philippines, another nation favorably disposed toward American goals in Eastern and Southeastern Asia, has also maintained warm relations with the United States. It has permitted retention of United States bases on its territory and has assisted the United States outside its borders.

On the Southeast Asian peninsula, American policy encountered warm support, stinging criticism, and calm indifference. South Vietnam, in large part a product of United States power and resources, and Thailand, formal ally in the SEATO pact, worked very closely with the United States. On the other hand, Cambodia, led by Prince Norodom Sihanouk often bitterly condemned United States interference in Cambodian internal affairs and attempted to maintain friendly relations with China. In Laos, where rival factions competed for prestige and power, and indigenous traditions and customs prevented a sophisticated view of international politics, the United States found Laotian leaders eager to accept American aid when Communist or rival factions gained political strength though they had little sympathy for American goals in Southeast Asia.

Indonesia accepted American aid but until the overthrow of President Sukarno thought of itself as the nation of destiny in the area, attempted an adventuresome foreign policy toward Malaysia, and was among the leaders of the neutralist bloc of nations. Until 1965 when a Chinese-led coup resulted in bloodshed and stronger Indonesian-American ties, Indonesia had attempted to steer a middle course in the Cold War.

Similarly, India, while it accepted American assistance, attempted to maintain a neutralist position by establishing friendly relations with the Soviet Union, China, and the United States. Though often frustrating to the United States, the policy worked fairly well for India until the border war with China in 1962 resulted in closer Indian-American military and economic cooperation. Pakistan, by contrast, accepted the Chinese and Soviet ideological and national threat as real and joined the Central Treaty Organization and the Southeast Asia Treaty Organization.

This volume contains the major available documents in United States relations since 1945 with the following Asian countries: Japan, China, Korea, Vietnam, Laos, the Philippines, Indonesia, Cambodia, Thailand, and India and Pakistan. Documents pertaining to other Asian states were omitted only because of problems of space and because their relative importance necessitated giving priority to those relating to the above named countries.

Since much of the documentation of American foreign policy since 1945 is not yet available to scholars either in the National Archives or in the most valued State Department publication, the *Foreign Relations* series, the editor had to search in a variety of other areas for representative documents. Those sources most often used were the *Department of State Bulletin, United States Relations with China, American Foreign Policy: Current Documents,* all published by the State Department, and *Documents on American Foreign Relations* published by the Council on Foreign Relations. In addition, many valuable materials were extracted from the record of various Congressional hearings of the period, especially the *Military Situation in the Far East,* 1951, the Hearings on the Institute of Pacific Relations and those of 1965 and 1966 on China and of 1968 regarding Vietnam. Memoirs and Diaries of leading statesmen proved valuable as well, as did *The New York Times* and other news publications.

In assembling the materials, I have sought to include those items which in my view are most basic to an understanding of American policy and though I have exercised an editorial prerogative in making deletions, the texts are published in full wherever possible. Like anyone engaged in a project of this nature, I have naturally contracted debts of gratitude to many people. I owe a special word of appreciation, however, to Miss Opal Carr and Mrs. Eunice Edmunds of the University of Oklahoma libraries for assistance in locating and copying documents, and to my former colleague Gilbert C. Fite, for his numerous helpful suggestions and criticisms.

Russell D. Buhite
Associate Professor
University of Oklahoma

December, 1971

THE UNITED STATES

AND JAPAN

THE UNITED STATES AND JAPAN

Commentary

United States association with Japan since 1945 ranges from the victor-vanquished relationship of the immediate postwar period to alliance and mutual cooperation in the 1950's and 1960's. In a relatively short time Japan, a much despised enemy whose aggression in the previous two decades rested on an authoritarian, military-industrial base, became a peaceful, democratic and friendly state by and large favorably disposed toward American goals in Asia. This transformation occurred at least in part because of a wise and generous postwar American foreign policy.

The United States, in concert with its wartime allies, began to shape the destiny of Japan prior to the War's end—at the Cairo Conference, at Yalta and at Potsdam. The powers agreed to divest Japan of all Pacific islands acquired since 1914, to secure the independence of Korea, to return Formosa, Manchuria and the Pescadores Islands to China, to cede the Kurile Islands and the southern part of Sakhalin Island as well as Japanese concessions in Manchuria to the Soviet Union, and to seek Japan's unconditional surrender. The effect of these decisions was to reduce Japan to four main islands—her territorial domain at the time of the Meiji restoration.

With the end of the War, the United States, informing its allies of its decision but acting alone and with dispatch, occupied Japan and established control over its territory. Subsequent to protests by the Soviet Union, which hoped to have a major voice in the occupation, the United States in December, 1945, agreed to the establishment of the Far Eastern Advisory Commission with headquarters in Washington and the Allied Council for Japan stationed in Tokyo. But while ostensibly a policy-making organization, the Commission exercised little power and the Council did nothing but advise; power rested with the United States and more specifically with General Douglas MacArthur, Supreme Allied Commander.

The United States, reacting to adverse postwar developments in Europe, rejected Russian intrusions and remained the arbiter of Japan's affairs. Its goals in the occupation were four-fold: demilitarization, democratization, economic reorganization and social and educational reform. Pursuant to these objectives, the United States sytematically destroyed the Japanese war machine and, at least temporarily, wiped out attendant industries like aircraft and synthetic rub-

3

ber, and along with ten other nations, tried and convicted Japan's "war cri-minals." The United States also wrote a new constitution, which it dictated to the Japanese Emperor in 1947. It provided for renunciation of war, popular control, equality of the sexes, and contained a bill of rights. The Emperor was divested of his divine status and nearly all of his power, save that of ceremonial head of state. In order to guarantee a democratic direction, educational changes patterned on American models were imposed, and it was hoped that this would alter old social patterns. The great familial industrial combines or *Zaibatsu* were also dissolved and wealth diffused, the right of collective bargaining guaranteed and land reform promulgated.

Contrary to what one might expect, the Japanese response to the American program was generally friendly. A high degree of introspection made the Japan-ese people critical of past policies, and desire for westernization and economic reconstruction made them intellectually receptive to change. The American deci-sion to retain the Japanese emperor as a symbol undoubtedly helped, as did the choosing of General MacArthur as Supreme Commander. The General's regal bearing, firm authority and benevolent policies impressed the Japanese.

The end of the 1940's saw a change in United States policy. Subsequent to the accession of the Communists to power in China and the beginning of the Korean War, the United States began to terminate the occupation and to associate Japan with its anti-Communist position in Asia. In September, 1950, negotiations were begun to this end, and on September 8, 1951, at San Francisco, Japan signed a peace treaty with the United States and some forty-seven other nations with whom she had been at war. As a result of the treaty formal occupa-tion ended on April 28, 1952. Significantly, however, on the same day of the signing of the peace treaty, the United States and Japan signed a security agree-ment, under which American forces were to remain indefinitely in Japan to provide for her defense. More concerned with the Communist menace in Asia than with consistency in its attitude toward a demilitarized Japan, the United States in the 1950's began urging Japanese rearmament. To the chagrin of Japan-ese left-wing students, Communists and neutralist-pacifists, Japan established a National Defense Force, and in March, 1954, signed a Mutual Defense Assis-tance arrangement with the United States providing for increased United States military aid and restriction on trade with Communist China. In 1960 the two countries signed a second mutual security agreement which revised the earlier pact.

Closely related to American assumption of a defense burden was Japan's economic development. The increased United States military buildup in the Far East, both during and after the Korean War, provided a ready market for indus-trial products and jerked Japan's economy out of its postwar doldrums. The United States presence also allowed Japan to reduce her defense expenditures, thus releasing more capital for reinvestment in industry. The result of these and other factors has been a steady economic growth far surpassing that of any other Asian nation and rivaling those in Western Europe; it has also led to an expanding United States-Japanese trade. In fact, Japan constitutes Amer-ica's second most important market, and the United States imports more Japanese goods than any other country by a decisive margin.

Items associated with the American presence comprised the major divisive issues between the two countries in the late 1950's and 1960's. The Japanese government had to remain sensitive to relatively strong pacifist and Marxist opinion, which, rising out of the ashes of the Second World War, advocated a neutralist role for Japan in world affairs, urged elimination of American bases, led opposition to United States testing of nuclear weapons in the Pacific and protested the signing of the security agreements. At the same time, many other Japanese expressed the hope that one day the Ryukyu Islands and especially Okinawa, under American control since the War, would be returned to Japan. Notwithstanding these issues, the Japanese-American relationship, based on mutual economic and political interest, has been essentially one of partnership, particularly since 1960. Japan shares many of the American goals for East Asia: political change without violent upheaval, economic advance achieved mainly through regulated private enterprise, increased commerce within the region, and prevention of hegemony by a hostile power.

WARTIME DECLARATIONS

A. The Cairo Declaration*

December 1, 1943

The several military missions have agreed upon future military operations against Japan. The Three Great Allies expressed their resolve to bring unrelenting pressure against their brutal enemies by sea, land, and air. This pressure is already rising.

The Three Great Allies are fighting this war to restrain and punish the aggression of Japan. They covet no gain for themselves and have no thought of territorial expansion. It is their purpose that Japan shall be stripped of all the islands in the Pacific which she had seized or occupied since the beginning of the first World War in 1914, and that all the territories Japan has stolen from the Chinese, such as Manchuria, Formosa, and the Pescadores, shall be restored to the Republic of China. Japan will also be expelled from all other territories which she has taken by violence and greed. The aforesaid three great powers, mindful of the enslavement of the people of Korea, are determined that in due course Korea shall become free and independent.

With these objects in view the three Allies, in harmony with those of the United Nations at war with Japan, will continue to persevere in the serious and prolonged operations necessary to procure the unconditional surrender of Japan.

B. The Potsdam Proclamation*

July 26, 1945

1. We—the President of the United States, the President of the National Government of the Republic of China, and the Prime Minister of Great Britain, representing the hundreds of millions of our countrymen, have conferred and agree that Japan shall be given an opportunity to end this war.

2. The prodigious land, sea and air forces of the United States, the British Empire and of China, many times reinforced by their armies and air fleets from the west, are poised to strike the final blows upon Japan. This military power is sustained and inspired by the determination of all the Allied Nations to prosecute the war against Japan until she ceases to resist.

3. The result of the futile and senseless German resistance to the might of the aroused free peoples of the world stands forth in awful clarity as an example to the people of Japan. The might that now converges on Japan is immeasurably greater than that which, when applied to the resisting Nazis, necessarily laid

---

*Report of Government Section, Supreme Commander for the Allied Powers, *Political Reorientation of Japan, September 1945 to September 1948*, Appendix A, p. 441.

Department of State Bulletin, Vol. XIII, pp. 137-38.

waste to the lands, the industry and the method of life of the whole German people. The full application of our military power, backed by our resolve, *will* mean the inevitable and complete destruction of the Japanese armed forces and just as inevitably the utter devastation of the Japanese homeland.

4. The time has come for Japan to decide whether she will continue to be controlled by those self-willed militaristic advisers whose unintelligent calculations have brought the Empire of Japan to the threshold of annihilation, or whether she will follow the path of reason.

5. Following are our terms. We will not deviate from them. There are no alternatives. We shall brook no delay.

6. There must be eliminated for all time the authority and influence of those who have deceived and misled the people of Japan into embarking on world conquest, for we insist that a new order of peace, security and justice will be impossible until irresponsible militarism is driven from the world.

7. Until such a new order is established and until there is convincing proof that Japan's war-making power is destroyed, points in Japanese territory to be designated by the Allies shall be occupied to secure the achievement of the basic objectives we are here setting forth.

8. The terms of the Cairo Declaration shall be carried out and Japanese sovereignty shall be limited to the islands of Honshu, Hokkaido, Kyushu, Shikoku and such minor islands as we determine.

9. The Japanese military forces, after being completely disarmed, shall be permitted to return to their homes with the opportunity to lead peaceful and productive lives.

10. We do not intend that the Japanese shall be enslaved as a race or destroyed as a nation, but stern justice shall be meted out to all war criminals, including those who have visited cruelties upon our prisoners. The Japanese Government shall remove all obstacles to the revival and strengthening of democratic tendencies among the Japanese people. Freedom of speech, of religion, and of thought, as well as respect for the fundamental human rights shall be established.

11. Japan shall be permitted to maintain such industries as will sustain her economy and permit the exaction of just reparations in kind, but not those which would enable her to re-arm for war. To this end, access to, as distinguished from control of, raw materials shall be permitted. Eventual Japanese participation in world trade relations shall be permitted.

12. The occupying forces of the Allies shall be withdrawn from Japan as soon as these objective have been accomplished and there has been established in accordance with the freely expressed will of the Japanese people a peacefully inclined and responsible government.

13. We call upon the government of Japan to proclaim now the unconditional surrender of all Japanese armed forces, and to provide proper and adequate assurances of their good faith in such action. The alternative for Japan is prompt and utter destruction.

C. Statement by President Harry S. Truman on Japanese Acceptance of Surrender Terms*

August 14, 1945

I have received this afternoon a message from the Japanese Government in reply to the message forwarded to that Government by the Secretary of State on August 11. I deem this reply a full acceptance of the Potsdam Declaration which specifies the unconditional surrender of Japan. In the reply there is no qualification.

Arrangements are now being made for the formal signing of surrender terms at the earliest possible moment.

General Douglas MacArthur has been appointed the Supreme Allied Commander to receive the Japanese surrender. Great Britain, Russia, and China will be represented by high-ranking officers.

Meantime, the Allied armed forces have been ordered to suspend offensive action.

The proclamation of V-J Day must wait upon the formal signing of the surrender terms by Japan.

Following is the Japanese Government's message accepting our terms:

Communication of the Japanese Government of August 14, 1945, addressed to the Governments of the United States, Great Britain, the Soviet Union, and China:

With reference to the Japanese Government's note of August 10 regarding their acceptance of the provisions of the Potsdam declaration and the reply of the Governments of the United States, Great Britain, the Soviet Union, and China sent by American Secretary of State Byrnes under the date of August 11, the Japanese Government have the honor to communicate to the Governments of the four powers as follows:

1. His Majesty the Emperor has issued an Imperial rescript regarding Japan's acceptance of the provisions of the Potsdam declaration.

2. His Majesty the Emperor is prepared to authorize and ensure the signature by his Government and the Imperial General Headquarters of the necessary terms for carrying out the provisions of the Potsdam declaration. His Majesty is also prepared to issue his commands to all the military, naval, and air authorities of Japan and all the forces under their control wherever located to cease active operations, to surrender arms and to issue such other orders as may be required by the Supreme Commander of the Allied Forces for the execution of the above-mentioned terms.

*Ibid., p. 225.

UNITED STATES OCCUPATION OF JAPAN, 1945-1951

A. United States Initial Post-Surrender Policy for Japan*

August 29, 1945

PURPOSE OF THIS DOCUMENT

This document is a statement of general initial policy relating to Japan after surrender. It has been approved by the President and distributed to the Supreme Commander for the Allied Powers and to appropriate U.S. departments and agencies for their guidance. It does not deal with all matters relating to the occupation of Japan requiring policy determinations. Such matters as are not included or are not fully covered herein have been or will be dealt with separately.

Part I
Ultimate Objectives

The ultimate objectives of the United States in regard to Japan, to which policies in the initial period must conform, are:

(a) To insure that Japan will not again become a menace to the United States or to the peace and security of the world.

(b) To bring about the eventual establishment of a peaceful and responsible government which will respect the rights of other states and will support the objectives of the United States as reflected in the ideals and principles of the Charter of the United Nations. The United States desires that this government should conform as closely as may be to principles of democratic self-government but it is not the responsibility of the Allied Powers to impose upon Japan any form of government not supported by the freely expressed will of the people.

These objectives will be achieved by the following principal means:

(a) Japan's sovereignty will be limited to the islands of Honshu, Hokkaido, Kyushu, Shikoku and such minor outlying islands as may be determined, in accordance with the Cairo Declaration and other agreements to which the United States is or may be a party.

(b) Japan will be completely disarmed and demilitarized. The authority of the militarists and the influence of militarism will be totally eliminated from her political, economic, and social life. Institutions expressive of the spirit of militarism and aggression will be vigorously suppressed.

(c) The Japanese people shall be encouraged to develop a desire for individual liberties and respect for fundamental human rights, particularly the freedoms of religion, assembly, speech, and the press. They shall also be encouraged to form democratic and representative organizations.

(d) The Japanese people shall be afforded opportunity to develop for themselves an economy which will permit the peacetime requirements of the population to be met.

Department of State Bulletin, Vol. XIII, pp. 423-30.

Part II
Allied Authority

Military Occupation

There will be a military occupation of the Japanese home islands to carry into effect the surrender terms and further the achievement of the ultimate objectives stated above. The occupation shall have the character of an operation in behalf of the principal allied powers acting in the interests of the United Nations at war with Japan. For that reason, participation of the forces of other nations that have taken a leading part in the war against Japan will be welcomed and expected. The occupation forces will be under the command of a Supreme Commander designated by the United States.

Although every effort will be made, by consultation and by constitution of appropriate advisory bodies, to establish policies for the conduct of the occupation and the control of Japan which will satisfy the principal Allied powers, in the event of any differences of opinion among them, the policies of the United States will govern.

Relationship to Japanese Government

The authority of the Emperor and the Japanese Government will be subject to the Supreme Commander, who will possess all powers necessary to effectuate the surrender terms and to carry out the policies established for the conduct of the occupation and the control of Japan.

In view of the present character of Japanese society and the desire of the United States to attain its objectives with a minimum commitment of its forces and resources, the Supreme Commander will exercise his authority through Japanese governmental machinery and agencies, including the Emperor, to the extent that this satisfactorily furthers United States objectives. The Japanese Government will be permitted, under his instructions, to exercise the normal powers of government in matters of domestic administration. This policy, however, will be subject to the right and duty of the Supreme Commander to require changes in governmental machinery or personnel or to act directly if the Emperor or other Japanese authority does not satisfactorily meet the requirements of the Supreme Commander in effectuating the surrender terms. This policy, moreover, does not commit the Supreme Commander to support the Emperor or any other Japanese governmental authority in opposition to evolutionary changes looking toward the attainment of United States objectives. The policy is to use the existing form of Government in Japan, not to support it. Changes in the form of Government initiated by the Japanese people or government in the direction of modifying its feudal and authoritarian tendencies are to be permitted and favored. In the event that the effectuation of such changes involves the use of force by the Japanese people or government against persons opposed thereto, the Supreme Commander should intervene only where necessary to ensure the security of his forces and the attainment of all other objectives of the occupation.

Publicity as to Policies

The Japanese people, and the world at large, shall be kept fully informed of the objectives and policies of the occupation, and of progress made in their fulfilment.

Part III
Political

Disarmament and Demilitarization

Disarmament and demilitarization are the primary tasks of the military occupation and shall be carried out promptly and with determination. Every effort shall be made to bring home to the Japanese people the part played by the military and naval leaders, and those who collaborated with them, in bring about the existing and future distress of the people.

Japan is not to have an army, navy, air force, secret police organization, or any civil aviation. Japan's ground, air and naval forces shall be disarmed and disbanded and the Japanese Imperial General Headquarters, the General Staff and all secret police organizations shall be dissolved. Military and naval materiel, military and naval vessels and military and naval installations, and the military, naval and civilian aircraft shall be surrendered and shall be disposed of as required by the Supreme Commander.

High officials of the Japanese Imperial General Headquarters, and General Staff, other high military and naval officials of the Japanese Government, leaders of ultra-nationalist and militarist organizations and other important exponents of militarism and aggression will be taken into custody and held for future disposition. Persons who have been active exponents of militarism and militant nationalism will be removed and excluded from public office and from any other position of public or substantial private responsibility. Ultra-nationalistic or militaristic social, political, professional and commercial societies and institutions will be dissolved and prohibited.

Militarism and ultra-nationalism, in doctrine and practice, including paramilitary training, shall be eliminated from the educational system. Former career military and naval officers, both commissioned and non-commissioned, and all other exponents of militarism and ultra-nationalism shall be excluded from supervisory and teaching positions.

War Criminals

Persons charged by the Supreme Commander or appropriate United Nations agencies with being war criminals, including those charged with having visited cruelties upon United Nations prisoners or other nationals, shall be arrested, tried and, if convicted, punished. Those wanted by another of the United Nations for offenses against its nationals, shall, if not wanted for trial or as witnesses or otherwise by the Supreme Commander, be turned over to the custody of such other nation.

Encouragement of Desire for Individual Liberties and Democratic Processes

Freedom of religious worship shall be proclaimed promptly on occupation. At the same time it should be made plain to the Japanese that ultra-nationalistic and militaristic organizations and movements will not be permitted to hide behind the cloak of religion.

The Japanese people shall be afforded opportunity and encouraged to become familiar with the history, institutions, culture, and the accomplishments of the United States and the other democracies. Association of personnel of the occupation forces with the Japanese population should be controlled, only to the extent necessary, to further the policies and objectives of the occupation.

Democratic political parties, with rights of assembly and public discussion, shall be encouraged, subject to the necessity for maintaining the security of the occupying forces.

Laws, decrees and regulations which establish discriminations on ground of race, nationality, creed or political opinion shall be abrogated; those which conflict with the objectives and policies outlined in this document shall be repealed, suspended or amended as required; and agencies charged specifically with their enforcement shall be abolished or appropriately modified. Persons unjustly confined by Japanese authority on political grounds shall be released. The judicial, legal and police systems shall be reformed as soon as practicable to conform to the policies set forth in Articles 1 and 3 of this Part III and thereafter shall be progressively influenced, to protect individual liberties and civil rights.

Part IV
Economic

Economic Demilitarization

The existing economic basis of Japanese military strength must be destroyed and not be permitted to revive.

Therefore, a program will be enforced containing the following elements, among others; the immediate cessation and future prohibition of production of all goods designed for the equipment, maintenance, or use of any military force or establishment; the imposition of a ban upon any specialized facilities for the production or repair of implements of war, including naval vessels and all forms of aircraft; the institution of a system of inspection and control over selected elements in Japanese economic activity to prevent concealed or disguised military preparation; the elimination in Japan of those selected industries or branches of production whose chief value to Japan is in preparing for war; the prohibition of specialized research and instruction directed to the development of war-making power; and the limitation of the size and character of Japan's heavy industries to its future peaceful requirements, and restriction of Japanese merchant shipping to the extent required to accomplish the objectives of demilitarization.

The eventual disposition of those existing production facilities within Japan which are to be eliminated in accord with this programn, as between conversion to other uses, transfer abroad, and scrapping will be determined after inventory. Pending decision, facilities readily convertible for civilian production should not be destroyed, except in emergency situations.

Promotion of Democratic Forces

Encouragement shall be given and favor shown to the development of organizations in labor, industry, and agriculture, organized on a democratic basis. Policies shall be favored which permit a wide distribution of income and of the ownership of the means of production and trade.

Those forms of economic activity, organization and leadership, shall be favored that are deemed likely to strengthen the peaceful disposition of the Japanese people, and to make it difficult to command or direct economic activity in support of military ends.

To this end it shall be the policy of the Supreme Commander:

> (a) To prohibit the retention in or selection for places of importance in the economic field of individuals who do not direct future Japanese economic effort solely towards peaceful ends; and
> (b) To favor a program for the dissolution of the large industrial and banking combinations which have exercised control of a great part of Japan's trade and industry.

Resumption of Peaceful Economic Activity

The policies of Japan have brought down upon the people great economic destruction and confronted them with the prospect of economic difficulty and suffering. The plight of Japan is the direct outcome of its own behavior, and the Allies will not undertake the burden of repairing the damage. It can be repaired only if the Japanese people renounce all military aims and apply themselves diligently and with single purpose to the ways of peaceful living. It will be necessary for them to undertake physical reconstruction, deeply to reform the nature and direction of their economic activities and institutions, and to find useful employment for their people along lines adapted to and devoted to peace. The Allies have no intention of imposing conditions which would prevent the accomplishment of these tasks in due time.

Japan will be expected to provide goods and services to meet the needs of the occupying forces to the extent that this can be effected without causing starvation, widespread disease and acute physical distress.

The Japanese authorities will be expected, and if necessary directed, to maintain, develop and enforce programs that serve the following purposes:

> (a) To avoid acute economic distress.
> (b) To assure just and impartial distribution of available supplies.
> (c) To meet the requirements for reparations deliveries agreed upon by the Allied Governments.
> (d) To facilitate the restoration of Japanese economy so that the reasonable peaceful requirements of the population can be satisfied.

In this connection, the Japanese authorities on their own responsibility shall be permitted to establish and administer controls over economic activities, including essential national public services, finance, banking, and production and distribution of essential commodities, subject to the approval and review of the Supreme Commander in order to assure their conformity with the objectives of the occupation.

Reparations

Reparations for Japanese aggression shall be made:

(a) Through the transfer—as may be determined by the appropriate Allied authorities—of Japanese property located outside of the territories to be retained by Japan.

(b) Through the transfer of such goods or existing capital equipment and facilities as are not necessary for a peaceful Japanese economy or the supplying of the occupying forces. Exports other than those directed to be shipped on reparation account or as restitution may be made only to those recipients who agree to provide necessary imports in exchange or agree to pay for such exports in foreign exchange. No form of reparation shall be exacted which will interfere with or prejudice the program for Japan's demilitarization.

Restitution

Full and prompt restitution will be required of all identifiable looted property.

Fiscal, Monetary, and Banking Policies

The Japanese authorities will remain responsible for the management and direction of the domestic fiscal, monetary, and credit policies subject to the approval and review of the Supreme Commander.

International Trade and Financial Relations

Japan shall be permitted eventually to resume normal trade relations with the rest of the world. During occupation and under suitable controls, Japan will be permitted to purchase from foreign countries raw materials and other goods that it may need for peaceful purposes, and to export goods to pay for approved imports.

Control is to be maintained over all imports and exports of goods, and foreign exchange and financial transactions. Both the policies followed in the exercise of these controls and their actual administration shall be subject to the approval and supervision of the Supreme Commander in order to make sure that they are not contrary to the policies of the occupying authorities, and in particular that all foreign purchasing power that Japan may acquire is utilized only for essential needs.

Japanese Property Located Abroad

Existing Japanese external assets and existing Japanese assets located in territories detached from Japan under the terms of surrender, including assets owned in whole or part by the Imperial Household and Government, shall be revealed to the occupying authorities and held for disposition according to the decision of the Allied authorities.

Equality of Opportunity for Foreign Enterprise within Japan

The Japanese authorities shall not give, or permit any Japanese business organization to give, exclusive or preferential opportunity or terms to the enterprise of any foreign country, or cede to such enterprise control of any important branch of economic activity.

Imperial Household Property

Imperial Household property shall not be exempted from any action necessary to carry out the objectives of the occupation.

B. United States Demobilization Directive for Japan*

OFFICE OF THE SUPREME COMMANDER FOR THE ALLIED POWERS

September 2, 1945

Directive
Number I

Pursuant to the provisions of the Instrument of Surrender signed by the representatives of the Emperor of Japan and the Japanese Imperial Government and of the Japanese Imperial General Headquarters, 2 September 1945, the attached "General Order Number I, Military and Naval" and any necessary amplifying instructions, will be issued without delay to Japanese and Japanese-controlled Armed Forces and to affected civilian agencies, for their full and complete compliance.

By direction of the Supreme Commander for the Allied Powers:

R.K. Sutherland,
Lieutenant General, U.S. Army,
Chief of Staff

General Order No. I
Military and Naval

The Imperial General Headquarters by direction of the Emperor, and pursuant to the surrender to the Supreme Commander for the Allied Powers of all Japanese Armed Forces by the Emperor, hereby orders all of its Commanders in Japan and abroad to cause the Japanese Armed Forces and Japanese-controlled Forces under their command to cease hostilities at once, to lay down their arms, to remain in their present locations and to surrender unconditionally to Commanders acting on behalf of the United States, the Republic of China, the United Kingdom and the British Empire, and the Union of Soviet Socialist Republics, as indicated hereafter or as may be further directed by the Supreme

Political Reorientation of Japan, September 1945 to September 1948, Appendix B, pp. 442-44.

Commander for the Allied Powers. Immediate contact will be made with the indicated Commanders, or their designated representatives, subject to any changes in detail prescribed by the Supreme Commander for the Allied Powers, and their instructions will be completely and immediately carried out.

(a) The senior Japanese Commanders and all ground, sea, air and auxiliary forces within China (excluding Manchuria), Formosa, and French Indo-China North of 16 degrees North latitude, shall surrender to Generalissimo Chiang Kai-shek.

(b) The senior Japanese Commanders and all ground, sea, air and auxiliary forces within Manchuria, Korea North of 38 degrees North latitude, Karafuto, and the Kurile Islands, shall surrender to the Commander in Chief of Soviet Forces in the Far East.

(c) (1) The senior Japanese Commanders and all ground, sea, air and auxiliary forces within the Andamans, Nicobars, Burma, Thailand, French Indo-China South of 16 degrees North latitude, Malaya, Sumatra, Java, Lesser Sundas (including Bali, Lombok, and Timor) Boeroe, Ambon, Aroe, Tanimbar, and islands in the Arafura Sea, Celebes, Halmahera and Dutch New Guinea shall surrender to the Supreme Allied Commander, South East Asia Command.

(2) The senior Japanese Commanders and all ground, sea, air and auxiliary forces within Borneo, British New Guinea, the Bismarcs and the Solomons shall surrender to the Commander in Chief, Australian Military Forces.

(d) The senior Japanese Commanders and all ground, sea, air and auxiliary forces in the Japanese mandated Islands, Bonins, and other Pacific Islands shall surrender to the Commander in Chief, U.S. Pacific Fleet.

(e) The Imperial Headquarters, its senior Commanders, and all ground, sea, air and auxiliary forces in the main islands of Japan, minor islands adjacent thereto, Korea South of 38 degrees North latitude, Ryukyus, and the Philippines shall surrender to the Commander in Chief, U.S. Army Forces, Pacific.

(f) The above indicated Commanders are the only representatives of the Allied Powers empowered to accept surrender, and all surrenders of Japanese Forces shall be made only to them or to their representatives. . . .

C. Message Outlining Authority of General Douglas MacArthur as U.S. Supreme Commander*

September 6, 1945

1. The authority of the Emperor and the Japanese Government to rule the State is subordinate to you as Supreme Commander for the Allied powers. You will exercise your authority as you deem proper to carry out your mission. Our relations with Japan do not rest on a contractual basis, but on an unconditional surrender. Since your authority is supreme, you will not entertain any question on the part of the Japanese as to its scope.

2. Control of Japan shall be exercised through the Japanese Government to the extent that such an arrangement produces satisfactory results. This does not prejudice your right to act directly if required. You may enforce the orders issued by you by the employment of such measures as you deem necessary, including the use of force.

3. The statement of intentions contained in the Potsdam Declaration will be given full effect. It will not be given effect, however, because we consider ourselves bound in a contractual relationship with Japan as a result of that

*Occupation of Japan, Policy and Progress, Department of State Publication 2671, Far Eastern Series 17, p. 88.

document. It will be respected and given effect because the Potsdam Declaration forms a part of our policy stated in good faith with relation to Japan and with relation to peace and security in the Far East.

D. Agreement Establishing Far Eastern Commission and Allied Council for Japan*

Moscow, December 27, 1945

The Foreign Ministers of the Union of Soviet Socialist Republics, the United Kingdom, and the United States of America met in Moscow from December 16 to December 26, 1945, in accordance with the decision of the Crimea Conference, confirmed at the Berlin Conference, that there should be periodic consultation between them. At the meeting of the three Foreign Ministers, discussion took place on an informal and exploratory basis and agreement was reached on:

FAR EASTERN COMMISSION AND ALLIED COUNCIL FOR JAPAN

A. Far Eastern Commission

Agreement was reached, with the concurrence of China, for the establishment of a Far Eastern Commission to take the place of the Far Eastern Advisory Commission. The Terms of Reference for the Far Eastern Commission are as follows:

1. Establishment of the Commission
A Far Eastern Commission is hereby established composed of the representatives of the Union of Soviet Socialists Republics, United Kingdom, United States, China, France, The Netherlands, Canada, Australia, New Zealand, India, and the Philippine Commonwealth.

II. Functions
A. The functions of the Far Eastern Commission shall be:

(a) To formulate the policies, principles, and standards in conformity with which the fulfillment by Japan of its obligations under the Terms of Surrender may be accomplished.

(b) To review, on the request of any member, any directive issued by the Supreme Commander for the Allied Powers or any action taken by the Supreme Commander involving policy decisions within the jurisdiction of the Commission.

(c) To consider such other matters as may be assigned to it by agreement among the participating Governments reached in accordance with the voting procedure provided for in Article V-2 hereunder.

B. The Commission shall not make recommendations with regard to the conduct of military operations nor with regard to territorial adjustments.

Ibid., p. 69.

C. The Commission in its activities will proceed from the fact that there has been formed an Allied Council for Japan and will respect existing control machinery in Japan, including the chain of command from the United States Government to the Supreme Commander and the Supreme Commander's command of occupation forces.

III. Functions of the United States Government

1. The United States Government shall prepare directives in accordance with the policy decisions of the Commission and shall transmit them to the Supreme Commander through the appropriate United States Government agency. The Supreme Commander shall be charged with the implementation of the directives which express the policy decisions of the Commission.

2. If the Commission decides that any directive or action reviewed in accordance with Article II-A-2 should be modified, its decision shall be regarded as a policy decision.

3. The United States Goverment may issue interim directives to the Supreme Commander pending action by the Commission whenever urgent matters arise not covered by policies already formulated by the Commission; provided that any directives dealing with fundamental changes in the Japanese constitutional structure or in the regime of control, or dealing with a change in the Japanese Government as a whole will be issued only following consultation and following the attainment of agreement in the Far Eastern Commission.

4. All directives issued shall be filed with the Commission.

IV. Other Methods of Consultation

The establishment of the Commission shall not preclude the use of other methods of consultation on Far Eastern issues by the participating Governments.

V. Composition

1. The Far Eastern Commission shall consist of one representative of each of the States party to this agreement. The membership of the Commission may be increased by agreement among the participating Powers as conditions warrant by the addition of representatives of other United Nations in the Far East or having territories therein. The Commission shall provide for full and adequate consultations, as occasion may require, with representatives of the United Nations not members of the Commission in regard to matters before the Commission which are of particular concern to such nations.

2. The Commission may take action by less than unanimous vote provided that action shall have the concurrence of at least a majority of all the representatives including the representatives of the four following Powers: United States, United Kingdom, Union of Soviet Socialist Republics and China.

VI. Location and Organization

1. The Far Eastern Commission shall have its headquarters in Washington. It may meet at other places as occasion requires, including Tokyo, if and when it deems it desirable to do so. It may make such arrangements through the

Chairman as may be practicable for consultation with the Supreme Commander for the Allied Powers.

2. Each representative on the Commission may be accompanied by an appropriate staff comprising both civilian and military representation.

3. The Commission shall organize its secretariat, appoint such committees as may be deemed advisable, and otherwise perfect its organization procedure.

VII. Termination

The Far Eastern Commission shall cease to function when a decision to that effect is taken by the concurrence of at least a majority of all the representatives including the representatives of the four following Powers: United States, United Kingdom, Union of Soviet Socialist Republics and China. Prior to the termination of its functions the Commission shall transfer to any interim or permanent security organization of which the participating governments are members those functions which may appropriately be transferred.

It was agreed that the Government of the United States on behalf of the four Powers should present the Terms of Reference to the other Governments specified in Article I and invite them to participate in the Commission on the revised basis.

B. Allied Council for Japan

The following agreement was also reached, with the concurrence of China, for the establishment of an Allied Council for Japan:

1. There shall be established an Allied Council with its seat in Tokyo under the chairmanship of the Supreme Commander for the Allied Powers (or his Deputy) for the purpose of consulting with and advising the Supreme Commander in regard to the implementation of the Terms of Surrender, the occupation and control of Japan, and of directives supplementary thereto; and for the purpose of exercising the control authority herein granted.

2. The membership of the Allied Council shall consist of the Supreme Commander (or his Deputy) who shall be Chairman and United States member; a Union of Soviet Socialist Republics member; a Chinese member; and a member representing jointly the United Kingdom, Australia, New Zealand, and India.

3. Each member shall be entitled to have an appropriate staff consisting of military and civilian advisers.

4. The Allied Council shall meet not less often than once every two weeks.

5. The Supreme Commander shall issue all orders for the implementation of the Terms of Surrender, the occupation and control of Japan, and directives supplementary thereto. In all cases action will be carried out under and through the Supreme Commander who is the sole executive authority for the Allied Powers in Japan. He will consult and advise with the Council in advance of the issuance of orders on matters of substance, the exigencies of the situation permitting. His decisions upon these matters shall be controlling.

6. If, regarding the implementation of policy decisions of the Far Eastern

Commission on questions concerning a change in the regime of control, fundamental changes in the Japanese constitutional structure, and a change in the Japanese Government as a whole, a member of the Council disagrees with the Supreme Commander (or his Deputy), the Supreme Commander will withhold the issuance of orders on these questions pending agreement thereon in the Far Eastern Commission.

7. In cases of necessity the Supreme Commander may take decisions concerning the change of individual Ministers of the Japanese Government, or concerning the filling of vacancies created by the resignation of individual cabinet members, after appropriate preliminary consultation with the representatives of the other Allied Powers on the Allied Council.

E. Constitution of Japan*

Effective, May 3, 1947

We, the Japanese people, acting through our duly elected representatives in the National Diet, determined that we shall secure for ourselves and our posterity the fruits of peaceful cooperation with all nations and the blessings of liberty throughout this land, and resolved that never again shall we be visited with the horrors of war through the action of government, do proclaim that sovereign power resides with the people and do firmly establish this Constitution. Government is a sacred trust of the people, the authority for which is derived from the people, the powers of which are exercised by the representatives of the people, and the benefits of which are enjoyed by the people. This is a universal principle of mankind upon which this Constitution is founded. We reject and revoke all constitutions, laws, ordinances, and rescripts in conflict herewith.

We, the Japanese people, desire peace for all time and are deeply conscious of the high ideals controlling human relationship, and we have determined to preserve our security and existence, trusting in the justice and faith of the peace-loving peoples of the world. We desire to occupy an honored place in an international society striving for the preservation of peace, and the banishment of tyranny and slavery, oppression and intolerance for all time from the earth. We recognize that all peoples of the world have the right to live in peace, free from fear and want.

We believe that no nation is responsible to itself alone, but that laws of political morality are universal; and that obedience to such laws is incumbent upon all nations who would sustain their own sovereignty and justify their sovereign relationship with other nations.

We, the Japanese people, pledge our national honor to accomplish these high ideals and purposes with all our resources.

Political Reorientation of Japan, September 1945 to September 1948, Appendix C, pp. 671-77.

CHAPTER I

THE EMPEROR

Article 1

The Emperor shall be the symbol of the State and of the unity of the people, deriving his position from the will of the people with whom resides sovereign power.

Article 2

The Imperial Throne shall be dynastic and succeeded to in accordance with the Imperial House Law passed by the Diet.

Article 3

The advice and approval of the Cabinet shall be required for all acts of the Emperor in matters of state, and the Cabinet shall be responsible therefor.

Article 4

The Emperor shall perform only such acts in matters of state as are provided for in this Constituion and he shall not have powers related to government.

The Emperor may delegate the performance of his acts in matters of state as may be provided by law.

Article 5

When, in accordance with the Imperial House Law, a Regency is established, the Regent shall perform his acts in matters of state in the Emperor's name. In this case, paragraph one of the preceding article will be applicable.

Article 6

The Emperor shall appoint the Prime Minister as designated by the Diet.

The Emperor shall appoint the Chief Judge of the Supreme Court as designated by the Cabinet.

Article 7

The Emperor, with the advice and approval of the Cabinet, shall perform the following acts in matters of state on behalf of the people:

Promulgation of amendments of the constitution, laws, cabinet orders and treaties.
Convocation of the Diet.
Dissolution of the House of Representatives.
Proclamation of general election of members of the Diet.
Attestation of the appointment and dismissal of Ministers of State and other officials as provided for by law, and of full powers and credentials of Ambassadors and Ministers.
Attestation of general and special amnesty, commutation of punishment, reprieve, and restoration of rights.
Awarding of honors.
Attestation of instruments of ratification and other diplomatic documents as provided for by law.
Receiving foreign ambassadors and ministers.
Performance of ceremonial functions.

Article 8

No property can be given to, or received by, the Imperial House, nor can any gifts be made therefrom, without the authorization of the Diet.

CHAPTER II
RENUNCIATION OF WAR

Article 9

Aspiring sincerely to an international peace based on justice and order, the Japanese people forever renounce war as a sovereign right of the nation and the threat or use of force as means of settling international disputes.

In order to accomplish the aim of the preceding paragraph, land, sea, and air forces, as well as other war potential, will never be maintained. The right of belligerency of the state will not be recognized.

CHAPTER III
RIGHTS AND DUTIES OF THE PEOPLE

Article 10

The conditions necessary for being a Japanese national shall be determined by law.

Article 11

The people shall not be prevented from enjoying any of the fundamental human rights. These fundamental human rights guaranteed to the people by this Constitution shall be conferred upon the people of this and future generations as eternal and inviolate rights.

Article 12

The freedoms and rights guaranteed to the people by this Constitution shall be maintained by the constant endeavor of the people, who shall refrain from any abuse of these freedoms and rights and shall always be responsible for utilizing them for the public welfare.

Article 13

All of the people shall be respected as individuals. Their right to life, liberty, and the pursuit of happiness shall, to the extent that it does not interfere with the public welfare, be the supreme consideration in legislation and in other governmental affairs.

Article 14

All of the people are equal under the law and there shall be no discrimination in political, economic or social relations, because of race, creed, sex, social status or family origin.

Peers and peerage shall not be recognized.

No privilege shall accompany any award of honor, decoration or any distinction, nor shall any such award be valid beyond the lifetime of the individual who now holds or hereafter may receive it.

Article 15

The people have the inalienable right to choose their public officials and to dismiss them.

All public officials are servants of the whole community and not of any group thereof.

Universal adult suffrage is guaranteed with regard to the election of public officials.

In all elections, secrecy of the ballot shall not be violated. A voter shall not be answerable, publicly or privately, for the choice he has made.

Article 16

Every person shall have the right of peaceful petition for the redress of damage, for the removal of public officials, for the enactment, repeal or amendment of laws, ordinances or regulations and for other matters; nor shall any person be in any way discriminated against for sponsoring such a petition.

Article 17

Every person may sue for redress as provided by law from the State or a public entity, in case he has suffered damage through illegal act of any public official.

Article 18

No person shall be held in bondage of any kind. Involuntary servitude, except as punishment for crime, is prohibited.

Article 19

Freedom of thought and conscience shall not be violated.

Article 20

Freedom of religion is guaranteed to all. No religious organization shall receive any privileges from the State, nor exercise any political authority.

No person shall be compelled to take part in any religious act, celebration, rite or practice.

The State and its organs shall refrain from religious education or any other religious activity.

Article 21

Freedom of assembly and association as well as speech, press and all other forms of expression are guaranteed.

No censorship shall be maintained, nor shall the secrecy of any means of communication be violated.

Article 22

Every person shall have freedom to choose and change his residence and to choose his occupation to the extent that it does not interfere with the public welfare.

Freedom of all persons to move to a foreign country and to divest themselves of their nationality shall be inviolate.

Article 23

Academic freedom is guaranteed.

Article 24

Marriage shall be based only on the mutual conset of both sexes and it shall be maintained through mutual cooperation with the equal rights of husband and wife as a basis.

With regard to choice of spouse, property rights, inheritance, choice of domicile, divorce and other matters pertaining to marriage and the family, laws shall be enacted from the standpoint of individual dignity and the essential equality of the sexes.

Article 25

All people shall have the right to maintain the minimum standards of wholesome and cultured living.

In all spheres of life, the State shall use its endeavors for the promotion and extension of social welfare and security, and of public health.

Article 26

All people shall have the right to receive an equal education correspondent to their ability, as provided by law.

All people shall be obligated to have all boys and girls under their protection receive ordinary education as provided for by law. Such compulsory education shall be free.

Article 27

All people shall have the right and the obligation to work.

Standards for wages, hours, rest and other working conditions shall be fixed by law.

Children shall not be exploited.

Article 28

The right of workers to organize and to bargain and act collectively is guaranteed.

Article 29

The right to own or to hold property is inviolable.

Property rights shall be defined by law, in conformity with the public welfare.

Private property may be taken for public use upon just compensation therefor.

Article 30

The people shall be liable to taxation as provided by law.

Article 31

No person shall be deprived of life or liberty, nor shall any other criminal penalty be imposed, except according to procedure established by law.

Article 32

No person shall be denied the right of access to the courts.

Article 33

No person shall be apprehended except upon warrant issued by a competent judicial officer which specifies the offense with which the person is charged, unless he is apprehended, the offense being committed.

Article 34

No person shall be arrested or detained without being at once informed of the charges against him or without the immediate privilege of counsel; nor shall he be detained without adequate cause; and upon demand of any person such cause must be immediately shown in open court in his presence and the presence of his counsel.

Article 35

The right of all persons to be secure in their homes, papers and effects against entries, searches and seizures shall not be impaired except upon warrant issued for adequate cause and particularly describing the place to be searched and things to be seized, or except as provided by Article 33.

Each search or seizure shall be made upon separate warrant issued by a competent judicial officer.

Article 36

The infliction of torture by any public officer and cruel punishments are absolutely forbidden.

Article 37

In all criminal cases the accused shall enjoy the right to a speedy and public trial by an impartial tribunal.

He shall be permitted full opportunity to examine all witnesses, and he shall have the right of compulsory process for obtaining witnesses on his behalf at public expense.

At all times the accused shall have the assistance of competent ccounsel who shall, if the accused is unable to secure the same by his own efforts, be assigned to his use by he State.

Article 38

No person shall be compelled to testify against himself.

Confession made under compulsion, torture or threat, or after prolonged arrest or detention shall not be admitted in evidence.

No person shall be convicted or punished in cases where the only proof against him is his own confession.

Article 39

No person shall be held criminally liable for an act which was lawful at the time it was committed, or of which he has been acquitted, nor shall he be placed in double jeopardy.

Article 40

Any person, in case he is acquitted after he has been arrested or detained, may sue the State for redress as provided by law.

CHAPTER IV

THE DIET

Article 41

The Diet shall be the highest organ of state power, and shall be the sole law-making organ of the State.

Article 42

The Diet shall consist of two Houses, namely the House of Representatives and the House of Councillors.

Article 43

Both Houses shall consist of elected members, representative of all the people. The number of the members of each House shall be fixed by law.

Article 44

The qualifications of members of both Houses and their electors shall be fixed by law. However, there shall be no discrimination because of race, creed, sex, social status, family origin, education, property or income.

Article 45

The term of office of members of the House of Representatives shall be four years. However, the term shall be terminated before the full term is up in case the House of Representatives is dissolved.

Article 46

The term of office of members of the House of Councillors shall be six years, and election for half the members shall take place every three years.

Article 47

Electoral districts, method of voting and other matters pertaining to the method of election of members of both Houses shall be fixed by law.

Article 48

No person shall be permitted to be a member of both Houses simultaneously.

Article 49

Members of both Houses shall receive appropriate annual payment from the national treasury in accordance with law.

Article 50

Except in cases provided by law, members of both Houses shall be exempt from apprehension while the Diet is in session, and any members apprehended before the opening of the session shall be freed during the term of the session upon demand of the House.

Article 51

Members of both Houses shall not be held liable outside the House for speeches, debates or votes cast inside the House.

Article 52

An ordinary session of the Diet shall be convoked once per year.

Article 53

The Cabinet may determine to convoke extraordinary sessions of the Diet. When a quarter or more of the total members of either House makes the demand, the Cabinet must determine on such convocation.

Article 54

When the House of Representatives is dissolved, there must be a general election of members of the House of Representatives within forty (40) days from the date of dissolution, and the Diet must be convoked within thirty (30) days from the date of the election.

When the House of Representatives is dissolved, the House of Councillors is closed at the same time. However, the Cabinet may in time of national emergency convoke the House of Councillors in emergency session.

Measures taken at such session as mentioned in the proviso of the preceding paragraph shall be provisional and shall become null and void unless agreed to by the House of Representatives within a period of ten (10) days after the opening of the next session of the Diet.

Article 55

Each House shall judge disputes related to qualifications of its members. However, in order to deny a seat to any member, it is necessary to pass a resolution by a majority of two-thirds or more of the members present.

Article 56

Business cannot be transacted in either House unless one-third or more of total membership is present.

All matters shall be decided, in each House, by a majority of those present, except as elsewhere provided in the Constitution, and in case of a tie, the presiding officer shall decide the issue.

Article 57

Deliberation in each House shall be public. However, a secret meeting may be held where a majority of two-thirds or more of those members present passes a resolution therefor.

Each House shall keep a record or proceedings. This record shall be published and given general circulation, excepting such parts of proceedings of secret session as may be deemed to require secrecy.

Upon demand of one-fifth or more of the members present, votes of the members on any matter shall be recorded in the minutes.

Article 58

Each House shall select its own president and other officials.

Each House shall establish its rules pertaining to meetings, proceedings and internal discipline, and may punish members for disorderly conduct. However, in order to expel a member, a majority of two-thirds or more of those members present must pass a resolution thereon.

Article 59

A bill becomes a law on passage by both Houses, except as otherwise provided by the constitution.

A bill which is passed by the House of Representatives, and upon which the House of Councillors makes a decision different from that of the House of Representatives, becomes a law when passed a second time by the House of Representatives by a majority of two-thirds or more of the members present.

The provision of the preceding paragraph does not preclude the House of Representatives from calling for the meeting of a joint committee of both Houses, provided for by law.

Failure by the House of Councillors to take final action within sixty (60) days after receipt of a bill passed by the House of Representatives, time in recess excepted, may be determined by the House of Representatives to constitute a rejection of the said bill by the House of Councillors.

Article 60

The budget must first be submitted to the House of Representatives.

Upon consideration of the budget, when the House of Councillors makes a decision different from that of the House of Representatives, and when no agreement can be reached even through a joint committee of both Houses, provided for by law, or in the case of failure by the House of Councillors to take final action within thirty (30) days, the period of recess excluded, after the receipt of the budget passed by the House of Representatives, the decision of the House of Representatives shall be the decision of the Diet.

Article 61

The second paragraph of the preceding article applies also to the Diet approval required for the conclusion of treaties.

Article 62

Each House may conduct investigations in relation to government, and may demand the presence and testimony of witnesses, and the production of records.

Article 63

The Prime Minister and other Ministers of State may, at any time, appear in either House for the purpose of speaking on bills, regardless of whether they are members of the House or not. They must appear when their presence is required in order to give answers or explanations.

Article 64

The Diet shall set up an impeachment court from among the members of both Houses for the purpose of trying those judges against whom removal proceedings have been instituted.

Matters relating to impeachment shall be provided by law.

CHAPTER V
THE CABINET

Article 65

Executive power shall be vested in the Cabinet.

Article 66

The Cabinet shall consist of the Prime Minister, who shall be its head, and other Ministers of State, as provided for by law.

The Prime Minister and other Ministers of State must be civilians.

The Cabinet, in the exercise of executive power, shall be collectively responsible to the Diet.

Article 67

The Prime Minister shall be designated from among the members of the Diet by a resolution of the Diet. This designation shall precede all other business.

If the House of Representatives and the House of Councillors disagree and if no agreement can be reached even through a joint committee of both Houses, provided for by law, or the House of Councillors fails to make designation within ten (10) days, exclusive of the period of recess, after the House of Representatives has made designation, the decision of the House of Representatives shall be the decision of the Diet.

Article 68

The Prime Minister shall appoint the Ministers of State. However a majority of their number must be chosen from among the members of the Diet.

The Prime Minister may remove the Ministers of State as he chooses.

Article 69

If the House of Representatives passes a non-confidence resolution, or rejects a confidence resolution, the Cabinet shall resign en masse, unless the House of Representatives is dissolved within ten (10) days.

Article 70

When there is a vacancy in the post of Prime Minister, or upon the first convocation of the Diet after a general election of members of the House of Representatives, the Cabinet shall resign en masse.

Article 71

In the cases mentioned in the two preceding articles, the Cabinet shall continue its functions until the time when a new Prime Minister is appointed.

Article 72

The Prime Minister, representing the Cabinet, submits bills, reports on general national affairs and foreign relations to the Diet and exercises control and supervision over various administrative branches.

Article 73

The Cabinet, in addition to other general administrative functions, shall perform the following functions:

Administer the law faithfully; conduct affairs of state.

Manage foreign affairs.

Conclude treaties. However, it shall obtain prior or, depending on circumstances, subsequent approval of the Diet.

Administer the civil service, in accordance with standards established by law.

Prepare the budget, and present it to the Diet.

Enact cabinet orders in order to execute the provisions of this Constitution and of the law. However, it cannot include penal provisions in such cabinet orders unless authorized by such law.

Decide on general amnesty, special amnesty, commutation of punishment, reprieve, and restoration of rights.

Article 74

All laws and cabinet orders shall be signed by the competent Minister of State and countersigned by the Prime Minister.

Article 75

The Ministers of State, during their tenure of office, shall not be subject to legal action without the consent of the Prime Minister. However, the right to take that action is not impaired hereby.

CHAPTER VI
JUDICIARY

Article 76

The whole judicial power is vested in a Supreme Court and in such inferior courts as are established by law.

No extraordinary tribunal shall be established, nor shall any organ or agency of the Executive be given final judicial power.

All judges shall be independent in the exercise of their conscience and shall be bound only by this Constitution and the laws.

Article 77

The Supreme Court is vested with the rule-making power under which it determines the rules of procedure and of practice, and of matters relating to attorneys, the internal discipline of the courts and the administration of judicial affairs.

Public procurators shall be subject to the rule-making power of the Supreme Court.

The Supreme Court may delegate the power to make rules for inferior courts to such courts.

Article 78

Judges shall not be removed except by public impeachment unless judicially declared mentally or physically incompetent to perform official duties. No disciplinary action against judges shall be administered by any executive organ or agency.

Article 79

The Supreme Court shall consist of a Chief Judge and such number of judges as may be determined by law; all such judges excepting the Chief Judge shall be appointed by the Cabinet.

The appointment of the judges of the Supreme Court shall be reviewed by the people at the first general election of members of the House of Representatives following their appointment, and shall be reviewed again at the first general election of members of the House of Representatives after a lapse of ten (10) years, and in the same manner thereafter.

In cases mentioned in the foregoing paragraph, when the majority of the voters favors the dismissal of a judge, he shall be dismissed.

Matters pertaining to review shall be prescribed by law.

The judges of the Supreme Court shall be retired upon the attainment of the age as fixed by law.

All such judges shall receive, at regular stated intervals, adequate compensation which shall not be decreased during their terms of office.

Article 80

The judges of the inferior courts shall be appointed by the Cabinet from a list of persons nominated by the Supremne Court. All such judges shall hold office for a term of ten (10) years with a privilege of reappointment, provided that they shall be retired upon the attainment of the age as fixed by law.

The judges of the inferior courts shall receive, at regular stated intervals, adequate compensation which shall not be decreased during their terms of office.

Article 81

The Supreme Court is the court of last resort with power to determine the constitutionality of any law, order, regulation or official act.

Article 82

Trials shall be conducted and judgment declared publicly.

Where a court unanimously determines publicity to be dangerous to public order or morals, a trial may be conducted privately, but trials of political offenses, offenses involving the press or cases wherein the rights of people as guaranteed in Chapter III of this Constitution are in question shall always be conducted publicly.

CHAPTER VII
FINANCE

Article 83

The power to administer national finances shall be exercised as the Diet shall determine.

Article 84

No new taxes shall be imposed or existing ones modified except by law or under such conditions as law may prescribe.

Article 85

No money shall be expended, nor shall the State obligate itself, except as authorized by the Diet.

Article 86

The Cabinet shall prepare and submit to the Diet for its consideration and decision a budget for each fiscal year.

Article 87

In order to provide for unforeseen deficiencies in the budget, a reserve fund may be authorized by the Diet to be expended upon the responsibility of the Cabinet.

The Cabinet must get subsequent approval of the Diet for all payments from the reserve fund.

Article 88

All property of the Imperial Household shall belong to the State. All expenses of the Imperial Household shall be appropriated by the Diet in the budget.

Article 89

No public money or other property shall be expended or appropriated for the use, benefit or maintenance of any religious institution or association, or for any charitable, educational or benevolent enterprises not under the control of public authority.

Article 90

Final accounts of the expenditures and revenues of the State shall be audited annually by a Board of Audit and submitted by the Cabinet to the Diet, together with the statement of audit, during the fiscal year immediately following the period covered.

The organization and competency of the Board of Audit shall be determined by law.

Article 91

At regular intervals and at least annually the Cabinet shall report to the Diet and the people on the state of national finances.

CHAPTER VIII
LOCAL SELF-GOVERNMENT

Article 92

Regulations concerning organization and operations of local public entities shall be fixed by law in accordance with the principle of local autonomy.

Article 93

The local public entities shall establish assemblies as their deliberative organs, in accordance with law.

The chief executive officers of all local public entities, the members of their assemblies, and such other local officials as may be determined by law shall be elected by direct popular vote within their several communities.

Article 94

Local public entities shall have the right to manage their property, affairs and administration and to enact their own regulations within law.

Article 95

A special law, applicable only to one local public entity, cannot be enacted by the Diet without the consent of the majority of the voters of the local public entity concerned, obtained in accordance with law.

CHAPTER IX
AMENDMENTS

Article 96

Amendments to this Constitution shall be initiated by the Diet, through a concurring vote of two-thirds or more of all the members of each House and shall thereupon be submitted to the people for ratification, which shall require the affirmative vote of a majority of all votes cast thereon, at a special referendum or at such election as the Diet shall specify.

Amendments when so ratified shall immediately be promulgated by the Emperor in the name of the people, as an integral part of this Constitution.

CHAPTER X
SUPREME LAW

Article 97

The fundamental human rights by this Constitution guaranteed to the people of Japan are fruits of the age-old struggle of man to be free; they have survived the many exacting tests for durability and are conferred upon this and future generations in trust, to be held for all time inviolate.

Article 98

This Constitution shall be the supreme law of the nation and no law, ordinance, imperial rescript or other act of government, or part thereof, contrary to the provisions hereof, shall have legal force or validity.

The treaties concluded by Japan and established laws of nations shall be faithfully observed.

Article 99

The Emperor or the Regent as well as Ministers of State, members of the Diet, judges, and all other public officials have the obligation to respect and uphold this Constitution.

CHAPTER XI
SUPPLEMENTARY PROVISIONS

Article 100

This Constitution shall be enforced as from the day when the period of six months will have elapsed counting from the day of its promulgation.

The enactment of laws necessary for the enforcement of this Constitution, the election of members of the House of Councillors and the procedure for the convocation of the Diet and other preparatory procedures necessary for the enforcement of this Constitution may be executed before the day prescribed in the preceding paragraph.

Article 101

If the House of Councillors is not constituted before the effective date of this Constitution, the House of Representatives shall function as the Diet until such time as the House of Councillors shall be constituted.

Article 102

The term of office for half the members of the House of Councillors serving in the first term under this Constitution shall be three years. Members falling under this category shall be determined in accordance with law.

Article 103

The Ministers of State, members of the House of Representatives and judges in office on the effective date of the Constitution, and all other public officials who occupy positions corresponding to such positions as are recognized by this Constitution shall not forfeit their positions automatically on account of the enforcement of this Constitution unless otherwise specified by law. When, however, successors are elected or appointed under the provisions of this Constitution, they shall forfeit their positions as a matter of course.

UNITED STATES CONTROL OVER JAPANESE FOREIGN RELATIONS

F. Relaxation of Control over Foreign Policy and Trade*

May 6, 1949

The Department of State has recommended to the Far Eastern Commission countries that, under SCAP's supervision, Japan be permitted to attend international meetings and conventions and to adhere to and participate in such international arrangements and agreements as other countries may be willing to conclude with Japan.

It is now over three and a half years since Japan surrendered and the Allied Powers began the process of establishing conditions in Japan which would lead finally to the restoration of that country ito a normal status in the family of nations. This is the pattern envisaged in the Potsdam Declaration and the Basic Post Surrender Policy for Japan which was approved by the Far Eastern Commission on June 19, 1947. The latter document states in part that one of the objectives to which policies for the post-surrender period for Japan should conform is "to bring about the earliest possible establishment of a democratic and peaceful government which will carry out its international responsibilities, respect the rights of other states, and support the objectives of the United Nations."

It is important from the point of view of developing responsible government in Japan that it should be given increasing direction of its own affairs in the international field as well as in the domestic field as at present. That this process should develop under the guiding hand of the occupation has obvious advantages in developing a healthy international outlook among the Japanese and in averting the confusion that might well arise from any abrupt removal of current restrictions after a peace treaty. The immediate resumption by Japan of some international responsibilities in such fields as trade promotion, citizenship and property problems, cultural relations, technical and scientific arrangements and exchanges would provide a substantial contribution to the economic recovery of Japan.

G. United States Encouragement of Japanese Participation in International Relations*

August 18, 1949

A basic objective of the occupation in Japan is to foster among the Japanese Government and people a respect for the rights of other nations and governments. It is clear to the United States Government that by facilitating the progressive resumption by Japan of international relationships mutually beneficial to other peoples as well as to the Japanese people, this objective can be materially furthered.

Such international relationships require good will on both sides. Relations

*Department of State Press Release, 331, May 6, 1949.
*Department of State Bulletin, Vol. XXI, p. 307.

between nations are a two-way street. Because Japan is a defeated country under military occupation and because the Far Eastern Commission is the international body which formulates the policies, principles, and standards in conformity with which the fulfillment by Japan of its obligations under the terms of surrender may be accomplished, expression of general willingness to enter into even limited relationships with Japan tends to await the leadership of that body.

It was against this background that the United States proposed to the Far Eastern Commission that it take positive action recognizing that SCAP subject to his discretion and continued control has the authority to permit Japan to participate in international relationships such as conventions, meetings, consular arrangements, or other bilateral accords as Japan may be invited to participate in and as SCAP considers to be in the interest of the occupation.

From an examination of the record it is clear that the Far Eastern Commission has not taken any action denying SCAP the authority to approve Japanese intercourse with the outside world. In fact, under the broad policies of the Far Eastern Commission SCAP is correctly allowing Japanese international relationships of a limited character. Not only will the Japanese through such participation acquire direct experience and knowledge of democratic practices, but also the vestiges of hatred and suspicion of the Japanese left over from the war will tend to be dissipated.

It is not the legal authority of the Far Eastern Commission which is important but rather the assumption of enlightened leadership by the Far Eastern Commission member governments. No matter what position the Far Eastern Commission takes any government may still refuse to enter into relationships with Japan or deny Japanese access to its territory.

Likewise, the determination of whether or not Japan should be invited to participate in international organizations or conferences lies with the member governments concerned.

Almost 4 years after the war it is obvious that increased participation by Japan in international relationships under the control of SCAP will be a measurable step toward achievement of the Allied objective to foster the growth of a democratic and peaceful Japan.

H. Statement by General Frank R. McCoy, U.S. Member of the Far Eastern Commission, on United States Reparation Policy*

May 12, 1949

The Japanese reparations problem has been one of the most important and pressing questions with which the Far Eastern Commission and its member countries have had to deal. The United States, on its part, has taken a long and continuing interest in this problem and has been keenly aware of the interest of the other FEC countries in finding a reasonable solution to it. It is to be regretted that this controversial issue which for such a long time has proved

*Department of State Press Release, 350, May 12, 1949.

incapable of solution by this Commission continues to retard the achievement of economic self-support by Japan, which is so greatly in the interest of our common objectives with respect to that country.

In our discussions of the matter here in the Commission we have proceeded from that agreement contained in the Potsdam Declaration that reparations would be exacted from Japan and that they should be in a form which would not impair the ability of the Japanese people to support themselves. From the earliest days of the Far Eastern Commission the United States has been guided by a desire that the victims of Japanese aggression receive as reparations such of Japan's resources as was possible without jeopardizing Japan's ability to meet its own peaceful needs. The United States has felt, further, that in order that the nations devastated by Japan might receive reparation while their need was greatest, in order that there might be removed from the mind of the Japanese Government and people uncertainty regarding the reparations question, and in order that as many as possible of Japan's post-war obligations might be disposed of during the period of the occupation, a reparations program should be worked out and put into effect at the earliest practical moment.

These factors led the United States Government to take the initiative in making a number of policy proposals to the Far Eastern Commission. In April, 1946, the United States submitted to the Far Eastern Commission a pattern of proposals providing that there should be made immediately available for reparations designated quantities of industrial facilities which were at that time considered to be clearly surplus to Japan's peaceful needs. Between May and December of that year the Commission adopted a series of Interim Reparations Policy decisions based upon these U.S. proposals, but the subsequent inability of the Commission to agree on a schedule of shares for division of the facilities among the claimant countries prevented implementation of the decisions. In April, 1947, the U.S. Government offered further proposals, which would have had the effect of making known to Japan precisely, and on a final basis, what industrial capacity should be considered by that country to be immune from removal as reparations and what should be eligible for removal. In the same month, the U.S. because of its desire to work toward a settlement of this matter issued an Advance Transfers interim directive, under authority granted in paragraph III, 3, of the Terms of Reference of the Far Eastern Commission, instructing the Supreme Commander to effect delivery to four of the FEC countries of 30 per cent of the facilities which the Far Eastern Commission itself had previously determined in the Interim Removals decisions to be available for reparations removal. Issuance of this directive was motivated in part by a desire to assist those countries which had in the course of fighting against Japan's aggression on their own territories suffered most grievously, but it was also motivated by a desire to prompt FEC countries to agree upon a reparations program from which all eleven countries might benefit.

In November, 1947, the United States Government took the initiative once more in an effort to end the stalemate within the Commission on the questions of reparations shares, a stalemate which continued to make it impossible for any of the Commission's decisions on the reparations problem to take practical effect. This U.S. proposal contained the provision that if the Far Eastern Commission countries would accept the schedule of percentages which had been worked out by the U.S. Government—on the basis of prolonged exchanges of views among Commission members as to the equities involved—the U.S. Government, on its part, would make available an important part of its own share for distribution among the countries which could accept the U.S. proposal as a whole. Sixteen months have passed and this proposal has not been accepted by the Commission.

I should like to emphasize at this point that the action of my Government, and, it is assumed, of the other Member Governments, in participating in the policy decisions which have been taken by the Commission on the questions of reparations was predicated upon two basic assumptions, namely, that the resources to be removed from Japan as reparations were clearly excess to the peaceful needs of a self-supporting Japanese economy, and that there would be a shares schedule acceptable to and agreed upon by the Far Eastern Commission countries which would determine in what proportions available reparations should be divided.

As I have already stated, and as the Commission well knows, the second of these assumptions has not been realized and there seems little prospect of its being realized. As regards the first assumption, that reparations removals should be limited to facilities clearly excess to the needs of a self-supporting Japanese economy, successive studies during the past eighteen months of Japan's future industrial requirements have necessitated progressive upward adjustments of earlier estimates of these requirements. The first of these studies was that of Overseas Consultants, Incorporated, whose report was made available to the Commission on March 2, 1948, and the second was that of the so-called Johnston Committee, whose report was made available to the Commission on may 19, 1948. Both of these reports came to the sober conclusion that the quantity of capital equipment in Japan which could be properly considered in excess of Japan's peaceful needs had been greatly over estimated. Both reports indicated that for a variety of reasons the Japanese economy was continuing to operate at a heavy deficit even though living standards remained at a minimum level, and that the end to these deficits is not in sight. The evidence contained in these reports, and the common knowledge of all Far Eastern Commission countries, leads to the inescapable conclusion that the Japanese economy can be made to bear additional economic burdens, beyond those directly related to meeting its own requirements, only by prolonging or increasing the staggering costs borne by the American taxpayer.

The United States has, since the time of the Japanese surrender, carried the burden of preventing such disease and unrest in Japan as might jeopardize the purposes of the occupation. The critical economic conditions with which, it is now apparent, Japan is faced, and the prospect of continuing deficits in Japan's international payments for some years to come, render measures of Japanese economic recovery of utmost importance. It is inescapable that if the basic purposes of the occupation are to be achieved, the Japanese people must be enabled to support themselves at a tolerable standard of living. No one could reasonably suggest that Japan should be abandoned to economic despair. So to abandon Japan would be to undo the costly victory in the Pacific.

I am sure that other Commission countries agree with my Government that the Japanese people themselves must exert maximum efforts for the attainment of recovery. For some months the U.S. Government has explored means whereby this objective could best be achieved. In issuing its directive of December 10 regarding Japan's economic stabilization, the U.S. Government took a major step towards requiring the Japanese people to exert their utmost energies in stabilizing their economy and reducing their dependence for subsistence on foreign subsidy. Under present circumstances in Japan the cost of dismantling, packing, and transporting reparations facilities would conflict with the program of Japan's economic stabilization and would constitute an additional financial burden upon the U.S. Government. I do not wish to emphasize this point unduly, but the U.S. Government would be lacking in candor if it did not point out that the resources at its disposal to meet demands from all parts of the world are limited.

It is now apparent to the U.S. Government that the first as well as the second of the two basic assumptions mentioned earlier, assumptions which underlay the policy decisions of the FEC having to do with reparations and are a precondition for an FEC reparations program, has not been realized. This fact has led my Government to several conclusions. Before stating them, however, I wish to emphasize that the U.S. Government maintains fully and categorically its support of the principle adopted by the Far Eastern Commision that Japan's war-making capacity should be eliminated. As you know, all of Japan's specialized war-making facilities have been destroyed. The U.S. Government believes that all other equipment used for war purposes in the past should, if retained in Japan, be fully converted to the purposes of and utilized in Japan's peaceful economy. Where this cannot be done, the U.S. Government believes that such equipment should be scrapped. The U.S. will not permit difficulties in reaching a solution of the reparations problem to be a means whereby Japan's war capacity might re-emerge.

It may not be amiss at this point to recall that Japan has already been deprived not only of all of its overseas territorial possessions, but also of substantial quantities of real property of Japanese ownership and origin in the former possessions and elsewhere abroad. This property constitutes a large payment which the Japanese have already made towards satisfaction of their reparations obligations. Unfortunately, from the standpoint of equity, some countries have benefited more than others in the reparations that they have obtained in this form. However, from the standpoint of Japan, the loss of these properties, whatever the proportions in which they happen to have been distributed, drastically reduces Japan's ability to support even at a minimum level the needs of its people.

In view of the above considerations, the United States is forced to the following conclusions:

(a) The deficit Japanese economy shows little prospect of being balanced in the near future and, to achieve eventual balance, will require all resources at its disposal.

(b) The burden of removing further reparations from Japan could detract seriously from the occupation objective of stabilizing the Japanese economy and permitting it to move towards self-support.

(c) There is little or no prospect of Near Eastern Commission agreement on a reparations shares schedule despite the repeated initatives by the United States over the past three years to assist the Commission in reaching such an agreement. Without agreement on a shares schedule the existing Far Eastern Commission policy decisions regarding reparations are incapable of implementation.

(d) Japan has already paid substantial reparations through expropriation of its former overseas assets and in smaller degree, under the Advance Transfer Program.

In light of these conclusions the United States Government is impelled to rescind its interim directive of April 4, 1947, bringing to an end the Advance Transfer Program called for by that directive. It is impelled also to withdraw its proposal of November 6, 1947, on Japanese reparations shares, and I am so informing the Secretary General. Finally, the U.S. Government takes this occasion to announce that it has no intention of taking further unilateral action under its interim directive powers to make possible additional reparations removals from Japan.

I earlier stated my Government's belief that maximum efforts should be exerted by the Japanese themselves for their economic recovery. It is the view of the United States that all facilities, including so-called "primary war facilities," presently designated as available for reparations which can contribute to Japanese recovery should be utilized as necessary in Japan's peaceful economy for recovery purposes.

With regard to "primary war facilities," all of which as I earlier stated were some time ago stripped of their special purpose equipment and thus of their "war facilities" characteristics, it is the view of the U.S. that SCAP, under the authority granted in paragraph 10 of the FEC decision on Reduction of Japanese Industrial War Potential, should as rapidly as practicable require the dismantlement, dispersion or other action for the utilization in Japan's peaceful economy of such of these facilities as are required to meet the needs of the occupation, which needs prominently include economic recovery. Remaining "primary war facilities" should continue to be protected, in the sense of preventing loss or scrapping of individual items, pursuant to the above-mentioned FEC decision requiring their "impounding." Impounding does not, however, include requirement that the facilities be kept in their present locations or that the Japanese devote resources to preserve their value or maintain them in working order.

The United States, it will be recalled, has repeatedly clarified its understanding that the "level of industry" proposals before the Commission, excepting those levels which will lapse by FEC decision on October 1, 1949, had application only to the question of the quantities of industrial facilities which could be spared for reparations, and had no bearing on the matter of future levels of industrial capacity in Japan. Turning now to this latter question, I have already emphasized my Government's support of the principle that Japan's capacity to make war should not be permitted to re-emerge. It is the considered view of the United States Government that this objective does not require that Japan's production for peaceful purposes be limited or that limitations be imposed on levels of Japanese productive capacity in industries devoted to peaceful purposes. This belief, coupled with the evidence of Japan's present economic plight and the difficult problems Japan will face in future in attaining levels of industrial production and foreign trade sufficient to support its people even at minimum levels, render it clearly advisable in my Government's view that Japan be permitted to develop its peaceful industries without limitation. The problem facing us is not one of limitation of Japan's peaceful industries but of reviving these industries to provide the people's barest wants.

The U.S. Government plans shortly to submit to the FEC for its consideration proposals for the rescission or amendment of existing and pending FEC reparations and level of industry policy papers so as to bring FEC policies on these matters, should the proposals be approved by the Commission, into conformity with the position which I have set forth. My Government earnestly hopes that the other Member Governments will appreciate the considerations underlying this position and will be able to concur in the new United States proposals.

UNITED STATES LABOR POLICY IN JAPAN

I. Letter from General Kuzma Derevyanko, Soviet Member of the Allied Council for Japan, to General Douglas A. MacArthur, Supreme Commander for the Allied Powers*

June 11, 1949

The ever-increasing pressure on the part of the present Japanese Government upon the democratic rights of the Japanese people, the suppression of the legal activities of trade unions and other democratic organizations, and also the arbitrariness and chastisement committed by the Japanese police in connection with trade union leaders, progressively minded persons, and participants of various labor demonstrations and meetings to the present time have become facts deserving serious attention.

Calling to attention also the fact that the illegal activities of the Government and police organs, intended to forcefully impede the democratization of the nation, are taking place before the eyes of the American occupation authorities, General Headquarters, SCAP does not take any measures to the prevention of these activities flagrantly violating the Potsdam Declaration and the policies of the Far Eastern Commission to the democratization of Japan. These facts explain the increasingly great concern in the broad Japanese public opinion for the fate of democratization of their nation.

The masses of the people are indignant at the activities of the present Japanese Government resorting to the brutal suppression of the democratic movements by analogous methods of violence and repression existing during the period of the militaristic domination of Japan.

The occurrence in Tokyo on 30 and 31 May of the brutal suppression by

*Documents on American Foreign Relations, 1949, pp. 182-83.

the Japanese police of the peaceful demonstration consisting of representatives of trade unions, students and other public organizations has aroused a just indignation in the entire nation and beyond its borders.

As is known, this suppression was inflicted upon participants of a peaceful demonstration of laborers, employees and students who gathered for the sole purpose of expressing their protest against the new "public safety regulations" which were preconceived for further limiting the rights of labor and public organizations to hold gatherings, meetings and demonstrations.

The Japanese police, attempting to disperse the demonstration, began ruthlessly clubbing them, as a result one member of the Tokyo City Transportation Union, Laborer Kinji Hashimoto was killed by the police. Demonstrators who were headed to the building of the Headquarters Tokyo Metropolitan Police with protests against this bloody suppression and with demands that punitive measures be taken against the ones guilty of the crime were not admitted there and were subjected to new beatings by the police. Gathering on the following day near the Tokyo Metropolitan Assembly Hall, the representatives of numerous trade unions and students organizations, with intentions to demand punishment of those guilty of the killing of the laborer Hashimoto, were again subjected to brutal beating by specially mobilized police numbering about 2,000 policemen. As a result of this one hundred demonstrators received wounds and injuries and more than sixty persons were arrested.

Bringing the above content to your attention I wish to express my hopes that, on your part, proper measures will be taken to prevent illegal activites and antilabor measures which are practiced at this time by the Japanese Government.

At the same time I wish to express my hope that you will take appropriate measures for punishing those guilty of the brutal suppressions of labor demonstrations and killing laborer Hashimoto.

J. Comment by General MacArthur on Derevyanko's Letter*

June 13, 1949

The Soviet letter, replete with inaccuracies and misrepresentations of fact, could be disregarded as routine Soviet propaganda did it not so completely unmask the Soviet role as an incitor of disorder and violence in an otherwise orderly Japanese society. The thorough duplicity of its apparent championship of fundamental human rights on the one hand and the Soviet callous indifference to the release for repatriation of Japanese prisoners of war on the other—its talk of greater liberality for Japanese workers and the Soviet practice of labor exploitation, is a shocking demonstration of inconsistent demagoguery.

The purpose of the letter is obviously twofold: To incite irresponsible and unruly minority elements in Japan to violent and disorderly resistance against the duly constituted government of Japan and the lawful orders and processes

Ibid., pp. 183-84.

thereof with a view to creating confusion, unrest and bewilderment in the ranks of the law-abiding Japanese masses, and to screen the Soviet unconscionable failure to abide by the requirements of International Law and specific Potsdam commitments in the return of over 400,000 Japanese citizens, long held in bondage, to their homeland.

This failure to meet international commitments and maintain normal standards of human decency in the disposition of captives finds little parallel in the history of modern civilization, and is calculated so to outrage normal sensibilities that even the Japanese Communists have been moved to register a bitter and indignant protest.

The burdened effort at this late date to challenge the number long publicly recorded as held in Soviet hands by charging mathematical error is small solace indeed to the hundreds of thousands of Japanese homes from whom no sophistry can conceal the fact that a family member in Soviet custody has failed to return; and as to whom, contrary to all international covenants respecting prisoners of war, no word whatsoever has been received during the long period of captivity.

For the Soviet to speak in derogation of the status of labor in Japan is hypocrisy compounded. This premise is based upon such fantastic exaggerations as to obviously to belie the truth. The Japanese labor laws match the most progressive in their liberality and advanced concept, and the labor movement here, despite its immaturity, has advanced more rapidly and with less friction than has its counterpart in many of the democratic countries of the world.

Incidents of violence have been rare indeed and no segment of Japanese society has made such democratic gains as labor which enjoys rights and liberties and safeguards largely unknown to the peoples of the Soviet Union, which following the totalitarian concept, holds under ruthless suppression individual liberty and personal dignity.

For the Soviet to speak of "democratic rights," "the suppression of legal activities," "arbitrariness and chastisement," is enough to challenge the late lamented Ripley at his imagination's best and leads one to conclude that now there must really be nothing new under the sun.

THE JAPANESE PEACE TREATY

K. United States Memorandum*

November 24, 1950

There is given below a brief general statement of the type of Treaty envisioned by the United States government proper to end the state of war with Japan. It is stressed that this statement is only suggestive and tentative and does not commit the United States Government to the detailed content or wording of any future draft. It is expected that after there has been an opportunity to

*Department of State Press Release, 1180, Nov. 24, 1950.

study this outline there will be a series of informal discussions designed to elaborate on it and make clear any points which may be obscure at first glance.

The United States proposes a treaty with Japan which would end the state of war, restore Japanese sovereignty and bring back Japan as an equal in the society of free peoples. As regards specific matters, the treaty would reflect the principles indicated below:

1. *Parties:* Any or all nations at war with Japan which are willing to make peace on the basis proposed and as may be agreed.

2. *United Nations:* Membership by Japan would be contemplated.

3. *Territory:* Japan would (a) recognize the independence of Korea; (b) agree to U.N. trusteeship, with the U.S. as administering authority, of the Ryukyu and Bonin Islands and (c) accept the future decision of the U.K., U.S.S.R., China and U.S. with reference to the status of Formosa, Pescadores, South Sakhalin and the Kuriles. In the event of no decision within a year after the Treaty came into effect, the U.N. General Assembly would decide, special rights and interests in China would be renounced.

4. *Security:* The Treaty would contemplate that, pending satisfactory alternative security arrangements such as U.N. assumption of effective responsibility, there would be continuing cooperative responsibility between Japanese facilities and U.S. and perhaps other forces for the maintenance of international peace and security in the Japan area.

5. *Political and Commercial Arrangements:* Japan would agree to adhere to multilateral treaties dealing with narcotics and fishing. Prewar bilateral treaties could be revived by mutual agreement. Pending the conclusion of new commercial treaties, Japan would extend most-favored nation treatment, subject to normal exceptions.

6. *Claims:* All parties would waive claims arising out of war acts prior to September 2, 1945, except that (a) the Allied Powers would, in general, hold Japanese property within their territory and (b) Japan would restore allied property or, if not restorable intact, provide yen to compensate for an agreed percentage of lost value.

7. *Disputes:* Claims disputes would be settled by a special neutral tribunal to be set up by the President of the International Court of Justice. Other disputes would be referred either to diplomatic settlement, or to the International Court of Justice.

L. Note From the Soviet Union to the United States*

November 20, 1950

On October 26 of this year, during his conversation with J.A. Malik, Mr. Dulles presented a memorandum on the question of the peace treaty with Japan, containing a brief general statement of the type of treaty which, in the opinion of the United States Government, would be suitable for ending the state of

---

Ibid.

war with Japan. In this connection the Soviet Government would like to obtain an explanation on several points of this memorandum.

1. It is a known fact that the United States of America, Great Britain, China, the U.S.S.R. and a number of other states, signatories of the Delcaration by United Nations in Washington on January 1, 1942, obligated themselves not to conclude a separate peace with the enemy states.

In as much as the above obligation exists, an explanation is desired as to whether a peace treaty with Japan is contemplated in which are meant to participate the U.S.A., Great Britain, China and the U.S.S.R., in whose name the surrender terms for Japan were signed, as well as any other country which took an active part in the war against Japan, or whether the possibility exists of concluding a separate peace with Japan with only a few of the above-mentioned powers participating.

2. By the Cairo Declaration of December 1, 1943, signed by the U.S.A., Great Britain and China, and the Potsdam Agreement of July 26, 1945, signed by these same countries, joined by the Soviet Union, the question of returning Formosa and the Pescadores to China was decided. In a similar manner the Yalta Agreement of February 11, 1945, signed by the U.S.A., Great Britain and the U.S.S.R., decided the question of returning the southern part of Sakhalin Island and the adjacent islands to the Soviet Union and handing over to her the Kurile Islands.

In as much as the above agreements exist, how should the proposal contained in the memorandum be interpreted which would make the status of Formosa, the Pescadores, Southern Sakhalin and the Kurile Islands subject to a new decision by the U.S.A., Great Britain, China and the U.S.S.R., and in case the states mentioned fail to reach an agreement in the course of a year, to a decision of the General Assembly of the United Nations.

3. Neither the Cairo Declaration nor the Potsdam Agreement mention that the Ryukyu and Bonin Islands should be taken out from under Japanese sovereignty; moreover, in signing those agreements the states announced that they "had no thoughts of territorial expansion."

In this connection the question arises as to what is the basis for the proposal contained in the memorandum to the effect that the Ryukyu and Bonin Islands should be placed under the trusteeship of the United Nations with the United States as the administrative power.

4. It is well known that the Japanese people display deep interest in whether the occupation forces would remain in Japan after the conclusion of the peace treaty, all the more so because in the Potsdam Declaration (paragraph 12) it was provided that the occupation troops would be withdrawn from Japan.

In connection with this, the Soviet Government desires to know whether it is contemplated that in the peace treaty with Japan a definite period of time must be provided for the withdrawal of the occupation forces from Japan's territory as provided in peace treaties already concluded with other states.

5. The decision of June 19, 1947, agreed upon between the states which are members of the Far Eastern Commission, adopted on the initiative of the United States of America, provides that Japan will not possess an army, a navy,

or an air force. However, in the memorandum which sets forth the position of the United States with respect to security in the region of Japan, there is mentioned "the joint responsibility of Japanese organs and of American, and possibly other troops, for the maintenance of international peace and security in the region of Japan."

In as much as in the memorandum is mentioned the above-indicated "joint responsibility" for the maintenance of international peace and security in the region of Japan, the Soviet Government desires to receive explanations on the following two questions:

Firstly, whether it is proposed in connection with the above-mentioned "joint responsibility," to create Japanese armed forces, that is, a Japanese army, a Japanese navy and a Japanese air force, as well as the corresponding Japanese staffs.

Secondly, whether the above-mentioned "joint responsibility" means that even after the conclusion of a peace treaty with Japan, American military, naval and air force bases will be maintained on the territory of Japan.

6. Nothing is said in the memorandum concerning the necessity of ensuring for the Japanese people an opportunity to develop freely its peacetime economy.

The Soviet Government desires to receive an explanation whether it is intended to include in the peace treaty provisions for the annulment of all limitations on the development of Japanese peacetime economy and for granting Japan access to the sources of raw materials, and also for Japan's participation in world trade with equal rights.

In as much as it is perfectly evident that in the matter of the peace treaty with Japan, China has a special interest, because China in particular was subjected for many years to aggression on the part of Japanese militarists, the Soviet Government desires to know what is being done to determine the point of view of the Government of the Chinese People's Republic on this matter.

It stands to reason that later it may be necessary to obtain explanations on other questions which may possibly arise, particularly after the position of other states with regard to the memorandum of the United States becomes known.

M. Note From the United States to the Soviet Union*

December 28, 1950

On November 20 of this year Mr. Malik presented to Mr. Dulles an aide-memoire expressing the desire of the Soviet Government for clarification of a number of points in a tentative United States statement of principles respecting a Japanese peace treaty given Mr. Malik by Mr. Dulles on October 26. After careful study of the Soviet aide-memoire of November 20, the United States Government has concluded that most of the questions raised by the Soviet Government have in fact been answered by the statement of principles given to Mr. Malik on October 26. However, in order to dispel any possible misunder-

*Ibid., 1267, Dec. 28, 1950.

standing, the points raised by the Soviet Government are further discussed as follows:

1. The United States Government hopes that all nations at war with Japan will participate in the conclusion of peace. The United States does not, however, concede that any one nation has a perpetual power to veto the conclusion by others of peace with Japan. The wartime declaration of January 1, 1942, referred to by the Soviet Union, was designed to assure that all nations at war with Japan, or with the other Axis powers or their associates, would continue to fight until victory had been won. That they did. The United States does not accept the thesis, often put forward by the Soviet Union, that there cannot be peace except on terms that one power dictates. Japan, after its defeat, has now for over five years loyally complied with the agreed terms of surrender and is entitled to peace. The United States should be glad to know whether it is the view of the Soviet Union that there can never be any peace with Japan unless terms can be found which are fully satisfactory to each one of the 47 nations which signed or adhered to the Declaration of January 1, 1942.

2. The Cairo Declaration of 1943 stated the purpose to restore 'Manchuria, Formosa and the Pescadores to the Republic of China.' That Declaration, like other wartime declarations such as those of Yalta and Potsdam, was in the opinion of the United States Government subject to any final peace settlement where all relevant factors should be considered. The United States cannot accept the view, apparently put forward by the Soviet Government, that the views of other Allies not represented at Cairo must be wholly ignored. Also the United States believes that declarations such as that issued at Cairo must necessarily be considered in the light of the United Nations Charter, the obligations of which prevail over any other international agreement.

3. The United States Government does not understand the reference by the Soviet Union to "territorial expansion" in connection with the suggestion that the Ryukyu and Bonin Islands might be placed under the United Nations trusteeship system, with United States as administering authority. Article 77 of the United Nations Charter expressly contemplated the extension of the trusteeship system to "territories which may be detached from enemy states as a result of the Second World War" and certainly the trusteeship system is not to be equated with "territorial expansion."

The Government of the United States also does not understand the suggestion of the Soviet Union that because the Ryukyu and Bonin Islands are not mentioned in either the Cairo Declaratin or the Potsdam Agreement, their consideration in the peace settlement is automatically excluded. The Government of the Soviet Union seems to have ignored the fact that the Potsdam Declaration provided that Japanese sovereignty should be limited to the four main islands, which were named, and "such minor islands as we determine." It is, therefore, strictly in accordance with the Potsdam Agreement that the peace settlement should determine the future status of these other islands.

4. It is the view of the United States Government that, upon conclusion of a peace settlement, the military occupation of Japan would cease. The fact that a "new order of peace, security, and justice," as envisaged in the Potsdam De-

claration, has not been established, and that irresponsible militarism has not been driven from the world, would at the same time make it reasonable for Japan to participate with the United States and other nations in arrangmenents for individual and collective self-defense, such as are envisaged by the United Nations Charter and particularly article 51 thereof. These arrangements could include provision for the stationing in Japan of troops of the United States and other nations.

Whereas Japan for its part declares its intention to apply for membership in the United Nations and in all circumstances to conform to the principles of the Charter of the United Nations; to strive to realize the objectives of the Universal Declaration of Human Rights; to seek to create within Japan conditions of stability and well-being as defined in Articles 55 and 56 of the Charter of the United Nations and already initiated by post-surrender Japanese legislation; and in public and private trade and commerce to conform to internationally accepted fair practices;

Whereas the Allied Powers welcome the intentions of Japan set out in the foregoing paragraph;

The Allied Powers and Japan have therefore determined to conclude the present Treaty of Peace, and have accordingly appointed the undersigned Plenipotentiaries, who, after presentation of their full powers, found in good and due form, have agreed on the following provisions:

CHAPTER I

PEACE

Article I

1. The state of war between Japan and each of the Allied Powers is terminated as from the date on which the present Treaty comes into force between Japan and the Allied Power concerned as provided for in Article 23.

2. The Allied Powers recognize the full sovereignty of the Japanese people over Japan and its territorial waters.

CHAPTER II

TERRITORY

Article 2

1. Japan, recognizing the independence of Korea, renounces all right, title and claim to Korea, including the islands of Quelpart, Port Hamilton and Dagelet.

2. Japan renounces all right, title and claim to Formosa and the Pescadores.

3. Japan renounces all right, title and claim to the Kurile Islands, and to that portion of Sakhalin and the islands adjacent to it over which Japan acquired

sovereignty as a consequence of the Treaty of Portsmouth of September 5, 1905.

4. Japan renounces all right, title and claim in connection with the League of Nations Mandate System, and accepts the action of the United Nations Security Council of April 2, 1947, extending the trusteeship system to the Pacific Islands formerly under mandate to Japan.

5. Japan renounces all claim to any right or title to or interest in connection with any part of the Antarctic area, whether deriving from the activities of Japanese nationals or otherwise.

6. Japan renounces all right, title and claim to the Spratly Islands and to the Paracel Islands.

Article 3

Japan will concur in any proposal of the United States to the United Nations to place under its trusteeship system, with the United States as the sole administering authority, Nansei Shoto south of 29° north latitude (including the Ryukyu Islands and the Daito Islands), Nanpo Shoto south of Sofu Gan (including the Bonin Islands, Rosario Island and the Volcano Islands) and Parece Vela and Marcus Island. Pending the making of such a proposal and affirmative action thereon, the United States will have the right to exercise all and any powers of administration, legislation and jurisdiction over the territory and inhabitants of these islands, including their territorial waters.

Article 4

1. Subject to the provisions of paragraph 2 of this Article, the disposition of property of Japan and of its nationals in the areas referred to in Article 2, and their claims, including debts, against the authorities presently administering such areas and the residents (including juridical persons) thereof, and the disposition in Japan of property of such authorities and residents, and of claims, including debts, of such authorities and residents against Japan and its nationals, shall be the subject of special arrangements between Japan and such authorities. The property of any of the Allied Powers or its nationals in the areas referred to in Article 2 shall, insofar as this has not already been done, be returned by the administering authority in the condition in which it now exists. (The term nationals whenever used in the present Treaty includes juridical persons.)

2. Japan recognizes the validity of dispositions of property of Japan and Japanese nationals made by or pursuant to directives of the United States Military Government in any of the areas referred to in Articles 2 and 3.

3. Japanese owned submarine cables connecting Japan with territory removed from Japanese control pursuant to the present Treaty shall be equally divided, Japan retaining the Japanese terminal and adjoining half of the cable, and the detached territory the remainder of the cable and connecting terminal facilities.

CHAPTER III
SECURITY

Article 5

1. Japan accepts the obligations set forth in Article 2 of the Charter of the United Nations, and in particular the obligations

(a) to settle its international disputes by peaceful means in such a manner that international peace and security, and justice, are not endangered;
(b) to refrain in its international relations from the threat or use of force against the territorial integrity or political independence of any State or in any other manner inconsistent with the Purposes of the United Nations;
(c) to give the United Nations every assistance in any action it takes in accordance with the Charter and to refrain from giving assistance to any States against which the United Nations may take preventive or enforcement action.

2. The Allied Powers confirm that they will be guided by the principles of Article 2 of the Charter of the United Nations in their relations with Japan.

3. The Allied Powers for their part recognize that Japan as a sovereign nation possesses the inherent right of individual or collective self-defense referred to in Article 51 of the Charter of the United Nations and that Japan may voluntarily enter into collective security arrangements.

Article 6

1. All occupation forces of the Allied Powers shall be withdrawn from Japan as soon as possible after the coming into force of the present Treaty, and in any case not later than 90 days thereafter. Nothing in this provision shall, however, prevent the stationing or retention of foreign armed forces in Japanese territory under or in consequence of any bilateral or multilateral agreements which have been or may be made between one or more of the Allied Powers, on the one hand, and Japan on the other.

2. The provisions of Article 9 of the Potsdam Proclamation of July 26, 1945, dealing with the return of Japanese military forces to their homes, to the extent not already completed, will be carried out.

3. All Japanese property for which compensation has not already been paid, which was supplied for the use of the occupation forces and which remains in the possession of those forces at the time of the coming into force of the present Treaty, shall be returned to the Japanese Government within the same 90 days unless other arrangements are made by mutual agreement.

CHAPTER IV
POLITICAL AND ECONOMIC CLAUSES

Article 7

1. Each of the Allied Powers, within one year after the present Treaty has come into force between it and Japan, will notify Japan which of its prewar bilateral treaties or conventions with Japan it wishes to continue in force or revive, and any treaties or conventions so notified shall continue in force or be revived subject to such amendments as may be necessary to ensure conformity with the present Treaty. The treaties and conventions so notified shall be considered as having been continued in force or revived three months after the date of notification and shall be registered with the Secretariat of the United Nations. All such treaties and conventions as to which Japan is not so notified shall be regarded as abrogated.

2. Any notification made under paragraph 1. of this Article may except from the operation or revival of a treaty or convention any territory for the international relations of which the notifying Power is responsible, until three months after the date on which notice is given to Japan that such exception shall cease to apply.

Article 8

1. Japan will recognize the full force of all treaties now or hereafter concluded by the Allied Powers for terminating the state of war initiated on September 1, 1939, as well as any other arrangements by the Allied Powers for or in connection with the restoration of peace. Japan also accepts the arrangements made for terminating the former League of Nations and Permanent Court of International Justice.

2. Japan renounces all such rights and interests as it may derive from being a signatory power of the Conventions of St. Germain-en-Laye of September 10, 1919, and the Straits Agreement of Montreux of July 20, 1936, and from Article 16 of the Treaty of Peace with Turkey signed at Lausanne on July 24, 1923.

3. Japan renounces all rights, title and interests acquired under, and is discharged from all obligations resulting from, the Agreement between Germany and the Creditor Powers of January 20, 1930, and its Annexes, including the Trust Agreement, dated May 17, 1930; the Convention of January 20, 1930, respecting the Bank for International Settlements; and the Statutes of the Bank for International Settlements. Japan will notify to the Ministry of Foreign Affairs in Paris within six months of the first coming into force of the present Treaty its renunciation of the rights, title and interests referred to in this paagraph.

Article 9

Japan will enter promptly into negotiations with the Allied Powers so desiring for the conclusion of bilateral and multilateral agreements providing for the regulation or limitation of fishing and the conservation and development of fisheries on the high seas.

Article 10

Japan renounces all special rights and interests in China, including all benefits and privileges resulting from the provisions of the final Protocol signed at Peking on September 7, 1901, and all annexes, notes and documents supplementary thereto, and agrees to the abrogation in respect to Japan of the said protocol, annexes, notes and documents.

Article 11

Japan accepts the judgments of the International Military Tribunal for the Far East and of other Allied War Crimes Courts both within and outside Japan, and will carry out the sentences imposed thereby upon Japanese nationals imprisoned in Japan. The power to grant clemency to reduce sentences and to parole with respect to such prisoners may not be exercised except on the decision of the Government or Governments which imposed the sentence in each instance, and on the recommendation of Japan. In the case of persons sentenced by the International Military Tribunal for the Far East, such power may not be exercised except on the decision of a majority of the Governments represented on the Tribunal, and on the recommedation of Japan.

Article 12

1. Japan declares its readiness promptly to enter into negotiations for the conclusion with each of the Allied Powers of treaties or agreements to place their trading, maritime and their commercial relations on a stable and friendly basis.

2. Pending the conclusion of the relevant treaty or agreement, Japan will, during a period of four years from the the first coming into force of the present Treaty

    (a) accord to each of the Allied Powers, its nationals, products and vessels.

        (1) most-favored-nation treatment with respect to customs duties, charges, restrictions and other regulations on or in connection with the importation and exploration of goods;

        (2) national treatment with respect to shipping, navigation and imported goods, and with respect to natural and juridical persons and their interests—such treatment to include all matters pertaining to the levying and collection of taxes,

access to the courts, the making and performance of contracts, rights to property (tangible and intangible), participation in juridical entities constituted under Japanese law, and generally the conduct of all kinds of business and professional activities;

(b) ensure that external purchases and sales of Japanese state trading enterprises shall be based solely on commercial considerations.

3. In respect to any matter, however, Japan shall be obliged to accord to an Allied Power national treatment, or most-favored-nation treatment, only to the extent that the Allied Power concerned accords Japan national treatment or most-favored-nation treatment, as the case may be, in respect of the same matter. The reciprocity envisaged in the foregoing sentence shall be determined, in the case of products, vessels and juridical entities of, and persons domiciled in, any non-metropolitan territory of an Allied Power, and in the case of juridical entities of, and persons domiciled in, any state or province of an Allied Power having a federal government, by reference to the treatment accorded to Japan in such territory, state or province.

4. In the application of this Article, a discriminatory measure shall not be considered to derogate from the grant of national or most-favored-nation treatment, as the case may be, if such measure is based on an exception customarily provided for in the commercial treaties of the party applying it, or on the need to safeguard that party's external financial position or balance of payments (except in respect to shipping and navigation), or on the need to maintain its essential security interests, and provided such measure is proportionate to the circumstances and not applied in an arbitrary or unreasonable manner.

5. Japan's obligations under this Article shall not be affected by the exercise of any Allied rights under Article 14 of the present Treaty; nor shall the provisions of this Article be understood as limiting the undertakings assumed by Japan by virtue of Article 15 of the Treaty.

Article 13

1. Japan will enter into negotiations with any of the Allied Powers, promptly upon the request of such Power or Powers, for the conclusion of bilateral or multilateral agreements relating to international civil air transport.

2. Pending the conclusion of such agreement or agreements, Japan will, during a period of four years from the first coming into force of the present Treaty, extend to such Power treatment not less favorable with respect to air-traffic rights and privileges than those exercised by any such Powers at the date of such coming into force, and will accord complete equality of opportunity in respect to the operation and development of air services.

3. Pending its becoming a party to the Convention on International Civil Aviation in accordance with Article 93 thereof, Japan will give effect to the provisions of that Convention applicable to the international navigation of aircraft, and will give effect to the standards, practices and procedures adopted as annexes to the Convention in accordance with the terms of the Convention.

CHAPTER V

CLAIMS AND PROPERTY

Article 14

It is recognized that Japan should pay reparations to the Allied Powers for the damage and suffering caused by it during the war. Nevertheless it is also recognized that the resources of Japan are not presently sufficient, if it is to maintain a viable economy, to make complete reparation for all such damage and suffering and at the same time meet its other obligations.

Therefore,

1. Japan will promptly enter into negotiations with Allied Powers so desiring, whose present territories were occupied by Japanese forces and damaged by Japan, with a view to assisting to compensate those countries for the cost of repairing the damage done, by making available the services of the Japanese people in production, salvaging and other work for the Allied Powers in question. Such arrangments shall avoid the imposition of additional liabilities on other Allied Powers, and, where the manufacturing of raw materials is called for, they shall be supplied by the Allied Powers in question, so as not to throw any foreign exchange burden upon Japan.

2. (I) Subject to the provisions of sub-paragraph (II) below, each of the Allied Powers shall have the right to seize, retain, liquidate or otherwise dispose of all property, rights and interests of

    (a) Japan and Japanese nationals,
    (b) persons acting for or on behalf of Japan or Japanese nationals, and
    (c) entities owned or controlled by Japan or Japanese nationals,

which on the first coming into force of the present Treaty were subject to its jurisdiction. The property, rights and interests specified in this sub-paragraph shall include those now blocked, vested or in the possession or under the control of enemy property authorities of Allied Powers, which belonged to, or were held or managed on behalf of, any of the persons or entities mentioned in (a), (b) or (c) above at the time such assets came under the controls of such authorities.

(II) The following shall be excepted from the right specified in sub-paragraph (I) above:

    (1) property of Japanese natural persons who during the war resided with the permission of the Government concerned in the territory of one of the Allied Powers, other than territory occupied by Japan, except property subjected to restrictions during the war and not released from such restrictions as of the date of the first coming into force of the present Treaty;

    (2) all real property, furniture and fixtures owned by the Government of Japan and used for diplomatic or consular purposes, and all personal furniture and furnishings and other private property not of an investment nature which was normally necessary for the carrying out of diplomatic and consular functions, owned by Japanese diplomatic and consular personnel;

(3) property belonging to religious bodies or private charitable institutions and used exclusively for religious or charitable purposes;

(4) property, rights and interests which have come within its jurisdiction in consequence of the resumption of trade and financial relations subsequent to September 2, 1945, between the country concerned and Japan, except such as have resulted from transactions contrary to the laws of the Allied Power concerned;

(5) obligations of Japan or Japanese nationals, any right, title or interest in tangible property located in Japan, interests in enterprises organized under the laws of Japan, or any paper evidence thereof; provided that this exception shall only apply to obligations of Japan and its nationals expressed in Japanese currency.

(III) Property referred to in exceptions (1) through (5) above shall be returned subject to reasonable expenses for its preservation and administration. If any such property has been liquidated the proceeds shall be returned instead.

(IV) The right to seize, retain, liquidate or otherwise dispose of property as provided in sub-paragraph (I) aobve shall be exercised in accordance with the laws of the Allied Power concerned, and the owner shall have only such rights as may be given him by those laws.

(V) The Allied Powers agree to deal with Japanese trademarks and literary and artistic property rights on a basis as favorable to Japan as circumstances ruling in each country will permit.

Except as otherwise provided in the present Treaty, the Allied Powers waive all reparations claims of the Allied Powers, other claims of the Allied Powers and their nationals arising out of any actions taken by Japan and its nationals in the course of the prosecution of the war, and claims of the Allied Powers for direct military costs of occupation.

Article 15

1. Upon application made within nine months of the coming into force of the present Treaty between Japan and the Allied Power concerned, Japan will, within six months of the date of such application, return the property, tangible and intangible, and all rights or interests of any kind in Japan of each Allied Power and its nationals which was within Japan at any time between December 7, 1941, and September 2, 1945, unless the owner has freely disposed thereof without duress or fraud. Such property shall be returned free of all encumbrances and charges to which it may have become subject because of the war, and without any charges for its return. Property whose return is not applied for by or on behalf of the owner or by his Government within the prescribed period may be disposed of by the Japanese Government as it may determine. In cases where such property was within Japan on December 7, 1941, and cannot be returned or has suffered injury or damage as a result of the war, compensation will be made on terms not less favorable than the terms provided in the draft Allied Powers Property Compensation Law approved by the Japanese Cabinet on July 13, 1951.

2. With respect to industrial property rights impaired during the war, Japan will continue to accord to the Allied Powers and their nationals benefits no

less than those heretofore accorded by Cabinet Orders No. 309 effective September 1, 1949, No. 12 effective January 28, 1950, and No. 9 effective February 1, 1950, all as now amended, provided such nationals have applied for such benefits within the time limits prescribed therein.

3. Japan acknowledges that the literary and artistic property rights which existed in Japan on December 6, 1941, in respect to the published and unpublished works of the Allied Powers and their nationals have continued in force since that date, and recognizes those rights which have arisen, or but for the war would have arisen, in Japan since that date, by the operation of any conventions and agreements to which Japan was a party on that date, irrespective of whether or not such conventions or agreements were abrogated or suspended upon or since the outbreak of war by the domestic law of Japan or of the Allied Power concerned.

Without the need for application by the proprietor of the right and without the payment of any fee or compliance with any other formality, the period from December 7, 1941, until the coming into force of the present Treaty between Japan and the Allied Power concerned shall be excluded from the running of the normal term of such rights; and such period, with an additional period of six months, shall be excluded from the time within which a literary work must be translated into Japanese in order to obtain translating rights in Japan.

Article 16

As an expression of its desire to indemnify those members of the armed forces of the Allied Powers who suffered undue hardships while prisoners of war of Japan, Japan will transfer its assets and those of its nationals in countries which were neutral during the war, or which were at war with any of the Allied Powers, or, as its option, the equivalent of such assets to the International Committee of the Red Cross which shall liquidate such assets and distribute the resultant fund to appropriate national agencies, for the benefit of former prisoners of war and their families on such basis as it may determine to be equitable. The categories of assets described in Article 14, 2(II) (2) through (5) of the present Treaty shall be excepted from transfer, as well as assets of Japanese natural persons not residents of Japan on the first coming into force of the Treaty. It is equally understood that the transfer provision of this Article has no application to the 19,770 shares in the Bank for International Settlements presently owned by Japanese financial institutions.

Article 17

1. Upon the request of any of the Allied Powers, the Japanese Government shall review and revise in conformity with international law any decision or order of the Japanese Prize Courts in cases involving ownership rights of nationals of that Allied Power and shall supply copies of all documents comprising

the records of these cases, including the decisions taken and orders issued. In any case in which such review or revision shows that restoration is due, the provisions of Article 15 shall apply to the property concerned.

2. The Japanese Government shall take the necessary measures to enable nationals of any of the Allied Powers at any time within one year from the coming into force of the present Treaty between Japan and the Allied Power concerned to submit to the appropriate Japanese authorities for review any judgment given by a Japanese court between December 7, 1941, and such coming into force, in any proceedings in which any such national was unable to make adequate presentation of his case either as plaintiff or defendant. The Japanese Government shall provide that, where the national has suffered injury by reason of any such judgment, he shall be restored in the position in which he was before the judgment was given or shall be afforded such relief as may be just and equitable in the circumstances.

Article 18

1. It is recognized that the intervention of the state of war has not affected the obligation to pay pecuniary debts arising out of obligations and contracts (including those in respect of bonds) which existed and rights which were acquired before the existence of a state of war, and which are due by the Government or nationals of Japan to the Government or nationals of one of the Allied Powers, or are due by the Government or nationals of one of the Allied Powers to the Government or nationals of Japan. The intervention of a state of war shall equally not be regarded as affecting the obligation to consider on their merits claims for loss or damage to property or for personal injury or death' which arose before the existence of a state of war, and which may be presented or re-presented by the Government of one of the Allied Powers to the Government of Japan, or by the Government of Japan to any of the Governments of the Allied Powers. The provisions of this paragraph are without prejudice to the rights conferred by Article 14.

2. Japan affirms its liability for the prewar external debt of the Japanese State and for debts of corporate bodies subsequently declared to be liabilities of the Japanese State, and expresses its intention to enter into negotiations at an early date with its creditors with respect to the resumption of payments on those debts; to encourage negotiations in respect to other prewar claims and obligations; and to facilitate the transfer of sums accordingly.

Article 19

1. Japan waives all claims of Japan and its nationals against the Allied Powers and their nationals arising out of the war or out of actions taken because of the existence of a state of war, and waives all claims arising from the presence, operations or actions of forces or authorities of any of the Allied Powers in

Japanese territory prior to the coming into force of the present Treaty.

2. The foregoing waiver includes any claims arising out of actions taken by any of the Allied Powers with respect to Japanese ships between September 1, 1939, and the coming into force of the present Treaty, as well as any claims and debts arising in respect to Japanese prisoners of war and civilian internees in the hands of the Allied Powers, but does not include Japanese claims specifically recognized in the laws of any Allied Power enacted since September 2, 1945.

3. Subject to reciprocal renunciation, the Japanese Government also renounces all claims (including debts) against Germany and German nationals on behalf of the Japanese Government and Japanese nationals, including intergovernmental claims and claims for loss or damage sustained during the war, but excepting (a) claims in respect of contracts entered into and rights acquired before September 1, 1939, and (b) claims arising out of trade and financial relations between Japan and Germany after September 2, 1945. Such renunciation shall not prejudice actions taken in accordance with Articles 16 and 20 of the present Treaty.

4. Japan recognizes the validity of all acts and omissions done during the period of occupation under or in consequence of directives of the occupation authorities or authorized by Japanese law at that time, and will take no action subjecting Allied nationals to civil or criminal liability arising out of such acts or omissions.

Article 20

Japan will take all necessary measures to ensure such disposition of German assets in Japan as has been or may be determined by those powers entitled under the Protocol of the proceedings of the Berlin Conference of 1945 to dispose of those assets, and pending the final disposition of such assets will be responsible for the conservation and administration thereof.

Article 21

Notwithstanding the provisions of Article 25 of the present Treaty, China shall be entitled to the benefits of Articles 10 and 14, 2; and Korea to the benefits of Articles 2, 4, 9 and 12 of the present Treaty.

CHAPTER VI
SETTLEMENT OF DISPUTES

Article 22

If in the opinion of any Party to the present Treaty there has arisen a dispute concerning the interpretation or execution of the Treaty, which is not settled by reference to a special claims tribunal or by other agreed means, the dispute shall, at the request of any party thereto, be referred for decision to the International Court of Justice. Japan and those Allied Powers which are not already parties to the Statute of the International Court of Justice will deposit with the Registrar of the Court, at the time of their respective ratifications of the present Treaty, and in conformity with the resolution of the United Nations Security Council, dated October 15, 1946, a general declaration accepting the jurisdiction, without special agreement, of the Court generally in respect to all disputes of the character referred to in this Article.

CHAPTER VII

FINAL CLAUSES

Article 23

1. The present Treaty shall be ratified by the States which sign it, including Japan, and will come into force for all the States which have then ratified it, when instruments of ratification have been deposited by Japan and by a majority, including the United States of America as the principal occupying Power, of the following States, namely Australia, Canada, Ceylon, France, Indonesia, the Kingdom of the Netherlands, New Zealand, Pakistan, the Republic of the Philippines, the United Kingdom of Great Britain and Northern Ireland, and the United States of America. The present Treaty shall come into force for each State which subsequently ratifies it, on the date of deposit of its instrument of ratification.
2. If the Treaty has not come into force within nine months after the date of the deposit of Japan's ratification, any State which has ratified it may bring the Treaty into force between itself and Japan by a notification to that effect given to the Governments of Japan and the United States of America not later than three years after the date of deposit of Japan's ratification.

Article 24

All instruments of ratification shall be deposited with the Government of the United States of America which will notify all the signatory States of each such deposit, of the date of the coming into force of the Treaty under paragraph 1. of Article 23, and of any notifications made under paragraph 2. of Article 23.

Article 25

For the purposes of the present Treaty the Allied Powers shall be the States at war with Japan, or any State which previously formed a part of the territory of a State named in Article 23, provided that in each case the State concerned has signed and ratified the Treaty. Subject to the provisions of Article 21, the present Treaty shall not confer any rights, titles or benefits on any State which is not an Allied Power as herein defined; nor shall any right, title or interest of Japan be deemed to be diminished or prejudiced by any provision of the Treaty in favor of a State which is not an Allied Power as so defined.

Article 26

Japan will be prepared to conclude with any State which signed or adhered to the United Nations Declaration of January 1, 1942, and which is at war with Japan, or with any State which previously formed a part of the territory of a State named in Article 23, which is not a signatory of the present Treaty, a bilateral Treaty of Peace on the same or substantially the same terms as are provided for in the present Treaty, but this obligation on the part of Japan will expire three years after the first coming into force of the present Treaty. Should Japan make a peace settlement or war claims settlement with any State granting that State greater advantages than those provided by the present Treaty, those same advantages shall be extended to the parties to the present Treaty.

Article 27

The present Treaty shall be deposited in the archives of the Government of the United States of America which shall furnish each signatory State with a certified copy thereof.

UNITED STATES AGREEMENT WITH SOVEREIGN JAPAN

A. United States-Japanese Security Treaty*

Signed, September 8, 1951
Effective, April 28, 1952

Japan has this day signed a Treaty of Peace with the Allied Powers. On the coming into force of that Treaty, Japan will not have the effective means to exercise its inherent right of self-defense because it has been disarmed.

There is danger to Japan in this situation because irresponsible militarism has not yet been driven from the world. Therefore Japan desires a Security Treaty with the United States of America to come into force simultaneously with the Treaty of Peace between the United States of America and Japan.

The Treaty of Peace recognizes that Japan as a sovereign nation has the right to enter into collective security arrangements, and further, the Charter of the United Nations recognizes that all nations possess an inherent right of individual and collective self-defense.

In exercise of these rights, Japan desires, as a provisional arrangement for its defense, that the United States of America should maintain armed forces of its own in and about Japan so as to deter attack upon Japan.

The United States of America in the interest of peace and security, is presently willing to maintain certain of its armed forces in and about Japan, in the expectation, however, that Japan will itself increasingly assume responsibility for its own defense against direct and indirect aggression, always avoiding any armament which could be an offensive threat or serve other than to promote peace and security in accordance with the purposes and principles of the United Nations Charter.

Accordingly, the two countries have agreed as follows:

Article I

Japan grants, and the United States of America accepts, the right, upon the coming into force of the Treaty of Peace and of this Treaty, to dispose United States land, air and sea forces in and about Japan. Such forces may be utilized to contribute to the maintenance of international peace and security in the Far East and to the security of Japan against armed attack from without, including assistance given at the express request of the Japanese Government to put down large scale internal riots and disturbances in Japan, caused through instigation or intervention by an outside power or powers.

---

* *American Foreign Policy 1950-1955: Basic Documents*, Vol. I, pp. 885-86.

Article II

During the exercise of the right referred to in Article I, Japan will not grant, without the prior consent of the United States of America, any bases or any rights, powers or authority whatsoever, in or relating to bases or the right of garrison or of maneuver, or transit of ground, air or naval forces to any third power.

Article III

The conditions which shall govern the disposition of armed forces of the United States of America in and about Japan shall be determined by administrative agreements between the two Governments.

Article IV

This Treaty shall expire whenever in the opinion of the Governments of the United States of America and Japan there shall have come into force such United Nations arrangements for such alternative individual or collective security dispositions as will satisfactorily provide for the maintenance by the United Nations or otherwise of international peace and security in the Japan Area.

Article V

This Treaty shall be ratified by the United States of America and Japan and will come into force when instruments of ratification thereof have been exchanged by them at Washington.

In witness whereof the undersigned Plenipotentiaries have signed this Treaty.

Done in duplicate at the city of San Francisco, in the English and Japanese languages, this eighth day of September, 1951.

B. United States-Japanese Mutual Defense Assistance Agreement*

Tokyo, March 8, 1954

The Government of the United States of America and the Government of Japan.

Desiring to foster international peace and security, within the framework of the Charter of the United Nations, through voluntary arrangements which will further the ability of nations dedicated to the purposes and principles of the Charter to develop effective measures for individual and collective self-defense in support of those purposes and principles:

*Department of State Bulletin, Apr. 5, 1954, pp. 520-22.

Reaffirming their belief, as stated in the Treaty of Peace with Japan signed at the city of San Francisco on September 8, 1951, that Japan as a sovereign nation possesses the inherent right of individual or collective self-defense referred to in Article 51 of the Charter of the United Nations;

Recalling the preamble of the Security Treaty between the United States of America and Japan, signed at the city of San Francisco on September 8, 1951, to the effect that the United States of America, in the interest of peace and security, would maintain certain of its armed forces in and about Japan as a provisional arrangement in the expectation that Japan will itself increasingly assume responsibility for its own defense against direct and indirect aggression, always avoiding any armament which could be an offensive threat or serve other than to promote peace and security in accordance with the purposes and principles of the Charter of the United Nations;

Recognizing that, in the planning of a defense assistance program for Japan, economic stability will be an essential element for consideration in the development of its defense capacities, and that Japan can contribute only to the extent permitted by its general economic condition and capacities;

Taking into consideration the support that the Government of the United States of America has brought to these principles by enacting the Mutual Defense Assistance Act of 1949, as amended, and the Mutual Security Act of 1951, as amended, which provides for the furtherance of the objectives referred to above; and

Desiring to set forth the conditions which will govern the furnishing of such assistance;

Have agreed as follows:

Article I

1. Each Government, consistently with the principle that economic stability is essential to international peace and security, will make available to the other and to such other governments as the two Governments signatory to the present Agreement may in each case agree upon, such equipment, materials, services, or other assistance as the Government furnishing such assistance may authorize, in accordance with such detailed arrangements as may be made between them. The furnishing and use of any such assistance as may be authorized by either Government shall be consistent with the Charter of the United Nations. Such assistance as may be made available by the Government of the United States of America pursuant to the present Agreement will be furnished under those provisions, and subject to all of those terms, conditions and termination provisions of the Mutual Defense Assistance Act of 1949, the Mutual Security Act of 1951, acts amendatory and supplementary thereto, and appropriation acts thereunder which may affect the furnishing of such assistance.

2. Each Government will make effective use of assistance received pursuant to the present Agreement for the purposes of promoting peace and security in a manner that is satisfactory to both Governments, and neither Government,

without the prior consent of the other, will devote such assistance to any other purpose.

3. Each Government will offer for return to the other, in accordance with terms, conditions and procedures mutually agreed upon, equipment or materials furnished under the present Agreement, except equipment and materials furnished on terms requiring reimbursement, and no longer required for the purposes for which it was originally made available.

4. In the interest of common security, each Government undertakes not to transfer to any person not an officer or agent of such Government, or to any other government, title to or possession of any equipment, materials, or services received pursuant to the present Agreement, without the prior consent of the Government which furnished such assistance.

Article II

In conformity with the principle of mutual aid, the Government of Japan agrees to facilitate the production and transfer to the Government of the United States of America for such period of time, in such quantities and upon such terms and conditions as may be agreed upon of raw and semi-processed materials required by the United States of America as a result of deficiencies or potential deficiencies in its own resources, and which may be available in Japan. Arrangements for such transfer shall give due regard to requirements for domestic use and commercial export as determined by the Government of Japan.

Article III

1. Each Government will take such security measures as may be agreed upon between the two Governments in order to prevent the disclosure or compromise of classified articles, services or information furnished by the other Government pursuant to the present Agreement.

2. Each Government will take appropriate measures consistent with security to keep the public informed of operations under the present Agreement.

Article IV

The two Governments will, upon the request of either of them, make appropriate arrangements providing for the methods and terms of the exchange of industrial property rights and technical information for defense which will expedite such exchange and at the same time protect private interests and maintain security safeguards.

Article V

The two Governments will consult for the purpose of establishing procedures whereby the Government of Japan will so deposit, segregate, or assure title to all funds allocated to or derived from any programs of assistance undertaken by the Government of the United States of America so that such funds shall not be subject to garnishment, attachment, seizure or other legal process by any person, firm, agency, corporation, organization or government, when the Government of Japan is advised by the Government of the United States of America that any such legal process would interfere with the attainment of the objectives of the program of assistance.

Article VI

1. The Government of Japan will grant

(a) Exemption from duties and internal taxation upon importation or exportation to materials, supplies or equipment imported into or exported from its territory under the present Agreement or any similar agreement between the Government of the United States of America and the Government of any other country receiving assistance, except as otherwise agreed to; and

(b) Exemption from and refund of Japanese taxes, as enumerated in the attached Annex E, so far as they may affect expenditures of or financed by the Government of the United States of America effected in Japan for procurement of materials, supplies, equipment and services under the present Agreement or any similar agreement between the Government of the United States of America and the Government of any other country receiving assistance.

2. Exemption from duties and exemption from and refund of Japanese taxes as enumerated in the attached Annex E will apply, in addition to any other expenditures of or financed by the Government of the United States of America for materials, supplies, equipment and services for mutual defense, including expenditures made in conformity with the Security Treaty betwen the United States of America and Japan or any foreign aid program of the Government of the United States of America under the Mutual Security Act of 1951, as amended, or any acts supplementary, amendatory or successory thereto.

Article VII

1. The Government of Japan agrees to receive personnel of the Government of the United States of America who will discharge in the territory of Japan the responsibilities of the latter Government regarding equipment, materials, and services furnished under the present Agreement, and who will be accorded facilities to observe the progress of the assistance furnished by the Government of the United States of America under the present Agreement. Such personnel who are nationals of the United States of America, including personnel temporarily assigned, will, in their relationships, with the Government of Japan, operate

as part of the Embassy of the United States of America under the direction and control of the Chief of the Diplomatic Mission, and will have the same privileges and immunities as are accorded to other personnel with corresponding rank in the Embassy of the United States of America.

2. The Government of Japan will make available, from time to time, to the Government of the United States of America funds in yen for the administrative and related expenses of the latter Government in connection with carrying out the present Agreement.

Article VIII

The Government of Japan, reaffirming its determination to join in promoting international understanding and good will, and maintaining world peace, to take such action as may be mutually agreed upon to eliminate causes of international tension, and to fulfill the military obligations which the Government of Japan has assumed under the Security Treaty between the United States of America and Japan, will make, consistent with the political and economic stability of Japan, the full contribution permitted by its manpower, resources, facilities and general economic condition to the development and maintenance of its own defensive strength and the defensive strength of the free world, take all reasonable measures which may be needed to develop its defense capacities, and take appropriate steps to ensure the effective utilization of any assistance provided by the Government of the United States of America.

Article IX

1. Nothing contained in the present Agreement shall be construed to alter or otherwise modify the Security Treaty between the United States of America and Japan or any arrangements concluded thereunder.

2. The present Agreement will be implemented by each Government in accordance with the constitutional provisions of the respective countries.

Article X

1. The two Governments will, upon the request of either of them, consult regarding any matter relating to the application of the present Agreement or to operations or arrangements carried out pursuant to the present Agreement.

2. The terms of the present Agreement may be reviewed at the request of either of the two Governments or amended by agreement between them at any time.

Article XI

1. The present Agreement shall come into force on the date of receipt by the Government of the United States of America of a written notice from the Government of Japan of ratification of the Agreement by Japan.

2. The present Agreement will thereafter continue in force until one year after the date of receipt by either Government of a written notice of the intention of the other to terminate it, provided that the provisions of Article I, paragraphs 2, 3 and 4, and arrangements entered into under Article III, paragraph 1, and Article IV shall remain in force unless otherwise agreed by the two Governments.

3. The Annexes to the present Agreement shall form an integral part thereof.

4. The present Agreement shall be registered with the Secretariat of the United Nations.

In witness whereof the representatives of the two Governments, duly authorized for the purpose, have signed the present Agreement.

Done in duplicate, in the English and Japanese languages, both equally authentic, at Tokyo, this eighth day of March, one thousand nine hundred fifty-four.

For the United States of America: John M. Allison
For Japan: Katsuo Okazaki

EXCHANGE OF VIEWS ON NUCLEAR WEAPONS TEST

C. Prime Minister of Japan, Nobusuke Kishi, to President Dwight D. Eisenhower*

September 24, 1957

My dear Mr. President: I have the honour to call Your Excellency's attention to the proposal submitted by the Japanese delegation to the present session of the General Assembly on 23 September, 1957 on the question of disarmament and nuclear test explosions.

Japan as a peace-loving nation ardently desires prompt realization of a general disarmament, particularly, prohibition of the manufacture, use and test of nuclear weapons as is clearly stated in the several resolutions of the Diet, which have been duly transmitted to Your Excellency's government. My government, recognizing the urgent necessity of ending all nuclear test explosions, has repeatedly requested your government to suspend such tests. But to our profound disappointment, none of the countries concerned has so far taken the initiative to suspend nuclear test explosions. But they all go on repeating their tests, creating a vicious circle of the most regrettable kind, which does nothing to lessen distrust among nations.

Ibid., Oct. 21, 1957, p. 636.

The recent Disarmament Conference, while giving indications of partial agreement among the powers concerned, came to an impasse on account of the disagrement of views as to whether suspension of nuclear test explosions should be carried out in connection with other aspects of disarmament, or it should take place separately from them. This difference in opinion is perhaps irreconcilable, and it may be extremely difficult to resolve the present impasse. But when we consider the proposition on the one hand that disarmament negotiation be carried on while continuing with nuclear test explosions, and the proposition on the other that the negotiation be continued after having first put a stop to nuclear tests, the preferability of the latter, from the standpoint of humanity, is obvious; it is sure to be welcomed by world public opinion, I, therefore, earnestly request Your Excellency to make a thorough study of the proposal of the Japanese Delegation. Acceptance will, my government believes, pave the way for the solution of the question of disarmament and nuclear test explosions, which is eagerly wished by the Japanese people and all peoples of the world.

I avail myself of this opportunity to extend to Your Excellency the assurances of my highest consideration.

D. President Eisenhower to Prime Minister Kishi*

October 3, 1957

Dear Mr. Prime Minister: I have for a long time given serious and thoughtful consideration to the issue you raise in your communication of September twenty-fourth regarding the continuation of nuclear testing, which has been the subject of discussion between us in the past.

Unfortunately, I have been able to reach no other conclusion than that for the time being and in the present circumstances, the security of the United States, and, I believe, that of the free world, depends to a great degree upon what we learn from the testing of nuclear weapons. We are at a stage when testing is required for the development of important defensive uses of nuclear weapons, particularly against missiles, submarines, and aircraft, as well as to reduce further the fallout yield from nuclear weapons. To stop these tests in the absence of effective limitations on nuclear weapons production and other elements of armed strength and without the opening up of all principal nations to a measure of inspection as a safeguard against surprise attack in which nuclear weapons could be used is a sacrifice which would be dangerous to accept.

We are aware of the preoccupations with the question of health hazards connected with nuclear testing. We believe that these are ill founded. However, we have pledged to conduct those tests which may be necessary only in such a manner as will keep world radiation from rising to more than a small fraction of the levels which might be hazardous. Also, as you know, the General Assembly has established a scientific committee to study this problem. This committee is due to report by July 1958, and its findings will no doubt be fully debated in the United Nations.

Ibid., pp. 635-36.

We believe that nuclear tests can and should be suspended if other limitations of the type I have mentioned are agreed upon. Accordingly, the United States has joined with the Governments of the United Kingdom, France, and Canada in presenting proposals which provide for the suspension of testing in this context. Of special importance, I think, is the proposal that further production of fissionable materials for weapons purposes be stopped and a beginning be made in the reduction of existing weapons stockpiles. We believe that if this proposal is widely supported in the General Assembly, it will be accepted by the Soviet Union. In this event, we would be assured that atomic energy in the future would be devoted to peaceful purposes everywhere in the world.

E. Treaty of Mutual Cooperation and Security between the United States and Japan*

[Extract]

Signed, January 19, 1960

The United States of America and Japan,

Desiring to strengthen the bonds of peace and friendship traditionally existing between them, and to uphold the principles of democracy, individual liberty, and the rule of law,

Desiring further to encourage closer economic cooperation between them and to promote conditions of economic stability and well-being in their countries,

Reaffirming their faith in the purposes and principles of the Charter of the United Nations, and their desire to live in peace with all peoples and all governments,

Recognizing that they have the inherent right of individual or collective self-defense as affirmed in the Charter of the United Nations,

Considering that they have a common concern in the maintenance of international peace and security in the Far East,

Having resolved to conclude a treaty of mutual cooperation and security,

Therefore agree as follows:

Article I

The Parties undertake, as set forth in the Charter of the United Nations, to settle any international disputes in which they may be involved by peaceful means in such a manner that international peace and security and justice are not endangered and to refrain in their international relations from the threat or use of force against the territorial integrity or political independence of any state, or in any other manner inconsistent with the purposes of the United Nations. The Parties will endeavor in concert with other peace-loving countries to strengthen the United Nations so that its mission of maintaining international peace and security may be discharged more effectively.

*Department of State, *Treaties and Other International Acts*, Series 4509, pp. 2-4.

Article II

The Parties will contribute toward the further development of peaceful and friendly international relations by strengthening their free institutions, by bringing about a better understanding of the principles upon which these institutions are founded, and by promoting conditions of stability and well being. They will seek to eliminate conflict in their international economic policies and will encourage economic collaboration between them.

Article III

The Parties, individually and in cooperation with each other, by means of continuous and effective self-help and mutual aid will maintain and develop, subject to their constitutional provisions, their capacities to resist armed attack.

Article IV

The Parties will consult together from time to time regarding the implementation of this Treaty, and, at the request of either Party, whenever the security of Japan or international peace and security in the Far East is threatened.

Article V

Each Party recognizes that an armed attack against either Party in the territories under the administration of Japan would be dangerous to its own peace and safety and declares that it would act to meet the commmon danger in accordance with its constitutional provisions and processes.

Any such armed attack and all measures taken as a result thereof shall be immediately reported to the Security Council of the United Nations in accordance with the provisions of Article 51 of the Charter. Such measures shall be terminated when the Security Council has taken the measures necessary to restore and maintain international peace and security.

Article VI

For the purpose of contributing to the security of Japan and the maintenance of international peace and security in the Far East, the United States of America is granted the use by its land, air and naval forces of facilities and areas in Japan.

The use of these facilities and areas as well as the status of United States armed forces in Japan shall be governed by a separate agreement, replacing the Administrative Agreement under Article III of the Security Treaty between the United States of America and Japan, signed at Tokyo on February 28, 1952, as amended, and by such other arrangements as may be agreed upon.

Article VII

This Treaty does not affect and shall not be interpreted as affecting in any way the rights and obligations of the Parties under the Charter of the United Nations or the responsibility of the United Nations for the maintenance of international peace and security.

Article VIII

This Treaty shall be ratified by the United States of America and Japan in accordance with their respective consitutional processes and will enter into force on the date on which the instruments of ratification thereof have been exchanged by them in Tokyo.

Article IX

The Security Treaty between the United States of America and Japan signed at the city of San Francisco on September 8, 1951 shall expire upon the entering into force of this Treaty.

Article X

This Treaty shall remain in force until in the opinion of the Governments of the United States of America and Japan there shall have come into force such United Nations arrangements as will satisfactorily provide for the maintenance of international peace and security in the Japan area.

However, after the Treaty has been in force for ten years, either Party may give notice to the other Party of its intention to terminate the Treaty, in which case the Treaty shall terminate one year after such notice has been given.

*　　　　　*　　　　　*

UNITED STATES POLICY TOWARD JAPAN, 1960-1970

A. Statement Issued on Postponement of President Eisenhower's Visit to Japan*

Manila, June 16, 1960

The President has been informed of the Japanese Government's request that he postpone his visit to Japan. Although he would have liked to fulfill his long-held ambition to pay his respects to the Emperor and to the people of this great sister democracy and ally of the United States, he, of course, fully accepts the decision of the Japanese authorities and therefore will not visit Japan at this time.

In so doing, the President wishes to express his full and sympathetic understanding of the decision taken by the Japanese Government. He would like also to express his regrets that a small organized minority, led by professional Communist agitators acting under external direction and control, have been able by resort to force and violence to prevent his good-will visit and to mar the celebration of this centennial in Japanese-American relations.

At the same time the President remains confident that the deliberate challenges to law and order which have caused the Japanese Government to reach its decision will not and cannot disrupt the abiding friendship and understanding which unite our two nations and our two peoples.

B. Joint Communiqué by President John F. Kennedy and Prime Minister Hayato Ikeda of Japan on United States-Japanese Relations*

Washington, June 22, 1961

President Kennedy and Prime Minister Ikeda concluded today a constructive and friendly exchange of views on the present international situation and on relations between the United States and Japan. Secretary Rusk, Foreign Minister Kosaka, and other U.S. and Japanese officials participated in the conversations.

The President and the Prime Minister discussed various problems confronting the peoples of the world who are resolved to defend their freedom, and they reaffirmed the determination of the two countries to intensify their efforts toward the establishment of world peace based on freedom and justice. The President and the Prime Minister stressed that the common policy of the two countries is to strengthen the authority of the United Nations as an organ for the maintenance of world peace.

The President and the Prime Minister expressed their concern over the unstable aspects of the situation in Asia and agreed to hold close consultations in the future with a view to discovering the ways and means by which stability and well-being might be achieved in that area. Their discussion of the Asian

*American Foreign Policy: Current Documents, 1960, pp. 677-78.

*American Foreign Policy: Current Documents, 1961, pp. 964-65.

situation included an examination of various problems relating to Communist China. They also exchanged views concernig the relations of their respective countries with Korea.

The President and the Prime Minister recognized the urgent need for an agreement on a nuclear test ban accompanied by effective inspection and control measures, agreeing that it is of crucial importance for world peace. They also expressed their conviction that renewed efforts should be made in the direction of general disarmament.

The President and the Prime Minister reviewed the world economic situation. They agreed on the need for continued close cooperation among the free countries of the world, particularly in promoting the growth of international trade and financial stability. They agreed that both countries should pursue liberal trade policies looking to an orderly expansion of trade between the two countries.

The President and the Prime Minister stressed the importance of development assistance to less developed countries. The Prime Minister expressed a particular interest in this connection in development assistance for East Asia. They agreed to exchange views on such assistance and agreed that both countries would make positive efforts to the extent of their respective capacities.

The President and the Prime Minister expressed satisfaction with the firm foundation on which the United States-Japanese partnership is established. To strengthen the partnership between the two countries, they agreed to establish a Joint United States-Japan Committee on Trade and Economic Affairs at the cabinet level, noting that this would assist in achieving the objectives of Articles II of the Treaty of Mutual Cooperation and Security. The President and the Prime Minister also recognized the importance of broadening educational, cultural and scientific cooperation between the two countries. They therefore agreed to form two United States-Japan committees, one to study expanded cultural and educational cooperation between the two countries, and the other to seek ways to strengthen scientific cooperation.

The President and the Prime Minister exchanged views on matters relating to the Ryukyu and Bonin Islands, which are under United States administration but in which Japan retains residual sovereignty. The President affirmed that the United States would make further efforts to enhance the welfare and well-being of the inhabitants of the Ryukyus and welcomed Japanese cooperation in these efforts; the Prime Minister affirmed that Japan would continue to cooperate with the United States to this end.

OKINAWA PROBLEM

C. Statement by President Kennedy on Measures to Strengthen Civil and Local Government in the Ryukyu Islands*

March 19, 1962

I have today signed an amendment to Executive Order 10713 dated June

*American Foreign Policy: Current Documents, 1962, pp. 1032-33.

5, 1957, providing for the administration of the Ryukyu Islands. The amendment to the Executive Order, as well as a number of other measures set forth below, are the result of recommendations of the interdepartmental Task Force appointed last year to investigate current conditions in the Ryukyu Islands and the United States policies and programs in force there.

The work of the Task Force underlines the importance the United States attaches to its military bases the Ryukyu Islands. The armed strength deployed at these bases is of the greatest importance in maintaining our deterrent power in the face of threats to the peace in the Far East. Our bases in the Ryukyu Islands help us assure our allies in the great arc from Japan through Southeast Asia not only of our willingness but also of our ability to come to their assistance in case of need.

The report of the Task Force examines in detail the problem of reconciling the military imperative for continued United States administration with the desires of the Ryukyuan people to assert their identity as Japanese, to obtain the economic and social welfare benefits available in Japan, and to have a greater voice in the management of their own affiars. The report has also considered in the same context the desire of the Japanese people to maintain close contact with their countrymen in the Ryukyus.

I recognize the Ryukyus to be a part of the Japanese homeland and look forward to the day when the security interests of the Free World will permit their restoration to full Japanese sovereignty. In the meantime we face a situation which must be met in a spirit of forbearance and mutual understanding by all concerned. I have directed that a number of specific actions be taken to give expression to this spirit by the United States, to discharge more effectively our responsibilities toward the people of the Ryukyus, and to minimize the stresses that will accompany the anticipated eventual restoration of the Ryukyu Islands to Japanese administration. These actions consist of:

1. Asking the Congress to amend the Price Act (PL 86-629) to remove the present $6 million ceiling on assistance to the Ryukyu Islands.

2. Preparing for submission to the Congress plans for the support of new programs in the Ryukyus to raise the levels of compensation for Ryukyuan employees of the U.S. Forces and the Government of the Ryukyu Islands and the levels of public health, educational and welfare services so that over a period of years they reach those obtaining in comparable areas in Japan.

3. Preparing proposals for the Congress to provide over future years a steady increase in loan funds available for the development of the Ryukyuan economy.

4. Entering into discussions with the Government of Japan with a view to working out precise arrangements to implement a cooperative relationship between the United States and Japan in providing assistance to promote the welfare and well-being of the inhabitants of the Ryukyu Islands and their economic development, as discussed between Prime Minister Ikeda and myself during his visit to Washington last year.

5. Carrying on a continuous review of governmental functions in the Ryukyu Islands to determine when and under what circumstances additional functions that need not be reserved to the United States as administering authority can

be delegated to the Government of the Ryukyu Islands.

6. Carrying on a continuous review of such controls as may be thought to limit unnecessarily the private freedoms of inhabitants of the Ryukyu Islands with a view to eliminating all controls which are not essential to the maintenance of the security of the United States military installations in the Ryukyus or of the islands themselves.

The amendments to Executive Order No. 10713 are designed to accomplish the following purposes:

1. Provide for nomination of the Chief Executive of the Government of the Ryukyu Islands by the legislature.

2. Restate the veto power of the High Commissioner, to emphasize its restricted purposes.

3. Lengthen the term of the legislature from two to three years.

4. Permit the legislature to alter the number and boundaries of election districts.

5. Provide that the Civil Administrator shall be a civilian.

6. Make certain technical changes in the provisions for criminal jurisdiction over certain Americans in the Ryukyus.

D. Statement by Secretary of State Dean Rusk on a Joint Program of Economic Assistance to the Ryukyu Islands*

November 1, 1962

Discussions will be resumed in Tokyo on November 2 between United States Ambassador Reischauer and Japanese Foreign Minister Ohira to work out arrangements for a cooperative relationship between the United States and Japan in providing increased economic assistance to the Ryukyu Islands. This is a further step in the implementation of an objective discussed by President Kennedy and Prime Minister Ikeda in June of 1961 and subsequently incorporated in the President's March 19 policy statement on Okinawa.

The United States, in the years since the end of World War II, has contributed very substantially to the economic rehabilitation and development of Okinawa. United States aid has steadily grown. This year the Congress increased to $12 million the ceiling on U.S. assistance—a 100 percent increase—and provided an appropriation appreciably larger than any in recent years. This will enable us to move forward in improving the economic and social conditions of the people of the Ryukyu Islands. We hope that, as a result of the discussions with the Japanese Government, greater Japanese assistance will also henceforth be available, which can be utilized in conjunction with United States and Ryukyuan funds for the maximum benefit of Okinawa.

We live in a period when the essential security interests of the free world require the continued United States administration of the Ryukyus; the policies enunciated by President Kennedy on March 19 provided for steps to be taken during this period which will minimize the stresses that will accompany the

*Ibid., pp. 1039-40.

anticipated eventual restoration of these islands to Japanese administration. We are now implementing these policies and will continue to do so. We are confident of the understanding of the people of Japan and Okinawa and of the Japanese and Ryukyuan governments, and we look forward to their support and close cooperation in the achievement of this common purpose.

E. Address by U. Alexis Johnson, Deputy Under Secretary of State for Political Affairs, on Japan's Role as a World Power*

[Extract]

March 28, 1963

*   *   *

Japan is emerging as a major world power at a time when, as it realizes, the national power of a single nation is not a sufficient basis for action. This is the lesson we have ourselves learned and had reimpressed upon us with each new turn of events. Each nation lives and works in a complex web of diverse relationships with other nations. To act effectively requires concerted effort.

The tasks confronting the free world in the decade ahead are truly enormous. All countries are faced by important problems of improving the quality of life in their own societies. Both Japan and the United States have their share of problems of this kind. There are problems of establishing more effective economic and political relationships between the developed nations. There are critical problems of insuring the security and independence of the developing countries and of promoting their economic and social progress. Finally, there are the broad problems of creating and sustaining a world environment of security within which these other constructive tasks can go forward.

The means employed will be as diverse as the problems to which they are addressed. If Japan is to achieve the secure place in the world to which its power entitles it; if Japan is to make the contribution to solution of these problems which it can make—and which it recognizes as its responsibility to make— its ties with other free nations will have to be further strengthened in a variety of ways. This is not something which Japan can do alone; Japan requires the cooperation of the other free countries, just as they require the cooperation of Japan.

*   *   *

As you well know, Japan's limited natural resources make expanding trade an essential condition to continuing growth. It is less well appreciated that Japanese prosperity promotes American prosperity. After Canada, Japan is our most important customer. Over the past 5 years United States exports to Japan

---

*American Foreign Policy: Current Documents, 1963, pp. 771-78.

exceeded imports from Japan by about $1 billion ($6.2 billion compared with $5.2 billion.) Of the $6.2 billion of United States exports to Japan during this period, $2.4 billion were agricultural products (including cotton, $760 million; grains, $495 million; soybeans, $450 million). During this 5-year period we also sold to Japan $1.2 billion of machinery and vehicles, $600 million of chemicals, $342 million of petroleum products, and $257 million of coking coal. There is now rightly much concern over the future of our large sales of agricultural products to the EEC [European Economic Community] countries. However, we should also not lose sight of the continuing importance of Japan as a market for our agricultural products. In fact, of course, that is why you are meeting here. Over the past 5 years our exports of these commodities to Japan alone have amounted to almost half our exports of agricultural commodities ot the five EEC [European Economic Community] countries.

If Japan is to buy from us, it must also be able to sell to us. We are the largest market in the world and a particularly important market for the high-quality luxury and semiluxury goods which are an important part of Japan's exports. Old ideas die very slowly. There is still a belief in this country that the Japanese are able to do so well in our markets only because theirs is a low-wage economy. This business of comparing labor costs is, of course, very difficult, and this is not the time or the place to enter into a debate on the subject. However, the practices of Japanese industry with respect to fringe benefits and the retention of workers in times of slack production or after a worker is no longer efficient, make it impossible to arrive at a picture of true labor costs solely on the basis of a comparison of hourly or daily base wages with those of the United States or Europe. Moreover, labor is only one of the production costs, and the costs of both raw materials and capital are high in Japan.

When trade is as large as our trade with Japan, it is highly likely that there will be problems. But these problems must be seen in perspective. A current controversy over that trade concerns Japanese exports to this country of certain cotton textile products. What is immediately at issue is trade of the value of a few million dollars out of a total trade approaching $3 billion.

*   *   *

We are not doctrinaire on the subject of the economic systems adopted by others, but Japan is an excellent example for the developing countries of the possibilities of progress through private enterprise. This is a private enterprise system in which the Government plays an important role in setting goals and in giving general guidance to the economy. It is a system which leaves a large sphere of freedom to the vigorous private entrepreneurs. The results have included a growth in per capita income from $261 in 1953 to $416 in 1961, with a planned target of $579 for 1970 (in 1958 prices). If recent rates of growth continue, that target will be considerably exceeded.

Japan is a model for the developing countries in certain aspects of social modernization. Though Japan has been an industrial country for many years, its social characteristics have basically followed traditional Asian patterns.

Nevertheless, under the impact of occupation policies, urbanization, development of mass communications, representative government, and economic progress, there has been a remarkable growth in civil freedom and in freedom from the bonds of traditional ways. Japanese society has developed an increasingly modern outlook. While the society is still in flux, the basis has been laid for an enduring democratic society.

Japan provides useful lessons for the developing countries in education. Whereas in many of the developing countries, and in some of the developed countries as well, the educational system is poorly related to the needs of the society, in Japan a quite effective effort is being made to relate education to such needs.

If Japan is in some important respects a model or example for the developing countries, a special burden of responsibility is placed upon the United States and Europe. We must demonstrate in our trade and other policies that countries which earn the right to acceptance as major industrial nations will be treated equally with other industrial nations. We must not through our policies weaken the attraction of this example by denying Japan full equality.

*   *   *

I turn now, more briefly, to Japan's role as a Pacific power. This is a special, though very important, aspect of Japan's world role which I have discussed. Much of what I have already said therefore applies. Japan has a special role to play as the only major industrial power in Asia. It is an example in a special sense to the developing countries of Asia and has particularly important trade and aid relationships with Asia.

Because it is the major industrial nation in Asia, an important part of the trade relationships of the area revolve around Japan. In 1962 Japan did 33 percent of its export trade and 28 percent of its import trade with free Asia. Expansion of this trade cannot be viewed as a substitute for expansion of trade with the United States and Europe, but such expansion is of great potential importance to both Japan and free Asia, for Japan is a very important source of modern technology for the area.

The entire free world has a strong interest in insuring the continued independence of Asian countries against the various Communist efforts to gain control of them. But Japan has a very special interest in their continued independence and in the growth of their prosperity. Although Japan's economic assistance program is worldwide in scope, it is understandably concentrated in Asia. Thus, in 1961 about 60 percent of all official bilateral Japanese assistance was disbursed to Asian countries. Japan has engaged in various cooperative ventures with other Asian countries for the development of their resources for their mutual benfit. These ventures include, for example, the Orissa iron-ore project in India, involving Japanese assistance to the development of Indian iron-ore deposits and related transport facilities.

While Japanese experience has worldwide application, it is a particular example for Asia. Thus Japanese rice-growing techniques have been widely adopted in Asia, and Japanese handicraft industry methods are also being introduced. Japanese technology is being transferred through technical cooperation programs. In 1962, 269 Japanese experts were sent abroad and 434 trainees were received by Japan. In addition more third-country training under United States assistance programs has been done in Japan than in any other country in Asia.

* * *

F. Joint Communiqué Issued by President Lyndon B. Johnson and Prime Minister Eisaku Sato of Japan on Matters of Mutual Interest*

[Extract]

January 13, 1965

* * *

The President and the Prime Minister reviewed the present international situation and reaffirmed the partnership of the two countries which grows out of common beliefs and the shared objective of a lasting peace based on justice, freedom and prosperity for all peoples. They expressed a firm determination that the two countries should cooperate more closely in seeking this common objective. They agreed that for this purpose the two countries should maintain the closest contact and consultation not only on problems lying between them but on problems affecting Asia and the world in general.

The President and the Prime Minister, recognizing the valuable role of the United Nations in the maintenance of the peace and prosperity of the world, exchanged frank views on the difficult questions now confronting the United Nations, and agreed to continue cooperative efforts to strengthen the functions of the United Nations and to enhance its authority.

The President and the Prime Minister recognized the desirability of promoting arms control and a reduction of the arms race as rapidly as possible, and strongly hoped that, following the partial test ban treaty, further steps can be made toward the realization of a total nuclear test ban.

The President and the Prime Minister, recognizing that the question of China is a problem having a vital bearing on the peace and stability of Asia, exchanged frank views on the positions of their respective countries and agreed to maintain close consultation with each other on this matter. The President emphasized the United States policy of firm support for the Republic of China and his grave concern that Communist China's militant policies and expansionist pressures against its neighbors endanger the peace of Asia. The Prime Minister stated that it is the fundamental policy of the Japanese Government to maintain friendly ties based on the regular diplomatic relationship with the Government of the Republic of China and at the same time to continue to promote private

*American Foreign Policy: Current Documents, 1965, pp. 769-71.

contact which is being maintained with the Chinese mainland in such matters as trade on the basis of the principle of separation of political matters from economic matters.

The President and the Prime Minister expressed their deep concern over the unstable and troubled situation in Asia, particularly in Vietnam, and agreed that continued perseverance would be necessary for freedom and independence in South Vietnam. They reaffirmed their belief that peace and progress in Asia are prerequisites to peace in the whole world.

The President and the Prime Minister recognized that the elevation of living standards and the advancement of social welfare are essential for the political stability of developing nations throughout the world and agreed to strengthen their economic cooperation with such countries. They agreed to continue to consult on the forms of such assistance. The Prime Minister expressed a particular interest in expanding Japan's role in developmental and technical assistance for Asia.

The President and the Prime Minister reaffirmed their belief that it is essential for the stability and peace of Asia that there be no uncertainty about Japan's security. From this viewpoint, the Prime Minister stated that Japan's basic policy is to maintain firmly the United States-Japan Mutual Cooperation and Security Treaty arrangements, and the President reaffirmed the United States determination to abide by its commitment under the Treaty to defend Japan against any armed attack from the outside.

The President and the Prime Minister affirmed the importance of constantly seeking even closer relationships between the two countries. In particular, they recognized the vital importance to both countries of the expansion of their economic relations sustained by the growth of their respective economies, and agreed that the two countries should cooperate with each other in the worldwide efforts for the expansion of world trade and for effective international monetary cooperation.

The President and the Prime Minister confirmed the desirability of maintaining and utilizing the Joint United States-Japan Committee on Trade and Economic Affairs where exchange of views takes place at the cabinet level, as well as the United States-Japan Committee on Scientific Cooperation and the Joint United States-Japan Conference on Cultural and Educational Interchange. They further agreed that the fourth meeting of the joint United States-Japan Committee on Trade and Economic Affairs would be held in July of this year.

The President and the Prime Minister recognized the importance of United States military installations on the Ryukyu and Bonin Islands for the security of the Far East. The Prime Minister expressed the desire that, as soon as feasible, the administrative control over these islands will be restored to Japan and also a deep interest in the expansion of the autonomy of the inhabitants of the Ryukyus and in further promoting their welfare. Appreciating the desire of the Government and people of Japan for the restoration of administration to Japan, the President stated that he looks forward to the day when the security interests of the free world in the Far East will permit the realization of this desire. They confirmed that the United States and Japan should continue substantial economic assistance to the Ryukyu Islands in order to advance further the welfare and well-being of the inhabitants of these islands. They expressed their satisfaction with the smooth operation of the cooperative arrangements between the United States and Japan concerning assistance to the Ryukyu Islands. They agreed in principle to broaden the functions of the existing Japan-United States Consultative Committee so as to enable the Committee to conduct consultations not only on economic assistance to the Ryukyu Islands but also on other matters on which the two countries can cooperate in continuing to promote the well-being of the inhabitants of the islands. The President agreed to give favorable consideration to an ancestral graves visit by a representative group of former residents of the Bonin Islands.

*   *   *

G. Statement by President Johnson on the Election of the Ryukyuan Chief Executive*

December 20, 1965

I have today signed an amendement to Executive Order 10713, as previously amended, which provides for the administration of Okinawa and other Ryukyu Islands. The new amendement specifies that the Ryukyuan Chief Executive, heretofore appointed by the U.S. High Commissioner, shall henceforth be elected by the legislative body of the Government of the Ryukyu Islands, as the popularly chosen representatives of the Ryukyuan people.

This amendment is another forward step in the continuing policy of the United States to afford the Ryukyuan people as great a voice in managing their own affairs as is compatible with the essential role of the Ryukyus in maintaining the security of Japan and the Far East.

I am happy to announce this change at this time so as to insure that the Ryukyuan Chief Executive for the next term can be elected directly by the representatives of the Ryukyuan People.

[Annex]
Executive Order 11263
Further Amending Executive Order No. 10713,
Providing for Administration of the Ryukyu Islands

By virtue of the authority vested in me by the Constitution, and as President of the United States and Commander in Chief of the armed forces of the United States, subsection (b) of Section 8 of Executive Order No. 10713 of June 5, 1957, as amended by Executive Order No. 11010 of March 19, 1962, is further amended to read as follows:

Ibid., pp. 777-78.

(b) (1) The Chief Executive shall be elected by a majority of the entire membership of the legislative body and shall serve until the end of the term of the legislative body that shall have elected him.

(2) In the event the legislative body does not, within a reasonable time as determined by the High Commissioner, elect a Chief Executive to succeed an incumbent or to fill a vacancy, the High Commissioner may appoint a Chief Executive who shall serve until a successor is elected by the legislative body.

(3) The incumbent Chief Executive at the end of the term of a legislative body shall continue in office until a successor takes office pursuant to either of the foregoing paragraphs.

H. Statements by Secretary of Defense Robert McNamara on Japan's Future Role in Asia*

[Extract]

July 15, 1966

I think your country [Japan] will and should play an increasing role in Asia, in organizing the nations of free Asia to defend themselves, to strengthen their ties one with another, and to gradually develop economic, cultural, and other ties with Red China. Hopefully, in the long run Red China will go through an evolutionary process in which any present aspirations she may have to carry out aggression beyond her borders will gradually disappear. I don't know any other nation in Asia which is better qualified by knowledge and economic and other capabilities to carry out a leadership role in that program than your own.

. . . . I believe that it would be a serious mistake for your country or any other nation on the periphery of Red China to develop its own nuclear force. I don't believe that force would be a protection against Chinese aggression. It would, without question, cause a diversion of resources from very necessary economic development projects.

It's not at all needed, because we have treaty commitments with you under the terms of which we are bound, within the limits of our constitutional processes, to come to your defense. Under no conceivable circumstances would you develop as large a nuclear force as we presently have; so it would be an utter waste for you and for others who are in a similar position.

Yes [Japan can rely absolutely on U.S. nuclear deterrence and assistance]. We have never at any time indicated that we would limit the type of weapon that we would use in fulfilling our treaty obligations and that simply means that those with whom we have treaties are protected by the full arsenal of our weaponry, both conventional and nuclear. For example, we have today on the soil of Western Europe over 5,000 nuclear warheads, and we have in our strategic forces today well over 1,400 ballistic missiles and about 600 heavy bombers armed with nuclear warheads. This is a tremendous nuclear force, larger by far than any other nuclear force in the world and larger by far than Red China could obtain for decades.

Without question [the credibility of U.S. nuclear deterrents will be maintained

* *American Foreign Policy: Current Documents, 1966,* pp. 700-01.

in the foreseeable future]. It's absolutely essential as a foundation for stability among nations, and it's the foundation of our security.

Our view of the relationship between the U.S. and Japan is founded on our belief that, strong as we are economically, politically, militarily, we're not strong enough to provide for our own security. Our security depends on relations with other nations, particularly with such nations as Japan. So a strong relationship with Japan, culturally, economically, politically, militarily, is very much in our own interest—our own selfish interest—and we are seeking to develop that interest.

We think our relation with you is strong. I attended a Cabinet meeting today, for example, at which Secretaries Rusk and Wirtz [W. Willard Wirtz, Secretary of Labor] and Connor [John T. Connor, Secretary of Commerce] reported on their recent meeting in Kyoto with members of your Cabinet. They said it was as though they were meeting with the rest of us in our own Cabinet. Over the past several years, because of exchange of these Cabinet members the relationships personally and officially have developed very strong indeed; and I see no reason why that should change in the future.

We recognized that Japan, with its own history and Asian environment, has differing attitudes, approaches, and policies on many common issues. However, we share the vital stake in maintaining and further developing favorable relations. I look upon it as a very selfish thing. We need a strong relationship with you; just as, frankly, I think you need a strong relationship with us.

Your defense policies must be matters for you to consider and not for me to comment on. I think the basic action required by you in your own security interests, and in ours as well, is to fashion a larger role for yourselves in the affairs of the Pacific and Asia, to take a larger role in organizing and leading the free nations of Asia in developing stronger ties amongst themselves, economically, politically, and otherwise. We were very pleased to see, for example, the recent meeting in Seoul of Asian nations. We hope you will take a leading part in continuing meetings of that kind in the future.

I think your role there [in assisting economic and social development of Asian countries needing aid], as I say, should be one of leadership; it should also be one of assistance—growing assistance, particularly economic assistance—to the developing nations of Asia. We were delighted at your willingness to participate fully in the Asian Development Bank. We were also delighted at your sponsorship of the recent ministerial conference on trade and development in Southeast Asia and at reports that you are planning to hold an agricultural development conference. We think in the future you should initiate more and more ventures of that kind and participate more and more fully in laying the foundation for an accelerated growth of the underdeveloped nations of Asia, of which there are many.

I think Japan can take a more significant role in arms control and arms reductions, nonproliferation, and, as a matter of fact, in United Nations affairs in general, including participation in a U.N. peacekeeping force.

I. Joint Communiqué Issued by President Johnson and Prime Minister Sato on Matters of Mutual Interest*

[Extract]

Washington, November 15, 1967

I

President Johnson and Prime Minister Sato met in Washington on November 14 and 15, 1967, to exchange views on the present international situation and on other matters of mutual interest to the United States and Japan.

II

The President and the Prime Minister declared that the United States and Japan, guided by common democratic principles of individual dignity and personal freedom, will continue to cooperate closely with each other in efforts to bring about world peace and prosperity. They took note of the importance of reinforcing the authority and role of the United Nations as a peace-keeping organization, of promoting arms control and a reduction of the arms race, including the early conclusion of a Non-Proliferation Treaty, as well as of rendering effective assistance to the developing countries, particularly those in Southeast Asia.

III

The President and the Prime Minister exchanged frank views on the recent international situation, with particular emphasis on developments in the Far East. They noted the fact that Communist China is developing its nuclear arsenal and agreed on the importance of creating conditions wherein Asian nations would not be susceptible to threats from Communist China. The President and the Prime Minister also agreed that, while it is difficult to predict at present what external posture Communist China may eventually assume, it is essential for the free world countries to continue to cooperate among themselves to promote political stability and economic prosperity in the area. Looking toward an enduring peace in Asia, they further expressed the hope that Communist China would ultimately cast aside its present intransigent attitude and seek to live in peace and prosper alongside other nations in the international community.

American Foreign Policy: Current Documents, 1967, pp. 771-74.

IV

The President reaffirmed the continuing United States determination to assist the South Vietnamese people in the defense of their freedom and independence. At the same time, he made it clear that he was prepared to enter into negotiations at any time to find a just and lasting solution to the conflict. The Prime Minister expressed support for the United States position of seeking a just and equitable settlement and reaffirmed Japan's determination to do all it can in the search for peace. He also expressed the view that reciprocal action should be expected of Hanoi for a cessation of the bombing of North Vietnam. The Prime Minister noted that he had found widespread support during his Southeast Asian trips for free world efforts to cope with Communist intervention and infiltration.

The President and the Prime Minister agreed that it is important that the new Government in South Vietnam continue its progress toward stable democratic institutions and the social and economic betterment of its people.

V

The President and the Prime Minister exchanged views frankly on the matter of security in the Far East including Japan. They declared it to be the fundamental policy of both countries to maintain firmly the Treaty of Mutual Cooperation and Security between the United States and Japan in order to ensure the security of Japan and the peace and security of the Far East. The President and the Prime Minister recognized the maintenance of peace and security rests not only upon military factors, but also upon political stability and economic development. The Prime Minister stated that Japan is prepared to make a positive contribution to the peace and stability of Asia in accordance with its capabilities. The President stated that such efforts on the part of Japan would be a highly valued contribution.

VI

Referring to his recent visits to the Southeast Asian countries, the Prime Minister explained the efforts these nations are making in a spirit of self-help toward achievement of greater welfare and prosperity for their peoples, but noted their continued need for assistance in their efforts. The Prime Minister stated that it is the intention of the Government of Japan, in meeting this need, to continue its efforts to provide more effective bilateral and multilateral assistance to the Southeast Asian region particularly in the fields of agriculture, fisheries, transportation and communication, by increasing the amount of assistance and liberalizing its conditions. The Prime Minister described the encouraging trends which he had observed particularly in Southeast Asia toward greater regional cooperation and he cited the promising prospects for the Asian Development Bank and its Special Funds. He further stated that it is the intention of the Government of Japan to make greater use of these institutions by assisting in further expanding their operations. Recognizing the need to strengthen economic assistance to the developing areas, particularly to the Southeast Asian countries, the President and the Prime Minister agreed to maintain closer consultation with each other in this field.

VII

The President and the Prime Minister frankly discussed the Ryukyu and the Bonin Islands. The Prime Minister emphasized the strong desire of the Government and people of Japan for the return of administrative rights over the Ryukyu Islands to Japan and expressed his belief that an adequate solution should promptly be sought on the basis of mutual understanding and trust between the Governments and people of the two countries. He further emphasized that an agreement should be reached between the two governments within a few years on a date satisfactory to them for the reversion of these islands. The President stated that he fully understands the desire of the Japanese people for the reversion of these Islands. At the same time, the President and the Prime Minister recognized that the United States military bases on these islands continue to play a vital role in assuring the security of Japan and other free nations in the Far East.

As a result of their discussion, the President and the Prime Minister agreed that the two Governments should keep under joint and continuous review the status of the Ryukyu Islands, guided by the aim of returning administrative rights over these Islands to Japan and in the light of these discussions.

The President and the Prime Minister further agreed that, with a view toward minimizing the stresses which will arise at such time as administrative rights are restored to Japan, measures should be taken to identify further the Ryukyuan people and their institutions with Japan proper and to promote the economic and social welfare of the Ryukyuan residents. To this end, they agreed to establish in Naha an Advisory Committee to the High Commissioner of the Ryukyu Islands. The Governments of Japan and the United States of America and the Government of the Ryukyu Islands will each provide a representative and appropriate staff to the Committee. The Committee will be expected to develop recommendations which should lead to substantial movement toward removing the remaining economic and social barriers between the Ryukyu Islands and Japan proper. The existing United States-Japan Consultative Committee in Tokyo will be kept informed by the High Commissioner of the progress of the work of the Advisory Committee. It was also agreed that the functions of the Japanese Government Liaison Office would be expanded as necessary to permit consultations with the High Commissioner and the United States Civil Administration on matters of mutual interest.

The President and the Prime Minister also reviewed the status of the Bonin Islands and agreed that the mutual security interests of Japan and the United States could be accommodated within arrangements for the return of administration of these islands to Japan. They therefore agreed that the two Governments will enter immediately into consultations regarding the specific arrangements for accomplishing the early restoration of these islands to Japan without detriment to the security of the area. These consultations will take into account the intention of the Government of Japan, expressed by the Prime Minister, gradually to assume much of the responsibility for defense of the area. The President and the Prime Minister agreed that the United States would retain under the terms of the Treaty of Mutual Cooperation and Security between the United States and Japan such military facilities and areas in the Bonin Islands as required in the mutual security of both countries.

The Prime Minister stated that the return of the administrative rights over the Bonin Islands would not only contribute to solidifying the ties of friendship between the two countries but would also help to reinforce the conviction of the Japanese people that the return of the administrative rights over the Ryukyu Islands will also be solved within the framework of mutual trust between the two countries.

*   *   *

J. Joint United States-Japanese Statement on Return of the Bonin Islands to Japanese Administration*

April 5, 1968

Foreign Minister Miki and Ambassador Johnson signed today in Tokyo an agreement for the return to Japanese administration of the Bonin and Volcano Island groups (together with Rosario Island, Parece Vela and Marcus Island) which had been administered by the United States under the provisions of Article 3 of the peace treaty with Japan. Upon completion by Japan of its legal procedures necessary for the entry into force of the agreement, the actual turnover of administration will take place after a thirty-day transitional period.

President Johnson and Prime Minister Sato agreed in November of 1967 in Washington that the two governments should enter immediately into consultations regarding the specific arrangements for accomplishing the early restoration of these islands to Japan without detriment to the security of the area. Today's agreement is the result of negotiations conducted within the framework of the President and Prime Minister's understanding.

After the entry into force of today's agreement, the United States will continue the use of LORAN navigational stations on Iwo Jima and Marcus under the terms of the Status of Forces Agreement between the two countries, but all other installations and sites will be transferred to Japan.

The Government of Japan has under consideration measures to facilitate the reintegration of the slightly over two hundred Japanese nationals who are now living on Chichi Jima into Japanese life, as well as the return of the former residents of the islands evacuated during the war.

*Department of State Bulletin, Apr. 29, 1968, pp. 570-71.

K. Comments by Secretary of State Rusk on the Ryukyu Islands*

May 17, 1968

The President had very frank and useful talks with Prime Minister Sato here in Washington last November about the Ryukyu Islands question. The Prime Minister told President Johnson of the desire of the Japanese people for restoration of administrative rights over the Ryukyus. The President informed the Prime Minister that he fully understands the desire of the Japanese people for the reversion of these islands. At the same time, they both recognized that the United States military bases on these islands continue to play a vital role in assuring the security not only of Japan but of other free nations in the Far East.

This question is closely linked to future developments in Asia, and therefore I cannot at this time give you a definite timetable for reversion. Nevertheless, we understand the Prime Minister's desire for reaching an agreement within a few years on a satisfactory date for reversion. Therefore, we agreed last year to keep this question under joint and continuing review. In the meantime, I am pleased by the agreement we have already reached for the return of the Bonin Islands.

Prime Minister Sato and President Johnson also recognized the need to take steps to promote the economic and social welfare of the people of the Ryukyus and to foster greater identification with Japan proper, in order to reduce the stresses which will come at such time as administrative rights are restored to Japan. They therefore agreed to establish an Advisory Committee to the High Commissioner of the Ryukyu Islands. This Committee is now operating in Naha, and I understand that in a few short months it has already come up with some very constructive actions.

L. Joint Communiqué Issued by President Richard M. Nixon and Prime Minister Sato on Restoration of Okinawa to Normal Status*

[Extract]

November 21, 1969

President Nixon and Prime Minister Sato met in Washington on Nov. 19, 20 and 21, 1969, to exchange views on the present international situation and on other matters of mutual interest to the United States and Japan.

*   *   *

The Prime Minister emphasized his view that the time had come to respond

---

*Ibid., June 24, 1968, pp. 821-25.
*Congressional Record, Nov. 25, 1969, pp. 515006-07.

to the strong desire of the people of Japan, of both the mainland and Okinawa, to have the administrative rights over Okinawa returned to Japan on the basis of the friendly relations between the United States and Japan and thereby to restore Okinawa to its normal status. The President expressed appreciation of the Prime Minister's view. The President and the Prime Minister also recognized the vital role played by United States forces in Okinawa in the present situation in the Far East. As a result of their discussion it was agreed that the mutual security interests of the United States and Japan could be accommodated within arrangements for the return of the administrative rights over Okinawa to Japan. They therefore agreed that the two Governments would immediately enter into consultations regarding specific arrangements for accomplishing the early reversion of Okinawa without detriment to the security of the Far East including Japan. They further agreed to expedite the consultations with a view to accomplishing the reversion during 1972, subject to the conclusion of these specific arrangements with the necessary legislative support. In this connection, the Prime Minister made clear the intention of his Government, following reversion, to assume gradually the responsibility for the immediate defense of Okinawa as part of Japan's defense efforts for her own territories. The President and the Prime Minister agreed also that the United States would retain, under the terms of the Treaty of Mutual Cooperation and Security, such military facilities and areas in Okinawa as required in the mutual security of both countries.

The President and the Prime Minister agreed that, upon return of the administrative rights, the Treaty of Mutual Cooperation and Security and its related arrangements would apply to Okinawa without modification thereof. In this connection, the Prime Minister affirmed the recognition of his Government that the security of Japan could not be adequately maintained without international peace and security in the Far East and, therefore, the security of countries in the Far East was a matter of serious concern for Japan. The Prime Minister was of the view that, in the light of such recognition on the part of the Japanese Government, the return of the administrative rights over Okinawa in the manner agreed above should not hinder the effective discharge of the international obligations assumed by the United States for the defense of countries in the Far East, including Japan. The President replied that he shared the Prime Minister's view.

The Prime Minister described in detail the particular sentiment of the Japanese people against nuclear weapons and the policy of the Japanese Government reflecting such sentiment. The President expressed his deep understanding and assured the Prime Minister that, without prejudice to the position of the United States Government with respect to the prior consultation system under the Treaty of Mutual Cooperation and Security, the reversion of Okinawa would be carried out in a manner consistent with the policy of the Japanese Government as described by the Prime Minister.

The President and the Prime Minister took note of the fact that there would be a number of financial and economic problems, including those concerning United States business interests in Okinawa, to be solved between the two countries in connection with the transfer of the administrative rights over Okinawa to Japan and agreed that detailed discussions relative to their solution would be initiated promptly.

The President and the Prime Minister, recognizing the complexity of the problems involved in the reversion of Okinawa, agreed that the two Governments should consult closely and cooperate on the measures necessary to assure a smooth transfer of administrative rights to the Japanese Government, in accordance with reversion arrangements to be agreed to by both Governments. They agreed that the United States-Japan Consultative Committee in Tokyo should undertake over-all responsibility for this preparatory work. The President and the Prime Minister decided to establish in Okinawa a preparation commission in place of the existing advisory committee to the High Commissioner of the Ryukyu Islands for the purpose of consulting and coordinating locally on measures relating to preparation for the transfer of administrative rights, including necessary assistance to the government of the Ryukyu Islands. The preparatory commission will be composed of a representative of the Japanese Government with ambassadorial rank and the High Commissioner of the Ryukyu Islands, with the chief executive of the government of the Ryukyu Islands acting as adviser to the commission. The commission will report and make recommendations to the two Governments through the United States-Japan Consultative Committee.

The President and the Prime Minister expressed their conviction that a mutually satisfactory solution of the question of the return of the administrative rights over Okinawa to Japan, which is the last of the major issues between the two countries arising from World War II, would further strengthen United States-Japan relations, which are based on friendship and mutual trust and would make a major contribution to the peace and security of the Far East.

M. Comments by Under Secretary Johnson on the Future of United States Relations with the Far East*

[Extract]

April 10, 1970

Much is said about Japan's "economic miracle." But we should not forget that Japan has established at home a solid base of political stability and democratic rights, including a vigorous press and an independent judiciary. Japan is, in fact, a striking illustration of the principle that a political democracy in Asia can produce political stability and an efficient economic system. While we Americans can take some pride in this because of our recent association with Japan under the occupation, we should not forget that the roots go back much further in the history of modern Japan. We should also remember that many years ago Japan was one of the first countries in the world to establish universal compulsory education and that today a higher proportion of its population is

---

*Department of State Bulletin, Apr. 27, 1970, pp. 537-42.

in colleges and universities than that of any country except our own.

All of this means that Japan has reached the stage where its leaders believe it can make new and more helpful contributions to stability and progress in Asia. In his speech at the National Press Club last November, Prime Minister Sato spoke of Japan's intention to contribute in a major way to the economic development and technical assistance of the Asian countries and their nation-building efforts.

This is a policy which we in Washington welcome. It coincides with the view expressed by the President at Guam last summer that the nations of Asia are capable of undertaking greater responsibility for the development of the region. The time has come for the United States to assume less of a leading and more of a supporting role in the area.

The President has stressed that this is not a policy of isolation from or indifference to events in Asia. From our far past we have been and will remain involved in Asia. We are in some ways more a Pacific than we are an Atlantic power. We have learned that peace for us is much less likely if there is no peace in Asia.

The importance of Japan in Asia is clear. As the President said in his state of the Union message on January 22, Japanese-American friendship and cooperation is the linchpin for peace in the Pacific. In sheer economic and industrial power terms it is clear that Japan is and will long remain the overwhelmingly most important fact in Asia. Against this background I want to discuss our policy in the area and to say as clearly as I can what it does mean and what it does not mean.

In this connection I might add that the Nixon doctrine and the President's foreign policy statement of February 18[1] met with favorable reception in Japan. The Japanese Foreign Office took the unusual step of releasing a commendatory statement on it. Even the Japanese press, which is as free and independent as any in the world, generally applauded the foreign policy line laid down by the President. I feel that this was by no means accidental. It reflects the actuality that these two great Pacific nations, bound by mutual security interests and by their growing and mutually profitable trade, tend to see things in much the same way.

At the same time, it should be stressed that we and Japan are both independent countries and we will decide on our actions in the light of our own conception of our own national interests. Japan, in particular, has achieved a state of strength and confidence which would make it foolhardy for the United States to seek to impose its will on the Japanese Government and people. We have not tried and will not try to do so. We can, nevertheless, take satisfaction in the fact that the Governments of both nations are seeking to achieve that understanding and common outlook necessary to keep our policies following compatible lines. The fate of both of our countries, and perhaps of Asia, depends on the success of these efforts.

*   *   *

[1] President Nixon's foreign policy report to the Congress on Feb. 18.

Looking at Japan's phenomenal economic growth, there are those who say it should be doing even more in the defense field, that Japan has been getting a "free ride." As indicated above, however, Japan has already assumed responsibility for its own conventional defense, and it is doubtful whether there is much more that it could do that would directly relieve United States military responsibilities in Japan, almost all of which are related to regional commitments. Nor do I believe Japan's modest degree of arming should create a threat to any of its neighbors. In part as a result of Japan's position as the economic colossus of Asia, other Asian countries understandably remain sensitive to the possibility of Japanese expansionism. But it is my observation that Japan also is very much aware of this sensitivity. And the United States, in reducing its military profile in Asia, has no intention of trying to push Japan into the assumption of security responsibilities for which Japan and its neighbors are not prepared.

The Japanese Government and people will, of course, decide the role they wish Japan to take in the security field. In my observation, the great majority of Japanese reject an overseas military role for Japan—for a variety of legal and political reasons derived from its recent history. As the President has said, the United States will not ask Japan to assume responsibilities inconsistent with the deeply felt concerns of the Japanese people.

Japan has decided that its most effective contribution under present circumstances may well be to continue to offer increasing economic cooperation with the other nations of Asia and to take care of the local and conventional defense of its territory, including Okinawa after reversion. We and Japan recognize that security in the area depends not only on military power but also—and just as important—on the political, social, and economic health of the countries of the region. To this Japan can make a large contribution.

*   *   *

Looking at the region as a whole, the ideal is a community of the free states of Asia cooperating together for their common interests in political, economic, and security fields, with which we are associated only to the degree that those states desire our association. This is the goal set by President Nixon. The growth of economic cooperation among the states of the area has been manifested in many ways: by the founding of the Asian Development Bank, which was genuinely at the initiative of the countries of the area rather than from any direction from the United States; by setting up the Southeast Asian Ministerial Conference on Economic Development, organized at the initiative of Japan and with which we have no formal association; and by the Mekong River Development Committee, which was created by ECAFE [Economic Commission for Asia and the Far East].

I think that I have made the point that in the economic field in particular, real progress is being made in regional cooperation and development. I would expect Japan to make an increasing contribution in these areas. During his visit to Washington last November, this was the goal set for Japan by Prime Minister Sato.

*   *   *

The United States made the decision a year ago that our relationship with Japan for the 1970's and beyond had to be founded on a mutual and increasingly interdependent concern for peace and security in the Far East. On the basis of this decision, agreement was made last November for the return of administrative control over the Ryukyu Islands to Japan in 1972. Our bases on Okinawa will, of course, take on the same status after reversion as our bases in Japan. The Nixon-Sato agreement was of historic importance and, we are confident, has laid a solid foundation for U.S.-Japan cooperation in the 1970's. This cooperation, and our good relations with the other countries of Asia, are keys to the success of the Nixon doctrine in Asia.

Our relationship will not be without its stresses. We have, for example, attained a large degree of harmony with Japan in our common understanding of security requirements, but this does not mean that we have total identity of views or that there will not be problems in the future. We also have to recognize that commercial competition, not only in our bilateral relations but also in third markets, is going to increase and there will be further frictions. These are in many ways the problems of success—success in achieving a two-way trade relationship of over $8 billion last year, with every prospect of further increases in the future.

Specific issues will no doubt continue to plague us, as is currently the case with the textile problem. These issues must and will be solved. Both Governments recognize that it is in their common interest to build up the relationship and to eliminate the frictions that are bound to occur out of the success we both have achieved. Another hopeful note is that Japanese, American, and Asian businessmen are coming to realize that Asia offers expanding opportunities for mutually beneficial cooperation. Businessmen on both sides of the Pacific are working together and meeting together to take advantage of these opportunities. Increased direct investment between the United States, Japan, and other nations, combined with the growth of multinational corporations, is also going to blur the more traditional distinctions of corporate identity and interests. We are confident that if Japan and the nations of Asia will recognize that foreign assistance and foreign investment can be beneficial rather than constituting exploitation, then working together we can improve the lot of every one of us.

I am sure that most of my friends in the Japanese business community will agree with me that the era has passed during which Japan could claim special privileges and that, if Japan is going to continue its spectacular economic development, Japan must be willing to grant to others that same freedom of economic enterprise within Japan that Japan is seeking and in large degree receiving in other economically developed countries, especially in the United States.

Prime Minister Sato has emphasized that the cooperation between Japan and the United States is not to be confined to our two countries or just to Asia.

He went on to say that, since this cooperation is between the first and second ranking economic powers of the free world, it should extend over a wide range of global problems in the 1970's, such as the easing of general tensions, the strengthening of the U.N., arms control and the realization of disarmament, preservation of the free-trade system, and the securing of a stable international monetary system. We and Japan are already working together in scientific development and space exploration. I think it is safe to guess that U.S.-Japan cooperation will encompass common efforts to surmount the problems of advanced industrial societies, such as urban congestion and damage to the environment.

It is a source of cautious optimism for the 1970's that there seems to be growing up a broad community of interests and perceptions between the United States and Japan. We have worked hard to lend substance to the U.S.-Japan partnership concept. The frontiers of our common interest and consultation are constantly being expanded in political, economic, scientific, and cultural fields. We meet often and fruitfully, both within and without government, with our partners to talk over the many matters of mutual interest.

I hope I have not left you with the impression that we have solved all our problems or that the future will be free of frictions. But, considering the breadth and depth of our relationship, I think that we can all take considerable satisfaction at how well we have managed our common interests up to now. I am sure we can do even better in the future. If we both keep trying, I am sure that we can do so.

N. United States Statement on U.S.-Japanese Treaty of Mutual Cooperation and Security*

June 22, 1970

Secretary Rogers noted, in his meeting this afternoon with Foreign Minister Aichi, that tomorrow, June 23, is the 10th anniversary of the U.S.-Japan Treaty of Mutual Cooperation and Security.

The Secretary expressed the conviction that this treaty has served both countries well and lies at the heart of the cooperative relationship which has developed between the United States and Japan and which is vital to the future well-being of both peoples.

Secretary Rogers reaffirmed, on behalf of the United States, the understanding reached last November by President Nixon and Prime Minister Sato that the two Governments intend to maintain the treaty, whose role they valued highly in maintaining the peace and security of the Far East including Japan.

On the basis of this firm foundation, the Secretary said, he was confident that the decade of the 1970's would see the further strengthening of the ties between the two countries and of their commitment to peace and prosperity for all mankind.

The Secretary said he was happy to note that the Government of Japan shared these views, as indicated in its statement of June 22.

*Ibid., July 13, 1970, p. 33.

THE UNITED STATES

AND CHINA

THE UNITED STATES AND CHINA

Commentary

From the turn of the nineteenth century to the Communist accession to power in 1949, United States concern for China was mainly twofold: a primary interest in commerce whereby the United States would sell its industrial products in what was presumed to be a vast China market, and a secondary interest in promoting and protecting missionary work, education, and other American cultural endeavors. Translated into policy, American concern manifested itself with the Open Door Policy, the objective of which was equality of commercial opportunity and respect for China's territorial integrity, and through which the United States hoped to prevent hegemony by the European powers and Japan and thus the exclusion of its nationals. The Open Door Policy was basically a statement of an American goal, and though the main thrust of American diplomacy was in defense of this goal, United States military action to secure equal commercial privileges or to preserve China's integrity was not implied. United States political involvement prior to 1941, was therefore slight. Between 1941 and 1949, however, the United States became much more actively involved in China's affairs: first, as an ally during the Second World War, it tried to keep China in the War and second, in the postwar period it hoped to bring stability to the nation through an ambiguous attempt to prevent the Communist overthrow of Chiang Kai-shek's government. After 1949 the United States refused to recognize the new government and worked to "contain" its power.

During the course of the Second World War, United States policy was predicated on the view that China had to be kept viable militarily and that at War's end it should be an independent, democratic state. Pursuant to this aim, the United States trained Chinese pilots, built airfields in China, gave massive military and economic aid, and assigned Generals Joseph Stilwell and later Albert Wedemeyer as Chiefs of Staff of Chiang Kai-shek's army. Politically, American officials worked to effect an accommodation between strong Communist forces, which were in control of large segments of rural, northern China, and Chiang Kai-shek's government, whose armies were trying to subjugate them. Such an agreement, it was believed, would not only contribute to more effective action against Japan but would have important postwar consequences as well. To achieve this end, President Roosevelt sent Patrick Hurley, former Secretary of War under Hoover and a roving emissary during the Second World War, to China as his personal representative in 1944.

Hurley worked at his assignment for over a year, succeeded in initiating serious Kuomintang-CCP discussions, but ultimately failed to reconcile forces that may well have been irreconcilable. Certainly the growing strength of the Communists among the Chinese peasants, their strengthened military posture, and Chiang's reluctance to achieve needed governmental reforms seemed to preclude a settlement through 1945. At any rate, Hurley returned to the United States disappointed and frustrated in the Fall of 1945, and because of earlier differences with American Foreign Service officers, angrily submitted his resignation, charging that the State Department was responsible for his failure.

Subsequently, President Truman sent General George Marshall to assist in working out an agreement between China's warring factions; but over a year later, after a series of frustrations with extremists on each side, he returned to the United States wishing a pox on both their houses. Later, General Albert Wedemeyer undertook a similar mission; he concluded that only massive advisory and material aid to save the Chiang government would suffice. In view of earlier decisions to rebuild Western Europe, and because there was little confidence in Chiang Kai-shek's ability to achieve a stable government, and little United States support for large-scale military intervention in China, this commitment was not made. In the meantime, in spite of some postwar American military and economic assistance, the civil war went badly for the government, and culminated in Communist control of the country in 1949.

The Communist victory and Chiang Kai-shek's flight to Formosa were cause for acrimonious post-mortems in the United States. Republicans quickly castigated President Truman for his "loss" of China; vicious attacks were made on Democratic Far Eastern policy dating back to the Yalta agreements of 1945. After the Alger Hiss case, which raised questions about Communists in the State Department, and after the beginning of the Korean War, a wave of hysteria swept the United States, and even more emotional charges were made concerning United States policy makers during the 1945-1949 period. Former Ambassador Hurley, long gone from a position of power and a bitter and disappointed man, added fuel to the fire with a new series of charges, which consisted heavily of innuendo and half-truths based on imperfect memory. Partially as a result of the intense feeling generated by these charges and the Korean War, the United States refused to recognize the People's Republic of China, and through the 1950's strengthened its defense commitments to the nationalist government on Taiwan.

During that decade there was little questioning of this policy, probably because of the residue of feeling resulting from Chinese intervention in Korea and crises created by Chinese pressure on Taiwan and the offshore islands. During the 1960's, however, opinion became more vocal that mainland China should not remain isolated, and the United States should establish diplomatic relations and stop opposing Chinese admission to the United Nations. Spokesmen for this position generally did not minimize the possibility of Chinese threats to the peace of Asia, but believed that the United States could best serve its interests with a policy of strength and flexibility. Meanwhile, one basic problem remained: what to do about the government of Chiang Kai-shek.

WORLD WAR II POLICY TOWARD
CHINESE NATIONALISTS AND CHINESE COMMUNISTS

A. Recommendation of U.S. Ambassador Patrick Hurley Against American Aid to the Chinese Communists*

January–February, 1945

Meanwhile, another problem had arisen shortly before the Ambassador's departure for Washington. This was the problem of supplying American arms and equipment to groups in China other than the National Government. The Ambassador recommended that "all such requests, no matter how reasonable they may seem to be, be universally refused until or unless they receive the sanction of the National Government and of the American Government." It was his "steadfast position that all armed warlords, armed partisans and the armed forces of the Chinese Communists must without exception submit to the control of the National Government before China can in fact have a unified military force or unified government." The Ambassador followed this policy in connection with a request from General Chu Teh in January 1945 that the United States Army lend the Communist forces 20 million dollars in United States currency for use in procuring the defection of officers and men of the Chinese puppet government together with their arms and for use in encouraging sabotage and demolition work by puppet troops behind the Japanese lines. General Chu informed General Wedemeyer that his forces would assume full responsibility for repayment of the loan following victory over Japan and in support of his request submitted a document claiming that during 1944 Communist forces won over 34,167 Chinese puppet troops with 20,850 rifles, sidearms, mortars, field pieces, etc. The document estimated that with American financial help puppet defections during 1945 could be increased to 90,000 men. In commenting on this proposal the Ambassador stated:

"While financial assistance of the type requested by General Chu might in the end prove to be more economical than importing a similar quantity of arms and ammunition from the United States for use against Japan, I am of the firm opinion that such help would be identical to supplying arms to the Communist armed Party and would, therefore, be a dangerous precedent. The established policy of the United States to prevent the collapse of the National Government and to sustain Chiang Kai-shek as president of the Government and Generalissimo of the Armies would be defeated by acceptance of the Communist Party's plan or by granting the lend-lease and monetary assistance requested by General Chu Teh."

---

*Department of State, *United States Relations with China*, (Washington, 1949), pp. 86-87.

B. Recommendations of George Atcheson, American Chargé d'Affaires, on Supplying Arms and Military Equipment to Chinese Communists*

[Extract]

February 28, 1945

Shortly after the arrival of General Hurley in Washington for consultation the question of supplying arms and military equipment to the Chinese Communist forces was raised by the American Chargé d'Affaires at Chungking, George Atcheson, in the communication to the Department of State paraphrased below. The Chargé had reported on February 26 that since the conclusion of negotiations with the Communists there had been a growing impression among observers there that for various reasons the Generalissimo had greatly stiffened his attitude toward the Communists and toward the continuing faint hopes held by some liberals that a settlement might still eventually be possible.

It appears that the situation in China is developing in some ways which are neither conducive to the future unity and peace of China nor to the effective prosecution of the war.

A necessary initial step in handling the problem was the recent American endeavor to assist compromise between the factions in China through diplomatic and persuasive means. Not only was unity correctly regarded as the essence of China's most effective conduct of the war, but also of the speedy, peaceful emergence of a China which would be united, democratic, and strong.

However, the rapid development of United States Army plans for rebuilding the armies of Chiang Kai-shek, the increase of additional aid such as that of the War Production Board, the cessation of Japanese offensives, the opening of the road into China, the expectation that the Central Government will participate at San Francisco in making important decisions, the conviction that we are determined upon definite support and strengthening of the Central Government alone and as the sole possible channel for assistance to other groups, the foregoing circumstances have combined to increase Chiang Kai-shek's feeling of strength greatly. They have resulted in lack of willingness to make any compromise and unrealistic optimism on the part of Chiang Kai-shek.

Among other things, this attitude is reflected in hopes of an early settlement with the Soviet Union without settlement of the Communist problem, when nothing was ultimately offered except an advisory inter-party committee without place or power in the Government, and in recent appointments of a military-political character, placing strong anti-Communists in strategic war areas, and naming reactionaries to high administrative posts, such as General Ho Kuo Kuang, previously Commander-in-Chief of Gendarmerie, as Chairman of Formosa; and Admiral Chan Chak, Tai Li subordinate, as mayor of Canton.

On their part, the Communists have arrived at the conclusion that we are definitely committed to the support of Chiang Kai-shek alone, and that Chiang's hand will not be forced by us so that we may be able to assist or cooperate

Ibid., pp. 87–92.

with the Communists. Consequently, in what is regarded by them as self-protection, they are adopting the course of action which was forecast in statements made by Communist leaders last summer in the event they were still excluded from consideration, of increasing their forces actively and expanding their areas to the south aggressively, reaching southeast China, regardless of nominal control by the Kuomintang. We previously reported to the Department extensive movements and conflicts with forces of the Central Government already occurring.

It is the intention of the Communists, in seizing time by the forelock, to take advantage of East China's isolation by the capture of the Canton-Hankow Railway by Japan to render themselves as nearly invincible as they can before the new armies of Chiang Kai-shek, which are being formed in Yunnan at the present time, are prepared; and to present to us the dilemma of refusing or accepting their assistance if our forces land at any point on the coast of China. There is now talk by Communists close to the leaders of the need of seeking Soviet aid. Active consideration is being given to the creation of a unified council of their various independent guerrilla governments by the party itself, which is broadcasting demands for Communist and other non-Kuomintang representations at San Francisco.

Despite the fact that our actions in our refusal to aid or deal with any group other than the Central Government have been diplomatically correct, and our intentions have been good, the conclusion appears clear that if this situation continues, and if our analysis of it is correct, the probable outbreak of disastrous civil conflict will be accelerated and chaos in China will be inevitable.

It is apparent that even for the present this situation, wherein we are precluded from cooperating with the strategically situated, large and aggressive armies and organized population of the Communist areas, and also with the forces like the Li Chi-shen-Tsai Ting-k'ai group in the southeast, is, from a military standpoint, hampering and unsatisfactory. From a long-range viewpoint, as set forth above, the situation is also dangerous to American interests.

If the situation is not checked, it is likely to develop with increasing acceleration, as the tempo of the war in China and the entire Far East is raised, and the inevitable resolution of the internal conflict in China becomes more imperative. It will be dangerous to permit matters to drift; the time is short.

In the event the high military authorities of the United States agree that some cooperation is desirable or necessary with the Communists and with other groups who have proved that they are willing and in a position to fight Japan, it is our belief that the paramount and immediate consideration of military necessity should be made the basis for a further step in the policy of the United States. A favorable opportunity for discussion of this matter should be afforded by the presence of General Wedemeyer and General Hurley in Washington.

The initial step which we propose for consideration, predicated upon the assumption of the existence of the military necessity, is that the President inform Chiang Kai-shek in definite terms that we are required by military necessity to cooperate with and supply the Communists and other suitable groups who can aid in this war against the Japanese, and that to accomplish this end, we are taking direct steps. Under existing conditions, this would not include forces which are not in actual position to attack the enemy, such as the Szechwan warlords. Chiang Kai-shek can be assured by us that we do not contemplate reduction of our assistance to the Central Government. Because of transport difficulties, any assistance we give to the Communists or to other groups must be on a small scale at first. It will be less than the natural increase in the flow of supplies into China, in all probability. We may include a statement that we will furnish the Central Government with information as to the type and extent of such assistance. In addition, we can inform Chiang Kai-shek that it will be possible for us to use our cooperation and supplies as a lever to restrict them to their present areas and to limit aggressive and independent action on their part. Also we can indicate the advantages of having the Communists assisted by the United States instead of seeking direct or indirect help or intervention from the Soviet Union.

Chiang Kai-shek might also be told, if it is regarded as advisable, at the time of making this statement to him, that while our endeavor to persuade the various groups of the desirability of unification has failed and it is not possible for us to delay measures for the most effective prosecution of the war any longer, we regard it as obviously desirable that our military aid to all groups be based upon coordination of military command and upon unity, that we are prepared, where it is feasible, and when requested, to lend our good offices to this end, and although we believe the proposals should come from Chiang Kai-shek, we would be disposed to support the following:

First, formation of something along the line of a war cabinet or supreme war council in which Communists and other groups would be effectively represented, and which would have some part in responsibility for executing and formulating joint plans for war; second, nominal incorporation of Communist and other forces selected into the armies of the Central Government, under the operational command of United States officers designated by Chiang Kai-shek upon General Wedemeyer's advice, upon agreement by all parties that these forces would operate only within their existing areas or areas which have been specifically extended. However, it should be clearly stated that our decision to cooperate with any forces able to assist the war effort will neither be delayed by nor contingent upon the completion of such internal Chinese arrangements.

It is our belief that such a *modus operandi* would serve as an initial move toward complete solution of the problem of final entire unity, and would bridge the existing deadlock in China. The principal and over-riding issues have become clear, as one result of the recent negotiations. At the present time, Chiang Kai-shek will not take any forward step which will mean loss of face, personal power, or prestige. Without guarantees in which they believe, the Communists will not take any forward step involving dispersion and eventual elimination of their forces, upon which depend their strength at this time and their political existence in the future. The force required to break this deadlock will be exerted on both parties by the step we propose to take. The *modus operandi* set forth in these two proposals should initiate concrete military cooperation, with political cooperation as an inevitable result, and consequently furnish a foundation for increasing development toward unity in the future.

The political consultation committee plan, which could function, if adopted, side by side with the Government and the war council, would not be excluded by these proposals. It should be anticipated that the committee would be greatly strengthened, in fact.

Of course, the statements to the Generalissimo should be made in private, but the possibility would be clearly understood, in case of his refusal to accept it, of the logical, much more drastic step of a public expression of policy such as that which was made by Churchill with reference to Yugoslavia.

The fact of our aid to the Communists and other forces would shortly become known throughout China, however, even if not made public. It is out belief that profound and desirable political effects in China would result from this. A tremendous internal pressure for unity exists in China, based upon compromise with the Communists and an opportunity for self-expression on the part of the now repressed liberal groups. Even inside the Kuomintang, these liberal groups such as the Sun Fo group, and the minor parties, were ignored in recent negotiations by the Kuomintang, although not by the Communists, with whom they present what amounts to a united front, and they are discouraged and disillusioned by what they regard as an American commitment to the Kuomintang's existing reactionary leadership. We would prove we are not so committed by the steps which we proposed, we would markedly improve the prestige and morale of these liberal groups, and the strongest possible influence would be exerted by us by means of these internal forces to impel Chiang Kai-shek to make the concessions required for unity and to put his own house in order.

Such a policy would unquestionably be greatly welcomed by the vast majority of the people of China, even though not by the very small reactionary minority by which the Kuomintang is controlled, and American prestige would be increased by it.

The statement has been made to a responsible American by Sun Fo himself that if Chiang Kai-shek were told, not asked, regarding United States aid to Communists and guerrillas, this would do more to make Chiang Kai-shek come to terms with them than any other course of action. It is believed by the majority of the people of China that settlement of China's internal problems is more a matter of reform of the Kuomintang itself than a matter of mutual concessions. The Chinese also state, with justification, that American non-intervention in China cannot avoid being intervention in favor of the conservative leadership which exists at the present time.

In addition, by a policy such as this, which we feel realistically accepts the facts in China, we could expect to obtain the cooperation of all the forces of China in the war; to hold the Communists to our side instead of throwing them into the arms of the Soviet Union, which is inevitable otherwise in the event the U.S.S.R. enters the war against Japan; to convince the Kuomintang that its apparent plans for eventual civil war are undesirable; and to bring about some unification, even if not immediately complete, that would furnish a basis for peaceful development toward complete democracy in the future.

General Hurley strongly opposed the course of action recommended above and it remained the policy of the United States to supply military material and financial support only to the recognized Chinese National Government.

*   *   *

C. Interview Between Ambassador Hurley and Marshal Joseph Stalin on Chinese Communists and Nationalists*

[Extract]

April 15, 1945

After consultation in Washington, the Ambassador departed on April 3, 1945, for Chungking. He travelled by way of London and Moscow in order to discuss American policy in China with British and Soviet leaders. He reported to the Department of State that on the night of April 15, 1945, he had concluded a conference with Marshal Stalin and Foreign Minister Molotov in which the Ambassador, Mr. Harriman, had also participated. With respect to this conference General Hurley reported to the Department that he had recited for Marshal Stalin in the presence of Mr. Molotov his analysis of Mr. Molotov's earlier statement respecting the Soviet attitude toward the Chinese Communist Party and the National Government. His report, dated April 17, continued:

"My analysis was briefly as follows: 'Molotov said at the former conference that the Chinese Communists are not in fact Communists at all. Their objective is to obtain what they look upon as necessary and just reformations in China. The Soviet Union is not supporting the Chinese Communist Party. The Soviet Union does not desire internal dissension or civil war in China. The Government of the Soviet Union wants closer and more harmonious relations in China. The Soviet Union is intensely interested in what is happening in Sinkiang and other places and will insist that the Chinese Government prevent discriminations against Soviet Nationals.' Molotov agreed to this analysis. I then outlined for Stalin and Molotov existing relations between the Chinese Government and the Chinese Communist Party. I stated with frankness that I had been instrumental in instituting conferences and negotiations between the Chinese Communist Party and the Chinese Government. I then presented in brief form an outline of the negotiations, of the progress which had been made and of the present status. I informed Stalin that both the Chinese Government and the Chinese Communist Party claimed to follow the principles of Sun Yat-sen for the establishment of a government of the people, by the people and for the people in China. I continued that the National Government and the Chinese Communist Party are both strongly anti-Japanese and that the purpose of both is to drive the Japanese from China. Beyond question there are issues between the Chinese Communist Party and the Chinese Government, but both are pursuing the same principal objective, namely, the defeat of Japan and the creating of a free, demo-

*Ibid., pp. 94-96.

cratic and united government in China. Because of past conflicts there are many differences on details existing between the two parties. I made clear American insistence that China supply its own leadership, arrive at its own decisions, and be responsible for its own policies. With this in mind, the United States had endorsed China's aspirations to establish a free, united government and supported all efforts for the unification of the armed forces of China. I informed him that President Roosevelt had authorized me to discuss this subject with Prime Minister Churchill and that the complete concurrence of Prime Minister Churchill and Foreign Secretary Eden had been obtained in the policy of endorsement of Chinese aspirations to establish for herself a united, free, and democratic government and for the unification of all armed forces in China in order to bring about the defeat of Japan. To promote the foregoing program it had been decided to support the National Government of China under the leadership of Chiang Kai-shek. Stalin stated frankly that the Soviet Government would support the policy. He added that he would be glad to cooperate with the United States and Britain in achieving unification of the military forces in China. He spoke favorably of Chiang Kai-shek and said that while there had been corruption among certain officials of the National Government of China, he knew that Chiang Kai-shek was 'selfless', 'a patriot' and that the Soviet in times past had befriended him . . ."

*   *   *

D. Instructions Given by Secretary of State E.R. Stettinius to Ambassador Hurley on Russian Intervention in China*

April 23, 1945

I attach great importance to Marshal Stalin's endorsement at the present time of our program for furthering the political and military unity of China under Generalissimo Chiang Kai-shek. However, at the same time I feel, as I have no doubt you do also, the necessity of facing the probability that Marshal Stalin's offer is given in direct relation to circumstances that are existing now and that may not long continue. The U.S.S.R. is at present preoccupied in Europe and the basis for her position in Asia following the war is not yet affected by the Communist-Kuomintang issue to an appreciable degree. In view of these circumstances I can well appreciate the logic of Marshal Stalin's readiness to defer to our leadership and to support American efforts directed toward military and political unification which could scarcely fail to be acceptable to the U.S.S.R. If and when the Soviet Union begins to participate actively in the Far Eastern theater, Chinese internal unity has not been established and the relative advantages of cooperation with one side or the other become a matter of great practical concern to the future position of the Soviet Union in Asia, it would be equally logical, I believe, to expect the U.S.S.R. to reexamine Soviet policy and to revise its policy in accordance with its best interests. Consequently I believe

* *Ibid.*, p. 98.

that it is of the utmost importance that when informing Generalissimo Chiang Kai-shek of the statements made by Marshal Stalin you take special pains to convey to him the general thought expressed in the preceding paragraph in order that the urgency of the situation may be fully realized by him. Please impress upon Generalissimo Chiang Kai-shek the necessity for early military and political unification in order not only to bring about the successful conclusion of the Japanese war but also to establish a basis upon which relations between China and the Soviet Union may eventually become one of mutual respect and permanent friendship.

E. Yalta Far Eastern Agreement*

February 11, 1945

The leaders of the three great powers—the Soviet Union, the United States of America and Great Britain—have agreed that in two or three months after Germany has surrendered and the war in Europe has terminated, the Soviet Union shall enter into the 'war against Japan on the side of the Allies on conditions that:

1) The status quo in Outer Mongolia (the Mongolian People's Republic) shall be preserved;

2) The former rights of Russia violated by the treacherous attack of Japan in 1904 shall be restored, vis:

> (a) the southern part of Sakhalin as well as the islands adjacent to it shall be returned to the Soviet Union;
> (b) the commercial port of Dairen shall be internationalized, the pre-eminent interests of the Soviet Union in this port being safeguarded and the lease of Port Arthur as a naval base of the U.S.S.R. restored;
> (c) the Chinese-Eastern Railroad and the South-Manchurian Railroad, which provide an outlet to Dairen, shall be jointly operated by the establishment of a joint Soviet-Chinese company, it being understood that the pre-eminent interests of the Soviet Union shall be safeguarded and that China shall retain full sovereignty in Manchuria;

3) The Kurile islands shall be handed over to the Soviet Union.

It is understood that the agreement concerning Outer Mongolia and the ports and railroads referred to above will require concurrence of Generalissimo Chiang Kai-shek. The President will take measures in order to obtain this concurrence on advice from Marshal Stalin.

The heads of the three great powers have agreed that these claims of the Soviet Union shall be unquestionably fulfilled after Japan has been defeated.

For its part, the Soviet Union expresses its readiness to conclude with the National Government of China a pact of friendship and alliance between the U.S.S.R. and China in order to render assistance to China with its armed forces for the purpose of liberating China from the Japanese yoke.

Joseph V. Stalin
Franklin D. Roosevelt
Winston S. Churchill

*Department of State, *Foreign Relations of the United States: The Conferences at Malta and Yalta, 1945* (Washington, 1955), p. 984.

F. Treaty of Friendship and Alliance Between the Republic of China and the U.S.S.R.*

August 14, 1945

The President of the National Government of the Republic of China, and the Presidium of the Supreme Soviet of the U.S.S.R.,

Desirous of strengthening the friendly relations that have always existed between China and the U.S.S.R., through an alliance and good neighborly post-war collaboration,

Determined to assist each other in the struggle against aggression on the part of enemies of the United Nations in this world war, and to collaborate in the common war against Japan until her unconditional surrender,

Expressing their unswerving aspiration to cooperate in the cause of maintaining peace and security for the benefit of the peoples of both countries and of all the peace-loving nations,

Acting upon the principles enunciated in the joint declaration of the United Nations of January 1, 1942, in the four power Declaration signed in Moscow on October 30, 1943, and in the Charter of the International Organization of the United Nations.

Have decided to conclude the present Treaty to this effect and appointed as their plenipotentiaries:

The President of the National Government of the Republic of China;

His Excellency Dr. Wang Shih-chieh, Minister for Foreign Affairs of the Republic of China,

The Presidium of the Supreme Soviet of the U.S.S.R.;

His Excellency Mr. V.M. Molotov, the People's Commissar of Foreign Affairs of the U.S.S.R.,

Who, after exchanging their Full Powers, found in good and due form, have agreed as follows:

Article I

The High Contracting Parties undertake in association with the other United Nations to wage war against Japan until final victory is won. The High Contracting Parties undertake mutually to render to one another all necessary military and other assistance and support in this war.

Article II

The High Contracting Parties undertake not to enter into separate negotiations with Japan and not to conclude, without mutual consent, any armistice or peace treaty either with the present Japanese Government or with any other government or authority set up in Japan which do not renounce all aggressive intentions.

*Department of State Bulletin, Feb. 10, 1946, pp. 201-02.

Article III

The high Contracting Parties undertake after the termination of the war against Japan to take jointly all measures in their power to render impossible a repetition of aggression and violation of the peace by Japan.

In the event of one of the High Contracting Parties becoming involved in hostilities with Japan in consequence of an attack by the latter against the said Contracting Party, the other High Contracting Party shall at once give to the Contracting Party so involved in hostilities all the military and other support and assistance with the means in its power.

This article shall remain in force until such time as the organization "The United Nations" may on request of the two High Contracting Parties be charged with the responsibility for preventing further aggression by Japan.

Article IV

Each High Contracting Party undertakes not to conclude any alliance and not to take any part in any coalition directed against the other High Contracting Party.

Article V

The High Contracting Parties, having regard to the interests of the security and economic development of each of them, agree to work together in close and friendly collaboration after the coming of peace and to act according to the principles of mutual respect for their sovereignty and territorial integrity and of non-interference in the internal affairs of the other contracting party.

Article VI

The High Contracting Parties agree to render each other every possible economic assistance in the post-war period with a view to facilitating and accelerating reconstruction in both countries and to contributing to the cause of world prosperity.

Article VII

Nothing in this treaty shall be so construed as may affect the rights or obligations of the High Contracting Parties as members of the organization "The United Nations".

Article VIII

The present Treaty shall be ratified in the shortest possible time. The exchange of the instruments of ratification shall take place as soon as possible in Chungking.

The Treaty comes into force immediately upon its ratification and shall remain in force for a term of thirty years.

If neither of the High Contracting Parties has given notice, a year before the expiration of the term, of its desire to terminate the Treaty, it shall remain valid for an unlimited time, each of the High Contracting Parties being able to terminate its operation by giving notice to that effect one year in advance.

In faith whereof the Plenipotentiaries have signed the present Treaty and affixed their seals to it.

Done in Moscow, the Fourteenth August, 1945, corresponding to the Fourteenth day of the Eighth month of the Thirty-fourth year of the Chinese Republic, in two copies, each one in the Russian and Chinese languages, both texts being equally authoritative.

The Plenipotentiary of the Supreme Soviet
of the U.S.S.R.

The Plenipotentiary of the President of the National
Government of the Republic of China

G. Comment by President Harry S. Truman on Ambassador Hurley's Resignation*

[Extract]

1956

Ambassador Hurley was engaged in an effort to get the Chinese Communists and the government of Chiang Kai-shek to sit down together and solve their differences peacefully. The Ambassador had sent me a series of long cables in which he gave me his views on the situation. He had gone to China at first not as our diplomatic representative but as President Roosevelt's personal representative. He was critical of the State Department, and in many of the cables and reports that I received from him he questioned the judgment and ability of the career diplomats. He felt very strongly, as I did, that America ought to be the champion of anti-imperialism in Asia. Hurley complained that the State Department did not give his reports and recommendations the priority he thought they deserved.

Finally, on September 10, 1945, he restated once again, as he had done on several previous occasions, what he understood to have been President Roosevelt's long-range aims in Asia. He recited what he had done to further these

*Harry S. Truman, *Memoirs: Years of Trial and Hope* (New York, 1958), pp. 64-66.

aims and quoted instances of decisions made in Washington which he thought differed in their aims from what he thought the wisest course. Then he asked for permission to return to Washington. "I would like," he cabled to the Secretary of State, "to have an opportunity to discuss the American Asiatic policy with you, sir, and the President."

After he had come back, Hurley called at the White House with Secretary Byrnes, and a week later both Hurley and Wedemeyer came in for a more extended discussion. I made it clear to them that it would be our policy to support Chiang Kai-shek but that we would not be driven into fighting Chiang's battles for him.

General Hurley reported to me that, in spite of all weaknesses which he and Wedemeyer recognized, the prospects for peaceful development in China were favorable. Economically, China's potential was not substantially different from the situation just before 1937. The main problem ahead seemed to be not production but distribution. Financially, our continued aid has placed China in a better position than she had known in years, and politically, General Hurley had just succeeded in bringing the Communist leader, Mao Tse-tung, to Chungking for direct discussion with the National Government leaders. Out of these discussions there came an agreement between the Chinese leaders which was published on October 11, just two days before Hurley first called at the White House. At that moment there was reason to hope that China's problems might be solved.

Hurley had witnessed the preliminary signing of this agreement, and he told me that it promised to lead to true peace in China. The agreement called for a constitutional convention, a national assembly that would write a new constitution, and included provisions that would enable all political parties to take part. Chiang Kai-shek, apparently, would have the strongest voice in this convention since more of his followers would be seated than Communists.

An interim council of forty, appointed by Chiang Kai-shek but with not more than half from his party, would run affairs until the new constitution could come into force. Chiang Kai-shek would have a veto over any of the council's decisions, although three fifths of the council could override such vetoes.

This was a good agreement, and I congratulated Hurley on the fine work that had made it possible. However, the agreement never bore results.

Chiang Kai-shek's forces were moving into areas held by the Japanese, with a large part of his troops being ferried north by our Air Force transports. We had also landed fifty thousand of our marines at several important ports so that, through these ports, the removal of the Japanese could be carried on. The Communists wanted the National Government to stop these troop movements, for they believed that Chiang was taking advantage of the situation to strengthen his positions against them. Nor were they passive about it. They cut the rail lines wherever they could, and the Chungking government soon began receiving reports that the Chinese Communists, contrary to the agreement, were moving into Manchuria. Resentment was rising on both sides as the charges and countercharges increased.

On November 4, our embassy in Chungking reported that civil war seemed to be threatening, and the Political Consultative Conference, which was scheduled to convene November 20, failed to meet. On November 25 Chou En-lai, the principal representative of the Communists in Chungking, left for Yenan, and the next day his first deputy followed him. By now there were reports of armed clashes. I discussed the seriousness of the situation with Hurley at the White House on November 27, and we agreed that it would be best if he returned to Chungking without delay. He assured me that he would only wind up a few personal matters and then return to China.

This conversation took place about 11:30 A.M., but less than two hours later, while the members of the Cabinet were with me for the weekly Cabinet luncheon, I was called to the telephone. One of the White House correspondents called from the National Press Club and to my astonishment told me that Ambassador Hurley, in a talk with newspapermen, had attacked the administration, the State Department, our foreign policy, and me personally.

To me, this was an utterly inexplicable about-face, and what had caused it I cannot imagine even yet. I realized, however, that Hurley would have to go, and the Cabinet concurred. The same day I learned to my surprise that a "letter of resignation" from Hurley was given by him to the press; but he would have been out, with or without that letter.

Hurley was an impetuous sort of person. A few weeks later—in January 1946—he made a special effort to see my press secretary, Charlie Ross. He explained to Ross that he was anxious to serve me anywhere and at any time, and he wanted Ross to tell me that nothing he had said at the time of his resignation had been intended as a personal criticism of me.

"He begged me to believe," Ross reported to me, "that he was 'in your corner.'"

Hurley went on to say to Ross, "Byrnes is a smart enough man . . . but he hasn't been given sufficient information by the 'flagpole sitters' in the State Department . . . There is no reason for Byrnes's agitation over Chinese-Russian relations because they are all spelled out in the agreement by the Chinese and the Russians signed last July or August . . . ." The reason Byrnes had no need to worry was that, according to Hurley, "Stalin keeps his word."

*   *   *

THE MISSION OF GENERAL GEORGE C. MARSHALL IN CHINA, 1945-1947

A. President Truman to General Marshall, Special Representative of the President to China*

[Extract]

Washington, December 15, 1945

My dear General Marshall:

On the eve of your departure for China I want to repeat to you my appreciation of your willingness to undertake this difficult mission.

I have the utmost confidence in your ability to handle the task before you but, to guide you in so far as you may find it helpful, I will give you some of the thoughts, ideas, and objectives which Secretary Byrnes and I have in mind with regard to your mission.

              *   *   *

The fact that I have asked you to go to China is the clearest evidence of my very real concern with regard to the situation there. Secretary Byrnes and I are both anxious that the unification of China by peaceful, democratic methods be achieved as soon as possible. It is my desire that you, as my Special Representative, bring to bear in an appropriate and practicable manner the influence of the United States to this end.

Specifically, I desire that you endeavor to persuade the Chinese Government to call a national conference of representatives of the major political elements to bring about the unification of China and, concurrently, to effect a cessation of hostilities, particularly in north China.

It is my understanding that there is now in session in Chungking a Peoples' Consultative Council made up of representatives of the various political elements, including the Chinese Communists. The meeting of this Council should furnish you with a convenient opportunity for discussions with the various political leaders.

Upon the success of your efforts, as outlined above, will depend largely, of course, the success of our plans for evacuating Japanese troops from China particularly north China, and for the subsequent withdrawal of our own armed forces from China. I am particularly desirous that both be accomplished as soon as possible.

In your conversations with Chiang Kai-shek and other Chinese leaders you are authorized to speak with the utmost frankness. Particularly, you may state in connection with the Chinese desire for credits, technical assistance in the economic field, and military assistance (I have in mind the proposed U.S. military advisory group which I have approved in principle), that a China disunited

*United States Relations with China, pp. 605-06.

and torn by civil strife could not be considered realistically as a proper place for American assistance along the lines enumerated.

I am anxious that you keep Secretary Byrnes and me currently informed of the progress of your negotiations and of obstacles you may encounter. You will have our full support and we shall endeavor at all times to be as helpful to you as possible.

B. Statement by President Truman on United States Policy Toward China*

December 15, 1945

The Government of this United States holds that peace and prosperity of the world in this new and unexplored era ahead depend upon the ability of the sovereign nations to combine for collective security in the United Nations organization.

It is the firm belief of this Government that a strong, united and democratic China is of the utmost importance to the success of this United Nations organization and for world peace. A China disorganized and divided either by foreign aggression, such as that undertaken by the Japanese, or by violent internal strife, is an undermining influence to world stability and peace, now and in the future. The United States Government has long subscribed to the principle that the management of internal affairs is the responsibility of the peoples of the sovereign nations. Events of this century, however, would indicate that a breach of peace anywhere in the world threatens the peace of the entire world. It is thus in the most vital interest of the United States and all the United Nations that the people of China overlook no opportunity to adjust their internal differences promptly by means of peaceful negotiation.

The Government of the United States believes it essential:

(1) That a cessation of hostilities be arranged between the armies of the National Government and the Chinese Communists and other dissident Chinese armed forces for the purpose of completing the return of all China to effective Chinese control, including the immediate evacuation of the Japanese forces.

(2) That a national conference of representatives of major political elements be arranged to develop an early solution to the present internal strife—a solution which will bring about the unification of China.

The United States and the other United Nations have recognized the present National Government of the Republic of China as the only legal government in China. It is the proper instrument to achieve the objective of a unified China.

The United States and the United Kingdom by the Cairo Declaration in 1943 and the Union of Soviet Socialist Republics by adhering to the Potsdam Declaration of last July and by the Sino-Soviet Treaty and Agreements of August 1945, are all committed to the liberation of China, including the return of Manchuria to Chinese control. These agreements were made with the National Government of the Republic of China.

*Department of State Bulletin, Dec. 16, 1945, p. 945.

In continuation of the constant and close collaboration with the national Government of the Republic of China in the prosecution of this war, in consonance with the Potsdam Declaration, and to remove possibility of Japanese influence remaining in China, the United States has assumed a definite obligation in the disarmament and evacuation of the Japanese troops. Accordingly the United States has been assisting and will continue to assist the National Government of the Republic of China in effecting the disarmament and evacuation of Japanese troops in the liberated areas. The United States Marines are in North China for that purpose.

The United States recognizes and will continue to recognize the National Government of China and cooperate with it in international affairs and specifically in eliminating Japanese influence from China. The United States is convinced that a prompt arrangement for a cessation of hostilities is essential to the effective achievement of this end. United States support will not extend to United States military intervention to influence the course of any Chinese internal strife.

The United States has already been compelled to pay a great price to restore the peace which was first broken by Japanese aggression in Manchuria. The maintenance of peace in the Pacific may be jeopardized, if not frustrated, unless Japanese influence in China is wholly removed and unless China takes her place as a unified, democratic and peaceful nation. This is the purpose of the maintenance for the time being of United States military and naval forces in China.

The United States is cognizant that the present National Government of China is a "one-party government" and believes that peace, unity and democratic reform in China will be furthered if the basis of this Government is broadened to include other political elements in the country. Hence, the United States strongly advocates that the national conference of representatives of major political elements in the country agree upon arrangements which would give those elements a fair and effective representation in the Chinese National Government. It is recognized that this would require modification of the one-party "political tutelage" established as an interim arrangement in the progress of the nation toward democracy by the father of the Chinese Republic, Doctor Sun Yat-sen.

The existence of autonomous armies such as that of the Communist army is inconsistent with, and actually makes impossible, political unity in China. With the institution of a broadly representative government autonomous armies should be eliminated as such and all armed forces in China integrated effectively into the Chinese National Army.

In line with its often expressed views regarding self-determination, the United States Government considers that the detailed steps necessary to the achievement of political unity in China must be worked out by the Chinese themselves and that intervention by any foreign government in these matters would be inappropriate. The United States Government feels, however, that China has a clear responsibility to the other United Nations to eliminate armed conflict within its territory as constituting a threat to world stability and peace—a responsibility which is shared by the National Government and all Chinese political and military groups.

As China moves toward peace and unity along the lines described above, the United States would be prepared to assist the National Government in every reasonable way to rehabilitate the country, improve the agrarian and industrial economy, and establish a military organization capable of discharging China's national and international responsibilities for the maintenance of peace and order. In furtherance of such assistance, it would be prepared to give favorable consideration to Chinese requests for credits and loans under reasonable conditions for projects which would contribute toward the development of a healthy economy throughout China and healthy trade relations between China and the United States.

C. President Truman to President Chiang Kai-shek*

Washington, August 10, 1946

I have followed closely the situation in China since I sent General Marshall to you as my Special Envoy. It is with profound regret that I am forced to the conclusion that his efforts have seemingly proved unavailing.

In his discussions with you, I am certain that General Marshall has reflected accurately the overall attitude and policy of the American Government and of informed American public opinion also.

The rapidly deteriorating political situation in China, during recent months, has been a cause of grave concern to the American people. While it is the continued hope to the United States that an influential and democratic China can still be achieved under your leadership, I would be less than honest if I did not point out that latest developments have forced me to the conclusion that the selfish interests of extremist elements, both in the Kuomintang and the Communist Party, are obstructing the aspirations of the people of China.

*   *   *

In the United States, there now exists an increasing school of thought which maintains that our whole policy toward China must be re-examined in the light of spreading strife, and notably by evidence of the increasing trend to suppress the expression of liberal views among intellectuals as well as freedom of the press. The assassinations of distinguished Chinese liberals at Kunming recently have not been ignored. Regardless of where responsibility may lie for these cruel murders, the result has been to cause American attention to focus on the China situation, and there is increasing belief that an attempt is being made to resort to force, military or secret police rather than democratic processes to settle major social issues.

American faith in the peaceful and democratic aspirations of the Chinese people has not been destroyed by recent events, but has been shaken. The firm desire of the people of the United States and of the American Government is still to help China achieve lasting peace and a stable economy under a truly

United States Relations with China, p. 652.

democratic government. There is an increasing awareness, however, that the hopes of the people of China are being thwarted by militarists and a small group of political reactionaries who are obstructing the advancement of the general good of the nation by failing to understand the liberal trend of the times. The people of the United States view with violent repugnance this state of affairs.

It cannot be expected that American opinion will continue in its generous attitude towards your nation unless convincing proof is shortly forthcoming that genuine progress is being made toward a peaceful settlement of China's internal problems. Furthermore, it will be necessary for me to redefine and explain the position of the United States to the people of America.

I earnestly hope that in the near future I may receive some encouraging word from you which will facilitate the achievement of our mutually declared aims.

D. Chinese Ambassador V.K. Wellington Koo To President Truman*

Washington, August 28, 1946

My dear Mr. President:

Referring to my acknowledgement of August 12 of your letter dated August 10 containing a message to President Chiang Kai-shek, I have the honor to transmit to your excellency, in accordance with instructions, the following reply:

"Referring to your· message of August 10, I wish to thank you cordially for your expressions of genuine concern for the welfare of my country.

"General Marshall has labored most unsparingly to achieve our common objective; namely, peace and democracy in China, since his arrival. Despite all obstacles, I, too, have done my utmost to cooperate with him in the accomplishment of his task.

"The desire for peace has to be mutual, therefore, it means the Communists must give up their policy to seize political power through the use of armed force, to overthrow the government and to install a totalitarian regime such as those with which Eastern Europe is now being engulfed.

"The minimum requirement for the preservation of peace in our country is the abandonment of such a policy. The Communists attacked and captured Changchun in Manchuria and attacked and captured Tehchow in Shantung after the conclusion of the January agreement. In June, during the cease-fire period, they attacked Tatung and Taiyuan in Shansi and Hsuchow in northern Kiangsu. They have opened a wide offensive on the Lunghai railway in the last few days, with Hsuchow and Kaifeng as their objectives.

"Mistakes have also been made by some subordinates on the government side, of course, but compared to the flagrant violations on the part of the Communists, they are minor in scale. We deal sternly with the offender whenever any mistake occurs on our Government side.

"In my V-J Day message on August 14, I announced the firm policy of the government to broaden speedily the basis of the government by the inclusion of all parties and non-partisans, amounting to the effectuation of the program

Ibid., p. 653.

of peaceful reconstruction adopted on January 13 by the political consultation conference. It is my sincere hope that our views will be accepted by the Chinese Communist party. On its part, the Government will do the utmost in the shortest possible time to make peace and democracy a reality in this country.

"I am cooperating with General Marshall with all my power in implementing that policy which has as its aim our mutually declared objective. Success must depend upon the sincerity of the Communists in response to our appeals. I am depending on your continued support in the realization of our goal. (Sgd.) Chiang Kai-shek."

E. General Marshall to President Chiang Kai-shek*

Nanking, October 1, 1946

Your Excellency:

Since our conversation of Monday morning, September 30, and General Yu Ta Wei's call on me the same afternoon, I have carefully considered all the factors involved in the present status of negotiations and military operations.

*   *   *

I am not in agreement either with the present course of the Government in regard to this critical situation or with that of the Communist Party. I disagree with the evident Government policy of settling the fundamental differences involved by force, that is by utilizing a general offensive campaign to force compliance with the Government point of view or demands. I recognize the vital necessity of safeguarding the security of the Government, but I think the present procedure has past well beyond that point.

On the part of the Communist Party, I deplore actions and statements which provide a basis for the contention on the part of many in the Government that the Communist's proposals can not be accepted in good faith, that it is not the intention of that Party to cooperate in a genuine manner in a reorganization of the Government, but rather to disrupt the Government and seize power for their own purposes.

I will not refer to the circumstances connected with the ineffective negotiations since last March. I wish merely to state that unless a basis for agreement is found to terminate the fighting without further delays or proposals and counter-proposals, I will recommend to the President that I be recalled and that the United States Government terminate its efforts of mediation.

F. President Chiang Kai-shek to General Marshall*

Nanking, October 2, 1946

Your Excellency's letter dated October 1, 1946, which was attached with

*Ibid., pp. 662-63.
*Ibid., pp. 663-64.

a letter from General Chou En-lai under date of September 30, 1946 handed to you by Mr. Tung Pi-wu, has been received. The Government is more eager than any other party for an early cessation of hostilities, but past experience shows that the Chinese Communist Party has been in the habit of taking advantage of negotiations to obtain respite and regroup their troops in order to launch fresh attacks on Government troops who have been abiding by truce agreements (attached is a list of important evidences of Communist troops attacking Government troops during the truce periods), and that conflicts only ceased temporarily but flared up again after a short interval. Therefore effective means should be devised to assure that cease fire is permanent and not temporary. The Government, having the responsibility of restoring and maintaining order and security in the country, can not allow the chaotic situation to be prolonged indefinitely.

With a view to saving time and showing its utmost sincerity, the Government hereby, with all frankness, expresses its maximum concessions in regard to the solution of the present problem:

(1) The Chinese Communist Party has been incessantly urging the reorganization of the National Government. This hinges on the distribution of the membership of the State Council. The Government originally agreed that the Chinese Communist Party be allocated eight seats and the Democratic League, four, with a total of twelve. The Chinese Communist Party, on the other hand, requested ten for themselves and four for the Democratic League with a total of fourteen. Now the Government makes a fresh concession by taking the mean and offering one seat for the independents to be recommended by the Chinese Communist Party and agreed upon by the Government, so that, added to the original twelve, it makes a total of thirteen seats. But the Communist Party should without delay produce the list of their candidates for the State Council as well as the list of their delegates to the National Assembly. This reassignment of seats should be decided by the proposed group of five to be confirmed by the Steering Committee of PCC.

(2) For immediate implementation of the program for reorganization of the army, the location of the eighteen Communist divisions should be immediately determined and the Communist troops should enter those assigned places according to agreed dates. The above should be decided by the Committee of Three and carried out under the supervision of the Executive Headquarters.

If the Communist Party has the sincerity for achieving peace and cooperating with the Government, and is willing to solve immediately the above-mentioned two problems, a cease fire order should be issued by both sides, when agreement has been reached thereon.

Kindly forward the above to the Communist Party and let me know your esteemed opinion about it.

G. Statement by General Marshall*

January 7, 1947

The President has recently given a summary of the developments in China

Ibid., pp. 686-89.

during the past year and the position of the American Government toward China. Circumstances now dictate that I should supplement this with impressions gained at first hand.

In this intricate and confused situation, I shall merely endeavor here to touch on some of the more important considerations—as they appeared to me—during my connection with the negotiations to bring about peace in China and a stable democratic form of government.

In the first place, the greatest obstacle to peace has been the complete, almost overwhelming suspicion with which the Chinese Communist Party and the Kuomintang regard each other.

On the one hand, the leaders of the Government are strongly opposed to a communistic form of government. On the other hand, the Communists frankly state that they are Marxists and intend to work toward establishing a communistic form of government in China, though first advancing through the medium of a democratic form of government of the American or British type.

The leaders of the Government are convinced in their minds that the Communist-expressed desire to participate in a government of the type endorsed by the political Consultative Conference last January had for its purpose only a destructive intention. The Communists felt, I believe, that the government was insincere in its apparent acceptance of the PCC resolutions for the formation of the new government and intended by coercion of military force and the action of secret police to obliterate the Communist Party. Combined with this mutual deep distrust was the conspicuous error by both parties of ignoring the effect of the fears and suspicions of the other party in estimating the reason for proposals or opposition regarding the settlement of various matters under negotiation. They each sought only to take counsel of their own fears. They both, therefore, to that extent took a rather lopsided view of each situation and were susceptible to every evil suggestion or possibility. This complication was exaggerated to an explosive degree by the confused reports of fighting on the distant and tremendous fronts of hostile military contact. Patrol clashes were deliberately magnified into large offensive actions. The distortion of the facts was utilized by both sides to heap condemnation on the other. It was only through the reports of American officers in the field teams from Executive Headquarters that I could get even a partial idea of what was actually happening and the incidents were too numerous and the distances too great for the American personnel to cover all of the ground. I must comment here on the superb courage of the officers of our Army and Marines in struggling against almost insurmountable and maddening obstacles to bring some measure of peace to China.

I think the most important factors involved in the recent breakdown of negotiations are these: On the side of the National Government, which is in effect the Kuomintang, there is a dominant group of reactionaries who have been opposed, in my opinion, to almost every effort I have made to influence the formation of a genuine coalition government. This has usually been under the cover of political or party action, but since the Party was the Government, this action, though subtle or indirect, has been devastating in its effect. They were quite frank in publicly stating their belief that cooperation by the Chinese

Communist Party in the government was inconceivable and that only a policy of force could defintely settle the issue. This group includes military as well as political leaders.

On the side of the Chinese Communist Party there are, I believe, liberals as well as radicals, though this view is vigorously opposed by many who believe that the Chinese Communist Party discipline is too rigidly enforced to admit of such differences of viewpoint. Nevertheless, it has appeared to me that there is a definite liberal group among the Communists, especially of young men who have turned to the Communists in disgust at the corruption evident in the local governments—men who would put the interest of the Chinese people above ruthless measures to establish a Communist ideology in the immediate future. The dyed-in-the-wool Communists do not hesitate at the most drastic measures to gain their end as, for instance, the destruction of communications in order to wreck the economy of China and produce a situation that would facilitate the overthrow or collapse of the Government, without any regard to the immediate suffering of the people involved. They completely distrust the eaders of the Kuomintang and appear convinced that every Government proposal is designed to crush the Chinese Communist Party. I must say that the quite evidently inspired mob actions of last February and March, some within a few blocks of where I was then engaged in completing negotiations, gave the Communists good excuse for such suspicions.

However, a very harmful and immensely provocative phase of the Chinese Communist Party procedure has been in the character of its propaganda. I wish to state to the American people that in the deliberate misrepresentation and abuse of the action, policies and purposes of our Government this propaganda has been without regard for the truth, without any regard whatsoever for the facts, and has given plain evidence of a determined purpose to mislead the Chinese people and the world and to arouse a bitter hatred of Americans. It has been difficult to remain silent in the midst of such public abuse and whole-sale disregard of facts, but a denial would merely lead to the necessity of daily denials; an intolerable course of action for an American official. In the interest of fairness, I must state that the Nationalist Government publicity agency has made numerous misrepresentations, though not of the vicious nature of the Communist propaganda. Incidentally, the Communist statements regarding the Anping incident which resulted in the death of three Marines and the wounding of twelve others were almost pure fabrication, deliberately representing a carefully arranged ambuscade of a Marine convoy with supplies for the maintenance of Executive Headquarters and some UNRRA supplies, as a defense against a Marine assault. The investigation of this incident was a tortuous procedure of delays and maneuvers to disguise the true and privately admitted facts of the case.

Sincere efforts to achieve settlement have been frustrated time and again by extremist elements of both sides. The agreements reached by the Political Consultative Conference a year ago were a liberal and forward-looking charter which then offered China a basis for peace and reconstruction. However, irreconcilable groups within the Kuomintang, interested in the preservation of their own feudal control of China, evidently had no real intention of implementing them. Though I speak as a soldier, I must here also deplore the dominating influence of the military. Their dominance accentuates the weakness of civil government in China. At the same time, in pondering the situation in China, one must have clearly in mind not the workings of small Communist groups or committees to which we are accustomed in America, but rather of millions of people and an army of more than a million men.

I have never been in a position to be certain of the development of attitudes in the innermost Chinese Communist circles. Most certainly, the course which the Chinese Communist Party has pursued in recent months indicated an unwillingness to make a fair compromise. It has been impossible even to get them to sit down at a conference table with Government representatives to discuss given issues. Now the Communists have broken off negotiations by their last offer which demanded the dissolution of the National Assembly and a return to the military positions of January 13th which the Government could not be expected to accept.

Between this dominant reactionary group in the Government and the irreconcilable Communists who, I must state, did not so appear last February, lies the problem of how peace and well-being are to be brought to the long-suffering and presently inarticulate mass of the people of China. The reactionaries in the Government have evidently counted on substantial American support regardless of their actions. The Communists by their unwillingness to compromise in the national interest are evidently counting on an economic collapse to bring about the fall of the Government, accelerated by extensive guerrilla action against the long lines of rail communications—regardless of the cost in suffering to the Chinese people.

The salvation of the situation, as I see it, would be the assumption of leadership by the liberals in the Government and in the minority parties, a splendid group of men, but who as yet lack the political power to exercise a controlling influence. Successful action on their part under the leadership of Generalissimo Chiang Kai-shek would, I believe, lead to unity through good government.

In fact, the National Assembly has adopted a democratic constitution which in all major respects is in accordance with the principles laid down by the all-party Political Consultative Conference of last January. It is unfortunate that the Communists did not see fit to participate in the Assembly since the constitution that has been adopted seems to include every major point that they wanted.

Soon the Government in China will undergo major reorganization pending the coming into force of the constitution following elections to be completed before Christmas Day 1947. Now that the form for a democratic China has been laid down by the newly adopted constitution, practical measures will be the test. It remains to be seen to what extent the Government will give substance to the form by a genuine welcome of all groups actively to share in the responsibility of government.

The first step will be the reorganization of the State Council and the Executive branch of Government to carry on administration pending the enforcement of the constitution. The manner in which this is done and the amount of representation accorded to liberals and to non-Kuomintang members will be significant. It is also to be hoped that during this interim period the door will remain open for Communists or other groups to participate if they see fit to assume their share of responsibility for the future of China.

It has been stated officially and categorically that the period of political tutelage under the Kuomintang is at an end. If the termination of one-party rule is to be a reality, the Kuomintang should cease to receive financial support from the Government.

I have spoken very frankly because in no other way can I hope to bring the people of the United States to even a partial understanding of this complex problem. I have expressed all these views privately in the course of negotiations; they are well known, I think, to most of the individuals concerned. I express them now publicly, as it is my duty, to present my estimate of the situation and its possibilities to the American people who have a deep interest in the development of conditions in the Far East promising an enduring peace in the Pacific.

H. Statement by President Truman on United States Policy Toward China*

[Extract]

December 18, 1946

Last December I made a statement of this Government's views regarding China. We believed then and do now that a united and democratic China is of the utmost importance to world peace, that a broadening of the base of the National Government to make it representative of the Chinese people will further China's progress toward this goal, and that China has a clear responsibility to the other United Nations to eliminate armed conflict within its territory as constituting a threat to world stability and peace. It was made clear at Moscow last year that these views are shared by our Allies, Great Britain and the Soviet Union. On December 27th, Mr. Byrnes, Mr. Molotov and Mr. Bevin issued a statement which said, in part:

"The three Foreign Secretaries exchanged views with regard to the situation in China. They were in agreement as to the need for a unified and democratic China under the National Government for broad participation by democratic elements in all branches of the national government, and for a cessation of civil strife. They affirmed their adherence to the policy of non-interference in the internal affairs of China."

The policies of this Government were also made clear in my statement of last December. We recognized the National Government of the Republic of China as the legal government. We undertook to assist the Chinese Government in reoccupation of the liberated areas and in disarming and repatriating the Japanese invaders. And finally, as China moved toward peace and unity along

* *Ibid.*, pp. 689-94.

the lines mentioned, we were prepared to assist the Chinese economically and in other ways.

I asked General Marshall to go to China as my representative. We had agreed upon my statement of the United States Government's views and policies regarding China as his directive. He knew full well in undertaking the mission that halting civil strife, broadening the base of the Chinese Government and bringing about a united, democratic China were tasks for the Chinese themselves. He went as a great American to make his outstanding abilities available to the Chinese.

During the war, the United States entered into an agreement with the Chinese Government regarding the training and equipment of a special force of 39 divisions. That training ended V-J Day and the transfer of the equipment had been largely completed when General Marshall arrived.

The United States, the United Kingdom and the Union of Soviet Socialist Republics all committed themselves to the liberation of China, including the return of Manchuria to Chinese control. Our Government had agreed to assist the Chinese Government in the reoccupation of areas liberated from the Japanese, including Manchuria, because of China's lack of shipping and transport planes. Three armies were moved by air and eleven by sea, to China, Formosa, north China and Manchuria. Most of these moves had been made or started when General Marshall arrived.

The disarming and evacuation of Japanese progressed slowly—too slowly. We regarded our commitment to assist the Chinese in this program as of overwhelming importance to the future peace of China and the whole Far East. Surrendered but undefeated Japanese armies and hordes of administrators, technicians and Japanese merchants, totalling about 3,000,000 persons, had to be removed under the most difficult conditions. At the request of the Chinese Government we had retained a considerable number of American troops in China, and immediately after V-J Day we landed a corps of Marines in north China. The principal task of these forces was to assist in the evacuation of Japanese. Only some 200,000 had been returned to Japan by the time General Marshall arrived.

General Marshall also faced a most unpropitious internal situation on his arrival in China. Communications throughout the country were badly disrupted due to destruction during the war and the civil conflicts which had broken out since. This disruption was preventing the restoration of Chinese economy, the distribution of relief supplies, and was rendering the evacuation of Japanese a slow and difficult process. The wartime destruction of factories and plants, the war-induced inflation in China, the Japanese action in shutting down the economy of occupied China immediately after V-J Day, and finally the destruction of communications combined to paralyze the economic life of the country, spreading untold hardship to millions, robbing the victory over the Japanese of significance to most Chinese and seriously aggravating all the tensions and discontents that existed in China.

Progress toward solution of China's internal difficulties by the Chinese themselves was essential to the rapid and effective completion of most of the programs in which we had already pledged our assistance to the Chinese Government. General Marshall's experience and wisdom were available to the Chinese in their efforts to reach such solutions.

Events moved rapidly upon General Marshall's arrival. With all parties availing themselves of his impartial advice, agreement for a country-wide truce was reached and announced on January 10th. A feature of this agreement was the establishment of a unique organization, the Executive Headquarters in Peiping. It was realized that due to poor communications and the bitter feelings on local fronts, generalized orders to cease fire and withdraw might have little chance of being carried out unless some authoritative executive agency, trusted by both sides, could function in any local situation.

The Headquarters operated under the leaders of three commissioners—one American who served as chairman, one Chinese Government representative, and one representative of the Chinese Communist Party. Mr. Walter S. Robertson, Charge d'Affaires of the American Embassy in China, served as chairman until his return to this country in the fall. In order to carry out its function in the field, Executive Headquarters formed a large number of truce teams, each headed by one American officer, one Chinese Government officer, and one Chinese Communist officer. They proceeded to all danger spots where fighting was going on or seemed impending and saw to the implementation of the truce terms, often under conditions imposing exceptional hardships and requiring courageous action. The degree of cooperation attained between Government and Communist officers in the Headquarters and on the truce teams was a welcome proof that despite two decades of fighting, these two Chinese groups could work together.

Events moved forward with equal promise on the political front. On January 10th, the Political Consultative Conference began its sessions with representatives of the Kuomintang or Government Party, the Communist Party and several minor political parties participating. Within three weeks of direct discussion these groups had come to a series of statesmanlike agreements on outstanding political and military problems. The agreements provided for an interim government of a coalition type with representation of all parties for revision of the Draft Constitution along democratic lines prior to its discussion and adoption by a National Assembly and for reduction of the Government and Communist armies and their eventual amalgamation into a small modernized truly national army responsible to a civilian government.

In March, General Marshall returned to this country. He reported on the important step the Chinese had made toward peace and unity in arriving at these agreements. He also pointed out that these agreements could not be satisfactorily implemented and given substance unless China's economic disintegration were checked and particularly unless the transportation system could be put in working order. Political unity could not be built on economic chaos. This Government had already authorized certain minor credits to the Chinese Government in an effort to meet emergency rehabilitation needs as it was doing for other war devastated countries throughtout the world. A total of approximately $66,000,000 was involved in six specific projects, chiefly for the purchase of raw cotton, and for ships and railroad repair material. But these emergency measures were inadequate. Following the important forward step made by the Chinese in the agreements as reported by General Marshall, the Export-Import Bank earmarked a total of $500,000,000 for possible additional credits on a project by project basis to Chinese Government agencies and private enterprises. Agreement to extend actual credits for such projects would obviously have to be based upon this Government's policy as announced December 15, 1945. So far, this $500,000,000 remains earmarked, but unexpended.

While comprehensive large scale aid has been delayed, this Government has completed its wartime lend-lease commitments to China. Lend-lease assistance was extended to China to assist her in fighting the Japanese, and later to fulfill our promise to assist in re-occupying the country from the Japanese. Assistance took the form of goods and equipment and of services. Almost half the total made available to China consisted of services, such as those involved in air and water transportation of troops. According to the latest figures reported, lend-lease assistance to China up to V-J Day totalled approximately $870,000,-000. From V-J Day to the end of February, shortly after General Marshall's arrival, the total was approximately $600,000,000 mostly in transportation costs. Thereafter, the program was reduced to the fulfillment of outstanding commitments, much of which was later suspended.

A considerable quantity of civilian goods has also been made available by our agreement with China for the disposal of surplus property which enabled us to liquidate a sizable indebtedness and to dispose of large quantities of surplus material. During the war the Chinese Government furnished Chinese currency to the United States Army for use in building its installations, feeding the troops, and other expenses. By the end of the war this indebtedness amounted to something like 150,000,000,000 Chinese dollars. Progressive currency inflation in China rendered it impossible to determine the exact value of the sum in Unied States currency.

China agreed to buy all surplus property owned by the United States in China and on seventeen Pacific Islands and bases with certain exceptions. Six months of negotiations preceded the agreement finally signed in August. It was imperative that this matter be concluded in the Pacific as had already been done in Europe, especially in view of the rapid deterioration of the material in open storage under tropical conditions and the urgent need for the partial alleviation of the acute economic distress of the Chinese people which it was hoped this transaction would permit. Aircraft, all non-demilitarized combat material, and fixed installations outside of China were excluded. Thus, no weapons which could be used in fighting a civil war were made available through this agreement.

The Chinese Government cancelled all but 30,000,000 United States dollars of our indebtedness for the Chinese currency, and promised to make available the equivalent of 35,000,000 United States dollars for use in paying United States governmental expenses in China and acquiring and improving buildings and properties for our diplomatic and consular establishments. An additional sum of 20,000,000 United States dollars is also designated for the fulfillment of a cultural and educational program.

Before General Marshall arrived in China for the second time, in April, there was evidence that the truce agreement was being disregarded. The sincere and unflagging efforts of Executive Headquarters and its truce teams have succeeded in many instances in preventing or ending local engagements and thus saved thousands of lives. But fresh outbreaks of civil strife continued to occur, reaching a crisis of violence in Manchuria with the capture of Changchun by the Communists and where the presence of truce teams had not been fully agreed to by the National Government.

A change in the course of events in the political field was equally disappointing. Negotiations between the Government and the Communists have been resumed again and again, but they have as often broken down. Although hope for final success has never disappeared completely, the agreements made in January and February have not been implemented, and the various Chinese groups have not since that time been able to achieve the degree of agreement reached at the Political Consultative Conference.

*   *   *

It is a matter of deep regret that China has not yet been able to achieve unity by peaceful methods. Because he knows how serious the problem is, and how important it is to reach a solution, General Marshall has remained at his post even though active negotiations have been broken off by the Communist Party. We are ready to help China as she moves toward peace and genuine democratic government.

The views expressed a year ago by this Government are valid today. The plan for political unification agreed to last February is sound. The plan for military unification of last February has been made difficult of implementation by the progress of the fighting since last April, but the general principles involved are fundamentally sound.

China is a sovereign nation. We recognize that fact and we recognize the National Government of China. We continue to hope that the Government will find a peaceful solution. We are pledged not to interfere in the internal affairs of China. Our position is clear. While avoiding involvement in their civil strife, we will persevere with our policy of helping the Chinese people to bring about peace and economic recovery in their country.

*   *   *

We believe that our hopes for China are identical with what the Chinese people themselves most earnestly desire. We shall therefore continue our positive and realistic policy toward China which is based on full respect for her national sovereignty and on our traditional friendship for the Chinese people and is designed to promote international peace.

I. Views of U.S. Ambassador to China, John Leighton Stuart, on the Chinese Communists*

July 1, 1947

Communist military successes, the shrinkage of railway mileage in Nationalist hands, the depreciation and depletion of Nationalist equipment and supplies, the increasing friction between southern military forces and civil administrators on one hand and northern troops and the local civil population on the other, reports of a projected withdrawal of Nationalist forces to intramural China and the abandonment of Manchuria to the Communists, rumors of the early return of Marshal Chang Hsueh-liang to Manchuria, and the expanding economic stagnation suggest the following observations:

The recent Communist drive has met with little Nationalist resistance. Northeast Combat Command sources and military observers admit that many Nationalist withdrawals were premature and without military necessity. The words "strategic retreat" have lost all significance. As a result the Communists possess almost complete initiative and are able to maneuver practically at will. If Ssupingkai with its garrison of 17,000 falls, the Communists should be able to proceed successfully against bypassed Changchun and Kirin and thereupon gain unimpared control over 90 percent of Manchuria. The fall of Yingkow would leave only ports on the west coast of the Liaotung Gulf in Nationalist hands. The only railway of any appreciable mileage in Nationalist hands is the Peiping-Liaotung main line. The Communist drive eastward through Jehol is threatening even these meager holdings and should this drive be successful and contact be established between these forces and those now in the vicinity of Yingkow, Manchuria will be effectively cut off from land and water communication with China, and Mukden itself will be virtually in a state of siege. Nationalist military intelligence has been outstandingly deficient. The Northeast Combat Command is seemingly in almost complete ignorance of Communist plans and is therefore being constantly outwitted. Northeast Combat Command headquarters officers admit they had no intelligence of the recent Communist drive on Changchun and then southwards, even though it is now known that such plans therefore had been formulated three months prior to the opening of the drive.

Rivalry (if not enmity) between General Hsiung Shih-hui, the Generalissimo's representative, and General Tu Li-ming, commanding the Northeast Combat Command, is openly discussed and the absence of closely integrated military and economic planning in Manchuria is attributed to it.

By holding the initiative, the Communists are able to keep the Nationalists scurrying over the countryside, thereby causing depreciation of Nationalist motorized mobile equipment and depletion of sorely needed supplies. Communist transport on the other hand consists almost wholly of draft animals. Persons in direct contact with the Nationalist troops in rural areas state there are insufficient small arms and ammunition to arm all combatant troops now in the field. These reports are so consistent, some, though not necessarily full, credence must

*Ibid., pp. 732-35.

be given them. The Communists also are underarmed, but by guerrilla tactics and surprise night attacks they are able to cause greater loss of weapons and expenditure of ammunition by the Nationalists than by themselves.

Nationalist southern military forces and civil administrators conduct themselves in Manchuria as conquerors, not as fellow countrymen, and have imposed a "carpet-bag" regime of unbridled exploitation upon areas under their control. If military and civil authorities of local origin were in control, they too would probably exploit the populace, but experience has shown that Chinese authorities of local origin, in general, never quite strangle a goose laying golden eggs, and furthermore, it is a human trait to be less resentful toward exploitation by one's own than toward that by outsiders. The result of this is that the countryside is so antagonistic toward outsiders as to affect the morale of non-Manchurian troops and at the same time arouse vindictiveness in southern military officers and civil administrators.

Nationalist withdrawals toward Mukden have progressively cut off Nationalist-held areas from the great food producing regions in Manchuria, thereby causing a potential Nationalist food shortage which was already apparent in extensive grain hoarding and speculation. Puerile efforts have been made toward price control and to combat hoarding, but in general, the results of these efforts have been largely to enforce the requisitioning of grain at bayonet point for controlled prices and to enable the resale of requisitioned grain at black market prices for the benefit of the pockets of rapacious military and civil officials. The common man is being crushed between the rising cost of living and the depreciating currency. (The cost of living index of May, 160 percent compared to 100 percent in April.) Local currency is pegged to Chinese National Currency and has not only fallen with CNC, but also because of the wholesale exodus of families of Nationalist officials and the resulting flight from local currency incidental to frenzied buying of CNC and gold bars. The black market value of the U.S. dollar at Mukden is now TP dollars 3,300 against TP dollars 1,000 March 1.

Little goods move between Mukden and its hinterland. Business is rapidly approaching a standstill, exports from Manchuria have practically disappeared and imports have reduced to a trickle of the normal. Almost all capital has been expended in long-range investment since the Nationalists took over Manchuria and no such capital, government or private, is being invested today. All commodity markets are purely speculative.

The evidence is growing daily that the people of Manchuria not only are prepared for but are keenly desirous of a change in the government. But what change? Most are undecided even though voluble in discontent of the present way of living and the trend of events. It is safe to state that the overwhelming majority in the nation are as dissatisfied with, dislike and would welcome freedom from the present Nationalist regime. A like majority fear and would therefore not welcome the Communist regime. Many talk "revolution" even aloud in public places, but few are able to define their conception of revolution other than as change from the present way of living and even fewer envisage revolution involving armed resistance. There seems no likelihood that an armed uprising would be more than abortive, at least until the national morale and military might has suffered devastating deterioration. One platform on which Manchus seem almost unanimous is "out with Heilien (outsider) Chinese and Manchuria for the Manchus." The return of Ma Chan-shan lent heart to those who look to restoration of Manchu rule under a "native son," but his relegation to figure-head status in a position of impotence has dampened their hopes. Eyes are today turned toward the possibility of the return of the young Marshall to power in Manchuria. His vices, weaknesses and "playboy" tendencies are known but he is nevertheless associated in the minds of the people with prosperity and progress which Manchuria enjoyed under Chang Tso-lin regime. He or some other pre-Manchu leader could serve as a central figure for rallying the Manchu people. Such a change would in all likelihood herald the return of warlordism to Manchuria, but even so Manchuria would remain Chinese with nominal allegiance at least to China and not a "Manchu peoples republic" as it may become if the Communists succeed in sweeping the Nationalists back into intramural China.

There is every reason to believe that punitive military action against the Communists, unless succeeded by overwhelming military occupation will not save Manchuria to China. It is high time for Nanking to be realistic and to replace its present impotent disliked regime in Manchuria with one which will be supported by the local population and would thereby serve to weaken the Communist movement. It may be, and some think that it is, too late to accomplish this purpose. Without some such effective measure there are many indications that it will be only a matter of some months, perhaps six to nine, before Manchuria will be lost.

THE MISSION OF U.S. GENERAL ALBERT C. WEDEMEYER IN CHINA

A. Remarks by General Wedemeyer on China*

[Extract]

August 22, 1947

Taxation

Approximately 80 percent of the people of China are hard working peasants, their crops are visible and officials can easily appraise the amounts the peasants are able to give toward government. Corrupt officials in many instances take more than the peasants are able to give and this results finally in the peasants leaving the land and forming bandit groups.

In contrast to the taxation of peasants, Chinese businessmen and rich Chinese resort to devious and dishonest methods to avoid payment of proper taxes to their government. It is commonly known that Chinese business firms maintain two sets of books, one showing the true picture of business transactions and the other showing a distorted picture so that they do not pay as much tax as they should.

Military

For the first year after the war, in my opinion it was possible to stamp out or at least to minimize the effect of Chinese Communists. This capability was predicated upon the assumption that the Central Government disposed its military forces in such a manner as to insure control of all industrial areas, food producing areas, important cities and lines of communication. It was also assumed that the Central Government appointed highly efficient and scrupulously honest officials as provincial governors, district magistratetes, mayors, and throughout the political and economic structure. If these assumptions had been accomplished, political and economic stability would have resulted, and the people would not have been receptive, in fact, would have strongly opposed the infiltration or penetration of communistic ideas. It would not have been possible for the Chinese Communists to expand so rapidly and acquire almost undisputed control of such vast areas. I believe that the Chinese Communist movement cannot be defeated by the employment of force. Today China is being invaded by an idea instead of strong military forces from the outside. The only way in my opinion to combat this idea successfully is to do so with another idea that will have stronger appeal and win the support of the people. This means that politically and economically the Central Government will have to remove

* *United States Relations with China*, pp. 758-62.

corruption and incompetence from its ranks in order to provide justice and equality and to protect the personal liberties of the Chinese people, particularly of the peasants. To recapitulate, the Central Government cannot defeat the Chinese Communists by the employment of force, but can only win the loyal, enthusiastic and realistic support of the masses of the people by improving the political and economic situation immediately. The effectiveness and timeliness of these improvements will determine in my opinion whether or not the Central Government will stand or fall before the Communist onslaught.

During the war while serving as the Generalissimo's Chief-of-Staff, I tried to impress upon all Chinese military officials the importance of reestablishing excellent relationships between officers and enlisted men. I explained that officers must show sincere interest in the welfare of their men both in times of war and in peace. Wounded must be evacuated from the battlefield and cared for in hospitals or aid stations. Officers should visit their men in the hospital and find out if they can visit them in any way. Officers should play games with their soldiers such as basketball and soccer. The junior officers should know all of their men in the unit by name. They should talk to them and encourage them to discuss their problems. Explain to them why they are fighting. Explain the objectives of their Government and encourage open discussions. This will create a feeling of mutual respect and genuine affection. Discipline acquired through fear is not as effective as discipline acquired through affection and mutual respect. It would be so easy for the Chinese officers to win the respect and admiration of their men who are simple, kindly and brave and who will gladly endure hardships and dangers if they are properly led and cared for.

Conscription

I have received many reports that the conscription of men for military service is not being carried out honestly or efficiently. Again, as in taxation peasants are expected to bear the brunt of conscription, although in the cities there are thousands and thousands of able-bodied men, who should be under the conscription laws eligible for military service. Rich men's sons by the payment of money avoid conscription and the sons of rich men are being sent to school abroad instead of remaining here to help their country in a time of great crisis.

Relationship Between Military and Civilians

I cannot emphasize too strongly the importance of establishing and maintaining good relationship between military forces and the civilian population. Officers and men in the army and air corps should be very careful to be courteous, friendly, cooperative and honest in all of their contacts with civilians. In Manchuria, I was told by many sources that the Central Government armies were welcomed enthusiastically by the people as deliverers from Japanese oppression.

Today, after several months of experience with these Central Government armies, the people experience a feeling of hatred and distrust because the officers and enlisted men were arrogant and rude. Also they stole and looted freely; their general attitude was that of conquerors instead of that of deliverers. In Formosa the reports are exactly the same, alienating the Formosans from the Central Government. All of this is a matter of discipline. Of course if the officers themselves are dishonest or discourteous, one can hardly expect the enlisted men to be otherwise. Good relations between the military forces and the civilians are absolutely essential if the Central Government expects to bring about successful conclusion of operations against the Communists. At first the Communist armies were also crude and destructive and made the people hate even, but in the past few weeks, they have adopted an entirely new approach which requires their officers and men to be very careful in all their relations with civilian communities. You can understand therefore how important it is that your own military forces adopt steps immediately to improve the conditions that I have mentioned.

Promotion in the military service should be by merit and merit alone. Older officers or incompetent ones should be retired and relieved. The retired officers should realize that they must make room for the younger ones and they must accept retirement patriotically and philosophically. There are entirely too many Generals in the Chinese Army. Most of them are not well-educated and are not well versed in modern combat. Generals should never be used in civilian posts of responsibility, for example, as governors, mayors and magistrates, except perhaps as Minister of Defense. Military men should not be permitted to belong to a particular political party. After the constitution goes into effect on December 25, they should be permitted to cast a vote, in other words, exercise the right of suffrage, but no military men should be permitted to hold government office or be active members of a political party.

*   *   *

Corruption

One hears reports on all sides concerning corruption among government officials, high and low and also throughout the economic life of the country. With spiralling inflation, the pay of government officials both in civil service and in military service is wholly inadequate. I am sure that persons who are presently practicing dishonest methods would never consider doing so were it not for the fact that they receive insufficient remuneration to meet the bare necessities of life. Many of them are not trying to acquire vast fortunes, but are just trying to provide a standard of living commensurate with their position. On the other hand, certain rich families, some of whom have relatives in high positions of the government, have been greatly increasing their fortunes. Nepotism is rife and in my investigations I have found that sons, nephews and brothers of government officials have been put in positions within the government, sponsored firms, or in private firms to enable them to make huge profits at the expense of their government and their people. It would be interesting and revealing if you would conduct an investigation into various large banking organizations and other newly created business organizations, to ascertain how much money has been made by such organizations and to what individuals or groups of individuals the money has been paid. To reduce corruption, it will be necessary to establish an index of the standard of living and as the exchange rises the pay of civil service and military service must be increased accordingly. I should emphasize that I am sure many patriotic and selfless Chinese are eking out a bare existence under difficult conditions. They are a great credit to China. However, it must be very discouraging to them to realize that many who already had amassed great fortunes have taken advantage of the present unfortunate situation in China to increase their wealth.

*   *   *

There are approximately ten million Chinese citizens living abroad. These Chinese in many instances are financially able to help their country in this time of dire necessity. Also there are many Chinese here in China who have vast sums of money invested abroad. They should be required to make a complete report on their holdings in securities and capital goods. It has been conservatively estimated in America that they could raise at least one billion United States dollars from these sources. China is far from bankrupt in a financial sense or with regard to material resources. China is practically bankrupt in spiritual resources. If the people of China really love their country and want it to emerge strong and united, they should be prepared to come forward and make any sacrifice, including their lives if necessary. Again I should like to emphasize that it is predominantly the poor people, the peasants, who are making great sacrifices and predominantly the rich class who are not coming forward to assist their country.

Punishment and Secret Police

I have had reported to me many instances of misdirection and abuse in meting out punishments to offenders political or otherwise. In Formosa there are many so-called political offenders who are still in prison without any charges or sentences. Some have been released but only after paying large sums of money and being required to sign a statement to the effect that they were guilty of an offense against the government. Actually in their hearts and minds they did not feel that they were guilty of such offense. Secret police operate widely, very much as they do in Russia and as they did in Germany. People disappear. Students are thrown into jail. No trials and no sentences. Actions of this nature do not win support for the government. Quite the contrary. Everyone lives with a feeling of fear and loses confidence in the government.

Final Remarks

The Government should not be worried about criticism. I think constructive criticism should be encouraged. It makes the people feel that they are participating in government; that they are members of the team. I have mentioned earlier the terrible economic conditions that exist in England. Criticism of the government is expressed freely in meetings on the streets, and in the press, and on the radio. This is in my opinion a healthy condition. The Government should point out that it is made up of human beings who are of course fallible and can make mistakes. The Government should emphasize, however, that once the mistakes are pointed out, effective steps will be taken to remedy them. The Government should publish information freely concerning expenditures, taxation. Let all the people know how much income tax each individual, particularly wealthy people and big business firms are paying. Announce publicly when any official or any individual has been guilty of some crime or offense and also indicate the punishment meted out. By the same token, announce publicly the accomplishment or good work of individual Government activities. All of these matters would contribute to confidence on the part of the people in the Government. They want to know what is going on and they have a right to know. Open and public official announcements on the part of the Government will also serve to stop malicious conjectures and adverse propaganda of opponents of the Government.

I realize that many of the ideas that I have expressed are quite contrary to Chinese tradition. However, I have carefully studied the philosophy of Confucius and I am sure that all of these ideas are in consonance with the fine principles of conduct that he prescribed. I have confidence in the good sound judgment and in the decency of the bulk of the Chinese peoples. I hope sincerely that you will accept my remarks in the same spirit in which they were given, namely, in the interest of China. Anything that I can do to help China become a strong, happy and prosperous nation, I would gladly do. Anything I could do to protect the sovereignty of China and to insure her a place of respect in the eyes of the world in the family of nations, I would gladly do.

B. Statement by General Wedemeyer on the Conclusion of His Mission in China*

August 24, 1947

As promised in the initial press release, the inquiry into economic, political, military and social conditions has been undertaken without commitment or prejudgment.

All members of the mission have striven for objectivity and impartiality. To that end we have traveled widely to escape influences peculiar to any one area, visiting Mukden and Fusan, Manchuria; Peiping, Tientsin, Tsingtao and Tsinan

*Ibid., pp. 763-64.

in North China; Nanking, Shanghai and Hankow in Central China; Canton in South China, and also Taiwan (Formosa).

Successful efforts were made to reach all classes and categories of people as measured by economic position, intellectual attainment and divergent political viewpoints. Foreign business men and officials were interviewed. We have seen officials of national and local governments, members of various political organizations, many of whom were frankly critical of the government and some of whom were far Left in their views.

We have approximately 2,000 letters, a small proportion of which were anonymous. These letters contained suggestions which we were able to follow up advantageously.

The last week of our stay in China was devoted chiefly to analyzing an enormous mass of data and in relating political, economic and other items together to reach sound judgments and conclusions.

Varied as were the views, there is one point on which all the hearts and minds of China unite: Throughout strife-torn China there is a passionate longing for peace, an early, lasting peace. I wish the means of attaining it were as easily discernible.

After V-J Day the Chinese people rightfully expected to enjoy the fruits of hard-earned victory. They endured hardships and dangers and suffered untold privations in their efforts to expel the ruthless invader.

In China today I find apathy and lethargy in many quarters. Instead of seeking solutions of problems presented, considerable time and effort are spent in blaming outside influences and seeking outside assistance.

It is discouraging to note the abject defeatism of many Chinese, who are normally competent and patriotic, and who instead should be full of hope and determination.

Weakened and disrupted by long years of war and revolution, China still possesses most of the physical resources needed for her own rehabilitation. Recovery awaits inspirational leadership and moral and spiritual resurgence which can only come from within China.

While I am fully aware of the interests and problems of particular individuals or groups within the country, I am profoundly concerned over the welfare of the Chinese people as a whole. It is my conviction that if the Chinese Communists are truly patriotic and interested primarily in the well-being of their country, they will halt the voluntary employment of force in efforts to impose ideologies. If they are sincere in a desire to help the Chinese people, they can better do so by peaceful means, in lieu of the violence and destruction which have marked these tragic months.

Equally important, the existing Central government can win and retain the undivided, enthusiastic support of the bulk of the Chinese people by removing incompetent and/or corrupt people who now occupy many positions of responsibility in the government, not only national but more so in provincial and municipal structures.

There are honorable officials who show high efficiency and devotion to duty, who strive to live within ridiculous salaries and such private means as they possess, just as there are conscientious businessmen who live up to a high code of commercial ethics. But no one will misunderstand my emphasis upon the large number whose conduct is notoriously marked by greed, incompetence or both.

To regain and maintain the confidence of the people, the Central government will have to effect immediately drastic, far-reaching political and economic reforms. Promises will no longer suffice. Performance is absolutely necessary. It should be accepted that military force in itself will not eliminate Communism.

On taking leave, all members of the mission join in expressing sincere gratitude for the assistance uniformly given by the Generalissimo and all patriotic Chinese with whom we had contact. All Americans hope and pray that China will achieve the unity, prosperity and happiness which her people so richly deserve and of which they have been unjustly deprived for so many years.

C. Report by General Wedemeyer to President Truman on His Mission in China*

[Extract]

September 19, 1947

CHINA

Part I
General Statement

China's history is replete with examples of encroachment, arbitrary action, special privilege, exploitation, and usurpation of territory on the part of foreign powers. Continued foreign infiltration, penetration or efforts to obtain spheres of influence in China, including Manchuria and Taiwan (Formosa), could be interpreted only as a direct infringement and violation of China's sovereignty and a contravention of the principles of the Charter of the United Nations. It is mandatory that the United States and those other nations subscribing to the principles of the Charter of the United Nations should combine their efforts to insure the unimpeded march of all peoples toward goals that recognize the dignity of man and his civil rights and, further, definitely provide the opportunity to express freely how and by whom they will be governed.

Those goals and the lofty aims of freedom-loving peoples are jeopardized today by forces as sinister as those that operated in Europe and Asia during the ten years leading to World War II. The pattern is familiar—employment of subversive agents; infiltration tactics; incitement of disorder and chaos to disrupt normal economy and thereby to undermine popular confidence in government and leaders; seizure of authority without reference to the will of the people—all the techniques skillfully designed and ruthlessly implemented in

Ibid., pp. 764-74.

order to create favorable conditions for the imposition of totalitarian ideologies. This pattern is present in the Far East, particularly in the areas contiguous to Siberia.

If the United Nations is to have real effect in establishing economic stability and in maintaining world peace, these developments merit high priority on the United Nations' agenda for study and action. Events of the past two years demonstrate the futility of appeasement based on the hope that the strongly consolidated forces of the Soviet Union will adopt either a conciliatory or a cooperative attitude, except as tactical expedients. Soviet practice in the countries already occupied or dominated completes the mosaic of aggressive expansion through ruthless secret police methods and through an increasing political and economic enslavement of peoples. Soviet literature, confirmed repeatedly by Communist leaders, reveals a definite plan for expansion far exceeding that of Nazism in its ambitious scope and dangerous implications. Therefore in attempting a solution to the problem presented in the Far East, as well as in other troubled areas of the world, every possible opportunity must be used to seize the initiative in order to create and maintain bulwarks of freedom.

Notwithstanding all the corruption and incompetence that one notes in China, it is a certainty that the bulk of the people are not disposed to a Communist political and economic structure. Some have become affiliated with Communism in indignant protest against oppressive police measures, corrupt practices and mal-administration of National Government officials. Some have lost all hope for China under existing leadership and turn to the Communists in despair. Some accept a new leadership by mere inertia.

Indirectly, the United States facilitated the Soviet program in the Far East by agreeing at the Yalta Conference to Russian re-entry into Manchuria, and later by withholding aid from the National Government. There were justifiable reasons for these policies. In the one case we were concentrating maximum Allied strength against Japanese in order to accelerate crushing defeat and thus save Allied lives. In the other, we were withholding unqualified support from a government within which corruption and incompetence were so prevalent that it was losing the support of its own people. Further, the United States had not yet realized that the Soviet Union would fail to cooperate in the accomplishment of world-wide plans for post-war rehabilitation. Our own participation in those plans has already afforded assistance to other nations and peoples, friends and former foes alike, to a degree unparalleled in humanitarian history.

Gradually it has become apparent that the World War II objectives for which we and others made tremendous sacrifices are not being fully attained, and that there remains in the world a force presenting even greater dangers to world peace than did the Nazi militarists and the Japanese jingoists. Consequently the United States made the decision in the Spring of 1947 to assist Greece and Turkey with a view to protecting their sovereignties, which were threatened by the direct or inspired activities of the Soviet Union. Charges of unilateral action and circumvention of the United Nations were made by members of that organization. In the light of its purposes and principles such criticisms seemed plausible. The United States promptly declared its intention of referring the matter to the United Nations when that organization would be ready to assume responsibility.

It follows that the United Nations should be informed of contemplated action with regard to China. If the recommendations of this report are approved, the United States should suggest to China that she inform the United Nations officially of her request to the United States for material assistance and advisory aid in order to facilitate China's post-war rehabilitation and economic recovery. This will demonstrate that the United Nations is not being circumvented, and that the United States is not infringing upon China's sovereignty, but contrary-wise is cooperating constructively in the interest of peace and stability in the Far East, concomitantly in the world.

The situation in Manchuria has deteriorated to such a degree that prompt action is necessary to prevent that area from becoming a Soviet satellite. The Chinese Communists may soon gain military control of Manchuria and announce the establishment of a government. Outer Mongolia, already a Soviet satellite, may then recognize Manchuria and conclude a "mutual support agreement" with a *de facto* Manchurian government of the Chinese Communists. In that event, the Soviet Union might accomplish a mutual support agreement with Communist-dominated Manchuria, because of her current similar agreement with Outer Mongolia. This would create a difficult situation for China, the United States and the United Nations. Ultimately it could lead to a Communist-dominated China.

The United Nations might take immediate action to bring about cessation of hostilities in Manchuria as a prelude to the establishment of a Guardianship or Trusteeship. The Guardianship might consist of China, Soviet Russia, the United States, Great Britain and France. This should be attempted promptly and could be initiated only by China. Should one of the nations refuse to partici-pate in Manchurian Guardianship, China might then request the General Assem-bly of the United Nations to establish a Trusteeship, under the provisions of the Charter.

Initially China might interpret Guardianship or Trusteeship as an infringement upon her sovereignty. But the urgency of the matter should encourage a realistic view of the ·situation. If these steps are not taken by China, Manchuria may be drawn into the Soviet orbit, despite United States aid, and lost, perhaps permanently, to China.

The economic deterioration and the incompetence and corruption in the polit-ical and military organizations in China should be considered against an all-inclusive background lest there be disproportionate emphasis upon defects. Co-mity requires that cognizance be taken of the following:

> Unlike other Powers since V-J Day, China has never been free to devote full attention to internal problems that were greatly confounded by eight years of war. The current civil war has imposed an overwhelming financial and eco-nomic burden at a time when resources and energies have been dissipated and when, in any event, they would have been strained to the utmost to meet the problems of recovery.
>
> The National Government has consistently, since 1927, opposed Communism.

Today the same political leader and same civil and military officials are determined to prevent their country from becoming a Communist-dominated State or Soviet satellite.

Although the Japanese offered increasingly favorable surrender terms during the course of the war, China elected to remain steadfast with her Allies. If China had accepted surrender terms, approximately a million Japanese would have been released for employment against American forces in the Pacific.

I was assured by the Generalissimo that China would support to the limit of her ability an American program for the stabilization of the Far East. He stated categorically that, regardless of moral encouragement or material aid received from the United States, he is determined to oppose Communism and to create a democratic form of government in consonance with Doctor Sun Yatsen's principles. He stated further that he plans to make sweeping reforms in the government including the removal of incompetent and corrupt officials. He stated that some progress has been made along these lines but, with spiraling inflation, economic distress and civil war, it has been difficult to accomplish fully these objectives. He emphasized that, when the Communist problem is solved, he could drastically reduce the Army and concentrate upon political and economic reforms. I retain the conviction that the Generalissimo is sincere in his desire to attain these objectives. I am not certain that he has today sufficient determination to do so if this requires absolute overruling of the political and military cliques surrounding him. Yet, if realistic United States aid is to prove effective in stabilizing the situation in China and in coping with the dangerous expansion of Communism, that determination must be established.

Adoption by the United States of a policy motivated solely toward stopping the expansion of Communism without regard to the continued existence of an unpopular repressive government would render any aid ineffective. Further, United States prestige in the Far East would suffer heavily, and wavering elements might turn away from the existing government to Communism.

In China [and Korea], the political, economic and psychological problems are inextricably mingled. All of them are complex and are becoming increasingly difficult of solution. Each has been studied assiduously in compliance with your directive. Each will be discussed in the course of this report. However, it is recognized that a continued global appraisal is mandatory in order to preclude disproportionate or untimely assistance to any specific area.

The following three postulates of United States foreign policy are pertinent to indicate the background of my investigations, analysis and report:

The United States will continue support of the United Nations in the attainment of its lofty aims, accepting the possible development that the Soviet Union or other nations may not actively participate.

Moral support will be given to nations and peoples that have established political and economic structures compatible with our own, or that give convincing evidence of their desire to do so.

Material aid may be given to those same nations and peoples in order to accelerate post-war rehabilitation and to develop economic stability, provided:

That such aid shall be used for the purposes intended.

That there is continuing evidence that they are taking effective steps to help themselves, or are firmly committed to do so.

That such aid shall not jeopardize American economy and shall conform to an integrated program that involves other international commitments and contributes to the attainment of political, economic and psychological objectives of the United States.

Part II
Political

Although the Chinese people are unanimous in their desire for peace at almost any cost, there seems to be no possibility of its realization under existing circumstances. On one side is the Kuomintang, whose reactionary leadership, repression and corruption have caused a loss of popular faith in the Government. On the other side, bound ideologically to the Soviet Union, are the Chinese Communists, whose eventual aim is admittedly a Communist state in China. Some reports indicate that Communist measures of land reform have gained for them the support of the majority of peasants in areas under their control, while others indicate that their ruthless tactics of land distribution and terrorism have alienated the majority of such peasants. They have, however, successfully organized many rural areas against the National Government. Moderate groups are caught between Kuomintang misrule and repression and ruthless Communist totalitarianism. Minority parties lack dynamic leadership and sizable following. Neither the moderates, many of whom are in the Kuomintang, nor the minority parties are able to make their influence felt because of National Government repression. Existing provincial opposition leading to possible separatist movements would probably crystallize only if collapse of the Government were imminent.

Soviet actions, contrary to the letter and spirit of the Sino-Soviet Treaty of 1945 and its related documents, have strengthened the Chinese Communist position in Manchuria, with political, economic and military repercussions of the National Government's position both in Manchuria and in China proper, and have made more difficult peace and stability in China. The present trend points toward a gradual disintegration of the National Government's control, with the ultimate possibility of a Communist-dominated China.

*   *   *

Economic

Under the impact of civil strife and inflation, the Chinese economy is disintegrating. The most probable outcome of present trends would be, not sudden collapse, but a continued and creeping paralysis and consequent decline in the authority and power of the National Government. The past ten years of war have caused serious deterioration of transportation and communication facilities, mines, utilities and industries. Notwithstanding some commendable efforts and large amounts of economic aid, their overall capabilities are scarcely half those of the pre-war period. With disruption of transportation facilities and the loss of much of North China and Manchuria, important resources of those rich areas are no longer available for the rehabilitation and support of China's economy.

*   *   *

Social—Cultural

Public education has been one of the chief victims of war and social and economic disruption. Schoolhouses, textbooks and other equipment have been destroyed and the cost of replacing any considerable portion cannot not be met. Teachers, like other public servants, have seen the purchasing power of a month's salary shrink to the market value of a few days' rice ration. This applies to the entire educational system, from primary schools, which provide a medium to combat the nation's grievous illiteracy, to universities, from which must come the nation's professional men, technicians and administrators. The universities have suffered in an additional and no less serious respect—traditional academic freedom. Students participating in protest demonstrations have been severely and at times brutally punished by National Government agents without pretense of trial or public evidence of the sedition charged. Faculty members have often been dismissed or refused employment with no evidence of professional unfitness, patently because they were politically objectionable to government officials. Somewhat similarly, periodicals have been closed down "for reasons of military security" without stated charges, and permitted to reopen only after new managements have been imposed. Resumption of educational and other public welfare activities on anything like the desired scale can be accomplished only by restraint of officialdom's abuses, and when the nation's economy is stabilized sufficiently to defray the cost of such vital activities.

Military

The overall military position of the National Government has deteriorated in the past several months and the current military situation favors Communist forces. The Generalissimo has never wavered in his contention that he is fighting for national independence against forces of an armed rebellion nor has he been completely convinced that the Communist problem can be resolved except by force of arms. Although the Nationalist Army has a preponderance of force, the tactical initiative rests with the Communists. Their hit-and-run tactics, adapted to their mission of destruction at points or in areas of their own selection, give them a decided advantage over Nationalists, who must defend many critical areas including connecting lines of communication. Obviously large numbers of Nationalist troops involved in such defensive roles are immobilized whereas Communist tactics permit almost complete freedom of action. The Nationalists' position is precarious in Manchuria, where they occupy only a slender finger of territory. Their control is strongly disputed in Shantung and Hopei

Provinces where the Communists make frequent dislocating attacks against isolated garrisons.

In order to improve materially the current military situation, the Nationalist forces must first stabilize the fronts and then regain the initiative. Further, since the Government is supporting the civil war with approximately seventy per cent of its national budget, it is evident that steps taken to alleviate the situation must point toward an improvement in the effectiveness of the armed forces with a concomitant program of social, political and economic reforms, including a decrease in the size of the military establishment. Whereas some rather ineffective steps have been taken to reorganize and revitalize the command structure, and more sweeping reforms are projected, the effectiveness of the Nationalist Army requires a sound program of equipment and improved logistical support. The present industrial potential of China is inadequate to support military forces effectively. Chinese forces under present conditions cannot cope successfully with internal strife or fulfill China's obligations as a member of the family of nations. Hence outside aid, in the form of munitions (most urgently ammunition) and technical assistance, is essential before any plan of operations can be undertaken with a reasonable prospect of success. Military advice is now available to the Nationalists on a General Staff level through American military advisory groups. The Generalissimo expressed to me repeatedly a strong desire to have this advice and supervision extended in scope to include field forces, training centers and particularly logistical agencies.

*   *   *

Part IV
Conclusions

The peaceful aims of freedom-loving peoples in the world are jeopardized today by developments as portentous as those leading to World War II.

The Soviet Union and her satellites give no evidence of a conciliatory or cooperative attitude in these developments. The United States is compelled, therefore, to initiate realistic lines of action in order to create and maintain bulwarks of freedom, and to protect United States strategic interests.

The bulk of the Chinese are not disposed to Communism and they are not concerned with ideologies. They desire food, shelter and the opportunity to live in peace.

The spreading internecine struggle within China threatens world peace. Repeated American efforts to mediate have proved unavailing. It is apparent that positive steps are required to end hostilities immediately. The most logical approach to this very complex and ominous situation would be to refer the matter to the United Nations.

A China dominated by Chinese Communists would be inimical to the interests of the United States, in view of their openly expressed hostility and active opposition to those principles which the United States regards as vital to the peace of the world.

The Communists have the tactical initiative in the overall military situation. The Nationalist position in Manchuria is precarious, and in Shantung and Hopei Provinces strongly disputed. Continued deterioration of the situation may result in the early establishment of a Soviet satellite government in Manchuria and ultimately in the evolution of a Communist-dominated China.

China is suffering increasingly from disintegration. Her requirements for rehabilitation are large. Her most urgent needs include governmental reorganization and reforms, reduction of the military budget and external assistance.

A program of aid, if effectively employed, would bolster opposition to Communist expansion, and would contribute to gradual development of stability in China.

Due to excesses and oppressions by government police agencies basic freedoms of the people are being jeopardized. Maladministration and corruption cause a loss of confidence in the Government. Until drastic political and economic reforms are undertaken United States aid can not accomplish its purpose.

Even so, criticism of results achieved by the National Government in efforts for improvement should be tempered by a recognition of the handicaps imposed on China by eight years of war, the burden of her opposition to Communism, and her sacrifices for the Allied cause.

A United States program of assistance could best be implemented under the supervision of American advisors in specified economic and military fields. Such a program can be undertaken only if China requests advisory aid as well as material assistance.

Part V
Recommendations

It is recommended:

That the United States Government provide as early as practicable moral, advisory, and material support to China in order to contribute to the early establishment of peace in the world in consonance with the enunciated principles of the United Nations, and concomitantly to protect United States strategic interests against militant forces which now threaten them.

That United States policies and actions suggested in this report be thoroughly integrated by appropriate government agencies with other international commitments. It is recognized that any foreign assistance extended must avoid jeopardizing the American economy.

That China be advised that the United States is favorably disposed to continue aid designed to protect China's territorial integrity and to facilitate her recovery, under agreements to be negotiated by representatives of the two governments, with the following stipulations:

That China inform the United Nations promptly of her request to the United States for increased material and advisory assistance.

That China request the United Nations to take immediate action to bring about a cessation of hostilities in Manchuria and request that Manchuria be placed under a Five-Power Guardianship or, failing that, under a Trusteeship in accordance with the United Nations Charter.

That China make effective use of her own resources in a program for economic reconstruction and initiate sound fiscal policies leading to reduction of budgetary deficits.

That China give continuing evidence that the urgently required political and military reforms are being implemented.

That China accept American advisors as responsible representatives of the United States Government in specified military and economic fields to assist China in utilizing United States aid in the manner for which it is intended.

D. Secretary of State George C. Marshall to President Truman*

Washington, September 25, 1947

I understand General Wedemeyer is presenting his report to you at noon today. It seems to me mandatory that we treat Wedemeyer's report strictly top secret and that no indication of its contents be divulged to the public. This will allow us time to review our policy in the light of the report, giving due consideration to it in balance with our policies in other parts of the world.

If you agree, I suggest Wedemeyer be informed by you accordingly.

If questioned by the press, you might state that a summary of the report cannot be issued until careful consideration has been given it by the various Departments of the Government concerned.

---

*Albert C. Wedemeyer, *Wedemeyer Reports* (New York, 1958), p. 446.

UNITED STATES POLICY IN CHINA, 1948-1949

A. Ambassador Stuart to Secretary Marshall*

Nanking, August 10, 1948

1. *Military:* The Communists continue to win the civil war. They have retained the initiative with all the advantage given by the offensive and government troops just do not seem to have the will or the ability to fight. There are many reports of defections to the Communists but none from Communist ranks. Occupying as they do most of north China east of Sian and north of the Yangtze River except for a few scattered urban centers such as Peiping and Tientsin and certain lines of communication the Communists now appear intent on removing the last vestiges of government strength from Shantung Province, a prelude possibly to full-scale attack south to Nanking or possibly to an all-out attack on Peiping-Tientsin area. In Central China south of the Yangtze scattered Communist bands operate throughout the countryside creating confusion and disorder with the obvious intent of further weakening the government and preparing the way for some future large-scale operation. In south China though less active Communist guerrilla units operate more or less at will and the government has no forces to employ against them.

It is a gloomy picture and one would expect the government to clutch at any means of improving the situation.

*   *   *

There is an awareness of the desperateness of the military situation yet no evidence of a will or capability to cope with it.

2. *Economic:* The inflationary spiral continues at an accelerated pace. Prices have become astronomical and their rise so rapid that the government has been unable to print sufficient money to meet day-by-day needs with the result that barter is becoming more and more the rule. Prices increasingly are quoted either in US dollars, silver or gold. In the interior silver dollars are coming back to use. Thus government has introduced measures to control inflation but the effects have been only temporary and palliative. The fact is that the government in the absence of assured continuing and massive loans from the United States cannot hope to find an answer as long as circumstances require the maintenance of the present military establishment. A renewed and concerted attack on the periphery of the central problem now impends but at best it can only provide a breathing spell.

3. *Psychological:* After years of war and destruction the all-consuming urge of the people today, and this includes both low and high ranking members of the government and Communist areas as well, is for peace. This urge becomes all the more insistent as most people can see no ray of hope under present conditions. A spirit of defeatism is prevalent throughout the country reaching

---

*United States Relations with China, pp. 885-87.

even men of cabinet rank. Almost without exception there is no longer faith that the present government can bring a return to even a bearable standard of living without some radical reorganization. With this frame of mind a cessation of hostilities is desired at almost any price. There is an overwhelming desire for peace yet the Generalissimo wants only military victory over the Communists and no one has yet found a way to surmount the Generalissimo's objections and win out to peace.

4. *The Generalissimo himself:* Universally the Generalissimo is criticized for his ineffective leadership and universally no one can suggest any one to take his place. He is the one who holds this vast country together. Without him disintegration seems inevitable yet long experience with him suggests that he is no longer capable of changing and reforming or of discarding inefficient associates in favor of competent ones and unless he can summon the resources to reverse the present trend he will inevitably and in time be discarded. Nevertheless the Generalissimo is a resourceful man and there are signs that he is trying to find a way to continue the fight against the Communists and at the same time prevent a return of the country to regionalism. He has sent former Prime Minister Chang Chun to the north and to the southwest offering regional autonomy in return for continued allegiance to Nanking and there is reason to believe Chang Chun's trip has not been entirely unproductive of results. There is active and violent agitation for reorganization of the Kuomintang which will permit liberal voices greater weight in government circles and there is evidence that under Wong Wen-hao the government is making a valiant effort toward economic and financial reform which may be announced shortly. Unless, however, these drastic measures which are contemplated produce a miracle and result in the retention of the Generalissimo and the Kuomintang in control we may expect to see some kind of an accommodation with the Communists or a regional breakup or a combination of the two. The third possibility seems the most likely.

Even though at present some form of coalition seems most likely we believe that from the standpoint of the United States it would be most undesirable. We say this because the history of coalitions including Communists demonstrates all too clearly Communist ability by political means to take over complete control of the government and in the process to acquire some kind of international recognition. We question whether a Communist government can in the foreseeable future come to full power in all China by means other than coalition. We would recommend therefore that American efforts be designed to prevent the formation of a coalition government and our best means to that end is continued and, if possible, increased support to the present government. Nevertheless deterioration has already progressed to the verge of collapse and it may already be too late for our support to change the course of events. To assure success we should likely have to involve ourselves in great responsibilities, military, economic, political for we should have to undertake the direction of Chinese affairs on a large scale and a scale in fact that would likely involve responsibilities beyond our resources.

B. Secretary Marshall's Policy Directives*

August 12 and 13, 1948

The Secretary of State on August 12, 1948, outlined the following points for the Embassy's general guidance:

1. The United States Government must not directly or indirectly give any implication of support, encouragement or acceptability of coalition government in China with Communist participation.

2. The United States Government has no intention of again offering its good offices as mediator in China.

Overt United States opposition to Chinese Government compromise with the Chinese Communists (or even secretly expressed opposition, which would likely become known) would at this juncture provide ammunition in China for propaganda alleging that the United States was encouraging and prolonging the civil war. It could also mislead the Chinese Government to expect unlimited aid which could not eventuate under the existing world situation and in any circumstances would require congressional action. Any informal expression of United States Government attitude toward these questions should, at this stage of developments in China, be confined to the two points outlined above. You should, of course, overlook no suitable opportunity to emphasize the pattern of engulfment which has resulted from coalition governments in eastern Europe.

On August 13 Secretary Marshall observed:

> While the Department will keep actively in mind the questions raised, it is not likely that the situation will make it possible for us at this juncture to formulate any rigid plans for our future policy in China. Developments in China are obviously entering into a period of extreme flux and confusion in which it will be impossible with surety to perceive clearly far in advance the pattern of things to come and in which this Government plainly must preserve a maximum freedom of action.

C. Policy Review*

October, 1948

Toward the end of October the Embassy again pointed out the continuing deterioration and inquired whether there had been any changes in Washington. To this the Secretary replied:

There is general agreement with your assumption that the United States purposes in the Far East would as in the past be best served by the existence of political stability in China under a friendly Government, and American policy and its implementation have been consistently directed toward that goal. However, underlying our recent relations with China have been the fundamental considerations that the United States must not become directly involved in the Chinese civil war and that the United States must not assume responsibility for underwriting the Chinese Government militarily and economically. Direct

*Ibid., pp. 279-80.

*Ibid., pp. 280-85.

armed intervention in the internal affairs of China runs counter to traditional American policy toward China . . ." Public statements in Congress by leaders of the Senate Foreign Relations Committee, which initiated Section 404 (b) of the China Aid Act, indicated that aid to China under the $125,000,000 grants must be completely clear of the implication of the United States underwriting the military campaign of the Chinese Government, since any such implication would be impossible over so vast an area.

Our China Aid Program was designed to give the Chinese Government a breathing spell to initiate those vital steps necessary to provide the framework within which the base for economic recovery might be laid and essential for its survival. It was clear that in the main solution of China's problems was largely one for the Chinese themselves and the aid was intended to give the Chinese Government further opportunity to take measures of self-help.

The general basic considerations governing our approach to the China problem were set forth in my statement before the Senate Foreign Relations and House Foreign Affairs Committees executive sessions, a copy of which was forwarded to you. The United States Government must be exceedingly careful that it does not become committed to a policy involving the absorption of its resources to an unpredictable extent as would be the case if the obligations are assumed of a direct responsibility for the conduct of the civil war in China or for the Chinese economy, or both. To achieve the objective of reducing the Chinese Communists to a completely negligible factor in China in the immediate future, it would be necessary for the United States virtually to take over the Chinese Government and administer its economic, military and governmental affairs. Strong Chinese sensibilities regarding infringement of China's sovereignty, the intense feeling of nationalism among all Chinese, and the unavailability of qualified American personnel in large numbers required argue strongly against attempting such a solution. It would be impossible to estimate the final cost of a course of action of this magnitude. It certainly would be a continuing operation for a long time to come. It would involve the United States Government in a continuing commitment from which it would practically be impossible to withdraw, and it would very probably involve grave consequences to this nation by making of China an arena of international conflict. Present developments make it unlikely that any amount of United States military or economic aid could make the present Chinese Government capable of reestablishing and then maintaining its control throughout all China. There is little evidence that the fundamental weaknesses of the Chinese Government can be basically corrected by foreign aid. These considerations were set forth in my statement in February and they are certainly no less true under present circumstances.

          *   *   *

In summary, adoption of a course of increased aid would violate all basic considerations underlying American policy toward China, would involve the United States directly in China's civil war, would commit this Government to underwriting the Chinese Government militarily and economically at a cost which it would be impossible to estimate at a time when the United States has heavy commitments throughout the world in connection with foreign aid programs and would not, in the light of appraisals of the situation submitted by the Embassy and consular offices in China over a period of several months, achieve its avowed objectives.

D. President Chiang Kai-shek to President Truman*

November 9, 1948

I have the honor to acknowledge receipt of Your Excellency's reply dated October 16, 1948, for which I am deeply grateful.

The Communist forces in Central China are now within striking distance of Shanghai and Nanking. If we fail to stem the tide, China may be lost to the cause of democracy. I am therefore compelled to send to Your Excellency again a direct and urgent appeal.

The general deterioration of the military situation in China may be attributed to a number of factors. But the most fundamental is the non-observance by the Soviet Government of the Sino-Soviet Treaty of Friendship and Alliance, which, as Your Excellency will doubtless recall, the Chinese Government signed as a result of the well-intentioned advice from the United States Government. I need hardly point out that, but for persistent Soviet aid, the Chinese Communists would not have been able to occupy Manchuria and develop into such a menace.

As a co-defender of democracy against the onrush and infiltration of Communism throughout the world, I appeal to you for speedy and increased military assistance and for a firm statement of American policy in support of the cause for which my Government is fighting. Such a statement would serve to bolster up the morale of the armed forces and the civilian population and would strengthen the Government's position in the momentous battle now unfolding in North and Central China.

My Government would be most happy to receive from you as soon as possible a high-ranking military officer who will work out in consultation with my Government a concrete scheme of military assistance, including the participation of American military advisers in the direction of operations.

As the situation demands your Excellency's full sympathy and quick decision, I shall appreciate an early reply.

E. President Truman to President Chiang Kai-shek*

November 11, 1948

My dear President Chiang:

This is in acknowledgment of your letter delivered to the White House on

Ibid., pp. 888-89.

Ibid., pp. 889-90.

November 9 through the good offices of your Ambassador, Dr. V.K. Wellington Koo.

As I stated in my letter of October 16, 1948, everything possible is being done to expedite the procurement and shipment to China of the weapons and ammunition being obtained in this country under the China Aid Program. I am again emphasizing to the appropriate officials the urgency of your needs and the necessity of prompt action. In this connection, I have just been informed that one shipment of arms and ammunition sailed from Guam on November 4 and another from Japan on November 7 en route to China. I have also been informed that a further shipment of ammunition sailed from the West Coast of the United States on November 9 and is scheduled to reach China about November 24.

A message of November 9 from the Secretary of State to Ambassador Stuart, containing Secretary Marshall's reply to a request from the Chinese Foreign Minister for military aid and the visit of a high-ranking United States officer to China, apparently crossed Your Excellency's message in transmission. The Secretary authorized Ambassador Stuart to inform the Foreign Minister that the United States National Military Establishment was making every effort to expedite shipments of military material purchased in this country under the China Aid Act. He also authorized Ambassador Stuart to point out the inherent difficulties involved in an attempt on the part of a newly appointed foreign official to advise the Chinese Government regarding its courses of action in the present dilemma, even if such an official would be completely conversant with all the numerous complexities of the situation, and to point out the even greater difficulties for a foreign official not familiar with China.

However, Major General Barr, Director of the Joint United States Military Advisory Group in China, is conversant with the current situation and his advice has always been available to you.

Your attention may have been called to my public statement on March 11, 1948, in which I stated that the United States maintained friendly relations with the Chinese Government and was trying to assist the recognized Government of China maintain peace. I also stated that I did not desire Communists in the Chinese Government. Secretary Marshall stated publicly on March 10, 1948, that the Communists were now in open rebellion against the Chinese Government and that the inclusion of the Communists in the Government was a matter for the Chinese Government to decide, not for the United States Government to dictate. I believe that these statements and the action of my Government in extending assistance to the Chinese Government under the China Aid Act of 1948 have made the position of the United States Government clear.

You will understand the desire of the United States Government to support the cause of peace and democracy throughout the world. It is this desire that has led this Government to extend assistance to many countries in their efforts to promote sound economies and stable conditions without which the peoples of the world cannot expect to have peace and the principles of democracy cannot grow. It was with that hope that the United States Government has extended assistance in various forms to the Chinese Government. I am most sympathetic with the difficulties confronting the Chinese Government and people at this time and wish to assure Your Excellency that my Government will continue to exert every effort to expedite the implementation of the program of aid for China which has been authorized by the Congress with my approval.

F. Ambassador Stuart to Secretary Marshall*

[Extract]

Nanking, December 21, 1948

May I outline below my personal views re political outlook in China and bearing of this on American policy. This is partly for record but chiefly in order to have full benefit of your instructions.

As you are well aware my original hope had been that by military aid to Chiang Government especially in form of advice upon which all else would be conditioned, it might have been possible to keep area south of Yangtse intact and clear coastal region from Nanking northward of militant Communism. It would have been expected that again with American technical advisers and economic aid there would be improvements in local Government and in people's livelihood which would compare favorably with conditions in Communist territory. National Government would guard its frontier but carry on no aggressive warfare against Communists. This would allow public opinion to take form in both sections and be basis for some sort of negotiated settlement. Whether this would have proven practicable and results have justified our efforts now is immaterial.

Dealing with present realities one must begin as always with President Chiang. It is distressing to observe how completely he has lost public confidence in recent months and how widespread is desire he retire. This sentiment is shared by most officials of all ranks in Government and is almost universal among politically conscious citizens. Opposition to him is primarily because of conviction that war as he has been conducting it is hopeless and is bringing upon people almost unendurable economic and other distress. View is not infrequently expressed that he is best asset Communists have. It is ironical therefore that he refuses to turn over active direction of affairs as he has been repeatedly advised to do because this would be in his opinion tantamount to allowing Communists overrun country. Issue is thus confused in his mind as apparently in case of many in U.S. as though American military aid to him were only alternative to complete Communist domination of China. But it would be in violation of basic principle of democracy to maintain in power man who has lost support of his own people. It would arouse greater sympathy for Communist cause and violent anti-American feeling.

In any case our military men all seem to be agreed that such aid would be too late, even under new leadership. It is probable that resistance groups will carry on for some time in south and west and may form a loose federation.

*Ibid., pp. 897-99.

But our military aid to these would at this state be in my opinion very unwise and would certainly complicate matters in coastal provinces and central area.

*   *   *

G. Secretary of State Dean Acheson to Senator Tom Connally, Chairman of the Senate Committee on Foreign Relations*

March 15, 1949

The following comments on S. 1063 are offered in response to your request as conveyed by Mr. O'Day, Clerk of the Committee on Foreign Relations, in his letter of February 28, 1949. It is the Department's view that the Bill proposes aid of a magnitude and character unwarranted by present circumstances in China.

Despite the present aid program authorized by the last Congress, together with the very substantial other aid extended by the United States to China since V-J Day, aggregating over $2 billion, the economic and military position of the Chinese Government has deteriorated to the point where the Chinese Communists hold almost all important areas of China from Manchuria to the Yangtze River and have the military capability of expanding their control to the populous areas of the Yangtze Valley and of eventually dominating south China. The National Government does not have the military capability of maintaining a foothold in south China against a determined Communist advance. The Chinese Government forces have lost no battles during the past year because of lack of ammunition and equipment, while the Chinese Communists have captured the major portion of military supplies, exclusive of ammunition, furnished the Chinese Government by the United States since V-J Day. There is no evidence that the furnishing of additional military material would alter the pattern of current developments in China. There is, however, ample evidence that the Chinese people are weary of hostilities and that there is an overwhelming desire for peace at any price. To furnish solely military material and advice would only prolong hostilities and the suffering of the Chinese people and would arouse in them deep resentment against the United States. Yet, to furnish the military means for bringing about a reversal of the present deterioration and for providing some prospect of successful military resistance would require the use of an unpredictably large American armed force in actual combat, a course of action which would represent direct United States involvement in China's fratricidal warfare and would be contrary to our traditional policy toward China and the interests of this country.

In these circumstances, the extension of as much as $1.5 billion of credits to the Chinese Government, as proposed by the Bill, would embark this Government on an undertaking the eventual cost of which would be unpredictable but of great magnitude, and the outcome of which would almost surely be catastrophic. The field supervision of United States military aid, the pledging of

Ibid., pp. 1053-54.

revenue of major Chinese ports in payment of United States aid, United States administration and collection of Chinese customs in such ports, and United States participation in Chinese tax administration, all of which are called for by the Bill, would without question be deeply resented by the Chinese people as an extreme infringement of China's sovereignty and would arouse distrust in the minds of the Chinese people with respect to the motives of the United States in extending aid. While the use of up to $500 million in support of the Chinese currency, as proposed in the Bill, would undoubtedly ease temporarily the fiscal problem of the Chinese Government, stabilization of the Chinese currency cannot be considered feasible so long as the Government's monetary outlays exceed its income by a large margin. After the first $500 million had been expended, the United States would find it necessary to continue provision of funds to cover the Chinese Government's budgetary deficit if the inflationary spiral were not to be resumed. That China could be expected to repay United States financial, economic and military aid of the magnitude proposed, which the Bill indicates should all be on a credit basis, cannot be supported by realistic estimates of China's future ability to service foreign debts even under conditions of peace and economic stability.

The United States has in the past sought to encourage the Chinese Government to initiate those vital measures necessary to provide a basis for economic improvement and political stability. It has recognized that, in the absence of a Chinese Government capable of initiating such measures and winning popular support, United States aid of great magnitude would be dissipated and United States attempts to guide the operations of the Chinese Government would be ineffective and probably lead to direct involvement in China's fratricidal warfare. General Marshall reflected these considerations when he stated in February 1948 that an attempt to underwrite the Chinese economy and the Chinese Government's military effort represented a burden on the United States economy and a military responsibility which he could not recommend as a course of action for this Government.

Despite the above observations, it would be undesirable for the United States precipitously to cease aid to areas under the control of the Chinese Government which it continues to recognize. Future developments in China, including the outcome of political negotiations now being undertaken, are uncertain. Consideration is being given, therefore, to a request for Congressional action to extend the authority of the China Aid Act of 1948 to permit commitment of unobligated appropriations for a limited period beyond April 2, 1949, the present expiration date of the Act. If during such a period, the situation in China clarified itself sufficiently, further recommendations might be made.

**H. Statement by Secretary Acheson on Basic Principles of United
  States Policy Toward the Far East***

[Extract]

August 5, 1949

As you are all aware, the United States is confronted by a situation in China
which will test to the full our unity of purpose, our ingenuity, and our adherence
to the basic principles which have for half a century governed our policy toward
China. The background of that situation and the extensive and persistent efforts
of the United States during the past 5 years to assist the Chinese people are
fully described in the document which the Department is issuing on August
5. They are summarized in my letter of transmittal to the President. Secretary
Marshall in February 1948 confidentially told the Senate Foreign Relations
Committee and the House Foreign Affairs Committee in executive session many
of the facts which are now being published as well as the conclusions drawn
from those facts. He made it clear why public disclosure at that time seemed
inadvisable, and I have pointed out in my letter to the President why we feel
the information should be made public now. As I said in that letter, the strength
of our system of government is based on an informed and critical public opinion,
and it is in order that our people may be fully informed in regard to the background of our Far Eastern policy that this record is now being published.

The situation in China serves to emphasize a vital factor in connection with
the question of United States aid to foreign nations—that is, that, while the
United States can with the best of intentions contribute substantial aid to a
foreign government, it cannot guarantee that that aid will achieve its purpose.
The achievement of that purpose must, in the final analysis, depend upon the
degree to which the recipient government and people make wise use of our
assistance and take effective measures of self-help. Without such action by the
recipient, no amount of American aid can avail. This is no less true in China
than in other parts of the world.

Our traditional policy of assisting the Chinese people to resist domination
by a foreign power or powers is now faced by the gravest difficulties. On the
one hand, there is in China a Communist regime which, while in fact serving
the imperialist interests of a foreign power, has for the present been able to
persuade large numbers of Chinese that it is serving their interests and has
been able to extend its sway in constantly widening circles. On the other hand,
there is the National Government of China which has been unable to rally
its people and has been driven out of extensive and important portions of the
country, despite very extensive assistance from the United States and advice
from eminent American representatives which subsequent events proved to be
sound.

This means that United States policy toward China is confronted by a situation
in which alternatives are very sharply limited. We must not base our policy

*Department of State Bulletin, Vol. XXI, p. 236.

on illusions or wishful thinking. I am convinced however that the basic elements of our traditional policy toward the Far East remain valid now as in the past, and I should like to state certain basic principles by which we should continue to be guided. These are:

1. The United States desires to encourage in every feasible way the development of China as an independent and stable nation able to play a role in world affairs suitable for a great and free people.

2. The United States desires to support the creation in China of economic and political conditions which will safeguard basic rights and liberties and progressively develop the economic and social well-being of its people.

3. The United States is opposed to the subjection of China to any foreign power, to any regime acting in the interest of a foreign power, and to the dismemberment of China by any foreign power, whether by open or clandestine means.

4. The United States will continue to consult with other interested powers, in the light of conditions in all countries concerned and in the Far East as a whole, on measures which will contribute to the continuing security and welfare of the peoples of that area.

5. The United States will encourage and support efforts of the United Nations to achieve these objectives and particularly to maintain peace and security in the Far East.

*   *   *

TREATY OF FRIENDSHIP, ALLIANCE AND MUTUAL ASSISTANCE BETWEEN THE U.S.S.R. AND THE PEOPLE'S REPUBLIC OF CHINA*

February 14, 1950

The Presidium of the Supreme Soviet of the Union of Soviet Socialist Republics and the Central People's Government of the People's Republic of China;

Filled with determination jointly to prevent, by the consolidation of friendship and cooperation between the Union of Soviet Socialist Republics and the People's Republic of China, the rebirth of Japanese imperialism and a repetition of aggression on the part of Japan or any other state which should unite in any form with Japan in acts of aggression. Imbued with the desire to consolidate lasting peace and universal security in the Far East and throughout the world in conformity with the aims and principles of the United Nations organization;

Profoundly convinced that the consolidation of good neighborly relations and friendship between the Union of Soviet Socialist Republics and the People's Republic of China meets the fundamental interests of the peoples of the Soviet Union and China;

Resolved for this purpose to conclude the present Treaty and appointed as their plenipotentiary and representatives;

The Presidium of the Supreme Soviet of the Union of Soviet Socialist Republics—Andrei Yanuaryevich Vyshinsky, Minister of Foreign Affairs of the Union of Soviet Socialist Republics;

The Central People's Government of the People's Republic of China—Chou En-lai, Prime minister of the State Administrative Council and Minister of Foreign Affairs of China;

Who, after exchange of their credentials, found in due form and good order, agreed upon the following:

Article I

Both High Contracting Parties undertake jointly to take all the necessary measures at their disposal for the purpose of preventing a repetition of aggression and violation of peace on the part of Japan or any other state which should unite with Japan, directly or indirectly, in acts of aggression. In the event of one of the High Contracting Parties being attacked by Japan or states allied with it, and thus being involved in a state of war, the other High Contracting Party will immediately render military and other assistance with all the means at its disposal.

The High Contracting Parties also declare their readiness in the spirit of sincere cooperation to participate in all international actions aimed at ensuring peace and security throughout the world, and will do all in their power to achieve the speediest implementation of these tasks.

Military Situation in the Far East, pt. 5, pp. 3172-73.

Article II

Both High Contracting Parties undertake by means of mutual agreement to strive for the earliest conclusion of a peace treaty with Japan, jointly with the other Powers which were allies during the Second World War.

Article III

Both the High Contracting Parties undertake not to conclude any alliance directed against the other High Contracting Party, and not to take part in any coalition or in actions or measures directed against the other High Contracting Party.

Article IV

Both High Contracting Parties will consult each other in regard to all important international problems affecting the common interests of the Soviet Union and China, being guided by the interests of the consolidation of peace and universal security.

Article V

Both the High Contracting Parties undertake, in the spirit of friendship and cooperation and in conformity with the principles of equality, mutual interests, and also mutual respect for the state sovereignty and territorial integrity and noninterference in internal affairs of the other High Contracting Party—to develop and consolidate economic and cultural ties between the Soviet Union and China, to render each other every possible economic assistance, and to carry out the necessary economic cooperation.

Article VI

The present Treaty comes into force immediately upon its ratification; the exchange of instruments of ratification will take place in Peking.

The present Treaty will be valid for 30 years. If neither of the High Contracting Parties gives notice one year before the expiration of this term of its desire to denounce the Treaty, it shall remain in force for another five years and will be extended in compliance with this rule.

Done in Moscow on Februrary 14, 1950, in two copies, each in the Russian and Chinese languages, both texts having equal force.

Signed:

By Authorization of the Presidium of the
Supreme Soviet of the Union of Soviet
Socialist Republics, A.Y. Vyshinsky

By Authorization of the Central People's
Government of the People's Republic of
China, Chou En-lai

DOCUMENTS RELATED TO LOYALTY OF STATE DEPARTMENT PERSONNEL INVOLVED WITH UNITED STATES CHINA POLICY

A. Investigation of Charges Against John Carter Vincent*

April 18, 1947

The Honorable Walter F. George, United States Senate

My dear Senator George: I refer to Senator Bridges' letter of April 7, 1947, to Senator Vandenberg, which you transmitted to me, and in which Senator Bridges encloses a memorandum submitted to him by someone whose name is not given setting forth a number of charges relative to the policies and record of Mr. John Carter Vincent, whose nomination for the promotion to Career Minister is under consideration by the Foreign Relations Committee. Although Senator Bridges does not express any opinion on the credibility or validity of the memorandum, he believes that an investigation into Mr. Vincent's fitness for the post is warranted.

I have made a careful investigation of all the charges made against Mr. Vincent and believe that they are wholly groundless.

I attach a point-by-point analysis of the allegations against Mr. Vincent. For the sake of convenience I have divided Senator Bridges' memorandum into 12 numbered paragraphs and have followed each paragraph with my answer or comments on the allegations contained in it. I have, in some places, rearranged slightly the text of the memorandum in order to shorten it and to make the charges stand forth more clearly. Inasmuch as the chronology and itinerary of Mr. Vincent's assignments and movements are substantially correct, I have omitted any reference to them from my summary.

I have known Mr. Vincent well throughout my service in the State Department. I recommended him for his present post and have worked intimately with him during my service as Under Secretary during which period he has reported directly to me. Increasing knowledge has brought increasing respect for his judgment and admiration for him as a gentleman and a disinterested and loyal servant of our Republic. He is a man of the finest intellectual quality and the highest character.

I am enclosing two copies of this letter, together with the analysis which you may want to submit to Senator Vandenberg.

Sincerely yours,
Dean Acheson, Acting Secretary

ANALYSIS OF ALLEGATIONS AGAINST MR. JOHN CARTER VINCENT
MADE IN MEMO TRANSMITTED WITH LETTER FROM SENATOR BRIDGES
OF APRIL 7, 1947 TO SENATOR VANDENBERG

1. It is alleged that the "actions, advice, and recommendations of Mr. Vincent"

Institute of Pacific Relations, Hearings Before the Subcommittee to Investigate the Administration of the Internal Security Act and other Internal Security Laws, Committee on the Judiciary, U.S. Senate, 82 Cong. 2nd sess., Part 13, pp. 4540-46.

have been coordinated with the steps outlined in two official Communist documents:

1. "The Program of the Communist International and its Constitution." Workers Library Publishers. 1928. 3d American Edition, 1936.

2. "The Revolutionary Movement in the Colonies and Semi-Colonies," adopted as a resolution by the 6th World Congress of the Comintern, Sept. 1, 1928.

Comment: Mr. Vincent advised me that he has never even read the two Communist documents under reference. I have never read them myself. I state categorically that any advice given by Mr. Vincent or any action taken by him was not coordinated, either intentionally or coincidentally, with these documents. The author of the memorandum presented to Senator Bridges does not quote from the documents and does not cite any specific instances in which Mr. Vincent's policies and actions have paralleled the supposed Communist line. The effect of citing these documents at the outset of a bill of particulars against Mr. Vincent is tendentious and unfair.

II. It is charged that while at the Embassy in Chungking in 1941 Mr. Vincent "expressed dislike for Ambassador Gauss," "a general dislike of the Chinese," and "an anti-Japanese viewpoint (prior to adoption of the Russo-Jap nonaggression pact in mid-April 1941)," and that he "expressed sympathy for Communist aims and ideology" and dislike for "alleged American exploitation of cheap Chinese labor."

Comment: The allegation regarding Mr. Vincent's personal feelings toward Ambassador Gauss or vice versa bears on Mr. Vincent's fitness for this promotion only in its imputation of disloyalty. The contrary is the case. Mr. Vincent lived with Ambassador Gauss for two years (from 1941 to 1943), and their relation appears to have been close and amicable. I discover in the record only loyalty on the part of Mr. Vincent, both to the person of Ambassador Gauss and to the policies and actions advocated by him.

The allegation that Mr. Vincent has expressed a "general dislike of the Chinese," I find wholly untrue. Mr. Vincent has dedicated a great part of his life to friendship with the Chinese, the betterment of conditions in China, and toward good relations between that country and the United States of America.

With respect to his alleged "anti-Japanese viewpoint" it is quite true that from the beginning of Japanese aggression—and entirely unaffected by the Russo-Japanese arrangements in 1941, a wholly tendentious insinuation—Mr. Vincent and many others, among whom I include myself, were actively advocating measures to counteract that aggression.

Mr. Vincent has no "sympathy for Communist aims and ideology" and I am willing to state that he has never expressed any such sympathy directly or indirectly.

Mr. Vincent tells me that he knows of no instances of American exploitation of cheap Chinese labor and has never discussed the subject.

III. It is charged that, in 1945 while Mr. Vincent was first Chief of the Division of Chinese Affairs and later Director of the Office of Far Eastern Affairs, personnel in the State Department engaged in private correspondence with personnel of the Embassy in Chungking, via diplomatic pouch, and that this private correspondence was "leaked" to the Communists. It is stated that General Hurley's resignation came two months later.

Comment: The implication is that Mr. Vincent conducted or permitted, a clandestine personal correspondence on official matters undermining the policies of General Hurley. It is further implied that the substance of this unapproved correspondence was being illicitly conveyed to the Communists. It is further implied that this was the cause for General Hurley's resignation.

In 1945, Mr. Vincent was at the San Francisco Conference from the middle of April to the end of May, at the Potsdam Conference from early June to early August, at the Moscow Conference from early December to the end of the year.

The entire subject of this alleged unofficial correspondence and contact with the Communists was thoroughly ventilated in the hearings of the Senate Foreign Relations Committee during December 1945 on the charges brought by former Ambassador Hurley against the loyalty of certain Foreign Service officers. Secretary Byrnes said before the Committee:

"The other complaint of Ambassador Hurley is that some official or employee did not merely express a different view of his superior officer, but advised someone associated with the Communist forces that the Ambassador did not accurately represent United States policy. For such action there would be no excuse. I would be the first to condemn it and to dismiss the person guilty of it. But Ambassador Hurley has not furnished me, nor do I understand that he has furnished this Committee, any specific evidence to prove that any employee was guilty of such conduct."

The Committee took no action whatsoever on General Hurley's charges and failed to find the matter worth a published report. Furthermore, Mr. Vincent has at no time engaged in or countenanced private correspondence on official matters. I think, therefore, that we may consider the case as without foundation.

However, for whatever interest it may have, I should like to point out that on the basis of records available to us, Mr. Vincent's name appears to have been mentioned only three times in the course of these hearings, and not at all in connection with the question of the alleged clandestine correspondence. Ambassador Hurley referred once to a letter addressed to the President by Mr. Maxwell Stewart finding fault with Mr. Hurley, which Mr. Vincent acknowledged on reference from the White House without commenting on the substance of the letter.

Secretary Byrnes in his testimony referred to a report from General Hurley, dated December 24, 1944, and said that "there was a message signed by Mr. Stettinius with the initials of Mr. Vincent in the corner stating that the position of Hurley was sound."

There was only one other reference to Mr. Vincent during the hearings. Ambassador Hurley stated that he did not know Mr. Vincent well in spite of the fact that he and Mr. Vincent shared an office in the Department for a month in the spring of 1945 and went on to say that Mr. Vincent was in sympathy with George Atcheson (now Ambassador and Political Adviser to General Mac-

Arthur) and the others who were trying to undermine U.S. policy in China.

IV. It is stated that "a statement issued by President Truman on December 15, 1945, at the time of the appointment of General Marshall as Ambassador, presumably drafted by Vincent, entirely overlooked the principles of the Open Door, made no mention of the November 26, 1941, note to Japan, and in brief invited the Republic of China to 'agree to the Communistic terms for a coalition government or get no more aid from us.' This constituted a repetition in China of the policy so disastrously followed in Yugoslavia and Poland previously."

Comment. This paragraph is a criticism of the policies enunciated in a statement issued by President Truman on December 15, 1945, and its apparent intent as well as the intent of the entire memorandum is to imply that Mr. Vincent had improperly exerted his influence to compel the Chinese authorities to incorporate Communists in the government. This implication is entirely false.

As to the Presidential statement, it was not drafted by Mr. Vincent, or under his supervision. It was prepared under the direction of Secretary Byrnes, General Marshall, and myself. It was revised and approved by the President. Mr. Vincent was in entire agreement with its contents.

The statement at no place indicates that Chinese Communists must be brought into the Chinese Government. The Communists are mentioned only twice. It is stated that the United States Government believes it essential that "a cessation of hostilities be arranged between the armies of the National Government and the Chinese Communists . . ." Further on in the document it is stated that "the existence of autonomous armies such as that of the Communist Army is inconsistent with, and actually makes impossible, political unity in China." Incidentally, I note that in the above-quoted paragraph of the memorandum under discussion, an internal quotation appears of which the source is not given. If this is intended to summarize the purport of the President's message, it is clearly a misrepresentation.

As is well known, the subsequent course of events prevented the establishment of internal unity in China. When General Marshall arrived in China in December 1945, he found that provision had been made by the National Government for a People's Consultative Council made up of representatives of the National Government party (Kuomintang), the Communists, and two other minority parties. There were also a number of nonparty members. This Council had not met due to inability of the authorities to arrange for a cessation of hostilities. General Marshall immediately exerted his influence to bring about a truce and was able to do so as of January 10. On the same day the People's Consultative Council met. This Council of its own initiative and with the approval of Chiang Kai-shek drew up a series of resolutions and agreements providing for representation by all parties in a State Council (the National Government party retained control over the Council), for the adoption of a constitution, for abolition of one-party government and representation by other parties in the government on a minority basis, and for unification of all armed forces in a nonpolitical national army. It was these resolutions and agreements, freely adopted by the Chinese, which General Marshall used as his guide in his subsequent efforts to assist the Chinese toward peace and unity. He became a member of a 3-man committee (a National Government representative, a Communist representative, and himself) to supervise a truce agreement and prepared for the amalgamation of the armed forces.

Subsequent developments in China gradually undermined and finally wrecked the chances of bringing about peace and unity in accordance with the People's Consultative Council resolutions and agreements. General Marshall has set forth clearly in his statement of January 7 the reasons for this disappointing development.

V. It is stated that "in September 1946, six members of the Military Affairs Committee of the House, visited General MacArthur in Tokyo. They issued (PM, N.Y., Sept. 10, 1946) 'an alarming statement about Soviet intentions in the Far East.' The next day General MacArthur issued a warning about the danger of communism in Japan. This 'was deeply resented by John Carter Vincent.' "

Comment: Mr. Vincent has given me the following account of the incident to which this paragraph apparently refers:

"The story regarding my alleged resentment over a statement made by General MacArthur is as follows: On September 2, 1946, a newspaperman (New York Herald Tribune) called to ask me what I thought of the statement that had just been issued by General MacArthur. I told him I had not read the statement. He asked whether there had been any change in policy regarding Japan. I told him there had been one and went on to explain that American policy towards Japan was expressed in the Potsdam Declaration, Terms of Surrender and certain papers of the State-War-Navy Committee that had been made public. The newspaperman manufactured out of whole cloth the story that 'an official of the State Department' took exception to General MacArthur's statement. The story was untrue; the newspaperman subsequently apologized to me. The fact that he was eventually discharged by the Herald Tribune proves nothing in this connection."

VI. It is charged that:

> (a) Mr. Vincent presented a draft statement to Secretary Byrnes "in the fall of 1946" which "recommended withdrawal of all aid to the National government." Senator Bridges' document then indicates that his alleged draft by Mr. Vincent could be compared to the act of the Soviet Union in continuing aid to the Communists in China despite its undertaking to support the Central government in the Sino-Soviet pacts of August 14, 1945.
>
> (b) Mr. Vincent on November 11, 1946, while Director of the Office of Far Eastern Affairs, delivered an address in which he said that it was "unsound to invest private or public capital in countries where there is widespread corruption in business and official circles; where a government is wasting its substance on excessive armament, where the fact or trend of Civil War exists."
>
> The memorandum in reference characterizes this speech as an "indirect expression of American foreign policy in China" and points to the editorial disapproval of the speech as expressed in the New York World Telegram and approval given it by the Daily Worker, the Chicago Star and Communist party dailies.

Comment: As to (a), I have not been able to find any record of any such recommendation or draft prepared by Mr. Vincent or anyone else. The only draft presented by Mr. Vincent to the Secretary in the fall of 1946 was the paper which subsequently became the basis of the President's statement of December 18, 1946. It was prepared at my request and approved by the Secretary of State, the Secretaries of War and Navy, and by General Marshall. In no draft of the statement was there any recommendation that we withdraw all aid to the National Government. On the contrary, the statement provided, in a paragraph drafted by Mr. Vincent, for aid to China under the indicated conditions: Mr. Vincent has consistently advocated the extension of credits to China when conditions in China are such that the credits can be effectively utilized to improve economic conditions and promote a revival of American-Chinese business relations. He was, furthermore, active in supporting the grant by the Export-Import Bank of the $500,000,000 credit to China in March 1946. This was in accord with the expressed view of General Marshall.

I believe that the best comment on the allegation in paragraph (b) above is the text itself of Mr. Vincent's speech. I attach a copy.

There are also attached for your information copies of two letters, one from the National Foreign Trade Council and the other from the China-American Council of Commerce and Industry, the two trade organizations most actively interested in commercial relations with China. You will note that the President of the National Foreign Trade Council states that Mr. Vincent's "enunciation of the attitude and policies of the United States with respect to our interests in the Far East was most impressive." The President of the China-America Council states that Mr. Vincent's speech was discussed at a meeting of the Executive Committee of the Council and "appreciation expressed for the clear-cut statement of policy of the Department of State as presented in his address." In addition to these two statements of approval, there have been received in the Department a large number of letters from businessmen, who heard or read Mr. Vincent's speech, expressing their appreciation and approval.

As to press reaction to Mr. Vincent's speech, criticism appears to have been confined to the Scripps-Howard press. It is reported that certain Communist dailies approved this speech but I might add to the list of those expressing approval the following: New York Journal of Commerce, New York Herald Tribune, Washington Post, Washington Times-Herald, etc.

VII. It is stated that Mr. Vincent accompanied "Owen Lattimore, member of the Editorial Board of Amerasia, pro-Communist magazine on Asia," and Henry Wallace on his trip to China in 1944. Mr. Wallace's report of his journey is said to have been "prepared with the direct assistance of Mr. Vincent" and it is alleged that it "should be examined for further indications of Mr. Vincent's approval of the Communist program in China, opposition to the support of the Nationalist Government and furtherance of extension of the influence of Russia in China."

Comment: Mr. Vincent was assigned by the Secretary of State to accompany Mr. Wallace, the Vice President of the United States, on the journey mentioned. Mr. Vincent did not prepare or assist in the preparation of the report and does not know what recommendations it contained. Mr. Vincent had never met Mr. Wallace prior to the trip to China, saw him only a few times on official business after their return, and has had no contact with him since his resignation from the Government.

VII. It is alleged that "examination of the top secret and secret documents required by General Hurley, and passing between the State Department (Mr. Vincent) and General Hurley at the time of his incumbency, would prove revealing of the policy and aims of Mr. Vincent, contrary to the best interests of this country and contrary to its avowed Foreign Policy in China."

Comment: The allegation does not cite any particular document or reference to support the charge that the aims and policies of Mr. Vincent were contrary to the best interests of this country and contrary to its foreign policy in China, and indeed could not do so. At no time have the policy and aims of Mr. Vincent been contrary to our best interests in China or to our foreign policy. No documents ever went directly from Mr. Vincent to General Hurley and any documents from the Department to General Hurley were prepared or approved by Mr. Ballantine, then Director of the Office of Far Eastern Affairs, or Under Secretary Grew who were responsible for the formulation of policy with regard to China at that time, subject to the close review of the Secretary of State and the President.

IX. It is charged that "at the Potsdam Conference in July 1945, Vincent, aware of the secret Yalta agreement with respect to agreement that Russia was to have certain rights in Manchura, failed to properly advise Mr. Byrnes of this text, made a great show of opposing Russian demands with respect to China, and furthered a final agreement (which still remains secret) which gave Russia even more than agreed at Yalta. Under date of Oct. 31, 1946, Mr. John M. Patterson, Acting Assistant Chief, Division of Public Liaison, Department of State, replied to the request of the American China Policy Association, Inc., for release that 'No secret agreements concerning China were concluded at the Potsdam Conference.' It is thought that Mr. Vincent instructed Mr. Patterson in the writing of this letter (Why did Mr. Vincent conceal (if he did) from President Truman and Secretary Byrnes at Potsdam, the precise nature and extent of the previous secret Yalta commitments? It would seem that only the Russians could have been benefited by the concealment, as they were thus able to squeeze more concession from our negotiators who were ignorant of the exact terms which had been squeezed from President Roosevelt).

Comment: Mr. Vincent had no knowledge of the Yalta Agreement until he reached Potsdam. Moreover, Mr. Byrnes was fully informed concerning the Yalta conversations. He attended the Conference and was thoroughly familiar with the full text of the Yalta Agreements before he departed for the Potsdam Conference. It is therefore absurd to suggest that there was anything which Mr. Vincent could have withheld from Mr. Byrnes even if he had known it.

As you are aware, the full texts of the Yalta and Potsdam Agreements have now been made public. The Potsdam Agreement does not contain any "final agreement which gave Russia even more than agreed to at Yalta."

Mr. Vincent does not know Mr. John M. Patterson and gave no instruction to him in the writing of any such letter as that referred to.

X. It is stated that "in late July or early August 1945, Ambassador Hurley finally secured clearance to show the Yalta text to the Chinese. He then exerted every effort to force T.V. Soong and Foreign Minister Wang Shi-hsueh to go to Moscow. When they got there, the Russians made additional demands and the Chinese Government appealed to Hurley to mediate. 'Somehow or other Washington learned of this' and Hurley received a cable believed to have read somewhat as follows: 'You will not advise, you will not mediate, you will not assist in Chinese Russian negotiations.' It was signed 'Grew,' but it is believed that Under Secretary Grew, who was then being forced out, did not compose it."

Comment: This allegation is completely inaccurate. There is no record of information reaching the Department at the time cited of any "additional demands" made by representatives of the U.S.S.R. during the Sino-Russian conversations nor of any appeal by the Chinese Government that General Hurley "mediate." The Chinese Government had been informed a year prior to that time that the United States did not desire to place itself in any position in which it might appear as a "mediator" between China and other countries and Ambassador Hurley had been apprised of this as early as six months prior to the alleged time. This policy had the full approval of Mr. Grew and of the President.

XI. It is charged that apparently in the summer of 1945 "Henry Luce of Time-Life-Fortune, who was represented in China by Theodore White, a strong pro-Communist, became uneasy about 'angled' dispatches and applied for a passport to fly out and see for himself. The State Department refused it. He appealed to General Hurley who cabled recommending the issuance. In reply Hurley received a reprimand advising him not to interfere. Mr. Luce finally obtained an official invitation from Chiang Kai-shek which brought the passport, investigated, and fired White for pro-Communist propaganda. White is a great admirer of Vincent and, like him, has been connected with the Institute of Pacific Relations."

Comment: Mr. Vincent has never been consulted or informed with respect to any grant or refusal of travel permission from Mr. Luce.

XII. It is charged that "during the past two years, the Far Eastern Division of the State Department has been denuded of its former heads who were not pro-Soviet. Hornbeck, former Far Eastern Division head, who has been advanced to Political Adviser to the Secretary, was packed off as Ambassador to the Netherlands; Grew was forced to retire, as was Dooman, Drumright, and the Chief of China Section was sent to London. Now in control of the Far East Division, Lattimore and Vincent (Lattimore having no official connection although he lectures to Department personnel, and to the War College, and is known to advise Dean Acheson and President Truman as well as Vincent) have sent to General MacArthur, as well as to China, men and women of Red sympathies. A few names sent MacArthur are John S. Service (ardent pro-Communist, arrested in 1945 for turning State Department papers over to Communist Philip Jaffe of *Amerasia*). Theodore Cohen (Labor Adviser), Miriam Farley, and T.A. Bisson of the Institute of Pacific Relations, listed as a Communist front by the Dies committee of 1944, of which Vincent and Lattimore are both trustees). Lattimore, close friend and associate of Vincent, is reported to have loaded the OWI with Reds (both Chinese and American) and helped to secure the appointment of a man without qualifications (also without a Communist record) as head of UNRRA for China and helped him staff this division of UNRRA with pro-Communists."

Comment: This allegation seeks to suggest a purpose and design behind the various personnel changed and transfers referred to which, I can say, from personal knowledge did not and does not exist. Insofar as Mr. Vincent is concerned he had nothing to do with the transfer of Mr. Hornbeck or the retirement of Mr. Grew and Mr. Dooman. Mr. Drumright had long desired an assignment to London which he eventually received.

I do not recollect ever having met Mr. Owen Lattimore; he has never advised me nor has he ever had anything to do with the operations of the Office of Far Eastern Affairs. I do not care at this time to go into the charges made against him which, in view of the above, are irrelevant to the present inquiry.

Mr. Vincent had nothing to do with the assignments of any of the persons whose names are listed as having been sent to General MacArthur. With respect to Mr. John S. Service, whose name is included, I would point out that, prior to his assignment to Tokyo, he was cleared of all charges which had been made against him.

Mr. Vincent is not a trustee of the Institute of Pacific Relations. He was elected to the post in 1944 with the permission of his superior, Mr. Joseph Grew. He was never able actively to serve in that capacity and was not reelected in subsequent years. It might be pointed out in this connection that such substantial citizens as Mr. Walter F. Dillingham, Mr. Henry F. Grady, Mr. Paul G. Hoffman, and Mr. Robert G. Sproul are trustees of the institution.

B. Investigation of Charges Against Owen Lattimore*

[Extract]

July 20, 1950

The Charge Before the Subcommittee

Senator McCarthy appeared before the subcommittee at an open session on March 13, 1950, and at an executive session on March 21, 1950, to give testimony concerning Owen Lattimore. The charges of Senator McCarthy consist of two principal components, namely, (1) Mr. Lattimore's alleged connection with the State Department, and (2) his "record as a pro-Communist," to use Senator McCarthy's words in public testimony and "top Russian spy," to use his words in executive-session testimony.

Senator McCarthy testified that Mr. Lattimore has been one of the State Department's most regular consultants, that he is the principal architect of our far eastern policy, that he has held numerous positions with the State Depart-

---

*State Department Employee Loyalty Investigation, Report of the Committee on Foreign Relations, 81 Cong., 2nd sess., pp. 49-74.

ment, and that he was one of the State Department's top advisers in developing our Asiatic program. In executive session, Senator McCarthy testified that he did not know when Lattimore had been on the payroll of the State Department but he understood that Lattimore has very free access to a desk in the Department and has access to all the files.

In his testimony, he described Mr. Lattimore as a man whose "record as a pro-Communist goes back many years," and then continued with the following material.

Senator McCarthy cited and read into the record an article from the June 6, 1946, issue of the Washington Times-Herald, commenting upon Lattimore, which mentioned the latter's connection with the editorial board of the magazine Amerasia, referred to his authorship of an article concerning the Moscow purge trials, and alleged that Lattimore opposed General MacArthur's policies in Japan. These same points, or the implications thereof, appear throughout in the Senator's testimony.

Senator McCarthy then quoted an article published in Columbia magazine, edition of September 1949, by Rev. James F. Kearney, S.J., dealing with the China question. In this article Father Kearney states, "There are those who believe, though, that no Americans deserve more credit for this Russian triumph and Sino-American disaster than Owen Lattimore and a small group of his friends . . . ."

Senator McCarthy alluded to Mr. Lattimore's writings generally in his testimony and specifically called attention to Lattimore's article in Pacific Affairs of September 1938, as describing the Moscow purge trials as a "triumph for democracy."

Senator McCarthy pointed out that Mr. Lattimore was a trustee of the Institute of Pacific Relations, the American Council of which was listed by the California Committee on Un-American Activities in its 1948 report as a Communist-front organization.

He asserted that Lattimore was a member of the editorial board of the magazine, Amerasia, the chairman of which was Frederick Vanderbilt Field; and that the managing editor of the magazine was Philip J. Jaffe, who was indicted and pleaded quilty to a charge of conspiracy to violate statutes penalizing the illegal obtaining and possession of Government documents.

Senator McCarthy testified that the Maryland Association for Democratic Rights was an affiliate of the National Emergency Conference for Democratic Rights, and that at a conference of the Maryland Association in Baltimore, early in 1944, Mr. and Mrs. Lattimore were sponsors. He testified that the House Special Committee on Un-American Activities cited the National Emergency Conference for Democratic Rights as a Communist-front organization

. . . .

During the executive session before which he testified, Senator McCarthy insisted that information concerning Lattimore in the FBI files would show "in detail not the case merely of a man who appears to favor Russia, not the case of a man who might disagree with what we think about Russia, but a man who is definitely an espionage agent."

He furthermore asserted: "This man is the top of the whole ring of which Hiss was a part," and "I think he is the top Russian spy."

*   *   *

Lattimore's Connection with the State Department

Reference is made to the allegations that Lattimore was one of the State Department's most regular consultants, that he was one of the principal architects of our far eastern policy, that he held numerous positions with the State Department, and that he was one of the State Department's top advisers in developing our Asiatic program. The State Department files reveal that Mr. Lattimore might be said to have served the State Department as follows:

1. Entered on duty October 15, 1945, with the United States Reparations Mission to Japan at the request of Edwin W. Pauley, and terminated February 12, 1946, at the completion of the assignment. He was paid from the Department of State's international Conference Fund.

2. June 6, 1946, Mr. Lattimore made a speech to a group of State Department employees. He received no remuneration.

3. October 6 to 8, 1949, Mr. Lattimore was a delegate to a conference on Chinese affairs at the State Department without compensation but reimbursed for expenses.

As to the first service in connection with the State Department, Mr. Lattimore was serving as an economic adviser to Mr. Pauley and was not making Chinese or far eastern policy in the State Department. Such influence as his views may have had would have been in the sphere of economic arrangements for the future via-á-vis the conquered nation, Japan.

As one of 28 persons, Mr. Lattimore made a speech on June 5, 1946, as part of a lecture program designed to bring before departmental personnel the viewpoints of various persons who were working on, or interested in, foreign affairs. The speakers are listed in a letter from Mr. Peurifoy, Deputy Under Secretary of State, dated April 17, 1950, set out as appendix 11 of this report.

Relative to the third capacity in which Mr. Lattimore is indicated to have served, he was one of 31 who expressed in writing their views on United States policy toward China to the State Department in response to a solicitation of private individuals. Some of these 31 individuals were among a group of 25 who participated in a roundtable discussion to exchange views.

*   *   *

As to Lattimore's having been one of the principal architects of our far-eastern policy, the comments of former Secretaries of State are most pertinent.

Former Secretary of State, Cordell Hull, wrote Chairman Tydings as follows:

In my opinion, he was in no sense the "principal architect" of our far-eastern policy during the period I served as Secretary of State. Although his position in academic circles as a student of and writer on some aspects of Chinese life and history was of course known to us, I am not aware that during this period he had any appreciable influence on our far-eastern policy. I do not remember having consulted with him on that subject or on any subject at any time.

Former Secretary of State, James F. Byrnes, advised the chairman by letter of April 24, 1950, as follows:

> I do not know Mr. Lattimore. If he ever wrote me about the far eastern policy the letter was not called to my attention. If, while I was Secretary of State, he discussed our far-eastern policy with any officials of the Department concerned with that policy, in their discussions with me, they did not quote him.
> Early in December 1945, Gen. George C. Marshall went to China and thereafter his reports to the President and me influenced our policies in China and the Far East. I do not think General Marshall was influenced by Mr. Lattimore.

Gen. George C. Marshall advised the chairman of the subcommittee by letter dated April 22, 1950;

> I have received your letter of April 17 in which you refer to a recent statement, in connection with the hearings of the Subcommittee on Foreign Relations under Senate Resolution 231, that "Owen Lattimore is the principal architect of our far eastern policy." Your letter then asks the extent to which, in my opinion, "Lattimore was the principal architect of our far eastern policy" during the period in which I served as Secretary of State.
> The statement referred to above is completely without basis in fact.
> So far as I and my associates can recall I never even met Mr. Lattimore.
> I take the liberty of commenting on the harmful effect on our foreign relations of such statements, charges, or insinuations broadcast with so little regard for the truth. They undoubtedly confuse our friends abroad, undermine and weaken our position before the world, and actually lend assistance to the powers that would destroy us.

Secretary of State Dean Acheson informed the chairman by letter dated April 27, 1950, as follows:

> . . . The far eastern policy of this Government, like all other foreign policy, is the responsibility of the Secretary of State and has been made by me in my administration subject, of course, to the direction of the President. I welcome this opportunity to state personally and categorically that during the period in which I have been Secretary, Mr. Lattimore, so far as I am concerned or am aware, has had no influence in the determination of our far eastern policy. There is clearly no basis in fact for describing Mr. Lattimore as the "principal architect" of our far eastern policy. I might add that, so far as I am aware, I have never met Mr. Lattimore.

*   *   *

Obviously the finding of the subcommittee must be that Mr. Lattimore was not a State Department employee nor one of its most regular consultants, either directly or indirectly. Certainly he has not held "numerous positions with the State Department" as Senator McCarthy testified. There is nothing which justifies describing him as an "architect" of our far-eastern policy . . . . If for no other reason, though as will appear later there are other reasons, the subcommittee must conclude that the case of Mr. Lattimore provides no basis for charging the State Department with having employed persons who are disloyal to the United States.

    *   *   *

It would seem to be of no value to labor the question of whether Lattimore's writings can or cannot prove him to be pro-Communist, since it does not appear that his writings had any appreciable influence on State Department policy making. There are many points in Lattimore's writings at which obviously he does not follow the Communist Party line. This is not to say that at times Lattimore's writings paralleled to a degree the Communist line. This fact is, of course, conclusive of nothing, since, to hold otherwise, would be to suggest, for example, that everyone who opposed the Marshall plan is pro-Communist because the Communist Party also opposed it.

In the case of Mr. Lattimore, we feel that it is highly significant that he staunchly supported Chiang Kai-shek long after the Communists had begun their attack upon him. Ultimately, Lattimore advocated abandonment of Chiang on the ground that he had lost the support of his people and that his Government had become corrupt and ineffective. Mr. Lattimore suggested that he was in "good company" since General Marshall appears to have come to a similar conclusion; and that his, Lattimore's, change occurred after and not before the Marshall report.

    *   *   *

Lattimore's Connection with Institute of Pacific Relations

Lattimore's principal connection with the Institute of Pacific Relations was his editorship of their magazine Pacific Affairs from 1934 to 1941. Pacific Affairs is the quarterly journal published by the international secretariat of the Institute of Pacific Relations. According to Mr. Lattimore's testimony, since this journal is international in scope it has always tried to present a variety of authors of different nationalities and different points of view. He chose authors on the basis of their professional competency, not on the basis of their political views or affiliations. Mr. Lattimore testified that he would make no apology for the fact that under his editorship some contributors were then, or subsequently, regarded as "leftist." He pointed out that no article in Pacific Affairs ever called the Chinese Communists "agrarian reformers," and that the Communist phrase if used in the magazine was "agrarian democracy" which appeared in a translation of a Chinese article, the introductory note to which pointed out that it represented a Chinese Communist point of view. Frederick V. Field had two articles in Pacific Affairs under Lattimore's editorship. Lattimore asserted that less than ½ percent of the total of 250 articles published were written by persons named by Senator McCarthy. He also pointed out that Pacific Affairs was not the only "well established" and "reputable" periodical to which these individuals contributed, naming many well-known periodicals to which they contributed. Ninety-four out of the two hundred and fifty contributions, according to Mr. Lattimore, were definitely to the right of center, politically.

The articles appearing in Pacific Affairs have, for the most part, been on social, economic, and technical subjects; the political articles that have been published therein appear to represent all shades of opinion.

It can be readily seen from these facts that the political views of the contributors to Pacific Affairs cannot be taken as evidence of the political views of Mr. Lattimore, because to do so would be to create Mr. Lattimore a man of either all possible views or no views at all. There having been no showing that Mr. Lattimore unfairly selected and published articles on only one side of the far eastern question, or other political questions, his experience as editor of Pacific Affairs is indicative of nothing in contemplation of the present discussion.

Lattimore was a trustee of the institute. It has been shown that this institute is supported by many well known and highly reputable individuals in various walks of life. It is a research and educational organization recommended by the Rockefeller Foundation as the most important single source of independent studies of the problems of the Pacific area and the Far East. Of the many thousands of dollars received as contributions supporting the organization, only a few thousand are shown to have come from allegedly pro-Communist contributors. It is obvious that contributions from persons, other than alleged leftists or pro-Communists, sustain the institute.

*   *   *

Lattimore's Connection with Amerasia

Mr. Lattimore was on the board of editors of the magazine Amerasia from its founding in 1937 until his resignation in 1941. Lattimore testified that he went on the board to show that Pacific Affairs welcomed other periodicals in the field, but that he was never an active board member. Mr. Lattimore resigned in 1941, 4 years prior to the arrest of its managing editor, Philip Jaffe.

*   *   *

Conclusion

We find that Owen Lattimore is not now and never has been in any proper sense an employee of our State Department. His connection with that Department in any capacity has been at most peripheral and that on a most sporadic basis.

Far from being the "architect of our Far Eastern policy," we find that Mr. Lattimore has had no controlling or effective influence whatever on that policy. His views have but been among those of hundreds of others that have gone into the cauldron from which emerges the source material that the policy-makers of our State Department employed in making their judgments.

We find no evidence to support the charge that Owen Lattimore is the "top Russian spy" or, for that matter, any other sort of spy.

*   *   *

Having found on the evidence before us that Mr. Lattimore is not an employee of our State Department, that he is not the architect of our Far Eastern policy, and that he is not a spy, our consideration of him should be concluded, since to do otherwise would place us in the anomalous position of passing judgment on the ideological disposition of a private citizen. We are constrained, however, to make some observations relative to the case in its entirety, not only as a matter of elementary fairness to Mr. Lattimore, who traveled half-way around the world to answer the charges against himself, but to scholars and writers throughout the country and to the American public generally.

Owen Lattimore is a writer and a scholar who has been charged with a record of procommunism going back many years. There is no legal evidence before us whatever to support this charge and the weight of all other information indicates that it is not true. For the greater portion of his life, Mr. Lattimore has made studies concerning Mongolia, a land little known to most Americans. These studies have brought him physically into contact with peoples whose lives have been influenced and conditioned, to a lesser or greater degree, by Sino-Russian influences. In making his studies, Mr. Lattimore has found it necessary perforce to come into contact with and study these influences. We find absolutely no evidence to indicate that his writings and other expressions have been anything but the honest opinions and convictions of Owen Lattimore. Similar opinions and convictions *vis-à-vis* the Far East are entertained by many Americans about whom no conceivable suggestion of Communist proclivities could be entertained. We do not find that Mr. Lattimore's writings follow the Communist or any other line, save as his very consistent position on the Far East may be called the Lattimore line.

Some of Mr. Lattimore's friends, associates, and contacts have been identified before us as Communists. On the other hand, many of his intimate associates are people of the highest repute. Certainly the former connections, when taken with the latter, are not such as to conclude that he is a Communist on the theory that "birds of a feather flock together," even were we prepared to accept such a theory under the circumstances. Perhaps in many of his contacts, Mr. Lattimore has not exercised the discretion which our knowledge of communism in 1950 indicates would have been wise, but we are impelled to comment that in no instance has Mr. Lattimore on the evidence before us been shown to have knowingly associated with Communists. The convenient theory suggested to us that *he must have known* has not yet become the criterion for judging a private citizen in this country.

We have received communications from scholars and research workers of the highest repute from all over the Nation dramatically revealing the danger to independent research and freedom of expression of attacks such as that leveled by Senator McCarthy against Owen Lattimore. We agree that the vigor of our democracy and the vitality of our institutions depend upon the free exercise by all our citizens of their right to think independently and to state and advocate fearlessly their conclusions. Recognition of this right is the very essence of democracy and freedom.

In our view, the Lattimore case affords an opportunity to reaffirm this Nation's determination to protect its citizens when they, not as minions or agents of a foreign power or subversive group but as independent researchers, writers, and speakers, express freely their honest views and convictions. We believe that the Lattimore case vividly illustrates the danger of promiscuous and specious attacks upon private citizens and their views, and the imperative necessity that inquiries relating to matters of such character, where deemed relevant to our national security, should be handled by the duly constituted agencies of our Government that are equipped to handle such matters by intelligent and proven methods designed to obtain the truth without injustice, character assassination, and a prostitution of the American concept of fair play. To do otherwise will be to breed fear, prejudice, and injustice and divide and confuse our people at a time when the necessity for a united America, strong in its faith in our heritage of freedom is needed as never before to meet the challenge of totalitarian aggression.

We would be remiss in not commenting on the manner in which the charges against Owen Lattimore have been presented. As in the case of other phases of our inquiry, we have seen a distortion of the facts on such a magnitude as to be truly alarming. Unfortunately, until now, it has been largely these distortions that have been before the American people.

C. Investigation of Charges Against John Stewart Service*

July 20, 1950

Senator McCarthy made his first charge against John Stewart Service on the floor of the Senate on January 5, 1950. Thereafter he delivered a speech at Wheeling, W. Va., on February 9, 1950, which he read to the Senate on February 20, 1950. A third speech was made in the Senate on March 30, 1950. In addition, he appeared as a witness before this subcommittee on March 14, 1950. As we have done in other cases, all of the Senator's allegations have been considered in this report although only the statements in our record are technically before us.

Allegations

The charges against John Stewart Service have a dual character: (1) That

---

* *Ibid.*, pp. 74-94.

[1] Phillip Jaffe, Editor of *Amerasia* magazine. Service was arrested on June 6, 1945 for giving documents to Jaffe. In early August, the Grand Jury returned "no true bill" against Jaffe.

he is pro-Communist as indicated by *(a)* his reports from China, during the period 1943 to April 1945, in which he allegedly advocated the cause of the Chinese Communists and *(b)* his associations during the same period; (2) that he was involved in the abstraction of Government documents in connection with the Amerasia case. The allegations under each category will be considered in order.

McCarthy charges of pro-Communist activities

(1) That Mr. Service is one of the dozen "top policy makers" in the entire State Department Far Eastern Division and has been a part of the pro-Soviet group that advocated the United States overthrow Chiang Kai-shek because the only hope of Asia was communism.

(2) That Gen. Patrick J. Hurley, who had testified before the Senate Foreign Relations Committee on December 5, 6, and 10, 1945, declared that Mr. Service was one of the pro-Communist group in the State Department who "sabotaged" the United States policy in China. Senator McCarthy referred to Service's Report No. 40:

> which, according to Hurley, was a plan for the removal of support from the Chiang Kai-shek government with the end result that the Communists would take over.

Associations

(1) That the Communist affiliations of Mr. Service are well known.

*   *   *

Amerasia

The connection of John Stewart Service with the Amerasia case was presented to the subcommittee by Senator McCarthy. He made the following allegations both as a witness, and on the floor of the Senate:

(1) That: "The FBI then took over and reported that in the course of its quest it was found that John Stewart Service was in communication from China with Jaffe."[1]

(2) That: "The substance of some of Service's confidential messages to the State Department reached the officers of Amerasia in New York before they arrived in Washington. One of the papers found in Jaffe's possession was Document No. 58, one of Service's secret reports entitled: 'Generalissimo Chiang Kai-shek—Decline of His Prestige and Criticism of and Opposition to His Leadership'."

*   *   *

Senator McCarthy concluded his testimony about Mr. Service by making the following charge:

> Again we have a known associate and collaborator with Communists and pro-Communists, a man high in the State Department, consorting with "admitted espionage agents."

*   *   *

Discussion of Allegations

"Pro-Communist" activities

(1) That Service is one of dozen top policy makers in the entire State Department Far Eastern Division and as part of the pro-Soviet group advocated that the United States overthrow Chiang Kai-shek because the only hope of Asia was communism.

This allegation, as well as that made by General Hurley to which reference will be made, is based almost exclusively upon an interpretation of the reports sent from China by John Stewart Service during the period 1943 to April 1945. He wrote a total of 125 reports during this time and it is impossible to make a fair and correct interpretation of these reports without reviewing them all. We have seen how one or two reports may be quoted out of context and unfairly utilized to create an impression of procommunism. Even in such instances, however, Mr. Service was able to point to explanatory sections in each report that completely overcame the purported Communist implications of those portions of the report quoted. While we have seen in the case of Mr. Service the unfairness and futility of analyzing portions of a man's reports and writings as a basis to support preconceived conclusions, this consideration does not appear to have deterred others. We do regard as highly significant the estimate of Mr. George Kennan, a State Department expert whose knowledge of communism is well known. Mr. Kennan reviewed all of Mr. Service's reports, concluding:

> My conclusion is the following: I find no evidence that the reports acquired their character from any ulterior motive or association or from any impulse other than the desire on the part of the reporting officer to acquaint the Department with the facts as he saw and interpreted them. I find no indication that the reports reported anything but his best judgment candidly stated to the Department. On the contrary the general level of thoughtfulness and intellectual flexibility which pervades the reporting is such that it seems to me out of the question that it could be the work of a man with a closed mind or with ideological preconceptions, and it is my conclusion that it was not.

     *   *   *

The other facet of this allegation is that Mr. Service is one of "the dozen top policy members" of the Far Eastern Division. Mr. Service himself, has clearly pointed out that while in China he was a junior member of General Stilwell's staff and served primarily as a reporter and not as a policy-forming officer. We also note that Mr. Service was in China on duty, or in California on leave, during the entire period from 1941 to April 12, 1945, except for a total of 62 days which he spent in Washington. At the time he wrote his reports, he was a Foreign Service officer grade VI or lower. The facts, therefore, clearly show that Mr. Service was one of many young Foreign Service officers who were reporting to the State Department what they found to exist in the field, and that the policy of the State Department was made by top officials in Washington based on a consideration of all information received.

(2) That Gen. Patrick J. Hurley charged that Mr. Service had sabotaged United States policy in China.

This allegation is part and parcel of the first allegation heretofore discussed. Yet there is one aspect in which they differ. This allegation infers that Mr. Service was subordinate to General Hurley and under his control, which is not true. Mr. Service was attached to General Stilwell's staff in the summer of 1943, and thereafter, he was responsible only to General Stilwell and his successor, General Wedemeyer. Even General Hurley admitted to the Senate Foreign Relations Committee that Mr. Service was not his subordinate. Not only was he never charged with insubordination by his superiors, but he was commended for his work by both. It is also noteworthy that Ambassador Gauss, under whom Mr. Service served for a year and one-half prior to his transfer to General Stilwell's staff, also commended him highly. We see, therefore, that all of Mr. Service's superiors during the period of his work in China were more than satisfied with his work, and that only General Hurley, for whom he did not work, has complained.

* * *

There is one fundamental aspect of this allegation that is never mentioned by those who attack Mr. Service's reports as being "pro-Communist." They assume that the reports were erroneous and misrepresented the true picture in China. In this connection, there is not one iota of evidence before us that these reports do not constitute objective reporting of a situation that then existed in China. On the contrary, men such as George Kennan who know the Chinese problem and communism intimately have stated that these reports do constitute impartial objective reporting.

We, therefore, have a picture of a blanket allegation being made against a man that his reports are "pro-Communist." Five years after the reports were written, it is proposed to penalize a Foreign Service officer by destroying his career and branding him as disloyal for writing what appears to have been the true facts as he saw them. It is manifestly clear to us that such a thesis, if permitted to go unchallenged, would destroy almost completely the integrity and reliability of the Foreign Service. No man may know when the facts as seen today may have a completely different implication 5 years later.

* * *

Amerasia

The most serious evidence against Mr. Service is his admitted association with the other subjects in the Amerasia case. The facts of that case are given in great detail in another portion of this report, and those facts applicable to all the subjects will not be repeated here. Only certain specific details that pertain primarily to Mr. Service will be discussed in this portion of the report.

* * *

Service's explanation

On April 18, I received a telephone call from Mark Gayn. I had never previously met him but had known a good deal of him as we shared a China background. I had read at least one of his books and seen articles on the Far East which he had written for Collier's. On this occasion, he told me that he was planning a series of articles for the Saturday Evening Post. During a lunch together, he said that he had an extra bed in his apartment in New York City which he would be glad to have me use if I ever visited that city.

About this time, I had received an invitation from Lt. Andrew Roth, whom I had met the previous November on an occasion when, at the request of my superiors in the State Department, I had given a talk on Chinese affairs at the Institute of Pacific Relations in Washington. Roth invited me for supper at his home on the evening of April 19. Roth was a naval officer and I knew him to be assigned to the Office of Naval Intelligence where he was engaged in intelligence work relating to the Far East. I had no reason to believe I should be suspicious of Lieutenant Roth or of any journalist to whom he might seek to introduce me.

During that day of April 19, he telephoned me, saying that Philip Jaffe was also going to be at his home that evening but was anxious to meet me before then, since there would be a number of people at the party and probably little opportunity to talk. Roth asked that I telephone Jaffe at his hotel and I did so. I knew of Jaffe as the editor of Amerasia but I had never previously met him nor had any contact by correspondence or otherwise with him. However, as he was the editor of a well-known specialist magazine on the Far East, I saw no reason why I should not meet and talk to him on a background basis as with any other reputable newspaperman or writer. The only time that we found convenient was for me to stop at his hotel in the late afternoon and go together to Roth's dinner.

In view of the later unhappy consequences of my meeting with Mr. Jaffe, I think I should emphasize at this point that my meeting with him was in no sense abnormal, since it was entirely conformable to the policy concerning relations with the press which I had pursued under instructions in the field attached to General Stilwell's headquarters and also the policy of the Department permitting Foreign Service officers to provide background information to members of the press.

When I prepared to leave the office before going over to Jaffe's hotel, I had on my desk a number of my personal copies of memoranda written during my last visit at Yenan. Among these was a report of an interview with Mao Tse-tung about the end of March, in which Mao had given details of the current Communist position and the probable line to be taken at the forthcoming Communist Party Congress . . . .

It occured to me that Jaffe would probably be especially interested in recent news from Yenan and particularly in recent statements of the Communist position in the controversy going on in China. I, therefore, took with me my personal copy of this memorandum which contained nothing except the Communists' own presentation of their position. During the conversation, Mr. Jaffe, as I expected, asked concerning the present Communist attitude and instead of trying to remember in detail, I let him read the memorandum which I had brought with me. Jaffe was extremely interested and asked at once if I did not have other similar reports about Yenan which it would be possible to show him. Since many of these memos were purely reportorial, containing only statements or observations available to and continually being obtained by newspapermen on the spot, I agreed to let Mr. Jaffe see some of this type of material. It was agreed that I would bring some of these with me the next day and that I would lunch with him at his hotel.

The following day, I went through my personal copies of my Yenan memoranda and selected several—I think about 8 or 10—which were purely descriptive and did not contain discussion of American military or political policy. These I considered it would be appropriate to allow Jaffe, as a writer on China, to see. I probably took these to the hotel in the early forenoon, expecting to pick them up at lunch. At lunch, Jaffe surprised me by saying that he had not had time to read the memoranda, that he was leaving Washington that afternoon and wished to take them with him for several days. After considerable discussion and in view of the nonpolicy and purely factual nature of the papers, I allowed Jaffe to retain them. It was arranged that I would pick them up when I expected to visit New York a few days later for another meeting with the Institute of Pacific Relations research staff there. I may add that this meeting was also authorized by my superiors in the Department of State and was one at which I discussed off-the-record the political background of affairs then prevailing in China.

These personal copies I refer to, and from among which I allowed Jaffe to see selected ones of a descriptive nonpolicy nature, were some of my file copies of memoranda which I had written in China over my own signature, recording my own observations and conversations as a reporter. They did not represent, nor purport to represent the views of the Embassy, the Army, or the Department of State. They bore only the unofficial classification which I placed on them when I wrote them, a classification which by this time was of no significance since the information contained in them had been extensively reported by American newspaper correspondents who had visited the Communist areas. They were not removed from any official files; they had never been in official files.

It was not unusual to allow writers to have access to this type of factual material for background purposes, since reading the material or taking notes on it was always more satisfactory from the viewpoint of accuracy than merely relying on one's memory and oral recital.

*   *   *

Conclusion

We have carefully considered the evidence and conclude that John Stewart Service is neither a disloyal person, a pro-Communist, nor a security risk. We have been particularly impressed with the frankness and cooperativeness of Mr. Service in his appearances before us. Many questions with hidden implications have been asked him about events that transpired many years ago. Never did he seek to avoid answering on the ground he could not remember but always gave his subcommittee the benefit of any recollection he might have. In addition, he waived his immunity and voluntarily appeared before the grand jury in August of 1945, after hearing all the facts, the grand jury unanimously voted not to indict Mr. Service. We could not fail to be impressed also by the most continuous scrutiny to which he has been subjected during the last 5 years. He has been cleared four times by either the State Department Personnel Board or the State Department Security and Loyalty Board . . . .

While not condoning it, we recognize that it was an accepted practice for State Department officials to impart some types of classified information to writers in order to give them background information for their articles. John S. Service was in an unusual position in China and, in accordance with General Stilwell's wishes, he maintained relations with the representatives in China of the American press in order to brief them on political and quasi-military developments in the China theater. He appears to have been allowed a greater freedom in contacts with the press than would an officer in a similar position in Washington. It should also be emphasized that both Mark Gayn and Philip Jaffe were considered reputable newsmen and writers by the public in the spring of 1945 when Service first met them. Mark Gayn was known for his articles in Collier's and the Saturday Evening Post and had also worked for Time and Fortune. Mr. Service was unaware of the changes in the editorial board of Amerasia and still considered it an impartial authority on far-eastern affairs. Because of the limited number of writers specializing on China, it was natural that he would expect experts in that field, like Gayn and Jaffe, to show a greater interest in his material than the average writer. In addition, it is undisputed that Mr. Service was seeing other correspondents during this same period.

We must conclude that Service was extremely indiscreet in his dealings with Gayn and Jaffe, a fact which he himself readily admits. Perhaps the State Department's administration process was at fault in failing to brief its employees coming into Washington on short consultations on how they should treat the press during their stay. But we cannot and do not conclude that his indiscretion in the Amerasia matter is sufficient to brand an otherwise competent and loyal employee of 17 years' service as disloyal, pro-Communist, or a security risk.

D. Report on Basis of Allegations Against State Department Personnel*

[Extract]

July 20, 1950

Three well-defined sources have been largely responsible for the charge that

Ibid., pp. 145-51.

disloyal individuals in our State Department have been responsible for the "failure of America's China policy."

The first of these sources is a distortion of the testimony of Patrick J. Hurley, former Ambassador to China, who on December 5, 6, and 10, 1945, testified before the Senate Foreign Relations Committee. This testimony has been employed in certain quarters to sustain a thesis that persons disloyal to the United States in our State Department have been responsible for the ascendancy of the Communist Party of China and the decline of the Nationalist Government. General Hurley himself, however, testified:

> They were disloyal to the American policy. I would not say they were disloyal to the United States Government.

An objective appraisal of General Hurley's testimony reflects that he did not charge the State Department career foreign officers with being disloyal Americans in that they sought to aid another nation to the injury of the United States; but rather that they disagreed with him, and were insubordinate in acting on their disagreement, as to the means whereby the Chinese situation could best be explained to aid our war against Japan and to the advantage of the United States. It has been established that the officers to whom General Hurley referred were not his subordinates; hence a charge of "insubordination" is ridiculous. General Hurley's essential point was that the "career men" were seeking to foster an American policy in China contrary to the American policy at the time, as General Hurley understood it. This fact has been entirely ignored by those who would use the so-called Hurley charges to support their claim that disloyal persons or traitors were or are in the State Department. In any event, the Senate Foreign Relations Committee heard General Hurley in 1945, made inquiry concerning the matter, and did not regard the charges as meriting further action.

The second source is Alfred Kohlberg, New York City importer whose wealth appears to have stemmed from contacts with representatives of the Nationalist Government of China. We do not propose to discuss Mr. Kohlberg at any length apart from observing that his name has repeatedly entered our hearings as the individual behind the scenes who has been responsible not only for a great deal of Senator McCarthy's assertions but for those of others as well. His principal theme manifestly has been that the Institute of Pacific Relations became the captive of the Communists and that, through the institute, the Communists influenced effectively the Far Eastern Division of the State Department and thereby American foreign policy. An illustration of the extension of the Kohlberg influence is found in the testimony of Mr. Louis F. Budenz before the subcommittee.

In seeking to document his testimony concerning Mr. Owen Lattimore, Mr. Budenz presented to us a photostatic copy of an article by Father James F. Kearney which indicated certain alleged Communist connections on the part of Mr. Lattimore. When Father Kearney was interviewed by agents of the Federal Bureau of Investigation concerning his article, he advised that the source of the information contained therein was Alfred Kohlberg.

Still a third source is an article entitled "The State Department Espionage Case," indicated to have been written by Emmanuel S. Larsen, one of the defendants in the Amerasia case. This article appeared in the October 1946, issue of Plain Talk, a magazine published in New York City of which Isaac Don Levine has been the editor and Ralph de Toledano, the managing editor. Mr. Kohlberg we have been reliably informed, has financed this publication. This article, attributed to Larsen has been repeatedly cited, paraphrased and referred to as the basis for charges that American far-eastern policy was "sold down the river" to Soviet Russia.

Without going into detail concerning the article, its theme, apart from setting forth an extremely perverted account of the Amerasia case, is essentially that certain foreign service officers of the State Department, particularly John S. Service, undermined the China Nationalist Government and generally conspired to bring the Communists into the ascendancy in China. For approaching 4 years, people in this country have either been reading or accepting this article as a truthful confession of one of the Amerasia defendants and an accurate account of "what really happened to our China policy."

Testifying before us, however, Larsen repudiated the Plain Talk article in all essential respects. To corroborate his repudiation, he submitted the draft of the article which he actually wrote, which is now an exhibit in our proceedings. The true draft bears little or no resemblance to the article which was published and, unlike the latter, contains none of the bases for charges of a plot to destroy American policy in the Far East which have greatly confused the American people.

Larsen gave the following account of the circumstances under which he came into contact with Plain Talk. Following the disposition of the Amerasia case, he went to St. Petersberg, Fla., where two respresentatives of Plain Talk proceeded from New York City to solicit him to write an article concerning the case. Being virtually penniless, Larsen agreed to write the article, he to receive $300 and expenses therefor. He went to New York City where he conferred with Messrs. Kohlberg, Levine, and Toledano. Larsen drafted the article which set forth his understanding of the facts, but was advised by Levine that "it won't do". Levine thereupon completely rewrote the article in the form in which it appeared in the magazine, and asked Larsen to initial it. Larsen testified that he objected to the article in its entirety, but that he had not as yet been paid as agreed and was desperate to get out of New York. In this situation he at length initialed the article and it was published.

If true, the action of Levine and his associates in connection with the Plain Talk article is one of the most despicable instances of a deliberate effort to deceive and hoodwink the American people in our history. Such conduct is beneath contempt. While Larsen's credibility generally is open to serious doubt, we cannot escape the fact that the draft of his article, which is before us in black and white, is a far cry from the actual Plain Talk article. Significantly, on the last day Larsen testified he stated, in the presence of a member of the subcommittee staff, that Levine telephoned him on the night before his appearance before us as a witness suggesting that he, Larsen, "go easy on the Plain Talk article." At the same time, Levine suggested that he would effect a lucrative arrangement on Larsen's behalf for the writing of some syndicated articles on the Far East.

Similarly, Larsen largely repudiated before us the testimony which he had given in appearing, not under oath, before the Hobbs committee at which time he endeavored to present the picture of an effort in the Far Eastern Division of the State Department to mold our China policy to a pro-Communist pattern. In explaining his repudiation of that testimony, Larsen stated that at the time he was under the impression that John S. Service had endeavored before the grand jury to make him the scapegoat in the Amerasia case and that he, Larsen, set out to "get even" with Service before the Hobbs committee. He testified that he had since found that Service did not attempt to prejudice his case before the grand jury and that in testifying before us he was endeavoring to tell the truth.

Seldom, if ever, in the history of congressional investigations has a committee been subjected to an organized campaign of vilification and abuse comparable to that with which we have been confronted throughout this inquiry. This campaign has been so acute and so obviously designed to confuse and confound the American people that an analysis of the factors responsible therefor is indicated.

The first of these factors was the necessity of creating the impression that our inquiry was not thorough and sincere in order to camouflage the fact that the charges made by Senator McCarthy were groundless and that the Senate and the American people had been deceived. No sooner were hearings started than the cry of "whitewash" was raised along with the chant "investigate the charges and not McCarthy." This chant we have heard morning, noon, and night for almost 4 months from certain quarters for readily perceptible motives. Interestingly, had we elected to investigate Senator McCarthy, there would have been ample basis therefor, since we have been reliably informed that at the time he made the charges initially he had no information whatever to support them, and, furthermore, it early appeared that in securing Senate Resolution 231 a fraud had been perpetrated upon the Senate of the United States.

From the very outset of our inquiry, Senator McCarthy has sought to leave the impression that the subcommittee has been investigating him and not "disloyalty in the State Department." The reason for the Senator's concern is now apparent. He had no facts to support his wild and baseless charges, and lived in mortal fear that this situation would be exposed.

Few people, cognizant of the truth in even an elementary way, have, in the absence of political partisanship, placed any credence in the hit-and-run tactics of Senator McCarthy. He has stooped to a new low in his cavalier disregard of the facts.

The simple truth is that in making his speech at Wheeling, Senator McCarthy was talking of a subject and circumstances about which he knew nothing. His extreme and irresponsible statements called for emergency measures. As Senator Wherry told Emmanuel S. Larsen:

Oh, Mac has gone out on a limb and kind of made a fool of himself and we have to back him up now.

Starting with nothing, Senator McCarthy plunged headlong forward, desperately seeking to develop some information, which colored with distortion and fanned by a blaze of bias, would forestall a day of reckoning.

*   *   *

In concluding our report, we are constrained to make observations which we regard as fundamental.

It is, of course, clearly apparent that the charges of Communist infiltration of and influence upon the State Department are false. This knowledge is reassuring to all Americans whose faith has been temporarily shaken in the security of their Government by perhaps the most nefarious campaign of untruth in the history of our Republic.

We believe, however, that this knowledge and assurance, while important, will prove ultimately of secondary significance in contemplating the salutary aspects of our investigation. For, we believe that, inherent in the charges that have been made and the sinister campaign to give them ostensible verity, are lessons from which the American people will find inspiration for a rededication to the principles and ideals that have made this Nation great.

We have seen the technique of the "Big Lie," elsewhere employed by the totalitarian dictator with devastating success, utilized here for the first time on a sustained basis in our history. We have seen how, through repetition and shifting untruths, it is possible to delude great numbers of people.

*   *   *

THE CHINA LOBBY

A. Comments by Secretary Acheson and Senator Wayne Morse on the Existence of a China Lobby in the United States*

June 7, 1951

Senator Morse: Mr. Secretary, I want to make a very brief statement in regard to allegations concerning the existence of a force in America known as the China lobby before I ask you questions relative thereto.

I would like to say for the record that behind the sincere differences of opinion in this country over the proper course of the United States to follow in China there has existed the more or less clandestine struggle between two extremist groups, each representing not America's interests but the interests of the two principal contenders for power in the Chinese civil war.

While American Communists and their fellow travelers have ardently backed the Chinese Communists and sought to turn American public and official opinion in favor of Communist ends in China, it was alleged that there has been operating at the other extreme a propaganda and pressure group working for the Nationalist Chinese, Kuomintang, Chiang Kai-shek interests. This latter group is generally referred to in the American press as the China lobby.

Although the vicious operations of the Communists have been widely exposed, to some extent, but I believe still not fully—and I am strongly in favor of a complete disclosure and exposé of Communist activities in the United States and elsewhere in the world—there never has been, however, a thorough public investigation of the so-called China lobby.

Yet often in the political struggle for domination over American opinion the best interests of the United States, it seems to me, have been lost sight of in the smoke arising from the behind-the-scenes battles of these two sets of agents in the United States, representing extreme factions in China.

It is widely alleged that the China lobby, or pro-Chiang group, in the United States has for several years been conducting a violent campaign against American policies in China, chiefly by charging that the State Department, and especially its Far Eastern Division, is a nest of Reds, controlled by Communists and fellow travelers.

These charges have gone along the line that the State Department has set up a foreign policy in Asia contrary to the long-time best interests of the United States, because of its alleged support of pro-Communist interests in China.

In addition, it is believed by many that the China lobby has been especially active in pressuring Congress for financial, economic, and military aid for the Chiang regime, both before and since it retired to Formosa.

It is believed by many that Chinese individuals related to the Soong family— Mrs. Chiang Kai-shek's relatives—have immense sums of money cached outside Chinese territory, some of it in the United States, some of it in European coun-

*Military Situation in the Far East, pt. 3, 2116-21; 2187-90; 2206-07.

tries and in England, some of it some people think in South Africa and some in South America.

It is rumored that T.V. Soong himself has many millions of dollars on deposit in the United States.

It is also alleged that prominent Nationalist officials and generals made fortunes in graft on American loans and grant-in-aid during and since the war against Japan. It is probably reasonable to assume that some of this money is being used to finance propaganda and similar operations in the United States chiefly to promote more money being given to Chiang and the Chiang forces.

This suggests to some a closed circuit of American dollars flowing from Congress to the Nationalists and back again in the form of lobbying activities for still more money for Chiang.

It is alleged that from 1946 to 1949 the Central News Agency, a wholly owned instrument of the Nationalist Government, spent in the neighborhood of $654,000,000 to influence American public opinion.

Paid Lobbyist for China

In March 1948 the counselor of the Chinese Embassy, Chen Chih-mai, hired William J. Goodwin as a lobbyist paid by the Natural Resources Commission of China, a wholly owned subsidiary of the Nationalist Government of China. It is alleged that Goodwin's contract paid him $40,000 a year.

His job called for interesting American investors in China. Goodwin switched to the Chinese News Service under contract starting July 7, 1949.

His new job required him to explain to leaders of thought in the United States, and including Members of Congress, the danger of the Communist movement to the security of the United States, and conversely to urge confidence in the Nationalist Government of China and to seek for it large measures of American support and material aid. It is reported that he received $25,000 a year for this work.

In an interview with Alfred Friendly of the Washington Post, in September 1949, Goodwin said he had converted at least 50 Congressmen, mostly Senators, to his way of thinking on China aid.

He added in a confidential whisper, "China will get anything she asked for," reports Friendly. "China is bound to get what she wants. Just think of the billboards next November if she doesn't," is the quote from Friendly's story of his interview with Goodwin.

Fortunes Allegedly Amassed by Chinese Individuals

T.V. Soong, Chiang's brother-in-law, resigned from the Kuomintang rather than go to Formosa, it was announced on June 9, 1950. Reputed to be one of the wealthiest men in the world, he left China shortly before the Government fled from Canton to Nanking, late in 1948. At that time an effort was made to have him donate part of his fortune, said to be scattered in banks, as I have pointed out, in France, North and South America, and South Africa. It is believed that he refused and left for Hong Kong, and then for Paris. He is now, I understand, living in the United States.

In January 1950 Madam Chiang ended a 14-month mission to the United States to obtain support in a military mission for the Nationalists, in which she failed.

Doris Fleeson wrote in the Evening Star on January 16, 1950, that the administration arsenals are crammed with facts about the entire Chiang circle—who they are, the wealth they have taken from China, the troubles we have had with them. "With such a story they can make a telling fight, if pushed to it. They prefer not to," she wrote, "because they don't want to lend aid and comfort to the Reds."

Now, it was reported by Robert Allen in a story in 1949 which he wrote for the press—and I quote:

> Note deleted from the white paper, as published, was a State Department list of several hundred top Nationalist officials and generals who made millions grafting on United States aid. The United States authorities know the whereabouts of the secret bank accounts of many of these officials. They are in London, Paris, Chicago, New York, San Francisco, Manila, and Bangkok. Certain multimillionaire Nationalists in the United States are highly fearful the Treasury may freeze their holdings. The Nationalists have demanded the return of these private fortunes.

Then I quote also from Marquis Child's article of May 5, 1950, in which he says:

Inquiry Once Urged Into "China Lobby"

> Both President Truman and Secretary of State Acheson have resolutely set themselves against any investigation of the so-called Nationalist China lobby. Urging and prodding from every quarter has met with a firm "No." The belief is that such an investigation would serve chiefly to further the bitter controversy now focused on American foreign policy in the Far East. Any benefits from showing the sources of paid propaganda and paid pressures would be purely incidental. No one who knows anything about the way things work here doubts that a powerful China lobby has brought extraordinary influence to bear on Congress and the Executive. It would be hard to find any parallel in diplomatic history for the agents and diplomatic representatives of a foreign power exerting such pressures. The methods used cannot, of course, be compared with those of Russian communism, since Russian communism works in each country through an internal conspiracy. Nationalist China has used the techniques of direct intervention on a scale rarely, if ever, seen. The lobby has gained adherents among some ex-Communists in America who have in some instances carried over into this new endeavor the conspiratorial fanaticism they gave to communism.
>
> Another reason for opposing a congressional inquiry is the difficulty—perhaps the impossibility—of digging up the underlying facts. That is particularly true with respect to sources of money. High officials here believe that Chinese Nationalists or members of their families have put in foreign banks considerably over a half billion dollars. But it is so carefully concealed that it could hardly be traced in Swiss and New York accounts to the real owners.
>
> A plane load of 21 American newspapermen has just left for Formosa as invited guests of the Chinese Central News Agency. The news agency is subsidized by the Nationalist Government. (Marquis Childs, May 5, 1950.)

Then I have many others, and one other newspaper story that I want to cite as the foundation for the first question I want to put to you.

This is a news story of the Washington Post by Benjamin Bradlee, September

18, 1949, under the headline "Chiang pays lobbyist here to get funds—former member of Christian Front gets $25,000 salary."

Bradlee writes:

Lobbyist Hired by Chinese

The Chinese Nationalists have hired a $25,000 a year lobbyist to get more money for Chiang Kai-shek and to sabotage administration plans to withhold funds. The international influence man is William J. Goodwin, of Roslyn, N.Y., and the Metropolitan Club in Washington, a registered lobbyist and foreign agent with a stormy background of Wall Street finance, Christian Front activity, Tammany Hall politics, and big-time public relations.

In less than 2 years, according to Justice Department records, Goodwin has contracted for $65,000 from the Nationalist Government, first to get help from the United States, then to influence leaders of thought and urge them to approve larger measures of American support and material aid.

With this money Goodwin has given intimate dinners in Washington's exclusive clubs and hotels for more than 100 Members of Congress. He has campaigned for legislators, even while registered as a foreign agent, contributed to their campaigns, and sent some of them flowers and at least one a congratulatory present . . . .

From the Washington Post, by Benjamin Bradlee, September 18, 1949, extract therefrom.

Now, Mr. Secretary, may I say that I have never had any contact or conversations or experience in any way with any person since I have been in the Senate that would justify my saying that I know anything about a China lobby from first-hand contact therewith, if such a lobby exists. But I do feel, Mr. Secretary, that there has been so much talk about the China lobby, so much has appeared in the press and so much criticism has been hurled at you and the State Department in respect to the same, as some of these articles I have quoted from indicate very clearly, that in the course of this hearing an opportunity ought to be presented to the State Department to make any statement that it wishes on the problem of a China lobby, if one exists. That is why I am pursuing this line of questioning this afternoon.

State Department Attitude Towards China Lobby

My first general question—and I will be more specific later—my first general question is this: Do you feel that the broad general account in respect to the existence of an alleged China lobby which is set forth in the statement I have just made for the record, and in which statement I have quoted from newspaper accounts that have appeared in the press in the past, sets forth in any degree whatsoever a factual statement in respect to the existence of what has generally been referred to as a China lobby which seeks to influence the policies of this Government in respect to support for the Nationalist Government regime?

Secretary Acheson: Senator Morse, I am not able to answer the question as to whether I do or do not feel that the facts are as represented in those statements.

Since you notified me that you were going to go into this subject, I have asked in the Department of State that whatever material we have bearing upon the possibility of illegal or improper use of funds should be collected so that I could look at it. I am told that it has been collected, but I have not had an opportunity to look at it, and I do not know what sort of thing it indicates at all.

I am told that, for the most part, this material is material which comes in in the regular course of affairs from some other agencies to the Department of State and that it is very fragmentary. As soon as I can get to it I will look at it.

I agree with what Senator McMahon has said and what I gather from your remarks that you also believe, and that is that if there is any improper use of funds to influence the foreign policy or any other policy of the United States Government, the people are entitled to know about it, and it is important that they should know about it, and that it would be a very serious and deleterious thing for the United States to have that happen.

The Department of State is not the agency which is charged by law with finding out these matters, nor is it equipped for that. We do not have the administration of the so-called Lobbying Act and the registration under the Lobbying Act. We do not have the administration of the foreign agents registration law.

We do not have an investigatory source of the sort which can be used for this kind of thing. We do not have powers of subpena. We do not have the power to administer oaths, and we do not have access to financial transactions which would reveal, or might reveal, some of these matters.

We are not in any way equipped nor are we charged with the administration of the laws in this respect. So far as I myself am concerned, I would not want to make charges against people under any circumstances unless it was in my line of duty and unless I believed that the charges had evidence, substantial evidence, behind them, which I had and which I could vouch for.

I should be particularly careful not to make any charges against people who could immediately respond that I was doing this because they were criticizing me. Criticism is something which I have to bear as an occupational hazard and I am quite ready to bear it, and therefore I cannot respond to the question because to do so goes beyond my knowledge and would be for me to imply that there are illegal activities going on when I do not have the responsibility for that nor do I have the adequate basis for knowledge.

State Department Knowledge of Facts on China Lobby

Senator Morse: Mr. Secretary, do you believe there is any basis of fact in the allegation in the Robert Allen article from which I read that the names of some considerable number of Nationalist Chinese were deleted from the white paper because of his claim that they were involved in transactions that showed their involvement in corrupt practices?

Secretary Acheson: No, sir; I do not believe that is true.

Senator Morse: Do you know of any names of Nationalist Chinese being deleted from the original manuscript of the white paper prior to its printing for any purpose whatsoever?

Secretary Acheson: I do not, but I shall have inquiry made as to whether any such thing was done.

Senator Morse: Is there any basis in fact, in your opinion, for the assertion made or implied in some of the newspaper articles from which I quoted that you as Secretary of State sought to prevent an investigation of what is referred to as the China Lobby?

Secretary Acheson: That is not correct, sir, in any respect whatever.

Senator Morse: And you know of no such activity of represssing such an investigation at the White House level; do you?

Secretary Acheson: No, sir; and I do not believe that represents the President's attitude.

Senator Morse: I am correct in my understanding, am I not, that your investigation of whatever the files of the State Department may show in regard to the information data which have been compiled by your subordinates on the broad question that I have raised as to the possible activity of Nationalists or Nationalist agents in this country will be studied and the study completed by you in time to report to this committee?

Secretary Acheson: I shall get at it just as soon as I can, Senator.

I am fairly occupied most of the day with these hearings and a good part of the evening carrying on my regular duties . . . .

Senator Morse: I wish to make very clear for the record that all I have sought to do in raising this matter is to offer the Department of State and, through the Department of State, the administration, an opportunity to put into the record of these hearings any information that they have in their files bearing upon any allegations of lobbying activities on the part of agents of the Nationalist Chinese regime to influence either appropriation legislation or other legislation or American public opinion.

There has been so much discussion of it and so many charges and counter-charges that as a lawyer it seems to me the only way to meet such an issue as that is to get it on the record if the information exists, and if this administration has any such information, I personally think that it owes it to the American people to bring the facts out.

If there is no such information, then I think that the American people ought to know that, too; and I repeat, I have no such information. I wouldn't have the facilities to get it if it existed. I have already stated that I have not been myself contacted by anyone in regard to Asiatic policy that would justify my pinning on them the label or the accusation that they were seeking to lobby me for the Nationalist Chinese cause.

But, I am disturbed about it, and I wanted to at least make a good faith attempt to find out what the Government files can disclose on it, if the information is in the file, and I shall await whatever information you are able to give us on the basis of your examination of the information that your subordinates have, I understand, compiled for you.

I think it is only fair, however, in view of what the Secretary has said, that he should be given an opportunity to look at the information which has been compiled for him in the State Department on the general subject, and report on it to this committee before I continue with my examination here, or elsewhere, on this issue.

I do not mean, by that, Mr. Chairman, that this is the last question that I shall ask on this general issue.

Therefore, I will turn to another issue, Mr. Secretary.

*　　　　　　*　　　　　　*

Soybean Speculations in 1950

Are you informed as to a corner that's supposed to have existed in the soybean market a year ago last June in the hands of certain Chinese in this country? Have you ever discussed that matter with the Secretary of Agriculture?

Secretary Acheson: Yes; I have discussed it with him.

Senator McMahon: Is there anything that you can say at this time concerning the personalities who were engaged in that operation and what action was taken by this Government to break up that operation?

Secretary Acheson: I don't know that I ever knew who the personalities involved were. There was, as I recall it, a very serious situation created by a group of Chinese buying and taking delivery of a certain amount of soybeans, which gave certain controls over the prices. That was a matter of concern to the Department of Agriculture, was discussed by Secretary Brannan with me, and he took certain remedial steps.

Now I can look into it again with him and refresh my memory about it, but that is all I recall on the thing now.

Senator McMahon: You do not know the personalities that were engaged in this attempt to corner the soybean market?

Secretary Acheson: No, sir; I don't.

Senator McMahon: But they were Chinese?

Secretary Acheson: Yes, sir; they were Chinese, as I recall it.

Senator McMahon: Was there, as you understood, any violation of the Commodity Exchange law involved?

Secretary Acheson: I don't recall that there was.

Senator McMahon: You do not know the source of the funds that were used in this speculation in soybeans?

Secretary Acheson: No sir; I do not.

Senator McMahon: You do not know the relationship at this time between the so-called China Lobby crowd and this operation?

Secretary Acheson: No, sir.

*　　　　　　*　　　　　　*

Nature of State Department Files on Lobby

Secretary Acheson: I should like to say that yesterday afternoon I spent the time going through the material which has been collected for me in the State Department on this subject.

The material consists of several categories. There is a very large collection of newspaper, magazine, and other public articles on the subject, all very much along the line of those which Senator Morse spoke of the other day.

There are reports from other agencies such as the CIA reporting things which have been said to them, and those are sent along to the other agencies of Government, including the State Department.

There are in that file reports of conferences and meetings between officers of the State Department and officers of other departments in the Government on that general subject, which are general summaries of what information the other departments have, but very sketchy in that regard.

There are reports from our own officers overseas as to what has been said to them by various people. There are reports which have been made to officers of the State Department by people who come in and say that someone has told them various things.

I read all of this material yesterday afternoon, and with one exception, to which I shall revert in a moment, these are all hearsay statements; that is, they are statements which are made not on the knowledge of the person making them, but reporting things which that informant, very often not identified, has been told by others. The exception to that—well, I will go on with that.

The exception to that is a considerable amount of information in the file which has to do not with the improper use of funds or proper use of funds to influence opinion, but with an alleged attempt to violate the law against recruiting in the United States for foreign armies. There is considerable direct evidence on that subject in the file.

On that point, however, the file ends up with the fact the person who was engaged in this allegedly illegal activity died, and that brought an end to that particular effort.

This information is not sufficient or would not warrant me in making charges of any sort. The information is such that if this hearsay is correct and can be believed, it would support the charge that there is very considerable use of foreign funds in the United States for the purpose of influencing opinion, and there is some reason, if this hearsay is believed, to say that some of these activities, at least, are sufficient in this file to prevent me from saying that there is not any use of funds.

As I say, the material does not warrant charges. The material is of the nature which, if supplemented by other material, would be useful to the investigating staff, either of an executive agency or a committee of Congress in looking forward into the activities of certain individuals and institutions.

It is not material which, in any fairness, ought to be made public, but it ought to be used by an investigating staff to pursue their investigation.

Already most, if not all, of this has been brought to the attention of such investigating staffs of the executive branch. If any committee of Congress has a staff which wishes to go into that, I would be glad to make this available to that committee.

Presidential Authorization of Lobby Investigation

Now I have also reported to the President of the United States the views of the members of this joint committee as expressed to me yesterday by the Senators who have spoken on the record, and I am authorized and directed by the President to say to the joint committee that he has instructed the agencies of the executive branch having powers and duties in regard to this matter to get together all their material and bring it together so that there can be an immediate, or as soon as possible, an appraisal of what is known in the executive branch, with a view to going forward to legal action if that is provable by what is known, or by conducting investigations further if that apppears to be the proper course to follow, or in making public the situation if that seems to be the proper course.

He has also authorized me and directed me to say that he will direct all these agencies of the Government to cooperate to the fullest possible extent with any committee or committees of the Congress which wish to go into this matter for the purpose of informing them what is known, for the purpose of helping any investigation, for the purpose of assisting them in coming to a conclusion as to whether or not they wish to have one.

That, I believe is a full statement on my activities yesterday afternoon in this regard.

B. Attempts to Influence Public Opinion in Behalf of Nationalist China*

[Extract]

March 25, 1963

TESTIMONY OF HAMILTON WRIGHT, JR. BEFORE SENATE COMMITTEE
ON FOREIGN RELATIONS

The Chairman: I show you a copy of a letter dated May 2, 1957, addressed to Dr. F.T. Tsiang, who, I believe, was Ambassador to the United Nations of the Republic of China and signed "Hamilton Wright" and titled "Proposal for a Publicity Campaign for Free China" and ask you if you wrote and sent this letter?

Mr. Wright, Senior: That is correct.

The Chairman: That is your letter?

Mr. Wright, Senior: Yes.

(A copy of this letter is as follows:)

Hamilton Wright Organization, Inc.
New York, N.Y., May 2, 1957

Re Proposal for a publicity campaign for Free China.
Dr. T.F. Tsiang,
Republic of Free China's Ambassador to the United Nations,
New York, N.Y.

Activities of Non-Diplomatic Representatives of Foreign Principals in the United States, Hearing Before the Committee on Foreign Relations. U.S. Senate, 88 Cong. 1st sess., pp. 684-91.

My dear Dr. Tsiang: We are very enthusiastic and excited over the possibility of an opportunity to tell the amazing story of "Free China" to the people of the United States, Canada, South America, and Europe.

Few nations in the world today enjoy the sympathetic understanding and good will that the people of Free China have among Americans. Their sufferings, their losses, the Communistic shame they have been subjected to, are beyond the telling.

But the lack of knowledge—the lack of information—the absence of news and pictures on the fantastic "comeback" of Free China, is most unfortunate.

A handful of people here are aware of the unbelievable progress in Taiwan during the past 10 years. But the way of life, the conduct of 10,000,000 Chinese on the 240 mile-long island, is virtually unknown in this country. Free China's success in developing a "new nation"—establishing new industries—creating a system of education—her self sufficiency in agriculture—her conduct of government—and her way of life, are powerful, penetrating subjects for world-wide publicity.

This is the material that makes dramatic, thought-provoking articles for news-papers and magazines. This is the truth when told through pictures and stories, that makes people think and remember. This material is perfect for newsreels, television, and motion picture short subjects. This is the way to tell the story of Free China to 175 million Americans and to other nations throughout the world.

How to Accomplish this Campaign

In order to get these stories, pictures, and movies, we would go to China with our own crew of experts. We would research, create, and manufacture feature news.

The secret of success is to gather this material from the American point of view. The objectives do not change. They always remain constant. But to get the story of Free China across to 175 million Americans, week in and week out—you have to tell it with human interest. American editors will publish stories and pictures free of charge if they are interesting enough for their readers.

I never have known of an opportunity that is so natural. Everything is in its favor. It is long overdue. This should have been started years ago.

How We Would Work

We would send our own camera car and a highly trained staff of writers, photographers, moving picture cameramen and a director to Taiwan, with all the equipment necessary for making black and white and color still pictures, television short subjects, newsreels and a cinemascope color moving picture. These men would travel from one end of Taiwan and the Islands to the other, making pictures, writing stories, gathering facts and figures—getting human in-terest stories and sparkling pictures on "Free Chinese at work in Taiwan."

This material would then be sent back to our New York office. Here it would be edited and released to thousands of newspapers, magazines, newsreels, televi-sion networks, and to the Hollywood distributors. In about 90 days after we started work in Taiwan you would begin to see the material appearing throughout the country.

Everything we release is given free-gratis to the press. We sell nothing. Our only source of income would be from this contract.

This work must go on day in and day out—non-stop. By the same token that you cannot plant a fruit tree and get fruit the first year—so too, you cannot start a campaign of this kind and expect immediate results. The campaign gathers momentum as it progresses.

Our Objectives

As you well know, every Senator, Representative, politician—even our President—is first, last and always ". . . the servant of the American people . . ." It is the votes of the people that put these men in office. It is their job to carry out what the voters want.

To inform the voters—to make them "Free China conscious"—to make the American people aware of the tremendous uphill fight the 10 million Chinese have won on Taiwan—to get across the "human interest" story—is the first step toward these objectives.

The entire effort behind this campaign would be to arouse public opinion in the United States, Canada, South America, and Europe and to create a sympathetic understanding of Free China that would have dramatic impact on members of the United Nations and prevent the seating of Red China in the United Nations and the lifting of trade sanctions against Red China. Too, this campaign will bring vociferous moral support from the American people when the day comes for a "return to the mainland."

Cost $300,000 United States per Year

As per your suggestion, $300,000 would be the minimum agreeable to us for the first year of the campaign. This would cover all costs—no extras.

I am enclosing a detailed proposal of exactly what we would do—how we would work—and our guarantees.

We could send our crews to Taiwan about 30 days after this contract was signed.

As I explained to you, I would be most happy to fly to Taipei to meet with Government officials and to take examples of our work along (newspapers, magazines, newsreels, television, motion picture short subjects).

We are sending you, with this proposal, a sample scrap book of our work. I think this is important so that members of the Government will better understand what this is all about. Publicity-public relations is an extremely difficult and complicated profession to people not familiar with U.S. news work.

To have the opportunity of serving the people of Free China and to work with you would be a signal honor and rare privilege, I assure you.

Very truly yours,

*   *   *

Letter of August 9, 1957

The Chairman: I now show you a copy of a letter dated August 9, 1957, addressed to Mr. Hamilton Wright and signed Sampson C. Shen and ask you if you received this letter?

Mr. Wright, Senior: Yes, we received it. Could I just read it to refresh my memory?

The Chairman: Certainly. I just wanted to identify it as a letter that was received by you.

Mr. Wright, Senior: O.K.

The Chairman: You did receive that letter?

Mr. Wright, Senior: Yes, sir.

(A copy of the letter is as follows:)

> Government Information Office,
> Republic of China,
> August 9, 1957

Mr. Hamilton Wright,
Grand Hotel, Taipei

Dear Mr. Wright: The following will serve as a summary of our comments on your proposal for a publicity campaign for the Republic of China.

We congratulate you for a forceful and vivid presentation of your ideas through the scrapbook and motion picture short subjects you brought along. It is my pleasure to inform you that the Government has in principle accepted your proposal of a 1-year contract at $300,000. Only the details remain to be worked out.

We don't believe, however, that the contract can be signed before your departure from Taipei. Further discussion on the terms of the agreement appears necessary. We shall carry on the correspondence with you until the contract is ready for signature.

The Government Information Office has been designated as the sponsoring agency of this project. You are requested to keep in contact with the head of our New York office, Mr. N. C. Nyi, whose address is Chinese News Service, 1270 Sixth Avenue, also in Rockefeller Plaza.

Objectives of the Campaign

Your suggestion to publicize the natural resources, industrial opportunities, agricultural developments, tourist attractions, public work projects, cultural advancement, and the work of the Government to help build the nation is of course laudable. But that is not all that we have in mind in launching this campaign.

In our publicity-public relations work in the United States, we have met with certain "sales resistance" on the part of the American public. These should be, in our opinion, the primary targets of this campaign. The "two Chinas" theory has never been totally discredited. There have been talks of admitting the Chinese Communists in the United Nations, of relaxing the embargo of strategic material to the Chinese mainland, and of taking another look at U.S. policy toward China.

It is for this reason that we want to avoid creating the impression that the building up of Taiwan is an end in itself, that the Government is content in just sitting here, and that we have given up the goal of recovering the mainland.

There are other fallacies we wish to correct, such as "Chiang's army is aging," and "Taiwanese are not Chinese." Naturally we are not asking you to distribute false propaganda in your country. The truth, when ably presented, will always defeat lies, and what we want you to do is simply to tell the truth to the American people, through means that are acceptable to their sense of justice and of objectivity.

Terms of The Agreement

For the lack of a draft agreement, we will use paragraphs 9 through 43 of the memorandum you submitted to Dr. T. F. Tsiang as the basis for our comments.

We would like to set the objectives outlined above be included in the final agreement. As the Government Information Office shall be the agency responsible for this operation, we suggest that the provision on subject matter and media be changed to read that the Hamilton Wright Organization shall decide what subjects it shall photograph, film, and write about and to select the proper media "in consultation and agreement with the Government Information Office of the Republic of China." Similarly, the proper person for you to contact in the United States should be Mr. N. C. Nyi of the Chinese News Service.

You did not specify whether the contract will go into effect when it is signed, when the downpayment is made by the Government, or when your crew arrives at Taiwan to begin the operations. This has definite bearings in calculating the duration of the contract. It is our hope that the contract will go into effect 2 months after it is signed, preferably commensurate with the arrival of your advance party.

Going over your proposition, we have found that performance guarantees are limited to motion picture short subjects and newsreels. No guarantee of use has been offered in regard to newspaper and popular magazine features, still pictures both color and black and white, syndicated full-page picture layouts, Sunday picture supplements, window display posters, and trade magazine stories. This makes it difficult for us to understand the exact meaning of paragraphs 38 and 39 on proof of good performance of this contract and on elasticity in fulfilling the guarantees. We are also left in the dark concerning your system of "six to one" in evaluating the publicity you will obtain for us in the course of the campaign.

Another point we would like to mention is the matter of copyright of all still pictures, newsreels, and motion picture short subjects. Except in the case of the Cinema Scope trailer, which we understand from you would belong to the studio distributing it, we wonder if it is possible for us to obtain a copy of all negatives and transparencies afterwards for our own use. The Government will not claim any copyright to the pictures if they should be used by any person or organization in the United States or elsewhere, but we certainly hope to have the liberty of using them later on in any manner and in any part of the world.

Preparations to Implementing the Contract

We would like to know at your earliest convenience, what you expect us to do in providing necessary assistance once the contract is signed. Among these are the size of the crew you intend to bring to Taiwan, their estimated date of arrival, and expected length of stay, what accommodations would be needed including hotel and office space, number of Chinese liaison, and technical personnel needed by your field team, etc.

Yours sincerely,
Sampson C. Shen,
Director, Government Information Office

The Chairman: This was also pertinent to the same contract, relating to the same contract discussed in the previous letter? It was in effect his reply, is that correct, one of his replies?

This also carries the subheading called "Objectives of the Campaign" corresponding to the other objectives, that you mentioned in your letter, is that not true?

He says here, and I quote, on page 2:

> In our publicity public relations work in the United States we have met with certain sales resistance on the part of the American public. These should be in our opinion the primary targets of this campaign. The two-Chinas theory has never been totally discredited. There have been talks of admitting the Chinese Communists in the United Nations, of relaxing the embargo of strategic material to the Chinese mainland and taking another look at U.S. policy toward China.
>
> It is for this reason that we want to avoid creating the impression that the building up of Taiwan is an end in itself, that the Government is content in just sitting here, that we have given up the goal of recovering the mainland.
>
> There are other fallacies we wish to correct such as "Chiang's army is aging" and "Taiwanese are not Chinese." Naturally, we are not asking you to distribute false propaganda in your country. The truth when ably presented will always defeat lies. What we want you to do is tell the truth to the American people through means that are sensible to their sense of justice and objectivity.

Is that not as stated by Mr. Shen, a political objective?

Mr. Wright, Junior: Yes.

The Chairman: It is, isn't it? Do you agree?

Mr. Wright, Junior: Of course.

The Chairman: That is all I wanted to know. In other words, the objectives as shown by both your original proposal and Mr. Shen's is essentially political.

Mr. Wright, Junior: Correct.

Agreement with Government of Free China, September 1957

The Chairman: I show you a copy of what purports to be an agreement, dated September 1957, between the Government of Free China and the Hamilton Wright Organization and ask if you can identify this document.

Mr. Wright, Senior: It is particularly understood that the services taken by our organization shall not be construed as political propaganda or intended to fall in that category but rather to enlighten and inform the American public opinion as to the efforts made by free China and in an effort to uphold the processes of a democratic way of life

The Chairman: This is the document?

Mr. Wright, Senior: Yes; this is a firm contract. This is what it finally was struck down to.

(A copy of the document is as follows:)

Agreement made and entered into this—day of September, 1957, between the Government of Free China, Taipei, Taiwan, hereinafter designated "Government" and Hamilton Wright Organization, Inc., a domestic corporation having its principal place of business at 30 Rockefeller Plaza, New York, New York, United States of America, hereinafter designated "Organization."

Witnesseth:

Whereas Government is desirous of having publicity representation in the United States of America; and

Whereas Organization is willing to undertake a publicity campaign for Government in the United States of America,

Now, therefore, in consideration of the sum of One Dollar ($1), lawful money of the United States, each to the other in hand paid, the receipt of which is hereby acknowledged and the mutual covenants hereinafter contained, it is agreed as follows:

1. Organization agrees to carry on an editorial publicity campaign in the newspapers, magazines, television, radio, newsreels, theaters and other media for Government, the details of such publicity more particularly hereinafter described, and Government agrees to employ Organization for such publicity campaign and to cooperate in carrying out such campaign, more fully hereinafter described, for the period of one (1) year, beginning October 1, 1957, and ending September 30, 1958.

2. Organization, in carrying out its publicity campaign for Government, will publicize the natural resources, industrial opportunities, agricultural developments, tourist attractions, public works projects, cultural advancement, and the work of Government to help build a vigorous, healthy economy in Taiwan. It will be the function of Organization to bring to the attention of the people of the United States and the free world the tremendous difficulties under which the people of Free China are working toward the ultimate goal of returning to the mainland of Asia. It is particularly understood that the services undertaken by Organization shall not be construed as "political propaganda" or intended to fall within that category, but rather to inform and enlighten American public opinion as to the efforts made by Free China to establish and uphold democratic processes and the democratic way of life.

3. During the discussions leading up to this agreement, various correspondence has passed between Government and Organization, in particular items

9 to 43, inclusive, hereto attached. It is agreed between Government and Organization that these particular items are made a part of this agreement, and Organization and Government agree to carry out, as nearly as possible, both the details and spirit of the plans making up this publicity campaign, set forth in these items.

A letter dated August 15, 1957, from Organization to Mr. Sampson C. Shen, Director, Government Information Office, Taipei, Taiwan, Republic of China, together with fourteen pages of suggested matter, from No. 1 to No. 21, is also annexed hereto and made a part hereof.

Each page of the said items 9 to 43, and the said letter of August 15, 1957 and its attached fourteen pages, are initialed by both the representatives of Government and Organization. Government has fully read and approved the matter contained in the papers hereto attached, and the parties hereto agree that they shall be read as part of this agreement as though fully embodied and set forth at length.

4. Government and Organization agree that the Information Office of Free China in Taipei shall be the official agency of Government, and Organization will submit for approval its pictures and news releases to the China News Service, 1270 Sixth Avenue, New York City. In the event, however, that releases cannot be approved immediately, due to holidays, weekends or absence of proper officials, Organization shall have the right, in its judgment, to release such material in order not to lose the news value of such subject matter. It is understood, however, that the submission of such material shall be for checking technical accuracy and Government policy and not editorial editing.

5. All negatives (stills in black and white, all motion picture negative) shall automatically become the property of Government upon the completion of this contract. Government also shall be entitled to the full use of any and all photographic material and all stories for its own use, so long as it does not compete with the releases of Organization through the established United States of America newsreel-television outlets and news photo syndicates, syndicated Sunday supplements, etc.

6. It is understood and agreed between Government and Organization that Government shall give complete co-operation at all times to Organization and its staff in Taiwan and the United States of America, more particularly the cities of New York and Washington, which shall include the introductions to government officials, arrangements to make certain photographs (Army, Navy, Air Force, etc.) and co-operation in the use of government airplanes, trucks, helicopters, boats, etc., and interpreters, etc.

7. Government agrees to pay to Organization the sum of Three hundred thousand dollars ($300,000.) U.S.A., as follows: One hundred thousand dollars ($100,000) upon the signing of this agreement; fifty thousand dollars ($50,000) on December 1, 1957; fifty thousand dollars ($50,000) on March 1, 1958; fifty thousand dollars ($50,000) on June 1, 1958; and fifty thousand dollars ($50,000) on September 30, 1958.

All payments are to be made to Hamilton Wright Organization, Inc., 30 Rockefeller Plaza, New York 20, N.Y., or Hamilton Wright Organization, Inc., in care of The Chase Manhattan Bank, 30 Rockefeller Plaza, New York 20, N.Y., or in care of the Irving Trust Company, Rockefeller Center, New York 20, N.Y.

8. It is understood and agreed that this agreement shall be automatically renewed from year to year, upon the same terms and conditions as herein set forth, unless Government or Organization notifies the other, in writing, by registered mail, sixty (60) days prior to the expiration of this agreement that it shall not be renewed.

9. It is further agreed by and between the parties hereto that either party shall have the privilege of cancelling this agreement after February 1, 1958, by giving to the other sixty (60) days' written notice, by registered mail.

In the event that Government cancels this agreement it will pay to Organization the proportionate amount of fees to the date of cancellation, but in no event less than one hundred and fifty thousand dollars ($150,000).

In the event that Organization cancels this agreement it will continue to render services to the date of cancellation, and its remuneration shall be in proportion to said date of cancellation.

In witness whereof, Government and Organization have caused these presents to be executed by their duly authorized officers or duly authorized representatives, and their seals to be hereunto affixed, the day and year first above written.

In the presence of:

> *Government of Free China*
> *By*

In the presence of:

> *Hamilton Wright Organization, Inc.*
> *By*

UNITED STATES POLICY IN CHINA, 1952-1960

A. United States-China Mutual Defense Treaty*

Washington, December 2, 1954

The Parties to this Treaty,

Reaffirming their faith in the purposes and principles of the Charter of the United Nations and their desire to live in peace with all peoples and all Governments, and desiring to strengthen the fabric of peace in the West Pacific Area.

Recalling with mutual pride the relationship which brought their two peoples together in a common bond of sympathy and mutual ideals to fight side by side against imperialist aggression during the last war,

Desiring to declare publicly and formally their sense of unity and their common determination to defend themselves against external armed attack, so that no potential aggressor could be under the illusion that either of them stands alone in the West Pacific Area, and

Desiring further to strengthen their present efforts for collective defense for the preservation of peace and security pending the development of a more comprehensive system of regional security in the West Pacific Area,

Have agreed as follows:

Article I

The Parties undertake, as set forth in the Charter of the United Nations, to settle any international dispute in which they may be involved by peaceful means in such a manner that international peace, security and justice are not endangered and to refrain in their international relations from the threat or use of force in any manner inconsistent with the purposes of the United Nations.

Article II

In order more effectively to achieve the objective of this Treaty, the Parties separately and jointly by self-help and mutual aid will maintain and develop their individual and collective capacity to resist armed attack and communist subversive activities directed from without against their territorial integrity and political stability.

Article III

The Parties undertake to strengthen their free institutions and to cooperate

*Council on Foreign Relations, *Documents on American Foreign Relations, 1954.* (New York, 1955), pp. 360-62.

with each other in the development of economic progress and social well-being and to further their individual and collective efforts toward these ends.

Article IV

The Parties, through their Foreign Ministers or their deputies, will consult together from time to time regarding the implementation of this Treaty.

Article V

Each Party recognizes that an armed attack in the West Pacific Area directed against the territories of either of the Parties would be dangerous to its own peace and safety and declares that it would act to meet the common danger in accordance with its constitutional processes.

Any such armed attack and all measures taken as a result thereof shall be immediately reported to the Security Council of the United Nations. Such measures shall be terminated when the Security Council has taken the measures necessary to restore and maintain international peace and security.

Article VI

For the purposes of Articles II and V, the terms "territorial" and "territories" shall mean in respect of the Republic of China, Taiwan and the Pescadores; and in respect of the United States of America the island territories in the West Pacific under its jurisdiction. The provisions of Articles II and V will be applicable to such other territories as may be determined by mutual agreement.

Article VII

The Government of the Republic of China grants, and the Government of the United States of America accepts, the right to dispose such United States land, air and sea forces in and about Taiwan and the Pescadores as may be required for their defense, as determined by mutual agreement.

Article VIII

This Treaty does not affect and shall not be interpreted as affecting in any way the rights and obligations of the Parties under the Charter of the United Nations or the responsibility of the United Nations for the maintenance of international peace and security.

Article IX

   This Treaty shall be ratified by the United States of America and the Republic of China in accordance with their respective constitutional processes and will come into force when instruments of ratification thereof have been exchanged by them at Taipei.

Article X

   This Treaty shall remain in force indefinitely. Either Party may terminate it one year after notice has been given to the other Party.
   In witness whereof the undersigned Plenipotentiaries have signed this Treaty.
   Done in duplicate, in the English and Chinese languages, at Washington on this second day of December of the Year One Thousand Nine Hundred and Fifty-four, corresponding to the second day of the twelfth month of the Forty-third Year of the Republic of China.

For the United States of America: John Foster Dulles
For the Republic of China: George K.C. Yeh

THE FORMOSA CRISIS

B. President Dwight D. Eisenhower to Congress on Defense of Formosa*

January 24, 1955

   The most important objective of our Nation's foreign policy is to safeguard the security of the United States by establishing and preserving a just and honorable peace. In the Western Pacific a situation is developing in the Formosa Straits that seriously imperils the peace and our security.
   Since the end of Japanese hostilities in 1945, Formosa and the Pescadores have been in the friendly hands of our loyal ally, the Republic of China. We have recognized that it was important that these islands should remain in friendly hands. In unfriendly hands, Formosa and the Pescadores would seriously dislocate the existing, even if unstable, balance of moral, economic, and military forces upon which the peace of the Pacific depends. It would create a breach in the island chain of the Western Pacific that constitutes, for the United States and other free nations, the geographical backbone of their security structure in that ocean. In addition, this breach would interrupt north-south communications between other important elements of that barrier, and damage the economic life of countries friendly to us.
   The United States and the friendly Government of the Republic of China,

* *Ibid.*, pp. 294-98.

and indeed all the free nations, have a common interest that Formosa and the Pescadores should not fall into the control of aggressive Communist forces.

Influenced by such considerations, our Government was prompt, when the Communists committed armed aggression in Korea in June 1950, to direct our Seventh Fleet to defend Formosa from possible invasion from the Communist mainland.

These considerations are still valid. The Seventh Fleet continues under Presidential directive to carry out that defensive mission. We also provide military and economic support to the Chinese Nationalist Government and we cooperate in every proper and feasible way with that Government in order to promote its security and stability. All of these military and related activities will be continued.

In addition, there was signed last December, a Mutual Defense Treaty between this Government and the Republic of China, covering Formosa and the neighboring Pescadores. It is a treaty of purely defensive character. That treaty is now before the Senate of the United States.

Meanwhile Communist China has pursued a series of provocative political and military actions, establishing a pattern of aggressive purpose. That purpose, they proclaim, is the conquest of Formosa.

In September 1954 the Chinese Communists opened up heavy artillery fire upon Quemoy Island, one of the natural approaches to Formosa, which had for several years been under the uncontested control of the Republic of China. Then came air attacks of mounting intensity against other free China islands, notably those in the vicinity of the Tachen group to the north of Formosa. One small island (Ichiang) was seized last week by air and amphibious operations after a gallant few fought bravely for days against overwhelming odds. There have been recent heavy air attacks and artillery fire against the main Tachen Islands themselves.

The Chinese Communists themselves assert that these attacks are a prelude to the conquest of Formosa. For example, after the fall of Ichiang, the Peiping radio said that it showed a—"determined will to fight for the liberation of Taiwan [Formosa]. Our people will use all their strength to fulfill that task."

Clearly, this existing and developing situation poses a serious danger to the security of our country and of the entire Pacific area and indeed to the peace of the world. We believe that the situation is one for appropriate action of the United Nations under its charter, for the purpose of ending the present hostilities in that area. We would welcome assumption of such jurisdiction by that body.

Meanwhile, the situation has become sufficiently critical to impel me, without awaiting action by the United Nations, to ask the Congress to participate now, by specific resolution, in measures designed to improve the prospects for peace. These measures would contemplate the use of the Armed Forces of the United States if necessary to assure the security of Formosa and the Pescadores.

The actions that the United States must be ready to undertake are of various kinds. For example, we must be ready to assist the Republic of China to redeploy and consolidate its forces if it should so desire. Some of these forces are scattered throughout the smaller offshore islands as a result of historical rather than military reasons directly related to defending Formosa. Because of the air situation in the area, withdrawals for the purpose of redeployment of Chinese Nationalist forces would be impractical without assistance of the Armed Forces of the United States.

Moreover, we must be alert to any concentration or employment of Chinese Communist forces obviously undertaken to facilitate attack upon Formosa, and be prepared to take appropriate military action.

I do not suggest that the United States enlarge its defensive obligations beyond Formosa and the Pescadores as provided by the treaty now awaiting ratification. But, unhappily, the danger of armed attack directed against that area compels us to take into account closely related localities and actions which, under current conditions, might determine the failure or the success of such an attack. The authority that may be accorded by the Congress would be used only in situations which are recognizable as parts of, or definite preliminaries to, an attack against the main positions of Formosa and the Pescadores.

Authority for some of the actions which might be required would be inherent in the authority of the Commander in Chief. Until Congress can act I would not hesitate, so far as my constitutional powers extend, to take whatever emergency action might be forced upon us in order to protect the rights and security of the United States.

However, a suitable congressional resolution would clearly and publicly establish the authority of the President as Commander in Chief to employ the Armed Forces of this Nation promptly and effectively for the purposes indicated if in his judgment it became necessary. It would make clear the unified and serious intentions of our Government, our Congress, and our people. Thus it will reduce the possibility that the Chinese Communists, misjudging our firm purpose and national unity, might be disposed to challenge the position of the United States, and precipitate a major crisis which even they would neither anticipate nor desire.

In the interest of peace, therefore, the United States must remove any doubt regarding our readiness to fight, if necessary, to preserve the vital stake of the free world in a free Formosa, and to engage in whatever operations may be required to carry out that purpose.

To make this plain requires not only Presidential action but also congressional action. In a situation such as now confronts us, and under modern conditions of warfare, it would not be prudent to await the emergency before coming to the Congress. Then it might be too late. Already the warning signals are flying.

I believe that the threatening aspects of the present situation, if resolutely faced, may be temporary in character. Consequently, I recommend that the resolution expire as soon as the President is able to report to the Congress that the peace and security of the area are reasonably assured by international conditions, resulting from United Nations action or otherwise.

Again I say that we would welcome action by the United Nations which might, in fact, bring an end to the active hostilities in the area. This critical situation has been created by the choice of the Chinese Communists, not by us. Their offensive military intent has been flaunted to the whole world by words and by deeds. Just as they created the situation, so they can end it if they so choose.

What we are now seeking is primarily to clarify present policy and to unite in its application. We are not establishing a new policy. Consequently, my recommendations do not call for an increase in the Armed Forces of the United States of any acceleration in military procurement or levels of defense production. If any unforeseen emergency arises requiring any change, I will communicate with the Congress. I hope, however, that the effect of an appropriate congressional resolution will be to calm the situation rather than to create further conflict.

One final point: The action I request is, of course, no substitute for the treaty with the Republic of China which we have signed and which I have transmitted to the Senate. Indeed, present circumstances make it more than ever important that this basic agreement should be promptly brought into force, as a solemn evidence of our determination to stand fast in the agreed treaty area and to thwart all attacks directed against it. If delay should make us appear indecisive in this basic respect, the pressures and dangers would surely mount.

Our purpose is peace. That cause will be served if, with your help, we demonstrate our unity and our determination. In all that we do we shall remain faithful to our obligations as a member of the United Nations to be ready to settle our international disputes by peaceful means in such a manner that international peace and security, and justice, are not endangered.

For the reasons outlined in this message, I respectfully request that the Congress take appropriate action to carry out the recommendations contained herein.

C. Joint Congressional Resolution on Defense of Formosa*

Adopted by the House of Representatives, January 25, 1955
Adopted by the Senate, January 28, 1955

Whereas the primary purpose of the United States, in its relations with all other nations, is to develop and sustain a just and enduring peace for all; and

Whereas certain territories in the West Pacific under the jurisdiction of the Republic of China are now under armed attack, and threats and declarations have been and are being made by the Chinese Communists that such armed attack is in aid of and in preparation for formed attack on Formosa and the Pescadores,

Whereas such armed attack if continued would gravely endanger the peace and security of the West Pacific Area and particularly of Formosa and the Pescadores; and

Whereas the secure possession by friendly governments of the Western Pacific Island chain, of which Formosa is a part, is essential to the vital interests of the United States and all friendly nations in or bordering upon the Pacific Ocean; and

Whereas the President of the United States on January 6, 1955, submitted

*Ibid., pp. 298-99.

to the Senate for its advice and consent to ratification a Mutual Defense Treaty between the United States of America and the Republic of China, which recognizes that an armed attack in the West Pacific area directed against territories, therein described, in the region of Formosa and the Pescadores, would be dangerous to the peace and safety of the parties to the treaty: Therefore be it

Resolved by the Senate and House of Representatives of the United States of America in Congress assembled, That the President of the United States be and he hereby is authorized to employ the Armed Forces of the United States as he deems necessary for the specific purpose of securing and protecting Formosa and the Pescadores against armed attack, this authority to include the securing and protection of such related positions and territories of that area now in friendly hands and the taking of such other measures as he judges to be required or appropriate in assuring the defense of Formosa and the Pescadores.

This resolution shall expire when the President shall determine that the peace and security of the area is reasonably assured by international conditions created by action of the United Nations or otherwise, and shall so report to the Congress.

TALKS BETWEEN THE UNITED STATES AND COMMUNIST CHINA, 1955

D. Statement by Secretary of State John Foster Dulles*

[Extract]

July 26, 1955

Last April at the Bandung conference Mr. Chou En-lai suggested that there should be bilateral talks with the United States. He said, "The Chinese people do not want to have war with the United States. We are willing to settle international disputes by peaceful means."

Immediately [on April 23, 1955] the Department of State responded by stating that "the United States always welcomes any efforts, if sincere, to bring peace to the world." Then at my subsequent press conference [April 26, 1955] I referred to Mr. Chou En-lai's statement and said, "Whether or not that was a sincere proposal remains to be seen. Perhaps the Chinese Communists are merely playing a propaganda game. But we intend to try to find out. In doing so we shall not, of course, depart from the path of fidelity and honor to our ally, the Republic of China."

Developments since then indicate the possibility of obtaining beneficial results from a continuance of the talks which have been going on at Geneva for the past year and their restoration to the original ambassadorial level.

*   *   *

Department of State Bulletin, Aug. 8, 1955, pp. 220-21.

The former belligerent Communist propaganda about Taiwan and against the United States has recently been somewhat subdued.

In addition, various governments which have diplomatic relations with the People's Republic of China have indicated their own belief in the desire of the Chinese Communists to pursue a peaceful path.

Under these circumstances the United States proposed on July 11 to Mr. Chou En-lai that the talks that had been going on at Geneva, recently at the consular level, should be somewhat raised in level and enlarged in scope. This proposal was made through the intermediary of the United Kingdom, which represents the interests of the United States in Communist China. There was prompt acceptance of this proposal and, after the date was agreed to, a mutually agreed communiqué with reference to it was arrived at and simultaneously issued in Peiping and in Washington yesterday morning.

It was made clear that the offer of the United States did not imply any diplomatic recognition whatsoever. It was also made clear that we were not prepared in any way in these talks to make arrangements which would prejudice the rights of our ally, the Republic of China.

The United States will be represented at Geneva on August 1 by our Ambassador to Czechoslovakia, U. Alexis Johnson. It was Ambassador Johnson who represented the United States in the Geneva talks with the Chinese Communists when these talks first began a year ago. Prior to that, as a Departmental officer, he devoted himself largely to the Korean Armistice negotiations.

The United States is concerned with getting back the American civilians still detained in Communist China. In this connection we are prepared to discuss with the Chinese Communists the status of the few Chinese students in the United States who desire to return to Communist China and who the Chinese Communists claim, without foundation, are prevented.

We also want to reinforce the efforts of the United Nations to get back the Americans who as members of the United Nations Command in Korea became prisoners of war and are still held by the Chinese Communists. . . .

Of course, the basic thing is that which I pointed out in my press conference of April 26, namely, "whether we must prepare for war in that area or whether there is apt to be a cease-fire in the area."

*   *   *

Both the Republic of China and the Chinese People's Republic claim that the area held by the other is part of China. But in connection with the mutual security treaty which the United States made with the Republic of China, it was agreed that the Republic of China would not use force except as a matter of joint agreement, subject to action of an emergency character which was clearly an exercise of the inherent right of self-defense.

We believe that the principle of nonrecourse to force is valid not merely for the United States and its allies but that it is valid for all.

We shall hope to find out in the forthcoming talks whether the Chinese Communists accept the concept of a cease-fire in accordance with the United Nations principle of avoiding any use or threat of force which could disturb the peace of nations.

No doubt the Chinese Communists will have matters of their own to bring up. We shall listen to hear what they are, and if they directly involve the United States and Communist China we will be disposed to discuss them with a view to arriving at a peaceful settlement.

*   *   *

E. Announcement of Mutual Return of Civilians to Their Respective Countries*

September 10, 1955

The Ambassadors of the United States of America and the People's Republic of China have agreed to announce measures which their respective governments have adopted concerning the return of civilians to their respective countries.

With respect to Chinese in the United States, Ambassador U. Alexis Johnson, on behalf of the United States, has informed Ambassador Wang Ping-nan that:

1. The United States recognizes that Chinese in the United States who desire to return to the People's Republic of China are entitled to do so and declares that it has adopted and will further adopt appropriate measures so that they can expeditiously exercise their right to return.

2. The Government of the Republic of India will be invited to assist in the return to the People's Republic of China of those who desire to do so as follows:

A. If any Chinese in the United States believes that contrary to the declared policy of the United States he is encountering obstruction in departure, he may so inform the Embasssy of the Republic of India in the United States and request it to make representations on his behalf to the United States Government. If desired by the People's Republic of China, the Government of the Republic of India may also investigate the facts in any such case.

B. If any Chinese in the United States who desires to return to the People's Republic of China has difficulty in paying his return expenses, the Government of the Republic of India may render him financial assistance needed to permit his return.

3. The United States Government will give wide publicity to the foregoing arrangements and the Embassy of the Republic of India in the United States may also do so.

With respect to Americans in the People's Republic of China, Ambassador Wang Ping-nan, on behalf of the People's Republic of China, has informed Ambassador U. Alexis Johnson that:

1. The People's Republic of China recognizes that Americans in the People's Republic of China who desire to return to the United States are entitled to do so, and declares that it has adopted and will further adopt appropriate measures so that they can expeditiously exercise their right to return.

*Ibid., Sept. 19, 1955, p. 456.

2. The Government of the United Kingdom will be invited to assist in the return to the United States of those Americans who desire to do so as follows:

A. If any American in the People's Republic of China believes that contrary to the declared policy of the People's Republic of China he is encountering obstruction in departure, he may so inform the Office of the Chargé d'Affaires of the United Kingdom in the People's Republic of China and request it to make representations on his behalf to the Government of the People's Republic of China. If desired by the United States, the Government of the United Kingdom may also investigate the facts in any such case.

B. If any American in the People's Republic of China who desires to return to the United States has difficulty in paying his return expenses, the Government of the United Kingdom may render him financial assistance needed to permit his return.

3. The Government of the People's Republic of China will give wide publicity to the foregoing arrangements and the Office of the Chargé d'Affaires of the United Kindgom in the People's Republic of China may also do so.

F. State Department Announcement on Return of Civilians*

January 21, 1956

Agreement to Repatriation of Civilians

On September 10, 1955, the representatives of both sides, by agreement, issued statements that civilians were entitled to return to their own countries.

The Communist declaration stated:

"The People's Republic of China recognizes that Americans in the People's Republic of China who desire to return to the United States are entitled to do so, and declares that it has adopted and will further adopt appropriate measures so that they can expeditiously exercise their right to return."

As of today, 4 months after this declaration was made, only 6 out of the 19 for whom representations were being made on September 10 have been released. Thirteen Americans are still in Communist prisons.

As for the United States, any Chinese is free to leave the United States for any destination of his choosing, and not a single one has been refused exit. The Indian Embassy, which was designated to assist any Chinese who wished to leave, has not brought to the attention of this Government any case of a Chinese who claims he is being prevented from leaving, nor has it stated that it is impeded in any way in carrying out its functions under the terms of the September 10 agreed announcement.

Discussion of Renunciation of Force

After this agreed announcement was made, the two sides proceeded to discuss "other practical matters at issue between them."

The Communists suggested the topics of the termination of the trade embargo

*Ibid., Jan. 30, 1956, pp. 164-66.

against Communist China and the holding of a meeting by the Foreign Ministers of both sides.

Ambassador Johnson at the October 8, 1955, meeting pointed out that progress in further discussions could not be expected in the face of continuing Communist threats to take Taiwan by military force and suggested that both sides agree to announce that they renounced the use of force generally and particularly in the Taiwan area and agree to settle their differences by peaceful means. The U.S. representatives made clear that this renunciation of the use of force was not designed to commit the Communists to renounce pursuit of their policies by peaceful means with respect to Taiwan. . . .

Three weeks after the U.S. proposal to renounce the use of force, the Communists on October 27 proposed a draft. . . .

In this proposal, the Communists pointedly omitted any reference to the Taiwan area or to the recognition of the right of self-defense, and inserted a provision for an immediate meeting of Foreign Ministers.

This proposal was unacceptable because it would have made it possible for the Communists to claim that the proposal did not apply to the Taiwan area, which is the very place against which the Communist threats are directed, and to claim further that the United States had renounced the right to use force in self-defense. Ambassador Johnson further pointed out that consideration of higher level meetings was neither appropriate nor acceptable under existing circumstances.

On November 10, 1955, Ambassador Johnson, in an attempt to reach an acceptable form of declaration, submitted a new draft declaration. This made clear that the renunciation of the use of force was without prejudice to the peaceful pursuit of its policies by either side; that it had general application but applied particularly to the Taiwan area; and that it did not deprive either side of the right of self-defense.

The U.S. proposal was rejected by the Communists, who, on December 1, 1955, made a counterproposal. This represented an advance over their previous proposal in that it dropped the provision for talks on the Foreign Minister level in favor of the continuance of ambassadorial talks but still pointedly omitted any reference to the Taiwan area and to recognition of the right of self-defense.

In a further effort to reach agreement, Ambassador Johnson, at the January 12 meeting, suggested two simple amendments to the Communist counterproposal. These were the insertion of the words "without prejudice to the inherent right of individual and collective self-defense" and of the words "in the Tawian area or elsewhere. . . ."

This was the status of the discussions when the Communists released their public statement of January 18.

The Communist statement apparently rejects the U.S. proposal. It states, "Taiwan is Chinese territory: there can be no question of defense, as far as the United States is concerned. . . . Yet the United States has demanded the right of defense of the Taiwan area. Is this not precisely a demand that China accept continued occupation of Taiwan and that the tension in the Taiwan area be maintained forever?" And further, it states: "The American side continues to demand that our side accept that the United States has 'the inherent right of individual and collective self-defense' in China's Taiwan area. This is what our side absolutely cannot accept."

Two points must be made clear. First, the United States is not occupying Taiwan and Taiwan has never been a part of Communist China. The claims of Communist China and the contentions of the United States with respect to this area are well known and constitute a major dispute between them. It is specifically with respect to this dispute that the United States has proposed the principle of renunciation of force and the settlement of differences by peaceful means. This is the principle which the Communists say they have accepted.

In this connection the United States has made completely clear that in renouncing the use of force neither side is relinquishing its objectives and policies but only the use of force to attain them.

Secondly, the United States has rights and responsibilities in the Taiwan area; also it has a mutual defense treaty. Accordingly it is present in the Taiwan area. The Communist refusal to state that the renunciation of force is without prejudice to the right of self-defense against armed attack can only be interpreted as an attempt to induce the United States to agree that if attacked it will forego the right to defend its lawful presence in this area.

The right of individual and collective self-defense against armed attack is inherent; it is recognized in international law; it is specifically affirmed in the charter of the United Nations. No country can be expected to forego this right. Indeed, the Communists should be as anxious to preserve this right as is the United States.

Conclusion

The present exchange makes clear that:

1. Four months after the Communists announced that they would adopt measures to permit Americans in China to return to the United States, 13 Americans are still held in Communist prisons.

2. The United States proposed that the parties renounce the use of force without prejudice to the right of individual and collective self-defense against armed attack, in order that the discussions might take place free from the threat of war.

3. The United States made clear that this renunciation would not prejudice either side in the pursuit of its objectives and policies by peaceful means.

4. The Communists, while stating that they accept the principle of the renunciation of force, have deprived such acceptance of its value by refusing to agree that it is without prejudice to the right of individual and collective self-defense against armed attack and that it is applicable to the Taiwan area.

In short, the Communists so far seem willing to renounce force only if they are first conceded the goals for which they would use force.

The United States, for its part, intends to persist in the way of peace. We seek the now overdue fulfillment by the Chinese Communists of their undertaking that the Americans now in China should be allowed expeditiously to return.

We seek this not only for humanitarian reasons but because respect for international undertakings lies at the foundation of a stable international order. We shall also seek with perseverance a meaningful renunciation of force, particularly in the Taiwan area.

EISENHOWER ADMINISTRATION POLICY TOWARD COMMUNIST CHINA

G. Statement by Secretary Dulles on United States Policy Toward Communist China*

March 13, 1957

The United States adheres steadfastly to the three main aspects of its China policy, which is to recognize the Republic of China; not to recognize the so-called People's Republic of China; and to oppose the seating of this People's Republic in the United Nations as the accredited representative of what the charter calls the Republic of China.

This policy is not merely an expression of sentimental loyalty to a Government which was loyal to the Allied cause throughout even the darkest days of the Second World War.

Our policy stems primarily from considerations of national interest and, we believe, of international interest. First of all we ask ourselves: Will the interests of the United States be advanced by according diplomatic recognition to the Chinese Communist regime?

The answer to that is in our opinion clearly negative. United States diplomatic recognition of the Chinese Communist regime would serve no national purpose but would strengthen and encourage influences hostile to us and our allies and further imperil lands whose independence is related to our own peace and security.

In this connection we recall that there are many millions of immigrant Chinese who form parts of the populations of free Asian countries. Today many of them, perhaps most of them, remain loyal to the Republic of China now seated at Taiwan, which symbolizes the China that they know. We can see only loss and no gain in action which would make these overseas Chinese more apt to serve the subversive policies of the Chinese Communist regime.

If we examine this matter from the standpoint of the United Nations, we come to a similar conclusion. The United Nations would not be strengthened if the Communists were there to represent China, and we cannot see that they have any right to this role.

The charter seeks that membership should be made up of peace-loving governments able and willing to carry out their obligations under the charter. There is no evidence that the Chinese Communist regime would represent China in

*Ibid., Apr. 1, 1957, pp. 531-32.

the spirit envisaged by the charter. It has fought the United Nations in Korea and still stands condemned as an aggressor against the United Nations. It seized Tibet by force. It promoted the war in Indochina. It refuses to renounce resort to war as an instrument of its policy in relation to Taiwan and the Penghus. Its conduct toward other nations and their citizens does not reflect the tolerance and good neighborliness which the members of the United Nations are supposed to practice.

If the Communist regime were allowed to represent the Republic of China in the United Nations, it would presumably sit on the Security Council as a permanent member with veto power. That Council is the body which by the charter is entrusted with primary responsibility for the maintenance of peace and security in conformity with the principles of justice and international law. It would be grotesque if that high responsibility were to be conferred upon a regime which itself stands condemned as an armed aggressor against the United Nations and which itself is a most conspicuous violator of justice and international law.

The United Nations is faced with growing responsibilities. These could not be more readily discharged by giving the Chinese Communists the opportunity to work mischief there.

We believe that United States policies are not merely in our own interest and in the interest of the free world but also that they are in the interest of the Chinese people themselves, with whom the American people have historic ties of friendship.

H. Address by Secretary Dulles on United States Policy Toward Communist China*

[Extract]

San Francisco, June 28, 1957

It is appropriate that in this great city of San Francisco, which faces the Far East, we should consider our policies toward communism in China.

The Situation Today

On the China mainland 600 million people are ruled by the Chinese Communist Party. That party came to power by violence and, so far, has lived by violence.

It retains power not by will of the Chinese people but by massive, forcible repression. It fought the United Nations in Korea; it supported the Communist war in Indochina; it took Tibet by force. It fomented the Communist Huk rebellion in the Philippines and the Communists' insurrection in Malaya. It does not disguise its expansionist ambitions. It is bitterly hateful of the United States, which it considers a principal obstacle in the way of its path of conquest.

In the face of this condition the United States has supported, morally and materially, the free nations of the Western Pacific and Southeast Asia. Our

*Ibid., July 15, 1957, pp. 91-95.

security treaties make clear that the violation of these nations by international communism would be considered as endangering our own peace and safety and that we would act accordingly.

Together we constitute a goodly company and a stout bulwark against aggression.

As regards China, we have abstained from any act to encourage the Communist regime—morally, politically, or materially. Thus:

We have not extended diplomatic recognition to the Chinese Communist regime;

We have opposed its seating in the United Nations;

We have not traded with Communist China or sanctioned cultural interchanges with it.

These have been, and are, our policies. Like all our policies, they are under periodic review.

The Precedent of Russia

As we review our China policy, we naturally and properly recall our recognition policy as regards Communist Russia.

The Bolsheviks seized power from Kerensky in 1917. Nevertheless, we continued for 16 years to treat the Kerensky representatives in exile as representing the lawful government of Russia. By 1933 it seemed that the Communist regime might be considered as a peaceful member of society. For more than a decade it had committed no act of armed aggression. It had accepted the independence of Estonia, Latvia, and Lithuania, and of Poland. It was not demonstrably maltreating American citizens. It promised to cease subversive activities in the United States, to respect American rights in Russia, and to settle Russia's public and private debts to the United States.

Also, by 1933, we desired to encourage the Soviet regime to resist Japanese aggressive policies in the Far East. The Republic of China, inspired by this same notion, had recognized the Soviet Government in December 1932, and we shortly followed suit.

We need not question that act of recognition under the circumstances which then prevailed. Recognition seemed indicated by many tests, and we did not read the future.

However, it can, I think, be said with confidence that recognition would not have been accorded to the Soviet Union even in 1933 had there been clear warning that the Soviet promises given in that connection were totally unreliable, that aggressive war would soon become an instrumentality of Soviet policy, and that it would be neutral toward Japanese aggression in Asia.

In the case of Communist China we are forewarned. That regime fails to pass even those tests which, after 16 years, the Soviet regime seemed to pass.

(1) Soviet Russia, in 1933, had had a decade of peaceful and nonaggressive relations with neighboring states; Communist China's past record is one of armed aggression.

(2) The Soviet regime seemed to want peace for the future. In the case of Communist China the situation is quite the reverse. Mr. Chou En-lai, at the

time of the Bandung conference, said that "the Chinese people do not want to have war with the United States and are willing to settle international disputes by peaceful means." But when the United States took him up and sought explicit reciprocal renunciations of force, his ambassador, after presenting various evasive formulas, finally stated frankly that his regime did intend to use armed force to take Taiwan (Formosa) unless they could get it in some other way.

(3) The Soviet Union in 1933 was not flagrantly violating its international engagements. The Chinese Communist regime is violating the 1953 Korean armistice and the 1954 Indochina armistice.

(4) There was reason to hope that the Soviet regime would treat our nationals with respect. The Chinese Communist regime violates the persons of our citizens in defiance of the elementary code of international decency, and it breaches its 1955 pledge to release them.

(5) It seemed, in 1933, that the Soviet regime and the United States had parallel interests in resisting Japanese aggression in the Far East. Today the political purposes of Communist China clash everywhere with our own.

The Consequences of Recognition

United States diplomatic recognition of Communist China would have the following consequences:

(1) The many mainland Chinese, who by Mao Tse-tung's own recent admission seek to change the nature of their government, would be immensely discouraged.

(2) The millions of overseas Chinese would feel that they had no Free China to which to look. Today increasing numbers of these overseas Chinese go to Free China to study. Six years ago there were less than 100 Chinese students from Southeast Asia and Hong Kong studying in Taiwan. Now there are nearly 5,000.

The number of Chinese students from overseas communities coming to Free China has increased year by year; the number going to Communist China has declined, and hundreds of disillusioned students have made their way out of mainland China in the past 2 years.

If the United States recognized the Chinese Communist regime, many of the millions of overseas Chinese in free Asian countries would, reluctantly, turn to acceptance of the guiding direction of the Communist regime. This would be a tragedy for them; and it would imperil friendly governments already menaced by Chinese Communist subversion.

(3) The Republic of China, now on Taiwan, would feel betrayed by its friend. That Government was our ally in the Second World War and for long bore alone the main burden of the Far Eastern war. It had many tempting opportunities to compromise with the Japanese on terms which would have been gravely detrimental to the United States. It never did so.

We condemn the Soviets for having dishonored their 20-year treaty pledge of 1945 to support the Chinese National Government as the central government of China. We are honor-bound to give our ally, to whom we are pledged by a mutual defense treaty, a full measure of loyalty.

(4) The free Asian governments of the Pacific and Southeast Asia would be gravely perplexed. They are not only close to the vast Chinese land mass, but geographically and, to some extent, politically, they are separated as among themselves. The unifying and fortifying influence is, above all, the spirit and resolution of the United States. If we seemed to waver and to compromise with communism in China, that would in turn weaken free Asia resistance to the Chinese Communist regime and assist international communism to score a great success in its program to encircle us.

China and the United Nations

United States recognition of Communist China would make it probable that the Communist regime would obtain the seat of China in the United Nations. That would not be in the interest either of the United States or of the United Nations.

The United Nations is not a reformatory for bad governments. It is supposedly an association of those who are already "peace-loving" and who are "able and willing to carry out" the charter obligations. The basic obligation is not to use force, except in defense against armed attack.

The Chinese Communist regime has a record of successive armed aggressions, including war against the United Nations itself, a war not yet politically settled but discontinued by an armistice. The regime asserts not only its right but its purpose to use force if need be to bring Taiwan under its rule.

*   *   *

Trade and Cultural Relations with Communist China

Let me turn now to the matter of trade and cultural relations, which could exist, to a limited degree, without recognition.

Normal peacetime trade with China, from which the American and Chinese peoples would benefit, could be in the common interest. But it seems that that kind of trade is not to be had in any appreciable volume.

Trade with Communist China is not a normal trade. It does not provide one country with what its people want but cannot well produce for themselves, in exchange for what other people want but cannot well produce for themselves. Trade with Communist China is wholly controlled by an official apparatus, and its limited amounts of foreign exchange are used to develop as rapidly as possible a formidable military establishment and a heavy industry to support it. The primary desire of that regime is for machine tools, electronic equipment, and, in general, what will help it produce tanks, trucks, planes, ammunition, and such military items.

Whatever others may do, surely the United States, which has heavy security commitments in the China area, ought not build up the military power of its potential enemy.

We also doubt the value of cultural exchanges, which the Chinese Communists are eager to develop. They want this relationship with the United States primarily because, once that example were given, it would be difficult for China's close neighbors not to follow it. These free nations, already exposed to intense Communist subversive activities, could not have the cultural exchanges that the Communists want without adding greatly to their danger.

These are the considerations which argue for a continuance of our present policies. What are the arguments on the other side?

The "De Facto" Argument

There are some who say that we should accord diplomatic recognition to the Communist regime because it has now been in power so long that it has won the right to that.

That is not sound international law. Diplomatic recognition is always a privilege, never a right.

Of course, the United States knows that the Chinese Communist regime exists. We know that very well, for it has fought us in Korea. Also, we admit of dealing with the Chinese Communists in particular cases where that may serve our interests. We have dealt with it in relation to the Korean and Indochina armistices. For nearly 2 years we have been, and still are, dealing with it in an effort to free our citizens and to obtain reciprocal renunciations of force.

But diplomatic recognition gives the recognized regime valuable rights and privileges, and, in the world of today, recognition by the United States gives the recipient much added prestige and influence at home and abroad.

Of course, diplomatic recognition is not to be withheld capriciously. In this matter, as others, the United States seeks to act in accordance with principles which contribute to a world society of order under law.

A test often applied is the ability of a regime actually to govern. But that is by no means a controlling factor. Nations often maintain diplomatic relations with governments-in-exile. And they frequently deny recognition to those in actual power.

Other customary tests are whether, as Thomas Jefferson put it, the recognized government reflects "the will of the nation, substantially declared"; whether the government conforms to the code of civilized nations, lives peacefully, and honors its international obligations.

Always, however, recognition is admitted to be an instrument of national policy, to serve enlightened self-interest.

One thing is established beyond a doubt. There is nothing automatic about recognition. It is never compelled by the mere lapse of time.

The "Inevitability" Argument

Another argument beginning to be heard is that diplomatic recognition is inevitable, so why not now?

First, let me say emphatically that the United States need never succumb to the argument of "inevitability." We, with our friends, can fashion our own destiny. We do not accept the mastery of Communist forces.

And let me go on to say: Communist-type despotisms are not so immutable as they sometimes appear. Time and circumstances work also upon them.

There is often an optical illusion which results from the fact that police states, suppressing differences, give an external appearance of hard permanency, whereas the democracies, with their opposition parties and often speaking through different and discordant voices, seem the unstable, pliable members of the world society.

The reality is that a governmental system which tolerates diversity has a long life expectancy, whereas a system which seeks to impose conformity is always in danger. That results from the basic nature of human beings. Of all the arguments advanced for recognition of the Communist regime in China, the least cogent is the argument of "inevitability."

China Versus Russia

There are some who suggest that, if we assist the Chinese Communists to wax strong, then they will eventually break with Soviet Russia and that that is our best hope for the future.

No doubt there are basic power rivalries between Russia and China in Asia. But also the Russian and Chinese Communist parties are bound together by close ideological ties.

Perhaps, if the ambitions of the Chinese Communists are inflated by successes, they might eventually clash with Soviet Russia. Perhaps, too, if the Axis Powers had won the Second World War, they would have fallen out among themselves. But no one suggested that we should tolerate and even assist an Axis victory because in the end they would quarrel over the booty—of which we would be part.

Conclusion

We seek to appraise our China policies with an open mind and without emotion, except for a certain indignation at the prolonged and cruel abuse of American citizens in China. We have no feeling whatsoever that change is to be avoided merely in the interest of consistency or because change might be interpreted as admitting past error.

We always take into account the possibility of influencing the Communist regime to better ways if we had diplomatic relations with it, or if, without that, we had commercial and cultural contacts with it. But the experience of those who now recognize and deal with the Chinese Communist regime convinces us that, under present conditions, neither recognition, nor trade, nor cultural relations, nor all three, would favorably influence the evolution of affairs in China. The probable result, internally, would be the opposite of what we hope for.

Internationally the Chinese Communist regime does not conform to the practices of civilized nations; does not live up to its international obligations; has not been peaceful in the past and gives no evidence of being peaceful in the future. Its foreign policies are hostile to us and our Asian allies. Under these circumstances it would be folly for us to establish relations with the Chinese Communists which would enhance their ability to hurt us and our friends.

*   *   *

We can confidently assume that international communism's rule of strict conformity is, in China as elsewhere, a passing and not a perpetual phase. We owe it to ourselves, our allies, and the Chinese people to do all that we can to contribute to that passing.

If we believed that this passing would be promoted by trade and cultural relations, then we would have such relations.

If we believed that this passing would be promoted by our having diplomatic relations with the present regime, then we would have such relations.

If we believed that this passing would be promoted by some participation of the present regime in the activities of the United Nations, then we would not oppose that.

We should be, and we are, constantly testing our policies, to be as certain as we can be that, in the light of conditions as they from time to time are, our policies shall serve the great purposes to which our Nation has been dedicated since its foundation—the cause of peace, justice, and human liberty.

Our policies are readily adjustable to meet the requirements of changing conditions. But there are occasions when not we but others should provide the change. Nothing could be more dangerous than for the United States to operate on the theory that, if hostile and evil forces do not quickly or readily change, then it is we who must change to meet them.

The United States exerts an immense influence in the world today, not only because it is powerful but because we stand for peace, for national independence, and personal liberty. Many free nations seek to coordinate their foreign policies with ours. Such coordination is indeed indispensable if the free world is to have the cohesion needed to make it safe. But United States policies will never serve as rallying points for free peoples if the impression is created that our policies are subject to change to meet Communist wishes for no reason other than that communism does not want to change. If communism is stubborn for the wrong, let us be steadfast for the right.

The capacity to change is an indispensable capacity. Equally indispensable is the capacity to hold fast that which is good. Given those qualities, we can hopefully look forward to the day when those in Asia who are yet free can confidently remain free and when the people of China and the people of America can resume their long history of cooperative friendship.

I. State Department Announcements on Trade with Communist China*

April 20, 1957

The United States has been repeatedly pressed by some of its allies to relax controls on trade with Communist China to the same level as those which apply to trade with the Soviet bloc.

We have been and are unwilling to agree to any relaxation which would result in an increased flow of strategic goods to Communist China. At the time of the Korean war, when the United Nations forces were attacked by the Chinese

*Ibid., May 13, 1957, pp. 722-23.

Communists, the United Nations established an embargo on shipment of strategic goods to Communist China. Communist China is still hostile, and controls have continued.

Heretofore, our allies have agreed to multilateral controls on trade with Communist China considerably more severe than on trade with the rest of the communist bloc.

In an effort to meet the views of its allies and at the same time continue to maintain effective multilateral trade controls, the United States has informed the 14 nations which participate with it in multilateral controls that it is prepared to discuss certain modifications in the existing system.

The U.S. proposal was made to the embassies of the 14 countries in Washington during the past week.

Under this proposal certain items for peaceful use which now are embargoed by the multilateral control system for shipment to Communist China would be removed from controls and would be placed on the same basis as in the case of trade with the European Soviet bloc. Certain other items now embargoed to Communist China would continue under embargo and would be transferred to the European Soviet-bloc list but under a lesser degree of control.

The proposal would also involve a tightening of the "exceptions" procedure now in use.

It was emphasized to our allies that there is no change in United States policy with respect to trade with Communist China. The United States will continue its unilateral embargo on all trade with Communist China.

May 30, 1957*

The United Kingdom has decided that it can no longer agree to maintain a level of security controls over its exports to Communist China more severe than the multilateral controls applied to the U.S.S.R. and the Soviet-bloc countries in Europe.

The United States is most disappointed by this action. It means that an agreement for the continuation of a differential trade control toward Communist China has not been reached, even though many of the nations which have been engaged in the recent talks on this subject expressed their support for such a program. For its part the United States contemplates no change in its policy of total embargo on trade with Communist China.

The recent discussions among the cooperating governments have revealed that there was a wish on the part of all countries to retain a unified approach on the question of trade controls on exports to Communist China. A majority of the countries, including the United States, sought a unanimous agreement on the maintenance of a differential. The United States believed that the security interests of the free world would be best promoted by the maintenance of a significant differential. After an initial difference of opinion on the precise extent of the differential, the United States agreed to a proposal developed by representatives of a number of the participating countries. This proposal obtained the support of a majority of the cooperating governments.

*   *   *

Ibid., June 17, 1957, pp. 967-68.

J. Comment by Acting Secretary of State Christian A. Herter on Travel by American Citizens in Communist China*

August 13, 1957

Dear Fellow Citizen: The Department of State has been informed that a number of United States citizens presently in Moscow have been invited to visit Communist China and that some of them have indicated an intention to accept the invitation. This letter is addressed only to those citizens of the United States who are contemplating such travel to or in Communist China.

The policy of the United States with respect to Communism in China, non-recognition of the Chinese Communist regime, and related matters has been recently restated by the Secretary of State in his address of June 28, 1957, at San Francisco. Generally speaking, it is not consistent with the policy of the United States, as approved by the President, that citizens of the United States travel to the areas of China under Communist control.

There are many reasons for this, and they are cumulative. They include the non-recognition of the regime; the existence of a quasi state of war and the continued application of the Trading with the Enemy Act; the refusal of Communist China to renounce the use of force; and the illegal jailing of Americans already in China despite promises to let them out.

Suffice it to say that those officials of your Government who are charged with responsibility in this matter have soberly and definitely come to the conclusion here expressed. Most of your fellow citizens—even those who may desire a change in some aspects of this policy—have accepted it. The Department of State has already received requests from parents requesting that their children be informed of their strong disapproval of any travel to Communist China.

For you to determine to travel to Communist China in violation of the declared policy of your Government is a serious matter, not to be undertaken lightly. By so doing, you will be violating the restriction plainly stamped in your passport. If you persist in violating this restriction, at the first possible opportunity your passport will be marked valid only for travel for direct return to the United States and your passport will be taken up when you do so return. In the event that you make application for a passport at a later date, your wilful violation of passport restrictions will be duly considered in connection with such application.

Your attention is further called to the fact that travel to and in Communist China at this time may well involve violation of regulations issued and enforced under the Trading with the Enemy Act, which constitutes a criminal offense under our law.

There may be some of you who feel that by going to Communist China and debating the position of Democracy as against Communism you may be doing a service in offsetting the propaganda efforts of others less well-intentioned. If you believe this, you are in error. By traveling to Communist China at this time you will, in the considered view of your Government, be acting as a willing

*Ibid., Sept. 2, 1957, p. 393.

tool of Communist propaganda intended, wherever possible, to subvert the foreign policy and the best interests of the United States, of which you are a citizen.

I request that you reconsider any intention or thought you may have had of going to Communist China at this time.

K. Department of State Memorandum on United States Policy Toward Communist China*

[Extract]

August 11, 1958

Policy toward Communist China has been an important issue since the Communists came to power there, and it is of critical significance to the United States and the free world today. In the United States the issue is a very real one to the vast majority of the people. As a result of Korean and Chinese Communist aggression in Korea, the United States suffered 142,000 casualties, bringing tragedy to communities all over the country. Nevertheless, despite the emotions thus engendered and the abhorrence of the American people for the brutality and utter lack of morality of Communist systems, the policy of the United States Government toward China has necessarily been based on objective considerations of national interest. It also reflects a continuing appraisal of all available facts.

Basically the United States policy of not extending diplomatic recognition to the Communist regime in China proceeds from the conviction that such recognition would produce no tangible benefits to the United States or to the free world as a whole and would be of material assistance to Chinese Communist attempts to extend Communist dominion throughout Asia. It is not an "inflexible" policy which cannot be altered to meet changed conditions. If the situation in the Far East were so to change in its basic elements as to call for a radically different evaluation of the threat Chinese Communist policies pose to United States and free-world security interests, the United States would of course readjust its present policies. However, the course of events in the Far East since the establishment of the Chinese Communist regime in 1949 has thus far confirmed the United States view that its interests and those of the free world are best served by withholding diplomatic recognition from the regime in Peiping.

The basic considerations on which United States policy toward China rests are twofold. First, the Soviet bloc, of which Communist China is an important part, is engaged in a long-range struggle to destroy the way of life of the free countries of the world and bring about the global dominion of communism. The Chinese Communist regime has made no secret of its fundamental hostility to the United States and the free world as a whole nor of its avowed intention to effect their downfall. Today its defiance of and attacks on the non-Communist

Ibid., Sept. 8, 1958, pp. 385-90.

world have reached a level of intensity that has not been witnessed since the Korean war. The second basic factor is that East Asia is peculiarly vulnerable to the Communist offensive because of the proximity of the free countries of that area to Communist China, the inexperience in self-government of those which have recently won their independence, their suspicions of the West inherited from their colonial past, and the social, political, and economic changes which inevitably accompany their drive toward modernization.

The Chinese Communists see the victory of communism in Asia as inevitable; and now that they control the vast population and territory of mainland China they are utilizing the advantages these give to encompass their ends. Chinese Communist leaders have shown by their words and their acts that they are not primarily interested in promoting the welfare of their people while living at peace with their neighbors. Their primary purpose is to extend the Communist revolution beyond their borders to the rest of Asia and thence to the rest of the world. Liu Shao-chi, the second-ranking member of the Chinese Communist Party has said: "The most fundamental and common duty of Communist Party members is to establish communism and transform the present world into a Communist world." Mao Tse-tung himself has said that his regime's policy is "to give active support to the national independence and liberation movements in countries in Asia, Africa, and Latin America." That these are not empty words was shown by Chinese Communist aggression in Korea and provision of arms and other assistance to the Communist rebels in Indochina.

United States policy in Asia, as elsewhere in the world, is to promote the domestic welfare and to strengthen the independence of free nations. Because of the proximity of many Asian nations to mainland China and the disparity in size and power between them and Communist China, this can be done only if the Communist threat is neutralized. The first need of United States policy in the Far East is to deter Communist aggression, else the free nations would be in grave danger of succumbing to Communist pressures before they had gathered the strength with which to resist them. The United States has sought to accomplish this by military assistance to the nations directly in the path of Chinese Communist expansion—Korea, Taiwan, and Viet-Nam—and by a system of mutual defense arrangements with other nations of the area. We have been successful in this effort, and since 1954 the Chinese Communists have not been able to make further gains through the open use of military force.

The measures the United States and its allies in Asia have taken to preserve the security of the free nations of the area are of vital interest to the other free nations of the world. Loss of the rest of East Asia to communism could have a disastrous effect on the free world's ability to resist effectively the encroachments of communism elsewhere. The consequences for Australia and New Zealand would be especially serious. Loss of the islands of the West Pacific and of the Southeast Asian peninsula would isolate these countries and place them in a strategically exposed and dangerous position.

Efforts to halt further Communist expansion cannot be confined to military deterrence alone. Countermeasures against Chinese Communist subversion and political infiltration are equally necessary. This is especially so as, since 1955,

Peiping has increasingly resorted to propaganda, subversion, "people's diplomacy," and political maneuvering in its dealings with its Asian neighbors. Peiping seeks to win by this means what it apparently does not dare attempt through military conquest. The United States therefore considers that in preserving the peace and security of Asia it is as important to be alert to the threat of subversion as to that of open military attack.

In the effort to block Peiping's attempts to extend Communist rule in Asia the withholding of diplomatic recognition is an important factor. The extension of diplomatic recognition by a great power normally carries with it not only increased access to international councils but enhanced international standing and prestige as well. Denial of recognition on the other hand is a positive handicap to the regime affected and one which makes it that much the more difficult for it to pursue its foreign policies with success. One basic purpose of United States nonrecognition of Communist China is to deny it these advantages and to that extent limit its ability to threaten the security of the area.

In the case of China there are special considerations which influence United States policy with regard to recognition. For one thing, although the Chinese Communists have seized the preponderant bulk of China, they have not completed their conquest of the country. The generally recognized legitimate Government of China continues to exist and in Taiwan is steadily developing its political, economic, and military strength. The Government of the Republic of China controls the strategic island of Taiwan and through its possession of a sizable military force—one of the largest on the side of the free world in Asia—presents a significant deterrent to renewed Chinese Communist aggression. Recognition of Communist China by the United States would seriously cripple, if not destroy altogether, that Government. On the other hand, continued United States recognition and support of the Republic of China enables it to challenge the claim of the Chinese Communists to represent the Chinese people and keeps alive the hopes of those Chinese who are determined eventually to free their country of Communist rule.

Recognition of Communist China by the United States would have an adverse effect on the other free governments of Asia which could be disastrous to the cause of the free world in that part of the world. Those nations which are closely allied to the United States and are striving to maintain their independence on the perimeter of Chinese Communist power, especially Korea and Viet-Nam, would be profoundly confused and demoralized. They would interpret such action as abandonment of their cause by the United States. They might reason that their only hope for survival lay in desperate measures, not caring whether these threatened the peace of the area and the world. Governments further removed from the borders of China would see in American recognition of Communist China the first step in the withdrawal of the United States from the Far East. Without the support of the United States they would be unable long to defy the will of Peiping; and some would probably conclude that their wisest course would be speedily to seek the best terms obtainable from Peiping. Needless to say, these developments would place the entire free world position in Asia in the gravest peril.

Another special consideration in the case of China is that large and influential "overseas" Chinese communities exist in most of the countries of Southeast Asia. The efforts of these countries to build healthy free societies and to develop their economies would be seriously retarded if these communities were to fall under the sway of the Chinese Communists; and a grave threat of Communist subversion through these overseas communities would arise. Recognition of Communist China by the United States and the decline in the fortunes of the Republic of China which would inevitably result would have such a profound psychological effect on the overseas Chinese that it would make inevitable the transfer of the loyalties of large numbers to the Communist side. This in turn would undermine the ability of the most countries to resist the pressures tending to promote the expansion of Chinese Communist influence and power.

Still another factor which must be considered in the case of China is the effect which recognition of the Communist regime would have on the United Nations. Recognition of Peiping by the United States would inevitably lead to the seating of Peiping in that body. In the view of the United States this would vitiate, if not destroy, the United Nations as an instrument for the maintenance of international peace. The Korean war was the first and most important effort to halt aggression through collective action in the United Nations. For Communist China, one of the parties against which the effort of the United Nations was directed, to be seated in the United Nations while still unpurged of its aggression and defying the will of the United Nations in Korea would amount to a confession of a failure on the part of the United Nations and would greatly reduce the prospects for future successful action by the United Nations against aggression. Moreover, the Republic of China is a charter member in good standing of the United Nations, and its representatives there have contributed importantly to the constructive work of that organization. If the representatives of the Chinese Communist regime were to be seated in their place and given China's veto in the Security Council, the ability of that body in the future to discharge the responsibility it has under the charter for the maintaining of international peace and security would be seriously impaired.

Those who advocate recognition of the Chinese Communists often assume that by the standards of international law applied to such cases the Peiping regime is "entitled" to diplomatic recognition. In the view of the United States diplomatic recognition is a privilege and not a right. Moreover, the United States considers that diplomatic recognition is an instrument of national policy which it is both its right and its duty to use in the enlightened self-interest of the nation. However, there is reason to doubt that even by the tests often cited in international law the Chinese Communist regime qualifies for diplomatic recognition. It does not rule all China, and there is a substantial force in being which contests its claim to do so. The Chinese Communist Party, which holds mainland China in its grip, a tiny minority comprising less than 2 percent of the Chinese people, and the regimentation, brutal repression, and forced sacrifices that have characterized its rule have resulted in extensive popular unrest. To paraphrase Thomas Jefferson's dictum, this regime certainly does not represent "the will of the populace, substantially declared." Finally, it has shown no intention to honor its international obligations. One of its first acts was to abrogate the treaties of the Republic of China, except those it chose to continue. On assuming power it carried out a virtual confiscation without compensation of the properties of foreign nationals, including immense British investments notwithstanding the United Kingdom's prompt recognition of it. It has failed to honor various commitments entered into since, including various provisions of the Korean armistice and the Geneva accord on Viet-Nam and Loas, as well as the agreed announcement of September 1955 by which it pledged itself to permit all Americans in China to return home "expeditiously."

The United States policy toward recognition of Communist China is then based on a carefully considered judgment of the national interest. Nonrecognition of Peiping coupled with continued recognition and support of the Republic of China facilitates the accomplishment of United States policy objectives in the Far East. Recognition of Peiping would seriously hinder accomplishment of these objectives and would facilitate the advance of Communist power in Asia.

In the process of determining its policy toward China the United States has taken into account the various statements and arguments advanced by proponents of extending diplomatic recognition to Peiping. One of the most commonly advanced reasons for recognition is that reality must be "recognized" and 600 million people cannot be "ignored." While superficially appealing, both statements themselves overlook the realities of the situation. United States policy is, of course, based on full appreciation of the fact that the Chinese Communist regime is currently in control of mainland China. However, it is not necessary to have diplomatic relations with a regime in order to deal with it. Without extending diplomatic recognition the United States has participated in extended negotiations with Chinese Communist representatives, in the Korean and Indochina armistice negotiations, and more recently in the ambassadorial talks in Geneva. Similarly, United States policy in no sense "ignores" the existence and the aspirations of the Chinese people. Its attitude toward the people of China remains what it historically has been, one of friendship and sympathetic understanding. It is nonetheless clear that our friendship for the Chinese people must not be permitted to blind us to the threat to our security which the Communist regime in China now presents. Moreover, the United States is convinced that the Chinese Communist regime does not represent the true will or aspirations of the Chinese people and that our policy of withholding recognition from it is in actuality in their ultimate interest.

*   *   *

An argument often heard is that the Chinese Communists are here "to stay"; that they will have to be recognized sooner or later; and that it would be the course of wisdom to bow to the inevitable now rather than be forced to do so ungracefully at a later date. It is true that there is no reason to believe that the Chinese Communist regime is on the verge of collapse; but there is equally no reason to accept its present rule in mainland China as permanent. In fact, unmistakable signs of dissatisfaction and unrest in Communist China have appeared in the "ideological remodeling" and the mass campaign against "rightists" which have been in progress during the past year. Dictatorships often create an illusion of permanence from the very fact that they suppress and still all opposition, and that of the Chinese Communists is no exception to this rule. The United States holds the view that communism's rule in China is not permanent and that it one day will pass. By withholding diplomatic recognition from Peiping it seeks to hasten that passing.

In public discussions of China policy one of the proposals that has attracted widest attention is that known as the "two Chinas solution'." Briefly, advocates of this arrangement propose that the Chinese Communist regime be recognized as the government of mainland China while the Government at Taipei remains as the legal government of Taiwan. They argue that this approach to the Chinese problem has the merit of granting the Communists only what they already control while retaining for the free world the militarily strategic bastion of Taiwan. However, it overlooks or ignores certain facts of basic importance. The Republic of China would not accept any diminution of its sovereignty over China and could be expected to resist such an arrangement with all the means at its disposal. If a "two Chinas solution" were to be forcefully imposed against its will, that Government's effectiveness as a loyal ally to the free-world-cause would be destroyed. Peiping, too, would reject such an arrangement. In fact, over the past year Chinese Communist propaganda has repeatedly and stridently denounced the "two Chinas" concept and, ironically, has been accusing the United States Government of attempting to put it into effect. Peiping attaches great importance to the eventual acquisition of Taiwan and has consistently reserved what it calls its "right" to seize Taiwan by force if other means fail. There is no prospect that it would ever acquiesce in any arrangements which would lead to the permanent detachment of Taiwan from China.

The "two Chinas" concept is bitterly opposed by both Peiping and Taipei. Hence, even if such a solution could be imposed by outside authority, it would not be a stable one. Constant policing would be required to avert its violent overthrow by one side or the other.

It is sometimes said that nonrecognition of Peiping tends to martyrize the Chinese Communists, thereby enabling them to pose, especially before Asian neutralists, as an innocent and injured party. It would be impossible to deny that there is some truth in this. But this disadvantage is far outweighed by the disadvantages that would result from following the opposite course. It is surely better that some neutralists, who are either unable or unwilling to comprehend the threat inherent in Chinese Communist policies, mistakenly consider Peiping unjustly treated than that the allies of the United States in Asia, who are the first line of defense against Chinese Communist expansion, should be confused and demoralized by what to them could only appear to be a betrayal of the common cause.

AMBASSADORIAL TALKS BETWEEN THE UNITED STATES AND COMMUNIST CHINA

L. Letter from U.S. Representative at the Geneva Talks to the Representative of the People's Republic of China*

March 12, 1958

I have received your letter of January 14, 1958, addressed to Ambassador Johnson. As Ambassador Johnson explained at his meeting with you on December 12, 1957, he has been transferred to a new post, and I have been designated as the United States representative.

You are correct in recollecting that the decision in 1955 to elevate the talks previously held between consular officers of the United States and the People's Republic of China to the ambassadorial level reflected the hope that the question of return of civilians of both countries would thereby be more easily resolved and that further discussion and settlement of other practical matters at issue between our two sides would be facilitated. I also fully concur in your assertion that for more than two years the talks have not been satisfactory. I must emphatically reject, however, your suggestion that the failure of the talks to fulfill the hope with which they were undertaken has been caused by the attitude of the United States. In actuality, it has been the attitude of your side and its unwillingness to live up to its pledged word that has resulted in the sterility of the talks.

On September 10, 1955, you and Ambassador Johnson agreed upon and made public an agreed announcement concerning the return of civilians of both sides, in which the People's Republic of China undertook to adopt appropriate measures so that Americans in that country who desired to do so could expeditiously exercise their right to return to the United States. At the time of this announcement, out of the group of 41 Americans whose return had been the subject of the discussions leading up to the announcement, 19 still remained to be freed from prison or house arrest. Today, almost two and one-half years later, your side continues to hold six American citizens against their will in clear contravention of its unmistakable commitment under the announcement. In marked contrast, the United States has permitted all Chinese in the United States who desired to return to the People's Republic of China to do so. Under the terms of the agreed announcement any Chinese in the United States who believes that he is being obstructed from returning to the People's Republic of China can so inform the Embassy of the Republic of India in the United States and request it to make representations on his behalf to the United States Government. The fact that not one single case of such representations by the Embassy of the Republic of India has occurred provides irrefutable evidence that no Chinese in the United States has been or is being obstructed from returning to the People's Republic of China.

As Ambassador Johnson stated on December 12, 1957, the United States

*American Foreign Policy: Current Documents, 1958, pp. 1131-32.

is not able at this time to designate a representative of ambassadorial rank. However, this matter is being given careful consideration, and I am confident that a United States representative of such rank will be designated as soon as feasible. Meanwhile, I stand ready as the designated United States representative to meet in Geneva at a mutually convenient time with you or such other representative as your government may desire to name.

M. Nationalist Chinese Statement on Resumption of Talks*

[Extract]

June 30, 1958

More than half a year has passed since the U.S. Government suspended the Sino-American ambassadorial talks. The Chinese Government considers that this state of affairs should not continue. The U.S. ruling circles have been playing all sorts of tricks in an attempt to create the false impression that the Sino-American talks are still continuing in order to cover up its continued occupation of China's territory of Taiwan and its activities to create world tension. Such sinister designs must not be allowed to bear fruit. The Chinese Government agreed to hold the Sino-American ambassadorial talks with the aim of settling questions. The U.S. Government must answer clearly whether it is sincere about the talks.

Since December 12, 1957, when the U.S. Government broke the agreement between China and the United States on holding talks on an ambassadorial level by refusing to designate a representative of ambassadorial rank, thereby suspending the talks, the Chinese side, on January 14 and March 26, 1958 repeatedly urged the U.S. Government to designate a representative with the rank of ambassador to resume the talks. The U.S. Government, however, not only refused to do this but did not even consider it necessary to reply to the March 26 letter of the Chinese side. Moreover, a spokesman of the State Department of the United States recently even remarked nonchalantly that a First Secretary of its foreign service was ready to hold talks with us at any time, as if there had never been an agreement between China and the United States on the holding of talks on an ambassadorial level. This cannot but rouse the indignation of the Chinese people.

The imperialistic attitude consistently maintained by the United States is proven by the record of nearly three years of the Sino-American ambassadorial talks. The U.S. occupation of China's territory of Taiwan created tension in the Taiwan area. This is a naked act of aggression against China and the Chinese people have every right to take any measures to repulse it. Nevertheless, the Chinese side, in order to relax the tension in the Taiwan area, expressed its willingness to sit down and talk matters over with the United States and, during the Sino-American ambassadorial talks, put forward a series of reasonable proposals for the peaceful settlement of the international disputes between China

*Peking Review, July 8, 1958, pp. 21-22.

and the United States in the Taiwan area. But the American side rejected all these proposals. They attempted to confuse China's domestic affair, a matter between the Chinese Government and the Taiwan local authorities, with the international disputes between China and the United States in the Taiwan area, and demanded that China give up its right of exercising sovereignty over its own territory and recognize the right of "self-defense" for the United States on China's territory. This demonstrates clearly that the aim of the United States is not to relax the tension in the Taiwan area at all, but to insist that China recognize the status quo of U.S. occupation of Taiwan and to maintain and heighten tension. It is due to the imperialist policy of the United States that discussion on this crucial question of Sino-American relations has bogged down since the latter part of 1956.

In order to break the deadlock and gradually improve Sino-American relations, the Chinese side further put forward a series of proposals on certain questions that are comparatively easy to settle, such as removing the trade barriers between the two countries, eliminating the obstacles in the way of mutual contacts and cultural exchange between the two peoples, exchanging correspondents for news coverage on an equal and reciprocal basis and rendering judicial assistance between the two countries. Although questions such as the entry of correspondents for news coverage and judicial assistance were first raised by those concerned on the American side to those concerned on the Chinese side, and all the proposals of the Chinese side were fully in accord with the principles of equality and mutual benefit, the U.S. Government nonetheless rejected them. What is even more intolerable is the fact that the United States, in disregard of the agreement reached in 1955 on the return of civilians of both sides, continues to detain thousands upon thousands of Chinese civilians in the United States and prevent them from returning to their motherland.

Irrefutable facts show that what the United States was after in the Sino-American ambassadorial talks was by no means a peaceful settlement of the international disputes between China and the United States on the basis of equality and mutual respect for territorial integrity and sovereignty, but to impose its imperialist will on the Chinese people and, failing that, to make use of the ambassadorial talks to deceive the people of the world and cover up its sinister designs to continue its aggression against China and to create international tension. During the past three years, the United States has been intensifying its interference and control of all aspects of life in Taiwan, establishing on it bases for guided missiles to threaten the Chinese people and utilizing the reactionary clique in Taiwan to carry out subversive activities and armed intervention against Southeast Asian countries. At the same time, the United States is endeavouring to bring about, at many international conferences and organizations, a situation of "two Chinas," to create eventually such a *fait accompli* in the international arena, and thereby to prolong its occupation of Taiwan. This is the crux of the reason for the failure of the Sino-American ambassadorial talks to make progress. U.S. Secretary of State Dulles recently declared that it is in the best interests of the United States to persist in its policy of enmity towards the People's Republic of China but that it will deal with China when its interest so demands. This demonstrates most clearly that, in the minds of the U.S. ruling circles, the Sino-American ambassadorial talks are but a means serving the imperialist policy of the United States. The reason China agreed to hold the ambassadorial talks was to try by peaceful means to eliminate armed aggression and the threat of force in the Taiwan area on the part of the United States. However, the Chinese people are by no means afraid of U.S. aggression, and there is no reason whatsoever why they should pine for talks with the United States. Building socialism with lightning speed, the Chinese people are perfectly strong enough to liberate their territory of Taiwan. No force on earth can stop the great cause of the Chinese people in building up and uniting their motherland. The handful of U.S. imperialists can only suffer isolation and defeat from their policy of enmity towards the 600 million Chinese people.

*   *   *

THE TAIWAN STRAITS CRISIS

N. Comment by Secretary Dulles*

September 4, 1958

I have reviewed in detail with the President the serious situation which has resulted from aggressive Chinese Communist military actions in the Taiwan (Formosa) Straits area. The President has authorized me to make the following statement.

1. Neither Taiwan (Formosa) nor the islands of Quemoy and Matsu have ever been under the authority of the Chinese Communists. Since the end of the Second World War, a period of over 13 years, they have continuously been under the authority of Free China, that is, the Republic of China.

2. The United States is bound by treaty to help to defend Taiwan (Formosa) from armed attack and the President is authorized by Joint Resolution of the Congress to employ the armed forces of the United States for the securing and protecting of related positions such as Quemoy and Matsu.

3. Any attempt on the part of the Chinese Communists now to seize these positions or any of them would be a crude violation of the principles upon which world order is based, namely, that no country should use armed force to seize new territory.

4. The Chinese Communists have, for about 2 weeks, been subjecting Quemoy to heavy artillery bombardment and, by artillery fire and use of small naval craft, they have been harassing the regular supply of the civilian and military population of the Quemoys, which totals some 125 thousand persons. The official Peiping radio repeatedly announces the purpose of these military operations to be to take by armed force Taiwan (Formosa), as well as Quemoy

**Department of State Bulletin*, Sept. 22, 1958, pp. 445-46.

and Matsu. In virtually every Peiping broadcast Taiwan (Formosa) and the off-shore islands are linked as the objective of what is called the "Chinese Peoples Liberation Army."

5. Despite, however, what the Chinese Communists say, and so far have done, it is not yet certain that their purpose is in fact to make an all-out effort to conquer by force Taiwan (Formosa) and the offshore islands. Neither is it apparent that such efforts as are being made, or may be made, cannot be contained by the courageous, and purely defensive, efforts of the forces of the Republic of China, with such substantial logistical support as the United States is providing.

6. The Joint Resolution of Congress, above referred to, includes a finding to the effect that "the secure possession by friendly governments of the Western Pacific Island chain, of which Formosa is a part, is essential to the vital interests of the United States and all friendly nations in and bordering upon the Pacific Ocean." It further authorizes the President to employ the Armed Forces of the United States for the protection not only of Formosa but for "the securing and protection of such related positions and territories of that area now in friendly hands and the taking of such other measures as he judges to be required or appropriate in assuring the defense of Formosa." In view of the situation outlined in the preceding paragraph, the President has not yet made any finding under that Resolution that the employment of the Armed Forces of the United States is required or appropriate in insuring the defense of Formosa. The President would not, however, hesitate to make such a finding if he judged that the circumstances made this necessary to accomplish the purposes of the Joint Resolution. In this connection, we have recognized that the securing and protecting of Quemoy and Matsu have increasingly become related to the defense of Taiwan (Formosa). This is indeed also recognized by the Chinese Communists. Military dispositions have been made by the United States so that a Presidential determination, if made, would be followed by action both timely and effective.

7. The President and I earnestly hope that the Chinese Communist regime will not again, as in the case of Korea, defy the basic principle upon which world order depends, namely, that armed force should not be used to achieve territorial ambitions. Any such naked use of force would pose an issue far transcending the offshore islands and even the security of Taiwan (Formosa). It would forecast a widespread use of force in the Far East which would endanger vital free world positions and the security of the United States. Acquiescence therein would threaten peace everywhere. We believe that the civilized world community will never condone overt military conquest as a legitimate instrument of policy.

8. The United States has not, however, abandoned hope that Peiping will stop short of defying the will of mankind for peace. This would not require it to abandon its chains, however ill-founded we may deem them to be. I recall that in the extended negotiations which the representatives of the United States and Chinese Communist regime conducted at Geneva between 1955 and 1958, a sustained effort was made by the United States to secure, with particular reference to the Taiwan area, a declaration of mutual and reciprocal renunciation of force, except in self-defense, which, however, would be without prejudice

to the pursuit of policies by peaceful means. The Chinese Communists rejected any such declaration. We believe, however, that such a course of conduct constitutes the only civilized and acceptable procedure. The United States intends to follow that course, so far as it is concerned, unless and until the Chinese Communists, by their acts, leave us no choice but to react in defense of the principles to which all peace-loving governments are dedicated.

O. Chinese Communist Comment*

[Extract]

September 6, 1958

Taiwan and the Penghu Islands [Pescadores] have been China's territories from ancient times. Following the Second World War, they were restored to China after being occupied by Japan for a period of time. It is entirely China's internal affair for the Chinese people to exercise their sovereign right to liberate these areas. This is the Chinese people's sacred and inviolable right. The United States Government itself also declared formally that it would not get involved in China's civil conflict in the Taiwan area. Were it not for the fact that the United States Government later went back on its own statement and carried out armed intervention, Taiwan and the Penghu Islands would have long been liberated and placed under the administration of the Government of the People's Republic of China. These are undeniable facts recognized by fair-minded world public opinion unanimously.

United States support of the Chiang Kai-shek clique entrenched on Taiwan and the Penghu Islands, which has long been repudiated by all the Chinese people, and its direct occupation of Taiwan and the Penghu Islands by armed force constitute unlawful interference in China's internal affairs and infringement of China's territorial integrity and sovereignty, and are in direct conflict with the United Nations Charter and all codes of international law.

*   *   *

P. Nikita Khrushchev, Chairman of the Council of Ministers of the U.S.S.R., to President Eisenhower*

[Extract].

September 7, 1958

Mr. President: I am addressing myself to you on a question of great importance which, we are sure, is now occupying the minds of all to whom the cause of peace is dear.

*Peking Review, Sept. 9, 1958, pp. 15-16.

*Department of State Bulletin, Sept. 29, 1958, pp. 499-503.

As a result of the policy being carried on by the USA in regard to China, and especially of the actions being undertaken at the present time by American Government in the area of the Chinese island of Taiwan and of the Taiwan Straits, a dangerous situation has arisen in the Far East. Humanity has again been put before the direct threat of the beginning of a military conflagration.

In this responsible moment, the Government of the Soviet Union has decided to turn to the Government of the USA with an appeal to show sense, not to permit steps which could entail irreparable consequences.

You well know, Mr. President, that the Soviet Union stands firmly on the position of the peaceful coexistence of all states, regardless of their social or state structure, and is in favor of not allowing the beginning of military conflicts, in order to assure conditions for a peaceful life for peoples on the whole globe. I think no one will dispute that the principles of peaceful coexistence have already received broad international recognition, and it can be said that for the overwhelming majority of states, they are the basis of their relations with other countries.

Nevertheless, in the postwar years, as a result of the policy of the USA, a deeply abnormal situation has been continuously maintained in the Far East, the cause of which is the aggressive policy of the Government of the USA, a policy of war. The main reason for the tense and, it must be directly said, very very dangerous situation which has arisen is that the USA has seized age-old Chinese territory—the island of Taiwan with the Pescadores Islands—by force, is continuing to occupy these territories, cloaking this occupation with references to its support of the traitor of the Chinese people, Chiang Kai-shek, and is also trying to extend its aggression to the offshore Chinese islands.

As the Soviet Government has already stated many times in the organization of the United Nations, as well as in correspondence with the Government of the USA and governments of other powers, the situation is also inadmissible that a great state—The Chinese People's Republic—as a result of the position taken by the Government of the USA, is deprived of the opportunity to participate in the work of the organization of the United Nations, and is not represented in that organization, although it has a legitimate right to this.

You also know as well as I do that the Chinese state is one of the founders of the UN and that by force of that circumstance alone the existing situation is absolutely abnormal and deeply unjust in regard to the Chinese people.

The situation which has now arisen as a result of the actions of the USA in the area of the island of Taiwan and of the Taiwan Straits seriously disturbs the Soviet Government and the people. Indeed, I think, it will not be an exaggeration to say that it disturbs the whole world, every country, regardless of at what distance it is located from the Taiwan area. If you look squarely at the truth, you must acknowledge that the USA is trying to assume the functions of some sort of world gendarme in this area too. We think that for any state, regardless how strong and influential it is, to take such a role on itself is an unworthy affair for a civilized state and quite risky.

The Government of the USA is carrying out military demonstrations trying to prevent the liberation of Taiwan and to keep this Chinese island as its military base, aimed above all against the Chinese People's Republic, and also to hinder the lawful actions of the CPR directed at the liberation of the offshore island on which Chiang Kai-shekists have ensconced themselves.

In the area of the Taiwan Straits, there is one of the strongest naval units of the American Navy—the Seventh Fleet of the USA. Hasty measures are being taken to strengthen this fleet, and military vessels and aviation are being transferred to the Far East from the USA, the Mediterranean Sea, and other areas. More than that, it has been announced that in the next few days "joint maneuvers" of the naval forces and marines of the USA and Chiang Kai-shek clique will be carried out in the Taiwan area, and that new contingents of American troops are being transferred to Taiwan on this pretext. The question arises whether such actions in the present situation can be assessed as other than an open provocation. It seems to us that with the most indulgent approach no other evaluation can be given to these actions.

It must be said that, in general, the practice of urgently transferring naval vessels of the USA from one place to another has become a frequent phenomena recently. In truth, by the direction of movement of the American Naval Fleet one can now judge almost without error to what place will be directed the spearhead of the next blackmail and provocations.

Very recently the world was a witness to similar demonstrations of the American Navy in the Mediterranean Sea when the armed intervention of the USA into Lebanon was carried out and when the Sixth Fleet of the USA held the capital of Lebanon, and indeed that whole country, under the muzzles of its guns. When today attempts are being made to rattle the saber and threaten China, then, it seems to us, one should not forget that China is not small Lebanon which recently fell victim to foreign intervention, which has met universal condemnation at the just concluded special session of the UN General Assembly. The great 600 million Chinese people are powerful and unconquerable not only for their inexhaustible resources, but also for their solidarity in support of the government, and are confidently and firmly moving on the path of the further development and strengthening of their country, the raising of their welfare, at which we, Soviet people, are truly happy and at which all those who wish the Chinese people well cannot but be happy. But I would want to emphasize not only this side of the matter, but also that China is not alone; it has true friends ready to go to its aid at any moment in case of aggression against China, since the interests of the security of People's China are inseparable from the interests of the security of the Soviet Union.

*　　　　　*　　　　　*

Nearly every day political and military leaders of the USA come out with threats addressed to People's China. Such and only such a meaning have the repeated statements of USA Secretary of State Dulles about the activities of the USA in the region of the Taiwan Straits and in particular the statement which he made in your and his name on 4 September. This statement cannot but evoke the most decisive condemnation. It represents an open attempt of crude and unceremoinious trampling of the sovereign rights of other states. The Government of the USA having no rights for this permits itself arbitrarily to establish some kind of boundary of its interests and the sphere of operations of its armed forces on the territory of China. Such activities it is impossible to qualify otherwise than as aggressive, which undoubtedly will be condemned by all peoples.

*   *   *

Military leaders in the USA try even, with the tacit agreement of the American Government, to resort to atomic blackmail in relation to China, acting evidently still on inertia under the impression of the moods governing in Washington in that short period in the course of which the USA had at its disposal a monopoly of the atomic weapons. As is known, even at that time the policy of atomic blackmail did not have and could not have any success. Is it necessary to say that in present conditions when the USA has long not been the possessor of a monopoly in the field of atomic armaments, attempts to intimidate other states by atomic weapons are a completely hopeless business.

*   *   *

The Chinese people wants peace and defends peace but it does not fear war. If war will be thrust on China, whose people are full of determination to defend its rightful cause, then we have not the slightest doubt that the Chinese people will give a worthy rebuff to the aggressor.

*   *   *

The American people in the past itself had to beat off attempts of foreign powers to interfere in its internal affairs and by force of arms to impose their will on it. It is well known that these attempts ended lamentably for those who undertook them. Would it not be right to draw the appropriate conclusions from this historical experience of the United States and end the policy of interference in the internal affairs of China? Indeed if national independence is dear to the American people, then why should it be less dear to the Chinese people, as well as to any other people?

It is possible you will find what I have said above as harsh. But I do not permit myself to agree with this. In this letter to you, as also on other occasions, I simply wish to express myself frankly and to emphasize the whole danger of the situation developing in the region of Taiwan and the Chinese offshore islands as a result of actions of the USA. If we were to hide our thoughts behind outwardly polite diplomatic formulations, then, I think it would be more difficult to understand each other. Moreover, we desire, that you, the Government of the USA and the whole American people with whom we wish only good relations and friendship should have a correct idea about those consequences which the present actions of the USA in the Far East might have. It would be a serious miscalculation if in the United States the conclusion were drawn that it was possible to deal with China in accordance with the example as it was done by certain powers in the past. Such kind of miscalculation might have serious consequences for the cause of peace in the whole world. Therefore let us introduce into the question full clarity because reservations and misunderstandings in such affairs are most dangerous.

An attack on the Chinese People's Republic, which is a great friend, ally and neighbor of our country, is an attack on the Soviet Union. True to its duty, our country will do everything in order together with People's China to defend the security of both states, the interests of peace in the Far East, the interest of peace in the whole world.

*   *   *

Q. Address by President Eisenhower*

[Extract]

September 11, 1958

My friends: Tonight I want to talk to you about the situation, dangerous to peace, which has developed in the Formosa Straits in the Far East. My purpose is to give you its basic facts and then my conclusions as to our Nations' proper course of action.

To begin, let us remember that traditionally this country and its Government have always been passionately devoted to peace and honor, as they are now. We shall never resort to force in settlement of differences except when compelled to do so to defend against aggression and to protect our vital interests.

This means that, in our view, negotiations and conciliation should never be abandoned in favor of force and strife. While we shall never timidly retreat before the threat of armed aggression, we would welcome in the present circumstances negotiations that could have a fruitful result in preserving the peace of the Formosa area and reaching a solution that could be acceptable to all parties concerned, including, of course, our ally, the Republic of China.

Bombardment of Quemoy and Matsu

On the morning of August 23d the Chinese Communists opened a severe bombardment of Quemoy, an island in the Formosan Straits off the China coast. Another island in the same area, Matsu, was also attacked. These two islands have always been a part of Free China—never under Communist control.

This bombardment of Quemoy has been going on almost continuously ever since. Also, Chinese Communists have been using their naval craft to try to break up the supplying of Quemoy with its 125,000 people. Their normal source of supply is by sea from Formosa, where the Government of Free China is now located.

*Ibid., pp. 481-84.

Chinese Communists say that they will capture Quemoy. So far they have not actually attempted a landing, but their bombardment has caused great damage. Over 1,000 people have been killed or wounded. In large part these are civilians.

This is a tragic affair. It is shocking that in this day and age naked force should be used for such aggressive purposes.

But this is not the first time that the Chinese Communists have acted in this way.

In 1950 they attacked and tried to conquer the Republic of Korea. At that time President Truman announced the intention of protecting Formosa, the principal area still held by Free China, because of the belief that Formosa's safety was vital to the security of the United States and the free world. Our Government has adhered firmly ever since 1950 to that policy.

In 1953 and 1954 the Chinese Communists took an active part in the war in Indochina against Viet-Nam.

In the fall of 1954 they attacked Quemoy and Matsu, the same two islands they are attacking now. They broke off that attack when, in January 1955, the Congress and I agreed that we should firmly support Free China.

Since then, for about 4 years, Chinese Communists have not used force for aggressive purposes. We have achieved an armistice in Korea which stopped the fighting there in 1953. There is a 1954 armistice in Viet-Nam; and since 1955 there has been quiet in the Formosa Straits area. We had hoped that the Chinese Communists were becoming peaceful—but it seems not.

So the world is again faced with the problem of armed aggression. Powerful dictatorships are attacking an exposed, but free, area.

What should we do?

Shall we take the position that, submitting to threat, it is better to surrender pieces of free territory in the hope that this will satisfy the appetite of the aggressor and we shall have peace?

Do we not still remember that the name of "Munich" symbolizes a vain hope of appeasing dictators?

At that time the policy of appeasement was tried, and it failed. Prior to the Second World War, Mussolini seized Ethiopia. In the Far East Japanese warlords were grabbing Manchuria by force. Hitler sent his armed forces into the Rhineland in violation of the Versailles Treaty. Then he annexed little Austria. When he got away with that, he next turned to Czechoslovakia and began taking it bit by bit.

In the face of all these attacks on freedom by the dictators, the powerful democracies stood aside. It seemed that Ethiopia and Manchuria were too far away and too unimportant to fight about. In Europe appeasement was looked upon as the way to peace. The democracies felt that, if they tried to stop what was going on, that would mean war. But, because of these repeated retreats, war came just the same.

If the democracies had stood firm at the beginning, almost surely there would have been no World War. Instead they gave such an appearance of weakness and timidity that aggressive rulers were encouraged to overrun one country after another. In the end the democracies saw that their very survival was at stake. They had no alternative but to turn and fight in what proved to be the most terrible war that the world has ever known.

I know something about that war, and I never want to see that history repeated. But, my fellow Americans, it certainly can be repeated if the peace-loving democratic nations again fearfully practice a policy of standing idly by while big aggressors use armed force to conquer the small and weak.

Let us suppose that the Chinese Communists conquer Quemoy. Would that be the end of the story? We know that it would not be the end of the story. History teaches that, when powerful despots can gain something through aggression, they try, by the same methods, to gain more and more and more.

Also, we have more to guide us than the teachings of history. We have the statements, the boastings, of the Chinese Communists themselves. They frankly say that their present military effort is part of a program to conquer Formosa.

It is as certain as can be that the shooting which the Chinese Communists started on August 23d had as its purpose not just the taking of the island of Quemoy. It is part of what is indeed an ambitious plan of armed conquest.

This plan would liquidate all of the free-world positions in the Western Pacific area and bring them under captive governments which would be hostile to the United States and the free world. Thus the Chinese and Russian Communists would come to dominate at least the western half of the now friendly Pacific Ocean.

So aggression by ruthless despots again imposes a clear danger to the United States and to the free world.

In this effort the Chinese Communists and the Soviet Union appear to be working hand in hand. Last Monday I received a long letter on this subject from Prime Minister Krushchev. He warned the United States against helping its allies in the Western Pacific. He said that we should not support the Republic of China and the Republic of Korea. He contended that we should desert them, return all of our naval forces to our home bases, and leave our friends in the Far East to face, alone, the combined military power of the Soviet Union and Communist China.

Does Mr. Khrushchev think that we have so soon forgotten Korea?

I must say to you very frankly and soberly, my friends, the United States cannot accept the result that the Communists seek. Neither can we show, now, a weakness of purpose—a timidity—which would surely lead them to move more aggressively against us and our friends in the Western Pacific area.

If the Chinese Communists have decided to risk a war, it is not because Quemoy itself is so valuable to them. They have been getting along without Quemoy ever since they seized the China mainland 9 years ago.

If they have now decided to risk a war, it can only be because they, and their Soviet allies, have decided to find out whether threatening war is a policy from which they can make big gains.

If that is their decision, then a Western Pacific "Munich" would not buy us peace or security. It would encourage the aggressors. It would dismay our friends and allies there. If history teaches anything, appeasement would make it more likely that we would have to fight a major war.

Security of Western Pacific Vital to U.S.

Congress has made clear its recognition that the security of the Western Pacific is vital to the security of the United States and that we should be firm. The Senate has ratified, by overwhelming vote, security treaties with the Republic of China covering Formosa and the Pescadores, and also the Republic of Korea. We have a mutual security treaty with the Republic of the Philippines, which could be next in line for conquest if Formosa fell into hostile hands. These treaties commit the United States to the defense of the treaty areas. In addition, there is a joint resolution which the Congress passed in January 1955 dealing specifically with Formosa and the offshore islands of Free China in the Formosa Straits.

At that time the situation was similar to what it is today.

Congress then voted the President authority to employ the armed forces of the United States for the defense not only of Formosa but of related positions, such as Quemoy and Matsu, if I believed their defense to be appropriate in assuring the defense of Formosa.

I might add that the mandate from the Congress was given by an almost unanimous bipartisan vote.

Today, the Chinese Communists announce, repeatedly and officially, that their military operations against Quemoy are preliminary to attack on Formosa. So it is clear that the Formosa Straits resolution of 1955 applies to the present situation.

If the present bombardment and harassment of Quemoy should be converted into a major assault, with which the local defenders could not cope, then we would be compelled to face precisely the situation that Congress visualized in 1955.

I have repeatedly sought to make clear our position in this matter so that there would not be danger of Communist miscalculation. The Secretary of State on September 4th made a statement to the same end. This statement could not, of course, cover every contingency. Indeed, I interpret the joint resolution as requiring me not to make absolute advance commitments but to use my judgment according to the circumstances of the time. But the statement did carry a clear meaning to the Chinese Communists and to the Soviet Union. There will be no retreat in the face of armed aggression, which is part and parcel of a continuing program of using armed force to conquer new regions.

I do not believe that the United States can be either lured or frightened into appeasement. I believe that, in taking the position of opposing aggression by force, I am taking the only position which is consistent with the vital interests of the United States and, indeed, with the peace of the world.

Some misguided persons have said that Quemoy is nothing to become excited about. They said the same about South Korea—about Viet-Nam, about Lebanon.

Now I assure you that no American boy will be asked by me to fight *just* for Quemoy. But those who make up our armed forces—and I believe the American people as a whole—do stand ready to defend the principle that armed force shall not be used for aggressive purposes.

Upon observance of that principle depends a lasting and just peace. It is that same principle that protects the Western Pacific free-world positions as well as the security of our homeland. If we are not ready to defend this principle, then indeed tragedy after tragedy would befall us.

Prospect for Negotiation

But there is a far better way than resort to force to settle these differences, and there is some hope that such a better way may be followed.

This is the way of negotiation.

That way is open and prepared because in 1955 arrangements were made between the United States and the Chinese Communists that an ambassador on each side would be authorized to discuss at Geneva certain problems of common concern. These included the matter of release of American civilians imprisoned in Communist China and such questions as the renunciation of force in the Formosa area. There have been 73 meetings since August 1955.

When our ambassador, who was conducting these negotiations, was recently transferred to another post, we named as successor Mr. [Jacob D.] Beam, our Ambassador to Poland. The Chinese Communists were notified accordingly the latter part of July, but there was no response.

The Secretary of State, in his September 4th statement, referred to these Geneva negotiations. Two days later, Mr. Chou En-lai, the Premier of the People's Republic of China, proposed that these talks should be resumed "in the interests of peace." This was followed up on September 8th by Mr. Mao Tse-tung, the Chairman of the People's Republic of China. We promptly welcomed this prospect and instructed our Ambassador at Warsaw to be ready immediately to resume these talks. We expect that the talks will begin upon the return to Warsaw of the Chinese Communist Ambassador, who has been in Peiping.

Perhaps our suggestion may be bearing fruit. We devoutly hope so.

Naturally, the United States will adhere to the position it first took in 1955, that we will not in these talks be a party to any arrangements which would prejudice rights of our ally, the Republic of China.

We know by hard experiences that the Chinese Communist leaders are indeed militant and aggressive. But we cannot believe that they would now persist in a course of military aggression which would threaten world peace, with all that would be involved. We believe that diplomacy can and should find a way out. There are measures that can be taken to assure that these offshore islands will not be a thorn in the side of peace. We believe that arrangements are urgently required to stop gunfire and to pave the way to a peaceful solution.

If the bilateral talks between ambassadors do not fully succeed, there is still the hope that the United Nations could exert a peaceful influence on the situation.

*   *   *

My friends, we are confronted with a serious situation. But it is typical of the security problems of the world today. Powerful and aggressive forces are constantly probing, now here, now there, to see whether the free world is weakening. In the face of this there are no easy choices available. It is misleading for anyone to imply that there are.

However, the present situation, though serious, is by no means desperate or hopeless.

There is not going to be any appeasement.

I believe that there is not going to be any war.

But there must be sober realization by the American people that our legitimate purposes are again being tested by those who threaten peace and freedom everywhere.

This has not been the first test for us and for the free world. Probably it will not be the last. But as we meet each test with courage and unity, we contribute to the safety and the honor of our beloved land—and to the cause of a just and lasting peace.

R. President Eisenhower to Chairman Khrushchev*

September 12, 1958

Dear Mr. Chairman: I have your letter of September 7. I agree with you that a dangerous situation exists in the Taiwan area. I do not agree with you as to the source of danger in this situation.

The present state of tension in the Taiwan area was created directly by Chinese Communist action, not by that of the Republic of China or by the United States. The fact is that following a long period of relative calm in that area, the Chinese Communists, without provocation, suddenly initiated a heavy artillery bombardment of Quemoy and began harassing the regular supply of the civilian and military population of the Quemoys. This intense military activity was begun on August 23rd—some three weeks after your visit to Peiping. The official Peiping radio has repeatedly been announcing that the purpose of these military operations is to take Taiwan (Formosa) as well as Quemoy and Matsu, by armed force. In virtually every Peiping broadcast, Taiwan (Formosa) and the offshore islands are linked as the objective of what is called the "Chinese Peoples Liberation Army."

The issue, then, is whether the Chinese Communists will seek to achieve their ambitions through the application of force, as they did in Korea, or whether they will accept the vital requisite of world peace and order in a nuclear age and renounce the use of force as the means for satisfying their territorial claims. The territory concerned has never been under the control of Communist China. On the contrary, the Republic of China—despite the characterizations you apply to it for ideological reasons—is recognized by the majority of the sovereign nations of the world and its government has been and is exercising jurisdiction over the territory concerned. United States military forces operate in the Taiwan

Ibid., pp. 498-99.

area in fulfillment of treaty commitments to the Republic of China to assist it in the defense of Taiwan (Formosa) and the Penghu (Pescadores) Islands. They are there to help resist aggression—not to commit aggression. No upside down presentation such as contained in your letter can change this fact.

The United States Government has welcomed the willingness of the Chinese Communists to resume the Ambassadorial talks, which were begun three years ago in Geneva, for the purpose of finding a means of easing tensions in the Taiwan area. In the past, the United States representative at these talks has tried by every reasonable means to persuade the Chinese Communist representative to reach agreement on mutual renunciation of force in the Taiwan area but the latter insistently refused to reach such agreement. The United States hopes that an understanding can be achieved through the renewed talks which will assure that there will be no resort to the use of force in the endeavor to bring about a solution of the issues there.

I regret to say I do not see in your letter any effort to find that common language which could indeed facilitate the removal of the danger existing in the current situation in the Taiwan area. On the contrary, the description of this situation contained in your letter seems designed to serve the ambitions of international Communism rather than to present the facts. I also note that you have addressed no letter to the Chinese Communist leaders urging moderation upon them. If your letter to me is not merely a vehicle for one-sided denunciation of United States actions but is indeed intended to reflect a desire to find a common language for peace, I suggest you urge these leaders to discontinue their military operations and to turn to policy of peaceful settlement of the Taiwan dispute.

If indeed, for the sake of settling the issues that tend to disturb the peace in the Formosa area, the Chinese Communist leaders can be persuaded to place their trust in negotiation and a readiness to practice conciliation, then I assure you the United States will, on its part, strive in that spirit earnestly to the same end.

S. Theodore F. Green, Chairman of the Senate Foreign Relations Committee, to President Eisenhower*

September 29, 1958

Dear Mr. President: There are many indications of a real danger that the United States may become involved in military hostilities in defense of Quemoy and Matsu. These indications comprise newspaper reports from the Far East, communications which I have received from very many Americans, dispatches from friendly nations throughout the world, as well as concern expressed publicly by many prominent Americans well informed in the field of foreign policy, and your own statements to the American people.

Recently I have expressed my own views stating that "it does not appear to me that Quemoy is vital to the defense of either Formosa or the United

*Ibid., Oct. 20, 1958, pp. 605-06.

States." I have suggested that military action in the area should not be ordered unless you, Mr. President, are sure beyond any reasonable doubt that the security of Formosa itself is in fact directly threatened. Subsequent to your address of September 11, I proposed that if there is danger of military involvement in this area—a danger which you indicated existed—Congress should be called immediately into session.

The purpose of this letter, Mr. President, is to bring to your attention my deep concern that the course of events in the Far East may result in military involvement at the wrong time, in the wrong place, and on issues not of vital concern to our own security, and all this without allies either in fact or in heart. Furthermore, it is my impression, confirmed by the press and by my own mail, that United States military involvement in defense of Quemoy would not command that support of the American people essential to successful military action.

My decision to send this letter to you has involved a great deal of soul-searching on my part. At one point, I seriously contemplated calling the Committee on Foreign Relations back to Washington so that it might meet with cabinet members to learn fully the nature of our possible involvement. That course was rejected for the present because I felt such a public act might interfere with the conduct of negotiations in which your representatives are now engaged. I also contemplated the advisability of seeking in advance of this letter the consensus of views of the members of the Committee so that our joint views might be brought to your attention. But that action was rejected because it would be time consuming and because of the possibility that such action might be construed as a political maneuver.

It is not my intention to make this letter to you public at this time. I am sending copies of it, however, to each member of the Committee on Foreign Relations with the thought that he may wish to provide you independently with his views, particularly with reference to those I have set forth in this letter. I am sending a copy also to Senator Lyndon Johnson.

With respect and deep concern, I remain

T. President Eisenhower to Senator Green*

October 2, 1958

Dear Senator Green: I acknowledge your letter of September twenty-ninth with reference to the situation in the Far East. I note that you are concerned that the United States might become involved in hostilities in defense of Quemoy and Matsu; that it does not appear to you that Quemoy is vital to the defense of Formosa, or the United States; that in such hostilities we would be without allies, and, finally, that military involvement in the defense of Quemoy would not command that support of the American people essential to successful military action.

Let me take up these points in order:

Ibid.

1. Neither you nor any other American need feel that the United States will be involved in military hostilities merely in defense of Quemoy or Matsu. I am quite aware of the fact that the Joint Resolution of Congress, which authorized the President to employ the armed forces of the United States in the Formosa area, authorized the securing and protection of such positions as Quemoy and Matsu only if the President judges that to be required or appropriate in assuring the defense of Formosa and the Pescadores.

I shall scrupulously observe that limitation contained in the Congressional authority granted me.

2. The Congressional Resolution had, of course, not merely negative but positive implications. I shall also observe these. I note that it does not appear to you that Quemoy is vital to the defense of Formosa or the United States. But the test which the Congress established was whether or not the defense of these positions was judged by the President to be required or appropriate in assuring the defense of Formosa. The Congressional Resolution conferring that responsibility on the President was adopted by almost unanimous vote of both Houses of the Congress. Since then the people of the United States reelected me to be that President. I shall, as President and Commander-in-Chief of the Armed Forces of the United States, exercise my lawful authority and judgment in discharging the responsibility thus laid upon me.

I welcome the opinions and counsel of others. But in the last analysis such opinions cannot legally replace my own.

The Chinese and Soviet Communist leaders assert, and have reason to believe, that if they can take Quemoy and Matsu by armed assault that will open the way for them to take Formosa and the Pescadores and, as they put it, "expel" the United States from the West Pacific and cause its Fleet to leave international waters and "go home."

I cannot dismiss these boastings as mere bluff. Certainly there is always the possibility that it may in certain contingencies, after taking account of all relevant facts, become necessary or appropriate for the defense of Formosa and the Pescadores also to take measures to secure and protect the related positions of Quemoy and Matsu.

I am striving to the best of my ability to avoid hostilities; to achieve a cease-fire, and a reasonable adjustment of the situation. You, I think, know my deep dedication to peace. It is second only to my dedication to the safety of the United States and its honorable discharge of obligations to its allies and to world order which have been assumed by constitutional process. We must not forget that the whole Formosa Straits situation is intimately connected with the security of the United States and the free world.

3. You say that in the event of hostilities we would be without allies "in fact or in heart." Of course, no nation other than the Republic of China has a treaty alliance with us in relation to the Formosa area. That is a well known fact—known to the Congress when it adopted the Formosa Joint Resolution and known to the Senate when it approved of our Treaty of Mutual Security with the Republic of China. But if you mean that the United States action in standing firm against armed Communist assault would not have the approval

of our allies, then I believe that you are misinformed. Not only do I believe that our friends and allies would support the United States if hostilities should tragically, and against our will, be forced upon us, I believe that most of them would be appalled if the United States were spinelessly to retreat before the threat of Sino-Soviet armed aggression.

4. Finally, you state that even if the United States should become engaged in hostilities, there would not be "that support of the American people essential to successful military action."

With respect to those islands, I have often pointed out that the only way the United States could become involved in hostilities would be because of its firm stand against Communist attempts to gain their declared aims by force. I have also often said that firmness in supporting principle makes war less, rather than more, likely of occurrence.

I feel certain, beyond the shadow of a doubt, that if the United States became engaged in hostilities on account of the evil and aggressive assaults of the forces of Communism, the American people would unite as one to assure the success and triumph of our effort.

I deeply deplore the effect upon hostile forces of a statement that if we became engaged in battle, the United States would be defeated because of disunity at home. If that were believed, it would embolden our enemies and make almost inevitable the conflict which, I am sure, we both seek to avoid provided it can be avoided consistently with the honor and security of our country.

Though in this letter I have explained the facts and the principles that guide the government in dealing with the critical Formosa Straits situation, I cannot close without saying that our whole effort is now, and has always been, the preservation of a peace with honor and with justice. After all, this is the basic aspiration of all Americans, indeed of all peoples.

Inasmuch as there have been public reports on the essence of your letter, I feel I should make this reply public.

With great respect and best wishes,

U. Comments by Secretary Dulles at a News Conference*

October 28, 1958

Q. Mr. Secretary, what do you think of the idea of having war every other day?

A. Well, it is part of this upside-down acting and talking to which we have had to grow accustomed, or try to grow accustomed. It seems to me the most shocking aspect of it is the complete demonstration that this shooting is not for military purposes but merely for the purpose of promiscuous killing. If you have a military purpose, you carry on your shooting for military objectives and your purpose is to destroy the capacity of your enemy to resist. When you do it only every other day and say, in between times you can bring in supplies—indeed, we will give them to you, so as to increase your capacity

*Ibid., Nov. 3, 1958, pp. 769-70.

to resist—and the next day you do your shooting, that shows the killing is done for political purposes and promiscuously. It is only designed to kill primarily the civilians, who are the ones most exposed. It is an extremely repugnant procedure according to our standards.

Q. Do you recall any precedent for any ceasefire arrangement such as this?

A. No, I think it has no precedent. I think it can be explained. My own interpretation of it is this: For 7 weeks they carried on a very extensive bombardment, together with interference by naval craft, to try to interdict the resupplying of the islands. At the end of that 7 weeks it became apparent that the techniques that had been developed jointly between the Chinese Nationalists and ourselves, and carried out primarily by the Chinese, were such that the island could not be cut off and made to wither on the vine, so to speak, through this level of fire. Therefore they had to confront a new situation. They knew that we could resupply the island; so in order to save face they said, "We will let you resupply the island every other day." Thus what we had demonstrated, the ability to do so against their will, they now made to appear as something that we did at their will. In that way they are trying to save themselves from a loss of face and a defeat in the effort which they had initiated but had been unable to conclude successfully.

Q. Mr. Secretary, do you suggest, then, that they will allow the firing to just wither away one of these days and be done with it?

A. That is a possibility. I wouldn't ever bank heavily, put all your bets, on just one theory of the Chinese Communists' action, because they can reverse themselves overnight. But it seems as though, at least for the moment, they do not want to raise up the level of their military effort, as by bringing in large amounts of airpower and the like; also they did not want to be exposed as having failed in the present level of effort. So, as I say, to save their face they seemed to devise this somewhat outlandish and rather uncivilized way of dealing with it. What they will do in the future I don't know. My belief is that they will not engage in a level of military effort which is likely to provoke a general war. . . .

UNITED STATES REACTION TO CHINESE COMMUNIST ACTIONS IN TIBET

V. Statement of Concern by Acting Secretary of State Herter*

March 26, 1959

I am deeply shocked at reports seeping out from Tibet about the ruthless suppression of human liberties there and the determined effort by the Chinese Communists to destroy the religion and culture of the people of Tibet.

It has been only 8 years since the Peiping regime agreed to respect Tibet's religious and cultural autonomy. Evidently the Communists have broken that

*Ibid., Apr. 13, 1959, pp. 514-15.

agreement as part of their ruthless drive to eliminate all individuality and human values within their empire. Once again the hypocrisy of the Communists is demonstrated. They constantly charge others with aggression and interference, but when a courageous people within their grasp seeks liberty their answer is ruthless repression.

We are saddened by the suffering of the Tibetan people, and yet we see in their resistance efforts one more heartening example of the indomitable spirit of man.

W. State Department Statement*

March 28, 1959

The order issued by Chou En-lai clearly reveals Peiping's intention to destroy the historical autonomy of the Tibetan people. This is a blatant violation of Peiping's solemn pledge of May 1951 guaranteeing the Tibetans political and religious autonomy.

In place of the legitimate Tibetan Government dissolved by the order the Communists have established direct military rule. As evidence we note that among the five Chinese appointees on the revised administrative control committee is a Deputy Political Commissar of the Red Chinese Army. The Communists' order states that the Panchen Lama will act as Chairman of the new Tibetan regime. The Panchen Lama has never been the primary religious leader of Tibet, and it is clear that the replacement of the Dalai Lama has been effected by foreign intervention without the consent of the Tibetan people. The Panchen Lama was brought up in China and came to Tibet in the wake of the Chinese Red Army.

A significant feature of the Chinese Communist statements this morning [March 28] is the admission that the Tibetan resistance to Chinese Communist rule is widespread and continuing. The statements admit that the Communists have been trying to suppress by force this Tibetan resistance since last May. By their count at least 20,000 Tibetan patriots are in arms against them. They also state that the entire Tibetan Army has joined the resistance movement.

The United States is profoundly sympathetic with the people of Tibet in the face of the barbarous intervention of the Chinese Communist imperialists to deprive a proud and brave people of their cherished religious and political autonomy and to pervert their institutions to Communist ends.

X. Speech by Senator Clair Engle on Revision of United States China Policy*

[Extract]

May 21, 1959

OUR CHINA POLICY NEEDS REVISION

Mr. President, I know there are political dangers in undertaking to discuss

Ibid., April 19, 1959, p. 515.
Congressional Record, May 21, 1959, pp. 8760-62.

our China foreign policy. I am aware of the fact that the State Department regards this area of our foreign policy as one that should not be touched.

I do not see why our policy in China should be any more sacrosanct than our policy in Europe, which has come under continuous discussion and analysis not only on the floor of the Senate, but also in the press and among the people generally in the United States. I know also that this is an extremely complicated and difficult field of foreign policy but it nevertheless requires some public airing. I am convinced that our China policy needs a critical reexamination. I am prepared to dispute the premise that our present policy is adequate and that nothing about it can or should be changed.

I undertake this discussion with the full knowledge that what I say may be misunderstood, misinterpreted and criticized. But we have to start somewhere and I think that this phase of our foreign policy is deserving of more attention and discussion on the floor of the U.S. Senate than it has received.

*   *   *

There was a time when the United States looked out upon the rest of the world through the front door and we did not see much beyond Europe. We looked at the Far East through the back door—when we bothered to look at it at all. Our knowledge of peoples and cultures and forces at work in the Far East and south Asia was meager.

*   *   *

To be sure, in a general way we are aware that the sleeping Asian giant has awakened; that colonialism is dead; that a revolution is in progress—a revolution basically to replace suppression with freedom, which is what the people really want, regardless of the form the revolution takes. They want to replace poverty with plenty and to replace inequality with equality. What we may not have understood too well is that regardless of the many forms this revolution has taken, there is an underlying community of interest among the peoples of Asia. Most of the peoples of Asia have the same hopes and aspirations. We cannot dispose of this community of interest by attaching labels to the effect that this or that country is Communist, or neutral, or a staunch ally. Irrespective of these labels the motivations of the people remain similar though the forms of government may differ.

Our problem has been to determine the best means by which we can identify ourselves with this upheaval, to aid and guide the processes of change. The assumption that we can and should guide this change in our own image in itself is a denial of the very equality and right of self-determination these nations of Asia are seeking. As we have faced this dilemma our policy has coined stock responses to stock labels. If the label is "staunch ally" the response is to subsidize the economy, give unequivocal support to the leadership and conclude a defense assistance agreement. If the label is "neutralist" the response is to toy along, give a restrained support, and alternate wooing with wrist slapping. If the label is "Communist" the response is to retreat into a defensive posture of containment and threats of massive retaliation. These widely diverse responses have become the stock policy formulas, irrespective of the fact that all Asian peoples in our pigeonholed categories are seeking nearly the same ultimate objectives, irrespective of the same underlying pressures, and irrespective of the fact that many of the countries of Asia are under authoritarian government, though with notable exceptions.

While our policy in all of Asia is interrelated, China policy is central, affecting not only the nature of our relationships throughout Asia but also affecting the balance of power and the potential peace of the world. Mr. President, since China policy has such an important bearing on our future in Asia, I should like to take that policy off the shelf where it has been gathering dust since 1949; take a look at it, and ask some questions about it.

I do this because of a conviction that this China policy is based on a reaction to the past, rather than a calculated look into the future. I am impressed with the fact that our present China policy is compounded of a lack of understanding of the processes which have been simmering in China since the Boxer Rebellion. To this is added our embarrassment emanating from not having been able to save China in 1949, and from our unwillingness to decisively defeat Communist China in Korea. Add to this our emotional and moral revulsion for mass executions on the mainland, the reprehensible brainwashings, the excess of revolution—add further the fact that a number of U.S. citizens have been held imprisoned in China—the net result of this affront to our moral sense and our prestige has been a China policy of absolute containment plus pressure. The policy calls for not recognizing the existence of the regime, for sealing off the regime and the 600 million people of China, for a ring of military defenses surrounding China, for an absolute trade embargo, and for a boycott on all travel and exchanges. The psychological warfare aspects of present policy call for measures not only to deter any aggression but to pose a threat of implied eventual liberation by a refugee government on an island 100 miles from the mainland. The presumed objective of this policy of containment, insulation and psychological compression is to serve the national interests of the United States.

My purpose is not to contend that these extremes of policy should be replaced by the opposite extremes. I do not contend that we can or should recognize the Mao government under the conditions of hostility which now prevail. Before any two-way recognition can take place many changes will have to be made in relationships between the United States and China. I cannot take the position that the Mao government should represent China in the United Nations until changes take place which now bar the Mao government from representing China. Instead of replacing the extreme of present policy with any policy of giving the Chinese everything they seek in the hope of winning their affection, I would suggest the need for examining the many possible alternative middle courses affecting the relationship—courses which may serve the national interest 10 years from now far better than our present policy.

*   *   *

To some extent the administration has fostered the view that the advocate of any policy other than the present rigid policy of total insulation is guilty of un-Americanism or appeasement. We have insulated ourselves from all direct knowledge of what is transpiring in China. Through this policy of insulation we not only deprive ourselves of intelligence and of the benefits of two-way communication, but we also make it possible for the Mao government to whip up the fears of the unknown—the fears of the U.S. colossus beyond the wall the Mao government and we, together, have built around China. Thus, the United States conveniently provides the external threat used by the regime to justify greater and greater demands upon the people. And if the lack of contact creates an exaggerated fear of the aggressive designs of the United States, I suggest that it may also contribute to our fear of the aggressive designs of China.

I am not among those who believe that simply by furthering exchanges we are going to convert the Chinese leaders to democracy, nor do I believe they would convert us to communism. Nor do I believe that such relations could wean China overnight from its present association with the Soviet Union. I do believe, however, that over a period of years contacts between the American and Chinese people would wear off the sharp edges. It would reduce our differences to the real differences, ruling out the specious, artificial, unrealistic images which many Americans hold of China and which the Chinese now hold of the United States.

I am fully aware of the fact that Americans who have suggested such a course have been charged with a lack of knowledge of the nature of communism. I can assure Senators that the evils of communism are well understood. On the evidence available, there can be little doubt that the capacity of China to cause mischief in the world will have expanded manyfold in 10 to 15 years. The issue is not whether China constitutes a potential danger. On this there is wide agreement. The question, rather, is: What is the best course of action the United States should take now to support our national and international interest 10 or 15 years hence?

It is simplicity itself to respond to a threat by attempting to build a military, economic and psychological wall around China. This response of containment, not supplemented by other positive measures, is the Maginot line response. It is the "moat" psychology of medieval days. It is a negative and defensive posture. It denies the United States the advantage of those relationships essential to affect change—and there is no reason why such active relationships could not be maintained concurrently with our present determined measures to deter China from committing aggression. I can see no incompatibility between a policy which would build up the capacity of the free countries of Asia to resist any Communist aggression while at the same time make an effort to reestablish relations with the people and government of China. It is said that such a course of action would involve calculated risks. I believe it is time for the American people to be alerted to the calculated risks if the present policy continues for another 10 years. We cannot dispose of the reality of Communist China through either a wall or a vacuum between us. The reality of China will still exist.

Adverse Effects of Present Policy

Mr. President, in questioning our present China policy in terms of where it may be leading us, may I state frankly some of the consequences as they appear to me.

Our present policy does not reduce China's present or potential power. It drives China into a closer relationship with the Soviet Union than otherwise might exist. It creates an economic dependence of China upon the Soviet Union which serves to amalgamate a relationship which otherwise in all probability would be one of differences and frictions. It maintains an atmosphere of war in which solutions in our interest remain impossible. It helps to keep the fires of anti-Americanism alive in China, permitting the regime to use the so-called American Threat as a justification for forcing the Chinese people into ever-increasing depths of bondage. Among most of our allies and the neutral nations of Asia it puts the United States in the ludicrous position of weakness and artificiality. We appear in the position of attempting to escape behind the flimsy curtain we have created, rather than facing the reality of Communist China and dealing with it with the manly forthrightness becoming the world's leading military and economic power. These allies seem embarrassed at being compelled to defer to the efforts of the United States to keep alive the myth that Communist China does not exist.

At the opposite extreme, two allies—the Republic of Korea and the Republic of China on Formosa—hold an interest in having the United States involved in a total war with Communist China. They not only benefit by the illusion that Communist China does not legally or factually exist, they employ every device and opportunity available to identify the United States with the eventual liberation of the mainland. The United States is placed in the position of being the dog wagged by the tail.

This present China policy not only alienates many of our allies, but it perpetuates a psychological state of war when our interest demands peace. It places on us the onus of preventing the relaxation of tensions necessary if there is ever to be a solution of such basic problems as the reunification of Korea and the permanent status of Formosa. But above all, it prevents the free world from making a concerted effort to open the windows of China. It prevents the people of China from seeing the non-Communist world as it is. It compels the United States to get its information from translations of the mainland censored press or from Canadian, Japanese, Indian or other foreign correspondents in China. The United States is in the pathetic position of depriving itself of direct information on what is happening in the most populous country in the world.

National security, and indeed international security in the Far East as in the Middle East, Europe and elsewhere, depends upon more than military defense. To be sure, military strength is necessary in the world in which we live. As a matter of national policy we prepare not only for the eventuality of total nuclear war but also for localized conventional war. However, we do not assume the inevitability of either kind of war to the extent that we rule out the use of other instruments to attain the national objectives. Among these other instruments employed is the constant effort to arrive at areas of mutual agreement with the Soviet Union. I do not refer only to the agreements for exchange of persons, cultural, agricultural exchanges, and so forth. While these undoubtedly are proving to be beneficial, we have not been reluctant to search for more substantive agreements affecting the world's security. I think the administration is to be highly commended for its patient negotiation with the Soviet Union and other powers seeking an enforceable inspection system as an integral part of any disarmament or arms control agreement. There has not been agreement, but we cannot say that the effort to reach agreement has been in vain. In the current negotiations on Berlin and European security we are pursuing the search for areas of mutual agreement at the Foreign Minister level, and, if necessary, at the head of state level. In sharp contrast, our China policy for all practical purposes rules out the use of instruments other than ultimate recourse to war. I say this in the belief that if any mutual understandings are to be reached with China, they must be reached with Mao Tse-tung, Chou En-lai or Chen Yi and not with Ambassador Wang Ping-nan in Warsaw.

*   *   *

Y. Address by Under Secretary of State Douglas Dillon on United States China Policy*

[Extract]

October 7, 1959

I am happy to be here with you tonight and to have this timely opportunity to review recent developments in the Far East. You have been privileged during your conference to hear some of Asia's most distinguished leaders talk of their policies and problems in frank and constructive terms. I, in turn, wish to discuss United States policies toward the Far East and to outline the manner in which they are helping to strengthen the foundations of freedom in that important area of the world.

One year ago, almost to the day, the late John Foster Dulles stood before this same Council during the height of the sustained Chinese Communist attacks in the Taiwan Straits. He defined with unmistakable clarity the stakes involved in that attack. He said, "What is involved is a Communist challenge to the basic principle of peace that armed force should not be used for aggression. Upon the observance and enforcement of that principle depends world order everywhere."

Secretary Dulles declared that the United States would stand firm and not retreat in the face of armed aggression. We, and our ally, the Government of the Republic of China, stood firm. The challenge was met, and the Communist resort to naked force failed of its goal. Ten million human beings on Taiwan were not delivered into slavery.

*   *   *

*Department of State Bulletin, Oct. 26, 1959, pp. 571-74.

Developments in Taiwan Area

Now, in retrospect, what was the net result of the tumultuous events in the Taiwan area during the autumn of 1958?

I would answer that a potential war was averted by our firm stand against the Chinese Communist use of force.

Since then the heavy Red bombardment of August 1958 has dwindled to token shelling on a senseless, alternate-day basis. While tensions have been somewhat relaxed, basic fears of irrational and explosive behavior by the Chinese Communists persist.

The Peiping regime has demonstrated absolutely no disposition to make the slightest move toward an agreement on a cease-fire or a renunciation of force. Its recalcitrance at the negotiating table has been maintained since the talks were resumed at Warsaw more than a full year ago. The depth of the Peiping regime's contempt for world opinion became fully apparent this past spring, when it cruelly and ruthlessly extinguished the last vestiges of freedom in Tibet. The Dalai Lama fled to India in order to preserve the symbol of the spiritual and temporal resistance of the courageous Tibetan people. This gross shock to Asian and world sensibilities was still reverberating when Peiping unleashed a torrent of abuse against one of the world's most dedicated men, India's Prime Minister Nehru. That action, coupled with incursions across the frontier into Indian territory, compounded the shocked dismay produced by the brutal massacres in Tibet.

Question of Peaceful Settlement of Disputes

Very recently we have had cause to hope that at long last the Communists were preparing to put aside the use of threats and force to achieve their objectives. We recall the joint communiqué at Camp David wherein President Eisenhower and Chairman Khrushchev agreed that "all outstanding international questions should be settled not by the application of force but by peaceful means through negotiation."

*   *   *

I regret having to report that the initial Chinese Communist reaction was not encouraging. For the Chinese Communist authorities appear to have heavily edited Chairman Khruschev's speeches in the initial domestic output of their controlled radio. Deleted were Khrushchev's strictures against "testing the capitalist system by force," against waging "predatory wars," and against "imposing socialism by force of arms" because "the people would not understand."

Instead, the population of mainland China and the Chinese Communist armed forces were treated to an order of the day by Chinese Communist Defense Minister Lin Piao, at the October 1 National Day parade in Peiping, in which Lin Piao attacked the alleged "aggressive schemes" of the United States. He then proclaimed that no foreign countries would be allowed to interfere in Peiping's so-called "liberation" of Taiwan. These words were echoed by other Chinese

Communist leaders, including Liu Shao-chi, the Chairman, or chief of state, of the Chinese Communist regime.

* * *

But in spite of all this we still must hope that the Chinese Communist overlords will, after reflection, heed the advice of the Soviet Union, whose leadership over the international Communist movement they themselves recognize, and adhere to Chairman Khrushchev's proposition that differences must be settled by negotiation and not by force.

* * *

The time has come for all of us, on both sides of the Iron and Bamboo Curtains, to face squarely the issue of whether we can afford to permit *any* dispute *anywhere* to be settled by recourse to arms. We firmly reject attempts by Communist leaders to justify what they call "just, revolutionary wars" or "wars of liberation." War is war, no matter where or why it may be fought. Peace also is indivisible. Peace is not the prerogative of the Communists alone, nor can it be applied only to areas outside the immediate concern of the Sino-Soviet bloc.

There can be no glossing over the danger that an attempt to seize Taiwan and the offshore islands is just as likely to embroil the world community in total war as is the launching of any other type of war.

There can be no exceptions in the matter of peaceful settlement of disputes.

Once this fact adequately impresses itself upon the thinking of our shrinking planet and is reflected in its actions and outlook everywhere, there will assuredly be an atmosphere conducive to the broad-scale disarmament and peaceful progress so fervently desired by all men of good will.

We earnestly hope Peiping will see the light.

The Asian Revolution

I am confident that our hope is shared by the peoples of free Asia, who are crying out today for economic and social progress. They are driving for greater freedom for the human spirit. They are reaching out for a larger share of the good things of life. They are at the beginning stage of the continuing Asian revolution, a profound social and political upheaval which has drawn much of its inspiration from our own liberal revolution. It is marked by a surging tide of nationalism which is wiping out old landmarks, casting aside outworn institutions, and eliminating social inequities. In their stead, free Asia's leaders, who are struggling to build new, just, and abundant societies, are adopting and adapting many of the social, intellectual, political, and material aspects of our own democratic tradition. With energy and tenacity of purpose the free nations of the area have vastly enlarged their possibility of achieving security, stability, and progress.

Their development is menaced by the new Chinese Communist imperialism.

The United States, through SEATO and other mutual defense arrangements, stands ready to help the free peoples of Asia throw back Communist aggression. But how much better if we could concentrate our efforts entirely on cooperative programs for their social and economic progress!

United States policy is designed to promote the independence of the free nations of Asia and to help them build strong and free societies. The basic purpose of this policy is to assure that the continuing Asian social revolution will not falter because of a lack of understanding or too feeble a response.

*   *   *

COMMUNIST CHINA AND THE UNITED NATIONS

Z. Statement by U.N. Ambassador James J. Wadsworth on the Admission of China to the United Nations*

[Extract]

October 1, 1960

The General Assembly has before it a draft resolution recommended by the General Committee which reads as follows:

The General Assembly

1. Decides to reject the request of the Union of Soviet Socialist Republics for the inclusion in the agenda of its fifteenth regular session of the item entitled 'Representation of China in the United Nations'.

2. Decides not to consider, at its fifteenth regular session, any proposals to exclude the representatives of the Government of the Republic of China or to seat representatives of the Central People's Government of the People's Republic of China.

Now, the effect of the adoption of this resolution by the General Assembly will be that without further debate at this session the proposal to expel the Republic of China from this organization and to seat in its place the People's Republic of China will once again be rejected, as it has been rejected every year since 1951.

In the General Committee we stated briefly our reasons for our strong opposition to the Soviet proposal. Now, before the entire membership of this great body, I should like to set forth our reasoning in more detail.

*   *   *

In Korea in the fall of 1950, when the United Nations forces had almost finished defeating the aggressor army of communist North Korea, a million Chinese Communist troops poured into Korea to renew the aggression. For this, in February 1951, Communist China was condemned by a vote of the

*U.S./U.N. Press Release, No. 3515, Oct. 1, 1960.

General Assembly which remains valid to this day. After two years of bitter war against the United Nations, an armistice was achieved. The Chinese Communists violated the armistice by callously refusing to account for thousands of prisoners of war in their hands—which they have never done to this day—and by illegally reinforcing their military forces in North Korea. They sabotaged the inspection system set up under the armistice agreement to prevent such violations. To this day, the only terms on which they have expressed willingness to see the Korean nation unified are such as to guarantee that the entire nation would be rendered helpless against their pressure and would fall into communist hands.

Throughout these years, they have drummed into the minds of helpless, captive Chinese people the myth that the United States was the aggressor in Korea, and that the United Nations action there was part of a United States plot "to strangle the New China in its cradle."

In the Taiwan Strait Communist China has been using armed forces intermittently since 1950 as part of its violent campaign to seize Taiwan and the Pescadores and thus to destroy the Republic of China. Twice, in 1955 and again in 1958, its acts of violence and threats against Taiwan reached such a pitch as to bring the specter of general war to the Western Pacific. To this day it continues its capricious and wanton bombardment of the offshore islands, causing death and injury to many civilians.

Since 1955 the United States has sought in over 100 ambassadorial meetings with representatives of Communist China to work out an agreement by which neither side would use force in the Taiwan Strait. They have stubbornly refused to make any such agreement.

In Southeast Asia also, Communist China's record is one of aggressive pressure. They began in February 1950 by calling on all the peoples of Southeast Asia to overthrow their governments. For many years they gave material support and propaganda encouragement to communist guerrillas who were trying to overthrow the governments of the Philippines and Malaya. In North Vietnam, a communist state which owes its existence in great measure to the Chinese Communists they have helped the regime to enlarge its army greatly both in troop strength and in weapons—all in violation of the armistice terms applying to that area.

The outrages of Communist China in Tibet are well known. As early as February 1950, within months of their accession to power, they sent an army to subdue the traditionally self-governing mountain kingdom of Tibet. In 1959 they tightened their control by summarily dissolving the Tibetan government and establishing a so-called "Tibetan autonomous region" which has no autonomy at all. It is a colonial despotism. Thousands of Tibetans were massacred. The Dalai Lama, the spiritual and temporal ruler of Tibet, was driven into asylum abroad. The war against the Tibetans has continued in 1960 with frequent reports of heavy fighting. The Chinese Communist troops have even violated international frontiers in their efforts to hunt down Tibetans trying to escape. This matter is so serious that the General Assembly will debate it this fall for the second year in succession.

In the past year the Chinese Communists have moved beyond Tibet and have made military incursions into the territory of the sovereign nations of South Asia. Prime Minister Nehru of India has described these incursions bluntly as "aggression." Official maps issued by Communist China show as Chinese large areas long regarded by other states as their territory. Characteristically, while conducting these aggressive moves the Chinese Communists make loud charges of aggression against the very states which they offend.

Thus, all along the borders between Communist China and non-Communist Asia there is trouble and discord. From Korea south and west along the 6,000 mile arc that ends in the Himalayas, we find a history of Chinese Communist complicity in military aggression, subversion and outright seizure of territory.

On the mainland of China, uncivilized acts against nationals of other countries are standard practice. Hundreds of foreign Christian missionaries have been arrested and many religious leaders killed. Hundreds of foreign civilians have been imprisoned. Countless members of the Moslem minority in China have been imprisoned for "carrying on counter-revolutionary activity under the cloak of religion."

Throughout the ten years of Communist China's violent career these actions have been accompanied by an official campaign of hate propaganda against foreign governments and peoples which in its massiveness and its viciousness must be unequaled in the history of the world. The chief target of this abuse has been the United States.

*   *   *

Such, then, is the actual record of behavior of the Chinese Communist regime which the Soviet Union proposes for admission to the United Nations.

*   *   *

UNITED STATES POLICY IN CHINA, 1960-1968

A. Address by Roger Hilsman, Assistant Secretary of State for Far Eastern Affairs, on Redefinition of United States China Policy*

[Extract]

December 13, 1963

I am honored to be invited to this distinguished forum. Here in San Francisco you stand at the gateway to the problems and promise of the Pacific. As one currently responsible for dealing with the problems and furthering the promise of this region, I feel a special obligation to you.

Asia is not on fire; but portions of it smolder with each morning's headlines— a new South Viet-Nam government struggling to defeat Communist terrorism, Indonesia in a period of "confrontation" with the new Malaysia, Cambodia seeking an altered power balance between East and West to preserve its neutrality and independence, and many lesser conflicts.

I could focus today on any one of these problems, and our time would be too little to do it justice. For the passions of nationalism—at its best and at its most vexing—are at floodtide in much of Asia. And out of the interaction of these passions and the threat of Communist aggression are emerging new national identities and new national purposes.

Of course, the paradox of nation building is that the ultimate guarantee of its success lies in the capacity of national leaders to transcend parochial nationalism and to understand the interdependence of all peoples. How to bring peaceful regional cooperation out of conflicting national revolutions—that is the key question.

In the Far East that question has a special significance. For the evolution of each Asian state is taking place today under the long shadows cast by China— by the China of history that was for so long the matrix of East Asian civilization, and by the mainland China of today, the torchbearer of a rigid totalitarian ideology that threatens all its neighbors.

For Americans, China presents a special problem in history. We first met Chinese civilization late in the decay of its imperial splendor. For a century we sent out to China our traders, our missionaries, our educators, our doctors, and our good will. In the turmoil that followed the Chinese revolution of 1911 we felt a special kinship with China's culture and people. In World War II we became the staunchest of allies.

Yet our involvement with China, while intense, was not wholly real; it was fed by illusions as well as good will. We knew little—and understood less—of imperial China's strength and unity. We had little understanding of the ferment and weakness created by the collapse of the Confucian state. And we were little aware of the depth and fervor of Chinese nationalism in reaction to a sense of repeated humiliation at the hands of the West.

*Department of State Bulletin, Jan. 6, 1964, pp. 11-17.

As a result Americans were totally unprepared for the tragedy of the Chinese revolution: its capture by Marxism-Leninism and its transformation into a fiercely hostile force—hostile to the West and menacing to its neighbors. Our reaction was anger and disbelief, a sense of personal betrayal.

Today, 14 years have passed since the establishment of the Communist government in Peiping. It is time to take stock—dispassionately—of the greatest and most difficult problem we face in our efforts to assist in the developments of a peaceful Far East.

U.S. Does Not "Ignore" China

Let me begin by disposing of a myth. It is frequently charged that the United States Government is "ignoring" China and its 700 million people.

This is simply untrue. We do not ignore our ally, the Government of the Republic of China. We do not ignore the 12 million people in Taiwan. Nor, in fact, do we ignore the people of the mainland. We are very much aware of them, and we have a deep friendship for them. Nor, finally, do we ignore the Communist leadership which has established itself on the mainland. We meet with them from time to time, as at the periodic talks between our ambassadors in Warsaw. We should like to be less ignorant of them and for them to be less ignorant of us. To this end we have been striving for years to arrange an exchange of correspondents; but we have been put off with the assertion that so long as the "principal issue"—which they define in terms of their absurd charge that we are "occupying" Taiwan—is unresolved, there can be no progress on "secondary issues."

If we have not persuaded the Chinese Communists to allow an exchange of correspondents and to lower the wall of secrecy with which they surround themselves, we have nevertheless spent considerable effort in trying to understand what manner of men the Chinese Communists are, what are their ambitions, and what are the problems which stand in their way. We have tried to be objective and to see to it that dislike of communism does not becloud our ability to see the facts.

Failure of the "Great Leap Forward"

What is the essence of our analysis? What sort of people are the Chinese Communists? What kind of power is at their disposal?

These are important questions. We shall be in danger if we let our policies be guided by emotionalism or our thought processes by cliches. Our policies flow from the answers to these questions, and it is not enough that we prove ourselves properly anti-Communist by repeating anti-Communist phrases.

First and foremost, the Chinese Communist leaders have shown themselves to be dangerously overconfident and wedded to outdated theories but pragmatic when their existence is threatened.

Take the example of the so-called "great leap forward" of 1958-1960. You have undoubtedly heard that it was a catastrophe, and so it was. The Chinese Communist leaders did not understand the laws of the economically possible, and they undertook to do what could not be done. The collapse was extraordinary. Agriculture has barely regained its 1957 level, but there may be 70 million more mouths to feed. Industrial production fell by perhaps one-half between 1959 and 1962. The Chinese Communists first blamed the weather, then blamed the Russians. But, as their educated men must know, they have above all else to blame their own attempt to rewrite economics. I am still astounded at the arrogance of a leadership which believed that what all others have learned about economics was wrong and that it had by some flash of illumination come upon the truth.

The failure of the "great leap" is not the only lesson which we may learn from this period of internal crisis. Though the economy collapsed, the regime did not. Nor was its authority effectively challenged. It retained firm command of the instruments of control.

Equally important, the leaders have learned, and·publicly admit, that it will take generations before China becomes a modern industrial power. They have finally shown an ability to temper their grandiose slogans and frenetic schemes.

To be sure, communism has yet to prove that it can make agriculture work. The Communists have swallowed their Marxism and allowed the return of small private plots, but they have not abandoned collectivized agriculture. This dogmatic contrariness in a land which is still overwhelmingly agricultural may yet bring them even greater troubles. Moreover, recent failures have eroded the morale and discipline of the movement.

Nevertheless the Communists did correct the most dangerous mistakes of the "great leap forward." When their survival depended upon it, they showed flexibility in meeting the threat, and we have no reason to believe that there is a present likelihood that the Communist regime will be overthrown.

A second major fact about Communist China's leaders is their parochialism: They have seen extraordinarily little of the outside world, and their world view is further constricted by their ideology. Thirty to forty years ago they took over certain Marxist economic assumptions and Lenin's technique for organizing a disciplined party. To these Mao Tse-tung added certain tactical innovations. Such methods worked in their struggle for power, and they expect them to work in their struggle for modernization. I believe, however, that there are men at the second echelon who know that the "great leap forward" reflected a stubborn addiction to theories which do not work in a modern world. Yet I wonder whether the leadership has absorbed the same lessons.

These are the "Marxist puritans"; they see all the world as a conflict between unblemished good and unredeemable evil. Few people consider themselves wrong and evil, but there are very few people on earth who are so sublimely confident as are the Chinese Communist leaders that they are always right and good. They have arrogated to themselves the right to present the "revolution." Those who disagree are automatically wrong and evil. This attitude is displayed in their quarrel with the Russians.

Unfortunately, in this world there is no assurance that people are good because they think they are good or that they are right because they think they are right. If the Chinese Communists are obsessed with their own goodness, rather than being consciously evil as they often appear to others, the threat which they pose to a peaceful world is not thereby diminished. Mao and his colleagues are simply unaware of some of the vital ideas which have moved civilization. For them there is no problem of the relationship between man and society: The individual *must* yield. These men know nothing of the genuine purposes of democracy or of constitutional government. These are men who say that "all progressive wars are just, and all wars that impede progress are unjust," and who then reserve the right to decide what is "progress." These are men who comfortably clothe their own dictatorship in a cloak of doctrinal righteousness. Where such men triumph, some of civilization's most precious values are eclipsed. And they have proclaimed their determination to spread their system everywhere.

Is this permanent? Must we live indefinitely with such men?

Perhaps I am too optimistic; but there is some evidence of evolutionary forces at work in mainland China. As I have said, the present leaders have seen remarkably little of the outside world. They have conquered mainland China. They must believe that, with concepts unchanged, they can go on to conquer the world. These leaders, however, were deep in rural China when the rest of the world was debating Keynes and sharpening the tools of economic analysis. They may not yet have absorbed all the lessons of the "great leap forward"; but the more sophisticated second echelon of leadership undoubtedly knows that it was simple ignorance of the techniques of administering a complex economy which led to many of the mistakes of 1958. This economic example is particularly striking; it could be repeated throughout the sciences and humanities. The leaders may not know it, but the intellectuals know that the official explanation is not adequate as a description of reality. As these ideas seep upward or as the present leaders retire, this awareness may eventually profoundly erode the present simple view with which the leadership regards the world.

Furthermore, an economy becomes geometrically more complex as it modernizes, as the stages of production multiply, and as wants become more diverse. Rule by command becomes progressively less effective than encouraging the exercise of personal initiative in running such a society. The Chinese Communists have shown that they see the problem; but they have not shown themselves willing to sacrifice their doctrinal orthodoxy, as will be required if they are to deal with the problem.

In China today the old gods have been struck down and Marx, Lenin, and Mao Tse-tung put in their place. We see no signs yet that a new credo is on the rise to replace this present pantheon. We may see a leadership professedly Marxist for some time, even if its values and priorities change. This process of change is not automatic, nor is it likely to happen very fast. Nevertheless, the present leaders have shown that they already fear it, in their efforts to resurrect "revolutionary awareness." We do not know which way these changes will go, but—and here is my point—neither do the Chinese Communists.

What about the appeal of the Chinese Communists to the new nations of the world? They have scored some successes with extremists everywhere in identifying themselves as the radical end of the Communist movement. Peiping has been alert to the worldwide opportunities for playing on nationalistic differences and prejudices and gaining toeholds within the so-called national liberation movements or among the dissatisfied and disgruntled. We may expect this process to continue. These successes, however, may be more apparent than real. As extremists approach power, they may become less radical and may weigh more heavily the questions as to who can offer them more support and more protection.

The Chinese Communists are "true believers," arrogant in the assumption that other countries will wish to do things their way and will see the world as they see it; they cannot see themselves and their own beliefs as the product of a special time and place. But if there is a tendency afoot in the world, it would seem to be in the opposite direction, as more countries look to their own national ideals and interests rather than to an unquestioning faith in Marxism-Leninism.

Thus the Chinese Communists have set themselves up as a model for the less developed nations. But, like the king in the fairy tale, they seem unaware that they have no clothes. Others see, though the Chinese Communists have not, that the failure of the "great leap forward" has shown the model to be gravely deficient.

Taiwan, a Model for Chinese Development

The tragedy of the closed and stagnant society of the mainland is dramatized by the robust survival of an alternative model for Chinese development: the record of the Government of the Republic of China on Taiwan.

Here the modernization of Chinese society has taken place outside the Communist straitjacket—and the results are extraordinarily impressive.

Of the Republic of China I can only say: "Go see for yourself." While Communist China has suffered the disaster of the "great leap forward," Taiwan has enjoyed a sustained and remarkable economic growth. The model of Taiwan's development in the past 15 years is of increasing interest to the less developed nations everywhere. In time the contrast with the mainland can hardly be lost upon those nations which have an opportunity to see it.

Stereotypes die hard, and Communist China by its sheer size exercises a fascination; but if the economic techniques used by the Republic of China over the next few years yield the great gains in economic and social welfare that we have reason to expect, the impact on other developing nations will be considerable. And we may see a diminution of the attractive power of industrialization carried out through the suffering which seems to be the inescapable companion of economic growth in Communist countries.

Not alone through economic accomplishment the Republic of China has the opportunity to preserve and vitalize the humane traditions and values of Chinese civilization in the course of its modernization. These are a legacy which the Chinese Communists are attempting to eradicate on the mainland.

U.S. Purposes Are Peaceful and Defensive

You have expected me to talk about American policy, and I have talked mostly about Communist China's prospects. I have had a reason for doing this.

Policies based upon a misapprehension of reality may lead us far from the goals we seek. There has perhaps been more emotion about our China policy than about our policy toward any single country since World War II. Yet our nation must look squarely at China, pursuing policies which will protect the interests of our country, of the free world, and of men of good will everywhere.

Our prime objective concerning Communist China is that it not subvert or commit aggression against its free-world neighbors. It must not be allowed to accomplish for communism through force of arms that success which it has rarely achieved at the ballot box.

President Kennedy called our purposes in the Far East peaceful and defensive. And so they remain.

If the free-world governments of Asia are responsive to the needs and wishes of their own peoples, and if they have developed the techniques and machinery for fulfilling the role of government in their countries, communism can endanger them only through the naked threat of military force. Most of the countries thus threatend are too small to stand alone against such a threat, and they need to use their resources for their people's welfare rather than for the creation of an elaborate war machine. We have undertaken in many cases to provide the protection against massive attack which will permit them to pursue their own destinies unafraid.

Our military assistance in the Far East has been given with the objective of permitting Asian nations to develop the forces to defend their own borders and to protect themselves against probing attacks and paramilitary challenges. This is a necessary and grave responsibility.

However, I think that our hearts lie in that assistance which we can give in another direction: in helping them to establish the economic and political conditions in which a free society can flourish. This is particularly agreeable to us, because these are the things which those countries would want to do, and which we would want to help them to do, whether or not communism existed.

Before I close, there is one other area in which questions have been raised about American policy and in which a clarification of this Government's position is timely. I refer to the apparent differences in the.policies which we are adopting toward the Soviet Union and toward Communist China. We maintain a policy of nonrecognition and trade embargo of Communist China—at a time when we are willing to broaden contact with the Soviet Union.

The Soviet Union and Communist China do share the goal of communizing the world. But we see important differences in the thinking and tactics of the two. In the U.S.S.R. the Communists were developing a modern industrial society precisely when in China they were conducting a guerrilla war from rural bases. The Soviet leadership seems to have absorbed certain lessons from its more extended development—as to the values and priorities which one may safely pursue on a small planet and as to the price of miscalculating the nature of the outside world.

We believe that the policies which have proved their worth with Moscow are equally valid for our long-term relations with Peiping. But we also believe that our approach should be adapted to the differences in behavior between the two, as they relate to our own national objectives.

First and foremost, we fully honor our close and friendly ties with the people of the Republic of China on Taiwan and with their Government. We conceive of this relationship not as an historical accident but as a matter of basic principle. So long as Peiping insists on the destruction of this relationship as the *sine qua non* for any basic improvement in relations between ourselves and Communist China, there can be no prospect for such an improvement.

Our differing policies toward the Soviet Union and Communist China derive, secondly, from their differing attitudes toward negotiations, as such, even in limited areas. Faced with the realities of the nuclear age, the Soviet Union appears to recognize that certain interests—notably survival—are shared by all mankind. Peiping, however, remains wedded to a fundamentalist form of communism which emphasizes violent revolution, even if it threatens the physical ruin of the civilized world. It refuses to admit that there are common interests which cross ideological lines.

Third, United States policy is influenced by Chinese communism's obsessive suspicion of the outside world, far exceeding even that of the Soviet Union. Whereas Moscow appears to have learned that free-world readiness to negotiate limited common interests is not a sign of weakness, Peiping regards any conciliatory gesture as evidence of weakness and an opportunity for exploitation.

Perhaps the best evidence of this paranoid view of the world came from Peiping's Foreign Minister Ch'en I, who declared, at the height of China's food crisis in 1962, that his government would never accept any aid from America because this would mean "handing our vast market over to America." Given the near-subsistence level of the society and the limited purchasing power of the government, this view of American intentions could only be conjured up by men possessed of an unremitting distrust of all external people and a naive sense of their own economic prospects.

Fourth are the differing circumstances and opportunities on the peripheries of the Soviet Union and Communist China. The Soviet Union and European members of its bloc border on long established, relatively stable states defended by powerful, locally based—as well as more distant—deterrent and defensive forces. Communist China's neighbors, on the other hand, include newly established states struggling to maintain their independence with very limited defense forces. There is a wider range of opportunities for aggression and subversion available to Peiping which renders it even more important that in dealing with Peiping we not permit that regime to underestimate free-world firmness and determination.

Much speculation has turned around the question of possible commercial relations between private American firms and Communist China, especially in view of the declining trade between Communist China and its Soviet bloc partners. Peiping's own policies, however, seem crystal clear on this point. Peiping apparently wants none of it. As one of its trade officials recently delcared, "We have a very clear attitude. We won't trade with the United States because the United States Government is hostile to us." The Chinese Communists follow

Mao's maxim that "politics and economics are inseparable." They made this clear in their unilateral rupture of contracts with Japanese firms in 1958 and their willingness to jeopardize major industrial projects as the price for carrying on their disputes with the Soviet Union in 1960.

In sum, while respecting the right of others to view the matter otherwise, we find important differences in the willingness and ability of the Soviet Union and Communist China, at the present stage of their respective development to reach limited agreements which can bring some reduction of the terrible dangers and tensions of our present-day world. We believe that policies of strength and firmness, accompanied by a constant readiness to negotiate—policies long and effectively pursued with the Soviet Union—will best promote the changes which must take place on the China mainland before we can hope to achieve long sought conditions of peace, security, and progress in this half of the globe.

*   *   *

We are confronted in Communist China with a regime which presently finds no ground of common interest with those whose ideals it does not share, which has used hatred as an engine of national policy. The United States is the central figure in their demonology and the target of a sustained fury of invective. After President Kennedy's assassination, while other nations—Communist and free—shared our grief, the Chinese Communist Daily Worker published a cartoon of a man sprawled on the ground with the caption "Kennedy Bites the Dust." If this speaks for the Chinese Communist leadership, I am confident that it does not speak for most Chinese.

Americans—businessmen, missionaries, diplomats—have long felt a particularly close rapport with the Chinese. In World War II American pilots downed in Communist areas came out with moving accounts of Chinese helpfulness and friendliness. The Communists had not destroyed those attitudes then. I doubt they have succeeded in destroying them now.

We do not know what changes may occur in the attitudes of future Chinese leaders. But if I may paraphrase a classic canon of our past, we pursue today toward Communist China a policy of the open door: We are determined to keep the door open to the possibility of change and not to slam it shut against any developments which might advance our national good, serve the free world, and benefit the people of China. Patience is not unique to the Chinese. We too can maintain our positions without being provoked to unseemly action or despairing of what the future may hold. We will not sow the dragon's seed of hate which may bear bitter fruit in future generations of China's millions. But neither will we betray our interests and those of our allies to appease the ambitions of Communist China's leaders.

We hope that, confronted with firmness which will make foreign adventure unprofitable, and yet offered the prospect that the way back into the community of man is not closed to it, the Chinese Communist regime will eventually forsake its previous venomous hatreds which spring from a rigid class view of society. We hope that they will rediscover the Chinese virtue of tolerance for a multitude of beliefs and faiths and that they will accept again a world of diversity in place of the gray monolith which seems to be communism's goal for human society.

*   *   *

B. Speech by J. William Fulbright, Chairman of the Senate Foreign Relations Committee, on United States China Policy*

[Extract]

March 25, 1964

FOREIGN POLICY: OLD MYTHS AND NEW REALITIES

*   *   *

The Far East is another area of the world in which American policy is handicapped by the divergence of old myths and new realities. Particularly with respect to China, an elaborate vocabulary of make-believe has become compulsory in both official and public discussion.

*   *   *

I do not think the United States can, or should, recognize Communist China, or acquiesce in its admission to the United Nations under present circumstances. It would be unwise to do so, because there is nothing to be gained by it so long as the Peiping regime maintains its attitude of implacable hostility toward the United States. I do not believe, however, that this state of affairs is necessarily permanent. As we have seen in our relations with Germany and Japan, hostility can give way in an astonishingly short time to close friendship; and, as we have seen in our relations with China, the reverse can occur with equal speed. It is not impossible that in time our relations with China will change again—if not to friendship, then perhaps to "competitive coexistence." It would therefore be extremely useful if we could introduce an element of flexibility, or, more precisely, of the capacity to be flexible, into our relations with Communist China.

We would do well, as former Assistant Secretary Hilsman has recommended, to maintain an "open door" to the possibility of improved relations with Communist China in the future. For a start, we must jar open our minds to certain realities about China, of which the foremost is that there really are not "two Chinas," but only one—mainland China; and that it is ruled by Communists, and is likely to remain so for the indefinite future. Once we accept this fact, it becomes possible to reflect on the conditions under which it might be possible for us to enter into relatively normal relations with mainland China. One condition, of course, must be the abandonment by the Chinese Communists, tacitly,

*Congressional Record, Mar. 25, 1964, pp. 6227-32.

if not explicitly, of their intention to conquer and incorporate Taiwan. This seems unlikely now; but far more surprising changes have occurred in politics, and it is quite possible that a new generation of leaders in Peiping and Taipei may put a quiet end to the Chinese civil war, thus opening the possibility of entirely new patterns of international relations in the Far East.

Should such changes occur, they will open important opportunities for American policy; and it is to be hoped that we shall be able and willing to take advantage of them. It seems possible, for instance, that an atmosphere of reduced tensions in the Far East might make it possible to strengthen world peace by drawing mainland China into existing East-West agreements in such fields as disarmament, trade, and educational exchange.

These are long-range prospects, which may or may not materialize. In the immediate future, we are confronted with possible changes in the Far East resulting from recent French diplomacy.

French recognition of Communist China, although untimely and carried out in a way that can hardly be considered friendly to the United States, may nonetheless serve a constructive long-term purpose, by unfreezing a situation in which many countries, none more than the United States, are committed to inflexible policies by long-established commitments and the pressures of domestic public opinion. One way or another, the French initiative may help generate a new situation in which the United States, as well as other countries, will find it possible to reevaluate its basic policies in the Far East.

*   *   *

C. Address by William P. Bundy, Assistant Secretary of State For Far Eastern Affairs, on United States Asian Policy*

[Extract]

September 29, 1964

*   *   *

Communist China's foreign policy is fashioned by men whose whole life has been one of struggle, who are thoroughly wedded to a fundamentalist concept of communism, who have grown rigid and intransigent even in the face of overwhelming proof that the 19th-century doctrines of Karl Marx are hopelessly inadequate to meet the 20th-century problems of China. Monumentally convinced of the correctness of their position, they view all who disagree with them, including even the Russians, as old and bad and decadent. Neutralists are tolerated only to the extent that they are moving in the direction desired by Peiping.

I do not claim to know what their precise goals are. Are these goals to be defined in territorial terms, and, if so, what territories? Or could their goals

*Department of State Bulletin, Oct. 19, 1964, pp. 534-40.

be better described in terms of their quest for power and status and of gaining control and influence over other nations? Or are their goals directed more at exploiting the divisions and the difficulties of the countries of the free world, especially those in bordering areas? I suspect that all these and other elements are involved. But in any event the record of Communist China's behavior in recent years—against the offshore islands [Quemoy and Matsu], Tibet, and India—should leave us in no doubt of her militant and expansionist outlook.

More recently we have evidence in the continuing statements of Chinese Communist leaders, expressed most forcefully in the course of their ideological dispute with the Soviet Union. They say (as in their June 14, 1964 [*sic*], letter to the Soviet Communist Party) that "two-thirds of the world's population need to make revolution." They add that the revolution must be violent: "Violent revolution is a universal law of proletarian revolution. To realize the transition to socialism the proletariat must wage armed struggle, smash the old state machine, and establish the dictatorship of the proletariat."

Now it may be argued that the leaders of Communist China do not really mean all that they say, but I think it is a good rule of thumb to believe most of what dictators say about their intentions.

Finally, we should note that the severest indictments of Chinese Communist bellicosity come from the Soviet Union itself and, because of the close relationship that until recently marked Moscow-Peiping affairs, the Soviet Union may be in a good position to judge what Communist China is up to.

To say that Communist China is fundamentally militant is not inconsistent with the view that she may be tactically cautious when confronted with major force. Unquestionably our United States strategic and conventional capabilities, supplementing the efforts of free Asian nations, have made Communist China reluctant to embark on the older forms of naked aggression. Instead they prefer what Premier Khrushchev has called "wars of national liberation"—support to guerrillas, training of saboteurs, and the creation of Communist-dominated "national fronts." Fortunately Japan and other countries with internal stability and strength are not susceptible to this type of aggression.

I do not say that this will always be the picture of the policy of the Asian Communist nations. They confront tremendous internal problems. Like Communist countries everywhere they have not yet found the answer to the basic problem of agricultural production, much less of carrying out a true industrial or scientific revolution along the lines on which you in Japan have led the way. If their leaders were reasonable, or even pragmatic, the Communist nations of Asia should recognize that they cannot afford to embark on outside adventures that draw upon resources so urgently needed at home.

Thus we do not rule out the possibility that the passage of time will bring about desirable changes in the outlook of Communist China, North Korea, and North Viet-Nam. But clearly this cannot come about unless Communist expansionism is deterred and completely frustrated and unless, too, the conduct of all our relationships with Communist China gives her no encouragement that a continued militant course can be accepted.

So long as Peiping, as well as Hanoi and Pyongyang, continue on their present course, I see no basic change in United States policy toward mainland China. It is inconceivable to me that, at a time when Communist China is stridently proclaiming a militant revolutionary thesis and bearing out its threats with actions that undermine the security of nations both in Asia and Africa and even in the Americas, we should relax our guard. It remains the first requirement of our policy to help maintain adequate free-world military strength in order to deter aggression or, where aggression or threats to the peace occur, to be able to cope with such threats effectively. Without such capability to keep the peace, there can be no peace.

*　　　　　　　*　　　　　　　*

We recognize the profound implications of the Sino-Soviet rift and the possibility that it may lead to greater tension between the U.S.S.R. and Communist China in the northern regions. But we doubt that the U.S.S.R. has yet abandoned her Communist expansionist aims, and certainly not to the point where in the foreseeable future she could be relied upon to play a constructive role in assisting other nations to defend themselves against Communist China. There may be a long-term hope in this direction, but let us recognize always that the differences between the U.S.S.R. and Communist China are still concerned primarily not with their basic objectives but rather with the degree of violence to be employed to achieve those objectives. And let us recognize too that, to the extent that Soviet policy has changed or may change in the future, this will be in large part due to the fact that we, in partnership with other free-world nations, have maintained a military posture adequate to deter and to defeat any aggressive action.

But I do not want to leave the impression that we regard communism as the only major problem facing Asia. Security is fundamental. But economic and social progress remains an equally important need for the welfare of nations and of the individuals who must always be our primary concern.

The headlines in the newspapers today sometimes create the impression that the whole of East Asia is in turmoil. It is true that we face serious problems in Southeast Asia today, but we faced at least equally serious ones 10 years ago after Dien Bien Phu, when the Huks were still active in the Philippines, and the jungle insurgents were in Malaya. Problems and dangers are always with us. They are a fact of life in our rapidly changing world.

Meanwhile, over the past several decades there has been progress in the Far East of a slow, steady, unsensational kind which will, I firmly believe, have far more long-range significance than the problems with which we are so deeply concerned today. In most of the countries of free Asia there has been a notable degree of improvement in what the economists call "human resources" but what I still like to call "people." People are, by and large, healthier. They are better educated. They live longer. Students have far more opportunities for advanced and specialized studies at home and abroad.

Within the last 15 years there have been some remarkable success stories—Japan, the Republic of China, and, despite some remaining weaknesses, the

Republic of Korea, the Philippines, Thailand, and even South Viet-Nam in the 1954-59 period.

Undoubtedly, however, Japan has provided the outstanding example of progress during the past 10 years. This progress extends well beyond the material things of life, beyond the economic growth which has surpassed that of any other nation in the postwar era. Japan's progress has also been in the arts, in health, education, and broadening intellectual horizons in all directions.

The United States has ties of friendship, confidence, and mutual interest with many Far Eastern countries but none of which we are prouder and which we cherish more than those with Japan. Our friendship began long before the war, survived the war, and is now almost unique between two great nations of different historical and cultural background.

Inevitably, in view of the breadth of our relations, we have problems. Sometimes United States actions run counter to what Japan considers its best interests. But neither of us, because of this reality of international life, loses sight of the larger picture of our common devotion to a world of freedom under law, of our vast and steadily growing trade, of our vital mutual security ties, and of our proven friendship. I have not the slightest doubt, as I hope that you do not, that the negotiation process, with each side taking account of the other's views, is simply an outward expression of this status.

*   *   *

COMMUNIST CHINA'S TEST OF A NUCLEAR WEAPON

D. Comment by Secretary of State Dean Rusk*

September 29, 1964

For some time it has been known that the Chinese Communists were approaching the point where they might be able to detonate a first nuclear device. Such an explosion might occur in the near future. If it does occur, we shall know about it and will make the information public.

It has been known since the 1950's that the Chinese Communists have been working to develop a nuclear device. They not only failed to sign but strongly opposed the nuclear test ban treaty which has been signed by over 100 countries. The detonation of a first device does not mean a stockpile of nuclear weapons and the presence of modern delivery systems. The United States has fully anticipated the possibility of Peiping's entry into the nuclear weapons field and has taken it into full account in determining our military posture and our own nuclear weapons program. We would deplore atmospheric testing in the face of serious efforts made by almost all other nations to protect the atmosphere from further contamination and to begin to put limitations upon a spiraling arms race.

*Ibid., Oct. 19, 1964, pp. 542-43.

E. Chinese Communist Announcement*

October 16, 1964

China exploded an atom bomb at 15:00 hours on October 16, 1964, and thereby conducted successfully its first nuclear test. This is a major achievement of the Chinese people in their struggle to increase their national defence capability and oppose the U.S. imperialist policy of nuclear blackmail and nuclear threats.

To defend oneself is the inalienable right of every sovereign state. And to safeguard world peace is the common task of all peace-loving countries. China cannot remain idle and do nothing in the face of the ever increasing nuclear threat posed by the United States. China is forced to conduct nuclear tests and develop nuclear weapons.

The Chinese Government has consistently advocated the complete prohibition and thorough destruction of nuclear weapons. Should this have been realized, China need not develop the nuclear weapon. But this position of ours has met the stubborn resistance of the U.S. imperialists. The Chinese Government pointed out long ago that the treaty on the partial halting of nuclear tests signed by the United States, Britain and the Soviet Union in Moscow in July 1963 was a big fraud to fool the people of the world, that it tried to consolidate the nuclear monopoly held by the three nuclear powers and tie up the hands and feet of all peace-loving countries, and that it not only did not decrease but had increased the nuclear threat of U.S. imperialism against the people of China and of the whole world. The U.S. Government declared undisguisedly even then that the conclusion of such a treaty does not at all mean that the United States would not conduct underground tests, or would not use, manufacture, stockpile, export or proliferate nuclear weapons. The facts of the past year and more fully prove this point.

During the past year and more, the United States has not stopped manufacturing various nuclear weapons on the basis of the nuclear tests which it had already conducted. Furthermore, seeking for ever greater perfection, the United States has during this same period conducted several dozen underground nuclear tests, thereby further perfecting the nuclear weapons it manufactures. In stationing nuclear submarines in Japan, the United States is posing a direct threat to the Japanese people, the Chinese people and the peoples of all other Asian countries. The United States is now putting nuclear weapons into the hands of the West German revanchists through the so-called multilateral nuclear force and thereby threatening the security of the German Democratic Republic and the other East European socialist countries. U.S. submarines carrying Polaris missiles with nuclear warheads are prowling the Taiwan Straits, the Tonkin Gulf, the Mediterranean Sea, the Pacific Ocean, the Indian Ocean and the Atlantic Ocean, threatening everywhere peace-loving countries and all peoples who are fighting against imperialism, colonialism and neo-colonialism. Under such circumstances, how can it be considered that the U.S. nuclear blackmail and nuclear threat against

*Peking Review, Oct. 16, 1964, Supplement.

the people of the world no longer exist just because of the false impression created by the temporary halting of atmospheric tests by the United States?

The atom bomb is a paper tiger. This famous saying by Chairman Mao Tse-tung is known to all. This was our view in the past and this is still our view at present. China is developing nuclear weapons not because we believe in the omnipotence of nuclear weapons and that China plans to use nuclear weapons. The truth is exactly to the contrary. In developing nuclear weapons, China's aim is to break the nuclear monopoly of the nuclear powers and to eliminate nuclear weapons.

The Chinese Government is loyal to Marxism-Leninism and proletarian internationalism. We believe in the people. It is the people who decide the outcome of a war, and not any weapon. The destiny of China is decided by the Chinese people and the destiny of the world by the peoples of the world, and not by the nuclear weapon. The development of nuclear weapons by China is for defence and for protecting the Chinese people from the danger of the United States launching a nuclear war.

The Chinese Government hereby solemnly declares that China will never at anytime and under any circumstances be the first to use nuclear weapons.

The Chinese people firmly support the struggles for liberation waged by all oppressed nations and people of the world. We are convinced that, by relying on their own struggles and also through mutual aid, the peoples of the world will certainly win victory. The mastering of the nuclear weapon by China is a great encouragement to the revolutionary peoples of the world in their struggles and a great contribution to the cause of defending world peace. On the question of nuclear weapons, China will neither commit the error of adventurism nor the error of capitulationism. The Chinese people can be trusted.

The Chinese Government fully understands the good wishes of peace-loving countries and people for the halting of all nuclear tests. But more and more countries are coming to realize that the more the U.S. imperialists and their partners hold on to their nuclear monopoly, the more is there danger of a nuclear war breaking out. They have it and you don't, and so they are very haughty. But once those who oppose them also have it, they would no longer be so haughty, their policy of nuclear blackmail and nuclear threat would no longer be so effective, and the possibility for a complete prohibition and thorough destruction of nuclear weapons would increase. We sincerely hope that a nuclear war would never occur. We are convinced that, so long as all peace-loving countries and people of the world make common efforts and persist in the struggle, a nuclear war can be prevented.

The Chinese Government hereby formally proposes to the governments of the world that a summit conference of all the countries of the world be convened to discuss the question of the complete prohibition and thorough destruction of nuclear weapons, and that as a first step, the summit conference should reach an agreement to the effect that the nuclear powers and those countries which may soon become nuclear powers undertake not to use nuclear weapons, neither to use them against non-nuclear countries and nuclear-free zones, nor against each other.

If those countries in possession of huge quantities of nuclear weapons are not even willing to undertake not to use them, how can those countries not yet in possession of them be expected to believe in their sincerity for peace and not to adopt possible and necessary defensive measures?

The Chinese Government will, as always, exert every effort to promote the realization of the noble aim of the complete prohibition and thorough destruction of nuclear weapons through international consultations. Before the advent of such a day, the Chinese Government and people will firmly and unswervingly march along their own road of strengthening their national defences, defending their motherland and safeguarding world peace.

We are convinced that nuclear weapons which are after all created by man, certainly will be eliminated by man.

F. Statement by President Lyndon B. Johnson*

October 16, 1964

The Chinese Communists have announced that they conducted their first nuclear test today. By our own detection system we have confirmed that a low-yield test actually took place in western China at about 3 a.m., e.d.t.

As Secretary Rusk noted on September 29, we have known for some time that the Chinese Communists had a nuclear development program which was approaching the point of a first detonation of a test device.

This explosion comes as no surprise to the United States Government. It has been fully taken into account in planning our own defense program and nuclear capability. Its military significance should not be overestimated. Many years and great efforts separate testing of a first nuclear device from having a stockpile of reliable weapons with effective delivery systems.

Still more basic is the fact that, if and when the Chinese Communists develop nuclear weapons systems, free-world nuclear strength will continue to be enormously greater.

The United States reaffirms its defense commitments in Asia. Even if Communist China should eventually develop an effective nuclear capability, that capability would have no effect upon the readiness of the United States to respond to requests from Asian nations for help in dealing with Communist Chinese aggression. The United States will also not be diverted from its efforts to help the nations of Asia to defend themselves and to advance the welfare of their people.

The Chinese Communist nuclear weapons program is a tragedy for the Chinese people, who have suffered so much under the Communist regime. Scarce economic resources which could have been used to improve the well-being of the Chinese people have been used to produce a crude nuclear device which can only increase the sense of insecurity of the Chinese people. Other Asian nations have wisely chosen instead to work for the well-being of their people through economic development and peaceful use of the atom. In this way they

*Department of State Bulletin, Nov. 2, 1964, p. 612.

have made a great contribution to the peace and security of the world.

The Chinese Communist nuclear detonation is a reflection of policies which do not serve the cause of peace. But there is no reason to fear that it will lead to immediate dangers of war. The nations of the free world will recognize its limited significance and will persevere in their determination to preserve their independence.

We join all humanity in regretting the contamination of the atmosphere caused by the Chinese Communist test. We will continue in our own efforts to keep the atmosphere clean. We will pursue with dedication and determination our purpose of achieving concrete practical steps on the road that leads away from nuclear armaments and war and toward a world of co-operation, development, and peace.

STATE DEPARTMENT POLICY STATEMENTS

G. Address by Marshall Green, Deputy Assistant Secretary of State for Far Eastern Affairs, on United States Policy Toward Communist China*

[Extract]

February 26, 1965

*   *   *

There are very strict and serious limits within which . . . (American policy toward Communist China) must be pursued.

We—and the outside world, for that matter—have little leverage on the course of developments in Communist China. The mainland of China is tightly controlled by a small group of men singularly impervious to ideas from abroad, and the continental scale and mass of mainland China lessens its reliance upon external relationships.

Our policy toward Communist China is not a policy toward that one country alone. It is inextricably connected with our policies toward China's neighbors, some of whom are very directly threatened by Communist expansionism. We have responsibilities toward these nations, and, having had a role of leadership thrust upon us, we must give clear and unwavering evidence as to our intentions, for those who seek our support. An effort to show flexibility and to better relationships with Communist China would be disastrous if not accompanied by a clear willingness to stand by our friendships, our principles, and our commitments in the Far East.

Finally, Peiping's policy toward the United States is very simple. It is one of avowed hostility. It does not allow even for the working out of lesser problems in our relations, to say nothing of an exploration of fundamental solutions of

American Foreign Policy: Current Documents, 1965, pp. 721-26.

issues between us. As a Chinese Communist document puts it: "We do not wish to settle our disputes with the United States on a piecemeal basis; else we will undermine the revolutionary fervor of our own people. When the time comes for a settlement, it will be done all at once."

This is not a climate in which one may look for quick or easy solutions.

We can be fairly certain that mainland China's fate today is largely controlled by some 70 top Communist leaders, most of whom have much in the way of common experience, who have gone through the cruel and annealing experience of the long march, the Yenan Caves, and the struggle against the Japanese, the Chinese Nationalists, and the United Nations in Korea. These are men who have grown tough and hard and intransigent in the course of this long struggle. They are men who are dedicated Maoists, who are Sinocentric in their outlook, and whose suspicions and inherent xenophobia have been fed by deep resentment of the indignities which China suffered at the hands of the West in the 19th century. In the course of this long common struggle the leaders of Communist China have experienced what in their eyes has been a triumphant success, and this flush of success has contributed to the absolute certainty they feel that the course on which they are embarked is the only one for China. They have a monumental conviction as to the rectitude of their position.

Through violence they successfully made a revolution; and they brought their revolution to success in the countryside and in locales isolated from the interchange of modern ideas. Perhaps this helps to explain their narrow, almost primitive division of the world into what they see as "good, rising progressive forces" like themselves and "bad, decadent imperialist forces" led by ourselves. For them the world is divided into two hostile camps. There is no tolerance of neutrals except insofar as neutrals may be moving in the direction desired by the Peiping leadership.

These leaders have publicly proclaimed a dogma which demands that all non-Communist states must be communized, that this process must be done violently, and that the "bourgeois state machine" must be "smashed." They argue that all the self-proclaimed Socialists who are not Communists are "bourgeois" and marked for destruction, though they may be used for a time to further the Communists' policies. All means are justified, and legal means are presumably the least attractive, since the Chinese say that they are the least likely to succeed. I am not making this up; I am paraphrasing Communist sources.

Being a simple man, I am prone to simplicity of formulations. Hence I am attracted to the "concentric circles" definition of Communist China's ambitions in foreign affairs. You will recall that this formulation sets forth three concentric circles, the innermost of which is China's desire to restore Peiping's control over all areas China regards as her own. The second circle represents Peiping's objective to regain control over areas adjacent to China's borders which at certain times in the past have been under Chinese dominion. Southeast Asia would be a case in point. The third and outer of the concentric circles would be the achievement of great-power status complete with nuclear weapons and becoming the dominant force in the world tomorrow. These objectives are simultaneously pursued.

Of course, such a pattern does not fully establish China's foreign policy goals, for obviously they transcend such narrow definition. For one thing, Peiping is bent upon redressing past indignities imposed on China. It aspires to leadership of the Socialist camp as well as the defeat of "modern revisionism," which it sees as corrupting the world Communist movement. Increasingly it craves leadership of the Afro-Asian world, identifying China with that majority of the world's population living in less privileged circumstances. Because China sees all these ambitions as challenged one way or another by American policy and American design, it is a fundamental objective of China's foreign policy to expel American power and presence from Asia and the West Pacific.

Peiping's tactics in pursuing the foregoing objectives are too well known—indeed painfully well known—to require review. The pursuit of its objectives is of course greatly facilitated by the many basic differences, divisions, and discords amongst China's neighbors. Peiping is also in a good position to exploit the many disappointments and frustrations of our times and to associate itself as the leader of less developed nations in a world where the gap between the have and have-not countries seems unfortunately to be growing.

It is difficult to separate out United States policies toward Communist China from United States policies toward Asia. China makes up a large slice of Asia, and it is China's central threat to its neighbors that poses such a problem for our policy there. Some of our policies, such as assisting nations to achieve economic and social progress, would be pursued even if China did not exist, but the presence of Communist China undoubtedly makes our programs larger and more urgent. These policies could be, for purposes of our discussion today, put under two general headings.

First are the policies directed toward strengthening the security of free-world countries, especially those menaced by Communist China; and of promoting the stability and economic growth of these countries; and of promoting unity and cohesion to the extent we can among the countries comprising the free world.

Then there are the policies that we pursue directly toward Communist China itself. In essence, these policies boil down to seeking to make clear to Communist China that its external adventures are risky and expensive, while at the same time doing what we can to make possible and attractive a process of change whereby mainland China will come to adopt a less intolerant view of others.

We avoid those actions which would tend to strengthen Communist China's position or contribute to the realization of its expansionist goals. Thus, we refuse to establish diplomatic relations with Communist China or to promote its seating in the United Nations. We see little to gain and much to lose through such action.

As to trade with mainland China, we maintain a complete embargo on trade and financial dealings. We do not prevail on others not to trade with mainland China, but we try to hold the line against trade in strategic items and we have urged our friends not to extend trading terms that amount to aid to Communist China.

A significant but ofttimes overlooked aspect of our current policy toward

Communist China is the fact that, while opposing Communist Chinese expansionism, we nevertheless would improve some of our contacts with Communist China. Under this general heading we have held more than 120 diplomatic-level talks with Peiping representatives in Geneva and Warsaw; we have participated with Peiping in international gatherings such as the Geneva talks of 1954 and 1962; we have authorized virtually every newspaperman who has so desired to travel to Communist China; we have authorized a number of other visits to Communist China by Americans for humanitarian or national interest reasons. The United States Post Office accepts letters for delivery to mainland China. There is no prohibition on correspondence to and from China or even on the export of films.

We are holding out the possibility and prospect of expanding such contacts. I for one would greatly hope that they could be expanded and that Peiping would not continue to reject this overture from our side for I believe it would be in our common interest to have wider knowledge of each other.

Is it possible simultaneously to pursue a policy, on the one hand, of seeking to thwart Chinese Communist ambitions and, on the other hand, of seeking to moderate those ambitions? I see the two as entirely complementary. Peiping is not likely to deviate from a course of expansionism if it feels that that course is succeeding. The laws of bureaucratic behavior suggest that no politburo group is likely to suggest a change if Peiping is moving from what it regards as success to success. Only if the costs and risks of expansionism are evident whilst alternative opportunities are available to devote themselves to purposes more at harmony with the rest of the world, only then are the Chinese Communists likely to decide to live in peace in a world with other peoples and other ideas.

Is this all we can do?

It takes two to tango. In part, our relatinship is inescapably established by Communist China's attitude toward us, and this attitude at this particular point of history is embedded in a singularly fierce and infelxible mood in Peiping. There is very little "give" to permit improvement in relations with these men.

*　　　　　*　　　　　*

H. Address by U.S. Ambassador-at-Large Averell Harriman on Chinese Communist Membership in the United Nations*

[Extract]

October 31, 1965

THE BLUEPRINT OF COMMUNIST CHINA IS UNMISTAKABLE

*　　　　　*　　　　　*

People who favor Communist Chinese membership in the United Nations

*Ibid., pp. 748-49.

argue that it would provide an opportunity to talk with the Chinese. But the fact is that there are already many opportunities. We talk to the Communist Chinese on a continuing basis in Warsaw. And our experience is that the only thing they ever want to talk about is our handing Taiwan over to them.

Furthermore, it is naive to suppose that one can moderate Chinese Communist aggressiveness merely by talking with them. The British have been talking with them since 1949 and have not yet even been able to get them to agree on an exchange of ambassadors.

                    *   *   *

If Communist China were to join the United Nations, the effect would be to disrupt the organization. If we doubt that, all we need do is listen to what Peiping itself has to say on this point. Peiping has made its views unmistakably clear.

Last month [September 29] the Foreign Minister of Communist China, Mr. Chen Yi, held an outspoken news conference. Nearly 300 newsmen were present, including many foreign correspondents. For reasons of its own, Peiping itself did not publish the text of the news conference until a week later. However, we now have an official Chinese version of what was said, a transcript reviewed and approved by the regime. So there can be no doubt as to the authenticity of Peiping's views.

Chen Yi was emphatic about the conditions Communist China poses before it will join the United Nations. He said:

> The United Nations must rectify its mistakes and undergo a thorough reorganization and reform. It must admit and correct all its past mistakes. Among other things, it should cancel its resolution condemning China and the Democratic People's Republic of Korea as aggressors, and adopt a resolution condemning the United States as the aggressor; the U.N. Charter must be reviewed and revised jointly by all countries, big and small; all independent states should be included in the United Nations; and all imperialist puppets should be expelled.
>
> If (he continues) the task of reforming the United Nations cannot be accomplished, conditions will no doubt gradually ripen for the establishment of a revolutionary United Nations.

The revolutionary concept of the Chinese Communists has been clearly defined by an exceptionally important Chinese Communist document that appeared less than 2 months ago. It was written by Lin Piao, the Minister of National Defense of Communist China. He is also the Vice Chairman of the Central Committee of the Chinese Communist Party and a Vice Premier of Communist China. The article is 18,000 words long but despite its length was published in full in all the Peiping papers, was carried in all the provincial and municipal newspapers throughout China, was broadcast over both the domestic and international services of Peiping radio, was published as a pamphlet by the people's Publishing House of China and translated into many languages.

There can be no doubt that the Communist Chinese themselves regard it as a document of the highest importance.

It spells out in unmistakable clarity and detail the Communist Chinese doctrine of world revolution. Its significance is similar to that of *Mein Kampf*. It states unequivocally what the intentions of Communist China are, what sort of world it wants, and how that world is to be created.

It is a document that everyone should read but particularly those who disagree with our Government's policy toward Communist China or are critical about our policy in Viet-Nam.

Lin Piao begins with a detailed analysis of the Communist revolution in China and goes on to state:

> It was on the basis of the lessons derived from the people's wars in China that Comrade Mao Tse-tung, using the simplest and most vivid language, advanced the famous thesis that "political power grows out of the barrel of a gun." He clearly pointed out: The seizure of power by armed force, the settlement of the issue by war, is the central task and highest form of revolution. This Marxist-Leninist principle of revolution holds good universally, for China and for all other countries.

He then explains that the Chinese Communist revolution had one essential difference from the Russian revolution. The Russian revolution, Lin notes,

> . . . began with armed uprisings in the cities, and then spread to the countryside; while the Chinese Revolution won nationwide victory through the encirclement of the cities from the rural areas, and the final capture of the cities.

This leads Lin to his central theme. the "rural areas of the world" today, he states, are Asia, Africa, and Latin America. The "cities of the world" are Western Europe and North America.

Hence, he concludes, just as communism in China succeeded by capturing first the countryside, and then encircling and defeating the cities, so the world Communist movement will succeed by first capturing Asia, Africa, and Latin America—thereby encircling Western Europe and North America—and then by finally and decisively defeating the United States and its Western allies.

And how is the countryside of the world—Asia, Africa, and Latin America—to be captured? It is to be captured, says Lin, by waging "wars of national liberation."

"In the last analysis," says Lin Piao bluntly, "the Marxist-Leninist theory of proletarian revolution is the theory of the seizure of state power by revolutionary violence, the theory of countering war against the people by people's war."

"Today," he adds, "the conditions are more favorable than ever before for the waging of people's wars by the revolutionary peoples of Asia, Africa, and Latin America."

Thus the blueprint of Communist China is unmistakable. Win Asia, Africa, and Latin America through "wars of national liberation," and the United States and its Western allies will be encircled and eventually overwhelmed.

And the whole "focus" of the revolutionary movement against the United States today, he states, is in Viet-Nam. No matter what action America may take in Viet-Nam, the Communist Chinese determination "to support and aid the Vietnamese people" is "unshakable"; and "the Chinese people will do everything in their power to support the Vietnamese people until every single one of the U.S. aggressors is driven out of Viet-Nam."

           *   *   *

THE SINO-SOVIET DISPUTE AND IMPLICATIONS FOR UNITED STATES CHINA POLICY

I. Statement of Roger Hilsman, Department of Law and Government, Columbia University, New York*

March 10, 1965

First, let me say it is a privilege and honor Mr. Chairman, to appear as a private citizen before this subcommittee before which I have testified so often as an official in the past. It is good to see all you again.

I think the Foreign Affairs Committee and the Far Eastern Subcommittee are tbe highly commended for their wisdom and foresight in holding these hearings on the Sino-Soviet dispute and its implications. A public discussion of these matters will be a great service to the American people and to the U.S. Government. For I would conjecture that future historians, looking back, will point to the Sino-Soviet dispute as one of the most portentous international political developments of our time.

Quite clearly, the dispute is fundamental in every rich sense of that word. First of all, it is concerned with ideology, with the nature of the Communist world, with their vision of the future world, and with what kind of interpretation shall be given to the "sacred" tests of Marx and Lenin.

It is also concerned with power—whether power shall be centered in Moscow, widely distributed in the Communist bloc in a formula of "polycentrism," or, perhaps, concentrated in Peiping. Communism is a doctrine for seizing and holding· power, and in a very real sense the Chinese Communists in their bid for leadership are really just behaving like Communists, although in this instance against other Communists.

The Sino-Soviet dispute is also concerned with strategy—grand, nuclear strategy toward the whole of the free world. The differences here are symbolized by Mao Tse-tung's statements, in the midst of the Cuban missile crisis, that the United States and the free world was only a paper tiger, and Khruschev's reply that this particular paper tiger had nuclear teeth.

It is also concerned with policy toward the in-between world. I was on the Harriman mission to New Delhi in the wake of the Chinese Communist attack on India, and it was quite clear to us at that time that the motive for the attack was as much to insult the Soviet Union as it was to humiliate India.

All of this—the sources of the dispute, its twists and turns, and its texture—has been the subject of thorough analysis inside the Government and in our great universities. The question now is how the dispute will develop in the future.

Speculating about the future of such esoteric matters as the Communists relations with each other is obviously risky. But enough is known of the nature

*Subcommittee on the Far East and the Pacific of the House Committee on Foreign Affairs, *Sino-Soviet Conflict, Report on Sino-Soviet Conflict and Its Implications* (Washington, U.S. Government Printing Office, 1965), pp. 2-6. Mr. Hilsman was a leading authority on foreign affairs and international politics as well as a distinguished scholar and leading public servant.

of the dispute to chance, perhaps, at least two predictions.

The first is that the dispute will probably not proceed rapidly either to a complete and final break or to a complete and perfect healing. Both sides will on different occasions undoubtedly make overtures to the other. At times the two sides will seem to come together. At other times they will seem to veer almost unbearably far apart. Yet I think that before either eventuality is consummated one or the other side will draw back.

My feeling is that the Chinese Communist price for healing the breach will be too high for the Soviets to pay. In the first place, the Chinese will undoubtedly insist on a very large share of the leadership of the bloc and a very large place for Chinese national interests, as opposed to Russian national interests, in deciding on bloc policy—in both cases probably too large a share. In the second place, the Chinese will also probably insist on abandoning the policy of easing international tensions that the Soviets adopted following the Cuban missile crisis and returning to a very aggressive, very Stalinist cold war. And I think the Soviet leaders, having rejected that alternative after the missile crisis, will be very reluctant to accept it now. Their policy of easing international tensions, signing the test ban treaty, and so on, does not mean, of course, that the Soviets have abandoned the goals of communism, but only that they hope to reach those goals by less risky means—by political means, subversion, and so on. In the Cuban missile crisis, the Soviet leaders looked down the gun barrel of nuclear war and decided that that road led to disaster. The people now heading the Soviet Union are the same ones who put the missiles into Cuba and the same ones who took them out. They understand the risks and consequences of nuclear war, and they are not likely to return to high-risk, cold war except for very weighty reasons—if we adopt policies that they feel force them into it, for example, or if the Chinese high-risk policies are so successful the Soviets are in danger of losing their position of leadership in the bloc.

The second speculation is that if the judgment is correct that the Sino-Soviet dispute will be around for some time as a dispute, then both Chinese and Soviet moves on the international scene will be done in terms more of the effect the particular move has on the dispute than in terms of the effect it has on the United States or the West—that the dispute, in other words, will be the single most important influence on both Soviet and Chinese behavior for at least the next several years.

The implications of all this for the United States are not necessarily all to the good. The breakup of what people thought of as a monolithic, single-willed Communist bloc is certainly not unwelcome—but this was inevitable anyway and started among the Eastern European satellites long before the Chinese and Soviets began to quarrel. But the Soviets will not, in my judgment, give up to the Chinese the right to speak for revolution and radicalism. Kosygin's recent visit to Hanoi, for example, seems more likely to result in increased Soviet aid for the war against South Vietnam and increased pressure for negotiations on Communist terms than a sudden outbreak of peaceful cooperation. It is not a happy thought that one possible outcome of the dispute is that we might find ourselves trying to deal with two highly competitive fomentors of subversion in Africa, Latin America, Asia, and the Middle East rather than just one.

What should our policy be? I think it would be a mistake to take sides in the dispute, as some have suggested, or to attempt to manipulate it as a way of scoring points in the cold war. Basically, we must deal with Communist China as an independent force in the world, and in the long run our policy must combine firmness with a willingness to provide the Chinese Communists with an honorable and acceptable alternative to continued hostility. This is the policy we have been following with the Soviet Union—when they put missiles in Cuba we dealt with them firmly, very firmly, but a few months later we had the flexibility to negotiate a test ban treaty without letting the emotion of the past cloud our vision of what was good for both the United States and the world. While still a Government official I had the privilege of enunciating such a policy toward Communist China, a policy of firmness combined with flexibility and dispassion, in San Francisco on December 13, 1963, and I think it continues to be the only sound approach for the long run.

Parenthetically, I might add that there are a number of initiatives we might now take to implement that policy statement, as I recently suggested also in a San Francisco speech. If we took these steps—arranging to have the Chinese invited to the arms control talks in Geneva, lifting U.S. travel restrictions, reexamining some of our trade policies, and proceeding to the recognition of Outer Mongolia—there would be no dramatic results; that is, the Chinese would continue to behave as Communists. But these steps would at least begin to put political pressure on the Chinese Communists, to get the United States off the hook it is now on, and to help persuade the peoples and nations of Asia that it is not we who are isolating the Chinese Communists but the Chinese Communists themselves through their pariah policies and attitudes.

But the real test of our capacity to deal with the Chinese Communists both firmly and wisely is in southeast Asia and South Vietnam. It is the supreme test for our determination to stop Chinese-inspired Communist expansion, which we must do. But it is also a test of our capacity to accommodate ourselves to the fact that the Chinese Communists effectively control the mainland with its vast manpower and resources and therefore to the fact of Communist China's continued existence, which we must also do. The Chinese, incidentally, must also learn to accommodate themselves to our continued power and presence in Asia, and those who press so hard for "peace initiatives" right now must realize that giving the Chinese opportunities to do so does not mean that they will have the foresight and wisdom to take those opportunities—by which I mean only that in international affairs it takes two to avoid disaster.

Implementing this general policy in the specific case of southeast Asia and South Vietnam requires first that we assess our goals there coldly and realistically. I do not think the United States needs or wants to make southeast Asia a bastion of anticommunism and a base for American power in Asia. Such ambitions, indeed, would lead only to war, for the Chinese Communists would undoubtedly make extraordinary sacrifices in blood and treasure to frustrate them. At the same time, I think the Chinese can be brought to recognize that we will not tolerate their making southeast Asia into a bastion of anti-westernism and a base for Chinese Communist power. And with the proper orchestration of military, political, and diplomatic instrumentalities, I think this task of bringing the Chinese to discipline their ambitions could be accomplished at a cost that most Americans would find reasonable.

The goal, then, is southeast Asia for the southeast Asians. This will mean a neutralized buffer zone including Laos, Cambodia, and South Vietnam and will require negotiations at a suitable time.

But what time is "suitable"? The time will be suitable, I fear, only when we have demonstrated our determination to be firm by an appropriate and creditable use of force in the furtherance of these goals, even though they are essentially limited and modest. I think having limited and modest goals is not enough, that our goals have to be backed up by American power even though they are limited.

One possible form this use of force might take is airpower. It must, of course, be used with circumspection. Using airpower against either Laos or North Vietnam violates the Geneva agreements of both 1954 and 1962 at a time when there is merit to the argument that if our goals in southeast Asia are indeed limited and modest, then we ought to be trying to preserve as much of the sanctity of the Geneva accords as we can—precisely to convey to the Communists that we regard the situation envisioned by the Geneva accords as an acceptable alternative for both of us. Airpower used across Communist borders also runs some risk of driving the Soviet back into the arms of the Chinese, but probably not a very high risk at least for the time being.

These are the costs of using airpower, but on balance the costs may be worth paying. For airpower might possibly work.

The greatest doubt about bombing is whether it will be effective in forcing the Communists to call it quits in a place like South Vietnam. Bombing or the threat of bombing might deter the Communists from doing something they had not yet begun, but will it cause them to stop something already going, and from their point of view going rather well? The kind of all-out bombing of North Vietnam that some have suggested would, it seems, almost surely bring the regular North Vietnamese armies into South Vietnam and possibly the Chinese Communists as well. The kind of limited, tailored bombing program the United States has recently inaugurated, on the other hand, runs only a very small risk of spiraling into a larger war. Although there is a real question whether such measured and limited attacks on North Vietnam will do enough damage to persuade the Communists we mean business, it is probably worth a try.

But what if measured retaliation does not work? What do we do then? The problem is that the use of airpower in any form is to Asians a weak response. Given the history of America's flirtation with ideas of "immaculate" war in Asia, the use of airpower looks too much like a bluff, like an attempt to use force "on the cheap." In the circumstances, the only thing we can really be sure will impress either Communist or non-Communist Asians are ground forces.

If we put ground forces into Thailand as a first step and later, if necessary, into South Vietnam, and couple these moves with a diplomatic offensive designed to bring about negotiations to reestablish the Geneva agreements, I think the Chinese and North Vietnamese Communists would get the message of our determination and begin to revise their ambitions downward. It was only after we put ground troops into Thailand in 1962, you will recall, that the Communists signed the Laos accords. After stalling for almost a year. And for many months thereafter they behaved themselves.

But we cannot bluff. If the Communists refuse to come to the negotiating table and insist on total victory, we must fight—and fight on the ground as well as in the air. I think both the Chinese and the North Vietnamese Communists have demonstrated by their caution that they respect American power and that the chances that they would insist on war are therefore very small. But we must face the possibility squarely.

Let me add here that I think that one of the greatest dangers is that a lot of people in the country think that they wouldn't really fight for southeast Asia, but they are going to try to bluff their way through with measures that are designed to look tough but that they don't really mean to follow up. If so, we may well find ourselves in a war because the Communists will see through the bluff. What I am arguing is, we have to make up our minds whether we want to save southeast Asia, or don't. If we want to save it, we have to face the possibility of fighting on the ground there. I don't think we will have to fight if we do this, but we must be prepared to. My greatest fear is if we try to win on the cheap, that we will get into a war that we might have deterred if we had made up our minds in time.

But here, indeed, is the rub. Both our people and our military leaders find limited wars distasteful, and they have recoiled especially from the thought of having again to fight on the ground, in the jungle muck of Asia.

But limited wars are a fact of life in the nuclear age. The Communists, and especially the Chinese Communists, will continue to present limited challenges—guerrilla terrorism, small-scale ground attack, and so on—and they will present these challenges in uninviting places in southeast Asia, and in Africa. Thus of one thing, at least, we can be certain. If we do not face the possibility of fighting on the ground now, in southeast Asia, then we will surely have to face it later—in Thailand or elsewhere—and in even more unfavorable circumstances.

If we are to meet the challenge posed by the Chinese Communists, in sum, and the perplexities, brought about through the Sino-Soviet dispute, of threats increasing in the midst of an easing of international tensions and a growing detente, then we must somehow find in ourselves the strength and maturity to stand firm against our enemies while at the same time taking positive initiatives in seeking ways of mutual accommodation. For lasting peace has always been dialectical, the product of both strength and conciliation.

J. Statement of Dr. Harold C. Hinton, Institute for Sino-Soviet Studies, George Washington University, Washington, D.C.*

March 10, 1965

Thank you, Mr. Chairman.

It seems logical to begin a discussion of the Chinese aspect of the Sino-Soviet dispute with a brief statement of what appears to be Communist China's policy goals. The first is security against strategic attack, and above all nuclear attack, by the United States or conceivably the Soviet Union, against local attack or border probing by either of those powers or by Nationalist China or India, and against the satellitization of any region of China by a power entrenched just across the frontier as happened more than once during China's modern history. The second goal is power, which includes such things as the maintenance of internal political control, the building of a heavy industrial system, and a modern military establishment, and the keeping alive abroad of a widespread belief in Communist China's willingness to use its power when and if necessary. The third goal is territorial unification, by which I refer not to the vast areas of Asia that Chinese sources sometimes allege to have been taken from imperial China by the "imperialist" powers in the 19th century but to Taiwan, which is important to Communist China mainly because it shelters a rival regime whose elimination would terminate the prolonged Chinese civil war and give the Communists sole custody of the symbols of China's sovereignty and status. The fourth goal is influence, under which are included such things as an ultimately predominant political position in at least the continental portion of eastern Asia, a leading role in the revolutionization of the underdeveloped areas, a prominent a position in the international Communist movement as the increasingly decentralized nature of that movement may permit, ultimate status as a superpower at least roughly comparable to the United States and the Soviet Union, and the eventual communization of the world.

The methods employed by Communist China to date in pursuit of these goals occupy a wide spectrum. At one extreme is overt violence, notably in the Korean war, which however taught the Chinese an effective lesson in the risks of such behavior. In general, Communist China has restricted the employment of overt violence to situations in which it considered its security to be threatened; to use overt violence primarily in pursuit of influence would entail not only military risks but serious political consequences. Subversion, or covert violence, is widely employed by the Chinese for purposes of both security and influence; Communist China also encourages and supports resort to subversion by foreign left-wing regimes under appropriate conditions, consistent with tailoring the Chinese role so that the military and political risks to Communist China do not become excessive. Communist China makes widespread use of threats and military maneuvers and demonstrations, which produce an effect without creating much genuine risk. Communist China also makes widespread, and on the whole, effective

Ibid., pp. 14-18. Mr. Hinton received a Ph.D. from Harvard University and taught at Oxford, Columbia, Harvard, Georgetown, Trinity College and John Hopkins, as well as George Washington University. He is the author of several books on Asian politics and foreign policy.

use of such more or less non-violent methods as diplomacy, cultural relations, economic penetration and attraction, liaison with foreign leftists, border disputes, and the harboring of political exiles from other countries.

The strictly ideological aspect of the issues in dispute between Communist China and the Soviet Union is less important than the jurisdictional: Mao Tse-tung believes that he had evolved a unique revolutionary strategy for the underd-eveloped world that was validated by his own victory in China in 1949, and that since the death of Stalin he has been the only living figure in the Communist world having the status of what Marxist-Leninists call a "continuator," or major prophet; hence he has claimed for the Chinese party a unique authority to define ideology and strategy for the entire movement. One of the major sources of Sino-Soviet political differences is the obvious Soviet preoccupation with Europe and the equally obvious Chinese preoccupation with the Far East. The two are clearly in a state of intense rivalry for influence within the international Communist movement. They favor differing revolutionary strategies for the un-derdeveloped areas. The Russians generally prefer a more or less peaceful pro-cess aided by the presumed economic attractiveness of the Communist bloc that will bring the country in question into the bloc in a relatively developed state, so that it will not be unduly dependent on foreign aid and will not be oriented toward Communist China; the Chinese, for both ideological and nationalistic reasons, generally favor a more active strategy of political and if possible military struggle. In the economic field, the Chinese believe that the Russians could and should have been more generous in the terms on which they have extended aid to and traded with Communist China. In addition, the Chinese consider that they themselves went too far during their first 5-year plan (1953-57) in applying the Stalinist Soviet model of economic development to China and have since been looking for an approach more suited to Chinese conditions. Among the most important social issues between Communist China and the Soviet Union are the enormous differences between their traditional cultures and between the stages of Communist-style modernization in which they now find themselves.

Since at least as long ago as 1953, the Chinese have increasingly resented what they regarded as a strong Soviet tendency to subordinate Chinese national and revolutionary interests to Soviet national interest, and in particular to consi-derations of Soviet national security. The obsessive anti-Americanism of the Communist Chinese feeds on a number of things, prominent among them the American policy of denying them Taiwan and of aiding and protecting the rival regime that makes it headquarters on the island. The Soviet Union has given little more than lipservice to the Communist Chinese ambition to control Taiwan and has no wish to become embroiled in a major Far Eastern war over Taiwan, or for that matter anything else. There is an obvious Sino-Soviet rivalry for influence in Asia, which takes such forms as a border dispute that seems to have approached a state of war during 1963 and 1964, a jockeying for position in the small Asian Communist states (Outer Mongolia, North Korea, and North Vietnam), and Soviet efforts to build counterweights to China in India and Indonesia. One of the very most basic Chinese objections to Khrushchev was his failure to behave as the leader of the Communist bloc, as Stalin had allegedly done to a considerably greater degree, or in other words to use the power and influence of the Soviet state to aid, support, and protect the other states of the Communist bloc. Since the Second World War the Soviet Union, for at least partly economic reasons, has never built its strategic military forces to a level where they could serve as much more than a minimum deterrent to the United States, and not to a level that would give it the kind of offensive leverage adequate to enable it to play the role demanded by the Chinese. Communist China would probably like to see the Soviet Union restore Stalinist controls, hold down consumption levels, and build up its strategic forces, provided of course that they were employed to exert pressure on the United States, not China.

The essential difference between Communist China and the Soviet Union over the question of war has not been over the results of a general nuclear war, which both wish to avoid, but over the chances that local war might escalate into general war. The Russians, who are dangerous enough so that the United States keeps its main military attention focused on them, feel correspondingly disinclined to assume that the chances of escalation are as small as the Chinese say they are. Since the middle 1950's, with some outstanding exceptions such as Berlin and Cuba, the Soviet Union has been impelled by its fear of American strategic military power to conciliate the United States to the extent it regarded as necessary to guarantee against general war. The Chinese have regarded this conciliation as not only unnecessary but politically wrong, since it has prevented the Soviet Union from giving them the support to which they felt entitled. Khrushchev found himself caught in a kind of vicious circle in which his gestures to the United States enraged the Chinese, who thereby drove him to move still closer to the United States so that he could have his hands free in the west to deal with his increasingly troublesome neighbor to the east. Since about 1960, when the Sino-Soviet dispute came out into the open, the Soviet Union has evidently wanted the United States to stay on in Okinawa, because an American withdrawal from that important base would seriously impair the ability of the United States to continue its military containment of Communist China, with results that might involve the Soviet Union in undesired risks and complications.

The effects of the Sino-Soviet dispute on Chinese policy have been very far reaching. The Chinese effort to incite revolutions anywhere and everywhere in the underdeveloped areas, which has been especially vigorous since 1958, stems not only from a desire to advance the cause of communism but from a conviction of the unreliability of Soviet aid and protection against the United States, Nationalist China, or the two together. The Chinese hope is that revolutions in other parts of the world will so distract and tie down the United States that the attainment of Communist China's objectives in the Far East will eventually become possible. It may be recalled that in the 1920's the Communist International also tried to stir up revolutions almost everywhere; this was done not only to advance the cause of communism but to shield the infant Soviet state. In the economic field, Communist China's fear of the United States and Nationalist China, in the light of Soviet unreliability, contributed greatly to the efforts at drastic self-strengthening represented by the collectivization drive of

1955 and the great leap forward of 1958. The Sino-Soviet dispute, and in particular the withdrawal of Soviet aid in 1960, has driven Communist China to adopt a policy that it calls self-sufficiency, which really means a reduction of economic relations with the Communist bloc and an increase of economic relations with the West, excluding the United States; the interesting implication is that the Chinese see trade with the West as carrying fewer irksome strings than does trade with the Soviet Union. In addition, the Chinese have deprecated Soviet aid programs in the underdeveloped areas and set up an aid program of their own which, although much smaller than the Soviet program, is not only differently designed but clearly intended to be competitive with it.

In the military field, the Sino-Soviet dispute has rendered the Sino-Soviet alliance almost meaningless, except in the extremely unlikely event that the United States launched a clearly unprovoked strategic attack on Communist China or landed troops on Chinese territory near the Soviet Union. This situation in turn has made the Chinese cautious in their overt military behavior, at any rate since 1951 and where the United States is concerned. They have begun since 1956 to acquire nuclear weapons and appropriate delivery systems of their own manufacture, for reasons of both prestige and security. As a long-range goal, they have advocated since about the same time a program of complete nuclear disarmament, without conventional disarmament, which if it should ever be adopted would obviously relieve China of the greatest threats to its security and would leave it the major military power in Asia. As the best means toward this goal, the Chinese encourage the creation of national nuclear forces, including non-Communist forces, apparently in the belief that this is the best way to create so much general concern that the United States and the Soviet Union will eventually be driven to agree to general nuclear disarmament.

The issues between Communist China and the Soviet Union that I have discussed unfolded during the decade of Khrushchev's ascendancy in the Soviet Union. His fall, in which I believe his excessive party and state pressures on Communist China to have played the precipitating role, eliminated from the Sino-Soviet relationship its most immediate tensions and its extreme urgency, but not the fundamental issues. The policy of marginally greater toughness toward the non-Communist world and marginally greater consideration for the Chinese that Khrushchev's successors have so far adopted is clearly not enough to satisfy the Chinese, who demand a far more sweeping repudiation of Khrushchev's policies. It is hard to see how the Russians can ever see their way to satisfying the Chinese, and the dispute is therefore almost certain to continue. It seems possible that some means will be found to carry on the dispute without overtly rupturing the formal unit of the international Communist movement beyond repair, but this possibility is of less importance than the persistence of the dispute and the opportunity it will offer to the United States, as in the past, to exacerbate Sino-Soviet differences by containing both the two great Communist powers, and in particular by continuing to frustrate Communist China's major objectives with respect to Taiwan and other areas of the Far East.

K. Statement of Dr. George E. Taylor, Director, Far Eastern and Russian Institute, The University of Washington*

[Extract]

March 16, 1965

I

First of all let us say something about the present position of the United States in Asia and the Western Pacific.

The main lines of our present approach were laid down by President Truman. They are to maintain sufficient military force in the western Pacific to discourage open aggression by the Communist powers and to assist those states that wish to maintain their independence. To further these policies we have concluded bilateral mutual security pacts, as with Japan, Korea, Taiwan, and the Philippines and multilateral arrangements such as the SEATO and ANZUS. Our military power in the western Pacific depends at least to some extent on the viability of these political arrangements, in other words, on the morale, the attitudes, and the endurance of our allies. Where appropriate this calls for U.S. assistance in the construction of the institutions and the spirit of the modern state and nation. More than ever before the various ways in which our policy is expressed—military, political, economic, psychological—are interdependent.

The weakest links in the chain are the new underdeveloped states, one can hardly call them nations, of southeast Asia. Where we deal with strong nation-states, such as Japan, the lack of integration in policy implementation is often concealed but not in our dealings with emerging nations, such as Vietnam, which have to collect the materials, choose the design, construct the house, live in it and defend it all at the same time. To some extent in the Philippines, to a larger degree in southeast Asia, we are inevitably involved in the intimate task of nation building, and as the problems of the new nations are all so interrelated, participation in their solution is no simple matter.

Let us remember that the United States brings a considerable amount of experience to the task. Under different conditions, but not so different as to be irrelevant, the United States has been engaged in the business of nation building in the Philippines since 1900 and in Japan since 1945. In the case of the Philippines we contributed the politically decisive concept of a self-liquidating colony, in the case of Japan the vital assistance in releasing revolutionary forces which were already in being in such a way as to change the internal balance of power in favor of representative government and a free economy. In the Philippines we helped to defeat the Communist-led attempt to seize power with political ideas and strategies, not by contributing large military forces. We have more recently been attempting to devise a body of theory to guide us in our efforts

*Ibid., pp. 170-73. Mr. Taylor received a D.Litt. degree from the University of Birmingham and later studied at Harvard, Johns Hopkins and in Peiping prior to joining the Far Eastern and Russian Institute at the University of Washington. He is the author of several books and articles on Asia.

to encourage economic growth in underdeveloped countries—and ideas in this field are likely to be as important as weapons of war. There is a good deal of solid history behind the emergence of these new dimensions in the implementation of policy, in fact, the two most important seedbeds—the Philippines and Japan—came before the direct impact of Communist power in eastern Asia.

The effect of the Sino-Soviet bloc, divided or not, upon the U.S. position is felt most keenly in those areas where the state structure and national sentiment are the weakest. The invasion of South Korea, for example, led to a continuing effort to fabricate a nation out of South Korea. It also led to the addition of a new psychological warfare device of nonforcible repatriation of prisoners of war—a valuable tool in combating Communist powers. To the Communists we also owe the clause in the SEATO which authorizes a member state to call for help not only against direct aggression but also against internal subversion—a very important addition to the legal armory and a timely recognition of the political facts of life.

Most significant of all, perhaps, the Communists have forced us to pay attention to what is now called counterinsurrection, a type of civil war which Mao Tse-tung has made famous and in which he has had some successes. The Communists have forced on us the most painful of all tasks, the task of creative thinking. The struggles against Communist terrorists in Malaya and the Philippines both succeeded because the governments saw the problem as a whole, as a sort of social, political, and military continuum. They formulated doctrines for countering civil war, they made military action an integral part of political and social action. They won because of the superiority of their ideas, institutions, and organizations. From these experiences, as from experience in Vietnam, we have learned that we have to clarify our objectives in order to coordinate the means by which they are to be achieved.

II

Does this conflict between Moscow and Peiping change the situation described above? Basically, in my opinion, it does not, but it leads to several modifications which are important. First of all let us say something about Chinese Communist policy, recently so ably discussed by Deputy Assistant Secretary Marshall Green at Princeton, February 26, 1965. Communist China has three main objectives—the first is to finish the civil war. It is essential for Peiping to eliminate the political influence of the National Government of China if control of the mainland is to be secure. She has tried to do this by force, by subversion, and by getting the U.N. General Assembly to do it for her. She has tried to get Moscow's assistance not only in the U.N. but also in the Taiwan Straits. It is possible that the conflict has reduced the chances of war in this area. Second, Peiping seeks to establish China as a great power, certainly on a regional basis, by industrialization, by development of nuclear capcity, and by expansion of her influence beyond her borders. Third, Peiping seeks to increase its own influence in the bloc, which means to decrease that of the Soviet Union. This she seeks to do by undermining the ideological prestige of the Soviet leaders, by an organizational drive to capture as many of the worldwide Communist parties as possible, and by opposing every sign of agreement between Moscow and the United States, however flimsy. As the facts of nuclear power force the Soviet Union, for its own safety, into some measures of arms control, Peiping has the propaganda advantage. Pursuit of the third objective has led to a vigorous expansion of Chinese activities in Asia, Africa, and Latin America.

III

The first consequence for the U.S. position is that the Soviet Union does not loom as large in eastern Asia and the western Pacific as it used to. We can expect to deal more and more exclusively with the Chinese. The second consequence is that the difficulties of anticipating Chinese and Soviet reactions have been increased. This is because both Moscow and Peiping use the flow of events to put pressures on each other. We have to guess how far the one is prepared to go in embarrassing the other. In my view it is wiser to assume that if the Communist regime in Peiping ever gets into a position where the future of the Chinese Communist Party itself is at stake Moscow can be counted on to come to its assistance. Unlikely as it appears to be at present, the reverse would also be true. Moscow and Peiping are playing dangerous politics with each other and this increases the potential irrational element in their relations with the West.

The Sino-Soviet conflict has an influence on the psychological-political forces at work in Asia. It gives to Peiping somewhat more of the stature of an independent nation-state than it had during the days of "leaning to one side." The claim to represent Chinese nationalism, to be correcting the humiliations of the past, and to expect, therefore, the loyalty of the oversea Chinese is all the more plausible. It is that much harder for many to remember the Communist element in this captive nationalism. In fact, one of the important side benefits to Peiping of the conflict with Moscow is its appeal to Chinese on Taiwan and abroad.

Evidence of the prevalence of the view that Chinese foreign policy can be interpreted entirely in terms of nationalism and great state interests can be seen in the diplomacy of France, the general willingness to trade with Peiping, and the rising pressures to admit her to the U.N. It is more difficult to get our allies to agree with our general line, as Marshall Green puts it, of avoiding those actions which would tend to strengthen Communist China's position or contribute to the realization of its expansionist goals. This spurious nationalism also reveals the shortcomings of the political policies of the National Government, which has not opposed the conquest of Tibet or the general treatment of minorities by Peiping on the grounds that it could not be less nationalist than Peiping.

We have seen how many Chinese analysts in this country consciously or unconsciously support Peiping against Moscow. The impact of the Peiping position on Taiwan must be watched very carefully. Others will speak on Japan, but it is obvious that the conflict helps the Chinese with the Japanese, whose long-standing fear of Russia is still a factor in their foreign policy.

*   *   *

This is no time to relax our efforts. The pressures which China and the Soviet Union are putting on the underdeveloped countries of southeast Asia are all the greater because of the success of U.S. policies in some other parts of Asia. We should remind ourselves that Japan is prosperous in large part because of the successful policies of the occupation, especially the land reform, which helped to revitalize industry and rob the Communists of a rural base. Taiwan is economically far ahead of the mainland also in part because of successful land reform. The Philippines has far to go but has avoided one Communist takeover and is well on the way to constructing a free economy. Malaya finally crushed a Communist-led civil war and came to terms with Singapore to set up Malaysia, largely owing to enlightened British policies. There is ample evidence, in other words, that where the Western style of economic development is adopted, especially on the land, the contrast with the Communist style is vastly to our advantage.

The Sino-Soviet conflict has shown that mainland China is not, by itself, a great power. It ranks low in naval and air power, and much of its large army is necessary to keep its own people in order. The only weapons it has to use in international affairs are subversion, a powerful enough weapon, and organizational infighting within Communist parties abroad. Unlike the Soviet Union, China is too poor to cover the mailed fist with a velvet glove. But unlike the Soviet Union she does not face the military and economic might of the West. She can take advantage of her opportunities, which are in the weak and disorganized societies of the world, because she does not have the responsibilities that go with great power.

The Sino-Soviet conflict, then, makes no fundamental difference to the U.S. position in Asia because we still have to deal with the bloc as a whole. Peiping and Moscow still have fundamental interests in common which, in a real crisis, outweigh their differences. In the meantime the conflict will complicate the resolution of problems such as Vietnam in a way that was not true of Korea, and possibly increase the difficulties of negotiation. But it is well to keep things in perspective; we are paying a great deal of attention to China. But there is the risk that in concentrating on the rift we may neglect the effective unity of the Communist bloc and think of Peiping and Moscow as two distinct antagonistic and utterly separate powers—which they are not.

L. Statement of Marshall Green, Deputy Assistant Secretary of State for Far Eastern Affairs*

March 23, 1965

Those who have dealt with Communist China are impressed by the remarkable

* *Ibid.*, pp. 318-21.

intransigence and arrogance of its leaders, who are at once sinocentrics and dedicated Communists. These are men who have had a long common struggle together during the years of the long march, exile in the Yenan caves, the fight against the Japanese, the Chinese Nationalists and the United Nations itself. By their lights they feel that this long struggle has been crowned with success, and this flush of success only makes them the more convinced about the course on which they are now embarked. They are not yet ready to admit that truth is shared, that other philosophies may have validity, and not just the philosophy which they have embraced. All the world to them is black and white. Those who agree with Peiping's leaders are regarded as good or progressive or rising; those who disagree with them are bad, decadent and reactionary. They see the world as a battlefield of struggling ideas, in which theirs must prevail.

Anyone who tries to deal with these Chinese Communist leaders is almost certain to find them rigid, suspicious, and maddeningly difficult. The Soviets, one can be sure, are no exception; and because of the very fact that they have had so many dealings with the Chinese Communists, few can be more smarting from the experience than the Soviets.

Ever since the Chinese moved openly onto the offensive in their campaign against Khrushchev and his colleagues, relations have moved steadily downhill. We have been presented just recently with a striking example of the extent to which the former Communist monolith has been weakend and fractured by this fratricidal infighting. After earlier demands by former Premier Khrushchev for a conference of Communist parties, which was to take formal action against the "splitting" activities of Communist China, the new Soviet leadership was obliged to downgrade the gathering into a "consultative" session, which met at the beginning of this month in Moscow. Far from reaching any conclusions as to how to handle relations between Communist China and other Communist countries, this conclave adjourned sine die after coming only to the most general agreement that unity as a goal was desirable. The conclave was comdemned by Peiping on March 19 as a schismatic meeting convoked by Moscow "unilaterally, illegally, and by scraping bits and pieces together." Central direction simply no longer exists in the Communist movement.

Before turning to an examination of some of the major elements in the Sino-Soviet conflict, I should like to introduce one note of caution. I often hear and read that differences between Moscow and Peiping represent an unqualified gain for the free world. I cannot agree that the gain is unqualified. Neither Moscow nor Peiping, in their struggles with each other, are siding with free nations or defending the sovereignty and rights of free people. Rather, they are disagreeing over how best to spread Communist doctrine and control abroad, of how best to communize the world. As each strives to prove its brand of communism correct, and particularly as Peiping seeks to gain victories for its more activist and militant support for "wars of national liberation," the threat to free men and nations is increased. The threat is not eased.

What have been some of the major factors in the Sino-Soviet dispute, as seen from Peiping's eyes?

1. For Mao and his colleagues, leadership of the world Communist movement

unquestionably stands at or near the fore. Following Stalin's death in 1953, the Chinese Communists progressively felt that Mao should assume the mantle of world Communist leadership. This sense of superiority has been evident in the vitriolic attacks on Khrushchev the "uncultured peasant," whose removal was accepted by Peiping as a vindication of its own attitudes.

The Chinese leaders do not seem to regard the new Kremlin leadership as much of an improvement. Increasingly the theme is developed that the new Soviet leaders represent no more than "Khrushchevism without Khrushchev." Peiping rejects Moscow's "modern revisionism" and sees the Soviet Union as going soft and bourgeois and as no longer a worthy follower of Lenin. Peiping also maintains its rejection of Soviet policies on "peaceful coexistence," and demands more active Soviet support for "wars of national liberation." Peiping has shown no inclination to end its efforts to split local Communist parties where the incumbent is pro-Moscow in orientation.

2. In similar fashion, Peiping continues to challenge Moscow for a leadership role in the underdeveloped world. Its appeal has at times been frankly racial. Peiping plays heavily on its alleged common heritage with many underdeveloped countries of exploitation by "colonialism" and "imperialism"—a theme particularly stressed by Premier Chou En-lai in his extended visit to Africa last year. The Chinese have given added impetus to this effort by laying great stress on the notion of "self-reliance." They acknowledge that their aid is limited in size, but point to the favorable terms under which it is granted and its alleged nonpolitical orientation. Communist China continues to seek the exclusion of the Soviet Union from Afro-Asian gatherings.

3. Also involved in the dispute are longstanding national differences. There is, for example, the continuing problem of conflicting border claims. Peiping periodically makes pointed reference to prerevolutionary "unequal treaties," under which considerable portions of the then-Chinese empire were ceded to Czarist Russia. Peiping does not consider this chapter of Chinese-Russian relations closed.

This nationalistic side to the conflict was dramatized by the flight in 1962 of thousands of nomads from the Chinese Province of Sinkiang to Soviet central Asia. Subsequently, the Chinese claimed that the nomads had been lured across by inflammatory broadcasts from the Soviet side of the border—a remarkable charge against a reputedly friendly government.

4. A particular source of friction has been Peiping's suspiciousness over any signs of improvement of Soviet relations with the United States. When Peiping castigates the Soviet policy of "peaceful coexistence" (as it does with monotonous regularity), it has this development uppermost in mind. Communist China saw in the Cuban missile crisis and in the conclusion of the partial nuclear test-ban treaty nothing less than capitulation to U.S. interests. I think we can expect to see any future positive steps in our dealings with Moscow treated in similar fashion by Communist China.

This listing of factors does not purport to be all-inclusive. Such intangibles as Chinese mandarin cultural superiority, noted earlier, have undoubtedly come into play. Communist China is sharply critical of domestic policies of the Soviet leadership. The Soviet withdrawal of technicians and cessation of technological aid in the nuclear field were considered to be a real "stab in the back." Other elements could undoubtedly be found.

As to the future, it seems to me highly doubtful that the Chinese Communists wish to find any real settlement of the dispute. The Chinese leaders—in the wake of their successful nuclear explosion and the purge of Khrushchev (which they interpret as a Chinese victory), and in the obvious failure of the March 1-5 meeting in Moscow of various Communist parties—see little reason to change their basically anti-Soviet tactics. They probably consider that things are moving rather well as far as they are concerned, and that further gains will accrue without any dramatic shift in their policy toward the Soviet Union.

Although Peiping has been endeavoring, with considerable success, to split local Communist parties where the leadership has shown itself amenable to Moscow control or direction, it has not yet pushed for the creation of a new, exclusively Peiping-oriented, international Communist organization. The Chinese are undoubtedly delighted with the weakened Soviet position within the Communist world (as exemplified by the March meeting in Moscow), but they probably do not see the time as yet ripe for such a move. Peiping probably also recognizes that a number of other parties would be skittish at the idea of exchanging Moscow's leadership for its own. It has, after all, played fast and loose with the polycentric trends within the Communist movement; it must realize that this trend cannot be reversed overnight. Meanwhile, one can imagine great potential for future friction in relations between the two in Africa, in Indonesia, and in other parts of the globe, or in international gatherings; such as, the forthcoming Second Afro-Asian Conference in Algiers.

The present Chinese Communist leadership has increasingly shown an almost morbid fear that revisionism exerts a real pull on many at home, particularly among the youth. Mao has expressed his concern over the need to find revolutionary successors, and it is evident that the leadership is deeply worried lest today's youth turns away from the revolutionary ideals held by the "Long March" veterans. Soviet policies—modern revisionism—represent the main focus of this Chinese fear. It seems virtually certain that anti-Soviet attitudes of the present leaders in Peiping will continue to be fanned by their worry over the appeal which these Soviet trends hold.

I think, in short, that we can expect to see the present leadership in Peiping continue to go its own way, in many areas pressing its case with vigor against the Soviet Union, convinced of its own superiority, and almost impervious to ideas from without. There is little reason to believe that the deep-seated prejudices against Moscow, refined over the past several years, are going to be quickly and easily resolved. The uncompromising outlook of the present leadership in Peiping makes it difficult to think otherwise.

TESTIMONY OF UNITED STATES SCHOLARS BEFORE THE SENATE FOREIGN RELATIONS COMMITTEE ON UNITED STATES POLICY TOWARD CHINA

M. Statement of A. Doak Barnett*

March 8, 1966

Sino-Soviet Dispute

The Sino-Soviet dispute as it has evolved in recent years is clearly one of the most important developments in the international politics of the 1960's—just as the formation of the Sino-Soviet alliance was in the 1930's. There can be no doubt that the conflicts between Peking and Moscow now are very real, very bitter, and very deep. The dispute has involved basic clashes of national interests as well as major ideological differences, and it has resulted in worldwide competition between the two countries.

In a fundamental sense the Sino-Soviet dispute has weakened Peking's international position, which has been to our advantage in many respects, since it imposes increased restraints on the Chinese Communist regime. But not all of the results of the dispute have been good from our point of view. It appears, for example, to have been a significant factor reinforcing Peking's tendency in recent years to maintain a highly militant posture.

We cannot, moreover, rely on the dispute to solve our own basic problems in relations with the Chinese. In certain situations, Soviet interests and policies may run parallel to ours, as appears to be the case even in Vietnam today, to a very limited degree. But we cannot expect such parallelism to be dependable or believe that it will result—as some suggest—in a kind of Soviet-American anti-Chinese axis.

*   *   *

Change in U.S. China Policy

Let me, at this point, return again to questions relating to U.S. policy.

On February 23, President Johnson clearly stated that our desire is to avoid major conflict with China. "Some ask," he said, "about the risks of wider war, perhaps against the vast land armies of Red China. And again, the answer is 'No.' Never by any act of ours—and not if there's any reason left behind the wild words from Peking. We have threatened no one, and we will not. We seek the end of no regime, and we will not." He declared that we will employ a "measured use of force," with "prudent firmness," and that "there will not be a mindless escalation."

This is a wise posture for us to adopt—although to insure against major war resulting from miscalculation we must firmly hold the line against further

*U.S. Policy with Respect to Mainland China, Hearings Before the Committee on Foreign Relations, U.S. Senate, 89 Cong., 2nd sess., March 8, 10, 16, 18, 21, 28, 30, 1966. pp. 3-16. Mr. Barnett, who was born and lived the first fifteen years of his life in China, is Director of Columbia's East Asian Institute. He has published several books and articles on U.S. relations with China.

escalation in practice as well as theory. This stand is excellent, as far as it goes. But in my opinion we should go still further, especially in regard to policy toward China, and, as I suggested earlier, we should alter our basic posture toward the Chinese Communist regime from one of containment plus isolation to one of containment without isolation.

I indicated earlier that such a change of posture would call for re-examination of many specific aspects of our current policy toward China, and I would like now to make just a few comments on some of these.

The China Issue In The UN

The China issue in the United Nations is in many respects an urgent question, since unless we can soon evolve a new and sounder position on this issue, we are likely to be defeated in the General Assembly, and then our entire policy of isolation of Peking will begin to unravel as a result of a major political defeat, even before we can, on our own initiative, attempt to redefine our posture.

Last fall, we were barely able to get enough votes to sustain our position. Conceivably we might do so once or twice again; but it is equally conceivable that next fall the General Assembly might, despite our opposition, vote to seat Peking in the present China seat occupied by the Chinese Nationalist regime. If this takes place there is little likelihood that the Nationalists could later be brought back into the United Nations, since this would then be a question of admitting a new member, which is subject to the veto.

It would be to our interest, therefore, to take the initiative in the General Assembly in promoting a solution in which the Assembly would declare that there are now two successor states ruling the territory of the original China which joined the United Nations when it was formed in 1945, and that both should have seats in the Assembly. Neither the Chinese Communists nor the Chinese Nationalists are presently willing to accept such a solution and conceivably both might boycott the United Nations for a period of time, if such a solution were adopted. Nevertheless, it is a realistic and reasonable position for the international community as a whole to adopt, and I believe that, if it were adopted, there would be numerous pressures operating over time to induce Peking and Taipei eventually to reexamine their positions and consider accepting seats even under these conditions.

If and when Communist China does assume a seat in the United Nations, its initial impact is likely to be disruptive, but I firmly believe that over the long run it is nonetheless desirable to involve Peking in this complicated political arena where it will have to deal on a day-to-day basis with such a wide variety of countries and issues. It will soon learn, I think, that dogmatic arrogance will result only in self-isolation and that even a major nation must make compromises to operate with any success in the present community.

Foreseeable Modification of U.S. Taiwan Policy

A shift of American policy on the United Nations issue—and, in fact, any significant change in our posture toward Peking—will inevitably require some modification of our policy toward the Nationalist regime on Taiwan. For many reasons—political, strategic, and moral—we should continue defending Taiwan against attack and should firmly support the principle of self-determination in regard to the 13 million inhabitants of the island. But we will not be able to continue sustaining the fiction that the Nationalist regime is the government of mainland China.

Our view of the Nationalist regime should be one in which we recognize it as the legal government of the territories it now occupies, essentially Taiwan and the Pescadores, rather than as the government of all China: this, one might note, is essentially the position which the Japanese Government already maintains in regard to the Nationalists. We should do all we can to obtain representation for the Taipei regime in the United Nations and to urge the international community to accept and support it as the government of its present population and territory. But we cannot indefinitely sustain the fiction that is is the government of all China.

Desirability of Contacts

The desirability of increased unofficial contacts with Communist China has already been accepted, at least to a limited degree, by the U.S. Government, and there is now a sizable number of American newsmen, and some doctors and medical scientists, who would be permitted to visit mainland China if the Chinese Communists would grant them visas. The present obstacles to limited contacts, in short, are created by Peking, not by us. But despite Peking's current intransigence, we should continue searching for every possible opportunity for contact, in the hope that Peking will eventually modify its present stand, and should encourage scholars, businessmen, and others, as well as newsmen and doctors, to try to visit mainland China.

As a part of our effort to increase unofficial contacts with Communist China we should, in my opinion, end our embargo on all trade and permit trade in nonstrategic items. The present significance of our embargo, it should be stressed, is wholly symbolic, since no other major trading nation maintains such an embargo, and Peking is able, therefore, to purchase in Japan, Germany, England, or elsewhere any goods that are denied to it by us. The ending of our embargo might well be largely symbolic, too, since the Chinese Communists are likely to prefer trading with countries other than the United States. Nevertheless, it is conceivable that over time some limited trade contacts might develop, and be desirable from our point of view.

De Facto Recognition

The question of de jure recognition of Communist China—which in some discussions of China policy is given more attention than it deserves—is really a question for the future rather than the present. Until Peking indicates a willingness to exchange diplomatic representatives with us, there are no strong arguments for our unilaterally extending official recognition that would not be reciprocated.

Our aim, certainly should be to work toward eventual establishment of normal diplomatic relations, but it is likely to be some time—even if we alter our own overall position—before that is possible. We can and should, however, clearly indicate now—in much more explicit fashion than we have to date—that we do recognize the Peking regime in a de facto sense. One might argue that our frequent ambassadorial meetings with the Chinese Communists in Warsaw already constitute a form of de facto recognition, but officially we have refused to acknowledge any sort of recognition—de jure or de facto—and we should now do so.

*   *   *

N. Statement of John K. Fairbank*

[Extract]

March 10, 1966

My conclusion is that the alternative to war with Peking, over Vietnam or elsewhere, lies along two lines of effort—one is to achieve a better balance between destruction and construction in our own effort in Vietnam, so that the non-Communist model of nation building there can compete more effectively with the Chinese Communist model of nation building. The other line of effort is to defuse or dampen Peking's militancy by getting China into greater contact with the outside world, more connected with the international scene and more interested in participating in it like other countries.

How to get the Peking leadership into the international order instead of their trying to destroy it according to their revolutionary vision, is primarily a psychological problem. Therapy for Peking's present, almost paranoid, state of mind must follow the usual lines of therapy; it must lead the rulers of China gradually into different channels of experience until by degrees they reshape their picture of the world and their place in it.

The remolding of Chairman Mao, the greatest remolder of others in history, is not something I would advocate as feasible. But I think it is high time we got ourselves ready to deal with his successors and with their successors in years ahead.

In practice this means getting Peking into a multitude of activities abroad. China should be included in all international conferences, as on disarmament, and in international associations, both professional and functional, in international sports, not just ping-pong, and in trade with everyone, including ourselves, except for strategic goods. One thinks naturally of the U.N. agencies and participation in the Security Council as well as the Assembly. Yet all this can come only step by step, with altercation all along the way—not an easy process but a lot more constructive than warfare.

American policy should work toward a gradual shift from trying to isolate

*Ibid., pp. 98-107. Mr. Fairbank is a professor of history and Director of the East Asian Research Center at Harvard.

Peking, which only worsens our problem, to a less exposed position where we can acquiesce in the growth of contact between Peking and other countries and let them suffer the impact of Peking's abrasiveness.

In gradually manipulating Peking into an acceptance of the international world, as an alternative to trying to subvert it, we must motivate Chinese behavior according to China's needs:

> (1) One of these is the craving for greater prestige in the world to redress the balance of the last century's humiliations. For China to be in the center of the world's councils would seem to a Chinese patriot only right and proper.
>
> (2) We can also use the Peking government's need for prestige to maintain itself domestically. It is still true that the virtue of the rulers, as advertised in their acknowledged achievements, is a vital element sustaining any regime in China.
>
> (3) In addition, the Chinese people positively need certain kinds of aid through exchanges of technology or of goods, like all developing countries.
>
> (4) Peking may also be motivated by the opportunity to manipulate foreigners against one another. This traditional way of dealing with outsiders can be attempted in any conclave like the United Nations. But any number can play this game, and, in fact, it is the essence of diplomacy.

As these types of motives come into play, we may expect the Peking regime to be involved in bilateral relationships and be influenced by others whose desire is for peace rather than violence. In the end all this may make coexistence more attractive and feasible.

Opening the door for China's participation in the world scene is only one part of an American policy. The other part is to hold the line. The Chinese are no more amenable to pure sweetness and light than other revolutionaries. Encouraging them to participate in the U.N. and other parts of the international scene has to be combined with a cognate attitude of firmness backed by force. Military containment on the Korean border, in the Taiwan Straits, and somehow in Vietnam cannot soon be abandoned and may have to be maintained for some time. But containment alone is a blind alley unless we add policies of constructive competition and of international contact.

In short, my reading of history is that Peking's rulers shout aggressively out of manifold frustrations, that isolation intensifies their ailment and makes it self-perpetuating, and that we need to encourage international contact with China on many fronts.

O. Statement of Hans Morgenthau*

[Extract]

March 30, 1966

I. The Interests and Policies of China

China poses for the United States three fundamental issues, which can be separated for purposes of analysis but in practice blend into each other. First,

---

*Ibid., pp. 556-61. Mr. Morgenthau is a professor of political science and history at the University of Chicago, and Director of the Center for the Study of American Foreign Policy.

China is the most powerful nation of the mainland of Asia and potentially the most powerful nation in the world. Second, China has been for at least a millennium a great power of a peculiar kind in that her outlook upon, and relations with, the outside world have been different from those of other great powers. Third, China is today the fountainhead of the most virulent kind of communism, proclaiming the inevitability of armed conflict and instigating and supporting Communist subversion throughout the world.

1. China as a Great Power

As a great Asian power, China seeks to restore the position she occupied before she was reduced to a semicolonial status about a century ago. That goal has been proclaimed by the Chinese leaders, and the policies actually pursued by them with regard to the offshore islands and Taiwan, Korea, Vietnam, Burma, Cambodia, Tibet, and India conform to a consistent pattern: restoration of the territorial boundaries and of the influence the Chinese Empire possessed before its modern decline. These boundaries are likely to comprise Taiwan and the offshore islands, Outer Mongolia, and the Asian territories claimed by China and annexed by the Soviet Union during the 19th century. Physically, considering the distribution of power on the Asian mainland, China could go much further, she could go virtually as far as she wanted to. But she has never done so in the past, and she is not likely to do so in the future.

*   *   *

II. The Interests and Policies of the United States

What are the interests of the United States with regard to China, and what are the policies most likely to serve those interests? The United States has two such interests maintenance or, if need be, the restoration of a viable balance of power in Asia and the maintenance of a world balance of power. We have tried to serve these interests for more than 15 years through two policies: the isolation and the peripheral military containment of China.

1. The Policy of Isolating China

The policy of isolating China seeks the downfall of its Communist government. It is intimately connected with the recognition of the Chiang Kai-shek government as the legitimate government of China and with the expectation of its return to the mainland. By maintaining close relations with the Chiang Kai-shek government and none with the Communist government, a policy in which we expected our allies to participate, we tried to destroy the legitimacy of the Communist government. By interdicting all personal and commercial relations with mainland China we expected to make it impossible for the Communist government to govern. This policy has obviously failed. Chiang Kai-shek will not return to the mainland and his government survives only by virtue of the presence of the 7th Fleet in the Straits of Taiwan. The Communist government of China enjoys diplomatic, cultural, and commercial relations with many nations, among which there are many allies of the United States, and it is the United States rather than Communist China which has been isolated in consequence of its policy of isolation. Insofar as China is isolated, as it is in the Communist world, that isolation is in good measure self-inflicted, and our policy of isolation has nothing to do with it.

Thus from the point of view of China, our policy of isolation is no longer an important issue. Therefore, no favorable response can be expected from China if the United States should give up the policy. The real issue is not isolation but containment. This is the crucial point at which the traditional national interests of China and the policy of the United States clash. The slogan "containment without isolation" obscures that crucial issue. It is a formula for continuing the unsuccessful policy of peripheral military containment by making it appear that the abandonment of the policy of isolation portends a significant change in American policy. It tends to make the policy of military containment palatable by tying it to an apparently real and benevolent change in our China policy. It also carries a suggestion of condescension—"We are going to be nice to you from now on"—which is not likely to impress a China that is mindful of its humiliations, past and present.

Similar considerations apply to the proposal to end the isolation of China by engaging in trade with her. The existence and the volume of trade between the United States and China are irrelevant to the basic issues that divide the two nations. Furthermore, China looks at foreign trade not as a series of transactions undertaken for commercial gain, but as an instrument of national policy. To engage in indiscriminate trade with China, apart from an overall political settlement, is self-defeating, for such trade strengthens China politically and militarily without giving an equivalent political or military advantage to the other partner.

Finally, the seating of the Communist government as the representative of China in the United Nations is not likely to be successful if it is conceived merely as the liquidation of the policy of isolation and not also and primarily as a settlement of the issue of Taiwan. It is virtually inconceivable that a representative of the Communist government should set foot in the United Nations while a representative of the Chiang Kai-shek government is present; for the idea of "two Chinas" is as repellent to Mao Tse-tung as it is to Chiang Kai-shek. If the General Assembly should vote this fall that the representative of the Communist government replace the representative of the Chiang Kai-shek government, the latter would no longer be represented in the General Assembly but would still occupy the seat of China as a permanent member of the Security Council. It is here that the issue would be joined.

If the Security Council should decide to emulate the General Assembly and install the representative of the Communist government in the permanent seat of China—a decision the United States could nullify by vetoing it—the Chiang Kai-shek government would be deprived of any representation in the United Nations. In consequence, its claim to be the legitimate government of China would be destroyed, and its claim to be the legitimate government of Taiwan would be considerably imparied. Thus our policy of containing Communist China, which we could continue behind the military shield of the 7th Fleet, would be politically undermined. For by weakening Chiang Kai-shek's claim, Communist China would have taken the first step toward achieving the recognition of its own. Thus it becomes obvious again that the real issue is not isolation but containment.

2. *The Policy of Peripheral Military Containment*

We thought that the policy of military containment which worked so well against the Soviet Union in Europe would work equally well elsewhere, and so we applied it to the Middle East through the Baghdad Pact and to Asia through SEATO, and have followed it in our policies vis-a-vis China. Yet what succeeded in Europe was bound to fail elsewhere. The reasons for that failure are twofold.

First, the threat that faced the nations of Western Europe in the aftermath of the Second World War was primarily military. It was the threat of the Red army marching westward. Behind the line of military demarcation of 1945 which the policy of containment declared to be the westernmost limits of the Soviet empire, there was an ancient civilization, only temporarily weak and able to maintain itself against the threat of Communist subversion.

The situation is different in the Middle East and Asia. The threat there is not primarily military but political in nature. Weak governments and societies provide opportunities for Communist subversion. Military containment is irrelevant to that threat and may even be counterproductive. Thus the Baghdad Pact did not protect Egypt from Soviet influence and SEATO has had no bearing on Chinese influence in Indonesia and Pakistan, to speak of Asia only.

Second, and more important, China is, even in her present underdeveloped state, the dominant power in Asia. She is this by virtue of the quality and quantity of her population, her geographic position, her civilization, her past power remembered and her future power anticipated. Anybody who has traveled in Asia with his eyes and ears open must have been impressed by the enormous impact which the resurgence of China has made upon all manner of men, regardless of class and political conviction, from Japan to Pakistan.

The issue China poses is political and cultural predominance. The United States can no more contain Chinese influence in Asia by arming Thailand and fighting in South Vietnam than China could contain American influence in the Western Hemisphere by arming, say, Nicaragua and fighting in Lower California. If we are convinced that we cannot live with a China predominant on the mainland of Asia, then we must strike at the heart of Chinese power—that is, rather than try to contain the power of China by nibbling at the periphery of her empire, we must try to destroy that power itself. Thus there is logic on the side of that small group of Americans who are convinced that war between the United States and China is inevitable and that the earlier it comes, the better will be the chances for the United States to win it.

Yet, while logic is on their side, practical judgment is against them. For while China is obviously no match for the United States in overall power, China is largely immune to the specific types of power in which the superiority of the United States consists—that is, nuclear, air, and naval power. Certainly, the United States has the power to destroy the nuclear installations and the major industrial and population centers of China, but this destruction would not defeat China; it would only set her development back. To be defeated, China has to be conquered.

Physical conquest would require the deployment of millions of American soldiers on the mainland of Asia. No American military leader has ever advocated a course of action so fraught with incalculable risks, so uncertain of outcome, requiring sacrifices so out of proportion to the interests at stake and the benefits to be expected. President Eisenhower declared on February 10, 1954, that he "could conceive of no greater tragedy than for the United States to become involved in an all-out war in Indochina." General MacArthur, in the congressional hearings concerning his dismissal and in personal conversation with President Kennedy, emphatically warned against sending American foot soldiers to the Asian mainland to fight China.

If we do not want to set ourselves goals which cannot be attained with the means we are willing to employ, we must learn to accommodate ourselves to the political and cultural predominance of China on the Asian mainland. It is instructive to note that those Asian nations which have done so—such as Burma and Cambodia—live peacefully in the shadow of the Chinese giant. On the other hand, those Asian nations which have allowed themselves to be transformed into outposts of American military power—such as Laos in the late fifties, South Vietnam and Thailand—have become the actual or prospective victims of Communist aggression and subversion. Thus it appears that peripheral military containment is counterproductive. Challenged at its periphery by American military power at its weakest—that is, by the proxy of client-states—China or its proxies are able to respond with locally superior military and political power.

Thus, even if the Chinese threat were primarily of a military nature, peripheral military containment would be ineffective in the long run in view of China's local military superiority. By believing otherwise, we have fallen heir to a misconception of our containment of the Soviet Union and of the reasons for its success. The Soviet Union has not been contained by the Armed Forces we have been able to put in the field locally in Europe. It has been contained by the near certainty that an attack upon these forces would be countered by the nuclear retaliation of the United States. If we are to assume that the Chinese armies stand, or one day will stand, poised to sweep over Asia, they will not be contained by the Armed Forces we or our allies can put into the field on the mainland of Asia. They will only be deterred by the near certainty that China as an organized society will be destroyed in the process of nuclear retaliation.

China is today protected from the full measure of our nuclear retaliation by her own technological backwardness; for she does not possess the number of industrial and population centers whose nuclear destruction would spell her defeat. It is for this reason that China is today more daring in words, and might well become more daring in action if her vital interests were sufficiently threatened, than would be justified in view of the overall distribution of power between the United States and China. However, in the measure that China develops her nuclear capability, she also becomes vulnerable to nuclear retaliation; for once China has developed into a modern nation with a high technological capability, she will also have developed a large number of vital industrial and population centers and will then have become as vulnerable to nuclear attack as are the United States and the Soviet Union today. Assuming a modicum of rationality in the government which will then govern China, fear of nuclear retaliation must be assumed to have the same restraining influence upon Chinese policies as it has had upon the policies of the United States and the Soviet Union since the beginning of the nuclear age. Thus the nuclear arms race, at least as long as it is carried on among a few great powers, carries within itself its own corrective, however tenuous: nuclear power and nuclear ulnerability go hand in hand, and so does the rational requirement of self-restraint.

3. The Worldwide Containment of China

The peripheral military containment of China is, however, being justified not only in local terms but also, and to an ever greater extent, in worldwide terms. We are told that by containing China in South Vietnam we are containing her everywhere, and that by frustrating a "war of national liberation" in southeast Asia, we frustrate all "wars of national liberation." This argument has the virtue of simplicity, but it is supported by no historic evidence. It brings to mind the statement which William Graham Sumner made at the beginning of the century: "The amount of superstition is not much changed, but it now attaches to politics, not to religion."

The so-called domino theory is indeed an echo of the Marxist dogma of historic inevitability which asserts that communism will inevitably spread from country to country until in the end it engulfs the world. Nothing of the kind has actually happened. After the Second World War, the nations of Eastern Europe went Communist, but Finland to this day has not. After the collapse of French rule in Indochina in 1954, North Vietnam went Communist, but nobody else did. For almost two decades, the fortunes of communism in Indonesia have fluctuated according to local conditions, not according to what happened or did not happen elsewhere. Can anyone seriously maintain that the fortunes of the guerrilla wars in Guatemala, Colombia, or Venezuela will depend upon what happens or does not happen in South Vietnam? It stands to reason that the triumph or defeat of communism in any particular country is not simply a byproduct of what happens or does not happen in other countries. What will happen in Vietnam can at the very best be no more than one factor among many, and most certainly not the decisive one, that will influence developments in other countries.

III. A New China Policy for the United States

What follows from this analysis for the policies of the United States vis-a-vis China? In view of the vital interests of the United States in the Asian and world balance of power, five basic principles ought to guide the policies of the United States with regard to China:

First, the policy of peripheral military containment ought to be gradually liquidated. This policy is not only irrelevant to the interests of the United States but actually runs counter to them.

Second, both the policy of isolating China and the policy of ending that isolation are essentially irrelevant to the issue at hand. One may aggravate, and the other ameliorate, the international climate; but they have no relevance, one way or the other, to the basic issue of containment.

Third, since the expansion of Chinese power and influence, threatening the Asian and world balance of power, proceeds by political rather than military means, it must be contained by political means. To that purpose, it is necessary to strengthen politically, socially, and economically, the nations of Asia which are within China's reach, without exacting in return political and military alinements directed against China. We ought to pursue a similar policy with regard to the uncommitted nations in which China in the recent past has attempted to gain a foothold.

Fourth, we ought to be clear in our minds that if we should continue the present policy of the peripheral military containment of China, we will find ourselves in all likelihood sooner or later at war with China. If we want to avoid such a war, we must change our policy. If we do not want to change our policy, we must be ready to go to war. That is to say, either we bring the means we are willing to employ into line with our objectives, or we cut down our objectives to the measure of the means we are willing to employ.

Fifth, the ultimate instrument for containing China is the same that has contained the Soviet Union: the retaliatory nuclear capability of the United States. It must be brought home to China, as it was brought home to the Soviet Union, that in the unlikely event that she should embark upon a policy of Asian or world conquest, she is bound to be at war with the United States.

JOHNSON ADMINISTRATION POLICY TOWARD CHINA

P. Statement by Secretary Rusk on United States Policy Toward China*

March 16, 1966

Mr. Chairman, during the last month and a half this distinguished committee and its corresponding members in the other House have heard testimony on

*American Foreign Policy: Current Documents, 1966, pp. 650-59.

Communist China from a number of prominent scholars and distinguished experts on Asia.

I welcome these hearings. For Communist China's policies and intentions, in all their aspects, need to be examined—and reexamined continually.

China Specialists in Government

The Department of State and other agencies of the Government do collect, study, and analyze continually with the greatest care all the information obtainable on Communist China in order to make—and, when the facts warrant, revise—judgments of Peiping's intentions and objectives. Highly trained Chinese-language officers here in Washington and overseas—men who specialize in Chinese history and communism—are working full time analyzing and appraising Peiping's moves. Numerous private scholars, some of whom have appeared before this committee in recent weeks, are consulted by the Department of State. And there are, of course, many specialists on Communist China in other agencies of the Government. These capable individuals—in and out of Government—systematically interchange and cross-check their analyses and estimates to provide what I believe is the most complete and most accurate picture of Communist China, its leaders, and its policies, available to any non-Communist government in the world.

Three Caveats

Before going further, I would like to enter three caveats:

First, the experts do not always agree, especially in their estimates of Chinese Communist intentions.

Second, the leaders we are discussing are both Chinese and Communist. Some of their words and acts can perhaps be best understood in terms of Chinese background—Chinese traits of historic Chinese ambitions. Others can perhaps be better understood in terms of their beliefs and ambitions as Communists. They are deeply committed to a body of Communist doctrine developed by Mao Tse-tung. Still other words and acts may be consistent with both the Chinese and doctrinaire Communist factors.

We have faced a similar problem over the years with respect to the Soviet leadership. Some of their words and acts could be explained chiefly in terms of historic Russian imperial ambitions or Russian traits or practices. Others have been clearly attributable to Marxist-Leninist doctrine, or to interpretations of that doctrine by Stalin and more recent leaders. Some sovietologists put more emphasis on the traditional nationalist or imperial factors, others put more on the Marxist-Leninist factors. There is no way to determine the exact weight which ought to be given to each of these two influences.

Likewise, with regard to the Chinese Communists, there has been considerable disagreement over the respective dimensions of the two streams of influence: Chinese and Marxist-Leninist-Maoist. Over the years some of the experts on China may not have appreciated adequately Marxist-Leninist-Maoist doctrine. Likewise, some of the experts on Chinese Communist doctrine may tend to underestimate the Chinese factors in the behavior and intentions of the Peiping regime.

The third caveat is this: Predicting what the Chinese Communists will do next may be even more hazardous than usual at this juncture. They themselves appear to be taking stock. We know that some high-level talks have been going on and that they have called some of their ambassadors back for consultation.

Chinese Communist Setbacks

We know—the whole world knows—that the Chinese Communists have suffered some severe setbacks internationally during the past 14 months. They were unable to persuade the Afro-Asians to accept their substantive views on the Second Bandung Conference. They have found themselves in difficulty in several African countries. Their diplomatic missions have been expelled from Burundi, Dahomey, and the Central African Republic. Their technicians have been expelled from Ghana. The Governments of Kenya and Tunisia have warned them against promoting revolution in Africa.

During the fighting between India and Pakistan, the Chinese Communists marched up hill and down again. They have been disappointed by the Tashkent agreement and the steps taken in accord with it. They were strongly opposed to the agreement between Japan and the Republic of Korea, which was ratified by both countries. They have suffered a major setback in Indonesia—the Indonesian Communist Party has been decimated.

Generally, in their struggle with Moscow for leadership of the world Communist movement, the Chinese Communists appear to have lost ground. Even their relations with Castro's Cuba have sunk to the level of mudslinging.

And, probably most important of all, Peiping sees the power of the United States committed in Southeast Asia to repel an aggression supported—and actively promoted—by Peiping.

Will the Chinese Communist reaction to all these setbacks be a wild lashing out? Or will it be a sober decision to draw back and even to move toward peaceful coexistence?

We, of course, hope it will be the latter. But we cannot be sure what Peiping intends to do. We do not expect the worst but we must be prepared for it.

Our Relations with Peiping

I will not try here today to review in detail the record of our relations with the Peiping regime. In the months after the Chinese Communist takeover in 1949 we watched to see whether the initial demonstration of intense hostility toward the United States and toward Americans who were still resident in China was momentary, or reflected a basic Peiping policy. Then came the aggression against the Republic of Korea, to which, at a second stage, the Chinese Communists committed large forces, thus coming into direct conflict with the United Nations and the United States.

We have searched year after year for some sign that Communist China was ready to renounce the use of force to resolve disputes. We have also searched for some indication that it was ready to abandon its premise that the United States is its prime enemy.

The Chinese Communist attitudes and actions have been hostile and rigid.

But a democracy, such as ours, does not accept rigidity. It seeks solutions to problems, however intractable they may seem.

Sino-United States Ambassadorial Talks

We have discussed various problems with the Chinese Communists at international conferences such as the Geneva conferences of 1954 and 1962.

In 1955 we began with them a series of bilateral conversations at the level of ambassadors, first in Geneva and later in Warsaw. It was our hope that by direct, systematic communication we might be able to reduce the sharpness of the conflict between us. There now have been 129 of these meetings, the latest of which took place in Warsaw today.

These exchanges have ranged widely, covering many subjects affecting our two countries. At first there was a little progress in dealing with small specific issues, such as the release of Americans being held in Communist China. Although an understanding was reached in this limited area, Peiping refused to fulfill its commitment to release all the Americans.

I think it is accurate to say that no other non-Communist nation has had such extensive conversations with the Peiping regime as we have had. The problem is not lack of contact between Peiping and Washington. It is what, with contact, the Peiping regime itself says and does.

Although they have produced almost no tangible results, these conversations have served and still serve useful purposes. They permit us to clarify the numerous points of difference between us. They enable us to communicate in private during periods of crisis. They provide an opening through which, hopefully, light might one day penetrate. But the talks have, so far, given no evidence of a shift or easing in Peiping's hostility toward the United States and its bellicose doctrines of world revolution. Indeed, the Chinese Communists have consistently demanded, privately as well as publicly, that we let them have Taiwan. And when we say that we will not abandon the 12 or 13 million people on Taiwan, against their will, they say that, until we change our minds about that, no improvement in relations is possible.

Today we and Peiping are as far apart on matters of fundamental policy as we were 17 years ago.

The Basic Issues

In assessing Peiping's policies and actions, and the problems they present to American foreign policy and to the free peoples of the world, we must ask ourselves certain key questions:

What does Peiping want, and how does it pursue its objectives?

How successful has it been, and how successful is it likely to be in the future?

Is it on a collision course with the United States?

What are the prospects for change in its policies?

What policies should the United States adopt, or work toward, in dealing with Communist China?

What Does Peiping Want?

First, the Chinese Communist leaders seek to bring China on the world stage as a great power. They hold that China's history, size, and geographic position entitle it to great-power status. They seek to overcome the humiliation of 150 years of economic, cultural, and political domination by outside powers.

Our concern is with the way they are pursuing their quest for power and influence in the world. And it is not only our concern but that of many other countries, including in recent years the Soviet Union.

Peiping is aware that it still lacks many of the attributes of great-power status, and it chafes bitterly under this realization.

Arming To Become a "Great Power"

The Chinese Communists are determined to rectify this situation. They already have one of the largest armies in the world. They are now developing nuclear weapons and missile delivery systems. They are pouring a disproportionately large proportion of their industrial and scientific effort into military and military-related fields.

What is all this military power for? Some believe it to be for defensive purposes alone:

To erect a token "deterrent" nuclear capability against the United States or the U.S.S.R.;

To demonstrate symbolically that "China must be reckoned with"; To react to an imaginary, almost pathological, notion that the United States and other countries around its borders are seeking an opportunity to invade mainland China and destroy the Peiping regime.

But such weapons need not serve a defensive role. They can be used directly by Peiping to try to intimidate its neighbors, or in efforts to blackmail Asian countries into breaking defense alliances with the United States, or in an attempt to create a nuclear "balance" in Asia in which Peiping's potentially almost unlimited conventional forces might be used with increased effect.

These weapons can ultimately be employed to attack Peiping's Asian neighbors and, in time, even the United States or the Soviet Union. This would be mad and suicidal, as Peiping must know, despite cavalier statements that mainland China can survive nuclear war. Nevertheless, a potential nuclear capability, on top of enormous conventional forces, represents a new factor in the equilibrium of power in Asia that this country and its friends and allies cannot ignore.

Peiping's use of power is closely related to what I believe are its second and third objectives: dominance within Asia and leadership of the Communist world revolution, employing Maoist tactics. Peiping is striving to restore traditional Chinese influence or dominance in South, Southeast, and East Asia. Its concept of influence is exclusive. Foreign Minister Ch'en Yi reportedly told Prince Sihanouk recently that his country's "friendship" with Cambodia would be incompatible with Cambodian ties with the United States. Peiping has tried to alienate North Viet-Nam and North Korea from the Soviet Union. It has had uneven success in such maneuvers. But it has not abandoned this objective. Where Peiping is present, it seeks to exclude all others. And this is not only true in its relations with its neighbors but in the Communist world as well.

Direct Aggression

Peiping has not refrained from the use of force to pursue its objectives. Following Korea, there were Tibet and the attacks on the offshore islands in the Taiwan Straits. There have been the attacks on India. It is true that, since Korea, Peiping has moved only against weaker foes and has carefully avoided situations which might bring it face to face with the United States. It has probed for weaknesses around its frontier but drawn back when the possibility of a wider conflict loomed.

While the massive and direct use of Chinese Communist troops in overt aggression cannot be ruled out, Peiping's behavior up to now suggests it would approach any such decision with caution.

If the costs and risks of a greater use of force were reduced by, for example, our unilateral withdrawal from the region, Peiping might well feel freer to use its power to intimidate or overwhelm a recalcitrant opponent or to aid directly insurgent forces.

Mao's Doctrine of World Revolution

As I have said, the Chinese Communist leaders are dedicated to a fanatical and bellicose Marxist-Leninist-Maoist doctrine of world revolution. Last fall, Lin Piao, the Chinese Communist Minister of Defense, recapitulated in a long article Peiping's strategy of violence for achieving Communist domination of the world. This strategy involves the mobilization of the underdeveloped areas of the world—which the Chinese Communists compare to the "rural areas"—against the industrialized or "urban" areas. It involves the relentless prosecution of what they call "people's wars." The final stage of all this violence is to be what they frankly describe as "wars of annihilation."

It is true that this doctrine calls for revolution by the natives of each country. In that sense it may be considered a "do-it-yourself kit." But Peiping is prepared to train and indoctrinate the leaders of these revolutions and to support them with funds, arms, and propaganda, as well as politically. It is even prepared to manufacture these revolutionary movements out of whole cloth.

Peiping has encouraged and assisted—with arms and other means—the aggressions of the North Vietnamese Communists in Laos and against South Viet-Nam. It has publicly declared its support for so-called national liberation forces in Thailand, and there are already terrorist attacks in the remote rural areas of northeast Thailand. There is talk in Peiping that Malaysia is next on the list. The basic tactics of these "wars of liberation" have been set forth by Mao and his disciples, including General Giap, the North Vietnamese Communist Minister of Defense. They progress from the undermining of independent governments and the economic and social fabrics of society by terror and assassination, through guerrilla warfare, to large-scale military action.

Peiping has sought to promote Communist coups and "wars of liberation" against independent governments in Africa and Latin America as well as in Asia.

Words Versus Actions

Some say we should ignore what the Chinese Communist leaders say and judge them only by what they do. It is true that they have been more cautious in action than in words—more cautious in what they do themselves than in what they have urged the Soviet Union to do. Undoubtedly, they recognize that their power is limited. They have shown, in many ways, that they have a healthy respect for the power of the United States.

But it does not follow that we should disregard the intentions and plans for the future which they have proclaimed. To do so would be to repeat the catastrophic miscalculation that so many people made about the ambitions of Hitler—and that many have made at various times in appraising the intentions of the Soviet leaders.

I have noted criticism of the so-called analogy between Hitler and Mao Tse-tung. I am perfectly aware of the important differences between these two and the countries in which they have exercised power. The seizure of Manchuria by Japanese militarists, of Ethiopia by Mussolini, and of the Rhineland, Austria, and Czechoslovakia by Hitler, were laboratory experiments in the anatomy and physiology of aggression. How to deal with the phenomenon of aggression was the principal problem faced in drafting the United Nations Charter, and the answer was: collective action. We do ourselves no service by insisting that each source of aggression or each instance of aggression is unique. My own view is that we have learned a good deal about this phenomenon and its potentiality for leading into catastrophe if the problem is not met in a timely fashion.

The bellicosity of the Chinese Communists has created problems within the Communist world as well as between Peiping and the non-Communist world.

Recently a leading official of a Communist state said to me that the most serious problem in the world today is how to get Peiping to move to a policy of "peaceful coexistence."

Chinese Communist Fear of Attack

At times the Communist Chinese leaders seem to be obsessed with the notion that they are being threatened and encircled. We have told them both publicly and privately, and I believe have demonstrated in our actions in times of crisis and even under grave provocation, that we want no war with Communist China. The President restated this only last month in New York. We do not seek to overthrow by force the Peiping regime; we do object to its attempt to overthrow other regimes by force.

How much Peiping's "fear" of the United States is genuine and how much it is artificially induced for domestic political purposes only the Chinese Communist leaders themselves know. I am convinced, however, that their desire to expel our influence and activity from the western Pacific and Southeast Asia is not motivated by fears that we are threatening them.

I wish I could believe that Communist China seeks merely a guarantee of friendly states around its borders, as some commentators have suggested. If it was as simple as this, they would have only to abandon their policies which cause their neighbors to seek help from the United States.

The trouble is that Peiping's leaders want neighboring countries to accept subordination to Chinese power. They want them to become political and economic dependencies of Peiping. If the United States can be driven from Asia this goal will be in their grasp. The "influence," therefore, that Peiping's present leaders seek in Asia is indeed far reaching.

Dominance in the Communist Movement

I had the privilege almost exactly a year ago of commenting at some length before this committee on the Sino-Soviet dispute. The essential nature of this conflict has not changed in this year. It has, if anything, intensified and widened. Its Russo-Chinese national aspects have become more conspicuous. Both sides have clearly given increased thought to the implications of a wider war in Southeast Asia for their mutual treaty obligations. I don't know what the Soviets would actually do with respect to their treaty with Communist China, but Peiping does not seem to be counting on Soviet support.

Peiping's Desire to Maintain Sharp Communist-U.S. Polarity

One of Peiping's most fundamental differences with Moscow centers on its desire to maintain the sharpest possible polarization between the Communist world and the United States. Peiping argues that we are the "enemy of all the people in the world." Its national interests in Asia are served by maximizing Communist (and world) pressure on us and by attempting to "isolate" us. For this reason alone the Chinese would probably have opposed any Soviet attempts to reach understandings with us. In addition there are ideological and psychological reasons for Sino-Soviet rivalry:

The intense and deadly antagonisms that have always characterized schisms in the Marxist world;

Mao's belief that after Stalin's death the mantle of world Communist leadership should rightfully have passed to him and the Chinese Communist party;

Peiping's obsession, also held or professed by the leaders of the Soviet Union during the 30 years after the Bolshevik revolution, with a fear of being threatened and encircled;

The mixture of the psychology of the veterans of the long march and Chinese traditional attitudes which has led Peiping's leaders to believe that through a combination of patience, struggle, and "right thinking" all obstacles can be conquered; and

Peiping's professed belief that the Soviets are joining with the United States in keeping China in a position of inferiority and subordination.

All these have merged to give the Sino-Soviet dispute a flavor and an intensity which rival even the current Chinese Communist antagonism for the United States itself.

How Successful has Peiping Been?

We can see that the Communist Chinese have set vast goals for themselves, both internally and externally. The disastrous results of the so-called great leap forward have forced them to acknowledge that it will take them generations to achieve their goals.

They have wrought considerable changes on the mainland of China. Perhaps their greatest feat has been to establish their complete political authority throughout the country. They have made some progress in industrialization, education, and public health—although at the expense of human freedom, originality, and creativity. But their efforts to improve agriculture and to mold the Chinese people into a uniform Marxist pattern have been far less successful.

The economic, political, and social problems still confronting the Chinese Communist leaders today are staggering.

Economic Problems

Peiping's economic power will almost certainly increase over the coming years. But even with relatively effective birth control programs the population of mainland China may reach 1 billion by 1985.

Where is the food to come from? Where are the resources for investment to come from? Can the rapidly increasing military and economic cost of great-power status be carried by Chinese society at the same time that other economic tasks vital to China's economic survival are carried out? I do not denigrate in the slightest native Chinese ingenuity and capacity for incredibly hard work when I suggest that the solutions to these problems are in the gravest doubt.

Internal Political Problems

Even more important to Peiping's leaders than these economic problems however, are the will and morale of their own people. The current leaders—Mao, Liu Shao-ch'i, Chou En-lai, and others—are an intensely committed group of men whose entire lives symbolize their willingness to postpone the satisfactions of the present for the promised glory of the future.

Every generation is suspicious that the youth of today is not what is was in the good old days. But this has become another obsession of Peiping's old men. Their domestic propaganda and their comments to visitors, as well as the reports of refugees, have all emphasized their distrust of the youth of the country. They fear that their grand designs and goals—both domestic and foreign—will not be pursued with zeal by the next generation.

I believe their concern may be both genuine and warranted. How pleased can young college graduates be to be sent off to rural China for years for ideological hardening? How attractive is it to the Chinese peasant and worker to be called on for years of sacrifice to bring revolution to Africa or Latin America? Will Chinese scientists accept the dogma that scientific truth can be found only in the pages of Mao Tse-tung's writings? How can professional Chinese Communist army officers and soldiers be persuaded that the words of Mao represent a "spiritual atomic bomb" more powerful than any material weapon?

I am unaware of any new revolution brewing on the Chinese mainland. I have no evidence that the current regime does not, in practical terms, control effectively all of mainland China. But there is evidence of a growing psychological weariness that in years to come could produce a significant shift in the policies of a new generation of leaders.

The dramatic succession of foreign policy failures during the last year, both in the Communist and non-Communist world, must be having some effect on the confidence of the people in the wisdom of their leaders and even on the leaders themselves.

I do not predict any quick changes in China. Nor are there simple solutions. Peiping's present state of mind is a combination of aggressive arrogance and obsessions of its own making. There are doubtless many reasons, cultural, historical, political, for this state of mind. Psychologists have struggled for years in an effort to characterize what is a normal personality. The definition of what a normal state personality might be is beyond my abilities. I would be inclined, however, to advance the view that a country whose behavior is as violent, irascible, unyielding, and hostile as that of Communist China is led by leaders whose view of the world and of life itself is unreal. It is said that we have isolated them. But to me they have isolated themselves—both in the non-Communist and Communist world.

We have little hope of changing the outlook of these leaders. They are products of their entire lives. They seem to be immune to agreement or persuasion by anyone, including their own allies.

It is of no help in formulating policy to describe Peiping's behavior as neurotic. Its present policies pose grave and immediate problems for the United States and other countries. These must be dealt with now. The weapons and advisers that Peiping exports to promote and assist insurections in other countries cannot be met by psychoanalysis. At the present time there is a need for a counterweight of real power to Chinese Communist pressures. This has had to be supplied primarily by the United States and our allies.

We should be under no illusion that by yielding to Peiping's bellicose demands today we would in some way ease the path toward peace in Asia. If Peiping reaps success from its current policies, not only its present leaders but those who follow will be emboldened to continue them. This is the path to increased tension and even greater dangers to world peace in the years ahead.

China as a Great Power

We expect China to become some day a great world power. Communist China is a major Asian power today. In the ordinary course of events, a peaceful China would be expected to have close relations—political, cultural and economic—with the countries around its borders and with the United States.

It is no part of the policy of the United States to block the peaceful attainment of these objectives.

More than any other Western people, we have had close and warm ties with the Chinese people. We opposed the staking out of spheres of influence in China. We used our share of the Boxer indemnity to establish scholarships for Chinese students in the United States. We welcomed the revolution of Sun Yat Sen. We took the lead in relinquishing Western extraterritorial privileges in China. We refused to recognize the puppet regime established by Japan in Manchuria. And it was our refusal to accept or endorse, even by implication, Japan's imperial conquests and further designs in China that made it impossible for us to achieve a *modus vivendi* with Japan in 1940-41.

We look forward hopefully—and confidently—to a time in the future when the government of mainland China will permit the restoration of the historic ties of friendship between the people of mainland China and ourselves.

Elements of Future Policy

What should be the main elements in our policy toward Communist China?

We must take care to do nothing which encourages Peiping—or anyone else— to believe that it can reap gains from its aggressive actions and designs. It is just as essential to "contain" Communist aggression in Asia as it was, and is, to "contain" Communist aggression in Europe.

At the same time, we must continue to make it plain that, if Peiping abandons its belief that force is the best way to resolve disputes and gives up its violent strategy of world revolution, we would welcome an era of good relations.

More specifically, I believe, there should be 10 elements in our policy.

First, we must remain firm in our determination to help those Allied nations which seek our help to resist the direct or indirect use or threat of force against their territory by Peiping.

Second, we must continue to assist the countries of Asia in building broadly based effective governments, devoted to progressive economic and social policies, which can better withstand Asian Communist pressures and maintain the security of their people.

Third, we must honor our commitments to the Republic of China and to the people on Taiwan, who do not want to live under communism. We will continue to assist in their defense and to try to persuade the Chinese Communists to join with us in renouncing the use of force in the area of Taiwan.

Fourth, we will continue our efforts to prevent the expulsion of the Republic of China from the United Nations or its agencies. So long as Peiping follows its present course it is extremely difficult for us to see how it can be held to fulfill the requirements set forth in the charter for membership, and the United States opposes its membership. It is worth recalling that the Chinese Communists have set forth some interesting conditions which must be fulfilled before they are even willing to consider membership:

The United Nations resolution of 1950 condemning Chinese Communist aggression in Korea must be rescinded.

There must be a new United Nations resolution condemning U.S. "aggression."

The United Nations must be reorganized.

The Republic of China must be expelled.

All other "imperialist puppets" must be expelled. One can only ask whether the Chinese Communists seriously want membership, or whether they mean to destroy the United Nations. We believe the United Nations must approach this issue with the utmost caution and deliberation.

Fifth, we should continue our efforts to reassure Peiping that the United States does not intend to attack mainland China. There are, of course, risks of war with China. This was true in 1950. It was true in the Taiwan Straits crises of 1955 and 1958. It was true in the Chinese Communist drive into Indian territory in 1962. It is true today in Viet-Nam. But we do not want war. We do not intend to provoke war. There is no fatal inevitability of war with Communist China. The Chinese Communists have, as I have already said, acted with caution when they foresaw a collision with the United States. We have acted with restraint and care in the past and we are doing so today. I hope that they will realize this and guide their actions accordingly.

Sixth, we must keep firmly in our minds that there is nothing eternal about the policies and attitudes of Communist China. We must avoid assuming the existence of an unending and inevitable state of hostility between ourselves and the rulers of mainland China.

Seventh, when it can be done without jeopardizing other U.S. interests, we should continue to enlarge the possibilities for unofficial contacts between Communist China and ourselves—contacts which may gradually assist in altering Peiping's picture of the United States.

In this connection, we have gradually expanded the categories of American citizens who may travel to Communist China. American libraries may freely purchase Chinese Communist publications. American citizens may send and receive mail from the mainland. We have in the past indicated that if the Chinese themselves were interested in purchasing grain we would consider such sales. We have indicated our willingness to allow Chinese Communist newspapermen to come to the United States. We are prepared to permit American universities to invite Chinese Communist scientists to visit their institutions.

We do not expect that for the time being the Chinese Communists will seize upon these avenues of contact or exchange. All the evidence suggests Peiping wishes to remain isolated from the United States. But we believe it is in our interests that such channels be opened and kept open. We believe contact and communication are not incompatible with a firm policy of containment.

Eighth, we should keep open our direct diplomatic contacts with Peiping in Warsaw. While these meetings frequently provide merely an opportunity for a reiteration of known positions, they play a role in enabling each side to communicate information and attitudes in times of crisis. It is our hope that they might at some time become the channel for a more fruitful dialog.

Ninth, we are prepared to sit down with Peiping and other countries to discuss the critical problems of disarmament and nonproliferation of nuclear weapons. Peiping has rejected all suggestions and invitations to join in such talks. It has attacked the test ban treaty. It has advocated the further spread of nuclear weapons to non-nuclear countries. It is an urgent task of all countries to persuade Peiping to change its stand.

Tenth, we must continue to explore and analyze all available information on Communist China and keep our own policies up to date. We hope that Peiping's policies may one day take account of the desire of the people of Asia and her own people for peace and security. We have said, in successive administrations, that when Peiping abandons the aggressive use of force and shows that it is not irrevocably hostile to the United States, then expanded contacts and improved relations may become possible. This continues to be our position.

These, I believe, are the essential ingredients of a sound policy in regard to Communist China.

I believe that they serve the interests not only of the United States and of the free world as a whole—but of the Chinese people. We have always known of the pragmatic genius of the Chinese people, and we can see evidence of it even today. The practices and doctrines of the present Peiping regime are yielding poor returns to the Chinese people. I believe that the Chinese people, no less their neighbors and the American people crave the opportunity to move toward the enduring goals of mankind: a better life, safety, freedom, human dignity, and peace.

Q. Statement by Secretary Rusk on the Situation in Communist China*

September 16, 1966

I think I have said before that I suspect what is going on [inside mainland China with regard to the cultural revolution and the Red Guards] is of some importance, but if I were to be frank with you I would have to say that I don't know what it is.

We have been interested in this phenomenon of the Red Guards, the efforts which they have made in some parts of the country to attack elements in the Communist Party apparatus. We noted the period of what seemed to be excesses, followed by attempts by the leadership to restrain those excesses.

But I think that I would be fraudulent if I were to try to say to you that I think we know the real significance of these recent events. My guess is that there are some very important issues at stake there inside China on these matters, but we will have to wait a little bit to find out just what those are.

R. Statement by Secretary Rusk on the Free Nations of Asia*

October 12, 1967

THE FREE NATIONS OF ASIA . . . DON'T WANT [COMMUNIST CHINA] TO OVERRUN THEM

Within the next decade or two, there will be a billion Chinese on the mainland, armed with nuclear weapons, with no certainty about what their attitude toward the rest of Asia will be.

Now, the free nations of Asia will make up at least a billion people. They don't want China to overrun them, on the basis of a doctrine of the world revolution. The militancy of China has isolated China, even within the Communist world, but they have not drawn back from it. They have reaffirmed it, as recently as their reception of their great and good friend, Albania, 2 days ago.

*Ibid., pp. 675-76.

*American Foreign Policy: Current Documents, 1967, pp. 753-54.

Now, we believe that the free nations of Asia must brace themselves, get themselves set, with secure, progressive, stable institutions of their own, with cooperation among the free nations of Asia stretching from Korea and Japan right around to the subcontinent, if there is to be peace in Asia over the next 10 or 20 years. We would hope that in China there would emerge a generation of leadership that would think seriously about what is called "peaceful coexistence," that would recognize the pragmatic necessity for human beings to live together in peace rather than on a basis of continuing warfare.

Now, from a strategic point of view, it is not very attractive to think of the world cut in two by Asian communism reaching out through Southeast Asia and Indonesia, which we know has been their objective, and that these hundreds of millions of people in the free nations of Asia should be under the deadly and constant pressure of the authorities in Peking, so that their future is circumscribed by fear.

Now, these are vitally important matters to us, who are both a Pacific and an Atlantic power. After all, World War II hit us from the Pacific, and Asia is where two-thirds of the world's people live. So we have a tremendous stake in the ability of the free nations of Asia to live in peace; and to turn the interests of people in mainland China to the pragmatic requirements of their own people and away from a doctrinaire and ideological adventurism abroad.

Yes, I think so [—the U.S. can fulfill this commitment of containment and still meet the commitment of the Manila Conference to withdraw within 6 months after a peace agreement has been reached in Viet-Nam].

That does not mean that we ourselves have nominated ourselves to be the policemen for all of Asia. We have, for good reasons, formed alliances with Korea and Japan, the Philippines, the Republic of China, Thailand, Australia, and New Zealand; and South Viet-Nam is covered by the Southeast Asia Treaty.

That doesn't mean that we are the general policemen. Today, the Laotian forces are carrying the burden in Laos on the ground; the Thais are carrying the burden in Thailand; the Burmese are carrying the burden in Burma; the Indians are carrying the burden upon their northeastern frontier—the Sikkim border—and what ever other threat there might be in that direction.

But we have our part; we have accepted a share, and we have accepted that share as a part of the vital national interest of the United States.

Now, what I don't understand is that Senators would declare in August 1964 that the United States considers it a vital national interest of this country that there be international peace and security of Southeast Asia, and then 2 years later, some of them seem to brush that aside as having no validity. Now, that wasn't a Tonkin Bay reaction. Paragraph 1 was Tonkin Bay. Paragraph 2 was Southeast Asia—was Southeast Asia.

Now, if people change their minds, then it is fair to ask the question, "on which occasion were they right?"

Now, I personally believe they were right in August 1964. And perhaps they will be right again if they come back to that position—1968 or '69.

But these are not matters that change with the wind. These have to do with the possibility of organizing a peace on a planet on which human beings can destroy each other. Now, perhaps we could at least agree that that is the central question, even though there could be some debate about how you do it.

And I believe that those who think that you can have peace by letting one small country after the other be overrun have got a tremendous burden of proof in the light of the history of the past four decades; and they have not sustained that burden of proof.

No [I would not describe the net objective as the containment of Chinese Communist militancy].

The central objective is an organized and reliable peace.

Now, if China pushes out against those with who we have alliances, then we have a problem; but so does China. If China pushes out against the Soviet Union, both China and the Soviet Union have a problem.

We are not picking out ourselves—we are not picking out Peking as some sort of special enemy. Peking has nominated itself by proclaiming a militant doctrine of the world revolution and doing something about it. This is not a theoretical debate; they are doing something about it.

Now, we can live at peace—we have not had a war with the Soviet Union in 50 years of coexistence since their revolution. We are not ourselves embarked upon an ideological campaign to destroy anybody who calls themselves Communist. But we are interested in the kind of world structure sketched in articles I and II of the United Nations Charter, in which all nations, large and small, have a right to live in peace. And the aggressors nominate themselves—we don't choose them—the aggressors nominate themselves by what they say and do. And when they do, then those who are genuinely interested in peace have a problem on their hands, and sometimes it gets tough; and sometimes we are tested and we find out what kind of people we are. And I think one of the most important historical facts in this postwar period has been that the almost unbelievable power of the United States has been harnessed to the simple notion of organizing a peace in the world.

S. Address by Under Secretary Nicolas Katzenbach on a Realistic View of Communist China*

[Extract]

May 21, 1968

I would like to talk to you today about our relations, or lack of them, with Communist China. I must warn you at the outset that I am not going to reveal any great new truths about China or enunciate any startling new policy. But mainland China is an ancient, populous, and powerful nation. Our relations with it are always of significance to us and always worthy or renewed consideration.

The evolution of our policy toward both mainland China and the Government of the Republic of China on Taiwan has been spelled out often. But misconcep-

*Department of State Bulletin, June 10, 1968, pp. 737-40.

tions and misunderstandings persist. I shall attempt to sort out a few of them and perhaps dispel some of the gray areas around the periphery.

We have, of course, followed with great interest the developments going on on the mainland in recent years. Many of these, and especially the ones coming under the heading of Mao Tse-tung's curiously misnamed "Cultural Revolution," have been fully reported by the press. We have, in general, refrained from commenting on these events, but I can summarize for you what we believe the situation there to be.

The Cultural Revolution, conceived by Mao as a means of eliminating individuals and viewpoints which deviated from the straight and true path he wanted China to follow, has now been raging for over 2 years. In that time hundreds of thousands, and perhaps even millions, of Communist Party and government officials and ordinary Chinese have come under criticism. Schools have been closed or disrupted. Key political, economic, and military officials have been dismissed. There has been intense political upheaval with major sectors of the economy and government thrown into confusion.

Since the major target of the Cultural Revolution was the organizational leadership of the Chinese Communist Party itself, the movement has had to rely primarily on *ad hoc* mass organizations of students or workers such as the famed Red Guards. At their worst these have spread terror and chaos. At a minimum they have created a vast disorganization throughout the country. By the middle of last year the leaders in Peking began to be alarmed by the degree to which the life of the country had been disrupted. They attempted to stem the violence and factionalism, which by this time had grown to enormous proportions, particularly in the cities.

At present Peking is attempting to reorganize and stabilize political and administrative organizations in the provinces. Tripartite revolutionary committees composed of army, party, and Red Guard-type representatives have been established in most of the provinces to take the place of the previous administrative units. In many areas, however, factional disputes have created deep antagonisms and the committees have been set up only with great difficulty.

While the major political forces operating in Peking are difficult to discern, Mao Tse-tung seems to retain his overwhelmingly preeminent position. Major issues—how best to carry out economic development, the role of material incentives versus ideological motivations, the allocation of limited resources to areas of need—remain, however, and will probably continue to create intense disagreements and conflicts. But for the moment the authorities in Peking—relying increasingly upon the military—remain in overall control.

This—in broad outline—is the situation that seems to exist on the mainland. It is Peking's foreign policy, however, not its domestic problems, that is of greatest interest to us. And unhappily, its foreign policy, unlike its domestic situation, has remained static in the last few years.

Communist China's Foreign Policy

We have followed Communist China's foreign policy closely ever since the Communist government came to power in 1949. Although right from the beginning we made efforts to maintain contacts and avoid hostile relations, the Communist authorities left little doubt that they wanted to eliminate any American representation from the Chinese mainland and to pursue a politically hostile policy toward this country.

Even after North Korea's invasion of the South in 1950 the United States avoided rigid restrictions on contact and trade with the Chinese mainland. Only after the massive Chinese intervention in Korea late in the fall of 1950 did we put such restrictions into effect.

For a brief period beginning in 1954 Peking attempted to improve its international image. It was during this period that it agreed to ambassadorial contacts with the United States. The original purpose of these meetings was to secure the release and exchange of Americans and Chinese who wanted to return home. An understanding was reached on the subject in September 1955; and we anticipated that it would, in the language of the public announcement, be "expeditiously" implemented.

But the Chinese suddenly changed their posture. Developments on the question, they said, were contingent on U.S. action on a wide range of other issues. One demand was that we abandon our commitment to the defense of Taiwan, which was not then and is not now open to negotiation. Some of the issues they raised, such as the exchange of journalists and related questions of travel and exchange, I think we might have pursued more energetically. Further progress might possibly have been achieved at that time. Still, in view of Peking's failure to follow through on the earlier commitment, skepticism about their good faith was understandable.

A year later, in 1957 when, after some prodding from members of your profession, the United States Government *did* indicate a willingness to explore the subject of journalists, China again reversed its position. In recent years, Peking has consistently turned down all proposals for increased contact.

Proposals for the exchange of newspapermen, of scholars or scientific information, have all been rejected. Hints that we might be willing to sell commodities such as grain or drugs were ignored or denounced as a trick.

Why do the Chinese Communists maintain this position? One can only speculate. One reason may be simply a continuation of the same bitterness reported on 46 years ago by four distinguished Americans—Charles Evans Hughes, Henry Cabot Lodge, Elihu Root, and Oscar W. Underwood. Reviewing the unhappy history of Chinese dealings with the West they concluded:

> A situation had thus been created in which the Chinese people nursed a sense of grievance and even of outrage; and the foreign nations found their relations complicated by mutual suspicion and resentment.

Internal political factors must, of course, be considered. The dominant element within the Chinese Communist leadership still apparently thinks that easing tensions with the United States would represent a betrayal of the revolution.

Furthermore, we (and increasingly the Soviet Union as well) are seen by the Chinese as prime examples of what should not happen in their country. Contact, exchange, *détente*—all threaten not only the objectives of Peking's foreign policy but the whole ideological fabric which this generation of leaders has woven together.

So long as such attitudes persist in Peking, the establishment of diplomatic relations becomes unrealistic. For the underlying premise of such a move—the desire for expanded and improved peaceful contacts between the two countries—appears still to be lacking on the Chinese side.

*   *   *

Peking's Isolation

It is often argued that we are isolating Peking from the international community by opposing its participation in the United Nations and other international groups and by discouraging other states from establishing diplomatic relations or conducting trade with it.

But once again, it is not the attitude of the United States but that of the People's Republic of China which isolates it. The United States, influential though it may be, does not control and govern the organs of the United Nations or of other international bodies.

The Government of the United States cannot accept Peking's demand for participation in international organizations to the exclusion of the Republic of China. This view is shared by a majority of the members of the United Nations.

Under present circumstances, Communist China's participation in the Security Council, particularly, would weaken that body's ability to deal constructively with international problems.

The Chinese mistreatment of diplomats and diplomatic missions in Peking since 1967, including the entry or sacking of several embassies, and the highly undiplomatic activities of many of Peking's own officials abroad have hardly helped its cause in the international community.

Peking has declined to participate even in totally nonpolitical international activities, such as the International Geophysical Year. It rarely permits its scientists to attend even those international scientific meetings in which national membership is not a factor.

The Chinese have quarreled even with fellow Communist nations, with consequences for international Communist unity that are familiar to you. They have withdrawn from most of the organizations which formerly were known under the general label of the "world peace movement" and attempted either to set up rival organizations or disrupt already existing ones.

The United States would welcome a change in Peking's position which might indicate a shift in its attitude on the general conduct of international affairs. Few signs of any shift are discernible. Under these circumstances, any isolation which Peking senses is of its own choosing.

Embargo on Trade With Communist China

But what about the embargo on U.S. trade with Peking? Are not the Chinese able to obtain virtually whatever they need from other countries anyway?

Since our present restrictions on trade were established, China has grown increasingly able to produce many industrial materials which it needs. And gradually more and more states, including many, such as Japan, Australia, and West

Germany, which do not recognize the Peking regime, have steadily increased their trade with mainland China in nonstrategic goods and commodities.

At the same time, Peking has shown little interest in trading with the United States. In 1961 it turned a cold shoulder on President Kennedy when he indicated that the United States would consider Chinese interest in the purchase of food grains. Last year it rejected out of hand this administration's indication of willingness to permit the export of drugs and medical supplies for the treatment of certain epidemic diseases.

We have from time to time reveiwed our trade policy to see if it would be feasible and in our interest to reduce the barriers on our side to mutually beneficial trade in nonstrategic goods with the mainland. We have undertaken this review to determine whether such peaceful trade might be possible without harming our interests in the area. In view of Peking's attitudes, however, I cannot be optimistic about any early or significant practical result in terms of trade.

We have said many times in recent years that we are willing to move toward reciprocal (or even unilateral) person-to-person contacts and exchanges with mainland China. Just last week Leonard Marks [Director, United States Information Agency] invited Communist Chinese journalists here to observe and report on this year's election campaign.

We have informed numerous nongovernmental organizations which wish to invite representatives from mainland China to meetings in this country that we have no objection. We would also be happy to see exchanges of cultural exhibits and articles.

We are prepared to issue visas to Chinese visitors from the mainland who may wish to come to the United States, subject only to legislation applying to all visitors.

Is is true that the degree of antagonism between the United States and Communist China is so great and so irreconcilable that there must inevitably take place a major military confrontation between our two countries?

Our entire policy and philosophy aims to avoid such a calamity. War is never inevitable. Given normal and sensible restraint on both sides, there is absolutely no reason why the United States and Communist China should come into conflict.

While hoping for better relations with Communist China, we are realistic enough to expect changes to come slowly. For our ability to influence the rate at which changes occur is limited. Many of them will result ultimately from altered perceptions and a more relaxed atmosphere within mainland China itself. The winds of change are blowing throughout the world. Sooner or later they must blow even over the Great Wall of China. When they do, if they bring about a Chinese wish for improved relations, the United States will be happy to respond positively.

In 1843 President John Tyler wrote a ltter to the Chinese Emperor. The spirit of one paragraph can still stand as our attitude today: "The Governments of two such great countries should be at peace. It is proper and according to the will of heaven that they should respect each other, and act wisely."

UNITED STATES POLICY IN CHINA, 1969-1970

A. Address by Under Secretary Elliot Richardson on Foreign Policy Aims and Strategy of the Nixon Administration*

[Extract]

September 5, 1969

*　　　　　*　　　　　*

In the case of Communist China, long-run improvement in our relations is in our own national interest. We do not seek to exploit for our own advantage the hostility between the Soviet Union and the People's Republic. Ideological differences between the two Communist giants are not our affair. We could not fail to be deeply concerned, however, with an escalation of this quarrel into a massive breach of international peace and security. Our national security would in the long run be prejudiced by associating ourselves with either side against the other. Each is highly sensitive about American effforts to improve relations with the other. We intend, nevertheless, to pursue a long-term course of progressively developing better relations with both. We are not going to let Communist Chinese invective deter us from seeking agreements with the Soviet Union where those are in our interest. Conversely, we are not going to let Soviet apprehensions prevent us from attempting to bring Communist China out of its angry, alienated shell.

*　　　　　*　　　　　*

B. State Department Statement on the Relaxing of Trade Restrictions with Communist China*

December 19, 1969

It has been decided to remove most Foreign Assets Control restrictions on United States foreign subsidiaries and on United States business participation in third-country trade in presumptive Chinese goods. It also has been decided to modify further the regulations on noncommercial imports from China. These revised regulations will be published, as is required, in the Federal Register on December 24.

These changes have been under consideration for some time. As is evident from their nature, their principal effect is to relax restrictions on American firms and private citizens abroad and thereby to remove administrative difficulties. The restrictions being removed have been a source of increasing irritation to United States citizens and have placed American firms abroad in a disadvanta-

*Department of State Bulletin, Sept. 22, 1969, pp. 257-60.

*Ibid., Jan. 12, 1970, pp. 31-32.

geous position. Additionally, existing Foreign Assets Control restraints on foreign subsidiaries of American firms have been a source of friction between the United States Government and friendly foreign governments, which resent the extraterritorial effect of such controls. While present actions will not relieve all United States restraints—particularly those relating to the Department of Commerce prohibition on the export of U.S.-origin goods and technology to mainland China—they should significantly reduce certain areas of friction.

Now, these changes bear out the previous remarks by Secretary Rogers that we planned to take other steps which we hope would improve relations with Communist China. They are, however, strictly unilateral and are not related to recent Warsaw contacts with Communist Chinese representatives.

Changes in China Trade Restrictions

Changes in the Foreign Assets Control Regulations were announced by the State Department on December 19. The changes are summarized as follows:

1. For foreign subsidiaries of U.S. firms, most FAC restrictions on transactions with China regarded as nonstrategic by COCOM [Coordinating Committee on export controls (Paris)] are removed. This is intended to permit American subsidiaries, insofar as FAC restrictions are concerned, to engage in trade with Communist China under regulations applicable to other firms in countries in which they operate and to remove restrictions which those countries view as interference in their domestic affairs. This action will not affect Commerce Department controls on export or re-export of U.S.-origin goods or of unpublished American technology.

2. Present restrictions on U.S. business participation in third-country trade in presumptive Chinese goods are eliminated. This will permit American firms (including banking, insurance, transport, and trading) to purchase and ship to third countries commodities of presumptive Chinese origin that they are now able to ship to the United States under certificates-of-origin procedures. Although certificates will not be required for third-country transactions, such goods still may not be shipped to the United States without them. This change is responsive to urgent requests of foreign branches of U.S. firms, and it is expected to improve the competitive position of American business concerns overseas.

3. The $100 ceiling on noncommercial purchases of Chinese Communist goods by Americans is removed, as is the requirement that noncommercial imports from China enter the United States as accompanied baggage. This will further relieve administrative difficulties of American citizens and is responsive to the desire of American tourists, collectors, museums, and universities to import Chinese products for their own account. It will not permit imports by persons or commercial organizations in the United States for resale.

C. State Department Statement on the Resumption of United States-Communist China Warsaw Meetings*

January 8, 1970

The Governments of the United States and the People's Republic of China have agreed to hold the 135th ambassadorial-level meeting in Warsaw January 20, 1970. The United States will be represented by Ambassador Walter J. Stoessel, Jr. The Chinese side will be represented by Chargé d'Affaires Lei Yang.

The meeting will be held at the Embassy of the People's Republic of China, with holdings of subsequent meetings alternating between the United States and the People's Republic of China Embassies.

Ibid., Jan. 26, 1970, p. 83.

THE UNITED STATES

AND KOREA

THE UNITED STATES AND KOREA

Commentary

American policy toward Korea in 1945 was simply support of the Cairo Declaration which called for Korean independence. Little consideration was given to the possibility that events would conspire to force the United States to make a lengthy military and economic commitment. Certainly no one expected that a quarter-century later American forces would remain on Korean soil.

The problem of Korea since the Second World War is a difficult one. Korea in the nineteenth century was a hermit kingdom, for some years a client state of China; but because of its peninsular geographic position, which thrust at the heart of Japan, it was very much an object of Japanese interest as well. Wars with China and Russia allowed Japan to increase its influence and finally to annex the country in 1910. Korea remained a part of Japan until the end of the Second World War. In 1945, in order to accept the surrender of Japanese troops, the country was divided at the 38th parallel, the Russians taking the surrender to the north of the line and the United States to the south. The choice of the 38th parallel had no logical geographical or social basis; it was an arbitrary boundary originating in the Pentagon, which viewed it as purely temporary.

In any event the Soviets, consistent with their practice in Eastern Europe, soon thereafter began establishing a Communist regime in the North, while the United States supported conservative, quasi-democratic governmental units in the South. In December, 1945, the foreign ministers of the two occupying countries met in Moscow to work out a formula for unification but failed, primarily because of Soviet insistence on predominant Communist representation in the new government. A later attempt at unification in 1947 also failed. Consequently, the United States submitted the matter to the United Nations, which then constituted a temporary commission to hold elections in the entire peninsula for a constitutional assembly. Though the commission was blocked in its attempt to include the North, elections were held in the South, a new constitution was drafted, and in August of 1948, the Republic of Korea, with Syngman Rhee as its first president, came into existence. The Soviets, meanwhile, created a "Peoples" Republic in the North under Kim Il Sung.

The Soviets then armed North Korea with heavy weapons, preparing it for

339

possible military reunification, and withdrew in 1948. The United States on the other hand, provided light defensive weapons for South Korea prior to its withdrawal in 1949. In January, 1950, Secretary of State Dean Acheson, speaking before the National Press Club in Washington, indicated that the "defensive perimeter" of the United States did not encompass Korea, but that its protection in case of attack would be the United Nations. This may have suggested to the Communist bloc that the United States was removing its protective umbrella. Whether it was in response to the Secretary's comments or not, the North Koreans with support from Moscow, launched an invasion of South Korea on June 25, 1950.

The result of the Communist action was a long and indecisive war, involving large numbers of American soldiers. Upon American initiatives, the United Nations Security Council with the Soviet delegate absent, demanded on June 25 and 27 the withdrawal of North Korean troops and voted to provide military assistance to the Republic of Korea. Because President Truman saw the Communist invasion as a threat to security in the Pacific and ultimately to the vital interests of the United States, he also authorized United States air support of South Korea, a naval blockade of North Korea, and responding to a directive from the U.N., appointed General Douglas MacArthur commander of all U.N. forces. The United States was to play the leading role in Korea. After initial setbacks, MacArthur engineered a daring landing at Inchon in the North, and by early October had cleared the aggressors from the South and advanced toward the Chinese border. Shortly thereafter, in November, Chinese armies entered the war in support of North Korea. Though quickly branded as aggressors by the U.N., the Chinese fought furiously and again pushed south of the 38th parallel. In July, 1951, the Soviet representative to the United Nations suggested the desirability of an armistice and negotiations began, but the fighting continued for two more years.

After the Chinese intervention, General MacArthur advocated the bombing of sites in China, the blockading of the China coast and all other actions needed to bring "victory." These proposals were rejected by Truman and the Joint Chiefs of Staff, who hoped to restrict the scope of the War and feared the possibility of Russian advances in Western Europe. Subsequently, the General made public his differences with the Administration and was removed from his command in April, 1951. The removal unleashed a furor in the United States which did not subside until after the armistice was signed in July, 1953.

The armistice, although it put an end to the shooting, brought little peace. South and North Korea glared at one another over a truce line supervised by a neutral commission. Attempts to achieve a permanent settlement at Geneva in 1954 failed, as the Communists repeatedly rejected suggestions on reunification through supervised elections. This was where the matter stood throughout the remainder of the 1950's and 1960's. Korea was a victim of the Cold War, seemingly permanently divided; the North, a military power in its own right, was backed by the forces of the Soviet Union and Communist China, and the South was supported by the power of the United States, with which it strengthened its security arrangements.

Events since 1967 have caused some concern in the United States that the North was preparing another attempt at reunification. In that year several efforts were made to infiltrate northern troops into the South, and one attempt was made to assassinate the South Korean president. In January, 1968, the United States intelligence ship *Pueblo* was captured in international waters and detained; in April, 1969, an American aircraft was shot down over the Sea of Japan. Some observers saw these acts as unilateral and somewhat irrational outbursts by North Korea; others interpreted them as in conjunction with events in Vietnam, American policy makers entertained some fear that North Korea was weighing pacifist and neo-isolationist opinion in the United States, preparatory to another invasion of the South. Whatever the meaning, one thing remains clear: permanent peace appears no nearer now than in 1953.

THE PARTITION OF KOREA

A. Report of the Meeting of Foreign Affairs Ministers of the U.S.S.R., the United States and the United Kingdom*

[Extract]

Moscow, December 27, 1945

*   *   *

1. With a view to the re-establishment of Korea as an independent state, the creation of conditions for developing the country on democratic principles and the earliest possible liquidation of the disastrous results of the protracted Japanese domination in Korea, there shall be set up a provisional Korean democratic government which shall take all the necessary steps for developing the industry, transport and agriculture of Korea and the national culture of the Korean people.

2. In order to assist the formation of a provisional Korean government and with a view to the preliminary elaboration of the appropriate measures, there shall be established a Joint Commission consisting of representatives of the United States command in southern Korea and the Soviet command in northern Korea. In preparing their proposals the Commission shall consult with the Korean democratic parties and social organizations. The recommendations worked out by the Commission shall be presented for the consideration of the Governments of the Union of Soviet Socialist Republics, China, the United Kingdom and the United States prior to final decision by the two Governments represented on the Joint Commission.

3. It shall be the task of the Joint Commission, with the participation of the provisional Korean democratic government and of the Korean democratic organizations to work out measures also for helping and assisting (trusteeship) the political, economic and social progress of the Korean people, the development of democratic self-government and the establishment of the national independence of Korea.

The proposals of the Joint Commission shall be submitted, following consultation with the provisional Korean Government for the joint consideration of the Governments of the United States, Union of Soviet Socialist Republics, United Kingdom and China for the working out of an agreement concerning a four-power trusteeship of Korea for a period of up to five years.

4. For the consideration of urgent problems affecting both southern and northern Korea and for the elaboration of measures establishing permanent coordination in administrative-economic matters between the United States command in southern Korea and the Soviet command in northern Korea, a conference of the representatives of the United States and Soviet commands in Korea shall be convened within a period of two weeks.

*   *   *

*Council on Foreign Relations, *Documents on American Foreign Relations*, 1948, Vol. VIII pp.836-37.

B. Communiqué No. 5 of the United States-Soviet Joint Commission*

Seoul, April 18, 1946

The U.S.-Soviet Joint Commission continued discussion on the question of conditions of consultation with democratic parties and social organizations. Col. Gen. T. F. Shtikov, Chief of the Soviet Delegation, was chairman on sessions held on April 8,9,11, and 13, 1946, in the Tuk Soo Palace, Seoul, Korea, and Maj. Gen. A. V. Arnold, chief of the U. S. delegation, was chairman at the session, April 17, 1946.

As a result of a thorough investigation and analysis of the points of view of the Soviet delegation and the delegation of the United States, the Joint Commission reached the following decision on the first point of the joint program of work covering the conditions of the consultation with democratic parties and social organizations:

Decision

The Joint Commission will consult with Korean democratic parties and social organizations which are truly democratic in their aims and methods and which will subscribe to the following declarations:

We . . . . declare that we will uphold the aims of the Moscow Decision on Korea as stated in paragraph 1 of this decision, namely:

The reestablishment of Korea as an independent state, the creation of conditions for developing the country on democratic principles, and the earliest possible liquidation of the disastrous results of the protracted Japanese domination in Korea. Further, we will abide by the decisions of the Joint Commission in its fulfilment of paragraph 2 of the Moscow decision in the formation of a Provisional Korean Democratic Government; further, we will cooperate with the Joint Commission in the working out by it with the participation of the Provisional Korean Democratic Government of proposals concerning measures foreseen by paragraph 3 of the Moscow decision.

Signed . . . .
Representing the . . . .
Party or Organization

The procedure for inviting representatives of Korean democratic parties and social organizations to consult with the Joint Commission is being worked out by Joint Sub-Commission No. 1. When details of the procedure are completed it will be announced publicly.

Department of State Bulletin, Vol. XVI, p. 173.

C. Secretary Marshall to Soviet Foreign Minister V. Molotov on Reconvening of the Joint Commission on Korea*

April 8, 1947

I wish to call your attention to the situation in Korea. The representatives of the Soviet Union and the United States on the Joint U.S.-U.S.S.R. Commission in Korea have been unable to make progress toward the establishment of a Korean Provisional Government. It has been nineteen months since the Japanese surrender, yet Korea has profited little. The country is divided into two zones. The Soviet Commander in Northern Korea has refused to permit freedom of movement and free economic exchange between these zones. This has precluded freely chosen political amalgamation of the Korean people and has resulted in grave economic distress.

The policy of the United States toward Korea has the following basic objectives:

(1) To assist in the establishment as soon as practicable of a self-governed sovereign Korea, independent of foreign control and eligible for membership in the United Nations.

(2) To insure that the national government so established shall be representative of the freely expressed will of the Korean people.

(3) To aid the Koreans in building a sound economy as an essential basis for their independent and democratic state.

The United States, in the Cairo Declaration of December 1, 1943, declared its determination that in due course Korea should become free and independent. The United Kingdom and the Republic of China were parties to the same declaration. The Cairo Declaration was specifically reaffirmed by the Three Powers in the Potsdam Declaration, which defined terms for the Japanese surrender. The U.S.S.R. in its declaration of war on Japan on August 8, 1945 declared its adherence to these declarations.

Upon the surrender of Japan, United States and Soviet forces accepted the surrender of Japanese forces in Korea in the areas respectively south and north of a line arbitrarily assigned for this purpose, the thirty-eighth degree parallel. This line of demarcation became in effect a boundary between zones of occupation. At the conference of the Foreign Ministers of the U.S., the U.K. and the U.S.S.R. in Moscow in December, 1945, the serious consequences of the bizonal division of Korea were discussed and an agreement regarding Korea was reached and published in part three of the communiqué of the conference. The Republic of China subsequently subscribed to this agreement.

On March 20, 1946, the Joint U.S.-U.S.S.R. Commission appointed under the terms of the Moscow Agreement met and began its task, as outlined in the agreement, of assisting in the formation of a provisional Korean democratic government as a first step in assuring the establishment of an independent and sovereign Korean nation.

It was the hope of the Government of the United States that speedy action

Ibid., Vol. XVI, p. 716.

would be taken by the Joint Commission, a provisional Korean government would rapidly be established, the unfortunate results of the line of demarcation between the United States and the Soviet forces would be overcome and Korea could be started on the way to attaining an independent and democratic government.

Unfortunately the work of the Joint Commission became stalemated after a short time through the failure to agree on the definition of the word "democratic" as it pertained to the representatives of the parties and social organizations mentioned in the Moscow Agreement to be consulted by the Joint Commission in its task of assisting in the formation of a provisional government. As it became evident that no agreement could be reached at the time, the Joint Commission adjourned *sine die* on May 8, 1946.

The United States Commander in Korea has several times suggested to the Soviet Commander that the Commission reconvene and get on with its work.

However, the Soviet Commander has insisted on a formula which would result in eliminating the majority of representative Korean leaders from consultation as representatives of Korean democratic parties and social organizations, and has reiterated this position in a letter to the American Commander as recently as February 28, 1947. It has therefore been impossible to agree upon a basis for reconvening the Commission.

Now in April 1947, almost sixteen months since the agreement pertaining to Korea was reached in Moscow, there has still been no real progress made toward the implementation of that agreement.

In fulfillment of the intent of the Agreement and Declaration made at Moscow in December 1945, the Government of the United States desires to further the work of establishing a free and independent Korea without additional delay.

To this end I ask that our Governments agree to instruct our respective Commanders in Korea to reconvene the Joint Commission as soon as possible and charge it with expediting its work under the terms of the Moscow Agreement on a basis of respect for the democratic right of freedom of opinion. I further suggest that a mutually acceptable date during the summer of 1947 be fixed for a review by the two Governments of the progress made to that date by the Joint Commission. In the meantime, the United States, mindful of its obligations under the Moscow Agreement, sees no alternative to taking without further delay such steps in its zone as will advance the purposes of that agreement.

I am furnishing copies of this letter to the British and Chinese Governments.

D. Secretary Marshall to Foreign Minister Molotov on the Moscow Agreement*

May 2, 1947

I have considered your letter of April 19, 1947 in which you accept our proposal to reconvene the U.S.-U.S.S.R. Joint Commission and suggest that the Commission resume its work on May 20 of this year. I have also noted your

*Ibid., p. 947.

statement that resumption of the Commission's work shall be "on the basis of an exact execution of the Moscow Agreement on Korea."

In order to avoid any future misunderstanding with respect to the phrase "exact execution" I wish to make clear my interpretation of the phrase. In my letter to you of April 8 I stated that the Joint Commission should be charged with expediting "its work under the terms of the Moscow Agreement on a basis of respect for the democratic right of freedom of opinion." In making this statement I had and have in mind the well-known position of the Government of the United States that Korean representatives of democratic parties and social organizations shall not be excluded from consultation with the Commission on the formation of a provisional Korean government because of opinions they might hold or may have expressed in the past concerning the furture government of their country, provided they are prepared to cooperate with the Commission.

You mention three points which the Soviet Government believes to be of primary importance in its policy towards Korea. Your statement concerning the importance of establishing a provisional democratic Korean government on the basis of wide-scale participation of Korean democratic parties and social organizations has from the beginning been accepted by the United States Government as basic to its policy of assisting in the establishment of a self-governing sovereign Korea, independent of foreign control and eligible for membership in the United Nations.

I interpret your second point with respect to the establishment of "democratic authority agencies" throughout Korea as referring to local, provincial and national government agencies chosen, as you state, by means of free elections on the basis of a general and equal electoral right.

I welcome the assurance contained in your third point with regard to the importance you attach to aiding in the restoration of Korea as an independent democratic state and in the development of its national economy and national culture. The United States Government has under consideration a constructive program for the rehabilitation of the economy of Korea and for its educational and political development.

In order that I may direct the United States Commander in Korea to make preparations for opening the sessions of the Joint Commission in Seoul on May 20, 1947, may I receive an early confirmation that we are mutually agreed as to the basis on which the Commission shall resume its important work?

I am furnishing copies of this letter to the Governments of China and the United Kingdom.

E. Acting Secretary of State Robert Lovett to Foreign Minister Molotov on the United States' Intention to Refer the Korean Question to the United Nations*

September 17, 1947

The decision of the Soviet Government as conveyed in your letter of Septem-
Ibid., Vol. XVII, p. 623.

ber 4, not to participate in Four Power discussions of proposals of the United States Government designed to achieve the speedy realization of the aims of the Moscow Agreement on Korea is deeply regretted. For almost two years the United States Government has been faithfully endeavoring to reach agreement with the Soviet Government to carry out the terms of the Moscow Agreement but with no appreciable success. It has even proved impossible for the Soviet and United States Delegations on the Joint Commission in Korea to agree upon a joint report of the status of their deliberations up to the present. There is no sign of the early setting up of a Korean Provisional Government. Korea remains divided and her promised independence unrealized.

The United States Government believes that this situation must not be permitted to continue indefinitely. In view of the fact that bilateral negotiations have not advanced Korean independence and that the Soviet Government does not agree to discussions among the powers adhering to the Moscow Agreement, there is but one course remaining. It is the intention, therefore, of my Government to refer the problem of Korean independence to the forthcoming session of the General Assembly of the United Nations. It is suggested that the members of the Joint Commission hold themselves in readiness to give such aid and assistance to the General Assembly as may be required during the Assembly's consideration of this problem.

It is the hope of my Government that consideration of this problem by the General Assembly may result in bringing about the early restoration of freedom and independence to the long suffering people of Korea.

Copies of this letter have been furnished to the Governments of the United Kingdom and China.

F. General Assembly Resolution on the Independence of Korea*

November 14, 1947

I

Inasmuch as the Korean question which is before the General Assembly is primarily a matter for the Korean people itself and concerns its freedom and independence; and

Recognizing that this question cannot be correctly and fairly resolved without the participation of representatives of the indigenous population:

The General Assembly,

1. Resolves that elected representatives of the Korean people be invited to take part in the consideration of the question;

2. Further resolves that in order to facilitate and expedite such participation and to observe that the Korean representatives are in fact duly elected by the Korean people and not mere appointees from military authorities in Korea, there be forthwith established a United Nations Temporary Commission on Korea, to be present in Korea, with right to travel, observe and consult throughout Korea.

*Ibid., p. 1031.

II

The General Assembly

Recognizing the urgent and rightful claims to independence of the people of Korea;

Believing that the national independence of Korea should be re-established and all occupying forces then withdrawn at the earliest practicable date;

Recalling its previous conclusion that the freedom and independence of the Korean people cannot be correctly or fairly resolved without the participation of representatives of the Korean people, and its decision to establish a United Nations Temporary Commission on Korea (hereinafter called the "Commission") for the purpose of facilitating and expediting such participation by elected representatives of the Korean people:

1. Decides that the Commission shall consist of representatives of Australia, Canada, China, El Salvador, France, India, Philippines, Syria, Ukrainian Soviet Socialist Republic;

2. Recommends that the elections be held not later than 31 March 1948 on the basis of adult suffrage and by secret ballot to choose representatives with whom the Commission may consult regarding the prompt attainment of the freedom and independence of the Korean people and which representatives, constituting a National Assembly, may establish a National Government of Korea. The number of representatives from each voting area or zone should be proportionate to the population and the elections should be under the observation of the Commission;

3. Further recommends that as soon as possible after the election, the National Assembly should convene and form a National Government and notify the Commission of its formation;

4. Further recommends that immediately upon the establishment of a National Government, that Government should, in consultation with the Commission (a) constitute its own national security forces and dissolve all military or semi-military formations not included therein; (b) take over the functions of government from the military commands and civilian authorities of north and south Korea; and (c) arrange with the occupying Powers for the complete withdrawal from Korea of their armed forces as early as practicable and if possible within ninety days;

5. Resolves that the Commission shall facilitate and expedite the fulfillment of the foregoing programme for the attainment of the national independence of Korea and withdrawal of occupying forces, taking into account its observations and consultations in Korea. The Commission shall report, with its conclusions, to the General Assembly and may consult with the Interim Committee (if one be established) with respect to the application of this resolution in the light of developments;

6. Calls upon the Member States concerned to afford every assistance and facility to the Commission in the fulfillment of its responsibilities;

7. Calls upon all Members of the United Nations to refrain from interfering in the affairs of the Korean people during the interim period preparatory to

the establishment of Korean independence, except in pursuance of the decisions of the General Assembly; and thereafter, to refrain completely from any and all acts derogatory to the independence and sovereignty of Korea.

G. Proclamation by U.S. Commander Hodge, Calling for General Elections in South Korea*

March 1, 1948

The General Assembly of the United Nations, having established a United Nations Temporary Commission on Korea, recommend that election be held to choose representatives with whom the commission may consult regarding prompt attainment of the freedom and independence of the Korean people, and which representatives, constituting a National Assembly, may establish a national government of Korea;

And the United Nations Temporary Commission on Korea having consulted the Interim Committee of the United Nations, which expressed the view that it is incumbent upon the United Nations Temporary Commission on Korea to implement the program as outlined in the Resolution of the General Assembly in that part of Korea which is accessible to the commission; and

The United Nations Temporary Commission on Korea having concluded to observe such elections in those parts of Korea accessible to it, and the territory occupied by the Armed Forces of the United States of America being accessible to the commission:

Now, therefore, by virtue of the power vested in me as Commanding General of the United States Army Forces in Korea, I do hereby proclaim as follows:

1. That election of the representatives of the Korean people, under the observance of the United Nations Temporary Commission on Korea, shall be held within the territory of this command on 9 May 1948.

2. That such election is being held under the terms and provisions of Public Act number 5, dated 3 September 1947, law for the election of members of the Korean Interim Legislative Assembly, with such changes, additions, and emendations as, after consultation with the United Nations Temporary Commission on Korea, may be deemed necessary.

Given under my hand at Seoul, Korea, on 1 March 1948.

H. Letter from Commander Hodge Congratulating Members of the Korean National Assembly*

May 27, 1948

I congratulate you upon your election as representative of the Korean people to participate in forming a government and in uniting the Korean nation. You carry great responsibilities of which I am sure you are well aware and which

*Ibid., Vol. XVIII, p. 344.
*Ibid., p. 800.

I am confident you will handle with great honor to yourself and the fine people you represent.

The most important feature of the election is that it puts the fate and future of Korea into Korean hands. The manner and method in which the elected representatives in South Korea make their approach to handling the affairs of their nation will have tremendous and lasting effect on the future of the Korean people.

The policy of the United States has always been that Korea shall be a united, independent nation under democratic government free of foreign domination. That same policy is reflected internationally in the forty-three to nothing vote of the United Nations General Assembly when it voted to observe elections in Korea as a step toward establishing a Korean national government and to advise Korean elected representatives in the formation of that government. This policy also reflects the wishes of the thirty million Korean people, and we all regret exceedingly that the free election could not be held in Korea north of the thirty-eight degree parallel at the same time as in South Korea. The United States and United Nations hope that this can be done and that representatives from North Korea can join those of South Korea in the establishment of a truly national Korean Government, joining North and South Korea together in one nation.

It is my hope, the hope of the United States Government, and the hope of the members of the United Nations Temporary Commission on Korea as expressed to me on numerous occasions, that the newly elected representatives will do everything in their power to form a truly democratic government and to unite Korea.

I am sure that members of the Assembly, both as individuals and as members of party groups, have ideas as to how these objectives can be accomplished. In that connection, I have three suggestions for your possible early consideration when you meet to begin your deliberations toward the formation of a government. They are as follows:

First, in order to pave the way for unification of North and South Korea, an early resolution might be adopted stating that one hundred seats (or a number as calculated on a proportional population basis) are always open in the Assembly for your brothers in North Korea when their representatives have been duly chosen.

Second, the Assembly might, early in its deliberations, appoint an able liaison committee to contact the United Nations Temporary Commission on Korea inasmuch as this Commission was specifically appointed for the purpose of facilitating and expediting the establishment of an independent Korean government. The government which you will form will certainly wish to have the approval of the United Nations of the world and such a committee would be most helpful to both the U.N. and the Korean Assembly in carrying out the remaining provisions of the U.N. resolution of November 14, 1947.

Third, that the Assembly avoid precipitant action in the adoption of any constitution providing a form of government that may not be suitable to Korean needs and psychology. The Constitution provides the basic foundation of the

state and its provisions should be the subject of most careful and serious considerations.

I wish you and all other elected representatives of the Korean people every
success. I assure you that as the senior United States representative in Korea
I will continue to do everything I can to assist the Korean people in maintaining
their life-long desire—namely, an independent Korean nation, united under its
own sovereign government.

I. State Department Announcement on the Withdrawal of Forces from Korea*

September 20, 1948

It has been the consistent view of this government that the best interests
of the Korean people would be served by the withdrawal of all occupying forces
from Korea at the earliest practicable date. This same view was embodied in
the UN General Assembly Resolution of November 14, 1947 in which provision
was made for such withdrawal as soon as practicable after the establishment
of the Korean Government which it was the intention of that Resolution to
bring into being. Had the Soviet Union cooperated in carrying out the provisions
of the Resolution of November 14, 1947 the question of troop withdrawal from
Korea would doubtless have been already resolved.

The United States Government regards the question of the withdrawal of
occupying forces as but one facet of the entire question of the unity and independence of Korea. The General Assembly of the UN has taken cognizance of
this larger question as evidenced by the Resolution referred to above, and may
be expected to give further consideration to the matter at its forthcoming meeting.

J. United States Statement on Korean Independence*

Paris, December 7, 1948

The committee now takes in hand the matter of securing the independence
of Korea. That is a momentous task and it is an exciting task—for it is a
task of creation. Five years ago the war victors promised independence and
unity to the thirty million people of Korea. But, as in other cases, the victors
have not been able to redeem their promises, so, the United Nations has had
to take up the task.

Last year we made a good beginning. Then, this Assembly voted, 43 to O
with 6 abstentions, to establish a United Nations Temporary Commission on
Korea. It was given a mandate to consult, on our behalf, with the "elected
representatives of the Korean people" and "to observe that the Korean representatives are, in fact, duly elected by the Korean people and not mere military
appointees in Korea". The commission was also authorized to supervise the

*Ibid., Vol. XIX, p. 440.
*Ibid., p.758.

establishment of a Korean Government on the basis of elections to a national assembly, which in turn, would establish a national government. That government, it was contemplated, would set up its own national security forces; would dissolve all military or semi-military formations not included therein; take over the functions of government from the military commands and civilian authorities of north and south Korea and arrange with the occupying powers for the complete withdrawal from Korea of their armed forces. Thus, independence would become a reality.

The members of the commission have worked well and hard under most difficult conditions. We now have before us their reports and we have heard from their rapporteur. We also have the report of the Interim Committee regarding its consultation in February of this year with the United Nations Temporary Commission on Korea.

The reports are in certain respects most gratifying. In other respects they are disheartening. The disheartening feature of the reports, to mention them first, is that in the area of Korea north of the 38th parallel, which constitutes the Soviet zone of occupation, the United Nations commission was defied. It was not permitted to "travel, observe and consult" as the Assembly requested. It was, indeed, excluded and not allowed to assure that free elections would be held and the people of that area permitted to participate in the formation of a national government. Instead, it seems that in the darkness of that area, closed to United Nations observation, there has been brought into being a Communist-controlled regime that asserts pretensions to govern all Korea and that threatens to back those pretentions by force and violence. Already it has incited acts of terrorism and cruelty that shock all decent people. Yet that regime, born in obscurity, in defiance of the United Nations has been recognized by three member states: The Soviet Union, Czechoslovakia and Poland, and is, it seems, supported morally and materially by the forces in north Korea of the Soviet Union.

It is for the Korean people a dreadful thing that after forty years of oppression from Japan, they should now be threatened with new violence and terrorism from the north., It is for the United Nations a disheartening and a disturbing fact that recommendations of this Assembly, adopted by a vote of 43 to O, should be flouted by some of our members. This Assembly should not, indeed it cannot, conceal the gravity of that situation, not alone for Korea, but for the United Nations itself.

That is the somber aspect of the problem. There is, however, another and brighter aspect. South of the 38th parallel, where two-thirds of the Korean people reside, the United Nations commission was given every facility to travel, observe and consult as requested by this Assembly. Furthermore, under the auspices of the commission, elections were held which constituted a magnificent demonstration of the capacity of the Korean people to establish a representative and responsible government. Despite widespread efforts to confuse and to intimidate, despite the actual murder of many would-be voters, approximately eighty percent of the eligible voters registered, and of these approximately ninety-five percent cast ballots.

The result was a balanced assembly, fairly reflective of the will of the people. The government created by that Assembly is now in authority; it is consolidating its position; it is building up security forces and local constabulary; it is maintaining law and order despite the efforts of some subversive elements; it is developing the economy of the country, and in that connection it is receiving, and will continue to receive, substantial economic aid from members of the United Nations.

In sum, there has been established a lawful government having effective control and jurisdiction over the part of Korea where the United Nations temporary commission was able to observe and consult, and in which the great majority of the people of Korea reside. That government was based on elections which were a valid expression of the free will of the electorate in that part of Korea and it is the only such government in Korea.

The United Nations can be proud of its efforts and of the response of the Korean people, who have shown that, given the opportunity, they are willing and able to help themselves.

We shall, no doubt, hear repeated last year's glowing statements about conditions in north Korea which our commission was prevented from observing. The unknown can always be made to appear glamorous and that is, perhaps, why north Korea is a forbidden land so far as United Nations observation is concerned. It would, however, be irresponsible for this committee to depend upon the reports of those who refused to permit of verification by the United Nations commission sent out to Korea for that purpose. We do have data, independently verified by our United Nations commission, that shows that there has now come into being, through a cooperative effort of the United Nations and the Korean people a government under whose auspices the Korean people may at last realize their oft-promised independence and unity.

It is, of course, obvious that neither independence nor unity are yet fully achieved and the United Nations cannot consider its task completed. Further measures are required of us.

First of all, the United Nations ought to put the seal of legitimacy on what has been done under its auspices. The government of the Republic of Korea needs that in order to maintain its prestige and authority at home and abroad. It would, indeed, be unthinkable that the United Nations should in any way disown the consequences of its own creative program.

In the second place, we believe that the United Nations should continue a commission on Korea in order to help the new government of Korea to end the wartime military occupation of Korea. There ought to be an observed withdrawal of occupation forces from all Korea as soon as practical. And that withdrawal should be a reality so complete and thorough that, in fact, the Korean people are truly the masters in their own home and not ruled or terrorized by elements that take their orders from without.

In the third place, we believe that the United Nations commission should help the Korean people to reunite and to end the economic dislocations, the fears of civil war, that now gravely disturb the life of the people. As in the case of Greece, Communist elements seek, by violence, to impose their will, and there is danger that these efforts will be supported in one form or another by neighboring Communist regimes. The presence of a United Nations commission with authority to observe will deter organized violence and tend to assure that the peoples of north and south Korea and their neighbors will, in the words of the charter, "practice tolerance and live together in peace with one another as good neighbors." We also believe the United Nations commission may be able through good offices to help break down peacefully the barrier to friendly intercourse caused by the present division of Korea.

The Governments of Australia, China and the United States are submitting to this committee a draft of resolution that, in our opinion, will enable the United Nations to move forward along these lines. I hope that that resolution will receive overwhelming support. It should, because the principle involved protects not only Korea, but all of us. The United Nations here faces a familiar pattern. We see violence, terrorism and internal division being stimulated from without by those who hope thereby to gain international objectives.

Every non-Communist government in the world is, to a greater or lesser extent, subject to these tactics.

There is one elemental defense, and that is, through the United Nations, to evidence at least a moral solidarity with those who in violation of our charter are subjected to such threats of violence.

A distinguished representative of one of the Communist states said a few days ago before the plenary assembly "we know that we are hated because of our form of government." That is not the case. What are hated are the methods of coercion, terrorism and violence that are often employed by Communist governments and taught to party members. It may be that the greatest service that the United Nations can render is to be the instrumentality for demonstrating that whenever those methods are used or threatened internationally, the rest of the world community closes ranks to prevent the success of these methods by whatever peaceful means are available either to the United Nations as an organization or to member states acting pursuant to the charter.

If that happens, then it may be learned that the use of force, coercion, terrorism and violence to achieve international objectives has consequences such that those methods cease to be expedient. That, in turn, may lead all the member nations to respect their charter undertaking to refrain in their international relations from the threat or use of force. Therein lies, in my opinion, the greatest hope of peace. So, in the interest of Korean independence, and also in the interest of the independence of each of us, let us demonstrate here solidarity with the newly formed but already threatened, Government of the Republic of Korea.

K. State Department Statement on United States Policy in Korea*

[Extract]

June 8, 1949

On January 1 of this year the United States Government extended full recogni-

Ibid., p. 781.

tion to the Government of the Republic of Korea. In so doing, the United States welcomed into the community of free nations a new republic, born of the efforts of the United Nations, and of the United States as a principally interested power, to give effect to the urgent and rightful claims of the Korean people to freedom and national independence.

The United States Government, inspired by its historic ties of friendship with the Korean people and by its sincere interest in the spread of free institutions and representative government among the peoples of the world, entertains a particularly deep and sympathetic concern for the welfare of the Republic of Korea. As evidence of this concern, the United States is currently carrying out in Korea a program of economic and technical assistance designed to provide the economic stability without which political stability would be impossible. A request for authorization to continue and to strengthen this program during the coming fiscal year has already been submitted to the Congress. The United States has, moreover, maintained in Korea a military training mission whose function it has been to advise and assist the Government of the Republic of Korea in the development of its own security forces, in consonance with the United Nations General Asembly's resolution of November 14, 1947, and has transferred to that government for those forces substantial amounts of military equipment and supplies under the authority of the Surplus Property Act. The transfer of such equipment and supplies is continuing, while the military training mission has recently been placed on a more formal basis with the establishment of a United States Military Advisory Group to the Republic of Korea. Other forms of assistance, such as that in the fields of education and vocational training, also have been and are being given to the Republic of Korea by the United States Government.

In pursuance of the recommendation contained in the General Assembly's resolution of December 12, 1948, to the effect that the occupying Powers should "withdraw their occupation forces from Korea as early as practicable," the United States Government will soon have completed the withdrawal of its occupation forces from that country. As is clear from the broad program of assistance outlined above, this withdrawal in no way indicates a lessening of United States interest in the Republic of Korea, but constitutes rather another step toward the normalization of relations with that republic and a compliance on the part of the United States with the cited provision of the December 12 resolution of the General Assembly.

While the United States has given unstintingly of its material assistance and political support in order that the Republic of Korea might grow and prosper, this government recognizes that the Korean problem remains one of international concern and that it is only through continued support by the entire community of nations to which that republic owes its existence that the security and stability of this new nation can be assured during the critical months and years that lie ahead. So long as the authority of the Republic of Korea continues to be challenged within its own territory by the alien tyranny which has been arbitrarily imposed upon the people ot North Korea, the need for such support will be a vital one.

*   *   *

MILITARY ASSISTANCE TO KOREA

A. John J. Muccio, U.S. Ambassador to Korea, to Syngman Rhee, President of the Republic of Korea, on U.S. Military Advisors for Korea*

May 2, 1949

I have the honor to refer to your request for a United States military and naval mission and to recent references thereto in our discussions looking towards setting a date for the early withdrawal of United States occupation forces.

As you know, there has been in existence on a provisional basis for more than eight months a United States military mission known as the Provisional Military Advisory Group whose function it has been to advise and assist the Korean Government in the development and training of its own security forces. It is the judgment of my Government that, due in no small part to the spirit of eager cooperation which has been shown by the Korean Government and its responsible officials, the work of the Provisional Military Advisory Group has contributed significantly to raising the capabilities of the security forces of the Republic of Korea. This judgment would seem to be substantiated by your own recent statement to the effect that Korean defense forces "are now rapidly approaching the point at which our security can be assured, provided the Republic of Korea is not called upon to face attack from foreign sources".

In order to assure the continuance of this progress without further dependence upon the presence of United States occupation forces in Korea, my Government has decided to establish an augmented Korean Military Advisory Group to function as a part of the American Mission in Korea, with responsibility for the training mission heretofore undertaken by the Provisional Military Advisory Group. Under my overall direction as Ambassador, the Korean Military Advisory Group will be headed by Brigadier General W. L. Roberts, presently Commanding General, United States Army Forces in Korea, and Commanding Officer of the Provisional Military Advisory Group. Further details concerning the composition of the New Military Advisory Group will be discussed at an appropriate time with the proper officials of your Government.

B. Speech by Secretary Acheson on a Review of United States Policy to 1950*
[Extract]

January 12, 1950

This afternoon I should like to discuss with you the relations between the Peoples of the United States and the peoples of Asia, and I used the words, "relations of the peoples of the United States and the peoples of Asia" advisedly.

*Department of State Bulletin, Vol. XX, pp. 106.
*Ibid., pp. 261-62.

I am not talking about governments or nations because it seems to me what I want to discuss with you is this feeling of mine that the relations depend upon the attitudes of the people; that there are fundamental attitudes, fundamental interests, fundamental purposes of the people of the United States, 150 million of them, and of the peoples of Asia, unnumbered millions, which determine and out of which grow the relations of our countries and the policies of our governments. Out of these attitudes and interests and purposes grow what we do from day to day.

Now, let's dispose of one idea right at the start and not bother with it any more. That is that the policies of the United States are determined out of abstract principles in the Department of State or in the White House or in the Congress. That is not the case. If these policies are going to be good, they must grow out of the fundamental attitudes of our people on both sides. If they are to be effective, they must become articulate through all the institutions of our national life, of which this is one of the greatest—through the press, through the radio, through the churches, through the labor unions, through the business organizations, through all the groupings of our national life, there must become articulate the attitudes of our people and the policies which we propose to follow. It seems to me that understanding is the beginning of wisdom and therefore, we shall begin by trying to understand before we announce what we are going to do, and that is a proposition so heretical in this town that I advance it with some hesitation.

Now, let's consider some of the basic factors which go into the making of the attitudes of the peoples on both sides. I am frequently asked: Has the State Department got an Asian policy? And it seems to me that that discloses such a depth of ignorance that it is very hard to begin to deal with it. The peoples of Asia are so incredibly diverse and their problems are so incredibly diverse that how could anyone, even the most utter charlatan believe that he had a uniform policy which would deal with all of them. On the other hand, there are very important similarities in ideas and in problems among the peoples of Asia and so what we come to, after we understand these diversities and these common attitudes of mind, is the fact that there must be certain similarities of approach, and there must be very great dissimilarities in action.

Let's come now to the matters which Asia has in common. There is in this vast area what we might call a developing Asian consciousness, and a developing pattern, and this, I think is based upon two factors which are pretty nearly common to the entire experience of all these Asian people.

One of these factors is a revulsion against the acceptance of misery and poverty as the normal condition of life. Throughout all of this vast area, you have that fundamental revolutionary aspect in mind and belief. The other common aspect that they have is the revulsion against foreign domination. Whether that foreign domination takes the form of colonialism or whether it takes the form of imperialism, they are through with it. They have had enough of it, and they want no more.

These two basic ideas which are held so broadly and commonly in Asia tend to fuse in the minds of many Asian peoples and many of them tend to believe that if you could get rid of foreign domination, if you could gain independence, then the relief from poverty and misery would follow almost in course. It is easy to point out that that is not true, and of course, they are discovering that it is not true. But underneath that belief, there was a very profound understanding of a basic truth and it is the basic truth which underlies all our democratic belief and all our democratic concept. That truth is that just as no man and no government is wise enough or disinterested enough to direct the thinking and the action of another individual, so no nation and no people are wise enough and disinterested enough very long to assume the responsibility for another people or to control another people's opportunities.

That great truth they have sensed, and on that great truth they are acting. They say and they believe that from now on they are on their own. They will make their own decisions. They will attempt to better their own lot, and on occasion they will make their own mistakes. But it will be their mistakes, and they are not going to have their mistakes dictated to them by anybody else.

The symbol of these concepts has become nationalism. National independence has become the symbol both of freedom from foreign domination and freedom from the tyranny of poverty and misery.

Since the end of the war in Asia, we have seen over 500 million people gain their independence and over seven new nations come into existence in this area.

We have the Philippines with 20 million citizens. We have Pakistan, India, Ceylon, and Burma with 400 million citizens, southern Korea with 20 million, and within the last few weeks, the United States of Indonesia with 75 million.

This is the outward and visible sign of the internal ferment of Asia. But this ferment and change is not restricted to these countries which are just gaining their independence. It is the common idea and the common pattern of Asia, and as I tried to suggest a moment ago, it is not based on purely political conceptions. It is not based purely on ideological conceptions. It is based on a fundamental and an earthy and a deeply individual realization of the problems of their own daily lives. This new sense of nationalism means that they are going to deal with those daily problems—the problems of the relation of man to the soil, the problem of how much can be exacted from them by the tax collectors of the state. It is rooted in those ideas. With those ideas they are going forward. Resignation is no longer the typical emotion of Asia. It has given way to hope, to a sense of effort, and in many cases, to a real sense of anger.

Let's consider for a moment another important factor in this relationship. That is the attitude of our own people to Asia. What is that fundamental attitude out of which our policy has grown? What is the history of it? Because history is very important, and history furnishes the belief on the one side in the reality and truth of the attitude.

What has our attitude been toward the peoples of Asia? It has been, I submit to you, that we are interested—that Americans as individuals are interested in the peoples of Asia. We are not interested in them as pawns or as subjects for exploitation but just as people.

Through all this period of time also, we had, and still have great interests in Asia. But let me point out to you one very important factor about our interests in Asia. That is that our interests have been parallel to the interests of the people of Asia. For 50 years, it has been the fundamental belief of the American people—and I am not talking about announcements of government but I mean a belief of people in little towns and villages and churches and missionary forces and labor unions throughout the United States—it has been their profound belief that the control of China by a foreign power was contrary to American interests. The interesting part about that is it was not contrary to the interests of the people of China. There was not conflict but parallelism in that interest. And so from the time of the announcement of the open door policy through the 9-power treaty to the very latest resolution of the General Assembly of the United Nations, we have stated that principle and we believe it. And similarly in all the rest of Asia—in the Philippines, in India, in Pakistan and Indonesia, and in Korea—for years and years and years, the interests of Americans through-out this country have been in favor of their independence. This is where their independence, [sic] societies, and their patriotic groups have come for funds and sympathy. The whole policy of our government insofar as we have responsi-bility in the Philippines was to bring about the accomplishment of this independ-ence and our sympathy and help. The very real help which we have given other nations in Asia has been in that direction, and it is still in that direction.

Now, I stress this, which you may think is a platitude, because of a very important fact: I hear almost every day someone say that the real interest of the United States is to stop the spread of communism. Nothing seems to me to put the cart before the horse more completely than that. Of course we are interested in stopping the spread of communism. But we are interested for a far deeper reason than any conflict between the Soviet Union and the United States. We are interested in stopping the spread of communism because commu-nism is a doctrine that we don't happen to like. Communism is the most subtle instrument of Soviet foreign policy that has ever been devised, and it is really the spearhead of Russian imperialism which would, if it could, take from these people what they have won, what we want them to keep and develop, which is their own national independence, their own individual independence, their own development of their own resources for their own good and not as mere tributary states to this great Soviet Union.

Now, it is fortunate that this point that I made does not represent any real conflict. It is an important point because people will do more damage and create more misrepresentation in the Far East by saying our interest is merely to stop the spread of communism than any other way. Our real interest is in those people as people. It is because communism is hostile to that interest that we want to stop it. But it happens that the best way of doing both things is to do just exactly what the peoples of Asia want to do and what we want to help them to do, which is to develop a soundness of administration of these new governments and to develop their resources and their technical skills so that they are not subject to penetration either through ignorance, or because they believe these false promises, or because there is real distress in their areas.

If we can help that development, if we can go forward with it, then we have brought about the best way that anyone knows of stopping this spread of communism.

It is important to take this attitude not as a mere negative reaction to communism but as the most positive affirmation of the most affirmative truth that we hold, which is in the dignity and right of every nation, of every people, and of every individual to develop in their own way, making their own mistakes, reaching their own triumphs but acting under their own responsibility. That is what we are pressing for in the Far East, and that is what we must affirm and not get mixed up with purely negative and inconsequential statements.

Soviet Attitude

Now, let me come to another underlying and important factor which determines our relations and, in turn, our policy with the peoples of Asia. That is the attitude of the Soviet Union toward Asia, and particularly towards those parts of Asia which are contiguous to the Soviet Union, and with great particularity this afternoon, to north China.

The attitude and interest of the Russians in north China, and in these other areas as well, long antedates communism. This is not something that has come out of communism at all. It long antedates it. But the Communist regime has added new methods, new skills, and new concepts to the thrust of Russian imperialism. This [These] Communistic concept[s] and techniques have armed Russian imperialism with a new and most insidious weapon of penetration. Armed with these new powers, what is happening in China is that the Soviet Union is detaching the northern provinces [areas] of China from China and is attaching them to the Soviet Union. This process is complete in Outer Mongolia. It is nearly complete in Manchuria, and I am sure that in inner Mongolia and in Sinkiang there are very happy reports coming from Soviet agents to Moscow. This is what is going on. It is the detachment of these whole areas, vast areas—populated by Chinese—the detachment of these areas from China and their attachment to the Soviet Union.

I wish to state this and perhaps sin against my doctrine of nondogmatism, but I should like to suggest at any rate that this fact that the Soviet Union is taking the four northern provinces of China is the single most significant, most important fact, in the relation of any foreign power with Asia.

*   *   *

The consequences of this Russian attitude and this Russian action in China are perfectly enormous. They are saddling all those in China who are proclaiming their loyalty to Moscow, and who are allowing themselves to be used as puppets of Moscow, with the most awful responsibility which they must pay for. Furthermore, these actions of the Russians are making plainer than any speech, or any utterance, or any legislation can make throughout all of Asia, what the true purposes of the Soviet Union are and what the true function of communism as an agent of Russian imperialism is. These I suggest to you are the fundamental factors, fundamental realities of attitude out of which our relations and policies must grow.

Now, let's in the light of that consider some of these policies. First of all, let's deal with the question of military security. I deal with it first because it is important and because, having stated our policy in that regard, we must clearly understand that the military menace is not the most immediate.

What is the situation in regard to the military security of the Pacific area, and what is our policy in regard to it?

In the first place, the defeat and the disarmament of Japan has placed upon the United States the necessity of assuming the military defense of Japan so long as that is required, both in the interest of our security and in the interests of the security of the entire Pacific area and, in all honor, in the interest of Japanese security. We have American—and there are Australian—troops in Japan. I am not in a position to speak for the Australians, but I can assure you that there is no intention of any sort of abandoning or weakening the defenses of Japan and that whatever arrangements are to be made either through permanent settlement or otherwise, that defense must and shall be maintained.

This defensive perimeter runs along the Aleutians to Japan and then goes to the Ryukyus. We hold important defense positions in the Ryukyu Islands, and those we will continue to hold. In the interest of the population of the Ryukyu Islands, we will at an appropriate time offer to hold these islands under trusteeship of the United Nations. But they are essential parts of the defensive perimeter of the Pacific, and they must and will be held.

The defensive perimeter runs from the Ryukyus to the Philippine Islands. Our relations, our defensive relations with the Philippines are contained in agreements between us. Those agreements are being loyally carried out and will be loyally carried out. Both peoples have learned by bitter experience the vital connections between our mutual defense requirements. We are in no doubt about that, and it is hardly necessary for me to say an attack on the Philippines could not and would not be tolerated by the United States. But I hasten to add that no one perceives the imminence of any such attack.

So far as the military security of other areas in the Pacific is concerned, it must be clear that no person can guarantee these areas against military attack. But it must also be clear that such a guarantee is hardly sensible or necessary within the realm of practical relationship.

Should such an attack occur—one hesitates to say where such an armed attack could come from—the initial reliance must be on the people attacked to resist it and then upon the commitments of the entire civilized world under the Charter of the United Nations which so far has not proved a weak reed to lean on by any people who are determined to protect their independence against outside aggression. But it is a mistake, I think, in considering Pacific and Far Eastern problems to become obsessed with military considerations. Important as they are, there are other problems that press, and these other problems are not capable of solution through military means. These other problems arise out of the susceptibility of many areas, and many countries in the Pacific area, to subversion and penetration. That cannot be stopped by military means.

Susceptibility to Penetration

The susceptibility to penetration arises because in many areas there are new governments which have little experience in governmental administration and have not become firmly established or perhaps firmly accepted in their countries. They grow, in part, from very serious economic problems, some of them growing out directly from the last war, others growing indirectly out of the last war because of the disruptions of trade with other parts of the world, with the disruption of arrangements which furnished credit and management to these areas for many years. That has resulted in dislocation of economic effort and in a good deal of suffering among the peoples concerned. In part this susceptibility to penetration comes from the great social upheaval about which I have been speaking, an upheaval which was carried on and confused a great deal by the Japanese occupation and by the propaganda which has gone on from Soviet sources since the war.

Here, then, are the problems in these other areas which require some policy on our part, and I should like to point out two facts to you and then discuss in more detail some of these areas.

The first fact is the great difference between our responsibility and our opportunities in the northern part of the Pacific area and in the southern part of the Pacific area. In the north, we have direct responsibility in Japan and we have direct opportunity to act. The same thing to a lesser degree is true in Korea. There we had direct responsibility, and there we did act, and there we have a greater opportunity to be effective than we have in the more southerly part.

In the southerly part of the area, we are one of many nations who can do no more than help. The direct responsibility lies with the peoples concerned. They are proud of their new national responsibility. You can not sit around in Washington, or London, or Paris, or The Hague, and determine what the policies are going to be in those areas. You can be willing to help, and you can help only when the conditions are right for help to be effective.

Limitations of U.S. Assistance

That leads me to the other thing that I wanted to point out, and that is the limitation of effective American assistance. American assistance can be effective when it is the missing component in a situation which might otherwise be solved. The United States cannot furnish all these components to solve the question. It can not furnish determination, it can not furnish the will, and it can not furnish the loyalty of a people to its government. But if the will and if the determination exists and if the people are behind their government, then, and not always then, is there a very good chance. In that situation, American help can be effective and it can lead to an accomplishment which could not otherwise be achieved.

*　　　　　　*　　　　　　*

So after this survey, what we conclude, I believe, is that there is a new day which has dawned in Asia. It is a day in which the Asian peoples are on their own, and know it, and intend to continue on their own.It is a day in which the old relationships between east and west are gone, relationships which at their worst were exploitation, and which at their best were paternalism. That relationship is over, and the relationship of east and west must now be in the Far East one of mutual respect and mutual helpfulness. We are their friends. Others are their friends. We and those others are willing to help, but we can help only where we are wanted and only where the conditions of help are really sensible and possible. So what we can see is that this new day in Asia, this new day which is dawning, may go on to a glorious noon or it may darken and it may drizzle out. But that decision lies within the countries of Asia and within the power of the Asian people. It is not a decision which a friend or even an enemy from the outside can decide for them.

NORTH KOREAN INVASION OF SOUTH KOREA

A. Security Council Resolution*

June 25, 1950

Resolution concerning the complaint of aggression upon the Republic of Korea, adopted at the four hundred and seventy-third meeting of the Security Council on June 25, 1950:

The Security Council,

Recalling the finding of the General Assembly in its resolution of 21 October 1949 that the Government of the Republic of Korea is a lawfully established government "having effective control and jurisdiction over that part of Korea where the United Nations Temporary Commission on Korea was able to observe and consult and in which the great majority of the people of Korea reside; and that this Government is based on elections which were a valid expression of the free will of the electorate of that part of Korea and which were observed by the Temporary Commission; and that this is the only such Government in Korea";

Mindful of the concern expressed by the General Assembly in its resolutions of 12 December 1948 and 21 October 1949 of the consequences which might follow unless Member States refrained from acts derogatory to the results sought to be achieved by the United Nations in bringing about the complete independence and unity of Korea; and the concern expressed that the situation described by the United Nations Commission on Korea in its report menaces the safety and well-being of the Republic of Korea and of the people of Korea and might lead to open military conflict there;

Noting with grave concern the armed attack upon the Republic of Korea by forces from North Korea,

Determines that this action constitutes a breach of the peace,

I. Calls for the immediate cessation of hostilities: and

Calls upon the authorities of North Korea to withdraw forthwith their armed forces to the thirty-eighth parallel;

II. Requests the United Nations Commission on Korea

> (a) To communicate its fully considered recommendations on the situation with the least possible delay;
> (b) To observe the withdrawal of the North Korean forces to the thirty-eighth parallel; and
> (c) To keep the Security Council informed on the execution of this resolution;

III. Calls upon all Members to render every assistance to the United Nations in the execution of this resolution and to refrain from giving assistance to the North Korean authorities.

(Voting for the resolution: China, Cuba, Ecuador, Egypt, France, India, Norway, United Kingdom, United States. Abstention: Yugoslavia. Absent: Soviet

*Military Situation in The Far East, Pt. 5, pp. 3368-69.

365

Union, the Soviet Delegate having boycotted meeting of the Council since Jan. 10, 1950.)

B. Statement by President Truman*

June 27, 1950

In Korea the Government forces, which were armed to prevent border raids and to preserve internal security, were attacked by invading forces from North Korea. The Security Council of the United Nations called upon the invading troops to cease hostilities and to withdraw to the thirty-eighth parallel. This they have not done, but on the contrary have pressed the attack. The Security Council called upon all members of the United Nations to render every assistance to the United Nations in the execution of this resolution. In these circumstances I have ordered United States air and sea forces to give the Korean Government troops cover and support.

The attack upon Korea makes it plain beyond all doubt that communism has passed beyond the use of subversion to conquer independent nations and will now use armed invasion and war. It has defied the orders of the Security Council of the United Nations issued to preserve international peace and security. In these circumstances the occupation of Formosa by Communist forces would be a direct threat to the security of the Pacific area and to United States forces performing their lawful and necessary functions in that area.

Accordingly I have ordered the Seventh Fleet to prevent any attack on Formosa. As a corollary of this action I am calling upon the Chinese Government on Formosa to cease all air and sea operations against the mainland. The Seventh Fleet will see that this is done. The determination of the future status of Formosa must await the restoration of security in the Pacific, a peace settlement with Japan, or consideration by the United Nations.

I have also directed that United States forces in the Philippines be strengthened and that military assistance to the Philippine Government be accelerated.

I have similarly directed acceleration in the furnishing of military assistance to the forces of France and the associated states in Indochina and the dispatch of a military mission to provide close working relations with those forces.

I know that all members of the United Nations will consider carefully the consequences of this latest aggression in Korea in defiance of the Charter of the United Nations. A return to the rule of force in international affairs would have far-reaching effects. The United States will continue to uphold the rule of law.

I have instructed Ambassador Austin, as the representative of the United States to the Security Council, to report these steps to the Council.

*Ibid., p. 3369.

C. Statement by Warren Austin, U.S. Representative to the United Nations*

June 27, 1950

The United Nations finds itself confronted today with the gravest crisis in its existence.

Forty-eight hours ago the Security Council, in an emergency session, determined that the armed invasion of the Republic of Korea by armed forces from northern Korea constituted a breach of the peace. Accordingly, the Security Council called for a cessation of hostilities forthwith and the withdrawal by the northern Korean authorities of their armed forces to the thirty-eighth parallel. The Security Council also requested the United Nations Commission on Korea to observe the withdrawal and to report. Finally, the Security Council called upon all members to render every assistance to the United Nations in the execution of the resolution and to refrain from giving assistance to the North Korean authorities.

The decision of the Security Council has been broadcast to the Korean authorities and is known to them. We now have before us the report of the United Nations Commission for Korea which confirms our worst fears. It is clear that the authorities in North Korea have completely disregarded and flouted the decision of the Security Council. The armed invasion of the Republic of Korea continues. The North Korean authorities have even called upon the established Government of the Republic to surrender.

It is hard to imagine a more glaring example of disregard for the United Nations and for all the principles which it represents.

The most important provisions of the Charter are those outlawing aggressive war. It is precisely these provisions which the North Korea authorities have violated.

It is the plain duty of the Security Council to invoke stringent sanctions to restore international peace.

The Republic of Korea has appealed to the United Nations for protection. I am happy and proud to report that the United States is prepared as a loyal member of the United Nations to furnish assistance to the Republic of Korea.

I have tabled a resolution which I ask the Council to consider favorably as the next step to restore world peace.

That resolution is as follows:

The Security Council,
    Having determined that the armed attack upon the Republic of Korea by forces from North Korea constitutes a breach of the peace,
    Having called for an immediate cessation of hostilities, and
    Having called upon the authorities of North Korea to withdraw forthwith their armed forces to the Thirty-eighth Parallel, and
    Having noted from the report of the United Nations Commission for Korea that the authorities in North Korea have neither ceased hostilities nor withdrawn their armed forces to the Thirty-eighth Parallel, and that urgent military measures are required to restore international peace and security, and

Ibid., pp. 3370-71

Having noted the appeal from the Republic of Korea to the United Nations
for immediate and effective steps to secure peace and security.

Recommends that the members of the United Nations furnish such assistance
to the Republic of Korea as may be necessary to repel the armed attack and to
restore international peace and security in the area.

This is the logical consequence of the resolution concerning the complaint
of aggression upon the Republic of Korea adopted at the four hundred and
seventy-third meeting of the Security Council on June 25, 1950, and the subsequent events recited in the preamble of this resolution. That resolution of June
25 called upon all members to render every assistance to the United Nations
in the execution of this resolution, and to refrain from giving assistance to the
North Korean authorities. This new resolution is the logical next step. Its significance is affected by the violation of the former resolution, the continuation
of aggression, and the urgent military measures required.

I wish now to read the statement which the President of the United States
made today on this critical situation.

The keynote of the resolution and my statement and the significant characteristic of the action taken by the President is support of the United Nations purposes and principles—in a word "peace."

D. The Second Security Council Resolution*

June 27, 1950

Resolution concerning the complaint of aggression upon the Republic of
Korea, adopted at the four hundred and seventy-fourth meeting of the Security
Council, on June 27, 1950:

The Security Council,

Having determined that the armed attack upon the Republic of Korea by forces
from North Korea constitutes a breach of the peace,

Having called for an immediate cessation of hostilities, and

Having called upon the authorities of North Korea to withdraw forthwith their
armed forces to the 38th parallel, and

Having noted from the report of the United Nations Commission for Korea
that the authorities in North Korea have neither ceased hostilities nor withdrawn
their armed forces to the 38th parallel and that urgent military measures are required to restore international peace and security, and

Having noted the appeal from the Republic of Korea to the United Nations
for immediate and effective steps to secure peace and security,

Recommends that the Members of the United Nations furnish such assistance
to the Republic of Korea as may be necessary to repel the armed attack and to
restore international peace and security in the area.

(Voting for the resolution: United States, United Kingdom, France, China, Norway, Ecuador, and Cuba. Voting against: Yugoslavia. Absention: Egypt, India (2
days later India accepted the resolution). Absent: Soviet Union.)

*Ibid., p. 3371.

**E. Statement by President Truman on Further Military Action
in Korea***

June 30, 1950

At a meeting with congressional leaders at the White House this morning, the President, together with the Secretary of Defense, the Secretary of State, and the Joint Chiefs of Staff, reviewed with them the latest developments of the situation in Korea.

The congressional leaders were given a full review of the intensified military activities.

In keeping with the United Nations Security Council's request for support to the Republic of Korea in repelling the North Korean invaders and restoring peace in Korea, the President announced that he had authorized the United States Air Force to conduct missions on specific military targets in Northern Korea wherever militarily necessary, and had ordered a naval blockade of the entire Korean coast.

General MacArthur has been authorized to use certain supporting ground units.

F. The Third Security Council Resolution*

July 7, 1950

The Security Council, having determined that the armed attack upon the Republic of Korea by forces from North Korea constitutes a breach of the peace, having recommended that members of the United Nations furnish such assistance to the Republic of Korea as may be necessary to repel the armed attack and to restore international peace and security in the area.

(1) Welcomes the prompt and vigorous support which governments and peoples of the United Nations have given to its resolutions of 25 and 27 June 1950 to assist the Republic of Korea in defending itself against armed attack and thus to restore international peace and security in the area;

(2) Notes that members of the United Nations have transmitted to the United Nations offers of assistance for the Republic of Korea;

(3) Recommends that all members providing military forces and other assistance pursuant to the aforesaid Security Council resolutions make such forces and other assistance available to a unified command under the United States;

(4) Requests the United States to designate the commander of such forces;

(5) Authorizes the unified command at its discretion to use the United Nations flag in the course of operations against North Korean forces concurrently with the flags of the various nations participating;

(6) Requests the United States to provide the Security Council with reports, as appropriate, on the course of action taken under the unified command.

(Voting for the resolution: United States, the United Kingdom, France, China, Cuba, Ecuador, and Norway. Abstention: Egypt, India, and Yugoslavia. Absent: Soviet Union.)

Ibid., p. 3372.
Ibid.

G. Account by President Truman on His Response to the North Korean Attack

[Extract]

1956

It was a little after ten in the evening, and we were sitting in the library of our home on North Delaware Street when the telephone rang. It was the Secretary of State calling from his home in Maryland.

"Mr. President," said Dean Acheson, "I have very serious news. The North Koreans have invaded South Korea."

My first reaction was that I must get back to the capital, and I told Acheson so. He explained, however, that details were not yet available and that he thought I need not rush back until he called me again with further information. In the meantime, he suggested to me that we should ask the United Nations Security Council to hold a meeting at once and declare that an act of aggression had been committed against the Republic of Korea. I told him that I agreed and asked him to request immediately a special meeting of the Security Council, and he said he would call me to report again the following morning, or sooner if there was more information on the events in Korea.

Acheson's next call came through around eleven-thirty Sunday morning, just as we were getting ready to sit down to an early Sunday dinner. Acheson reported that the U.N. Security Council had been called into emergency session. Additional reports had been received from Korea and there was no doubt that an all-out invasion was under way there. The Security Council, Acheson said, would probably call for a ceasefire, but in view of the complete disregard the North Koreans and their big allies had shown for the U.N. in the past, we had to expect that the U.N. order would be ignored. Some decision would have to be made at once as to the degree of aid or encouragement which our government was willing to extend to the Republic of Korea.

I asked Acheson to get together with the Service Secretaries and the Chiefs of Staff and start working on recommendations for me when I got back. Defense Secretary Louis Johnson and Chairman of the Chiefs of Staff General Omar Bradley were on their way back from an inspection tour of the Far East. I informed the Secretary of State that I was returning to Washington at once.

The crew of the presidential plane Independence did a wonderful job. They had the plane ready to fly in less than an hour from the time they were alerted, and my return trip got under way so fast that two of my aides were left behind. They could not be notified in time to reach the airport.

The plane left the Kansas City Municipal Airport at two o'clock and it took just a little over three hours to make the trip to Washington. I had time to think aboard the plane. In my generation, this was not the first occasion when the strong had attacked the weak. I recalled some earlier instances: Manchuria, Ethiopia, Austria. I remembered how each time that the democracies failed to act it had encouraged the aggressors to keep going ahead. Communism was

*Harry S. Truman, *Memoirs: Years of Trial and Hope* (New York, 1958), pp. 332-35.

acting in Korea just as Hitler, Mussolini, and the Japanese had acted ten, fifteen, and twenty years earlier. I felt certain that if South Korea was allowed to fall Communist leaders would be emboldened to override nations closer to our own shores. If the Communists were permitted to force their way into the Republic of Korea without opposition from the free world, no small nation would have the courage to resist threats and aggression by stronger Communist neighbors. If this was allowed to go unchallenged it would mean a third world war, just as similar incidents had brought on the second world war. It was also clear to me that the foundations and the principles of the United Nations were at stake unless this unprovoked attack on Korea could be stopped.

I had the plane's radio operator send a message to Dean Acheson asking him and his immediate advisers and the top defense chiefs to come to Blair House for a dinner conference.

When the Independence landed, Secretary of State Acheson was waiting for me at the airport, as was Secretary of Defense Johnson, who himself had arrived only a short while before. We hurried to Blair House, where we were joined by the other conferees. Present were the three service Secretaries, Secretary of the Army Frank Pace, Secretary of the Navy Francis Matthews, and Secretary of the Air Force Thomas Finletter. There were the Joint Chiefs of Staff, General of the Army Omar N. Bradley, the Army Chief General Collins, the Air Force Chief General Vandenberg, and Admiral Forrest Sherman, Chief of Naval Operations. Dean Acheson was accompanied by Under Secretary Webb, Deputy Under Secretary Dean Rusk and Assistant Under Secretary John Hickerson, and Ambassador-at-Large Philip Jessup.

It was late, and we went at once to the dining room for dinner. I asked that no discussion take place until dinner was served and over and the Blair House staff had withdrawn. I called on Dean Acheson first to give us a detailed picture of the situation. Acheson read us the first report that had been received by the State Department from our Ambassador in Seoul, Korea, at nine twenty-six the preceding evening:

> According Korean army reports which partly confirmed by KMAG field advisor reports North Korean forces invaded ROK territory at several points this morning. Action was initiated about 4 a.m. Ongjin blasted by North Korean artillery fire. About 6 a.m. North Korean infantry commenced crossing parallel in Ongjin area, Kaesong area, Chunchon area and amphibious landing was reportedly made south of Kangnung on east coast. Kaesong was reportedly captured at 9 a.m. with some 10 North Korean tanks participating in operation. North Korean forces, spearheaded by tanks, reportedly closing in on Chunchon. Details of fighting in Kangnung are unclear, although it seems North Korean forces have cut highway. Am conferring with KMAG advisors and Korean officials this morning re situation.
> It would appear from nature of attack and manner in which it was launched that it constitutes all out offensive against ROK.
>
> *Muccio*

There were additional messages from Ambassador Muccio, too, giving more details, but all confirmed that a full-fledged attack was under way, and the North Koreans had broadcast a proclamation that, in effect, was a declaration of war.

Earlier that Sunday evening, Acheson reported, the Security Council of the United Nations had, by a vote of 9 to 0, approved a resolution declaring that a breach of the peace had been committed by the North Korean action and ordering the North Koreans to cease their action and withdraw their forces.

I then called on Acheson to present the recommendations which the State and Defense Departments had prepared. He presented the following recommendations for immediate action:

1. That MacArthur should evacuate the Americans from Korea—including the dependents of the Military Mission—and, in order to do so, should keep open the Kimpo and other airports, repelling all hostile attacks thereon. In doing this, his air forces should stay south of the 38th parallel.

2. That MacArthur should be instructed to get ammunition and supplies to the Korean army by airdrop and otherwise.

3. That the Seventh Fleet should be ordered into the Formosa Straits to prevent the conflict from spreading to that area. The Seventh Fleet should be ordered from Cavite north at once. We should make a statement that the fleet would repel any attack on Formosa and that no attacks should be made from Formosa on the mainland.

At this point I interrupted to say that the Seventh Fleet should be ordered north at once but that I wanted to withhold making any statement until the fleet was in position.

After this report I asked each person in turn to state his agreement or disagreement and any views he might have in addition. Two things stand out in this discussion. One was the complete, almost unspoken acceptance on the part of everyone that whatever had to be done to meet this aggression had to be done. There was no suggestion from anyone that either the United Nations or the United States could back away from it. This was the test of all the talk of the last five years of collective security. The other point which stands out in my mind from the discussion was the difference in view of what might be called for. Vandenberg and Sherman thought that air and naval aid might be enough. Collins said that if the Korean army was really broken, ground forces would be necessary. But no one could tell what the state of the Korean army really was on that Sunday night. Whatever the estimates of the military might be, everyone recognized the situation as serious in the extreme.

I then directed that orders be issued to put the three recommendations into immediate effect.

*　　　　　　*　　　　　　*

H. Speech by Senator Robert Taft Criticizing Administration Policy*

[Extract]

June 28, 1950

THE KOREAN CRISIS CAUSED BY
WAVERING FOREIGN POLICIES OF ADMINISTRATION

An Outrageous Act of Aggression

Early on Sunday morning, June 25, the Communist-dominated Republic of North Korea launched an unprovoked aggressive military attack on the Republic of Korea, recognized as an independent nation by the United Nations. On the same day the Security Council of the United Nations adopted a resolution noting with grave concern the armed attack upon the Republic of Korea from forces from North Korea, and determining that this action constituted a breach of the peace. The resolution called for the immediate cessation of hostilities, for the withdrawal of the armed forces of North Korea to the thirty-eighth parallel, and for the United Nations Commission on Korea to make informational reports; and called "upon all members to render every assistance to the United Nations in the execution of this resolution and to refrain from giving assistance to the North Korean authorities." This resolution was adopted by a vote of nine members, Russia being absent, and Yugoslavia abstaining.

The attack did not cease, and on Tuesday, June 27, the President issued a statement announcing that he had "ordered United States air and sea forces to give the Korean Government troops cover and support." He also announced that he had ordered the Seventh Fleet to prevent any attack on Formosa, and that he had directed that United States forces in the Philippines be strengthened, and that military assistance to the Philippine Government and the forces of France and the associated states in Indochina be accelerated.

On the same day, last night, the United Nations adopted another resolution definitely recommending "that the members of the United Nations furnish such assistance to the Republic of Korea as may be necessary to repel the armed attack and restore international peace and security in the area." This vote was adopted by seven members of the Security Council; Yugoslavia voting "no," and India and Egypt refraining from voting, Russia still being absent. American air and sea forces have moved into Korea and are partaking in the war against the northern Korea Communists.

No one can deny that a serious crisis exists. The attack was as much a surprise to the public as the attack at Pearl Harbor, although, apparently, the possibility was foreseen by all our intelligence forces, and should have been foreseen by the administration. We are now actually engaged in a de facto war with the northern Korean Communists. That in itself is serious, but nothing compared to the possibility that it might lead to war with Soviet Russia. It is entirely

*Military Situation in The Far East, Pt. 5, pp. 3210-12.

possible that Soviet Russia might move in to help the North Koreans and that the present limited field of conflict might cover the entire civilized world. Without question, the attack of the North Koreans is an outrageous act of aggression against a friendly independent nation, recognized by the United Nations, and which we were instrumental in setting up. The attack in all probability was instigated by Soviet Russia. We can only hope that the leaders of that country have sufficient judgment to know that a world war will result in their own destruction, and will therefore refrain from such acts as might bring about such a tragic conflict.

A Fortunate Change of Policy

Mr. President, Korea itself is not vitally important to the United States. It is hard to defend. We have another instance of communism picking out a soft spot where the Communists feel that they can make a substantial advance and can obtain a moral victory without risking war. From the past philosophy and declarations of our leaders, it was not unreasonable for the North Koreans to suppose that they could get away with it and that we would do nothing about it.

The President's statement of policy represents a complete change in the programs and policies heretofore proclaimed by the administration. I have heretofore urged a much more determined attitude against communism in the Far East, and the President's new policy moves in that direction. It seems to me that the time had to come, sooner or later, when we would give definite notice to the Communists that a move beyond a declared line would result in war. That has been the policy which we have adopted in Europe. Whether the President has chosen the right time or the right place to declare this policy may be open to question. He was information which I do not have.

It seems to me that the new policy is adopted at an unfortunate time, and involves a very difficult military operation indeed—the defense of Korea. I sincerely hope that our Armed Forces may be successful in Korea. I sincerely hope that the policy thus adopted will not lead to war with Russia. In any event, I believe the general principle of the policy is right, and I see no choice except to back up wholeheartedly and with every available resource the men in our Armed Forces who have been moved into Korea.

If we are going to defend Korea, it seems to me that we should have retained our Armed Forces there and should have given, a year ago, the notice which the President has given today. With such a policy, there never would have been such an attack by the North Koreans. In short, this entirely unfortunate crisis has been produced first, by the outrageous, aggressive attitude of Soviet Russia, and second, by the bungling and inconsistent foreign policy of the administration.

Not a Bipartisan Policy

I think it is important to point out, Mr. President, that there has been no pretense of any bipartisan foreign policy about this action. The leaders of the Republican Party in Congress have never been consulted on the Chinese policy or Formosa or Korea or Indochina. Republican members of the Foreign Relations Committee and of the Armed Forces Committee were called to the White House at 10:30 a. m. on June 27, and were informed with regard to the President's statement, but, of course, they had no opportunity to change it or to consult Republican policy committees in either the House of Representatives or the Senate.

I hope at a later time to put into the Record a historical statement of the position of various Republican leaders on the general question of China policy, showing that it is very different indeed, from what the President has heretofore advocated, and that, in general, it is more in accord with what he is now proposing.

Congress Not Consulted

Furthermore, it should be noted that there has been no pretense of consulting the Congress. No resolution has ever been introduced asking for the approval of Congress for the use of American forces in Korea. I shall discuss later the question of whether the President is usurping his powers as Commander in Chief. My own opinion is that he is doing so; that there is no legal authority for what he has done. But I may say that if a joint resolution were introduced asking for approval of the use of our Armed Forces already sent to Korea and full support of them in their present venture, I would vote in favor of it.

The Attack Invited by Past Administration Policy

I have said that the present crisis is produced by the bungling and inconsistent policies of the administration.

First, we agreed to the division of Korea along the thirty-eithth parallel giving the Russians the northern half of the country, with most of the power and a good deal of the industry, and leaving a southern half which could not support itself, except on an agricultural basis. This was in line with a very foolish policy which paid for Russian assistance against Japan, which we did not need, by presenting Russia with the Kurile Islands, half of Sakhalin Island, and the control of Manchuria. The agreement was a part of the sympathetic acceptance of communism as a peace-loving philosophy, which has made Russia a threat to the very existence of the world.

Second, the Chinese policy of the administration gave basic encouragement to the North Korean aggression. If the United States was not prepared to use its troops and give military assistance to Nationalist China against Chinese Communists, why should it use its troops to defend Nationalist Korea against Korean Communists? That certainly must have seemed a fairly logical conclusion to those who have inaugurated this aggression. The Communists undoubtedly considered that Korea was very much less important than China to the United

States, and that they could get away with their grab of Korea, as the Chinese Communists got away with theirs in China. The general policy of doing nothing in China was reaffirmed by Secretary Acheson in a speech before the National Press Club as recently as January 12 of this year.

I read from the New York Herald Tribune's account of that speech:

"Secretary of State Dean Acheson accused the Soviet Union today of planning dismemberment of China. He said the United States could exploit the eventual resentment of Asian peoples over this aggression only by avoiding foolish adventures such as intervention on Formosa."

I might suggest that intervention in Korea from a military standpoint is a good deal more foolish an adventure than intervention on Formosa.

According to the New York Herald Tribune:

"Soviet Russia, using new methods, new skills, and new concepts to cloak imperialist aggression, already had swallowed Outer Mongolia and has nearly completed the absorption of Manchuria, Secretary Acheson said. He charged Moscow with similar designs on the areas of Inner Mongolia and Sinkiang.

"In a major policy speech before the National Press Club, Secretary Acheson said the United States was helpless to prevent this dismemberment. He made it clear that the State Department's future plans for checking the spread of Soviet influence through Asia would depend mainly on the righteous wrath and anger of Chinese and other Asiatics over Russian encroachments."

No doubt the North Korean Communists were quite prepared to take a chance on that "righteous wrath and anger'" of the Chinese and perhaps of other Koreans, which might perhaps develop some 10 years from today.

According to the account in the New York Herald Tribune, Secretary Acheson also said:

"For its own security the United States must and shall maintain armed forces in Japan, the Ryukyu Islands (Okinawa) and the Philippines. But no such line of containment could be drawn in southern and southeast Asia, where the United States had no direct responsibilities and only limited opportunities for action.

"He said we would fight if Japan, Okinawa, or the Philippines were attacked.

"But we could give no such guaranty to southern and southeast Asia."

In other places he made it equally clear that neither Formosa nor Korea was included behind the line upon which the United States would stand.

Just for my own satisfaction, I read:

"He jabbed sarcastically at Senator Robert A. Taft, Republican, of Ohio, who charged in the Senate yesterday that President Truman and Secretary Acheson had forsaken the policy of containing communism by their refusal to save Formosa."

This is quoting Secretary Acheson.

"To say that the main motive of American foreign policy was to halt the spread of communism was putting the cart before the horse. The United States was interested in stopping communism chiefly because it had become a subtle instrument of Soviet imperialism."

There is nothing, apparently, against communism.

*   *   *

I. Speech by Ambassador Austin on the Future of Korea*

September 30, 1950

I shall speak briefly, because events require us to act quickly.

I shall speak with restraint, because the death and destruction in Korea are themselves the tragic evidence of the evil and cost of aggression.

I shall speak frankly, because the issue before us involves more than the peace and security of Korea.

The United Nations was defied when the Commission created by this Assembly was prevented by the Soviet occupation authorities from observing elections in the northern area.

The United Nations was defied when Soviet occupation authorities installed a puppet regime which, according to the Assembly's Commission, ruled only by right of a mere transfer of power from the Soviet Government.

The ultimate defiance of the United Nations was aggression by the North Korean regime.

Defiance of the will and authority of the United Nations endangers the peace and security of every member nation.

The origin and nature of the North Korean regime cannot be disguised. That origin was justification for my Government, on June 27, asking the Soviet Government to use its influence to halt the invasion and restore the peace. That request was rejected. Instead, the representative of the Soviet Government, since the first of August, has used the Security Council of the United Nations as a forum in which to deny the aggression and justify the action of the North Korean authorities.

Preparation for aggression in North Korea could have been prevented. The launching of aggression from North Korea could have been stopped. The support of aggression from North Korea could have been withheld. None of this happened. The United Nations has had to suppress this aggression by force.

Now we must turn from the past and consider the future. As we do so, two facts should be emphasized. First, the people of the world will not accept the standards of conduct represented by the Korean aggression. Second, the Government and the people of the United States, for their part, wish to cooperate with the Soviet Government as well as the free members of the United Nations to build the kind of world community envisaged by the Charter.

Practical men face facts. These are two of the basic facts about the world in which we live. If these facts are faced, particularly by the Soviet Government, we can turn to the task before us with increased hope and confidence for the future of mankind.

Today, the forces of the United Nations stand on the threshold of military victory. The operations authorized by the Security Council have been conducted with vigor and skill. The price paid has been high. The sacrifice in anxiety, sorrow, wounded, and dead must be abundantly requited. A living political, social, and spiritual monument to the achievement of the first enforcement of the United Nations peace-making function must be erected.

*Department of State Bulletin, Vol. XXIII, pp. 579-80.

The opportunities for new acts of aggression, of course, should be removed. Faithful adherence to the United Nations objective of restoring international peace and security in the area counsels the taking of appropriate steps to eliminate the power and ability of the North Korean aggressor to launch future attacks. The aggressor's forces should not be permitted to have refuge behind an imaginary line because that would recreate the threat to the peace of Korea and of the world.

The political aspect of the problem identified with the 38th parallel becomes a matter of major concern for the United Nations. The question of whether this artificial barrier shall remain removed and whether the country shall be united now must be determined by the United Nations.

An ancient people has waited long and suffered much for freedom, independence, and unity. On three occasions, the General Assembly has registered its support of these objectives. The General Assembly sent Commissions to Korea to assist in carrying out these aims. Its Commissions have not been allowed to operate north of the 38th parallel, to observe elections, to ascertain whether the people were free to express their will, or to accomplish the peaceful unification of Korea.

The artificial barrier which has divided North and South Korea has no basis for existence either in law or in reason. Neither the United Nations, its Commission on Korea, nor the Republic of Korea recognizes such a line. Now, the North Koreans, by armed attack upon the Republic of Korea, have denied the reality of any such line.

Whatever ephemeral separation of Korea there was for purposes relating to the surrender of the Japanese was so volatile that nobody recognizes it. Let us not, at this critical hour and on this grave event, erect such a boundary. Rather, let us set up standards and means, principles and policies, according to the Charter, by which all Koreans can hereafter live in peace among themselves and with their neighbors.

The great opportunity given by victory inspires dedication rather than rejoicing; responsibility rather than revenge, consecration rather than recrimination. In that spirit, we should consider the political action required of us that will contribute to enduring peace.

The Korean people should have the right to live free from pressure and intimidation. We should seek here a solution that will not further the interests of any one country but which would be for the benefit of the Korean people and the whole United Nations.

The United States, therefore, welcomes the declaration in the draft resolution before you that United Nations Forces would remain in Korea only as long as is necessary to carry out the General Assembly's recommendations. My Government hopes, in fact, the the major portion of this effort will be carried out by units of the United Nations Forces from countries other than the United States. We would be pleased if Asian states would contribute the greatest share.

The United States does not wish to evade its duty as a member state. I have been authorized to state that my Government seeks no special privilege or position in Korea. We withdrew our forces once before from Korea in connection with the General Assembly's efforts to achieve the unification of that country. As an earnest of our cooperation toward that objective, we will do the same again.

The draft resolution clearly states one of the most determined objectives of the United Nations—the unity and independence of Korea. At this moment, we cannot foresee the precise circumstances in which unification is to be accomplished. Even if this were not the case, we would be ill-advised to try to develop here detailed blueprints for such a complex operation. Therefore, we endorse the idea of establishing in Korea a strong United Nations Commission empowered to devise practical and effective measures for achieving United Nations objectives.

The Commission would, of course, consult with the Unified Command and with the democratically selected representatives of the Korean people. At an appropriate time, elections by secret ballot, free from fraud and intimidation, under the auspices of the United Nations Commission would have to be arranged.

Free, democratic elections already have been held south of the 38th parallel. The General Assembly has formally declared the Government of the Republic of Korea, formed as a result of those elections, to be the lawfully constituted Government in that part of Korea in which the United Nations Commission was able to observe elections.

It is the territory and people of this Government that have been ravaged by war; it is the soldiers of this Government whose valor and patriotism have been strengthened by the United Nations Forces. The manner and procedures required to unify the country are functions for the United Nations to perform, but the Government of the Republic of Korea has unquestionably earned the right to be consulted in all matters relating to the future of Korea.

The future of Korea is, in a special and unique sense, the responsibility of the United Nations. That is why Secretary Acheson, in his address at the opening of this Assembly, placed particular emphasis on the task of reconstruction.

"Just as Korea has become the symbol of resistance against aggression," he stated, "so can it become also the vibrant symbol of the renewal of life."

We cannot limit our horizons to removing the scars of war. One of the fundamental purposes of our association in the United Nations is self-help and mutual assistance to remove the causes of conflict among men. We live in a world in which most of our fellow men eat too little, live too wretchedly, and die too young. We also live in a world in which misery and disease can be ameliorated if we can only learn how to marshal our knowledge and our resources properly.

The maintenance of enduring peace in Korea, and anywhere else in our world community, does not mean merely the absence of military operations. It means pushing ahead with our efforts to advance human well-being. And, as Secretary Acheson states, Korea is the place in which to make an historic beginning.

Establishing a free and independent nation in Korea will require a United Nations program to rebuild the economy of Korea and reestablish its educational, health, and social institutions. The responsibilities proposed for the United Nations Unification and Rehabilitation Commission in the field of reconstruction and recovery are, in the view of the United States, particularly important. Urgent action is required so that plans can be made to mobilize the resources and equipment needed from the member states to aid the Korean people to rebuild their factories, their transportation system, their schools, and their homes.

The problem of relief and emergency rehabilitation in Korea is upon us now. We feel that the Economic and Social Council should be requested to proceed immediately to draw up a program. Urgent action also is required to prepare a program of reconstruction. The Economic and Social Council, therefore, should submit to the Assembly at the earliest possible moment, recommendations for a general program of reconstruction and rehabilitation and for the machinery to implement it.

Let us join together in Korea to develop a pattern of coordinated economic and social action which we can employ in other places where the need is not to repair the ravages of war but is for development. By focusing on one place of extreme need, the United Nations and its specialized agencies can gain strength from experience to aid peoples everywhere to combat disease, build hospitals and schools, train teachers and public administrators, build and operate factories, and obtain more food from the land.

In Korea we have learned new lessons in how to act collectively to promote security. The lessons give endless promise. Let us now learn new lessons in how to act collectively to promote well-being. Here is our great opportunity to put into practical effect the basic economic and social precepts of the Covenant on Human Rights.

Let us make the United Nations the world's construction agency.

An enduring solution of the Korean problem should, in the view of the United States, include these elements:

First: Establishment of a free, independent, and united country.

Second: Establishment of a strong United Nations Commission to consult with all appropriate authorities and individuals and to make recommendations for carrying out the unification process.

Third: Selection of representatives of the Korean people in free elections conducted under the auspices of the United Nations Commission.

Fourth: Consultation with the Government of the Republic of Korea in all matters pertaining to the future of Korea.

Fifth: Vigorous United Nations efforts to assist the reconstruction and development of Korea.

Sixth: The retention of United Nations forces in Korea only as long as is necessary for the achievement of United Nations objectives.

Seventh: Elimination of special privileges for any nation and the development of friendly relations with all.

And eighth: Admission of Korea to the United Nations and assumption by her of the obligations, duties, and privileges of membership.

These elements for an enduring solution of the Korean problem are all contained in the draft resolution submitted by the delegations of the United Kingdom, the Philippines, Australia, Norway, Netherlands, Brazil, Cuba, and Pakistan. My Government is glad to declare its wholehearted support of that resolution.

J. General Assembly Resolution Declaring Communist China an Aggressor*

February 1, 1951

The General Assembly,

Noting that the Security Council, because of lack of unanimity of the permanent members, has failed to exercise its primary responsibility for the maintenance of international peace and security in regard to Chinese Communist intervention in Korea,

Noting that the Central People's Government of the People's Republic of China has not accepted United Nations proposals to bring about a cessation of hostilities in Korea with a view to peaceful settlement, and that its armed forces continue their invasion of Korea and their large-scale attacks upon United Nations forces there,

1. Finds that the Central People's Government of the People's Republic of China, by giving direct aid and assistance to those who were already committing aggression in Korea and by engaging in hostilities against United Nations forces there, has itself engaged in aggression in Korea;

2. Calls upon the Central People's Government of the People's Republic of China to cause its forces and nationals in Korea to cease hostilities against the United Nations forces and to withdraw from Korea;

3. Affirms the determination of the United Nations to continue its action in Korea to meet the aggression;

4. Calls upon all States and authorities to continue to lend every assistance to the United Nations action in Korea;

5. Calls upon all States and authorities to refrain from giving any assistance to the aggressors in Korea;

6. Requests a Committee composed of the members of the Collective Measures Committee as a matter of urgency to consider additional measures to be employed to meet this aggression and to report thereon to the General Assembly, it being understood that the Committee is authorized to defer its report if the Good Offices Committee referred to in the following paragraph reports satisfactory progress in its efforts;

7. Affirms that it continues to be the policy of the United Nations to bring about a cessation of hostilities in Korea and the achievement of United Nations objectives in Korea by peaceful means, and requests the President of the General Assembly to designate forthwith two persons who would meet with him at any suitable opportunity to use their good offices to this end.

Military Situation in The Far East, Pt. 5, pp. 3513-14.

THE TRUMAN-MACARTHUR CONTROVERSY

A. President Harry S. Truman to Ambassador Austin on United States Action Relative to Formosa*

August 28, 1950

As I told you on the telephone this morning I want to congratulate you on your able presentation of the views of the United States Government in the Security Council of the United Nations from the first onset of the aggression against the Republic of Korea. Throughout the entire course of the proceedings you have represented this Government with great effectiveness and in full accordance with my directions.

The letter which you addressed to the Secretary General of the United Nations on August 25 on the subject of Formosa admirably sums up the fundamental position of this Government as it had been stated by me on June 27 and in my Message to the Congress on July 19. You have clearly set forth in that letter the heart and essence of the problem. You have faithfully set down my views as they were then and as they are now.

To the end that there be no misunderstanding concerning the position of the government of the United States with respect to Formosa, it may be useful to repeat here the seven fundamental points which you so clearly stated in your letter to Mr. Lie.

"1. The United States has not encroached on the territory of China, nor has the United States taken aggressive action against China.

"2. The action of the United States in regard to Formosa was taken at a time when that island was the scene of conflict with the mainland. More serious conflict was threatened by the public declaration of the Chinese Communist authorities. Such conflict would have threatened the security of the United Nations forces operating in Korea under the mandate of the Security Council to repel the aggression of the Republic of Korea. They threatened to extend the conflict through the Pacific area.

"3. The action of the United States was an impartial neutralizing action addressed both to the forces on Formosa and to those on the mainland. It was an action designed to keep the peace and was, therefore, in full accord with the spirit of the Charter of the United Nations. As President Truman has solemnly declared, we have no designs on Formosa, and our action was not inspired by any desire to acquire a special position for the United States.

"4. The action of the United States was expressly stated to be without prejudice to the future political settlement of the status of the island. The actual status of the island is that it is territory taken from Japan by the victory of the Allied forces in the Pacific. Like other such territories, its legal status cannot be fixed until there is international action to determine its future. The Chinese Government was asked by the Allies to take the surrender of the Japanese forces on the island. That is the reason the Chinese are there now.

Military Situation in The Far East, Pt. 5, pp. 3476-77.

"5. The United States has a record through history of friendship for the Chinese people. We still feel the friendship and know that millions of Chinese reciprocate it. We took the lead with others in the last United Nations General Assembly to secure approval of a resolution on the integrity of China. Only the Union of the Soviet Socialist Republics and its satellites did not approve the resolution.

"6. The United States would welcome United Nations consideration of the case of Formosa. We would approve full United Nations investigation here, or on the spot. We believe that United Nations consideration would contribute to a peaceful, rather than a forceable solution of that problem.

"7. We do not believe that the Security Council need be, or will be, diverted from its consideration of the aggression against the Republic of Korea. There was a breach of the peace in Korea. The aggressor attacked, has been condemned, and the combined forces of the United Nations are now in battle to repel the aggression.

"Formosa is now at peace and will remain so unless someone resorts to force.

"If the Security Council wishes to study the question of Formosa we shall support and assist that study. Meanwhile, the president of the Security Council should discharge the duties of his office and get on with the item on the agenda, which is the complaint of aggression against the Republic of Korea, and specifically, the recognition of the right of the Korean Ambassador to take his seat and the vote on the United States resolution for the localization of the Korean conflict."

These seven points accurately record the position of the United States.

In the forthcoming discussion of the problem in the Security Council you will continue to have my complete support.

B. Message of General MacArthur to Veterans of Foreign Wars*

August, 1950

*   *   *

A New Battle Line

In view of misconceptions currently being voiced concerning the relationship of Formosa to our strategic potential in the Pacific, I believe it in the public interest to avail myself of this opportunity to state my views thereon to you, all of whom, having fought overseas, understand broad strategic concepts.

To begin with, any appraisal of that strategic potential requires an appreciation of the changes wrought in the course of the past war. Prior thereto the western strategic frontier of the United States lay on the littoral line of the Americas with an exposed island salient extending out through Hawaii, Midway, and Guam to the Philippines.

That salient was not an outpost of strength but an avenue of weakness along which the enemy could and did attack us. The Pacific was a potential area

*Ibid., pp. 3477-80.

of advancement for any predatory force intent upon striking at the bordering land areas.

All of this was changed by our Pacific victory. Our strategic frontier then shifted to embrace the entire Pacific Ocean, which has become a vast moat to protect us as long as we hold it.

Indeed, it acts as a protective shield to all of the Americas and all free lands of the Pacific Ocean area we control to the shores of Asia by a chain of islands extending an an are from the Aleutians to the Marianas held by us and our free Allies. From this island chain we can dominate with air power every Asiatic port from Vladivostock to Singapore and prevent any hostile movement into the Pacific.

Any predatory attack from Asia must be an amphibious effort. No amphibious force can be successful with our control of the sea lanes and the air over these lanes in its avenue of advance. With naval and air supremacy and modern ground elements to defend bases, any major attack from continental Asia toward us or our friends of the Pacific would come to failure.

A Peaceful Lake

Under such conditions the Pacific no longer represents menacing avenues of approach for a prospective invader—it assumes instead the friendly aspect of a peaceful lake. Our line of defense is a natural one and can be maintained with a minimum of military effort and expense.

It envisions no attack against anyone nor does it provide the bastions essential for offensive operations, but properly maintained would be an invincible defense against aggression. If we hold this line we may have peace—lose it and war is inevitable.

The geographic location of Formosa is such that in the hand of a power unfriendly to the United States it constitutes an enemy salient in the very center of this defensive perimeter, 100 to 150 miles closer to the adjacent friendly segments—Okinawa and the Philippines—than any point in continental Asia.

At the present time there is on Formosa a concentration of operational air and naval bases which is potentially greater than any similar concentration of the Asiatic mainland between the Yellow Sea and the Strait of Malacca. Additional bases can be developed in a relatively short time by an aggressive exploitation of all World War II Japanese facilities.

An enemy force utilizing those installations currently available could increase by 100 per cent the air effort which could be directed against Okinawa as compared to operations based on the mainland and at the same time could direct damaging air attacks with fighter-type aircraft against friendly installations in the Philippines, which are currently beyond the range of fighters based on the mainland. Our air supremacy at once would become doubtful.

Strategic Formosa

As a result of its geographic location and base potential, utilization of Formosa by a military power hostile to the United States may either counter-balance or overshadow the strategic importance of the central and southern flank of the United States front line position.

Formosa in the hands of such a hostile power could be compared to an unsinkable aircraft carrier and submarine tender ideally located to accomplish offensive strategy and at the same time checkmate defensive or counter-offensive operations by friendly forces based on Okinawa and the Philippines.

This unsinkable carrier-tender has the capacity to operate from ten to twenty air groups of types ranging from jet fighters to B-29 type bombers as well as to provide forward operating facilities for short-range coastal submarines.

In acquiring this forward submarine base, the efficacy of the short-range submarine would be so enormously increased by the additional radius of activity as to threaten completely sea traffic from the south and interdict all set lanes in the Western Pacific. Submarine blockade by the enemy with all its destructive ramifications would thereby become a virtual certainty.

Should Formosa fall and bases thereafter come into the hands of a potential enemy of the United States, the latter will have acquired an additional "fleet" which will have been obtained and can be maintained at an incomparably lower cost than could its equivalent in aircraft carriers and submarine tenders.

Current estimates of air and submarine resources in the Far East indicate the capability of such a potential enemy to extend his forces southward and still maintain an imposing degree of military strength for employment elsewhere in the Pacific area.

A Historical Function

Historically, Formosa has been used as a springboard for just such military aggression directed against areas to the south. The most notable and recent example was the utilization of it by the Japanese in World War II. At the outbreak of the Pacific War in 1941, it played an important part as a staging area and supporting base for the various Japanese invasion convoys. The supporting air forces of Japan's Army and Navy were based on fields situated along southern Formosa.

From 1942 through 1944 Formosa was a vital link in the transportation and communication chain which stretched from Japan through Okinawa and the Philippines to Southeast Asia. As the United States carrier forces advanced into the Western Pacific, the bases on Formosa assumed an increasingly greater role in the Japanese defense scheme.

Should Formosa fall into the hands of a hostile power, history would repeat itself. Its military potential would again be fully exploited as the means to breach and neutralize our Western Pacific defense system and mount a war of conquest against the free nations of the Pacific basin.

Nothing could be more fallacious than the threadbare argument by those who advocate appeasement and defeatism in the Pacific that if we defend Formosa we alienate continental Asia.

Those who speak thus do not understand the Orient. They do not grant that it is in the pattern of the Oriental psychology to respect and follow aggressive, resolute and dynamic leadership—to quickly turn on a leadership characterized by timidity or vacillation—and they underestimate the Oriental mentality. Nothing in the last five years has so inspired the Far East as the American determination to preserve the bulwarks of our Pacific Ocean strategic position from future encroachment, for few of its people fail accurately to appraise the safeguard such determination brings to their free institutions.

To pursue any other course would be to turn over the fruits of our Pacific victory to a potential enemy. It would shift any future battle area 5,000 miles eastward to the coasts of the American continents, our own home coast; it would completely expose our friends in the Philippines, our friends in Australia and New Zealand, our friends in Indonesia, our friends in Japan, and other areas, to the lustful thrusts of those who stand for slavery against liberty, for atheism as against God.

The decision of President Truman on June 27 lighted into flame a lamp of hope throughout Asia that was burning dimly toward extinction. It marked for the Far East the focal and turning point in this area's struggle for freedom. It swept aside in one great monumental stroke all of the hypocrisy and the sophistry which has confused and deluded so many people distant from the actual scene.

C. Message from Secretary of Defense Louis A. Johnson to General MacArthur*

August 26, 1950

The President of the United States directs that you withdraw your message for National Encampment of Veterans of Foreign Wars, because various features with respect to Formosa are in conflict with the policy of the United States and its position in the United Nations.

D. Message of President Truman to General MacArthur*

August 29, 1950

I am sending you for your information the text of a letter which I sent to Ambassador Austin dated Aug 27. I am sure that when you examine this letter, and the letter which Ambassador Austin addressed to Trygve Lie on Aug. 25 (a copy of which I am told was sent to your headquarters that night), you will understand why my action of the 26th in directing the withdrawal of your message to the Veterans of Foreign Wars was necessary . . .

*Ibid, p. 3480.
*Ibid.

E. Comment by President Truman on Differences over Formosa*

[Extract]

1956

General MacArthur's visit to Formosa on July 31 had raised much speculation in the world press. Chiang Kai-shek's aids let it be known that the Far East commander was in fullest agreement with their chief on the course of action to be taken. The implication was—and quite a few of our newspapers said so—that MacArthur rejected my policy of neutralizing Formosa and that he favored a more aggressive method.

After Harriman explained the administration's policy to MacArthur he had said that he would accept it as a good soldier. I was reassured. I told the press that the general and I saw eye to eye on Formosa policy.

To make doubly sure, on August 14 the Joint Chiefs of Staff informed General MacArthur, with my approval, that the intent of the directive to him to defend Formosa was to limit United States action there to such support operations as would be practicable without committing any forces to the island itself. No commitments were to be made to the National Government for the basing of fighter squadrons on Formosa, and no United States forces of any kind were to be based ashore on Formosa except with the specific approval of the Joint Chiefs of Staff.

I assumed that this would be the last of it and that General MacArthur would accept the Formosa policy laid down by his Commander in Chief. But I was mistaken. Before the month ended—on August 26—the White House Press Room brought me a copy of a statement which General MacArthur had sent to the commander in chief of the Veterans of Foreign Wars. This document was not to be read until August 28, but MacArthur's public relations office in Tokyo had handed it to the papers several days in advance, and when I first heard about it, on the morning of August 26, a weekly magazine was already in the mails with the full text.

The substance of the long message was that, "in view of misconceptions being voiced concerning the relationship of Formosa to our strategic potential in the Pacific," the general thought it desirable to put forth his own views on the subject. He argued that the oriental psychology required "aggressive, resolute and dynamic leadership," and "nothing could be more fallacious than the thread-bare argument by those who advocate appeasement and defeatism in the Pacific that if we defend Formosa we alienate continental Asia." In other words, he called for a military policy of aggression, based on Formosa's position. The whole tenor of the message was critical of the very policy which he had so recently told Harriman he would support. There was no doubt in my mind that the world would read it that way and that it must have been intended that way.

*Truman, *Memoirs*, pp. 354-55.

It was my opinion that this statement could only serve to confuse the world as to just what our Formosa policy was, for it was at odds with my announcement of June 27, and it also contradicted what I had told the Congress. Furthermore, our policy had been reaffirmed only the day before in a letter which, on my instructions, Ambassador Austin had addressed to the Secretary General of the United Nations, Trygve Lie.

The subject of Formosa had been placed before the Security Council by the Russian delegation, which charged us with acts of aggression in our aid to Chiang Kai-shek, and I had approved a State Department proposal that we counter this charge with a declaration that we were entirely willing to have the United Nations investigate the Formosa situation. Mr. Malik, the Russian delegate, was trying to persuade the Security Council that our action in placing the Seventh Fleet in the Formosa Strait amounted to the incorporation of Formosa within the American orbit. Austin's letter to Trygve Lie had made it plain that we had only one intention: to reduce the area of conflict in the Far East. General MacArthur's message—which the world might mistake as an expression of American policy—contradicted this.

Of course, I would never deny General MacArthur or anyone else the right to differ with me in opinions. The official position of the United States, however, is defined by decisions and declarations of the President. There can be only one voice in stating the position of this country in the field of foreign relations. This is of fundamental constitutional significance. General MacArthur, in addition to being an important American commander, was also the United Nations commander in Korea. He was, in fact, acting for and on behalf of the United Nations. That body was then debating the question of Formosa, and its members—even those outside the Soviet bloc—differed sharply in their views regarding Formosa. It was hardly proper for the U.N.'s agent to argue a case then under discussion by that body.

I realized that the damage had been done and that the MacArthur message was in the hands of the press.

I gave serious thought to relieving General MacArthur as our military field commander in the Far East and replacing him with General Bradley.

*   *   *

F. General MacArthur's Surrender Demand to North Korean Forces*

October 9, 1950

This is to inform you of the action taken by the United Nations General assembly on Oct. 8 [Oct. 7, United States time], 1950, in adopting the resolution appended thereto.

In order that the decisions of the United Nations may be carried out with a minimum of further loss of life and destruction of property, I, as United

**Military Situation in The Far East*, Pt. 5, p. 3483.

Nations Commander in Chief, for the last time, call upon you and the forces under your command, in whatever part of Korea situated, forthwith to lay down your arms and cease hostilities.

And I call upon all North Koreans to cooperate fully with the United Nations in establishing a unified independent democratic government of Korea assured that they will be treated justly and that the United Nations will act to relieve and rehabilitate all parts to a unified Korea.

Unless immediate response is made by you in the name of the North Korean Government I shall at once proceed to take such military action as may be necessary to enforce the decrees of the United Nations.

G. Announcement by President Truman Relative to his Meeting with General MacArthur at Wake Island*

[Extract]

October 15, 1950

I have met with General of the Army Douglas MacArthur for the purpose of getting first hand information and ideas from him. I did not wish to take him away from the scene of action in Korea any longer than necessary, and, therefore. I came to meet him at Wake. Our conference has been highly satisfactory.

The very complete unanimity of view which prevailed enabled us to finish our discussions rapidly in order to meet General MacArthur's desire to return at the earliest possible moment. It was apparent that the excellent coordination which has existed between Washington and the field, to which General MacArthur paid tribute, greatly facilitated the discussion.

*   *   *

Primarily, we talked about the problems in Korea which are General MacArthur's most pressing responsibilities. I asked him for information on the military aspects.

I got from him a clear picture of the heroism and high capacity of the United Nations forces under his command. We also discussed the steps necessary to bring peace and security to the area as rapidly as possible in accordance with the intent of the resolution of the United Nations General Assembly and in order to get our armed forces out of Korea as soon as their United Nations mission is completed.

We devoted a good deal of time to the major problem of peaceful reconstruction of Korea which the United Nations is facing and to the solution of which we intend to make the best contribution of which the United States is capable.

This is a challenging task which must be done properly if we are to achieve the peaceful goals for which the United Nations has been fighting.

Ibid., pp. 3484-85.

The success which has attended the combined military effort must be supplemented by both spiritual and material rehabilitation. It is essentially a task of helping the Koreans to do a job which they can do for themselves better than anyone else can do it for them.

*   *   *

H. Comment by President Truman on his Meeting at Wake Island with General MacArthur*

[Extract]

1956

We discussed the Japanese and the Korean situations.

The general assured me that the victory was won in Korea. He also informed me that the Chinese Communists would not attack and that Japan was ready for a peace treaty.

Then he brought up the subject of his statement about Formosa to the Veterans of Foreign Wars. He said that he was sorry if he had caused any embarrassment. I told him that I considered the incident closed. He said he wanted me to understand that he was not in politics in any way—that he had allowed the politicians to make a "chump" (his word) of him in 1948 and that it would not happen again.

I told him something of our plans for the strengthening of Europe, and he said he understood and that he was sure it would be possible to send one division from Korea to Europe in January 1951. He repeated that the Korean conflict was won and that there was little possibility of the Chinese Communists coming in.

The general seemed genuinely pleased at this opportunity to talk with me, and I found him a most stimulating and interesting person. Our conversation was very friendly—I might say much more so than I had expected.

A little after seven-thirty we went to another small building, where other members of our parties had gathered. The others at this meeting, besides General MacArthur and myself, were Admiral Radford, Ambassador Muccio, Secretary of the Army Pace, General Bradley, Philip Jessup and Dean Rusk from the State Department, Averell Harriman, and Colonel Hamblen of Bradley's staff.

It was not until much later that I learned that Miss Vernice Anderson, the secretary to Ambassador Jessup, was next door and, without instructions from anyone, took down stenographic notes. This fact later became known during the hearings following General MacArthur's recall, and there was a good deal of noise about it. I can say that neither I nor Mr. Jessup nor anyone else had given Miss Anderson instructions to take notes; as a matter of fact, she was not brought along to take notes but merely to have a secretary available for the drafting of the communiqué that would have to be issued at the end of the meeting.

In any case, Miss Anderson's note-taking became known later on, and the record of what was said in this larger meeting at Wake Island has been printed in the newspapers and in some books as well. I will therefore relate here only the high points of the discussion—those things that so impressed me at the time that I remember them even without notes.

General MacArthur stated his firm belief that all resistance would end, in both North and South Korea, by Thanksgiving. This, he said, would enable him to withdraw the Eighth Army to Japan by Christmas. He would leave two divisions and the detachments of the other United Nations in Korea until elections had been held there. He thought this might be done as early as January and that it would then be possible to take all non-Korean troops out of the country.

Quite a bit of discussion followed about the aid Korea would need for rehabilitation once the conflict had been concluded, and both General MacArthur and Ambassador Muccio answered questions which were put to them by me and other members of my party. When Secretary Pace asked General MacArthur what the Army or ECA could do to help him, the general said, without any hesitation, that he did not know of any commander in the history of war who had ever had more complete and adequate support than he had received from all agencies in Washington.

I remember that we talked about the prisoners our forces had taken, and the general said that they were the happiest Koreans in all Korea. They were well fed and clean, and though they had been captured as North Korean "Communists," they were really no different from other Koreans.

Then I gave MacArthur an opportunity to repeat to the larger group some of the things he had said to me in our private meeting.

"What are the chances," I asked, "for Chinese or Soviet interference?"

The general's answer was really in two parts. First he talked about the Chinese. He thought, he said, that there was very little chance that they would come in. At the most they might be able to get fifty or sixty thousand men into Korea, but, since they had no air force, "if the Chinese tried to get down to Pyongyang, there would be the greatest slaughter."

Then he referred to the possibilities of Russian intervention. He referred to the Russian air strength, but he was certain that their planes and pilots were inferior to ours. He saw no way for the Russians to bring in any sizable number of ground troops before the onset of winter. This would leave the possibility of combined Chinese-Russian intervention, he observed, with Russian planes supporting Chinese ground units. This, he thought, would be no danger. "It just wouldn't work," he added, "with Chinese Communist ground and Russian air."

       *   *   *

I. Comment by General MacArthur on the Meeting with President Truman at Wake Island*

[Extract]

1964

I knew nothing of the purpose of the meeting, my only information being that Averell Harriman would be there. A number of American correspondents in Tokyo requested permission to accompany me. In view of the number of Washington correspondents announced as coming, I assumed that the Tokyo representatives would be permitted to attend also, especially as my plane could accommodate a large representation. I passed their requests along to the Pentagon, recommending approval, and was surprised when the request was promptly and curtly disapproved.

The President's party arrived in three planes with thirty-five reporters and photographers. As I shook hands with Mr. Truman, he remarked, "I've been a long time meeting you, General."

I replied, "I hope it won't be so long next time." But there was never to be a next time.

I had been warned about Mr. Truman's quick and violent temper and prejudices, but he radiated nothing but courtesy and good humor during our meeting. He has an engaging personality, a quick and witty tongue, and I liked him from the start. At the conference itself, he seemed to take great pride in his historical knowledge, but, it seemed to me that in spite of his having read much, it was of a superficial character, encompassing facts without the logic and reasoning dictating those facts. Of the Far East he knew little, presenting a strange combination of distorted history and vague hopes that somehow, some way, we could do something to help those struggling against Communism.

His advisers were numerous and distinguished: Admiral Arthur Radford, commander of the Pacific Fleet: Army Secretary Frank Pace: Press Secretary Charles Ross: U.N. Ambassador Philip Jessup; Joint Chiefs Chairman Omar Bradley; State Department Far Eastern Chief Dean Rusk; Special Adviser Averell Harriman; and Legal Adviser Charles Murphy. There were numerous other Truman aides and aides' aides. I had with me my military secretary, my aide-de-camp, and my pilot. Press Secretary Ross announced that no record was to be made of the talks.

Wake Island's heat caused the President to remove his coat. I pulled out a new briar pipe and inquired: "Do you mind if I smoke, Mr. President?"

Truman replied, "No. I suppose I've had more smoke blown in my face than any other man alive." He seemed to enjoy the laugh that followed.

The conference itself was innocuous enough. The sketchy agenda contained nothing upon which Washington did not already have my fullest views as they affected my responsibilities either as supreme commander for the Allied powers in Japan or as commander-in-chief for the United Nations in Korea. They dealt

*Douglas MacArthur, *Reminiscences*, (New York, 1964), pp. 360-62.

with such matters as the administration of Korea when united, its rehabilitation, the treatment of prisoners of war, the economic situation in the Philippines, the security of Indo-China, the progress of a treaty of peace with Japan, routine details of supply logistics for Japan and Korea—nothing on which my views were not known. No new policies, no new strategy of war or international politics, were proposed or discussed. Formosa was not on the agenda.

Near the end of the conference, the possibility of Chinese intervention was brought up almost casually. It was the general consensus of all present that Red China had no intention of intervening. This opinion had previously been advanced by the Central Intelligence Agency and the State Department. General Bradley went so far as to bring up the question of transferring troops in the Far East to Europe, and said he would like to have two divisions from Korea home by Christmas for this purpose.

My views were asked as to the chance of Red China's intervention. I replied that the answer could only be speculative; that neither the State Department through its diplomatic listening posts abroad, nor the Central Intelligence Agency to whom a field commander must look for guidance as to a foreign nation's intention to move from peace to war, reported any evidence of intent by the Peiping government to intervene with major forces; that my own local intelligence, which I regarded as unsurpassed anywhere, reported heavy concentrations near the Yalu border in Manchuria whose movements were indeterminate; that my own military estimate was that with our largely unopposed air forces, with their potential capable of destroying, at will, bases of attack and lines of supply north as well as south of the Yalu, no Chinese military commander would hazard the commitment of large forces upon the devastated Korean peninsula. The risk of their utter destruction through lack of supply would be too great. There was no disagreement from anyone. This episode was later completely misrepresented to the public through an alleged but spurious report in an effort to pervert the position taken by me. It was an ingeniously fostered implication that I flatly and unequivocally predicted that under no circumstances would the Chinese Communists enter the Korean War. This is prevarication.

The entire conference lasted only an hour and thirty-six minutes, and I then drove with the President to the airfield to see him off. The discussion of Far Eastern problems was at an end. Instead, he turned the conversation to American politics. Rather impertinently, I asked him if he intended to run for re-election. The Emperor had asked me about this in a recent visit in Tokyo. The President, long accustomed to dodging this question in press conferences, immediately countered by asking me if I had any political ambitions along such lines. I had no need to duck the question, and I replied: "None whatsoever. If you have any general running against you, his name will be Eisenhower, not MacArthur."

*   *   *

J. General MacArthur's Report to the Security Council on Entry of the Chinese Communists into the Korean War*

November 5, 1950

I herewith submit a special report of the United Nations Command operations in Korea which I believe should be brought to the attention of the United Nations.

The United Nations Forces in Korea are continuing their drive to the North and their efforts to destroy further the effectiveness of the enemy as a fighting force are proving successful. However, presently in certain areas of Korea, the United Nations Forces are meeting a new foe. It is apparent to our fighting forces, and our intelligence agencies have confirmed the fact, that the United Nations are presently in hostile contact with Chinese Communist military units deployed for action against the forces of the United Command.

Hereafter, in summary form, are confirmed intelligence reports substantiating the fact that forces other than Korean are resisting our efforts to carry out the resolutions of the United Nations:

A. 22 August: Approximately 50 bursts heavy anti-aircraft fire from Manchurian side of Yalu River against RB-29 flying at 7,000 feet over Korea in the vicinity of the Sui-Ho reservoir; damage, none; time 1600K; weather, 10 miles visibility, high broken clouds.

B. 24 August: Approximately 40 bursts heavy anti-aircraft fire from Manchurian side of Yalu River against RB-29 flying at 10,000 feet over Korea in the vicinity of Sinuiju; damage, none; time 1500K; weather, 20 miles visibility.

C. 15 October: Anti-aircraft fire from the Manchurian side of Yalu River against a flight of 4 F-51's flying near the Sinuiju airfield on the Korean side of the river; damage, 1 aircraft total loss; time, 1445I; weather, overcast at 8,000 feet; 8 to 10 miles visibility.

D. 16 October: The 370th Regiment of the 124th Division of the Chinese Communist 42nd Army, consisting of approximately 2,500 troops, crossed the Yalu River (Korean border) at Wan Po Jin, and proceeded to the area of Chosen and Fusen Dams in North Korea where they came in contact with U.N. forces approximately 40 miles north of Hamhung.

E. 17 October: Approximately 15 bursts heavy anti-aircraft fire from Manchurian side of Yalu River against RB-29 flying at 10,000 feet over Korea in the vicinity of Sinuiju; damage, none; time 1200I; weather, 8 miles visibility, low clouds 2,300 feet.

F. 20 October: A Chinese Communist Task Force known as the "56th" unit, consisting of approximately 5,000 troops, crossed the Yalu River (Korean border) at Antung and deployed to positions in Korea south of the Sui-Ho Dam. A captured Chinese Communist soldier of this Task Force states that his group was organized out of the regular Chinese Communist 40th Army stationed at Antung, Manchuria.

*Military Situation in The Far East, Pt. 5, pp. 3492-93.

G. 1 November: A flight of F-51's was attacked early in the afternoon by 6 to 9 Jet aircraft which flew across the Yalu River into Manchuria. No damage was done to US aircraft. A red star was observed on the top of the right wing on one of the Jet aircraft.

H. 1 November: Anti-aircraft fire from the Manchurian side of the Yalu River directed against a flight of 13 F-80 aircraft was observed in the vicinity of Sinuiju at 1345 hours. This resulted in the total loss of 1 U. N. aircraft.

I. 30 October: Interrogation of 19 Chinese prisoners of war identified two additional regiments of 124 CCF Division, the 371 and the 372 in the vicinity of Changjin.

J. 2 November: Interrogation of prisoners of war indicates the 54 CCF unit in Korea. This unit is reported to have same organization as 55 and 56 units, but to be drawn from the 112,113, and 114 Divisions of the 38 CCF Army.

K. 3 November: Further interrogation of Chinese prisoners of war indicates 56 CCF unit organized from elements of 118, 119, and 120 CCF Divisions of the 40 CCF Army.

L. 4 November: As of this date, a total of 35 CCF prisoners had been taken in Korea.

The continued employment of Chinese Communist forces in Korea and the hostile attitude assumed by such forces, either inside or outside Korea, are matters which it is incumbent upon me to bring at once to the attention of the U.N.

K. Statement of President Truman*

November 16, 1950

The Security Council has before it a resolution concerning the grave situation caused by the Chinese Communist intervention in Korea. This resolution, introduced by the representatives of Cuba, Ecuador, France, Norway, the United Kingdom and the United States, reaffirms that it is the policy of the United Nations to hold the Chinese frontier with Korea inviolate, to protect fully legitimate Korean and Chinese interests in the frontier zone, and to withdraw the United Nations forces from Korea as soon as stability has been restored and a unified, independent and democratic government established throughout Korea.

This resolution further calls upon all states and authorities to withdraw immediately from Korea all individuals or units which are assisting the North Korean forces. I am sure that all members of the Security Council genuinely interested in restoring peace in the Far East will not only support this resolution but also use their influence to obtain compliance with it.

United Nations forces now are being attacked from the safety of a privileged sanctuary. Planes operating from bases in China cross over into Korea to attack United Nations ground and air forces and then flee back across the border. Chinese Communist and North Korean Communist forces are being reinforced,

*Ibid., p. 3994.

supplied and equipped from bases behind the safety of the Sino-Korean border.

The pretext which the Chinese Communists advance for taking offensive action against United Nations forces in Korea from behind the protection afforded by the Sino-Korean border is their professed belief that these forces intend to carry hostilities across the frontier into Chinese territory.

The resolutions and every other action taken by the United Nations demonstrate beyond any doubt that no such intention has ever been entertained. On the contrary, it has been repeatedly stated that it is the intention of the United Nations to localize the conflict and to withdraw its forces from Korea as soon as the situation permits.

Speaking for the United States Government and people, I can give assurance that we support and are acting within the limits of United Nations policy in Korea, and that we have never at any time entertained any intention to carry hostilities into China.

So far as the United States is concerned, I wish to state unequivocally that because of our deep devotion to the cause of world peace and our long-standing friendship for the people of China we will take every honorable step to prevent any extension of the hostilities in the Far East.

If the Chinese Communist authorities or people believe otherwise, it can only be because they are being deceived by those whose advantage it is to prolong and extend hostilities in the Far East against the interests of all Far Eastern people.

Let it be understood, however, that a desire for peace, in order to be effective, must be shared by all concerned. If the Chinese Communists share the desire of the United Nations for peace and security in the Far East they will not take upon themselves the responsibility for obstructing the objectives of the United Nations in Korea.

L. Special Communiqué Issued by General MacArthur*

November 28, 1950

Enemy reactions developed in the course of our assault operations of the past four days disclose that a major segment of the Chinese continental armed forces in army, corps and divisional organization of an aggregate strength of over 200,000 men is now arrayed against the United Nations forces in North Korea.

There exists the obvious intent and preparation for support of these forces by heavy reinforcements now concentrated within the privileged sanctuary north of the international boundary and constantly moving forward.

Consequently, we face an entirely new war. This has shattered the high hopes we entertained that the intervention of the Chinese was only of a token nature on a volunteer and individual basis as publicly announced, and that therefore the war in Korea could be brought to a rapid close by our movement to the international boundary and the prompt withdrawal thereafter of United Nations forces, leaving Korean problems for settlement by the Koreans themselves.

It now appears to have been the enemy's intent, in breaking off contact with

*Ibid., p. 3495.

our forces some two weeks ago, to secure the time necessary surreptitiously to build up for a later surprise assault upon our lines in overwhelming force, taking advantage of the freezing of all rivers and roadbeds which would have materially reduced the effectiveness of our air interdiction and permitted a greatly accelerated forward movement of enemy reinforcements and supplies. This plan has been disrupted by our own offensive action, which forced upon the enemy a premature engagement.

General MacArthur later issued this additional paragraph to the communiqué:

This situation, repugnant as it may be, poses issues beyond the authority of the United Nations military council—issues which must find their solution within the councils of the United Nations and chancelleries of the world.

M. Statement of President Truman*

November 30, 1950

Recent developments in Korea confront the world with a serious crisis. The Chinese Communist leaders have sent their troops from Manchuria to launch a strong and well-organized attack against the United Nations forces in North Korea. This has been done despite prolonged and earnest efforts to bring home to the Communist leaders of China the plain fact that neither the United Nations nor the United States has any aggressive intentions toward China. Because of the historic friendship between the people of the United States and China, it is particularly shocking to us to think that Chinese are being forced into battle against our troops in the United Nations command.

The Chinese attack was made in great force, and it still continues. It has resulted in the forced withdrawal of large parts of the United Nations command. The battlefield situation is uncertain at this time. We may suffer reverses as we have suffered them before. But the forces of the United Nations have no intention of abandoning their mission in Korea.

The forces of the United Nations are in Korea to put down an aggression that threatens not only the whole fabric of the United Nations but all human hopes of peace and justice. If the United Nations yields to the forces of aggression, no nation will be safe or secure. If aggression is successful in Korea, we can expect it to spread through Asia and Europe to this hemisphere. We are fighting in Korea for our own national security and survival.

N. Message from Joint Chiefs of Staff to General MacArthur*

December 6, 1950

"1. The President, as of 5 December, forwarded a memo to all Cabinet members and to the Chairman, N. S. R. B.; Administrator, E. C. A.; Director, C. I. A.; Administrator, E. S. A.; and Director, Selective Service, which reads as follows:

* *Ibid.,* p. 3496
* *Ibid.,* p. 3180.

" 'In the light of the present critical international situation, and until further written notice from me, I wish that each one of you would take immediate steps to reduce the number of public speeches pertaining to foreign or military policy made by officials of the departments and agencies of the Executive Branch. This applies to officials in the field as well as those in Washington.

" 'No speech, press release, or other public statement concerning foreign policy should be released until it has received clearance from the Department of State.

" 'No speech, press release, or other statement concerning military policy should be released until it has received clearance from the Department of Defense.

" 'In addition to the copies submitted to the Departments of State or Defense for clearance, advance copies of speeches and press releases concerning foreign policy or military policy should be submitted to the White House for information.

" 'The purpose of this memorandum is not to curtail the flow of information to the American people, but rather to insure that the information made public is accurate and fully in accord with the policies of the United States Government.

"2. He also forwarded the following to the Secretary of State and Secretary of Defense:

" 'In addition to the policy expressed in my memorandum of this date to the heads of departments, concerning the clearance of speeches and statements, I wish the following steps to be taken:

" 'Officials overseas, including military commanders and diplomatic representatives, should be ordered to exercise extreme caution in public statements, to clear all but routine statements with their departments, and to refrain from direct communication on military or foreign policy with newspapers, magazines or other publicity media in the United States.'

"3. The above is transmitted to you for guidance and appropriate action."

O. Message from Joint Chiefs of Staff to General MacArthur*

March 20, 1951

State planning Presidential announcement shortly that, with clearing of bulk of South Korea of aggression, United Nations now prepared to discuss conditions of settlement in Korea. Strong UN feeling persists that further diplomatic effort toward settlement should be made before any advance with major forces north of 38th Parallel. Time will be required to determine diplomatic reactions and permit new negotiations that may develop. Recognizing that parallel has no military significance, State has asked JCS what authority you should have to permit sufficient freedom of action for next few weeks to provide security for U. N. forces and maintain contact with enemy. Your recommendations desired.

Ibid.

P. Statement of General MacArthur*

March 24, 1951

Operations continue according to schedule and plan. We have now substantially cleared South Korea of organized Communist forces. It is becoming increasingly evident that the heavy destruction along the enemy's lines of supply caused by our 'round-the-clock massive air and naval bombardment, has left his troops in the forward battle area deficient in requirements to sustain his operations.

This weakness is being brilliantly exploited by our ground forces. The enemy's human wave tactics definitely failed him as our own forces become seasoned to this form of warfare; his tactics of infiltration are but contributing to his piecemeal losses, and he is showing less stamina than our own troops under rigors of climate, terrain, and battle.

Of even greater significance than our tactical success has been the clear revelation that this new enemy, Red China, of such exaggerated and vaunted military power, lacks the industrial capacity to provide adequately many critical items essential to the conduct of modern war.

He lacks manufacturing bases and those raw materials needed to produce, maintain, and operate even moderate air and naval power, and he cannot provide the essentials for successful ground operations, such as tanks, heavy artillery, and other refinements science has introduced into the conduct of military campaigns.

Formerly his great numerical potential might well have filled this gap, but with the development of existing methods of mass destruction, numbers alone do not offset vulnerability inherent in such deficiencies. Control of the sea and air, which in turn means control over supplies, communications, and transportation are no less essential and decisive now than in the past.

When this control exists, as in our case, and is coupled with the inferiority of ground firepower, as in the enemy's case, the resulting disparity is such that it cannot be overcome by bravery, however fanatical, or the most gross indifference to human loss.

These military weaknesses have been clearly and definitely revealed since Red China entered upon its undeclared war in Korea. Even under inhibitions which now restrict activity of the United Nations forces and the corresponding military advantages which accrue to Red China, it has been shown its complete inability to accomplish by force of arms the conquest of Korea.

The enemy therefore must by now be painfully aware that a decision of the United Nations to depart from its tolerant effort to contain the war to the area of Korea through expansion of our military operations to his coastal areas and interior bases would doom Red China to the risk of imminent military collapse.

These basic facts being established, there should be no insuperable difficulty arriving at decisions on the Korean problem if the issues are resolved on their own merits without being burdened by extraneous matters not directly related

*Ibid., p. 3181.

to Korea, such as Formosa and China's seat in the United Nations.

The Korean nation and people which have been so cruelly ravaged must not be sacrificed. That is the paramount concern. Apart from the military area of the problem where the issues are resolved in the course of combat, the fundamental questions continue to be political in nature and must find their answer in the diplomatic sphere.

Within the area of my authority as military commander, however, it should be needless to say I stand ready at any time to confer in the field with the commander in chief of the enemy forces in an earnest effort to find any military means whereby the realization of the political objectives of the United Nations in Korea, to which no nation may justly take exceptions, might be accomplished without further bloodshed.

Q. Message from Joint Chiefs of Staff to General MacArthur*

March 24, 1951

The President has directed that your attention be called to his order as transmitted 6 December 1950. In view of the information given you 20 March 1951 any further statements by you must be coordinated as prescribed in the order of 6 December.

The President has also directed that in the event Communist military leaders request an armistice in the field, you immediately report that fact to the JCS for instructions.

R. Letters Exchanged by Hon. Joseph W. Martin, Jr., and General MacArthur*

March, 1951

Office of the Minority Leader,
House of Representatives,
Washington, D. C., March 8, 1951

General of the Army Douglas MacArthur,
    Commander in Chief, Far Eastern Command.

My Dear General: In the current discussions of foreign policy and over-all strategy many of us have been distressed that, although the European aspects have been heavily emphasized. we have been without the views of yourself as Commander in Chief of the Far Eastern Command.

I think it is imperative to the security of our Nation and for the safety of the world that policies of the United States embrace the broadest possible strategy and that in our earnest desire to protect Europe we not weaken our position in Asia.

Enclosed is a copy of an address I delivered in Brooklyn, N. Y., February 12, stressing this vital point and suggesting that the forces of Generalissimo Chiang Kai-shek on Formosa might be employed in the opening of a second Asiatic front to relieve the pressure on our forces in Korea.

* *Ibid.*, pp. 3181-82.
* *Ibid.*, p. 3182.

I have since repeated the essence of this thesis in other speeches, and intend to do so again on March 21, when I will be on a radio hook-up.

I would deem it a great help if I could have your views on this point, either on a confidential basis or otherwise. Your admirers are legion, and the respect you command is enormous. May success be yours in the gigantic undertaking which you direct.

Sincerely yours.

Joseph W. Martin, Jr.

General Headquarters,
Supreme Commander for the Allied Powers,
Tokyo, Japan, March 20, 1951

Hon. Jospeh W. Martin, Jr.,
House of Representatives, Washington, D. C.

Dear Congressman Martin: I am most grateful for your note of the 8th forwarding me a copy of your address of February 12. The latter I have read with much interest, and find that with the passage of years you have certainly lost none of your old-time punch.

My views and recommendations with respect to the situation created by Red China's entry into war against us in Korea have been submitted to Washington in most complete detail. Generally these views are well known and clearly understood, as they follow the conventional pattern of meeting force with maximum counterforce, as we have never failed to do in the past. Your view with respect to the utilization of the Chinese forces on Formosa is in conflict with neither logic nor this tradition.

It seems strangely difficult for some to realize that here in Asia is where the Communist conspirators have elected to make their play for global conquest, and that we have joined the issue thus raised on the battlefield; that here we fight Europe's war with arms while the diplomatic there still fight it with words; that if we lose the war to communism in Asia the fall of Euorpe is inevitable, win it and Europe most probably would avoid war and yet preserve freedom. As you pointed out, we must win. There is no substitute for victory.

With renewed thanks and expressions of most cordial regard, I am

Faithfully yours,

Douglas MacArthur

S. President Truman's Recall of General MacArthur*

April 10, 1951

MESSAGE RELIEVING GENERAL MACARTHUR OF COMMAND

I deeply regret that it becomes my duty as President and Commander in Chief of the United States military forces to replace you as Supreme Com-

* *Ibid.*, p. 3179-80.

mander, Allied Powers; Commander in Chief, United Nations Command; Commander in Chief, Far East; and Commanding General, United States Army, Far East.

You will turn over your commands, effective at once, to Lt. Gen. Matthew B. Ridgway. You are authorized to have issued such orders as are necessary to complete desired travel to such place as you select.

My reasons for your replacement will be made public concurrently with the delivery to you of the foregoing order, and are contained in the next following message.

STATEMENT OF THE PRESIDENT RELATIVE
TO THE RELIEF OF GENERAL MACARTHUR

With deep regret I have concluded that General of the Army Douglas MacArthur is unable to give his wholehearted support to the policies of the United States Government and of the United Nations in matters pertaining to his official duties. In view of the specific responsibilities imposed upon me by the Constitution of the United States and the added responsibility which has been entrusted to me by the United Nations, I have decided that I must make a change of command in the Far East. I have, therefore, relieved General MacArthur of his commands and have designated Lt. Gen. Matthew B. Ridgway as his successor.

Full and vigorous debate on matters of national policy is a vital element in the constitutional system of our free democracy. It is fundamental, however, that military commanders must be governed by the policies and directives issued to them in the manner provided by our laws and Constitution. In time of crisis, this consideration is particularly compelling.

General MacArthur's place in history as one of our greatest commanders is fully established. The Nation owes him a debt of gratitude for the distinguished and exceptional service which he has rendered his country in posts of great responsibility. For that reason I repeat my regret at the necessity for the action I feel compelled to take in his case.

T. Comment by President Truman on His Dismissal of General MacArthur*

1956

The time had come to draw the line. MacArthur's letter to Congressman Martin showed that the general was not only in disgreement with the policy of the government but was challenging this policy in open insubordination to his Commander in Chief.

I asked Acheson, Marshall, Bradley, and Harriman to meet with me on Friday

*Truman, *Memoirs,* pp. 447-48.

morning, April 6, to discuss MacArthur's action. I put the matter squarely before them. What should be done about General MacArthur? We discussed the question for an hour. Everyone thought that the government faced a serious situation.

Averell Harriman was of the opinion that I should have fired MacArthur two years ago. In the spring of 1949, as in 1948, MacArthur had pleaded that he could not come home because of the press of business in Tokyo, and it had been necessary for the Secretary of the Army, Kenneth Royall, to intervene urgently from Washington in order to get MacArthur to withhold his approval from a bill of the Japanese Diet which was completely contrary to the economic policy for the occupation as prescribed by the governmental authorities in Washington.

Secretary of Defense Marshall advised caution, saying he wished to reflect further. He observed that if I relieved MacArthur it might be difficult to get the military appropriations through Congress.

General Bradley approached the question entirely from the point of view of military discipline. As he saw it, there was a clear case of insubordination and the general deserved to be relieved of command. He did wish, however, to consult with the Chiefs of Staff before making a final recommendation.

Acheson said that he believed that General MacArthur should be relieved, but he thought it essential to have the unanimous advice of the Joint Chiefs of Staff before I acted. He counseled that the most careful consideration be given to this matter since it was of the utmost seriousness. He added, "If you relieve MacArthur, you will have the biggest fight of your administration."

We then joined the Cabinet for the regularly scheduled meeting. There was comment all around the table, of course, about the letter to Martin but there was no discussion of the probelm of what to do with MacArthur. After the Cabinet meeting, Acheson, Marshall, Bradley, and Harriman returned with me to my office, and we continued our discussion.

I was careful not to disclose that I had already reached a decision. Before the meeting adjourned, I suggested to Marshall that he go over all the messages in the Pentagon files that had been exchanged with General MacArthur in the past two years. Then I asked all four to return the following day at 9 a. m.

The next morning, Saturday, April 7, we met again in my office. This meeting was short. General Marshall stated that he had read the messages and that he had now concluded that MacArthur should have been fired two years ago. I asked General Bradley to make a final recommendation to me of the Joint Chiefs of Staff on Monday.

On Sunday, the eighth of April, I sent for Acheson to come to Blair House, and I discussed the situation further with him. I informed him that I had already that morning consulted with Snyder. I then told Acheson that I would be prepared to act on Monday when General Bradley made his report on the recommendations of the Joint Chiefs of Staff.

At nine o'clock Monday morning I again met with Marshall, Bradley, Acheson, and Harriman. General Bradley reported that the Joint Chiefs of Staff had met with him on Sunday, and it was his and their unanimous judgment that General MacArthur should be relieved.

General Marshall reaffirmed that this was also his conclusion. Harriman restated his opinion of Friday. Acheson said he agreed entirely to the removal of MacArthur.

*　　　　　*　　　　　*

TRUCE ARRANGEMENTS

A. Special United Nations Report on Korea*

[Extract]

October 18, 1952

FOREWORD

The Unified Command transmits herewith a special report on the present status of the military action and the armistice negotiations in Korea, for the information of the General Assembly in connection with its discussion of the problem of Korea.

The Security Council resolution of July 7, 1950 established a Unified Command under the United States and entrusted to it the responsibility for the conduct of the military operations in Korea necessitated by the aggression of the North Korean Forces on June 25, 1950. The military action of the United Nations is now in its twenty-eighth month. For fifteen months the United Nations Command has conducted armistice negotiations with representatives of the armed forces of the Chinese Communist and North Korean regimes with a view to bringing the fighting in Korea to an end on a basis consistent with United Nations objectives and principles. In this period a tentative draft armistice agreement has been worked out by both sides, covering all agreed points. The text of this draft agreement forms an appendix to this report. (See Annex A) [not printed].

The differences between the United Nations Command and the Communists which have prevented the conclusion of an armistice were narrowed by the end of April 1952, to one question: whether all prisoners of war should be returned, by force if necessary. Final conclusion of an armistice under the terms of the present draft agreement now depends upon Communist acceptance of a solution to the prisoner of war question consistent with humanitarian principles.

The question of prisoner of war repatriation has been under discussion for more than eight months. The issue arose because the United Nations Command learned, at an early stage of the hostilities, that many prisoners of war were violently opposed to being returned to the Communists. The United Nations Command is willing to return all prisoners excepting those who would violently resist repatriation. The Communists, however, have insisted on the return of all prisoners by force if necessary.

An issue of principle has thus been posed on which the Unified Command cannot yield without disregard for the fundamental principles of human rights and individual freedom embodied in the Charter.

The United Nations Command has negotiated in good faith and has made every effort to achieve an armistice. It has indicated a willingness to consider any reasonable proposal for solution of the prisoner-of-war question consistent

*United Nations Document A/2228, Oct. 18, 1952.

with the principle that prisoners-of-war shall not be returned by force. The United Nations Command has offered numerous proposals for settling the question, but all these proposals have been categorically rejected by the Communists. Not a single constructive proposal has been put forward by the Communists. For months the Communists have not in fact been negotiating but have merely exploited the negotiation sessions for propaganda purposes.

As recently as September 28, the United Nations Command made three new proposals. On October 8, the Communists flatly rejected these suggestions and again insisted on the forced repatriation of prisoners. The United Nations Command Delegation, therefore, called a recess. The duration of the recess is entirely up to the Communists, the negotiations are not terminated. Meetings will resume as soon as the Communists are ready to negotiate in good faith. The United Nations Delegation is prepared to meet with the Communists whenever they come forward with a constructive proposal, or accept any one of the numerous outstanding United Nations Command proposals. The United Nations Command will leave no stone unturned, no promising avenue unexplored, in its effort to conclude an armistice on honorable terms consistent with United Nations objectives in Korea.

*   *   *

Armistice Negotiations

Background

From the outset of the Korean hostilities, the United Nations Command has at all times demonstrated its willingness to end the fighting in Korea on an honorable basis. It has taken steps to this end on its own initiative and in response to proposals of others. The United Nations Command has insisted, of course, that the cessation of hostilities must be on a basis consistent with the United Nations objective of repelling aggression and restoring peace and security in Korea. As early as July, 1950, the United States Government directed its Ambassador to the Soviet Union, Mr. Kirk, to ask the Soviet Government to "use its influence with the North Korean authorities to withdraw their invading forces immediately." In addition, the United Nations Command has on several occasions directed appeals to the Communists to halt the fighting. Fullest cooperation was given to United Nations and other diplomatic efforts to halt the fighting and negotiate a settlement, such as the proposals made by the Cease-Fire Group and the Good Offices Committee established by the General Assembly.

On June 23, 1951, Jacob Malik, Soviet representative on the Security Council, suggested in a radio address: "The Soviet peoples . . . believe that the most acute problem of the present day, the problem of the armed conflict in Korea could also be settled . . . . The Soviet peoples believe that as a first step discussions should be started between the belligerents for a cease-fire and an armistice . . . ." The United States Government, always prepared to follow up any proposals that might lead to an end to the fighting, immediately sought clarification of certain aspects of Mr. Malik's statement. The United States Ambassador in Moscow called on Soviet Deputy Foreign Minister Gromyko who explained that in his view an armistice would:

1. include a cease-fire;
2. be limited to strictly military questions without involving any political or territorial matters.

The United Nations Command thereupon undertook to establish direct contact with the Communist Command and arrangements were made for the initiation of armistice negotiations.

The United Nations Command entered into the armistice negotiations hopeful of quickly concluding an agreement which would stop the fighting. The United Nations Command was determined, however, that the armistice agreement must assure the achievement of the basic purposes of the United Nations military action in Korea—to repel the aggression against the Republic of Korea and restore peace and security in the area. From the basic purpose of the United Nations action in Korea flowed the principal United Nations requirements for an armistice agreement:

1. a line of demarcation consistent with the United Nations objective of repelling aggression, based upon military realities, and affording defensible positions for the opposing forces;
2. other provisions offering maximum reasonable assurance against a renewal of the aggression;
3. appropriate arrangements for an exchange of prisoners of war;
4. avoidance of political issues as not properly related to armistice negotiations.

The United Nations Command negotiators have steadfastly refused to compromise the basic requirements within this framework, and the United Nations Command has at the same time maintained the broadest flexibility in seeking agreement.

*   *   *

The Military Demarcation Line

The initial substantive agreement reached between the United Nations Command and Communist negotiators was the fixing of a military demarcation line between both sides so as to establish a demilitarized zone. At the outset of negotiations on the demarcation line, the Communists proposed the 38th parallel while the United Nations Command suggested a line directly related to the actual line of contact between the forces of both sides and a demilitarized zone 20 miles wide. The objective of the United Nations Command proposals was to provide maximum defensive safeguards against a possible renewal of aggression. The United Nations Command contended that since an armistice involved military, rather than political, decisions the demarcation line should be based on military requirements. Specifically, a line related to the line of contact and taking advantage of terrain features was considered essential to provide relatively defensible positions. The line of contact was furthermore considered by the United

Nations Command as consistent with the United Nations objective of repelling the aggression.

After extended negotiations and following the resumption of meetings in the new conference site of Panmunjom, the Communists accepted in principle the United Nations position that the demarcation line should be based on the line of contact. On November 27, final agreement was reached whereby the existing lines of contact between the two sides should be the demarcation line if an armistice agreement were signed within thirty days; otherwise it should be the line of contact as of the signing of the armistice. The agreement also specified that upon the coming into effect of the armistice both sides were to withdraw two kilometers from this line, creating a four-kilometer demilitarized zone between the military forces so as to minimize the possibility of incidents which could lead to a resumption of hostilities.

*   *   *

The area of agreement reached by March 1952 may thus be summarized as follows:

1. There will be a cease-fire within twelve hours of the signing of an armistice.

2. Both sides will withdraw their forces from the demilitarized zone within seventy-two hours after the signing of an armistice.

3. All military forces will be withdrawn from rear areas and the coastal islands and waters of Korea within five days after the signing of an armistice.

4. Both sides shall cease the introduction into Korea of reinforcing military personnel. However, the rotation of 35,000 military personnel a month shall be permitted. Rotated personnel shall enter Korea only through designated ports of entry, under the supervision and inspection of the teams of the Neutral Nations Supervisory Commission.

5. Both sides shall cease the introduction into Korea of reinforcing combat aircraft, armored vehicles, weapons and ammunition. However, the replacement of destroyed, damaged, worn out or used up equipment on the basis of piece-for-piece of the same effectiveness and the same type is permitted. Such replacement shall take place only through designated ports of entry, under the supervision and inspection of teams of the Neutral Nations Supervisory Commission.

6. A military Armistice Commission, with headquarters at Panmunjom composed of military officers of the United Nations Command and the Communist Forces and aided by joint observer teams will:

    (a) supervise the implementation of the armistice agreement;
    (b) deal with alleged armistice violations and settle through negotiations any such violations;
    (c) report all violations of the armistice agreement to the Commanders of the opposing sides;

7. A Neutral Nations Supervisory Commission, with headquarters in proximity to those of the Military Armistice Commission, composed of four senior officers, two of whom shall be appointed by neutral nations nominated by the

United Nations Command and two of whom shall be appointed by neutral nations nominated jointly by the Supreme Commander of the Korean People's Army and the Commander of the Chinese People's Volunteers will supervise, observe, inspect, and investigate adherence to the terms of the armistice agreement relative to the introduction into Korea of reinforcing military personnel and equipment. At the request of the Military Armistice Commission or senior member of either side, it can conduct special observation and inspection at places outside the demilitarized zone where violations have been reported. Twenty inspection teams, ten of which will be located at the designated ports of entry, five in North Korea and five in South Korea, with ten mobile teams in reserve, will assist the Commission.

Prisoners of War

Background
The prisoner of war issue, from the very beginning of the Korean hostilities has been a major problem for the United Nations Command. There has been a notable difference between the United Nations Command and Communist treatment of prisoners. The United Nations Command has from the beginning of the Korean war scrupulously lived up to the principles of the Geneva Convention relative to the humane treatment of prisoners of war. It sent lists of captured personnel to the International Committee of the Red Cross (ICRC) which in turn transmitted them to the Communists. It admitted the ICRC to its prisoner-of-war camps and gave them every facility for inspection and reporting on the treatment of prisoners of war. The humane treatment of the prisoners was especially noteworthy in view of the provocative actions of some Communist prisoners, and their repeated efforts to foment disorders. The reports of the ICRC on the conditions in United Nations Command camps have been almost uniformly favorable. In those few instances where the ICRC had criticism to offer, the United Nations Command was prompt to correct the situation.

On the other hand, the Communists, while stating they are abiding by the Convention, have failed to live up to it in virtually every important respect. They have never informed the ICRC of captured personnel, except for a token list of 110 names transmitted to the ICRC in the early days of hostilities. The Communists failed to appoint a protecting power or a benevolent organization such as the ICRC and rejected the efforts of the ICRC to obtain entry into the Communist prisoner-of-war camps; they refused to exchange relief packages and even, until recently on a very limited basis, mail; they have not reported on the health of prisoners of war and have refused to exchange seriously sick and wounded; they have failed to give the accurate location of their prisoner-of-war camps and to mark them properly; and they have situated their camps in positions of danger in proximity to legitimate military targets.

Exchange of Prisoners Lists
When the prisoner of war question was first considered, the United Nations Command still had not received any lists of the United Nations and Republic

of Korea prisoners in Communist custody, while the Communists had received lists totalling approximately 170,000 names through the ICRC. Subsequently, it was found that during the period of large scale North Korean surrenders and of mass movements of refugees from the North that some 37,500 persons had erroneously been included on these lists as prisoners of war. These persons were reclassified as civilian internees and later released to their homes in the Republic of Korea. The ICRC was informed of this action. When the Communists finally agreed to exchange lists at Panmunjom the United Nations Command gave the Communists a list containing approximately 132,000 names. At a later date, upon further investigation an additional 11,000 persons were also reclassified as civilian internees and are in process of release. Consequently, the United Nations Command has currently in its custody about 121,000 persons.

The list provided by the Communists contained only some 11,500 United Nations Command and Republic of Korea prisoners, although the Communists had themselves indicated earlier in Pyongyang radio broadcasts on February 9 and April 8, 1951, that they had captured 65,000 persons in just the first nine months of the hostilities. The Communists stated at Panmunjom that large numbers of the captured persons had been "reeducated" and released at the front where many of them joined North Korean forces and that the process was so rapid they had no opportunity to obtain their names.

Extent of Agreement on Prisoner of War Exchange

In subsequent discussions, agreement was reached on a number of points relating to the exchange of prisoners. The two delegations agreed that:

1. Prisoners of war, when released from custody, will not again be employed in acts of war in the Korean conflict.

2. Sick and injured prisoners will be repatriated first.

3. The exchange of prisoners of war will be completed within two months.

4. A committee of Communist and United Nations Command officers will supervise the exchange of prisoners of war.

5. This committee will be assisted by joint Red Cross teams composed of representatives of United Nations Red Cross societies and Communist Red Cross societies.

6. Korean civilians will be permitted to return to their homes on either side of the demarcation line.

7. Foreign civilians will be permitted to return to their homes.

United Nations Command Efforts to Settle Prisoner of War Question

As increasing numbers of enemy personnel deserted to or were otherwise captured by the United Nations Command, it became evident that a substantial number of the prisoners of war felt that they would suffer death or injury if returned to the Communists. Many prisoners of war, it became clear, would violently resist such return. Therefore, decent respect for the rights of these individuals and the recognized humanitarian principles to which the United Nations is dedicated rendered it unthinkable that United Nations Command forces under the United Nations banner should compel these resisting prisoners of war to return to the other side. Many other governments particularly those with troops in Korea, indicated that they shared this view. The magnitude of the problem, however, was not fully appreciated by the United Nations Command. It was not until the attitudes of the prisoners of war were examined in April 1952 that it was recognized how many prisoners of war would resist repatriation.

*   *   *

The United Nations Command screened in early April only those prisoners of war consenting to be interviewed, some 106,000, and to its surprise found that only about 70,000 wanted repatriation. No attempt was made to screen the prisoners of war in Communist-dominated camps which refused to cooperate. However, since the Communists pressed for an early reply on a round number, the United Nations Command obtained the 70,000 figure by including all prisoners of war who in interviews indicated that they would not resist repatriation, and an estimate covering the prisoners of war who were not screened; in making the latter estimate the United Nations Command assumed that in the camps refusing to be interviewed most prisoners of war would desire repatriation. (It may be noted that out of the camps which were Communist controlled and refused to cooperate in screening, more than a thousand individuals sought at the earliest opportunity and at the risk of their lives to escape from the camps and proclaim their resistance to being returned to the Communists. A considerable number of such individuals were murdered by their Communist fellow prisoners in attempting such escapes.)

Subsequently, the United Nations Command completed the interviewing of those who were not previously screened. The results indicated that a total of approximately 83,000 (76,600 Koreans and 6,400 Chinese) could be repatriated without the use of force.

When the Communists were informed of the results of the first screening and realized the large numbers of prisoners resisting repatriation, they insisted upon the full repatriation of all prisoners of war and at the same time sought to discredit the screening undertaken by the United Nations Command. It was thus during and after the April screening of the prisoners of war that a series of incidents occurred in the prisoner of war camps, particularly on Koje island. On investigation it was found that these incidents were deliberately provoked by Communist prisoners at the instigation of the Communist Command in order to intimidate the prisoners who did not desire repatriation and in order to obscure the results of the screening. Subsequently, following these incidents the compounds on Koje were reorganized and brought under control.

In support of their position, the Communists cited the Geneva Convention. The Communists cited in particular Article 118 which provides: "Prisoners of war shall be released and repatriated without delay after cessation of hostilities." The United Nations Command, however, has pointed out to the Communists that forcible repatriation was inconsistent with the humanitarian basis and thus the spirit of the Geneva Convention. Furthermore, Article 6 provides: ". . . the High Contracting Parties may conclude other special agreements for all matters concerning which they may deem it suitable to make separate provision. No special agreement shall adversely affect the situation of prisoners of war, as defined by the present Convention, nor restrict the rights which it confers upon them. . . ." The United Nations Command pointed out to the Communists that a special agreement on non-forcible repatriation protected the rights of the individual prisoner to elect not to be repatriated to his home and was consistent with the Convention.

Following the Communist refusal to agree to an exchange of prisoners on the basis of the 70,000 estimate, the United Nations Command, on April 28, offered a package proposal. The proposal covered the differences on the arrangements for supervising the armistice, namely rehabilitation and construction of military airfields and the composition of the Neutral Nations Supervisory Commission, and the question of repatriation of prisoners of war. The United Nations Command proposed that:

> 1. There shall not be forced repatriation of prisoners of war.
> 2. The United Nations Command will not insist on prohibiting reconstruction and rehabilitation of airfields.
> 3. The United Nations Command agrees to accept Poland and Czechoslovakia as members of the Neutral Nations Supervisory Commission if the Communists agree to accept Sweden and Switzerland (thus withdrawing their demand for the inclusion of the Soviet Union).

In making the above proposal the United Nations Command made it clear that the proposal must be accepted in whole. Accordingly, Communist acceptance of only the second and third points of the proposal in fact constituted a rejection of the proposal. However, this proposal remains open.

During the five months of fruitless negotiation on the prisoner repatriation issue following Communist rejection of the package proposal, the United Nations Command has indicated to the Communist negotiators, that, while it is firm on the issue of non-forcible repatriation, it is prepared to consider any reasonable suggestion for resolving the deadlock.

The United Nations Command negotiators have also assured the Communists of their willingness to consider any reasonable means for an impartial verification of the wishes of the prisoners of war or for implementing the actual exchange of prisoners so as to avoid embarrassment to the Communists.

Specifically, on April 23, the United Nations Command negotiators proposed that joint Red Cross teams from both sides with, or without military observers of both sides, be admitted to the prisoner of war camps of both sides to verify the fact that non-repatriates would forcibly resist return to the side from which they came. It was also proposed that all prisoners of war of both sides be delivered in groups to the demilitarized zone and be given an opportunity to express their preference on repatriation. The verification would be carried out as one or a combination of (a) the ICRC, (b) teams from impartial nations, (c) joint teams of military observers, or (d) Red Cross representatives from each side.

On September 28, the United Nations Command delegation made its broadest proposals in another effort to meet Communist objections to the principle of non-forcible repatriation and Communist allegations that the previous screening was unfair and that the United Nations Command is forcibly restraining and coercing the non-repatriates. The United Nations Command put forward three alternative proposals:

1. Both sides would agree that as soon as the armistice agreement goes into effect all prisoners of war of each side shall be entitled to release and repatriation, both sides agreeing that the obligation to exchange and repatriate prisoners of war is fulfilled by having them brought to an agreed exchange point in the demilitarized zone where the prisoner of war will be identified and his name checked against the agreed list of prisoners of war. However, both sides would agree that any prisoner of war who at the time of his identification states that he wishes to return to the side by which he had been detained shall immediately be permitted to do so and that that side will transport him from the demilitarized zone and not detain him as a prisoner of war but permit him to regain civilian status.

2. Prisoners not resisting repatriation would be expeditiously exchanged. All prisoners of war who have indicated to the United Nations Command that they would forcibly resist repatriation will be delivered to the demilitarized zone in small groups where they will be entirely freed from the military control of either side and interviewed by representatives of mutually agreed country or countries not participating in the Korean hostilities and free to go to the side of their choice as indicated by those interviews.

3. Prisoners not resisting repatriation would be expeditiously exchanged. Prisoners of war who have indicated to the United Nations Command that they will forcibly resist repatriation will be delivered in groups to the demilitarized zone and there entirely freed from the military control of either side and without questioning, interviewing or screening of any kind to be released and free to go to the side of their choice.

The United Nations Command delegation also made it clear that the procedures contained in the three proposals could be carried out in the presence of or under the observation of one or a combination of (a) the ICRC, (b) joint Red Cross teams, or (c) joint teams of military observers of both sides.

These proposals were rejected by the Communists. At that time, the United Nations Command called a recess in the negotiations. No constructive proposals have been forthcoming from the Communists either since this rejection or in the more than six months prior to it. The months of meetings have been used for purely propaganda purposes by the Communists.

The United Nations Command does not desire to break off negotiations and is not doing so; it has merely called a recess. The United Nations Command desires to continue to negotiate in good faith. The numerous proposals it has made remain open. When the Communist delegation is ready to accept any one of the proposals or to make a constructive proposal of its own which could lead to an honorable armistice, the United Nations Command delegation is prepared to meet with it again at Panmunjom and make all possible progress towards an armistice. The United Nations Command liaison officers remain available for consultation and for the performance of their customary duties. That is the present situation in the armistice negotiations in Korea. It remains the sincere hope of the United Nations Command that an honorable armistice can be realized.

CORRESPONDENCE BETWEEN PRESIDENT EISENHOWER AND PRESIDENT RHEE ON THE KOREAN ARMISTICE

B. President Eisenhower to President Rhee*

June 6, 1953

Dear Mr. President:

I received on June 2 the cabled text of your communication dated May 30. I have given it the careful and sympathetic consideration it deserves.

The Republic of Korea has engaged all of its resources, human and material, in a struggle which will go down in history as one of the epic struggles of all time. You have dedicated your all without reservation to the principle that human liberty and national liberty must survive against Communist aggression, which tramples upon human dignity and which replaces national sovereignty with a humiliating satellite status. The principles for which your nation has fought and for which so many of your youth have died are principles which defend free men and free nations everywhere.

The United States has stood with you, and with you we have fought for those principles, as part of the United Nations Command. The blood of your youth and our youth has been poured out on the altar of common sacrifice. Thereby we have demonstrated not only our dedication to the cause of human freedom and political liberty, but also our dedication to an equally important principle which is that there cannot be independence without interdependence, and there cannot be human liberty except as men recognize that they are bound together by ties of common destiny.

The moment has now come when we must decide whether to carry on by warfare a struggle for the unification of Korea or whether to pursue this goal by political and other methods.

The enemy has proposed an armistice which involves a clear abandonment of the fruits of aggression. The armistice would leave the Republic of Korea in undisputed possession of substantially the territory which the Republic administered prior to the aggression, indeed this territory will be somewhat enlarged.

The proposed armistice, true to the principle of political asylum, assured that the thousands of North Koreans and Communist Chinese prisoners in our hand, who have seen liberty and who wish to share it, will have the opportunity to do so and will not be forcibly sent back into Communist areas. The principle of political asylum is one which we could not honorably surrender even though we thereby put an earlier end to our own human and material losses. We have suffered together many thousands of casualties in support of this principle.

It is my profound conviction that under these circumstances acceptance of the armistice is required of the United Nations and the Republic of Korea. We would not be justified in prolonging the war with all the misery it involves in the hope of achieving, by force, the unification of Korea.

The unification of Korea is an end to which the United States is committed, not once but many times, through its World War II declarations and through

*Department of State Bulletin, June 15, 1953, pp. 835-36.

its acceptance of the principles enunciated in reference to Korea by the United Nations. Korea is unhappily not the only country which remains divided after World War II. We remain determined to play our part in achieving the political union of all countries divided. But we do not intend to employ war as an instrument to accomplish the worldwide political settlements to which we are dedicated and which we believe to be just. It was indeed a crime that those who attacked from the north invoked violence to unite Korea under their rule. Not only as your official friend but as a personal friend I urge that your country not embark upon a similar course.

There are three major points I would like to make to you:

1. The United States will not renounce its efforts by all peaceful means to effect the unification of Korea. Also as a member of the United Nations we shall seek to assure that the United Nations continues steadfast in its determination in this respect. In the political conference which will follow an armistice that will be our central objective. The United States intends to consult with your Government both before and during such a conference and expects the full participation of your Government in that conference.

2. You speak of a mutual defense pact. I am prepared promptly after the conclusion and acceptance of an armistice to negotiate with you a mutual defense treaty along the lines of the treaties heretofore made between the United States and the Republic of the Philippines, and the United States and Australia and New Zealand. You may recall that both of these treaties speak of "the development of a more comprehensive system of regional security in the Pacific area." A security pact between the United States and the Republic of Korea would be a further step in that direction. It would cover the territory now or hereafter brought peacefully under the administration of the ROK. Of course you realize that under our constitutional system any such treaty would be made only with the advice and consent of the Senate. However, the action which the United States has heretofore taken, and the great investment of blood and treasure which has already been made for the independence of Korea are certainly clear indications of American temper and intentions not to tolerate a repetition of unprovoked aggression.

3. The United States Government, subject to requisite Congressional appropriations, will be prepared to continue economic aid to the Republic of Korea which will permit in peace a restoration of its devastated land. Homes must be rebuilt. Industries must be re-established. Agriculture must be made vigorously productive.

The preamble of the Constitution of the United States states the goals of our people, which I believe are equally the goals of the brave people of Korea, namely, "to form a more perfect union, establish justice, insure domestic tranquillity, provide for the common defense, promote the general welfare, and secure the blessings of liberty." Manifestly, not all of these conditions now prevail in Korea. Moreover, in existing circumstances they cannot be achieved either by prolongation of the present conflict or by reckless adventure with a new one. Only by peaceful means can these things be achieved.

With the conclusion of an armistice the United States is prepared to join with the Republic of Korea to seek for Korea these ends. We believe that in Korea there should be a more perfect union and, as I say, we shall seek to achieve that union by all peaceful methods. We believe that there should be domestic tranquillity and that can come from the end of fighting. There should be provision for the defense of Korea. That will come from the mutual security treaty which we are prepared to make. The general welfare should be advanced and that will come from your own peacetime efforts and from economic assistance to your war-torn land. Finally, a peaceful settlement will afford the best opportunity to bring to your people the blessings of liberty.

I assure you, Mr. President, that so far as the United States is concerned, it is our desire to go forward in fellowship with the Republic of Korea. Even the thought of a separation at this critical hour would be a tragedy. We must remain united.

C. President Rhee to President Eisenhower*

June 19, 1953

Dear Mr. President:

First of all, I must apologize for my long delay in answering your good letter of June 6, 1953.

To confess the truth, I made more than one draft, but I could not express myself clearly without appearing to be argumentative, which I wanted to avoid. I do hope you will read this letter in the same friendly spirit in which it is written.

From the beginning, we repeatedly tried to make clear to all friendly nations that if an armistice permitting the Chinese aggressors to remain in Korea should be concluded we could not survive. This apprehensiveness has not abated.

Evidently our friendly nations seem to take it for granted that the withdrawal of the Chinese Communists from Korea and the subsequent unification of Korea can be accomplished by the political conference scheduled to follow the armistice. I do not wish to enter detailed argument over this point but I feel I must say, at least, that we do not believe in the possibility.

It is true that is a matter of opinion. Our opinion is, however, supported by facts which we can never ignore or forget. The experiences we have gone through ourselves will remain a guiding factor in forming our judgments until something happens which convincingly counterattacks them.

Now that the United Nations is to conclude a cease-fire agreement with the Communist aggressors regardless of what may happen to Korea, in practical terms we are constantly haunted by the question of how we can survive as a nation at all. The following passages will, I hope, give you some idea of our reactions to the situation.

We desire to remain friendly to the United States to the last, remembering what it has done for us, both militarily and economically, in our struggle against aggression.

If the United States forces have to stand by, for some reason, ceasing to participate in any further struggle or to withdraw from Korea altogether as

Ibid., July 6, 1953, pp. 13-14.

an aftermath of the impending armistice, we have nothing to say against it.

Whenever they find it necessary or desirable to leave Korea they can do so with a friendly feeling toward us, just as we are trying to remain their friends. So long as either party does not interfere with the plans of the other, both can maintain the cordial relations between them.

In the first year of this three-year-old war, both the United States and the United Nations alternately and repeatedly announced, as the war objectives, the establishment of a united, independent and democratic Korea and the punishment of the aggressors. It was at the time of the United Nations drive to the Yalu that they made these announcements so that we naturally took them as their declared war objectives. But later, when the Communist forces proved to be stronger than expected, the United Nations statesmen took to the interpretation that it had never been intended to unify Korea by war. That was an open confession of weakness; very few people took it at its face value. Nowadays we hear no more about the unification of Korea or the punishment of the Communist aggressors, as if either we had achieved these objectives or abandoned them.

All we hear about is an armistice. There is grave doubt that an armistice reached in such an atmosphere of appeasement can lead to a permanent peace acceptable and honorable to us. Personally, I do not believe that the Communists will agree, at a conference table, to what they have never been made to agree to on the battlefield.

Your generous offers of economic aid and an increase of the R.O.K. defense forces are highly appreciated by all Korean people, for they are what we badly need. But when such offers come as a price for our acceptance of the armistice as we know it, they cannot but have little inducement, because, as I have said before, to accept such an armistice is to accept a death warrant.

Nothing would be of much avail to Korea, to say the least, after that fatal blow should have been dealt it.

We do not question the sincerity with which you kindly promised to use your authority to bring about a mutual defense pact between our two nations, after the conclusion of the armistice. As a matter of fact, a mutual defense pact is what we have constantly sought, and we are behind it heart and soul; but if it is tied up with the armistice its efficacy would be diminished almost to a vanishing point.

Mr. President, you will easily imagine what a hard situation we confront. We committed everything, including our arms and forces to the United Nations action in Korea, incurring frightful losses in manpower as well as material destruction, in the sole belief that we and our friends had the self-same objectives of unifying sundered Korea and punishing the Communist aggressors. Now the United Nations seems to stop short of its original aims and to come to terms with the aggressors which we cannot accept, not because we have never been consulted but because those terms would mean sure death for the Korean nation. Moreover, the United Nations is now putting pressure on us in cooperating with it, and is joining hands, it seems, with the enemy in this matter of armistice terms.

We cannot avoid seeing the cold fact that the counsels of appeasers have prevailed in altering the armistice position of the United States. In our view, this perilous trend, if perpetuated by the conclusion of this fatal armistice, will eventually endanger the remainder of the free world, including the United States, which millions of both free and enslaved hope and pray from the bottom of their hearts will lead them in liberation of the peoples in chains behind the Iron Curtain.

At this very moment, the Communist forces are launching a large-scale offensive when the armistice talks have scarcely left anything except the affixing of signatures by the parties concerned. This should be a warning for our immediate future. The terms of the armistice being what they are, the Communist build-up will go on unhampered until it is capable of overwhelming South Korea with one swoop at a moment of the Communists' own choosing. What is to follow for the rest of the Far East? And the rest of Asia? And the rest of the free world?

Still looking to your wise leadership for a remedy in this perilous hour.

D. Summary of the Major Provisions of the Korean Armistice*

Signed, July 27, 1953

The Military Demarcation Line

The Communists delayed negotiations for some time by insisting that the demarcation line between both sides should be the 38th parallel. Finally, however, they recognized the merit of the United Nations Command position that the line should be determined strictly on military grounds and should correspond to the actual line of contact between the opposing forces. The objective of the United Nations Command in insisting on such a line was to provide maximum defensive safeguards against possible renewal of the aggression.

The line of demarcation was first marked out on 27 November 1951, on the basis of the line of contact as of that time. It was then agreed that this should be the final demarcation line, provided an armistice was achieved within thirty days; otherwise the line should be redrawn on the basis of the line of contact at the time of the armistice. In fact, tentative agreement was reached on a new line in June 1953, when it seemed that an armistice could be signed within a very few days, but the Communists insisted that it be redrawn again to take account of the results of the offensive they launched on 13-14 July 1953. The Demarcation Line was finally agreed on the basis indicated in the map attached to the Armistice Agreement.

The Demilitarized Zone was established in accordance with the agreement, each side withdrawing its forces two kilometers north and south of the Demarcation Line respectively.

Documents on American Foreign Relations, 1953, pp. 289-97.

Arrangements for Implementing the Armistice

With the exception of the continuing disagreement on the rehabilitation of airfields, the arrangements for implementing the armistice were virtually completed by March 1952. The United Nations Command finally gave up its insistence on the limitation of articles when it signed the armistice. The agreements on this subject may be summarized as follows:

1. There will be a cease-fire within twelve hours of the signing of an armistice.

2. Both sides will withdraw forces from the Demilitarized Zone within seventy-two hours after the signature of an armistice.

3. All military forces will be withdrawn from rear areas and the coastal islands and waters of Korea within five days after the signing of an armistice.

4. Both sides shall cease the introduction into Korea of reinforcing military personnel. However, the rotation of 35,000 military personnel a month shall be permitted. Rotated personnel shall enter Korea only through designated ports of entry, under the supervision and inspection of the teams of the Neutral Nations Supervisory Commission.

5. Both sides shall cease the introduction into Korea of reinforcing combat aircraft, armoured vehicles, weapons and ammunition. However, the replacement of destroyed, damaged, worn-out or used up equipment on the basis of piece-for-piece of the same effectiveness and the same type is permitted. Such replacement shall take place through designated ports of entry, under the supervision and inspection of teams of the Neutral Nations Supervisory Commission.

6. A Military Armistice Commission, with headquarters at Panmunjom, composed of military officers of the United Nations Command and the Communist forces and aided by Joint Observer Teams, will:

    (a) Supervise the implementation of the Armistice Agreement;
    (b) Deal with alleged armistice violations and settle through negotiations any such violations;
    (c) Report all violations of the Armistice Agreement to the Commanders of the opposing sides.

7. A Neutral Nations Supervisory Commission, with headquarters in proximity to those of the Military Armistice Commission, composed of four senior officers, two of whom shall be appointed by neutral nations nominated by the United Nations Command and two of whom shall be appointed by neutral nations nominated jointly by the Supreme Commander of the Korean People's Army and the Commander of the Chinese People's Volunteers will supervise, observe, inspect, and investigate adherence to the terms of the armistice agreement relative to the introduction into Korea of reinforcing military personnel and equipment. At the request of the Military Armistice Commission or senior member of either side, it can conduct special observation and inspection at places outside the demilitarized zone where violations have been reported. Twenty inspection teams, ten of which will be located at the designated ports of entry, five in North Korea and five in South Korea, with ten mobile teams in reserve, will assist the Commission.

The Political Conference Following an Armistice

In order to counter the constant efforts of the Communists to inject political questions into the Korean armistice negotiations, and to prevent such extraneous issues from delaying armistice negotiations, the United Nations Command agreed to dispose of political questions by recommending their consideration at a political conference following an armistice. The United Nations Command Delegation accepted a revised Communist proposal now contained in article 60 of the Armistice agreement, which provides:

"In order to insure the peaceful settlement of the Korean question, the military Commanders of both sides hereby recommend to the governments of the countries concerned on both sides that, within three (3) months after the Armistice Agreement is signed and becomes effective, a political conference of a higher level of both sides be held by representatives appointed respectively to settle through negotiation the questions of the withdrawal of all foreign forces from Korea, the peaceful settlement of the Korean question, etc."

Excerpts from Article III ("Arrangements Relating to Prisoners of War") of the Armistice Agreement

51. The release and repatriation of all prisoners of war held in the custody of each side at the time this armistice agreement becomes effective shall be effected in conformity with the following provisions agreed upon by both sides prior to the signing of this armistice agreement.

(a) Within sixty (60) days after this armistice agreement becomes effective each side shall, without offering any hindrance, directly repatriate and hand over in groups all those prisoners of war in its custody who insist on repatriation to the side to which they belonged at the time of capture . . . .

(b) Each side shall release all those remaining prisoners of war, who are not directly repatriated, from its military control and from its custody and hand them over to the Neutral Nations Repatriation Commission for disposition in accordance with the provisions in the annex hereto: "Terms of Reference for Neutral Nations Repatriation Commission."

*   *   *

55. Panmunjom is designated as the place where prisoners of war will be delivered and received by both sides . . . .

*   *   *

58. (a) The Commander of each side shall furnish to the Commander of the other side as soon as practicable, but not later than ten (10) days after this Armistice Agreement becomes effective, the following information concerning prisoners of war:

(1) Complete data pertaining to the prisoners of war who escaped since the effective date of the data last exchanged.

2. Insofar as practicable, information regarding . . . those prisoners of war who died while in his custody.

(b) If any prisoners of war escape or die after the effective date of the supplementary information specified above, the detaining side shall furnish to the other sides. . . the data pertaining thereto in accordance with the provisions of subparagraph 58(a) hereof. Such data shall be furnished at 10-day intervals until the completion of the program of delivery and reception of prisoners of war.

(c) Any escaped prisoner of war who returns to the custody of the detaining side after the completion of the program of delivery and reception of prisoners of war shall be delivered to the Military Armistice Commission for disposition.

59. (a) All civilians who, at the time this armistice agreement becomes effective, are in territory under the military control of the Commander in Chief, United Nations Command, and who, on 24 June 1950, resided north of the military demarcation line established in this armistice agreement shall, if they desire to return home, be permitted and assisted by the Commander in Chief, United Nations Command, to return to the area north of the military demarcation line; and (similar provisions covering South Koreans north of the armistice line). The commander of each side shall be responsible for publicizing widely throughout territory under his military control the contents of the provisions of this subparagraph, and for calling upon the appropriate civil authorities to give necessary guidance and assistance to all such civilians who desire to return home.

(b) (Similar provisions are made for civilians of foreign nationality.)

*   *   *

Excerpts from the Agreement on Prisoners of War, Signed at Panmunjom on June 8, 1953, and Annexed to the Armistice Agreement, under the Title "Terms of Reference for Neutral Nations Repatriation Commission"

I. General

1. In order to ensure that all prisoners of war have the opportunity to exercise their right to be repatriated following an armistice, Sweden, Switzerland, Poland, Czechoslovakia and India shall each be requested by both sides to appoint a member to a Neutral Nations Repatriation Commission which shall be established to take custody in Korea of those prisoners of war who, while in the custody of the detaining powers, have not exercised their right to be repatriated . . . . Representatives of both sides shall be permitted to observe the operations of the Repatriation Commission and its subordinate bodies, to include explanations and interviews.

2. Sufficient armed forces and any other operating personnel required to assist the Neutral Nations Repatriation Commission in carrying out its functions and responsibilities shall be provided exclusively by India, whose representative shall be the umpire in accordance with the provisions of Article 132 of the Geneva

Convention, and shall also be chairman and executive agent of the Neutral Nations Repatriation Commission . . . .

3. No force or threat of force shall be used against the prisoners of war specified in paragraph 1 above to prevent or effect their repatriation, and no violence to their persons or affront to their dignity or self-respect shall be permitted in any manner for any purpose whatsoever (but see paragraph 7 below). This duty is enjoined on and entrusted to the Neutral Nations Repatriation Commission. This Commission shall ensure that prisoners of war shall at all times be treated humanely in accordance with the specific provisions of the Geneva Convention, and with the general spirit of that convention.

II. Custody of Prisoners of War

4. All prisoners of war who have not exercised their right of repatriation following the effective date of the armistice agreement shall be released from the military control and from the custody of the detaining side as soon as practicable and, in all cases, within sixty (60) days subsequent to the effective date of the armistice agreement, to the Neutral Nations Repatriation Commission at locations in Korea to be designated by the detaining side.

5. At the time the Neutral Nations Repatriation Commission assumes control of the prisoner of war installations, the military forces of the detaining side shall be withdrawn therefrom, so that the locations specified in the preceding paragraph shall be taken over completely by the armed forces of India.

6. Notwithstanding the provisions of paragraph 5 above, the detaining side shall have the responsibility for maintaining and ensuring security and order in the areas around the locations where the prisoners of war are in custody and for preventing and restraining any armed forces (including irregular armed forces) in the area under its control from any acts of disturbance and intrusion against the locations where the prisoners of war are in custody.

7. Notwithstanding the provisions of paragraph 3 above, nothing in this agreement shall be construed as derogating from the authority of the Neutral Nations Repatriation Commission to exercise its legitimate functions and responsibilities for the control of the prisoners of war under its temporary jurisdiction.

III. Explanation

8. The Neutral Nations Repatriation Commission, after having received and taken into custody all those prisoners of war who have not exercised their right to be repatriated, shall immediately make arrangements so that within ninety (90) days after the Neutral Nations Repatriation Commission takes over the custody, the nations to which the prisoners of war belong shall have freedom and facilities to send representatives to the locations where such prisoners of war are in custody to explain to all the prisoners of war depending upon these nations their rights and to inform them of any matters relating to their return to their homelands, particularly of their full freedom to return home to lead a peaceful life, under the following provisions:

A. The number of such explaining representatives shall not exceed seven (7) per thousand prisoners of war held in custody by the Neutral Nations Repatriation

Commission; and the minimum authorized shall not be less than a total of five (5).

B. The hours during which the explaining representatives shall have access to the prisoners shall be as determined by the Neutral Nations Repatriation Commission and generally in accord with Article 53 of the Geneva Convention relative to the treatment of prisoners of war.

C. All explanations and interviews shall be conducted in the presence of a representative of each member nation of the Neutral Nations Repatriation Commission and a representative from the detaining side.

D. Additional provisions governing the explanation work shall be prescribed by the Neutral Nations Repatriation Commission, and will be designed to employ the principles enumerated in paragraph 3 above and in this paragraph.

E. The explaining representatives, while engaging in their work, shall be allowed to bring with them necessary facilities and personnel for wireless communications....

9. Prisoners of war in its custody shall have freedom and facilities to make representations and communications to the Neutral Nations Repatriation Commission and to representatives and subordinate bodies of the Neutral Nations Repatriation Commission and to inform them of their desires on any matter concerning the prisoners of war themselves, in accordance with arrangements made for the purpose by the Neutral Nations Repatriation Commission.

IV. Disposition of Prisoners of War

10. Any prisoner of war who, while in the custody of the Neutral Nations Repatriation Commission, decides to exercise the right of repatriation, shall make an application requesting repatriation to a body consisting of a representative of each member nation of the Neutral Nations Repatriation Commission. Once such an application is made, it shall be considered immediately by the Neutral Nations Repatriation Commission or one of its subordinate bodies so as to determine immediately by majority vote the validity of such application. Once such an application is made to and validated by the Commission or one of its subordinate bodies, the prisoner of war concerned shall immediately be transferred to and accommodated in the tents set up for those who are ready to be repatriated. Thereafter, he shall, while still in the custody of the Neutral Nations Repatriation Commission, be delivered forthwith to the prisoner of war exchange point at Panmunjom for repatriation under the procedure prescribed in the armistice agreement.

11. At the expiration of ninety (90) days after the transfer of custody of the prisoners of war to the Neutral Nations Repatriation Commission, access of representatives to captured personnel, as provided for in paragraph 8 above, shall terminate, and the question of disposition of the prisoners of war who have not exercised their right to be repatriated shall be submitted to the political conference recommended to be convened in paragraph 60, draft armistice agreement, which shall endeavor to settle this question within thirty (30) days, during which period the Neutral Nations Repatriation Commission shall continue to retain custody of those prisoners of war. The Neutral Nations Repatriation Commission shall declare the relief from the prisoner of war status to civilian status of any prisoners of war who have not exercised their right to be repatriated and for whom no other disposition has been agreed to by the political conference within one hundred and twenty (120) days after the Neutral Nations Repatriation

Commission has assumed their custody. Thereafter, according to the application of each individual, those who choose to go to neutral nations shall be assisted by the Neutral Nations Repatriation Commission and the Red Cross Society of India. This operation shall be completed within thirty (30) days, and upon its completion, the Neutral Nations Repatriation Commission shall immediately cease its functions and declare its dissolution. After the dissolution of the Neutral Nations Repatriation Commission, whenever and wherever any of those above-mentioned civilians who have been relieved from the prisoner of war status desire to return to their fatherlands, the authorities of the localities where they are shall be responsible for assisting them in returning to their fatherlands.

* * *

IX. Publication

22. After the armistice agreement becomes effective, the terms of this agreement shall be made known to all prisoners of war who, while in the custody of the detaining side, have not exercised their right to be repatriated.

* * *

XI. Procedural Matters

24. The interpretation of this agreement shall rest with the Neutral Nations Repatriation Commission. The Neutral Nations Repatriation Commission, and/or any subordinate bodies to which functions are delegated or assigned by the Neutral Nations Repatriation Commission, shall operate on the basis of majority vote.

* * *

26. When this agreement has been acceded to by both sides and by the 5 powers herein, it shall become effective upon the date the armistice becomes effective.

27. Done at Panmunjom, Korea, at 1400 hours on the 8th day of June, 1953, in English, Korean, and Chinese, all texts being equally authentic.

Signed: Nam Il, General, Korean People's Army Senior Delegate, Delegation of the Korean People's Army and the Chinese People's Volunteers

Signed: William K. Harrison, Jr. Lieutenant General, United States Army, Senior Delegate, United Nations Command Delegation

E. Treaty of Mutual Defense Between the United States and South Korea*

October 1, 1953

The Parties to this Treaty, reaffirming their desire to live in peace with all peoples and all governments, and desiring to strengthen the fabric of peace in the Pacific Area, desiring to declare publicly and formally their common determination to defend themselves against external armed attack so that no potential aggressor could be under the illusion that either of them stands alone in the Pacific Area, desiring further to strengthen their efforts for collective defense for the preservation of peace and security pending the development of a more comprehensive and effective system of regional security in the Pacific Area, have agreed as follows:

Article I

The Parties undertake to settle any international disputes in which they may be involved by peaceful means in such a manner that international peace and security and justice are not endangered and to refrain in their international relations from the threat or use of force in any manner inconsistent with the purposes of the United Nations, or obligations assumed by any Party toward the United Nations.

Article II

The Parties will consult together whenever, in the opinion of either of them, the political independence or security of either of the Parties is threatened by external armed attack. Separately and jointly, by self-help and mutual aid, the Parties will maintain and develop appropriate means to deter armed attack and will take suitable measures in consultation and agreement to implement this Treaty and to further its purposes.

Article III

Each Party recognizes that an armed attack in the Pacific Area on either of the Parties in territories now under their respective administrative control, or hereafter recognized by one of the Parties as lawfully brought under the administrative control of the other, would be dangerous to its own peace and safety and declares that it would act to meet the common danger in accordance with its constitutional processes.

Ibid., pp. 312-13.

Article IV

The Republic of Korea grants, and the United States of America accepts, the right to dispose United States land, air and sea forces in and about the territory of the Republic of Korea as determined by mutual agreement.

Article V

This Treaty shall be ratified by the Republic of Korea and the United States of America in accordance with their respective constitutional processes and will come into force when instruments of ratification thereof have been exchanged by them at————————.

Article VI

This Treaty shall remain in force indefinitely. Either Party may terminate it one year after notice has been given to the other Party.

In witness whereof the undersigned plenipotentiaries have signed this Treaty.

Done in duplicate at _____ this _____ day of _____.

F. Declaration by the Sixteen Nations Participating in the United Nations Action in Korea Regarding a Korean Settlement*

June 15, 1954

Pursuant to the resolution of August 28, 1953, of the United Nations General Assembly, and the Berlin communiqué of February 18, 1954, we, as nations who contributed military forces to the United Nations Command in Korea, have been participating in the Geneva Conference for the purpose of establishing a united and independent Korea by peaceful means.

We have made a number of proposals and suggestions in accord with the past efforts of the United Nations to bring about the unification, independence, and freedom of Korea; and within the framework of the following two principles which we believe to be fundamental.

1. The United Nations, under its Charter, is fully and rightfully empowered to take collective action to repel aggression, to restore peace and security, and to extend its good offices to seeking a peaceful settlement in Korea.

2. In order to establish a unified, independent and democratic Korea, genuinely free elections should be held under UN supervision for representatives in the national assembly, in which representation shall be in direct proportion to the indigenous population in Korea.

We have earnestly and patiently searched for a basis of agreement which would enable us to proceed with Korean unification in accordance with these fundamental principles.

*Documents on American Foreign Relations, 1954, pp. 267-68.

The Communist delegations have rejected our every effort to obtain agreement. The principal issues between us, therefore, are clear. Firstly, we accept and assert the authority of the United Nations. The Communists repudiate and reject the authority and competence of the United Nations in Korea and have labelled the United Nations itself as the tool of aggression. Were we to accept this position of the Communists, it would mean the death of the principle of collective security and of the UN itself. Secondly, we desire genuinely free elections. The Communists insist upon procedures which would make genuinely free elections impossible. It is clear that the Communists will not accept impartial and effective supervision of free elections. Plainly, they have shown their intention to maintain Communist control over North Korea. They have persisted in the same attitudes which have frustrated United Nations efforts to unify Korea since 1947.

We believe, therefore, that it is better to face the fact of our disagreement than to raise false hopes and mislead the peoples of the world into believing that there is agreement where there is none.

In the circumstances, we have been compelled reluctantly and regretfully to conclude that so long as the Communist delegations reject the two fundamental principles which we consider indispensable, further consideration and examination of the Korean question by the conference would serve no useful purpose. We reaffirm our continued support for the objectives of the United Nations in Korea.

In accordance with the resolution of the General Assembly of the United Nations of August 28, 1953, the member states parties to this declaration will inform the United Nations concerning the proceedings at this conference.

Geneva, 15 June 1954

> *For Australia: R.G. Casey*
> *For Belgium: P.H. Spaak*
> *For Canada: C.A. Ronning*
> *For Colombia: Francisco Urrutia*
> *For Ethiopia: Z.G. Heywot*
> *For France: Jean Chauvel*
> *For Greece: Jean Kindynis*
> *For Luxembourg: J. Sturm*
> *For The Netherlands: A. Bentinck*
> *For New Zealand: A.D. McIntosh*
> *For The Philippines: Carlos P. Garcia*
> *For The Republic of Korea: Y.T. Pyun*
> *For Thailand: Wan Waithayakon*
> *For Turkey: M.C. Acikalin*
> *For The United Kingdom: Anthony Eden*
> *For The United States of America: Walter Bedell Smith*

UNITED STATES POLICY TOWARD KOREA, 1960-1970

A. Communiqué Issued Subsequent to Talks Between Chairman Chung Hee Park of South Korea and President John F. Kennedy*

November 14, 1961

Chairman Park and President Kennedy concluded today a friendly and constructive exchange of views on the current situation in Korea and the Far East and the various matters of interest to the governments and peoples of the Republic of Korea and the United States of America. Foreign Minister Choi [Choe Tok-sin], Secretary Rusk and other officials of the two governments participated in the conversations.

The two leaders reaffirmed the strong bonds of friendship traditionally existing between the two countries and their determination to intensify their common efforts toward the establishment of world peace based on freedom and justice.

The Chairman reviewed the situation in Korea which led to the military revolution of May 16 and set forth the achievements made by the revolutionary Government. He emphasized the positive steps taken by the Government for social reform and economic stability, particularly the new Government's actions to reform the civil service, rationalize tax collections, abolish usury in local areas, increase employment opportunities, stimulate investment, and expand both domestic and foreign trade. He emphasized as well the positive steps taken by the Government in strengthening the nation against Communism and in eliminating corruption and other social evils.

The President welcomed Chairman Park's full exposition of the current situation in the Republic of Korea and expressed his gratification at the many indications of progress made by the new Government of the Republic.

The Chairman reiterated the solemn pledge of the revolutionary government to return the government to civilian control in the summer of 1963, as he declared in the statement made on August 12, 1961. The President particularly expressed his satisfaction with the Korean government's intention to restore civilian government at the earliest possible date.

The two leaders discussed the position of Korea in the maintenance of peace and security in the Far East, and in this connection reviewed the continuing contribution of United States economic and military assistance to the strengthening of the Korean nation. Recognizing that the successful achievement of Korean economic development in accordance with a long-range plan is indispensable to build a democratic foundation and to maintain a strong anti-Communist posture in Korea, the President expressed great interest in Korea's draft Five Year Economic Development Plan. In this connection, he assured the Chairman that the United States Government would continue to extend all possible economic

*Department of State Bulletin, Dec. 4, 1961, pp. 928-29.

aid and cooperation to the Republic of Korea, in order to further such long range economic development.

The Chairman and the President discussed the problem of mutual defense against the threat of external armed aggression in the Pacific area. They recognized that the common interest of their two countries as bulwarks of the Free World against Communist expansion is deepened and reinforced by the fact that Korean and United States troops are brothers-in-arms, standing side by side in the United Nations Command for the defense of Korean soil. The President reaffirmed the determination of the United States to render forthwith and effectively all possible assistance to the Republic of Korea, in accordance with the Mutual Defense Treaty between the Republic of Korea and the United States of America signed on October 1, 1953, including the use of armed forces, if there is a renewal of armed attack.

The two leaders recalled that Korea had been successfully defended against armed aggression by the first collective military measures pursuant to the call of the United Nations. They recalled the declarations by United Nations members whose military forces participated in the Korean action, including their affirmation that in the interests of world peace, "if there is a renewal of the armed attack, challenging again the principles of the United Nations, we should again be united and prompt to resist." The Chairman and the President reaffirmed their faith in the United Nations, and their determination to seek the unification of Korea in freedom through peaceful means under the principles laid down and reaffirmed by the United Nations General Assembly.

Chairman Park and President Kennedy expressed their deep satisfaction with their meeting and discussions and reiterated their resolve to continue to serve the cause of freedom and democracy, and to strengthen the friendly ties between their two peoples.

NORTH KOREAN SEIZURE OF THE U.S.S. PUEBLO

B. Defense Department Statement*

January 23, 1968

The U.S.S. *Pueblo*, a Navy intelligence collection auxiliary ship, was surrounded by North Korean patrol boats and boarded by an armed party in international waters in the Sea of Japan shortly before midnight e.s.t. last night [January 22].

The United States Government acted immediately to establish contact with North Korea through the Soviet Union.

When the *Pueblo* was boarded, its reported position was approximately 25 miles from the mainland of North Korea.

*Ibid., Feb. 12, 1968, pp. 189-90.

The ship reported the boarding took place at 127 degrees, 54.3 minutes east longitude; 39 degrees, 25 minutes north latitude. The time was 11:45 p.m. e.s.t.

The ship's complement consist of 83, including six officers and 75 enlisted men and two civilians.

At approximately 10 p.m. e.s.t., a North Korean patrol boat approached the *Pueblo*. Using international signals, it requested the *Pueblo's* nationality. The *Pueblo* identified herself as a U.S. ship. Continuing to use flag signals, the patrol boat said: "Heave to or I will open fire on you." The *Pueblo* replied: "I am in international waters." The patrol boat circled the *Pueblo*.

Approximately 1 hour later, three additional patrol craft appeared. One of them ordered: "Follow in my wake; I have a pilot aboard." The four ships closed in on the *Pueblo*, taking different positions on her bow, beam, and quarter. Two MIG aircraft were also sighted by the *Pueblo* circling off the starboard bow.

One of the patrol craft began backing toward the bow of the *Pueblo*, with fenders rigged. An armed boarding party was standing on the bow.

The *Pueblo* radioed at 11:45 p.m. that she was being boarded by North Koreans.

At 12:10 a.m. e.s.t. today [January 23] the *Pueblo* reported that she had been requested to follow the North Korean ships into Wonsan and that she had not used any weapons.

The final message from the *Pueblo* was sent at 12:32 a.m. It reported that it had come to "all stop" and that it was "going off the air."

The *Pueblo* is designated the AGER-2. It is a modified auxiliary light cargo ship (AKL).

The *Pueblo* is 179 feet long and 33 feet wide, with a displacement of 906 tons. It has a 10.2-foot draft. Its maximum speed is 12.2 knots.

C. State Department Statement*

January 23, 1968

You've all seen or had the statement by the Department of Defense this morning about the boarding in international waters of a U.S. naval vessel by North Koreans. I'm authorized to state that the United States Government views this action by North Korea with utmost gravity. We have asked the Soviet Union to convey to the North Koreans our urgent request for the immediate release of the vessel and crew.

The matter will also be raised directly with the North Koreans in a meeting of the Military Armistice Commission. We will, of course, use any other channels which might be helpful.

I wish to reemphasize the seriousness with which we view this flagrant North Korean action against the United States naval vessel on the high seas.

Ibid., p. 190.

D. Statement by Arthur Goldberg, U.S. Ambassador to the United Nations *

[Extract]

January 26, 1968

The United States has requested this meeting, as I stated in my letter to you, to consider the grave threat to peace which the authorities of North Korea have brought about by their increasingly dangerous and aggressive military actions in violation of the Korean Armistice Agreement of 1953, of the United Nations Charter, and of international law.

We have asked that the Council be convened at an hour when peace is in serious and imminent danger—when firm and forthwith action is required to avert that danger and preserve peace.

A virtually unarmed vessel of the United States Navy, sailing on the high seas, has been wantonly and lawlessly seized by armed North Korean patrol boats and her crew forcibly detained. This warlike action carries a danger to peace which should be obvious to all.

A party of armed raiders, infiltrated from North Korea, has been intercepted in the act of invading the South Korean Capital City of Seoul with the admitted assignment of assassinating the President of the Republic of Korea. This event marks the climax of a campaign by the North Korean authorities, over the past 18 months, of steadily growing infiltration, sabotage, and terrorism in flagrant violation of the Korean Armistice Agreement.

Mr. President, these two lines of action are manifestly parallel. Both stem from North Korea. Both are completely unwarranted and unjustified. Both are aimed against peace and security in Korea. Both violate the United Nations Charter, solemn international agreements, and time-honored international law. And both pose a grave threat to peace in a country whose long search for peace and reunification in freedom has been an historic concern to the United Nations and my country.

We bring these grave developments to the attention of the Security Council in the sincere hope that the Council will act promptly to remove the danger to international peace and security. For, Mr. President, it must be removed, and without delay. And it will be removed only if action is taken forthwith to secure the release of the U.S.S. *Pueblo* and its 83-man crew and to bring to an end the pattern of armed transgressions by North Korea against the Republic of Korea. My Government has stated at the highest level our earnest desire to settle this matter promptly and peacefully and, if at all possible, by diplomatic means.

It is testimony to this desire that, in fidelity to the charter, my Government has brought this matter to the Security Council, which has the primary responsibility for the maintenance of international peace and security and which, together with other organs of the United Nations, has a special and historic concern for peace and security in Korea.

Ibid., pp. 194-97.

It is imperative, therefore, that the Security Council act with the greatest urgency and decisiveness. The existing situation cannot be allowed to stand. It must be corrected, and the Council must face up to its responsibility to see it corrected. This course is far more preferable to other remedies which the charter reserves to member states.

Let me now turn to the facts concerning these two aspects of North Korean aggressive conduct on which the Council's action is urgently required.

Seizure of the U.S.S. Pueblo

At 12 noon on January 23, Korean time, the United States ship *Pueblo,* manned by a crew of six officers, 75 enlisted men, and two civilians and sailing in international waters off the North Korean coast, was confronted by a heavily armed North Korean patrol boat identified as submarine chaser No. 35.

The strict instructions under which the *Pueblo* was operating required it to stay at least 13 nautical miles from the North Korean coast. While my country adheres to the 3-mile rule of international law concerning territorial waters, nevertheless the ship was under order whose effect was to stay well clear of the 12-mile limit which the North Korean authorities have by long practice followed.

*   *   *

Now with your permission, Mr. President, I should like to refer to this map provided for the convenience of the Council and show the exact location of the *Pueblo* as given in these coordinates. If the members of the Council will look at the map, you will see a number 3 blue. Number 3 blue is approximately 25 nautical miles from the port of Wonsan. It is 16.3 nautical miles from the nearest point of the North Korean mainland, on the Peninsula of Hodo-Pando, and 15.3 nautical miles from the Island of Ung-Do.

Now, at exactly the same time, the North Korean submarine chaser No. 35, which intercepted the *Pueblo,* reported its own location in the number 3 red—and this is a report now from the North Korean submarine chaser No. 35 monitored by us—and that location was 39 degrees 25 minutes north latitude and 127 degrees 56 minutes east longitude. You will note the positions. In other words, these two reported positions are within a mile of one another and show conclusively that according to the North Korean report, as well as our own, the *Pueblo* was in international waters.

The report of its location by the North Korean craft, made by international Morse code, was followed 10 minutes later by the following oral message from the North Korean craft to its base, and I quote it: "We have approached the target here, the name of the target is GER 1-2."

Now, we talk about the *Pueblo* and that is the name by which the ship is, of course, known. But the technical name for this ship is GER-2, and this name was painted on the side of the ship.

The message continued, and I again quote the Korean radio message in Korean words: "Get it? GER 1-2: did you get it? So our control target is GER 1-2. I will send it again. Our control target is GER 1-2."

Inasmuch as the location of the *Pueblo* is, of course, a matter of vital importance, it is important to the Council to know that the information available to the United States as reported by our vessel to our authorities and to the North Korean authorities as reported by its vessel and transmitted by its own ship was virtually identical, with only this small margin of difference. And interestingly enough, the North Korean ship reported the *Pueblo* to be about a mile farther away from the shoreline than the United States fix of its position. That distance between the blue and the red is about a mile. So you see, the North Korean broadcast monitored was reporting what I have stated to this Council.

Mr. President, we have numerous other reports during this encounter consistent with the location I have described. And information other than coordinates corroborative of what I have said is by voice monitor; information on coordinates, as I said, was by international Morse code.

The North Korean patrol boat, having made its approach, used international flag signals to request the *Pueblo's* nationality. The *Pueblo*, replying with the same signal system, identified herself as a United States vessel. The North Korean vessel then signaled: "Heave to or I will open fire on you." The *Pueblo* replied: "I am in international waters."

The reply was not challenged by the North Korean vessel, which, under international law, if there had been an intrusion—which there was not—should have escorted the vessel from the area in which it was. However, that vessel then proceeded for approximately an hour to circle the *Pueblo*, which maintained its course and kept its distance from the shore. At that point three additional North Korean armed vessels appeared, one of which ordered the *Pueblo*: "Follow in my wake." As this order was issued, the four North Korean vessels closed in on the *Pueblo* and surrounded it. At the same time two MIG aircraft appeared overhead and circled the *Pueblo*. The *Pueblo* attempted peacefully to withdraw from this encirclement but was forcibly prevented from doing so and brought to a dead stop. It was then seized by an armed boarding party and forced into the North Korean port of Wonsan.

Now, reports from the North Korean naval vessels on their location and on the seizure of the *Pueblo* at this point show that the *Pueblo* was constantly in international waters.

At 1:50 p.m. Korean time, within a few minutes of the reported boarding of the *Pueblo*, North Korean vessels reported their position at 39-26 NL 128-02 EL, or about 21.3 miles from the nearest North Korean land. This is the point on the map here. And we would be very glad, Mr. President, to make this map available for the records of the Security Council.

Now, Mr. President, I want to lay to rest—completely to rest—some intimations that the *Pueblo* had intruded upon the territorial waters and was sailing away from territorial waters and that the North Korean ships were in hot pursuit. This is not the case at all, and I shall demonstrate it by this map.

Now, we will show by times and the course of the vessel exactly what occurred, and you will see from this that the location of the *Pueblo* was constantly far away from Korean shores, always away from the 12-mile limit until it was taken into Wonsan by the North Korean vessels. The locations of the *Pueblo* are shown on the blue line, and the location of the SO-135, the first North Korean vessel, on the red line.

Now, the *Pueblo,* far from having sailed from inside territorial waters to outside territorial waters, was cruising in an area—in this area—and this will be demonstrated by the time sequence—and when I say, "this area," I mean the area that is east and south of any approach to the 12-mile limit.

At 0830 Korean local time, the *Pueblo* was at the location I now point to on the map. It had come to that point from the southeast, not from anywhere in this vicinity. And that is point 1 on the map, so that our record will be complete. Point 2 on the map shows the position of the North Korean submarine chaser No. 35 as reported by her at 10:55, and you will see that she is close to—the North Korean vessel, not the *Pueblo*—the 12-mile limits.

Point No. 3 is the position reported by the *Pueblo* at 12 o'clock noon, and you will see that she is a considerable distance from the 12-mile limit, which is the dotted line.

Red point No. 3 is the position reported by the North Korean submarine chaser No. 35 at 12 o'clock noon when it signaled the *Pueblo* to stop. In other words, this is the position of the North Korean vessel, this is the position of the *Pueblo*; and the position of the North Korean vessel that I point to, the red line, the position reported audibly by the North Korean vessel. There is very little difference in these two reports.

Point No. 4 is the position reported by the North Korean vessel at 1350—1:50 p.m.—when she reported boarding the *Pueblo*. And you will recall that I just told the Council that the *Pueblo*, seeking to escape the encirclement, did not move in the direction which would have transgressed the 12-mile limit.

Now, all of this is verified not by reports solely from the *Pueblo*; all of this is verified by reports from the North Korean vessels which were monitored; and I think it is a very clear picture of exactly what transpired.

Here, too, Mr. President, with your permission, we will make this available.

Mr. President, it is incontrovertible from this type of evidence, which is physical evidence of international Morse code signals and voice reports, that the *Pueblo* when first approached and when seized was in international waters well beyond the 12-mile limit and that the North Koreans knew this.

Offense Against International Law

Further compounding this offense against international law, and the gravity of this warlike act, is the fact that the North Koreans clearly intended to capture the *Pueblo*, knowing that it was in international waters, and force it to sail into the port of Wonsan. This aim is made clear by messages exchanged among the North Korean vessels themselves which we monitored, including the following: "By talking this way, it will be enough to understand according to present instructions we will close down the radio, tie up the personnel, tow it, and enter port at Wonsan. At present we are on our way to boarding. We are coming in." This is an exact voice broadcast from the ship which acknowledges the instructions that it was following.

Now, Mr. President, in light of this, this was no mere incident, no case of mistaken identity, no case of mistaken location. It was nothing less than a deliberate, premeditated armed attack on a United States naval vessel on the high seas, an attack whose gravity is underlined by these simple facts which I should now like to sum up.

The location of the *Pueblo* in international waters was fully known to the North Korean authorities since the broadcasts were not only between its own ships but were directed to its shore installations.

The *Pueblo* was so lightly armed that the North Koreans in one of the conversations which we have monitored even reported it as unarmed.

The *Pueblo* was therefore in no position to engage in a hostile, warlike act toward the territory or vessels of North Korea; and the North Koreans knew this.

Nevertheless, the *Pueblo,* clearly on the high seas, was forcibly stopped, boarded, and seized by North Korean armed vessels. This is a knowing and willful aggressive act—part of a deliberate series of actions in contravention of arrangements designed to keep peace in the area, which apply not only to land forces but to naval forces as well. It is an action which no member of the United Nations could tolerate.

I might add, in light of the comments of the distinguished Soviet representative on the adoption of the agenda, that Soviet ships engage in exactly the same activities as the *Pueblo* and sail much closer to the shores of other states. And one such Soviet ship right now is to be found in the Sea of Japan and currently is not far from South Korean shores.

*   *   *

E. Address by Secretary of State Dean Rusk*

[Extract]

February 10, 1968

The *Pueblo* is an intelligence-gathering ship, one of a number of such vessels which we and the Soviet Union and others have long had on the high seas. The Soviet Union has had such ships operating along both our east and our west coasts, off Guam, and near our naval task forces in the Mediterranean, the Western Pacific, and elsewhere.

In a genuinely peaceful and open world these operations would not be needed. In the world of today they are essential. They are especially important to us because our adversaries have closed societies. They don't publish the sort of facts that the Communists know about our military disposition simply from reading newspapers and department and committee reports.

There is not a scrap of evidence to indicate that the *Pueblo* was at any time inside the 12-mile limit which North Korea claims as territorial waters. It was

*Ibid., pp. 301-02.

under strict orders to stay outside the 12-mile limit. It was outside that limit when it was intercepted and seized. We know that not only from our own data but from intercepted North Korean messages.

The most essential fact is that, under accepted international law, North Korea had no right to seize the *Pueblo* either on the high seas or in territorial waters. The convention on the law of the sea, adopted in 1958, makes it entirely clear that, if any warship comes inside territorial waters, the coastal state can require it to leave but does not have the right to seize it. At least three times in recent years Soviet war vessels have come inside our territorial limit of only three miles. We didn't seize them; we simply required them to depart.

So this North Korean action was a very grave violation of the law and practice of nations.

The President's first concern has been to recover the crew and the ship. And he has hoped to avoid a renewal of major warfare in Korea. So, while taking various precautionary measures, he has been seeking to obtain the return of the crew and ship by peaceful means.

We asked the International Red Cross to intercede on behalf of the crew, and it agreed to do so.

We have asked many other nations to cooperate with our efforts to recover the crew and ship by peaceful means.

At our suggestion, an emergency session of the United Nations Security Council was convened.

Then the North Koreans said the matter was not within the jurisdiction of the United Nations but should be discussed through the Military Armistice Commission at Panmunjom. We have been meeting with them there, so far with very little result. They have given us the name of the one member of the crew who was killed and of three who were injured—that is all.

There are 50,000 American troops in the Republic of Korea. The President has taken steps to strengthen our forces in the area, without diminishing our forces in South Viet-Nam.

North Korea will make a grave error if it interprets our restraint as a lack of determination or deludes itself into thinking that the American commitment to defend the Republic of Korea has weakened in the slightest.

F. State Department Statement on the Release of the U.S.S. *Pueblo* Crew*

December 22, 1968

The crew of the U.S.S. *Pueblo* was freed today at Panmunjom. They will immediately be given medical examinations and returned to the United States. Their families will meet them in San Diego.

The agreement to free the men involved the acceptance by both sides of the following procedure. General Woodward, our negotiator, signed a document prepared by the North Koreans. He made a formal statement for the record

Ibid., Jan. 6, 1969, p. 1.

just before signing. The text of his statement had earlier been transmitted to the North Koreans and they had accepted our requirement that this statement be coupled with the signature of their document. Our statement read:

> The position of the United States Government with regard to the *Pueblo*, as consistently expressed in the negotiations at Panmunjom and in public, has been that the ship was not engaged in illegal activity, that there is no convincing evidence that the ship at any time intruded into the territorial waters claimed by North Korea, and that we could not apologize for actions which we did not believe took place. The document which I am going to sign was prepared by the North Koreans and is at variance with the above position, but my signature will not and cannot alter the facts. I will sign the document to free the crew and only to free the crew.

General Woodward then signed the North Korean document and received the custody of the crew.

As he said, General Woodward placed his name on the false North Korean document for one reason only: to obtain the freedom of the crew who were illegally seized and have been illegally held as hostages by the North Koreans for almost exactly 11 months. He made clear that his signature did not imply the acceptance by the United States of the numerous false statements in that document. Indeed, the prior acceptance by the North Koreans of the statement which General Woodward read into the record just before signing shows clearly their recognition of our position that the facts of the case call for neither an admission of guilt nor for an apology.

G. Statement by President Lyndon B. Johnson*

December 22, 1968

I am deeply gratified that after a long 11 months of totally unjustified detention by the North Koreans, the crew of the U.S.S. *Pueblo* have been freed. They should be reunited with their families in time for Christmas, and I am happy for them that their time of ordeal ends on a note of joy.

I want to pay tribute also to the patience and courage of these relatives while their husbands, fathers, and sons were held by the North Koreans.

Ths negotiations at Panmunjom were cruelly drawn out, and I am grateful for the understanding which the *Pueblo* families showed through the long and painful period during which their Government has sought to free the crew.

I must express my deep sorrow over the death of one crew member, Seaman Duane D. Hodges, who was killed while endeavoring to carry out his duties during the seizure of the ship.

I also want to thank our negotiator at Panmunjom, Major General Gilbert H. Woodward. He carried out his difficult and successful assignment with distinction and has preserved the integrity of the United States while obtaining the release of the men of the *Pueblo*.

*Ibid., pp. 1-2.

H. Statement by Secretary Rusk*

December 22, 1968

President Johnson and I are pleased to report that the United States representative at Panmunjom has just obtained the release of the 82 officers and men of the U.S.S. *Pueblo* who last January were illegally seized with their ship on the high seas.

The men will stop first at an American Army hospital near Seoul and will fly from there to San Diego after any immediate medical needs have been met. The body of Seaman Duane D. Hodges, who lost his life at the time the ship was captured, has also been returned.

The men were released after long and difficult negotiations. The North Korean negotiator insisted from the beginning that the men would not be released unless the United States falsely confessed to espionage and to violations of North Korean territory and apologized for such alleged actions.

We necessarily refused these demands. We repeatedly offered to express our regrets if shown valid evidence of a transgression. But this Government had— and has now—no reliable evidence that the *Pueblo* in any way violated her sailing orders and intruded into waters claimed by North Korea.

After 10 months of negotiations during which we made every sort of reasonable offer, all of which were harshly rejected, we had come squarely up against a most painful problem: how to obtain the release of the crew without having this Government seem to attest to statements which simply are not true. Then within the past week, a way which does just that was found, and a strange procedure was accepted by the North Koreans. Apparently the North Koreans believe there is propaganda value even in a worthless document which General Woodward publicly labeled false before he signed it.

General Woodward said:

> The position of the United States Government with regard to the *Pueblo*, as consistently expressed in the negotiations at Panmunjom and in public, has been that the ship was not engaged in illegal activity, that there is no convincing evidence that the ship at any time intruded into the territorial waters claimed by North Korea, and that we could not apologize for actions which we did not believe took place. The document which I am going to sign was prepared by the North Koreans and is at variance with the above position, but my signature will not and cannot alter the facts. I will sign the document to free the crew and only to free the crew.

If you ask me why these two contradictory statements proved to be the key to effect the release of our men, the North Koreans would have to explain it. I know of no precedent in my 19 years of public service. The simple fact is that the men are free and our position on the facts of the case is unchanged.

We regret that the ship itself, U.S.S. *Pueblo*, has not yet been returned; that will have to be pursued further.

During these painful months I met with the families of a number of the crew. I want to pay tribute to the understanding which relatives have shown

Ibid., p. 2.

toward our efforts to free the men, even at times when it seemed that these efforts were getting nowhere.

And the American people deserve a word of thanks. This has been a most frustrating episode. There have been a few among us who counseled either violent reprisals, which could not save the men, or abject surrender to North Korean demands. But the great majority of our people have kept their heads. And the crew has now been released in time to have Christmas with their loved ones.

I. North Korean Document Signed by the United States*

Panmunjom, December 22, 1968

To the Government of the Democratic People's Republic of Korea,

The Government of the United States of America,

Acknowledging the validity of the confessions of the crew of the USS Pueblo and of the documents of evidence produced by the Representative of the Government of the Democratic People's Republic of Korea to the effect that the ship, which was seized by the self-defense measures of the naval vessels of the Korean People's Army in the territorial waters of the Democratic People's Republic of Korea on January 23, 1968, had illegally intruded into the territorial waters of the Democratic People's Republic of Korea.

Shoulders full responsibility and solemnly apologizes for the grave acts of espionage committed by the U.S. ship against the Democratic People's Republic of Korea after having intruded into the territorial waters of the Democratic People's Republic of Korea.

And gives firm assurance that no U.S. ships will intrude again in the future into the territorial waters of the Democratic People's Republic of Korea.

Meanwhile, the Government of the United States of America earnestly requests the Government of the Democratic People's Republic of Korea to deal leniently with the former crew members of the USS Pueblo confiscated by the Democratic People's Republic of Korea side, taking into consideration the fact that these crew members have confessed honestly to their crimes and petitioned. the Government of the Democratic People's Republic of Korea for leniency.

Simultaneously with the signing of this document, the undersigned acknowledges receipt of 82 former crew members of the Pueblo and one corpse.

On behalf of the Government of the United
States of America
Gilbert H. Woodward, Major General, USA

J. United States Statement on the American Reconnaissance Plane Shot down by North Korea*

Panmunjom, April 17, 1969

General Yi: Three days ago your armed forces committed an unprovoked

*Ibid., pp. 2-3.
*Ibid., May 5, 1969, p. 388.

attack on an unarmed U.S. aircraft. An EC-121, flying a routine reconnaissance track parallel to North Korea over the Sea of Japan, was reported missing at around 1400 hours, Korean time, on April 15. About 2 hours later, at 1555 hours, April 15, your radio announced that North Korean military forces had shot down a "large-sized plane of the U.S."

This aircraft was flying a routine reconnaissance track similar to a large number of missions which have been flown over international waters in that area regularly since 1950. The aircraft commander was under orders to maintain a distance of 50 nautical miles from the coast of North Korea. All evidence confirms that the plane remained far outside your claimed territorial airspace.

When shot down, the aircraft was at point approximately 41 degrees 12 minutes North and 131 degrees 48 minutes East. Debris from the aircraft was initially sighted and subsequently recovered in the vicinity of 41 degrees 14 minutes North and 131 degrees 50 minutes East. These points are approximately 90 miles from North Korea. There appear to have been no survivors from the 31 men on board the aircraft.

From the foregoing facts about your attack on U.S. aircraft it is clear that:

1. At no time did our aircraft penetrate or even closely approach North Korean airspace. Since it was at all times clearly within international airspace, you had no right to threaten or interfere with it, let alone shoot it down.

2. Our aircraft was engaged in completely legitimate reconnaissance operations. These operations are made necessary by your repeated acts and threats of aggression. So long as such flights are conducted outside your territorial limits you have no right to interfere with them. I note that your authorities seem, in some respects, to share this view, since they felt compelled to allege falsely that the aircraft was within your airspace.

3. No one can believe that a single unarmed propeller-driven aircraft can represent a threat to North Korea. It was not attacking you or preparing to attack you or supporting an attack on you. The shooting down of this U.S. plane was not an act of self-defense. It was a calculated act of aggression.

4. This act cannot be justified under international law. On the contrary, the centuries-old tradition of freedom of the seas and the newer principle regarding freedom of the airspace over international waters clearly make your action illegal. International law and custom call you to account for the consequences of your violation of these principles.

This incident was not an isolated act. You have repeatedly regularly violated both the letter and the spirit of the Armistice Agreement and the rules of international law. I need only cite the attempt in January 1968 to assassinate President Pak, your lawless seizure of the U.S.S. *Pueblo*, your brutal mistreatment of her crew, your innumerable infiltrations into the Republic of Korea, and your other violations of the demilitarized zone.

The peace of this area is constantly being disturbed by your actions. The proper course for you to take in this instance is to acknowledge the true facts of the case: that you shot down our aircraft over international waters at a point approximately 90 miles from your coast and that this plane at no time entered your airspace. We, of course, expect that you will take appropriate measures to prevent similar incidents in the future.

I have nothing further to say at this time.

THE UNITED STATES

AND VIETNAM

THE UNITED STATES AND VIETNAM

Commentary

Since 1960, Vietnam has been edged to the center of the world stage. The small Asian country, about which most Americans once knew considerably less than William McKinley knew of the Philippines in 1898, has become a tragic battleground on which Americans and Vietnamese have slaughtered one another in a seemingly endless war. All too poignantly, recent events have shifted what was once a French colonial problem to the predominant position in United States foreign policy.

The area of Vietnam came under French colonial control in the latter half of the nineteenth century. In a series of moves beginning in 1857 and culminating in 1883, France either annexed or established protectorates over Cochin China, Tonkin and Annam. She then exploited the regions for her own economic benefit with a harsh and hierarchical administration. Even so, it was not until the First World War that nationalism developed as a significant force. Thousands of young Vietnamese were taken to France to fight and to work in French factories. Many of them became infected with socialist and anti-colonial ideas and returned determined to achieve independence. Ho Chi Minh, like many of his countrymen, spent the war years in Europe; later he became active in the French Communist Party, studied in Moscow, worked in China, and returned to Vietnam in the mid-1920's to organize the Indochinese Communist Party. Ho's party had good discipline and good leadership—thus it was able to withstand severe French harassment throughout the 1930's.

During the Second World War Ho, then in South China, organized the Viet Minh to fight the Japanese who had occupied his homeland. In 1942 the Chinese arrested him, but later released him to return to Indochina, where he led the Viet Minh in waging war against the Japanese, thus enlarging his following. Just prior to the end of the war Japan granted Vietnam its "independence," though the French sought to retain control through a puppet head of state, Bao Dai. Japan's move allowed Ho Chi Minh to establish his control over a large segment of the country and eventually to declare the existence of the Democratic Republic of Vietnam in September, 1945.

However, pursuant to allied agreement, at war's end the Chinese accepted the Japanese surrender in northern Indochina and the British did so in the

445

south. The British, colonialists themselves and unwilling to stand in the way of the reassertion of French authority, promptly turned the southern part of the country over to the French. France then was confronted with the fact of a popular, nationalistic, independent, albeit Communist, government led by Ho Chi Minh, which it had to subdue somehow if it were to establish its authority. The French first tried negotiation and in 1946 signed an agreement with Ho Chi Minh, which, if carried out, would have made Vietnam part of a French Union with independence on most domestic questions. Extremists on both sides prevented the execution of the agreement; sporadic fighting broke out, and ultimately French bombardment of the city of Haiphong and Viet Minh attacks on French positions triggered a long, bloody war.

The war for French imperialism in Indochina lasted from 1946 through 1954. During this period several events drew American attention to the conflict and led eventually to active United States involvement. Soviet activity in Europe in the post-1945 period convinced American policy makers of the Soviet interest in expanding Communist imperialism. China "fell" to Communist revolutionaries in December, 1949. And, in 1950 the Korean War broke out. These facts convinced the United States of the serious nature of the Communist threat, tended to indicate the monolithic nature of the Communist bloc, and consequently led President Truman in 1950 to agree to give large amounts of American aid to the French in their own struggle against the Viet Minh. The policy, most observers would now agree, was unwise. Ho Chi Minh was clearly a Communist, but he was also a nationalist who had the loyal support of his countrymen in his effort to unify his homeland. Had the United States not made the commitment to the French, it seems likely that it could have worked with Ho's government and perhaps, capitalizing on traditional Sino-Vietnamese hostility, made Vietnam the Yugoslavia of Asia. On the other hand, aid to France associated the United States with moribund French imperialism and thus angered Vietnamese nationalists. It also had the effect of driving the Vietnamese Communists into closer association with China

Meanwhile, the Viet Minh achieved the ascendancy in the fighting. Then, in 1954 the Soviet Union and China pressured Ho into negotiating a settlement at Geneva which, while it spelled doom for French interests, generally constituted a diplomatic victory for the West. Viet Minh forces defeated the French at Dienbienphu while the conference was in session and could have gone on to ultimate military victory. On advice from Moscow and Peking, the Communist forces chose instead to agree to divide the country at the 17th parallel, to consolidate their control over the North, and to use elections specified for 1956 in the Geneva accords to unify the country. The United States and the puppet government of the French in South Vietnam refused to sign the Geneva agreements, but the United States stated that it would abide by the terms.

After 1954, the United States, which previously had borne the major cost of the French effort, assumed the support of a South Vietnamese government led by the Catholic Ngo Dinh Diem. It also helped block the elections which were to be held in 1956, believing that such elections would be "rigged" in the North to achieve Communist success—though it was clear to many that

Ho Chi Minh might win an entirely free election. Again, the American decision was based on assumptions about the monolithic nature of world Communism and on a desire to "contain" China. It was believed that North Vietnam was an agent of Chinese expansion and, since 1954, had very little freedom of action in the Communist bloc. From 1955 to 1957 the Diem government dealt successfully with many of the problems in the South and seemed a satisfactory non-Communist alternative. In 1957, however, Hanoi, furious over the failure to unify the country through elections, began to call for intensified terrorist raids in the South and the overthrow of the Diem government. Between 1957 and 1962 Presidents Eisenhower and Kennedy sent more American troops as "advisers," but this did not stem the tide. In 1963 in the hope that a new government would bring political reform and thus viability to the non-Communist forces in the South, the United States encouraged a *coup d'etat* which overthrew Diem. It then increased American aid.

In 1964-1965 United States policy entered a new phase. The summer of 1964 saw the North Vietnamese attack American ships in the Gulf of Tonkin, a congressional resolution permitting the President to respond as such incidents warranted, and United States retaliatory attacks on the Vietnamese gunboats. In 1965, as North Vietnam applied additional pressure on the government in the South, President Johnson approved American bombing in the North in an attempt to force the Vietnamese to the bargaining table; he also sent American combat units to South Vietnam for the first time. After 1965 the war became increasingly Americanized, with the introduction of hundreds of thousands of American troops and the expansion of the number of air missions over the North. The action certainly delayed and perhaps prevented North Vietnam's unification of the country, but also led to a cruel, bloody, prolonged and indecisive conflict.

Because of rising world criticism and increasingly impassioned objections within the United States, as well as the great cost of the war in lives and money, President Johnson attempted several times in the 1967-1968 period to move toward negotiations. Both North Vietnamese unwillingness to discuss a settlement except on their own terms and the President's reluctance to sacrifice American objectives led to a continuation of the bombing attacks on the North and prevented meaningful discussions. Finally, in 1968, as domestic protest against the war built up and it became clear to the President that he had failed to articulate his objectives in terms that convinced Americans they were worth the cost, he offered to partially stop the bombing and begin talks. To underscore his point, he removed himself from contention for the presidential nomination. Preliminary talks then began in Paris preparatory to more formal discussions which began after the President acted to halt all bombing attacks on the North on October 31.

President Nixon continued American participation in the Paris talks, at first optimistic about the prospect of getting a settlement through Soviet assistance. When this did not materialize, the President, cognizant of the great domestic pressure to end the conflict and eschewing escalation of the United States military effort, implemented a new plan. He indicated to the North Vietnamese that the United States was going to begin a process of "Vietnamization" of the war—that is, withdrawal of American forces and more rapid military preparation of the South Vietnamese themselves to take over the fighting. Still hoping for a negotiated settlement but without any other significant bargaining power, the President then suggested he would use this Vietnamizing process as his "hole card." If the North Vietnamese would negotiate an end of the war promptly, he would speed up the process of American withdrawal; otherwise he would simply proceed on his own schedule.

To bolster his position the President took the plan to the Nation in a nationally televised speech, appealing to the great "silent majority" of Americans to allow him time to end the war with American honor intact. The appeal seemed to mute, at least temporarily, much of the domestic criticism. In the meantime, in the winter of 1969-70 the President appeared to downgrade the Paris meetings by failing to replace retiring United States delegate Henry Cabot Lodge with a representative of high rank. And the war was far from being "over."

In the sense that the war has led to great loss of life, has had a most divisive effect on the American people, and has triggered manifestations of unrest in major United States cities and university campuses, it must be considered one of the most catastrophic events in American history. Yet, several facts should be considered in viewing the war. For a good part of the twentieth century, the United States has considered Southeast Asia and the Pacific region vital to its national interest and security. American reaction to Japanese aggression in Asia in the form of economic sanctions in 1940 and 1941 came primarily not in behalf of China but only when Japan began to move southward to threaten Southeast Asia and the Pacific. In this respect the Asian part of the Second World War must be seen as being in part about Southeast Asia.

In 1964 and 1965, the United States was concerned about Chinese expansion and her creation of client states in Southeast Asia. In the view of some, China had already demonstrated expansionist ideas—in annexing Tibet, in threatening Formosa and the offshore islands, and in attacking India. Moreover, in 1964 China developed the atomic bomb and in the fall of 1965 Defense Minister Lin Piao spoke belligerently of Chinese aspirations for Southeast Asia. In view of these events and the fact that China had once ruled Vietnam for a thousand years, American policy makers were convinced of the threat in the contiguous territory. In addition, they feared that if all Vietnam became a Communist state, the subversion of the other Southeast Asian countries of which Lin Piao spoke in 1965 would be that much easier. It seemed that because all Southeast Asian nations possessed huge Chinese populations, China's influence or control could soon become paramount. China's actions in Indonesia in the fall of 1965 in attempting to overthrow the government, which, though ill-timed and ultimately a failure, tended to prove the American assessment of Chinese intentions.

Developments since 1967, however, have indicated that China has become increasingly diplomatically isolated, and, because of internal turmoil and the Sino-Soviet dispute, no longer a serious threat to the region—if indeed she ever was. In other words, circumstances achieved the major objective sought by the United States. This lends support to the argument that the United States should have long ago concluded a settlement with North Vietnam and withdrawn—or withdrawn unilaterally if that was the only way to achieve it. Because the war had been articulated to the American people in moralistic and idealistic terms, and because the United States has always found it difficult to pursue *realpolitik* to the extent that would have been necessary in the quick abandonment of its South Vietnamese ally, its policy had a degree of built-in inflexibility. Moreover, during the Johnson administration there seemed to be little awareness of changed conditions which would necessitate a reassessment of the American position. The Nixon administration seems to recognize the changes; indeed it appears to be making a reappraisal of the American posture in all of Asia as it withdraws forces from Vietnam. Whether, in the case of Vietnam, Nixon is acting with sufficient dispatch remains the major question.

AMERICAN POLICY TOWARD FRENCH PRESENCE IN VIETNAM

A. Communiqué Issued on United States-French Discussions on Indochina*

June 18, 1952

Mr. Jean Letourneau, Minister in the French Cabinet for the Associated States in Indochina, has just concluded a series of conversations with U. S. Government officials from the Department of State, Department of Defense, the Office of Director for Mutual Security, the Mutual Security Agency, and Department of the Treasury. The Ambassadors of Cambodia and Viet-Nam have also participated in these talks.

The principle which governed this frank and detailed exchange of views and information was the common recognition that the struggle in which the forces of the French Union and the Associated States are engaged against the forces of Communist aggression in Indochina is an integral part of the world-wide resistance by the Free Nations to Communist attempts at conquest and subversion. There was unanimous satisfaction over the vigorous and successful course of military operations, in spite of the continuous comfort and aid received by the Communist forces of the Viet-Minh from Communist China. The excellent performance of the Associated States' forces in battle was found to be a source of particular encouragement. Special tribute was paid to the 52,000 officers and men of the French Union and Associated States' armies who have been lost in this six years' struggle for freedom in Southeast Asia and to the 75,000 other casualties.

In this common struggle, however, history, strategic factors, as well as local and general resources require that the free countries concerned each assume primary responsibility for resistance in the specific areas where Communism has resorted to force of arms. Thus the United States assumes a large share of the burden in Korea while France has the primary role in Indochina. The partners, however, recognize the obligation to help each other in their areas of primary responsibility to the extent of their capabilities and within the limitations imposed by their global obligations as well as by the requirements in their own areas of special responsibility. It was agreed that success in this continuing struggle would entail an increase in the common effort and that the United States for its part will, therefore, within the limitations set by Congress, take steps to expand its aid to the French Union. It was further agreed that this increased assistance over and above present U. S. aid for Indochina, which now approximates one third of the total cost of Indochina operations, would be especially devoted to assisting France in the building of the national armies of the Associated States.

Mr. Letourneau reviewed the facts which amply demonstrate the determination of the Associated States to pursue with increased energy the strengthening

* *Department of State Bulletin*, June 30, 1952, p. 1010.

of their authority and integrity both against internal subversion and against external aggression.

In this connection Mr. Letourneau reminded the participants that the accords of 1949, which established the independence within the French Union of Cambodia, Laos and Viet-Nam, have been liberally interpreted and supplemented by other agreements, thus consolidating this independence. Mr. Letourneau pointed out that the governments of the Associated States now exercise full authority except that a strictly limited number of services related to the necessities of the war now in progress remain temporarily in French hands. In the course of the examination of the Far Eastern economic and trade situation, it was noted that the Governments of the Associated States are free to negotiate trade treaties and agreements of all kinds with their neighbors subject only to whatever special arrangements may be agreed between members of the French Union.

It was noted that these states have been recognized by thirty-three foreign governments.

The conversations reaffirmed the common determination of the participants to prosecute the defense of Indochina and their confidence in a free, peaceful and prosperous future for Cambodia, Laos, and Viet-Nam.

Mr. Letourneau was received by the President, Mr. Acheson, and Mr. Foster, as Acting Secretary of Defense. Mr. John Allison, Assistant Secretary of State for Far Eastern Affairs, acted as Chairman of the U.S. Delegation participating in the conversations.

B. Replies by Ho Chi Minh, President of The Democratic Republic of Vietnam, to Questions Submitted by the Swedish Newspaper *Expressen**

Published, November 29, 1953

First question: Recent debates in the French National Assembly have shown that many French statesmen want to reach a settlement of the Indochina conflict via direct negotiations with your government. Can it be expected that this desire, which is even stronger among the French people as a whole, will be favorably received by you and your government?

Answer: The French government imposed the war on the people of Vietnam, who were forced to take up arms and fight heroically for seven or eight years, defending their national independence and their desire to live in peace. If the French colonizers continue their predatory war the Vietnam people will be filled with determination to wage the patriotic war to a triumphant conclusion. If the French government, having learnt the lesson of several years of war, wants to declare a truce and reach a negotiated settlement of the Indochina question, the government and people of the Democratic Republic of Vietnam are prepared to discuss the French proposal.

Second question: Is there any chance at present for a truce and on what terms?

Pravda and *Izvestia*, Dec. 1, 1953.

Answer: The French government must cease hostilities. Then truce will be a reality. Such a truce must be based on genuine respect on the part of the French government for the independence of Vietnam.

Third and fourth questions: Would you be willing to accept the good offices of a neutral state to arrange a meeting with the other side? Could Sweden assume such a mission?

Answer: If neutral states desire cessation of the war in Vietnam and want to initiate negotiations, a favorable reception will be given such initiative. However, truce negotiations are largely a matter which must be handled by the governments of France and the Democratic Republic of Vietnam.

Fifth question: In that case, would you agree to the calling of a conference which would enable you to put an end to the present hostilities?

Answer: The war has been an incredible ordeal for our people. The French people too have suffered greatly. And this is why the French people are opposing the war in Vietnam.

Ho Chi Minh continued: "I have always felt great sympathy and admiration for the French people and the French peace partisans. At present, it is not just Vietnam's independence which is subject to crude aggression. Serious danger also threatens the independence of France: American imperialism is pushing the French colonizers into prolonging and continually expanding the war to reconquer Vietnam so as to weaken France more and more and take its place in Vietnam. On the other hand American imperialism is compelling France to sign the European Defense Community treaty, which entails the restoration of German militarism. The French people's struggle for independence, democracy and peace and for an end to the war in Vietnam is one of the important factors which could solve the problem of Vietnam."

C. French Declaration on Indochina*

July 3, 1953

The Government of the French Republic, meeting in Council of Ministers, has reviewed the relations of France with the Associated States of Indochina.

It considers that the time has come to adapt the agreements concluded by them with France to the position which they have succeeded in acquiring, with her full support, in the community of free peoples.

Respectful of national traditions and human freedoms, France, in the course of nearly a century of cooperation, has led Cambodia, Laos and Vietnam to the full expression of their personality and has maintained their national unity.

By the Agreements of 1949, she recognized their independence and they agreed to associate themselves with her within the French Union.

The Government of the Republic wishes today to make a solemn declaration.

In the four years which have elapsed since the signing of the agreements, the brotherhood of arms between the armies of the French Union and the national armies of the Associated States has been further strengthened thanks to

*Press and Information Service of the French Embassy, *Press Release,* July 1953.

the development of the latter, which are taking a daily increasing part in the struggle against the common enemy.

In the same period, the civil institutions of the three nations have put themselves in a position to assume all the powers incumbent upon modern States, while the voice of their Governments has been heard by the majority of countries constituting the United Nations Organization.

France considers that, under these conditions, there is every reason to complete the independence and sovereignty of the Associated States of Indochina by ensuring, in agreement with each of the three interested Governments, the transfer of the powers that she had still retained in the interests of the States themselves, because of the perilous circumstances resulting from the state of war.

The French Government has decided to invite each of the three Governments to agree with it on the settlement of questions which each of them may deem necessary to raise in the economic, financial, judicial, military and political fields, in respect of and safeguarding the legitimate interests of each of the contracting parties.

The Government of the Republic expresses the wish that agreement on these various points may strengthen the friendship which unites France and the Associated States within the French Union.

D. Communiqué Issued by France and the United States Relative to French Aims and American Aid in Indochina*

September 30, 1953

The forces of France and the Associated States in Indochina have for 8 years been engaged in a bitter struggle to prevent the engulfment of Southeast Asia by the forces of international communism. The heroic efforts and sacrifices of these French Union allies in assuring the liberty of the new and independe states of Cambodia, Laos and Vietnam has earned the admiration and support of the free world. In recognition of the French Union effort the United States Government has in the past furnished aid of various kinds to the Governments of France and the Associated States to assist in bringing the long struggle to an early and victorious conclusion.

The French Government is firmly resolved to carry out in full its declaration of July 3, 1953 by which is announced its intention of perfecting the independence of the three Associated States in Indochina, through negotiations with the Associated States.

The Governments of France and the United States have now agreed that, in support of plans of the French Government for the intensified prosecution of the war against the Viet Minh, the United States will make available to the French Government prior to December 31, 1954 additional financial resources not to exceed $385 million. This aid is in addition to funds already earmarked by the United States for aid to France and the Associated States.

*Department of State Press Release, 529, Sept. 30, 1953.

The French Government is determined to make every effort to break up and destroy the regular enemy forces in Indochina. Toward this end the government intends to carry through, in close cooperation with the Cambodian, Laotian and Vietnamese Governments, the plans for increasing the Associated States forces while increasing temporarily French forces to levels considered necessary to assure the success of existing military plans. The additional United States aid is designed to help make it possible to achieve these objectives with maximum speed and effectiveness.

The increased French effort in Indochina will not entail any basic or permanent alteration of the French Government's plans and programs for its NATO forces.

THE GENEVA CONFERENCE

E. Communiqué Issued Subsequent to Talks between Secretary of State John Foster Dulles and French Foreign Minister M. Bidault*

April 14, 1954

Following their conversations in Paris on April 14th, the United States Secretary of State, Mr. John Foster Dulles, and the French Minister of Foreign Affairs, M. Bidault, issued the following statement:

For nearly two centuries it has been the practice for representatives of our two nations to meet together to discuss the grave issues which from time to time have confronted us.

In pursuance of this custom, which we hope to continue to the benefit of ourselves and others, we have had an exchange of views on Indochina and Southeast Asia.

Mr. Dulles expressed admiration for the gallant fight of the French Union forces, who continue with unshakeable courage and determination to repel Communist aggression.

We deplore the fact that on the eve of the Geneva Conference this aggression has reached a new climax in Viet-Nam, particularly at Dien-Bien-Phu, and has been renewed in Laos and extended to Cambodia.

The independence of the three Associated States within the French Union, which new agreements are to complete, is at stake in these battles.

We recognize that the prolongation of the war in Indochina, which endangers the security of the countries immediately affected, also threatens the entire area of Southeast Asia and of the Western Pacific. In close association with other interested nations, we will examine the possibility of establishing, within the framework of the United Nations Charter, a collective defense to assure the peace, security and freedom of this area.

We recognize that our basic objective at the Geneva Conference will be to seek the re-establishment of a peace in Indochina which will safeguard the freedom of its people and the independence of the Associated States. We are convinced that the possiblity of obtaining this objective depends upon our solidarity.

*Ibid., 197, Apr. 14, 1954.

F. The Indochina Armistic Agreements*

Geneva, July 20, 1954

AGREEMENT ON THE CESSATION OF HOSTILITIES IN VIETNAM
WITH ANNEXES

CHAPTER I
PROVISIONAL MILITARY DEMARCATION LINE
AND DEMILITARIZED ZONE

Article 1

A provisional military demarcation line shall be fixed, on either side of which the forces of the two parties shall be regrouped after their withdrawal, the forces of the People's Army of Viet-Nam to the north of the line and the forces of the French Union to the south.

The provisional military demarcation line is fixed as shown on the map attached.

It is also agreed that a demilitarized zone shall be established on either side of the demarcation line, to a width of not more than 5 kilometers from it, to act as a buffer zone and avoid any incidents which might result in the resumption of hostilities.

Article 2

The period within which the movement of all the forces of either party into its regrouping zone on either side of the provisional military demarcation line shall be completed shall not exceed three hundred (300) days from the present Agreement's entry into force.

Article 3

When the provisional military demarcation line coincides with a waterway, the waters of such waterway shall be open to civil navigation by both parties wherever one bank is controlled by one party and the other bank by the other party. The Joint Commission shall establish rules of navigation for the stretch of waterway in question. The merchant shipping and other civilian craft of each party shall have unrestricted access to the land under its military control.

Article 4

The provisional military demarcation line between the two final regrouping

*Senate Foreign Relations Committee, *Report on Indochina: Report of Senator Mike Mansfield on a Study Mission to Vietnam, Cambodia, Laos,* Oct. 15, 1954, 83 Cong., 2d sess., pp. 16-26.

zones is extended into the territorial waters by a line perpendicular to the general line of the coast.

All coastal islands north of this boundary shall be evacuated by the armed forces of the French Union, and all islands south of it shall be evacuated by the forces of the People's Army of Viet-Nam.

Article 5

To avoid any incidents which might result in the resumption of hostilities, all military forces, supplies and equipment shall be withdrawn from the demilitarized zone within twenty-five (25) days of the present Agreement's entry into force.

Article 6

No person, military or civilian, shall be permitted to cross the provisional military demarcation line unless specifically authorized to do so by the Joint Commission.

Article 7

No person, military or civilian, shall be permitted to enter the demilitarized zone except persons concerned with the conduct of civil administration and relief and persons specifically authorized to enter by the Joint Commission.

Article 8

Civil administration and relief in the demilitarized zone on either side of the provisional military demarcation line shall be the responsibility of the Commanders-in-Chief of the two parties in their respective zones. The number of persons, military or civilian, from each side who are permitted to enter the demilitarized zone for the conduct of civil administration and relief shall be determined by the respective Commanders, but in no case shall the total number authorized by either side exceed at any one time a figure to be determined by the Trung Gia Military Commission or by the Joint Commission. The number of civil police and the arms to be carried by them shall be determined by the Joint Commission. No one else shall carry arms unless specifically authorized to do so by the Joint Commission.

Article 9

Nothing contained in this chapter shall be construed as limiting the complete freedom of movement, into, out of or within the demilitarized zone, of the Joint Commission, its joint groups, the International Commission to be set up as indicated below, its inspection teams and any other persons, supplies or equipment specifically authorized to enter the demilitarized zone by the Joint Commission. Freedom of movement shall be permitted across the territory under the military control of either side over any road or waterway which has to be taken between points within the demilitarized zone when such points are not connected by roads or waterways lying completely within the demilitarized zone.

CHAPTER II
PRINCIPLES AND PROCEDURE GOVERNING IMPLEMENTATION OF THE PRESENT AGREEMENT

Article 10

The Commanders of the Forces on each side, on the one side the Commander-in-Chief of the French Union forces in Indo-China, and on the other side the Commander-in-Chief of the People's Army of Viet-Nam, shall order and enforce the complete cessation of all hostilities in Viet-Nam by all armed forces under their control, including all units and personnel of the ground, naval and air forces.

Article 11

In accordance with the principle of a simultaneous cease-fire throughout Indo-China, the cessation of hostilities shall be simultaneous throughout all parts of Viet-Nam, in all areas of hostilities and for all the forces of the two parties.

Taking into account the time effectively required to transmit the cease-fire order down to the lowest echelons of the combatant forces on both sides, the two parties are agreed that the cease-fire shall take effect completely and simultaneously for the different sectors of the country as follows:

Northern Viet-Nam, at 8:00 A.M. (local time) on 27 July 1954.
Central Viet-Nam at 8:00 A.M. (local time) on 1 August 1954.
Southern Viet-Nam, at 8:00 A.M. (local time) on 11 August 1954.

It is agreed that Pekin mean time shall be taken as local time.

From such time as the cease-fire becomes effective in Northern Viet-Nam, both parties undertake not to engage in any large-scale offensive action in any part of the Indo-Chinese theatre of operations and not to commit the air forces based on Northern Viet-Nam outside that sector. The two parties also undertake to inform each other of their plans for movement from one regrouping zone to another within twenty-five (25) days of the present Agreement's entry into force.

Article 12

All the operations and movements entailed in the cessation of hostilities and regrouping must proceed in a safe and orderly fashion:

(a) Within a certain number of days after the cease-fire Agreement shall have become effective, the number to be determined on the spot by the Trung Gia Military Commission, each party shall be responsible for removing and neutralizing mines (including river- and sea-mines), booby traps, explosives and any other dangerous substances placed by it. In the event of its being impossible to complete the work of removal and neutralization in time, the party concerned shall mark the spot by placing visible signs there. All demolitions, mine fields, wire entanglements and other hazards to the free movement of the personnel of the Joint Commission and its joint groups, known to be present after the withdrawal of the military forces, shall be reported to the Joint Commission by the Commanders of the opposing forces;

(b) From the time of the cease-fire until regrouping is completed on either side of the demarcation line:

(1) The forces of either party shall be provisionally withdrawn from the provisional assembly areas assigned to the other party.

(2) When one party's forces withdraw by a route (road, rail, waterway, sea route) which passes through the territory of the other party (see Article 24), the latter party's forces must provisionally withdraw three kilometers on each side of such route, but in such a manner as to avoid interfering with the movements of the civil population.

Article 13

From the time of the cease-fire until the completion of the movements from one regrouping zone into the other, civil and military transport aircraft shall follow air-corridors between the provisional assembly areas assigned to the French Union forces north of the demarcation line on the one hand and the Laotian frontier and the regrouping zone assigned to the French Union forces on the other hand.

The position of the air-corridors, their width, the safety route for single-engined military aircraft transferred to the south and the search and rescue procedure for aircraft in distress shall be determined on the spot by the Trung Gia Military Commission.

Article 14

Political and administrative measures in the two regrouping zones, on either side of the provisional military demarcation line:

(a) Pending the general elections which will bring about the unification of Viet-Nam, the conduct of civil administration in each regrouping zone shall be in the hands of the party whose forces are to be regrouped there in virtue of the present Agreement.

(b) Any territory controlled by one party which is transferred to the other party by the regrouping plan shall continue to be administered by the former party until such date as all the troops who are to be transferred have completely left that territory so as to free the zone assigned to the party in question. From then on, such territory shall be regarded as transferred to the other party, who shall assume responsibility for it.

Steps shall be taken to insure that there is no break in the transfer of responsibilities. For this purpose adequate notice shall be given by the withdrawing party to the other party, which shall make the necessary arrangements, in particular by sending administrative and police detachments to prepare for the assumption of administrative responsibility. The length of such notice shall be determined by the Trung Gia Military Commission. The transfer shall be effected in successive stages for the various territorial sectors.

The transfer of the civil administration of Hanoi and Haiphong to the authorities of the Democratic Republic of Viet-Nam shall be completed within the respective time-limits laid down in Article 15 for military movements.

(c) Each party undertakes to refrain from any reprisals or discrimination against persons or organizations on account of their activities during the hostilities and to guarantee their democratic liberties.

(d) From the date of entry into force of the present Agreement until the movement of troops is completed, any civilians residing in a district controlled by one party who wish to go and live in the zone assigned to the other party shall be permitted and helped to do so by the authorities in that district.

Article 15

The disengagement of the combatants, and the withdrawls and transfers of military forces, equipment and supplies shall take place in accordance with the following principles:

(a) The withdrawals and transfers of the military forces, equipment and supplies of the two parties shall be completed within three hundred (300) days, as laid down in Article 2 of the present Agreement;

(b) Within either territory successive withdrawals shall be made by sectors, portions of sectors or provinces. Transfers from one regrouping zone to another shall be made in successive monthly installments proportionate to the number of troops to be transferred;

(c) The two parties shall undertake to carry out all troop withdrawals and transfers in accordance with the aims of the present Agreement, shall permit no hostile act and shall take no step whatsoever which might hamper such withdrawals and transfers. They shall assist one another as far as this is possible.

(d) The two parties shall permit no destruction or sabotage of any public property and no injury to the life and property of the civil population. They shall permit no interference in local civil administration;

(e) The Joint Commission and the International Commission shall ensure that steps are taken to safeguard the forces in the course of withdrawal and transfer;

(f) The Trung Gia Military Commission, and later the Joint Commission, shall determine by common agreement the exact procedure for the disengagement of the combatants and for troop withdrawals and transfers, on the basis of the principles mentioned above and within the framework laid down below:

(1) The disengagement of the combatants, including the concentration of the armed forces of all kinds and also each party's movements into the provisional assembly areas assigned to it and the other party's provisional withdrawal from it, shall be completed within a period not exceeding fifteen (15) days after the date when the cease-fire becomes effective.

The general delineation of the provisional assembly areas is set out in the maps annexed to the present Agreement.

In order to avoid any incidents, no troops shall be stationed less than 1,500 metres from the lines delimiting the provisional assembly areas.

During the period until the transfers are concluded, all the coastal islands west of the following lines shall be included in the Haiphong perimeter:
—meridian of the southern point of Kebao Island
—northern coast of Ile Rousse (excluding the island), extended as far as the meridian of Campha-Mines
—meridian of Campha-Mines.
(2) The withdrawals and transfers shall be effected in the following order and within the following periods (from the date of the entry into force of the present Agreement):

Forces of the French Union

Hanoi perimiter . . . . .80 days
Haiduong perimiter . . . . .100 days
Haiphong perimiter . . . . .300 days

Forces of the People's Army of Viet-Nam

Ham Tan and Xuyenmoc provisional assembly area .80 days
Central Viet-Nam provisional assembly area, first
    instalment . . . . .80 days
Plaine des Joncs provisional assembly area . . . . .100 days
Central Viet-Nam provisional assembly area, second
    instalment . . . . .100 days
Point Camau provisional assembly area . . . . .200 days
Central Viet-Nam provisional assembly area, last
    instalment . . . . .300 days

CHAPTER III

BAN ON INTRODUCTION OF FRESH TROOPS, MILITARY PERSONNEL, ARMS AND

MUNITIONS, MILITARY BASES

Article 16

With effect from the date of entry into force of the present Agreement, the introduction into Viet-Nam of any troop reinforcements and additional military personnel is probhibited.

It is understood, however, that the rotation of units and groups of personnel, the arrival in Viet-Nam of individual personnel on a temporary duty basis and the return to Viet-Nam of individual personnel after short periods of leave or temporary duty outside Viet-Nam shall be permitted under the conditions laid down below:

(a) Rotation of units (defined in paragraph (c) of this Article) and groups of personnel shall not be permitted for French Union troops stationed north of the provisional military demarcation line laid down in Article 1 of the present Agreement, during the withdrawal period provided for in Article 2.

However, under the heading of individual personnel not more than fifty (50) men, including officers, shall during any one month be permitted to enter that part of the country north of the provisional military demarcation line on a termporary duty basis or to return there after short periods of leave or temporary duty outside Viet-Nam.

(b) "Rotation" is defined as the replacement of units or groups of personnel by other units of the same echelon or by personnel who are arriving in Viet-Nam territory to do their overseas service there;

(c) The units rotated shall never be larger than a battalion—or the corresponding echelon for air and naval forces;

(d) Rotation shall be conducted on a man-for-man basis, provided, however, that in any one quarter neither party shall introduce more than fifteen thousand five hundred (15,500) members of its armed forces into Viet-Nam under the rotation policy;

(e) Rotation units (defined in paragraph (c) of this Article) and groups of personnel, and the individual personnel mentioned in this Article, shall enter and leave Viet-Nam only through the entry points enumerated in Article 20 below:

(f) Each party shall notify the Joint Commission and the International Commission at least two days in advance of any arrivals or departures of units, groups of personnel and individual personnel in or from Viet-Nam. Reports on the arrivals or departures of units, groups of personnel and individual personnel in or from Viet-Nam shall be submitted daily to the Joint Commission and the International Commission.

All the above-mentioned notifications and reports shall indicate the places and dates of arrival or departure and the number of persons arriving or departing.

(g) The International Commission, through its Inspection Teams, shall supervise and inspect the rotation of units and groups of personnel and the arrival and departure of individual personnel as authorized above, at the points of entry enumerated in Article 20 below.

Article 17

(a) With effect from the date of entry into force of the present Agreement, the introduction into Viet-Nam of any reinforcements in the form of all types of arms, munitions and other war material, such as combat aircraft, naval craft, pieces of ordnance, jet engines and jet weapons and armoured vehicles, is prohibited.

(b) It is understood, however, that war material, arms and munitions which have been destroyed, damaged, worn out or used up after the cessation of hostilities may be replaced on the basis of piece-for-piece of the same type and with similar characteristics. Such replacements of war material, arms and munitions shall not be permitted for French Union troops stationed north of the provisional military demarcation line laid down in Article 1 of the present Agreement, during the withdrawal period provided for in Article 2.

Naval craft may perform transport operations between the regrouping zones.

(c) The war material, arms and munitions for replacement purposes provided for in paragraph (b) of this Article, shall be introduced into Viet-Nam only through the points of entry enumerated in Article 20 below. War material, arms and munitions to be replaced shall be shipped from Viet-Nam only through the points of entry enumerated in Article 20 below;

(d) Apart from the replacements permitted within the limits laid down in paragraph (b) of this Article, the introduction of war material, arms and munitions of all types in the form of unassembled parts for subsequent assembly is prohibited;

(e) Each party shall notify the Joint Commissin and the International Commission at least two days in advance of any arrivals or departures which may take place of war material, arms and munitions of all types.

In order to justify the requests for the introduction into Viet-Nam of arms, munitions and other war material (as defined in paragraph (a) of this Article) for replacement purposes, a report concerning each incoming shipment shall be submitted to the Joint Commission and the International Commission. Such reports shall indicate the use made of the items so replaced.

(f) The International Commission, through its Inspection Teams, shall supervise and inspect the replacements permitted in the circumstances laid down in this Article, at the points of entry enumerated in Article 20 below.

Article 18

With effect from the date of entry into force of the present Agreement, the establishment of new military bases is prohibited throughout Viet-Nam territory.

Article 19

With effect from the date of entry into force of the present Agreement, no military base under the control of a foreign State may be established in the regrouping zone of either party; the two parties shall ensure that the zones assigned to them do not adhere to any military alliance and are not used for the resumption of hostilities or to further an aggressive policy.

Article 20

The points of entry into Viet-Nam for rotation personnel and replacements of material are fixed as follows:

—Zones to the north of the provisional military demarcation line: Laokay, Langson, Tien-Yen, Haiphong, Vinh, Dong-Hoi, Muong-Sen;
—Zones to the south of the provisional military demarcation line: Tourane, Quinhon, Nhatrang, Bangoi, Saigon, Cap St. Jacques, Tanchau.

CHAPTER IV

PRISONERS OF WAR AND CIVILIAN INTERNEES

Article 21

The liberation and repatriation of all prisoners of war and civilian internees detained by each of the two parties at the coming into force of the present Agreement shall be carried out under the following conditions:

(a) All prisoners of war and civilian internees of Viet-Nam, French and other nationalities captured since the beginning of hostilities in Viet-Nam during military operations or in any other circumstances of war and in any part of the territory of Viet-Nam shall be liberated within a period of thirty (30) days after the date when the cease-fire becomes effective in each theatre.

(b) The term "civilian internees" is understood to mean all persons who, having in any way contributed to the political and armed struggle between the two parties, have been arrested for that reason and have been kept in detention by either party during the period of hostilities.

(c) All prisoners of war and civilian internees held by either party shall be surrendered to the appropriate authorities of the other party, who shall give them all possible assistance in proceeding to their country of origin, place of habitual residence or the zone of their choice.

CHAPTER V

MISCELLANEOUS

Article 22

The Commanders of the Forces of the two parties shall ensure that persons under their respective commands who violate any of the provisions of the present Agreement are suitably punished.

Article 23

In cases in which the place of burial is known and the existence of graves has been established, the Commander of the Forces of either party shall, within a specific period after the entry into force of the Armistice Agreement, permit the graves service personnel of the other party to enter the part of Viet-Nam territory under their military control for the purpose of finding and removing the bodies of deceased military personnel of that party, including the bodies of deceased prisoners of war. The Joint Commission shall determine the procedures and the time limit for the performance of this task. The Commanders of the Forces of the two parties shall communicate to each other all information in their possession as to the place of burial of military personnel of the other party.

Article 24

The present Agreement shall apply to all the armed forces of either party. The armed forces of each party shall respect the demilitarized zone and the territory under the military control of the other party, and shall commit no act and undertake no operation against the other party and shall not engage in blockade of any kind in Viet-Nam.

For the purposes of the present Article, the word "territory" includes territorial waters and air space.

Article 25

The Commanders of the Forces of the two parties shall afford full protection and all possible assistance and co-operation to the Joint Commission and its joint groups and to the International Commission and its inspection teams in the performance of the functions and tasks assigned to them by the present Agreement.

Article 26

The costs involved in the operations of the Joint Commission and joint groups and of the International Commission and its Inspection Teams shall be shared equally between the two parties.

Article 27

The signatories of the present Agreement and their successors in their functions shall be responsible for ensuring the observance and enforcement of the terms and provisions thereof. The Commanders of the Forces of the two parties shall, within their respective commands, take all steps and make all arrangements necessary to ensure full compliance with all the provisions of the present Agreement by all elements and military personnel under their command.

The procedures laid down in the present Agreement shall, whenever necessary, be studied by the Commanders of the two parties, and, if necessary, defined more specifically by the Joint Commission.

CHAPTER VI

JOINT COMMISSION AND INTERNATIONAL COMMISSION FOR SUPERVISION AND CONTROL IN VIET-NAM

Article 28

Responsibility for the execution of the agreement on the cessation of hostilities shall rest with the parties.

Article 29

An International Commission shall ensure the control and supervision of this execution.

Article 30

In order to facilitate, under the conditions shown below, the execution of provisions concerning joint actions by the two parties a Joint Commission shall be set up in Viet-Nam.

Article 31

The Joint Commission shall be composed of an equal number of representatives of the Commanders of the two parties.

Article 32

The Presidents of the delegations to the Joint Commission shall hold the rank of General.

The Joint Commission shall set up joint groups the number of which shall be determined by mutual agreement between the parties. The joint groups shall be composed of an equal number of officers from both parties. Their location on the demarcation line between the re-grouping zones shall be determined by the parties whilst taking into account the powers of the Joint Commission.

Article 33

The Joint Commission shall ensure the execution of the following provisions of the Agreement on the cessation of hostilities:

(a) A simultaneous and general cease-fire in Viet-Nam for all regular and irregular armed forces of the two parties.

(b) A re-groupment of the armed forces of the two parties.

(c) Observance of the demarcation lines between the re-grouping zones and of the demilitarized sectors.

Within the limits of its competence it shall help the parties to execute the said provisions, shall ensure liaison between them for the purpose of preparing and carrying out plans for the application of these provisions, and shall endeavor to solve such disputed questions as may arise between the parties in the course of executing these provisions.

Article 34

An International Commission shall be set up for the control and supervision over the application of the provisions of the agreement on the cessation of hostilities in Viet-Nam. It shall be composed of representatives of the following States: Canada, India and Poland.

It shall be presided over by the Representative of India.

Article 35

The International Commission shall set up fixed and mobile inspection teams, composed of an equal number of officers appointed by each of the above-mentioned States. The fixed teams shall be located at the following points: Lao-kay, Langson, Tien-Yen, Haiphong, Vinh, Dong-Hoi, Muong-Sen, Tourane, Quinhon, Nhatrang, Bangoi, Saigon, Cap St. Jacques, Tranchau. These points of location may, at a later date, be altered at the request of the Joint Commission, or of one of the parties, or of the International Commission itself, by agreement between the International Commission and the command of the party concerned. The zones of action of the mobile teams shall be the regions bordering the land and sea frontiers of Viet-Nam, the demarcation lines between the re-grouping zones and the demilitarized zones. Within the limits of these zones they shall have the right to move freely and shall receive from the local civil and military authorites all facilities they may require for the fulfilment of their tasks (provision of personnel, placing at their disposal documents needed for supervision, summoning witnesses necessary for holding enquiries, ensuring the security and freedom of movement of the inspection teams, etc. . . .). They shall have at their disposal such modern means of transport, observation and communication as they may require. Beyond the zones of action as defined above, the mobile teams may, by agreement with the command of the party concerned, carry out other movements within the limits of the tasks given them by the present agreement.

Article 36

The International Commission shall be responsible for supervising the proper execution by the parties of the provisions of the agreement. For this purpose it shall fulfil the tasks of control, observation, inspection and investigation connected with the application of the provisions of the agreement on the cessation of the hostilities, and it shall in particular:

(a) Control the movement of the armed forces of the two parties, effected within the framework of the regroupment plan.

(b) Supervise the demarcation lines between the regrouping areas, and also the demilitarized zones.

(c) Control the operations of releasing prisoners of war and civilian internees.

(d) Supervise at ports and airfields as well as along all frontiers of Viet-Nam the execution of the provisions of the agreement on the cessation of hostilities, regulating the introduction into the country of armed forces, military personnel and of all kinds of arms, munitions and war material.

Article 37

The International Commission shall, through the medium of the inspection teams mentioned above, and as soon as possible either on its own initiative, or at the request of the Joint Commission, or of one of the parties, undertake the necessary investigations both documentary and on the ground.

Article 38

The inspection teams shall submit to the International Commission the results of their supervision, their investigation and their observations; furthermore, they shall draw up such special reports as they may consider necessary or as may be requested from them by the Commission. In the case of a disagreement within the teams, the conclusions of each member shall be submitted to the Commission.

Article 39

If any one inspection team is unable to settle an incident or considers that there is a violation or a threat of a serious violation, the International Commission shall be informed; the latter shall study the reports and the conclusions of the inspection teams and shall inform the parties of the measures which should be taken for the settlement of the incident, ending of the violation or removal of the threat of violation.

Article 40

When the Joint Commission is unable to reach an agreement on the interpretation to be given to some provision or on the appraisal of a fact, the International Commission shall be informed of the disputed question. Its recommendations shall be sent directly to the parties and shall be notified to the Joint Commission.

Article 41

The recommendations of the International Commission shall be adopted by majority vote, subject to the provisions contained in article 42. If the votes are divided the chairman's vote shall be decisive.

The International Commission may formulate recommendations concerning amendments and additions which should be made to the provisions of the agreement on the cessation of hostilities in Viet-Nam, in order to ensure a more effective execution of that agreement. These recommendations shall be adopted unanimously.

Article 42

When dealing with questions concerning violations, or threats of violations, which might lead to a resumption of hostilities, namely:

(a) Refusal by the armed forces of one party to effect the movements provided for in the regroupment plan;
(b) Violation by the armed forces of one of the parties of the regrouping zones, territorial waters, or air space of the other party;

the decisions of the International Commission must be unanimous.

Article 43

If one of the parties refuses to put into effect a reommendation of the International Commission, the parties concerned or the Commission itself shall inform the members of the Geneva Conference.

If the International Commission does not reach unanimity in the cases provided for in Article 42, it shall submit a majority report and one or more minority reports to the members of the Conference.

The International Commission shall inform the members of the Conference in all cases where its activity is being hindered.

Article 44

The International Commission shall be set up at the time of the cessation of hostilities in Indo-China in order that it should be able to fulfil the tasks provided for in Article 36.

Article 45

The International Commission for Supervision and Control in Viet-Nam shall act in close co-operation with the International Commissions for Supervision and Control in Cambodia and Laos.

The Secretaries-General of these three Commissions shall be responsible for co-ordinating their work and for relations between them.

Article 46

The International Commission for Supervision and Control in Viet-Nam may, after consultation with the International Commissions for Supervision and Control in Cambodia and Laos, and having regard to the development of the situation in Cambodia and Laos, progressively reduce its activities. Such a decision must be adopted unanimously.

Article 47

All the provisions of the present Agreement, save the second sub-paragraph of Article 11, shall enter into force at 2400 hours (Geneva time) on 22 July 1954.

Done in Geneva at 2400 hours on the 20th of July 1954 in French and in Viet-Namese, both texts being equally authentic.

For the Commander-in-Chief of the People's
Army of Viet-Nam
Ta-Quang-Buu, Vice-Minister of National
Defence of the Democratic Republic of Viet-Nam

For the Commander-in-Chief of the French
Union Forces in Indo-China
Brigadier-General Delteil

Annex I
Delineation of the Provisional Military Demarcation Line and the Demilitarized Zone
(Reference: Article 1 of the Agreement)

(a) The provisional military demarcation line is fixed as follows, reading from east to west:

the mouth of the Song Ben Hat (Cua Tung River) and the course of that river (known as the Rao Thanh in the mountains) to the village of Bo Ho Su, then the parallel of Bo Ho Su to the Laos-Viet-Nam frontier.

(b) The demilitarized zone shall be delimited by Trung Gia Military Commission in accordance with the provisions of Article 1 of the Agreement on the cessation of hostilities in Viet-Nam.

Annex II
General Delineation of the Provisional Assembly Area
(Reference: Article 15 of the Agreement)

(a) North Viet-Nam

Delineation of the boundary of the provisional assembly area of the French Union forces:

1. The perimiter of Hanoi is delimited by the arc of a circle with a radius of 15 kilometres, having as its center the right bank abutment of Doumer Bridge

and running westwards from the Red River to the Rapids Canal in the north-east.

> In this particular case no forces of the French Union shall be stationed less than 2 kilometres from this perimeter, on the inside thereof.

2. The perimeter of Haiphong shall be delimited by the Song-Van Uc as far as Kim Thanh and a line running from the Song-Van Uc three kilometres north-east of Kim Thanh to cut Road No. 18 two kilometres east of Mao-Khé. Thence a line running three kilometres north of Road 18 to Cho-Troi and a straight line from Cho-Troi to the Mong-Duong ferry.

3. A corridor contained between:

> In the south, the Red River from Thanh-Tri to Bang-Nho, thence a line joining the latter point to Do-My (south-west of Kesat), Gia-Loc and Tien Kieu;
> In the north, a line running along the Rapids Canal at a distance of 1,500 metres to the north of the Canal, passing three kilometres north of Pha-Lai and Seven Pagodas and thence parallel to Road No. 18 to its point of intersection with the perimeter of Haiphong.
> *Note:* Throughout the period of evacuation of the perimeter of Hanoi, the river forces of the French Union shall enjoy complete freedom of movement on the Song-Van Uc. And the forces of the People's Army of Viet-Nam shall withdraw three kilometres south of the south bank of the Song-Van Uc.

Boundary between the perimeter of Hanoi and the perimeter of Haiduong:
A straight line running from the Rapids Canal three kilometres west of Chi-Ne and ending at Do-My (eight kilometres southwest of Kesat).

(b) Central Viet-Nam

Delineation of the boundary of the provisional assembly area of the forces of the Viet-Nam People's Army south of the Col des Nuages parallel:

The perimeter of the Central Viet-Nam area shall consist of the administrative boundaries of the provinces of Quang-Nagi and Binh-Dinh as they were defined before the hostilities.

(C) South Viet-Nam

Three provisional assembly areas shall be provided for the forces of the People's Army of Viet-Nam.

The boundaries of these areas are as follows:

> 1. *Xuyen-Moc, Ham-Tan Area*
> Western boundary: The course of the Song-Ray extended northwards as far as Road No. 1 to a point thereon eight kilometres east of the intersection of Road No. 1 and Road No. 3.
> Northern boundary: Road No. 1 from the above-mentioned intersection to the intersection with Route Communale No. 9 situated 27 kilometres west-south-west of Phanthiet and from that intersection a straight line to Kim Thanh on the coast.

> 2. *Plaine des Joncs Area*
> Northern boundary: The Viet-Nam-Cambodia frontier.
> Western boundary: A straight line from Tong-Binh to Binh-Thanh.
> Southern boundary: Course of the Fleuve Antérieur (Mekong) to ten Kilometres south-east of Cao Lanh. From that point, a straight line as far as Ap-My-Dien,

and from Ap-My-Dien a parallel to and three kilometres east and then south of the Tong Doc-Loc Canal, this line reaches My-Hanh-Dong and thence Hung-Thanh-My.

Eastern boundary: A straight line from Hung-Thanh-My running northwards to the Cambodian frontier south of Doi-Bao-Voi.

3. *Point Camau Area*
Northern boundary: The Song-Cai-lon from its mouth to its junction with the Rach-Nuoc-Trong, thence the Rach-Nuoc-Trong to the bend five kilometres northeast of Ap-Xeo-La. Thereafter a line to the Ngan-Dua Canal and following that Canal as far as Vinh-Hung. Finally, from Vinh-Hung a north-south line to the sea.

G. Protest by the South Vietnamese Delegation Against the Geneva Agreements*

July 21, 1954

The delegation of the State of Viet-Nam has presented a proposal designed to obtain an armistice without division, even provisional, of the territory of Viet-Nam, through the disarmament of all the belligerent forces after their withdrawal to the smallest possible zones of regroupment and the institution of a provisional control by the United Nations over the entire territory, pending the reestablishment of peace and arrangements permitting the Vietnamese people to determine its destiny through free elections. The delegation protests the summary rejection of this proposal, the only one which respects the aspirations of the Vietnamese people. It insists that, at least, the demilitarization and neutralization of the Catholic religious communities in the delta of northern Viet-Nam be accepted by the conference.

It protests solemnly: (a) the hasty conclusion of the armistice agreement, contracted only by the high authority of France and the Vietminh notwithstanding the fact that the French High Command controls the Vietnamese troops only through a delegation of authority by the Chief of State of Viet-Nam, and especially notwithstanding the fact that many clauses of this agreement are of such a nature as gravely to compromise the political future of the Vietnamese people; (b) the fact that this armistice agreement abandons to the Vietminh territories, many of which are still in the possession of Vietnamese troops and thus essential to the defense of Viet-Nam in opposing a larger expansion of Communism and virtually deprives Viet-Nam of the imprescriptible right to organize its defense otherwise than by the maintenance of a foreign army on its territory; (c) the fact that the French High Command has arrogated to itself without preliminary agreement with the delegation of the State of Viet-Nam the right to fix the date of future elections, notwithstanding that a matter of a clearly political character is concerned.

Consequently, the Government of the State of Viet-Nam requests that note be made of its solemn protest against the manner in which the armistice has been concluded and against the condtions of the armistice which take no account

*Relazioni Internazionali, Series 2, XVIII, No. 31, July 31, 1954, p. 926.

of the profound aspirations of the Vietnamese people, and of the fact that it reserves to itself complete freedom of action to guarantee the sacred right of the Vietnamese people to territorial unity, national independence and freedom.

H. Statement by Under Secretary of State Walter B. Smith on the Final Declaration of the Geneva Conference*

July 21, 1954

As I stated on July 18, my Government is not prepared to join in a delcaration by the Conference such as is submitted. However, the United States makes this unilateral declaration of its position in these matters:

DECLARATION

The Government of the United States, being resolved to devote its efforts to the strengthening of peace in accordance with the principles and purposes of the United Nations, takes note of the agreements concluded at Geneva on July 20, and 21, 1954 between (a) the Franco-Laotian Command and the Command of the Peoples Army of Viet-Nam, (b) the Royal Khmer Army Command of the Peoples Army of Viet-Nam, (c) the Franco-Vietnamese Command and the Command of the Peoples Army of Viet-Nam and of paragraphs 1 to 12 inclusive of the declaration presented to the Geneva Conference on July 21, 1954, declares with regard to the aforesaid agreements and paragraphs that (i) it will refrain from the threat or the use of force to disturb them, in accordance with Article 2 (4) of the Charter of the United Nations dealing with the obligation of members to refrain in their international relations from the threat or use of force; and (ii) it would view any renewal of the aggression in violation of the aforesaid agreements with grave concern and as seriously threatening international peace and security.

In connection with the statement in the declaration concerning free elections in Viet-Nam my Government wishes to make clear its position which it has expressed in a declaration made in Washington on June 29, 1954, as follows:

> In the case of nations now divided against their will, we shall continue to seek to achieve unity through free elections supervised by the United Nations to insure that they are conducted fairly.

With respect to the statement made by the representative of the State of Viet-Nam, the United States reiterates its traditional position that peoples are entitled to determine their own future and that it will not join in an arrangement which would hinder this. Nothing in its declaration just made is intended to or does indicate any departure from this traditional position.

We share the hope that the agreements will permit Cambodia, Laos and Viet-Nam to play their part, in full independence and sovereignty, in the peaceful community of nations, and will enable the peoples of that area to determine their own future.

*Department of State Press Release, 394, July 21, 1954.

SEATO TREATY AND DEFENSE OF VIETNAM, 1954-1961

A. The Southeast Asia Collective Defense Treaty*

Signed, Manila, September 8, 1954
Approved by Senate, February 1, 1955
Ratified by President Eisenhower, February 4, 1955
Effective, February 19, 1955

The Parties to this Treaty,

Recognizing the sovereign equality of all the Parties,

Reiterating their faith in the purposes and principles set forth in the Charter of the United Nations and their desire to live in peace with all peoples and all governments,

Reaffirming that, in accordance with the Charter of the United Nations, they uphold the principle of equal rights and self-determination of peoples, and declaring that they will earnestly strive by every peaceful means to promote self-government and to secure the independence of all countries whose peoples desire it and are able to undertake its responsibilities,

Desiring to strengthen the fabric of peace and freedom and to uphold the principles of democracy, individual liberty and the rule of law, and to promote the economic well-being and development of all peoples in the treaty area,

Intending to declare publicly and formally their sense of unity, so that any potential aggressor will appreciate that the Parties stand together in the area, and

Desiring further to coordinate their efforts for collective defense for the preservation of peace and security,

Therefore agree as follows:

Article I

The Parties undetake, as set forth in the Charter of the United Nations, to settle any international disputes in which they may be involved by peaceful means in such a manner that international peace and security and justice are not endangered, and to refrain in their international relations from the threat or use of force in any manner inconsistent with the purposes of the United Nations.

Article II

In order more effectively to achieve the objectives of this Treaty the Parties, separately and jointly, by means of continuous and effective self-help and mutual aid will maintain and develop their individual and collective capacity to resist

*Documents on American Foreign Relations, 1954, pp. 319-23.

473

armed attack and to prevent and counter subversive activities directed from without against their territorial integrity and political stability.

Article III

The Parties undertake to strengthen their free institutions and to cooperate with one another in the further development of economic measures, including technical assistance, designed both to promote economic progress and social well-being and to further the individual and collective efforts of governments toward these ends.

Article IV

1. Each Party recognizes that aggression by means of armed attack in the treaty area against any of the Parties or against any State or territory which the Parties by unanimous agreement may hereafter designate, would endager its own peace and safety, and agrees that it will in that event act to meet the common danger in accordance with its constitutional processes. Measures taken under this paragraphs shall be immediately reported to the Security Council of the United Nations.

2. If, in the opinion of any of the Parties, the inviolability or the integrity of the territory or the sovereignty or political independence of any Party in the treaty area or of any other State or territory to which the provisions of paragraph 1 of this Article from time to time apply is threatened in any way other than by armed attack or is affected or threatened by any fact or situation which might endanger the peace of the area, the Parties shall consult immediately in order to agree on the measures which should be taken for the common defense.

3. It is understood that no action on the territory of any State designated by unanimous agreement under paragraph 1 of this Article or on any territory so designated shall be taken except at the invitation or with the consent of the government concerned.

Article V

The Parties hereby establish a Council, on which each of them shall be represented, to consider matters concerning the implementation of this Treaty. The Council shall provide for consltation with regard to military and any other planning as the situation obtaining in the treaty area may from time to time require. The Council shall be so organized as to be able to meet at any time.

Article VI

This Treaty does not affect and shall not be interpreted as affecting in any way the rights and obligations of any of the Parties under the Charter of the United Nations or the responsibility of the United Nations for the maintenance of international peace and security. Each Party declares that none of the international engagements now in force between it and any other of the Parties or any third party is in conflict with the provisions of this Treaty, and undertakes not to enter into any international engagement in conflict with this Treaty.

Article VII

Any other State in a position to further the objectives of this Treaty and to contribute to the security of the area may, by unanimous agreement of the Parties, be invited to accede to this Treaty. Any State so invited may become a Party to the Treaty by depositing its instrument of accession with the Government of the Republic of the Philippines. The Government of the Republic of the Philippines shall inform each of the Parties of the deposit of each such instrument of accession.

Article VIII

As used in this Treaty, the "treaty area" is the general area of Southeast Asia, including also the entire territories of the Asian Parties, and the general area of the Southwest Pacific not including the Pacific area north of 21 degrees 30 minutes north latitude. The Parties may, by unanimous agreement, amend this Article to include within the treaty area the territory of any State acceding to this Treaty in accordance with Article VII or otherwise to change the treaty area.

Article IX

1. This Treaty shall be deposited in the archives of the Government of the Republic of the Philippines. Duly certified copies thereof shall be transmitted by that government to the other signatories.

2. The Treaty shall be ratified and its provisions carried out by the Parties in accordance with their respective constitutional processes. The instruments of ratification shall be deposited as soon as possible with the Government of the Republic of the Philippines, which shall notify all of the other signatories of such deposit.

3. The Treaty shall enter into force between the States which have ratified it as soon as the instruments of ratification of a majority of the signatories shall have been deposited, and shall come into effect with respect to each other State on the date of the deposit of its instrument of ratification.

Article X

This Treaty shall remain in force indefinitely, but any Party may cease to be a Party one year after its notice of denunciation has been given to the Government of the Republic of the Philippines, which shall inform the Governments of the other Parties of the deposit of each notice of denunciation.

Article XI

The English text of this Treaty is binding on the Parties, but when the Parties have agreed to the French text thereof and have so notified the Government of the Republic of the Philippines, the French text shall be equally authentic and binding on the Parties.

Understanding of the United States of America

The United States of America in executing the present Treaty does so with the understanding that its recognition of the effect of aggression and armed attack and its agreement with reference thereto in Article IV, paragraph 1, apply only to communist aggression but affirms that in the event of other aggression or armed attack it will consult under the provisions of Article IV, paragraph 2.

In witness whereof, the undersigned Plenipotentiaries have signed this Treaty.

Done at Manila, this eighth day of September 1954.

Protocol

Designation of states and territory as to which provisions of Article IV and Article III are to be applicable:

The Parties to the Southeast Asia Collective Defense Treaty unanimously designate for the purposes of Article IV of the Treaty the States of Cambodia and Laos and the free territory under the jurisdiction of the State of Vietnam.

The Parties further agree that the above-mentioned states and territory shall be eligible in respect of the economic measures contemplated by Article III.

This Protocol shall enter into force simultaneously with the coming into force of the Treaty.

In witness whereof, the undersigned Plenipotentiaries have signed this Protocol to the Southeast Asia Collective Defense Treaty.

Done at Manila, this eighth day of September 1954.

B. Communiqué Issued on United States-French Talks on Indochina*

[Extract]

September 29, 1954

*   *   *

The representatives of France and the United States reaffirm the intention of their governments to support the complete independence of Cambodia, Laos, and Viet-Nam. Both France and the United States will continue to assist Cambodia, Laos and Viet-Nam in their efforts to safeguard their freedom and independence and to advance the welfare of their peoples. In this spirit France and the United States are assisting the Government of Viet-Nam in the resettlement of the Vietnamese who have of their own free will moved to free Viet-Nam and who already number some 300,000.

In order to contribute to the security of the area pending the further development of national forces for this purpose, the representatives of France indicated that France is prepared to retain forces of its Expeditionary Corps, in agreement with the government concerned, within the limits permitted under the Geneva agreements and to an extent to be determined. The United States will consider the question of financial assistance for the forces of each of the three Associated States. These questions vitally affect each of the three Associated States and are being fully discussed with them.

The channel for French and United States economic aid, budgetary support, and other assistance to each of the Associated States will be direct to that state. The United States representatives will begin discussions soon with the respective governments of the Associated States regarding direct aid. The methods for efficient coordination of French and United States aid programs to each of the three Associated States are under consideration and will be developed in discussions with each of these states.

After the bilateral talks, the chiefs of diplomatic missions in Washington of Cambodia, Laos and Viet-Nam were invited to a final meeting to have an exchange of views and information on these matters. The representatives of all five countries are in complete agreement on the objectives of peace and freedom to be achieved in Indochina.

C. Letter From President Eisenhower to Ngo Dinh Diem, President of the Council of Ministers of Vietnam, on United States Aid*

October 23, 1954

Dear Mr. President:

I have been following with great interest the course of developments in Viet-Nam, particularly since the conclusion of the conference at Geneva. The implica-

*Department of State Press Release, 542, Sept. 29, 1954.
*Department of State Bulletin, Nov. 15, 1954, pp. 735-36.

tions of the agreement concerning Viet-Nam have caused grave concern regarding the future of a country temporarily divided by an artificial military grouping, weakened by a long and exhausting war and faced with enemies without and by their subversive collaborators within.

Your recent requests for aid to assist in the formidable project of the movement of several hundred thousand loyal Vietnamese citizens away from areas which are passing under a *de facto* rule and political ideology which they abhor, are being fulfilled. I am glad that the United States is able to assist in this humanitarian effort.

We have been exploring ways and means to permit our aid to Viet-Nam to be more effective and to make a greater contribution to the welfare and stability of the Government of Viet-Nam. I am, accordingly, instructing the American Ambassador to Viet-Nam to examine with you in your capacity as Chief of Government, how an intelligent program of American aid given directly to your Government can serve to assist Viet-Nam in its present hour of trial, provided that your Government is prepared to give assurances as to the standards of performance it would be able to maintain in the event such aid were supplied.

The purpose of this offer is to assist the Government of Viet-Nam in developing and maintaining a strong, viable state, capable of resisting attempted subversion or aggression through military means. The Government of the United States expects that this aid, will be met by performance on the part of the Government of Viet-Nam in undertaking needed reforms. It hopes that such aid combined with your own continuing efforts, will contribute effectively toward an independent Viet-Nam endowed with a strong government. Such a government would, I hope, be so responsive to the nationalist aspirations of its people, so enlightened in purpose and effective in performance, that it will be respected both at home and abroad and discourage any who might wish to impose a foreign ideology on your free people.

D. Letters of Congratulations From President Eisenhower to President Diem on Progress Made in South Vietnam*

July 6, 1956

Dear Mr. President: At this time I wish to extend to you and to your associates my warmest congratulations. The people of my country and of the entire Free World admire the devotion, the courage and determination which you have shown in surmounting the difficulties which confronted your newly independent country.

We recall, in particular, your success in inspiring a sense of national unity among your people; the courage of the Vietnamese nation in withstanding the pressures of aggressive Communism; and the notable progress made by your country toward the great goal of constitutional government.

I am proud that the Government and the people of the United States have been able to contribute to your successful efforts to restore stability and security to your country, and to help lay a solid basis for social and economic reconstruction.

*Ibid., July 23, 1956, pp. 150-51; Nov. 12, 1956, p. 765.

I speak for the people of the United States in our well wishes today to you and your countrymen and I look to many years of partnership in the achievement of our common goals.

October 22, 1956

Dear Mr. President: The admiration with which I have watched the progress of the Republic of Viet-Nam during the past year prompts me to send you the warmest congratulations of the American people on the occasion of the first anniversary of the Republic and upon the promulgation of the Vietnamese Constitution.

The American people have observed the remarkable struggle of the Vietnamese people during the past years to achieve and to maintain their independence. The successes of the Republic of Viet-Nam in thwarting the aggressive designs of Communism without, and in surmounting the most difficult obstacles within, have shown what can be achieved when a people rally to the cause of freedom.

We in America pray that those now still living in the enslaved part of your country may one day be united in peace under the free Republic of Viet-Nam.

The achievements of the Vietnamese people will long remain a source of inspiration to free peoples everywhere. As Viet-Nam enters this new period of national reconstruction and rehabilitation, my fellow countrymen and I are proud to be sharing some of the tasks which engage you.

May the Vietnamese people inspired by your dedicated leadership and the high principles of their democratic institutions, enjoy long years of prosperity in justice and in peace.

E. Statement Issued Following Talks Between President Eisenhower and President Diem*

May 11, 1957

His Excellency Ngo Dinh Diem, President of the Republic of Viet-Nam, and President Eisenhower have held discussions during President Ngo Dinh Diem's state visit as the guest of President Eisenhower during May 8—10.

Their discussions have been supplemented by meetings between President Ngo Dinh Diem and his advisers and Secretary of State Dulles and other American officials. These meetings afforded the occasion for reaffirming close mutual friendship and support between the Republic of Viet-Nam and the United States. The two Presidents exchanged views on the promotion of peace and stability and the development and consolidation of freedom in Viet-Nam and in the Far East as a whole.

President Eisenhower complimented President Ngo Dinh Diem on the remarkable achievements of the Republic of Viet-Nam under the leadership of President Ngo Dinh Diem since he took office in July 1954. It was noted that in less than three years a chaotic situation resulting from years of war had been changed into one of progress and stability.

*Ibid., May 27, 1957, pp. 851-52.

Nearly one million refugees who had fled from Communist tyranny in North Viet-Nam had been cared for and resettled in Free Viet-Nam.

Internal security had been effectively established.

A constitution had been promulgated and a national assembly elected.

Plans for agrarian reform have been launched, and a constructive program developed to meet long-range economic and social problems to promote higher living standards for the Vietnamese people.

President Ngo Dinh Diem reviewed with President Eisenhower the efforts and means of the Vietnamese Government to promote political stability and economic welfare in the Republic of Viet-Nam. President Eisenhower assured President Ngo Dinh Diem of the willingness of the United States to continue to offer effective assistance within the constitutional processes of the United States to meet these objectives.

President Eisenhower and President Ngo Dinh Diem looked forward to an end of the unhapy division of the Vietnamese people and confirmed the determination of the two Governments to work together to seek suitable means to bring about the peaceful unification of Viet-Nam in freedom in accordance with the purposes and principles of the United Nations Charter. It was noted with pleasure that the General Assembly of the United Nations by a large majority had found the Republic of Viet-Nam qualified for membership in the Unted Nations, which has been prevented by Soviet opposition.

President Eisenhower and President Ngo Dinh Diem noted in contrast the large build-up of Vietnamese Communist military forces in North Viet-Nam during the past two and one-half years, the harsh suppression of the revolts of the people of North Viet-Nam in seeking liberty, and their increasing hardships. While noting the apparent diminution during the last three years of Communist-inspired hostilites in Southeast Asia except in the Kingdom of Laos, President Eisenhower and President Ngo Dinh Diem expressed concern over continuing Communist subversive capabilities in this area and elsewhere. In particular, they agreed that the continued military build-up of the Chinese Communists, their refusal to renounce the use of force, and their unwillingness to subscribe to standards of conduct of civilized nations constitute a continuing threat to the safety of all free nations in Asia. To counter this threat, President Ngo Dinh Diem indicated his strong desire and his efforts to seek closer cooperation with the free countries of Asia.

Noting that the Republic of Viet-Nam is covered by Article IV of the Southeast Asia Collective Defense Treaty, President Eisenhower and President Ngo Dinh Diem agreed that aggression or subversion threatening the political independence of the Republic of Viet-Nam would be considered as endangering peace and stability. The just settlement of problems of the area by peaceful and legitimate means within the framework of the United Nations Charter will continue to be the mutual concern of both Governments. Finally, President Eisenhower and President Ngo Dinh Diem expressed the desire and determination of the two Governments to cooperate closely together for freedom and independence in the world.

KENNEDY ADMINISTRATION POLICY IN VIETNAM

A. Statement by Secretary Rusk on the Communist Threat to South Vietnam*

[Extract]

May 4, 1961

I thought that it might be useful if I were to make some comments on the background of the situation in Viet-Nam—that is, not background comments but comments on the background.

Since late in 1959 organized Communist activity in the form of guerrilla raids against army and security units of the Government of Viet-Nam, terrorist acts against local officials and civilians, and other subversive activities in the Republic of Viet-Nam have increased to levels unprecedented since the Geneva agreements of 1954. During this period the organized armed strength of the Viet Cong, the Communist apparatus operating in the Republic of Viet-Nam, has grown from about 3,000 to over 12,000 personnel. This armed strength has been supplemented by an increase in the numbers of political and propaganda agents in the area.

During 1960 alone, Communist armed units and terrorists assassinated or kidnaped over 3,000 local officials, military personnel, and civilians. Their activities took the form of armed attacks against isolated garrisons, attacks on newly established townships, ambushes on roads and canals, destruction of bridges, and well-planned sabotage against public works and communication lines. Because of Communist guerrilla activity 200 elementary schools had to be closed at various times, affecting over 25,000 students and 800 teachers.

This upsurge of Communist guerrilla activity apparently stemmed from a decision made in May 1959 by the Central Committee of the Communist Party of north Viet-Nam which called for the reunification of Viet-Nam by all "appropriate means." In July of the same year the Central Committee was reorganized and charged with intelligence duties and the "liberation" of south Viet-Nam. In retrospect this decision to step up guerrilla activity was made to reverse the remarkable success which the Government of the Republic of Viet-Nam under President Ngo Dinh Diem had achieved in consolidating its political position and in attaining significant economic recovery in the 5 years between 1954 and 1959.

Remarkably coincidental with the renewed Communist activity in Laos, the Communist Party of North Viet-Nam at its Third Congress on September 10, 1960, adopted a resolution which declared that the Vietnamese revolution has as a major strategic task the liberation of the south from the "rule of U.S. imperialists and their henchmen." This resolution called for the direct overthrow of the government of the Republic of Viet-Nam.

*Department of State Bulletin, May 22, 1961, pp. 757-58.

The most recent gains by the Pathet Lao in the southern part of Laos have given added seriousness to the security situation in Viet-Nam. Communist control over Lao territory bordering Viet-Nam south of the 17th parallel makes more secure one of the three principal routes by which north Vietnamese armed units have been able to infiltrate the Republic of Viet-Nam. The other two routes are, as is well known, directly across the 17th parallel and by sea along the coastline of the Republic of Viet-Nam. In addition to the obvious fact that the strength of the Pathet Lao has been tremendously increased by the importation of light and heavy arms from the outside, we have no reason to doubt that the north Vietnamese armed units not [*sic:* now?] operating in Laos have been similarly reequipped and strengthened from the same outside source.

The increased Communist activity in the Republic of Viet-Nam and countermeasures to meet this threat have been matters of urgent and recent discussions, both by the officials of Viet-Nam and the United States. In connection with these the President has authorized an increase in the amount of military assistance, and a number of other measures have been determined upon. Furthermore the United States has undertaken training and advisory measures which are designed to strengthen both materially and militarily the ability of the Viet-Nam armed forces to overcome this increased Communist threat. A part of the effort, of course, must include in a situation of this sort a vigorous civil program as well in the economic and social field.

*   *   *

B. Letter from President Kennedy to President Diem on the Communist Threat*

December 14, 1961

Dear Mr. President: I have received your recent letter in which you described so cogently the dangerous condtion caused by North Viet-Nam's efforts to take over our country.[1] The situation in your embattled country is well known to me and to the American people. We have been deeply disturbed by the assault on your country. Our indignation has mounted as the deliberate savagery of the Communist program of assassination, kidnapping and wanton violence became clear.

Your letter underlines what our own information has convincingly shown—that the campaign of force and terror now being waged against your people and your Government is supported and directed from the outside by the authorities at Hanoi. They have thus violated the provisions of the Geneva Accords designed to ensure peace in Viet-Nam and to which they bound themselves in 1954.

At that time, the United States, although not a party to the Accords, declared that it "would view any renewal of the aggression in volation of the agreements with grave concern and as seriously threatening international peace and security." We continue to maintain that view.

_____
* *Ibid.*, Jan. 1, 1952, p. 13.
[1] *Ibid.*, pp. 13-14.

In accordance with that declaration, and in response to your request, we are prepared to help the Republic of Viet-Nam to protect its people and to preserve its independence. We shall promptly increase our assistance to your defense effort as well as help relieve the destruction of the floods which you describe. I have already given the orders to get these programs underway.

The United States, like the Republic of Viet-Nam, remains devoted to the cause of peace and our primary purpose is to help your people maintain their independence. If the Communist authorities in North Viet-Nam will stop their campaign to destroy the Republic of Viet-Nam, the measures we are taking to assist your defense efforts will no longer be necessary. We shall seek to persuade the Communists to give up their attempts of force and subversion. In any case, we are confident that the Vietnamese people will preserve their independence and gain the peace and prosperity for which they have sought so hard and so long.

C. Interview between President Kennedy and Walter Cronkite of CBS-TV News on Vietnam*

[Extract]

September 2, 1963

*   *   *

Mr. Cronkite: Mr. President, the only hot war we've got running at the moment is of course the one in Viet-Nam, and we have our difficulties there, quite obviously.

President Kennedy: I don't think that unless a greater effort is made by the Government to win popular support that the war can be won out there. In the final analysis, it is their war. They are the ones who have to win it or lose it. We can help them, we can give them equipment, we can send our men out there as advisers, but they have to win it—the people of Viet-Nam—against the Communists. We are prepared to continue to assist them, but I don't think that the war can be won unless the people support the effort, and, in my opinion, in the last 2 months the Government has gotten out of touch with the people.

The repressions against the Buddhists, we felt, were very unwise. Now all we can do is to make it very clear that we don't think this is the way to win. It is my hope that this will become increasingly obvious to the Government, that they will take steps to try to bring back popular support for this very essential struggle.

Mr. Cronkite: Do you think this Government has time to regain the support of the people?

President Kennedy: I do. With changes in policy and perhaps with personnel, I think it can. If it doesn't make those changes, I would think that the chances of winning it would not be very good.

Mr. Cronkite: Hasn't every indication from Saigon been that President [Ngo

*Ibid., Sept. 30, 1963, pp. 498-99.

Dinh] Diem has no intention of changing his pattern?

President Kennedy: If he does not change it, of course, that is his decision. He has been there 10 years, and, as I say, he has carried this burden when he has been counted out on a number of occasions.

Our best judgment is that he can't be successful on this basis. We hope that he comes to see that; but in the final analysis it is the people and the Government itself who have to win or lose this struggle. All we can do is help, and we are making it very clear. But I don't agree with those who say we should withdraw. That would be a great mistake. That would be a great mistake. I know people don't like Americans to be engaged in this kind of an effort. Forty-seven Americans have been killed in combat with the enemy, but this is a very important struggle even though it is far away.

We took all this—made this effort to defend Europe. Now Europe is quite secure. We also have to participate—we may not like it—in the defense of Asia.

D. Interview between President Kennedy and NBC-TV Newsmen Chet Huntley and David Brinkley on Vietnam*

[Extract]

September 9, 1963

*   *   *

Mr. Huntley: Are we likely to reduce our aid to South Viet-Nam now?

The President: I don't think we think that would be helpful at this time. If you reduce your aid, it is possible you could have some effect upon the government structure there. On the other hand, you might have a situation which could bring about a collapse. Strongly in our mind is what happened in the case of China at the end of World War II, where China was lost—a weak government became increasingly unable to control events. We don't want that.

Mr. Brinkley: Mr. President, have you had any reason to doubt this so-called "domino theory," that if South Viet-Nam falls, the rest of Southeast Asia will go behind it?

The President: No, I believe it. I believe it. I think that the struggle is close enough. China is so large, looms so high just beyond the frontiers, that if South Viet-Nam went, it would not assault on Malaya but would also give the impression that the wave of the future in Southeast Asia was China and the Communists. So I believe it.

*   *   *

*Ibid., Sept. 30, 1963, pp. 499-500.

E. White House Statement on the Vietnamese Situation*

October 2, 1963

Secretary [of Defense Robert S.] McNamara and General [Maxwell D.] Taylor reported to the President this morning and to the National Security Council this afternoon. Their report included a number of classified findings and recommendations which will be the subject of further review and action. Their basic presentation was endorsed by all members of the Security Council and the following statement of United States policy was approved by the President on the basis of recommendations received from them and from Ambassador [Henry Cabot] Lodge.

1. The security of South Viet-Nam is a major interest of the United States as [of] other free nations. We will adhere to our policy of working with the people and Government of South Viet-Nam to deny this country to communism and to suppress the externally stimulated and supported insurgency of the Viet Cong as promptly as possible. Effective performance in this undertaking is the central objective of our policy in South Viet-Nam.

2. The military program in South Viet-Nam has made progress and is sound in principle, though improvements are being energetically sought.

3. Major U.S. assistance in support of this military effort is needed only until the insurgency has been suppressed or until the national security forces of the Government of South Viet-Nam are capable of suppressing it.

Secretary McNamara and General Taylor reported their judgment that the major part of the U.S. military task can be completed by the end of 1965, although there may be a continuing requirement for a limited number of U.S. training personnel. They reported that by the end of this year, the U.S. program for training Vietnamese should have progressed to the point where 1,000 U.S. military personnel assigned to South Viet-Nam can be withdrawn.

4. The political situation in South Viet-Nam remains deeply serious. The United States has made clear its continuing opposition to any repressive actions in South Viet-Nam. While such actions have not yet significantly affected the military effort, they could do so in the future.

5. It remains the policy of the United States, in South Viet-Nam as in other parts of the world, to support the efforts of the people of that country to defeat aggression and to build a peaceful and free society.

*Ibid., Oct. 21, 1963, p. 624.

JOHNSON ADMINISTRATION POLICY TOWARD VIETNAM

INCREASED MILITARY AID

A. Letter from President Johnson to General Duong Van Minh, Chairman of the Military Revolutionary Council in Vietnam, Assuring U.S. Support to South Vietnam*

December 31, 1963

Dear General Minh: As we enter the New Year of 1964, I want to wish you, your Revolutionary Government, and your people full success in the long and arduous war which you are waging so tenaciously and bravely against the Viet Cong forces directed and supported by the Communist regime in Hanoi. Ambassador Lodge and Secretary McNamara have told me about the serious situation which confronts you and of the plans which you are developing to enable your armed forces and your people to redress this situation.

This new year provides a fitting opportunity for me to pledge on behalf of the American Government and people a renewed partnership with your government and people in your brave struggle for freedom. The United States will continue to furnish you and your people with the fullest measure of support in this bitter fight. We shall maintain in Viet-Nam American personnel and material as needed to assist you in achieving victory.

Our aims are, I know, identical with yours: to enable your government to protect its people from the acts of terror perpetrated by Communist insurgents from the north. As the forces of your government become increasingly capable of dealing with this aggression, American military personnel in South Viet-Nam can be progressively withdrawn.

The United States Government shares the view of your government that "neutralization" of South Viet-Nam is unacceptable. As long as the Communist regime in North Viet-Nam persists in its aggressive policy, neutralization of South Viet-Nam would only be another name for a Communist takeover. Peace will return to your country just as soon as the authorities in Hanoi cease and desist from their terrorist aggression.

Thus, your government and mine are in complete agreement on the political aspects of your war against the forces of enslavement, brutality, and material misery. Within this framework of political agreement we can confidently continue and improve our cooperation.

I am pleased to learn from Secretary McNamara about the vigorous operations which you are planning to bring security and an improved standard of living to your people.

I wish to congratulate you particularly on your work for the unity of all your people, including the Hoa Hao and Cao Dai, against the Viet Cong. I know from my own experience in Viet-Nam how warmly the Vietnamese people respond to a direct human approach and how they have hungered for this in

*Department of State Bulletin, Jan. 27, 1964, pp. 121-22.

486

their leaders. So again I pledge the energetic support of my country to your government and your people.

We will do our full part to ensure that under your leadership your people may win a victory—a victory for freedom and justice and human welfare in Viet-Nam.

B. Appeal by President Johnson for More Aid to South Vietnam*

[Extract]

May 18, 1964

To the Congress of the United States:

Last January, in my budget message to the Congress, I pointed out that this budget made no provision for any major new requirements that might emerge later for our mutual defense and development program. I stated then that if such requirements should arise I would request prompt action by the Congress to provide additional funds.

That need has emerged in Vietnam. I now request that the Congress provide $125 million in additon to the $3.4 billion already proposed for foreign assistance; $70 million is required for economic and $55 million for military uses in Vietnam.

Since the 1965 budget was prepared, two major changes have occurred in Vietnam:

First, the Viet Cong guerrillas, under orders from their Communist masters in the north, have intensified terrorist actions against the peaceful people of South Vietnam. This increased terrorism requires increased response.

Second, a new government under Prime Minister [Nguyen] Khanh has come to power, bringing new energy and leadership and new hope for effective action. I share with Ambassador [Henry Cabot] Lodge the conviction that this new government can mount a successful campaign against the Communists.

*   *   *

The vigorous decisions taken by the new Government of Vietnam to mobilize the full resources of the country merit our strongest support. Increased Communist terror requires it.

By our words and deeds in a decade of determined effort, we are pledged before all the world to stand with the free people of Vietnam. Sixteen thousand Americans are serving our country and the people of Vietnam. Daily they face danger in the cause of freedom. Duty requires, and the American people demand,. that we give them the fullest measure of support.

*   *   *

Ibid., June 8, 1964, pp. 891-93.

THE GULF OF TONKIN INCIDENT

C. Message by President Johnson to the American People*

August 4, 1964

My fellow Americans: As President and Commander in Chief, it is my duty to the American people to report that renewed hostile actions against United States ships on the high seas in the Gulf of Tonkin have today required me to order the military forces of the United States to take action in reply.

The initial attack on the destroyer *Maddox,* on August 2, was repeated today by a number of hostile vessels atacking two U.S. destroyers with torpedoes. The destroyers and supporting aircraft acted at once on the orders I gave after the initial act of aggression. We believe at least two of the attacking boats were sunk. There were no U.S. losses.

The performance of commanders and crews in this engagement is in the highest tradition of the United States Navy. But repeated acts of violence against the Armed Forces of the United States must be met not only with alert defense but with positive reply. That reply is being given as I speak to you tonight. Air action is now in execution against gunboats and certain supporting facilities in North Viet-Nam which have been used in these hostile operations.

In the larger sense this new act of aggression, aimed directly at our own forces, again brings home to all of us in the United States the importance of the struggle for peace and security in Southeast Asia. Aggression by terror against the peaceful villagers of South Viet-Nam has now been joined by open aggression on the high seas against the United States of America.

The determination of all Americans to carry out our full commitment to the people and to the Government of South Viet-Nam will be redoubled by this outrage. Yet our response, for the present, will be limited and fitting. We Americans know, although others appear to forget, the risks of spreading conflict. We will seek no wider war.

I have instructed the Secretary of State to make this position totally clear to friends and to adversaries and, indeed to all. I have instructed Ambassador [Adlai E.] Stevenson to raise this matter immediately and urgently before the Security Council of the United Nations. Finally, I have today met with the leaders of both parties in the Congress of the United States, and I have informed them that I shall immediately request the Congress to pass a resolution making it clear that our Government is united in its determination to take all necessary measures in support of freedom and in defense of peace in Southeast Asia.

I have been given encouraging assurance by these leaders of both parties that such a resolution will be promptly introduced, freely and expeditiously debated, and passed with overwhelming support. And just a few minutes ago I was able to reach Senator Goldwater, and I am glad to say that he has expressed his support of the statement that I am making to you tonight. It is a solemn responsibility to have to order even limited military action by forces whose

Ibid., Aug. 24, 1964, p. 259.

overall strength is as vast and as awesome as those of the United States of America, but it is my considered conviction, shared throughout your Government, that firmness in the right is indispensable today for peace. That firmness will always be measured. Its mission is peace.

D. Message of President Johnson to Congress*

August 5, 1964

Last night I announced to the American people that the North Vietnamese regime had conducted further deliberate attacks against U.S. naval vessels operating in international waters, and that I had therefore directed air action against gunboats and supporting facilities used in these hostile operations. This air action has now been carried out with substantial damage to the boats and facilities. Two U.S. aircraft were lost in the action.

After consultation with the leaders of both parties in the Congress, I further announced a decision to ask the Congress for a resolution expressing the unity and determination of the United States in supporting freedom and in protecting peace in southeast Asia.

These latest actions of the North Vietnamese regime have given a new and grave turn to the already serious situation in southeast Asia. Our commitments in the area are well known to the Congress. They were first made in 1954 by President Eisenhower. They were further defined in the Southeast Asia Collective Defense Treaty approved by the Senate in February 1955.

This treaty with its accompanying protocol obligates the United States and other members to act in accordance with their constitutional processes to meet Communist aggression against any of the parties or protocol states.

Our policy in southeast Asia has been consistent and unchanged since 1954. I summarized it on June 2 in four simple propositions:

1. America keeps her word. Here as elsewhere, we must and shall honor our commitments.
2. The issue is the future of southeast Asia as a whole. A threat to any nation in that region is a threat to all, and a threat to us.
3. Our purpose is peace. We have no military, political, or territorial ambitions in the area.
4. This is not just a jungle war, but a struggle for freedom on every front of human activity. Our military and economic assistance to South Vietnam and Laos in particular has the purpose of helping these countries to repel aggression and strengthen their independence.

The threat to the free nations of southeast Asia has long been clear. The North Vietnamese regime has constantly sought to take over South Vietnam and Laos. This Communist regime has violated the Geneva accords for Vietnam. It has systematically conducted a campaign of subversion, which includes the direction, training, and supply of personnel and arms for the conduct of guerrilla warfare in South Vietnamese territory. In Laos, the North Vietnamese regime has maintained military forces, used Laotian territory for infiltration into South

Ibid., pp. 261-63.

Vietnam and most recently carried out combat operations—all in direct violation of the Geneva agreements of 1962.

In recent months, the actions of the North Vietnamese regime have become steadily more threatening. In May, following new acts of Communist aggression in Laos, the United States undertook reconnaissance flights over Laotian territory, at the request of the Government of Laos. These flights had the essential mission of determining the situation in territory where Communist forces were preventing inspection by the International Control Commission. When the Communists attacked these aircraft, I responsed by furnishing escort fighters with instructions to fire when fired upon. Thus, these latest North Vietnamese attacks on our naval vessels are not the first direct attack on armed forces of the United States.

As President of the United States I have concluded that I should now ask the Congress, on its part, to join in affirming the national determination that all such attacks will be met, and that the United States will continue in its basic policy of assisting the free nations of the area to defend their freedom.

As I have repeatedly made clear, the United States intends no rashness, and seeks no wider war. We must make it clear to all that the United States is united in its determination to bring about the end of Communist subversion and aggression in the area. We seek the full and effective restoration of the international agreements, signed in Geneva in 1954, with respect to South Vietnam, and again in Geneva in 1962, with respect to Laos.

I recommend a resolution expressing the support of the Congress for all necessary action to protect our Armed Forces and to assist nations covered by the SEATO Treaty. At the same time, I assure the Congress that we shall continue readily to explore any avenues of political solution that will effectively guarantee the removal of Communist subversion and the preservation of the independence of the nations of the area.

The resolution could well be based upon similar resolutions enacted by the Congress in the past—to meet the threat to Formosa in 1955, to meet the threat to the Middle East in 1957, and to meet the threat in Cuba in 1962. It could state in the simplest terms the resolve and support of the Congress for action to deal appropriately with attacks against our Armed Forces and to defend freedom and preserve peace in southeast Asia in accordance with the obligations of the United States under the Southeast Asia Treaty. I urge the Congress to enact such a resolution promptly and thus to give convincing evidence to the aggressive Communist nations, and to the world as a whole, that our policy in southeast Asia will be carried forward—and that the peace and security of the area will be preserved. . . .

E. Joint Resolution of Congress: Public Law 88—408*

Approved, August 10, 1964

To promote the maintenance of international peace and security in southeast Asia.

Ibid., p. 268.

Whereas naval units of the Communist regime in Vietnam, in violation of the principles of the Charter of the United Nations and of international law, have deliberately and repeatedly attacked United States naval vessels lawfully present in international waters, and have thereby created a serious threat to international peace; and

Whereas these attacks are part of a deliberate and systematic campaign of aggression that the Communist regime in North Vietnam has been waging against its neighbors and the nations joined with them in the collective defense of their freedom; and

Whereas the United States is assiting the peoples of southeast Asia to protect their freedom and has no territorial, military or political ambitions in that area, but desires only that these peoples should be left in peace to work out their own destinies in their own way: Now, therefore be it

Resolved by the Senate and House of Representatives of the United States of America in Congress assembled, That the Congress approves and supports the determination of the President, as Commander in Chief, to take all necessary measures to repel any armed attack against the forces of the United States and to prevent further aggression.

Sec. 2. The United States regards as vital to its national interest and to world peace the maintenance of international peace and security in southeast Asia. Consonant with the Constitution of the United States and the Charter of the United Nations and in accordance with its obligations under the Southeast Asia Collective Defense Treaty, the United States is therefore, prepared, as the President determines, to take all necessary steps, including the use of armed force, to assist any member or protocol state of the Southeast Asia Collective Defense Treaty requesting assistance in defense of its freedom.

Sec. 3 This resolution shall expire when the President shall determine that the peace and security of the area is reasonably assured by international conditions created by action of the United Nations or otherwise, except that it may be terminated earlier by concurrent resolution of the Congress.

AIR ATTACKS ON NORTH VIETNAM

F. White House Statement*

February 7, 1965

On February 7, U.S. and South Vietnamese air elements were directed to launch retaliatory attacks against barracks and staging areas in the southern area of North Viet-Nam which intelligence has shown to be actively used by Hanoi for training and infiltration of Viet Cong personnel into South Viet-Nam.

Results of the attack and further operational details will be announced as soon as they are reported from the field.

Today's action by the U.S. and South Vietnamese Governments was in response to provocations ordered and directed by the Hanoi regime.

Ibid., Feb. 22, 1965, pp. 238-39.

Commencing at 2 A.M. on February 7th, Saigon time (1 P.M. yesterday, eastern standard time), two South Vietnamese airfields, two U.S. barracks areas, several villages, and one town in South Viet-Nam were subjected to deliberate surprise attacks. Substantial casualties resulted.

Our intelligence has indicated, and this action confirms, that Hanoi has ordered a more aggressive course of action against both South Vietnamese and American installations.

Moreover, these attacks were only made possible by the continuing infiltration of personnel and equipment from North Viet-Nam. This infiltration markedly increased during 1964 and continues to increase.

To meet these attacks the Government of South Viet-Nam and the U.S. Government agreed to appropriate reprisal action against North Vietnamese targets. The President's approval of this action was given after the action was discussed with and recommended by the National Security Council last night [February 6].

Today's joint response was carefully limited to military areas which are supplying men and arms for attacks in South Viet-Nam. As in the case of the North Vietnamese attacks in the Gulf of Tonkin last August. The response is appropriate and fitting.

As the U.S. Government has frequently stated, we seek no wider war. Whether or not this course can be maintained lies with the North Vietnamese aggressors. The key to the situation remains the cessation of infiltration from North Viet-Nam and the clear indication by the Hanoi regime that it is prepared to cease aggression against its neighbors.

G. White House Statement*

February 11, 1965

On February 11, U.S. air elements joined with the South Vietnamese Air Force in attacks against military facilities in North Viet-Nam used by Hanoi for the training and infiltration of Viet Cong personnel into South Viet-Nam.

These actions by the South Vietnamese and United States Governments were in response to further direct provocations by the Hanoi regime.

Since February 8, a large number of South Vietnamese and U.S. personnel have been killed in an increased number of Viet Cong ambushes and attacks. A district town in Phuoc Long Province has been overrun, resulting in further Vietnamese and U.S. casualties. In Qui Nhon, Viet Cong terrorists in attack on an American military billet murdered Americans and Vietnamese. In addition, there have been a number of mining and other attacks on the railway in South Viet-Nam as well as assassinations and ambushes involving South Vietnamese civil and military officials.

The United States Government has been in consultation with the Government of South Viet-Nam on this continuation of aggressions and outrages. While maintaining their desire to avoid spreading the conflict, the two Governments felt compelled to take the action described above.

*Ibid., Mar. 1, 1965, p. 290.

H. Statement by President Johnson on U.S. Policy toward Vietnam*

March 25, 1965

1. It is important for us all to keep a cool and clear view of the situation in Viet-Nam.

2. The central cause of the danger there is aggression by Communists against a brave and independent people. There are other difficulties in Viet-Nam, of course, but if that aggression is stopped, the people and Government of South Viet-Nam will be free to settle their own future, and the need for supporting American military action there will end.

3. The people who are suffering from this Communist aggression are Vietnamese. This is no struggle of white men against Asians. It is aggression by Communist totalitarians against their independent neighbors. The main burden of resistance has fallen on the people and soldiers of South Viet-Nam. We Americans have lost hundreds of our own men there, and we mourn them. But the free Vietnamese have lost tens of thousands, and the aggressors and their dupes have lost still more. These are the cruel costs of the conspiracy directed from the North. This is what has to be stopped.

4. The United States still seeks no wider war. We threaten no regime and covet no territory. We have worked and will continue to work for a reduction of tensions on the great stage of the world. But the aggression from the North must be stopped. That is the road to peace in Southeast Asia.

5. The United States looks forward to the day when the people and governments of all Southeast Asia may be free from terror, subversion, and assassination—when they will need not military support and assistance against aggression but only economic and social cooperation for progress in peace. Even now, in Viet-Nam and elsewhere, there are major programs of development which have the cooperation and support of the United States. Wider and bolder programs can be expected in the future from Asian leaders and Asian councils— and in such programs we would want to help. This is the proper business of our future cooperation.

6. The United States will never be second in seeking a settlement in Viet-Nam that is based on an end of Communist aggression. As I have said in every part of the Union, I am ready to go anywhere at any time and meet with anyone whenever there is promise of progress toward an honorable peace. We have said many times—to all who are interested in our principles for honorable negotiation—that we seek no more than a return to the essentials of the agreements of 1954—a reliable arrangement to guarantee the independence and security of all in Southeast Asia. At present the Communist aggressors have given no sign of any willingness to move in this direction, but as they recognize the costs of their present course, and their own true interest in peace, there may come a change—if we all remain united.

Meanwhile, as I said last year and again last week. "It is and it will remain

Ibid., April 12, 1965, pp. 527-28.

the policy of the United States to furnish assistance to support South Viet-Nam for as long as is required to bring Communist aggression and· terrorism under control." The military actions of the United States will be such, and only such, as serve that purpose—at the lowest possible cost in human life to our allies, to our own men, and to our adversaries too.

I. Speech by President Johnson on "Pattern for Peace in Southeast Asia"*

[Extract]

April 7, 1965

Last week 17 nations sent their views to some two dozen countries having an interest in Southeast Asia. We are joining those 17 countries and stating our American policy tonight, which we believe will contribute toward peace in this area of the world.

I have come here to review once again with my own people the views of the American Government.

Tonight Americans and Asians are dying for a world where each people may choose its own path to change. This is the principle for which our ancestors fought in the valleys of Pennsylvania. It is a principle for which our sons fight tonight in the jungles of Viet-Nam.

Viet-Nam is far away from this quiet campus. We have no territory there, nor do we seek any. The war is dirty and brutal and difficult. And some 400 young men, born into an America that is bursting with opportunity and promise, have ended their lives on Viet-Nam's steaming soil.

Why must we take this painful road? Why must this nation hazard its ease, its interest, and its power for the sake of a people so far away?

We fight because we must fight if we are to live in a world where every country can shape its own destiny, and only in such a world will our own freedom be finally secure.

This kind of world will never be built by bombs or bullets. Yet the infirmities of man are such that force must often precede reason and the waste of war, the works of peace. We wish that this were not so. But we must deal with the world as it is, if it is ever to be as we wish.

The world as it is in Asia is not a serene or peaceful place.

The first reality is that North Viet-Nam has attacked the independent nation of South Viet-Nam. Its object is total conquest. Of course, some of the people of South Viet-Nam are participating in attack on their own government. But trained men and supplies, orders and arms, flow in a constant stream from North to South.

This support is the heartbeat of the war.

And it is a war of unparalleled brutality. Simple farmers are the targets of assassination and kidnaping. Women and children are strangled in the night because their men are loyal to their government. And helpless villages are

Ibid., Apr. 26, 1965, pp. 606-10.

ravaged by sneak attacks. Large-scale raids are conducted on towns, and terror strikes in the heart of cities.

The confused nature of this conflict cannot mask the fact that it is the new face of an old enemy.

Over this war—and all Asia—is another reality, the deepening shadow of Communist China. The rules in Hanoi are urged on by Peiping. This is a regime which has destroyed freedom in Tibet, which has attacked India, and has been condemned by the United Nations for aggression in Korea. It is a nation which is helping the forces of violence in almost every continent. The contest in Viet-Nam is part of a wider pattern of aggressive purposes.

Why are We in South Viet-Nam?

Why are these realities our concern? Why are we in South Viet-Nam?

We are there because we have a promise to keep. Since 1954 every American President has offered support to the people of South Viet-Nam. We have helped to build, and we have helped to defend. Thus, over many years, we have made a national pledge to help South Viet-Nam defend its independence.

And I intend to keep that promise.

To dishonor that pledge, to abandon this small and brave nation to its enemies, and to the terror that must follow, would be an unforgivable wrong.

We are also there to strengthen world order. Around the globe, from Berlin to Thailand, are people whose well-being rests in part on the belief that they can count on us if they are attacked. To leave Viet-Nam to its fate would shake the confidence of all these people in the value of an American commitment and in the value of America's word. The result would be increased unrest and instability, and even wider war.

We are also there because there are great stakes in the balance. Let no one think for a moment that retreat from Viet-Nam would bring an end to conflict. The battle would be renewed in one country and then another. The central lesson of our time is that the appetite of aggression is never satisfied. To withdraw from one battlefield means only to prepare for the next. We must say in Southeast Asia—as we did in Europe—in the words of the Bible: "Hitherto shalt thou come, but no further."

There are those who say that all our effort there will be futile—that China's power is such that it is bound to dominate all Southeast Asia. But there is no end to that argument until all of the nations of Asia are swallowed up.

There are those who wonder why we have a responsiblity there. Well, we have it there for the same reason that we have a responsibility for the defense of Europe. World War II was fought in both Europe and Asia, and when it ended we found ourselves with continued responsibility for the defense of freedom.

Our objective is the independence of South Viet-Nam and its freedom from attack. We want nothing for ourselves—only that the people of South Viet-Nam be allowed to guide their own country in their own way. We will do everything necessary to reach that objective, and we will do only what is absolutely necessary.

In recent months attacks on South Viet-Nam were stepped up. Thus it became necessary for us to increase our response and to make attacks by air. This is not a change of purpose. It is a change in what we believe that purpose requires.

We do this in order to slow down aggression.

We do this to increase the confidence of the brave people of South Viet-Nam who have bravely borne this brutal battle for so many years with so many casualties.

And we do this to convince the leaders of North Viet-Nam—and all who seek to share their conquest—of a simple fact:

We will not be defeated.

We will not grow tired.

We will not withdraw, either openly or under the cloak of a meaningless agreement.

We know that air attacks alone will not accomplish all of these purposes. But it is our best and prayerful judgment that they are a necessary part of the surest road to peace.

*　　　　　*　　　　　*

We will never be second in the search for such a peaceful settlement in Viet-Nam.

There may be many ways to this kind of peace: in discussion or negotiation with the governments concerned; in large groups or in small ones; in the reaffirmation of old agreements or their strengthening with new ones.

We have stated this position over and over again 50 times and more to friend and foe alike. And we remain ready with this purpose for unconditional discussions.

And until that bright and necessary day of peace we will try to keep conflict from spreading. We have no desire to see thousands die in battle—Asians or Americans. We have no desire to devastate that which the people of North Viet-Nam have built with toil and sacrifice. We will use our power with restraint and with all the wisdom that we can command.

But we will use it.

A Cooperative Effort For Development

This war, like most wars, is filled with terrible irony. For what do the people of North Viet-Nam want? They want what their neighbors also desire—food for their hunger, health for their bodies, a chance to learn, progress for their country, and an end to the bondage of material misery. And they would find all these things far more readily in peaceful association with others than in the endless course of battle.

These countries of Southeast Asia are homes for millions of impoverished people. Each day these people rise at dawn and struggle through until the night to wrest existence from the soil. They are often wracked by diseases, plagued by hunger, and death comes at the early age of 40.

*　　　　　*　　　　　*

. . . I would hope tonight that the Secretary-General of the United Nations could use the prestige of his great office and his deep knowledge of Asia to initiate, as soon as possible, with the countries of that area, a plan for cooperation in increased development.

For our part I will ask the Congress to join in a billion-dollar American investment in this effort as soon as it is underway. And I would hope that all other industrialized countries, including the Soviet Union, will join in this effort to replace despair with hope and terror with progress.

The task is nothing less than to enrich the hopes and existence of more than a hundred million people. And there is much to be done.

The vast Mekong River can provide food and water and power on a scale to dwarf even our own TVA. The wonders of modern medicine can be spread through villages where thousands die every year from lack of care. Schools can be established to train people in the skills needed to manage the process of development. And these objectives, and more, are within the reach of a cooperative and determined effort.

I also intend to expand and speed up a program to make available our farm surpluses to assist in feeding and clothing the needy in Asia. We should not allow people to go hungry and wear rags while our own warehouses overflow with an abundance of wheat and corn and rice and cotton. . .

The Dream of Our Generation

This will be a disorderly planet for a long time. In Asia, and elsewhere, the forces of the modern world are shaking old ways and uprooting ancient civilizations. There will be turbulence and struggle and even violence. Great social change—as we see in our own country—does not always come without conflict.

We must also expect that nations will on occasion be in dispute with us. It may be because we are rich, or powerful, or because we have made some mistakes, or because they honestly fear our intentions. However, no nation need ever fear that we desire their land, or to impose our will, or to dictate their institutions.

But we will always oppose the effort of one nation to conquer another nation.

We will do this because our own security is at stake.

But there is a more to it than that. For our generation has a dream. It is a very old dream. But we have the power, and now we have the opportunity to make that dream come true.

For centuries nations have struggled among each other. But we dream of a world where disputes are settled by law and reason. And we will try to make it so.

For most of history men have hated and killed one another in battle. But we dream of an end to war. And we will try to make it so.

For all existence most men have lived in poverty, threatened by hunger. But we dream of a world where all are fed and charged with hope. And we will help to make it so.

The ordinary men and women of North Viet-Nam and South Viet-Nam, of

China and India, of Russia and America, are brave people. They are filled with the same proportions of hate and fear, of love and hope. Most of them want the same things for themselves and their families. Most of them do not want their sons to ever die in battle, or to see their homes, or the homes of others, destroyed.

Well, this can be their world yet. Man now has the knowledge—always before denied—to make this planet serve the real needs of the people who live on it.

I know this will not be easy. I know how difficult it is for reason to guide passion, and love to master hate. The complexities of this world do now bow easily to pure and consistent answers.

But the simple truths are there just the same. We must all try to follow them as best we can.

* * *

J. Address by Secretary Rusk on "Steps to Peace"*

[Extract]

June 23, 1965

* * *

The other side is obviously not yet ready for peace. In these last months, the friends of peace of many lands have sought to move this dangerous matter to the conference table. But one proposal after another has been contemptuously rejected.

We and others, for example, have sought to clear a way for a conference on Laos, and a conference on Cambodia—two neighboring countries where progress toward peace might be reflected in Viet-Nam itself. But these efforts have been blocked by North Viet-Nam and by Communist China.

Twice there-has been an effort at discussions through the United Nations—first in the Security Council after the August attacks in the Tonkin Gulf, and later this April, when Secretary-General U Thant considered visits to Hanoi and Peiping to explore the possibilities of peace. But in August there was a refusal by Hanoi to come to the Security Council. And in April both Hanoi and Peiping made it clear that they would not receive U Thant, and both regimes made plain their view that the United Nations is not competent to deal with that matter.

Repeatedly our friends in Britain, as a co-chairman of the Geneva conference, have sought a path to settlement—first by working toward a new conference in Geneva and then by a visit of a senior British statesman. But the effort for a conference in Geneva was blocked, and the distinguished British traveler was told that he should stay away from Peiping and Hanoi.

**Ibid.*, July 12, 1965, pp. 50-55.

Twice in April we made additional efforts of our own. In Baltimore the President offered unconditional discussions with the governments concerned. Hanoi and Peiping call this offer a "hoax." At that time the 17 nonalined nations had appealed for a peaceful solution, by negotiations without preconditions. This proposal was accepted on our side. It was rejected by Hanoi and by Peiping. And some of its authors were labeled "monsters and freaks."

The President of India made constructive proposals—for an end of hostilities and an Afro-Asian patrol force. To us this proposal was full of interest and hope. But by Hanoi and Red China it was rejected as a betrayal.

Our own Government and the Government of South Viet-Nam, in May, suspended air attacks on North Viet-Nam. This action was made known to the other side to see if there would be a response in kind. This special effort for peace was denounced in Hanoi as a "wornout trick" and denounced in Peiping as a "swindle." To those who complain that that so-called "pause" was not long enough, I would simply report that the harsh reaction of the other side was fully known before the attacks were resumed. And I would also recall that we held our hand for more than 4 years while tens of thousands of armed men invaded the South and every attempt at peaceful settlement failed.

Hanoi's Response

Reports in the first half of June have confirmed that all these violent rejections are in fact what they appear to be—clear proof that what is wanted today in Hanoi is a military victory, not peace, and that Hanoi is not even prepared for discussions unless it is accepted in advance that there will be a Communist-dominated government in Saigon and unless too—so far as we can determine—American forces are withdrawn in advance.

So this record is clear. And there is substance in Senator [J. William] Fulbright's conclusion that "It seems clear that the Communist powers still hope to achieve a complete victory in South Viet-Nam and for this reason are at present uninterested in negotiations for a peaceful settlement." For the simple truth is that there is no lack of diplomatic procedures, machinery, or process by which a desire for peace can be registered—that there is no procedural miracle through which peace can be obtained if one side is determined to continue the war.

As I have said, Hanoi is presently adamant against negotiation or any avenue to peace. Peiping is even more so, and one can plainly read the declared doctrine and purpose of the Chinese Communists. They are looking beyond the current conflict to the hope of domination in all of Southeast Asia—and indeed beyond.

But one finds it harder to understand Hanoi's aversion to discussion. More immediately than the Chinese, the North Vietnamese face the costs and dangers of conflict. They, too, must fear the ambitions of Communist China in Southeast Asia. Yet they are still on the path of violence, insisting upon the forceful communization of South Viet-Nam and refusing to let their brothers in the South work out their own destiny in peace.

*　　　　　　*　　　　　　*

K. Statement by President Johnson: "We Will Stand in Vietnam"*

July 28, 1965

My fellow Americans: Not long ago I received a letter from a woman in the Midwest. She wrote,

> Dear Mr. President: In my humble way I am writing to you about the crisis in Viet-Nam. I have a son who is now in Viet-Nam. My husband served in World War II. Our country was at war, but now, this time, it is just something that I don't understand. Why?

Why must young Americans, born into a land exultant with hope and with golden promise, toil and suffer and sometimes die in such a remote and distant place?

The answer, like the war itself, is not an easy one, but it echoes clearly from the painful lessons of half a century. Three times in my lifetime, in two world wars and in Korea, Americans have gone to far lands to fight for freedom. We have learned at a terrible and brutal cost that retreat does not bring safety and weakness does not bring peace.

It is this lesson that has brought us to Viet-Nam. This is a different kind of war. There are no marching armies or solemn declarations. Some citizens of South Viet-Nam, at times with understandable grievances, have joined in the attack on their own government.

But we must not let this mask the central fact that this is really war. It is guided by North Viet-Nam, and it is spurred by Communist China. Its goal is to conquer the South, to defeat American power, and to extend the Asiatic dominion of communism.

There are great stakes in the balance.

Most of the non-Communist nations of Asia cannot, by themselves and alone, resist growing might and the grasping ambition of Asian communism.

Our power, therefore, is a very vital shield. If we are driven from the field in Viet-Nam, then no nation can ever again have the same confidence in American promise or in American protection.

In each land the forces of independence would be considerably weakened and an Asia so threatened by Communist domination would certainly imperil the security of the United States itself.

We did not choose to be the guardians at the gate, but there is no one else.

Nor would surrender in Viet-Nam bring peace, because we learned from Hitler at Munich that success only feeds the appetite of aggression. The battle would be renewed in one country and then another country, bringing with it perhaps even larger and crueler conflict, as we have learned from the lessons of history.

Moreover, we are in Viet-Nam to fulfill one of the most solemn pledges of the American nation. Three Presidents—President Eisenhower, President Kennedy, and your present President—over 11 years have committed themselves

Ibid., Aug. 16, 1965, pp. 262-65.

and have promised to help defend this small and valiant nation.

Strengthened by that promise, the people of South Viet-Nam have fought for many long years. Thousands of them have died. Thousands more have been crippled and scarred by war. We just cannot now dishonor our word, or abandon our commitment, or leave those who believed us and who trusted us to the terror and repression and murder that would follow.

This, then, my fellow Americans, is why we are in Viet-Nam.

PEACE EFFORTS

L. Statement by North Vietnamese Prime Minister Pham Van Dong on Terms for Negotiations*

[Extract]

April 8, 1965

*   *   *

It is the unswerving policy of the Government of the Democratic Republic of Vietnam to strictly respect the 1954 Geneva Agreements on Vietnam, and to correctly implement their basic provisions as embodied in the following points:

1. Recognition of the basic national rights of the Vietnamese people: peace, independence, sovereignty, unity and territorial integrity. According to the Geneva Agreements, the U.S. government must withdraw from South Vietnam all U.S. troops, military personnel and weapons of all kinds, dismantle all U.S. military bases there, cancel its "military alliance" with South Vietnam. It must end its policy of intervention and aggression in South Vietnam. According to the Geneva Agreements, the U.S. government must stop its acts of war against North Vietnam, completely cease all encroachments on the territory and sovereignty of the Democratic Republic of Vietnam.

2. Pending the peaceful reunification of Vietnam, while Vietnam is still temporarily divided into two zones the military provisions of the 1954 Geneva Agreements on Vietnam must be strictly respected: the two zones must refrain from joining any military alliance with foreign countries, there must be no foreign military bases, troops and military personnel in their respective territory.

3. The internal affairs of South Vietnam must be settled by the South Vietnamese people themselves, in accordance with the programme of the South Vietnam National Front for Liberation, without any foreign interference.

4. The peaceful reunification of Vietnam is to be settled by the Vietnamese people in both zones, without any foreign interference.

This stand unquestionably enjoys the approval and support of all peace and justice-loving Governments and peoples in the world.

The Government of the Democratic Republic of Vietnam is of the view that the above expounded stand is the basis for the soundest political settlement

*Documents on American Foreign Relations, 1965, pp. 147-49.

of the Vietnam problem. If this basis is recognized, favourable conditions will be created for the peaceful settlement of the Vietnam problem and it will be possible to consider the reconvening of an international conference along the pattern of the 1954 Geneva Conference on Vietnam.

The Government of the Democratic Republic of Vietnam declares that any approach contrary to the above stand is inappropriate; any approach tending to secure a U.N. intervention in the Vietnam situation is also inappropriate because such approaches are basically at variance with the 1954 Geneva Agreements on Vietnam.

M. Restatement of U.S. Position on Vietnam in "Fourteen Points"*

December, 1965

UNITED STATES OFFICIAL POSITION ON VIETNAM

The following statements are on the public record about elements which the United States believes can go into peace in Southeast Asia:

1. The Geneva Agreements of 1954 and 1962 are an adequate basis for peace in Southeast Asia;

2. We would welcome a conference on Southeast Asia or on any part thereof;

3. We would welcome "negotiations without preconditions" as the 17 nations put it;

4. We would welcome unconditional discussions as President Johnson put it;

5. A cessation of hostilities could be the first order of business at a conference or could be the subject of preliminary discussions;

6. Hanoi's four points could be discussed along with other points which others might wish to propose;

7. We want no U.S. bases in Southeast Asia;

8. We do not desire to retain U.S. troops in South Viet-Nam after peace is assured;

9. We support free elections in South Viet-Nam to give the South Vietnamese a government of their own choice;

10. The question of reunification of Viet-Nam should be determined by the Vietnamese through their own free decision;

11. The countries of Southeast Asia can be non-aligned or neutral if that be their option;

12. We would much prefer to use our resources for the economic reconstruction of Southeast Asia than in War. If there is peace, North Viet-Nam could participate in a regional effort to which we would be prepared to contribute at least one billion dollars;

13. The President has said "The Viet Cong would not have difficulty being represented and having their views represented if for a moment Hanoi decided

*Department of State Press Release, 4, January 7, 1966.

she wanted to cease aggression. I don't think that would be an insurmountable problem."

14. We have said publicly and privately that we could stop the bombing of North Viet-Nam as a step toward peace although there has not been the slightest hint or suggestion from the other side as to what they would do if the bombing stopped.

N. U.S. Ambassador Arthur J. Goldberg to U.N. Secretary General U Thant on Peace Efforts*

[Extract]

January 4, 1966

My government has during the past two weeks been taking a number of steps in pursuit of peace which flow in part from our obligations under the United Nations Charter of which we are most mindful, and in part from the appeals which His Holiness, the Pope, and you addressed just before Christmas to us and to others. I believe it would be of interest to you, in addition to what we have already communicated to you privately, and to all States Members of the United Nations to know more precisely what we have done, and what we have in mind.

You will observe that we have already responded in terms which go somewhat beyond the appeals earlier addressed to us. President Johnson dispatched messages, and in several cases personal representatives, to His Holiness the Pope, to the Secretary General of the United Nations, and to a considerable number of Chiefs of State or Heads of Government, reaffirming our desire promptly to achieve a peaceful settlement of the conflict in Viet Nam and to do all in our power to move that conflict from the battlefield to the conference table. In this connection, our bombing of North Viet Nam has not been resumed since the Christmas truce.

Among the points made in our messages conveyed to a number of governments are the following: that the United States is prepared for discussions or negotiations without any prior conditions whatsoever or on the basis of the Geneva Accords of 1954 and 1962, that a reciprocal reduction of hostilities could be envisaged and that a cease fire might be the first order of business in any discussions or negotiations, that the United States remains prepared to withdraw its forces from South Viet Nam as soon as South Viet Nam is in a position to determine its own future without external interference, that the United States desires no continuing military presence or bases in Viet Nam, that the future political structure in South Viet Nam should be determined by the South Viet Namese people themselves through democratic processes, and that the question of the reunification of the two Viet Nams should be decided by the free decisions of their two peoples.

* * *

Weekly Compilation of Presidential Documents, Jan. 10, 1966, pp. 9-10.

**O. Letter to Certain Heads of State From North Vietnamese President
Ho Chi Minh, Restating Conditions for Negotiations***

[Extract]

January 24, 1966

Dear Comrade President: I have the honor to call your attention to the war
of aggression waged by the U.S. imperialists in our country, Vietnam.

As is known to you, over the past 11 years and more, the U.S. imperialists
have been seriously sabotaging the 1954 Geneva agreements and preventing the
peaceful reunification of Vietnam in an attempt to turn South Vietnam into
a U.S. new-type colony and military base. They are now waging a war of aggression and barbarously repressing the patriotic struggle of our fellow countrymen
in the south. At the same time, they try to draw experiences from this war
to repress the national liberation movement in other countries.

In an endeavor to get out of the quagmire in South Vietnam, the U.S. imperialists have massively increased the strength of the U.S. expeditionary corps and
sent in troops from a number of their satellites to wage direct aggression in
South Vietnam. They have also launched air attacks on the DRV [Democratic
Republic of Vietnam], an independent and sovereign country and a member
of the socialist camp. While intensifying and extending the war of aggression
in Vietnam, the U.S. imperialists are clamoring about their desire for peace
and their readiness to engage in unconditional discussions, in the hope of fooling
world public opinion and the American people.

Recently, the Johnson administration has initiated a so-called search for peace
and put forward a 14-point proposal. As an excuse for its war of aggression
in South Vietnam, it claims that it is keeping its commitments to the Saigon
puppet administration; it slanders the patriotic struggle of the people of South
Vietnam, calling it an aggression by North Vietnam. This deceitful contention
can in no way rub out the solemn declaration made by the United States in
Geneva in 1954 that it will refrain from the threat or the use of force to disturb
them (i.e. the Geneva agreements). Still less can President Johnson's hypocritical
allegations conceal the U.S. crimes in Vietnam.

The United States talks about respecting the Geneva agreements. But one
of the main provisions of the said agreements bans the introduction of foreign
troops into Vietnam. If the United States really respects the agreements, it must
withdraw all U.S. and satellite troops from South Vietnam.

It is crystal clear that the United States is the aggressor who is trampling
underfoot the Vietnamese soil. The people of South Vietnam are the victim
of aggression and are fighting in self-defense. If the United States really wants
peace it must recognize the NFLSV [National Front for the Liberation of South
Vietnam] as the sole genuine representative of the people of South Vietnam
and engage in negotiations with it.

In accordance with the aspirations of the people of South Vietnam and the
spirit of the 1954 Geneva agreements on Vietnam, the National Front for Liber-

Documents on American Foreign Relations, 1966, pp. 199-202.

ation is fighting to achieve independence, democracy, peace, and neutrality in South Vietnam, and advance toward the peaceful reunification of the fatherland. If the United States really respects the right to self-determination of the people of South Vietnam, it cannot but approve this correct program of the National Front for Liberation. The 14 points of the United States boil down in essence to this: The United States is trying hard to cling to South Vietnam, to maintain there the puppet administration rigged up by it, and to perpetuate the partition of Vietnam.

*   *   *

The Vietnamese people will never submit to the U. S. imperialists' threats. At the very moment when the U.S. Government puts forward the so-called new peace efforts, it is frantically increasing the U.S. strength in South Vietnam. It is stepping up the terrorist raids, resorting to the scorched earth policy, burning all, destroying all, killing all, using napalm bombs, poison gases, and toxic chemicals to burn down villages and massacre the civilian population in vast areas of South Vietnam.

I strongly protest such extremely barbarous methods of warfare. I earnestly call on all peace-loving governments and peoples the world over to resolutely stay the hands of the U.S. war criminals.

The United States keeps sending its planes on espionage flights in preparation for new air attacks on the DRV. On the other hand, it is launching air attacks on many areas in the Kingdom of Laos and multiplying armed provocations against the Kingdom of Cambodia, thus posing an even more serious menace to peace in Indochina.

Obviously, the U.S. search for peace is only designed to conceal its schemes for intensified war of aggression. The Johnson administration's stand remains: aggression and expansion of the war. To settle the Vietnam questions the DRV Government has put forward the four-point stand which is an expression of the essential provisions of the 1954 Geneva agreements on Vietnam.

*   *   *

P. Statement by President Johnson on Resumption of Bombing North Vietnam*

[Extract]

January 31, 1966

For 37 days, no bombs fell on North Viet-Nam. During that time, we have made a most intensive and determined effort to enlist the help and the support of all the world in order to persuade the Government in Hanoi that peace

**Weekly Compilation of Presidential Documents*, Feb 7, 1966, pp. 147-49.

is better than war, that talking is better than fighting, and that the road to peace is open.

Our effort has met with understanding and support throughout most of the world, but not in Hanoi and Peking. From those two capitals have come only denunciation and rejection.

In these 37 days, the efforts of our allies have been rebuffed. The efforts of neutral nations have come to nothing. We have sought, without success, to learn of any response to efforts made by the governments of Eastern Europe. There has been no answer to the enlightened efforts of the Vatican. Our own direct private approaches have all been in vain.

The answer of Hanoi to all is the answer that was published 3 days ago. They persist in aggression. They insist on the surrender of South Viet-Nam to communism. It is, therefore, very plain that there is no readiness or willingness to talk, no readiness for peace in that regime today.

And what is plain in words is also plain in acts. Throughout these 37 days, even at moments of truce, there has been continued violence against the people of South Viet-Nam, against their Government, against their soldiers, and against our own American forces.

We do not regret the pause in the bombing. We yield to none in our determination to seek peace. We have given a full and decent respect to the opinions of those who thought that such a pause might give new hope for peace in the world.

Some said that 10 days might do it. Other said 20. Now, we have paused for twice the time suggested by some of those who urged it. And now the world knows more clearly than it has ever known before who it is that insists on aggression and who it is that works for peace.

*   *   *

So on this Monday morning [January 31] in Viet-Nam, at my direction, after complete and thorough consultation and agreement with the Government of South Viet-Nam, United States aircraft have resumed action in North Viet-Nam.

They struck the lines of supply which support the continuing movement of men and arms against the people and the Government of South Viet-Nam.

Our air strikes on North Viet-Nam from the beginning have been aimed at military targets and have been controlled with the greatest of care. Those who direct and supply the aggression really have no claim to immunity from military reply.

The end of the pause does not mean the end of our own pursuit of peace. That pursuit will be as determined and as unremitting as the pressure of our military strength on the field of battle.

*   *   *

Q. Address by French President Charles de Gaulle on Vietnam*

[Extract]

Pnompenh, Cambodia, September 1, 1966

*   *   *

Well, France considers that the fighting that is ravaging Indochina, by and of itself, offers no end. In France's view, if it is unthinkable that the American war apparatus will be annihilated on the spot, there is, on the other hand, no chance that the peoples of Asia will subject themselves to the law of the foreigner who comes from the other shores of the Pacific, whatever his intentions, however powerful his weapons. In short, as long and cruel as the ordeal must be, France holds for certain that it will have no military solution.

For the world not to head toward a catastrophe, only a political agreement could therefore restore peace. Now, since the conditions for such an agreement are quite clear and well known, there is still time to hope. The agreement, just like the one of 1954, would have the goal of establishing and guaranteeing the neutrality of the peoples of Indochina and their right to dispose of themselves, as they really are, and leaving each of them full responsibility for its affairs. The contracting parties would therefore be the real powers being exercised there and among the other powers, at least the five world powers. But the possibility and, even more, the opening of such broad and difficult negotiations would depend obviously, on the decision and the commitment which America would have wanted to take beforehand to repatriate its forces within a suitable and determined period of time. Without a doubt, such an outcome is not at all ripe today, assuming that it may ever be. But France considers it necessary to assert that, in her view, there exists no other, except to condemn the world to ever growing misfortunes. France is saying this out of her experience and disinterestedness. She is saying this by reason of the task she once accomplished in this region of Asia, the ties she has maintained there, the interest she continues to have for the peoples living there and which she knows they return to her. She is saying this because of the exceptional and two-century-old friendship that, on the other hand, she has for America, because of the idea she has up to now had of her—like the one America has of herself—that is, the idea of a country championing the concept that we must allow people to determine their own destiny in their own way. She is saying this in consideration of the warnings which Paris long repeated to Washington when nothing irreparable had yet been done.

*   *   *

*Documents on American Foreign Relations, 1966, pp. 239-42.

R. Joint Statement Issued on the Manila Conference*

[Extract]

October 25, 1966

Introduction

1. In response to an invitation from the President of the Republic of the Philippines, after consultations with the President of the Republic of Korea and the Prime Ministers of Thailand and the Republic of Vietnam, the leaders of seven nations in the Asian and Pacific region held a summit conference in Manila on October 24 and 25, 1966, to consider the conflict in South Vietnam and to review their wider purposes in Asia' and the Pacific. The participants were Prime Minister Harold Holt of Australia, President Park Chung Hee of the Republic of Korea, Prime Minister Keith Holyoake of New Zealand, President Ferdinand E. Marcos of the Philippines, Prime Minister Thanom Kittikachorn of Thailand, President Lyndon B. Johnson of the United States of America, and Chairman Nguyen Van Thieu and Prime Minister Nugyen Cao Ky of the Republic of Vietnam.

Basic Policy

2. The nations represented at this conference are united in their determination that the freedom of South Vietnam be secured, in their resolve for peace, and in their deep concern for the future of Asia and the Pacific. Some of us are now close to the actual danger, while others have learned to know its significance through bitter past experience. This conference symbolizes our common purposes and high hopes.

3. We are united in our determination that the South Viet-Namese people shall not be conquered by aggressive force and shall enjoy the inherent right to choose their own way of life and their own form of government. We shall continue our military and all other efforts, as firmly and as long as may be necessary, in close consultation among ourselves until the aggression is ended.

4. At the same time our united purpose is peace—peace in South Vietnam and in the rest of Asia and the Pacific. Our common commitment is to the defense of the South Vietnamese people. Our sole demand on the leaders of North Vietnam is that they abandon their aggression. We are prepared to pursue any avenue which could lead to a secure and just peace, whether through discussion and negotiation or through reciprocal actions by both sides to reduce the violence.

5. We are united in looking to a peaceful and prosperous future for all of Asia and the Pacific. We have therefore set forth in a separate declaration

*Weekly Compilation of Presidential Documents, Oct. 31, 1966, pp. 1556-60.

a statement of the principles that guide our common actions in this wider sphere.

6. Actions taken in pursuance of the policies herein stated shall be in accordance with our respective constitutional processes.

*   *   *

CORRESPONDENCE BETWEEN AMBASSADOR GOLDBERG AND SECRETARY GENERAL U THANT ON UNITED STATES POLICY IN VIETNAM

S. Goldberg to U Thant*

December 19, 1966

My Dear Mr. Secretary General: Two world leaders who command the respect of the entire international community have recently voiced the desire for a cease-fire in Vietnam. On December 8, Pope Paul VI noted the temporary Christmas truce arranged in Vietnam and beseeched all concerned to transform this temporary truce into a cessation of hostilities which would become the occasion for sincere negotiations. And you, Mr. Secretary General, expressed the sincere hope on the same day that the parties directly concerned would heed the Pope's appeal.

In the fourteen points my Government has put forward as elements of a peaceful settlement in Vietnam, you will recall, the United States has explicitly stated: A cessation of hostilities could be the first order of business at a conference or could be the subject of preliminary discussions. I herewith reaffirm our commitment to that proposal—a proposal which is in keeping with the appeal of the Pope as endorsed by you. Our objective remains the end of all fighting, of all hostilities and of all violence in Vietnam—and an honorable and lasting settlement there, for which, as we have repeatedly said, the Geneva Agreements of 1954 and 1962 would be a satisfactory basis.

President Johnson has time and again stressed his desire for a peaceful settlement of the Vietnam conflict. Other United States leaders have spoken in a similar vein. In speaking before the General Assembly on behalf of my Government on September 22, I noted there are differences between our aims as to the basis for such a settlement and the stated position of North Vietnam. I went on to say that: ". . . no differences can be resolved without contact, disccusions or negotiations." This holds equally true with regard to arrangements for a mutual cessation of hostilities.

We turn to you, therefore, with the hope and the request that you will take whatever steps you consider necessary to bring about the necessary discussions which could lead to such a cease-fire. I can assure you that the Government of the United States will cooperate fully with you in getting such discussions started promptly and in bring them to a successful completion.

*Department of State Bulletin, Jan. 9, 1967, pp. 63-64.

I request that this letter be circulated as an official document of the Security Council.

T.   U Thant to Goldberg*

December 30, 1966

My dear Ambassador, I have very carefully studied your letter to me dated 19 December 1966 on the subject of Viet-Nam. May I say how appreciative I am of your Government's request that I might take whatever steps I "consider necessary to bring about the necessary discussions which could lead to such a cease-fire", and especially of the assurance that "the Government of the United States will cooperate fully. . .in getting such discussions started promptly and in bringing them to a successful completion."

You are, of course, aware of my preoccupation with the question of Viet-Nam during the last three years. This preoccupation stems not merely from my recognition of the serious risk that the continuation of this war poses to international peace and security. To a very large extent it is influenced even more by my deep sympathy, and indeed anguish, over the untold suffering of the people of Viet-Nam who have known no peace for a generation, the tragic loss of lives on all sides, the increasing number of civilian casualties, the appalling destruction of property and the vast and mounting sums being spent on the prosecution of the war.

In this context may I also stress my strong feeling, publicly expressed more than once, that what is really at stake in Viet-Nam, unles an early end to the hostilities is brought about, is the independence, the identity and the survival of the country itself.

I have already referred to the serious risk to international peace and security that the continuance of the war in Viet-Nam poses. There is an ever present danger that the war in Viet-Nam may spread, and even spill over its frontiers. Already the war has poisoned relations amongst States and has, as I said earlier, brought to a halt the great enterprise of cooperation and understanding between nations which had barely made a modest start in recent years.

This is how I see the over-all situation. It is a situation in which a powerful nation like the United States should take the initiative in the quest for peace and show an enlightened and humanitarian spirit. I believe that in the circumstances only action deliberately undertaken in such spirit which, because of its power and position, the United States can afford to undertake, can halt the escalation and enlargement of this war, and thus bring about a turning of the tide towards peace.

Let me take this opportunity of reiterating my three-point programme, to which I still firmly adhere:

   1. The cessation of the bombing of North Viet-Nam;
   2. The scaling down of all military activities by all sides in South Viet-Nam;
   3. The willingness to enter into discussions with those who are actually fighting.

*Ibid., Jan. 23, 1967, pp. 138-39.

I strongly believe that this three-point programme, of which the cessation of the bombing of North Viet-Nam is the first and essential part, is necessary to create the possibility of fruitful discussions leading to a just and honorable settlement of the problem of Viet-Nam on the basis of the Geneva Agreements of 1954.

I also wish to recall that in the course of the twenty-first session, in the debate of the General Assembly, the majority of the delegations have endorsed the three-point programme. Many more heads of delegations also specifically pleaded for the cessation of the bombing of North Viet-Nam. It seems to me that this is a very clear indication of the public opinion of the world at large on this issue.

Leaders of religious faiths all over the world have also expressed their anxiety about the continuance and escalation of the war in Viet-Nam. Only a few days ago the General Secretary of the World Council of Churches expressed a similar concern.

When His Holiness the Pope made his plea for an extended cease-fire, I endorsed it and I urged all parties to heed his appeal. In my statement of 2 December I said: "Is it too much to hope that what is made possible for just a couple of days by the occurrence of common holidays may soon prove feasible for a longer period by the new commitments that peace requires, so that an atmosphere may be created which is necessary for meaningful talks to be held in the quest for a peaceful solution?"

This is what I have in mind when I refer to the need for a humanitarian approach. If action in such a spirit could be undertaken, even without conditions, by the United States to stop the bombing of North Viet-Nam, and if the New Year cease-fire could be extended by all the parties I feel hopeful that thereafter some favourable developments may follow. I am reminded in this context that in 1954 negotiations for a peaceful settlement were conducted even without a formal cease-fire and while fighting was going on. Even though there may be sporadic breaches of the cease-fire on account of lack of control and communication, I believe that this would provide a welcome respite for private contacts and diplomatic explorations so that, in time, formal discussions can take place on the basis of the Geneva Agreements of 1954.

I am writing this letter to you after long deliberation. I would like to close by assuring you and your Government that, in my personal and private capacity, I shall continue to exert my utmost efforts and to explore every avenue which may lead to a just, honourable and peaceful solution of the problem of Viet-Nam.

U. Goldberg to U Thant*

[Extract]

December 31, 1966

My dear Mr. Secretary-General: I appreciate your thoughtful reply to my letter of December 19 concerning Vietnam. The subject at issue—peace in

*Ibid., pp. 137-38.

Vietnam—is of such vital importance to my Government and to world peace that we have given your reply immediate attention and are sending you herewith our reply.

We share your deep concern about the development and effects of the conflict in Vietnam: the risk it poses to international peace, the ill effects upon relations between states, and—more than anything else—the tragic toll in death and destruction.

I can assure you without reservation that the preeminent desire of the United States Government is to bring all hostilities in Vietnam to a prompt and honorable end consistent with the United Nations Charter, which affirms for all peoples the right of self-determination, the right to decide their own destiny free of force.

We have carefully reflected on your ideas, expressed in your December 30 letter and on previous occasions, about the cessation of bombing of North Vietnam. As you rightly point out, Mr. Secretary-General, our size and power impose special responsibilities upon us. And it is with these responsibilities in mind that I wish to assure you categorically that my Government is prepared to take the first step toward peace: specifically, we are ready to order a prior end to all bombing of North Vietnam the moment there is an assurance, private or otherwise, that there would be a reciprocal response toward peace from North Vietnam.

I am, thus, reaffirming herewith an offer made before the General Assembly—on September 22 and again on October 18. We hope and trust that you will use every means at your disposal to determine what tangible response there would be from North Vietnam in the wake of such a prior step toward peace on our part.

While reaffirming our offer, I would also express our conviction that the goal which, I am sure, we both share—an end to all fighting, to all hostilities, to all organized terror and violence—cannot be attained by either appeals for or the exercise of restraint by only one side in the Vietnam conflict. We therefore welcome the idea in your letter that there be an extended cease-fire, which would obviously include a cessation of the bombing of North Vietnam as well as an end to all hostilities and organized violence in the south. We believe the temporary truces already arranged in Vietnam offer opportunities for initiatives in that direction—though we cannot but regret that the other parties concerned have shown no interest so far in such a cease-fire.

*   *   *

V. Speech by President Johnson on U.S. Policy in Asia*

[Extract]

July 12, 1966

*   *   *

Asia is now the crucial arena of man's striving for independence and order, and for life itself.

Weekly Compilation of Presidential Documents, July 18, 1966, pp. 924-29.

This is true because three out of every five people in all this world live in Asia tonight.

This is true because hundreds of millions of them exist on less than 25 cents a day.

This is true because Communists in Asia tonight still believe in force in order to achieve their Communist goals.

So if enduring peace can ever come to Asia, all mankind will benefit. But if peace fails there, nowhere else will our achievements really be secure.

By peace in Asia I do not mean simply the absence of armed hostilities. For wherever men hunger and hate there can really be no peace.

I do not mean the peace of conquest. For humiliation can be the seedbed of war.

I do not mean simply the peace of the conference table. For peace is not really written merely in the words of treaties, but peace is the day-by-day work of builders.

The peace we seek in Asia is a peace of conciliation between Communist states and their non-Communist neighbors; between rich nations and poor; between small nations and large; between men whose skins are brown and black and yellow and white; between Hindus and Moslems and Buddhists and Christians.

It is a peace that can only be sustained through the durable bonds of peace: through international trade; through the free flow of peoples and ideas; through full participation by all nations in an international community under law; and through a common dedication to the great tasks of human progress and economic development.

Is such a peace possible?

With all my heart I believe it is. We are not there yet. We have a long way to journey. But the foundations for such a peace in Asia are being laid tonight as never before. They must be built on these essentials:

[1]

First is the determination of the United States to meet our obligations in Asia as a Pacific power.

You have heard arguments the other way. They are built on the old belief that "East is East and West is West and never the twain shall meet;"

 —that we have no business but business interests in Asia;
 —that Europe, not the Far East, is really our proper sphere of interest;
 —that our commitments in Asia are not worth the resources they require;
 —that the ocean is vast, the cultures alien, the languages strange, and the races different;
 —that these really are not our kind of people.

But all of these arguments have been thoroughly tested. And all of them, I think, have really been found wanting.

They do not stand the test of geography—because we are bounded not by one, but by two oceans. And whether by aircraft or ship, by satellite or missile, the Pacific is as crossable as the Atlantic.

They do not stand the test of commonsense. The economic network of this shrinking globe is too intertwined—the basic hopes of men are too interrelated—the possibility of common disaster is too real for us to ever ignore threats to peace in Asia.

They do not stand the test of human concern, either. The people of Asia do matter. We share with them many things in common. We are all persons. We are all human beings.

And they do not stand the test of reality, either. Asia is no longer sitting outside the door of the 20th century. She is here, in the same world with all of us, to be either our partner or our problem.

Americans entered this century believing that our own security had no foundation outside our own continent. Twice we mistook our sheltered position for safety. Twice we were dead wrong.

And if we are wise now, we will not repeat our mistakes of the past. We will not retreat from the obligations of freedom and security in Asia.

[2]

The second essential for peace in Asia is this: to prove to aggressive nations that the use of force to conquer others is a losing game.

There is no more difficult task, really, in a world of revolutionary change—where the rewards of conquest tempt ambitious appetites.

As long as the leaders of North Viet-Nam really believe that they can take over the people of South Viet-Nam by force, we must not let them succeed.

We must stand across their path and say: "You will not prevail. But turn from the use of force and peace will follow."

Every American must know exactly what it is that we are trying to do in Viet-Nam. Our greatest resource, really, in this conflict—our greatest support for the men who are fighting out there—is your understanding. It is your willingness to carry—perhaps for a long time—the heavy burden of a confusing and costly war.

We are not trying to wipe out North Viet-Nam.

We are not trying to change their government.

We are not trying to establish permanent bases in South Viet-Nam.

And we are not trying to gain one inch of new territory for America.

Then, you say, "Why are we there?" Why?

Well, we are there because we are trying to make the Communists of North Viet-Nam stop shooting at their neighbors;

—because we are trying to make this Communist aggression unprofitable;

—because we are trying to demonstrate that guerrilla warfare, inspired by one nation against another nation, can never succeed. Once that lesson is learned, a shadow that hangs over all of Asia tonight will, I think begin to recede.

       *   *   *

PROPOSALS FOR PEACE NEGOTIATIONS

A. Pope Paul VI to President Johnson*

February 7, 1967

Our heartfelt appeals for the return of peace in Southeast Asia have always found a favourable reaction on your part, Mr. President, and that of your countrymen and this fact strengthens our hope in this hour of anxious waiting. We sincerely wish that the celebrations of the New Lunar Year so dear to the Vietnamese people with the suspension of the hostilities by all the parties engaged in the conflict, may open finally the way to the negotiations for a just and stable peace putting an end to the great sacrifices brought on by a war protracted now for years. We know quite well the obstacles to achieving such a goal but we have no doubt in your dedication, Mr. President, to a constant search for a way to peace. Therefore, we ask you to increase even more your noble effort in these days of truce for this great cause and we pray Almighty God to crown your endeavors for peace with every success. We assure you, Mr. President, of our sentiments of highest consideration.

B. President Johnson to Pope Paul*

February 8, 1967

I deeply appreciate your message, which is a great source of spiritual support. I devoutly share your wish that the suspension of hostilities over the Lunar New Year may be extended and may open the way to negotiations for a just and stable peace.

The governments of the United States and the Republic of Vietnam, together with others, are devoting intensive efforts to this end. As you know, the government of Vietnam has twice signified its readiness to discuss an extension of the truce with representatives of the other side.

We are prepared to talk at any time and place, in any forum, with the object of bringing peace to Vietnam; however, I know you would not expect us to reduce military action unless the other side is willing to do likewise.

We are prepared to discuss the balanced reduction in military activity, the cessation of hostilities, or any practical arrangements which could lead to these results.

We shall continue our efforts for a peaceful and honorable settlement until they are crowned with success.

*Weekly Compilation of Presidential Documents, Feb. 13, 1967, p. 212.
* Ibid., pp. 211-12.

C. Pope Paul to President Ho Chi Minh*

February 8, 1967

Noting with satisfaction the sentiments of sympathy and confidence shown by Your Excellency during meetings with religious personalities for our action in favor of peace, we feel encouraged to renew to you our appeal to do all that is in your power to hasten the solution, so much desired, of the conflict. We nourish the hope that neither of the two parties will trouble the serenity of the celebrations of Tet by actions which could lead to a renewal of hostilities. We hope to the contrary that this period of truce, in inspiring all with peaceful sentiments, will offer the occasion to establish mutual suspension of acts of war and to make possible the definition of fundamental points for sincere negotiations for peace. We raise our prayers to God and our wishes for all the Vietnamese people so dear to us, that there open finally an era of concord and prosperity and the respect of justice and liberty.

D. President Ho Chi Minh to Pope Paul*

February 13, 1967

I wish to thank Your Holiness for his message of Feb. 8, 1967. In his message Your Holiness expressed the wish to see an early peaceful solution to the Vietnam question.

Our people sincerely love peace in order to build our country in independence and freedom. However, the U.S. imperialists have sent to South Vietnam half a million U.S. and satellite troops and used more than 600,000 puppet troops to wage a war against our people.

They have committed monstrous crimes. They have use [d] the most barbarous arms such as napalm, chemical products and toxic gases, to massacre our compatriots and burn down our villages, pagodas, churches, hospitals, schools. Their acts of aggression have grossly violated the 1954 Geneva agreements on Vietnam and seriously menaced peace in Asia and the world.

To defend their independence and peace the Vietnamese people are resolutely fighting against the aggressors. They are confident that justice will triumph. The U.S. imperialists must put an end to their aggression in Vietnam, end unconditionally and definitively the bombing and all other acts of war against the Democratic Republic of Vietnam, withdraw from South Vietnam all American and satellite troops, recognize the South Vietnam National Front for Liberation and let the Vietnamese people settle themselves their own affairs. Only in such conditions can real peace be restored in Vietnam.

It is my hope that Your Holiness, in the name of humanity and justice, will use his high influence to urge that the U.S. Government respect the national rights of the Vietnamese people, namely peace, independence, sovereignty, unity and territorial integrity as recognized by the 1954 Geneva agreements on Vietnam.

*U.S. Senate Committee on Foreign Relations, *United States Armament and Disarmament Problems: Hearings Before The Subcommittee on Disarmament* (Washington, 1967), p. 173.
**The New York Times*, Feb. 14, 1967.

E. President Johnson to President Ho Chi Minh*

February 8, 1967

Dear Mr. President: I am writing to you in the hope that the conflict in Vietnam can be brought to an end. That conflict has already taken a heavy toll—in lives lost, in wounds inflicted, in property destroyed, and in simple human misery. If we fail to find a just and peaceful solution, history will judge us harshly.

Therefore, I believe that we both have a heavy obligation to seek earnestly the path to peace. It is in response to that obligation that I am writing directly to you.

We have tried over the past several years, in a variety of ways and through a number of channels, to convey to you and your colleagues our desire to achieve a peaceful settlement. For whatever reasons, these efforts have not achieved any results.

It may be that our thoughts and yours, our attitudes and yours, have been distorted or misinterpreted as they passed through these various channels. Certainly that is always a danger in indirect communication.

There is one good way to overcome this problem and to move forward in the search for a peaceful settlement. That is for us to arrange for direct talks between trusted representatives in a secure setting and away from the glare of publicity. Such talks should not be used as a propaganda exercise but should be a serious effort to find a workable and mutually acceptable solution.

In the past two weeks, I have noted public statements by representatives of your government suggesting that you would be prepared to enter into direct bilateral talks with representatives of the U.S. Government, provided that we ceased "unconditionally" and permanently our bombing operations against your country and all military actions against it. In the last day, serious and responsible parties have assured us indirectly that this is in fact your proposal.

Let me frankly state that I see two great difficulties with this proposal. In view of your public position such action on our part would inevitably produce worldwide speculation that discussions were under way and would impair the privacy and secrecy of those discussions. Secondly, there would inevitably be grave concern on our part whether your government would make use of such action by us to improve its military position.

With these problems in mind I am prepared to move even further towards an ending of hostilities than your Government has proposed in either public statements or through private diplomatic channels. I am prepared to order a cessation of bombing against your country and the stopping of further augmentation of U.S. forces in South Viet-Nam as soon as I am assured that infiltration into South Viet-Nam by land and by sea has stopped. These acts of restraint on both sides would, I believe, make it possible for us to conduct serious and private discussions leading toward an early peace.

I make this proposal to you now with a specific sense of urgency arising from the imminent New Year holidays in Viet-Nam. If you are able to accept

*Department of State Bulletin, Apr. 10, 1967, pp. 595-96.

this proposal I see no reason why it could not take effect at the end of the New Year, or Tet, holidays. The proposal I have made would be greatly strengthened if your military authorities and those of the Government of South Viet-Nam could promptly negotiate an extension of the Tet truce.

As to the site of the bilateral discussions I propose, there are several possibilites. We could, for example, have our representatives meet in Moscow where contacts have already occurred. They could meet in some other country such as Burma. You may have other arrangements or sites in mind and I would try to meet your suggestions.

The important thing is to end a conflict that has brought burdens to both our peoples, and above all to the people of South Viet-Nam. If you have any thoughts about the actions I propose, it would be most important that I receive them as soon as possible.

F. President Ho Chi Minh to President Johnson*

February 15, 1967

Excellency, on February 10, 1967, I received your message. Here is my response.

Viet Nam is situated thousands of miles from the United States. The Vietnamese people have never done any harm to the United States. But, contrary to the commitments made by its representative at the Geneva Conference of 1954, the United States Government has constantly intervened in Viet-Nam, it has launched and intensified the war of aggression in South Viet-Nam for the purpose of prolonging the division of Viet-Nam and of transforming South Viet-Nam into an American neo-colony and an American military base. For more than two years now, the American Government, with its military aviation and its navy, has been waging war against the Democratic Republic of Viet-Nam, an independent and sovereign country.

The United States Government has committed war crimes, crimes against peace and against humanity. In South Viet-Nam a half-million American soldiers and soldiers from the satellite countries have resorted to the most inhumane arms and the most barbarous methods of warfare, such as napalm, chemicals, and poison gases in order to massacre our fellow countrymen, destroy the crops, and wipe out the villages. In North Viet-Nam thousands of American planes have rained down hundreds of thousands of tons of bombs, destroying cities, villages, mills, roads, bridges, dikes, dams and even churches, pagodas, hospitals, and schools. In your message you appear to deplore the suffering and the destruction in Viet-Nam. Permit me to ask you: Who perpetrated these monstrous crimes? It was the American soldiers and the soldiers of the satellite countries. The United States Government is entirely responsible for the extremely grave situation in Viet-Nam.

The American war of aggression against the Vietnamese people constitutes a challenge to the countries of the socialist camp, a threat to the peoples' independent movement, and a grave danger to peace in Asia and in the world.

Ibid., pp. 596-97.

The Vietnamese people deeply love independence, liberty, and peace. But in the face of the American aggression they have risen up as one man, without fearing the sacrifices and the privations. They are determined to continue their resistance until they have won real independence and liberty and true peace. Our just cause enjoys the approval and the powerful support of peoples throughout the world and of large segments of the American people.

The United States Government provoked the war of aggression in Viet-Nam. It must cease that aggression, it is the only road leading to the re-establishment of peace. The United States Government must halt definitively and unconditionally the bombings and all other acts of war against the Democratic Republic of Viet-Nam, withdraw from South Viet-Nam all American troops and all troops from the satellite countries, recognize the National Front of the Liberation of South Viet-Nam, and let the Vietnamese people settle their problems themselves. Such is the basic content of the four-point position of the Government of the Democratic Republic of Viet-Nam, such is the statement of the essential principles and essential arrangements of the Geneva agreements of 1954 on Viet-Nam. It is the basis for a correct political solution of the Vietnamese problem. In your message you suggested direct talks between the Democratic Republic of Viet-Nam and the United States. If the United States Government really wants talks, it must first halt unconditionally the bombings and all other acts of war against the Democratic Republic of Viet-Nam. It is only after the unconditional halting of the American bombings and of all other American acts of war against the Democratic Republic of Viet-Nam that the Democratic Republic of Viet-Nam and the United States could begin talks and discuss questions affecting the two parties.

The Vietnamese people will never give way to force, it will never accept conversation under the clear threat of bombs.

Our cause is absolutely just. It is desirable that the Government of the United States act in conformity to reason.

G. Speech by President Johnson Reaffirming U.S. Policy in Vietnam*

[Extract]

National Legislative Conference, September 29, 1967

I deeply appreciate this opportunity to appear before an organization whose members contribute every day such important work to the public affairs of our State and of our country.

This evening I came here to speak to you about Vietnam.

I do not have to tell you that our people are profoundly concerned about that struggle.

There are passionate convictions about the wisest course for our Nation to follow. There are many sincere and patriotic Americans who harbor doubts about sustaining the commitment that three Presidents and a half a million of our young men have made.

*Weekly Compilation of Presidential Documents, Oct. 9, 1967, pp. 1372-77.

Doubt and debate are enlarged because the problems of Vietnam are quite complex. They are a mixture of political turmoil—of poverty—of religious and factional strife—of ancient servitude and modern longing for freedom. Vietnam is all of these things.

Vietnam is also the scene of a powerful aggression that is spurred by an appetite for conquest.

It is the arena where Communist expansionism is most aggressively at work in the world today—where it is crossing international frontiers in violation of international agreements; where it is killing and kidnaping; where it is ruthlessly attempting to bend free people to its will.

Into this mixture of subversion and war, of terror and hope, America has entered—with its material power and with its moral commitment.

Why?

Why should three Presidents and the elected representatives of our people have chosen to defend this Asian nation more than 10,000 miles from American shores?

We cherish freedom—yes. We cherish self-determination for all people—yes. We abhor the political murder of any state by another, and the bodily murder of any people by gangster of whatever ideology. And for 27 years—since the days of lend-lease we have sought to strengthen free people against domination by aggressive foreign powers.

But the key to all we have done is really our own security. At times of crisis—before asking Americans to fight and die to resist aggression in a foreign land—every American President has finally had to answer this question:

Is the aggression a threat—not only to the immediate victim—but to the United Sates of America and to the peace and security of the entire world of which we in America are a very vital part?

That is the question which Dwight Eisenhower and John Kennedy and Lyndon Johnson had to answer in facing the issue in Vietnam.

That is the question that the Senate of the United States answered by a vote of 82 to 1 when it ratified and approved the SEATO treaty in 1955, and to which the Members of the United States Congress responded in a resolution that it passed in 1964 by a vote of 504 to 2, "the United States is, therefore, prepared, as the President determines, to take all necessary steps, including the use of armed force, to assist any member, or protocol state of the Southeast Asia Collective Defense Treaty requesting assistance in defense of its freedom."

Those who tell us now that we should abandon our commitment—that securing South Vietnam from armed domination is not worth the price we are paying—must also answer this question. And the test they must meet is this: What would be the consequence of letting armed aggression against South Vietnam succeed? What would follow in the time ahead? What kind of world are they prepared to live in 5 months or 5 years from tonight?

*   *   *

I cannot tell you tonight as your President—with certainty—that a Communist conquest of South Vietnam would be followed by a Communist conquest of Southeast Asia. But I do know there are North Vietnamese troops in Laos. I do know that there are North Vietnamese trained guerrillas tonight in northeast Thailand. I do know that there are Communist-supported guerrilla forces operating in Burma. And a Communist coup was barely averted in Indonesia, the fifth largest nation in the world.

So your American President cannot tell you—with certainty—that a Southeast Asia dominated by Communist power would bring a third world war much closer to terrible reality. One could hope that this would not be so.

But all that we have learned in this tragic century strongly suggests to me that it would be so. As President of the United States, I am not prepared to gamble on the chance that it is not so. I am not prepared to risk the security—indeed, the survival—of this American Nation on mere hope and wishful thinking. I am convinced that by seeing this struggle through now, we are greatly reducing the chances of a much larger war—perhaps a nuclear war. I would rather stand in Vietnam, in our time, and by meeting this danger now, and facing up to it, thereby reduce the danger for our children and for our grandchildren.

*   *   *

I know there are other questions on your minds, and on the minds of many sincere, troubled Americans: "Why not negotiate now?" so many ask me. The answer is that we and our South Vietnamese allies are wholly prepared to negotiate tonight.

I am ready to talk with Ho Chi Minh, and other chiefs of state concerned, tomorrow.

I am ready to have Secretary Rusk meet with their foreign minister tomorrow.

I am ready to send a trusted representative of America to any spot on this earth to talk in public or private with a spokesman of Hanoi.

We have twice sought to have the issue of Vietnam dealt with by the United Nations—and twice Hanoi has refused.

Our desire to negotiate peace—through the United Nations or out—has been made very, very clear to Hanoi—directly and many times through third parties.

As we have told Hanoi time and time and time again, the heart of the matter really is this: The United States is willing to stop all aerial and naval bombardment of North Vietnam when this will lead promptly to productive discussions. We, of course, assume that while discussions proceed, North Vietnam would not take advantage of the bombing cessation or limitation.

But Hanoi has not accepted any of these proposals.

*   *   *

H. Statement by President Johnson*

December 23, 1967

I have come around the world to call on His Holiness Pope Paul in the spirit of his offer of "unarmed cooperation . . . toward the reestablishment of true peace."

No man can avoid being moved to try harder for peace at Christmas time.

We discussed possible paths to peace, and the efforts that have been made in recent years, so far without success.

We agree with His Holiness that "an honorable settlement of the painful and threatening dispute is still possible." I received his judgment to this end, and I deeply appreciate the full and free manner in which it was given.

His Holiness has suggested a principle of mutual restraint. If this principle was accepted by both sides, there would be rapid and solid progress toward peace.

We would be willing to stop the bombing and proceed promptly to serious and productive discussions.

A total end to the violence would be our urgent objective.

We support informal talks with the South.

We are ready for formal talks with the North.

We will agree to any proposal that would substitute the word and the vote for the knife and the grenade in bringing honorable peace to Vietnam.

We shall keep closely in touch with His Holiness in the days ahead, as we shall with others who are searching to lift the scourge of war from Vietnam and Southeast Asia.

I. Statement by Foreign Minister Trinh of the Democratic Republic of Vietnam*

[Extract]

December 29, 1967

Though suffering heavy defeats, the U.S. imperialists have not yet given up their aggressive schemes. They have barbarously bombed Hanoi capital and Haiphong port city, feverishly sent more U.S. and satellite troops to South Vietnam, and at the same time threatened to expand the war to Cambodia and Laos. In his bellicose speech delivered at San Antonio and his recent brazen statements, U.S. President L.B. Johnson while pretending to be desirous of peace talks used the pretext of defending the security of the United States to intensify the war and cling to South Vietnam. The U.S. imperialists are also scheming to bring the Vietnam question before the Security Council of the United Nations.

Ibid., Jan. 1, 1968, p. 1773.
Documents on American Foreign Relations, 1967, pp. 250-51.

It is necessary to point out that the United Nations has no right to discuss the Vietnam question. Whatever resolution on the Vietnam question adopted by the U.N. Security Council is null and void. . . .

The U.S. Government has unceasingly claimed that it wants to talk with Hanoi but has received no response. If the U.S. Government truly wants to talk, it must, as was made clear in our statement on 28 January 1967, first of all stop unconditionally the bombing and all other acts of war against the DRV. After the United States has ended unconditionally the bombing and all other acts of war against the DRV, the DRV will hold talks with the United States on questions concerned.

*   *   *

COMMENTS REGARDING VIETNAM BY MEMBERS OF THE SENATE

A. Testimony of Senator J. William Fulbright (Ark.), Chairman of Committee*

[Extract]

March 11, 1968

*　　　　　*　　　　　*

It goes without saying—or should go without saying—that our disagreements have nothing to do with whether one is for or against America. We are all for America and for America's interests, but we disagree as to what those interests are and how they can best be advanced. We are all for America's prosperity at home and for its prestige abroad, but we disagree as to which requires precedence in these critical days. We are all for our fighting men in Vietnam, but we disagree as to whether they ought to be fighting there—as to whether the cause to which we have committed them is worth their lives and their terrible sacrifices. These are not trivial disagreements, and it would be a disservice to the country to pretend they were insignificant.

The focus is Vietnam, where the issue has become very much more than the fate of a poor, small and war-torn Asian nation.

The question is also the fate of America, not because it had to be so but because our leaders have made it so. By committing half a million of our young men to bloody and endless combat in those distant jungles, our leaders have converted a struggle between Vietnamese for possession of the Vietnamese land into a struggle between Americans for possession of the American spirit.

Discrepancies About War in Vietnam

The crisis over the war at home is the result of certain, striking discrepancies—discrepancies between events and the description of them by the Administration, between current Administration policies and traditional American values, such discrepancies as the following:

The war is described as an exemplary war, a war, that is, which will prove to the Communists once and for all that so-called "wars of national liberation" cannot succeed. In fact, we are not proving that. What, indeed, are we proving in Vietnam except that, even with an army of half a million men and expenditures which approach $30 billion a year, we cannot win a civil war for a regime which is incapable of inspiring the patriotism of its own people.

It is said that if we were not fighting in Vietnam we would have to be fighting much closer to home, in Hawaii or even California. I regard this contention as a slander on the U.S. Navy and Air Force. In the words of the plain-spoken

*U.S. Senate Committee on Foreign Relations, *Hearings on the Foreign Assistance Act of 1968*, 90 Cong., 1st sess., 1968, pt. 1, pp. 8-9; 12-13.

former Marine Commandant General David M. Shoup, the contention is "pure, unadulterated poppycock."

It is said that we are fighting for freedom in Vietnam and when someone objects that the Saigon government is corrupt, dictatorial, and incapable of inspiring either the loyalty of its people or the fighting spirit of its soldiers, we are told that there is also corruption in Boston and Beaumont, Tex., the relevancy of which escapes me.

There are finally the discrepancies concerning the Gulf of Tonkin resolution of August 1964, regarded by the Administration as the "functional equivalent" of a declaration of war, and the intent and expectation of Congress in adopting that famous resolution. As the Senate debate of August 6 and 7, 1964, makes abundantly clear, Congress, and certainly I, believed at the time that it was acting not to authorize a war but to prevent one. In addition it has recently become clear that much of the information on which Congress acted in adopting the Tonkin resolution was inaccurate.

*   *   *

Differences About Organizing the Peace

Mr. Secretary, I will comment briefly on your comment. Of course, I had hoped that this and other discussions, particularly those on the floor of the Senate, would persuade the Administration to evaluate its policies generally. There is no question about our all wanting to organize the peace, but there is a difference of opinion about how it should be done.

You correctly stated that the United Nations was the method agreed upon even before the end of World War II. It has not been as successful as we would like. But neither has our own unilateral intrusion into Southeast Asia which, it seems to me, could well be considered to have incited a number of the developments to which you have just referred.

For example, regarding the so-called Southeast Asia resolution, it seems to me that the North Vietnamese, knowing very well that the case that was presented to the Senate was not true, could well have concluded that we were determined to attack them without real provocation, because the provocation in question was, to say the least, extremely slight, as has been admitted. There was no damage whatever to our forces, hwatever else might be said, and I think the North Vietnamese could well have decided that we were determined to attack them regardless of what they did.

It is a fact we have intruded with vast numbers of forces there. I don't wish to go into all this at the moment because I want the other members to proceed. I do want to say that I do not accept your version of what happened in the Gulf of Tonkin. I do not accept your version as to why there may be an intrusion of Communist forces into Thailand. Thailand is very intimately associated with us. As you well know, we have some enormous bases there. We are using Thailand as a base to attack North Vietnam.

After all, as long as the war is going on, isn't this fact an incitement to intrusion by the other side? I am not seeking to excuse the Communists, I have said very often that I am sorry they did not accept the offers made long ago to settle this matter, but I can also understand—since it is their country, they live there and have no place else to go—that they can be stubborn about any foreign country intruding. They had the experience of the French for some 75 years, and they are perhaps not sophisticated enough to make a distinction between the French and ourselves, although we make such a distinction or at least appear to them to do so.

I am, at the moment, only suggesting that I do not accept your statement at face value, as an accurate description of what we are doing in Vietnam or whether what we are doing is designed to accomplish the purpose of organizing the peace, a purpose on which we all agree.

As I said in my opening statement, I do not think that your objective and the objective of this committee are any different, but we seriously disagree as to how we accomplish this objective.

As to taxes, I agree with you, but the real difficulty people have with taxes relates to the purposes for which taxes are levied. It is not the taxes per se to which the people—or at least some of them—are objecting.

*   *   *

B. Testimony of Senator Wayne Morse (Ore.)*

[Extract]

March 11, 1968

I want to say that there is not the slightest question, and history will so show, that we were a provocateur, and that is why on August 5, 1964, and again on August 6, 1964, I made two speeches on the history of the *Maddox*[1] and tried to warn the Senate we were a provocateur because I had had a call from a high official in the Pentagon building the night before asking me to call for the logs, asking me to ask what the *Maddox* was doing.

For the Secretary of Defense to say she was on a routine patrol just does not square with the facts. She was on a provocateur patrol. Of course she was on the high seas.

I happen to believe that on the night of August 2 there was an engagement. I think it was a minor engagement, but I think at least one torpedo was fired, according to the records we have had put into the record, maybe more. No damage was done, as Senator Fulbright has pointed out. No debris was found, not even an oil skim when daylight came. I think there was certainly an incident on the night of August 2. I have grave doubts that there was one on the night of August 4, but the cablegrams speak for themselves and when history reads those cablegrams, it will be seen that the Navy not only knew about it, the Navy was participating in it from the beginning.

Ibid., pp. 31-33.
[1] The North Vietnamese attack on this U.S. destroyer prompted the Tonkin Bay Resolution.

In fact, let me say the record also shows that the Navy knew of the plans and participated in the development of the plans for the bombardment of North Vietnam. That was an act of aggression of the United States against North Vietnam. That was our first act, through the Navy, of aggression against North Vietnam, and it was after that, as the testimony and the record made by you people in the Administration has shown time and time again, the major infiltration went into South Vietnam, the major infiltration of North Vietnamese forces.

Containment of China

Mr. Secretary, you and I do agree to a major premise. We have to find a way out. But do not forget, if I am correctly informed, that in a press interview not so long ago, not so many weeks ago, you said one of the reasons we were in Vietnam was to contain China. That is the first time you stated it publicly, and I think you ought to tell the committee this morning what you mean by containing China.

Do you mean militarily containing China, and, if so, for how long? And do you think that you can contain China militarily and not eventually go to war with China when China is ready to go to war because of that kind of unilateral action on our part?

Proposed U.N. Security Council Resolution

These are some of the broad brush strokes, Mr. Secretary, that show the great differences between you and some of us on this committee. But the common objective we ought to join on—and that is to find a way honorably to get a peace over there. And so I ask you again, as I have so many times, have you ever sent to the Security Council a resolution asking the Security Council to take over jurisdiction, with our pledge that we will abide by their jurisdiction if it will, in turn, carry out its corollary obligation to enforce the peace over there. For the resolution that was sent up in March 1966 was not that kind of a resolution; but only a resolution that we put the issue on the agenda. You know my position and the position of Senator Mansfield too. We ought to ask them to take jurisdiction and pledge that we will support their jurisdiction.

If they do not—and I am through with this and you are certainly welcome to make any comments you want—you know what I think our course of action should be. For we have to stop this killing in an undeclared war. We cannot sit here in our security, in our safety, while American boys are dying in the jungles of North Vietnam in a war we do not dare declare. We just cannot continue because—let me say, Senator Mansfield is right—there is an incipient uprising in this country in opposition to this war, and it is going to get worse.

This talk about sending over 100,000 or 200,000 more troops—you are going to create a very serious difficulty in this country if you people in the Administration go through with that.

*　　　　　*　　　　　*

I want you to know, grieving me as it does, that is the position the senior Senator from Oregon is going to take. The time has come for this Administration to be told that they have now to plan for a withdrawal, if they cannot get help from other nations. To say that we are in there to preserve peace in Asia—we cannot be the policeman of the world to preserve peace around the world. It will destroy us because the rest of the world is not going to support us in our unilateral assumption that we can be the policeman of the world.

In a nutshell, that is my case against you and against the Administration. I am not going to vote for foreign aid until we first take care of Vietnam.

C. Testimony of Senator Karl Mundt (S. Dak.)*

[Extract]

March 11, 1968

Mr. Secretary, continuing this educational forum, let me turn to what I am mostly interested in and that is the trouble in Vietnam. I shall direct my questions to that problem and the one particular aspect on which it seems to me is the one thing on which we all do agree upon today; I allude to the unhappy and unprecedented amount of division among our American compatriots concerning what is the wisest course to follow in Vietnam. Never before in all the wars that I have studied have we had quite this degree of divisiveness, quite this extent of debate in public places, in the Congress and around the country by prominent people as we are having in connection with this war.

A lot of people give a lot of reasons for that dissension. Some would attribute it to the fact that it isn't God that is dead, it's patriotism that is dead. I cannot believe that. I do not believe either is dead. I believe that basically our people are as patriotic as they have been in previous wars. That they would rally behind this cause once they are convinced that it is necessary to our security and to our democratic system and once they are convinced that the cause is right and that the need is real.

Some place along the line I think we have failed collectively as public officials, as representatives of the communications media, people generally, to eliminate the confusion which I think is a basic cause for this great and growing dissension which has to me reached very alarming degrees because if we are going to win the war in Vietnam and lose the war at home or if we are going to lose the war at home so we can't win it in Vietnam this is scarcely the orthodox or proper way in which to achieve the conclusion of a conflict.

Fighting Two Wars in Vietnam

I want to explore with you what I think are some of the reasons for this dissension. Senator Carlson mentioned one this morning when he said we were

* *Ibid.*, pp. 58-59; 74.

fighting two wars at the same time in Vietnam. I have no particular individual judgment as to whether it is wise or unwise to fight an economic war and a military war at the same place, at the same time. But it is one difference that makes this a different type of war from any that we have ever fought before.

Customarily we have gone on with winning the war after which we have given economic aid, very frequently not only to the victor, but to the vanquished, and sometimes with excellent results, such as we have had in West Germany, for example, and in Japan and, to the vanquished and in some of the European areas where we have also helped the victors with good results, but we have never tried before, as far as I know, anything about to try to do it at the same time as we fight the war and this has people disturbed. No good and clear-cut valid and persuasive reason has ever been given to a lot of people I talked with as to why this time we fight the two wars in the same place and at the same time.

*   *   *

U.S. Security Reasons for Being in Vietnam

I do hope in the interests of bringing about some kind of united opinion in this country, and you are aware of it as we are, that the shift of opinion is in the wrong direction, that if we expect to achieve enduring peace and success for our vital situation something more convincing than has been said, has to come from the Administration in terms of telling the people what this war is all about. Many people are unwilling to accept, and I can understand their reluctance, the amount of sacrifice we have made if the goal is simply free elections in South Vietnam and the right of people to select their own mayor in Saigon. That is too small a goal for the amount of sacrifice that we are making. While that can well be a part of it and should be a part of it, it seems to me at this stage of the game, it is by far the lesser reason for staying there than the fact that if we fail we would open up the doors of Communist aggression; we jeopardize our security and decrease the likelihood of having an enduring peace. I hope you agree with that and if not you may say so.

*   *   *

D. Testimony of Senator Frank Church (Idaho)*

[Extract]

March 11, 1968

Mr. Secretary, you mentioned President Kennedy. I suppose none of us can say with any degree of reliability what he might have done had he lived in

*Ibid., pp. 80-81.

facing up to the situation that has developed in Vietnam, but I recall that shortly before his death, in a nationwide television interview, he made 'a statement concerning Vietnam that seemed to me to contain much wisdom. He said: "We must remember that it is their war; not ours. It is their country; not ours. Only they can win their war. There is no way that we can win it for them."

When our policy was confined to giving aid to anti-Communist elements in Vietnam, fighting pro-Communist elements in Vietnam, I supported the policy. But when we began to substitute American troops for Vietnamese and increasingly assumed the full burden of the fighting, when we began to convert a Vietnamese struggle into an American war, I could no longer support the policy and began to speak out against it.

I did so because I felt that President Kennedy had been correct, that this is their war, and it is their country, and unless they are willing and able to do those things that are necessary to win, then it will be a dreadful waste of American lives, and in the end it will avail us nothing.

Now, the events since have tended to confirm my worst fears, and the question that really arises, it seems to me, is: Are they ready and willing to undertake to do those things that are necessary in order to win?

I have in mind, for example, the recent disclosure that during the fighting in Hue a thousand Vietnamese soldiers were in the city on Tet leave, but instead of joining the fighting for their own city they disguised themselves as refugees and stayed at the university ground for three weeks. Among them was a full colonel of the South Vietnamese Army. They were at all times behind U.S. lines yet they made no effort to rejoin their units or to join in the battle to save their own city.

Now, my question is: How can we win with allies like these?

*   *   *

Military Casualties

Mr. Secretary, may I interrupt to say when you say it is not accurate to say that we are assuming the main burden of the fighting, I find that difficult to accept, because just last week the casualties in Vietnam were 542 American dead, and South Vietnamese combat dead were 139. And in reviewing the casualties for last year, we suffered greater casualties on their battlefield in dead, wounded, mangled, and maimed Americans, we suffered nearly twice the casualties as the South Vietnamese they drafted into their own armed services during the same period.

Now, when it reaches that point, I think that the policy is sick. And that one is quite justified in saying that American fighting men have assumed the major burden of the fighting in Vietnam.

*   *   *

E. Testimony of Senator Clifford Case (N.J.)*

[Extract]

March 11, 1968

Mr. Secretary, I guess I have nothing more to ask you. I wish that I could continue to agree. But I am more and more convinced that what we are doing is wrong now. I find myself almost exactly in the position that Peregrine Worsthorne announced himself as being in just a short time ago. He writes for the London Sunday Telegraph, and up to now he says that he has defended the war, but on the 25th of February he said this, and I would just like to close, Mr Chairman, with a couple of paragraphs from him because it is stated so well, without rancor, and with the greatest sympathy for the United States:

> The case for and against the war was always highly debatable. But in my judgment, until recently, the balance of the argument just tipped in favor of the hawks. It is not easy to go on making that case today. In the light of the Vietcong's sensational reemergence, how many of South Vietnam's neighbors are still impressed by the value of American protection?
>
> Are they not more likely to be drawing the conclusion, after the events of the last 3 weeks, that the American giant is tragically unable—however willing—to succeed in guerrilla war, except at a price in destruction which makes no possible sense.
>
> Instead of America's impressing the world with their strength and virtue, they are making themselves hated by some for what they are doing, and despised by the remainder for not doing it more efficaciously.
>
> This all could change . . . but I do not believe any longer there is *enough* ground to justify what the Americans are being forced to do. . . . It is not easy to exaggerate the harm being done to American public values, and even to the quality of American private life, by what he is being forced to do in Vietnam. It looks less and less certain that this intense internal, moral strain can be sustained without doing irreparable damage to the American body politic.
>
> For my part, I no longer find it possible to be certain that fighting on—at such terrible cost in degradation—will prove a less debilitating experience for the United States than suffering the humiliation of withdrawal.

I would like, Mr. Chairman, to put the rest of this article in the record, if I may, at this point. . . .

I do not do it for any purpose except that I have myself come very close to the feeling that there is nothing necesary in what we have done that requires us to continue to do it if the result will be more and more destruction in South Vietnam, and more and more degradation here at home. I leave the question of the facts as to whether this is happening for another occasion.

I just hope that the Administration is not so committed to a course that if it should be persuaded on the facts that it is wrong, it will not be able to change the policy.

*   *   *

Ibid., pp. 92-93.

F. Testimony of Senator Stuart Symington (Mo.)*

[Extract]

March 11, 1968

Mr. Secretary, many people believe that we must achieve a victory in Vietnam. Would you give us a brief summary of what you think would be "victory"—a definition of the word at this point?

*   *   *

I want to be frank. In my own mind and heart there have been increasing doubts over a period.

People say we must win. I ask with sincerity, what do we win if we win? It is clear what we are losing, but what do we win if we win?

*   *   *

What War Has Done to Concept of U.S. Capability

I know you have been given a lot of advice this afternoon, and I would give you three brief thoughts of mine: One of the reasons I have changed my position is because it has become clear we underestimated the durability and patriotism of the Vietcong and the North Vietnamese. Second, we have overestimated the stability, the concept of nationhood, of the South Vietnamese Government. In that I associate myself with some of the remarks of Senator Church. Finally, this adoption of a military policy of gradualism—hit them hard, and if that doesn't work, hit them harder—which has resulted in this one-for-one operation in the jungles of Asia. It has been a most unfortunate decision, whoever is responsible for it, because it is now clear also that it was wrong.

One of the ablest men in this town said recently that deterrence was "capability times will times belief." As one who has traveled many times to Vietnam in recent years, then back through the Middle East and Europe, I believe what is going on now in Vietnam has hurt the concept of our capability in the minds of our friends and allies as well as our enemies. It has hurt the national will in this country, because of increasing dissension, and I am afraid it has made people who are opposed to us reduce their belief in our capacity. It is hard for them to understand—an I am quoting them—why a country with an $800 billion gross national product and 200 million people can, whatever the reason, be so consistently stalemated over a period of years by a country with little or no gross national product and 17 million people.

If you would care to comment, Mr. Secretary, I would be glad, to have you do so on my time. If not, Mr. Chairman, that is all I have to say.

Ibid., pp. 100-01.

G. Testimony of Senator Clairborne Pell (R.I.)*

[Extract]

March 11, 1968

*   *   *

I will just conclude with two points, if I may. One, returning to the basic one of Vietnam, I know you recognize the depth of feeling of those of us who really see our present course as one of disaster. I continue to think we should disentangle. I am glad certain reexaminations are going on in the Administration. I pray and hope that they may come out in the direction that men like myself have felt should be the case, and have said so privately and increasingly publicly in the last two or three years.

*   *   *

H. Testimony of Senator Albert Gore (Tenn.)*

[Extract]

March 12, 1968

*   *   *

Now, I lay this as a background to a question whether we genuinely and truly offer to negotiate without conditions. I think it more nearly amounts to an offer to talk to anybody, any time, anywhere, if they are willing to accept defeat on a prime point in contention, the establishment of a pro-Western democracy in South Vietnam.

Let me repeat, lest I be misunderstood: Ho Chi Minh is not my champion. I would that he would not be in position of government leadership. But what I am trying to get at is not whether I am going to help Ho Chi Minh or encourage him—I believe that is the popular phrase—by raising these questions. I want to find a way to settle this horrible controversy which is so costly in life and blood and prestige of our country, and threatens, as all wars threaten, to become a world conflagration.

I think the first great mistake was made under the Eisenhower administration not to accept the Geneva accords but instead to undertake to create in South Vietnam something in our own image, a pro-Western democracy.

We undertook by persuasion, by aid, by propaganda, by politics, national and international, to establish this. When in 1965 this effort had failed, the second great mistake was made when President Johnson decided to use force

*Ibid., p. 132.

*Ibid., pp. 158-59.

to achieve what we had been unable to achieve by other means.

All of us make mistakes, as I said earlier. I do not excuse myself. I should have raised questions earlier. I acknowledge my own error, although it is not important in this context. This is but background, however, to inquire of you, if, in fact, you really mean that the United States would be willing to withdraw her 500,000-plus troops, and North Vietnam would withdraw her 70-some thousand, coupled with the cessation of hostilities, and whether you really mean this point 11, which is that the countries of Southeast Asia can be nonalined if they so choose.

*   *   *

I. Testimony of Senator Joseph Clark (Pa.)*

[Extract]

March 12, 1968

*   *   *

I would like to shift now and read to you, Mr. Secretary, a brief summary of my own conclusions and ask you to comment on them:

> The war in Vietnam is at a stalemate which neither side can convert into a military victory without leaving the country—and perhaps the world—in ruins.
>
> Vietnam is a cancer which is devouring our youth, our morals, our national wealth, and the energies of our leadership. The casualty list from this war only begins on the battlefield. As victims we must also count the programs of the Great Society, the balance of payments, a sound budget, a stable dollar, the world's good will, detente with the Soviet Union, and hopes for a durable world peace. The toll of this war can never be measured in terms of lives lost and dollars spent—they are only the tip of a vast iceberg whose bulk can never be accurately measured.
>
> We are not likely to end the war by a military victory. This has been amply demonstrated by the recent VC offensive. This is primarily a political war, a war which cannot be won by bullets and bombs short of annihilation of both the enemy and the people for whom we fight.
>
> Nor can we get out by unilateral withdrawal . . .

And I stress that because my position, like the positions of some of my colleagues, has been so grossly misrepresented in the press and elsewhere, and I have never been for scuttle and run.

> Nor is the only alternative to do more of what we are doing—on both the political and military side . . . . To continue our current policy of bombing the North, of search and destroy, of failure to press for political accommodations within South Vietnam, will inevitably lead to a wider war, spilling over as it already has begun to do—into Laos and Cambodia, and ending eventually in a confrontation in North Vietnam with China and the Soviet Union—which might well lead to World War III.

*_Ibid._, p. 190.

There are other alternatives. And unless we pursue them we will soon find that our policies inexorably become captives of the Saigon Government which is bent, in its folly and its reliance on American military might, on a total military victory. We must not allow the Saigon tail to wag the U.S. dog. There is freedom to maneuver left, but not much.

Not only the military but also the political war is at a stalemate, distasteful though that word is to the Administration—a stalemate which becomes more apparent with every day of continued bitter and costly fighting.

*   *   *

PEACE TALKS

A. Address by President Johnson on New Steps Toward Peace in Vietnam*

[Extract]

March 31, 1968

*   *   *

Tonight I renew the offer I made last August—to stop the bombardment of North Viet-Nam. We ask that talks begin promptly, that they be serious talks on the substance of peace. We assume that during those talks Hanoi will not take advantage of our restraint.

We are prepared to move immediately toward peace through negotiations.

So tonight, in the hope that this action will lead to early talks, I am taking the first step to deescalate the conflict. We are reducing—substantially reducing—the present level of hostilities. And we are doing so unilaterally and at once.

Tonight I have ordered our aircraft and our naval vessels to make no attacks on North Viet-Nam, except in the area north of the demilitarized zone where the continuing enemy buildup directly threatens Allied forward positions and where the movements of their troops and supplies are clearly related to that threat.

The area in which we are stopping our attacks includes almost 90 percent of North Viet-Nam's population and most of its territory. Thus there will be no attacks around the principal populated areas or in the food-producing areas of North Viet-Nam.

Even this very limited bombing of the North could come to an early end if our restraint is matched by restraint in Hanoi. But I cannot in good conscience stop all bombing so long as to do so would immediately and directly endanger the lives of our men and our allies. Whether a complete bombing halt becomes possible in the future will be determined by events.

Our purpose in this action is to bring about a reduction in the level of violence that now exists.

It is to save the lives of brave men and to save the lives of innocent women and children. It is to permit the contending forces to move closer to a political settlement.

And tonight I call upon the United Kingdom and I call upon the Soviet Union, as cochairmen of the Geneva conferences and as permanent members of the United Nations Security Council, to do all they can to move from the unilateral act of deescalation that I have just announced toward genuine peace in Southeast Asia.

Now, as in the past, the United States is ready to send its representatives to any forum, at any time, to discuss the means of bringing this ugly war to an end.

*   *   *

*Department of State Bulletin, Apr. 15, 1968, pp. 481-86.

Finally, my fellow Americans, let me say this:

Of those to whom much is given, much is asked. I cannot say, and no man could say, that no more will be asked of us.

Yet, I believe that now, no less than when the decade began, this generation of Americans is willing to "pay any price, bear any burden, meet any hardship, support any friend, oppose any foe to assure the survival and the success of liberty." Since those words were spoken by John F. Kennedy, the people of America have kept that compact with mankind's noblest cause.

And we shall continue to keep it.

Yet I believe that we must always be mindful of this one thing, whatever the trials and the tests ahead: The ultimate strength of our country and our cause will lie not in powerful weapons or infinite resources or boundless wealth but will lie in the unity of our people.

This I believe very deeply.

Throughout my entire public career I have followed the personal philosophy that I am a free man, an American, a public servant, and a member of my party, in that order always and only.

For 37 years in the service of our nation, first as a Congressman, as a Senator and as Vice President and now as your President, I have put the unity of the people first. I have put it ahead of any divisive partisanship.

And in these times as in times before, it is true that a house divided against itself by the spirit of faction, of party, of region, of religion, of race, is a house that cannot stand.

There is division in the American house now. There is divisiveness among us all tonight. And holding the trust that is mine, as President of all the people, I cannot disregard the peril to the progress of the American people and the hope and the prospect of peace for all peoples.

So I would ask all Americans whatever their personal interests or concern, to guard against divisiveness and all its ugly consequences.

Fifty-two months and 10 days ago, in a moment of tragedy and trauma the duties of this Office fell upon me. I asked then for your help and God's, that we might continue America on its course, binding up our wounds, healing our history, moving forward in new unity, to clear the American agenda and to keep the American commitment for all of our people.

United we have kept that commitment. United we have enlarged that commitment.

Through all time to come, I think America will be a stronger nation, a more just society, and a land of greater opportunity and fulfillment because of what we have all done together in these years of unparalleled achievement.

Our reward will come in the life of freedom, peace, and hope that our children will enjoy through ages ahead.

What we won when all of our people united just must not now be lost in suspicion, distrust, selfishness, and politics among any of our people.

Believing this as I do, I have concluded that I should not permit the Presidency to become involved in the partisan divisions that are developing in this political year.

With America's sons in the fields far away, with America's future under challenge right here at home, with our hopes and the world's hopes for peace in the balance every day, I do not believe that I should devote an hour or a day of my time to any personal partisan causes or to any duties other than the awesome duties of this Office—the Presidency of your country.

Accordingly, I shall not seek, and I will not accept, the nomination of my party for another term as your President.

But let men everywhere know, however, that a strong, a confident, and a vigilant America stands ready tonight to seek an honorable peace—and stands ready tonight to defend an honored cause—whatever the price, whatever the burden, whatever the sacrifices that duty may require.

Thank you for listening.

Good night and God bless all of you.

B. Address by President Johnson on the Bombing Halt of North Vietnam*

[Extract]

October 31, 1968

Good evening, my fellow Americans: I speak to you this evening about very important developments in our search for peace in Viet-Nam.

We have been engaged in discussions with the North Vietnamese in Paris since last May. The discussions began after I announced on the evening of March 31st in a television speech to the Nation that the United States, in an effort to get talks started on a settlement of the Viet-Nam war, had stopped the bombing of North Viet-Nam in the area where 90 percent of the people live.

When our representatives, Ambassador [W. Averell] Harriman and Ambassador [Cyrus R.] Vance, were sent to Paris, they were instructed to insist throughout the discussions that the legitimate elected government of South Viet-Nam must take its place in any serious negotiations affecting the future of South Viet-Nam.

Therefore, our Ambassadors Harriman and Vance made it abundantly clear to the representatives of North Viet-Nam in the beginning that, as I had indicated on the evening of March 31st, we would stop the bombing of North Vietnamese territory entirely when that would lead to prompt and productive talks—meaning by that, talks in which the Government of Viet-Nam was free to participate.

Our Ambassadors also stressed that we could not stop the bombing so long as by doing so we would endanger the lives and the safety of our troops.

For a good many weeks, there was no movement in the talks at all. The talks appeared to really be deadlocked. Then, a few weeks ago, they entered a new and a very much more hopeful phase.

*Ibid., Nov. 18, 1968, pp. 517-19.

As we moved ahead, I conducted a series of very intensive discussions with our allies and with the senior military and diplomatic officers of the United States Government on the prospects for peace. The President also briefed our congressional leaders and all of the presidential candidates.

Last Sunday evening, and throughout Monday, we began to get confirmation of the essential understanding that we had been seeking with the North Vietnamese on the critical issues between us for some time. I spent most of all day Tuesday reviewing every single detail of this matter with our field commander, General [Creighton W.] Abrams, whom I had ordered home and who arrived here at the White House at 2:30 in the morning and went into immediate conference with the President and the appropriate members of his Cabinet. We received General Abrams' judgment and we heard his recommendations at some length.

Now, as a result of all of these developments, I have now ordered that all air, naval, and artillery bombardment of North Viet-Nam cease as of 8 a.m., Washington time, Friday morning [November 1].

I have reached this decision on the basis of the developments in the Paris talks, and I have reached it in the belief that this action can lead to progress toward a peaceful settlement of the Vietnamese war.

I have already informed the three presidential candidates, as well as the congressional leaders of both the Republican and the Democratic Parties, of the reasons that the Government has made this decision.

This decision very closely conforms to the statements that I have made in the past concerning a bombing cessation.

It was on August 19th that the President said:

"This administration does not intend to move further until it has good reason to believe that the other side intends seriously"—seriously—"to join us in deescalating the war and moving seriously toward peace."

Then again on September 10th, I said:

". . . the bombing will not stop until we are confident that it will not lead to an increase in American casualties."

The Joint Chiefs of Staff, all military men, have assured me—and General Abrams very firmly asserted to me on Tuesday in that early 2:30 a.m. meeting—that in their military judgment this action should be taken now and this action would not result in any increase in American casualties.

A regular session of the Paris talks is going to take place next Wednesday, November 6th, at which the representatives of the Government of South Viet-Nam are free to participate. We are informed by the representatives of the Hanoi Government that the representatives of the National Liberation Front will also be present. I emphasize that their attendance in no way involves recognition of the National Liberation Front in any form. Yet it conforms to the statements that we have made many times over the years that the NLF would have no difficulty making its views known.

What we now expect—what we have a right to expect—are prompt, productive, serious, and intensive negotiations in an atmosphere that is conducive to progress.

We have reached the stage where productive talks can begin. We have made clear to the other side that such talks cannot continue if they take military advantage of them. We cannot have productive talks in an atmosphere where the cities are being shelled and where the demilitarized zone is being abused.

I think I should caution you, my fellow Americans, that arrangements of this kind are never foolproof. For that matter, even formal treaties are never foolproof, as we have learned from our experience.

But in the light of the progress that has been made in recent weeks, and after carefully considering and weighing the unanimous military and diplomatic advice and judgment rendered to the Commander in Chief, I have finally decided to take this step now and to really determine the good faith of those who have assured us that progress will result when bombing ceases and to try to ascertain if an early peace is possible. The overriding consideration that governs us at this hour is the chance and the opportunity that we might have to save human lives, save human lives on both sides of the conflict. Therefore, I have concluded that we should see if they are acting in good faith.

We could be misled—and we are prepared for such a contingency. We pray God it does not occur.

*   *   *

C. Vietnam Reappraisal by Clark M. Clifford, Former Secretary of Defense*

[Extract]

July, 1969

THE PERSONAL HISTORY OF ONE MAN'S VIEW AND HOW IT EVOLVED

Viet Nam remains unquestionably the transcendent problem that confronts our nation. Though the escalation has ceased, we seem to be no closer to finding our way out of this infinitely complex difficulty. The confidence of the past has become the frustration of the present. Predictions of progress and of military success, made so often by so many, have proved to be illusory as the fighting and the dying continue at a tragic rate. Within our country, the dialogue quickens and the debate sharpens. There is a growing impatience among our people, and questions regarding the war and our participation in it are being asked with increasing vehemence.

*   *   *

At the time of our original involvement in Viet Nam, I considered it to be based upon sound and unassailable premises, thoroughly consistent with our

*Clark M. Clifford, "A Vietnam Reappraisal: The Personal History of One Man's View and How It Evolved," *Foreign Affairs*, XVII (July 1969), pp. 601-22.

self-interest and our responsibilities. There has been no change in the exemplary character of our intentions in Viet Nam. We intervened to help a new and small nation resist subjugation by a neighboring country—a neighboring country, incidentally, which was being assisted by the resources of the world's two largest communist powers.

I see no profit and no purpose in any divisive national debate about whether we were right or wrong initially to become involved in the struggle in Viet Nam. Such debate at the present time clouds the issue and obscures the pressing need for a clear and logical evaluation of our present predicament, and how we can extricate ourselves from it.

Only history will be able to tell whether or not our military presence in Southeast Asia was warranted. Certainly the decisions that brought it about were based upon a reasonable reading of the past three decades. We had seen the calamitous consequences of standing aside while totalitarian and expansionist nations moved successively against their weaker neighbors and accumulated a military might which left even the stronger nations uneasy and insecure. We had seen in the period immediately after World War II the seemingly insatiable urge of the Soviet Union to secure satellite states on its western periphery. We had seen in Asia itself the attempt by open invasion to extend communist control into the independent South of the Korean Peninsula. We had reason to feel that the fate averted in Korea through American and United Nations military force would overtake the independent countries of Asia, albeit in somewhat subtler form, were we to stand aside while the communist North sponsored subversion and terrorism in South Viet Nam.

The transformation that has taken place in my thinking has been brought about, however, by the conclusion that the world situation has changed dramatically, and that American involvement in Viet Nam can and must change with it. Important ingredients of this present situation include the manner in which South Viet Nam and its Asian neighbors have responded to the threat and to our own massive intervention. They also include internal developments both in Asian nations and elsewhere, and the changing relations among world powers.

The decisions which our nation faces today in Viet Nam should not be made on interpretations of the facts as they were perceived four or five or fifteen years ago, even if, through compromise, a consensus could be reached on these interpretations. They must instead be based upon our present view of our obligations as a world power; upon our current concept of our national security; upon our conclusions regarding our commitments as they exist today; upon our fervent desire to contribute to peace throughout the world; and, hopefully, upon our acceptance of the principle of enlightened self-interest.

But these are broad and general guidelines, subject to many constructions and misconstructions. They also have the obvious drawback of being remote and impersonal.

The purpose of this article is to present to the reader the intimate and highly personal experience of one man, in the hope that by so doing there will be a simpler and clearer understanding of where we are in Viet Nam today, and what we must do about it. I shall go back to the beginning and identify, as well as I can, the origins of my consciousness of the problem, the opportunities I had to obtain the facts, and the resulting evolution of what I shall guardedly refer to as my thought processes.

*   *   *

In the late summer of 1967, President Johnson asked me to go with his Special Assistant, General Maxwell Taylor, to review the situation in South Viet Nam, and then to visit some of our Pacific allies. We were to brief them on the war and to discuss with them the possibility of their increasing their troop commitments. Our briefings in South Viet Nam were extensive and encouraging. There were suggestions that the enemy was being hurt badly and that our bombing and superior firepower were beginning to achieve the expected results.

Our visits to the allied capitals, however, produced results that I had not foreseen. It was strikingly apparent to me that the other troop-contributing countries no longer shared our degree of concern about the war in South Viet Nam. General Taylor and I urged them to increase their participation. In the main, our plea fell on deaf ears.

*   *   *

I returned home puzzled, troubled, concerned. Was it possible that our assessment of the danger to the stability of Southeast Asia and the Western Pacific was exaggerated? Was it possible that those nations which were neighbors of Viet Nam had a clearer perception of the tides of world events in 1967 than we? Was it possible that we were continuing to be guided by judgments that might once have had validity but were now obsolete? In short, although I still counted myself a staunch supporter of our policies, there were nagging, not-to-be-suppressed doubts in my mind.

*   *   *

In mid-January 1968, President Johnson asked me to serve as Secretary of Defense, succeeding Secretary McNamara, who was leaving to become President of the World Bank. .   .   .

*   *   *

I took office on March 1, 1968. The enemy's Tet offensive of late January and early February had been beaten back at great cost. the confidence of the American people had been badly shaken. The ability of the South Vietnamese Government to restore order and morale in the populace, and discipline and esprit in the armed forces, was being questioned. At the President's direction, General Earle G. Wheeler, Chairman of the Joint Chief of Staff, had flown to Viet Nam in late February for an on-the-spot conference with General Westmoreland. He had just returned and presented the military's request that over 200,000 troops be prepared for deployment to Viet Nam. These troops would be in addition to the 525,000 previously authorized. I was directed, as my first assignment, to chair a task forced named by the President to determine how this new requirement could be met. We were not instructed to assess the need for substantial increases in men and material; we were to devise the means by which they could be provided.

My work was cut out. The task force included Secretary Rusk, Secretary Henry Fowler, Under Secretary of State Nicholas Katzenbach, Deputy Secretary of Defense Paul Nitze, General Wheeler, CIA Director Richard Helms, the President's Special Assistant, Walt Rostow, General Maxwell Taylor and other skilled and highly capable officials. All of them had had long and direct experience with Vietnamese problems. I had not. I had attended various meetings in the past several years and I had been to Viet Nam three times, but it was quickly apparent to me how little one knows if he has been on the periphery of a problem and not truly in it. Until the day-long sessions of early March, I had never had the opportunity of intensive analysis and fact-finding. Now I was thrust into a vigorous, ruthlessly frank assessment of our situation by the men who knew the most about it. Try though we would to stay with the assignment of devising means to meet the military's requests, fundamental questions began to recur over and over.

*   *   *

"Will 200,000 more men do the job?" I found no assurance that they would.

"If not, how many more might be needed—and when?" There was no way of knowing.

"What would be involved in committing 200,000 more men to Viet Nam?" A reserve call-up of approximately 280,000, an increased draft call and an extension of tours of duty of most men then in service.

"Can the enemy respond with a build-up of his own?" He could and he probably would.

"What are the estimated costs of the latest requests?" First calculations were on the order of $2 billion for the remaining four months of that fiscal year, and an increase of $10 to $12 billion for the year beginning July 1, 1968.

"What will be the impact on the economy?" So great that we would face the possibility of credit restrictions, a tax increase and even wage and price controls. The balance of payments would be worsened by at least half a billion dollars a year.

"Can bombing stop the war?" Never by itself. It was inflicting heavy personnel and material losses, but bombing by itself would not stop the war.

"Will stepping up the bombing decrease American casualties?" Very little, if at all. Our casualties were due to the intensity of the ground fighting in the South. We had already dropped a heavier tonnage of bombs than in all the theaters of World War II. During 1967, an estimated 90,000 North Vietnamese had infiltrated into South Viet Nam. In the opening weeks of 1968, infiltrators were coming in at three to four times the rate of a year earlier, despite the ferocity and intensity of our campaign of aerial interdiction.

"How long must we keep on sending our men and carrying the main burden of combat?" The South Vietnamese were doing better, but they were not ready yet to replace our troops and we did not know when they would be.

When I asked for a presentation of the military plan for attaining victory in Viet Nam, I was told that there was no plan for victory in the historic American sense. Why not? Because our forces were operating under three major political restrictions: The President had forbidden the invasion of North Viet Nam because this could trigger the mutual assistance pact between North Viet Nam and China; the President had forbidden the mining of the harbor at Haiphong, the principal port through which the North received military supplies because a Soviet vessel might be sunk; the President had forbidden our forces to pursue the enemy into Laos and Cambodia, for to do so would spred the war, politically and geographically, with no discernible advantage. These and other restrictions which precluded an all-out, no-holds-barred military effort were wisely designed to prevent our being drawn into a larger war. We had no inclination to recommend to the President their cancellation.

"Given these circumstances, how can we win?" We would, I was told, continue to evidence our superiority over the enemy; we would continue to attack in the belief that he would reach the stage where he would find it inadvisable to go on with the war. He could not afford the attrition we were inflicting on him. And we were improving our posture all the time.

I then asked, "What is the best estimate as to how long this course of action will take? Six months? One year? Two years?" There was no agreement on an answer. Not only was there no agreement, I could find no one willing to express any confidence in his guesses. Certainly, none of us was willing to assert that he could see "light at the end of the tunnel" or that American troops would be coming home by the end of the year.

After days of this type of analysis, my concern had greatly deepened. I could not find out when the war was going to end; I could not find out the manner in which it was going to end; I could not find out whether the new requests for men and equipment were going to be enough, or whether it would take more and, if more, when and how much; I could not find out how soon the South Vietnamese forces would be ready to take over. All I had was the statement, given with too little self-assurance to be comforting, that if we persisted for an indeterminate length of time, the enemy would choose not to go on.

And so I asked, "Does anyone see any diminution in the will of the enemy after four years of our having been there, after enormous casualties and after massive destruction from our bombing?"

The answer was that there appeared to be no diminution in the will of the enemy. This reply was doubly impressive, because I was more conscious each day of domestic unrest in our own country. Draft card burnings, marches in the streets, problems on school campuses, bitterness and divisiveness were rampant. Just as disturbing to me were the economic implications of a struggle to be indefinitely continued at ever-increasing cost. The dollar was already in trouble, prices were escalating far too fast and emergency controls on foreign investment imposed on New Year's Day would be only a prelude to more stringent controls, if we were to add another $12 billion to Viet Nam spending—with perhaps still more to follow.

I was also conscious of our obligatins and involvements elsewhere in the world. There were certain hopeful signs in our relations with the Soviet Union, but both nations were hampered in moving toward vitally important talks on the limitation of strategic weapons so long as the United States was committed to a military solution in Viet Nam. We could not afford to disregard our interests in the Middle East, South Asia, Africa, Western Europe and elsewhere. Even accepting the validity of our objective in Viet Nam, that objective had to be viewed in the context of our overall national interest, and could not sensibly be pursued at a price so high as to impair our ability to achieve other, and perhaps even more important, foreign policy objectives.

Also, I could not free myself from the continuing nagging doubt left over from that August trip, that if the nations living in the shadow of Viet Nam were not now persuaded by the domino theory, perhaps it was time for us to take another look. Our efforts had given the nations in that area a number of years following independence to organize and build their security. I could see no reason at this time for us to continue to add to our commitment. Finally, there was no assurance that a 40 percent increase in American troops would place us within the next few weeks, months or even years in any substantially better military position than we were in then. All that could be predicted accurately was that more troops would raise the level of combat and automatically raise the level of casualties on both sides.

And so, after these exhausting days, I was convinced that the military course we were pursuing was not only endless, but hopeless. A further substantial increase in American forces could only increase the devastation and the Americanization of the war, and thus leave us even further from our goal of a peace that would permit the people of South Viet Nam to fashion their own political and economic institutions. Henceforth, I was also convinced, our primary goal should be to level off our involvement, and to work toward gradual disengagement.

To reach a conclusion and to implement it are not the same, especially when one does not have the ultimate power of decision. It now became my purpose to emphasize to my colleagues and to the President, that the United States had entered Viet Nam with a limited aim—to prevent its subjugation by the North and to enable the people of South Viet Nam to determine their own future. I also argued that we had largely accomplished that objective. Nothing required us to remain until the North had been ejected from the South, and the Saigon government had been established in complete military control of all South Viet Nam. An increase of over 200,000 in troop strength would mean that American forces would be twice the size of the regular South Vietnamese Army at that time. Our goal of building a stronger South Vietnamese Government, and an effective military force capable of ultimately taking over from us, would be frustrated rather than furthered. The more we continued to do in South Viet

Nam, the less likely the South Vietnamese were to shoulder their own burden.

> *   *   *

The fact is that the creation of strong political, social and economic institutions is a job that the Vietnamese must do for themselves. We cannot do it for them, nor can they do it while our presence hangs over them so massively. President Thieu, Vice President Ky, Prime Minister Huong and those who may follow them have the task of welding viable political institutions from the 100 or more splinter groups that call themselves political parties. It is up to us to let them get on with the job. Nothing we might do could be so beneficial or could so add to the political maturity of South Viet Nam as to begin to withdraw our combat troops. Moreover, in my opinion, we cannot realistically expect to achieve anything more through our military force, and the time has come to begin to disengage. That was my final conclusion as I left the Pentagon on January 20, 1969.

It remains my firm opinion today. It is based not only on my personal experiences, but on the many significant changes that have occurred in the world situation in the last four years.

In 1965, the forces supported by North Viet Nam were on the verge of a military take-over of South Viet Nam. Only by sending large numbers of American troops was it possible to prevent this from happening. The South Vietnamese were militarily weak and politically demoralized. They could not, at that time, be expected to preserve for themselves the right to determine their own future. Communist China had recently proclaimed its intention to implement the doctrine of "wars of national liberation." Khruschev's fall from power the preceding October and Chou En-lai's visit to Moscow in November 1964 posed the dire possibility of the two communist giants working together to spread disruption throughout the underdeveloped nations of the world. Indonesia, under Sukarno, presented a posture of implacable hostility toward Malaysia, and was a destabilizing element in the entire Pacific picture. Malaysia itself, as well as Thailand and Singapore, needed time for their governmental institutions to mature. Apparent American indifference to developments in Asia might, at that time, have had a disastrous impact on the independent countries of that area.

During the past four years, the situation has altered dramatically. The armed forces of South Viet Nam have increased in size and proficiency. The political situation there has become more stable, and the governmental institutions more representative. Elsewhere in Asia, conditions of greater security exist. The bloody defeat of the attempted communist coup in Indonesia removed Sukarno from power and changed the confrontation with Malaysia to cooperation between the two countries. The governments of Thailand and Singapore have made good use of these four years to increase their popular support. Australia and New Zealand have moved toward closer regional defense ties, while Japan, the Republic of Korea and Taiwan have exhibited a rate of economic growth and an improvement in living standards that discredit the teachings of Chairman Mao.

Of at least equal significance is that fact that, since 1965, relations between

Russia and China have steadily worsened. The schism between these two powers is one of the watershed events of our time. Ironically, their joint support of Hanoi has contributed to the acrimony between them. It has brought into focus their competition for leadership in the communist camp. Conflicting positions on the desirability of the peace negotiations in Paris have provided a further divisive factor. In an analogous development, increased Soviet aid to North Korea had made Pyongyang less dependent on China. The Cultural Revolution and the depredations of the Red Guards have created in China a situation of internal unrest that presently preoccupies China's military forces. The recent border clashes on the Ussuri River further decrease the likelihood that China will, in the near future, be able to devote its attention and resources to the export of revolution.

These considerations are augmented by another. It seems clear that the necessity to devote more of our minds and our means to our pressing domestic problems requires that we set a chronological limit on our Vietnamese involvement.

*   *   *

A first step would be to inform the South Vietnamese Government that we will withdraw about 100,000 troops before the end of this year. We should also make it clear that this is not an isolated action, but the beginning of a process under which all U.S. ground combat forces will have been withdrawn from Viet Nam by the end of 1970. The same information should, of course, be provided to the other countries who are contributing forces for the defense of South Viet Nam.

Strenuous political and military objections to this decision must be anticipated. Arguments will be made that such a withdrawal will cause the collapse of the Saigon governmment and jeopardize the security of our own and allied troops. Identical arguments, however, were urged against the decisions to restrict the bombing on March 31 of last year and to stop it completely on October 31. They have proven to be unfounded. There is, in fact, no magic and no specific military rationale for the number of American troops presently in South Viet Nam. The current figure represents only the level at which the escalator stopped.

*   *   *

Concurrently with the decision to begin withdrawal, orders should be issued to our military commanders to discontinue efforts to apply maximum military pressure on the enemy and to seek instead to reduce the level of combat. The public statements of our officials show that there has as yet been no change in our policy of maximum military effort. The result has been a continuation of the high level of American casualties, without any discernible impact on the peace negotiations in Paris.

While our combat troops are being withdrawn, we would continue to provide the armed forces of the Saigon government with logistic support and with our air resources. As the process goes on, we can appraise both friendly and enemy reactions. The pattern of our eventual withdrawal of non-combat troops and personnel engaged in air lift and air support can be determined on the basis of political and military developments. So long as we retain our air resources in South Viet Nam, with total air superiority, I do not believe that the lessening in the military pressure exerted by the ground forces would permit the enemy to make any significant gains. There is, moreover, the possibility of reciprocal reduction in North Vietnamese combat activity.

Our decision progressively to turn over the combat burden to the armed forces of South Viet Nam would confront the North Vietnamese leaders with a painful dilemma. Word that the Americans were beginning to withdraw might at first lead them to claims of victory. But even these initial claims could be expected to be tinged with apprehension. There has, in my view, long been considerable evidence that Hanoi fears the possibility that those whom they characterize as "puppet forces" may, with continued but gradually reduced American support, prove able to stand off the communist forces.

As American combat forces are withdrawn, Hanoi would be faced with the prospect of a prolonged and substantial presence of American air and logistics personnel in support of South Viet Nam's combat troops, which would be constantly improving in efficiency. Hanoi's only alternative would be to arrange, tacitly or explicitly, for a mutual withdrawal of all external forces. In either eventuality, the resulting balance of forces should avert any danger of a blood bath which some fear might occur in the aftermath of our withdrawal.

Once our withdrawal of combat troops commences, the Saigon government would recognize, probably for the first time, that American objectives do not demand the perpetuation in power or any one group of South Vietnamese. So long as we appear prepared to remain indefinitely, there is no pressure on Saigon to dilute the control of those presently in positions of power by making room for individuals representative of other nationalist elements in South Vietnamese society.

*   *   *

In the long run, the security of the Pacific region will depend upon the ability of the countries there to meet the legitimate growing demands of their own people. No military strength we can bring to bear can give them internal stability or popular acceptance. In Southeast Asia, and elsewhere in the less developed regions of the world, our ability to understand and to control the basic forces that are at play is a very limited one. We can advise, we can urge, we can furnish economic aid. But American military power cannot build nations, any more than it can solve the social and economic problems that face us here at home.

*   *   *

NIXON ADMINISTRATION POLICY TOWARD VIETNAM

A. Statement by Ambassador Henry Cabot Lodge, Head of U.S. Delegation at First Plenary Session of Vietnam Meetings, on the Task of Peace*

Paris, January 25, 1969

Ladies and gentlemen: This is a unique moment in history. Today, in this new meeting in Paris, the search for peace in Viet-Nam enters a new stage. Today we begin together the search for an honorable and enduring settlement to the conflict which divides us. The world will be watching these proceedings with close attention. They will expect progress, not propaganda. They will expect agreement, not acrimony. The United States is determined to do everything it can to assure that these meetings will lead us to peace.

Last Monday, a new President was inaugurated, committed to an honorable peace and dedicated to an equitable solution. In his inaugural address he stated:

> . . . the peace we seek to win is not victory over any other people but the peace that comes "with healing in its wings"; with compassion for those who have suffered; with understanding for those who have opposed us; with the opportunity for all the peoples of this earth to choose their own destiny.

I ask you to ponder these words.

No purpose is served by repeating the list of familiar charges or to recite once more the chronology which brought us here. Our responsibility is to the future, not the past. The problems we have settled have been procedural; the bulk of our substantive work is still ahead. The United States will enter these talks with a profound sense of responsibility and an open mind. It will put forth carefully considered proposals and hopes that the other side will do the same.

Undoubtedly we have many difficult sessions ahead of us. A good way to begin our task would be to deal with concrete proposals. The search for peace can begin in the DMZ. We believe that the demilitarized status of the zone between North and South Viet-Nam should be restored immediately. Specifically, the United States Government proposes that the DMZ should be:

> —Free of all regular and irregular military and subversive forces and personnel, military installations, military supplies and equipment.
> —An area in which, from which, and across which all acts of force are prohibited.
> —A zone temporarily separating North and South Viet-Nam pending their reunification through the free expression of the will of the people of the North and of the people of the South.
> —An area the same in size and definition as that provided in the 1954 Geneva accords.
> —Subject to an effective system of international inspection and verification.

We therefore propose that each side publicly declare its readiness to respect the provisions of the 1954 Geneva accords relating to the DMZ, and abide by those provisions.

*Department of State Bulletin, Feb. 10, 1969, pp. 124-25.

We stand ready to begin today to work out the details for transforming this proposal for a DMZ into a practical move toward peace. We are prepared to give serious and openminded consideration to all proposals directed to this end by your side. Nothing could be more auspicious for our work here than an agreement today to begin urgent consideration of this matter.

We will put forward other concrete proposals at subsequent meetings. Our proposal today with respect to the DMZ is advanced as a practical first step on the road to peace.

Of course, our real task is not a partial but a complete peace. The United States goal can be stated simply: to preserve the right of the South Vietnamese people to determine their own future without outside interference or coercion.

For this reason, the United States believes that all external forces should be withdrawn from South Viet-Nam and that all military and subversive forces of North Viet-Nam must be withdrawn into North Viet-Nam. We are ready to work toward the implementation of the objective of such mutual withdrawal.

The United States Government seeks no permanent establishment of troops, no permanent military bases, and no permanent military alliance. We have no desire to threaten or harm the people of North Viet-Nam or to invade that country or to overthrow its government. What we do seek is a South Viet-Nam that is free from attacks or subversion from without.

We seek peace not only in Viet-Nam but in the entire area of Southeast Asia. We believe that the Geneva agreements of 1962 on Laos must be observed. We consider it necessary that the sovereignty, independence, unity, and territorial integrity of Cambodia be fully respected.

The United States has, on more than one occasion, expressed its conviction that the essential elements of the Geneva accords of 1954 provide a basis for peace in Viet-Nam. We reaffirm this today.

The Geneva accords provided for international supervision. Experience has demonstrated the shortcomings of existing methods. One of our principal tasks will be to work out more effective ways of supervising any agreement and to insure equitable and effective investigation of complaints. We believe that the nations of the area, which have the most crucial interest in peace and stability in the region, should be involved in the system of monitoring of the agreement at which we may arrive.

We seek the early release of prisoners of war on both sides so they can return to their homes and rejoin their families. We would be prepared to discuss this at an early date so as to arrange for the prompt release of prisoners held by both sides.

The United States is present here because we seek a permanent peace. The United States Government considers that it has a mandate for a fresh look. We know that peace cannot be achieved unless both sides can take part in its achievement.

Ladies and gentlemen, we here will be judged ultimately by history, not tomorrow's headlines. Let us talk without rancor and recrimination. President Nixon in his inaugural address stated in another context: "We cannot learn from one another until we stop shouting at one another—until we speak quietly enough so that our words can be heard as well as our voices." And he added: "Let us take as our goal: Where peace is unknown, make it welcome; where peace is fragile, make it strong; where peace is temporary, make it permanent."

Ladies and gentlemen, in that spirit let us—together—take up the task of peace.

B. Speech by President Richard M. Nixon on Vietnam*

May 14, 1969

Good evening, my fellow Americans.

I have asked for this television time tonight to report to you on our most difficult and urgent problem—the war in Vietnam.

Since I took office four months ago, nothing has taken so much of my time and energy as the search for a way to bring lasting peace to Vietnam. I know that some believe I should have ended the war immediatley after the inauguration by simply ordering our forces home from Vietnam.

This would have been the easy thing to do. It might have been a popular move. But I would have betrayed my solemn responsibility as President of the United States if I had done so.

I want to end this war. The American people want to end this war. The people of South Vietnam want to end this war. But we want to end it permanently so that the younger brothers of our soldiers in Vietnam will not have to fight in the future in another Vietnam someplace else in the world.

The fact that there is no easy way to end the war does not mean that we have no choice but to let the war drag on with no end in sight.

For four years American boys have been fighting and dying in Vietnam. For 12 months our negotiators have been talking with the other side in Paris. And yet the fighting goes on. The destruction continues. Brave men still die.

The time has come for some new initiatives. Repeating the old formulas and the tired rhetoric of the past is not enough. When Americans are risking their lives in war, it is the responsibility of their leaders to take some risks for peace.

I would like to report to you tonight on some of the things we have been doing in the past four months to bring true peace, and then I would like to make some concrete proposals to speed that day.

Our first step began before inauguration. This was to launch an intensive review of every aspect of the Nation's Vietnam policy. We accepted nothing on faith, we challenged every assumption and every statistic. We made a systematic, serious examination of all the alternatives open to us. We carefully considered recommendations offered both by critics and supporters of past policies.

From the review, it became clear at once that the new Administration faced a set of immediate operational problems.

The other side was preparing for a new offensive.

There was a wide gulf of distrust between Washington and Saigon.

In eight months of talks in Paris, there had been no negotiations directly concerned with a final settlement.

*Congressional Record, May 15, 1969.

Therefore, we moved on several fronts at once.

We frustrated the attack which was launched in late February. As a result, the North Vietnamese and the Viet Cong failed to achieve their military objectives.

We restored a close working relationship with Saigon. In the resulting atmosphere of mutual confidence, President Thieu and his Government have taken important initiatives in the search for a settlement.

We speeded up the strengthening of the South Vietnamese forces. I am glad to report tonight, that as a result, General Abrams told me on Monday that progress in the training program had been excellent, and that apart from any developments that may occur in the negotiations in Paris, that time is approaching when South Vietnamese forces will be able to take over some of the fighting fronts now being manned by Americans.

In weighing alternate courses, we have had to recognize that the situation as it exists today is far different from what it was two years ago or four years ago or ten years ago.

One difference is that we no longer have the choice of not intervening. We have crossed that bridge. There are now more than a half million American troops in Vietnam and 35,000 Americans have lost their lives.

We can have honest debate about whether we should have entered the war in Vietnam. We can have honest debate about how the war has been conducted. But the urgent question today is what to do now that we are there.

Against that background, let me discuss first what we have rejected, and second, what we are prepared to accept.

We have ruled out attempting to impose a purely military solution on the battlefield.

We have also ruled out either a one-sided withdrawal from Vietnam, or the acceptance in Paris of terms that would amount to a disguised American defeat.

When we assumed the burden of helping defend South Vietnam, millions of South Vietnamese men, women and children placed their trust in us. To abandon them now would risk a massacre that would shock and dismay everyone in the world who values human life.

Abandoning the South Vietnamese people, however, would jeopardize more than lives in South Vietnam. It would threaten our long-term hopes for peace in the world. A great nation cannot renege on its pledges. A great nation must be worthy of trust.

When it comes to maintaining peace, "prestige" is not an empty word. I am not speaking of false pride or bravado—they should have no place in our policies. I speak, rather, of the respect that one nation has for another's integrity in defending its principles and meeting its obligations.

If we simply abandoned our effort in Vietnam, the cause of peace might not survive the damage that would be done to other natons' confidence in our reliability.

Another reason for not withdrawing unilaterally stems from debates within the Communist world between those who argue for a policy of containment of confrontation with the United States, and those who argue against it.

If Hanoi were to succeed in taking over South Vietnam by force—even after the power of the United States had been engaged—it would greatly strengthen those leaders who scorn negotiation, who advocate aggression, who minimize the risks of confrontation with the United States. It would bring peace now but it would enormously increase the danger of a bigger war later.

If we are to move successfully from an era of confrontation to an era of negotiation, then we have to demonstrate—at the point at which confrontation is being tested—that confrontation with the United States is costly and unrewarding.

Almost without exception, the leaders of non-Communist Asia have told me that they would consider a one-sided American withdrawal from Vietnam to be a threat to the security of their own nations.

In determining what choices would be acceptable, we have to understand our essential objective in Vietnam: What we want is very little, but very fundamental. We seek the opportunity for the South Vietnamese people to determine their own political future without outside interference.

Let me put it plainly: What the United States wants for South Vietnam is not the important thing. What North Vietnam wants for South Vietnam is not the important thing. What is important is what the people of South Vietnam want for South Vietnam.

The United States has suffered over a million casualties in four wars in this century. Whatever faults we may have as a nation, we have asked nothing for ourselves in return for those sacrifices. We have been generous toward those whom we have fought. We have helped our former foes as well as our friends in the task of reconstruction. We are proud of this record, and we bring the same attitude in our search for a settlement in Vietnam.

In this spirit, let me be explicit about several points:

We seek no bases in Vietnam.

We seek no military ties.

We are willing to agree to neutrality for South Vietnam if that is what the South Vietnamese people freely choose.

We believe there should be an opportunity for full participation in the political life of South Vietnam by all political elements that are prepared to do so without the use of force or intimidation.

We are prepared to accept any government in South Vietnam that results from the free choice of the South Vietnamese people themselves.

We have no intention of imposing any form of government upon the people of South Vietnam, nor will we be a party to such coercion.

We have no objection to reunification, if that turns out to be what the people of North Vietnam and the people of South Vietnam want; we ask only that the decision reflect the free choice of the people concerned.

At this point, I would like to add a personal word based on many visits to South Vietnam over the past five years. This is the most difficult war in American history, fought against a ruthless enemy. I am proud of our men who have carried the terrible burden of this war with dignity and courage, despite the division and opposition to the war in the United States. History will record that never have America's fighting men fought more bravely for more unselfish goals than our men in Vietnam. It is our responsibility to see that they have not fought in vain.

In pursuing our limited objective, we insist on no rigid diplomatic formats. Peace could be achieved by a formal negotiated settlement. Peace could be achieved by an informal understanding, provided that the understanding is clear, and that there were adequate assurances that it would be observed. Peace on paper is not as important as peace in fact.

This brings us to the matter of negotiations.

We must recognize that peace in Vietnam cannot be achieved overnight. A war that has raged for many years will require detailed negotiations and cannot be settled by a single stroke.

What kind of a settlement will permit the South Vietnamese people to determine freely their own political future? Such a settlement will require the withdrawal of all non-South Vietnamese forces, including our own, from South Vietnam, and procedures for political choice that give each significant group in South Vietnam a real opportunity to participate in the political life of the nation.

To implement these principles, I reaffirm now our willingness to withdraw our forces on a specified timetable. We ask only that North Vietnam withdraw its forces from South Vietnam, Cambodia and Laos into North Vietnam, also in accordance with a timetable.

We include Cambodia and Laos to insure that these countries would not be used as bases for a renewed war. Our offer provides for a simultaneous start on withdrawal by both sides; for agreement on a mutually acceptable timetable; and for the withdrawal to be accomplished quickly.

The North Vietnamese delegates have been saying in Paris that political issues should be discussed along with military issues, and there must be a political settlement in the South. We do not dispute this, but the military withrawal involves outside forces, and can, therefore, be properly negotiated by North Vietnam and the United States, with the concurrence of its allies.

The political settlement is an internal matter which ought to be decided among the South Vietnamese, themselves and not imposed by outsiders. However, if our presence at these political negotiations would be helpful, and if the South Vietnamese concerned agreed, we would be willing to participate along with the representatives of Hanoi, if that also were desired.

Recent statements by President Thieu have gone far toward opening the way to a political settlement. He has publicly declared his government's willingness to discuss a political solution with the National Liberation Front, and has offered free elections. This was a dramatic step forward, a reasonable offer that could lead to a settlement. The South Vietnamese Government has offered to talk without preconditions. I believe the other side should also be willing to talk without preconditions.

The South Vietnamese government recognizes, as we do, that a settlement must permit all persons and groups that are prepared to renounce the use of force to participate freely in the poltitical life of South Vietnam. To be effective, such a settlement would require two things: First, a process that would allow the South Vietnamese people to express their choice; and, second, a guarantee that this process would be a fair one.

We do not insist on a particular form of guarantee. The important thing is that the guarantees should have the confidence of the South Vietnamese people, and that they should be broad enough and strong enough to protect the interests of all major South Vietnamese groups.

This, then, is the outline of the settlement that we seek to negotiate in Paris. Its basic terms are very simple: Mutual withdrawl of non-South Vietnamese forces from South Vietnam, and free choice for the people of South Vietnam. I believe that the long-term interests of peace require that we insist on no less, and that the realities of the situation require that we seek no more.

And now to make very concrete what I have said. I propose the following specific measures which seem to me consistent with the principles of all parties. These proposals are made on the basis of full consultation with President Thieu.

As soon as agreement can be reached, all non-South Vietnamese forces would begin withdrawals from South Vietnam.

Over a period of twelve months, by agreed upon stages, the major portions of all U.S., Allied, and other non-South Vietnamese forces would be withdrawn. At the end of this twelve month period, the remaining U.S., Allied and other non-South Vietnamese forces would move into designated base areas and would not engage in combat operations.

The remaining U.S. and Allied forces would complete their withdrawals as the remaining North Vietnamese forces were withdrawn and returned to North Vietnam.

An international supervisory body, acceptable to both sides, would be created for the purpose of verifying withdrawals, and for any other purposes agreed upon between the two sides.

This international body would begin operating in accordance with an agreed timetable and would participate in arranging supervised cease fires in Vietnam.

As soon as possible after the international body was functioning, elections would be held under agreed procedures and under the supervision of the international body.

Arrangements would be made for the release or prisoners of war on both sides at the earliest possible time.

All parties would agree to observe the Geneva Accords of 1954 regarding South Vietnam and Cambodia, and the Laos Accords of 1962.

I believe this proposal for peace is realistic, and takes account of the legitimate interests of all concerned. It is consistent with President Thieu's six points. It can accommodate the various programs put forth by the other side. We and the Government of South Vietnam are prepared to discuss its details with the other side.

Secretary Rogers is now in Saigon and he will be discussing with President Thieu how, together, we may put forward these proposed measures most usefully in Paris. He will, as well, be consulting with our other Asian allies on these measures while on his Asian trip. However, I would stress that these proposals are not offered on a take-it-or-leave-it basis. We are quite willing to consider other approaches consistent with our principles.

We are willing to talk about anybody's program—Hanoi's four points, the NLF's 10 points—provided it can be made consistent with the very few basic principles I have set forth here.

Despite our disagreement with several of its points, we welcome the fact that the NLF has put forward its first comprehensive program. We are studying that program carefully. However, we cannot ignore the fact that immediately after the offer, the scale of enemy attacks stepped up and American casualties in Vietnam increased.

Let me make one point clear. If the enemy wants peace with the United States, that is not the way to get it.

I have set forth a peace program tonight which is generous in its terms. I have indicated our willingness to consider other proposals. But no greater mistake could be made than to confuse flexibility with weakness or of being reasonable with lack of resolution. I must also make clear, in all candor, that if the needless suffering continues, this will affect other decisions. Nobody has anything to gain by delay.

Reports from Hanoi indicate that the enemy has given up hope for a military victory in South Vietnam, but is counting on a collapse of American will in the United States. There could be no greater error in judgment.

Let me be quite blunt. Our fighting men are not going to be worn down; our mediators are not going to be talked down; and our allies are not going to be let down.

My fellow Americans, I have seen the ugly face of war in Vietnam. I have seen the wounded in field hospitals—American boys, South Vienamese boys, North Vietnamese boys. They were different in many ways—the color of their skins, their religions, their races, some were enemies; some were friends.

But the differences were small, compared with how they were alike. They were brave men and they were so young. Their lives—their dreams for the future—had been shattered by a war over which they had no control.

With all the moral authority of the office which I hold, I say that America could have no greater and prouder role than to help to end this war in a way which will bring nearer that day in which we can have a world order in which people can live together in peace and friendship.

I do not criticize those who disagree with me on the conduct of our peace negotiations. And I do not ask unlimited patience from a people whose hopes for peace have too often been raised and then cruelly dashed over the past four years.

I have tried to present the facts about Vietnam with complete honesty, and I shall continue to do so in my reporrts to the American people.

Tonight, all I ask is that you consider these facts, and, whatever our differences, that you support a program which can lead to a peace we can live with and a peace we can be proud of. Nothing could have a greater effect in convincing the enemy that he should negotiate in good faith than to see the American people united behind a generous and reasonable peace offer.

In my campaign for the Presidency, I pledged to end this war in a way that would increase our chances to win true and lasting peace in Vietnam, in the Pacific, and in the world. I am determined to keep that pledge. If I fail to do so, I expect the American people to hold me accountable for that failure.

But while I will never raise false expectations my deepest hope, as I speak to you tonight, is that we shall be able to look back on this day, at this critical turning point when American initiative moved us on dead center and forward to the time when this war would be brought to an end and when we shall be able to devote the unlimited energies and dedication of the American people to the exciting challenges of peace.

Thank you, and good night.

C. Address by President Nixon on the Pursuit of Peace in Vietnam*

[Extract]

November 3, 1969

Good evening, my fellow Americans: Tonight I want to talk to you on a subject of deep concern to all Americans and to many people in all parts of the world—the war in Viet-Nam.

I believe that one of the reasons for the deep division about Viet-Nam is that many Americans have lost confidence in what their Government has told them about our policy. The American people cannot and should not be asked to support a policy which involves the overriding issues of war and peace unless they know the truth about that policy.

Tonight, therefore, I would like to answer some of the questions that I know are on the minds of many of you listening to me.

How and why did America get involved in Viet-Nam in the first place!

How has this administration changed ithe policy of the previous administration!

What has really happened in the negotiations in Paris and on the battlefront in Viet-Nam!

What choices do we have if we are to end the war!

What are the prospects for peace!

Let me begin by describing the situation I found when I was inaugurated on January 20.

—The war had been going on for 4 years.
31,000 Americans had been killed in action.
—The training program for the South Vietnamese was behind schedule.
—540,000 Americans were in Viet-Nam, with no plans to reduce the number.
—No progress had been made at the negotiations in Paris and the United States had not put forth a comprehensive peace proposal.
—The war was causing division at home and criticism from many of our friends, as well as our enemies, abroad.

In view of these circumstances there were some who urged that I end the

*Department of State Bulletin, Nov. 24, 1969, pp. 437-46.

war at once by ordering the immediate withdrawal of all American forces.

From a political standpoint this would have been a popular and easy course to follow. After all, we became involved in the war while my predecessor was in office. I could blame the defeat which would be the result of my action on him and come out as the peacemaker. Some put it to me quite bluntly: This was the only way to avoid allowing Johnson's war to become Nixon's war.

But I had a greater obligation than to think only of the years of my administration and the next election. I had to think of the effect of my decision on the next generation and on the future of peace and freedom in America and in the world.

Let us all understand that the question before us is not whether some Americans are for peace and some Americans are against peace. The question at issue is not whether Johnson's war becomes Nixon's war.

The great question is: How can we win America's peace!

History of U.S. Involvement in Vietnam

Let us turn now to the fundamental issue. Why and how did the United States become involved in Viet-Nam in the first place!

Fifteen years ago North Viet-Nam, with the logistical support of Communist China and the Soviet Union, launched a campaign to impose a Communist government on South Viet-Nam by instigating and supporting a revolution.

In response to the request of the Government of South Viet-Nam, President Eisenhower sent economic aid and military equipment to assist the people of South Viet-Nam in their efforts to prevent a Communist takeover. Seven years ago President Kennedy sent 16,000 military personnel to Viet-Nam as combat advisers. Four years ago President Johnson sent American combat forces to South Viet-Nam.

Now, many believe that President Johnson's decision to send American combat forces to South Viet-Nam was wrong. And many others, I among them, have been strongly critical of the way the war has been conducted.

But the question facing us today is: Now that we are in the war, what is the best way to end it?

Consequences of Precipitate Withdrawal

In January I could only conclude that the precipitate withdrawal of American forces from Viet-Nam would be a disaster not only for South Viet-Nam but for the United States and for the cause of peace.

For the South Vietnamese, our precipitate withdrawal would inevitably allow the Communists to repeat the massacres which followed their takeover in the North 15 years before.

—They then murdered more than 50,000 people, and hundreds of thousands more died in slave labor camps.

—We saw a prelude of what would happen in South Viet-Nam when the Communists entered the city of Hue last year. During their brief rule there, there was a bloody reign of terror in which 3,000 civilians were clubbed, shot to death, and buried in mass graves.

—With the sudden collapse of our support, these atrocities of Hue would become the nightmare of the entire nation—and particularly for the million and a half Catholic refugees who fled to South Viet-Nam when the Communists took over in the North.

For the United States, this first defeat in our nation's history would result in a collapse of confidence in American leadership not only in Asia but throughout the world.

Three American Presidents have recognized the great stakes involved in Viet-Nam and understood what had to be done.

In 1963 President Kennedy, with his characteristic eloquence and clarity, said: " . . . we want to see a stable government there, carrying on a struggle to maintain its national independence.

We believe strongly in that. We are not going to withdraw from that effort. In my opinion, for us to withdraw from that effort would mean a collapse not only of South Viet-Nam, but Southeast Asia. So we are going to stay there."

President Eisenhower and President Johnson expressed the same conclusion during their terms of office.

For the future of peace, precipitate withdrawal would thus be a disaster of immense magnitude.

—A nation cannot remain great if it betrays its allies and lets down its friends.

—Our defeat and humiliation in South Viet-Nam without question would promote recklessness in the councils of those great powers who have not yet abandoned their goals of world conquest.

—This would spark violence wherever our commitments help maintain the peace—in the Middle East, in Berlin, eventually even in the Western Hemisphere.

Ultimately, this would cost more lives. It would not bring peace; it would bring more war.

For these reasons I rejected the recommendation that I should end the war by immediately withdrawing all our forces. I chose instead to change American policy on both the negotiating front and the battlefront.

U.S. Peace Proposals

In order to end a war fought on many fronts, I initiated a pursuit for peace on many fronts.

In a television speech on May 14, in a speech before the United Nations, and on a number of other occasions, I set forth our peace proposals in great detail.

—We have offered the complete withdrawal of all outside forces within 1 year.

—We have proposed a cease-fire under international supervision.

—We have offered free elections under international supervision, with the Communists participating in the organization and conduct of the elections as an organized political force. The Saigon Government has pledged to accept the result of the elections.

We have not put forth our proposals on a take-it-or-leave-it basis. We have indicated that we are willing to discuss the proposals that have been put forth by the other side. We have declared that anything is negotiable, except the right of the people of South Viet-Nam to determine their own future. At the Paris peace conference, Ambassador Lodge has demonstrated our flexibility and good faith in 40 public meetings.

Hanoi has refused even to discuss our proposals. They demand our unconditional acceptance of their terms, which are that we withdraw all American forces immediately and unconditionally and that we overthrow the Government of South Viet-Nam as we leave.

Private Initiatives Undertaken

We have not limited our peace initiatives to public forums and public statements. I recognized in January that a long and bitter war like this usually cannot be settled in a public forum. That is why, in addition to the public statements and negotiations, I have explored every possible private avenue that might lead to a settlement.

*   *   *

But the effect of all the public, private, and secret negotiations which have been undertaken since the bombing halt a year ago and since this administration came into office on January 20 can be summed up in one sentence: No progress whatever has been made except agreement on the shape of the bargaining table.

Now, who is at fault?

It has become clear that the obstacle in negotiating an end to the war is not the President of the United States. It is not the South Vietnamese Government.

The obstacle is the other side's absolute refusal to show the least willingness to join us in seeking a just peace. It will not do so while it is convinced that all it has to do is to wait for our next concession, and our next concession after that one, until it gets everything it wants.

There can now be no longer any question that progress in negotiation depends only on Hanoi's deciding to negotiate, to negotiate seriously.

I realize that this report on our efforts on the diplomatic front is discouraging to the American people, but the American people are entitled to know the truth—the bad news as well as the good news—where the lives of our young men are involved.

New Direction in U.S. Foreign Policy

Now let me turn, however, to a more encouraging report on another front.

At the time we launched our search for peace, I recognized we might not succeed in bringing an end to the war through negotiation.

I therefore put into effect another plan to bring peace—a plan which will bring the war to an end regardless of what happens on the negotiating front. It is in line with a major shift in U.S. foreign policy which I described in my press conference at Guam on July 25.

Let me briefly explain what has been described as the Nixon doctrine—a policy which not only will help end the war in Viet-Nam but which is an essential element of our program to prevent future Viet-Nams.

We Americans are a do-it-yourself people. We are an impatient people. Instead of teaching someone else to do a job, we like to do it ourselves. And this trait has been carried over into our foreign policy.

In Korea and again in Viet-Nam, the United States furnished most of the money, most of the arms, and most of the men to help the people of those countries defend their freedom against Communist aggression.

Before any American troops were comtitted to Viet-Nam, a leader of another Asian country expressed this opinion to me when I was traveling in Asia as a private citizen. He said: "When you are trying to assist another nation defend its freedom, U.S. policy should be to help them fight the war, but not to fight the war for them."

Well, in accordance with this wise counsel, I laid down in Guam three principles as guidelines for future American policy toward Asia:

—First, the United States will keep all of its treaty commitments.

—Second, we shall provide a shield if a nuclear power threatens the freedom of a nation allied with us or of a nation whose survival we consider vital to our security.

—Third, in cases involving other types of aggression, we shall furnish military and economic assistance when requested in accordance with our treaty commitments. But we shall look to the nation directly threatened to assume the primary responsibility of providing the manpower for its defense.

After I announced this policy, I found that the leaders of the Philippines, Thailand, Viet-Nam. South Korea, and other nations which might be threatened by Communist aggression welcomed this new direction in American foreign policy.

The Vietnamization Plan

The defense of freedom is everybody's business—not just America's business. And it is particularly the responsibility of the people whose freedom is threatened. In the previous administration we Americanized the war in Viet-Nam. In this administration we are Vietnamizing the search for peace.

The policy of the previous administration not only resulted in our assuming the primary responsibility for fighting the war but, even more significantly, did not adequately stress the goal of strengthening the South Vietnamese so that they could defend themselves when we left.

The Vietnamization plan was launched following Secretary [of Defense Melvin R.] Laird's visit to Viet-Nam in March. Under the plan, I ordered first a substantial increase in the training and equipment of South Vietnamese forces.

In July, on my visit to Viet-Nam, I changed General Abrams' orders so that they were consistent with the objectives of our new policies. Under the new orders, the primary mission of our troops is to enable the South Vietnamese forces to assume the full responsibility for the security of South Viet-Nam.

Our air operations have been reduced by over 20 percent.

And now we have begun to see the results of this long-overdue change in American policy in Viet-Nam:

—After 5 years of Americans going into Viet-Nam, we are finally bringing American men home. By December 15, over 60,000 men will have been withdrawn from South Viet-Nam, including 20 percent of all of our combat forces.

—The South Vietnamese have continued to gain in strength. As a result, they have been able to take over combat responsibilities from our American troops.

Two other significant developments have occurred since this administration took office:

—Enemy infiltration, infiltration which is essential if they are to launch a major attack, over the last 3 months is less than 20 percent of what it was over the same period last year.

—Most important, United States casualties have declined during the last 2 months to the lowest point in 3 years.

Our Program for the Future

Let me now turn to our program for the future.

We have adopted a plan which we have worked out in cooperation with the South Vietnamese for the complete withdrawal of all U.S. combat ground forces and their replacement by South Vietnamese forces on an orderly scheduled timetable. This withdrawal will be made from strength and not from weakness. As South Vietnamese forces become stronger, the rate of American withdrawal can become greater.

I have not and do not intend to announce the timetable for our program. There are obvious reasons for this decision, which I am sure you will understand. As I have indicated on several occasions, the rate of withdrawal will depend on developments on three fronts.

One of these is the progress which can be, or might be, made in the Paris talks. An announcement of a fixed timetable for our withdrawal would completely remove any incentive for the enemy to negotiate an agreement. They would simply wait until our forces had withdrawn and then move in.

The other two factors on which we will base our withdrawal decisions are the level of enemy activity and the progress of the training program of the South Vietnamese forces. I am glad to be able to report tonight progress on both of these fronts has been greater than we anticipated when we started the program in June for withdrawal. As a result, our timetable for withdrawal is more optimistic now than when we made our first estimates in June.

This clearly demonstrates why it is not wise to be frozen in on a fixed timetable. We must retain the flexibility to base each withdrawal decision on the situation as it is at that time rather than on estimates that are no longer valid.

Along with this optimistic estimate, I must in all candor leave one note of caution: If the level of enemy activity significantly increases, we might have to adjust our timetable accordingly.

However, I want the record to be completely clear on one point.

At the time of the bombing halt just a year ago, there was some confusion as to whether there was an understanding on the part of the enemy that if we stopped the bombing of North Viet-Nam, they would stop the shelling of cities in South Viet-Nam. I want to be sure that there is no misunderstanding on the part of the enemy with regard to our withdrawal program.

We have noted the reduced level of infiltration, the reduction of our casualties, and are basing our withdrawal decisions partially on those facors.

If the level of infiltration or our casualties increase while we are trying to scale down the fighting, it will be the result of a conscious decision by the enemy.

Hanoi could make no greater mistake than to assume that an increase in violence will be to its advantage. If I conclude that increased enemy action jeopardizes our remaining forces in Viet-Nam, I shall not hesitate to take strong and effective measures to deal with that situation.

This is not a threat. This is a statement of policy which as Commander in Chief of our Armed Forces I am making in meeting my responsibility for the protection of American fighting men wherever they may be.

My fellow Americans, I am sure you can recognize from what I have said that we really only have two choices open to us if we want to end this war:

—I can order an immediate, precipitate withdrawal of all Americans from Viet-Nam without regard to the effects of that action.

—Or we can persist in our search for a just peace, through a negotiated settlement if possible or through continued implementation of our plan for Vietnamization if necessary—a plan in which we will withdraw all of our forces from Viet-Nam on a schedule in accordance with our program, as the South Vietnamese become strong enough to defend their own freedom.

I have chosen this second course. It is not the easy way. It is the right way. It is a plan which will end the war and serve the cause of peace, not just in Viet-Nam but in the Pacific and in the world.

In speaking of the consequences of a precipitate withdrawal, I mentioned that our allies would lose confidence in America.

Far more dangerous, we would lose confidence in ourselves. Oh, the immediate reaction would be a sense of relief that our men were coming home. But as we saw the consequences of what we had done, inevitable remorse and divisive recrimination would scar our spirit as a people.

We have faced other crises in our history and have become stronger by rejecting the easy way out and taking the right way in meeting our challenges. Our greatness as a nation has been our capacity to do what had to be done when we knew our course was right.

I recognize that some of my fellow citizens disagree with the plan for peace I have chosen. Honest and patriotic Americans have reached different conclusions as to how peace should be achieved.

In San Francisco a few weeks ago I saw demonstrators carrying signs reading: "Lose in Viet-Nam, bring the boys home."

Well, one of the strengths of our free society is that any American has a right to reach that conclusion and to advocate that point of view. But as President of the United States, I would be untrue to my oath of office if I allowed the policy of this nation to be dictated by the minority who hold that point of view and who try to impose it on the Nation by mounting demonstrations in the street.

For almost 200 years, the policy of this nation has been made under our Constitution by those leaders in the Congress and in the White House elected by all of the people. If a vocal minority, however fervent its cause, prevails over reason and the will of the majority, this nation has no future as a free society.

And now I would like to address a word, if I may, to the young people of this nation who are particularly concerned—and I understand why they are concerned—about this war.

I respect your idealism.

I share your concern for peace.

I want peace as much as you do.

There are powerful personal reasons I want to end this war. This week I will have to sign 83 letters to mothers, fathers, wives, and loved ones of men who have given their lives for America in Viet-Nam. It is very little satisfaction to me that this is only one-third as many letters as I signed the first week in office. There is nothing I want more than to see the day come when I do not have to write any of those letters.

—I want to end the war to save the lives of those brave young men in Viet-Nam.

—But I want to end it in a way which will increase the chance that their younger brothers and their sons will not have to fight in some future Viet-Nam someplace in the world.

—And I want to end the war for another reason.

I want to end it so that the energy and dedication of you, our young people, now too often directed into bitter hatred against those responsible for the war, can be turned to the great challenges of peace: a better life for all Americans, a better life for all people on this earth.

I have chosen a plan for peace. I believe it will succeed.

If it does succeed, what the critics say now won't matter. If it does not succeed, anything I say then won't matter.

I know it may not be fashionable to speak of patriotism or national destiny these days. But I feel it is appropriate to do so on this occasion.

Two hundred years ago this nation was weak and poor. But even then, America was the hope of millions in the world. Today we have become the strongest and richest nation in the world. The wheel of destiny has turned so that any hope the world has for the survival of peace and freedom will be determined by whether the American people have the moral stamina and the courage to meet the challenge of free-world leadership.

Let historians not record that when America was the most powerful nation in the world we passed on the other side of the road and allowed the last hopes for peace and freedom of millions of people to be suffocated by the forces of totalitarianism.

And so tonight—to you, the great silent majority of my fellow Americans—I ask for your support.

I pledged in my campaign for the Presidency to end the war in a way that we could win the peace. I have initiated a plan of action which will enable me to keep that pledge.

The more support I can have from the American people, the sooner that pledge can be redeemed; for the more divided we are at home, the less likely the enemy is to negotiate at Paris.

Let us be united for peace. Let us also be united against defeat. Because let us understand: North Viet-Nam cannot defeat or humiliate the United States. Only Americans can do that.

Fifty years ago, in this room and at this very desk, President Woodrow Wilson spoke words which caught the imagination of a war-weary world. He said: "This is the war to end wars."

His dream for peace after World War I was shattered on the hard realities of great-power politics, and Woodrow Wilson died a broken man.

Tonight I do not tell you that the war in Viet-Nam is the war to end wars. But I do say this: I have initiated a plan which will end this war in a way that will bring us closer to that great goal to which Woodrow Wilson and every American President in our history has been dedicated—the goal of a just and lasting peace.

As President I hold the responsibility for choosing the best path to that goal and then leading the Nation along it.

I pledge to you tonight that I shall meet this responsibility with all of the strength and wisdom I can command in accordance with your hopes, mindful of your concerns, sustained by your prayers.

THE UNITED STATES

AND LAOS

THE UNITED STATES AND LAOS

Commentary

United States concern for the Kingdom of Laos dates essentially from the Geneva Conference of 1954. Laos, a part of French Indochina, was granted status as an independent state in July, 1953 by France, though it was still to be part of the French Union. Because the Indochina War took place in part on Laotian soil and because Laos had comprised a segment of France's Southeast Asian colony, it therefore appeared on the agenda at Geneva. At Geneva a cease fire was declared in the tiny country, withdrawal of most French and Vietnamese forces was to be effected, and the introduction of new forces or weapons prohibited; Laos was to be neutral in the struggle between the Communist bloc and the West.

But neutrality was easier to define than to guarantee. One of the early problems was that the Pathet Lao or pro-Communist forces, which in the Geneva accords were allowed sanctuary in two Laotian provinces bordering on North Vietnam, with Viet Minh assistance continued to try to "liberate" the country. Finally, in November, 1957 the Royal Government, headed by Prince Souvanna Phouma, achieved a satisfactory accommodation with the rebels. In July, 1958 the Prince announced that unification was completed and the International Control Commission could leave. Shortly thereafter, Souvanna Phouma resigned as Prime Minister—his successor being Phoui Sananikone. The new Minister quickly established a decidedly anti-Communist government, which in January, 1959 acted to subdue the Pathet Lao and all "dangerous ideology" in the country.

The result of the anti-Communist action was increased Communist aid to the rebels and additional American involvement. Between 1954 and 1958, North Vietnam, China, and the Soviet Union had sent supplies and weapons to the Pathet Lao, and North Vietnam helped recruit and train guerrilla forces in the country. In 1959, they stepped up the aid drastically and the Viet-Minh occupied a couple of Laotian provinces to put pressure on the government at Vientiane. Meanwhile, the United States, which had provided assistance to the neutralist government, sent supplies, military equipment and American technicians and instructors to bolster the government then in power. Fortunately, the crisis did not bring a serious clash necessitating a major United States decision as the Laotian government appealed to the United Nations, which sent an investigatory team to the scene; the fighting slackened in the fall of 1959.

Internal politics led to a new crisis in 1960-1962. Initially a pro-Western faction secured control of the government and cemented the country more closely to the United States. This faction was removed from power by a military coup in the summer of 1960 and the neutralist leader, Prince Souvanna Phouma, became Prime Minister—his intention being to sustain a government composed of the various Laotian factions. The pro-Western, pro-American group then began a counter-revolt in the South and by the end of the year drove the neutralist premier to seek exile in Cambodia, thus securing control in Vientiane. The Western nations recognized the new government but the Communist countries refused, insisting that Souvanna Phouma was the legitimate head of state and aided the Pathet Lao in securing military control over a good portion of the kingdom. This was how the matter stood in early 1961.

When President Kennedy assumed office he decided that support for the pro-American group was futile and in a speech in March, 1961 called for an internationally controlled ceasefire and a truly neutral Laos. The Communists agreed to the proposal for an international conference to deal with the question, and after achieving most of their military goals, to the ceasefire. Subsequently, in May a fourteen nation conference began at Geneva but the conference stalemated and the Pathet Lao failed to honor the truce; the United States and the Soviet Union agreed on neutralization of the country but it soon became clear that this meant a predominant position for the Communists. In May, 1962 the ceasefire completely broke down as the Pathet Lao proceeded to secure control over the large majority of the country. This prompted President Kennedy to send American troops to Thailand and part of the Seventh Fleet to Southeast Asian waters—a show of force designed to bring renewed negotiations.

Apparently in response to outside pressure, the Pathet Lao called a truce and in June the Laotian forces, neutralist, pro-Communist, and pro-American, agreed to form a coalition government. Then in July 1962, at Geneva, the fourteen nation commission signed an accord which reestablished Laotian independence and neutrality, the status to be guaranteed by a new International Control Commission.

By agreeing to support neutralization, the United States was fully cognizant that Pathet Lao strength in the country could lead to Communist control. But political apathy on the part of the indigenous population, the nature of the country itself and the military *fait accompli* by the pro-Communist forces prevented the United States from making further efforts in 1962 to "contain" Communism in Laos. The United States was to "take its stand" in South Vietnam instead.

Shortly after the Geneva agreement, the Pathet Lao boycotted the government and in 1963 fighting broke out again. This was followed by an increased flow of North Vietnamese army forces into the country to secure the supply routes known collectively as the Ho Chi Minh Trail. As the United States stepped up its involvement in Vietnam after 1965, additional North Vietnamese were transported over the trail into South Vietnam. To stop this flow of supplies and men, the United States then began bombing attacks along the route; to preserve the neutralist government of Laos in 1968 and 1969 it also provided millions of dollars in technical and military aid to Souvanna Phouma who had become a virtual ally. After 1968 United States bombing attacks increased as did the number of North Vietnamese troops, until by early 1970 North Vietnam had about 67,000 men there.

For reasons of their own, apparently in part at least to reactivate ebbing dissent in the United States, these North Vietnamese forces in early 1970 combined with the Pathet Lao to retake the strategically valuable Plain of Jars, which had been captured by CIA supported Meo tribesmen in September, 1969. The Communist forces continued their advance to the point that they threatened Luang Probang and Vientianne. In response, the United States sent additional "advisers"; but in March, 1970 President Nixon listed the total number of Americans in Laos as only 1,040 and vowed not to be involved further.

Meanwhile, Prince Souvanna Phouma, though the neutralist head of state, has protested strongly these Communist violations of the territory to North Vietnam, the International Control Commission and the United Nations, and has urged the continuation of American bombing of Communist positions.

INDEPENDENCE OF LAOS

A. Treaty of Amity and Association Between the French Republic and the Kindgom of Laos*

Paris, October 22, 1953

M. Vincent Auriol, President of the French Republic, President of the French Union, and His Majesty Sisavang Vong, King of Laos, noting that France has entirely fulfilled the commitments she had made for the purpose of ensuring to Laos the exercise of full sovereignty and independence, confirmed by the declaration of July 3, 1953.

Both equally desirous to maintain and strengthen the bonds of traditional friendship which unite the two countries and which were previously confirmed and strengthened when the Kingdom of Laos joined the French Union,

Have agreed to the following:

Article 1

The French Republic recognizes and declares that the Kingdom of Laos is a fully independent and sovereign State. Consequently, the latter shall replace the French Republic in the exercise of all rights and the fulfillment of all obligations resulting from any international treaty or special convention contracted by France on behalf of the Kingdom of Laos or of French Indochina, prior to the present convention.

Article 2

The Kingdom of Laos freely reaffirms its membership in the French Union, an association of independent and sovereign peoples, with freedom and equality of rights and duties, in which all the associates place in common their resources in order to guarantee the defense of the Union as a whole.

It reaffirms its decision to sit in the High Council, which, under the chairmanship of the President of the French Union, ensures the coordination of these resources and the general conduct of the affairs of the Union.

Article 3

France pledges herself to support and uphold the sovereignty and independence of Laos before all international bodies.

---

*Documents on American Foreign Relations, 1953, pp. 348-50.

Article 4

France and Laos pledge themselves to participate jointly in any eventual negotiation designed to modify the conventions currently binding the Associated States.

Article 5

Each of the High Contracting Parties pledges itself, on its own territory, to guarantee to the nationals of the other the same treatment as reserved to its own nationals.

Article 6

Should the agreements currently governing their economic relations come to be modified, the two High Contracting Parties mutually pledge themselves to grant to each other certain privileges, especially in the form of preferential tariffs.

Article 7

Special Conventions shall define the modalities of the association between the French Republic and the Kingdom of Laos. The Treaty and the Special Conventions shall cancel and replace all similar acts previously concluded between the two States.

Article 8

The present Treaty and the Special Conventions—unless other stipulations are made concerning the latter—shall go into effect on the date of their signature. The instruments of ratification of the present Treaty shall be exchanged as soon as the Treaty is approved by the French and Laotian constitutional bodies.

B. Geneva Agreement on the Cessation of Hostilities in Laos*

[Extract]

Geneva, July 20, 1954

CHAPTER I
CEASEFIRE AND EVACUATION OF FOREIGN ARMED FORCES
AND FOREIGN MILITARY PERSONNEL

Article 1

The Commanders of the armed forces of the parties in Laos shall order and enforce the complete cessation of all hostilities in Laos by all armed forces under their control, including all units and personnel of the ground, naval and air forces.

Article 2

In accordance with the principle of a simultaneous cease-fire throughout Indo-china the cessation of hostilities shall be simultaneous throughout the territory of Laos in all combat areas and for all forces of the two parties.

In order to prevent any mistake or misunderstanding and to ensure that both the cessation of hostilities and the disengagement and movements of the opposing forces are in fact simultaneous:

> (a) Taking into account the time effectively required to transmit the cease-fire order down to the lowest echelons of the combatant forces on both sides, the two parties are agreed that the complete and simultaneous cease-fire throughout the territory of Laos shall become effective at 8 hours (local time) on 6 August 1954. It is agreed that Peking mean time shall be taken as local time.
> (b) The Joint Commission for Laos shall draw up a schedule for the other operations resulting from the cessation of hostilities.

(Note: The cease-fire shall become effective 15 days after the entry into force of the present Agreement.)

Article 3

Provides for removal of military hazards in each regrouping area prior to evacuation and assurance of safe routes for evacuation. It corresponds to Article 12 of the Vietnam agreement.

Article 4

The withdrawals and transfers of military forces, supplies and equipment shall be effected in accordance with the following principles:

*Documents on American Foreign Relations, 1954, pp. 302-07.

(a) The withdrawals and transfers of the military forces, supplies and equipment of the two parties shall be completed within a period of 120 days from the day on which the Armistice Agreement enters into force. . . .

(b) The withdrawals of the Vietnamese People's Volunteers from Laos to Vietnam shall be effected by provinces. The position of those volunteers who were settled in Laos before the hostilities shall form the subject of a special convention . . . . There follow administrative provisions covering persons and property similar to those in Article 14 of the Vietnam agreement.

Article 5

During the days immediately preceding the cease-fire each party undertakes not to engage in any large-scale operation between the time when the Agreement on the cessation of hostilities is signed at Geneva and the time when the cease-fire comes into effect.

CHAPTER II

PROHIBITIONS OF THE INTRODUCTION OF FRESH TROOPS, MILITARY PERSONNEL ARMAMENTS AND MUNITIONS

Article 6

With effect from the proclamation of the cease-fire the introduction into Laos of any reinforcements of troops or military personnel from outside Laotian territory is prohibited.

Article 7

Upon the entry into force of the present Agreement, the establishment of new military bases is prohibited throughout the territory of Laos.

Article 8

The High Command of the French forces shall maintain in the territory of Laos the personnel required for the maintenance of two French military establishments, the first at Seno and the second in the Mekong valley, either in the province of Vientiane or downstream from Vientiane.

The effectives maintained in these military establishments shall not exceed a total of three thousand five hundred (3,500) men.

Article 9

Upon the entry into force of the present Agreement and in accordance with the declaration made at the Geneva Conference by the Royal Government of Laos on 20 July 1954, the introduction into Laos of armaments, munitions and military equipment of all kinds is prohibited, with the exception of a specified quantity of armaments in categories specified as necessary for the defence of Laos.

Article 10

The new armaments and military personnel permitted to enter Laos in accordance with the terms of Article 9 above shall enter Laos at the following points only: Luang-Prabang, Xieng-Khouang, Vientiane, Seno, Pakse, Savannakhet and Tchepone.

CHAPTER III
DISENGAGEMENT OF THE FORCES—ASSEMBLY AREAS—CONÇENTRATION AREAS

Article 11

The disengagement of the armed forces of both sides, including concentration of the armed forces, movements to rejoin the provisional assembly areas allotted to one party and provisional withdrawal movements by the other party, shall be completed within a period not exceeding fifteen (15) days after the cease-fire.

Article 12

The Joint Commission in Laos shall fix the site and boundaries:

—of the five (5) provisional assembly areas for the reception of the Vietnamese People's Volunteer Forces,
—of the five (5) provisional assembly areas for the reception of the French forces in Laos,
—of the twelve (12) provisional assembly areas, one to each province, for the reception of the fighting units of "Pathet Lao."

The forces of the Laotian National Army shall remain *in situ* during the entire duration of the operations of disengagement and transfer of foreign forces and fighting units of "Pathet Lao."

Article 13

The foreign forces shall be transferred outside Laotian territory as follows:

(1) French Forces: The French forces will be moved out of Laos by road (along routes laid down by the Joint Commission in Laos) and also by air and inland waterway;

(2) Vietnamese People's Volunteer forces: These forces will be moved out of Laos by land, along routes and in accordance with a schedule to be determined by the Joint Commission in Laos in accordance with the principle of simultaneous withdrawal of foreign forces.

Article 14

Pending a political settlement, the fighting units of "Pathet Lao," concentrated in the provisional assembly areas, shall move into the Provinces of Phongsaly and Sam-Neua, except for any military personnel who wish to be demobilised where they are. They will be free to move between these two Provinces in a corridor along the frontier between Laos and Vietnam bounded on the south by the line Sop Kin, Na Mi-Sop Sang, Muong Son.

Concentration shall be completed within one-hundred-and-twenty (120) days from the date of entry into force of the present Agreement.

Article 15

Each party undertakes to refrain from any reprisals or discrimination against persons or organizations for their activities during the hostilities and also undertakes to guarantee their democratic feedoms.

CHAPTER IV
PRISONERS OF WAR AND CIVILIAN INTERNEES

Article 16

Makes provisions similar to those contained in Article 21 of the agreement on Vietnam.

CHAPTER V
MISCELLANEOUS

Articles 17-23

Make arrangements similar to those in Article 22-27 of the Vietnam agreement.

CHAPTER VI
JOINT COMMISSION AND INTERNATIONAL COMMISSION
FOR SUPERVISION AND CONTROL IN LAOS

Articles 24-39

Provide for a Mixed Commission and an International Commission on a basis similar to that established in Chapter VI of the agreement on Vietnam.

CHAPTER VII

Article 40

All the provisions of the present Agreement, save paragraph (a) of Article 2, shall enter into force at 24 hours (Geneva time) on 22 July 1954.

Article 41

Done in Geneva (Switzerland) on 20 July 1954, at 24 hours, in the French language.

AMERICAN SUPPORT OF ROYAL GOVERNMENT

A. United States Statement on the Communist Military Threat to Laos*

August 1, 1959

It is obvious that the former Pathet Lao rebels and their north Vietnamese Communist patrons wish to deny to the Kingdom of Laos the period of tranquillity this small young nation desires. Evidently the Communist regimes in China and north Viet-Nam do not look with favor on any normalization of the situation along their boundaries. Instead they would prefer to keep southeast Asia in turmoil.

It is for this reason that, despite commitments at Geneva in 1954 and despite their further agreements with the Royal Lao Government for peaceful integration in 1957, the former Pathet Lao, backed by their Communist coconspirators across the jungle borders of Laos, have never ceased intriguing and agitating to prevent the consolidation of a non-Communist neutral Laos. They have consistently violated their own engagements whereby they obtained generous concessions from the Government of a country which desired only unity and peace. Now it appears they are again resorting to force in an effort to succeed where other measures short of the use of force have failed. With this new outbreak of fighting it may be that the Communist imperialists in the Far East are seeking to provoke a serious crisis. The United States does not believe that the use of force should be rewarded by concessions contrary to the will of the Royal Lao Government.

It would be absurd to maintain that Laos, with its sparse and scattered population of about 2 million, is a menace to the 650 million of Red China or the 14 million of north Vietnam. Each of these regimes maintains large modern forces which dwarf the 25,000-man army of Laos. It would be ludicrous to suppose that the Government of Laos would be guilty of aggression or aggressive designs against its neighbors.

The United States respects the policy of neutrality to which the Royal Lao Government has consistently adhered. The United States also respects the will of Laos to remain independent and to live in peace. It therefore views with concern what may be a deliberate effort of insurgent elements, apparently backed by Communists from outside, to provoke a crisis in Laos, a sovereign nation and member of the United Nations.

B. United States Response to Soviet Charges of American Aggression in Laos*

August 19, 1959

The Soviet Foreign Ministry's August 17 statement on the situation in Laos is replete with false charges.[1] It distorts the facts regarding recent events in Laos and suggests Soviet complicity in the Communist interference in Laos' internal affairs. Contrary to implications in the Soviet statement, the Lao Army

---

*Department of State Bulletin, Aug. 24, 1959, pp. 278-79.
*Ibid., Sept. 7, 1959, p. 344.
[1] Pravda, Aug. 18, 1959.

is controlled exclusively by the sovereign Government of Laos. It is not under the direction of United States military personnel. The few American technicians in Laos are there at the request of the French and Lao Governments. Their function is to help the French military mission by training the Lao National Army in the use and maintenance of World War II type American equipment. We also have a few clerical and fiscal personnel assisting the Lao Army's administration. No American personnel are commanding, advising, or serving with Lao units. No American personnel are directing military operations. We have no troops in Laos. We do not have in Laos, nor have we provided that country, any heavy or modern equipment. We have no bases in Laos, nor airstrips, as any of the dozen foreign correspondents who are in Laos will attest.

The Governments of Laos and the United States have made no attempt to conceal the arrangements under which American personnel are in Laos. These are all on the public record. The Soviet charges the Royal Lao Government with responsibility for a threat of civil war hanging over Laos. This again is directly contradictory to the facts. Pursuant to the agreement of November 1957, the Royal Lao Government integrated the former Pathet Lao provinces into its administration and the Pathet Lao battalions into the Lao Army. Subsequently, the Communist-dominated Neo Lao Hak Xat Party, which was the successor to the Pathet Lao movement, was recognized as legal. The Royal Lao Government has abided by the 1957 agreement. However, in May 1959 one of the former Pathet Lao battalions revolted and part of it escaped to north Viet-Nam thus providing further evidence to the link between the Pathet Lao and north Viet-Nam. These Communist organizations betrayed the trust of the Lao Government and people. In mid-July 1959 they perpetrated insurrection with outside help and direction. It is this Communist-directed action which has broken the peace in Laos. The "dangerous tension" in the area is of Communist origin.

The Department notes the expression of hope in the Soviet Government's latest statement that "talks on measures for the normalization of the situation in Laos now being held between the two co-Chairmen of the Geneva Conference on Indochina will have a positive issue." The United States also hopes these dicsussions will have some beneficial result. However, there may be some disagreement on what constitutes a beneficial result. If by a "positive issue" the Soviet Union means some new measures which will promote further civil disturbances in Laos, then we are opposed to such measures. On the other hand, the United States would welcome any measures which would help tranquilize the situation provided they fully recognize the legitimate sovereign desire of Laos to live peacefully within its borders and to progress in its own way, free of outside intervention in the conduct of its internal affairs.

C. State Department Statement on the United States Agreement to Increase Military Aid to Laos*

August 26, 1959

The United States strongly supports the determination of the Royal Lao Government to resist Communist efforts to undermine the security and stability

*Department of State Bulletin Sept. 14, 1959, p. 374.

of Laos. Contrary to repetitious allegations from Hanoi, Peiping, and Moscow, the United States reiterates that it has no military bases, airstrips, or other military installations in Laos. The few American technicians in Laos are there at the request of the French and Lao Governments to help in the training of the Lao National Army in the use and maintenance of certain World War II type equipment.

The United States will continue to support reasonable approaches to achieve a peaceful solution to the current situation in Laos. Unlike the Sino-Soviet bloc, the United States does not believe that there should be recourse to the use of force in resolving this matter. However, the Communists have posed their threat to Laos in terms that require adequate military and police counter-measures if that nation's integrity is to be preserved. The United States has, therefore, responded to specific requests from the Lao Government for improving its defense position by authorizing sufficient additional aid to permit temporary emergency increases in the Lao National Army and in the village militia which provides local police protection. The additional aid will permit the specific increases desired by the Government of Laos. The United States has also in the course of the past week taken steps to help improve the mobility of the Royal Lao Army and to otherwise help give that small nation better means to withstand what appears even more clearly to be an extensive Communist design to disrupt and subvert Laos.

D. United States Pledge to Support Laos*

September 5, 1959

The United States as a member of the United Nations will fulfill in good faith the obligations assumed by it under the charter. One of these obligations is to take appropriate measures in support of the charter. To this end the United States will support United Nations consideration of the Royal Lao Government's appeal.

The United States Government has repeatedly announced its strong support of the Royal Lao Government in its determination to resist Communist efforts to undermine the security and stability of Laos. On August 26, 1959, the United States announced that, in response to specific and urgent requests from the Lao Government for improving its defense position, additional aid was being authorized to permit emergency increases in the Lao Army and Militia to cope with the threat posed to that Government by the Communists. The United States announced at the same time that it would continue to support reasonable approaches to achieve a peaceful solution of the current situation in Laos.

On August 30 a strong attack from the northeast was launched against Royal Lao Army units in the northeastern border area of Sam Neua Province. The small Lao forces in this province had been reinforced and had begun to push back an earlier communist salient which had extended about 50 miles from the North Viet-Nam border in an area northwest of the town of Sam Neua. The August 30 attack against the northeastern border area provides further evidence of the active support of Communist rebel forces within Laos from

Ibid., Sept. 21, 1959, p. 414.

Communist north Viet-Nam. The attack could not have been supported nor coordinated without such outside collaboration.

It is now clear that the Communist bloc does not intend to permit the sovereign Lao Government to remain at peace. The Communist bloc apparently intends to foment and direct a rebellion within Laos and to give extensive support to the attempt to seize important areas and otherwise to prevent the establishment of those peaceful conditions necessary to implement basic economic and social programs. In short the Communist intervention is apparently aimed at preventing the Lao people from realizing their just hopes for a better life.

That outside Communist intervention exists is demonstrated by (1) the assistance evidently being received by the Communist forces within Laos, including supplies and military weapons that could be provided only from Communist territory; (2) the false—and ridiculous—Communist propaganda emanating simultaneously from Hanoi, Peiping, and Moscow to the effect that the Lao Government has been instigated by the United States to "stir up a civil war" within its boundaries; (3) the continuing flow from Moscow, Peiping and Hanoi of propaganda and false information about the situation in Laos aimed at confusing world opinion and stating that the U.S. is using Laos as a military base; and (4) the fact that the military outbreak in Laos has followed conferences in Moscow and Peiping between Ho Chi Minh and Soviet and Chinese Communist leaders and also conferences in Moscow between two members of the north Viet-Nam Politburo and Deputy Prime Minister Anastas Mikoyan.

The latest attack upon the Lao Army in Sam Neua Province has resulted in an appeal by the Royal Lao Government for United Nations assistance. It is appropriate that this matter be thus brought to the world's attention. It is obvious that any further augmentation of the invading force or continued material support thereof by Communists in north Viet-Nam will require a major change in the nature and magnitude of the Royal Lao Government's need for support. The United States is confident that the free world would recognize such a new danger to peace and would take the action necessary. For its part the United States supports that view.

EXCHANGE OF NOTES BETWEEN THE UNITED STATES AND THE SOVIET UNION ON LAOS

E. Soviet Note to the United States*

December 13, 1960

The Government of the Union of Soviet Socialist Republics considers it necessary to state the following to the United States Government.

In the declaration of September 22, 1960 concerning events in Laos, the Soviet Government already drew attention to the serious threat to peace in this area of Southeast Asia arising from the unceremonious intervention of the United States and several of its partners in the aggressive SEATO bloc in Laos internal affairs. However, if two or three months ago the United States Govern-

*Ibid., Jan 2, 1961, pp. 16-17.

ment somehow tried to camouflage its illegal action in Laos, recently the United States has in fact become a direct participant in military operations on the side of the rebels against the legal government of Laos and the Laotian people.

Flouting the sovereign rights of the Laotian government headed by Prince Souvanna Phouma, the United States now extends overt support to the rebel group of Nosavan, supplies it with arms, military equipment, military stores, and money. Rebel troops have proved to be supplied with such arms as have never until the present been in the Laotian Army: 105mm howitzers, 120mm mortars, heavy tanks, military aircraft, helicopters, armored launches, and other equipment.

The rebels have been trained in the use of these arms by numerous American advisers and instructors, whom the United States Government has sent and continues to send to their camp. Moreover, near the town of Pakadin there was shot down by government troops a reconnaissance aircraft No. 830 on board which were four American officers. During engagements between government troops and the rebels, American helicopters of "Sikorsky" type regularly fly over Thailand territory, directing the artillery fire of the rebels. From this it is evident that American military advisers and instructors not only train the rebels, but also directly lead their military actions against troops of the legal government of Laos. The United States Government also widely uses its ally in the SEATO military pact, Thailand, which makes available the territory of the country for active military operations against government units and carries out a tight economic blockade of Laos.

As the facts show, the United States Government completely ignores the repeated appeals and also the official demand of the legal government of Prince Souvanna Phouma, expressed in the December 5 declaration, that the United States cease delivery of weapons and military supplies to the rebels.

All this is a glaring violation on the part of the United States Government of Article 12 of the final declaration of the 1954 Geneva Conference on Indo-China, in which is contained the obligation of each participant of the conferences, including the United States, to respect the sovereignty, independence, unity and territorial integrity of Laos, and refrain from any interference in its internal affairs.

With its overt actions against the legal Laotian government of Prince Souvanna Phouma, which has proclaimed as its program a policy of peace, neutrality, and national unity, the United States Government seeks to compel the Laotian people to leave this path which it has chosen, and to put Laos again in the service of a policy of military pacts and aggressive preparations, foreign to the people of Laos.

However, it is appropriate to recall that once such a policy already suffered failure in Laos. The Laotian people overthrew the government which carried out the policy of turning Laos into a United States military base and semi-colony. Realization of the legitimate striving of the Laotian people for cessation at last of fratricidal war and for national unity in conditions excluding any foreign intervention must not be hindered.

Being one of the participants and chairmen of the Geneva Conference on

Indo-China, the Soviet Government decisively protests the United States intervention in the internal affairs of Laos and condemns this intervention. This undermines the Geneva agreements and is directed against the freedom and independence of the Laotian people, against its inalienable right to conduct a policy of peace, neutrality, and friendship with all peoples.

The Soviet Government cannot ignore the threat to peace and security in Southeast Asia arising from the crude United States interference in the internal affairs of Laos, and places on the United States Government all responsibility for the consequences which can arise as a result of the aggressive actions of the United States and some of its allies in the SEATO military bloc in relation to the Laotian people.

F. United States Note to the Soviet Union*

December 17, 1960

The Government of the United States acknowledges the receipt of the note of the Government of the Union of Soviet Socialist Republics dated December 13, 1960.

The Government of the United States categorically rejects the charges leveled against it in the Soviet Government's note. The United States condemns as a violation of every standard of legal conduct the recent Soviet action in airlifting weapons and ammunition in Soviet planes to rebel military forces fighting the loyal armed forces of the Royal Government in Vientiane. Thus the responsibility for the present fraticidal war in Laos, about which the Soviet Government claims to be concerned, rests squarely and solely upon the Soviet Government and its partners.

The United States had repeatedly made clear its consistent policy of supporting the Kingdom of Laos in its determination to maintain its independence and integrity. Such support will continue. The United States has warned against efforts to seize control of or to subvert that free nation.

The Soviet allegation that Lao Army troops have been recently armed with weapons which they have not had before is completely false. Such supplies as have been furnished by the United States to the forces in Laos, in whatever region, have been provided pursuant to a long-standing agreement with Laos, and with the approval of the legal Government of Laos. The Lao Army had been equipped with M-24 tanks and 105 millimeter howitzers long before the August 9, 1960 rebellion against the Royal Lao Government. The United States has not in fact supplied any equipment of this type to Laos since 1957. The United States has never supplied 120 millimeter mortars, armed aircraft, or armed or armored vessels to Laos. The United States has not brought any arms or ammunition into Laos since the end of November. No United States-supplied helicopters have been used to direct artillery fire. Furthermore, such American advisers as have been in the country either administering the American Military Aid Program or in the Franco-American training program are located at various

Ibid., pp. 15-16.

training sites and supply depots and have not led any military actions.

It is communist and communist-fostered subversive activities, the guerrilla warfare of the Pathet Lao forces, and now the Soviet airlift of weapons which have led directly to the suffering and chaos which have befallen Laos. The Soviet Government and its agents have attempted to carry out this latest, grave action clandestinely, under the cover of delivering food and petroleum products. However, their haste to strengthen the rebel forces in Laos has resulted in widespread knowledge of these Soviet arms deliveries, which have included the howitzers which the rebels are now using against loyal troops of the Lao Government, a government formed at Royal request pursuant to the National Assembly's action. The destruction which these Soviet weapons have brought to the capital city of Laos and the suffering and loss to its people is the direct result of this Soviet intervention.

At the same time, communist-controlled north Viet-Nam, which has long aided and furnished direction to the Pathet Lao guerrillas in Laos, has been making war-like preparations, calling up additional troops and moving military units westward toward the Lao border.

In the light of these facts the Government of the United States, in rejecting the false charges of the Soviet Government in its note of December 13, places the responsibility for the current strife in Laos where that responsibility properly belongs—squarely upon the U.S.S.R. and its agents. The Government of the United States, furthermore, condemns in strongest terms the illegal Russian delivery of military equipment to the rebels in Laos.

It has always been the objective of the United States to assist the people of Laos in developing their free political institutions, in improving their social and economic well being and in preserving their national integrity. The policy of the United States towards Laos remains the same today.

G. Statement by President Kennedy on Laos*

March 23, 1961

I want to talk about Laos. It is important, I think, for all Americans to understand this difficult and potentially dangerous problem. In my last conversation with General Eisenhower, the day before the inauguration, we spent more time on this hard matter than on any other one thing. And since then it has been steadily before the administration as the most immediate of the problems we found on taking office.

Our special concern with the problem in Laos goes back to 1954. That year, at Geneva, a large group of powers agreed to a settlement of the struggle for Indochina. Laos was one of the new states which had recently emerged from the French Union, and it was the clear premise of the 1954 settlement that this new country would be neutral, free of external domination by anyone. The new country contained contending factions, but in its first years real progress was made toward a unified and neutral status. But the efforts of a Communist-

---

*Ibid., Apr. 17, 1961, pp. 543-44.

dominated group to destroy this neutrality never ceased, and in the last half of 1960 a series of sudden maneuvers occurred and the Communists and their supporters turned to a new and greatly intensified military effort to take over

In this military advance the local Communist forces, known as the Pathet Lao, have had increasing support and direction from outside. Soviet planes, I regret to say, have been conspicuous in a large-scale airlift into the battle area—over 1,000 sorties since December 13, 1960, and a whole supporting set of combat specialists, mainly from Communist north Viet-Nam—and heavier weapons have been provided from outside, all with the clear object of destroying by military action the agreed neutrality of Laos. It is this new dimension of externally supported warfare that creates the present grave problem.

The position of this administration has been carefully considered, and we have sought to make it just as clear as we know how to the governments concerned. First: We strongly and unreservedly support the goal of a neutral and independent Laos, tied to no outside power or group of powers, threatening no one, and free from any domination. Our support for the present duly constituted Government is aimed entirely and exclusively at that result, and if in the past there has been any possible ground for misunderstanding of our support for a truly neutral Laos, there should be none now.

Secondly, if there is to be a peaceful solution, there must be a cessation of the present armed attacks by externally supported Communists. If these attacks do not stop, those who support a genuinely neutral Laos will have to consider their response. The shape of this necessary response will of course be carefully considered not only here in Washington but in the SEATO conference with our allies which begins next Monday, March 27. SEATO—the Southeast Asia Treaty Orgnization—was organized in 1954 with strong leadership from our last administration, and all members of SEATO have undertaken special treaty responsibilities toward an aggression against Laos.

No one should doubt our own resolution on this point. We are faced with a clear threat of a change in the internationally agreed position of Laos. This threat runs counter to the will of Laotian people, who wish only to be independent and neutral. It is posed rather by the military operations of internal dissident elements directed from outside the country. This is what must end if peace is to be kept in southeast Asia.

Third, we are earnestly in favor of constructive negotiation—among the nations concerned and among the leaders of Laos—which can help Laos back to the pathway of independence and genuine neutrality. We strongly support the present British proposal of a prompt end of hostilities and prompt negotiation. We are always conscious of the obligation which rests upon all members of the United Nations to seek peaceful solutions to problems of this sort. We hope that others may be equally aware of this responsibility.

My fellow Americans, Laos is far away from America, but the world is small. Its 2 million peaceful people live in a country three times the size of Austria. The security of all of southeast Asia will be endangered if Laos loses its neutral independence. Its own safety runs with the safety of us all—in real neutrality observed by all.

I want to make it clear to the American people, and to all the world, that all we want in Laos is peace, not war—a truly neutral government, not a cold-war pawn—a settlement concluded at the conference table, not on the battlefield. Our response will be in close cooperation with our allies and the wishes of the Laotian Government. We will not be provoked, trapped, or drawn into this or any other situation. But I know that every American will want his country to honor its obligations to the point that freedom and security of the free world and ourselves may be achieved.

Careful negotiations are being conducted with many countries in order to see that we take every possible course to insure a peaceful solution. Yesterday the Secretary of State informed the Members of the Congress and brought them up to date. We will continue to keep the country fully informed.

H. British Aide Memoire to The Soviet Union on Laos*

[Extract]

March 23, 1961

          *   *   *

Her Majesty's Government now wish to make the following proposals. An essential prerequisite for the successful execution of the proposals which follow is that there should be an immediate cessation of all active military operations in Laos. To this end the two co-Chairmen[1] should issue an immediate request for a *de facto* cease fire. If this can be accomplished Her Majesty's Government would agree to the suggestions of the Soviet Government that a message from the co-Chairmen should be sent to the Prime Minister of India asking Mr. Nehru to summon the International Commission for Supervision and Control in Laos to meet in New Delhi as soon as possible. The task of the Commission at this stage would be to verify the effectiveness of the cease fire and report thereon to the co-Chairmen.

Her Majesty's Government are also willing to accept the suggestion of the Soviet Government that an international conference should be convened to consider a settlement of the Laotian problem. To this end they believe that the Geneva Conference should be recalled by the co-Chairmen and they strongly endorse the suggestion made by His Royal Highness Prince Sihanouk of Cambodia that certain other nations should join the Conference and take part in its deliberations as full members. Her Majesty's Government suggest that this Conference should meet as soon as the International Commission can report that the cease fire is effective. They very much hope that this could be brought about without delay say within a period of two weeks.

Finally Her Majesty's Government consider that the question of a neutral

---

Ibid., Apr. 17, 1961, p. 545.
[1] The co-Chairmen of the Geneva Conference, 1954, Great Britain and the Soviet Union.

Laotian Government of national unity will have to be resolved as soon as possible before an international conference can reach any decisions. Her Majesty's Government cannot recognize the so-called "government of Prince Souvanna Phouma" as being competent to represent Laos at an international conference. They therefore hope that the various parties in Laos will immediately resume the discussions which were started in Phnom Penh, Cambodia with a view to agreeing on a national government which could represent Laos at the proposed International Conference. If no Government of national unity has been formed by the time the International Conference convenes it is clear that the Laotian Government cannot be represented as such and that the Conference will have to address itself as its first task to helping the parties of Laos to reach agreement on this point.

GENEVA CONFERENCE ON LAOS AND AGREEMENT ON NEUTRALITY

A. British-Soviet Message for a Ceasefire in Laos*

April 24, 1961

1. The co-Chairmen of the Geneva Conference on Indo-China, represented by the Governments of the Soviet Union and Great Britain, are following with great concern the situation which has developed in Laos.

2. They proceed from the fact that if this situation is not changed the position in Laos may become a serious threat to peace and security in Southeast Asia. They note at the same time that real conditions exist for normalizing the situation in Laos in accordance with the national interests of the Laotian people, on the basis of the Geneva Agreements of 1954. The co-Chairmen have in view the understanding already reached that an International Conference to settle the Laotian problem is to be called in Geneva on the 12th of May this year.

3. The co-Chairmen call on all Military Authorities, parties and organizations in Laos to cease fire before the convening of the International Conference on Laos, and they call on appropriate representatives to enter into negotiations for concluding an agreement of questions connected with the cease-fire.

4. The co-Chairmen call on the people of Laos to co-operate with the International Commission for Supervision and Control in Laos and to render it assistance, when it arrives in the country on their instructions, in exercising supervision and control over the cease-fire.

B. Statement by Secretary Rusk on the Opening of the Geneva Conference on Laos*

May 17, 1961

In late April we received an invitation to an international conference on the Laotian question. On Monday evening May 15 last, the co-Chairmen announced the opening of the conference and stated that "this conference is solely concerned with the international aspects of the Laotian question." We are here to take part on that basis because the Laotian question is urgent, in relation both to the people of that troubled country and to the peace of southeast Asia. We wish to say at the beginning how gratified we were that His Royal Highness Prince Sihanouk of Cambodia was able to open our sessions last evening with wise words aimed at moderation and a genuine attempt to reach a satisfactory solution.

At the outset, Mr. Chairman, I believe it necessary to raise a matter which we believe to be the first order of business in this conference. A number of invited governments, including the united States, considered that this conference could not meet with any hope of success unless there had been achieved a

*Department of State Bulletin, May 15, 1961, pp. 710-11.
*Ibid., June 5, 1961, pp. 844-48.

prompt and effective cease-fire. We received on May 12, the date proposed for the opening of our sessions, a report from the ICC, International Control Commission, which said that the Commission is satisfied that a general *de facto* cease-fire exists and such breaches as have been informally complained of are either due to misunderstanding or to factors such as the terrain, the nature of disposition of forces, both regular and irregular, of all parties.

Information from Laos indicated that rebel forces continue to attack in a number of localities and that rebel troop movements are occurring which are prejudicial to an effective cease-fire. The most serious of these violations have taken place in the Ban Padong area near Xieng Khouang, where artillery and infantry attacks are continuing against Government forces. The Royal Lao Government has made formal complaint to the ICC chairman.

Surely, Mr. Chairman, the cease-fire and proper instructions to the ICC are matters of first importance. This is something which cannot be postponed. An effective cease-fire is a prerequisite to any constructive result from our proceedings; a failure of a cease-fire would result in a highly dangerous situation which it is the purpose of the conference to prevent. I would urge that the co-Chairmen take this up immediately in order that the situation be clarified and the ICC given the necessary authorizations and instructions.

There is another point which affects our ability to come to a satisfactory result. We do not believe that this conference is properly constituted without due provision for the delegates of the constitutional government of Laos. The Royal Laotian Government, empowered by the King and Parliament to govern Laos, represents that country in the United Nations and in other international bodies. It is the only authority resting upon that nation's constitution and the means established by law for registering the wishes of its King and people. We do not see how we can make good progress without the presence here of the Government of Laos, and we regret, though understand, why it does not consider that it can be here under existing circumstances. We believe that this, too, is a matter which requires the immediate attention of the co-Chairmen in order that this conference of governments may have the benefit of the participation of the Government of the very country which we are discussing.

Before I turn to what I had intended to say about the questions before the conference, I should like to thank the Secretary of State for Foreign Affairs of the United Kingdom, Lord Home, for his constructive and helpful contribution of last evening. We find ourselves in general agreement with his suggestions and hope that the conference can settle down quickly to the detailed provisions required to give them effect.

The Real Threat to Peace in Southeast Asia

I also listened with interest to the remarks of the representative from Peiping, Chen Yi. He made certain statements about the United States which were not true and not new. We have heard them often before. Indeed, I rather thought that his statement of them on this occasion was less violent than language to which we have become accustomed. To leave open the possibility that those at this table are prepared to find some common basis for the settlement of the Laotian question, I shall comment upon his remarks with the restraint enjoined upon us by Prince Sihanouk.

There is only one problem of peace in southeast Asia and, indeed, in many other parts of the world: It is whether those who have wrapped around themselves the doctrine of the historical inevitability of world domination by their own particular political system merely believe it or will attempt to impose it upon others by all the means at their disposal. The real issue is whether peaceful coexistence is what normal language would indicate it means, or whether it means an all-out and continuous struggle against all those not under Communist control. The real threat to peace in southeast Asia is not from south to north, nor from across the Pacific Ocean. The threats are from north to south and take many forms. If these threats should disappear, SEATO would wither away, for it has no purpose but to maintain the peace in southeast Asia.

We cannot settle this argument in this conference, for it involves commitments of the Communist world which they would undoubtedly not yield in this discussion, just as it involves the commitments of free peoples who are determined to perfect and cherish freedoms still evolving from more than 2,000 years of struggle against tyranny in all forms. What we can do here is to discover whether we can agree that the people of Laos should be permitted to live in their own country without interference and pressures from the outside.

We note the statement made by the representative from Peiping that he "is ready to work jointly with the delegations of all the other countries participating in this conference to make contributions to the peaceful settlement of the Laotian question." We ourselves are prepared to work diligently to discover whether there *is* agreement in the conference on the questions before us.

Promptly after assuming office President Kennedy said: "We strongly and unreservedly support the goal of a neutral and independent Laos, tied to no outside power or group of powers, threatening no one, and free from any domination." In early exchanges with Chairman Khrushchev, the latter affirmed his commitment to a neutral and independent Laos, and there was useful discussion of the example of Austria. Other spokesmen of other governments, including a number represented here, have declared their desire for a neutral Laos.

The King of that country, on February 19 of this year, declared: "We desire to proclaim once more the policy of true neutrality that Laos has always sought to follow . . . . Once again we appeal to all countries to respect the independence, sovereignty, territorial integrity and neutrality of Laos."

I have already indicated that we believe the most immediate problem is to insure an effective cease-fire, to give the ICC the necessary and relevant instructions and to give it the resources required to carry out its vital task.

Task of Insuring a Neutral Laos

Next we must turn to the problem of insuring a genuinely neutral Laos. In this task, of course, most of us in this conference act as outsiders. We cannot impose on Laos anything which that country and its people do not truly want for themselves. In this particular instance we are fortunate that the expressed desires of the international community seem to coincide with what the people of Laos themselves want. Almost every nation here has expressed itself in favor of a neutral Laos.

But what does this mean? Neutrality is not simply a negative concept. A neutral Laos should be a dynamic, viable Laos, making progress toward more stable political institutions, economic well-being, and social justice. A truly neutral Laos must have the right to choose its own way of life in accordance with its own traditions, wishes, and aspirations for the future.

It is, of course, too early in the conference to present detailed proposals for achieving this end. But it is not too early to begin considering the broad outlines of a program directed to the goal.

As my Government sees it, such an outline would involve three separate points.

First: A definition of the concept of neutrality, as it applies to Laos, which all of us gathered here could pledge ourselves to respect. This definition must go beyond the classical concept of nonalinement and include positive assurance of the integrity of the elements of national life.

Second: The development of effective international machinery for maintaining and safeguarding that neutrality against threats to it from within as well as without.

Third: Laos will need, if it wishes to take its place in the modern world, a substantial economic and technical aid program. We believe that such aid could be most appropriately administered by neutral nations from the area and that it should be supported by contributions from many states and agencies. We do not believe that a neutral Laos should become a field of rivalries expressed through foreign aid programs on a national or bloc basis. But we do believe that the Laotians should benefit from the enlarged possibilities of better health, broader education, increased productivity which are opening up for mankind in all parts of the world.

A word more is perhaps in order about each of these points.

Respecting the Neutrality of Laos

First, neutrality. To be neutral, in the classical sense, means not to be formally alined with contending parties. Certainly we want this classical neutrality for Laos. But in today's world, with modern modes by which one government may subtly impose its will upon another, mere nonalinement is not enough.

Foreign military personnel, except for those specified in the Geneva Accords, should be withdrawn from Laos. But we mean all, not just those assisting the forces of the constituted Government of the country at its request. There is no problem about the withdrawal of the limited U.S. military personnel assisting with the training and supply of Government forces if the "Viet Minh brethren" and other elements who have entered Laos from the northeast return to their homes.

We have no desire to send military equipment into Laos; if international arrangements can be reached about forces and equipment, there would be no problem on our side.

We have no military bases in Laos and want none. We have no military alliances with Laos and want none. We have no interest in Laos as a staging area or as a thoroughfare for agents of subversion, saboteurs, or guerrilla bands to operate against Laos' neighbors.

If all those at this table can make the same commitments and support international machinery to protect Laos and its neighbors against such activities, we shall have taken an important step toward peace in southeast Asia.

Finally, neutrality must be consistent with sovereignty. It involves safeguards against subversion of the elements of the state which is organized, directed, or assisted from beyond its borders. In the end we must find a way to let the people of Laos live their own lives under conditions of free choice—and under conditions which permit the continuing exercise of choice to adapt institutions, policies, and objectives to the teachings of experience.

In the Final Declaration of the Geneva Conference of 1954, the parties pledged themselves to respect the sovereignty, the independence, the unity, and the territorial integrity of Laos. The intervening years since 1954 have demonstrated as a practical reality that, for Laos, sovereignty, independence, unity, and territorial integrity cannot long be maintained unless others also are willing to respect the neutrality of Laos.

We invite the nations of this conference to join in a solemn recognition and pledge of respect for Laotian neutrality. We invite all here to join in developing adequate machinery for protecting this status and with it the sovereignty, independence, unity, and territorial integrity of Laos as well.

Machinery for Keeping the Peace

Second, machinery for keeping the peace. The Geneva Conference of 1954 spent most of its time in discussing international machinery to supervise and control the introduction of arms and military personnel into the southeast Asian area. Despite those labors, that machinery has not proved effective in controlling military activity and in keeping the peace in the area. It has, however, given us a body of experience upon which we can draw in an effort to build better than our predecessors.

That experience suggests a set of principles or criteria by which we and the world will be able to judge whether the international controls developed here will effectively serve the ends for which they are designed.

The control machinery must have full access to all parts of the country without the need for the consent of any civil or military officials, national or local.

It must have its own transportation and communication equipment sufficient to the task. These must be constantly available to and under the sole orders of the control body.

It must be able to act on any complaints from responsible sources, including personnel of the control body itself, responsible military and civil officials in Laos, the governments of neighboring countries and of the members of this conference.

The control body should act by majority rule with the right to file majority and minority reports. It should not be paralyzed by a veto.

There should be some effective method of informing governments and the world at large about a finding by the control body that the conditions of peace and neutrality, as defined, have been violated.

If we are successful in giving practical meaning to the idea of a neutral Laos with international assurances against aggression and intervention, Lao armed forces could be reduced to the level necessary to maintain its own security.

This is the yardstick by which we can measure the prospective effectiveness of any control machinery for Laos. This is the yardstick which will influence the attitude of the United States toward the work of this conference. In short, pledges and promises must be backed by effective controls, effectively applied to maintain a genuinely neutral Laos.

Collective Assistance Efforts

Third, economic and technical development for Laos. The energies of the Lao people have too long been diverted from the constructive work of establishing for themselves and their children a better society and a better life. Schools, hospitals, agricultural improvement, industry, transport and communications, improved civil administration—all are needed, and urgently, if the promise which the 20th century holds out to all men is to be realized for Laos. Such improvement in their way of life is not only the right of the Laotians. It is also, I am convinced, a necessary condition of an independent and neutral Laos.

Unfortunately the resources necessary to permit such improvement at the required speed are not available in Laos itself. It is necessary that as many countries as possible supply the resources needed.

The United States would be willing to contribute to such a program. The United States has already contributed sizable amounts in material support and effort to assist the people of Laos in this program of economic and social development. It is a matter of regret that any portion of this effort has had to be expended to meet the threat of the security of Laos. Certainly one of the prime tasks for this conference is to devise means so that collective assistance efforts for Laos can be dedicated to the peaceful pursuits of people and to bringing the benefits of modern science and technology to the masses.

We believe that such assistance might usefully be administered by an organization of neutral nations of the area. We invite the U.S.S.R. to join with us in underwriting the cost of such assistance. Let us make Laos the scene of a cooperative effort for peaceful construction.

Mr. Chairman, I wish to inform the conference that I am one of several ministers who plan to return to our posts toward the end of this week. It was my announced intention when I first arrived. Our delegation will be led by Ambassador at Large W. Averell Harriman, one of our most distinguished public servants and most experienced diplomats. But official propaganda has begun to say that my departure means an attempt to sabotage this conference. It is not important that such propaganda is false; it is important that such propaganda bears upon the bona fides of those at the table.

In conclusion, Mr. Chairman, I do hope that all of us at the conference can keep our minds upon the Laotian people, who have suffered much and endured much during the past two decades. Let us find ways to let them lead their own lives in peace. They are few in number and need not be caught up in larger issues. Let us affirm that it is their country and not an appropriate target for ambitions with which they need not be involved. We shall contribute what we can to the success of this conference; if each can contribute, a good result can be accomplished.

EXCHANGE OF CORRESPONDENCE BETWEEN CHAIRMAN KHRUSHCHEV AND PRESIDENT KENNEDY ON A COALITION AGREEMENT IN LAOS

C. Chairman Khrushchev to President Kennedy*

June 12, 1962

Good news has come from Laos. As a result of the successful completion of negotiations involving the three political forces of Laos, it has been possible to form a coalition government of national unity headed by Prince Souvanna Phouma. Without question, this act may become the pivotal event both in the life of the Laotian people themselves and in the cause of strengthening peace in southeast Asia.

Formation of a coalition government of national unity in Laos opens the way toward completing in the near future the work done at the Geneva conference toward a peaceful settlement of the Laotian problem and giving life to the agreements worked out at that conference, which constitute a good basis for the development of Laos as a neutral and independent state.

The example of Laos indicates that, provided there is a desire to resolve difficult international problems on the basis of cooperation with mutual account of regard for the interests of all sides, such cooperation bears fruit. At the same time, the results achieved in the settlement of the Laotian problem strengthen the conviction that success in solving other international problems which now divide states and create tension in the world can be achieved on the same road as well.

As for the Soviet Government, it has always adhered, as it does now, to this line, which in present conditions is the only correct policy in international affairs in accordance with the interests of peace.

I avail myself of the occasion to express satisfaction over the fact that the mutual understanding we achieved while meeting in Vienna last June on the support of a neutral and independent Laos is beginning to be translated into life.

D. President Kennedy to Chairman Khrushchev*

I share your view that the reports from Laos are very encouraging. The formation of this government of national union under Prince Souvanna Phouma marks

Ibid., July 2, 1962, p. 12.
Ibid.,

a milestone in the sustained efforts which have been put forward toward this end, especially since our meeting in Vienna.

It is of equal importance that we should now press forward, with our associates in the Geneva Conference, to complete these agreements and to work closely together in their execution. We must continue also to do our best to persuade all concerned in Laos to work together to this same end. It is very important that no untoward actions anywhere be allowed to disrupt the progress which has been made.

I agree that continued progress in the settlement of the Laotian problem can be most helpful in leading toward the resolution of other international difficulties. If together we can help in the establishment of an independent and neutral Laos, securely sustained in this status through time, this accomplishment will surely have a significant and positive effect far beyond the borders of Laos. You can count on the continued and energetic efforts of the Government of the United States toward this end.

E. Declaration on The Neutrality of Laos*

[Extract]

Geneva, July 23, 1962

The Governments of the Union of Burma, the Kingdom of Cambodia, Canada, the People's Republic of China, the Democratic Republic of Viet-Nam, the Republic of France, the Republic of India, the Polish People's Republic, the Republic of Viet-Nam, the Kingdom of Thailand, the Union of Soviet Socialist Republics, the United Kingdom of Great Britain and Northern Ireland and the United States of America, whose representatives took part in the International Conference on the Settlement of the Laotian Question, 1961-1962;

Welcoming the presentation of the statement of neutrality by the Royal Government of Laos of July 9, 1962, and taking note of this statement, which is with the concurrence of the Royal Government of Laos, incorporated in the present Declaration as an integral part thereof, and the text of which is as follows:

The Royal Government of Laos,

Being resolved to follow the path of peace and neutrality in conformity with the interests and aspirations of the Laotian people, as well as the principles of the Joint Communique of Zurich dated June 22, 1961, and of the Geneva Agreements of 1954, in order to build a peaceful, neutral, independent, democratic, unified and prosperous Laos,

Solemnly declares that:

(1) It will resolutely apply the five principles of peaceful co-existence of foreign relations, and will develop friendly relations and establish diplomatic relations with all countries, the neighbouring countries first and foremost, on the basis of equality and of respect for the independence and sovereignty of Laos;

(2) It is the will of the Laotian people to protect and ensure respect for the sovereignty, independence, neutrality, unity, and territorial integrity of Laos;

Ibid., Aug. 13, 1962, pp. 259-61.

(3) It will not resort to the use or threat of force in any way which might impair the peace of other countries, and will not interfere in the internal affairs of other countries;

(4) It will not enter into any military alliance or into any agreement, whether military or otherwise, which is inconsistent with the neutrality of the Kingdom of Laos; it will not allow the establishment of any foreign military base on Laotian territory, nor allow any country to use Laotian territory for military purposes or for the purposes of interference in the internal affairs of other countries, nor recognize the protection of any alliance or military coalition, including SEATO;

(5) It will not allow any foreign interference in the internal affairs of the Kingdom of Laos in any form whatsoever;

(6) Subject to the provisions of Article 5 of the Protocol, it will require the withdrawal from Laos of all foreign troops and military personnel, and will not allow any foreign troops or military personnel to be introduced into Laos;

(7) It will accept direct and unconditional aid from all countries that wish to help the Kingdom of Laos build up an independent and autonomous national economy on the basis of respect for the sovereignty of Laos;

(8) It will respect the treaties and agreements signed in conformity with the interests of the Laotian people and of the policy of peace and neutrality of the Kingdom, in particular with Geneva Agreements of 1962, and will abrogate all treaties and agreements which are contrary to those principles.

This statement of neutrality by the Royal Government of Laos shall be promulgated constitutionally and shall have the force of law.

The Kingdom of Laos appeals to all the States participating in the International Conference on the Settlement of the Laotian Question, and to all other States, to recognize the sovereignty, independence, neutrality, unity, and territorial integrity of Laos, to conform to these principles in all respects, and to refrain from any action inconsistent therewith.

Confirming the principles of respect for the sovereignty, independence, unity and territorial integrity of the Kingdom of Laos and non-interference in its internal affairs which are embodied in the Geneva Agreements of 1954;

Emphasising the principle of respect for the neutrality of the Kingdom of Laos;

Agreeing that the above-mentioned principles constitute a basis for the peaceful settlement of the Laotian question;

Profoundly convinced that the independence and neutrality of the Kingdom of Laos will assist the peaceful democratic development of the Kingdom of Laos and the achievement of national accord and unity in that country, as well as the strengthening of peace and security in Southeast Asia:

1. Solemnly declare, in accordance with the will of the Government and people of the Kingdom of Laos, as expressed in the statement of neutrality by the Royal Government of Laos of July 9, 1962, that they recognize and will respect and observe in every way the sovereignty, independence, neutrality, unity and territorial integrity of the Kingdom of Laos.

2. Undertake, in particular, that

(a) they will not commit or participate in any way in any act which might directly or indirectly impair the sovereignty, independence, neutrality, unity or territorial integrity of the Kingdom of Laos;

(b) they will not resort to the use or threat of force or any other measures which might impair the peace of the Kingdom of Laos;

(c) they will refrain from all direct or indirect interference in the internal affairs of the Kingdom of Laos;

(d) they will not attach conditions of a political nature to any assistance which they may offer or which the Kingdom of Laos may seek;

(e) they will not bring the Kingdom of Laos in any way into any military alliance or any other agreement, whether military or otherwise, which is inconsistent with her neutrality, nor invite or encourage her to enter into any such alliance or to conclude any such agreement;

(f) they will respect the wish of the Kingdom of Laos not to recognize the protection of any alliance or military coalition, including SEATO;

(g) they will not introduce into the Kingdom of Laos foreign troops or military personnel in any form whatsoever, nor will they in any way facilitate or connive at the introduction of any foreign troops or military personnel;

(h) they will not establish nor will they in any way facilitate or connive at the establishment in the Kingdom of Laos of any foreign military base, foreign strong point or other foreign military installation of any kind;

(i) they will not use the territory of the Kingdom of Laos for interference in the internal affairs of other countries;

(j) they will not use the territory of any country, including their own, for interference in the internal affairs of the Kingdom of Laos.

3. Appeal to all other States to recognize, respect and observe in every way the sovereignty, independence and neutrality, and also the unity and territorial integrity, of the Kingdom of Laos and to refrain from any action inconsistent with these principles or with other provisions of the present Declaration.

4. Undertake, in the event of a violation or threat of violation of the sovereignty, independence, neutrality, unity or territorial integrity of the Kingdom of Laos, to consult jointly with the Royal Government of Laos and among themselves in order to consider measures which might prove to be necessary to ensure the observance of these principles and the other provisions of the present Declaration.

5. The present Declaration shall enter into force on signature and together with the statement of neutrality by the Royal Government of Laos of July 9, 1962 shall be regarded as constituting an international agreement. The present Declaration shall be deposited in the archives of the Governments of the United Kingdom and the Union of Soviet Socialist Republics, which shall furnish certified copies thereof to the other signatory States and to all the other States of the world.

*   *   *

F. Protocol to Declaration on Neutrality of Laos*

July 23, 1962

The Governments of the Union of Burma, the Kingdom of Cambodia, Canada, the People's Republic of China, the Democratic Republic of Viet-Nam, the Republic of France, the Republic of India, the Kingdom of Laos, the Polish People's Republic, the Republic of Viet-Nam, the Kingdom of Thailand, the Union of Soviet Socialist Republics, the United Kingdom of Great Britain and Northern Ireland and the United States of America;

Having regard to the Declaration on the Neutrality of Laos of July 23, 1962;

Have agreed as follows:

Article 1

For the purposes of this Protocol

(a) the term "foreign military personnel" shall include members of foreign

---

Ibid., Aug. 13, 1962, pp. 261-63.

military missions, foreign military advisers, experts, instructors, consultants, technicians, observers and any other foreign military persons, including those serving in any armed forces in Laos, and foreign civilians connected with the supply, maintenance, storing and utilization of war materials;

(b) the term "the Commission" shall mean the International Commission for Supervision and Control in Laos set up by virtue of the Geneva Agreements of 1954 and composed of the representatives of Canada, India and Poland, with the representative of India as Chairman;

(c) the term "the Co-Chairmen" shall mean the co-Co-Chairmen of the International Conference for the Settlement of the Laotian Question, 1961-1962, and their successors in the offices of Her Britannic Majesty's Principal Secretary of State for Foreign Affairs and Minister for Foreign Affairs of the Union of Soviet Socialist Republics respectively;

(d) the term "the members of the Conference" shall mean the Governments of countries which took part in the International Conference for the Settlement of the Laotian Question, 1961-1962.

Article 2

All foreign regular and irregular troops, foreign para-military formations and foreign military personnel shall be withdrawn from Laos in the shortest time possible and in any case the withdrawal shall be completed not later than thirty days after the Commission has notified the Royal Government of Laos that in accordance with Articles 3 and 10 of this Protocol its inspection teams are present at all points of withdrawal from Laos. These points shall be determined by the Royal Government of Laos in accordance with Article 3 within thirty days after the entry into force of this Protocol. The inspection teams shall be present at these points and the Commission shall notify the Royal Government of Laos thereof within fifteen days after the points have been determined.

Article 3

The withdrawal of foreign regular and irregular troops, foreign para-military formations and foreign military personnel shall take place only along such routes and through such points as shall be determined by the Royal Government of Laos in consultation with the Commission. The Commission shall be notified in advance of the point and time of all such withdrawals.

Article 4

The introduction of foreign regular and irregular troops, foreign para-military formations and foreign military personnel into Laos is prohibited.

Article 5

Note is taken that the French and Laotian Governments will conclude as soon as possible an arrangement to transfer the French military installations in Laos to the Royal Government of Laos.

If the Laotian Government considers it necessary, the French Government may as an exception leave in Laos for a limited period of time a precisely limited number of French military instructors for the purpose of training the armed forces of Laos.

The French and Laotian Governments shall inform the members of the Conference, through the Co-Chairmen, of their agreement on the question of the transfer of the French military installations in Laos and of the employment of French instructors by the Laotian Government.

Article 6

The introduction into Laos of armaments, munitions and war material generally, except such quantities of conventional armaments as the Royal Government of Laos may consider necessary for the national defense of Laos, is prohibited.

Article 7

All foreign military persons and civilians captured or interned during the course of hostilities in Laos shall be released within thirty days after the entry into force of this Protocol and handed over by the Royal Government of Laos to the representatives of the Governments of the Countries of which they are nationals in order that they may proceed to the destination of their choice.

Article 8

The Co-Chairmen shall periodically receive reports from the Commission. In addition the Commission shall immediately report to the Co-Chairmen any violations or threats of violations of this Protocol, all significant steps which it takes in pursuance of this Protocol, and also any other important information which may assist the Co-Chairmen in carrying out their functions. The Commission may at any time seek help from the Co-Chairmen in the performance of its duties, and the Co-Chairmen may at any time make recommendations to the Commission exercising general guidance.

The Co-Chairmen shall circulate the reports and any other important information from the Commission to the members of the Conference.

The Co-Chairmen shall exercise supervision over the observance of this Protocol and the Declaration on the Neutrality of Laos.

The Co-Chairmen will keep the members of the Conference constantly informed and when appropriate will consult with them.

Article 9

The Commission shall, with the concurrence of the Royal Government of Laos, supervise and control the cease-fire in Laos.

The Commission shall exercise these functions in full co-operation with the Royal Government of Laos and within the framework of the Cease-Fire Agreement or cease-fire arrangements made by the three political forces in Laos, or the Royal Government of Laos. It is understood that responsibility for the execution of the cease-fire shall rest with the three parties concerned and with the Royal Government of Laos after its formation.

Article 10

The Commission shall supervise and control the withdrawal of foreign regular and irregular troops, foreign para-military formations and foreign military personnel. Inspection teams sent by the Commission for these purposes shall be present for the period of the withdrawal at all points of withdrawal from Laos determined by the Royal Government of Laos in consultation with the Commission in accordance with Article 3 of this Protocol.

Article 11

The Commission shall investigate cases where there are reasonable grounds for considering that a violation of the provisions of Article 4 of this Protocol has occurred.

It is understood that in the exercise of this function the Commission is acting with the concurrence of the Royal Government of Laos. It shall carry out its investigations in full co-operation with the Royal Government of Laos and shall immediately inform the Co-Chairmen of any violations or threats of violations of Article 4, and also of all significant steps which it takes in pursuance of this Article in accordance with Article 8.

Article 12

The Commission shall assist the Royal Government of Laos in cases where the Royal Government of Laos considers that a violation of Article 6 of this Protocol may have taken place. This assistance will be rendered at the request of the Royal Government of Laos and in full co-operation with it.

Article 13

The Commission shall exercise its functions under this Protocol in close co-operation with the Royal Government of Laos. It is understood that the Royal

Government of Laos at all levels will render the Commission all possible assistance in the performance by the Commission of these functions and also will take all necessary measures to ensure the security of the Commission and its inspection teams during their activities in Laos.

Article 14

The Commission functions as a single organ of the international Conference for the Settlement of the Laotian Question, 1961-1962. The members of the Commission will work harmoniously and in co-operation with each other with the aim of solving all questions within the terms of reference of the Commission.

Decisions of the Commission on questions relating to violations of Articles 2, 3, 4 and 6 of this Protocol or of the cease-fire referred to in Article 9, conclusions on major questions sent to the Co-Chairmen and all recommendations by the Commission shall be adopted unanimously. On other questions, including procedural questions, and also questions relating to the initiation and carrying out of investigations (Article 15), decisions of the Commission shall be adopted by majority vote.

Article 15

In the exercise of its specific functions which are laid down in the relevant articles of this Protocol the Commission shall conduct investigations (directly or by sending inspection teams), when there are reasonable grounds for considering that a violation has occurred. These investigations shall be carried out at the request of the Royal Government of Laos or on the initiative of the Commission, which is acting with the concurrence of the Royal Government of Laos.

In the latter case decisions on initiating and carrying out such investigations shall be taken in the Commission by majority vote.

The Commission shall submit agreed reports on investigations in which differences which may emerge between members of the Commission on particular questions may be expressed.

The conclusions and recommendations of the Commission resulting from investigations shall be adopted unanimously.

Article 16

For the exercise of its functions the Commission shall, as necessary, set up inspection teams, on which the three member-States of the Commission shall be equally represented. Each member-State of the Commission shall ensure the presence of its own representatives both on the Commission and on the inspection teams, and shall promptly replace them in the event of their being unable to perform their duties.

It is understood that the dispatch of inspection teams to carry out various specific tasks takes place with the concurrence of the Royal Government of Laos. The points to which the Commission and its inspection teams go for the purposes of investigation and their length of stay at those points shall be determined in relation to the requirements of the particular investigation.

Article 17

The Commission shall have at its disposal the means of communication and transport required for the performance of its duties. These as a rule will be provided to the Commission by the Royal Government of Laos for payment on mutually acceptable terms, and those which the Royal Government of Laos cannot provide will be acquired by the Commission from other sources. It is understood that the means of communication and transport will be under the administrative control of the Commission.

Article 18

The costs of the operations of the Commission shall be borne by the members of the Conference in accordance with the provisions of this Article.

(a) The Governments of Canada, India and Poland shall pay the personal salaries and allowances of their nationals who are members of their delegations to the Commission and its subsidiary organs.

(b) The primary responsibility for the provision of accommodation for the Commission and its subsidiary organs shall rest with the Royal Government of Laos, which shall also provide such other local services as may be appropriate. The Commission shall charge to the Fund referred to in sub-paragraph (c) below any local expenses not borne by the Royal Government of Laos.

(c) All other capital or running expenses incurred by the Commission in the exercise of its functions shall be met from a Fund to which all the members of the Conference shall contribute in the following proportions:

The Governments of the People's Republic of China, France, the Union of Soviet Socialist Republics, the United Kingdom and the United States of America shall contribute 17.6 per cent each.

The Governments of Burma, Cambodia, the Democratic Republic of Viet-Nam, Laos, the Republic of Viet-Nam and Thailand shall contribute 1.5 per cent each.

The Governments of Canada, India and Poland as members of the Commission shall contribute 1 per cent each.

Article 19

The Co-Chairmen shall at any time, if the Royal Government of Laos so requests, and in any case not later than three years after the entry into force of this Protocol, present a report with appropriate recommendations on the question of the termination of the Commission to the members of the Conference for their consideration. Before making such a report the Co-Chairmen shall hold consultations with the Royal Government of Laos and the Commission.

Article 20

This Protocol shall enter into force on signature.

It shall be deposited in the archives of the Governments of the United Kingdom and the Union of Soviet Socialist Republics which shall furnish certified copies thereof to the other signator States and to all other States of the world.

In witness whereof, the undersigned Plenipotentiaries have signed this Protocol.

Done in two copies in Geneva this twenty-third day of July one thousand nine hundred and sixty-two in the English, Chinese, French, Laotian and Russian languages, each text being equally authoritative.

CONTINUED THREAT TO LAOS

A. Address by Secretary Rusk on the Importance of Laos*

[Extract]

June 14, 1964

    *   *   *

Why àre we concerned about Laos? First, because of its location. On the north and northeast it has nearly 1,100 miles of border with Communist China and Communist North Viet-Nam. It also shares 1,750 miles of border with four non-Communist countries, including Thailand, the heartland of Southeast Asia, and South Viet-Nam, which is resisting an aggression directed and supplied by Communist North Viet-Nam with the support of Communist China.

In 1949 the French granted Laos independence within the French Union. But the North Vietnamese Communists managed to attract a few Lao dissidents by pledges of military help and technical advice. In September 1950 the North Viet-Nam radio announced formation of the "resistance government of the Pathet Lao." Later broadcasts claimed that this government had a "national assembly," had picked a "prime minister," and had formed a "people's liberation army." All this occurred not in Laos but in North Viet-Nam.

In 1953 North Vietnamese forces invaded Laos, taking with them their puppet Pathet Lao government and troops. When the Indochinese war was brought to an end by the Geneva agreements of 1954, the Communists controlled two provinces of Laos. But under those agreements Laos was to be one country, the Pathet Lao forces were to be integrated into the Royal Lao Army, and all foreign military forces were to be withdrawn, excepting limited forces and two bases reserved for France. Those pledges were signed by the Communist regimes of North Viet-Nam and mainland China as well as by the Soviet Union and Poland.

But, because of Pathet Lao intransigence, those agreements did not bring peace and unity to Laos. And, in 1960, fighting among non-Communist elements gave the Communists new opportunities. When President Kennedy took office, the Soviet Union was airlifting arms and ammunition from Hanoi to Communist and neutralist forces in northeast Laos and on the strategic Plaine des Jarres. And we were supporting the Government forces in the Mekong Valley.

The 1962 Geneva Accords

The Soviet Union, however, indicated that it desired an independent and neutral Laos. And we had no wish beyond a free Laos that could live at peace with its neighbors. Subject to a cease-fire we agreed to negotiate. Finally, new accords were signed in Geneva in July 1962.

All participants "solemnly declared" their respect for the sovereignty, neutral-

*Documents on American Foreign Relations, 1964, pp. 220-23.

ity, and territorial integrity of Laos. They agreed, among other things, to: (1) withdraw all foreign troops in the presence of international inspectors; (2) prohibit introduction of military forces in any capacity; (3) withhold any war material from Laos except as "the Royal Government of Laos may consider necessary"; (4) not use the territory of Laos to intervene in the internal affairs of other countries.

Responsibility for general supervision of the accords was given to an International Control Commission (ICC) composed of representatives of Canada and Poland with India as chairman.

And all agreed also to support a Government of National Union composed of three factions, with the neutral leader Prince Souvanna Phouma as Premier.

The 14 governments which made these pledges included Communist China. and Communist North Viet-Nam as well as the Soviet Union and Poland.

Record of Communist Aggression and Deception

What happened? The non-Communist nations complied with the agreements. North Viet-Nam and its Pathet Lao puppets did not. We promptly withdrew our 600-man military aid mission. North Viet-Nam kept several thousand troops and military technicians in Laos. North Vietnamese cadres are the backbone of almost every Pathet Lao battalion. This was, and is, of course, a major violation of the Geneva accords.

Later, North Viet-Nam sent additional forces back into Laos—some of them in organized battalions—a second major violation.

The North Vietnamese have continued to use, and improve the corridor through Laos to reinforce and supply the Viet Cong in South Viet-Nam—a third major violation.

The Communists have continued to ship arms into Laos as well as through it—another major violation.

The Pathet Lao and the North Vietnamese Communists have compounded these international felonies by denials that they were committing them.

But there was another major violation which they could not deny. They barred freedom of access to the areas under their control, both to the Lao Government and to the International Control Commission. The Royal Lao Government, on the other hand, opened the areas under its control to access not only by the ICC but by all Lao factions.

The Communists repeatedly fired at personnel and aircraft on legitimate missions under the authority of the Royal Lao Government. They even fired on ICC helicopters. They repeatedly violated the cease-fire agreement. And this Spring they launched an assault on the neutralist forces of General Kong Le, driving them off the Plaine des Jarres, where they had been since early 1961.

This, in bare summary, is the Communist record of aggression, bad faith, and deception in Laos.

A Communist takeover in Laos would be as unacceptable as a Communist takeover in South Viet-Nam. The rest of Southeast Asia would be in jeopardy, and saving it would be much more costly, in blood and treasure, than turning back the aggressors in Laos and South Viet-Nam. The loss of Southeast Asia as a whole to the Communists would be intolerable.

Need for Compliance with Present Agreements

The Communist assault on Laos, like that on South Viet-Nam, involves the larger question of whether anyone is to be permitted to succeed in aggression by terror, guerrilla warfare, and the infiltration of arms and military personnel across national frontiers. If they are allowed to gain from these assaults in Southeast Asia, the Communist advocates of militance everywhere will feel encouraged.

Also at stake is the fundamental question of whether solemn international contracts are to be performed. All who believe in peace and in building a decent world order and rule of law have an interest in seeing that no government be allowed to gain from breaking its promises.

There is talk of negotiating new political settlements in Southeast Asia. But political settlements were reached in 1954 and 1962. The Geneva accords of 1962 were precisely agreements to neutralize Laos. No new agreements are required. All that is needed is compliance with the agreements already made.

The prescription for peace in Laos and Viet-Nam is simple: Leave your neighbors alone. It is in the vital interest of the free world that Peiping and Hanoi— and all Communists everywhere—learn, once and for all, that they cannot reap rewards from militancy, aggression by seepage, and duplicity. For our part, we certainly do not intend to abandon the peoples of Laos or Viet-Nam or other countries who are trying to remain free from Communist domination.

STATEMENTS BY THE UNITED STATES AND THE SOVIET UNION ON THE SITUATION IN LAOS

B. Statement by the Soviet Union*

July 26, 1964

In connection with the continued deterioration of the situation in Laos the Soviet Government, as one of the parties to the Geneva accords on Laos, feels obligated to call the attention of all the states which are parties to the above-mentioned accords to the following.

Lately it has become increasingly obvious that certain states have embarked on a course of flagrant intervention in the internal affairs of Laos and violation of the Geneva accords, which, as is well known, obligate the states which are signatories thereto to respect the independence and neutrality of Laos.

Contrary to the Geneva accords the United States has left its military personnel and various military and semimilitary organizations and services in Laos, continuing to give unilateral military aid to the reactionary forces of the country. With the support of the United States these forces carried out a military coup in Vientiane last April, which brought about an extreme aggravation of the domestic conditions in the country and paralyzed the operation of the coalition government, the establishment of which was in itself an advance on the road to realization of those principles which are laid down in the Geneva accords.

*Department of State Bulletin, Aug. 17, 1964, p. 220.

As a result there arose the threat of a complete breakdown of the accords signed at Geneva.

In flagrant violation of the sovereignty of Laos, United States aircraft are conducting reconnaissance flights above the territory of the country and are exposing to bombing and bombardment the areas controlled by the Pathet Lao. The numerous representations made by the Soviet Government, as co-Chairman of the Geneva Conference on Laos, to the Government of the U.S.A., with an appeal to discontinue interference in the internal affairs of Laos and violations of the Geneva accords, have not achieved their purpose. In spite of the repeated representations of the co-Chairmen, resumption of negotiations between the three political forces of Laos for a peaceful settlement in the country in accordance with the Geneva accords has still not been implemented.

The Soviet Government was the first to support the proposal of Prince Norodom Sihanouk, Chief of State of Cambodia, for convening a new international conference of 14 states concerning Laos. Considering the tense situation in Laos, the Soviet Government proposed that such a conference be held at Geneva in June 1964. However, the proposal for calling a conference at that time has not met with the support of the U.S.A. and certain other states.

Under various unfounded pretexts the proposal of the Polish People's Republic for conducting consultations with the participation of the three political forces for the purpose of planning a new international conference on Laos has also been rejected.

The Soviet Government can no longer reconcile itself to such a situation when the Geneva accords on Laos are thwarted, when certain states, which have signed the accords, evade the discussion of the dangerous situation in Laos which has been created and which threatens the peace and security not only of that country but of the entire area of Southeast Asia as well. Such a position is also dictated by the fact that in the situation thus created the co-Chairmen of the Geneva Conference have been placed in a false position, preventing them from fulfilling the functions imposed upon them.

The Soviet Government therefore addresses a proposal to the governments of all countries which signed the Geneva accords on Laos to convene in August of this year an international conference of 14 states on Laos to discuss urgent measures which would insure a peaceful settlement in Laos in accordance with the Geneva accords of 1962, strict and unswerving fulfillment of these accords by all the states concerned. Such a conference could be held in Geneva or in another city acceptable to all the participants of the conference. This new proposal has been dictated by the sincere desire to contribute to the implementation of the Geneva accords.

For its part, the Soviet Union is prepared, just as before, to contribute to the efforts directed toward expediting the convening of the said international conference. A negative attitude toward this proposal on the part of other states will place the Soviet Government in a position where it will be compelled to consider in general the question of the possibility of fulfillment by the Soviet Union of the functions of co-Chairman, since under the conditions of gross and systematic violation of the Geneva accords by certain states, the role of co-Chairman loses all useful significance and becomes fictitious.

C. United States Statement*

July 30, 1964

The Government of the United States shares the concern of the Government of the Union of Soviet Socialist Republics over the deteriorating situation in Laos, as expressed in the Soviet statement handed to the United States Government on July 26.

As the Soviet Government is aware, the United States Government placed great store in understandings regarding Laos reached by President Kennedy and Premier Khrushchev at Vienna in June 1961 and the Geneva Agreements on Laos which followed. The United States Government believed that peace could be restored to Laos if foreign interference were ended there and the people of that country were left alone to work out their own destinies on the basis of a policy of neutrality. The Geneva Agreements provided a sound basis for such a policy and placed responsibility upon the International Control Commission and the Co-Chairmen of the Geneva Conference to see to it that the parties lived up to their obligations.

From the very beginning, however, the Pathet Lao and North Viet-Nam, backed by the Chinese Communists, refused to comply with their obligations. North Vietnamese military forces were not withdrawn from Laos under ICC supervision. North Viet-Nam continued to use and, indeed, increased their use of Laotian territory to infiltrate military personnel and supplies into South Viet-Nam. The Pathet Lao, with North Vietnamese support, have repeatedly violated the cease-fire, most recently in their unprovoked attacks against and seizure of neutralist positions on the Plain of Jars, which were the subject of a report to the Co-Chairmen by the International Control Commission dated June 20. The Pathet Lao has refused to cooperate with the International Control Commission and with the Government of National Union.

These repeated violations of the Geneva Agreements have occurred in the face of the special responsibility which Article 8 of the Protocol to the Declaration on the Neutrality of Laos places on the Co-Chairmen to exercise supervision over the observance of the Agreements. At the same time, the International Control Commission has been unable effectively to deal with these violations largely because of the refusal of the Pathet Lao to allow the Commission to exercise free access to areas under Pathet Lao control and also the failure of its Polish member to participate in the Commission's activities in a positive manner.

The Soviet Government's statement makes certain allegations regarding United States activities in Laos which are contrary to fact. The United States withdrew all 666 of its military advisory personnel from Laos under ICC supervision in accordance with Articles 2 and 3 of the Geneva Protocol. In the face of the aggressive attacks launched by the Pathet Lao and North Vietnamese in May on the Plain of Jars in flagrant violation of the Geneva Agreements, the United States responded to Prime Minister Souvanna Phouma's request for

Ibid., pp. 218-20.

assistance by initiating reconnaissance flights. These flights were undertaken to obtain information not otherwise available as to the intentions and dispositions of the attacking forces in view of the forced withdrawal of the International Control Commission from the Plain of Jars and the imminent threat which the attacks posed to the whole of Laos including the Government of National Union and the entire Geneva settlement.

Not only did the United States not support the military coup attempted in April, but it took immediate and effective steps to support the Government of National Union under Prime Minister Souvanna Phouma. The United States Ambassador [Leonard Unger] in Vientiane worked in close harmony with the Soviet Ambassador at that time; and the attitude and actions of the United States Government with respect to the attempted coup are well known to the Soviet Government.

The United States continues to exert every effort to resolve the Laotian problem by peaceful means in accordance with the 1962 Agreements. In this connection, the United States Government participated in consultations at Vientiane called for by Prime Minister Souvanna Phouma under paragraph 4 of the Declaration on the Neutrality of Laos. The United States regrets that the Soviet Government did not join in those consultations. In addition, as the Soviet Government will recall, the United States has given its support to the proposal of the Polish Government for diplomatic talks among the Lao parties, the Co-Chairmen and members of the International Control Commission. The United States Government has been disturbed to note the rejection of these proposals by the Pathet Lao, the North Vietnamese and the Chinese Communists. The United States continues to believe that a preliminary conference of the general type suggested by the Polish Government offers the best hope of dealing with the current problems on the diplomatic level.

The United States Government notes that, in its statement, the Soviet Government proposes the convening of an international conference on Laos in August. As the Soviet Government is undoubtedly aware, Prime Minister Souvanna Phouma, in a communique of May 24, 1964, addressed himself to a similar proposal. In his statement, the Prime Minister expressed a willingness to attend such a conference if, first, a cease-fire were effected in Laos under International Control Commission supervision and the Pathet Lao withdrew from those areas which it illegally occupied by virtue of its May attacks. The United States Government believes the position of the Prime Minister is justified and fully supports this position.

In sum, the United States Government remains of the view that the 1962 Geneva Agreements provide a sound basis for resolution of the Laotian question. What is needed above all is compliance with those Agreements by those who have thus far ignored their commitments. Nevertheless, the United States is prepared to attend a conference such as that proposed by the Soviet Government if Prime Minister Souvanna Phouma's preconditions are met and it is thus demonstrated that there is some reason to believe that such a conference may serve a useful purpose.

D. State Department Statement Reaffirming Support of Geneva Agreements on Laos*

January 18, 1965

We continue to support the Geneva Agreements and the independence and neutrality of Laos which they are intended to achieve. Our actions are designed to preserve the Geneva settlement. We have for some time been assisting the Royal Lao Government, at its request, to help defend the independence, territorial integrity, and neutrality of Laos. This assistance has been made necessary by the repeated and blatant violations of the Geneva Agreements by the North Vietnamese and the Pathet Lao forces since the agreements were signed on July 23, 1962. In view of the serious Communist violations of the Geneva Agreements, we believe that this assistance to help Laos defend itself is entirely justified.

E. Address by Prince Souvanna Phouma, Prime Minister of Laos, on "The North Vietnamese Have Carried the War to Laos"*

[Extract]

October 18, 1966

*   *   *

Unfortunately, along with this trend towards a relaxation of tension and peace, there is in Asia a source of grave conflict—one which is localized to be sure, in the Indo-Chinese peninsula, especially in Viet-Nam and to a lesser degree in Laos, but which, tomorrow, could encompass all of Asia and perhaps the entire world. I think that world opinion regards matters in these regions in the following manner.

There is every reason to believe that, by degrees, by the insidious process of the wars called "wars of national liberation," if this process is not stopped in time, a third world war will burst into flames and destroy us all. It is by accelerating this process that some find benefits for their dream of hegemony, while others use it to try out principles and practices of the warfare of the future. General staffs are putting their theories to the test of fire; leaders are being trained; but the process of "de-escalation" has not yet been found.

It is said that the balance of terror makes war impossible. No one can really believe that. We for our part are skeptical, and we think that on the day when the die is cast the world will go up in smoke.

In Laos we have been suffering for years the immediate effects of the war in Viet-Nam. Through the intermediary of the so-called Pathet Lao forces and in collusion with them, the North Viet-Namese have carried the war to Laos. The famous "Ho Chi-Minh Trail," over which foreign weapons and troops pass,

* *American Foreign Policy: Current Documents, 1965*, p. 789.
* *American Foreign Policy, 1966*, pp. 720-21.

is in our territory. It is no longer a secret to anyone that entire North Viet-Namese battalions are operating in our country, attacking our forces, killing our women and children, carrying off our crops and our cattle. A number of North Viet-Namese prisoners belonging to regular units have been captured in engagements with our troops on various battlefields in Laos. Documents taken from the dead and interrogations of prisoners have enabled the Royal Government to furnish incontestable proof of the presence of increasingly greater numbers of North Viet-Namese troops in Lao territory, and their interference in the domestic affairs of our country—all in spite of the Geneva Agreements of 1962 on the neutrality of Laos.

*   *   *

F. Statement by U.S. Ambassador W. Averell Harriman Reviewing North Vietnamese Violations of Agreement on Laos*

[Extract]

Paris, June 5, 1968

Your Excellency, I want to stress again what I have said in every meeting. We are ready now—today—to discuss the question of the cessation of bombing and related matters. You have asked that we acknowledge or determine our responsibility for the cessation of all bombing. As we have stated, this has never presented an insurmountable obstacle for us, and we are prepared in fact to cease bombardment at the appropriate time and circumstance. Accordingly, I hope we can proceed forthwith to discuss related matters, I hope this will start before the close of our meeting today. But first I must call your attention to the situation in Laos.

On May 30 the Prime Minister of Laos, Prince Souvanna Phouma, spoke to his Parliament of the crushing burden imposed on his nation by the presence of the North Vietnamese Army in Laos. His small country now has to maintain an army of more than 60,000 men to defend against the invaders and has to support over half a million refugees who have fled Communist-controlled areas. The Prime Minister stressed that the aggression had turned Laos into an "active transit route" for North Vietnamese troops headed for South Viet-Nam. The same day that the Prime Minister spoke, the Royal Laotian Government released proof that there were some 40,000 North Vietnamese soldiers in Laos. These include 25,000 North Vietnamese regular soldiers in 57 battalions of the North Vietnamese Army and 12,000 other North Vietnamese in Laos maintaining and securing the lines of communication of the North Vietnamese Army which pass through Laos to South Viet-Nam. Additionally, some 3,000 North Vietnamese now serve in mixed North Vietnamese and Pathet Lao military units.

As you well know, the Government of North Viet-Nam committed itself not to "use the territory of the Kingdom of Laos for interference in the internal

**Department of State Bulletin*, June 24, 1968, pp. 817-18.

affairs of other countries" and to "respect and observe in every way the sovereignty, independence, neutrality, unity and territorial integrity of the Kingdom of Laos." These are the actual words from the Geneva Declaration of 1962, signed by the Democratic Republic of Viet-Nam. The deeds of North Viet-Nam belied the words to which it committed itself.

During the negotiations in Geneva in 1961-62, North Viet-Nam consistently refused to concede that North Vietnamese troops were in fact in Laos. At that time about 10,000 North Vietnamese troops were there. Yet, only 40 North Vietnamese were withdrawn under ICC [International Control Commission] observation.

The United States, obeying in every detail the agreements, dismantled its military advisory mission, withdrawing 666 American military personnel and 403 Filipino civilian technicians through ICC checkpoints.

But substantial numbers of North Vietnamese military personnel remained. Beginning in 1963, additional North Vietnamese Army units began to enter Laos in increasing numbers. Today North Vietnamese forces in Laos are at an all-time high—some 40,000.

Considering the size of that country, there are proportionately even more North Vietnamese soldiers in Laos than in South Viet-Nam. Since there can be no justification for the presence of those troops, you try to deny that they are there. But the facts speak too loudly to be denied. I will briefly review some of those facts.

It is a fact that North Viet-Nam is waging not one war but several wars in Laos; in the south of that country North Viet-Nam has built a complex of roads, paths, storage areas, and depots which had previously been known as the Ho Chi Minh Trail. In addition, there are military bases and camps from which North Vietnamese troops attack South Viet-Nam across international borders. In other military operations, North Vietnamese troops are attacking troops of the Royal Government of Laos, not only in south Laos but also in the center and in the north.

We offer the following eight categories of proof of North Viet-Nam's violations of the Geneva Agreement of 1962.

First, the International Control Commission has rendered three reports based on incontrovertible proof, including the interrogation of North Vietnamese soldiers who were either captured or surrendered to the Royal Lao Army.

The International Control Commission was asked by the Royal Lao Government on many other occasions to investigate violations. It was unable to perform the function assigned to it in the Geneva Agreements because access to the areas in question was refused by the Pathet Lao, acting in collusion with North Vietnamese.

Second, there are the complaints lodged by the Royal Government of Laos about specific violations of the 1962 Geneva agreements which resulted in no reports by the International Control Commission because of Poland's opposition to investigations. These complaints are of the greatest interest. Among the most recent communications to the ICC made public by the Royal Lao Government was one of December 30, 1967, about the role of the North Vietnamese Army in attacks upon Lao Government defenders of Nam Bac, Phalane, Lao Ngam, and Yangeteuil. On February 29, 1968, another communication to the ICC, which has not yet been made public, described North Vietnamese Army participation in offensives in Tha Thom, Atopeu, Lao Ngam, Phalane, and Saravane.

Third, there is the communique issued after consultations in Vientiane, called in 1964 by the British Co-Chairman of the Geneva conference. Those consultations took place under article 4 of the 1962 Agreement. They resulted in a call on June 29, 1964, for a cease-fire and withdrawal of all North Vietnamese forces from Lao territory.

Fourth, the Royal Lao Government has issued two White Books on North Vietnamese interference in Laos in violation of the Geneva Agreement. Those White Books contain extensive documentation based on the interrogation of North Vietnamese prisoners and other evidence. They are dated December 3, 1964, and August 25, 1966.

Fifth, the Royal Lao Government has made specific complaints about North Vietnamese aggression to the United Nations General Assemblies in every year since 1963. They establish the record of continuous violations of the 1962 Geneva agreement ever since North Viet-Nam affixed its signature to it. The World has not paid sufficient attention to the appeals for help from the Prime Minister of Laos. The war in that unhappy country has been too long the "forgotten war." It is time the world became more aware of this war—and that the states which have undertaken responsibilities for the neutrality of Laos live up to those responsibilities.

Sixth, the Ho Chi Minh Trail—which has become a vast complex of roads, trails, and waterways in Laos—has been under constant aerial surveillance since mid-1964. We have helped in this at the request of the Royal Lao Government. A vast amount of photographic evidence attests to the constant improvement and extension of this logistic network over the years. This evidence also proves that military supplies have moved and are continuing to move southward. These photographs and other evidence are available and can be provided to you if you wish to review them.

Seventh, there is the testimony, as supplied by the Lao Government, of members of the Lao Armed Forces as well as Lao civilians who have seen this logistic system and the North Vietnamese bases. Some of these witnesses have been held prisoner by North Vietnamese forces. Numerous eyewitness reports of these North Vietnamese violations are therefore available.

Eighth, the greatest mass of incontrovertible evidence of the North Vietnamese presence in south Laos comes from the personnel who have been captured or who have rallied to the Government of Viet-Nam in South Viet-Nam. From these reports, the movement of specific units of the North Vietnamese Army through Laos can be documented by dates and precise routes. For example, the activities of the 927th North Vietnamese Army Battalion or the 59th Transportation Group are fully documented in a series of reports.

*   *   *

G. Statement by President Nixon on the Scope of United States Involvement in Laos*

March 6, 1970

In light of the increasingly massive presence of North Vietnamese troops and their recent offensives in Laos, I have written letters today to British Prime Minister Wilson and Soviet Premier Kosygin asking their help in restoring the 1962 Geneva agreements for that country.

As co-Chairmen of that conference, the United Kingdom and the Soviet Union have particular responsibilities for seeing that its provisions are honored. My letters note the persistent North Vietnamese violations of the accords and their current offensives, support the Laotian Prime Minister's own current appeal to the co-Chairmen for consultations, urge the co-Chairmen to work with other signatories of the Geneva accords, and pledge full United States cooperation.

Hanoi's most recent military buildup in Laos has been particularly escalatory. They have poured over 13,000 additional troops into Laos during the past few months, raising their total in Laos to over 67,000. Thirty North Vietnamese battalions from regular division units participated in the current campaign in the Plain of Jars with tanks, armored cars, and long-range artillery. The indigenous Laotian Communists, the Pathet Lao, are playing an insignificant role.

North Viet-Nam's military escalation in Laos has intensified public discussion in this country. The purpose of this statement is to set forth the record of what we found in January 1969 and the policy of this administration since that time.

1. What We Found

A. The 1962 Accords

When we came into office, this administration found a highly precarious situation in Laos. Its basic legal framework had been established by the 1962 accords entered into by the Kennedy administration.

Laos has been a battleground for most of the past 20 years. In 1949 it became a semi-independent state within the French Union. The Pathet Lao Communists rebelled against the government in the early 1950's and fighting continued until the 1954 Geneva settlements ended the Indochina war. Laos at that time became an independent neutral state. The indigenous Communists, the Pathet Lao, nevertheless retained control of the two northern provinces.

Since then, this small country has been the victim of persistent subversion, and finally invasion, by the North Vietnamese.

By 1961, North Vietnamese involvement became marked, the Communist forces made great advances, and a serious situation confronted the Kennedy administration. In his news conference of March 1961, President Kennedy said, "Laos is far away from America, but the world is small . . . . The security

---

Ibid., Mar. 30, 1970, pp. 405-09.

of all Southeast Asia will be endangered if Laos loses its neutral independence."

In May 1961, negotiations for a Laotian settlement opened in Geneva, with Governor [W. Averell] Harriman as the chief American negotiator. During the course of those long negotiations, fighting continued and the Communists made further advances. Faced with a potential threat to Thailand, President Kennedy ordered 5,000 marines to that country in May 1962.

Finally, in July 1962, after 14 months of negotiations, 14 nations signed the Geneva accords providing for the neutralization of Laos. Other signatories besides the United States included the Soviet Union, Communist China, North Viet-Nam, the United Kingdom, France, the Southeast Asian nations most directly involved, and the members of the International Control Commission, Canada, India, and Poland.

These accords came 1 month after the three contending forces within Laos announced agreement on the details of a coalition government composed of the three major political factions and headed by the neutralist, Prince Souvanna Phouma. North Viet-Nam claimed that it favored a coalition government. Both North Viet-Nam and the Soviet Union backed Prince Souvanna for his new post. The present government of Laos thus has been the one originally proposed by the Communists. In approving the 1962 arrangements, the Kennedy administration in effect accepted the basic formulation which has been advanced by North Viet-Nam and the Soviet Union for a Laotian political settlement.

B. The Record 1962-1969

Before the ink was dry on the 1962 Geneva documents, and despite the fact that they embodied most of its own proposals, North Viet-Nam started violating them. In compliance with the accords, the 666 Americans who had been assisting the Royal Lao Government withdrew under ICC supervision. In contrast, the North Vietnamese passed only a token 40 men through ICC checkpoints and left over 6,000 troops in the country.

A steadily growing number of North Vietnamese troops have remained there ever since, in flagrant violation of the Geneva accords. They climbed to about 33,000 in mid-1967, 46,000 in mid-1968, and 55,000 in mid-1969. Today they are at an all-time high of some 67,000 men.

These are not advisers or technicians or attachés. They are line units of the North Vietnamese Army conducting open aggression against a neighbor that poses no threat to Hanoi.

In addition, since 1964 over a half million North Vietnamese troops have crossed the "Ho Chi Minh Trail" in Laos to invade South Viet-Nam. This infiltration route provides the great bulk of men and supplies for the war in South Viet-Nam.

The political arrangements for a three-way government survived only until April 1963, when the Pathet Lao Communist leaders departed from the capital and left their cabinet posts vacant. Fighting soon resumed, and since then there have been cycles of Communist offensives and Royal Laotian Government counter-offensives. The enemy forces have been led and dominated throughout by the North Vietnamese. In recent years Hanoi has provided the great majority of Communist troops in Laos.

North Viet-Nam appears to have two aims in Laos. The first is to ensure its ability to use Laos as a supply route for North Vietnamese forces in South Viet-Nam. The second is to weaken and subvert the Royal Lao Government—originally established at its urging—to hinder it from interfering with North Vietnamese use of Laotian territory, and to pave the way for the eventual establishment of a government more amenable to Communist control.

Prime Minister Souvanna Phouma has tried a variety of diplomatic efforts to restore peace in Laos. He has repeatedly appealed to the co-Chairmen and others to help arrange for restoration of the 1962 accords. He and the International Control Commission, hampered by lack of authority, have reported and publicized North Vietnamese violations of the accords. And Prime Minister Souvanna Phouma has made several attempts to achieve political reconciliation with the Pathet Lao and to reconstitute a tripartite government.

None of these efforts has borne fruit. Frustrated in his diplomatic efforts and confronted with continuing outside aggression, Souvanna has called upon three American administrations to assist his government in preserving Laotian neutrality and integrity.

By early 1963 the North Vietnamese and Pathet Lao had openly breached the 1962 agreements by attacking the neutralist government forces in north Laos and by occupying and fortifying the area in southeast Laos along what came to be known as the Ho Chi Minh Trail. In these circumstances, the Laotian Prime Minister requested American aid in the form of supplies and munitions. The Kennedy administration provided this assistance in line with the Laotian Government's right under the Geneva accords to seek help in its self-defense.

In mid-May 1964 the Pathet Lao, supported by the North Vietnamese, attacked Prime Minister Souvanna Phouma's neutralist military forces on the Plain of Jars. North.Viet-Nam also began to increase its use of the Ho Chi Minh Trail to further its aggression against South Viet-Nam. The Johnson administration responded to Royal Laotian Government requests to meet this escalation by increasing our training and logistic support to the Royal Lao Government. In May 1964, as North Vietnamese presence increased, the United States, at Royal Lao Government request, began flying certain interdictory missions against invaders who were violating Lao neutrality.

Thus, when this administration came into office we faced a chronically serious situation in Laos. There had been 6 years of seasonal Communist attacks and growing U.S. involvement at the request of the Royal Laotian Government. The North Vietnamese had steadily increased both their infiltration through Laos into South Viet-Nam and their troop presence in Laos itself. Any facade of native Pathet Lao independence has been stripped away. In January 1969 we thus had a military assistance program reaching back over 6 years, and air operations dating over 4 years.

II. The Policy of This Administration

Since this administration has been in office, North Vietnamese pressure has continued. Last Spring, the North Vietnamese mounted a campaign which threatened the royal capital and moved beyond the areas previously occupied by Communists. A counter-attack by the Lao Government forces, intended to relieve this military pressure and cut off supply lines, caught the enemy by surprise and succeeded beyond expectations in pushing them off the strategic central plain in north Laos known as the Plain of Jars.

The North Vietnamese left behind huge stores of arms, ammunition, and other supplies cached on the plain. During their operations in the Plain of Jars last summer and fall, Lao Government forces captured almost 8,000 tons of Communist equipment, supplies, and weapons, including tanks, armored cars, artillery pieces, machine guns, and thousands of individual weapons, including about 4,000 tons of ammunition. The size and nature of these supply caches the Communists had emplaced on the plain by the summer of 1969 show clearly that many months ago the North Vietnamese were preparing for major offensive actions on Laotian territory against the Royal Lao Government.

During the final months of 1969 and January 1970, Hanoi sent over 13,000 additional troops into Laos and rebuilt their stocks and supply lines. They also introduced tanks and long-range artillery.

During January and February, Prime Minister Souvanna Phouma proposed to the other side that the Plain of Jars be neutralized. The Communists' response was to launch their current offensive, which has recaptured the Plain of Jars and is threatening to go beyond the furthest line of past Communist advances.

The Prime Minister is now once again trying to obtain consultations among all the parties to the Geneva accords, envisaged under article 4 when there is a violation of Lao sovereignty, independence, neutrality, or territorial integrity.

In this situation our purposes remain straightforward.

We are trying above all to save American and Allied lives in South Viet-Nam, which are threatened by the continual infiltration of North Vietnamese troops and supplies along the Ho Chi Minh Trail. Hanoi has infiltrated over 100,000 men through Laos since this administration took office, and over 500,000 altogether. Our airstrikes have destroyed weapons and supplies over the past 4 years which would have taken thousands of American lives.

We are also supporting the independence and neutrality of Laos as set forth in the 1962 Geneva agreements. Our assistance has always been at the request of the legitimate government of Prime Minister Souvanna Phouma, which the North Vietnamese helped establish; it is directly related to North Vietnamese violations of the agreements.

We continue to be hopeful of eventual progress in the negotiations in Paris. But serious doubts are raised as to Hanoi's intentions if it is simultaneously violating the Geneva agreements on Laos, which we reached with them largely on the basis of their own proposals. What we do in Laos has thus as its aim to bring about conditions for progress toward peace in the entire Indochinese Peninsula.

I turn now to the precise nature of our aid to Laos.

In response to press conference questions on September 26, December 8, and January 30, I have indicated:

—that the United States has no ground combat forces in Laos.

—that there were 50,000 North Vietnamese troops in Laos and that "more perhaps are coming."

—that at the request of the Royal Laotian Government, which was set up by the Geneva accords of 1962, we have provided logistical and other assistance to that Government for the purpose of helping it to prevent the Communist conquest of Laos.

—that we have used airpower for the purpose of interdicting the flow of North Vietnamese troops and supplies on that part of the Ho Chi Minh Trail which runs through Laos.

—that at the request of the Royal Laotian Government, we have flown reconnaissance missions in northern Laos in support of the Loatian Government's efforts to defend itself against North Vietnamese aggression and that we were engaged in "some other activities."

It would, of course, have posed no political problem for me to have disclosed in greater detail those military support activities which had been initiated by two previous administrations and which have been continued by this administration.

I have not considered it in the national interest to do so because of our concern that putting emphasis on American activities in Laos might hinder the efforts of Prime Minister Souvanna Phouma to bring about adherence to the Geneva agreements by the Communist signatories.

In recent days, however, there has been intense public speculation to the effect that the United States involvement in Laos has substantially increased, in violation of the Geneva accords; that American ground forces are engaged in combat in Laos; and that our air activity has had the effect of escalating the conflict.

Because these reports are grossly inaccurate, I have concluded that our national interest will be served by putting the subject into perspective through a precise description of our current activities in Laos.

These are the facts:

—There are no American ground combat troops in Laos.

—We have no plans for introducing ground combat forces into Laos.

—The total number of Americans directly employed by the U.S. Government in Laos is 616. In addition, there are 424 Americans employed on contract to the Government or to Government contractors. Of these 1,040 Americans, the total number, military and civilian, engaged in a military advisory or military training capacity numbers 320. Logistics personnel number 323.

—No American stationed in Laos has ever been killed in ground combat operations.

—U.S. personnel in Laos during the past year has not increased, while during the past few months North Viet-Nam has sent over 13,000 additional combat ground troops into Laos.

When requested by the Royal Laotian Government, we have continued to provide military assistance to regular and irregular Laotian forces in the form of equipment, training, and logistics. The levels of our assistance have risen in response to the growth of North Vietnamese combat activities.

—We have continued to conduct air operations. Our first priority for such operations is to interdict the continued flow of troops and supplies across Laotian territory on the Ho Chi Minh Trail. As Commander in Chief of our Armed Forces, I consider it my responsibility to use our airpower to interdict this flow of supplies and men into South Viet-Nam and thereby avoid a heavy toll of American and Allied lives.

—In addition to these air operations on the Ho Chi Minh Trail, we have continued to carry out reconnaissance flights in northern Laos and to fly combat support missions for Laotian forces when requested to do so by the Royal Laotian Government.

—In every instance our combat air operations have taken place only over those parts of Laos occupied and contested by North Vietnamese and other Communist forces. They have been flown only when requested by the Laotian Government. The level of our air operations has been increased only as the number of North Vietnamese in Laos and the level of their aggression has increased.

Our goal in Laos has been and continues to be to reduce American involvement and not to increase it, to bring peace in accordance with the 1962 accords and not to prolong the war.

That is the picture of our current aid to Laos. It is limited. It is requested. It is supportive and defensive. It continues the purposes and operations of two previous administrations. It has been necessary to protect American lives in Viet-Nam and to preserve a precarious but important balance in Laos.

III. The Future

Peace remains the highest priority of this administration. We will continue our search for it in Viet-Nam. I hope my appeal today to the Geneva conference co-Chairmen will help in Laos. Our policy for that torn country will continue to rest on some basic principles:

—We will cooperate fully with all diplomatic efforts to restore the 1962 Geneva agreements.

We will continue to support the legitimate government of Prime Minister Souvanna Phouma and his efforts to de-escalate the conflict and reach political understandings.

—Our air interdiction efforts are designed to protect American and Allied lives in Viet-Nam. Our support efforts have the one purpose of helping prevent the recognized Laotian government from being overwhelmed by larger Communist forces dominated by the North Vietnamese.

—We will continue to give the American people the fullest possible information on our involvement, consistent with national security.

I hope that a genuine quest for peace in Indochina can now begin. For Laos, this will require the efforts of the Geneva conference co-Chairmen and the signatory countries.

But most of all it will require realism and reasonableness from Hanoi. For it is the North Vietnamese, not we, who have escalated the fighting. Today there are 67,000 North Vietnamese troops in this small country. There are no American troops there. Hanoi is not threatened by Laos; it runs risks only when it moves its forces across borders.

We desire nothing more in Laos than to see a return to the Geneva agreements and the withdrawal of North Vietnamese troops, leaving the Lao people to settle their own differences in a peaceful manner.

In the search for peace we stand ready to cooperate in every way with the other countries involved. That search prompted my letters today to the British Prime Minister and the Soviet Premier. That search will continue to guide our policy.

THE UNITED STATES

AND CAMBODIA

THE UNITED STATES AND CAMBODIA

Commentary

The major issues in United States-Cambodian relations are closely associated with the American presence in Vietnam. Prince Norodom Sihanouk, who led the tiny nation from independence until March 18, 1970, attempted a delicate balancing act between the major powers involved in Southeast Asia. Wary of the Chinese and fearful of engendering their wrath, he generally maintained a friendly pose toward that country, and similarly, in part to underscore his position, in 1963 rejected American economic assistance and in 1965 broke off diplomatic relations with the United States. When South Vietnamese and American troops violated the sanctity of Cambodian borders, as they did on numerous occasions, the Cambodian leader protested vigorously. At the same time, Viet Cong and North Vietnamese troops used Cambodian soil as a sanctuary, thus eliciting protest from the United States and South Vietnam. Although this problem seemed insoluble in view of the circumstances, events of 1969 brought a less acrimonious climate and finally in July, 1969 resumption of formal Cambodian-American relations.

On March 18, 1970, while Sihanouk was out of the country on a mission to Moscow and Peking—ostensibly to negotiate the reduction of North Vietnamese activity in his nation—the Cambodian National Assembly at the bidding of General Lon Nol, Commander in Chief of the Army, Sisowath Sirik Matak, Deputy Prime Minister, and Acting Chief of State Chen Heng, deposed him. Headed by Lon Nol as Prime Minister, the new government apparently wanted a neutrality sympathetic to the United States and South Vietnam rather than the pro-Communist variety followed by Sihanouk. It also demanded that North Vietnamese and Viet Cong troops leave Cambodian soil. The United States quickly extended diplomatic recognition to the new regime. Shortly thereafter American and South Vietnamese troops invaded Cambodia to end the Viet Cong sanctuary in that country.

INDEPENDENCE OF CAMBODIA

A. Geneva Agreement on the Cessation of Hostilities in Cambodia*

[Extract]

July 20, 1954

CHAPTER I
PRINCIPLES AND CONDITIONS GOVERNING EXECUTION OF THE CEASE-FIRE

Article I

As from twenty-third July 1954 at 1800 hours (Peking mean time) complete cessation of all hostilities throughout Cambodia shall be ordered and enforced by the Commanders of the Armed Forces of the two parties for all troops and personnel of the land, naval and air forces under their control.

Articles 2-3

[Make provisions similar to those of Articles 2, 3 and 5 of the agreement on Laos: August 7 being the date of the cease-fire in Cambodia.]

CHAPTER II
PROCEDURE FOR THE WITHDRAWAL OF THE FOREIGN ARMED FORCES AND FOREIGN MILITARY PERSONNEL FROM THE TERRITORY OF CAMBODIA

Article 4

1. The withdrawal outside the territory of Cambodia shall apply to:

   (a) the armed forces and military combatant personnel of the French Union;
   (b) the combatant formations of all types which have entered the territory of Cambodia from other countries or regions of the peninsula;
   (c) all the foreign elements (or Cambodians not natives of Cambodia) in the military formations of any kind or holding supervisory functions in all political or military, administrative, economic, financial or social bodies, having worked in liaison with the Vietnam military units.

[The remaining provisions of this article are similar to those of Chapter II of the agreement on Laos.]

Documents on American Foreign Relations, 1954, pp. 307-10.

CHAPTER III

OTHER QUESTIONS

Article 5

A. The Khmer Armed Forces, Natives of Cambodia

The two parties shall undertake that within thirty days after the cease-fire order has been proclaimed, the Khmer Resistance Forces shall be demobilised on the spot; simultaneously, the troops of the Royal Khmer Army shall abstain from taking any hostile action against the Khmer Resistance Forces.

Article 6

The situation of these nationals shall be decided in the light of the Declaration made by the Delegation of Cambodia at the Geneva Conference, reading as follows:

> The Royal Government of Cambodia,
> In the desire to ensure harmony and agreement among the peoples of the Kingdom,
> Declares itself resolved to take the necessary measures to integrate all citizens, without discrimination, into the national community and to guarantee them the enjoyment of the rights and freedoms for which the Constitution of the Kingdom provides;
> Affirms that all Cambodian citizens may freely participate as electors or candidates in general elections by secret ballot.

No reprisals shall be taken against the said nationals or their families, each national being entitled to the enjoyment, without any discrimination as compared with other nationals, of all constitutional guarantees concerning the protection of person and property and democratic freedoms.

Applicants therefore may be accepted for service in the Regular Army or local police formations if they satisfy the conditions required for current recruitment of the Army and Police Corps.

The same procedure shall apply to those persons who have returned to civilian life and who may apply for civilian employment on the same terms as other nationals.

Article 7

B. Ban on the Introduction of Fresh Troops, Military Personnel, Armaments and Munitions. Military Bases

In accordance with the Declaration made by the Delegation of Cambodia at 2400 hours on 20 July 1954 at the Geneva Conference of Foreign Ministers:

> The Royal Government of Cambodia will not join in any agreement with other States, if this agreement carries for Cambodia the obligation to enter into a military

alliance not in conformity with the principles of the Charter of the United Nations, or, as long as its security is not threatened, the obligation to establish bases on Cambodian territory for the military forces of foreign powers.

During the period which will elapse between the date of the cessation of hostilities in Vietnam and that of the final settlement of political problems in this country, the Royal Government of Cambodia will not solicit foreign aid in war material, personnel or instructors except for the purpose of the effective defense of the territory.

Articles 8-9

C. Civilian Internees and Prisoners of War—Burial
[Make provisions similar to those in Articles 21 and 23 of the agreement on Vietnam and Articles 16 and 18 of that on Laos.]

CHAPTER IV
JOINT COMMISSION AND INTERNATIONAL COMMISSION
FOR SUPERVISION AND CONTROL IN CAMBODIA

Articles 10-25

[Make provisions similar to those in Chapter VI of the agreement on Vietnam.]

CHAPTER V
IMPLEMENTATION

Articles 26-32

[Provide for punishment of violations, exchange of dead, burial, cooperation with the Mixed and International Commissions, composition and payment of these commissions.]

Article 33

All the provisions of the present Agreement shall enter into force at 0001 hours (Geneva time) on 23 July 1954.

Done at Geneva on 20 July 1954.

For the Commander-in-Chief of the
Units of the Khmer Resistance Forces and
for the Commander-in-Chief of the
Vietnamese Military Units: Ta-Quang-Buu,
Vice-Minister of National Defence of the
Democratic Republic of Vietnam
For the Commander-in-Chief of the Khmer National
Armed Forces: General Nhiek Tioulong

B. Letter from Secretary Dulles to Cambodian Foreign Minister Nong Kimny on United States Policy Toward Cambodia*

[Extract]

April 19, 1956

Dear Mr. Foreign Minister: I am disturbed to learn that recent statements from various quarters have given increasing publicity to allegations that the United States has been attempting to coerce Cambodia into the SEATO alliance under the penalty of withholding economic aid, and that the United States has obliged the independent and friendly nations of Viet-Nam and Thailand to impose measures of economic warfare upon Cambodia for the same alleged end.

I regret that these allegations have been made since they are utterly false and could harm the friendly relations existing between our two countries.

The American Ambassador on April 2 officially advised Their Majesties the King and Queen of Cambodia that the United States at no time had made any official public observation on Cambodian foreign policy. United States policy in Cambodia is based on a simple precept: That is, the United States through its military and economic aid programs seeks to assist the Cambodian Government in its endeavor to maintain the sovereign independence of the Kingdom. This assistance is extended only at the wish of the Royal Cambodian Government, which officially requested military aid on May 20, 1954 and military and economic aid on September 1, 1954.

Although the United States believes that the free nations can most effectively meet the threat of Communist aggression through collective defense, nevertheless United States policy recognizes that certain countries, though determined to defend themselves against aggression or subversion of their independence, have preferred not to join regional security arrangements. That choice we respect. The United States does not seek ties of mutual defense with any country unless that country believes that this application of the principle of collective security will better assure its independence.

Recognition of the position of these countries in no way prevents the maintenance of close and cordial relations with them. In giving economic and military assistance to friendly countries to improve their capacity to defend themselves against aggression or subversion, the United States is guided primarily by consideration of its own national interests. It considers it to be in its national interest to help in the economic and social advancement of all free nations.

I trust that this letter will dispose of the false allegations concerning our policy, which, I venture to repeat, aims only at assisting free nations to preserve their liberty and independence.

*   *   *

*Department of State Bulletin, April 30, 1956, p. 727.

VIOLATION OF NEUTRALITY

A. Letter from Prince Norodom Sihanouk, Cambodian Chief of State, to President Kennedy on Recognition and Guarantee of Neutrality and Territorial Integrity*

August 20, 1962

Mr. President: I have the honor to call Your Excellency's attention particularly to the very serious threat that has for years been hanging over my country, which has constantly been subjected to threats, plots, sabotage, blockades, and aggression by neighboring powers that are very much stronger militarily, concerning whose annexationist aims there is no longer any doubt. Territorial claims supported by the use of armed forces, the crossing of frontiers, flights over our territory, and its recent occupation by foreign troops cause me to fear that, in a short time, an insoluble situation will be created which could lead to an international conflict with unforeseeable consequences.

Cambodia can no longer endure this constant provocation and aggression, or the official or unofficial accusations made repeatedly by these same neighbors, to the effect that it is encouraging and promoting subversion in their countries; this is not and has never been true.

Sincerely desiring peace, but resolved to defend its honor and what remains of its national territory after numerous "amputations," Cambodia sees no other reasonable solution of this situation than to claim for itself the benefit of the international protection provisions that have been granted to Laos.

I take the liberty of reminding you that it is thanks to Cambodian initiative that Laos has been spared from greater sacrifices and that the western and socialist camps have not clashed.

Actually, my country has been making valuable contributions to the maintenance of peace and stability in Asia since 1954.

Today, before making decisions of prime importance in order to protect its existence, Cambodia requests of Your Excellency's Government and the other powers which met last month in Geneva the official recognition and guarantee of its neutrality and territorial integrity. It is ready to accept any appropriate control for that purpose.

The beneficial international accomplishments in Laos would not be lasting and the balance of forces in Southeast Asia would not long be maintained if Cambodia should in turn become a battle field, a prospect which appears to me to be inevitable if the powers concerned with the security of this region should fail to reach an agreement to neutralize it.

I venture to say to Your Excellency that my country is entitled to this consideration.

All foreign statesmen and observers of good faith have recognized that it formed a peaceful, closely united nation that abided by the United Nations Charter and met its international obligations; that practiced genuine neutrality;

*American Foreign Policy: Current Documents, 1962, pp. 1002-03.

and that was faithful to the principles of peaceful co-existence. They have also recognized that Cambodia succeeded in following this just and equitable policy through its own efforts, without aid from anyone and by surmounting innumerable difficulties.

I take the liberty of suggesting that Your Excellency be good enough to take an active interest in our fate and agree that an international conference on Cambodia be held as soon as possible in a large neutral capital or city of your choice (Geneva, New Delhi, Stockholm, etc.). . . .

B. Letter from President Kennedy to Prince Sihanouk on Cambodian Border Areas*

August 31, 1962

Your Royal Highness, it always gives me great pleasure to receive a personal communication from Your Royal Highness and I only regret that the reason for your letter of August 20 was to express your worry over the security of Cambodia. For, as you know, the fundamental and abiding objective of the United States is that each country, large and small, live in peace and independence so that its people may prosper, enjoy the fruits of its own endeavors, and pursue a course of international relations of its own choosing. This applies especially to countries with which we have such close friendly relations as we have with Cambodia.

In this spirit and in view of the present preoccupations of Your Royal Highness, I assure you that the United States respects the neutrality, territorial integrity and independence of Cambodia. I am sure you will recognize that this attitude is the foundation of United States relations with your Government and people. We recognize and respect the high aims you have set for Cambodia, and we wholeheartedly desire to further them. Our economic cooperation has aimed at supplementing Cambodia's own intensive efforts at economic and social progress, while our military assistance has been designed to help your people maintain the security of their beloved country.

The contribution of Cambodia and that of Your Royal Highness in person to peace in the world is known to all. I have in mind particularly your sponsorship of the recent conference on the Lao question. If for no other reason, therefore, Cambodia has the right to live in peace and tranquillity. The United States stands ready to do whatever it can to assure this, not only for Cambodia, but for its neighbors in Southeast Asia, all friends of the United States.

There are various methods by which nations achieve a state of peaceful harmony with each other. One, which you mentioned in your letter, is the idea of an international conference to recognize the neutrality and territorial integrity of Cambodia. Another, which you suggested to Ambassador Philip D. Sprouse in your conversation with him on August 28, is the issuance of "official letters" by interested governments declaring their respect for Cambodia's independence, neutrality and territorial integrity. This second method appears to me to be

---

Ibid., pp. 1003-04.

a wise suggestion, and a more expeditious and effective means of achieving the objectives cited in your letter. I should be glad to write such a formal letter for the United States. It is my hope that other governments interested in peace and stability in the area would likewise affirm these principles in an appropriate manner. Noting that your letter expresses willingness to accept whatever controls are necessary to insure Cambodia's aims as set forth therein, I would be interested in your ideas regarding the instrumentality for bringing the desired stability to Cambodia's border areas.

Ambassador Sprouse has also reported to me the statement that Your Royal Highness does not intend to be at New York for the next regular session of the United Nations General Assembly. This I regret, for I took great pleasure in our conversation during your visit last year. However, I hope, as I mentioned then, that you may find it possible to make a more leisurely visit to our country. My trusted military adviser, General Maxwell Taylor, whom I have chosen to be Chairman of our Joint Chiefs of Staff, will soon be visiting your country, and I have asked him to discuss with Your Royal Highness, as well as with other leaders in the area, the general question of peace in Southeast Asia.

Please accept the assurance of my highest consideration and personal esteem.

C. Note from Cambodia to the United States on Discontinuing American Aid*

[Extract]

November 20, 1963

          *   *   *

As the Government of the United States of America is aware, Prince Norodom Sihanouk, Chief of State, in full agreement with the Royal Government and the Cambodian people, solemnly declared on 5 November 1963 that Cambodia would find itself obliged to renounce the aid accorded it by [the] United States if the radio-broadcasting station of the rebels known as "Khmer Serei," installed in South Viet-Nam, did not end its broadcasts before 31 December 1963. In doing this the chief of the Cambodian state emphasized that [the] United States inevitably bore a considerable share of responsibility in the acts of "pro-Western" subversion directed from a neighboring country which they closely controlled.

The public revelations of an emissary of these "Khmer Serei" who has come from South Viet-Nam, have now provided proof that American agents were in fact the direct suppliers of arms, propaganda material, and money to that movement, which was fabricated to destroy Cambodia's national regime, its independence and its neutrality. From now on the Cambodian people cannot understand how official American declarations of respect for our sovereignty and

* *American Foreign Policy: Current Documents, 1963*, pp. 741-42.

our national policy can find expression in such flagrant American participation in a plot against our people and our liberties.

In response to popular wish and after having studied the new situation created by these very grave revelation[s], the Royal Government considers that the most elementary dignity prevents Cambodia from accepting the continuation of any form of American aid, however small. Consequently, the Royal Government has the honor to inform the American Government that Cambodia asks the cessation of aid accorded her by the United States in the military, economic, technical and cultural fields, and the initiation without delay of bilateral conversations on the liquidation of current programs in accordance with the existing agreements.

The Royal Government avails itself of this opportunity to express to the Government of the United States the profound gratitude of the Cambodian people towards the American people, for whom the Cambodian people retains all its friendships. Its generous aid in the course of recent years has contributed effectively to the modernization of our country. We cannot forget that. The Royal Government and the Cambodian people keenly hope that the great people of the United States, whose democratic sentiments they recognize, will understand that a soverign state such as ours cannot tolerate in silence the intrigues of American officials and agents working relentlessly to undermine its independence.

It is because our friendship for the American people remains intact that the Royal Government will maintain its diplomatic relations with the Government of the United States in the hope that a day will come when that friendship can bloom again in a climate of confidence and good faith.

*   *   *

D. State Department Statement Rejecting Allegations of United States Plotting Against Cambodia*

November 21, 1963

The American Ambassador to Cambodia, Philip D. Sprouse, has conveyed the United States reply to the Cambodian note of yesterday. In our reply we categorically reject the allegation that the United States is involved in any plotting against Cambodia. We state that officials of the American Embassy are prepared to begin immediately bilateral discussions of the termination of current aid programs as provided under the terms of the existing agreements. We note with satisfaction the expression of gratitude for American aid received in the past. We also welcome, in view of the long-standing friendship between the American and Cambodian peoples, the desire of the Royal Government of Cambodia to maintain diplomatic relations and state our intention to reciprocate.

*Ibid., p. 742.

E. Statement by Adlai E. Stevenson, U.S. Ambassador to the U.N., on United States and South Vietnamese Relations with Cambodia*

[Extract]

May 21, 1964

*   *   *

The facts about the incidents at issue are relatively simple and clear.

The Government of the Republic of Viet-Nam already has confirmed that, in the heat of battle, forces of the Republic of Viet-Nam did, in fact, mistakenly cross an ill-marked frontier between their country and Cambodia in pursuit of armed terrorists on May 7 and May 8, and on earlier occasions. That has been repeated and acknowledged here again today by the representative of Viet-Nam.

The Government of Viet-Nam has expressed its regrets that these incidents occurred with some tragic consequences. It has endeavored to initiate bilateral discussions with the Cambodian Government to remove the causes of these incidents.

But these incidents can only be assessed intelligently in the light of the surrounding facts: namely, the armed conspiracy which seeks to destroy not only the Government of Viet-Nam but the very society of Viet-Nam itself.

Mr. President, it is the people of the Republic of Viet-Nam who are the major victims of armed aggression. It is they who are fighting for their independence against violence directed from outside their borders. It is they who suffer day and night from the terror of the so-called Viet Cong. The prime targets of the Viet Cong for kidnaping, for torture, and for murder have been local officials, schoolteachers, medical workers, priests, agricultural specialists, and any others whose position, profession, or other talents qualified them for service to the people of Viet-Nam—plus, of course, the relatives and children of citizens loyal to their Government.

The chosen military objectives of the Viet Cong—for gunfire or arson or pillage—have been hospitals, schoolhouses, agricultural stations, and various improvement projects by which the Government of Viet-Nam for many years has been raising the living standards of the people. The Government and people of Viet-Nam have been struggling for survival, struggling for years for survival in a war which has been as wicked, as wanton, and as dirty as any waged against an innocent and peaceful people in the whole cruel history of warfare. So there is something ironic in the fact that the victims of this incessant terror are the accused before this Council and are defending themselves in daylight while terrorists perform their dark and dirty work by night throughout their land.

*   *   *

Department of State Bulletin, June 8, 1964, pp. 907-13.

The Cambodia—Viet-Nam Frontier

Now, Mr. President, if we can return to the more limited issue before this Council today: the security of the frontier between Cambodia and the Republic of Viet-Nam. My Government is in complete sympathy with the concern of the Government of Cambodia for the sanctity of its borders and the security of its people. Indeed, we have been guided for nearly a decade, in this respect, by the words of the final declaration of the Geneva conference of July 21, 1954:

> In their relations with Cambodia, Laos and Viet-Nam, each member of the Geneva Conference undertakes to respect the sovereignty, the independence, the unity, and the territorial integrity of the above-mentioned states, and to refrain from any interference in their internal affairs.

With respect to the allegations now made against my country, I shall do no more than reiterate what Ambassador [Charles W.] Yost, the United States delegate, said to this Council on Tuesday morning: The United States has expressed regret officially for the tragic results of the border incidents in which an American adviser was present; our careful investigations so far have failed to produce evidence that any Americans were present in the inadvertent crossing of the Cambodian frontier on May 7 and May 8; and there is, of course, no question whatever of either aggression or aggressive intent against Cambodia on the part of my country.

Let me emphasize, Mr. President, that my Government has the greatest regard for Cambodia and its people and its Chief of State, Prince Norodom Sihanouk, whom I have the privilege of knowing. We believe he has done a great deal for his people and for the independence of his country. We have demonstrated our regard for his effort on behalf of his people in very practical ways over the past decade. We have no doubt that he wants to assure conditions in which his people can live in peace and security. My Government associates itself explicitly with this aim. If the people of Cambodia wish to live in peace and security and independence—and free from external alinement if they so choose—then we want for them precisely what they want for themselves. We have no quarrel whatsoever with the desire of Cambodia to go its own way.

The difficulty, Mr. President, has been that Cambodia has not been in a position to carry out, with its own unaided strength, its own desire to live in peace and tranquillity. Others in the area have not been prepared to leave the people of Cambodia free to pursue their own ends independently and peacefully. The recent difficulties along the frontier which we have been discussing here in the Council are only superficially and accidentally related to the Republic of Viet-Nam. They are deeply and directly related to the fact that the leaders and armed forces of North Viet-Nam, supported by Communist China, have abused the right of Cambodia to live in peace by using Cambodian territory as a passageway, a source of supply, and a sanctuary from counterattack by the forces of South Viet-Nam, which is trying to maintain its right to live in peace and go its own way, too. Obviously Cambodia cannot be secure, her territorial integrity cannot be assured, her independence cannot be certain, as long as outsiders direct massive violence within the frontiers of her neighboring states. This is the real reason for troubles on the Cambodian border; this is the real reason we are here today.

Now it is suggested that the way to restore security on the Cambodian-Vietnamese border is to reconvene the Geneva conference which 10 years ago reached the solemn agreement which I just read to you.

Mr. President, we can surely do better than that. There is no need for another such conference. A Geneva conference on Cambodia could not be expected to produce an agreement any more effective than the agreements we already have. This Council is seized with a specific issue. The Cambodians have brought a specific complaint to this table. Let us deal with it. There is no need to look elsewhere.

We can make, here and now, a constructive decision to help meet the problem that has been laid before us by the Government of Cambodia—to help keep order on her frontier with Viet-Nam and thus to help eliminate at least one of the sources of tension and violence which afflict the area as a whole.

Let me say, Mr. President, that my Government endorses the statement made by the distinguished representative of Cambodia [Voeunsai Sonn] to the Council on Tuesday when he pointed out that states which are not members of the United Nations are not thereby relieved of responsibility for conducting their affairs in line with the principles of the charter of this organization. We could not agree more fully. Yet the regimes of Peiping and Hanoi, which are not members of this organization, are employing or supporting the use of force against their neighbors. This is why the borders of Cambodia have seen violence. And this is why we are here today. And that is why the United Nations has a duty to do what it can do to maintain order along the frontier between Cambodia and Viet-Nam—to help uphold the principles of the charter in Southeast Asia.

As for the exact action which this Council might take, Mr. President, my Government is prepared to consider several possibilities. We are prepared to discuss any practical and constructive steps to meet the problem before us.

One cannot blame the Vietnamese for concluding that the International Control Commission cannot do an effective job of maintaining frontier security. The "troika" principle of the International Control Commission, which is to say the requirement under article 42 of the Geneva agreement on Viet-Nam that decisions dealing with questions concerning violations which might lead to resumption of hostilities can be taken only by unanimous agreement, has contributed to the frustration of the ICC.

The fact that the situation in South Viet-Nam has reached the crisis stage is itself dramatic testimony of the frustration to which the International Control Commission has been reduced. With the exception of the special report on June 2, 1962 to which I referred, condemning Communist violations of the Geneva accords, the Commission has taken no action with respect to the Communist campaign of aggression and guerrilla warfare against South Viet-Nam.

The representative of Cambodia has suggested that a commission of inquiry investigate whether the Viet Cong has used Cambodian territory. We have no fundamental objection to a committee of inquiry. But we do not believe it addresses itself to the basic problem that exists along the Viet-Nam-Cambodian border. More is needed in order to assure that problems do not continue to arise.

Several practical steps for restoring stability to the frontier have been suggested, and I shall make brief and preliminary general remarks about them. I should like to reiterate what Ambassador Yost said, that we have never rejected any proposal for inspection of Cambodian territory.

One suggestion is that the Council request the two parties directly concerned to establish a substantial military force on a bilateral basis to observe and patrol the frontier and to report to the Secretary-General.

Another suggestion is that such a bilateral force be augmented by the addition of United Nations observers and possibly be placed under United Nations command to provide an impartial third-party element representing the world community. We also could see much merit in this idea.

A third suggestion is to make it an all-United Nations force. This might also be effective. It would involve somewhat larger U.N. expenditures than the other alternatives. But if this method should prove desirable to the members of the Council, the United States will be prepared to contribute.

We would suggest, Mr. President, that whether one of these or some other practical solution is agreed [upon], it would be useful to ask the Secretary-General of the United Nations to offer assistance to Cambodia and the Republic of Viet-Nam in clearly marking the frontiers between the two countries. One of the difficulties is that there are places where one does not know whether he stands on one side of the frontier or the other. Certainly it would help reduce the possibility of further incidents if this uncertainty were to be removed.

In conclusion, Mr. President, let me repeat that I am prepared to discuss the policy and the performance of my Government throughout Southeast Asia. But the issue before us is the security of the Cambodian-Viet-Nam border. I have expressed my Government's views on that subject. I hope other members of the Council also will express their views on that subject and that the Council, which is the primary world agency for peace and security, can quickly take effective steps to remedy a situation which could threaten peace and security.

F. Letter from Ambassador Stevenson to Sivert A. Nielsen, President of U.N. Security Council, Denying Cambodian Charges of Spreading Poisonous Chemicals in Cambodia*

[Extract]

August 14, 1964

I have the honour to refer to the letter to you from the Deputy United States Permanent Representative of 3 August 1964, which contained the United States Government's categorical rejection of the charges listed by the Foreign Minister of the Royal Government of Cambodia in his telegram of 28 July 1964. As you know, the United States has been charged by the Royal Government of

---

* *American Foreign Policy: Current Documents, 1964,* pp. 863-64.

Cambodia with spreading poisonous chemicals by aircraft on the Cambodian province of Ratanakiri, reportedly resulting in a loss of life.

My Government wishes to point out that the Royal Government of Cambodia, in its broadcasts and official press statements, continues to air these charges in spite of the letters sent to the President of the Security Council by my Government and by the Government of the Republic of Viet-Nam. These letters clearly stated that no Republic of Viet-Nam or American aircraft had conducted chemical operations of any character whatever, whether adjacent to the Cambodian territory indicated, or over Cambodian territory, on any of the dates or at any time in the period cited by the Royal Government of Cambodia. My Government has also instructed me to state that similar charges recently made by representatives of the Royal Cambodian Government concerning the spreading of poisonous chemicals in the Cambodian province of Svay Rieng are equally unsubstantiated and untrue.

In view of the serious nature of these allegations and their repetition following categorical denials from my Government and from the Government of the Republic of Viet-Nam, my Government has instructed me to reaffirm the statement made in its letter of 3 August that the United States Government would welcome an impartial international investigation of the Cambodian charges.

G. Statement by Secretary Rusk on the Neutrality and Territorial Integrity of Cambodia*

April 25, 1965

It has been proposed that an international conference composed of the government of the countries which took part in the Geneva conference of 1965 be called to consider the question of the neutrality and territorial integrity of Cambodia.

After reviewing this proposal with the President last week, and at his direction, we have informed a number of interested governments that if such a conference is called we will gladly participate. The President would appoint Ambassador Averell Harriman as our representative to the discussions.

Cambodia desires independence and neutrality. Here, as elsewhere in Asia, the United States wholeheartedly supports the right of each nation to shape its own course. To support this right for Cambodia is fully consistent with the purpose of the United States to support the right of every nation in Southeast Asia to lead a free and independent existence.

H. Letter from Secretary Rusk to Cambodian Foreign Minister Koun Wick Severing Diplomatic Relations with Cambodia*

May 6, 1965

Excellency: I have the honor to acknowledge receipt of Your Excellency's

*American Foreign Policy: Current Documents, 1965, p. 716.
*Ibid., pp. 716-17.

message of May 4 in which you explain the Cambodian position on the maintenance of consular relations. I wish, on my side, to clarify the position of the United States.

The United States not only accepts but supports the safety, independence, neutrality and prosperity of Cambodia and of the Cambodian people. We have demonstrated that through the postwar period in many ways, including through substantial resources placed at the disposal of the Royal Cambodian Government. We have further, in response to the proposal of your government, indicated our readiness to attend a conference of the governments attending the 1954 Geneva Conference for the purpose of providing Cambodia further international assurances on these matters. Whether or not such a conference takes place, the United States will continue to respect the neutrality of Cambodia. We trust that the Royal Cambodian Government for its part accepts the responsibilities incumbent on this neutral status.

I know of no issues affecting Cambodia which cannot be resolved through the normal processes of diplomacy, whether bilaterally or through such a conference. We take note of the fact that the Royal Cambodian Government has not maintained diplomatic representation in Washington since April 1964 and that it has now moved to break relations, a step requiring the withdrawal of the American Embassy from Phnom Penh. The Royal Government of Cambodia must therefore accept the consequences of the disappearance of the normal bilateral diplomatic machinery through which states of the international community attempt to resolve their differences and increase the range of common interest and cooperation.

It seems quite clear that the maintenance of consular relations, subject to the unilateral conditions imposed by the Royal Government of Cambodia, is not consistent with general international practice. Nor would such an attitude on the part of the Royal Government of Cambodia serve such activities as tourism and trade, for the benefit of which the Cambodian Government has suggested that consular relations be maintained.

The United States Government, for its part, desires normal relations with the Royal Government of Cambodia, but it is manifest that such relations are not possible in the absence of mutuality and reciprocity. Since reciprocity unfortunately is not present, we have no alternative but to accept the conclusions of the Royal Cambodian Government and to withdraw all official representation from your country.

Let me conclude, Excellency, by saying that the Government of the United States is prepared at any time to consider with the Royal Cambodian Government the restoration of relations on a mutually acceptable basis.

Please accept, Excellency, assurances of my high consideration.

I. Letter From Ambassador Goldberg to Secretary-General U Thant on the United States Desire to See Cambodia "Pursue Its Chosen Path in Peace"*

January 3, 1966

Dear Mr. Secretary General: The Permanent Representative of Cambodia to the United Nations recently requested the circulation of three statements from

* *American Foreign Policy: Current Documents, 1966*, p. 644.

his government dated December 25, 26, and 28 concerning the situation along the frontier between Cambodia and the Republic of Viet-Nam.

I should like to recall to the members of the Security Council that on May 21, 1964, during the Council's consideration of the Cambodian Government's complaint, Ambassador Adlai Stevenson summarized my Government's policy toward Cambodia in these words;

> "If the people of Cambodia wish to live in peace and security and independence— and free from external alinement if they so choose—then we want for them precisely what they want for themselves. We have no quarrel whatsoever with the desire of Cambodia to go its own way in peace and security."

Ambassador Stevenson added that Cambodia cannot be secure so long as the North Vietnamese Government continues to direct massive violence within the frontiers of Cambodia's neighbor, South Viet-Nam. The United States, he said, was prepared to discuss any practical and constructive steps to meet the problem of maintaining peace and order along the frontier between Cambodia and South Viet-Nam.

My Government's policy toward Cambodia and its people remains today as set forth by Mr. Stevenson in 1964. My Government remains ready to consider any constructive proposals to enable Cambodia to pursue its chosen path in peace.

In this connection, the United States Government has noted with interest the proposal made by the Cambodian Chief of State that the International Control Commission assume an increased supervisory role in Cambodia. My Government sincerely hopes that this initiative on the part of Prince Norodom Sihanouk will be given close and careful attention by all countries concerned with peace and security in Southeast Asia and will lead to the development of effective measures to prevent any possible abuse of Cambodian territory.

I respectfully request that this letter be circulated to all members as a Security Council document.

J. United States Note to Cambodia on Violation of Territory*

December 4, 1967

The United States has regretted the impairment of its relations with Cambodia. Despite differences, however, the United States continues to respect the neutrality, sovereignty, independence and territorial integrity of Cambodia.

A particularly distressing problem dividing the United States and Cambodia arises out of incidents in the Cambodia-South Viet-Nam border area. The United States wishes to emphasize that American forces operating in South Viet-Nam are engaged in conflict with Viet Cong-North Vietnamese forces committing aggression against South Viet-Nam. The American forces have no hostile intentions toward Cambodia or Cambodian territory. The root cause of incidents affecting Cambodian territory is the Viet Cong and North Vietnamese presence in the frontier region, and their use of Cambodian territory in violation of the neutrality of Cambodia.

*Department of State Bulletin, Jan. 22, 1968, p. 124.

The United States has offered to cooperate in seeking a solution to this problem. Following the suggestion of His Royal Highness Prince Sihanouk for more effective action by the International Control Commission, made most notably in December of 1965, the United States has consistently supported such action and has indicated its willingness to consider sympathetically any request for specific assistance to this end.

At the time, the Royal Cambodian Government suggested that the International Control Commission might undertake continuing and effective review of activities in the Port of Sihanoukville, and it was further suggested that the Commission might be expanded so that it could more effectively monitor the border areas between Cambodia and South Viet-Nam.

In addition, the United States has supported an International Conference on Cambodia, and it has also suggested direct, informal talks with Cambodian officials in order to seek an alternative remedy.

The United States is deeply concerned over the critical issue of Viet Cong-North Vietnamese use of Cambodian territory and it wishes to emphasize once more its willingness to cooperate on any reasonable method of controlling this problem.

The Royal Cambodian Government may not be aware of the extent of Viet Cong-North Vietnamese use of its territory, and the United States therefore wishes to provide it with the attached summary[1] of some of the evidence available. The documents and interrogations from which this evidence has been compiled are fully available if desired. Additional evidence received in more recent periods is being assessed, and may be presented to the Royal Cambodian Government at a later time.

The United States believes that the Royal Cambodian Government will share its concern over Viet Cong-North Vietnamese use of neutral Cambodian territory. It is in the spirit of assisting the Royal Cambodian Government in its efforts to prevent violations of its neutral territory that this evidence is presented.

K. White House Announcement on the Appointment of Ambassador Chester Bowles to Cambodia*

January 4, 1968

The United States Government is sending a representative to Cambodia in response to the indication given by His Highness Prince Norodom Sihanouk, Chief of State of Cambodia, that he would agree to receive an emissary of President Johnson. Ambassador Chester Bowles [U.S. Ambassador to India] has been selected for this mission, and the Governments of Cambodia and the United States are in agreement that Mr. Bowles should arrive in Phnom Penh within the next few days.

---

[1] The summary was not made public.
* *Ibid.*, p. 119.

L. Joint Communiqué on Talks Between Ambassador Bowles and Cambodian Officials*

January 12, 1968

The Honorable Chester Bowles, Special Representative of the President of the United States, accompanied by other officials of the United States Government, visited Phnom Penh from January 5 to January 12, 1968 to discuss matters of mutual interest with the Royal Cambodian Government.

During his visit Ambassador Bowles was received by His Royal Highness Prince Norodom Sihanouk, the Chief of State of Cambodia, and participated in several working meetings with His Excellency M. Son Sann, Prime Minister, assisted by high officials of the Royal Cambodian Government.

During the discussions, Ambassador Bowles renewed American assurance of respect for Cambodian soverignty, neutrality and territorial integrity. He expressed the hope that the effective functioning of the International Control Commission would avert violations of Cambodia's territory and neutrality by forces operating in Vietnam. Moreover, he declared that the Government of the United States of America is prepared to provide material assistance to the International Control Commission to enable it to increase its ability to perform its mission.

His Royal Highness Prince Sihanouk clearly expressed his Government's desire to keep the war in Vietnam away from his borders. He stressed Cambodia's desire that its territory and its neutrality be respected by all countries, including the belligerents in Vietnam. The Royal Government is determined to prevent all violation of the present borders of Cambodia. For this reason, the Royal Government is exerting every effort to have the present frontiers of the Kingdom recognized and respected.

Ambassador Bowles, convinced of Cambodia's good faith, emphasized that the United States of America has no desire or intention to violate Cambodian territory. He assured the Royal Cambodian Government that the United States will do everything possible to avoid acts of aggression against Cambodia, as well as incidents and accidents which may cause losses and damage to the inhabitants of Cambodia.

His Royal Highness Prince Norodom Sihanouk recalled that the Royal Government has since 1961 proposed the strengthening of the International Control Commission by the provision of additional means, by the creation of mobile teams, and by the establishment of fixed posts at various points in the country, and that this proposal still remains valid. The Royal Government is prepared to confirm anew to the International Control Commission that it still favors the strengthening of that organization so that it may be able, within the framework of its competence as defined by the Geneva Agreements of 1954, to investigate, confirm, and report all incidents as well as all foreign infiltrations on Cambodian territory.

In the course of these conversations, there was also a frank ·exchange of views on the general situation in Southeast Asia and on other subjects of mutual interest.

*Ibid., Jan. 29, 1968, pp. 133-34.

The working sessions took place in an atmosphere of reciprocal respect, comprehension, and good faith. The two sides expressed their satisfaction as well as their willingness to participate in similar meetings in the future.

At the end of his visit, Ambassador Bowles expressed for himself and the members of the American delegation the deepest gratitude for the cordial reception and warm hospitality accorded by His Royal Highness Prince Norodom Sihanouk of Cambodia and the Royal Government.

M. Statement by Secretary of State William Rogers on the Resumption of Diplomatic Relations Between the United States and Cambodia*

[Extract]

July 2, 1969

Ladies and gentlemen, I have a couple of brief announcements to make.

First, I am pleased to announce that the United States Government and the Royal Cambodian Government have agreed to the immediate resumption of diplomatic relations. I believe that the normalization of our diplomatic relations with the Kingdom of Cambodia is a positive step looking toward peace in Southeast Asia. It symbolized our overall policy in that area of favoring the independence and territorial integrity of all countries in Southeast Asia.

I will shortly be receiving Mr. Thay Sok, who has been designated by the Royal Cambodian Government as its Chargé d'Affaires in Washington. We expect very soon to designate an American Chargé d'Affaires in Phnom Penh. Pending his arrival and reception by the Cambodian Government, the Australian Embassy will continue to represent the United States interests in Cambodia.

*   *   *

*Ibid., July 21, 1969, pp. 41-49.

INVASION OF CAMBODIAN TERRITORY

A. Initial United States Response to the Cambodian Coup*

[Extract]

March 19, 1970

. . . The State Department spokesman, Carl Bartch, told newsmen: "Our position is that the question of recognition does not arise."

In response to questions, Mr. Bartch said that United States Recognition of Cambodia continued "for constitutional reasons." This meant that the new Government headed by Acting Chief of State Cheng Heng and Premier Lon Nol is seen by the United States to be the legal successor to that of the deposed Prince Norodom Sihanouk.

*   *   *

Secretary of Defense Melvin R. Laird was one of the few officials here who gave a public judgment on the stance of the new Cambodian regime. Mr. Laird, in an impromptu news conference at the Pentagon, said:

"I would think that whichever government finally comes out of this present turmoil that's taking place, there will be a likelihood that they will be somewhat tougher as far as the North Vietnamese influence in Cambodia."

"I'm sure that there will be some attempts in Cambodia to limit North Vietnamese activity," he continued. "There have been indications over the last few months that they are more and more concerned about this."

*   *   *

B. Press Conference Comments by President Nixon on the Cambodian Situation*

March 23, 1970

Q: Mr. President, will you entertain a question on Southeast Asia?

The President: Yes, I am not limiting this to the four subjects. I will take all of your questions.

Q: I am wondering how you feel about the recent developments in Cambodia, and how it relates to our activities in Vietnam.

The President: These developments in Cambodia are quite difficult to appraise. As you know from having been out there yourself on different occasions, the Cambodian political situation, to put it conservatively, is quite unpredictable and quite fluid.

The New York Times, Mar. 20, 1970.
Weekly Compilation of Presidential Documents, Mar. 23, 1970, p. 399.

However, we have, as you note, established relations on a temporary basis with the government which has been selected by the Parliament and will continue to deal with that government as long as it appears to be the government of the nation. I think any speculation with regard to which way this government is going to turn, what will happen to Prince Sihanouk when he returns, would both be premature and not helpful.

I will simply say that we respect Cambodia's neutrality. We would hope that North Vietnam would take that same position in respecting its neutrality. And we hope that whatever government eventually prevails there, that it would recognize that the United States interest is the protection of its neutrality.

C. Address by President Nixon on the American Military Strike Into Cambodia*

April 30, 1970

Good evening, my fellow Americans. Ten days ago, in my report to the Nation on Viet-Nam, I announced a decision to withdraw an additional 150,000 Americans from Viet-Nam over the next year. I said then that I was making that decision despite our concern over increased enemy activity in Laos, in Cambodia, and in South Viet-Nam.

At that time, I warned that if I concluded that increased enemy activity in any of these areas endangered the lives of Americans remaining in Viet-Nam, I would not hesitate to take strong and effective measures to deal with that situation.

Despite that warning, North Viet-Nam has increased its military aggression in all these areas, and particularly in Cambodia.

After full consultation with the National Security Council, Ambassador Bunker, General Abrams, and my other advisers, I have concluded that the actions of the enemy in the last 10 days clearly endanger the lives of Americans who are in Viet-Nam now and would constitute an unacceptable risk to those who will be there after withdrawal of another 150,000.

To protect our men who are in Viet-Nam and to guarantee the continued success of our withdrawal and Vietnamization programs, I have concluded that the time has come for action.

Tonight I shall describe the actions of the enemy, the actions I have ordered to deal with that situation, and the reasons for my decision.

Cambodia, a small country of 7 million people, has been a neutral nation since the Geneva agreement of 1954—an agreement, incidentally, which was signed by the Government of North Viet-Nam.

American policy since then has been to scrupulously respect the neutrality of the Cambodian people. We have maintained a skeleton diplomatic mission of fewer than 15 in Cambodia's capital, and that only since last August. For the previous 4 years, from 1965 to 1969, we did not have any diplomatic mission

*Department of State Bulletin, May 18, 1970, pp. 617-21.

whatever in Cambodia. And for the past 5 years, we have provided no military assistance whatever and no economic assistance to Cambodia.

North Viet-Nam, however, has not respected that neutrality.

For the past 5 years, as indicated on this map that you see here, North Viet-Nam has occupied military sanctuaries all along the Cambodian frontier with South Viet-Nam. Some of these extend up to 20 miles into Cambodia. The sanctuaries are in red, and as you note, they are on both sides of the border. They are used for hit-and-run attacks on American and South Vietnamese forces in South Viet-Nam.

These Communist-occupied territories contain major base camps, training sites, logistics facilities, weapons and ammunition factories, airstrips, and prisoner of war compounds.

For 5 years neither the United States nor South Viet-Nam has moved against these enemy sanctuaries, because we did not wish to violate the territory of a neutral nation. Even after the Vietnamese Communists began to expand these sanctuaries 4 weeks ago, we counseled patience to our South Vietnamese allies and imposed restraints on our own commanders.

In contrast to our policy, the enemy in the past 2 weeks has stepped up his guerrilla actions, and he is concentrating his main forces in these sanctuaries that you see on this map, where they are building up to launch massive attacks on our forces and those of South Viet-Nam.

North Viet-Nam in the last 2 weeks has stripped away all pretense of respecting the sovereignty or the neutrality of Cambodia. Thousands of their soldiers are invading the country from the sanctuaries; they are encircling the Capital of Phnom Penh. Coming from these sanctuaries, as you see here, they have moved into Cambodia and are encircling the Capital.

Cambodia, as a result of this, has sent out a call to the United States, to a number of other nations, for assistance. Because if this enemy effort succeeds, Cambodia would become a vast enemy staging area and a springboard for attacks on South Viet-Nam along 600 miles of frontier, a refuge where enemy troops could return from combat without fear of retaliation.

North Vietnamese men and supplies could then be poured into that country, jeopardizing not only the lives of our own men but the people of South Viet-Nam as well.

Three Options

Now, confronted with this situation, we have three options.

First, we can do nothing. Well, the ultimate result of that course of action is clear. Unless we indulge in wishful thinking, the lives of Americans remaining in Viet-Nam after our next withdrawal of 150.000 would be gravely threatened.

Let us go to the map again. Here is South Viet-Nam. Here is North Viet-Nam. North Viet-Nam already occupies this part of Laos. If North Viet-Nam also occupied this whole band in Cambodia, or the entire country, it would mean that South Viet-Nam was completely outflanked and the forces of Americans in this area, as well as the South Vietnamese, would be in an untenable military position.

Our second choice is to provide massive military assistance to Cambodia itself. Now, unfortunately, while we deeply sympathize with the plight of 7 million Cambodians, whose country is being invaded, massive amounts of military assistance could not be rapidly and effectively utilized by the small Cambodian Army against the immediate threat.

With other nations, we shall do our best to provide the small arms and other equipment which the Cambodian Army of 40,000 needs and can use for its defense. But the aid we will provide will be limited to the purpose of enabling Cambodia to defend its neutrality and not for the purpose of making it an active belligerent on one side or the other.

Our third choice is to go to the heart of the trouble. That means cleaning out major North Vietnamese and Viet Cong occupied territories—these sanctuaries which serve as bases for attacks on both Cambodia and American and South Vietnamese forces in South Viet-Nam. Some of these, incidentally, are as close to Saigon as Baltimore is to Washington. This one, for example [indicating], is called the Parrot's Beak. It is only 33 miles from Saigon.

Attacks on Enemy Sanctuaries

Now, faced with these three options, this is the decision I have made.

In cooperation with the armed forces of South Viet-Nam, attacks are being launched this week to clean out major enemy sanctuaries on the Cambodian-Viet-Nam border.

A major responsibility for the ground operations is being assumed by South Vietnamese forces. For example, the attacks in several areas, including the Parrot's Beak that I referred to a moment ago, are exclusively South Vietnamese ground operations under South Vietnamese command, with the United States providing air and logistical support.

There is one area, however, immediately above Parrot's Beak, where I have concluded that a combined American and South Vietnamese operation is necessary.

Tonight American and South Vietnamese units will attack the headquarters for the entire Communist military operation in South Viet-Nam. This key control center has been occupied by the North Vietnamese and Viet Cong for 5 years in blatant violation of Cambodia's neutrality.

This is not an invasion of Cambodia. The areas in which these attacks will be launched are completely occupied and controlled by North Vietnamese forces. Our purpose is not to occupy the areas. Once enemy forces are driven out of these sanctuaries and once their military supplies are destroyed, we will withdraw.

These actions are in no way directed at the security interests of any nation. Any government that chooses to use these actions as a pretext for harming relations with the United States will be doing so on its own responsibility and on its own initiative, and we will draw the appropriate conclusions.

Now, let me give you the reasons for my decision.

A majority of the American people, a majority of you listening to me, are for the withdrawal of our forces from Viet-Nam. The action I have taken tonight is indispensable for the continuing success of that withdrawal program.

A majority of the American people want to end this war rather than to have it drag on interminably. The action I have taken tonight will serve that purpose.

A majority of the American people want to keep the casualties of our brave men in Viet-Nam at an absolute minimum. The action I take tonight is essential if we are to accomplish that goal.

We take this action not for the purpose of expanding the war into Cambodia, but for the purpose of ending the war in Viet-Nam and winning the just peace we all desire. We have made and we will continue to make every possible effort to end this war through negotiation at the conference table rather than through more fighting on the battlefield.

The Record of North Viet-Nam's Intransigence

Let us look again at the record. We have stopped the bombing of North Viet-Nam. We have cut air operations by over 20 percent. We have announced withdrawal of over 250,000 of our men. We have offered to withdraw all of our men if they will withdraw theirs. We have offered to negotiate all issues with only one condition—and that is that the future of South Viet-Nam be determined not by North Viet-Nam, not by the United States, but by the people of South Viet-Nam themselves.

The answer of the enemy has been intransigence at the conference table, belligerence in Hanoi, massive military aggression in Laos and Cambodia, and stepped-up attacks in South Viet-Nam designed to increase American casualties.

This attitude has become intolerable. We will not react to this threat to American lives merely by plaintive diplomatic protests. If we did, the credibility of the United States would be destroyed in every area of the world where only the power of the United States deters aggression.

Tonight I again warn the North Vietnamese that if they continue to escalate the fighting when the United States is withdrawing its forces, I shall meet my responsibility as Commander in Chief of our Armed Forces to take the action I consider necessary to defend the security of our American men.

The action that I have announced tonight puts the leaders of North Viet-Nam on notice that we will be patient in working for peace, we will be conciliatory at the conference table, but we will not be humiliated. We will not be defeated. We will not allow American men by the thousands to be killed by an enemy from privileged sanctuaries.

The time came long ago to end this war through peaceful negotiations. We stand ready for those negotiations. We have made major efforts, many of which must remain secret. I say tonight that all the offers and approaches made previously remain on the conference table whenever Hanoi is ready to negotiate seriously.

But if the enemy response to our most conciliatory offers for peaceful negotiation continues to be to increase its attacks and humiliate and defeat us, we shall react accordingly.

My fellow Americans, we live in an age of anarchy, both abroad and at home. We see mindless attacks on all the great institutions which have been created by free civilizations in the last 500 years. Even here in the United States, great universities are being systematically destroyed. Small nations all over the world find themselves under attack from within and from without.

If, when the chips are down, the world's most powerful nation, the United States of America, acts like a pitiful, helpless giant, the forces of totalitarianism and anarchy will threaten free nations and free institutions throughout the world.

It is not our power but our will and character that is being tested tonight. The question all Americans must ask and answer tonight is this: Does the richest and strongest nation in the history of the world have the character to meet a direct challenge by a group which rejects every effort to win a just peace, ignores our warning, tramples on solemn agreements, violates the neutrality of an unarmed people, and uses our prisoners as hostages?

If we fail to meet this challenge, all other nations will be on notice that despite its overwhelming power the United States, when a real crisis comes, will be found wanting.

During my campaign for the Presidency, I pledged to bring Americans home from Viet-Nam. They are coming home.

I promised to end this war. I shall keep that promise.

I promised to win a just peace. I shall keep that promise.

We shall avoid a wider war. But we are also determined to put an end to this war.

In this room Woodrow Wilson made the great decisions which led to victory in World War I. Franklin Roosevelt made the decisions which led to our victory in World War II. Dwight D. Eisenhower made decisions which ended the war in Korea and avoided war in the Middle East. John F. Kennedy. in his finest hour, made the great decision which removed Soviet nuclear missiles from Cuba and the Western Hemisphere.

I have noted that there has been a great deal of discussion with regard to this decision that I have made, and I should point out that I do not contend that it is in the same magnitude as these decisions that I have just mentioned. But between those decisions and this decision, there is a difference that is very fundamental. In those decisions the American people were not assailed by counsels of doubt and defeat from some of the most widely known opinion leaders of the Nation.

I have noted, for example, that a Republican Senator has said that this action I have taken means that my party has lost all chance of winning the November elections. And others are saying today that this move against enemy sanctuaries will make me a one-term President.

No one is more aware than I am of the political consequences of the action I have taken. It is tempting to take the easy political path: to blame this war on previous administrations and to bring all of our men home immediately, regardless of the consequences, even though that would mean defeat for the United States; to desert 18 million South Vietnamese people who have put their trust in us and to expose them to the same slaughter and savagery which the leaders of North Viet-Nam inflicted on hundreds of thousands of North Vietnamese who chose freedom when the Communists took over North Viet-Nam in 1954; to get peace at any price now, even though I know that a peace of humiliation for the United States would lead to a bigger war or surrender later.

I have rejected all political considerations in making this decision.

Whether my party gains in November is nothing compared to the lives of 400,000 brave Americans fighting for our country and for the cause of peace and freedom in Viet-Nam. Whether I may be a one-term President is insignificant compared to whether by our failure to act in this crisis the United States proves itself to be unworthy to lead the forces of freedom in this critical period in world history. I would rather be a one-term President and do what I believe is right than to be a two-term President at the cost of seeing America become a second-rate power and to see this nation accept the first defeat in its proud 190-year history.

I realize that in this war there are honest and deep differences in this country about whether we should have become involved, that there are differences as to how the war should have been conducted.

But the decision I announce tonight transcends those differences. For the lives of American men are involved. The opportunity for 150,000 Americans to come home in the next 12 months is involved. The future of 18 million people in South Viet-Nam and 7 million people in Cambodia is involved. The possibility of winning a just peace in Viet-Nam and in the Pacific is at stake.

It is customary to conclude a speech from the White House by asking support for the President of the United States. Tonight I depart from that precedent. What I ask is far more important. I ask for your support for our brave men fighting tonight halfway around the world, not for territory, not for glory, but so that their younger brothers and their sons and your sons can have a chance to grow up in a world of peace and freedom and justice.

Thank you and good night.

D. Report by President Nixon on the Conclusion of the Cambodian Operation*

[Extract]

June 30, 1970

Together with the South Vietnamese, the armed forces of the United States have just completed successfully the destruction of enemy base areas along the Cambodian-South Viet-Nam frontier. All American troops have withdrawn from Cambodia on the schedule announced at the start of the operation.

The allied sweeps into the North Vietnamese and Viet Cong base areas along the Cambodian-South Vietnamese border:

> —will save American and allied lives in the future;
> —will assure that the withdrawal of American troops from South Viet-Nam can proceed on schedule;
> —will enable our program of Vietnamization to continue on its current timetable;
> —should enhance the prospects for a just peace.

*Ibid., July 20, 1970, pp. 65-75.

At this time, it is important to review the background for the decision, the results of the operation, their larger meaning in terms of the conflict in Indochina—and to look down the road to the future.

It is vital to understand at the outset that Hanoi left the United States no reasonable option but to move militarily against the Cambodian base areas. The purpose and significance of our operations against the Cambodian sanctuaries can only be understood against the backdrop of what we are seeking to accomplish in Viet-Nam—and the threat that the Communist bases in Cambodia posed to our objectives. Nor can that military action of the last 2 months be divorced from its cause—the threat posed by the constant expansion of North Vietnamese aggression throughout Indochina.

A Record of Restraint

America's purpose in Viet-Nam and Indochina remains what it has been—a peace in which the peoples of the region can devote themselves to development of their own societies, a peace in which all the peoples of Southeast Asia can determine their own political future without outside interference.

When this administration took office, the authorized strength of American troops in South Viet-Nam was 549,000—the high-water mark of American military presence in Southeast Asia. The United States had been negotiating at Paris for 10 months, but nothing had been agreed upon other then the shape of the bargaining table. No comprehensive allied peace proposal existed. There was no approved plan to reduce America's involvement in the war—in the absence of a negotiated settlement.

Since January of 1969, we have taken steps on all fronts to move toward peace. Along with the Government of South Viet-Nam, we have put forward a number of concrete and reasonable proposals to promote genuine negotiations. These proposals were first outlined by me 13 months ago, on May 14, 1969, and by President Thieu on July 11, 1969. Through both public and private channels, our proposals have been repeated and amplified many times since.

*   *   *

Background of the April 30 Decision

In assessing the April 30 decision to move against the North Vietnamese and Viet Cong sanctuaries in Cambodia, four basic facts must be remembered.

It was North Viet-Nam—not we—which brought the Viet-Nam war into Cambodia.

For 5 years, North Viet-Nam has used Cambodian territory as a sanctuary from which to attack allied forces in South Viet-Nam. For 5 years, American and allied forces—to preserve the concept of Cambodian neutrality and to confine the conflict in Southeast Asia—refrained from moving against those sanctuaries.

It was the presence of North Vietnamese troops on Cambodian soil that contributed to the downfall of Prince Sihanouk. It was the indignation of the Cambodian people against the presence of Vietnamese Communists in their country that led to riots in Phnom Penh which contributed to Prince Sihanouk's ouster—an ouster that surprised no nation more than the United States. At the end of Sihanouk's rule, the United States was making efforts to improve relations with his government and the Prince was taking steps against the Communist invaders on his national soil.

It was the government appointed by Prince Sihanouk and ratified by the Cambodian National Assembly—not a group of usurpers—which overthrew him with the approval of the National Assembly. The United States had neither connection with, nor knowledge of, these events.

It was the major expansion of enemy activity in Cambodia that ultimately caused allied troops to end 5 years of restraint and attack the Communist base areas.

The historical record is plain.

Viet Cong and North Vietnamese troops have operated in eastern Cambodia for years. The primary objective of these Communist forces has been the support of Hanoi's aggression against South Viet-Nam. Just as it has violated the 1962 Geneva accords on Laos, North Viet-Nam has consistently ignored its pledge, in signing the 1954 Geneva accords, to respect Cambodian neutrality and territorial integrity.

In a May 1967 Phnom Penh radio broadcast, Prince Sihanouk's following remarks were reported to the Cambodian people:

> I must tell you that the Vietnamese communists and the Viet Cong negotiated with us three or four times but that absolutely nothing comes out of the negotiations . . . After I expelled the French and after the French troops left Cambodia, Viet Minh remained in our country in order to conquer it. How can we have confidence in the Viet Minh? . . . If we side with the Viet Minh we will lose our independence.

Late in 1969, Prince Sihanouk ordered Cambodia's underequipped and weak armed forces to exercise some measure of control over North Vietnamese and Viet Cong Communist forces occupying Cambodian territory.

*   *   *

This Government had no advance warning of the ouster of Sihanouk, with whom we had been attempting to improve relations. Our initial response was to seek to preserve the status quo with regard to Cambodia and to try to prevent an expansion of Communist influence. The immunity of the Cambodian sanctuaries had been a serious military handicap for us for many years. But we had refrained from moving against them in order to contain the conflict. We recognized both the problems facing Sihanouk and the fact that he had exercised some measure of control over Communist activities, through regulation of the flow of rice and military supplies into the sanctuaries from coastal ports. We considered that a neutral Cambodia outweighed the military benefits of a move against the base areas.

This is why diplomatically our first reaction to Sihanouk's overthrow was to encourage some form of accommodation in Cambodia. We spoke in this sense to interested governments. And we made clear through many channels that we had no intention of exploiting the Cambodian upheaval for our own ends.

*   *   *

. . . In the face of our restraint and our warnings, the North Vietnamese continued to expand their territorial control, threatening to link up their base areas. From a series of isolated enclaves, the base areas were rapidly becoming a solid band of self-sustaining territory stretching from Laos to the sea from which any pretense of Cambodian sovereignty was rapidly being excluded.

> —On April 20, North Vietnamese forces temporarily captured Saang, only 18 miles south of Phnom Penh.
> —On April 22, Communist forces assaulted the town of Snuol east of Phnom Penh.
> —On April 23, they attacked the town of Mimot and an important bridge linking the town of Snuol and the capital of Kratie Province on Route 13.
> —On April 24, they moved on the resort city of Kep.
> —On April 26, they attacked some ships on the Mekong and occupied the town of Angtassom, a few miles west of Takeo.
> —They then attacked the city of Chhlong, on the Mekong River north of Phnom Penh, and the port city of Kampot.
> —During this same period, they cut almost every major road leading south and east out of Phnom Penh.

The prospect suddenly loomed of Cambodia's becoming virtually one large base area for attack anywhere into South Viet-Nam along the 600 miles of the Cambodian frontier. The enemy in Cambodia would have enjoyed complete freedom of action to move forces and supplies rapidly across the entire length of South Viet-Nam's flank to attack our forces in South Viet-Nam with impunity from well-stocked sanctuaries along the border.

We thus faced a rapidly changing military situation from that which existed on April 20.

The possibility of a grave new threat to our troops in South Viet-Nam was rapidly becoming an actuality.

The pattern of Communist action prior to our decision of April 30 makes it clear the enemy was intent both on expanding and strengthening its military position along the Cambodian border and overthrowing the Cambodian Government. The plans were laid, the orders issued, and already being implemented by Communist forces.

Not only the clear evidence of Communist actions—but supporting data screened from more than 6 tons of subsequently captured Communist documents—leaves no doubt that the Communists' move against the Cambodian Government preceded the U.S. action against the base areas.

*   *   *

The Military Operations

Ten major operations were launched against a dozen of the most significant base areas with 32,000 American troops and 48,000 South Vietnamese participating at various times. As of today, all Americans, including logistics personnel and advisers, have withdrawn, as have a majority of the South Vietnamese forces.

Our military response to the enemy's escalation was measured in every respect. It was a limited operation for a limited period of time with limited objectives.

We have scrupulously observed the 21-mile limit on penetration of our ground combat forces into Cambodian territory. These self-imposed time and geographic restrictions may have cost us some military advantages, but we knew that we could achieve our primary objectives within these restraints. And these restraints underscored the limited nature of our purpose to the American people.

* * *

The Future

Now that our ground forces and our logistic and advisory personnel have all been withdrawn, what will be our future policy for Cambodia?

The following will be the guidelines of our policy in Cambodia:

1. There will be no U.S. ground personnel in Cambodia except for the regular staff of our Embassy in Phnom Penh.

2. There will be no U.S. advisers with Cambodian units.

3. We will conduct—with the approval of the Cambodian Government—air interdiction missions against the enemy efforts to move supplies and personnel through Cambodia toward South Viet-Nam and to reestablish base areas relevant to the war in Viet-Nam. We do this to protect our forces in South Viet-Nam.

4. We will turn over material captured in the base areas in Cambodia to the Cambodian Government to help it defend its neutrality and independence.

5. We will provide military assistance to the Cambodian Government in the form of small arms and relatively unsophisticated equipment in types and quantitites suitable for their army. To date we have supplied about $5 million of these items, principally in the form of small arms, mortars, trucks, aircraft parts, communications equipment, and medical supplies.

6. We will encourage other countries of the region to give diplomatic support to the independence and neutrality of Cambodia. We welcome the efforts of the Djakarta group of countries[1] to mobilize world opinion and encourage Asian cooperation to this end.

7. We will encourage and support the efforts of third countries who wish to furnish Cambodia with troops or material. We applaud the efforts of Asian nations to help Cambodia preserve its neutrality and independence.

I will let the Asian governments speak for themselves concerning their future policies. I am confident that two basic principles will govern the actions of those nations helping Cambodia:

> —They will be at the request of, and in close concert with, the Cambodian Government.
> —They will not be at the expense of those nations' own defense—indeed they will contribute to their security, which they see bound up with events in Cambodia.

[1]Australia, Indonesia, Japan, Korea, Laos, Malaysia, New Zealand, the Philippines, Singapore, South Viet Nam, Thailand [Footnote in original.]

The South Vietnamese plan to help. Of all the countries of Southeast Asia, South Viet-Nam has most at stake in Cambodia. A North Vietnamese takeover would, of course, have profound consequences for its security. At the same time, the leaders of South Viet-Nam recognize that the primary focus of their attention must be on the security of their own country. President Thieu has reflected these convictions in his major radio and TV address of June 27. Our understanding of Saigon's intentions is as follows:

1. South Vietnamese forces remain ready to prevent reestablishment of base areas along South Viet-Nam's frontier.

2. South Vietnamese forces will remain ready to assist in the evacuation of Vietnamese civilians and to respond selectively to appeals from the Cambodian Government should North Vietnamese aggression make this necessary.

3. Most of these operations will be launched from within South Viet-Nam. There will be no U.S. air or logistics support. There will not be U.S. advisers on these operations.

4. The great majority of South Vietnamese forces are to leave Cambodia.

5. The primary objective of the South Vietnamese remains Vietnamization within their country. Whatever actions are taken in Cambodia will be consistent with this objective.

*   *   *

THE UNITED STATES

AND THAILAND

THE UNITED STATES AND THAILAND

Commentary

Circumstances during the years since 1945 have made Thailand a formal ally of the United States. Wishing to retain her independence during the Second World War, Thailand allowed Japan to cross her territory to attack Malaya and declared war on the United States, Britain and France. But this declaration was never taken very seriously by the United States though it was by Great Britain—because a resistance movement led by former Thai officials operated against Japan throughout the period. When the war ended, the United States quickly accepted a Thai nullification of the state of war and worked diligently to prevent punitive action against that country by Great Britain.

Subsequently in 1950 the United States and Thailand concluded agreements primarily for American technical and economic aid as well as military equipment—assistance aimed at insulating Thailand from the feared Communist threat to the region. In 1954, Thailand became a formal member of SEATO; in 1962, in a joint Thai-American statement the two countries agreed that the United States obligation to help Thailand in the event of aggression did not require the support of the other alliance members. The United States considered the preservation of Thai independence as "vital" to its own national interest. Since 1962, and with the expansion of the Vietnam War, the United States has sent a number of troops to Thailand, built large bases there, and has enlisted the support of Thai troops in ground fighting in Vietnam.

POSTWAR SETTLEMENTS

A. Proclamation by Thailand Nullifying The 1942 Declaration of War Against the United States*

August 17, 1945

Whereas Thailand had pursued a fixed policy of maintaining strict neutrality and of combating foreign aggression by all means, as is clearly evident from the enactment in B.E. 2484 (1941) of the Law "Defining the Duties of the Thais in Time of War," this fixed determination was made clear, when Japan moved her forces into Thai territory on the 8th December B.E. 2484 (1941), by acts combating aggression everywhere, and numerous soldiers, police and civilians lost their lives thereby.

This circumstance, which stands as evidence in itself, shows clearly that the declaration of war on Great Britain and the United States of America on the 25th January B.E. 2485 (1942), as well as all acts adverse to the United Nations are acts contrary to the will of the Thai people and constitute an infringement of the provisions of the Constitution and the laws of the land. The Thai people inside as well as outside the country, who were in a position to help and support the United Nations who are lovers of peace in the world, have taken action by every means to assist the United Nations as most of the United Nations are already aware. This shows once again that the will of the Thai people does not approve of the declaration of war and of acts adverse to the United Nations as already mentioned.

Now that Japan has agreed to comply with the declaration of the United States of America, Great Britain, China and the Soviet Union which was made at Potsdam, peace is restored to Thailand as is the wish of the Thai people.

The Regent, in the name of His Majesty the King, hereby openly proclaims on behalf of the Thai people that the declaration of war on the United States of America and Great Britain is null and void and not binding on the Thai people as far as the United Nations are concerned. Thailand has resolved that the good friendly relations existing with the United Nations prior to the 8th December B.E. 2484 (1941) shall be restored and Thailand is ready to cooperate fully in every way with the United Nations in the establishment of stability in the world. . . .

As for any other provisions of law having effects adverse to the United States of America, Great Britain and the British Empire, their repeal will be considered hereafter. All damages of any kind resulting from those laws will be legitimately made good.

In conclusion, all the Thai people as well as aliens who are in the Thai kingdom are requested to remain in tranquility and not to commit any act which will constitute a disturbance of public order. They should hold steadfastly to the ideals which have been laid down in the resolutions of the United Nations at San Francisco.

*Documents on American Foreign Relations, 1945-1946, p. 824.

B. Statement by Secretary of State James F. Byrnes on United States Relations with Thailand*

August 20, 1945

The Minister of Thailand M.R. Seni Pramoj, has communicated to the Department of State the text of the proclamation issued by the Regent of Thailand in the name of His Majesty the King on August 16. As regards Thai relations with this country, the proclamation declared null and void, as unconstitutional and contrary to the will of the Thai people, the declaration of war by Thailand on January 25, 1942 against the United States; announced Thai determination to restore the friendly relations which existed with the United Nations before the Japanese occupation; promised that repeal of laws prejudicial to our interests would be considered; assured just compensation for damages resulting from such laws; and pledged full Thai cooperation with the United Nations in establishing world stability.

The action of the Thai Government is a welcome step in American-Thai relations. The Japanese occupation of Thailand took place at the same time as the Japanese attack on Pearl Harbor. The Thai declaration of war was made seven weeks later. The Thai Government was then completely controlled by the Japanese. The American Government has always believed that the declaration did not represent the will of the Thai people. Accordingly we disregarded that declaration and have continued to recognize the Thai Minister in Washington as the Minister of Thailand, although, of course, we did not recognize the Thailand Government in Bangkok as it was under Japanese control.

Immediately following the Japanese occupation of Thailand, the Minister of Thailand in Washington organized a Free Thai movement among those Thai who were outside their country when the Japanese blow fell. The Free Thai have since contributed substantially to the Allied cause.

Soon after the Japanese occupation a resistance movement developed within Thailand. Our Government and the British Government have both given to and received from the resistance movement important aid and for some time past have been in constant communication with its leaders. For a number of months the resistance movement has been prepared to commence overt action against the Japanese. For operational reasons this Government and the British Government requested that such action be deferred. It was only because of this express request that the resistance movement did not begin open fighting for the liberation of their country before Japanese surrender made such action unnecessary.

Before the war Thailand and the United States had a long history of close friendship. We hope that friendship will be even closer in the future. During the past four years we have regarded Thailand not as an enemy but as a country to be liberated from the enemy. With that liberation now accomplished we look to the resumption by Thailand of its former place in the community of nations as a free, sovereign, and independent country.

*Ibid., pp. 824-25.

AMERICAN AID TO THAILAND

A. Statement by Secretary of State John Foster Dulles on United States Military Aid to Laos and Thailand in Face of Viet Minh Aggression*

[Extract]

May 9, 1953

In view of the recent, rapid sequence of events in the Far East, I believe it would be appropriate to summarize for you our actions concerning developments in Laos and Thailand.

Communist Viet Minh forces began their movement toward the Royal Capital City of Luang Prabang in Laos on April 12.

Following an appeal from the Government of Laos on April 13 to the free world to condemn the aggression, the United States issued a statement of support and sympathy.

*   *   *

The Ambassador from Thailand, Pote Sarasin, came to my office at 3:30 p.m. on Tuesday of this week, May 5, to discuss the problems confronting his country as a result of the Viet Minh invasion of Laos.

The Ambassador expressed his country's urgent need for small arms ammunition and for various military items urgently required by the Thai Navy, Army, and Air Force, which requests had simultaneously been made through the U.S. Military Assistance Advisory Group and our Embassy at Bangkok. Within 24 hours of the Ambassador's request certain amounts of such ammunition were in the air on their way to Bangkok from the Pacific area, and action was taken to expedite delivery of the other military items.

These two instances illustrate a capacity for decision and performance and of cooperative teamwork between the Departments of State and Defense, which should, I believe, be gratifying to the American people. Also, they should be impressive to others, whether they be friends or aggressors.

B. Department of Defense Statement On Increased Military Aid to Thailand*

July 13, 1954

The Department of Defense on July 13 announced a new program of increased military aid and technical assistance to the Government of Thailand.

American Foreign Policy, 1950-1955: Basic Documents, pp. 2369-70.
Ibid., p. 2396.

As a result of staff talks recently concluded between Department of Defense officials and a Thai military mission headed by Gen. Srisdt Dhanarajata, Deputy Defense Minister and Commander in Chief of the Royal Thai Army, a new and additional military-assistance program has been approved for the Thais so as to increase the capability of the Thai armed forces to resist aggression.

Additional emphasis will also be placed on the accelerated development of junior officers, noncommissioned officers, and technical personnel, the announcement stated. The program calls for additional support for Thai training activities, including the provision of weapons, equipment, and technical and training assistance in their use.

In addition to the military-aid grant, the Department of Defense also announced that approximately $3 million was being made available to the Thai Government for the construction of a highway from Saraburi, in Central Thailand, through Korat to Ban Phai, a distance of 297 miles.

While this highway will be of strategic value in case of military operations in Thailand, its value to the economy of the country will be considerable, the announcement stated.

The program will be administered in Thailand by a Joint U.S. Military Aid Group headed by Maj. Gen. W.N. Gillmore, U.S. Army.

C. Joint Communiqué Issued by the United States and Thailand on Peace in Southeast Asia*

Bangkok, May 18, 1961

The Vice President of the United States and the Prime Minister of Thailand have completed a series of meetings during the Vice President's visit to Thailand over the past two days. Their discussions covered many subjects of common interest, and reflected mutual objectives and undertakings of both Governments.

The Vice President stressed that the President of the United States had sent him on this mission to inform the Prime Minister personally and directly of the United States Government's complete understanding of Thailand's concern over the threats to peace and security in Southeast Asia, and conveyed the President's intense interest in the preservation of the independence and political integrity of Thailand and the other free countries of Southeast Asia.

Vice President Johnson also stressed that he had come at the personal request of President Kennedy to obtain the counsel of Prime Minister Sarit on what should be done in the immediate future to meet our common problems. Further, he stressed that he would report the views of the Prime Minister to President Kennedy.

The Vice President expressed his great appreciation for the amount of time, as well as the serious attention, which the Prime Minister and his colleagues devoted to these discussions. He also expressed gratitude for the warmth of the reception of the people of Thailand.

The Vice President noted that Thailand has made great social and economic

---

American Foreign Policy: Current Documents, 1961, pp. 1036-37.

progress. He cited the advances of Thailand in the fields of education, health, finance and economic development.

The Vice President expressed his interest in the challenge of the development of northeast Thailand where opportunities for development are being sought under the leadership of the Prime Minister.

At the conclusion of their talks, the Prime Minister and the Vice President agreed to the release of a joint communique covering the following points:

(1) Both Governments found mutual understanding regarding the serious situation existing in parts of Southeast Asia. They reached full accord on Thai-United States objectives of peace and independence, and agreed that both Governments should work for these objectives.

(2) Both Governments recognize that the foundation of Freedom rests on the adequate education of the young, the health of the people, and the improvement in the standards of livelihood of the people. Both Governments pledged their diligent efforts to the advance of education. health, communications, and other fields of modern progress in Thailand.

(3) The United States Government expressed its determination to honor its treaty commitments to support Thailand—its ally and historic friend—in defense against subversion and Communist aggression.

(4) Both Governments recognize the utmost importance of preserving the integrity and independence of Thailand.

(5) Both Governments reiterated their determination to fulfill their SEATO commitments and to go forward in steadfast partnership.

(6) Both Governments examined possible ways to strengthen Thai defense capabilities, agreed to explore ways in which this might be achieved through greater joint efforts and mutual sacrifices and the military assistance program involving the armed forces.

(7) Both Governments expressed approval of specific joint economic projects such as irrigation projects in the northeast and the new thermal power plant, which are being developed in Thailand, as well as the planning, and the setting up of projects under the Peace Corps program. .

The Vice President and the Prime Minister rededicated themselves to work for an honorable peace in Southeast Asia, and to intensify the efforts of their countries for the defense and progress of the free nations of this region.

Finally, they agreed on the desirability of regular consultation with as much frequency as may be practicable.

D. Joint Statement By Secretary Rusk and Foreign Minister Thanat Khoman on United States Policy Toward Thailand*

March 6, 1962

The Foreign Minister of Thailand, Thanat Khoman, and the Secretary of State, Dean Rusk, met on several occasions during the past few days for discus-

*Department of State Bulletin, Mar. 26, 1962, pp. 498-99.

sions on the current situation in Southeast Asia, the Southeast Asia Collective Defense Treaty and the security of Thailand.

The Secretary of State reaffirmed that the United States regards the preservation of the independence and integrity of Thailand as vital to the national interest of the United States and to world peace. He expressed the firm intention of the United States to aid Thailand, its ally and historic friend, in resisting Communist aggression and subversion.

The Foreign Minister and the Secretary of State reviewed the close association of Thailand and the United States in the Southeast Asia Collective Defense Treaty and agreed that such association is an effective deterrent to direct Communist aggression against Thailand. They agreed that the Treaty provides the basis for the signatories collectively to assist Thailand in case of Communist armed attack against that country. The Secretary of State assured the Foreign Minister that in the event of such aggression, the United States intends to give full effect to its obligations under the Treaty to act to meet the common danger in accordance with its constitutional processes. The Secretary of State reaffirmed that this obligation of the United States does not depend upon the prior agreement of all other parties to the Treaty, since this Treaty obligation is individual as well as collective.

In reviewing measures to meet indirect aggression, the Secretary of State stated that the United States regards its commitments to Thailand under the Southeast Asia Collective Defense Treaty and under its bilateral economic and military assistance agreements with Thailand as providing an important basis for United States actions to help Thailand meet indirect aggression. In this connection the Secretary reviewed with the Foreign Minister the actions being taken by the United States to assist the Republic of Viet-Nam to meet the threat of indirect aggression.

The Foreign Minister assured the Secretary of State of the determination of the Government of Thailand to meet the threat of indirect aggression by pursuing vigorously measures for the economic and social welfare and the safety of its people.

The situation in Laos was reviewed in detail and full agreement was reached on the necessity for the stability of Southeast Asia, of achieving a free, independent and truly neutral Laos.

The Foreign Minister and the Secretary of State reviewed the mutual efforts of their governments to increase the capabilities and readiness of the Thai armed forces to defend the Kingdom. They noted also that the United States is making a significant contribution to this effort and that the United States intends to accelerate future deliveries to the greatest extent possible. The Secretary and the Foreign Minister also took note of the work of the Joint Thai-United States Committee which has been established in Bangkok to assure effective cooperation in social, economic and military measures to increase Thailand's national capabilities. They agreed that this Joint Committee and its sub-committees should continue to work toward the most effective utilization of Thailand's resources and those provided by the United States to promote Thailand's development and security.

The Foreign Minister and the Secretary were in full agreement that continued economic and social progress is essential to the stability of Thailand. They reviewed Thailand's impressive economic and social progress and the Thai Government's plans to accelerate development, particularly Thailand's continuing determination fully to utilize its own resources in moving toward its development goals.

The Foreign Minister and the Secretary of State also discussed the desirability of an early conclusion of a treaty of friendship, commerce and navigation between the two countries which would bring into accord with current conditions the existing treaty of 1937.

E. Statement by President Kennedy on the Dispatch of Troops to Thailand*

May 15, 1962

Following joint consideration by the Governments of the United States and Thailand of the situation in Southeast Asia, the Royal Thai Government has invited, and I have today ordered, additional elements of the United States military forces, both ground and air, to proceed to Thailand and to remain there until further orders. These forces are to help insure the territorial integrity of this peaceful country.

The dispatch of United States forces to Thailand was considered desirable because of recent attacks in Laos by Communist forces and the subsequent movement of Communist military units toward the border of Thailand.

A threat to Thailand is of grave concern to the United States. I have, therefore, ordered certain additional American military forces into Thailand in order that we may be in a position to fulfill speedily our obligations under the Manila Pact of 1954, a defense agreement which was approved overwhelmingly by the U.S. Senate and to which the Secretary of State and Foreign Minister of Thailand referred in their joint statement of March 6, 1962. We are in consultation with SEATO governments on the situation.

I emphasize that this is a defensive act on the part of the United States and wholly consistent with the United Nations Charter, which specifically recognizes that nations have an inherent right to take collective measures for self-defense. In the spirit of that charter I have directed that the Secretary-General of the United Nations be informed of the actions that we are taking.

There is no change in our policy towards Laos, which continues to be the reestablishment of an effective cease-fire and prompt negotiations for a government of national union.

Ibid., June 4, 1962, pp. 904-05.

F. Address by Marshall Green, Deputy Assistant Secretary of State for Far Eastern Affairs, on Thai Countermeasures to the Threat of Communist Subversion*

March 14, 1965

We hear much these days about Communist aggression in Southeast Asia. For very obvious reasons the focus is on Viet-Nam and to some extent on Laos, but I would like to draw your attention to another area in Southeast Asia where Communist China and other Asian Communists are involved in expansionism and subversion. I refer to the northeast area of Thailand, where there is an impressive and growing array of evidence that Thailand may become an important target for the Communists. However, this is something that the Thai Government has long foreseen and, with our assistance, has taken effective measures to counteract. Here are some of the facts:

Communist subversive activity within Thailand has centered primarily on the northeastern province of Nakhon Phanom, close to Communist-held areas of Laos. There have been acts of terror. There has been a step-up in attempted recruitment of Communist-type cadres among the villagers and a reported increase in the number of meetings called by Communists and Communist sympathizers, who parrot the Communist line and hand out propaganda materials.

There has also been a step-up in the radio propaganda effort. The voices of Radio Peiping and Radio Hanoi are strongly heard in northeast Thailand. They are supplemented by a clandestine radio, located in Communist-held areas of Laos (and at times in North Viet-Nam), which calls itself the "Voice of the Thai People."

G. Joint Communiqué Issued on Thai-United States Discussions on Southeast Asia*

[Extract]

February 15, 1966

The Vice President of the United States and the Prime Minister of Thailand have concluded a most useful discussion and review of the common struggle against Communist aggression in Southeast Asia, including the results of the recently concluded conference in Hawaii.

The Vice President paid tribute to the strong and unhesitating stand which Thailand and her leaders have taken against the many forms of Communist aggression, the disguised as well as the blatant ones. He expressed the gratitude of his Government for Thailand's initiatives in seeking a larger regional framework for the peaceful achievement of social and economic progress. He emphasized the determination of the United States to provide all necessary assistance

*American Foreign Policy: Current Documents, 1965, pp. 817-18.
*American Foreign Policy: Current Documents, 1966, p. 732.

to enable Thailand and the other countries of Southeast Asia threatened by Communist aggression to defend themselves and to achieve in peace their just economic and social aims.

The Prime Minister concurred with the principle underlying the Declaration of Honolulu: that the war in Southeast Asia must be waged on two fronts simultaneously—the military front and the struggle to improve the social, economic, and physical well-being of the people.

Recognizing Thailand's commitment to defend itself against Communist aggression both from within and from without, the Vice President reaffirmed the United States pledge to assist in programs for the improvement of individual well-being and security in Thailand. Despite the progress already made in the development of rural areas, a need was clearly identified for greater efforts to provide more ample water supply, further expansion of rural credit for agriculture and related small industry, irrigation of farmlands, expansion of rural electrification, an expanded road system to connect outlying areas to markets, better medical care extended to presently isolated villages and the provision of more schools to educate the populace and to insure that they will be better equipped to share in the progress of their country and contribute to its strength and stability.

H. Comments by William P. Bundy, Assistant Secretary of State for Far Eastern Affairs, on United States Assistance to the Thai Counter-Insurgency Program*

[Extract]

September 4, 1966

We have a treaty relationship with Thailand, of course, in that they are a member of the SEATO treaty, the Southeast Asia Treaty Organization, so that we have a fully complete treaty relationship there. Now that applies to action in accordance with our constitutional processes in the event of external aggression and for consultation in the event of subversion.

What you have now is some kind of—well, a real threat of insurgency, particularly in the northeast area of Thailand. The Thai are dealing with that themselves, and our role is to supply them equipment and to assist them in training as they may desire.

*   *   *

. . . There is really no secret about the basic relationship we have with Thailand or about the basic measures we have taken there. The basic strength, which is about 25,000 of our forces who are there, principally Air Force units, is certainly a matter that has been widely reported and is understood, I think,

---

Ibid., p. 733.

in the Congress and has been fully discussed with the congressional leaders. There is really no secret about this.

*   *   *

With respect to the whole of the insurgency in Thailand, it is on a very limited scale. It is on a scale that on the Vietnamese benchmark would be perhaps on the level of '59 or '60 rather than any of the later periods. In numbers involved it is probably only in the hundreds; so it is a very different order of magnitude. And the Thai are absolutely determined to deal with this themselves. We do give them equipment and assistance and that kind of thing, but it is their job to deal with it as they see it, and surely I think we would all agree it is much sounder—and this is the way they see it—to have a nation deal with its own problems of this type.

I. White House Statement on Thai-United States Discussions on Economic Development and International Security *

October 7, 1966

The President met today (October 7) with two distinguished statesmen from Thailand, Minister of National Development Pote Sarasin and Foreign Minister Thanat Khoman. The discussion centered on the economic development programs of Thailand.

Minister Pote Sarasin reviewed Thailand's rapid economic progress. Some 60 percent of the Thai budget is devoted to economic development.

The President made clear that the United States would continue to join with other interested countries in assisting the economic development of Thailand and noted that the soundness and effectiveness of Thai programs had resulted during the last 5 years in substantial participation by the World Bank and other nations. The President further indicated that the United States would continue to supply equipment and training to assist actions already undertaken by Thailand to stamp out insurgency instigated by outside forces.

The President repeated to the Thai Ministers that the United States continued to adhere fully to its commitments to Thailand under the Southeast Asia Treaty of 1954, ratified by the Senate, and reaffirmed that this treaty represented an individual obligation of the United States in accordance with its terms and as stated in the communique between Foreign Minister Thanat and Secretary Rusk in 1962. The President made clear that these commitments had the full support of the American people, who recognized the firm Thai resolve to defend their own independence and freedom, and the major contribution Thailand was making to the security of the area.

---

* *Ibid.*, p. 734.

J. State Department Comment on a Secret Defense Paper Signed with Thailand in 1965*

July 10, 1969

The State Department acknowledged today that the United States signed a secret defense paper with Thailand in 1965, but a spokesman presented it as no more than a "military contingency plan" within the framework of previous commitments to come to Thailand's defense.

Robert J. McCloskey, the State Department spokesman, took issue with charges this week by Senator J. W. Fulbright, Democrat of Arkansas, that the secret arrangement had broadened American commitments to Thailand. He also asserted that the contingency plan specifically required United States consent before being implemented.

Mr. McCloskey indicated that it was customary to have such agreements with countries with which the United States has security pacts.

When newsmen suggested that there might be something unusual in having United States officials sign such contingency plans, Mr. McCloskey said that this approach had been adopted "to certify that this is the result of consultation between representatives of the two Governments and that it became a paper of record in the two Governments."

But Mr. McCloskey steadfastly refused to go into any details of the agreement though other sources indicated that it spelled out in core details the use of American troops in Thailand's defense under terms of the Southeast Asia Treaty Organization.

The sources also asserted that the special arrangement was designed to calm the fears of Thailand's anti-Communist leaders at a time when the Communist-led insurgency in northeastern Thailand was reported to be receiving increased aid from North Viet-Nam.

The Thai Government was reported to have taken the secret paper as reassurance that the United States would provide all the American troops necessary to combat an armed attack. But Administration sources insisted that it did not offer an "open-ended" commitment of American troops for Thai defense.

It was not clear whether Washington agreed in the paper to interpret mass, secret infiltration into Thailand as an armed attack committing the use of American forces, or merely pledged to react to an overt offensive across the Thai borders.

Mr. McCloskey, asked about such points, told newsmen: "I am not going to get into the details of what is involved in a classified contingency planning paper."

He said the secret paper had been signed by Premier Thanom Kittikachorn of Thailand, who was then the Defense Minister, and by Lieut. Gen. Richard Stilwell, who was then a major general in charge of the American military advisory mission to Thailand.

Senator Fulbright, chairman of the Foreign Relations Committee, was re-

*The New York Times, July 11, 1969.

ported to have received a top-secret Defense Department summary of the secret paper, but the Senator's aides said he wanted the entire arrangement made public.

K. Comment by Premier Thanom Kittikachorn of Thailand on the Existence of a Secret Agreement Between the United States and Thailand*

July 11, 1969

Marshal Thanom Kittikachorn, the Premier of Thailand, has denied that there is a secret agreement between the United States and this country that goes beyond the Southeast Asia Treaty Organization.

Marshal Thanom made the statement at a news conference yesterday in reply to questions about a Washington Report of a secret agreement.

Marshal Thanom said: "There is no such agreement." On further questioning he mentioned an agreement, negotiated in March, 1962, in which the United States pledged to "give full effect to its obligations under the SEATO treaty" and declared that the United States obligation to Thailand did not depend upon the prior agreement of all other parties to the treaty.

A reporter noted that the Washington report referred to a secret agreement. Marshal Thanom then said that there was yet another agreement on military cooperation reached with the representative of the Joint United States Military Advisory Group in Thailand.

He said, "It was three or four years ago. I can't remember exactly when."

This agreement, he said, "gives us the certainty and confidence that the United States will not desert us and let us fight against the Communists on our own." He did not elaborate.

United States Embassy sources here declined to comment on the Marshal's statements.

L. Statement by President Nixon on United States Relations with Thailand*

[Extract]

July 28, 1969

In returning once again to Thailand, I am deeply conscious of the fact that Thailand has a special interest in the strength of America's determination to honor its commitments in Asia and the Pacific. We will honor those commitments—not only because we consider them solemn obligations but, equally importantly, because we fully recognize that we and the nations of Southeast Asia share a vital stake in the future peace and prosperity of this region.

Both geography and common interest link the United States with the nations

---

*Ibid., July 12, 1969..
*Department of State Bulletin, Aug. 25, 1969, p. 154.

of Southeast Asia. We recognize the Pacific Ocean not as a barrier but as a bridge. We recognize also that whether peace can be maintained in Asia and the Pacific will determine whether peace can be maintained in the world, and we recognize here in Asia the beginnings of patterns of dynamic development that can be of enormous significance.

Our determination to honor our commitments is fully consistent with our conviction that the nations of Asia can and must increasingly shoulder the responsibility for achieving peace and progress in the area. The challenge to our wisdom is to support the Asian countries' efforts to defend and develop themselves, without attempting to take from them the responsibilities which should be theirs. For if domination by the aggressor can destroy the freedom of a nation, too much dependence on a protector can eventually erode its dignity.

What we seek for Asia is a community of free nations able to go their own way and seek their own destiny with whatever cooperation we can provide—a community of independent Asian countries, each maintaining its own traditions and yet each developing through mutual cooperation. In such an arrangement, we stand ready to play a responsible role in accordance with our commitments and basic interests.

*   *   *

Thailand is one of the foremost examples of the promise that the future holds in Asia—in terms of its economic development, its commitment to advancing the welfare of its people, and its larger view of new patterns of regional cooperation that can benefit all the nations and peoples of Asia. We are proud to consider Thailand our friend.

*   *   *

M. Joint Statement Issued by the United States and Thailand on Reduction of U.S. Forces*

Bangkok, August 26, 1969

The Royal Thai Government and the United States Government today announced the opening of talks to arrange for a gradual reduction of level of U.S. forces in Thailand consistent with assessment of both governments of the security situation.

The talks will be held in the first instance between the Foreign Minister of Thailand, H.E. Thanat Khoman, and the U.S. Ambassador to Thailand, Leonard Unger, in Bangkok beginning on or about September 1st. More detailed conversations in which Thai and U.S. representatives will participate will follow to plan for any reductions it is considered desirable to make over a period of time assuming there is no significant alteration in the security situation in Southeast Asia.

*Ibid., Sept. 15, 1969, p. 245.

THE UNITED STATES

AND INDONESIA

THE UNITED STATES AND INDONESIA

Commentary

Consistent with its practice *vis-a-vis* India, Pakistan, Ceylon, Burma, and the Philippines, the United States in 1945 supported Indonesian nationalist forces in their struggle for independence from the Dutch. These nationalist forces had gained some strength before the Second World War and during the War were used by the Japanese in the administration of the country; in 1945, as had occurred in Indochina, the Japanese granted the Indonesians "independence," thus allowing creation of the Indonesian Republic. When the Dutch tried to re-establish control over the islands by negotiations and later by force, they met with strong resistance and were frustrated by the Indonesian forces in their attempt. In the meantime, the Republic appealed to the United Nations to bring about cessation of hostilities, and the United States also exerted considerable influence behind the scenes to pressure the Dutch into accepting the Republic position. After difficult negotiations which brought about a *modus vivendi,* known as the Hague Agreement, complete Indonesian independence resulted in August, 1950.

After 1950 the United States provided huge amounts of military and economic assistance to the Republic led by President Sukarno who for some years devoted himself to urgent internal problems. By the 1960's, however, much of the aid was being used in military confrontations with the Dutch over West Irian and with Malaysia, which the Indonesian president expressed a desire to destroy. These facts and Sukarno's seemingly pro-Peking neutralism in foreign policy led to United States-Indonesian difficulty and the termination of American assistance. A *coup d'etat* engineered by Indonesian generals in 1965-1966 after an attempted takeover of the country by Chinese-backed Communists removed the charismatic president from office and established a military regime. Since then Indonesian-American relations have again become more normal though many problems have yet to be resolved.

POLICY TOWARD INDONESIAN INDEPENDENCE

A. United Nations Security Council Resolution on the Indonesian Question*

January 28, 1949

The Security Council,

Recalling its resolutions of 1 August 1947, 25 August 1947, and 1 November 1947, with respect to the Indonesian Question:

Taking note with approval of the Reports submitted to the Security Council by its Committee of Good Offices for Indonesia;

Considering that its resolutions of 24 December 1948 and 28 December 1948 have not been fully carried out;

Considering that continued occupation of the territory of the Republic of Indonesia by the armed forces of the Netherlands is incompatible with the restoration of good relations between the parties and with the final achievement of a just and lasting settlement of the Indonesian dispute;

Considering that the establishment and maintenance of law and order throughout Indonesia is a necessary condition to the achievement of the expressed objectives and desires of both parties;

Noting with satisfaction that the parties continue to adhere to the principles of the Renville Agreement[1] and agree that free and democratic elections should be held throughout Indonesia for the purpose of establishing a constituent assembly at the earliest practicable date, and further agree that the Security Council should arrange for the observation of such elections by an appropriate agency of the United Nations; and that the representative of the Netherlands has expressed his government's desire to have such elections held not later than 1 October 1949;

Noting also with satisfaction that the Government of the Netherlands plans to transfer sovereignty to the United States of Indonesia by 1 January 1950, if possible, and, in any case, during the year 1950;

Conscious of its primary responsibility for the·maintenance of international peace and security, and in order that the rights, claims and position of the parties may not be prejudiced by the use of force;

1. Calls upon the Government of the Netherlands to insure the immediate discontinuance of all military operations, calls upon the Government of the Republic simultaneously to order its armed adherents to cease guerrilla warfare, and calls upon both parties to co-operate in the restoration of peace and the maintenance of law and order throughout the area affected.

2. Calls upon the Government of the Netherlands to release immediately and unconditionally all political prisoners arrested by them since 17 December 1948 in the Republic of Indonesia; and to facilitate the immediate return of officials of the Government of the Republic of Indonesia to Jogjakarta in order that

*Documents on American Foreign Relations, 1949, pp. 574-78.
[1]A truce brought about by the U.N., signed on the U.S. Transport, *Renville*.

they may discharge their responsibilities under paragraph 1 above and in order to exercise their appropriate functions in full freedom, including administration of the Jogjakarta area, which shall include the city of Jogjakarta and its immediate environs. The Netherlands authorities shall afford to the Government of the Republic of Indonesia such facilities as may reasonably be required by that Government for its effective function in the Jogjakarta area and for communication and consultation with all persons in Indonesia.

3. Recommends that, in the interest of carrying out the expressed objectives and desires of both parties to establish a federal, independent, and sovereign United States of Indonesia at the earliest possible date, negotiations be undertaken as soon as possible by representatives of the Government of the Netherlands and representatives of the Republic of Indonesia with the assistance of the Commission referred to in paragraph 4 below on the basis of the principles set forth in the Linggadjati and Renville Agreements, and taking advantage of the extent of agreement reached between the parties regarding the proposals submitted to them by the United States representative on the Committee of Good Offices on 10 September 1948; and in particular, on the basis that:

> (a) The establishment of the Interim Federal Government which is to be granted the powers of internal government in Indonesia during the interim period before the transfer of sovereignty shall be the result of the above negotiations and shall take place not later than 15 March 1949;
> (b) The elections which are to be held for the purpose of choosing representatives to an Indonesian Constituent Assembly should be completed by 1 October 1949; and
> (c) The transfer of sovereignty over Indonesia by the Government of the Netherlands to the United States of Indonesia should take place at the earliest possible date and in any case not later than 1 July 1950;

Provided that if no agreement is reached by one month prior to the respective dates referred to in sub-paragraphs (a), (b), and (c) above, the Commission referred to in paragraph 4 (a) below or such other United Nations agency as may be established in accordance with paragraph 4 (c) below, shall immediately report to the Security Council with its recommendations for a solution of the difficulties.

4. (a) The committee of Good Offices shall henceforth be known as the United Nations Commission for Indonesia. The Commission shall act as the representative of the Security Council in Indonesia and shall have all of the functions assigned to the Committee of Good Offices by the Security Council since 18 December, and the functions conferred on it by the terms of this resolution. The Commission shall act by majority vote, but its reports and recommendations to the Security Council shall present both majority and minority views if there is a difference of opinion among the members of the Commission.

(b) The Consular Commission is requested to facilitate the work of the United Nations Commission for Indonesia by providing military observers and other staff and facilities to enable the Commission to carry out its duties under the Council's resolutions of 24 and 28 December 1948 as well as under the present resolution, and shall temporarily suspend other activities.

(c) The Commission shall assist the parties in the implementation of this resolution, and shall assist the parties in the negotiations to be undertaken under paragraph 3 above and is authorized to make recommendations to them or to the Security Council on matters within its competence. Upon agreement being reached in such negotiations the Commission shall make recommendations to the Security Council as to the nature, powers, and functions of the United Nations agency which should remain in Indonesia to assist in the implementation of the provisions of such agreement until sovereignty is transferred by the Government of the Netherlands to the United States of Indonesia.

(d) The Commission shall have authority to consult with representatives of areas in Indonesia other than the Republic, and to invite representatives of such areas to participate in the negotiations referred to in paragraph 3 above.

(e) The Commission or such other United Nations agency as may be established in accordance with its recommendation under paragraph 4 (c) above is authorized to observe on behalf of the United Nations the elections to be held throughout Indonesia and is further authorized, in respect of the Territories of Java, Madura and Sumatra, to make recommendations regarding the conditions necessary (a) to ensure that the elections are free and democratic, and (b) to guarantee freedom of assembly, speech and publication at all times, provided that such guarantee is not construed so as to include the advocacy of violence or reprisals.

(f) The Commission should assist in achieving the earliest possible restoration of the civil administration of the Republic. To this end it shall, after consultation with the parties, recommend the extent to which, consistent with reasonable requirements of public security and the protection of life and property, areas controlled by the Republic under the Renville Agreement (outside of the Jogjakarta area) should be progressively returned to the administration of the Government of the Republic of Indonesia, and shall supervise such transfers. The recommendations of the Commission may include provision for such economic measures as are required for the proper functioning of the administration and for the economic well-being of the population of the areas involved in such transfers. The Commission shall, after consultation with the parties, recommend which if any Netherlands forces shall be retained temporarily in any area (outside of the Jogjakarta area) in order to assist in the maintenance of law and order. If either of the parties fails to accept the recommendations of the Commission mentioned in this paragraph, the Commission shall report immediately to the Security Council with its further recommendations for a solution of the difficulties.

(g) The Commission shall render periodic reports to the Council, and special reports whenever the Commission deems necessary.

(h) The Commission shall employ such observers, officers and other persons as it deems necessary.

5. Requests the Secretary-General to make available to the Commission such staff, funds and other facilities as are required by the Commission for the discharge of its function.

6. Calls upon the Government of the Netherlands and the Republic of Indonesia to co-operate fully in giving effect to the provisions of this resolution.

**B. Statement by Warren Austin, U.S. Representative to the U.N.
Security Council, on Implementation of the January 28
Resolution on Indonesia***

March 10, 1949

I should like to state that the United States Government continues to believe that the Security Council's resolution of 28 January represents a sound and practical basis for a just and lasting solution of the Indonesian question, and we continue to support it fully.

Five weeks have passed since the Security Council adopted this resolution. During those five weeks, it must be admitted, little progress has been made in the implementation of the provisions of the Council's resolution. There has been neither actual nor complete cessation of hostilities in Indonesia, and active warfare, both guerilla and organized, is continuing to a variable extent in different areas. This has been reported to us by the United Nations Commission's Military Executive Board in the Commission's report of 1 March.

It is true that the Netherlands has decided to lift the restrictions on the freedom of movement of the leaders of the Republic of Indonesia and that the Netherlands has stated that the lifting of these restrictions is not dependent on the Republican leaders' participation in the proposed conference at The Hague. We have yet to see, however, the practical results of this decision and the leaders of the Republic are, as far as is known, still in residence at Bangka and Prapat. In the Netherland's Memorandum III contained in Appendix E of the Commission's report of 1 March it is stated that the Republican leaders will be subject to the same restrictions as everybody else, or, in other words, that they will be permitted the same freedom as other civilians enjoy in the areas under Netherlands control. It does not appear, however, that they are free to visit their own territory under Republican control or to have contact with their adherents in those areas. It is apparent that the Dutch have not offered the unconditional freedom which was contemplated in the Council resolution. For instance, the Republican leaders are not allowed to return to Jogjakarta.

Furthermore, the Netherlands has indicated that it is not prepared to restore the Government of the Republic to its capital at Jogjakarta, as provided in the Council's resolution of 28 January.

We are unable to understand the attitude of the Government of the Netherlands on this question, for two reasons; first, the provisions of the Security Council resolution in this respect are intrinsically sound and reasonable; secondly, the proposed accelerated transfer of sovereignty would give the Republic the power to restore the capital of Jogjakarta.

We have listened [sic] today to what the representative of the Netherlands had to say, and, among other things, he said the following: "It is hoped that by a supreme concerted effort of all parties it should be possible for such a conference to reach an agreement in about six weeks on the main principle

---

*Ibid., pp. 578-81.

for the subjects I have mentioned before. After that, another six weeks will probably be needed, as far as the Netherlands are concerned, for the ratification of the agreements, after which the transfer of sovereignty could take place. From that moment onward, responsibility for the affairs of Indonesia would rest with the Indonesians; they would be responsible for the elections, the maintenance of law and order etc. We shall be prepared to continue to render them assistance for a short while, but only if expressly requested to do so."

I now ask whether the Republicans would be competent to maintain law and order in twelve weeks, as stated. Is it clear that they are not competent to do so now? Again, is it clear that the anarchy described to us in this address would follow on restoration if it were effected now instead of twelve weeks later?

The Security Council resolution of 28 January considers the earliest practicable date for that transfer of sovereignty, but it puts the deadline off until 1 July 1950; that is to say, admittedly a year later, a year after that accelerated deadline. Therefore, the serious question arises whether the dangers spoken of here as probable aftermaths of the restoration of the Republic to power at its capital in Jogjakarta, are real. In other words, does not this address to which we have listened admit that they are not, that they are merely fancied dangers?

What were the reasons which led the Security Council to order the restoration of the Government of the Republic to its former seat of authority? My Government believed at the time of the adoption of the resolution, and continues to believe now, that military action cannot be permitted to eliminate one of the parties before the Council. We continue to believe that until the Republican Government can resume governmental responsibility at Jogjakarta, it cannot be expected to assume the responsibilities which negotiation for a just and lasting political settlement require and entail. For the Republican leaders to take part in any negotiations which are meaningful, must they not have the opportunity to assemble as a government in their own territory, to re-establish the contact of that government with its members who are dispersed by the military action, and to be able to represent accurately the wishes of political adherents?

This is not a question of form or rhetoric; it is a vital question. We have always understood, as has the Netherlands, that any agreement for a settlement of the political future of Indonesia would have to be reached with the Government of the Republic. The Linggadjati and Renville Agreements amply bear out this point. I am glad also to note that the Netherlands has confirmed its point of view in this respect in connection with the proposed conference at The Hague. There would be little of permanent value in any plan which would fail to take this central fact into account.

In order to negotiate an agreement with the Government of the Republic, there must be responsible heads of an organized Republican Government with whom to deal. An agreement resulting from negotiations undertaken without reference to such requirements seems necessarily doomed to futility. For these reasons it was apparent to my Government, and I believe to the majority of the members of the Security Council, when we were considering this matter in January, that a necessary first step in the solution of the Indonesian question was the re-establishment of the Republican Government at Jogjakarta. Unfortunately, this provision of the resolution of 28 January has not been carried out, as the Commission informed us in its report, which states: "The Netherlands Government has not complied with the basic prerequisites of further action under the resolution." The basic factor in the present political deadlock in Indonesia is the refusal of the Netherlands Government to permit the re-establishment of the Republican Government at Jogjakarta.

In the second memorandum submitted by the Netherlands to the Commission the Netherlands maintains that to allow the return of the Republican Government to Jogjakarta would be tantamount to precluding the possibility of achieving the speedy transfer of sovereignty as envisaged by the Netherlands because with the Republican Government restored to Jogjakarta, the maintenance of law and order by the Netherlands would be impossible. But they also say here that it would be possible within twelve weeks after this accelerated transfer of sovereignty.

This seems to be a very extreme position. I believe that the records of the Committee of Good Offices during the past year indicate that unstable conditions in Indonesia were not the result of the Republican Government's existence at Jogjakarta, but were directly attributable to the fact that the negotiations for a political settlement failed to produce any concrete results.

The extensive guerrilla warfare now being carried on in Indonesia is the direct consequence of the Netherlands' abandonment of negotiations in favour of military action. Is it entirely consistent to propose, as the Netherlands proposes, the transfer of sovereignty three or four months hence to an Indonesian Government which will include the Republic as a member State while at the same time maintaining that the immediate restoration of the Republic in the limited area of Jogjakarta would result in chaos?

It seems to my Government that if Indonesia is to receive early independence, as envisaged by the Netherlands plan, a beginning must be made now by the re-establishment of the Republic. Since the Security Council last considered this matter [410th meeting], the Netherlands Government has made a new proposal that a round table conference be held at The Hague to discuss the conditions for and the means by which the earliest possible transfer of sovereignty could be effectuated, with simultaneous establishment of the Netherlands-Indonesian Union and arrangements for the transition period, including the setting up of a federal interim government, these provisions being considered in their relation to the accelerated transfer of sovereignty.

The Netherlands has issued invitations to the President of the Republic, to other non-Republican Indonesian leaders and to the United Nations Commission for Indonesia to attend this conference. Some information on the Netherlands proposal was given by the United Nations Commission in its report of 1 March and also in a letter to the President of the Security Council from the Netherlands representative dated 2 March. This proposal is in general terms and is regarded by our Commission as a counter-proposal or as a substitute for the provisions of the resolution of 28 January. Our Commission has asked for instructions as to what its position should be towards the invitation which has been extended to it.

We are also informed by the supplementary report of the Commission [S/1270 Add. 1] that the President of the Republic, Mr. Soekarno, has indicated to the Netherlands authorities that he is not at present in a position to accept the invitation. He has, however, stated that he could agree in principle with the purpose of such a conference, and that if certain prior conditions were fulfilled his Government might be prepared to send a delegation. The principal condition is the restoration of the Republican Government at Jogjakarta in accordance with the provisions of the Security Council's resolution. There is an indication in the second appendix to the Commission's supplementary report [S/1270 Add. 1] that the non-Republican Indonesian leaders represented in the Federal Assembly for Consultation are in agreement with the President of the Republic on the necessity for the restoration of the Republican Government at Jogjakarta in accordance with the Security Council's resolution.

The second prerequisite for the acceptance by the Republican Government of the invitation to attend the conference at The Hague is that the position of the United Nations Commission as provided in the resolution of 28 January should not be prejudiced thereby. It is our understanding that the Netherlands has invited the participation of the Commission in accordance with the terms of the Council's resolution, and there would, therefore, appear to be no difficulty on this point. It would be unfortunate, in our view, if agreement could not be reached by the parties concerned on the preliminary step, the restoration of the Government of the Republic of Jogjakarta in accordance with the provisions of the Security Council's resolution, in order to remove an obstacle to further free negotiations between the parties.

If the parties came to such an agreement on the terms and conditions for holding the proposed conference at The Hague, we believe that negotiations between them at such a conference would be consistent with the basic purposes and objectives of the Council's resolution of 28 January which, of course, would remain in full force and effect. We believe that it would be appropriate for the Security Council's Commission to consult with the respresentatives of the Netherlands, the Government of the Republic and the leaders of the Federal Assembly for Consultation, and to assist them in reaching such agreement. If agreement were reached and the conference held, our Commission could participate therein in accordance with its terms of reference.

ECONOMIC AND MILITARY ASSISTANCE

NEW GUINEA PROBLEM

A. Comment by Secretary Dulles on United States Policy and Indonesia*

[Extract]

April 3, 1956

As far as economic assistance is concerned, the United States has no desire or intention of taking over the Dutch industrial position in Indonesia . . . Indonesia was a colony, and there was a very large amount of Netherlands capital . . . there. There is no desire or purpose on the part of the United States, governmentally or through encouraging private business, to take over that dominant economic position which the Dutch enjoyed.

We are giving a certain amount of economic assistance to Indonesia. Just before I was there[1] we signed a Public Law 480 arrangement with Indonesia which involved approximately $95 million worth of agricultural surplus goods.[2] So we are sympathetic to assisting Indonesia where it desires such assistance. But certainly we do not expect to take over the Dutch commercial position in Indonesia . . .

[With reference to the question of Netherlands New Guinea—West Irian] we expect to continue to take a position of neutrality because that is our general policy with relation to these highly controversial matters which involve countries both of whom are friends and where we ourselves are not directly involved.

B. Comment by Secretary Dulles Concerning the United States Position on the Status of New Guinea*

November 19, 1957

Our position on that matter [the status and future development of West New Guinea] is similar to that which we took last year. That is a position of neutrality. The arguments pro and con are closely balanced. We do not see a clear case to be made for either side sufficient, we think, to enable us to take a positive position on one side or another. So that we will continue, I expect, this year to abstain on the resolution. That depends, of course, to some extent on what the ultimate form of the resolution is. But that's our present disposition: to take the same position we did in previous years.

American Foreign Policy: Current Documents, 1956, p. 812.

[1] The Secretary of State visited Djakarta Mar. 12-13, 1956.

[2] Agreement of Mar. 2, 1956

American Foreign Policy: Current Documents, 1957, p. 1138.

C. Comment by Secretary Dulles on Recent Political Developments in Indonesia*

[Extract]

February 11, 1958

. . . You asked about the trend in recent months in Indonesia. I think that there has been a growing feeling among the Muslims, particularly in the islands other than Java—a feeling of concern at growing Communist influence in the Government in Java and in the feeling that the economic resources of these outer islands, like Sumatra, are being exploited contrary to the best interests of the entire Indonesian people.[1] That unrest has made itself manifest. The working out of these problems is primarily an internal problem for the Indonesian people and their Government. Actually, we observe what has gone on with interest, but we don't take any part in or interfere with these internal governmental problems.

We would like to see in Indonesia a government which is constitutional and which reflects the real interest and desires of the people of Indonesia. As you know, there is a kind of a "guided democracy" trend there now which is an evolution which may not quite conform with the provisional constitution and apparently does not entirely satisfy large segments of the population.

We doubt very much that the people of Indonesia will ever want a Communist-type or a Communist-dominated government. Most of them are Muslims, and they would not want, I think, to be subjected to a type of government which everywhere, I would say, where it does have power, maintains itself only by coercive methods and does not respond to the will of the people.

D. Comment by Secretary Dulles on United States Policy Regarding Arms Shipments to Indonesia*

[Extract]

April 8, 1958

The United States has a broad policy with respect to arms, which, I am sorry to say, seems not to be shared by the Soviet-bloc countries. We believe that arms should be supplied to a country from without only in accordance with certain fairly well-defined principles. One of these is the need of a country to have defense against possible aggression from without. The other is to have

*American Foreign Policy: Current Documents, 1958, p. 1208.

[1]The day before the Secretary's news conference—i.e., on Feb. 10, 1958—the non-Communist Revolutionary Council on West Sumatra issued a 5-day ultimatum to the Indonesian Government demanding the resignation of Premier Djuanda, the formation of a new cabinet in which the Communists would not be represented, and an end to the "guided democracy" program of President Sukarno. The Indonesian Government rejected the ultimatum and, upon its expiration on Feb. 15, the Revolutionary Council proclaimed itself the new Government of Indonesia. With the return of President Sukarno from a 6-weeks tour abroad, the regular Government of Indonesia began retaliatory air action on Feb. 21 against the rebel group.

*Ibid., pp. 1209-10.

small arms which would be required for a normal police force and the forces required to maintain internal order against subversive activities and the like which would not be of great proportions and not stimulated from abroad. But we do not believe that the promiscuous spreading of large amounts of major armaments around the world is a sound or a healthy practice. We try not to indulge in that ourselves. And we would be glad if others followed the same practice. That is the principle that has guided us in general in different parts of the world. I would not say that there is any principle that I can define here with sufficient elaboration to cover every possible contingency, and perhaps every rule has its exception. But, broadly speaking, those are our principles. A spreading of arms, which may be primarily designed for offensive operations, is not something that we approve of.

*   *   *

There is, I think, a report of a new request from the Indonesian Government for arms, but that has not yet been actually received. We got a request back last July, as I recall, for a very large amount of arms indeed. We asked the Indonesian Government for certain clarifications about that request. It turned out that what they were requesting was an amount of arms of the value between $600 million and $700 million. Shortly after that there were statements made about the West New Guinea or West Irian situation, whichever you call it, which came with the failure of Indonesia to get a two-thirds vote for a United Nations resolution which they wanted. These statements indicated that they might want to use force to produce the result which they had failed to get through the peaceful processes of the United Nations. In the light of those indications which came from Indonesia it did not seem that it would fit in with the United States policy to allow the export of any such vast quantity of arms as the Indonesian Government has referred to, nor did it seem to be any likelihood at all that there was in any quarter a threat of aggression against Indonesia which would require any such quantity of arms. That was the situation which continued until later on when the revolt broke out, and it did not seem wise to the United States to be in the position of supplying arms to either side of that civil revolution. That conforms, generally speaking, to our policy.

*   *   *

I am sure it is still our view that the situation there [in Indonesia] is primarily an internal one, and we intend to conform scrupulously to the principles of international law that apply to such a situation. It is quite true that the Soviet bloc is now supplying large amounts of arms under conditions which we hardly think is good international practice. But I use "good" in the sense of standards of judgment which are beyond those of accepted international law at the present time. We do not question that what is going on is within the compass of accepted principles of international law. They do not conform to what would be and has been United States policy with respect to the disposal of arms around the world.

E. Comment by Secretary Dulles on United States Policy of Nonintervention in the Indonesian Rebellion*

May 20, 1958

The United States believes that the situation in Indonesia can be and should be dealt with as an Indonesian problem. The United States itself is a nation which has suffered civil war, and we have sympathy and regret when another country undergoes the losses in life and the economic dislocations that are incidental to civil war. But we do believe that the situation can be and should be dealt with as an Indonesian matter by the Indonesians without intrusion from without, and we do hope that there will be quickly restored peace and stability in the Indonesian Republic.

AGREEMENT BETWEEN THE UNITED STATES AND INDONESIA ON THE SALE OF MILITARY EQUIPMENT AND SERVICES TO INDONESIA

F. Howard P. Jones, U.S. Ambassador to Indonesia, to Dr. Raden Soebandrio, Indonesian Minister of Foreign Affairs*

Djakarta, August 13, 1958

Excellency:

I have the honor to refer to recent conversations between representatives of our two governments, concerning the sale of military equipment, materials, and services to the Government of Indonesia, as a result of which the following understandings have been reached:

1. The Government of the United States, subject to applicable United States laws and regulations, shall make available to the Government of Indonesia on terms of payments in rupiahs or dollars such equipment, materials, and services as may be requested by the Government of Indonesia and approved by the Government of the United States. Such equipment, materials, and services as may be made available hereunder shall be designated by the Government of the United States in supplementary memoranda, which shall specify the pertinent terms of sale as they are mutually agreed upon.

2. The following assurances provided by the Government of Indonesia on March 14, 1957, shall be applicable to such equipment, materials, and services as may be made available hereunder:

> (a) Any weapons or other military equipment or services purchased by the Government of Indonesia from the Government of the United States shall be used by the Government of Indonesia solely for legitimate national self-defense, and it is self-evident that the Government of Indonesia, as a member of the United Nations Organization, interprets the term "legitimate national self-defense" within the scope of the United Nations Charter as excluding an act of aggression against any other state.

*Ibid., p. 1210.
*Ibid., pp. 1211-12.

(b) Any weapons or other military equipment or services purchased by the Government of Indonesia from the Government of the United States shall not be sold or otherwise disposed of to third parties.

3. In addition to the use provided for in subsection (a) of paragraph 2 of this note, the Government of Indonesia may use such equipment, materials, and services as may be made available hereunder to maintain its internal security.

I have the honor to propose that, if these understandings are acceptable to Your Excellency's Government, this note and Your Excellency's note in reply concurring therein shall constitute an agreement between our two governments, effective on the date of Your Excellency's note.

Accept, Excellency, the renewed assurances of my highest consideration.

G. Dr. Soebandrio to Ambassador Jones*

Djakarta, August 13, 1958

Excellency:

I have the honour to acknowledge receipt of Your Excellency's note No. 107 dated August 13, which reads as follows:

[Text as printed above]

I have the honor to confirm that the Government of the Republic of Indonesia concurs in the understandings as stated in the above-quoted note and that this reply and Your Excellency's note will constitute an agreement between our two governments effective on the date of exchange.

Accept, Excellency, the assurances of my highest consideration.

INDONESIAN DISPUTES WITH NEIGHBORING COUNTRIES

H. Statement by Jonathan B. Bingham, U.S. Representative to the U.N. General Assembly, on the West New Guinea Question*

[Extract]

November 22, 1961

*   *   *

The dispute over the territory of West New Guinea provides this Assembly with a great challenge and an unusual opportunity. I shall not attempt to review the tangled history of this dispute nor presume to pronounce judgment on the conflicting claims of the Governments of Indonesia and the Netherlands. However, hopefully the barren confrontation of claims and counterclaims is nearing its end. Provided the Assembly acts with judicious realism, this territory may

*Ibid. pp. 961-63.
*Ibid.

soon cease to be focus of international disputation. Indeed, it may well serve as a model for responsible decolonization.

My Government regards as imaginative and constructive the initiative which the Government of the Netherlands has taken in proposing its relinquishment of control over West New Guinea, with a United Nations administration for an interim period. The basic condition set by the Government of the Netherlands is that the inhabitants of the territory be afforded the right to exercise freedom of choice with regard to the ultimate disposition of the area. The position of the United States on the principle of self-determination is well known, and we perceive no valid reason why an appropriate expression of the will of the people should be denied the inhabitants of West New Guinea.

On the other hand, while we welcome the general nature of the Netherlands proposal, in our opinion the Netherlands draft resolution represents completely the point of view of its sponsor and does not sufficiently recognize the intense Indonesian interest in the territory. We believe that there is no purpose to be gained by attempting to ignore, as does the Netherlands draft, the claim of Indonesia to sovereignty over the territory the latter calls Irian Barat. The Assembly should, in our view, not be asked to accept either the Dutch claim to sovereignty or the Indonesian claim. Whatever it does should be without prejudice to either side. In the light of the dispute that exists, the proper course, in accordance with the United Nations Charter, would seem to be to assure the people of the area an opportunity at the proper time to express their own choice as to their political future, under the aegis of the United Nations.

In order to assure this result, we believe that any resolution adopted by the Assembly should make perfectly clear that the administration of the area would be turned over by the Dutch to the U.N. by a certain date. The conditions for the transfer would be laid down by the 17th General Assembly, after receiving the recommendations of a small commission comprised of disinterested member states.

We believe that such a U.N. administration, leading to the expression of choice by the people of the area, should provide to Indonesia every reasonable opportunity to pursue its objective of achieving the integration of West New Guinea with Indonesia. During the interim period, Dutch control would have been ended and an impartial U.N. administration would be in complete control. We would assume that under such an administration Indonesia would have access to the area.

* * *

One final point: We have every reason to hope and believe that the Indonesian Government can and will accept the idea of self-determination for West New Guinea, provided that the administration of the process is impartial and provided that Indonesia would have every appropriate access to the area. We believe that it would clearly be in Indonesia's interest to accept the prospective Dutch withdrawal from West New Guinea and then to pursue Indonesia's objectives through peaceful means.

* * *

I. United States Proposals for the Settlement of the West New Guinea Dispute*

May 26, 1962

1. The Governments of Indonesia and the Netherlands would each sign separate agreements or a single agreement which would be presented to the Acting Secretary-General of the United Nations.

2. The Government of the Netherlands would stipulate the transfer of administrative authority over West New Guinea to a temporary executive authority under the Acting Secretary-General of the United Nations at a specified date. The Acting Secretary-General of the United Nations would appoint a mutually acceptable, non-Indonesian administrator who would undertake to administer the territory for a period of not less than one year but not more than two. This administrator would arrange for the termination of Netherlands administration under circumstances that will provide the inhabitants of the territory the opportunity to exercise freedom of choice in accordance with paragraph 4 below. This administrator would replace top Dutch officials with short-term, one year non-Indonesian and non-Dutch officials hired on a contract basis.

3. The temporary executive authority under the Acting Secretary-General of the United Nations would administer West New Guinea during the first year with the assistance of non-Indonesian and non-Dutch personnel. Beginning the second year the Acting Secretary-General of the United Nations would replace United Nations officials with Indonesian officials, it being understood that by the end of the second year full administrative control would be transferred to Indonesia. United Nations technical assistance personnel will remain in an advisory capacity and to assist in preparation for carrying out the provisions of paragraph 4.

4. Indonesia agrees to make arrangements, with the assistance and participation of the Acting Secretary-General of the United Nations and United Nations personnel, to give the people of the territory the opportunity to exercise freedom of choice not later than——years after Indonesia has assumed full administrative responsibility for West New Guinea. The Government of the Netherlands would agree to transfer administration in accordance with this proposal on condition that the Government of the Netherlands would receive, as a result of formal negotiations, adequate guarantees for safeguarding the interests, including the right of self-determination, of the Papuans.

5. Indonesia and the Netherlands agree to share the costs of the foregoing.

6. Once this agreement has been signed, the Government of Indonesia and the Netherlands will resume normal diplomatic relations.

*American Foreign Policy: Current Documents, 1962, pp. 1120-21. These proposals, drawn up by former Ambassador Ellsworth Bunker, acting as Representative of the U.N. Acting Secretary-General in this matter, had been communicated to the Governments of Indonesia and the Netherlands considerably prior to their release to the public. Indonesia had tentatively accepted the proposals as a basis "in principle" for negotiations with the Netherlands; the Government of the Netherlands accepted them with a similar understanding, May 26.

J. Statement by Attorney General Robert F. Kennedy on His Mission to the Far East Concerning the Malaysia Dispute*

January 28, 1964

I have reported to the President, the members of the Cabinet, and the Members of Congress on the fact that the Governments of Malaysia, Indonesia, and the Philippines have agreed to sit down at a conference which will be called by Thanat Khoman, the Foreign Minister of Thailand, which conference will start the first week of February. They will sit down at this conference and make an effort to try to resolve their difficulties.

During that period of time a cease-fire will take place in that part of the world. President Sukarno has issued a cease-fire order in Indonesia, and already the regular military units of Indonesia have been called off in their efforts against Malaysia. The Guerrilla activity against Malaysia cannot be brought under control because some of the guerrillas are in areas where they cannot be contacted for a period of days; so it is not expected that the cease-fire will actually go into existence until the end of the month. This is understood by the Malaysians, by the Indonesians, and by the Filipinos.

The conference will take place in Bangkok. If there is a violation of the cease-fire it will be investigated by Thailand, and Thailand will then make a report to all of the parties involved, as well as to the world in general.

It is a step forward. There are obviously great problems still ahead. There are antagonisms, and there is mistrust between the various nations. There are differences of approach and differences on positions. But I think with good will and with genuine effort that the conference has a chance of success.

The alternative, really, of the conference is the continued war in the jungle. The conference has a better chance for peace. If the conference is not successful in solving the various antagonisms, the countries involved will go back into the jungle and back to killing one another. I think it is quite clear that if that happens, it will escalate and very possibly involve other nations. The United States has certain treaty obligations and other certain responsibilities in that part of the world; so it is a very serious matter. This country and this Government look on the situation with great concern.

Although this is an Asiatic dispute and it must in the last analysis be decided by Asian nations, this country and other countries of the free world will watch this conference with great concern.

K. Comment by Secretary Rusk on Continuation of the United States Aid Program to Indonesia*

April 3, 1964

. . . We have a very limited aid program there [in Indonesia] at the present time. Some of it is of great importance almost regardless of any particular polit-

*American Foreign Policy: Current Documents, 1964, pp. 896-97.
*Ibid., p. 898.

ical situation. For instance, the antimalarial program. This is the kind of thing that must not be allowed to lapse, because, it if lapses, then a large investment of some $30-40 million or more of effort goes down the drain and neighboring countries then become the victims of the failure of an antimalarial campaign in a place like Indonesia. So there is some aid progress.

But, on the other hand, questions of future aid and enlargement of aid turn very much on not only the measures that Indonesia is prepared to take inside the country but also the adjustment of their relations with their own immediate neighbors. We hope this can move forward.

L. Department of State Comment Opposing Legislation to Terminate United States Aid to Indonesia*

August 14, 1964

The Department considers that it would be unwise for Congress to terminate U.S. aid to Indonesia, thereby reducing the administration's flexibility in the conduct of U.S. relations with that country. Our present aid program consists of malaria eradication, certain technical assistance, and training of selected groups of Indonesians in the United States and through U.S. university and other American specialists in Indonesia.

We hope that, after a full presentation of all the facts bearing on the question, the conference committee of the House and the Senate will eliminate or modify this provision prior to final passage of the assistance act.[1]

M. Statement by Ambassador Stevenson on the United States Position in the Malaysian-Indonesian Dispute*

September 10, 1964

My delegation and my Government take a very serious view of the complaint before the Security Council in this case. The Government of Indonesia, a member of the United Nations, has sanctioned the use of force in the pursuit of its quarrel with the sovereign state of Malaysia, which is also a member of the United Nations. The distinguished representative of Indonesia has, indeed, expressed pride in the guerrillas and suggested that his Government will continue to use force until there is a settlement of its quarrel with Malaysia. And we are all aware of the announced objective of Indonesia to "crush Malaysia"—a fellow member of the United Nations.

But Indonesia's quarrel seems to be with the United Kingdom because it sponsored the independence and federation of its dependent territories in the area and is committtted to their defense. And the settlement proposed by Indonesia seems to be that Malaysia must change its paternity in a manner satisfactory to Indonesia.

Ibid., p. 901.

[1] The provision prohibiting foreign aid to Indonesia was stricken in the Senate House conference committee on the foreign aid authorization bill (see *The New York Times*, Oct. 2, 1964).

Department of State Bulletin, Sept. 28, 1964, pp. 448-50.

But, Mr. President, this is not a paternity case. This is an accusation by Malaysia that Indonesia has violated its territorial integrity by force. And the fact, which has not been denied, is that on the night of September 2, 1964, an armed band of significant size—equipped and transported by Indonesia and intended for violence—landed on the sovereign territory of Malaysia.

This incursion is the complaint before this Council. And it is this specific act of violence which my delegation specifically deplores.

Malaysia is a member of the United Nations which at the time of its creation voluntarily submitted its territories to examination by the United Nations to make certain that it was indeed the desire of their inhabitants to join the new state. Malaysia is therefore to an unusual degree a child of the United Nations.

Mr. President, the deterioration of relations between Indonesia and Malaysia must be distressing to every member of the United Nations. None is more distressed than my Government.

My Government recognizes both Indonesia and Malaysia as independent nations; we have tried to maintain friendly relations with both—relations based on mutual respect and seeking no more than mutual benefit. The test of our intentions does not depend upon faith in words: It is certified by a long record of useful and cooperative deeds.

We were an active member of the United Nations commission which helped bring about the birth of the Indonesian nation; we welcomed the independence of Malaya in 1957 and the proclamation of Malaysia just over a year ago this month. We welcomed Malaysia's admission to the United Nations just as we earlier welcomed the admission of Indonesia. With both of these ancient peoples we have sought to work in friendly harmony from the very moment they joined the lengthening list of newly independent nations. We have participated with both of them on the tangible tasks of nation building—the construction of roads and industries, the development of university education, the modernization of agriculture, the improvement of health and child welfare, the training of security forces. And we have been proud to be associated with military contingents from both of these nations in U.N. peacekeeping operations in other parts of the world.

Hence we are all the more distressed by the spectacle of one of these countries organizing and employing force as an instrument of its policy toward the other. We have welcomed the efforts of these neighbors, together with the assistance of the Philippines and Thailand, to work out a peaceful resolution of their differences. Our President has even sent out a personal representative [Attorney General Robert F. Kennedy] to help bring about a cease-fire, to get the conflict out of the jungles and back to the negotiating table.

My Government has believed from the beginning that if there is any legitimate dispute between these two states, which share common problems and enjoy a close ethnic and cultural affinity, it should be settled by negotiation between themselves, with the assistance of whatever good offices they may find mutually helpful.

Against this background, Mr. President, out attitude on the complaint before us grows directly from the obligation each member of this organization has under the charter.

This Council cannot condone the use of force in international relations outside the framework of the charter.

This Council must try to re-create the conditions of peace and security in the area of conflict, to enable the processes of peaceful settlement to move these two nations away from the precipice of war.

Yesterday the distinguished representative of Indonesia was very frank about the fact that force had in fact been used by his Government. He argued that in dealing with neighbors whose policies Indonesia does not like, the use of force on the territory of those neighbors was justified.

He made all too clear that the announced goal to "crush Malaysia" leads in practice to the arming of military units to operate in the territories of a neighboring nation. This is a new and dangerous doctrine of international law, outside the Charter of the United Nations and foreign to everything that man has learned about the danger of escalation from little wars to big wars and the crucial importance of maintaining the peace.

In the world about us there are, this very afternoon, half a hundred active disputes between neighbors—23 of them in Asia, 10 in Africa, 3 in Europe, and 12 in the Western Hemisphere. If other nations involved in these disputes were to take the law into their own hands and drop armed forces on the territory of their neighbors, the precarious peace of our inflammable world would soon go up in smoke.

The distinguished representative of Indonesia said we are faced here with a political problem, not a legal one. But you cannot separate politics and law— and the first law of politics is that there must be some minimum agreement to abide by the rules of the game. The way in which the Indonesian case has been stated here makes it even more necessary that this Council, which is entrusted by the charter with the maintenance of peace and security, clearly identify as inadmissible the armed action of the Indonesian Government against Malaysia on September 2.

The Government of Malaysia, while exercising its inherent right of self-defense also has met its obligation under the charter to bring this matter to the Security Council while there is yet time to escape the fateful consequences of violence and counter-violence.

It is now the duty of this Council to fulfill its obligations to the world community.

Let us focus on the fact that a collision has occurred—a collision which is part of a pattern of hostility which promises to recur and which threatens to expand.

Let us then get on with our duty. And our duty, Mr. President, goes far beyong the angry pointing of a finger at a violation of the charter. Our larger duty is to devise measures to keep these flames from spreading. For it is unmistakably clear that the outer limits of restraint have been reached. And we are face to face with all the dread prospect of escalating violence, with unforeseeable consequences for us all.

Mr. President, this Council can do two practical things. I suggest we get right to work on them.

First, the Council should call for the cessation of armed attack of Malaysia.

Second, the Council should help the parties to this dispute establish the condition and climate in which a negotiation on the merits of the disputed issues can be pursued with any prospect of success. This Council and the Secretary-General may well have a role to play in the establishment of such conditions. And the first condition is, of course, compliance with the call of the Security Council to cease hostilities. Once this improved climate has been created, efforts could then be made to resolve the entire dispute by nonviolent means.

Instruments for peaceful settlement are available. Our task under the charter as members of this Council is to see to it that an agreed instrument is chosen at the earliest possible date and that the parties take steps to pave the way for a return to diplomacy.

The United States delegation has no interest in recriminations about what has happened in the past; we are concerned with the present and the future of peace, and the means of restoring peace and keeping peace in this case. The United States is ready to work constructively and promptly with a deep sense of concern and a sharp sense of urgency for action by the Security Council to put a stop to violence, to create the conditions for peaceful settlement. And I am sure that, as in so many previous cases, there are practical and effective measures available to the United Nations and the Secretary-General to help attain these objectives.

COOLING OF RELATIONS

N. United States Information Agency Statement on Closing of Their Libraries and Reading Rooms in Indonesia*

March 4, 1965

U.S. Information Agency Director Carl T. Rowan announced on March 4 that the United States was closing immediately all USIA libraries and reading rooms in Indonesia, and that USIA personnel involved would be withdrawn promptly from that country.

"This is a decision that we take most reluctantly," said Mr. Rowan. "These libraries have been a symbol of man's search for knowledge, and for the mutual understanding without which peace is difficult, if not impossible, to achieve. That they were valued and appreciated is indicated by the fact that attendance at these libraries rose from 24,000 in 1948 to more than half a million in 1964. We have made it clear that we regard book burnings and the banishing of films and music as a step backward.

"In this instance, however, the Indonesian Government has left us no choice but to close these libraries. Not only has it failed to restrain those who have attacked the libraries periodically, but it has now seized the libraries and placed the whole USIA operation under conditions that we find intolerable. Until such time as our libraries and personnel can function under conditions that meet an acceptable standard of international conduct, USIA will cease to operate in Indonesia."

*American Foreign Policy: Current Documents, 1965, p. 755.

O. Comment by Secretary Rusk on Improving United States Relations with Indonesia*

[Extract]

March 7, 1965

*   *   *

Now, in the case of Indonesia, we have as you know, recently announced that we were withdrawing our information libraries and our information activities there.

They made it practically impossible for those in libraries to operate. They did not throw us out. We withdrew under the conditions in which they were forcing us or trying to force us to operate.

Now, we would like to see good relations with countries like Indonesia. But this requires some effort on both sides.

I think at the present time it is fair to say that our relations are being reduced: they are becoming, to use a diplomatic word, simplified.

We think that Indonesia needs to make a real effort on its side if our relations are to be improved in the months ahead. We hope that it can be, but I cannot assure you that they will be.

*   *   *

P. Statement by Secretary Rusk, Made Before Senate Foreign Relations Committee, on the Status of United States Assistance to Indonesia*

[Extract]

March 9, 1965

. . . The [United States] technical assistance program in Indonesia is currently under review. The United States and Indonesian Governments have been at odds on certain policies and courses of action pursued by the Indonesians. Over the past 2 years there has been a significant change in our assistance program in Indonesia. No loans have been made during this period. No shipments under the Public Law 480 sales agreements for surplus food have been made to Indonesia for nearly a year, and the agreement itself has now expired. In the same period, the technical assistance program, largely for universities, training, and malaria eradication, has dwindled. Under present circumstances it is questionable that a basis will exist for further technical assistance in fiscal year 1966.

*   *   *

-**Ibid.*, p. 755.
**Ibid.*, p. 756.

Q. Joint Communiqué Issued at Meetings Between Ambassador Ellsworth Bunker, And Indonesian Officials on United States-Indonesian Relations *

Djakarta, April 15, 1965

During his visit in Indonesia, Ambassador Ellsworth Bunker, representing President Johnson, has had several meetings with His Excellency President Sukarno, and has met with First Deputy Prime Minister Dr. Subandrio and other Ministers of the Government of Indonesia. These meetings have produced a full and frank exchange of views on the attitudes and desires of the two governments toward the question of the relationship between them.

Both governments have recognized that friendly relations between Indonesia and the United States are of the greatest importance to the people of both countries. Ambassador Bunker has assured President Sukarno that the United States has the objectives of attaining the freedom, welfare and security of all countries. While it is true that on a range of matters of foreign policy the views of Indonesia and those of the United States are divergent, they have agreed that these differences should not be allowed to affect unduly the general pattern of friendship which has existed for so many years between them.

President Sukarno emphasized that Indonesia regards the issue between Indonesia and Malaysia as being of the greatest importance, and that he wishes to see it settled on the basis of the Manila and Tokyo agreements. Ambassador Bunker reaffirmed that the United States deeply regrets that the problem exists, and hopes that a peaceful solution to it can be brought about by Asian powers through these or any other means acceptable to those concerned.

At the same time His Excellency the President and Ambassador Bunker recognized that these differences have produced certain tensions between Indonesia and the United States, and that as a result the programs of assistance to Indonesia which the United States has undertaken in recent years should be reviewed and revised on a continuing basis to be sure that they conform to the desires of the two governments. In specific, Ambassador Bunker informed his Excellency the President that the United States would be willing to continue its program of technical assistance to certain Indonesian universities, and the President assured Ambassador Bunker that this program was welcome to and had the full support of the Government of Indonesia.

On the other hand, His Excellency the President and Ambassador Bunker agreed that in light of the current situation the Peace Corps should cease operations in Indonesia. The Peace Corps Volunteers will, accordingly, take the necessary steps to terminate their programs in an orderly fashion and will depart from Indonesia during the next few weeks.

His Excellency the President and Ambassador Bunker concluded that personal communication between President Sukarno and President Johnson was of great importance to both countries, and undertook to see that it will be maintained.

Ibid., pp. 756-57.

OUSTER OF SUKARNO

R. Report by the Hsinhua News Agency (of the People's Republic of China) on Political Changes in Indonesia*

[Extract]

October 19, 1965

Sudden and drastic political changes have taken place in Indonesia since the night of September 30. At present, in the capital, Djarkarta, and some other cities under the military control of the Indonesian army authorities, Communists and other progressives are being arrested. The headquarters of the Indonesian Communist Party and offices of many mass organizations have been burnt down or wrecked, numerous Leftwing or middle-of-the-road newspapers, including *Harian Rakjat,* organ of the Central Committee of the Indonesian Communist Party have been banned, many colleges and other institutions have been closed down, and the Indonesian Communist Party and many progressive mass organizations outlawed.

    *   *   *

S. Comment by Secretary Rusk on Noninvolvement in the Indonesia Situation*

November 5, 1965

Quite frankly, as far as the facts are concerned, you gentlemen are getting just about all that we have in terms of what is happening in Indonesia.

I think it would not be right for me to attempt any evaluation. I think it is better for the United States not to involve itself directly by comment or by action in that situation. So that a judgment by me at this time I think would be untimely. I just prefer not to attempt that.

T. Joint Statement Issued on United States-Indonesian Matters of Mutual Interest*

September 27, 1966

The Secretary of State of the United States of America, Mr. Dean Rusk, and the Presidium Minister for Political Affairs and Foreign Minister of the Republic of Indonesia, Mr. Adam Malik, met today [September 27] to discuss a wide range of topics of mutual interest. They reviewed U.S. Indonesian rela-

*Ibid., pp. 758-64.
*Ibid., p. 764.
*American Foreign Policy: Current Documents, 1966, p. 694.

tions, the current Indonesian economic situation, Indonesia's position in the world community of nations, and the problem of achieving political stability and economic growth throughout the Far East, including Viet-Nam.

They discussed the improvements in relations between their governments during recent months, and expressed the determination of the two governments to expand areas of agreement and cooperation between Indonesia and the United States.

In discussions of economic matters, the Foreign Minister and the Secretary of State noted Indonesia's recent moves to resume normal relations with agencies of the United Nations, other international organizations and Indonesia's creditors, and recognized the necessity of a multilateral approach to a solution of Indonesian problems of debt relief and foreign assistance.

At the same time, the Government of the United States in recognition of Indonesia's need for immediate emergency assistance has in past months supplied rice and cotton, and is prepared to furnish additional quantities of these commodities as well as spare parts. Training of Indonesian personnel in the United States will also be resumed. The Indonesian Foreign Minister expressed the appreciation of the Indonesian people for help which was given earlier this year and for the willingness of the United States to provide additional emergency assistance.

THE UNITED STATES

AND THE PHILIPPINES

THE UNITED STATES AND THE PHILIPPINES

Commentary

American policy toward the Philippine Islands since 1945 has been mainly concerned with three issues: withdrawal of the vestiges of American sovereignty, economic rehabilitation and stability, and defense against aggression. Because of its nearly half-century of control in the islands, the United States even after independence has assumed special responsibility for the Philippines.

Pursuant to legislation enacted in the United States in 1934, a Philippine Commonwealth was created preparatory to independence. Though the Japanese interlude from 1941-1945 intruded on this period of preparation, on July 4, 1946 a presidential proclamation gave the islands status as an independent republic. Then, in part because Filipinos insisted that they were a target of Japanese aggression due to their connection with the United States, and also because of a feeling of moral obligation, the American Government undertook to restore the national economy. In 1946 Congress passed a Rehabilitation Act providing for $400 million, a sum which was later to be enlarged to cover many of the problems. Also in 1946 Congress enacted the Bell Act under which presumably the Philippine transition from its protected economic position in the American market to a completely free position would be made easier. In addition, the United States concluded defense agreements with the new Republic permitting continuation of American military bases and pledged itself to defend the island nation; it also gave large amounts of military aid and assisted in putting down the Huk rebellion. In 1954 Manila was the site of a conference which created the Southeast Asia Treaty Organization with the Philippines as a charter member.

During the course of events in the 1950's and 1960's American and Filipino policy makers have not always seen eye to eye. One of the major conflicts has been over the degree of American presence in the Philippines as manifested by United States bases. There have also been some economic disagreements. Generally, however, there has been sufficient mutuality of interest in the region to overcome the problems, and Philippine leaders have usually supported United States policies in Asia.

PHILIPPINE INDEPENDENCE

A. Act to Provide American Military Assistance to The Philippines*

June 26, 1946

PUBLIC LAW 454, 79 CONG. 2ND SESS.

Be it enacted by the Senate and House of Representatives of the United States of America in Congress assembled, That this Act may be cited as the "Republic of the Philippines Military Assistance Act."

Sec. 2.

Notwithstanding the provisions of any other law, the President is authorized, upon application by the Republic of the Philippines, and whenever in his discretion the public interest renders such course advisable, to provide: (a) for the instruction and training of military and naval personnel of the Republic of the Philippines; (b) for the maintenance, repair, and rehabilitation of military or navel equipment in the possession of the said country; and (c) for the transfer to the said country of any arms, ammunition, and implements of war as defined in the President's proclamation 2549 of April 9, 1942, or any superseding proclamations; any other aircraft; naval vessels except those in the category of battleships, cruisers, aircraft carriers, destroyers, and submarines; any stores, supplies, services, technical information, material, and equipment: Provided, That such transfer shall be consistent with military and naval requirements of the United States and with the national interest.

Sec. 3.

The President is authorized to provide such assistance or transfer property or information pursuant to section 2, by sale, loan, exchange, lease, gift, or transfer for cash, credit, or other property with or without warranty and upon such other terms and conditions as he shall find proper.

Sec. 4.

As a condition precedent to the receipt of any assistance, information, or property pursuant to this Act the Government of the Republic of the Philippines shall undertake (a) that it will not, without the consent of the President of the United States, transfer title to or possession of any property transferred to it pursuant to this Act, (b) that it will not permit use of any property so received or disclosure of any plan, specification, or other information pertaining thereto or any technical information furnished, by or to anyone not an officer, employee, or agent of the Republic of the Philippines, or for any purpose other than those set forth in this Act, and (c) that the Government of the Republic of the Philippines will make provisions comparable to those customarily made by the United States for the security of any article, plan, or information received under the terms of this Act.

*Documents on American Foreign Relations, 1946, pp. 817-19.

Sec. 5.

The President of the United States is authorized, upon application from the Republic of the Philippines, and whenever in his discretion the public interest renders such a course advisable, to detail officers and enlisted men of the Army of the United States, and the United States Navy and Marine Corps to assist that Government: Provided, That the officers and enlisted men so detailed are authorized to accept from the Republic of the Philippines offices and such compensation and emoluments thereunto appertaining as may be first approved by the Secretary of War, or by the Secretary of the Navy, as the case may be: Provided further, That such compensation may be accepted by the United States Government for remittance to the individual if in the opinion of the Secretary of War, or of the Secretary of the Navy, as the case may be, such a course appears desirable: Provided further, That while so detailed such officers and enlisted men shall receive, in addition to the compensation and emoluments allowed them by that Government, the pay and allowances thereto entitled in the Army of the United States, or the United States Navy, and Marine Corps, and shall be allowed the same credit for longevity, retirement, and for all other purposes that they would receive if they were serving with the forces of the United States: And provided further, That in addition to or in the absence of such compensation from that Government, the officers and enlisted men so detailed shall receive such additional compensation as may be determined by the Secretary of War, or the Secretary of the Navy, as the case may be, and approved by the President.

Sec. 6.

There is hereby authorized to be appropriated, out of any money in the Treasury not otherwise appropriated, such sums as may be necessary to carry out the provisions of this Act: Provided, That articles or services furnished pursuant to the provisions of this Act shall be within the limits of appropriations made specifically for that purpose or to the extent of availability of items which are surplus to the needs of the United States Government.

Sec. 7.

The President may from time to time promulgate such rules and regulations as may be necessary and proper to carry out any of the provisions of this Act; and he may exercise any power or authority conferred upon him by this Act through such department, agency, or officer as he shall direct: Provided, That no property shall be transferred by such department, agency, or officer pursuant to this Act except after consultation with the Secretary of State, and the Secretaries of War and Navy as their respective interests may appear.

Sec. 8.

The provisions of this Act become effective on the 4th day of July 1946 and continue in effect for a period of five years.

B. Proclamation by President Truman on Philippine Independence*

July 4, 1946

Whereas the United States of America by the Treaty of Peace with Spain of December 10, 1898, commonly known as the Treaty of Paris, and by the Treaty with Spain of November 7, 1900, did acquire sovereignty over the Philippines, and by the Convention of January 2, 1930, with Great Britain did delimit the boundary between the Philippine Archipelago and the State of North Borneo; and

Whereas the United States of America has consistently and faithfully during the past forty-eight years exercised jurisdiction and control over the Philippines and its people; and

Whereas it has been the repeated declaration of the legislative and executive branches of the Government of the United States of America that full independence would be granted the Philippines as soon as the people of the Philippines were prepared to assume this obligation; and

Whereas the People of the Philippines have clearly demonstrated their capacity for self-government; and

Whereas the Act of Congress approved March 24, 1934, known as the Philippine Independence Act, directed that, on the 4th Day of July immediately following a ten-year transitional period leading to the independence of the Philippines, the President of the United States of America should by proclamation withdraw and surrender all rights of possession, supervision, jurisdiction, control, or sovereignty of the United States of America in and over the territory and people of the Philippines, except certain reservations therein or thereafter authorized to be made, and, on behalf of the United States of America, should recognize the independence of the Philippines:

Now, therefore, I, Harry S. Truman, President of the United States of America, acting under and by virtue of the authority vested in me by the aforesaid act of Congress, do proclaim that, in accord with and subject to the reservations provided for in the applicable statutes of the United States,

The United States of America hereby withdraws and surrenders all rights of possession, supervision, jurisdiction, control, or sovereignty now existing and exercised by the United States of America in and over the territory and people of the Philippines; and,

On behalf of the United States of America, I do hereby recognize the independence of the Philippines as a separate and self-governing nation and acknowledge the authority and control over the same of the government instituted by the people thereof, under the constitution now in force.

In witness whereof, I have hereunto set my hand and caused the seal of the United States of America to be affixed.

Done at the City of Washington this Fourth day of July in the year of our Lord, nineteen hundred and forty-six, and of the Independence of the United States of America the one hundred and seventy-first.

*Department of State Bulletin, Vol. XV, p. 66.

C. Treaty Defining Relations Between the United States and The Philippines*

Manila, July 4, 1946
Effective, October 22, 1946

The United States of America and the Republic of the Philippines, being animated by the desire to cement the relations of close and long friendship existing between the two countries, and to provide for the recognition of the independence of the Republic of the Philippines as of July 4, 1946 and the relinquishment of American sovereignty over the Philippine Islands, have agreed upon the following articles:

Article I

The United States of America agrees to withdraw and surrender, and does hereby withdraw and surrender, all right of possession, supervision, jurisdiction, control or sovereignty existing and exercised by the United States of America in and over the territory and the people of the Philippine Islands, except the use of such bases, necessary appurtenances to such bases, and the rights incident thereto, as the United States of America, by agreement with the republic of the Philippines, may deem necessary to retain for the mutual protection of the United States of America and of the Republic of the Philippines. The United States of America further agrees to recognize, and does hereby recognize, the independence of the Republic of the Philippines as a separate self-governing nation and to acknowledge, and does hereby acknowledge, the authority and control over the same of the Government instituted by the people thereof, under the Constitution of the Republic of the Philippines.

Article II

The diplomatic representatives of each country shall enjoy in the territories of the other the privileges and immunities derived from generally recognized international law and usage. The consular representatives of each country, duly provided with exequatur, will be permitted to reside in the territories of the other in the places wherein consular representatives are by local laws permitted to reside; they shall enjoy the honorary privileges and the immunities accorded to such officers by general international usage; and they shall not be treated in a manner less favorable than similar officers of any other foreign country.

Article III

Pending the final establishment of the requisite Philippine Foreign service establishments abroad, the United States of America and the Republic of the

Department of State, Treaties and other International Acts Series 1568.

Philippines agree that at the request of the Republic of the Philippines the United States of America will endeavor, in so far as it may be practicable, to represent through its Foreign Service the interests of the Republic of the Philippines in countries where there is no Philippine representation. The two countries further agree that any such arrangements are to be subject to termination when in the judgment of either country such arrangements are no longer necessary.

Article IV

The Republic of the Philippines agrees to assume, and does hereby assume, all the debts and liabilities of the Philippine Islands, its provinces, cities, municipalities and instrumentalities, which shall be valid and subsisting on the date hereof. The Republic of the Philippines will make adequate provision for the necessary funds for the payment of interest on and principal of bonds issued prior to May 1, 1934 under authority of an Act of Congress of the United States of America by the Philippine Islands, or any province, city or municipality therein, and such obligations shall be a first lien on the taxes collected in the Philippines.

Article V

The United States of America and the Republic of the Philippines agree that all cases at law concerning the Government and people of the Philippines which, in accordance with Section 7 (6) of the Independence Act of 1934, are pending before the Supreme Court of the United States of America at the date of the granting of the independence of the Republic of the Philippines shall continue to be subject to the review of the Supreme Court of the United States of America for such period of time after independence as may be necessary to effectuate the disposition of the cases at hand. The contracting parties also agree that following the disposition of such cases the Supreme Court of the United States of America will cease to have the right of review of cases originating in the Philippine Islands.

Article VI

In so far as they are not covered by existing legislation, all claims of the Government of the United States of America or its nationals against the Government of the Republic of the Philippines and all claims of the Government of the Republic of the Philippines and its nationals against the Government of the United States of America shall be promptly adjusted and settled. The property rights of the United States of America and the Republic of the Philippines shall be promptly adjusted and settled by mutual agreement, and all existing property rights of citizens and corporations of the United States of America in the Republic of the Philippines and of citizens and corporations of the Republic of the Philippines in the United States of America shall be acknowledged, respected and safeguarded to the same extent as property rights of citizens and corporations of the Republic of the Philippines and of the United States of America respectively. Both Governments shall designate representatives who may in concert agree on measures best calculated to effect a satisfactory and expeditious disposal of such claims as may not be covered by existing legislation.

Article VII

The Republic of the Philippines agrees to assume all continuing obligations assumed by the United States of America under the Treaty of Peace between the United States of America and Spain concluded at Paris on the 10th day of December, 1898, by which the Philippine Islands were ceded to the United States of America, and under the Treaty between the United States of America and Spain concluded at Washington on the 7th Day of November 1900.

Article VIII

This Treaty shall enter into force on the exchange of instruments of ratification.

This Treaty shall be submitted for ratification in accordance with the constitutional procedures of the United States of America and of the Republic of the Philippines; and instruments of ratification shall be exchanged and deposited at Manila.

Signed at Manila this fourth day of July, one thousand nine hundred forty-six.

Protocol

It is understood and agreed by the High Contracting Parties that this Treaty is for the purpose of recognizing the independence of the Republic of the Philippines and for the maintenance of close and harmonious relations between the two Governments.

It is understood and agreed that this Treaty does not attempt to regulate the details of arrangements between the two Governments for their mutual defense; for the establishment, termination or regulation of the rights and duties of the two countries, each with respect to the other, in the settlement of claims, as to the ownership or control of real or personal property, or as to the carrying out of provisions of law of either country; or for the settlement of rights or claims of citizens or corporations of either country with respect to or against the other.

It is understood and agreed that the conclusion and entrance into force of this Treaty is not exclusive of further treaties and executive agreements providing for the specific regulation of matters broadly covered herein.

It is understood and agreed that pending final ratification of this Treaty, the provisions of Article II and III shall be observed by executive agreement.

Signed at Manila this fourth day of July, one thousand nine hundred forty-six.

ECONOMIC AND MILITARY ASSISTANCE

A. Report of the Bell Commission on an Economic Survey of the Philippines*

[Extract]

October 9, 1950

At the request of the President of the Philippine Republic, President Truman appointed a United States Economic Survey Mission to consider the economic and financial problems of that country and to recommend measures that will enable the Philippines to become and to remain self-supporting. The Mission was instructed to survey all aspects of the Philippine economy, including agriculture, industry, internal and external finances, domestic and foreign trade, and public administration. The Mission was asked to give special consideration to immediate measures to help raise production and living standards in the Philippines. The Mission has had the full cooperation of the Philippine Government and of many individuals and organizations outside the Governments. Their help has been invaluable in providing the Mission with the data necessary for its work.

Economic conditions in the Philippines are unsatisfactory. The economic situation has been deteriorating in the past 2 years and the factors that have brought this about cannot be expected to remedy themselves. Unless positive measures are taken to deal with the fundamental causes of these difficulties, it must be expected that the economic situation will deteriorate further and political disorder will inevitably result. Whatever is to be done to improve economic conditions in the Philippines must be done promptly, for if the situation is allowed to drift there is no certainty that moderate remedies will suffice.

*   *   *

The mission recommends that the following measures be taken:

1. That the finances of the Government be placed on a sound basis in order to avoid further inflation; that additional tax revenues be raised immediately in as equitable a manner as possible to meet the expenditures of the Government; that the tax structure be revised to increase the proportion of taxes collected from high incomes and large property holdings; that the tax collecting machinery be overhauled to secure greater efficiency in tax collection; that a credit policy be adopted which will encourage investment in productive enterprises; and that fiscal, credit and investment policy be better coordinated to prevent inflation.

2. That agricultural production be improved by applying known methods of increasing the yield from all basic crops; that the Department of Agriculture and Natural Resources be adequately supplied with funds and the agricultural extension service expanded; that the agricultural college at Los Banos be rehabilitated and the central experiment station located there, with other stations at

*American Foreign Policy, 1950-1955: Basic Documents, pp. 2355-57.

appropriate places throughout the country; that rural banks be established to provide production credit for small farmers; that the opening of new lands for settlement in homesteads be expedited and the clearance of land titles promptly assured; that a program of land redistribution be undertaken through the purchase of large estates for resale to small farmers; and that measures be undertaken to provide tenants with reasonable security on their land and an equitable share of the crops they produce.

3. That steps be taken to diversify the economy of the country by encouraging new industries; that adequate power and transportation facilities be provided as needed for further economic development; that a Philippine Development Corporation be established to coordinate all government corporations and enterprises and liquidate those that are ineffective; that financial assistance be made available to productive enterprises by the Corporation acting in cooperation with private banks; that the natural resources of the country be systematically explored to determine their potentialities for economic development; and that the present laws and practices with respect to the use of the public domain be re-examined.

4. That to avoid a further deterioration in the international payments position and to reduce the excessive demand for imports, a special emergency tax of 25 percent be levied for a period not to exceed two years on imports of all goods other than rice, corn, flour, canned fish, canned milk and fertilizer; that if such an emergency import levy is not possible under the Trade Agreement with the United States, either very heavy excise taxes should be imposed or a tax of 25 percent should be levied on all sales of exchange; that, as a safety measure, the present exchange and import controls be retained but their administration be simplified and liberalized and the full remittance of current earnings be permitted; that a Treaty of Friendship, Commerce and Navigation be concluded between the Philippines and the United States and the present Trade Agreement re-examined in the light of the new conditions.

5. That an adequate program of public health and improved education be undertaken, and better facilities for urban housing be provided; that the right of workers to organize free trade unions to protect their economic interests be established through appropriate legislation; that abuses in present employment practices depriving the workers of their just earnings be eliminated by legislation making mandatory direct payment of wages and retroactive monetary awards to workers; that a minimum wage for agricultural and other workers be established to provide subsistence standards of living.

6. That public administration be improved and reorganized so as to insure honesty and efficiency in Government; that the civil service be placed on a merit basis and civil service salaries raised to provide a decent standard of living; that the Philippine Government remove barriers to the employment of foreign technicians and take steps to improve training facilities for technicians in the Philippines; and that in accordance with the request of the Philippine Government, the United States send a Technical Mission to assist the Philippine Government in carrying out its agricultural and industrial development, fiscal controls, public administration, and labor and social welfare program.

7. That the United States Government provide financial assistance of 250 million dollars through loans and grants, to help in carrying out a 5-year program of economic development and technical assistance; that this aid be strictly conditioned on steps being taken by the Philippine Government to carry out the recommendations outlined above; including the immediate enactment of tax legislation and other urgent reforms; that expenditure of United States funds under this recommendation, including pesos derived from United States loans and grants, be subject to continued supervision and control of the Technical Mission; that the use of funds provided by the Philippine Government for economic and social development be co-ordinated with the expenditure of the United States funds made available for this purpose; and that an agreement be made for final settlement of outstanding financial claims between the United States and the Philippines, including funding of the Reconstruction Finance Corporation loan of 60 million dollars.

B. Report by Myron M. Cowan, U.S. Ambassador to the Philippines, on Progress and Developments in The Philippines*

[Extract]

June 15, 1951

I should like to give you a progress report on developments in the Philippines and our relations with that gallant ally of ours. As a result of 50 years of American tutelage and out of loyalty to and affection for the United States, the Philippines unfalteringly stood by us when Japan embarked on its program to conquer Asia. The surrender of Japan found the Philippines destroyed and laid waste to an extent which has happened to few countries in modern history, and of which few Americans can even begin to conceive.

Against this background of death and destruction, the United States, in compliance with its undertakings transferred sovereignty to the Philippines on July 4, 1946, and agreed to assist in its rehabilitation. It was to be expected that the first 5 years of Philippine independence would encounter the most serious difficulties, particularly in view of the growing menace of the international Communist conspiracy.

*   *   *

I believe this is as good a time as any to dispel once and for all the misconceptions about this 2 billion dollars worth of American aid. The best way to do it is to show what the United States has done and what this 2 billion dollars really consists of.

In the first place, the United States paid out 400 million dollars for private war damage claims, of which the majority were in amounts of less than 500 dollars each, and for the reconstruction of public buildings. At the same time,

Ibid., pp. 2357-59.

the United States spent roughly 118 million dollars in the reconstruction of such essential public services as roads and bridges, ports and harbors, public health, fisheries, weather services, coast surveys, interisland shipping, and civil air facilities.

Another category of American payments during the first 5 years of independence fell into a more strictly military category. An amount of 822 million dollars was paid out by the American armed forces as back pay for Philippine armed forces, civilian claims against the military, civil relief, redemption of the guerrilla currency, missing persons benefits, and other items for military pay and construction materials and services.

The Veterans Administration paid out 181 million dollars as compensation to Filipino veterans.

An arrangement was also made to transfer surplus property estimated at a fair value of 100 million dollars. Other kinds of equipment and material and technical assistance to the amount of 200 million dollars were also made available.

The foregoing adds up to a dollar value of less than 1.9 billion but it should be noted that it was all in the form of goods and services and payments to individuals. Not a single centavo of this total was paid to the Philippine Government in cash. The only direct financial aid has been an RFC budgetary loan of 60 million dollars and 89.5 million dollars of processing and excise taxes which the United States had collected on behalf of the Philippine Commonwealth.

Two billion dollars can be made to sound like a lot of aid if you interpret it to suit your own purposes. Honest analysis makes it look like something else. It is true that what the United States has done for the Philippines did make available to it substantial amounts of United States dollar exchange, much of which could undoubtedly have been spent more wisely than it was. We should remember, however, that the end of hostilities found the Philippines stripped of all consumer goods. It will still take many long years to replace what was destroyed.

The Philippine Government itself realized the danger of its position when its dollar reserves, during 1949, decreased from 400 million dollars to 248 million dollars. To remedy this situation the Philippine Government imposed the most stringent import regulations with the result that its reserves are now back to the 400 million dollars level. In addition, improved collection of taxes and the imposition of new taxes in the face of serious political opposition give us confidence that the Philippine budget will be balanced this year.

And lastly, Philippine production, particularly of such strategic and important commodities as copra, abaca, sugar, lumber, and minerals is now encouragingly close to the prewar level. I maintain that in view of the obstacles which had to be overcome and those which still remain, the record of Philippine self-help and American assistance is a good one. The purpose of the United States now is to extend the assistance necessary to preserve and extend the gains which have been made.

*   *   *

With American military assistance, the rejuvenated Philippine armed forces are now making significant inroads on the strength and capabilities of the Communist-dominated Huk movement. The presence of the Seventh Fleet in Philippine waters has contributed significantly to Philippine morale. American naval and air bases are being expanded. These specific measures are giving the Philippine people confidence that President Truman and the Secretary of State have meant exactly what they said when they categorically stated publicly that the United States would never tolerate aggression against the Philippines.

*   *   *

C. Mutual Defense Treaty Between the United States and the Republic of The Philippines*

August 30, 1951

The Parties to this Treaty,

Reaffirming their faith in the purposes and principles of the Charter of the United Nations and their desire to live in peace with all peoples and all Governments, and desiring to strengthen the fabric of peace in the Pacific Area,

Recalling with mutual pride the historic relationship which brought their two peoples together in a common bond of sympathy and mutual ideals to fight side-by-side against imperialist aggression during the last war,

Desiring to declare publicly and formally their sense of unity and their common determination to defend themselves against external armed attack, so that no potential aggressor could be under the illusion that either of them stands alone in the Pacific Area,

Desiring further to strengthen their present efforts for collective defense for the preservation of peace and security pending the development of a more comprehensive system of regional security in the Pacific Area,

Agreeing that nothing in this present instrument shall be considered or interpreted as in any way or sense altering or diminishing any existing agreements or understandings between the United States of America and the Republic of the Philippines,

Have agreed as follows:

Article I

The Parties undertake, as set forth in the Charter of the United Nations, to settle any international disputes in which they may be involved by peaceful means in such a manner that international peace and security and justice are not endangered and to refrain in their international relations from the threat or use of force in any manner inconsistent with the purposes of the United Nations.

Ibid., pp. 873-75.

Article II

In order more effectively to achieve the objective of this Treaty, the Parties separately and jointly by self-help and mutual aid will maintain and develop their individual and collective capacity to resist armed attack.

Article III

The Parties, through their Foreign Ministers or their deputies, will consult together from time to time regarding the implementation of this Treaty and whenever in the opinion of either of them the territorial integrity, political independence or security of either of the Parties is threatened by external armed attack in the Pacific.

Article IV

Each Party recognizes that an armed attack in the Pacific Area on either of the Parties would be dangerous to its own peace and safety and declares that it would act to meet the common dangers in accordance with its constitutional processes.

Any such armed attack and all measures taken as a result thereof shall be immediately reported to the Security Council of the United Nations. Such measures shall be terminated when the Security Council has taken the measures necessary to restore and maintain international peace and security.

Article V

For the purpose of Article IV, an armed attack on either of the Parties is deemed to include an armed attack on the metropolitan territory of either of the Parties, or on the island territories under its jurisdiction in the Pacific or on its armed forces, public vessels or aircraft in the Pacific.

Article VI

This Treaty does not affect and shall not be interpreted as affecting in any way the rights and obligations of the Parties under the Charter of the United Nations or the responsibility of the United Nations for the maintenance of international peace and security.

Article VII

This Treaty shall be ratified by the United States of America and the Republic of the Philippines in accordance with their respective constitutional processes and will come into force when instruments of ratification thereof have been exchanged by them at Manila.[1]

Article VIII

This Treaty shall remain in force indefinitely. Either Party may terminate it one year after notice has been given to the other Party.

In witness whereof the undersigned Plenipotentiaries have signed this Treaty. Done in duplicate at Washington this thirtieth day of August 1951.

D. Note from Secretary Dulles to the Philippine Chargé d'Affaires on Establishment of a Council Under the United States-Philippine Mutual Defense Treaty*

June 23, 1954

Sir: I refer to my conversation with General Carlos P. Romulo, Personal and Special Representative of the President of the Philippines, on June 15, 1954, in regard to implementation of the Mutual Defense Treaty between the United States of America and the Republic of the Philippines, and to an aide-memoire handed to the Acting Secretary of State by the Personal and Special Representative of the President of the Philippines on June 3, 1954.

During the discussions on June 15, between the Personal and Special Representative of the President of the Philippines and me, we were in agreement that, pursuant to the provisions of the United States-Philippine Mutual Defense Treaty, and in the light of international developments, it would be useful to establish a Council consisting of the Secretary of State, or his Deputy, and the Secretary of Foreign Affairs of the Republic of the Philippines, or his Deputy; that each member of the Council would designate a military representative; that consultations will be held upon the request of either party; and that the time and place of such meetings will be determined by mutual agreement . . . .

E. State Department Statement on the Revised United States-Philippine Trade Agreement*

[Extract]

September 4, 1955

The Department of State announced on September 6 (press release 529) that a revised agreement between the Republic of the Philippines and the United States regarding trade arrangements and related matters was signed on that date at the Department. The agreement was signed on behalf of the Philippines by

[1] Instruments of ratification were exchanged Aug. 27, 1952.
* *Ibid.*, p. 2360.
* *Ibid.*, pp. 2360-61.

Gen. Carlos P. Romulo, Special and Personal Envoy of the President of the Philippines; James M. Langley, Special Representative of the President of the United States of America, signed on behalf of the United States. It will enter into force on January 1, 1956.

The title of the agreement is "Agreement between the United States of America and the Republic of the Philippines concerning Trade and Related Matters during a Transitional Period following the Institution of Philippine Independence, signed at Manila on July 4, 1946, as revised." The authorizing legislation of the U.S. Congress is Public Law 196, 84th Congress, the Philippine Trade Agreement Revision Act of 1955.

The 1946 trade agreement was entered into at the time the Philippines gained its independence. At that time there were no precedents to indicate exactly how the problems of the new relationship which was to exist between the Philippines and the United States might best be met. During the 9 years of operation of this agreement, problems arose on both sides suggesting the need for revisions. These revisions, affecting every article of the agreement, provide for adjustments which better accommodate the current and future economic interests of both nations and effect changes in their relationships which were mutually felt desirable as a result of the experiences of the Philippines in handling its political and economic problems since the Philippines became independent in 1946. The modification of transitional tariff schedules coupled with the elimination of an exchange tax in the Philippines is an important element of the revised agreement.

The further economic development of the Philippines is one of the objectives of the new agreement. Such development, in addition to enhancing the importance of the Philippines as a trading partner of the United States, serves to strengthen a staunch friend and close ally.

*   *   *

F. Statement Issued Subsequent to Talks Between Vice President Richard M. Nixon and Philippine President Ramon Magsaysay on Military Bases*

July 3, 1956

Vice-President Nixon has discussed with President Magsaysay the necessity for strengthening military bases in the Philippines in order to bolster the common defense of the two countries as well as that of the Free World in this area. President Magsaysay concurred in the need for such a step for the mutual benefit of both countries. The President and the Vice President agreed that the two Governments will hold formal negotiations on military bases in the near future, and that these negotiations will be conducted on the basis of the following general principles:

(1)   The existence of a system of United States bases in the Philippines has been, and continues to be, a matter of mutual interest and concern to the two countries, for the purpose of insuring their common defense pursuant to the principles of the United Nations.

*Department of State Bulletin, July 16, 1956, pp. 95-96.

(2) In consonance with this mutuality of interest and concern, certain land areas in the Philippines have been and are being used by the United States as bases. The Philippine Government will contribute, for use in accordance with the terms of the Military Bases Agreement, the additional land which is deemed necessary by both Governments for the strengthening of the base system; the United States will turn over to the Philippine Government those areas listed in the Military Bases Agreement which the parties may hereafter agree are no longer needed. In addition, the United States has contributed and will contribute such personnel, equipment and physical facilities as may be necessary for the effective maintenance of such bases for the defense of the Philippines and the United States in this area.

(3) The United States has, since the independence of the Philippines, always acknowledged the sovereignty of the Philippines over such bases; and expressly reaffirms full recognition of such Philippine sovereignty over the bases. Further, the United States will transfer and turn over to the Philippines all title papers and title claims held by the United States to all land areas used either in the past or presently as military bases, except those areas which may now or will be used by the United States for its diplomatic and consular establishment. Such transfer of title papers and title claims will not affect use of the bases in accordance with the terms of the Military Bases Agreement.

G. Joint United States-Philippine Announcement of a Mutual Defense Board*

May 15, 1958

The Philippine and United States Governments today announced agreement on the establishment of a Philippine-United States Mutual Defense Board and the assignment of a Philippine military liaison officer to the staff of the Base Commander in major United States military bases in the Philippines.

One of a continuing series of actions implementing existing security and defense agreements between the two countries, today's exchange of notes marks a major step in securing effective collaboration between the two countries in the joint effort to improve and enhance the common defense.

As stated in the Exchange of Notes "the purpose of this (Mutual Defense) Board is to provide continuing inter-governmental machinery for direct liaison and consultation between appropriate Philippine and United States authorities on military matters of mutual concern so as to develop and improve, through continuing military cooperation, the common defense of the two sovereign countries." The Board will have Philippine and United States co-chairmen.

The Philippine military liaison officer, who will be assigned to a major United States military base, will cooperate with the Base Commander by advice, suggestion, and/or other appropriate action to assure observance of Philippine law and regulations within the base, will advise the Base Commander concerning problems involving Philippine nationals and residents on the base, and the day-to-day relationships between the base, Base Commander and such nationals and

Ibid., June 2, 1958, p. 913.

residents. These officers will be appointed by the Chief of Staff, Armed Forces of the Philippines, will be under the Administration of the Philippine Co-Chairman of the Mutual Defense Board, and will submit reports to the Board.

The agreements announced today are designed to enable the two governments to carry out more effectively the specified purposes and objectives of the Mutual Defense Agreement, and are part of the continuing effort of both governments to further strengthen their mutual defense and to contribute to international peace and security.

H. Note From George M. Abbott, U.S. Chargé d'Affaires, to Felixberto M. Serrano, Philippine Secretary of Foreign Affairs, on Transfer of Portions of Subic Bay, a U.S. Naval Base, to Philippine Authority*

Manila, December 7, 1959

I have the honor to refer to Part I of the Memorandum of Agreement signed by Your Excellency and Ambassador Bohlen on August 14, 1959 and the recent discussions between representatives of our two governments concerning relinquishment of the community of Olongapo and certain areas adjacent thereto which are now located within the United States Naval Base, Subic Bay.

I have been advised that the agreed report of recommendations of the Philippine-United States Olongapo Committee have been accepted by my Government as terms for the relinquishment and is appended hereto as an annex. In accordance with the aforesaid report and in implementation of Part I of the Memorandum of Agreement of August 14, 1959, my Government hereby relinquishes to the Philippine Government the entire area north of the northern boundary line of the Naval Base as delineated in red on the map designated Map No. 4 in the Memorandum of Agreement[1] and specifically described in the document dated September 27, 1959 appended to that map. The exact metes and bounds of this boundary line will be those determined by the Metes and Bounds Committee of the Mutual Defense Board. It is understood that the United States Government will transfer to the Philippine Government at the earliest possible date title to any terms of property listed in the aforesaid agreed report to which title cannot be transferred today. In the interim, the Philippine Government shall have the use of such items of property.

It is further understood that the Philippine Government will hold the United States Government harmless from any claims which may arise from the use by others than the United States of the areas released today, except for those meritorious claims paid by the United States.

If the foregoing is acceptable to your Government, I have the honor to propose that this note with its annex and Your Excellency's reply thereto indicating such acceptance shall constitute the agreement of our two Governments with respect to relinquishment of the Community of Olongapo and adjacent areas to the Philippine Government.

Accept, Excellency, renewed assurances of my highest consideration.

*American Foreign Policy: Current Documents, 1959, pp. 1247-48.
[1]Not printed.

I. Joint Statement Issued by President Eisenhower and Philippine President Carlos Garcia on Matters of Mutual Interest*

June 16, 1960

President Eisenhower, at the invitation of President Carlos Garcia, paid a state visit to the Philippines on June 14 to 16, 1960, returning the visit of President Garcia to the United States two years ago.

President Eisenhower recalled his personal association with the Philippines extending over a period of many years. As the first President of the United States to visit the Philippines while in office, he expressed his deep sense of satisfaction that he had been afforded this opportunity to attest to the admiration and affection which the government and people of the United States feel toward their Philippine allies.

President Garcia, on his part, viewed the affection shown to President Eisenhower by the Filipino people as a grateful remembrance of the latter's tour of duty in the Philippines some twenty-five years ago and their admiration for his military leadership in the second world war and his dedicated labors for a just and lasting world peace.

The visit afforded President Garcia and President Eisenhower, together with other officials of both governments, an opportunity for a frank and cordial exchange of views on matters of mutual interest. In a review of the international situation and of the bilateral relations of the two countries, the two Presidents:

1. Reaffirmed the bonds of friendship and mutual understanding which have historically joined the Filipino and American governments and peoples.

2. Noted the problems facing the free world at the beginning of the new decade and discussed the possibility of increased tensions in view of recent statements by Communist leaders in Moscow and Peiping. They renewed their determination to support the work of the United Nations and the objectives of the United Nations' Charter in the interest of true international peace and progress based on justice and the dignity of the individual.

3. Assessed the continuing threat to peace in the Far East posed by Communist China. They reaffirmed the importance of regional cooperation in insuring the independence of the nations of Southeast Asia. They emphasized the important role of the Southeast Asia Treaty Organization in furthering such cooperation and in developing a sense of regional solidarity; and they noted with satisfaction the contribution being made by the Philippines toward strengthening its ties with its Asian neighbors.

4. Noted that President Eisenhower's visit and the warm response thereto by the Filipino people provided renewed evidence of the strength and vitality of the alliance between the Philippines and the United States and of its essential contribution to the security of Southeast Asia. To promote the continuing strength of the alliance and to enable the Philippines to discharge its obligation thereunder, they emphasized the importance of close military collaboration and planning between the appropriate authorities of their countries. They further expressed the view that this close military collaboration and planning should

*American Foreign Policy: Current Documents, 1960, pp. 688-90.

be aimed at the maximum effectiveness in formulating and executing United States military assistance programs and in furthering Philippine defensive capability in the light of modern requirements.

5. Noted the recent meeting of the Council of Foreign Ministers of the SEATO held in Washington and expressed satisfaction with the continuing effectiveness of the SEATO as a deterrent to Communist aggression in Southeast Asia. They were also gratified that the Washington conference had given attention to the economic objectives of the SEATO, recognizing the importance of economic cooperation between and among the members.

6. Recalled the provisions of the Mutual Defense Treaty. President Eisenhower, on his part, renewed the assurance he had made to President Garcia in Washington that under the provisions of this treaty and other defensive agreements between the Philippines and the United States and in accordance with the deployments and dispositions thereunder, any armed attack against the Philippines would involve an attack against the United States Forces stationed there and against the United States and would instantly be repelled. It was noted that this understanding was included in the agreement reached between the Secretary of Foreign Affairs of the Philippines and the Ambassador of the United States on October 12, 1959.

7. Noted with satisfaction the considerable progress that had been made in talks between the Secretary of Foreign Affairs of the Philippines and the Ambassador of the United States towards settlement of problems arising from the presence of United States bases in the Philippines. They expressed confidence that the few remaining problems will be similarly resolved to the mutual satisfaction of the two governments.

8. Reemphasized the importance of strong, stable economies in furthering the objectives of peaceful development in the free world. President Eisenhower expressed his gratification at the evident progress which has been made in the Philippine economy, including notable advances in industrialization. The contribution which the United States aid programs have made and will continue to make to Philippine economic development was emphasized. In recognition of the economic interdependence of all nations in the modern world, they discussed opportunities for increased private investment and expanded trade between the two countries in a climate favorable to free enterprise and to the free movement of capital.

President Garcia and President Eisenhower concluded that the exchange of views and the renewal of personal associations made possible by President Eisenhower's visit will further strengthen the traditional ties between the two countries and will contribute significantly to the advancement of their cooperative efforts of behalf of peace and progress in this vital part of the world.

J. Statement by President Kennedy on the Postponement of Philippine President Diosdado Macapagal's Visit to the United States*

May 15, 1962

It is with deep regret that I learned of the decision of President Diosdado

*American Foreign Policy: Current Documents, 1962, p. 1088.

Macapagal of the Philippines to postpone his visit to the United States next month. I understand that President Macapagal's decision resulted from his country's disappointment over the failure of the Congress on May 9 to enact the Philippine War Damage Bill.

A new bill designed to fulfill this obligation has now been introduced in Congress with bipartisan sponsorship. The congressional leadership has assured me that it will again give its full support for the legislation, and I am hopeful that the new bill will pass. I am hopeful, too, that this disappointment will not be allowed to alter the harmonious relations between our countries and our profound and lasting friendship.

I sincerely hope that the many expressions of good will and sympathy by our people and our press will be accepted by the people of the Philippines as the true measure of our friendship and understanding. We continue to look forward with pleasure and anticipation to welcoming President Macapagal to the United States in the near future.

K. United States Authorization for the Appropriation of $73 Million for Philippine War Damage Claims*

August 30, 1962

PUBLIC LAW 87—616

Be it enacted by the Senate and House of Representatives of the United States of America in Congress assembled, That the Foreign Claims Settlement Commission (hereafter in this Act referred to as the "Commission") shall provide, out of funds appropriated pursuant to this Act, for the payment of the unpaid balance of awards heretofore made by the Philippine War Damage Commission under title I of the Philippine Rehabilitation Act of 1946. No payment shall be made under this Act to any person, or to his successors in interest, on account of any award unless payment was made on such award under the Philippine Rehabilitation Act of 1946, and the maximum amount paid under this Act, when added to amounts paid under the Philippine Rehabilitation Act of 1946 and section 7 of the War Claims Act of 1948 on account of any claim shall not exceed the aggregate amount of claims approved in favor of such claimant after reduction under the last proviso of section 102 (a) of the Philippine Rehabilitation Act of 1946. All payments under this Act in amounts over 25,000 pesos or equivalent value in dollars shall be subject to the provisions of section 104 (c) of the Philippine Rehabilitation Act of 1946.

Sec. 2.

Within sixty days after the enactment of this Act, or of legislation appropriating for administration expenses incurred in carrying out this act, whichever is later, the Commission shall prescribe and publish in the Federal Register and give appropriate publicity in the Republic of the Philippines concerning the period, not in excess of twelve additional months, within which application

Ibid., p. 1109.

must be filed under this Act. The Commission shall complete its determination and take final action with respect to applications filed under this Act not later than one year after the last date on which applications may be filed.

L. Joint Communiqué Issued by President Johnson and President Macapagal on Matters of International and Mutual Significance*

[Extract]

October 6, 1964

The President of the United States and the President of the Philippines today concluded the fruitful discussions they have held over the past days. These talks dealt with Philippine-American relations and matters of international significance to both countries. They were the latest in the long history of exchanges between Presidents of the two countries, and reflected the spirit of special friendship and cooperation which has existed between the Philippines and the United States over the years. The two Presidents expressed their confidence that the American and Philippine peoples would continue to benefit from this close association in the future.

The two Presidents exchanged views on the situation in Southeast Asia and pledged themselves to maintain the unity of commitment and purpose between their countries in defense of the right of the free nations of Southeast Asia to determine their own future.

President Johnson noted with deep appreciation the response by the Philippines to the request of the Government of Viet-Nam for aid in its defense against communist subversion and aggression. The two Presidents agreed that it is of the utmost importance to free men throughout the world that communist force not be permitted to dictate their future. Noting the struggle of the people of South Viet-Nam against communist aggression and its implication for all free people, the Two Presidents reaffirmed their intention to stand by the people of South Viet-Nam and reiterated their commitment to the defense of Southeast Asia under the SEATO Treaty. President Macapagal noted that prompt and decisive action by the United States in the Gulf of Tonkin had once again confirmed American readiness and determination to resist aggression in Southeast Asia to help assure its progress under freedom.

President Johnson expressed his appreciation to President Macapagal for the latter's efforts to bring about a peaceful settlement of the dispute between Indonesia and Malaysia. Both Presidents agreed that it is vitally important that this dispute, which now threatens the peace and stability of the Southwest Pacific area, be resolved.

The two Presidents recognized that the aggressive intentions and activities of Communist China continue to present an imminent threat in the Far East and in Southeast Asia. They reviewed, in this connection, the importance of the Mutual Defense Treaty between the Philippines and the United States in maintaining the security of both countries, and reaffirmed their commitment

* *American Foreign Policy: Current Documents,* 1964, pp. 946-49.

to meet any threat that might arise against their security. President Johnson made it clear that, in accordance with these existing alliances and the deployment and dispositions thereunder, any armed attack against the Philippines would be regarded as an attack against United States forces stationed there and against the United States and would instantly be repelled.

The United States and the Philippines agreed to study their mutual requirements for security, to review existing programs, and to consider changes needed to achieve increased capability and flexibility in the Philippine response to aggression and threats of aggression.

The two Presidents agreed that the relationship between their respective countries was a dynamic and flexible association with a history of past achievement and a heavy stake in a common future. In the spirit of this alliance, the two Presidents agreed that any matter of interest to either party related thereto should be the subject of friendly and frank discussion, and each President invited the views of the other in this regard.

The two Presidents likewise took cognizance of matters pertaining to Philippine veterans of World War II and agreed on the establishment of a joint commission to study this subject further.

President Macapagal reviewed the economic progress made by the Philippines in recent years. President Johnson commended the land reform program, initiated by President Macapagal this year, as holding out renewed hope to the Philippine people for the solution of the land tenure problems which, for decades, had beset a major sector of its economy. President Johnson noted past United States support for Philippine agrarian reform and expressed his hope that American assistance could continue in the future, particularly in the realization of the land reform objectives of the Philippines.

Both Presidents discussed the disposition of the Special Fund for education, provided for in the Philippine War Damage legislation. They agreed to consider plans including the possible formation of a joint committee which would ensure use of this fund to further educational programs to the mutual advantage of the Philippines and the United States, among which educational programs pertaining to land reform would be eligible.

President Macapagal explained the goals of his Socio-Economic Program and its objective of alleviating the plight of the common man in the Philippines. President Johnson reiterated his belief that it was the responsibility of this generation everywhere to join the campaign against poverty and the ills associated with it and pledged American support for worthy projects contributing to the economic development of the Philippines. The two Presidents noted that one area of particular interest which could bring great benefit to the Philippine people was rural electrification. President Macapagal said that Philippine Government plans envisage the establishment of generating and distribution electric systems in 607 towns and 400 selected barrios. President Johnson observed that a team of American experts has arrived in the Philippines, and, working with private and public Philippine energy experts, would cooperate in developing plans for this nationwide system of expanding power generation and distribution with its special attention to rural areas.

The two Presidents looked to developments in the trade between their respective countries and in the world trading community that could assure expanding markets for the leading exports of the Philippines, including sugar, coconut products, abaca, lumber, minerals and others. The Philippines expressed their readiness and willingness to supply additional sugar to the American market.

*   *   *

M. Department of State Announcement on an Amendment to the United States-Philippine Military Bases Agreement*

August 10, 1965

The Department of State announced on August 10 that the United States and the Philippines have agreed on a revision of the criminal jurisdiction arrangement now a part of the military bases agreement of 1947 which governs the presence of U.S. forces and bases in the Philippines.

The new arrangement, patterned after the NATO status-of-forces formula, provides for U.S. primary jurisdiction over American servicemen present in the Philippines in connection with U.S. bases there in cases involving offenses arising from acts or omission done in performance of official duty, offenses solely against the property or security of the United States, and offenses solely against the person or property of U.S. personnel.

The Philippines has primary jurisdiction in all other cases, including those on U.S. bases. Each country has exclusive jurisdiction regarding offenses punishable under its own laws but not by laws of the other country.

N. Joint Communiqué Issued by President Johnson and Philippine President Ferdinand Marcos on International Developments of Common Significance*

[Extract]

September 15, 1966

At the invitation of President Johnson, President Marcos made a state visit to Washington September 14 to 16, 1966. This afforded an opportunity for the two Presidents to engage in the friendly and fraternal talks which have become traditional between the two countries.

President Johnson and President Marcos had a frank and cordial exchange of views on international developments of common significance as well as the cooperative arrangements which gave substance to Philippine-American relations.

President Marcos set forth his vision of the Philippine future. He described the many frontiers that mankind faces—in space and in the ocean depths, on the farm and in the laboratory, in economic development and in expanding

*American Foreign Policy: Current Documents, 1965, pp. 794-95.
*American Foreign Policy: Current Documents, 1966, pp. 726-29.

the capabilities of the young. He expressed his determination to move his country forward across these frontiers, with the exertion of Philippine energy and initiative and with the cooperation of friendly nations, especially the United States.

*   *   *

Future Economic Relations. The two Presidents agreed that an expansion of trade between the Philippines and the United States would also contribute to the development and stability of both countries.

*   *   *

Offshore Procurement. The two Presidents agreed that the Philippines should participate on a full and equitable basis in supplying U.S. offshore procurement needs in Vietnam.

Mutual Security. Both Presidents recognized the strategic role which the Philippines plays in the network of allied defenses and agreed to strengthen their mutual defense capabilities. Both Presidents recognized that such defense construction projects as are presently under way and may be required in the future contribute to this end. President Marcos informed President Johnson of recent indications of resurgence of subversive activities, especially in Central Luzon. President Johnson pledged the continued assistance of the United States in the concerted drive of the Marcos Administration to improve the well-being of the people and strengthen its capabilities for internal defense.

The two Presidents reviewed the current requirements of the Philippine armed forces for external assistance. In accordance with President Marcos' program to expand the Army's civic action capability, President Johnson was pleased to inform him that the United States would within this fiscal year provide equipment for five engineer construction battalions to be engaged in civic action projects contributing to internal security, and would consider furnishing equipment for five more such battalions in the next fiscal year. President Johnson also informed President Marcos that delivery of a Destroyer Escort for the Philippine Navy was anticipated next year. The two Presidents agreed to keep the U.S. Military Assistance Program under continuing review in order to ensure that the materiel and training supplied to the Philippine armed forces were kept appropriate to the changing requirements and missions of these forces.

The two Presidents pledged themselves to strengthen the unity of the two countries in meeting any threat to their security. In this regard, they noted the continuing importance of the Mutual Defense Treaty between the Philippines and the United States in maintaining the security of both countries. President Johnson reiterated to President Marcos the policy of the United States regarding mutual defense as stated by him and by past U.S. Administrations to the Philippine Government since 1954.

The two Presidents noted that in the forthcoming Rusk-Ramos Agreement, the U.S. accepts President Marcos' proposal to reduce the term of the military bases agreement from 99 to 25 years. The two Presidents reaffirmed that the bases are necessary for both countries and their mutual defense, and were gratified with the progress being made in the negotiation and resolution of various issues related to the Bases Agreement in the spirit of harmony, friendship and mutual accommodation. They agreed that the base negotiations should be continued with a view to earliest possible resolution of remaining issues in the spirit of good will and cooperation which has characterized these negotiations to date.

The two Presidents noted the benefits to be ·gained if countries can share and profit from their common experiences in meeting Communist infiltration and subversion in all its forms in Southeast Asia. In this connection, the accomplishments of SEATO and of individual countries were discussed as well as means by which the Philippines and the United States might make an added contribution to this significant work. The two Presidents concluded that the usefulness of a center in the Philippines which might serve as a focal point for this work should be explored and proper actions pursued.

*   *   *

O. Joint Announcement by the United States and the Philippines on Reduction of the Duration of the Military Bases Agreement*

September 16, 1966

Secretary of State Dean Rusk and Philippine Secretary of Foreign Affairs Narciso Ramos signed and exchanged diplomatic notes today [September 16] dealing with United States bases in the Philippines and on which understandings had been reached in 1959. The United States agreed to amend the Philippine-U.S. Military Bases Agreement of 1947 by reducing the term of Agreement from the original period of 99 years to a period of 25 years from the exchange of notes. It also confirmed the understanding reached in 1959 concerning consultation, and reaffirmed its policy on mutual defense.

Ibid., p. 730.

THE UNITED STATES

AND INDIA AND PAKISTAN

THE UNITED STATES
AND INDIA AND PAKISTAN

Commentary

Since 1947 when India acquired its independence from Great Britain, and internal conflicts necessitated partition of the Hindu and Moslem sections of the sub-continent, United States policy has had three main objectives: preservation of the independence and political integrity of each of the new states; the rapid solution of domestic problems like food shortages, inadequate medical facilities, and insufficient technology to permit industrial advances; and the maintenance of peaceful relations between India and Pakistan.

In the case of Pakistan, that nation chose to join the Central Treaty Organization and the Southeast Asia Treaty Organization, thus relying on formal treaty arrangements to promote her security; the United States welcomed Pakistan's non-Communist, non-neutralist stance. India, on the other hand, through the 1950's eschewed formal alliances, pursued a neutralist course in foreign relations, often attacked the intransigent anti-Communist position of the United States, and professed to be on friendly terms with both the Soviet Union and China. Nevertheless, both Pakistan and India were recipients of American aid in the 1950's and 1960's, with India having received the huge sum of $4 billion by 1963. Border difficulties with China, culminating in China's invasion of Indian territory in October, 1962, altered India's neutralist posture somewhat and prompted the expansion of United States aid to include military arms and equipment. This increased commitment to India then led to a corresponding United States reassurance to Pakistan that it had no intention of strengthening India for any test with Pakistan.

American assurances were essential because of a long smoldering feud between the two nations over Kashmir. In this matter, the United States, viewing with apprehension any action which threatened to disrupt its friendly relations with either of these two important nations, frequently urged both sides to work to settle their differences, but to no avail. In 1965, when fighting broke out, the United States cut off arms shipments to both countries. After the conflict was stopped through the mediation of the Soviet Union, large-scale American aid was resumed, but United States apprehension remained. Although the two belligerents had temporarily shelved a major difference, fundamental problems,

733

both internal and external, confronted each country. And American policy was predicated on the view that India and Pakistan, comprising as they do huge populations and a large land mass, constitute vital areas in the international picture.

INDEPENDENCE

A. Message from President Truman to Governor General Mountbatten of India on the Creation of the Dominion*

August 15, 1947

On this memorable occasion, I extend to you, to Prime Minister Jawaharlal Nehru, and to the people of the Dominion of India the sincere best wishes of the Government and the people of the United States of America. We welcome India's new and enhanced status in the world community of sovereign independent nations, assure the new Dominion of our continued friendship and good will, and reaffirm our confidence that India, dedicated to the cause of peace and to the advancement of all peoples, will take its place at the forefront of the nations of the world in the struggle to fashion a world society founded in mutual trust and respect. India faces many grave problems, but its resources are vast, and I am confident that its people and leadership are equal to the tasks ahead. In the years to come the people of this great new nation will find the United States a constant friend. I earnestly hope that our friendship will in the future, as in the past, continue to be expressed in close and fruitful cooperation in international undertakings and in cordiality in our relations one with the other.

B. Message from President Truman to Governor General Jinnah of Pakistan on the Creation of the Dominion*

August 15, 1947

On this auspicious day which marks the emergence among the family of nations of the new Dominion of Pakistan, I extend on behalf of the American people sincere best wishes to you, and through you, to Prime Minister Liaquat Ali Khan and the people of Pakistan. To you who have labored so steadfastly for this day, and to the other leaders and the people of Pakistan fall profound responsibilities. I wish to assure you that the new Dominion embarks on its course with the firm friendship and good will of the United States of America. The American Government and people anticipate a long history of close and cordial relations with your country. We rejoice with you in the prospect for rapid progress toward the advancement of the welfare of the people of Pakistan, and look forward to the constructive participation of the new Dominion in world affairs for the welfare of all mankind.

---

*Documents on American Foreign Relations, 1945-1946, p. 581.
*Ibid., p. 582.

MILITARY AID TO PAKISTAN

A. Message From President Eisenhower to Indian Prime Minister Jawaharlal Nehru on the Defensive Purpose of United States Military Aid to Pakistan*

[Extract]

February 24, 1954

Dear Mr. Prime Minister: I send you this personal message because I want you to know about my decision to extend military aid to Pakistan before it is public knowledge and also because I want you to know directly from me that this step does not in any way affect the friendship we feel for India. Quite the contrary. We will continually strive to strengthen the warm and enduring friendship between our two countries.

*　　　　　　　*　　　　　　　*

What we are proposing to do, and what Pakistan is agreeing to, is not directed in any way against India. And I am confirming publicly that if our aid to any country, including Pakistan, is misused and directed against another in aggression I will undertake immediately, in accordance with my constitutional authority, appropriate action both within and without the UN to thwart such agression. . . .

I know that you and your Government are keenly aware of the need for economic progress as a prime requisite for stability and strength. This Government has extended assistance to India in recognition of this fact, and I am recommending to Congress a continuation of economic and technical aid for this reason. We also believe it in the interest of the free world that India have a strong military defense capability and have admired the effective way your Government has administered your military establishment. If your Government should conclude that circumstances require military aid of a type contemplated by our mutual security legislation, please be assured that your request would receive my most sympathetic consideration.

B. Mutual Defense Assistance Agreement Between the United States and Pakistan*

May 19, 1954

The Government of the United States of America and the Government of Pakistan,

Desiring to foster international peace and security within the framework of the Charter of the United Nations through measures which will further the ability of nations dedicated to the purposes and principles of the Charter to participate

*Department of State Bulletin, May 15, 1954, pp. 400-01.
*American Foreign Policy, 1950-1955: Basic Documents, pp. 2194-98.

effectively in arrangements for individual and collective self-defense in support of those purposes and principles;

Reaffirming their determination to give their full co-operation to the efforts to provide the United Nations with armed forces as contemplated by the Charter and to participate in United Nations collective defense arrangements and measures, and to obtain agreement on universal regulation and reduction of armaments under adequate guarantee against violation or evasion;

Taking into consideration the support which the Government of the United States has brought to these principles by enacting the Mutual Defense Assistance Act of 1949, as amended, and the Mutual Security Act of 1951, as amended;

Desiring to set forth the conditions which will govern the furnishing of such assistance;

Have agreed:

Article I

1. The Government of the United States will make available to the Government of Pakistan such equipment, materials, services or other assistance as the Government of the United States may authorize in accordance with such terms and conditions as may be agreed. The furnishing and use of such assistance shall be consistent with the Charter of the United Nations. Such assistance as may be made available by the Government of the United States pursuant to this Agreement will be furnished under the provisions and subject to all the terms, conditions and termination provisions of the Mutual Defense Assistance Act of 1949 and the Mutual Security Act of 1951, acts amendatory or supplementary thereto, appropriation acts thereunder, or any other applicable legislative provisions. The two Governments will, from time to time, negotiate detailed arrangements necessary to carry out the provisions of this paragraph.

2. The Government of Pakistan will use this assistance exclusively to maintain its internal security, its legitimate self-defense, or to permit it to participate in the defense of the area, or in United Nations collective security arrangements and measures, and Pakistan will not undertake any act of aggression against any other nation. The Government of Pakistan will not, without the prior agreement of the Government of the United States, devote such assistance to purposes other than those for which it was furnished.

3. Arrangements will be entered into under which equipment and materials furnished pursuant to this Agreement and no longer required or used exclusively for the purposes for which originally made available will be offered for return to the Government of the United States.

4. The Government of Pakistan will not transfer to any person not an officer or agent of that Government, or to any other nation, title to or possession of any equipment, materials, property, information, or services received under this Agreement, without the prior consent of the Government of the United States.

5. The Government of Pakistan will take such security measures as may be

agreed in each case between the two Governments in order to prevent the disclosure or compromise of classified military articles, services or information furnished pursuant to this Agreement.

6. Each Government will take appropriate measures consistent with security to keep the public informed of operations under this Agreement.

7. The two Governments will establish procedures whereby the Government of Pakistan will so deposit, segregate or assure title to all funds allocated to or derived from any programme of assistance undertaken by the Government of the United States so that such funds shall not, except as may otherwise be mutually agreed, be subject to garnishment, attachment, seizure or other legal process by any person, firm, agency, corporation, organization or government.

Article II

The two Governments will, upon request of either of them, negotiate appropriate arrangements between them relating to the exchange of patent rights and technical information for defense which will expedite such exchanges and at the same time protect private interests and maintain necessary security safeguards.

Article III

1. The Government of Pakistan will make available to the Government of the United States rupees for the use of the latter Government for its administrative and operating expenditures in connection with carrying out the purposes of this Agreement. The two Governments will forthwith initiate discussions with a view to determining the amount of such rupees and to agreeing upon arrangements for the furnishing of such funds.

2. The Government of Pakistan will, except as may otherwise be mutually agreed, grant duty-free treatment on importation or exportation and exemption from internal taxation upon products, property, materials or equipment imported into its territory in connection with this Agreement or any similar Agreement between the Government of the United States and the Government of any other country receiving military assistance.

3. Tax relief will be accorded to all expenditures in Pakistan by, or on behalf of, the Government of the United States for the common defense effort, including expenditures for any foreign aid programme of the United States. The Government of Pakistan will establish procedures satisfactory to both Governments so that such expenditures will be net of taxes.

Article IV

1. The Government of Pakistan will receive personnel of the Government

of the United States who will discharge in its territory the responsibilities of the Government of the United States under this Agreement and who will be accorded facilities and authority to observe the progress of the assistance furnished pursuant to this Agreement. Such personnel who are United States nationals, including personnel temporarily assigned, will, in their relations with the Government of Pakistan, operate as part of the Embassy of the United States of America under the direction and control of the Chief of the Diplomatic Mission, and will have the same privileges and immunities as are accorded other personnel with corresponding rank of the Embassy of the United States who are United States nationals. Upon appropriate notification by the Government of the United States the Government of Pakistan will grant full diplomatic status to the senior military member assigned under this Article and the senior Army, Navy and Air Force officers and their respective immediate deputies.

2. The Government of Pakistan will grant exemption from import and export duties on personal property imported for the personal use of such personnel or of their families and will take reasonable administrative measures to facilitate and expedite the importation and exportation of the personal property of such personnel and their families.

Article V

1. The Government of Pakistan will:

(a) join in promoting international understanding and goodwill, and maintaining world peace;
(b) take such action as may be mutually agreed upon to eliminate causes of international tension;
(c) make, consistent with its political and economic stability, the full contribution permitted by its manpower, resources, facilities and general economic condition to the development and maintenance of its own defensive strength and the defensive strength of the free world;
(d) take all reasonable measures which may be needed to develop its defense capacities; and
(e) take appropriate steps to insure the effective utilisation of the economic and military assistance provided by the United States.

2. (a) The Government of Pakistan will, consistent with the Charter of the United Nations, furnish to the Government of the United States, or to such other governments as the Parties hereto may in each case agree upon, such equipment, materials, services or other assistance as may be agreed upon in order to increase their capacity for individual and collective self-defense and to facilitate their effective participation in the United Nations system for collective security.

(b) In conformity with the principle of mutual aid, the Government of Pakistan will facilitate the production and transfer to the Government of the United States, for such period of time, in such quantities and upon such terms and conditions as may be agreed upon, of raw and semi-processed materials required by the United States as a result of deficiencies or potential deficiencies in its own resources, and which may be available in Pakistan. Arrangements for such transfers shall give due regard to reasonable requirements of Pakistan for domestic use and commercial export.

Article VI

In the interest of their mutual security the Government of Pakistan will co-operate with the Government of the United States in taking measures designed to control trade with nations which threaten the maintenance of world peace.

Article VII

1. This Agreement shall enter into force on the date of signature and will continue in force until one year after the receipt by either party of written notice of the intention of the other party to terminate it, except that the provisions of Article 1, paragraphs 2 and 4, and arrangements entered into under Article 1, paragraphs 3, 5 and 7, and under Article II, shall remain in force unless otherwise agreed by the two Governments.

2. The two Governments will, upon the request of either of them, consult regarding any matter relating to the application or amendment of this Agreement.

3. This Agreement shall be registered with the Secretariat of the United Nations.

Done in two copies at Karachi the 19th day of May one thousand nine hundred and fifty four.

C. Joint Communiqué Issued by President Eisenhower and Prime Minister Hussein Shahud Sahrawardy of Pakistan on United States-Pakistan Relations*

[Extract]

July 13, 1957

*   *   *

The President and the Prime Minister reviewed the steady growth of close, cooperative relations between their two countries. These relations are securely founded on mutual respect and trust between equal sovereign nations determined to maintain their independence by working together for peace and progress. They examined various joint programs which serve further to strengthen these ties.

---

*American Foreign Policy: Current Documents, 1957, pp. 1029-31.

The President and the Prime Minister agreed that international communism continues to pose the major threat to the security of the free world. They reaffirmed their determination to support the systems of collective security which have been forged in Asia. They reiterated their determination to oppose aggression. It was recognized that this determination, expressed in such organizations as the Southeast Asia Treaty Organization and the Baghdad Pact, as well as through the Mutual Security Agreement between Pakistan and the United States, has acted as a powerful deterrent to Communist aggression and has promoted stability in the treaty areas.

They expressed the belief that an effective international agreement on disarmament under adequate and effective international safeguards would contribute not only to the security of the world but also to its material progress.

They discussed the threat to the security and integrity of the nations of the Middle East resulting from the intrusion of Communist influence and subversion in that area. It was agreed that the United States and Pakistan would continue to exert their influence to promote conditions in the Middle East which will permit the nations of the area to work out their national destinies in freedom and peace.

The Prime Minister referred to Pakistan's disputes with India over Kashmir and the distribution of the waters of the Indus River and its tributaries. The Prime Minister said that Pakistan desires to settle such disputes peacefully and in conformity with international law and the decisions of the United Nations. The President expressed the hope that such regional disputes may be solved speedily, equitably, and permanently, in accordance with the principles of the United Nations.

*　　　　　*　　　　　*

D. Statement by Secretary Dulles on United States Financial Aid to India*

March 4, 1958

At 12:30 today the Eximbank and the Development Loan Fund together with Indian representatives will meet with the press to announce the results of discussion with representatives of the Government of India on the implementation of the $225 million of loans offered India by the United States to assist in meeting its current economic difficulties.

These discussions have been mutually satisfactory and the announcement today will indicate the uses to which it is intended that the Eximbank and the DLF loan be put.

We recognize that the Indian problem of maintaining economic growth is one of great magnitude. It is the expectation of both parties that the funds from these $225 million of loans will be expended for requirements of the

**Department of State Bulletin*, Mar. 24, 1958, pp. 464-65.

next 12 to 18 months. We recognize that the free world has a tremendous interest in the outcome of India's efforts to improve its economic well-being in the framework of its democratic political institutions. As I indicated some weeks ago...we hope that we, together with other free-world countries and the World Bank, can give the foreign exchange requirements of the Indian program enough support in the form of loans so it will be possible for that program to continue in an adequate form.

ECONOMIC AID TO INDIA

A. Comment by Secretary Dulles on United States Policy with India*

[Extract]

October 17, 1958

I think we can play a very considerable part [in helping India], and indeed we are. We have given a tremendous assistance to India. And India is neutralist in only one sense of the word. India is neutralist in the sense that it has not joined up in any of the collective security organizations. I think they may be wrong, but I think on the whole the free nations are more apt to stay free if they unite in collective security. But each country can make that decision for itself. We don't quarrel with the Indian decision. India is not neutral in the sense that it is indifferent to the threat of communism. It is fighting it, fighting it vigorously, hard, and is attempting to demonstrate for its own people that a free way of life can improve human welfare. And in that struggle, that competition with communism, we are all for it, and we believe it is extremely important that it should succeed.

. . . I think that this Indian second 5-year program is going to be carried through. It has had very great help from various free-world countries, most of all from the United States; considerable help from you and from others. And I believe it will succeed, and, as I have said before, I think it is extremely important that it should succeed. Because while I attach the greatest importance to the maintenance of the spiritual values—the moral values of the free world, in terms of the right of individuals to think as they wish, to believe as they wish, to get information, and so forth—one cannot realistically expect that human values will be preserved in an atmosphere of squalor and misery. . . .

B. Statement by U.N. Representative Stevenson on the United States View of the Indian Invasion of Goa*

[Extract]

December 18, 1961

I should like to express the view of the United States at this fateful hour in the life of the United Nations. I will not detain you long but long enough, I hope, to make clear our anxiety for the future of this Organization as a result of this incident.

When acts of violence take place between nations in this dangerous world, no matter where they occur or for what cause, there is reason for alarm. The

* *American Foreign Policy: Current Documents, 1958*, p. 1207.
* *American Foreign Policy: Current Documents, 1961*, pp. 956-59.

news from Goa tells of such acts of violence. It is alarming news, and in our judgment the Security Council has an urgent duty to act in the interests of international peace and security.

We know, as the world knows and as has been said countless times in the General Assembly and the Security Council, that the winds of change are blowing all over the world. But the winds of change are man made, and man can and must control them. They must not be allowed to become the bugles of war.

Our charter begins with the determination "to save succeeding generations from the scourge of war" and pledges its members to "practice tolerance and live together with one another as good neighbors."

*   *   *

These facts make the step which has been taken today all the harder to understand and to condone. The fact is—and the Indian Government has announced it—that Indian armed forces early this morning (December 18) marched into the Portuguese territories of Goa, Damao and Diu. Damao and Diu have been occupied, and there is fighting at this moment within the territory of Goa.

Here we are, Mr. President, confronted with the shocking news of this armed attack and that the Indian Minister of Defense [V.K. Krishna Menon], so well known in these halls for his advice on matters of peace and his tireless enjoinders to everyone else to seek the way of compromise, was on the borders of Goa inspecting his troops at the zero hour of invasion.

Let us be perfectly clear what is at stake here, gentlemen. It is the question of the use of armed force by one state against another and against its will, an act clearly forbidden by the charter. We have opposed such action in the past by our closest friends as well as by others. We opposed it in Korea in 1950, in Suez and in Hungary in 1956, in the Congo in 1960, and we do so again in Goa in 1961.

The facts in this case are unfortunately all too clear. These territories have been under Portuguese dominion for over four centuries. They have been invaded by Indian armed forces. The Government of India regards these territories as having the same status as the territories of Britain and France on the subcontinent from which those countries have voluntarily withdrawn. The Government of India has insisted that Portugal likewise withdraw. Portugal has refused, maintaining that it has a legal and moral right to these territories.

Mr. President, we have repeatedly urged both of the parties to this dispute to seek by peaceful processes the resolution of a problem which has its roots in the colonial past.

I do not at this time propose to concern myself with the merits of this dispute. We are not meeting here today to decide the merits of this case. We are meeting to decide what attitude should be taken in this body when one of the members of these United Nations casts aside the principles of the charter and seeks to resolve a dispute by force.

But, Mr. President, what is at stake today is not colonialism. It is a bold violation of one of the most basic principles of the United Nations Charter . . .

We realize fully the depths of the differences between India and Portugal concerning the future of Goa. We realize that India maintains that Goa by rights should belong to India. Doubtless India would hold, therefore, that its action today is aimed at a just end. But if our charter means anything it means that states are obligated to renounce the use of force, are obligated to seek a solution of their differences by peaceful means, are obligated to utilize the procedures of the United Nations when other peaceful means have failed. Prime Minister Nehru himself has often said that no right end can be served by a wrong means. The Indian tradition of nonviolence has inspired the whole world, but this act of force with which we are confronted today mocks the faith of India's frequent declarations of exalted principle. It is a· lamentable departure not only from the charter but from India's own professions of faith.

What is the world to do if every state whose territorial claims are unsatisfied should resort with impunity to the rule of armed might to get its way? The Indian subcontinent is not the only place in the world where such disputes exist.

*　　　　　*　　　　　*

THE SINO-INDIAN BORDER WAR OF 1962

C. Address by Prime Minister Nehru to the Indian Nation on the Chinese Invasion*

[Extract]

October 22, 1962

...A situation has arisen which calls upon all of us to meet it effectively. We are men and women of peace in this country, unused to the necessities of war. Because of this, we endeavored to follow a policy of peace even when aggression took place on our territory in Ladakh five years ago. We explored avenues for an honorable settlement by peaceful methods. That was our policy all over the world, and we tried to apply it in our own country...

But all our efforts have been in vain as far as our own frontier is concerned. A powerful and unscrupulous opponent, not caring for peace or peaceful methods, has continuously threatened us and even carried these threats into action. The time has therefore come for us to realize fully this menace that threatens the freedom of our people and the independence of our country.... To conserve that freedom and the integrity of our territory, we must gird up our loins to face the greatest menace that has come to us since we became independent. I have no doubt· that we shall succeed. Everything else is secondary to the freedom of our motherland, and, if necessary, everything has to be sacrificed in this great crisis.

I do not propose to give the long history of continuous aggression by the Chinese during the last five years, and how they have tried to justify it by

*American Foreign Policy: Current Documents, 1962, pp. 1015-16.

speeches, arguments, the repeated assertion of untruths and a campaign of calumny and vituperation against our country. Perhaps there are not many instances in history where one country—that is, India—has gone out of her way to be friendly and cooperative with the Chinese Government and people and to plead their cause in the councils of the world, and then for the Chinese Government to return evil for good, even to the extent of committing aggression and invading our sacred land. No self-respecting country, and certainly not India, with her love of freedom, can submit to this.

*   *   *

D. Letter from Prime Minister Nehru to Premier Chou En-lai of the People's Republic of China, Preconditioning Negotiations*

[Extract]

October 27, 1962

*   *   *

Nothing in my long political career has hurt and grieved me more than the fact that the hopes and aspirations for peaceful and friendly neighborly relations which we entertained, and to promote which my colleagues in the Government of India and myself worked so hard ever since the establishment of the People's Republic of China, should have been shattered by the hostile and unfriendly twist given in India-China relations during the past few years. The current clashes on the India-China border arising out of what is in effect a Chinese invasion of India, which you have described as "most distressing," are the final culmination of the deterioration in relations between India and China.

*   *

E. Note from Secretary Rusk to Prime Minister Nehru on Military Aid to India*

November 14, 1962

Excellency:. . . In response to requests from the Government of India, my Government is prepared to furnish assistance to the Government of India for the purpose of defense against the outright Chinese aggression directed from Peking now facing your country. It is the understanding of my Government that, with regard to defense articles made available to the Government of India under special arrangements to be concluded between representatives of our two Governments, and including defense articles provided between November 3 and November 14, 1962, the Government of India considers the assurances contained

*Ibid., pp. 1017-18.
*Ibid., pp. 1018-19.

in the Agreement effected by the exchange of notes of March 7 and 16, 1951 to be applicable and that the government of India is prepared:

> (1) to offer necessary facilities to representatives of the Government of the United States of America attached to the United States Embassy in India for the purpose of observing and reviewing the use of such articles and to provide them with such information as may be necessary for that purpose; and
> (2) to offer for return to the Government of the United States of America such articles furnished by the Government of the United States of America which are no longer needed for the purposes for which originally made available.

A reply to the effect that these understandings are correct will constitute an agreement between the Government of India and the Government of the United States of America, which shall come into force on the date of the note of reply from the Government of India.

Accept, Excellency, the renewed assurances of my highest consideration.

For the Secretary of State:
Phillips Talbot

F. State Department Statement on Military Aid to India and Pakistan*

November 17, 1962

The Department of State released today the text of an exchange of notes concerning the provision of defense assistance by the Government of the United States of America to the Government of India. In the exchange of notes it is stated that the assistance will be furnished for the purpose of defense against outright Chinese Communist aggression now facing India.

In 1954 when the United States decided to extend military aid to Pakistan, the Government of India was assured that if our aid to any country, including Pakistan, was misused and directed against another in aggression, the United States would undertake immediately, in accordance with constitutional authority, appropriate action both within and without the United Nations to thwart such aggression.

The Government of the United States of America has similarly assured the Government of Pakistan that, if our assistance to India should be misused and directed against another in aggression, the United States would undertake immediately, in accordance with constitutional authority, appropriate action both within and without the United Nations to thwart such aggression.

Needless to say, in giving these assurances the United States is confident that neither of the countries which it is aiding harbors aggressive designs.

G. Statement by President Kennedy on the Harriman-Nitze Mission to India*

[Extract]

November 20, 1962

Over the last weekend the Chinese have made great advances in northeastern

*Ibid., p. 1019
*Ibid., p. 1020.

India. Now they have offered some kind of cease-fire proposal, and we are in touch with the Indian Government to detemine their assessment of it. In order to better assess Indian needs, we are sending a team to New Delhi, headed by Assistant Secretary [of State for Far Eastern Affairs] Averell Harriman, including Assistant Secretary of Defense Paul Nitze and other representatives of the Defense Department and State Department. It will leave tomorrow.

In providing military assistance to India, we are mindful of our alliance with Pakistan. All of our aid to India is for the purpose of defeating Chinese Communist subversion. Chinese incursions into the subcontinent are a threat to Pakistan as well as India, and both have a common interest in opposing it.

We have urged this point in both governments. Our help to India in no way diminishes or qualifies our commitment to Pakistan, and we have made this clear to both governments as well.

*   *   *

There's been no indication of that [—a need to send American troops to India]. I think we can get a more precise idea of what the Indians need to protect their territorial integrity when Governor Harriman returns, and, also, I understand a similar mission may be being sent from London. And I think by the end of the week we ought to have a clearer idea of what the cease-fire offer means, what the military pressures are in India, and what assistance they would like to receive from us, but, as of today, I've heard nothing about American troops being requested.

. . . We can't tell precisely what the Indians require, and that's why this mission is going tomorrow, composed of representatives of State and Defense.

H. Comment by Secretary Rusk on the Significance of a Chinese Attack*

[Extract]

November 28, 1962

. . . In accordance with the announcement made by Peiping about their so-called "cease-fire," December 1 is a fairly important date.

As you know, China has had for many years, before the Communists came to power, certain territorial claims along that southern frontier. But the thing that has most concerned us is that the authorities in Peiping should have used violence in an attempt to settle a question which ought to be settled, if possible, by a course of negotiation; and the scale of their violence holds open the prospect that their intentions go far beyond the border issues.

Now, I think the events in India have alerted many Afro-Asian countries to the threat which has come from Peiping. They understand that these are

*Ibid., pp. 1023-24.

not issues that just turn upon some sort of cold war between Moscow and Washington, that there are other elements here that threaten their independence. And the rallying around of world opinion behind India in this situation, I think, must be a signal to the other side that India not only is a country with great potential of its own, great industrial strength, and is not to be easily tampered with, despite these immediate and short-term military reverses, but also that India, in the event of aggression, serious aggression, would have the support of the rest of the world. And this is something that Peiping must think seriously about.

I. Comment by President Kennedy on Aid to India*

February 21, 1963

There was an original request [for air defense assistance] made [by the Indian Government] in November, and then the British Government and the United States Government have sent a mission out at the present time to explore this matter of air security with the Indian Government. The mission has not completed its task or made recommendations. We are anxious to help India maintain itself against an attack, if such an attack should come again, and I think it's a matter which we ought to explore with the Indians in the next 4 or 5 weeks. India is a key area of Asia—500,000,000 people. It was attacked without warning after trying to follow a policy of friendship with countries on its border. We will find ourselves, I think, severely—the balance of power in the world would be very adversely affected if India should lose its freedom. . . .

J. Remarks by W. Averell Harriman, Under Secretary of State for Political Affairs, on Soviet Aid to India*

[Extract]

April 18, 1963

*   *   *

Why the Chinese Reds attacked India one cannot fully tell, but it must be beyond the reason of settling this border dispute. They built a road from Sinkiang Province into Tibet, which is the best way to get into the west and, of course, part of the territory which the Indians claim and which the Chinese claim. Their attack could not only have related to that because they were winning the particular local engagement which related to that area of Ladakh. They can get in by road or the Indians get in by air or by foot. But they attacked in the NEFA, the Northeast Frontier Area, where there was no real serious

**American Foreign Policy: Current Documents, 1963*, p. 763.
**Ibid.*, pp. 763-65.

difference over the border. Although there was technically, there was not a very basic difference. They must have had in mind the desire to destroy the image of India as a great country, to humiliate India, and to build up their own prestige, which they had lost to a very considerable extent by the collapse of the "great leap forward."

Now they have gained those objectives. On the other hand I think they have been rather surprised at the violent reaction within India itself, and I think we have a right to be encouraged. Nehru himself said this is not an attack on us nor a border dispute. It is an attack on our way of life. Others have said it is an attack on our existence as a nation of freedom and they look upon it, both the Government, Prime Minister Nehru and his colleagues, and the Indian people, as a long-term struggle, and they want to strengthen themselves in order to succeed in meeting it.

The area which Red China has perhaps the most immediate desire to gain control of—they don't indicate that they are willing to send military but they are attempting to subvert; that is the area in Southeast Asia, in Burma, Thailand, Cambodia, Viet-Nam. That is the great surplus rice producing area and is an area that, with greater development of their river resources, could support a very substantially larger population. I would think that you could see increased pressure on that area from time to time as the situation develops.

Now, as I say, this difference between Moscow and Peiping is extremely interesting and one which can have a very vital effect. I think we ought to understand some of the things we should not do. There are some people who think we should not give aid to India unless they break with Moscow. I think that is a very stupid thing. I think it is pleasant to see Mr. Khrushchev on the horns of a dilemma between his friend India and his eternal brother China. Why should we relieve him of that embarrassment? I think that it is very much in our interest that the Soviet Union continue to give economic assistance to India.

*   *   *

KASHMIR AND THE CONFLICT BETWEEN INDIA AND PAKISTAN

A. Statement by U.N. Representative Stevenson: "The Problem of Kashmir Cannot be Settled Unilaterally by Either Pakistan or India"*

[Extract]

February 14, 1964

So much has been said on the Kashmir case in this Council over the past 16 years that I shall not impose on your patience by reviewing the case again.

It is a matter of greatest regret to my Government, as it is to so many governments here represented, that India and Pakistan have been unable to reach a settlement either through mechanism set up by the Security Council or in bilateral talks, and that this dispute continues to occupy so much time of the international community. We are also profoundly concerned with the recurring communal disturbances in India and Pakistan which have caused such appalling loss of life, destruction of property, and displacement of peoples and human misery. It is hard for us to understand why these two countries have not found it possible during all of these years of bloodshed and of violence to take joint action to calm this situation and to allay the suffering, to stem the panic and migration of thousands of frightened human beings. Until there is a far greater effort to resolve these problems, they will continue to threaten the integrity and the prosperity of both countries.

*   *   *

Throughout the history of this issue it has been the desire of the United States to do what it could to compose the differences between the two friends. In doing so, we have started from the point of agreement between them because it was an equitable compromise based upon the sound principle that the people whose political affiliation and national status was subject to dispute have the right to express their will. We continue to support this principle as providing a sound basis upon which a political compromise of the dispute between India and Pakistan can be achieved through peaceful means.

If India and Pakistan are genuinely desirous of composing their difference, which is a prior condition of any political compromise, a fresh attempt must be made in light of today's realities to see how the basic principles can be applied to achieve such a political settlement. India, and indeed part of the very area in dispute, is under threat of Chinese Communist military attack. For this reason, as well as because of our long standing concern that the Kashmir question be peacefully resolved, we urged bilateral talks between the parties last year. While these talks did not bring an agreement, neither were they useless. Exploration of disputes through negotiation is a fundamental principle of the

*Department of State Bulletin, Mar. 16, 1964, pp. 425-26.

United Nations. It is the only way agreement can be achieved short of imposition by force. An agreement cannot be imposed from outside.

We recognize that the legitimate security interests of both India and Pakistan involve intricate internal problems of law and order and political consent. However, the international community, has a right to expect that these two great and ancient countries—a right to expect of them what we expect of all members of the United Nations community and that is to say a diligent and unrelenting effort to resolve their differences peacefully through negotiations. It must be recognized by both countries that the problem of Kashmir cannot be settled unilaterally by either party. It can only be settled, as I say, by agreement and by compromise, taking into account the free expression of the will of the people concerned. The United Nations was created to assist member states in this regard, and its resources are available to help the parties in the search for a solution. Friends of both countries also stand ready to help.

*   *   *

B. Statement by U.N. Ambassador Goldberg on a Ceasefire*

[Extract]

September 4, 1965

*   *   *

We are meeting here, as is apparent, in a spirit of grave concern for peace on the Asian subcontinent. The reverberations of fighting between the forces of India and Pakistan are reaching us in increasing volume. As the Secretary-General has reported so well and so objectively, the cease-fire line has been broken and there have been serious breaches of the cease-fire line in Jammu and Kashmir. Armed personnel as well as military units of the regular forces of both India and Pakistan have now crossed the cease-fire line established by agreement on July 27, 1949. And I shall not attempt to recapitulate the facts which have been reported in the report of the Secretary-General but shall only share his concern for future peace between India and Pakistan.

The United States and, as has been evident here today, all other members of this Council have viewed these events with the greatest apprehension and concern. Since the birth of India and Pakistan, my Government has developed close and friendly relations with their Governments, relations which we wish with all sincerity to continue. The people of the United States have many ties based on friendship, common interest, and shared goals with the peoples of both India and Pakistan. These are expressed not only in the broad programs which my Government has pursued and is pursuing to assist the development and security of these countries but also in the form of many nongovernmental exchanges and programs particularly in the fields of health, education, and economic development. And we know intimately from our close relations with both countries the intricacies of the underlying problem which is at the root of today's conflict, a problem which has been emphasized in the discussions which have taken place here today.

The immediate task at hand, however, is the cessation of conflict, a conflict, unfortunately, which has been threatening since early this year—and regrettably threatening. And we have, every one of us here today—governments and individuals—been watching with apprehension the upward trend in the temperature in this area on the subcontinent during the past year.

C. Statement by U.N. Ambassador Goldberg on Arms Shipments to India and Pakistan*

[Extract]

September 17, 1965

*   *   *

The United States enjoys and hopes to continue to enjoy friendly relations with both India and Pakistan. I should like to emphasize that we have suspended arms shipments to both countries, since we want, in support of the Security Council's resolutions calling for a cease-fire, to help bring about an end to this conflict and not to escalate it. It is the sense of the Security Council's resolutions that there be a prompt end and not an intensification of hostilities.

We deplore the use of arms supplied by us in this conflict in contravention of solemn agreements.

*   *   *

D. Statement by President Johnson on Acceptance of the Ceasefire*

[Extract]

September 22, 1965

I speak for every American when I commend the statesmanship and restraint shown by the leaders of Pakistan and India in their acceptance of the cease-fire call of the United Nations Security Council. The leadership shown in both nations thus takes us a long step away from the terrible dangers which have threatened the subcontinent of Asia.

On behalf of the American People I want to express our deep appreciation and gratitude to Secretary-General U Thant for his fairness and firmness in

*American Foreign Policy: Current Documents, 1965, pp. 804-05.
*Ibid., pp. 810-11.

the service of peace in these last weeks. I am especially proud of our own gifted Ambassador Arthur Goldberg and members of his new U.N. team. As President of the Security Council, he has given his able and untiring support to the efforts of the Secretary-General.

E. The Declaration of Tashkent*

January 10, 1966

The Prime Minister of India and the President of Pakistan having met at Tashkent and having discussed the existing relations between India and Pakistan, hereby declare their firm resolve to restore normal and peaceful relations between their countries and to promote understanding and friendly relations between their peoples. They consider the attainment of these objectives of vital importance for the welfare of the 600 million people of India and Pakistan.

I

The Prime Minister of India and the President of Pakistan agree that both sides will exert all efforts to create good neighbourly relations between India and Pakistan in accordance with the United Nations Charter. They reaffirm their obligation under the Charter not to have recourse to force and to settle their dispute through peaceful means. They considered that the interests of peace in their region and particularly in the Indo-Pakistan Sub-Continent and, indeed, the interests of the peoples of India and Pakistan were not served by the continuance of tension between the two countries. It was against this background that Jammu and Kashmir was discussed, and each of the sides set forth its respective position.

II

The Prime Minister of India and the President of Pakistan have agreed that all armed personnel of the two countries shall be withdrawn not later than 25 February 1966 to the positions they held prior to 5 August 1965, and both sides shall observe the cease-fire terms on the cease-fire line.

III

The Prime Minister of India and the President of Pakistan have agreed that relations between India and Pakistan shall be based on the principle of non-interference in the internal affairs of each other.

*American Foreign Policy: Current Documents, 1966, pp. 681-82.

IV

The Prime Minister of India and the President of Pakistan have agreed that both sides will discourage any propaganda directed against the other country, and will encourage propaganda which promotes the development of friendly relations between the two countries.

V

The Prime Minister of India and the President of Pakistan have agreed that the High Commissioner of India to Pakistan and the High Commissioner of Pakistan to India will return to their posts and that the normal functioning of diplomatic missions of both countries will be restored. Both Governments shall observe the Vienna Convention of 1961 on Diplomatic Intercourse.

VI

The Prime Minister of India and the President of Pakistan have agreed to consider measures towards the restoration of economic and trade relations, communications, as well as cultural exchanges between India and Pakistan, and to take measures to implement the existing agreements between India and Pakistan.

VII

The Prime Minister of India and the President of Pakistan have agreed that they give instructions to their respective authorities to carry out the repatriation of the prisoners of war.

VIII

The Prime Minister of India and the President of Pakistan have agreed that the sides will continue the discussion of questions relating to the problems of refugees and evictions of illegal immigrations. They also agreed that both sides will create conditions which will prevent the exodus of people. They further agreed to discuss the return of the property and assets taken over by either side in connection with the conflict.

IX

The Prime Minister of India and the President of Pakistan have agreed that the sides will continue meetings both at the highest and at other levels on matters of direct concern to both countries. Both sides have recognized the need to set up joint Indian-Pakistani bodies which will report to their Governments in order to decide what further steps should be taken.

The Prime Minister of India and the President of Pakistan record their feelings of deep appreciation and gratitude to the leaders of the Soviet Union, the Soviet Government and personally to the Chairman of the Council of Ministers of the U.S.S.R. for their constructive, friendly and noble part in bringing about the present meeting which has resulted in mutually satisfactory results. They also express to the Government and friendly people of Uzbekistan their sincere thankfulness for their overwhelming reception and generous hospitality.

They invite the Chairman of the Council of Ministers of the U.S.S.R. to witness this Declaration.

Lal Bahadur
Prime Minister of India

M.A. Khan, F.M.
President of Pakistan

F. Resolution on United States Participation in Relieving Victims of Hunger in India*

JOINT RESOLUTIONS

April 19, 1966

To support United States participation in relieving victims of hunger in India and to enhance India's capacity to meet the nutritional needs of its people.

Whereas the Congress has declared it to be the policy of the United States to make maximum efficient use of this Nation's agricultural abundance in furtherance of the foreign policy of the United States;

Whereas the Congress is considering legislation to govern the response of the United States to the mounting world food problem;

Whereas critical food shortages in India threatening the health if not the lives of tens of millions of people require an urgent prior response: Therefore be it

Resolved by the Senate and House of Representatives of the United States of America in Congress assembled,

That the Congress endorse and supports the President's initiative in organizing substantial American participation in an urgent international effort designed to:

(a) Help meet India's pressing food shortages by making available to India under Public Law 480 agricultural commodities to meet India's normal import needs plus added quantities of agricultural commodities as the United States share in the international response to the Indian emergency;

Ibid., p. 688.

(b) Help combat malnutrition, especially in mothers and children, via a special program;

(c) Encourage and assist those measures which the Government of India is planning to expand India's own agricultural production;

That the Congress urges the President to join India in pressing on other nations the urgency of sharing appropriately in a truly international response to India's critical need.

The Congress urges that to the extent necessary the food made available by this program be distributed in such manner that hungry people without money will be able to obtain food.

APPENDICES

APPENDIX A

Commentary

Since the completion of this volume, several important developments have occurred in American Asian policy: in the Spring, 1971 the Peoples Republic of China invited an American Table Tennis Team to Peking, inaugurating what was referred to initially as "Ping Pong Diplomacy"; in July, President Nixon announced that he would visit China in the near future; and in October, in spite of American support for a "two Chinas" policy, the U.N. expelled the Nationalist Chinese and seated Mainland China. Meanwhile, in February, 1971, the United States provided air and material support for a South Vietnamese attack on North Vietnamese troop concentrations in Laos; and during the remainder of the year, continued to withdraw troops from Vietnam while attempting to negotiate the release of American prisoners in Hanoi. In 1971 the United States also discussed trade differences with Japan and concluded a treaty granting the return of Okinawa to Japanese control. Though professing neutrality, in December, the Nixon administration also "tilted" in favor of Pakistan in the India-Pakistan war.

It would be manifestly presumptuous to suggest that one could include much of the significant documentation of these developments in a short appendix, even if the documents were all available. It is possible, however, to print some of those materials which reveal the basic thrust and direction of American policy.

JAPAN

Report by Secretary of State William Rogers Concerning the Agreement with Japan on the Ryukyu and Daito Islands*

September 5, 1971

The President: I have the honor to submit the Agreement between the United States of America and Japan concerning the Ryukyu Islands and the Daito Islands signed at Washington and Tokyo on June 17, 1971, with the recommendation that you transmit it to the Senate for its advice and consent to ratification.

The Secretary of Defense and the Chairman of the Joint Chiefs of Staff join in this recommendation and in the hope for early and favorable Senate action.

I also submit the following related documents for the information of the Senate:

Agreed Minutes,

Memorandum of Understanding concerning Article III,

Exchange of notes concerning the Voice of America facility on Okinawa,

Exchange of notes concerning submerged lands,

Letter from Minister for Foreign Affairs Kiichi Aichi to Ambassador Meyer concerning treatment of foreign nationals and firms,

Memorandum of Understanding on air services to and through Okinawa, and

The Arrangement concerning Assumption by Japan of the Responsibility for the Immediate Defense of Okinawa.

The United States authority over the Ryukyu Islands and the Daito Islands derives from Article 3 of the Treaty of Peace with Japan, signed September 8, 1951, which provided the United States with the right to exercise all powers of administration, legislation and jurisdiction over the territory and inhabitants of the islands referred to in Article 3. While Article 3 contemplated that these islands might ultimately be placed under United Nations trusteeship, the United States delegate to the Peace Treaty Conference, John Foster Dulles, stated that the United States considered that the article permitted Japan to retain "residual sovereignty" over the islands. The United States returned a part of the group, the Amami Islands, to Japan on December 25, 1953. Subsequently, successive American Presidents reaffirmed Japan's residual sovereignty over the remaining islands and stated the intention of the United States eventually to return them to Japan. In 1967 President Johnson and Prime Minister Sato agreed that the two Governments should keep under joint and continuous review the status of the Ryukyu Islands guided by the aim of returning administrative rights over these islands to Japan. They also agreed on the return to Japan of several additional islands mentioned in Article 3 of the Peace Treaty, including the Bonin Islands. These were returned on June 26, 1968.

In November, 1969 you and Prime Minister Sato agreed that the two Governments should enter immediately into consultations regarding specific arrange-

*Department of State Bullentin, Oct. 18, 1971, pp. 433-35.

ments for accomplishing the early reversion of Okinawa without detriment to the security of the Far East including Japan. You and Prime Minister Sato further agreed to expedite the consultations with a view to accomplishing the reversion during 1972 subject to the conclusion of these specific arrangements with the necessary legislative support.

As a result, negotiations between the United States and Japan began in March 1970 and culminated in the signature on June 17, 1971, of the Agreement and certain related documents I am submitting to you today. The negotiations were conducted for the United States by Ambassador Armin H. Meyer in Tokyo, with the support and assistance of United States military authorities and of the High Commissioner of the Ryukyu Islands. Instructions to the negotiators came from the Departments of State, Treasury and Defense. The Department of Commerce also participated in the formulation of these instructions when its interests were involved.

The Agreement consists of a preamble and nine articles. The preamble recalls President Nixon's meeting with Prime Minister Sato in November 1969 and notes that the two Governments have reaffirmed that the reversion of Okinawa is to be carried out on the basis of the Joint Communiqué issued on November 21, 1969. A copy of that Communiqué is enclosed. It expresses *inter alia* the intention of both Governments to maintain the United States-Japan Treaty of Mutual Cooperation and Security (which will also apply to Okinawa after reversion), Japan's recognition of its stake in the security of the Far East, and Japan's view that Okinawa reversion should not hinder the effective discharge of the international obligations assumed by the United States for the defense of countries in the Far East including Japan.

The preamble also recites the willingness of the United States to relinquish its rights and interests under Article 3 of the Treaty of Peace and Japan's willingness to assume full responsibility and authority over the Ryukyu Islands and the Daito Islands.

Under paragraph 1 of Article I the United States relinquishes in favor of Japan its rights and interests with respect to the Ryukyu Islands and the Daito Islands under Article 3 of the Peace Treaty, and Japan assumes full responsibility and authority for the exercise of all governmental powers over these islands. Paragraph 2 of Article I defines these islands for the purpose of the Agreement. An agreed minute to Article I describes the territory by geographical coordinates.

Article II confirms that treaties and other agreements between the United States and Japan become applicable to the Islands upon reversion.

Paragraph 1 of Article III commits Japan to grant the United States upon reversion the use of military facilities and areas in Okinawa in accordance with the 1960 United States-Japan Treaty of Mutual Cooperation and Security and its related arrangements. By a Memorandum of Understanding concerning Article III, the two Governments have agreed upon the specific facilities and areas to be granted for use by the United States armed forces upon reversion, pursuant to the provisions of the Agreement under Article VI of the Treaty of Mutual Cooperation and Security, regarding Facilities and Areas and the Status of

United States Armed Forces in Japan (the so-called SOFA).

Paragraph 2 of Article III refers to the provision of the SOFA which exempts the United States from any obligation to restore facilities and areas to their original condition upon their return and which exempts Japan from any obligation to compensate the United States for any improvements made by the United States on facilities and areas which are returned to the Government of Japan. This paragraph fixes the condition of the property for purposes of these exemptions as that existing at the time United States armed forces first used the facilities and areas. It also clarifies that Japan need make no specific compensation to the United States for improvements in facilities and areas made prior to reversion.

Under Article IV Japan waives all claims of Japan and its nationals against the United States and its nationals and against local authorities arising out of the United States administration of the Islands, except for certain claims specifically recognized under United States law or local laws applicable during the United States administration (which include the claims set forth in the Agreed Minute to Article IV). Paragraph 2 of Article IV grants authority to the United States to maintain a claims office on Okinawa to settle any claims remaining after reversion. Paragraph 3 of Article IV provides that the United States will make *ex gratia* contributions to Japanese nationals whose lands in the Islands were damaged prior to July 1, 1950, and were released from the use of United States authorities after June 30, 1961. In paragraph 4 of Article IV Japan recognizes the validity of all official acts and omissions of the United States during the period of its administration.

Article V concerns civil and criminal jurisdiction. Paragraph 1 provides Japanese recognition of the validity of final judgments rendered before reversion in civil cases. It obligates Japan to continue such judgments in full force and effect. Paragraphs 2 and 3 provide for the assumption by Japan of jurisdiction over civil and criminal cases pending at the time of reversion without in any way affecting the substantive rights involved. Paragraph 4 provides that Japan may continue the execution of any final criminal judgments rendered prior to reversion. An agreed minute to Article V deals with the question of exercise of criminal jurisdiction over members of United States armed forces with respect to offenses committed prior to reversion; Japan will not exercise jurisdiction over such cases.

Article VI transfers to the Government of Japan certain properties of the United States. The major part of such properties consists of public utility corporations. During the period of its administration the United States created certain new lands by reclamation from the sea, or otherwise acquired such lands. These reclaimed lands will also become the property of the Government of Japan upon reversion. The United States is not obliged to compensate Japan or its nationals for any alteration made prior to reversion to lands upon which properties to be transferred to the Government of Japan are located.

Article VII constitutes the payment provision of the Agreement. Considering, *inter alia,* the transfer of assets to the Government of Japan under Article VI, the fact that reversion will be carried out in a manner consistent with the policy of the Government of Japan as described in paragraph 8 of the Joint Communiqué of November 21, 1969, and certain extra costs borne by the Government of the United States resulting from reversion, the Japanese Government will pay the United States $320 million in stated installments within five years of reversion. The first installment of $100 million is to be paid within one week after reversion.

Article VIII contains authority for the Voice of America relay station on Okinawa to continue in operation for a period of five years after reversion, with consultations regarding future operation of the station to begin two years after reversion. Additional details regarding the operation of the Voice of America station are contained in an exchange of notes concerning the Voice of America facility on Okinawa.

Article IX provides for ratification of the Agreement and for its entry into force two months after the instruments of ratification are exchanged. In accordance with Article I, reversion will take place on the date the Agreement enters into force.

Certain important arrangements involved in Okinawa reversion are dealt with in the other documents submitted herewith. These include arrangements concerning the treatment of foreign nationals and firms on Okinawa, the assumption by Japan of the responsibility for the immediate defense of Okinawa, and commercial air services to and through Okinawa.

The arrangement concerning the treatment of foreign nationals and firms is contained in a letter of June 17, 1971, from then Foreign Minister Kiichi Aichi to Ambassador Meyer. The letter sets forth the policies decided upon by the Japanese Government respecting points that were of major concern to American business and professional interests in Okinawa. The provisions of the letter were worked out after close consultations with the representatives of the business and professional community on Okinawa, and we believe that the arrangement should provide a satisfactory basis for the post-reversion period.

The Arrangement concerning Assumption by Japan of the Responsibility for the Immediate Defense of Okinawa, signed on June 29, 1971 on behalf of the United States Department of Defense and the Japan Defense Agency, sets forth the agreed modalities for necessary coordination in connection with the deployment of Japanese Self Defense Forces in Okinawa after reversion. The Arrangement provides for Japanese takeover or joint use of certain installations or sites now used by United States forces on Okinawa, describes generally the missions and strengths of the Japanese forces to be deployed to Okinawa following reversion, and sets timetables for full assumption of the missions described.

A Memorandum of Understanding of June 17, 1971 concerning air services to and through Okinawa after reversion preserves existing traffic rights for American commerical air carriers now serving Okinawa. In addition there will be a five year "no charge" period following reversion during which the benefits American carriers receive by serving Okinawa will not be taken into account in calculating the overall balance of benefits which the United States receives under the bilateral air transport agreement with Japan.

The Agreement and related documents take account of essential American interests in Okinawa and the Far East. Under the Agreement the United States will retain its essential military bases on Okinawa under provisions of the United States-Japan Treaty of Mutual Cooperation and Security, which has proved very satisfactory in Japan proper. The treaty arrangements and Japan's recognition of its own stake in the security of the Far East should ensure effective operation of our bases on Okinawa and contribute to peace and security in the region.

More fundamentally, Okinawa's reversion will resolve the last remaining issue between the United States and Japan arising from World War II. Reversion is essential to the preservation and further development of relations with Japan. It will fulfill our pledge to the people of Japan and Okinawa and will enable them to realize their goal of reunifying Okinawa with Japan. It will, in short, be a unique historic act reflecting both the strength of the ties between the United States and Japan and the character of both nations.

Because of the unusual importance of the Agreement, I hope that the Senate will give it early and favorable consideration.

Address by U. Alexis Johnson, Under Secretary for Political Affairs on Trends in United States-Japan Relations*

October 18, 1971

I am very pleased to be here with you today in Los Angeles and am particularly pleased to share with you a few thoughts on U.S.-Japan relations—a subject close to my heart both professionally and personally. The title you have suggested for my talk, "Trends in United States-Japan Relations," is very timely. Some of the issues and frictions in the relations between our two countries which have arisen lately have tended to be overemphasized in the public media, as compared with those many broad areas, including the U.N., where we are working closely and effectively together. But it is clear that we stand at an important crossroads in U.S.-Japan relations.

*　　　　　　*　　　　　　*

It is the economic area to which both countries need to pay increasing attention, for unless this area is properly handled the consequences will be reflected in the political and security areas. A part of the problem is that the growth of the Japanese economy has been so fast. Over the past 10 years, Japan has tripled its GNP, quadrupled its exports, and tripled its foreign exchange reserves. Its balance of trade shifted firmly from a tenuous deficit to a sustained surplus. That Japan ranks third in the world in GNP is well known. What is less well known is that per capita income now approaches that of the United Kingdom. Our total trade with Japan is now greater than with any country except Canada.

Yet Japan has been slow to change those policies which were appropriate to its previous status of a weak and developing nation. I have often said to

*Ibid., Nov. 8, 1971. pp. 513-17.

my Japanese friends that it seems to me that policies of economic nationalism are no longer compatible with Japan's interests, for such policies can only result in other countries adopting similar policies directed against Japan.

In turn, we must be prepared to treat Japan with that consideration and respect that is appropriate to its status as a great power. We ask Japan for equality of treatment of our economic interests, and in turn, we must be prepared to accord equality of treatment to Japan.

Americans obviously like the price and quality of many Japanese products, for when given the opportunity they buy them at a high rate. This is good, for the American consumer is obtaining something he needs and wants. However, the speed and growth of Japanese exports to this country have created two problems. First, the development has in some areas taken place too fast for the American enterprises concerned to make the necessary adjustments without severe dislocations not only to earnings but also to labor. Secondly, there has not been a corresponding growth in American exports to Japan, so that there has been a massive increase in our adverse balance of payments with Japan.

It was due to the recognition by both countries of the first problem that last Friday we entered into an agreement on textiles. It is in recognition of the second problem that Japan has permitted a limited float of the yen, and the two governments are continuing to discuss not only monetary adjustments but also how the Japanese market can be further opened to American goods and investment. We want to solve these problems not by decreasing trade but rather by increasing trade in a manner that is healthy and sound for all parties.

Dramatic changes in the East Asian international environment are also under-way and will, of course, profoundly affect U.S.-Japan bilateral relations. The Nixon doctrine calls for a lower United States profile in Asia and assumes that regional powers will tackle their own problems without extensive United States involvement. The Sino-Soviet split continues to interject new elements in regional affairs. Intensely nationalistic governments among the smaller countries of the region seem to have emerged from the early confusion of the post-colonial period and are acquiring greater maturity and sophistication in their dealings with the major powers. The People's Republic of China has now been responsive to our overtures to establish better communication between us, and as you know, President Nixon will be visiting Peking. In short, a complicated multinational system is taking shape in East Asia, to which many of the old cliches are not applicable.

President Nixon's announced trips to Peking and Moscow and the bold steps he took in the economic sphere have been called by the Japanese press "Nixon shocks." I personally, however, find it difficult to understand why any in Japan would object to steps designed to lessen the tensions in Asia and diminish the chances of an outbreak of armed conflict. Similarly, the steps we have taken to strengthen our economy and the international monetary and trading system would seem to me to be in Japan's own interest. On this latter subject I note to my Japanese friends that we are not asking our foreign friends to bear the full brunt of our economic adjustments. We are also being very tough on ourselves.

We must recognize, however, that these bold moves have struck at two underpinnings of the world view held by many Japanese: first, that hostility between the United States and mainland China was somehow an unchanging law of nature, and second, that the United States is economically omnipotent. In fact, these so-called "shocks" may be more psychological than substantive. Many nations, and to some extent we ourselves, had come to believe in the postwar era that we were capable of doing virtually anything we wanted to do. It comes as a shock to those holding this view to observe the United States having to ask others for help rather than giving it.

*   *   *

CHINA

Announcement by Department of State Press Officer Charles W. Bray on Steps Taken on Contacts With Mainland China*

March 15, 1971

I have an announcement concerning the restriction on the use of American passports for travel to certain areas. With regard to the People's Republic of China, we have decided not to renew the restriction. With regard to the three other areas, North Viet-Nam, North Korea, and Cuba, the restriction remains in effect for another 6 months, at which time the matter will be considered again. Removing a restriction on the use of American passports for travel to the People's Republic of China is consistent with the President's publicly stated desire to improve communication with the mainland.

I could, if you would like, very briefly summarize the unilateral steps we have taken in recent years on the subject of trade and travel.

In July of 1969, we permitted noncommercial tourist purchases of up to $100 of Chinese goods. At the same time, we relaxed restrictions relating to travel to permit almost anyone with a legitimate purpose to travel to mainland China on an American passport. If I recall the figures correctly, we have validated on the order of 1,000 passports, including 270 in 1970.

In December 1969, we permitted unlimited purchases of Chinese goods to enable tourists, collectors, museums, universities, to import Chinese products for their own account. In the same month, that is, December of 1969, we permitted American-controlled subsidiaries abroad to conduct trade in nonstrategic goods with mainland China.

In April of 1970, we announced selective licensing of American-made components and related spare parts for nonstrategic foreign goods exported to China.

In August of 1970, we lifted the restriction on American oil companies abroad bunkering free-world ships bearing nonstrategic cargoes to Chinese ports on the mainland.

State Department Reaction to China's Invitation to an American Table Tennis Team to Visit Mainland China*

April 7, 1971

The State Department today described the Chinese invitation to an American table tennis team to visit Communist China as an "encouraging development" and said it would welcome reciprocal visits by Chinese athletic teams to this country.

The department spokesman, Charles W. Bray 3d, said the United States would "envisage no difficulties" in granting visas to a Chinese team.

The Chinese invitation, he said, is "clearly consistent with the hopes expressed by the President and Secretary of State that there could be greater contact between the American and Chinese peoples."

*Department of State Bulletin, Apr. 12, 1971, p. 510.
*The New York Times, Apr. 8, 1971.

Privately, ranking State Department officials described themselves as "very encouraged" by the Chinese invitation, which they regard as a conscious if limited diplomatic initiative by Peking.

One offical described the invitation as a "clear manifestation of China's changing and more flexible attitude toward the world."

"Such an invitation would never be issued casually or without Government approval," the official said. "There can be no question that this is meant to indicate at least a slight relaxation of their attitude toward the United States."

During the last two years the Nixon Administration has taken a series of tentative, unilateral steps to improve this country's relations with Peking. Trade restrictions have been modified and three weeks ago the last remaining curbs on travel by Americans to the Chinese mainland were lifted.

These gestures have been ignored by the Chinese, but officials here believe the table tennis invitation may well be Peking's way of indirectly welcoming the American overtures.

State Department sources said the American team would be encouraged to extend a reciprocal invitation to its Chinese hosts for a visit to this country "if they wish to do so." Among other problems, the unofficial American team presumably would have to find the funds to finance a Chinese visit to America, since their expenses in China are being paid at least nominally by their hosts.

U.N. Issue Under Review

The Chinese invitation comes at a time when the Nixon Administration is in the final stages of a full-scale review of its China policy and the question of the Peking Government's admission to the United Nations. A Presidential decision is expected shortly.

The Chinese overture may well strengthen the argument of officials within the Administration who have been calling for further unilateral American steps to improve relations, such as the authorization of non-strategic trade with China.

The White House added its tacit support for the American team's visit to China late today. Ronald L. Ziegler, the Presidential press secretary, noted Mr. Nixon's stated interest in improving communication with China and said that the team's planned visit conformed to that policy.

"It is a private visit and there is no official Government involvement," he added.

Comments by President Nixon on China*

April 29, 1971

Mr. Cormier [Frank Cormier, Associated Press].

Q. Mr. President, the Commission on the United Nations that you appointed, headed by your 1960 vice-presidential running mate, has come out rather strongly for a two-China policy. The last time we saw you you weren't prepared

*Department of State Bulletin, May 17, 1971, pp. 629-30.

to talk about that. I wonder if tonight you could say how you feel about those proposals.

The President: Well, Mr. Cormier, that recommendation by that very distinguished committee, of course, is being given consideration in the high councils of this Government, and I am, of course, considering it along with recommendations which move in the other direction.

I think, however, that your question requires that I put, perhaps, in perspective much of this discussion about our New China policy. I think that some of the speculation that has occurred in recent weeks since the visit of the table tennis team to Peking has not been useful.

I want to set forth exactly what it is and what it is not.

First, as I stated at, I think, one of my first press conferences in this room, the long-range goal of this administration is a normalization of our relationships with mainland China, the People's Republic of China, and the ending of its isolation from the other nations of the world. That is a long-range goal.

Second, we have made some progress toward that goal. We have moved in the field of travel; we have moved in the field of trade. There will be more progress made. For example, at the present time I am circulating among the departments the items which may be released as possible trade items in the future, and I will be making an announcement on that in a very few weeks.

But now when we move from the field of travel and trade to the field of recognition of the Government, to its admission to the United Nations, I am not going to discuss those matters, because it is premature to speculate about that.

We are considering all those problems. When I have an announcement to make, when a decision is made—and I have not made it yet—I will make it.

But up until that time we will consider all of the proposals that are being made. We will proceed on the path that we have been proceeding on. And that is the way to make progress. Progress is not helped in this very sensitive area by speculation that goes beyond what the progress might achieve.

I would just summarize it this way: What we have done has broken the ice. Now we have to test the water to see how deep it is.

I would finally suggest that—I know this question may come up if I don't answer it now—I hope and, as a matter of fact, I expect to visit mainland China sometime in some capacity—I don't know what capacity. But that indicates what I hope for the long term. And I hope to contribute to a policy in which we can have a new relationship with mainland China.

*   *   *

Q. Mr. President, you spoke of your intention to travel to mainland China. Is that at the invitation of Chairman Mao?

The President: I am not referring to any invitation. I am referring only to a hope and an expectation that at some time in my life and in some capacity, which, of course, does not put any deadline on when I would do it, that I would hope to go to mainland China.

*   *   *

Q. Sir, in your first answer on China, you said that you were considering suggestions for a two-China policy, along with suggestions that move in the other direction. Could you expound a little bit on what you mean by that? What is the range of alternatives?

The President: Mr. Bailey [Charles W. Bailey 2d, Minneapolis Tribune, Minneapolis Star], what I meant to convey was that both within the administration and from sources outside the administration, there are those who favor a two-China policy; there are those who favor universaility in the United Nations; there are those who favor a one-China policy, either mainland China or Taiwan China.

Now, all of these are positions that are taken. I am not suggesting that they are lively options as far as I am concerned. What I am saying is that this is a very complex problem. I will make the decision after advising with the Secretary of State and my other chief advisers in this field, and when I make it I will announce it; but I am not going to speculate on it now, because, I emphasize, this is a very sensitive area and too much speculation about it might destroy or seriously imperil what I think is the significant progress we have made, at least in the travel area, and possibly in the trade area, looking to the future.

Statement by President Nixon Announcing Acceptance of the Invitation to Visit People's Republic of China*

July 15, 1971

I have requested this television time tonight to announce a major development in our efforts to build a lasting peace in the world.

As I have pointed out on a number of occasions over the past 3 years, there can be no stable and enduring peace without the participation of the People's Republic of China and its 750 million people. That is why I have undertaken initiatives in several areas to open the door for more normal relations between our two countries.

In pursuance of that goal, I sent Dr. Kissinger, my Assistant for National Security Affairs, to Peking during his recent world tour for the purpose of having talks with Premier Chou En-lai.

The announcement I shall now read is being issued simultaneously in Peking and in the United States:

> "Premier Chou En-lai and Dr. Henry Kissinger, President Nixon's Assistant for National Security Affairs, held talks in Peking from July 9 to 11, 1971. Knowing of President Nixon's expressed desire to visit the People's Republic of China, Premier Chou En-lai on behalf of the Government of the People's Republic of China has extended an invitation to President Nixon to visit China at an appropriate date before May, 1972.
>
> "President Nixon has accepted the invitation with pleasure.

* *Ibid.*, Aug. 2, 1971. p. 121

"The meeting between the leaders of China and the United States is to seek the normalization of relations between the two countries and also to exchange views on questions of concern to the two sides."

In anticipation of the inevitable speculation which will follow this announcement, I want to put our policy in the clearest possible context. Our action in seeking a new relationship with the People's Republic of China will not be at the expense of our old friends.

It is not directed against any other nation. We seek friendly relations with all nations. Any nation can be our friend without being any other nation's enemy.

I have taken this action because of my profound conviction that all nations will gain from a reduction of tensions and a better relationship between the United States and the People's Republic of China.

It is in this spirit that I will undertake what I deeply hope will become a journey for peace—peace not just for our generation but for future generations on this earth we share together.

Statement by Secretary Rogers on the U.N. Decision on Chinese Representation*

October 26, 1971

Last night's decision to admit the People's Republic of China as a member of the United Nations, of course, is consistent with the policy of the United States. President Nixon hopes that this action, which will bring into the United Nations representatives of more than 700 million people, will result in a reduction of tensions in the Pacific area.

At the same time, the United States deeply regrets the action taken by the United Nations to deprive the Republic of China of representation in that organization. We think that this precedent, which has the effect of expelling 14 million people on Taiwan from representation in the United Nations, is a most unfortunate one which will have many adverse effects in the future.

We and the cosponsors of our resolution made an all-out effort to prevent the expulsion of the Republic of China. We are particularly grateful to all of our cosponsors for the very dedicated and determined effort that was made to retain a place for the Republic of China in the United Nations.

The Republic of China, of course, continues to be a respected and valued member of the international community, and the ties between us remain unaffected by the action of the United Nations.

Although we believe that a mistake of major proportion has been made in expelling the Republic of China from the United Nations, the United States recognizes that the will of a majority of the members has been expressed. We, of course, accept that decision.

We hope that the United Nations will not have been weakened by what it has done. We continue to believe in its principles and purposes and hope that ways can be found to make it more effective in the pursuit of peace in the future.

* * *

*Ibid., Nov. 15, 1971, p. 54.

Communiqué Issued by President Nixon and Premier Chou En-lai at the Conclusion of Their Meetings in China*

February 27, 1972

President Richard Nixon of the United States of America visited the People's Republic of China at the invitation of Premier Chou En-lai of the People's Republic of China from Feb. 21 to Feb. 28, 1972. Accompanying the President were Mrs. Nixon, U.S. Secretary of State William Rogers, Assistant to the President Dr. Henry Kissinger, and other American officials.

President Nixon met with Chairman Mao Tse-tung of the Communist Party of China on Feb. 21. The two leaders had a serious and frank exchange of views on Sino-U.S. relations and world affairs.

During the visit, extensive, earnest and frank discussions were held between President Nixon and Premier Chou En-lai on the normalization of relations between the United States of America and the People's Republic of China, as well as on other matters of interest to both sides. In addition, Secretary of State William Rogers and Foreign Minister Chi Peng-fei held talks in the same spirit.

President Nixon and his party visited Peking and viewed cultural, industrial and agricultural sites, and they also toured Hangchow and Shanghai where, continuing discussions with Chinese leaders, they viewed similar places of interest.

The leaders of the People's Republic of China and the United States of America found it beneficial to have this opportunity, after so many years without contact, to present candidly to one another their views on a variety of issues. They reviewed the international situation in which important changes and great upheavals are taking place and expounded their respective positions and attitudes.

The U. S. side stated:

Peace in Asia and peace in the world requires efforts both to reduce immediate tensions and to eliminate the basic causes of conflict. The United States will work for a just and secure peace: just, because it fulfills the aspirations of peoples and nations for freedom and progress; secure, because it removes the danger of foreign aggression. The United States supports individual freedom and social progress for all the peoples of the world, free of outside pressure or intervention.

The United States believes that the effort to reduce tensions is served by improving communications between countries that have different ideologies so as to lessen the risks of confrontation through accident, miscalculation or misunderstanding. Countries should treat each other with mutual respect and be willing to compete peacefully, letting performance be the ultimate judge. No country should claim infallibility and each country should be prepared to reexamine its own attitudes for the common good.

The United States stressed that the peoples of Indochina should be allowed to determine their destiny without outside intervention; its constant primary objective has been a negotiated solution; the eight-point proposal put forward by the Republic of Vietnam and the United States on Jan. 27, 1972, represents the basis for the attainment of that objective; in the absence of a negotiated settlement the United States envisages the ultimate withdrawal of all U.S. forces from the region consistent with the aim of self-determination for each country of Indochina.

*The New York Times, Feb. 28, 1972.

The United States will maintain its close ties with and support for the Republic of Korea. The United States will support efforts of the Republic of Korea to seek a relaxation of tension and increase communications in the Korean peninsula. The United States places the highest value on its friendly relations with Japan; it will continue to develop the existing close bonds. Consistent with the United Nations Security Council Resolution of Dec. 21, 1971, the United States favors the continuation of the cease-fire between India and Pakistan and the withdrawal of all military forces to within their own territories and to their own sides of the cease-fire line in Jammu and Kashmir; the United States supports the right of the peoples of South Asia to shape their own future in peace, free of military threat, and without having the area become the subject of big-power rivalry.

The Chinese side stated:

Wherever there is oppression, there is resistance. Countries want independence, nations want liberation and the people want revolution—this has become the irresistible trend of history. All nations, big or small, should be equal; big nations should not bully the small and strong nations should not bully the weak. China will never be a superpower and it opposes hegemony and power politics of any kind.

The Chinese side stated that it firmly supports the struggles of all oppressed people and nations for freedom and liberation and that the people of all countries have the right to choose their social systems according to their own wishes and the right to safeguard the independence, sovereignty and territorial integrity of their own countries and oppose foreign aggression, interference, control and subversion. All foreign troops should be withdrawn to their own countries.

The Chinese side expressed its firm support to the peoples of Vietnam, Laos and Cambodia in their efforts for the attainment of their goals and its firm support to the seven-point proposal of the Provisional Revolutionary Government of the Republic of South Vietnam and the elaboration of February this year on the two key problems in the proposal, and to the Joint Declaration of the Summit Conference of the Indochinese Peoples.

It firmly supports the eight-point program for the peaceful unification of Korea put forward by the Government of the Democratic People's Republic of Korea on April 12, 1971, and the stand for the abolition of the "U.N. Commission for the Unification and Rehabilitation of Korea." It firmly opposes the revival and outward expansion of Japanese militarism and firmly supports the Japanese people's desire to build an independent, democratic, peaceful and neutral Japan. It firmly maintains that India and Pakistan should, in accordance with the United Nations resolutions on the India-Pakistan question, immediately withdraw all their forces to their respective territories and to their own sides of the cease-fire line in Jammu and Kashmir and firmly supports the Pakistan Government and people in their struggle to preserve their independence and sovereignty and the people of Jammu and Kashmir in their struggle for the right of self-determination.

There are essential differences between China and the United States in their social systems and foreign policies. However, the two sides agreed that countries, regardless of their social systems, should conduct their relations on the principles of respect for the sovereignty and territorial integrity of all states, nonaggression against other states, noninterference in the internal affairs of other states, equality and mutual benefit, and peaceful coexistence. International disputes should be settled on this basis, without resorting to the use or threat of force. The United States and the People's Republic of China are prepared to apply these principles to their mutual relations.

With these principles of international relations in mind the two sides stated that:

Progress toward the normalization of relations between China and the United States is in the interests of all countries.

Both wish to reduce the danger of international military conflict.

Neither should seek hegemony in the Asia-Pacific region and each is opposed to the efforts by any other country or group of countries to establish such hegemony; and

Neither is prepared to negotiate on behalf of any third party or to enter into agreements or understandings with the other directed at other states.

Both sides are of the view that it would be against the interests of the peoples of the world for any major country to collude with another against other countries, or for major countries to divide up the world into spheres of interest.

The sides reviewed the long-standing serious disputes between China and the United States.

The Chinese side reaffirmed its position: The Taiwan question is the crucial question obstructing the normalization of relations between China and the United States; the Government of the People's Republic of China is the sole legal government of China; Taiwan is a province of China which has long been returned to the motherland; the liberation of Taiwan is China's internal affair in which no other country has the right to interfere; and all U.S. forces and military installations must be withdrawn from Taiwan. The Chinese government firmly opposes any activities which aim at the creation of "one China, one Taiwan," "one China, two governments," "two Chinas" and "independent Taiwan" or advocate that "the status of Taiwan remains to be determined."

The U.S. side declared: The United States acknowledges that all Chinese on either side of the Taiwan Strait maintain there is but one China and that Taiwan is a part of China. The United States Government does not challenge that position. It reaffirms its interest in a peaceful settlement of the Taiwan question by the Chinese themselves. With this prospect in mind, it affirms the ultimate objective of the withdrawal of all U.S. forces and military installations from Taiwan. In the meantime, it will progressively reduce its forces and military installations on Taiwan as the tension in the area diminishes.

The two sides agreed that it is desirable to broaden the understanding between the two peoples. To this end, they discussed specific areas in such fields as science, technology, culture, sports and journalism, in which people-to-people contacts and exchanges would be mutually beneficial. Each side undertakes to facilitate the further development of such contacts and exchanges.

Both sides view bilateral trade as another area from which mutual benefits can be derived, and agree that economic relations based on equality and mutual benefit are in the interest of the peoples of the two countries. They agree to facilitate the progressive development of trade between their two countries.

The two sides agree that they will stay in contact through various channels, including the sending of a senior U.S. representative to Peking from time to time for concrete consultations to further the normalization of relations between the two countries and continue to exchange views on issues of common interest.

The two sides expressed the hope that the gains achieved during this visit would open up new prospects for the relations between the two countries. They believe that the normalization of relations between the two countries is not only in the interest of the Chinese and American peoples but also contributes to the relaxation of tension in Asia and the world.

President Nixon, Mrs. Nixon and the American party express their appreciation for the gracious hospitality shown them by the government and people of the People's Republic of China.

VIETNAM

Address by President Nixon on a New Peace Initiative for All Indochina*

October 7, 1970

Good evening, my fellow Americans. Tonight I would like to talk to you about a major new initiative for peace.

When I authorized operations against the enemy sanctuaries in Cambodia last April, I also directed that an intensive effort be launched to develop new approaches for peace in Indochina.

In Ireland on Sunday, I met with the chiefs of our delegation to the Paris talks. This meeting marked the culmination of a Government-wide effort begun last spring on the negotiation front. After considering the recommendations of all my principal advisers, I am tonight announcing new proposals for peace in Indochina.

This new peace initiative had been discussed with the Governments of South Viet-Nam, Laos, and Cambodia. All support it. It has been made possible in large part by the remarkable success of the Vietnamization program over the past 18 months. Tonight I want to tell you what these proposals are and what they mean.

First, I propose that all armed forces throughout Indochina cease firing their weapons and remain in the positions they now hold. This would be a "cease-fire-in-place." It would not in itself be an end to the conflict, but it would accomplish one goal all of us have been working toward: an end to the killing.

I do not minimize the difficulty of maintaining a cease-fire in a guerrilla war where there are no front lines. But an unconventional war may require an unconventional truce; our side is ready to stand still and cease firing.

I ask that this proposal for a cease-fire-in-place be the subject for immediate negotiation. And my hope is that it will break the logjam in all the negotiations.

This cease-fire proposal is put forth without preconditions. The general principles that should apply are these:

A cease-fire must be effectively supervised by international observers, as well as by the parties themselves. Without effective supervision a cease-fire runs the constant risk of breaking down. All concerned must be confident that the cease-fire will be maintained and that any local breaches of it will be quickly and fairly repaired.

A cease-fire should not be the means by which either side builds up its strength by an increase in outside combat forces in any of the nations of Indochina.

And a cease-fire should cause all kinds of warfare to stop. This covers the full range of actions that have typified this war, including bombing and acts of terror.

A cease-fire should encompass not only the fighting in Viet-Nam but in all of Indochina. Conflicts in this region are closely related. The United States

*Department of State Bulletin, Oct. 26, 1970, pp. 465-67.

has never sought to widen the war. What we do seek is to widen the peace.

Finally, a cease-fire should be part of a general move to end the war in Indochina.

A cease-fire-in-place would undoubtedly create a host of problems in its maintenance. But it has always been easier to make war than to make a truce. To build an honorable peace, we must accept the challenge of long and difficult negotiations.

By agreeing to stop the shooting, we can set the stage for agreements on other matters.

A second point of the new initiative for peace is this:

I propose an Indochina peace conference. At the Paris talks today, we are talking about Viet-Nam. But North Vietnamese troops are not only infiltrating, crossing borders, and establishing bases in South Viet-Nam—they are carrying on their aggression in Laos and Cambodia as well.

An international conference is needed to deal with the conflict in all three states of Indochina. The war in Indochina has been proved to be of one piece; it cannot be cured by treating only one of its areas of outbreak.

The essential elements of the Geneva accords of 1954 and 1962 remain valid as a basis for settlement of problems between states in the Indochina area. We shall accept the results of agreements reached between these states.

While we pursue the convening of an Indochina peace conference, we will continue the negotiations in Paris. Our proposal for a larger conference can be discussed there as well as through other diplomatic channels.

The Paris talks will remain our primary forum for reaching a negotiated settlement, until such time as a broader international conference produces serious negotiations.

The third part of our peace initiative has to do with the United States forces in South Viet-Nam.

In the past 20 months, I have reduced our troop ceilings in South Viet-Nam by 165,000 men. During the spring of next year, these withdrawals will have totaled more than 260,000 men—about one-half the number that were in South Viet-Nam when I took office.

As the American combat role and presence have decreased, American casualties have also decreased. Our casualties since the completion of the Cambodian operation were the lowest for a comparable period in the last 4½ years.

We are ready now to negotiate an agreed timetable for complete withdrawals as part of an overall settlement.

We are prepared to withdraw all our forces as part of a settlement based on the principles I spelled out previously and the proposals I am making tonight.

Fourth, I ask the other side to join us in a search for a political settlement that truly meets the aspirations of all South Vietnamese.

Three principles govern our approach:

—We seek a political solution that reflects the will of the South Vietnamese people.

—A fair political solution should reflect the existing relationship of political forces in South Viet-Nam.

—And we will abide by the outcome of the political process agreed upon.

Let there be no mistake about one essential point: The other side is not merely objecting to a few personalities in the South Vietnamese Government. They want to dismantle the organized non-Communist parties and insure the takeover by their party. They demand the right to exclude whomever they wish from government.

This patently unreasonable demand is totally unacceptable.

As my proposals today indicate, we are prepared to be flexible on many matters. But we stand firm for the right of all the South Vietnamese people to determine for themselves the kind of government they want.

We have no intention of seeking any settlement at the conference table other than one which fairly meets the reasonable concerns of both sides. We know that when the conflict ends, the other side will still be there. And the only kind of settlement that will endure is one that both sides have an interest in preserving.

Finally, I propose the immediate and unconditional release of all prisoners of war held by both sides.

War and imprisonment should be over for all these prisoners. They and their families have already suffered too much.

I propose that all prisoners of war, without exception, without condition, be released now to return to the place of their choice.

And I propose that all journalists and other innocent civilian victims of the conflict be released immediately as well.

The immediate release of all prisoners of war would be a simple act of humanity.

But it could be even more. It could serve to establish good faith, the intent to make progress, and thus improve the prospects for negotiation.

We are prepared to discuss specific procedures to complete the speedy release of all prisoners.

The five proposals that I have made tonight can open the door to an enduring peace in Indochina.

Ambassador Bruce will present these proposals formally to the other side in Paris tomorrow. He will be joined in that presentation by Ambassador Lam representing South Viet-Nam.

Let us consider for a moment what the acceptance of these proposals would mean.

Since the end of World War II, there has always been a war going on somewhere in the world. The guns have never stopped firing. By achieving a cease-fire in Indochina, and by holding firmly to the cease-fire in the Middle East, we could hear the welcome sound of peace throughout the world for the first time in a generation.

We could have some reason to hope that we had reached the beginning of the end of war in this century. We might then be on the threshold of a generation of peace.

The proposals I have made tonight are designed to end the fighting throughout Indochina and to end the impasse in negotiations in Paris. Nobody has anything to gain by delay and only lives to lose.

There are many nations involved in the fighting in Indochina. Tonight, all those nations, except one, announce their readiness to agree to a cease-fire. The time has come for the Government of North Viet-Nam to join its neighbors in a proposal to quit making war and to start making peace.

As you know, I have just returned from a trip which took me to Italy, Spain, Yugoslavia, England, and Ireland.

Hundreds of thousands of people cheered me as I drove through the cities of those countries. They were not cheering for me as an individual. They were cheering for the country I was proud to represent—the United States of America. For millions of people in the free world, the nonaligned world, and the Communist world, America is the land of freedom, of opportunity, of progress.

I believe there is another reason they welcomed me so warmly in every country I visited, despite their wide differences in political systems and national backgrounds.

In my talks with leaders all over the world, I find that there are those who may not agree with all of our policies. But no world leader to whom I have talked fears that the United States will use its great power to dominate another country or to destroy its independence. We can be proud that this is the cornerstone of America's foreign policy.

There is no goal to which this nation is more dedicated, and to which I am more dedicated, than to build a new structure of peace in the world where every nation, including North Viet-Nam as well as South Viet-Nam, can be free and independent with no fear of foreign aggression or foreign domination.

I believe every American deeply believes in his heart that the proudest legacy the United States can leave during this period when we are the strongest nation of the world is that our power was used to defend freedom, not to destroy it; to preserve the peace, not to break the peace.

It is in that spirit that I make this proposal for a just peace in Viet-Nam and in Indochina.

I ask that the leaders in Hanoi respond to this proposal in the same spirit. Let us give our children what we have not had in this century: a chance to enjoy a generation of peace.

Remarks by Ambassador David K.E. Bruce, Head of U.S. Delegation at the 95th Plenary Session of the Meetings on Vietnam*

December 17, 1970

At last week's session, considerable time was devoted to the subjects of cease-fire and prisoners of war. That discussion demonstrated clearly the difference between the attitude of our two sides toward these negotiations. For even on such urgent subjects as these, you set up preconditions as an obstacle to genuine discussion by insisting that we must accept your one-sided demands before there can be any real negotiations between us.

Thus, you repeated as preconditions your longstanding demands that we agree to the withdrawal of all American and allied forces from South Viet-Nam by

*Ibid., Jan. 4, 1971, pp. 13-14.

June 30, 1971, and to the replacement of the present Government of the Republic of Viet-Nam. You asked us once again for a serious and direct reply. We have already given you such a reply many times. But let me state unequivocally again that we do not accept either of these preconditions. We will not accept any arbitrary deadline set by you for the withdrawal of our troops. However, we are quite prepared to negotiate an agreed timetable for complete troop withdrawals as part of an overall settlement. Such a settlement would have to include resolution of the question of North Vietnamese forces in Cambodia and Laos as well as South Viet-Nam. On a political settlement, we do not accept a solution predetermined in advance by you. This is a matter to be worked out by the South Vietnamese parties among themselves, not by outside parties.

In contrast to your position on cease-fire and prisoners of war, our proposals on these two issues are put forward for discussion without any preconditions whatsoever. We have called for immediate negotiations on an internationally supervised cease-fire-in-place throughout all of Indochina. In other words, we are ready to stop the fighting now and resolve the other issues in an atmosphere free from the use of force. We have not only proposed the immediate and unconditional release of all prisoners of war held by both sides, but at last week's session we suggested a specific way in which such a release could begin. We made another specific proposal at the 93d session that there be impartial inspection of prisoner camps in both North and South Viet-Nam in order to insure the proper treatment of prisoners while they are still held. These are specific, practical proposals which can be discussed and put into effect immediately. They deserve more serious consideration than you have apparently given them so far.

State Department Statement on United States Assistance for the South Vietnamese Operation in Laos*

February 8, 1971

Last evening the Government of the Republic of Viet-Nam announced in Saigon that elements of its armed forces have crossed into enemy-occupied territory of Laos to attack North Vietnamese forces and military supplies which have been assembled in sanctuaries close to the border of South Viet-Nam. These sanctuaries lie between the 15th and 17th parallels and comprise concentrations which are an important part of the Ho Chi Minh Trail system. Our Military Command in Viet-Nam has announced the limits of the U.S. military participation.

The decision of the United States to assist is based on the following policy considerations:

1. No American ground combat forces or advisers will cross into Laos.

2. The operation will be a limited one both as to time and area. The Vietnamese Government has made it clear that its objective will be to disrupt those

*Ibid., Mar. 1, 1971, pp. 256-57.

forces which have been concentrated in this region for use against South Vietnamese and U.S. forces located in the northern military regions of South Viet-Nam and to intercept or choke off the flow of supplies and men during the dry season which are designed for use further south on the Ho Chi Minh Trail in South Viet-Nam and Cambodia.

3. The operation will promote the security and safety of American and allied forces in South Viet-Nam and is consistent with statutory requirements. It will make the enemy less able to mount offensives and strengthen South Viet-Nam's ability to defend itself as U.S. forces are withdrawn from South Viet-Nam. It will protect American lives.

4. This ground operation by the South Vietnamese against the sanctuaries thus will aid in the Vietnamization program. The withdrawal of American forces from Viet-Nam will continue. During the month of April President Nixon will announce further withdrawals.

5. The measures of self-defense being taken by the Republic of Viet-Nam are fully consistent with international law. A report to this effect is being made by the Republic of Viet-Nam to the President of the Security Council of the United Nations, to the Geneva Cochairmen, and to the governments which comprise the International Control Commission.

6. This limited operation is not an enlargement of the war. The territory involved has been the scene of combat since 1965. The principal new factor is that South Viet-Nam forces will move against the enemy on the ground to deny him the sanctuaries and disrupt the main artery of supplies which he has been able to use so effectively against American and South Vietnamese forces in the past.

7. The United States has consistently sought to end the conflict in Indochina through negotiations. President Nixon specifically proposed last October that there be (a) a cease-fire throughout Indochina, (b) a negotiated timetable for the withdrawal of all forces, (c) immediate release of all prisoners of war, (d) an international peace conference for all of Indochina, and (e) a political settlement. This continues to be the policy of the United States.

8. The Royal Lao Government has issued a statement, which, while critical of the current military action, points out that the "primary responsibility for this development rests on the Democratic Republic of Viet-Nam which has violated international law and the 1962 Geneva Agreements. The Democratic Republic of Viet-Nam has violated and is continuing to violate the neutrality and territorial integrity of the Kingdom of Laos." The U.S. Government continues to favor the neutrality of Laos and the restoration of the situation contemplated by the 1962 Geneva accords in which all foreign forces would be withdrawn from Lao territory. A new Indochina conference as proposed by President Nixon could accomplish this objective.

KOREA

Joint Statement by the United States and Korea on U.S. Troop Reduction and Korean Modernization*

February 6, 1971

The Government of the Republic of Korea and the United States Government have completed satisfactory talks on the program for the modernization of the Korean armed forces and arrangements for the reduction of U.S. forces in Korea.

The United States has agreed to assist the Government of the Republic of Korea in its effort to modernize its defense forces, through a long range military assistance program on the basis of joint United States-Republic of Korea military recommendations. The Korean Government notes with satisfaction that the United States Congress has approved $150 million as supplemental funds for the first year portion of the said modernization program.

Consultations between the two governments on the reduction of U.S. troop strength in Korea by 20,000 and on the consequent repositioning of Korean and U.S. troops also have been concluded in a spirit of mutual understanding and close cooperation.

Reductions in the level of United States troops in Korea do not affect in any way the determination of the United States Government to meet armed attack against the Republic of Korea in accordance with the Mutual Defense Treaty of 1954 between the Republic of Korea and the United States.

Annual security consultative meetings to be attended by foreign and defense officials of both governments at a high level will be held to assess the nature of the military threat directed against the Republic of Korea. In such discussions, over-all capabilities to defend against the threat will be evaluated.

*Department of State Bulletin, Mar. 1, 1971, p. 263.

PAKISTAN AND INDIA

State Department Statement on the Situation in East Pakistan*

April 7, 1971

Since the beginning of the present crisis, we have on several occasions expressed concern over the loss of life and damage which have occurred in East Pakistan, and we have expressed the hope that peaceful conditions will be restored.

While we have pointed out the difficulty of obtaining reliable information on the situation, it is increasingly clear that there have been substantial casualties and damage, although we still have no way of estimating the extent of the casualties and damage with any precision.

Our sympathy goes out to the victims of recent events. Normal life in East Pakistan has been seriously disrupted. We continue to believe it is important that every feasible step be taken to end the conflict and achieve a peaceful accommodation.

We hope that it will be possible soon to alleviate the suffering caused by recent events. In this connection, we also hope the Government of Pakistan will avail itself of offers of assistance from the international community. The United States is prepared to assist in any international humanitarian effort of this kind.

We have discussed these matters with the Government of Pakistan, and we will continue to do so.

United States Position on the India-Pakistan War*

December 3,4,6, 1971

During last month's war between India and Pakistan, Henry Kissinger repeatedly convened WSAG—the Washington Special Action Group. At these secret sessions, officials of major government departments brought along assistants to take minutes of the give-and-take. It was minutes of this kind on three WSAG meetings that were released last week by Jack Anderson. Below, excerpts:

MEETING OF DEC. 3

Henry Kissinger: I am getting hell every half hour from the President that we are not being tough enough on India. He has just called me again. He does not believe we are carrying out his wishes. He wants to tilt in favor of Pakistan. He feels everything we do comes out otherwise.

Richard M. Helms [Director, Central Intelligence Agency]: . . . The Paks say the Indians are attacking all along the border; but the Indian officials say

* *Department of State Bulletin,* Apr. 26, 1971, p. 554.

**Newsweek,* Jan. 17, 1972, pp.14-15

this is a lie. In the east wing, the action is becoming larger and the Paks claim there are now seven separate fronts involved.

Kissinger: [Is India] seizing territory?

Helms: Yes, small bits of territory.

Joseph J. Sisco [Assistant Secretary of State]: It would help if you [Helms] could provide a map with a shading of the areas occupied by India. What is happening in the west—is a full-scale attack likely?

Adm. Thomas H. Moorer [chairman, Joint Chiefs of Staff]: . . . The Pak attack is not credible. It has been made during late afternoon, which doesn't make sense.

Kissinger: Is it possible that the Indians attacked first, and the Paks simply did what they could before dark in response?

Moorer: This is certainly possible.

Kissinger: . . . If the U.N. can't operate in this kind of situation effectively, its utility has come to an end and it is useless to think of U.N. guarantees in the Middle East . . . We have to take action. The President is blaming me, but you people are in the clear.

Sisco: That's ideal!

Kissinger: The earlier draft statement for [U.S. ambassador to the U.N. George] Bush is too evenhanded.

Sisco: . . . We will update the draft speech for Bush.

Maurice J. Williams [deputy administrator, Agency for International Development]: Are we to take economic steps with Pakistan also?

Kissinger: Wait until I talk with the President. He hasn't addressed the problem in connection with Pakistan yet.

Sisco: If we act on the Indian side, we can say we are keeping the Pakistan situation "under review."

Kissinger: It's hard to tilt toward Pakistan if we have to match every Indian step with a Pakistan step. If you wait until Monday, I can get a Presidential decision.

MEETING OF DEC. 4

Helms: The Indians have begun their 'no holds barred' offensive in East Pakistan. There is no evidence of ground action in the west. Yahya's speech today referred to the 'final' war with India and the need to drive back and destroy the enemy. Moscow is supporting Delhi throughout.

Kissinger: If the Indians announced full-scale invasion, this must be reflected in our U.N. statement this afternoon. By Monday morning, I [want] to get a full chronology of the sequence of events in both East and West Pakistan.

Samuel De Palma [Assistant Secretary of State]: Both Yahya and Mrs. Gandhi are making bellicose statements. If we refer to Mrs. Gandhi's in our statement, do we not also have to refer to Yahya's?

Kissinger: The President says either the bureaucracy should put out the right statements on this, or the White House will do it. Can the U.N. object to Yahya's statements about defending his country?

De Palma: We will have difficulty in the U.N. because most of the countries who might go with us do not want to tilt toward Pakistan to the extent we do.

Kissinger: Whoever is doing the backgrounding at State is invoking the President's wrath. Please try to follow the President's wishes.

De Palma: . . . As other countries will quibble with our statement, we need to decide how far we can bend.

Kissinger: We have told the Paks we would make our statement. Let's go ahead . . . regardless of what other countries want to do. We need now to make our stand clear even though it has taken us two weeks of fiddling . . . Nothing will happen at the Security Council because of Soviet vetoes. The whole thing is a farce.

Christopher Van Hollen [Deputy Assistant Secretary of State]: The Soviet tactic will be to stall, as they do not want a cease-fire yet.

De Palma: The Indians can delay by long speeches, and then the Soviets will use the same approach.

Kissinger: On AID [Agency for International Development] matters, the President wants to proceed against India only. We need to develop a public statement to explain our action.

Williams: The Department of Agriculture says the price of vegetable oil is weakening and it would help us domestically . . . to ship oil to India.

Kissinger: I will have an answer for you by the opening of business Monday. What is the military situation?

Adm. Elmo R. Zumwalt Jr. [Chief of Naval Operations]: The Pak logistics system can last one to two weeks only, if they are not overrun sooner. East Pakistan will soon be occupied except for the areas they leave to the Mukti Bahini. The Soviet military ambition in this exercise is to obtain permanent usage of the port at Visakhapatnam.

G. Warren Nutter [Assistant Secretary of Defense]: It goes without saying that the entire press is slanting this war to place the entire blame on the Pakistanis and to show that they attacked India.

Kissinger: This has been a well-done political campaign for which we will pay.

MEETING OF DEC. 6

Unlike the minutes of the two previous meetings, this memorandum contained only paraphrases of the Washington Special Action Group meeting.

Dr. Kissinger . . . directed that henceforth we show a certain coolness to the Indians; the Indian ambassador [to the United States] is not to be treated at too high a level.

Dr. Kissinger then asked whether we have the right to authorize Jordan or Saudi Arabia to transfer military equipment to Pakistan. Mr. Van Hollen stated the United States cannot permit a third country to transfer arms which we have provided them when we, ourselves, do not authorize sale direct to the ultimate recipient, such as Pakistan. As of last January we made a legislative decision not to sell to Pakistan.

Mr. Sisco said that the Jordanians would be weakening their own position by such a transfer and would probably be grateful if we could get them off the hook. [He said] that, as the Paks increasingly feel the heat, we will be getting emergency requests from them.

Dr. Kissinger said that the President may want to honor those requests. The matter has not been brought to Presidential attention but it is quite obvious that the President is not inclined to let the Paks be defeated. [Deputy Secretary of Defense David] Packard then said that we should look at what could be done. Mr. Sisco agreed but said it should be done very quietly.

GENERAL

Address by Marshall Green, Assistant Secretary for East Asian and Pacific Affairs on the Nixon Doctrine*

January 19, 1971

After being many times your guest at the Far East-America Council, it is now my pleasure and honor to be your speaker. In casting about for what might be the most appropriate subject to speak on today, I concluded that it might be well to give a progress report on the Nixon doctrine, which the President enunciated at Guam in the summer of 1969. This doctrine is, after all, the key aspect of United States foreign policy today, especially toward East Asia; and it would seem appropriate now, at the start of the new year, to review where we stand in putting this doctrine into effect. The record, I believe, is impressive—far more so than most observers realize. Many of the achievements have been quiet gains attracting little public attention, but these changes have nonetheless had profound importance for East Asia and for our relations with this important region.

The scope of the Nixon doctrine is widely known. Basically this doctrine as applied to East Asia sets a state of mind, a style of diplomacy, a way of conducting our programs abroad, which reduces our direct responsibility and calls upon the nations of the area, individually and collectively, to assume an increasing role in providing for their own internal defense.

Simply stated, the Nixon doctrine contains three basic propositions:

1. The United States will keep its treaty commitments;

2. We will provide a shield if a nuclear power threatens the freedom of a nation allied to us or of a nation whose survival we consider vital to our security or to the security of the region as a whole; and

3. In cases involving other types of aggression, the United States will furnish aid and economic assistance when requested and appropriate. But we shall look to the nation directly threatened to assume the primary responsibility of providing the manpower for its defense.

This new approach does not mean in any sense that the United States will cease to be a Pacific power or that we will not continue to play a significant role in East Asia. We can do so and we must. What it seeks is to establish a sound basis upon which we can continue to carry out this role in a manner compatible with Asia's own aspirations and which can command the essential support of the American people.

Having been present at the creation—as Dean Acheson would say—I can vividly recall the immediate circumstances in which the President gave his now-famous backgrounder at the Top of the Mar Hotel in Guam on July 25, 1969. It was an informal affair, called at the last moment by the President, attended by the hundred or more newsmen who accompanied him on his around-the-world

*Department of State Bulletin, Feb. 8, 1971, pp. 161-65.

789

trip. The President's backgrounder emphasized the great progress that had taken place in East Asia this past decade or so and stressed that the East Asian countries could now take on a large share of their own defense.

Indeed, the countries of East Asia, though they continued to seek our assistance and to need it, were by 1969 far better able to fend for themselves. Equally important, they were becoming more and more anxious to take their own initiatives and to find "Asian solutions for Asian problems." Likewise, the American people were coming to feel that we had taken on far more than our due share of the burdens of military security and economic assistance abroad. Our people were asking what other developed countries were doing to help East Asia, since those countries also had a stake in the security, stability, and progress of that area.

Meanwhile, of primary importance is the fact that throughout the region there has been steady and, in some cases, spectacular economic growth. The remarkable performance of Japan, Korea, and others is well known. Indonesia, only a few short years ago teetering on the brink of bankruptcy, has now stabilized its currency and is embarked at long last on the road toward economic development. In 1960 the gross national product of free East Asia, excluding Australia and New Zealand, stood at $82 billion. At the end of 1969 it was estimated in constant 1967 dollars at $220 billion. Assuming present growth rates continue, this figure should approach $300 billion by the end of this year.

Coupled with this remarkable economic growth has been a corresponding increase among Asians of a pool of technical skills, managerial competence, and entrepreneurial energy ready to tackle Asia's problems. But in many cases they lack the tools.

With this growth has also come a new sense of confidence and an improved ability to assume a larger share of the burden of their own defense. The sum total of the armed forces of our various East Asian allies has risen from about a million men a decade ago to 2 million today. These forces are better trained and better organized, although much still needs to be done in modernizing their equipment. Growth in effective reserve forces has been equally striking.

Our objective under the Nixon doctrine is to insure U.S. national security and that of our allies while at the same time permitting the reduction of U.S. forces abroad and reducing the likelihood of having to commit combat ground forces in the future.

In January 1969 we had 740,000 U.S. military personnel in East Asia. This figure now stands at 500,000, and it will be reduced on the basis of withdrawals already announced to 420,000 by the end of the current fiscal year. In short, our troop strength in East Asia will have been cut almost in half during the past 2 years, with the nations of Asia themselves assuming the additional responsibilities. 264,000 of these troops are coming out of Viet-Nam—a dramatic example of the success of the Vietnamization program—but significant cuts are also taking place in Korea, Thailand, Japan, and elsewhere. Meanwhile, South Viet-Nam has increased its own military forces from 800,000 2 years ago to more than 1 million today.

The greatest benefit from our troop withdrawals from South Viet-Nam has been the sharp reduction in U.S. casualties. In 1969 more than 14,000 Americans lost their lives in Viet-Nam; in 1970 the figure was 4,000. In the several months before our actions against the North Vietnamese sanctuaries in Cambodia the monthly rate was 347; now it stands at 149. These figures speak for themselves.

Our troop reductions and our changing role in South Viet-Nam have also produced financial savings for the U.S. taxpayer. The costs of the war have been reduced from $29 billion in fiscal year 1969 to $14.5 billion this fiscal year at current rates of expenditure. I should point out, however, that not all of this represents net savings (though the great bulk of it does). As we reduce our own presence it is essential that we actually step up aid to our friends and allies to enable them to take over missions we have been performing. Thus our withdrawal of a U.S. division from Korea will save us some $500 million per year, but we will have to help modernize the Korean armed forces if there is to be no gap in allied defenses in Korea.

                        *   *   *

My emphasis has been on the need for the countries of East Asia to maximize their contributions to their own security and development as well as to support the security and development of their neighbors. I have also stressed the need for other developed countries, notably Japan, to carry more of the burden of economic assistance to the developing countries of East Asia.

But there are at least three areas in which continuing U.S. support is essential:

First, if the reduction of our own military and other presence in East Asia is not to create unacceptable risks, then we must assist those nations in their efforts to strengthen their own defenses. Our economic and military aid may actually have to increase for a few years to achieve this objective. But we will be saving billions of dollars through our troop reductions, while our requirements for new aid will be counted in the millions.

I am convinced that Congress appreciates this point, as demonstrated by the prompt action it took in passing our supplemental aid appropriation last month. Nearly $500 million in that appropriation was earmarked to further these objectives in East Asia. This included funds to begin the modernization of Korea's armed forces, a move which must go hand in hand with our own troop withdrawals; funds to help equip Cambodia's troops, which have increased fourfold within the past 6 months and which, I might add, show a dedication and a fighting spirit far deeper than many observers originally expected; and funds to further the Vietnamization program, which also is basic to success of the Nixon doctrine.

Secondly, we will need to insure that our policies, particularly in the economic field, do not undercut the ability of these nations to stand on their own feet. In this connection, we have asked the Congress for legislation to make it possible for developing countries to export more to the United States, and we have encouraged other developed countries to provide preferential tariff arrangements for the exports of the developing nations. Care must also be taken in disposing of products from our surplus stockpiles in order that we not adversely affect the foreign exchange earnings of those very countries which we are asking to undertake an increasing share of the burden of their own defense. This is particularly true in the case of nations which rely heavily on earnings from the export of single basic commodities.

Finally, and of particular importance, I wish to emphasize that a reduced official American presence and involvement in East Asia should not, and I hope will not, mean a reduction in the overseas activities of our private sector or the presence of our commercial and investment interests, or indeed of American travelers. On the contrary, the new approach to our assistance and other programs looks toward greater flexibility in the programs that support and stimulate the flow of American investment into developing areas. These investments will play a key role in helping achieve the objectives envisaged under the Nixon doctrine.

To summarize, without reducing the credibility of our East Asian commitment, we are undertaking to assist our friends and allies in this area to develop a better capability to defend themselves individually and collectively. They welcome and accept this challenge, for they, too, want Asian solutions for Asian problems. The basic decisions to improve their lot can only be made by these nations themselves, but the policies we are following under the Nixon doctrine have, I believe, contributed significantly to achieving the objectives which both we and they seek. Much remains to be done, but we have made an encouraging beginning.

APPENDIX B

Commentary

Whether the settlement of the Vietnam War becomes a dramatic watershed in American foreign policy, only the perspective of history can determine. Nevertheless, a documentary record of United States relations with Asia, no matter how incomplete in other respects, would seem terribly inconclusive without reference to statements, accords, and protocols attending the termination of American involvement in a conflict that has touched the nation so deeply.

In this respect, 1972 was a critical year. On January 25, President Richard Nixon made public the essence of an American peace plan calling for the withdrawal of all U.S. forces from South Vietnam, the exchange of prisoners of war, a ceasefire in all of Indochina, and an internationally supervised presidential election in South Vietnam. The proposal also included an offer by President Thieu to resign one month prior to the holding of the election. These terms were not accepted and for reasons of their own—at least in part because the withdrawal of American troops made victory now seem conceivable—North Vietnam, on March 30, launched a full-scale invasion of the South. President Nixon responded to this attack with a resumption of the bombing of North Vietnam and on May 8 by mining North Vietnamese ports. At the same time, he reiterated American terms for ending the war and, significantly, did not demand the withdrawal of North Vietnamese troops from South Vietnam. On October 8, North Vietnam indicated that it would not insist on the installation of a coalition government in the South as a condition for negotiation of other points; the discussions then accelerated so rapidly that on October 26 National Security Adviser Henry Kissinger announced that "peace was at hand" with only a few details remaining to be settled.

After this announcement, however, South Vietnam raised objections to the presence of North Vietnamese troops in the South while both linguistic and substantive differences developed in the negotiations with North Vietnam. Subsequently, in mid-December the United States claimed the North Vietnamese were acting in bad faith and resumed the bombing of Hanoi and Haiphong with greater intensity than ever before. Finally, in January 1973, serious discussions resumed; on January 23 the parties concluded an agreement to end the War. The documents that follow include the basic substance of the American position during 1972 and early 1973 as revealed in press conferences by Henry Kissinger and a statement by President Nixon, as well as the terms of the formal agreement signed on January 27, 1973.

The accord, reflecting what remained the unresolved military conflict between North and South Vietnam, contained several ambiguities—in such areas as recognition of South Vietnam's sovereignty, the functioning of a National Council in the South, and future unification of the two Vietnams. American policymakers apparently believed, however, that new international realities, including the Soviet Union's desire for trade with the United States, the Sino-Soviet schism, the improving ability of South Vietnamese forces, and destruction in North Vietnam would give the agreement durability. Administration officials also defended the accord as far more favorable than any previously possible of negotiation. The terms appeared to confirm this assessment, but the question remained whether they justified the cost in lives, money, and the compromising of American ideals—in view of the national interests involved.

VIETNAM

News Conference Statement by Henry A. Kissinger, U.S. Representative at the Paris Peace Talks, on the Status of the Vietnam Ceasefire*

October 26, 1972

We have now heard from both Vietnams and it is obvious that the war that has been raging for 10 years is drawing to a conclusion, that this is a traumatic experience for all of the participants.

The President thought that it might be helpful if I came out here and spoke to you about what we have been doing, where we stand, and to put the various allegations and charges into perspective.

First, let me talk about the situation in three parts: where do we stand procedurally; what is the substance of the negotiations and where do we go from here?

We believe peace is at hand. We believe that an agreement is within sight on the May 8 proposals of the President and some adaptations of our Jan. 25 proposals, which is just to all parties.

It is inevitable that in a war of such complexity that there should be occasional difficulties in reaching a final solution. But we believe that by far the longest part of the road has been traversed and what stands in the way of an agreement now are issues that are relatively less important than those that have already been settled.

Let me first go through the procedural points.

The argument with respect to particular dates for signing the agreement.

As you know, we have been negotiating in these priviate sessions with the North Vietnamese for nearly four years. We resumed the discussions on July 19 of this year. Up to now the negotiations had always foundered on the North Vietnamese insistence that a political settlement be arrived at before a military solution be discussed, and on the companion demand of the North Vietnamese that the political settlement make arrangements which, in our view, would have predetermined the political outcome.

We had taken the view, from the earliest private meetings on, that rapid progress could be made only if the political and military issues were separated. That is to say, if the North Vietnamese and we would negotiate about methods to end the war and if the political solution of the war were left to the Vietnamese parties to discuss among themselves.

During the summer, through many long private meetings, these positions remained essentially unchanged.

As Radio Hanoi correctly stated today, on Oct. 8 the North Vietnamese for the first time made a proposal which enabled us to accelerate the negotiations. Indeed, for the first time they made a proposal which made it possible to negotiate concretely at all.

This proposal has been correctly summarized in the statements from Hanoi. That is to say, it proposed that the United States and Hanoi, in the first instance, concentrate on bringing an end to the military aspects of the war—that they agree on some very general principles within which the South Vietnamese parties could then determine the

The New York Times, Oct. 27, 1972.

political evolution of South Vietnam—which was exactly the position which we had always taken.

They dropped their demand for a coalition government which would absorb all existing authorities. They dropped their demand for a veto over the personalities and the structure of the existing government.

They agreed for the first time to a formula which permitted simultaneous discussion of Laos and Cambodia.

In short, we had for the first time a framework where, rather than exchange general propositions, and measuring our progress by whether dependent clauses of particular sentences had been minutely altered, we could examine concretely and precisely where we stood and what each side was prepared to give.

I want to take this opportunity to point out that from that time on the North Vietnamese negotiators behaved with goodwill and with great seriousness—and so did we.

And we have no complaint with the general description of events as it was given by Radio Hanoi.

However, there existed—there grew up—the seeds of one particular misunderstanding. The North Vietnamese negotiators made their proposal conditional on the solution of the problem by Oct. 31. And they constantly insisted that we give some commitment that we would settle the war and complete the negotiations by Oct. 31.

I want to stress that these dates were not dates that we invented or proposed. I would like to stress that my instructions from the President were exactly those that were stated by him at a press conference—that is to say, that we should make a settlement that was right, independent of any arbitrary deadlines that were established by our domestic processes.

In order to avoid an abstract debate on deadlines which at that time still seemed highly theoretical, we did agree that we would make a major effort to conclude the negotiations by Oct. 31. And it is true that we did from time to time give schedules by which this might be accomplished.

It was, however, always clear, at least to us, and we thought we made it clear in the records of the meetings, that obviously we could not sign an agreement in which details remain to be worked out simply because in good faith we had said we would make an effort to conclude it by a certain date.

It was always clear that we would have to discuss anything that was negotiated first in Washington and then in Saigon.

There has been a great deal of discussion whether Saigon has a veto over our negotiations, and I would like to explain our position with respect to that clearly.

The people of South Vietnam who have suffered so much and the Government of South Vietnam with which we have been allied and who will be remaining in that country after we have departed have every right to participate in the making of their own peace. They have every right to have their views heard and taken extremely seriously.

We, of course, preserve our own freedom of judgment and we will make our own decisions as to how long we believe a war should be continued.

But one source of misunderstanding has been that Hanoi seemed to be of the view that we could simply impose any solution on Saigon and that their participation was not required.

But I also want to make clear that the issues that remain to be settled have a number of sources and I will get into them in some detail.

Saigon, as is obvious from the public record, has expressed its views with its customary forcefulness, both publicly and privately. We agreed with some of their views; we didn't agree with all of them and we made clear which we accepted and which we could not join.

In addition, while my colleagues and I were in Saigon we visited other countries of Southeast Asia and we had extensive conversations with American officials, and it appeared there that there were certain concerns and certain ambiguities in the draft agreement that we believed required modification and improvement.

But I want to stress that what remains to be done is the smallest part of what has already been accomplished, and as charges and countercharges fill the air we must remember that having come this far we cannot fail, and we will not fail over what still remains to be accomplished.

Now let me first go briefly over the main provisions of the agreement as we understand them and then let me say what in our view still remains to be done.

We believe incidentally what remains to be done can be settled in one more negotiating session with the North Vietnamese negotiators, lasting, I would think, no more than three or four days, so we are not talking of a delay of a very long period of time.

Let me, however, before I go into the issues that still remain, cover those that we have—that are contained in the draft agreement, of which on the whole a very fair account has been given in the radio broadcast from Hanoi. I don't refer to the last two pages of rhetoric. I'm referring to the description of the agreement.

The principal provisions were and are that a cease-fire would be observed in South Vietnam at a time to be mutually agreed upon.

It would be a cease-fire in place.

But U.S. forces would be withdrawn within 60 days of the signing of the agreement.

There would be a total prohibition on the reinforcement of troops—that is to say that infiltration into South Vietnam from whatever area and from whatever country would be prohibited.

Existing military equipment within South Vietnam could be replaced on a one-to-one basis by weapons of the same characteristic and of similar characteristics and properties under international supervision.

The agreement provides that all captured military personnel and foreign civilians be repatriated within the same time period as the withdrawal—that is to say, there will be a return of all American prisoners—military or civilian—within 60 days after the agreement comes into force.

North Vietnam has made itself responsible for accounting of our prisoners and missing-in-actions throughout Indochina and for the repatriation of American prisoners throughout Indochina.

There is a separate provision that South Vietnamese civilians detained in South Vietnam—their future should be determined through negotiations among the South Vietnamese parties.

So the return of our prisoners is not conditional on the disposition of Vietnamese prisoners in Vietnamese jails on both sides of the conflict.

With respect to the political provisions, there is an affirmation of general principles guaranteeing the right of self-determination of the South Vietnamese people and that the South Vietnamese people should decide their political future through free and democratic elections under international supervision.

As was pointed out by Radio Hanoi, the existing authorities with respect to both internal and external politics would remain in office. The two parties in Vietnam would negotiate about the timing of elections, the nature of the elections and the offices for which these elections were to be held.

There would be created an institution called the National Council of National Reconciliation and Concord whose general task would be to help promote the maintenance of the cease-fire and to supervise the elections on which the parties might agree.

That council would be formed by appointment and it would operate on the basis of unanimity. We view it as an institutionalization of the election commission that we proposed on Jan. 25 in our plan.

There are provisions that the disposition of Vietnamese armed forces in the South should also be settled through negotiations among the South Vietnamese parties.

There are provisions that the unification of Vietnam also be achieved by negotiation among the parties without military pressure and without foreign interference, without coercion and without annexation. There is a very long and complex section on international supervision which will no doubt occupy graduate students for many years to come and which as far as I can tell only my colleague, Ambassador Sullivan, understands completely.

But, briefly, it provides for joint commission of the participants—either two-party or four-party—for those parts of the agreement that are applicable either to two parties or to four parties. It provides for an international supervisory commission to which disagreements of the commission composed of the parties would be referred, but which also had a right to make independent investigations.

And an international conference to meet within 30 days of the signing of the agreement to develop the guarantees and to establish the relationship of the various parties to each other in greater detail.

And, finally, a section on Cambodia and Laos in which the parties to the agreement agree to respect and recognize the independence and sovereignty of Cambodia and Laos; in which they agree to refrain from using the territory of Cambodia and the territory of Laos to encroach on the sovereignty and security of other countries.

There is an agreement that foreign countries shall withdraw their forces from Laos and Cambodia.

And there is a general section about a future relationship between the United States and the Democratic Republic of Vietnam in which both sides express their conviction that this agreement will usher in a new period of reconciliation between the two countries and in which the United States expresses its view that it will in the postwar period contribute to the reconstruction of Indochina and that both countries will develop their relationship on a basis of mutual respect and noninterference in each other's affairs, and that they move from hostility to normalcy.

Now, ladies and gentlemen, in the light of where we are, it is obvious that most of the most difficult problems have been dealt with. And if you'll consider what many of us—or what many of you might have thought possible some months ago compared to where we are, we have to say that both sides have approached this problem with a long-term point of view, with the attitude that we want to have not an armistice but peace.

And it is this attitude which will govern our actions despite occasional ups and downs which are inevitable in a problem of this complexity.

Now what is it then that prevents the completion of the agreement? Why is it that we have asked for one more meeting with the North Vietnamese to work out a final text? The principal reason is that in a negotiation that was stalemated for five years and which did not really make a breakthrough until Oct. 8, many of the general principles were clearly understood before the breakthrough.

But as one elaborated the text, many of the nuances on which the implementation will ultimately depend become more and more important.

It was obvious, it was natural, that when we were talking about the abstract desirability of a cease-fire that neither side was perhaps as precise as it had to become later about the timing and spacing of the cease-fire in a country in which there are no clear front lines. And also the acceptance on our part of the North Vietnamese insistence on an accelerated schedule meant that texts could never be conformed; that English and Vietnamese texts tended to lag behind each other and let ambiguities and formulations arise that require one more meeting to straighten out.

Let me give you a few examples and I think you will understand that we are talking here of a different problem than what occupied us in the many sessions I have had with you ladies and gentlemen about the problem of peace in Vietnam—sessions which concerned abstract theories of what approach might succeed. We are talking here about six or seven very concrete issues that with anything like the goodwill that has already been shown can easily be settled.

For example, it has become apparent to us that there will be a great temptation for the cease-fire to be paralleled by a last effort to seize as much territory as possible and perhaps to extend operations for long enough to establish political control over a given area.

We would like to avoid the dangers of the loss of life and perhaps in some areas even of the massacre that may be inherent in this, and we therefore want to discuss methods by which the international supervisory body can be put in place at the same time that the cease-fire is promulgated. And the Secretary of State has already had preliminary conversations with some of the countries that are to join this body in order to speed up this process.

Secondly, because of the different political circumstances in each of the Indo-chinese countries the relationship of military operations there to the end of the war in Vietnam, or cease-fire there in relation to the end of the war in Vietnam, is somewhat complex, and we would like to discuss more concretely how to compress the time as much as possible.

There were certain ambiguities that were raised by the interview that the North Vietnamese Prime Minister, Pham Van Dong, gave to one of the weekly journals in which he seemed to be, with respect to one or two points, under a missapprehension as to what the agreement contained, and at any rate we would like to have that clarified.

There are linguistic problems in which for example, we call the National Council of Reconciliation an administrative structure in order to make clear that we do not see it as anything comparable to a coalition government. We want to make sure that the

Vietnamese text conveys the same meaning. I must add that the word "administrative structure" was given to us in English by the Vietnamese, so this is not a maneuver on our part.

There are some technical problems as to what clauses of the Geneva accord to refer to in certain sections of the document and there is a problem which was never settled in which the North Vietnamese, as they have pointed out in their broadcast, have proposed that the agreement be signed by the United States and North Vietnam—we on behalf of Saigon; they on behalf of their allies in South Vietnam.

We have always held the view that we would leave it up to our allies whether they wanted a two-power document or whether they wanted to sign themselves a document that establishes peace in their country. Now they prefer to participate in the signing of the peace.

And it seems to us not an unreasonable proposal that a country on whose territory a war has been fought and whose population has been uprooted and has suffered so greatly that it should have the right to sign its own peace treaty.

This again strikes us as a not-insuperable difficulty, but its acceptance will require the redrafting of certain sections of the document, and that again is a job that will require several hours of work.

We have asked the North Vietnamese to meet with us on any date of their choice. We have, as has been reported, restricted our bombing in effect to the battle area in order to show our goodwill and to indicate that we are working within the framework of existing agreements.

We remain convinced that the issues that I have mentioned are soluble in a very brief period of time. We have undertaken, and I repeat it here publicly, to settle them at one more meeting and to remain at that meeting for as long as is necessary to complete the agreement.

*   *   *

News Conference Statement by Henry Kissinger on the Status of the Vietnam Ceasefire*

December 16, 1972

As you know, I have been reporting to the President and meeting with the Secretary of State, the Vice President, Secretary of Defense, Chairman of the Joint Chiefs and other senior officials and I'm meeting with you today because we wanted to give you an account of the negotiations as they stand today.

I'm sure you will appreciate that I cannot go into details of particular issues but I will give you as fair and honest a description of the general trend of the negotiations as I can.

First let me do this in three parts:

What led us to believe at the end of October that peace was imminent;

Second, what has happened since;

Third, where do we go from here?

*The New York Times, Dec. 17, 1972.

At the end of October we had just concluded three weeks of negotiations with the North Vietnamese. As you all know, on Oct. 8 the North Vietnamese presented to us a proposal which as it later became elaborated appeared to us to reflect the main principles that the President has always enunciated as being part of the American position.

These principles were that there had to be an unconditional release of American prisoners throughout Indochina.

Secondly, that there should be a cease-fire in Indochina brought into being by various means suitable to the conditions of the countries concerned.

Third, that we were prepared to withdraw our forces under these conditions in a time period to be mutually agreed upon.

Fourth, that we would not prejudge the political outcome of the future of South Vietnam. We would not impose a particular solution. We would not insist on our particular solution.

The agreement as it was developed during October seemed to us to reflect these principles precisely.

Then towards the end of October we encountered a number of difficulties. Now at the time, because we wanted to maintain the atmosphere leading to a rapid settlement we mentioned them at our briefings but we did not elaborate on them.

But let me sum up what the problems were at the end of October.

It became apparent that there was in preparation a massive Communist effort to launch an attack throughout South Vietnam to begin several days before the cease-fire would have been declared and to continue for some weeks after the cease-fire came into being.

Second, there was an interview by the North Vietnamese Prime Minister which implied that the political solution that we always insisted was part of our principles, namely that we would not impose a coalition government, was not as clearcut as our record of the negotiations indicated.

And thirdly, as no one could miss, we encountered some specific objections from Saigon.

In these conditions we proposed to Hanoi that there should be one other round of negotiations to clear up these difficulties.

We were convinced that with goodwill on both sides these difficulties could be relatively easily surmounted.

And that if we conducted ourselves, on both sides, in the spirit of the October negotiations, a settlement would be very rapid. It was our conviction that if we were going to bring to an end 10 years of warfare, we should not do so with an armistice, but with a peace that had a chance of lasting.

And therefore we proposed three categories of clarification in the agreement:

First, we wanted the so-called linguistic difficulties cleared up so that they would not provide the seed for unending disputes and another eruption of the war. I will speak about those in a minute.

Secondly, the agreement always had provided that international machinery be put in place immediately after the cease-fire was declared. We wanted to spell out the operational meaning of the word "immediately" by developing the protocols that were required to bring the international machinery into being simultaneously with the cease-fire agreement. This, to us, seemed a largely technical matter.

And, thirdly, we wanted some reference in the agreement—however vague, however elusive, however indirect—which did not, which would make clear that the two parts of Vietnam would live in peace with each other and that neither side would impose its solution on the other by force.

These seemed to us modest requirements, relatively easily achievable.

Let me now tell you the sequence of events since that time.

We all know of the disagreements that have existed between Saigon and Washington. These disagreements are to some extent understandable. It is inevitable that a people on whose territory the war has been fought and that for 25 years has been exposed to devastation and suffering and assassination would look at the prospects of a settlement in a more, in a more detailed way and in a more anguished way than we who are 10,000 miles away.

Many of the provisions of the agreement, inevitably, were seen in a different context in Vietnam than in Washington. And I think it is safe to say that we faced, with respect to both Vietnamese parties, this problem. The people of Vietnam, North and South, have fought for so long that the risks and perils of war, however difficult, seem sometimes more bearable to them than the uncertainties and the risks and perils of peace.

Now it is no secret either that the United States has not agreed with all the objections that were raised by Saigon. In particular, the United States position with respect to the cease-fire had been made clear in October, 1970. It has been reiterated in the President's proposals of Jan. 25, 1972.

It was repeated again in the President's proposal of May 8, 1972. None of these proposals had asked for a withdrawal of North Vietnamese forces.

And therefore we could not agree with our allies in South Vietnam when they added conditions to the established position after an agreement had been reached that reflected these established positions.

And as was made clear in the press conference here on Oct. 26, as the President has reiterated in his speeches, the United States will not continue the war one day longer than it believes is necessary to reach an agreement we consider just and fair.

So we want to leave no doubt about the fact that if an agreement is reached that meets the stated conditions of the President—if an agreement is reached that we consider just—that no other party will have a veto over our action.

But I am also—today this question is moot because we have not yet reached an agreement that the President considers just and fair.

And therefore I want to explain to you the process of the negotiations since they resumed on Nov. 20 and where we are.

The three objectives that we were seeking in these negotiations were stated in the press conference of Oct. 26, in many speeches by the President afterwards and in every communication to Hanoi since.

They could not have been a surprise.

Now let me say a word first about what were called linguistic difficulties, which were called these in order not to inflame the situation. How did they arise?

They arose because the North Vietnamese presented us a document in English which we then discussed with them, and in many places throughout this document the original wording was changed as the negotiations proceeded and the phrases were frequently weakened compared to the original formulation.

It was not until we received the Vietnamese text after those negotiations were concluded that we found that while the English terms had been changed the Vietnamese terms had been left unchanged and so we suddenly found ourselves engaged in two negotiations, one about the English text, the other about the Vietnamese text.

Having conducted many negotiations, I must say this was a novel procedure and it led to the view that perhaps these were not simply linguistic difficulties but substantive difficulties.

Now I must say that all of these except one have now been eliminated.

The second category of problems concerned bringing into being the international machinery so that it could operate simultaneously with the cease-fire and so as to avoid a situation where the cease-fire rather than bring peace would unleash another frenzy of warfare.

To that end we submitted on Nov. 20, the first day that the negotiations resumed, a list of what are called protocols—technical instruments to bring this machinery into being.

These protocols—I will not go into the details of these protocols and they're normally technical documents—and ours were certainly intended to conform to normal practice despite the fact that this occurred four weeks after we had made clear that this was our intention and three weeks after Hanoi had pressed us to sign a cease-fire agreement. The North Vietnamese refused to discuss our protocols and refused to give us their protocols, so that the question of bringing the international machinery into being could not be addressed.

The first time we saw the North Vietnamese protocols was on the evening of Dec. 12, the night before I was supposed to leave Paris, six weeks after we had stated what our end was, five weeks after the cease-fire was supposed to be signed—a cease-fire which called for this machinery to be set up immediately.

These protocols reopened—they're not technical instruments—but reopened a whole list of issues that had been settled—or we thought had been settled—in the agreement. They contained provisions that were not in the original agreement and they excluded provisions that were in the original agreement.

They are now in the process of being discussed by the technical experts in Paris, but some effort will be needed to remove the political provisions from them, and to return them to a technical status.

Secondly, I think it is safe to say that the North Vietnamese perception of international machinery and our perception of international machinery is at drastic variance. And that, ladies and gentlemen, is an understatement.

We had thought that an effective machinery required, in effect, some freedom of movement. And our estimate was that several thousand people were needed to monitor the many provisions of the agreement.

The North Vietnamese perception is that the total force should be no more than 250, of which nearly half should be located at headquarters; that it would be dependent for its communication, logistics and even physical necessities, entirely on the party in whose area it was located. So it would have no jeeps, no telephones, no radios of its own; that it could not move without being accompanied by liaison officers of the party that was to be investigated—if that party decided to give it the jeeps to get to where the violation was taking place, and if that party would then let it communicate what it found.

It is our impression that the members of this commission will not exert themselves in frenzies of activity if this procedure were adopted.

Now, thirdly, the substance of the agreement. The negotiations since Nov. 20 really have taken place in two phases: the first phase, which lasted for three days, continued the spirit and the attitude of the meetings in October. We presented our proposals— some were accepted, others were rejected. But by the end of the third day we had made very substantial progress.

And we thought—all of us thought—that we were within a day or two of completing the arrangements.

We do not know what decisions were made in Hanoi at that point, but from that point on the negotiations have had the character where a settlement was always just within our reach, and was always pulled just beyond our reach when we attempted to grasp it.

I do not think it is proper for me to go into the details of the specific issues, but I think I should give you a general atmosphere and a general sense of the procedures that were followed.

When we returned on Dec. 4, we were—we of the American team—thought that the meetings could not last more than two or three days because there were only two or three issues left to be resolved.

You all know that the meetings lasted nine days. They began with Hanoi withdrawing every change that had been agreed to two weeks previously. We then spent the rest of the week getting back to where we had already been two weeks before, and by Saturday we thought we had narrowed the issues sufficiently. Where, if the other side had accepted again one section that they had already agreed to two weeks previously, the agreement could have been completed.

At that point the President ordered General Haig to return to Washington so that he would be available for the mission that would then follow of presenting the agreement to our ally.

At that point we thought we were sufficiently close so that experts could meet to conform the texts so that we would not again encounter the linguistic difficulties which we had experienced previously and so that we could make sure that the changes that had been negotiated in English would also be reflected in Vietnamese.

When the experts met they were presented with 17 new changes in the guise of linguistic changes. When I met again with the special adviser the one problem which we thought remained on Saturday had grown to two and a new demand was presented.

When we accepted that it was withdrawn the next day and sharpened up. So we spent our time going through the 17 linguistic changes and reduced them again to two.

Then on the last day of the meeting we asked our experts to meet to compare whether the 15 changes that had been settled of the 17 that had been proposed, whether those now conformed in the two texts. At that point we were presented with 16 new changes including four substantive ones, some of which now still remain unsettled.

Now I will not go into the details or into the merits of these changes. The major difficulty that we now face is that provisions that were settled in the agreement appear again in a different form in the protocols, that matters of technical implementation which were implicit in the agreement from the beginning have not been addressed and were not presented to us until the very last day of a series of sessions that had been specifically designed to discuss them.

And that as soon as one issue was settled a new issue was raised. It was very tempting for us to continue the process which is so close to everybody's heart implicit in the many meetings of indicating great progress.

But the President decided that we could not engage in a charade with the American people.

And we are now in this curious position. Great progress has been made in the talks. The only thing that is lacking is one decision in Hanoi to settle the remaining issues in terms that two weeks previously they had already agreed to.

So we are not talking of an issue of principle that is totally unacceptable and secondly to complete the work that is required to bring the international machinery into being in the spirit that both sides have an interest of not ending the war in such a way that it is just the beginning of another round of conflict.

So we are in a position where peace can be near but peace requires a decision.

And this is why we wanted to restate once more what our basic attitude is.

With respect to Saigon we have sympathy and compassion for the anguish of their people and for the concerns of their Government.

But if we can get an agreement that the President considers just we will proceed with it.

With respect to Hanoi our basic objective was stated in the press conference of Oct. 26. We want an end of the war that is something more than an armistice. We want to move from hostilities to normalization and from normalization to cooperation.

But we will not make a settlement which is a disguised form of continued warfare and which brings about by indirection what we have always said we would not tolerate.

We have always stated that a fair solution cannot possible give either side everything that it wants. We have—we are not continuing a war in order to give total victory to our allies. We want to give them a reasonable opportunity to participate in a political settlement. But we also will not make a settlement which is a disguised form of victory for the other side.

Therefore we are at a point where we are again—perhaps we are closer to an agreement than we were at the end of October if the other side is willing to deal with us in good faith and with goodwill.

But it cannot do that every day an issue is settled a new one is raised, that when an issue is settled in an agreement it is raised again as an understanding and if it is settled in an understanding it is raised again as a protocol.

We will not be blackmailed into an agreement. We will not be stampeded into an agreement. And, if I may say so, we will not be charmed into an agreement, until its conditions are right.

For the President, and for all of us who have been engaged in these negotiations, nothing that we have done has meant more than attempting to bring an end to the war in Vietnam. Nothing that I have done since I am in this position has made me feel more the trustee of so many hopes as the negotiations which I have—in which I have recently participated.

And it was painful at times to think of the hopes of millions—and indeed of the hopes of many of you ladies and gentlemen who were standing outside these various meeting places—expecting momentous events to be occurring, while inside one frivolous issue after another was surfaced in the last three days.

And so what we are saying to Hanoi is: We are prepared to continue in the spirit of the negotiations that were started in October. We are prepared to maintain an agreement that provides for the unconditional release of all American and allied prisoners, that imposes no political solution on either side, that brings about an international supervised cease-fire and the withdrawal of all American forces within 60 days.

It is a settlement that is just to both sides, and that requires only a decision to maintain provisions that had already been accepted, and an end to procedures that can only mock the hopes of humanity.

And on that basis we can have a peace that justifies the hopes of mankind and the sense of justice of all participants.

Address by President Nixon Announcing the End of the Vietnam War*

January 23, 1973

Good evening. I have asked for this radio and television time tonight for the purpose of announcing that we today have concluded an agreement to end the war and bring peace with honor in Vietnam and Southeast Asia.

The following statement is being issued at this moment in Washington and Hanoi:

"At 12:30 Paris time today, Jan. 23, 1973, the agreement on ending the war and restoring peace in Vietnam was initialed by Dr. Henry Kissinger on behalf of the United States and Special Adviser Le Duc Tho on behalf of the Democratic Republic of Vietnam.

"The agreement will be formally signed by the parties participating in the Paris Conference on Vietnam on Jan. 27, 1973, at the International Conference Center in Paris. The cease-fire will take effect at 2400 Greenwich mean time, Jan. 27, 1973. The United States and the Democratic Republic of Vietnam express the hope that this agreement will insure stable peace in Vietnam and contribute to the preservation of lasting peace in Indochina and Southeast Asia."

That concludes the formal statement.

Throughout the years of negotiations, we have insisted on peace with honor.

In my addresses to the nation from this room on Jan. 25 and May 8, I set forth the goals that we considered essential for peace with honor. In the settlement that has now been agreed to, all the conditions that I laid down then have been met—a cease-fire internationally supervised will begin at 7 P.M. this Saturday, Jan. 27, Washington time. Within 60 days from this Saturday all Americans held prisoners of war throughout Indochina will be released.

There will be the fullest possible accounting for all of those who are missing in action.

*The New York Times, Jan. 24, 1973.

During the same 60-day period all American forces will be withdrawn from South Vietnam.

The people of South Vietnam have been guaranteed the right to determine their own future without outside interference.

By joint agreement, the full text of the agreement and the protocols to carry it out will be issued tomorrow.

Throughout these negotiations we have been in the closest consultation with President Thieu and other representatives of the Republic of Vietnam.

This settlement meets the goals and has the full support of President Thieu and the Government of the Republic of Vietnam as well as that of our other allies who are affected.

The United States will continue to recognize the Government of the Republic of Vietnam as the sole legitimate government of South Vietnam. We shall continue to aid South Vietnam within the terms of the agreement, and we shall support efforts for the people of South Vietnam to settle their problems peacefully among themselves.

We must recognize that ending the war is only the first step toward building the peace.

All parties must now see to it that this is a peace that lasts and also a peace that heals, and a peace that not only ends the war in Southeast Asia but contributes to the prospects of peace in the whole world. This will mean that the terms of the agreement must be scrupulously adhered to. We shall do everything the agreement requires of us, and we shall expect the other parties to do everything it requires of them. We shall also expect other interested nations to help insure that the agreement is carried out and peace is maintained.

As this long and very difficult war ends I would like to address a few special words to each of those who have been parties in the conflict.

First, to the people and Government of South Vietnam. By your courage, by your sacrifice, you have won the precious right to determine your own future and you have developed the strength to defend that right.

We look forward to working with you in the future, friends in peace as we have been allies in war.

To the leaders of North Vietnam: As we have ended the war through negotiations, let us now build a peace of reconciliation.

For our part, we are prepared to make a major effort to help achieve that goal. But just as reciprocity was needed to end the war, so too will it be needed to build and strengthen the peace.

To the other major powers that have been involved, even indirectly: Now is the time for mutual restraint so that the peace we have achieved can last.

And finally, to all of you who are listening, the American people: Your steadfastness in supporting our insistence on peace with honor has made peace with honor possible.

I know that you would not have wanted that peace jeopardized.

With our secret negotiations at the sensitive stage they were in during this recent period, for me to have discussed publicly our efforts to secure peace would not only have violated our understanding with North Vietnam, it would have seriously harmed and possibly destroyed the chances for peace.

Therefore I know that you now can understand why during these past several weeks I have not made any public statements about those efforts. The important thing was not to talk about peace but to get peace and to get the right kind of peace.

This we have done.

Now that we have achieved an honorable agreement let us be proud that America did not settle for a peace that would have betrayed our allies, that would have abandoned our prisoners of war or that would have ended the war for us but would have continued the war for the 50 million people of Indochina.

Let us be proud of the two and a half million young Americans who served in Vietnam, who served with honor and distinction in one of the most selfless enterprises in the history of nations.

And let us be proud of those who sacrificed, who gave their lives, so that the people of South Vietnam might live in freedom, and so that the world might live in peace.

In particular, I would like to say a word to some of the bravest people I have ever met—the wives, children, the families of our prisoners of war and the missing in action.

When others called on us to settle on any terms, you had the courage to stand for the right kind of peace, so that those who died and those who suffered would not have died and suffered in vain and so that where this generation knew war, the next generation would know peace. Nothing means more to me at this moment than the fact that your long vigil is coming to an end.

Just yesterday, a great American who once occupied this office died. In his life, President Johnson endured the vilification of those who sought to portray him as a man of war, but there was nothing he cared about more deeply than achieving a lasting peace in the world.

I remember the last time I talked with him. It was just the day after New Year's.

He spoke then of his concern with bringing peace, with making it the right kind of peace. And I was grateful that he once again expressed his support for my efforts to gain such a peace.

No one would have welcomed this peace more than he.

And I know he would join me in asking for those who died and for those who live, let us consecrate this moment by resolving together to make the peace we have achieved a peace that will last.

Thank you, and good evening.

The Vietnam Agreement and Protocols*

January 27, 1973

The parties participating in the Paris conference on Vietnam,

With a view to ending the war and restoring peace in Vietnam on the basis of respect for the Vietnamese people's fundamental national rights and the South Vietnamese people's right to self-determination, and to contributing to the consolidation of peace in Asia and the world,

Have agreed on the following provisions and undertake to respect and to implement them:

*The New York Times, Jan. 25, 1973. This was released on Jan. 24, 1973.

CHAPTER I
THE VIETNAMESE PEOPLE'S
FUNDAMENTAL NATIONAL RIGHTS

Article 1

The United States and all other countries respect the independence, sovereignty, unity and territorial integrity of Vietnam as recognized by the 1954 Geneva Agreements on Vietnam.

CHAPTER II
CESSATION OF HOSTILITIES,
WITHDRAWAL OF TROOPS

Article 2

A cease-fire shall be observed throughout South Vietnam as of 2400 hours G.M.T., on Jan. 27, 1973.

At the same hour, the United States will stop all its military activities against the territory of the Democratic Republic of Vietnam by ground, air and naval forces, wherever they may be based, and end the mining of the territorial waters, ports, harbors and waterways of the Democratic Republic of Vietnam. The United States will remove, permanently deactivate or destroy all the mines in the territorial waters, ports, harbors and waterways of North Vietnam as soon as this agreement goes into effect.

The complete cessation of hostilities mentioned in this article shall be durable and without limit of time.

Article 3

The parties undertake to maintain the cease-fire and to insure a lasting and stable peace.

As soon as the cease-fire goes into effect:

(a) The United States forces and those of the other foreign countries allied with the United States and the Republic of Vietnam shall remain in place pending the implementation of the plan of troop withdrawal. The Four-Party Joint Military Commission described in Article 16 shall determine the modalities.

(b) The armed forces of the two South Vietnamese parties shall remain in place. The Two-Party Joint Military Commission described in Article 17 shall determine the areas controlled by each party and the modalities of stationing.

(c) The regular forces of all services and arms and the irregular forces of the parties in South Vietnam shall stop all offensive activities against each other and shall strictly abide by the following stipulations:

¶All acts of force on the ground, in the air and on the sea shall be prohibited.

¶All hostile acts, terrorism and reprisals by both sides will be banned.

Article 4

The United States will not continue its military involvement or intervene in the internal affairs of South Vietnam.

Article 5

Within 60 days of the signing of this agreement, there will be a total withdrawal from South Vietnam of troops, military personnel, including technical military personnel and military personnel associated with the pacification program, armaments, munitions and war material of the United States and those of the other foreign countries mentioned in Article 3 (a). Advisers from the above-mentioned countries to all para-military organizations and the police force will also be withdrawn within the same period of time.

Article 6

The dismantlement of all military bases in South Vietnam of the United States and of the other foreign countries mentioned in Article 3 (a) shall be completed within 60 days of the signing of this agreement.

Article 7

From the enforcement of the cease-fire to the formation of the government provided for in Articles 9 (b) and 14 of this agreement, the two South Vietnamese parties shall not accept the introduction of troops, military advisers and military personnel, including technical military personnel, armaments, munitions and war material into South Vietnam.

The two South Vietnamese parties shall be permitted to make periodic replacement of armaments, munitions and war material which have been destroyed, damaged, worn out or used up after the cease-fire, on the basis of piece-for-piece, of the same characteristics and properties, under the supervision of the Joint Military Commission of Control and Supervision.

CHAPTER III
THE RETURN OF CAPTURED MILITARY PERSONNEL AND FOREIGN CIVILIANS, AND CAPTURED AND DETAINED VIETNAMESE CIVILIAN PERSONNEL

Article 8

(a) The return of captured military personnel and foreign civilians of the parties shall be carried out simultaneously with and completed not later than the same day as the troop withdrawal mentioned in Article 5. The parties shall exchange complete lists of the above-mentioned captured military personnel and foreign civilians on the day of the signing of this agreement.

(b) The parties shall help each other to get information about those military personnel and foreign civilians of the parties missing in action, to determine the location and take care of the graves of the dead so as to facilitate the exhumation and repatriation of the remains, and to take any such other measures as may be required to get information about those still considered missing in action.

(c) The question of the return of Vietnamese civilian personnel captured and detained in South Vietnam will be resolved by the two South Vietnamese parties on the basis of the principles of Article 21 (b) of the Agreement on the Cessation of Hostilities in Vietnam of July 20, 1954. The two South Vietnamese parties will do so in a spirit of national reconciliation and concord, with a view to ending hatred and enmity, in order to ease suffering and to reunite families. The two South Vietnamese parties will do their utmost to resolve this question within 90 days after the cease-fire comes into effect.

CHAPTER IV
THE EXERCISE OF THE SOUTH
VIETNAMESE PEOPLE'S RIGHT
TO SELF-DETERMINATION

Article 9

The Government of the United States of America and the Government of the Democratic Republic of Vietnam undertake to respect the following principles for the exercise of the South Vietnamese people's right to self-determination:

(a) The South Vietnamese people's right to self-determination is sacred, inalienable and shall be respected by all countries.

(b) The South Vietnamese people shall decide themselves the political future of South Vietnam through genuinely free and democratic general elections under international supervision.

(c) Foreign countries shall not impose any political tendency or personality on the South Vietnamese people.

Article 10

The two South Vietnamese parties undertake to respect the cease-fire and maintain peace in South Vietnam, settle all matters of contention through negotiations and avoid all armed conflict.

Article 11

Immediately after the cease-fire, the two South Vietnamese parties will:

¶ Achieve national reconciliation and concord, end hatred and enmity, prohibit all acts of reprisal and discrimination against individuals or organizations that have collaborated with one side or the other.

¶ Insure the democratic liberties of the people: personal freedom, freedom of speech, freedom of the press, freedom of meeting, freedom of organization, freedom of political activities, freedom of belief, freedom of movement, freedom of residence, freedom of work, right to property ownership and right to free enterprise.

Article 12

(a) Immediately after the cease-fire, the two South Vietnamese parties shall hold consultations in a spirit of national reconciliation and concord, mutual respect and mutual nonelimination to set up a National Council of National Reconciliation and

Concord of three equal segments. The council shall operate on the principle of unanimity. After the National Council of National Reconciliation and Concord has assumed its functions, the two South Vietnamese parties will consult about the formation of councils at lower levels. The two South Vietnamese parties shall sign an agreement on the internal matters of South Vietnam as soon as possible and do their utmost to accomplish this within 90 days after the cease-fire comes into effect, in keeping with the South Vietnamese people's aspirations for peace, independence and democracy.

(b) The National Council of National Reconciliation and Concord shall have the task of promoting the two South Vietnamese parties' implementation of this agreement, achievement of national reconciliation and concord and insurance of democratic liberties. The National Council of National Reconciliation and Concord will organize the free and democratic general elections provided for in Article 9 (b) and decide the procedures and modalities of these general elections. The institutions for which the general elections are to be held will be agreed upon through consultations between the two South Vietnamese parties. The National Council of National Reconciliation and Concord will also decide the procedures and modalities of such local elections as the two South Vietnamese parties agree upon.

Article 13

The question of Vietnamese armed forces in South Vietnam shall be settled by the two South Vietnamese parties in a spirit of national reconciliation and concord, equality and mutual respect, without interference, in accordance with the postwar situation. Among the questions to be discussed by the two South Vietnamese parties are steps to reduce their military effectives and to demobilize the troops being reduced. The two South Vietnamese parties will accomplish this as soon as possible.

Article 14

South Vietnam will pursue a foreign policy of peace and independence. It will be prepared to establish relations with all countries irrespective of their political and social systems on the basis of mutual respect for independence and sovereignty and accept economic and technical aid from any country with no political conditions attached. The acceptance of military aid by South Vietnam in the future shall come under the authority of the government set up after the general elections in South Vietnam provided for in Article 9 (b).

CHAPTER V
THE REUNIFICATION OF VIETNAM
AND THE RELATIONSHIP
BETWEEN NORTH AND SOUTH
VIETNAM

Article 15

The reunification of Vietnam shall be carried out step by step through peaceful means on the basis of discussions and agreements between North and South Vietnam, without coercion or annexation by either party, and without foreign interference. The time for reunification will be agreed upon by North and South Vietnam.

Pending reunification:

(a) The military demarcation line between the two zones at the 17th Parallel is only provisional and not a political or territorial boundary, as provided for in paragraph 6 of the Final Declaration of the 1954 Geneva Conference.

(b) North and South Vietnam shall respect the demilitarized zone on either side of the provisional military demarcation line.

(c) North and South Vietnam shall promptly start negotiations with a view to re-establishing normal relations in various fields. Among the questions to be negotiated are the modalities of civilian movement across the provisional military demarcation line.

(d) North and South Vietnam shall not join any military alliance or military bloc and shall not allow foreign powers to maintain military bases, troops, military advisers and military personnel on their respective territories, as stipulated in the 1954 Geneva Agreements on Vietnam.

CHAPTER VI
THE JOINT MILITARY COMMISSIONS, THE INTERNATIONAL COMMISSION OF CONTROL AND SUPERVISION, THE INTERNATIONAL CONFERENCE

Article 16

(a) The parties participating in the Paris conference on Vietnam shall immediately designate representatives to form a Four-Party Joint Military Commission with the task of insuring joint action by the parties in implementing the following provisions of this agreement:

¶The first paragraph of Article 2, regarding the enforcement of the cease-fire throughout South Vietnam.

¶Article 3 (a), regarding the cease-fire by U.S. forces and those of the other foreign countries referred to in that article.

¶Article 3 (c), regarding the cease-fire between all parties in South Vietnam.

¶Article 5, regarding the withdrawal from South Vietnam of U.S. troops and those of the other foreign countries mentioned in Article 3 (a).

¶Article 6, regarding the dismantlement of military bases in South Vietnam of the United States and those of the other foreign countries mentioned in Article 3 (a).

¶Article 8 (a), regarding the return of captured military personnel and foreign civilians of the parties.

¶Article 8 (b), regarding the mutual assistance of the parties in getting information about those military personnel and foreign civilians of the parties missing in action.

(b) The Four-Party Joint Military Commission shall operate in accordance with the principle of consultations and unanimity. Disagreements shall be referred to the International Commission of Control and Supervision.

(c) The Four-Party Military Commission shall begin operating immediately after the signing of this agreement and end its activities in 60 days, after the completion of the withdrawal of U.S. troops and those of the other foreign countries mentioned in Article 3 (a) and the completion of the return of captured military personnel and foreign civilians of the parties.

(d) The four parties shall agree immediately on the organization, the working procedure, means of activity and expenditures of the Four-Party Joint Military Commission.

Article 17

(a) The two South Vietnamese parties shall immediately designate representatives to form a Two-Party Joint Military Commission with the task of insuring joint action by the two South Vietnamese parties in implementing the following provisions of this agreement:

¶The first paragraph of Article 2. regarding the enforcement of the cease-fire throughout South Vietnam, when the Four-Party Joint Military Commission has ended its activities.

¶Article 3 (b), regarding the cease-fire between the two South Vietnamese parties.

¶Article 3 (c), regarding the cease-fire between all parties in South Vietnam, when the Four-Party Joint Military Commission has ended its activities.

¶Article 7, regarding the prohibition of the introduction of troops into South Vietnam and all other provisions of this article.

¶Article 8 (c), regarding the question of the return of Vietnamese civilian personnel captured and detained in South Vietnam;

¶Article 13, regarding the reduction of the military effectives of the two South Vietnamese parties and the demobilization of the troops being reduced.

(b) Disagreements shall be referred to the International Commission of Control and Supervision.

(c) After the signing of this agreement, the Two-Party Joint Military Commission shall agree immediately on the measures and organization aimed at enforcing the cease-fire and preserving peace in South Vietnam.

Article 18

(a) After the signing of this Agreement, an International Commission of Control and Supervision shall be established immediately.

(b) Until the international conference provided for in Article 19 makes definitive arrangements, the International Commission of Control and Supervision will report to the four parties on matters concerning the control and supervision of the implementation of the following provisions of this agreement:

¶The first paragraph of Article 2, regarding the enforcement of the cease-fire throughout South Vietnam.

¶Article 3 (a), regarding the cease-fire by U.S. forces and those of the other foreign countries referred to in that article.

¶Article 3 (c), regarding the cease-fire between all the parties in South Vietnam.

¶Article 5, regarding the withdrawal from South Vietnam of U.S. troops and those of the other foreign countries mentioned in Article 3 (a).

¶Article 6, regarding the dismantlement of military bases in South Vietnam of the United States and those of the other foreign countries mentioned in Article 3 (a).

¶Article 8 (a), regarding the return of captured military personnel and foreign civilians of the parties.

The International Commission of Control and Supervision shall form control teams for carrying out its tasks. The four parties shall agree immediately on the location and operation of these teams. The parties will facilitate their operation.

(c) Until the international conference makes definitive arrangements, the International Commission of Control and Supervision will report to the two South Vietnamese parties on matters concerning the control and supervision of the implementation of the following provisions of this agreement:

¶The first paragraph of Article 2, regarding the enforcement of the cease-fire throughout South Vietnam, when the Four-Party Joint Military Commission has ended its activities.

¶Article 3 (b), regarding the cease-fire between the two South Vietnamese parties.

¶Article 3 (c), regarding the cease-fire between all parties in South Vietnam, when the Four-Party Joint Military Commission has ended its activities.

¶Article 7, regarding the prohibition of the introduction of troops into South Vietnam and all other provisions of this article.

¶Article 8 (c), regarding the question of the return of Vietnamese civilian personnel captured and detained in South Vietnam.

¶Article 9 (b), regarding the free and democratic general elections in South Vietnam.

¶Article 13, regarding the reduction of the military effectives of the two South Vietnamese parties and the demobilization of the troops being reduced.

The International Commission of Control and Supervision shall form control teams for carrying out its tasks. The two South Vietnamese parties shall agree immediately on the location and operation of these teams. The two South Vietnamese parties will facilitate their operation.

(d) The International Commission of Control and Supervision shall be composed of representatives of four countries: Canada, Hungary, Indonesia and Poland. The chairmanship of this commission will rotate among the members for specific periods to be determined by the commission.

(e) The International Commission of Control and Supervision shall carry out its tasks in accordance with the principle of respect for the sovereignty of South Vietnam.

(f) The International Commission of Control and Supervision shall operate in accordance with the principle of consultations and unanimity.

(g) The International Commission of Control and Supervision shall begin operating when a cease-fire comes into force in Vietnam. As regards the provisions in Article 18 (b) concerning the four parties, the International Commission of Control and Supervision shall end its activities when the commission's tasks of control and supervision regarding these provisions have been fulfilled. As regards the provisions in Article 18 (c) concerning the two South Vietnamese parties, the International Commission of

Control and Supervision shall end its activities on the request of the government formed after the general elections in South Vietnam provided for in Article 9 (b).

(h) The four parties shall agree immediately on the organization, means of activity and expenditures of the International Commission of Control and Supervision. The relationship between the international commission and the international conference will be agreed upon by the International Commission and the International Conference.

Article 19

The parties agree on the convening of an international conference within 30 days of the signing of this agreement to acknowledge the signed agreements; to guarantee the ending of the war, the maintenance of peace in Vietnam, the respect of the Vietnamese people's fundamental national rights and the South Vietnamese people's right to self-determination; and to contribute to and guarantee peace in Indochina.

The United States and the Democratic Republic of Vietnam, on behalf of the parties participating in the Paris conference on Vietnam, will propose to the following parties that they participate in this international conference: the People's Republic of China, the Republic of France, the Union of Soviet Socialist Republics, the United Kingdom, the four countries of the International Commission of Control and Supervision, and the Secretary General of the United Nations, together with the parties participating in the Paris conference on Vietnam.

CHAPTER VII
REGARDING CAMBODIA
AND LAOS

Article 20

(a) The parties participating in the Paris conference on Vietnam shall strictly respect the 1954 Geneva Agreements on Cambodia and the 1962 Geneva Agreements on Laos, which recognized the Cambodian and the Lao peoples' fundamental national rights, i.e., the independence, sovereignty, unity and territorial integrity of these countries. The parties shall respect the neutrality of Cambodia and Laos.

The parties participating in the Paris conference on Vietnam undertake to refrain from using the territory of Cambodia and the territory of Laos to encroach on the sovereignity and security of one another and of other countries.

(b) Foreign countries shall put an end to all military activities in Cambodia and Laos, totally withdraw from and refrain from reintroducing into these two countries troops, military advisers and military personnel, armaments, munitions and war material.

(c) The internal affairs of Cambodia and Laos shall be settled by the people of each of these countries without foreign interference.

(d) The problems existing between the Indochinese countries shall be settled by the Indochinese parties on the basis of respect for each other's independence, sovereignty and territorial integrity, and noninterference in each other's internal affairs.

CHAPTER VIII
THE RELATIONSHIP BETWEEN
THE UNITED STATES AND
THE DEMOCRATIC REPUBLIC
OF VIETNAM

Article 21

The United States anticipates that this agreement will usher in an era of reconciliation with the Democratic Republic of Vietnam as with all the peoples of Indochina. In pursuance of its traditional policy, the United States will contribute to healing the wounds of war and to postwar reconstruction of the Democratic Republic of Vietnam and throughout Indochina.

Article 22

The ending of the war, the restoration of peace in Vietnam and the strict implementation of this agreement will create conditions for establishing a new, equal and mutually beneficial relationship between the United States and the Democratic Republic of Vietnam on the basis of respect for each other's independence and sovereignty and noninterference in each other's internal affairs. At the same time this will insure stable peace in Vietnam and contribute to the preservation of lasting peace in Indochina and Southeast Asia.

CHAPTER IX
OTHER PROVISIONS

Article 23

This agreement shall enter into force upon signature by plenipotentiary representatives of the parties participating in the Paris Conference on Vietnam. All the parties concerned shall strictly implement this agreement and its protocols.

Done in Paris this 27th day of January, 1973, in Vietnamese and English. The Vietnamese and English texts are official and equally authentic.

For the Government of the
United States of America
William P. Rogers
Secretary of State

For the Government of the
Democratic Republic of Vietnam
Nguyen Duy Trinh
Minister for Foreign Affairs

For the Government of the
Republic of Vietnam
Tran Van Lam
Minister for Foreign Affairs

For the Provisional Revolutionary
Government of the Republic of
South Vietnam
Nguyen Thi Binh
Minister for Foreign Affairs

2-PARTY VERSION
AGREEMENT ON ENDING THE WAR
AND RESTORING PEACE IN VIETNAM

The Government of the United States of America, with the concurrence of the Government of the Republic of Vietnam,

The Government of the Democratic Republic of Vietnam, with the concurrence of the Provisional Revolutionary Government of the Republic of South Vietnam,

With a view to ending the war and restoring peace in Vietnam on the basis of respect for the Vietnamese people's fundamental national rights and the South Vietnamese people's right to self-determination, and to contributing to the consolidation of peace in Asia and the world,

Have agreed on the following provisions and undertake to respect and to implement them:

[Text of agreement Chapters I-VIII same as above]

CHAPTER IX
OTHER PROVISIONS

The Paris agreement on Ending the War and Restoring Peace in Vietnam shall enter into force upon signature of this document by the Secretary of State of the Government of the United States of America and the Minister for Foreign Affairs of the Government of the Democratic Republic of Vietnam, and upon signature of a document in the same terms by the Secretary of State of the Government of the United States of America, the Minister for Foreign Affairs of the Government of the Republic of Vietnam, the Minister for Foreign Affairs of the Government of the Democratic Republic of Vietnam and the Minister for Foreign Affairs of the Provisional Revolutionary Government of the Republic of South Vietnam. The agreement and the protocols to it shall be strictly implemented by all the parties concerned.

Done in Paris this 27th day of January, 1973, in Vietnamese and English. The Vietnamese and English texts are official and equally authentic.

For the Government of the	*For the Government of the*
United States of America	*Democratic Republic of Vietnam*
William P. Rogers	*Nguyen Duy Trinh*
Secretary of State	*Minister for Foreign Affairs*

PROTOCOL ON CLEARING SEA MINES
PROTOCOL TO THE AGREEMENT ON ENDING THE WAR AND RESTORING PEACE IN VIETNAM CONCERNING THE REMOVAL, PERMANENT DEACTIVATION OR DESTRUCTION OF MINES IN THE TERRITORIAL WATERS, PORTS, HARBORS AND WATERWAYS OF THE DEMOCRATIC REPUBLIC OF VIETNAM

The Government of the United States of America,

The Government of the Democratic Republic of Vietnam,

In implementation of the second paragraph of Article 2 of the Agreement on Ending the War and Restoring Peace in Vietnam signed on this date,

Have agreed as follows:

Article I

The United States shall clear all mines it has placed in the territorial waters, ports, harbors and waterways of the Democratic Republic of Vietnam. This mine-clearing operation shall be accomplished by rendering the mines harmless through removal, permanent deactivation or destruction.

Article 2

With a view to insuring lasting safety for the movement of people and watercraft and the protection of important installations, mines shall, on the request of the Democratic Republic of Vietnam, be removed or destroyed in the indicated area; and whenever their removal or destruction is impossible, mines shall be permanently deactivated and their emplacement clearly marked.

Article 3

The mine-clearing operation shall begin at twenty-four hundred (2400) hours G.M.T. on Jan. 27, 1973. The representatives of the two parties shall consult immediately on relevant factors and agree upon the earliest possible target date for the completion of the work.

Article 4

The mine-clearing operation shall be conducted in accordance with priorities and timing agreed upon by the two parties. For this purpose, representatives of the two parties shall meet at an early date to reach agreement on a program and a plan of implementation. To this end:

(a) The United States shall provide its plan for mine-clearing operations, including maps of the minefields and information concerning the types, numbers and properties of the mines.

(b) The Democratic Republic of Vietnam shall provide all available maps and hydrographic charts and indicate the mined places and all other potential hazards to the mine-clearing operations that the Democratic Republic of Vietnam is aware of.

(c) The two parties shall agree on the timing of implementation of each segment of the plan and provide timely notice to the public at least 48 hours in advance of the beginning of mine-clearing operations for that segment.

Article 5

The United States shall be reponsible for the mine clearance on island waterways of the Democratic Republic of Vietnam. The Democratic Republic of Vietnam shall, to the full extent of its capabilities, actively participate in the mine clearance with the means of surveying, removal and destruction, and technical advice supplied by the United States.

Article 6

With a view to insuring the safe movement of people and watercraft on waterways and at sea, the United states shall in the mine-clearing process supply timely information about the progress of mine clearing in each area, and about the remaining mines to be destroyed. The United States shall issue a communiqué when the operations have been concluded.

Article 7

In conducting mine-clearing operations, the U.S. personnel engaged in these operations shall respect the sovereignty of the Democratic Republic of Vietnam and shall engage in no activities inconsistent with the Agreement on Ending the War and Restoring Peace in Vietnam and this protocol. The U.S. personnel engaged in the mine-clearing operations shall be immune from the jurisdiction of the Democratic Republic of Vietnam for the duration of the mine-clearing operations.

The Democratic Republic of Vietnam shall insure the safety of the U.S. personnel for the duration of their mine-clearing activities on the territory of the Democratic Republic of Vietnam, and shall provide this personnel with all possible assistance and the means needed in the Democratic Republic of Vietnam that have been agreed upon by the two parties.

Article 8

This protocol to the Paris Agreement on Ending the War and Restoring Peace in Vietnam shall enter into force upon signature by the Secretary of State of the Government of the United States of America and the Minister for Foreign Affairs of the Government of the Democratic Republic of Vietnam. It shall be strictly implemented by the two parties.

Done in Paris this 27th day of January, 1973, in Vietnamese and English. The Vietnamese and English texts are official and equally authentic.

For the Government of the	*For the Government of the*
United States of America	*Democratic Republic of Vietnam*
William P. Rogers	*Nguyen Duy Trinh*
Secretary of State	*Minister for Foreign Affairs*

PROTOCOL ON THE CEASE-FIRE
PROTOCOL TO THE AGREEMENT ON ENDING THE WAR AND RESTORING PEACE IN VIETNAM CONCERNING THE CEASE-FIRE IN SOUTH VIETNAM AND THE JOINT MILITARY COMMISSIONS

The parties participating in the Paris conference on Vietnam.

In implementation of the first paragraph of Article 2, Article 3, Article 5, Article 6, Article 16 and Article 17 of the Agreement on Ending the War and Restoring Peace in Vietnam signed on this date which provides for the cease-fire in South Vietnam and the establishment of a Four-Party Joint Military Commission and a Two-Party Joint Military Commission,

Have agreed as follows:

CEASE-FIRE IN SOUTH VIETNAM

Article 1

The high commands of the parties in South Vietnam shall issue prompt and timely orders to all regular and irregular armed forces and the armed police under their command to completely end hostilities throughout South Vietnam, at the exact time stipulated in Article 2 of the Agreement and insure that these armed forces and armed police comply with these orders and respect the cease-fire.

Article 2

(a) As soon as the cease-fire comes into force and until regulations are issued by the Joint Military Commissions, all ground, river, sea and air combat forces of the parties in South Vietnam shall remain in place; that is, in order to insure a stable cease-fire, there shall be no major redeployments or movements that would extend each party's area of control or would result in contact between opposing armed forces and clashes which might take place.

(b) All regular and irregular armed forces and the armed police of the parties in South Vietnam shall observe the prohibition of the following acts:

(1) Armed patrol in to areas controlled by opposing armed forces and flights by bomber and fighter aircraft of all types, except for unarmed flights for proficiency training and maintenance;

(2) Armed attacks against any person, either military or civilian, by any means whatsoever, including the use of small arms, mortars, artillery, bombing and strafing by airplanes and any other type of weapon or explosive device;

(3) All combat operations on the ground, on rivers, on the sea and in the air;

(4) All hostile acts, terrorism or reprisals; and

(5) All acts endangering lives or public or private property.

Article 3

(a) The above-mentioned prohibitions shall not hamper or restrict:

(1) Civilian supply, freedom of movement, freedom to work and freedom of the people to engage in trade, and civilian communication and transportation between and among all areas in South Vietnam.

(2) The use by each party in areas under its control of military support elements, such as engineer and transportation units, in repair and construction of public facilities and the transportation and supplying of the population.

(3) Normal military proficiency conducted by the parties in the areas under their respective control with due regard for public safety.

(d) The Joint Military Commissions shall immediately agree on corridors, routes and other regulations governing the movement of military transport aircraft, military transport vehicles and military transport vessels of all types of one party going through areas under the control of other parties.

Article 4

In order to avert conflict and insure normal conditions for those armed forces which are in direct contact, and pending regulation by the Joint Military Commissions, the commanders of the opposing armed forces at those places of direct contact shall meet as soon as the cease-fire comes into force with a view to reaching an agreement on temporary measures to avert conflict and to insure supply and medical care for these armed forces.

Article 5

(a) Within 15 days after the cease-fire comes into effect, each party shall do its utmost to complete the removal or deactivation of all demolition objects, minefields, traps, obstacles or other dangerous objects placed previously, so as not to hamper the population's movement and work, in the first place on waterways, roads and railroads in South Vietnam. Those mines which cannot be removed or deactivated within that time shall be clearly marked and must be removed or deactivated as soon as possible.

(b) Emplacement of mines is prohibited, except as a defensive measure around the edges of military installations in places where they do not hamper the population's movement and work, and movement on waterways, roads and railroads. Mines and other obstacles already in place at the edges of military installations may remain in place if they are in place where they do not hamper the population's movement and work, and movement on waterways, roads and railroads.

Article 6

Civilian police and civilian security personnel of the parties in South Vietnam, who are responsible for the maintenance of law and order, shall strictly respect the prohibitions set forth in Article 2 of this protocol. As required by their responsibilities, normally they shall be authorized to carry pistols, but when required by unusual circumstances, they shall be allowed to carry other small individual arms.

Article 7

(a) The entry into South Vietnam of replacement armaments, munitions and war material permitted under Article 7 of the agreement shall take place under the supervision and control of the Two-Party Joint Military Commission and of the International Commission of Control and Supervision and through such points of entry only as are designated by the two South Vietnamese parties. The two South Vietnamese parties shall agree on these points of entry within 15 days after the entry into force of the cease-fire. The two South Vietnamese parties may select as many as six points of entry which are not included in the list of places where teams of the International Commission of Control and Supervision are to be based contained in Article 4 (d) of the protocol concerning the international commission. At the same time, the two South Vietnamese parties may also select points of entry from the list of places set forth in Article 4 (d) of that protocol.

(b) Each of the designated points of entry shall be available only for that South Vietnamese party which is in control of that point. The two South Vietnamese parties shall have an equal number of points of entry.

Article 8

(a) In implementation of Article 5 of the agreement, the United States and the other foreign countries referred to in Article 5 of the agreement shall take with them all their armaments, munitions and war material. Transfers of such items which would leave them in South Vietnam shall not be made subsequent to the entry into force of the agreement except for transfers of communications, transport and other noncombat material to the Four-Party Joint Military Commission or the International Commission of Control and Supervision.

(b) Within five days after the entry into force of the cease-fire, the United States shall inform the Four-Party Joint Military Commission and the International Commission of Control and Supervision of the general plans for timing of complete troop withdrawals which shall take place in four phases of 15 days each. It is anticipated that the numbers of troops withdrawn in each phase are not likely to be widely different, although it is not feasible to insure equal numbers. The approximate numbers to be withdrawn in each phase shall be given to the Four-Party Joint Military Commission and the International Commission of Control and Supervision sufficiently in advance of actual withdrawals so that they can properly carry out their tasks in relation thereto.

Article 9

(a) In implementation of Article 6 of the agreement, the United States and the other foreign countries referred to in that article shall dismantle and remove from South Vietnam or destroy all military bases in South Vietnam of the United States and of the other foreign countries referred to in that article, including weapons, mines and other military equipment at these bases, for the purpose of making them unusable for military purposes.

(b) The United States shall supply the Four-Party Joint Military Commission and the International Commission of Control and Supervision with necessary information on plans for base dismantlement so that those commissions can properly carry out their tasks in relation thereto.

THE JOINT MILITARY COMMISSIONS

Article 10

(a) The implementation of the agreement is the responsibility of the parties signatory to the agreement.

The Four-Party Joint Military Commission has the task of insuring joint action by the parties implementing the agreement by serving as a channel of communication among the parties, by drawing up plans and fixing the modalities to carry out, coordinate, follow and inspect the implementation of the provisions mentioned in Article 16 of the agreement, and by negotiating and settling all matters concerning the implementation of those provisions.

(b) The concrete tasks of the Four-Party Joint Military Commission are:

(1) To coordinate, follow and inspect the implementation of the above-mentioned provisions of the agreement by the four parties.

(2) To deter and detect violations, to deal with cases of violation, and to settle conflicts and matters of contention between the parties relating to the above-mentioned provisions.

(3) To dispatch without delay one or more joint teams as required by specific cases, to any part of South Vietnam, to investigate alleged violations of the agreement and to assist the parties in finding measures to prevent recurrence of similar cases.

(4) To engage in observation at the places where this is necessary in the exercise of its functions.

(5) To perform such additional tasks as it may, by unanimous decisions, determine.

Article 11

(a) There shall be a Central Joint Military Commission located in Saigon. Each party shall designate immediately a military delegation of 59 persons to represent it on the central commission. The senior officer designated by each party shall be a general officer, or equivalent.

(b) There shall be seven Regional Joint Military Commissions located in the regions shown on the annexed map and based at the following places:

Regions	Places
I	Hue
II	Da Nang
III	Pleiku
IV	Phan Thiet
V	Bien Hoa
VI	My Tho
VII	Can Tho

Each party shall designate a military delegation of 16 persons to represent it on each regional commission. The senior officer designated by each party shall be an officer from the rank of lieutenant colonel to colonel, or equivalent.

(c) There shall be a joint military team operating in each of the areas shown on the annexed map and based at each of the following places in South Vietnam:

Region I	Bao Loc
Quang Tri	Phan Rang
Phu Bai	
	Region V
Region II	An Loc
Hoi An	Xuan Loc
Tam Ky	Ben Cat
Chu Lai	Cu Chi
	Tan An
Region III	
Kontum	Region VI
Hau Bon	Moc Hoa
Phu Cat	Giong Trom
Tuy An	
Ninh Hoa	Region VII
Ban Me Thuot	Tri Ton
	Vinh Long
Region IV	Vi Thanh
Da Lat	Khanh Hung
	Quan Long

Each party shall provide four qualified persons for each joint military team. The senior person designated by each party shall be an officer from the rank of major to lieutenant colonel, or equivalent.

(d) The Regional Joint Military Commissions shall assist the Central Joint Military Commission in performing its tasks and shall supervise the operations of the military teams. The region of Saigon-Gia Dinh is placed under the responsibility of the central commission, which shall designate joint military teams to operate in this region.

(e) Each party shall be authorized to provide support and guard personnel for its delegations to the Central Joint Military Commission and Regional Joint Military Commissions, and for its members of the joint military teams. The total number of support and guard personnel for each party shall not exceed 550.

(f) The Central Joint Military Commission may establish such joint subcommissions, joint staffs and joint military teams as circumstances may require. The central commission shall determine the numbers of personnel required for any additional subcommissions, staff or teams it establishes, provided that each party shall designate one-fourth of the number of personnel required and that the total number of personnel for the Four-Party Joint Military Commission, to include its staffs, teams and support personnel, shall not exceed 3,300.

(g) The delegations of the two South Vietnamese parties may, by agreement, establish provisional subcommissions and joint military teams to carry out the tasks specifically assigned to them by Article 17 in the agreement. With respect to Article 7 of the agreement, the two South Vietnamese parties' delegations to the Four-Party Joint Military Commission shall establish joint military teams at the points of entry into South Vietnam used for replacement of armaments, munitions and war material which are designated in accordance with Artical 7 of this protocol. From the time the cease-fire comes into force to the time when the Two-Party Joint Military Commission becomes operational, the two South Vietnamese parties' delegations to the Four-Party Joint Military Commission shall form a provisional subcommission and provisional joint military teams to carry out its tasks concerning captured and detained Vietnamese civilian personnel. Where necessary for the above purposes, the two parties may agree to assign personnel additional to those assigned to the two South Vietnamese delegations to the Four-Party Joint Military Commission.

Article 12

(a) In accordance with Article 17 of the agreement, which stipulates that the two South Vietnamese parties shall immediately designate their respective representatives to form the Two-Party Joint Military Commission, 24 hours after the cease-fire comes into force, the two designated South Vietnamese parties' delegations to the Two-Party Joint Military Commission shall meet in Saigon so as to reach an agreement as soon as possible on organization and operation of the Two-Party Joint Commission, as well as the measures and organization aimed at enforcing the cease-fire and preserving peace in South Vietnam.

(b) From the time the cease-fire comes into force to the time when the Two-Party Joint Military Commission becomes operational, the two South Vietnamese parties' delegations to the Four-Party Joint Military Commission at all levels shall simultaneously assume the tasks of the Two-Party Joint Military Commission at all levels, in addition to their functions as delegations to the Four-Party Joint Military Commission.

(c) If, at the time the Four-Party Joint Military Commission ceases its operation in accordance with Article 16 of the agreement, agreement has not been reached on organization of the Two-Party Joint Military Commission, the delegations of the two South Vietnamese parties serving with the Four-Party Joint Military Commission at all levels shall continue temporarily to work together as a provisional two-party joint military commission and to assume the tasks of the Two-Party Joint Military Commission at all levels until the Two-Party Joint Military Commission becomes operational.

Article 13

In application of the principle of unanimity, the Joint Military Commissions shall have no chairmen, and meetings shall be convened at the request of any representative. The Joint Military Commissions shall adopt working procedures appropriate for the effective discharge of their functions and responsibilities.

Article 14

The Joint Military Commissions and the International Commission of Control and Supervision shall closely cooperate with and assist each other in carrying out their respective functions. Each Joint Military Commission shall inform the international commission about the implementation of those provisions of the agreement for which that Joint Military Commission has responsibility and which are within the competence of the international commission. Each Joint Military Commission may request the international commission to carry out specific observation activities.

Article 15

The Central Four-Party Joint Military Commission shall begin operating 24 hours after the cease-fire comes into force. The Regional Four-Party Joint Military Commissions shall begin operating 48 hours after the cease-fire comes into force. The joint military teams based at the places listed in Article 11 (c) of this protocol shall begin operating no later than 15 days after the cease-fire comes into force. The delegations of the two South Vietnamese parties shall simultaneously begin to assume the tasks of the Two-Party Joint Military Commission as provided in Article 12 of this protocol.

Article 16

(a) The parties shall provide full protection and all necessary assistance and cooperation to the Joint Military Commissions at all levels, in the discharge of their tasks.

(b) The Joint Military Commissions and their personnel, while carrying out their tasks shall enjoy privileges and immunities equivalent to those accorded diplomatic missions and diplomatic agents.

(c) The personnel of the Joint Military Commissions may carry pistols and wear special insignia decided upon by each Central Joint Military Commission. The personnel of each party while guarding commission installations or equipment may be authorized to carry other individual small arms, as determined by each Central Joint Military Commission.

Article 17

(a) The delegation of each party to the Four-Party Joint Military Commission and the Two-Party Joint Military Commission shall have its own offices, communication, logistics and transportation means, including aircraft when necessary.

(b) Each party, in its areas of control, shall provide appropriate office and accommodation facilities to the Four-Party Joint Military Commission and the Two-Party Joint Military Commission at all levels.

(c) The parties shall endeavor to provide to the Four-Party Joint Military Commission and the Two-Party Joint Military Commission, by means of loan, lease or gift, the common means of operation, including equipment for communication, supply and transport, including aircraft when necessary. The Joint Military Commissions may purchase from any source necessary facilities, equipment and services which are not supplied by the parties. The Joint Military Commissions shall possess and use these facilities and this equipment.

(d) The facilities and the equipment for common use mentioned above shall be returned to the parties when the Joint Military Commissions have ended their activities.

Article 18

The common expenses of the Four-Party Joint Military Commission shall be borne equally by the four parties, and the common expenses of the Two-Party Joint Military Commission in South Vietnam shall be borne equally by these two parties.

Article 19

This protocol shall enter into force upon signature by plenipotentiary representatives of all the parties participating in the Paris conference on Vietnam. It shall be strictly implemented by all the parties concerned.

Done in Paris this 27th day of January, 1973, in Vietnamese and English. The Vietnamese and English texts are official and equally authentic.

For the Government of the
United States of America
William P. Rogers
Secretary of State

For the Government of the
Republic of Vietnam
Tran Van Lam
Minister for Foreign Affairs

For the Government of the
Democratic Republic of
Vietnam
Nguyen Duy Trinh
Minister for Foreign Affairs

For the Provisional
Revolutionary Government of
the Republic of South Vietnam
Nguyen Thi Binh
Minister for Foreign Affairs

2-PARTY VERSION
PROTOCOL TO THE AGREEMENT ON ENDING THE WAR AND RESTORING PEACE IN VIETNAM CONCERNING THE CEASE-FIRE IN SOUTH VIETNAM AND THE JOINT MILITARY COMMISSIONS

The Government of the United States of America, with the concurrence of the Government of the Republic of Vietnam,

The Government of the Democratic Republic of Vietnam, with the concurrence of the Provisional Revolutionary Government of the Republic of South Vietnam,

In implementation of the first paragraph of Article 2, Article 3, Article 5, Article 6, Article 16 and Article 17 of the Agreement on Ending the War and Restoring Peace in Vietnam signed on this date which provide for the cease-fire in South Vietnam and the establishment of a Four-Party Joint Military Commission and a Two-Party Joint Military Commission,

Have agreed as follows:

[Text of protocol Articles 1-18 same as above]

Article 19

The protocol to the Paris Agreement on Ending the War and Restoring Peace in Vietnam Concerning the Cease-fire in South Vietnam and the Joint Military Commissions shall enter into force upon signature of this document by the Secretary of State of the Government of the United States of America and the Minister for Foreign Affairs of the Government of the Democratic Republic of Vietnam, and upon signature of a document in the same terms by the Secretary of State of the Government of the United States of America, the Minister for Foreign Affairs of the Government of the Republic of Vietnam, the Minister for Foreign Affairs of the Democratic Republic of Vietnam and the Minister for Foreign Affairs of the Provisional Revolutionary Government of the Republic of South Vietnam. The protocol shall be strictly implemented by all the parties concerned.

Done in Paris this 27th day of January, 1973, in Vietnamese and English. The Vietnamese and English texts are official and equally authentic.

For the Government of the
United States of America
William P. Rogers
Secretary of State

For the Government of the
Democratic Republic of Vietnam
Nguyen Duy Trinh
Minister for Foreign Affairs

PROTOCOL ON CONTROL COMMISSION
PROTOCOL TO THE AGREEMENT ON ENDING THE WAR AND RESTORING PEACE IN VIETNAM CONCERNING THE INTERNATIONAL COMMISSION OF CONTROL AND SUPERVISION

The parties participating in the Paris conference on Vietnam,

In implementation of Article 18 of the Agreement on Ending the War and Restoring Peace in Vietnam signed on this data providing for the formation of the International Commission of control and Supervision,

Have agreed as follows:

Article 1

The implementation of the agreement is the responsibility of the parties signatory to the agreement.

The functions of the international commission are to control and supervise the implementation of the provisions mentioned in Article 18 of the agreement. In carrying out these functions, the international commission shall:

(a) Follow the implementation of the above-mentioned provisions of the agreement through communication with the parties and on-the-spot observation at the places where this is required.

(b) Investigate violations of the provisions which fall under the control and supervision of the commission.

(c) When necessary, cooperate with the Joint Military Commissions in deterring and detecting violations of the above-mentioned provisions.

Article 2

The international commission shall investigate violations of the provisions described in Article 18 of the agreement on the request of the Four-Party Joint Military Commission, or of the Two-Party Joint Military Commission or of any party, or, with respect to Article 9 (b) of the agreement on general elections, of the National Council of National Reconciliation and Concord, or in any case where the international commission has other adequate grounds for considering that there has been a violation of those provisions. It is understood that, in carrying out this task, the international commission shall function with the concerned parties' assistance and cooperation as required.

Article 3

(a) When the international commission finds that there is a serious violation in the implementation of the agreement or a threat to peace against which the commission can find no appropriate measure, the commission shall report this to the four parties to the agreement so that they can hold consultations to find a solution.

(b) In accordance with Article 18 (f) of the agreement, the international commission's reports shall be made with the unanimous agreement of the representatives of all the four members. In case no unanimity is reached, the commission shall forward the different views to the four parties in accordance with article 18 (b) of the agreement, or to the two South Vietnamese parties in accordance with Article 18 (c) of the agreement, but these shall not be considered as reports of the commission.

Article 4

(a) The headquarters of the international commission shall be at Saigon.

(b) There shall be seven regional teams located in the regions shown on the annexed map and based at the following places:

Regions	Places
I	Hue
II	Danang
III	Pleiku
IV	Phan Thiet
V	Bien Hoa
VI	My Tho
VII	Can Tho

The international commission shall redesignate three teams for the region of Saigon-Gia Dinh.

(c) There shall be 26 teams operating in the areas shown on the annexed map and based at the following places in South Vietnam:

Region I	Region II
Quang Tri	Hoi An
Phu Bai	Tam Ky
	Chu Lai

Region III	Ben Cat
Region	Cu Chi
Kontum	Tan An
Hau Bon	
Phu Cat	Region VI
Tinh Hoa	Moc Hoa
Ninh Hoa	Giong Trom
Ban Me Thuot	
	Region VI
Region IV	Tri Ton
Da Lat	Vinh Long
Bao Loc	Vi Thanh
Phan Rang	Khanh Hung
	Quan Long
Region V	
An Loc	
Xuan Loc	

d) There shall be 12 teams located as shown on the annexed map and based at the following places:
Gio Linh (to cover the area south of the provisional military demarcation line)

Lao Bao	Vung Tau
Ben Het	Xa Mat
Duc Co	Bien Hoa Airfield
Chu Lai	Hong Ngu
Qui Nhon	Can Tho
Nha Trang	

(e) There shall be seven teams, six of which shall be available for assignment to the points of entry which are not listed in paragraph (d) above and which the two South Vietnamese parties choose as points for legitimate entry to South Vietnam for replacement of armaments, munitions and war material permitted by Article 7 of the agreement. Any team or teams not needed for the above-mentioned assignment shall be available for other tasks, in keeping with the commission's responsibility for control and supervision.

(f) There shall be seven teams to control and supervise the return of captured and detained personnel of the parties.

Article 5

(a) To carry out its task concerning the return of the captured military personnel and foreign civilians of the parties as stipulated by Article 8 (a) of the agreement, the international commission shall, during the time of such return send one control and supervision team to each place in Vietnam where the captured persons are being returned, and to the last detention places from which these persons will be taken to the places of return.

(b) To carry out its tasks concerning the return of the Vietnamese civilian personnel captured and detained in South Vietnam mentioned in Article 8 (c) of the agreement, the international commission shall, during the time of such return, send one control and supervision team to each place in South Vietnam where the above-mentioned captured and detained persons are being returned, and to the last detention places from which these persons shall be taken to the places of return.

Article 6

To carry out its tasks regarding Article 9 (b) of the agreement on the free and democratic general elections in South Vietnam, the international commission shall organize additional teams, when necessary. The international commission shall discuss this question in advance with the National Council of National Reconciliation and Concord. If additional teams are necessary for this purpose, they shall be formed 30 days before the general elections.

Article 7

The international commission shall continually keep under review its size, and shall reduce the number of its teams, its representatives or other personnel, or both, when those teams, representatives or personnel have accomplished the tasks assigned to them and are not required for other tasks. At the same time, the expenditures of the international commission shall be reduced correspondingly.

Article 8

Each member of the international commission shall make available at all times the following numbers of qualified personnel:
(a) One senior representative and 26 others for the headquarters staff.
(b) Five for each of the seven regional teams.
(c) Two for each of the other international control teams, except for the teams at Gio Linh and Vung Tau, each of which shall have three.
(d) One hundred sixteen for the purpose of providing support to the commission headquarters and its teams.

Article 9

(a) The international commission, and each of its teams, shall act as a single body comprising representatives of all four members.
(b) Each member has the responsibility to insure the presence of its representatives at all levels of the international commission. In case a representative is absent, the member concerned shall immediately designate a replacement.

Article 10

(a) The parties shall afford full cooperation, assistance and protection to the international commission.
(b) The parties shall at all times maintain regular and continuous liaison with the international commission. During the existence of the Four-Party Joint Military Com-

mission, the delegations of the parties to that commission shall also perform liaison functions with the international commission. After the Four-Party Joint Military Commission has ended its activities, such liaison shall be maintained through the Two-Party Joint Military Commission, liaison missions or other adequate means.

(c) The international commission and the Joint Military Commissions shall closely cooperate with and assist each other in carrying out their respective functions.

(d) Wherever a team is stationed or operating, the concerned party shall designate a liaison officer to the team to cooperate with and assist it in carrying out without hindrance its task of control and supervision. When a team is carrying out an investigation, a liaison officer from each concerned party shall have the opportunity to accompany it, provided the investigation is not thereby delayed.

(e) Each party shall give the international commission reasonable advance notice of all proposed actions concerning those provisions of the agreement that are to be controlled and supervised by the international commission.

(f) The international commission, including its teams, is allowed such movement for observation as is reasonably required for the proper exercise of its functions as stipulated in the agreement. In carrying out these functions, the international commission, including its teams, shall enjoy all necessary assistance and cooperation from the parties concerned.

Article 11

In supervising the holding of the free and democratic general elections described in Articles 9 (b) and 12 (b) of the agreement in accordance with modalities to be agreed upon between the National Council of National Reconciliation and Concord and the international commission, the latter shall receive full cooperation and assistance from the national council.

Article 12

The international commission and its personnel who have the nationality of a member state shall, while carrying out their tasks, enjoy privileges and immunities equivalent to those accorded diplomatic missions and diplomatic agents.

Article 13

The international commission may use the means of communication and transport necessary to perform its functions. Each South Vietnamese party shall make available for rent to the international commission appropriate office and accommodation facilities and shall assist it in obtaining such facilities. The international commission may receive from the parties, on mutually agreeable terms, the necessary means of communication and transport and may purchase from any source necessary equipment and services not obtained from the parties. The international commission shall possess these means.

Article 14

The expenses for the activities of the international commission shall be borne by the parties and the members of the international commission in accordance with the provisions of this article:

(a) Each member country of the international commission shall pay the salaries and allowances of its personnel.

(b) All other expenses incurred by the international commission shall be met from a fund to which each of the four parties shall contribute twenty-three per cent (23%) and to which each member of the international commission shall contribute two per cent (2%).

(c) Within 30 days of the date of entry into force of this protocol, each of the four parties shall provide the international commission with an initial sum equivalent to four million five hundred thousand (4,500,00) French francs in convertible currency, which sum shall be credited against the amounts due from that party under the first budget.

(d) The international commission shall prepare its own budgets. After the international commission approves a budget, it shall transmit it to all parties signatory to the agreement for their approval. Only after the budgets have been approved by the four parties to the agreement shall they be obliged to make their contributions. However, in case the parties to the agreement do not agree on a new budget, the international commission shall temporarily base its expenditures on the previous budget, except for the extraordinary, one-time expenditures for installation or for the acquisition of equipment, and the parties shall continue to make their contributions on that basis until a new budget is approved.

Article 15

(a) The headquarters shall be operational and in place within 24 hours after the cease-fire.

(b) The regional teams shall be operational and in place, and three teams for supervision and control of the return of the captured and detained personnel shall be operational and ready for dispatch within 48 hours after the cease-fire.

(c) Other teams shall be operational and in place within 15 to 30 days after the cease-fire.

Article 16

Meetings shall be convened at the call of the chairman. The international commission shall adopt other working procedures appropriate for the effective discharge of its functions and consistent with respect for the sovereignty of South Vietnam.

Article 17

The members of the international commission may accept the obligations of this protocol by sending notes of acceptance to the four parties signatory to the agreement. Should a member of the international commission decide to withdraw from the international commission, it may do so by giving three months' notice by means of notes to the four parties to the agreement, in which case those four parties shall consult among themselves for the purpose of agreeing upon a replacement member.

Article 18

This protocol shall enter into force upon signature by plenipotentiary representatives of all the parties participating in the Paris conference on Vietnam. It shall be strictly implemented by all the parties concerned.

Done in Paris this 27th day of January, 1973, in Vietnamese and English. The Vietnamese and English texts are officially and equally authentic.

For the Government of the *United States of America* *William P. Rogers* *Secretary of State*	*For the Government of the* *Democratic Republic of Vietnam* *Nguyen Duy Trinh* *Minister for Foreign Affairs*
For the Government of the *Republic of Vietnam* *Tran Van Lam* *Minister for Foreign Affairs*	*For the Provisional* *Revolutionary Government of* *the Republic of South Vietnam* *Nguyen Thi Binh* *Minister for Foreign Affairs*

2-PARTY VERSION
PROTOCOL TO THE AGREEMENT
ON ENDING THE WAR AND
RESTORING PEACE IN VIETNAM
CONCERNING THE
INTERNATIONAL COMMISSION OF
CONTROL AND SUPERVISION

The Government of the United States of America, with the concurrence of the Government of the Republic of Vietnam,

The Government of the Democratic Republic of Vietnam, with the concurrence of the Provisional Revolutionary Government of the Republic of South Vietnam,

In implementation of Article 18 of the Agreement on Ending the War and Restoring Peace in Vietnam signed on this date providing for the formation of the International Commission of Control and Supervision,

Have agreed as follows:

[Text of protocol Articles 1-17 same as above]

Article 18

The Protocol to the Paris Agreement on Ending the War and Restoring Peace in Vietnam concerning the International Commission of Control and Supervision shall enter into force upon signature of this document by the Secretary of State of the Government of the United States of America and the Minister for Foreign Affairs of the Government of the Democratic Republic of Vietnam, and upon signature of a document in the same terms by the Secretary of State of the Government of the

United States of America, the Minister for Foreign Affairs of the Government of the Republic of Vietnam, the Minister for Foreign Affairs of the Government of the Democratic Republic of Vietnam and the Minister for Foreign Affairs of the Provisional Revolutionary Government of the Republic of South Vietnam. The protocol shall be strictly implemented by all the parties concerned.

Done in Paris this 27th day of January, 1973, in Vietnamese and English. The Vietnamese and English texts are official and equally authentic.

<table>
<tr><td>For the Government of the
United States of America
William P. Rogers
Secretary of State</td><td>For the Government of the
Democratic Republic of Vietnam
Nguyen Duy Trinh
Minister for Foreign Affairs</td></tr>
</table>

PROTOCOL ON THE PRISONERS
PROTOCOL TO THE AGREEMENT ON ENDING THE WAR AND RESTORING PEACE IN VIETNAM CONCERNING THE RETURN OF CAPTURED MILITARY PERSONNEL AND FOREIGN CIVILIANS AND CAPTURED AND DETAINED VIETNAMESE CIVILIAN PERSONNEL

The parties participating in the Paris conference on Vietnam,

In implementation of Article 8 of the Agreement on Ending the War and Restoring Peace in Vietnam signed on this data providing for the return of captured military personnel and foreign civilians, and captured and detained Vietnamese civilian personnel,

Have agreed as follows:

THE RETURN OF CAPTURED MILITARY PERSONNEL AND FOREIGN CIVILIANS

Article 1

The parties signatory to the agreement shall return the captured military personnel of the parties mentioned in Article 8 (a) of the agreement as follows:

¶All captured military personnel of the United States and those of the other foreign countries mentioned in Article 3 (a) of the agreement shall be returned to United States authorities.

¶All captured Vietnamese military personnel, whether belonging to regular or irregular armed forces, shall be returned to the two South Vietnamese parties; they shall be returned to that South Vietnamese party under whose command they served.

Article 2

All captured civilians who are nationals of the United States or of any other foreign countries mentioned in Article 3 (a) of the agreement shall be returned to United

States authorities. All other captured foreign civilians shall be returned to the authorities of their country of nationality by any one of the parties willing and able to do so.

Article 3

The parties shall today exchange complete lists of captured persons mentioned in Article 1 and 2 of this protocol.

Article 4

(a) The return of all captured persons mentioned in Articles 1 and 2 of this protocol shall be completed within 60 days of the signing of the agreement at a rate no slower than the rate of withdrawal from South Vietnam of United States forces and those of the other foreign countries mentioned in Article 5 of the agreement.

(b) Persons who are seriously ill, wounded or maimed, old persons and women shall be returned first. The remainder shall be returned either by returning all from one detention place after another or in order of their dates of capture, beginning with those who have been held the longest.

Article 5

The return and reception of the persons mentioned in Articles 1 and 2 of this protocol shall be carried out at places convenient to the concerned parties. Places of return shall be agreed upon by the Four-Party Joint Military Commission. The parties shall insure the safety of personnel engaged in the return and reception of those persons.

Article 6

Each party shall return all captured persons mentioned in Articles 1 and 2 of this protocol without delay and shall facilitate their return and reception. The detaining parties shall not deny or delay their return for any reason, including the fact that captured persons may, on any grounds, have been prosecuted or sentenced.

THE RETURN OF CAPTURED AND DETAINED VIETNAMESE CIVILIAN PERSONNEL

Article 7

(a) The question of the return of Vietnamese civilian personnel captured and detained in South Vietnam will be resolved by the two South Vietnamese parties on the basis of the principles of Article 21 (b) of the agreement on the Cessation of Hostilities in Vietnam of July 20, 1954, which reads as follows:

"The term 'civilian internees' is understood to mean all persons who, having in any way contributed to the political and armed struggle between the two parties, have been arrested for that reason and have been kept in detention by either party during the period of hostilities."

(b) The two South Vietnamese parties will do so in a spirit of national reconciliation and concord with a view to ending hatred and enmity in order to ease suffering and to reunite families. The two South Vietnamese parties will do their utmost to resolve this question within 90 days after the cease-fire comes into effect.

(c) Within 15 days after the cease-fire comes into effect, the two South Vietnamese parties shall exchange lists of the Vietnamese civilian personnel captured and detained by each party and lists of the places at which they are held.

TREATMENT OF CAPTURED
PERSONS DURING DETENTION

Article 8

(a) All captured military personnel of the parties and captured foreign civilians of the parties shall be treated humanely at all times, and in accordance with international practice.

They shall be protected against all violence to life and person, in particular against murder in any form, mutilation, torture and cruel treatment, and outrages upon personal dignity. These persons shall not be forced to join the armed forces of the detaining party.

They shall be given adequate food, clothing, shelter and the medical attention required for their state of health. They shall be allowed to exchange postcards and letters with their families and receive parcels.

(b) All Vietnamese civilian personnel captured and detained in South Vietnam shall be treated humanely at all times, and in accordance with international practice.

They shall be protected against all violence to life and person, in particular against murder in any form, mutilation, torture and cruel treatment, and outrages against personal dignity. The detaining parties shall not deny or delay their return for any reason including the fact that captured persons may, on any grounds, have been prosecuted or sentenced. These persons shall not be forced to join the armed forces of the detaining party.

They shall be given adequate food, clothing, shelter and the medical attention required for their state of health. They shall be allowed to exchange postcards and letters with their families and receive parcels.

Article 9

(a) To contribute to improving the living conditions of the captured military personnel of the parties and foreign civilians of the parties, the parties shall, within 15 days after the cease-fire comes into effect, agree upon the designation of two or more national Red Cross societies to visit all places where captured military personnel and foreign civilians are held.

(b) To contribute to improving the living conditions of the captured and detained Vietnamese civilian personnel, the two South Vietnamese parties shall, within 15 days after the cease-fire comes into effect, agree upon the designation of two or more national Red Cross societies to visit all places where the captured and detained Vietnamese civilian personnel are held.

Have agreed as follows:
[Text of protocol Articles 1-13 same as above]

Article 14

The protocol to the Paris Agreement on Ending the War and Restoring Peace in Vietnam concerning the Return of Captured Military Personnel and Foreign Civilians and Captured and Detained Vietnamese Civilian Personnel shall enter into force upon signature of this document by the Secretary of State of the Government of the United States of America and the Minister for Foreign Affairs of the Government of the Democratic Republic of Vietnam, and upon signature of a document in the same terms by the Secretary of State of the Government of the United States of America, the Minister for Foreign Affairs of the Government of the Republic of Vietnam, the Minister for Foreign Affairs of the Government of the Democratic Republic of Vietnam and the Minister for Foreign Affairs of the Provisional Revolutionary Government of the Republic of South Vietnam. The protocol shall be strictly implemented by all the parties concerned.

Done in Paris this 27th day of January, 1973, in Vietnamese and English. The Vietnamese and English texts are official and equally authentic.

For the Government of the
United States of America
William P. Rogers
Secretary of State

For the Government of the
Democratic Republic of Vietnam
Nguyen Duy Trinh
Minister for Foreign Affairs

ACKNOWLEDGEMENTS

"United States Position on India-Pakistan War," Copyright © 1972 by Newsweek Inc., reprinted by permission.

Reminiscences, Copyright © 1964 by Douglas MacArthur. Reprinted by permission of McGraw-Hill Book Company.

"A Viet Nam Reappraisal: The Personal History of One Man's View and How It Evolved," by Clark M. Clifford. Copyright © 1969 by the Council on Foreign Relations, Inc., New York. Reprinted by permission of Foreign Affairs.

INDEX

A

Abbott, George M., 722
Abrams, Gen. Creighton W., 539, 552, 562, 646
Acheson, Dean, 158, 160, 172, 191, 370-79,
    passim, 402-03, 451, 789
  on China, Communist (1941-49), 106-07
  on China Lobby, 191-99
  on China, Nationalist (1941-49), 158-59
  on Lattimore, 176
  on U.S.-Asian foreign policy, 357-64
  on Vincent, John Carter, 165
Aichi, Kiichi, 100, 762, 765
Aleutians, 362, 384
Ali Kahn, Liaquat, 735
Allied Council for Japan, 3, 18-21, *passim*
Allison, John, 73, 451
Amami Islands, 762
Amendment to the United States-Philippine
    Military Bases Agreement *see*
    Philippines, U.S.
Amerasia, 170-89, *passim*
American China Policy Association, Inc., 171
Anderson, Jack, 785
Anderson, Vernice, 390-91
Annam, 445
arms control, arms limitations, and disarmament
  Japan, 8
Arnold, A.V., 344
Asia
  Nixon Doctrine, 99
  and U.S.S.R., 361
  and U.S.
    Acheson on, 357-64
    Bundy on, 276
    Green on, 789-92
    Johnson, L.B. on, 512-14
    Johnson, U.A. on, 97
    Rusk on, 327

Asian Development Bank, 98
Associated States of Indochina, 452-53
Atcheson, George, 167
  on China, Communist (1941-49), 106-10
Auriol, Vincent, 573
Austin, Warren, 366, 682
  on Korea, 367-68
Australia, 370, 380, 386, 546
  and Korea, 355

B

Baghdad Pact, 741
  see also India, U.S.
Bahadur, Lal, 756
Bailey, Charles W., 772
Bao Dai, 445
Barnett, A. Doak, 305
Bartch, Carl, 645
Berlin Conference, 18, 64
Bevin, Ernest, 128-29
Bidault, M., 454
Bingham, Jonathan B., 690
Bisson, T.A., 172
Bonin Islands, 51, 53, 79-94, *passim,* 762
  and Japan, 93
Bowles, Chester, 642-43
Bradley, Gen. Omar, 370-71, 388-403, *passim*
Bray, Charles W., 769
Brazil, 380
Bridges
  on Vincent, John Carter, 165-73
Brinkley, David, 484
Bruce, David K.E., 780-81
Bundy, William P., 276, 669
Bunker, Ellsworth, 646, 699

Burma, 359
Bush, George, 786
Byrnes, James, 9, 116-19, *passim,* 128, 167,
    171, 662
  on Lattimore, 176
Buddhists, 483
Bundenz, Louis F., 187

C

Cairo Declaration (1943), 7, 51, 53, 119
  on China, Nationalist (1941-49), 7-8, 51, 119
  on Japan, 7-8
  on Korea, 7, 8, 339, 345
  on Manchuria, 7
  on Pescadores Islands, 7
  on Taiwan, 7
Cambodia, 453, 472, 476, 477, 570
  border areas
    Kennedy, J.F. on, 632-34
  and China, Communist (1950-59), 625
  and French Union, 451
  and French Union and Associated States, 477
  Geneva Conference (1954), 627-29
  neutrality
    Nixon on, 645
    Rusk on, 639
    Sihanouk on, 631-32
  Southeast Asia Treaty Organization, 630
  and U.S., 633-35, 641-42
    Bowles on, 643-44
    Dulles on, 630
    Goldberg on, 640-41
    Nixon on, 646-56
    Rogers on, 644
    Rusk on, 639-40
    Stevenson on, 635-38
    see also Vietnam war
  and Vietnam, South, 625, 633
    Vietnam war, Stevenson on, 638-39
Canada, 82
Case, Clifford, 531
Central Treaty Organization *see* Pakistan
Ceylon, 359
Chan Chak, 106
Chang Chun, 152
Chang Hsueh-liang, 133
Chang Tso-liu, 135
Chen Yi, 261, 591
Cheng Heng, 625, 645
Chiang Kai-shek, 17, 103-23, *passim,* 127, 137,
    145, 155, 168, 172, 177, 181-82,
    387-88, 400
  Stuart on, 152, 157
Chiang Kai-shek, Madam, 191
China, central government *see* China, Nationalist
    (1941-49)
China
  civil war *see* China, Communist (1941-49);
    China, Nationalist (1941-49)

  see also United States and China, Com-
    munist (1941-49), U.S. and China,
    Nationalist (1941-49)
  and Korea, 339
  and India, 448
  and Indonesia, 448
  internal problems, 103, 109, 122, 129-30
    see also China, Communist (1941-49);
      China, Nationalist (1941-49); U.S.
      and China, Communist (1941-49);
      U.S. and China, Nationalist (1941-49)
  Japanese evacuation, 129
  Japanese occupation, 109
  and U.S., Open Door Policy, 103
China Aid Act *see* U.S., China Aid Program
China, Communist (1941-49)
  and Cambodia, 625
  Chiang Kai-shek on, 124
  and Laos, 569
  and Manchuria, Koo on, 122-23
  Marshall on, 153-55
  P.C.C. *see* Political Consultative Conference
  Stuart on, 133
  and U.S.S.R., 108-09
    Acheson on, 107-09
    Chiang Kai-shek on, 155
  and U.S.,
    Acheson on, 106-10
    Marshall on, 123, 153-55
    Truman on, 119-21, 121-22, 128-32, 132
  and Vietnam, North, 480
  Wedemeyer on, 136-37, 142-50
    see also U.S. and China, Communist (1941-49)
China, Communist (1950-59), 495, 499, 582
  Eisenhower on, 211
  and India, 448, 746
  and Indonesia, 448
  and Japan, U.S.S.R. on, 52
  and Korea, U.N. on, 381
  and Korean war, 375, 381, 391, 393, 394-95
  and Laos, U.S. on, 580-83, *passim*
  Sino-Indian Border war, 745-46
  and Taiwan, 440
  and Taiwan Straits Crisis, 241
  and Tibet, 448
  and U.S.S.R.
    Treaty of Friendship and Alliance, 162-64
  and U.S.
    ambassadorial talks, 236-39
    mutual exchange of civilians, 216-20
  and Viet Minh, 450
  and Vietnam war, 495, 499, 500
    see also U.S. and China, Communist (1950-59)
China, Communist (1960-68)
  and India,
    Harriman on, 749-50
    Johnson, L.B. on, 495
    Stevenson on, 751
  and Japan, 79
  Johnson, L.B. on, 85
  nuclear weapons
    Johnson on, 90, 282-83
    Rusk on, 279

Sato on, 90
and Tibet, 448
U.S. on, 495
and U.S.
   admission to U.N. question, 104
   and Vietnam war
      Clifford on, 546
      Rusk on, 498-99
   see also U.S. and China, Communist (1960-68)
China, Communist (1971), 768
   and India, 775
   and Japan, 775
   and Korea, North, 775
   and Pakistan, 775
   and Taiwan, 776
   and U.N., admission question, U.S. on, 770
   and U.S.
      exchange of athletic teams, 769-70
      Nixon on, 771-72
      Nixon visit, 767
      Nixon visit, Nixon on, 772-73
      "Ping Pong Diplomacy," 769
      U.N. question, Rogers on, 773
   see also U. S. and China, Communist (1971)
China, Communist (1972)
   and U.S.
      Nixon visit, Nixon on, Chou En-lai on,
         774-77
China lobby see U.S.
China, Nationalist (1941-49), 106-10, passim
   Cairo Declaration, 7-8, 51, 119, 345
   and China, Communist, Chiang Kai-shek on,
      124
   and Japan, 53
   and Manchuria
      Cairo Declaration on, 7
      P.C.C. see Political Consultative
         Conference
   and Pescadores Islands
      Cairo Declaration on, 7
   Potsdam Proclamation, 119
   President see Chiang Kai-shek
   Sino-Soviet Treaty, 119
   and Taiwan, Cairo Declaration on, 7
   Treaty of Friendship with U.S.S.R., 113-15
   and U.S.S.R., 113
      Treaty of Friendship, 113-15
   and U.S., 53
      Acheson on, 158-59, 160-61
      Chiang Kai-shek on, 124, 155
      Marshall on, 153-55
      Political Consultative Conference,
         Truman on, 132
      Stuart on, 133, 151, 157-58
      Truman on, 119-121, 121-22, 128-32,
         156-57
      Wedemeyer on, 136-40, 142-50
   see also U.S. and China, Nationalist (1941-49)
China, Nationalist (1950-59)
   Truman on, 387-88
   and U.S.
      China Lobby, 199-207
      Eisenhower on, 210-13

see also U.S. and China, Nationalist (1950-59)
China, Nationalist (1971)
   and U.S., Nixon on, 772
China, People's Republic of see China,
      Communist (1950-59), (1960-68),
      (1970-71)
China, Republic of Free see China, Nationalist
      (1950-59), (1960-68), (1970-71)
Choe Tok-sin, 428
Chou En-lai, 117, 124, 162, 164, 214, 215, 256,
      261, 546, 746, 772, 774
Chung Hee Park
   on Korea, South, 428
Church, Frank, 529
Churchill, Winston, 109, 111-112
Chu Teh, 105
Clark, Joseph, 534
Clifford, Clark M., 540
Cochin China, 445
Cohen, Theodore, 172
communism
   China, 103-10, passim, 116-17, 126, 130,
      Johnson, L.B. on, Sato on, 85
   Indochina, 445
   Indonesia, 677
   Japan, 4, 78
   U.S.S.R., 360
Connally, Tom, 158
Connor, John T., 89
Convention of St. Germain-en-Lave, 57
Cormier, Frank, 770-71
Council Under the United States-Philippine
      Mutual Defense Treaty see
      Philippines, U.S.
Cowan, Myron M., 715
Crimea Conference see Yalta Conference
Cronkite, Walter, 483
Cuba, 380, 490

D

Daito Islands, 762-63
Dalai Lama, 256, 262
Declaration of Honolulu see Thailand, U.S.
Declaration on the Neutrality of Laos, 597-99
Declaration of Tashkent, 754-56
   see also India, Pakistan
"De Facto" Argument see U.S. and China,
      Communist (1950-59)
de Gaulle, Charles
   on U.S. in Vietnam war, 507
De Palma, Samuel, 786-87
Derevyanko, Kuzma
   on U.S. labor policy in Japan, 47-48
de Toledano, Ralph, 188
Dhanarajata Srisdt, 664
Diem, Ngo Dinh, 446-47, 477-84, passim
   on U.S. aid to Vietnam, South, 479-80
Dienbienphu, 454
Dillingham, Walter F., 173

Dillon, Douglas, 261
Djarkata *see* Indonesia
DMZ *see* demilitarized zone
"domino theory," 484, 545
    see also Vietnam, South
DRV (Democratic Republic of Vietnam) *see*
    Vietnam, North
Dulles, John Foster, 50, 52, 210, 214, 220-21,
    254, 261, 454, 479, 663, 686, 687,
    689, 714, 719, 743, 762
    on Cambodia, 630

E

Economic Commission for Asia and the Far
    East, 98
Eden, Anthony, 111
Eisenhower, Dwight D., 210, 220, 250, 252,
    393, 473, 489, 520, 586, 650, 723,
    736, 740
    on China, Nationalist (1950-59), 209-13
    on Kishi's views on nuclear weapons test, 74
    on Korea, 414-16
    on Taiwan Crisis, 210-13
    on Vietnam, South, 447, 477-80, 500
Engle, Clair, 256
Ethiopia, 370
European Economic Community, 83
Export-Import Bank, 131

F

Fairbank, John K., 308
Far Eastern Advisory Commission, 3, 18-20,
    passim, 41-51, *passim*
Farley, Miriam, 172
Field, Frederich, 174, 177
Finletter, Thomas, 371
Formosa *see* Taiwan
Formosa Crisis *see* Taiwan Crisis; China,
    Nationalist (1950-59)
Four Power Discussion on Korea *see* Korean
    war
Fowler, Henry, 543
France, 366, 450, 569
    and Associated States of Indochina, 452-53,
        477
    Geneva Conference (1954), 471
    and Ho Chi Minh, 446
    and Indochina, 454
    and Indochina war, 446
    and Laos, 569, 573
        Treaty of Amity with Laos, 573-74
        French Union and Laos, 573, 586
    and Vietnam, 445-46

"Free China," *see* China, Nationalist (1950-59)
French Union and Associated States, 450-54
    and U.S.
        Eisenhower on, 477-79
French Union of Cambodia, Laos, and Vietnam
        see French Union of Associated States
Fulbright, J. William, 275, 499, 524, 671

G

Garcia, Carlos, 723
Gayn, Mark, 184, 186
General Assembly *see* United Nations
Geneva Conference (1954), 409, 411-12, 422,
    454, 471, 477, 481, 490, 509, 511,
    518, 569, 575
Geneva Conference on Cambodia (1954), 627-
    29, 636
Geneva Conference on Indochina (1954), 584-85
    and U.K., 590
    and U.S.S.R., 590
Geneva Conference on Laos (1954), 575-79,
    597, 598, 600
    Rusk on, 590-96
Geneva Conference on Vietnam (1954), 501-02,
    504-05, 516, 549
    Smith, W.B. on, 472
Geneva Conference (1962), 490, 509
Geneva Conference on Laos (1962), 570, 597-
    99, 599-605, 606, 616, 620
    U.S. on, 612
Geneva Conference on Vietnam (1962), 550
Geneva Conference (1964), 555
George, Walter F., 165
Ghandhi, Indira, 786
Gillmore, Gen. W.N., 664
Goa
    and India
        Stevenson on, 743-45
Goldberg, Arthur, 509, 640, 752, 753
    on India-Pakistan dispute, 752-53
    on U.S.S. *Pueblo,* 431-35
    on Vietnam, 503
Goldwater, Barry, 488
Gore, Albert, 533
Grady, Henry F., 173
Great Britain *see* United Kingdom
Greece, 354
Green, Marshall, 283, 301, 668
Green, Theodore F., 251
Grew, Joseph, 171-73
Gromyko, Andrei
    on Korea, 407
Guam, 383
Gulf of Tonkin Incident, 488, 525
Gulf of Tonkin Resolution, 447
    Fulbright on, 525

H

Hague Agreement *see* Indonesia, Netherlands
Hamilton Wright Organization, Inc., 199, 205, 207
Harriman, W. Averell, 110, 286, 387, 390, 392, 402-03, 595, 613, 617, 748-49
Harriman-Nitze Mission to India, 747-48
Harrison, William K., 424
Hashimoto, Kinji, 48
Hawaii, 383
Helms, Richard M., 543, 785-88, *passim*
Herter, Christian, 229, 255
Hickerson, John, 371
Hilsman, Roger, 267, 289
Hinton, Harold C., 294
Hirohito, Emperor, 9, 17, 78
Hiss, Alger, 104, 175
Hitler, Adolph, 371
Hoa Hao, 486
Ho Chi Minh, 445-47, *passim,* 521, 583, 782
  and Indochinese Communist Party, 445
  on truce with France, 451
  on U.S. policy in Vietnam war, 505
  and Viet Minh, 445
  on Vietnam war, 504
Ho Chi Minh Trail, 570, 612-21, *passim*
Hoffman, Paul G., 173
Hokkaido, 8
Ho Kuo Kuang, 106
Holt, Harold, 508
Holyoake, Keith, 508
Honshu, 8
Hsinhua News Agency
  on Sukarno, ouster of, 700
Hsiung Shih-hui, 133
Hull, Cordell, 175
Hurley, Gen. Patrick, 103-07, 110-11, 117, 167, 171-72, 181-87, *passim*
  on China, Communist (1941-49), 105, 110
  on China, Nationalist (1941-49), 110
  interview with Joseph Stalin on China problem, 110-11
  resignation, 115, 117
    Truman on, 115-17
  on U.S. State Department, 115
Huk Rebellion *see* Philippines
Huntley, Chet, 484
Huong, 546

I

I.C.R.C. *see* International Committee of the Red Cross
Ikeda, Hayato, 81
  Joint Communiqué on U.S.-Japanese relations, 78

Inchon, 340
India, 359, 360, 448
  Baghdad Pact, 741
  and China, Communist, 746, 749-50, 775
    Rusk on, 748
  Declaration of Tashkent, 754-56
  and Goa
    Stevenson on, 743-45
  Harriman-Nitze Mission, 747-48
  independence
    Mountbatten on, 735
    Truman on, 735
  and Pakistan
    Johnson, L.B. on, 753-54
  and Pakistan-Kashmir dispute, 733
  Pakistan-Kashmir dispute
    Goldberg on, 752
    Stevenson on, 751-52
  Sino-Indian Border war
    Nehru on, 745-46
  Southeast Asia Treaty Organization, 741
  and U.S.S.R.
    Harriman on, 749-50
  and U.S., 756-57, 775
    Dulles on, 741-43
    Kennedy on, 749
    Rusk on, 746-47
India-Pakistan war
  and Jordan, 787
  Pakistan, East
    U.S. on, 785-88
  and Saudi Arabia, 787
  U.S. on, 785-88
Indochina, 366, 373, 375, 393, 445, 446, 450-54, *passim,* 507
  Armistice Agreements (1954), 455-71
  Associated States, 452-53
  Communist Party, 445
  and France, 446
  and U.S., 774
  and U.S., Nixon on, 778-81
Indochina war, 569
Indonesia, 359-60, 386, 448, 546
  communists, 677
  Hague Agreement, 677
  Linggadjati Agreement, 680
  and Malaysia, 677
  Manila Agreement, 699
  and Netherlands, 677
  Peace Corps, 699
  Renville Agreement, 680-83, *passim*
  Tokyo Agreement, 699
  and U.N., 677, 679
  U.N. Commission for, 680-81
  and U.S., 700-01
    Austin on, 682-85
    Bunker on, 699
    closing of U.S.I.A. Libraries, 697
    Rusk on, 693-94, 698
    Soebandrio on, 690

Indonesia (*cont.*)
    West New Guinea dispute, 692
    Bingham on, 690-91
    and West Irian, 677
    West New Guinea Question, Bingham on,
       690-91
"inevitability" argument *see* U.S. and China,
    Communist (1950-59), 225
Inner Mongolia, 376
Institute of Pacific Relations, 172-77, *passim*,
    184-87, *passim*
International Commission for Supervision and
    Control in Laos, 588, 590, 600
International Committee of the Red Cross, 409
International Control Commission Vietnam
    war, 490, 571, 607, 618, 637, 643
International Court of Justice, 65

J

Jaffe, Philip, 172-86, *passim*
Japan, 113-14, 362, 376, 382-93, *passim*, 448,
    546
    Allied Council for Japan, 3
    allied occupation, 8
    armed forces, after World War II, 16
    arms control, arms limitation, and
       disarmament, 4
    and Asia, 84-85, 448
    and Bonin Islands, 86-91, *passim*
    and China, Communist (1960-68), 79
    and China, Communist (1972)
       Nixon on, 775
    constitution, 4, 22-40
    economy, 13-14, 44-46, 83
    evacuation of China, 129
    Far Eastern Advisory Commission, 3
    and Korea, 339, 345, 353
    and Manchuria, 7
    nuclear weapons tests, 73
    occupation of China, 109
    and Okinawa, 94-95
    and Pescadores Islands, 7
    reparations, 42, 45, 60-61
    and Ryukyu Islands, 86-93, *passim*
    surrender terms, 9
    and Taiwan, 7, 385
    and Thailand, 662
    Treaty of Friendship between China,
       Nationalist-U.S.S.R., 113
    and U.N., 55-56
    and U.S., 100
       agreement on Ryukyu and Daito Islands
          Rogers on, 762-66
       Derevyanko on, 47-48, Ikeda on, 78,
          Johnson, U.A. on, 766-68
       initial post-surrender policy, 10-12

Treaty of Mutual Cooperation and
    Security, 100
    and Vietnam, 445
    war crimes and trials, 8, 12, 58
Japanese Peace Treaty, 49
Java *see* United Nations
Jessup, Philip, 390-92
Jogjakarta *see* Indonesia
Johnson, Louis, 370-71
Johnson, Lyndon B., 93-94, 282, 538, 542,
    664, 699, 726, 728, 753, 762
    on Asia, 512-14
    on election of Ryukyuan Chief Executive, 87
    joint communiqué with Eisaku Sato, 85,
       90-93
    and Paul VI, Pope, 522
    refusal of re-nomination, 538
    on U.S.S. *Pueblo*, 437
    on Vietnam, South, 486-87
    on Vietnam war, 447, 488-90, 491-98, 500-
       01, 505-06, 519-22, 536-38
Johnson, U. Alexis, 215-218, *passim*, 766
    on Japan, 82-85
    on U.S. relations with the Far East, 96-100
Joint Thai-United States Committee *see*
    Thailand, United States
Jones, F. Howard P., 689-90

K

Katzenbach, Nicholas, 329, 543
Kearney, James F., 187
Kennan, George, 182, 183
Kennedy, John F., 81, 482, 484, 520, 529,
    530, 596, 610, 631, 650, 664, 667,
    695, 747, 749
    on Cambodia border areas, 632-34
    joint communiqué on U.S.-Japanese
       relations, 78
    on Korea, South, 428
    on Laos, 570, 587, 592
    on Macapagal's visit to U.S., 724-25
    on Ryukyu Islands, 79
    on Vietnam, South, 447, 482, 483-84, 485,
       500
Kennedy, Robert F., 693, 695
Khan, M.A., 756
Khanh, Nguyen, 487
"Khmer Serei," 633
Khrushchev, Nikita, 241, 546, 592, 596, 610,
    750
Kim Il Sung, 339
Kishi, Nobusuke, 73
Kissinger, Henry, 772, 774, 786-88, *passim*
Kittikachorn, Thanom, 508, 671-72
Kohlberg, Alfred, 187
Koo, V.K. Wellington, 122, 156

on Marshall's mission to China, 122
Korea, 7, 54, 64, 79, 360, 375, 389-90, 450
    Cairo Declaration, 345
    elections, 349
    Japan, 339, 353
    independence problem, 348-55, *passim*
    Potsdam Proclamation (Declaration), 345
    U.S.-U.S.S.R. Joint Commission on, 344,
        348
Korea, Democratic People's Republic of *see*
        Korea, North
Korea, North, 356. 373, 375, 439-40
    and China, Communist (1971), 775
    elections, 351
    on prisoners of war, 409-13
    and U.S.S. *Pueblo* 429-30, 438-39, 541
    see also Pueblo, U.S.S.
    and U.S.S.R., 339
        U.S.S.R. zone of occupation, 353
    and U.N., 354, 367
    and U.S., 354
    and Vietnam, 341
Korea, Republic of *see* Korea, South
Korea, South, 355-75, *passim,* 410, 414, 429,
        440, 546
    constitution, 339
    elections, 339-40, 350-54, *passim,* 379
    Five Year Economic Development Plan, 428
    Treaty of Mutual Defense with the U.S.,
        425-26
    and U.S., 339, 775, 784
    U.S.-U.S.S.R. Joint Commission on, 344, 348
Korean National Assembly *see* Korea, South,
        elections
Korean war, 104, 340, 365, 373, 446
    armistice, 340, 418-24, 431, 440
        procedural matters, 424
        publication of terms, 424
    and China, Communist, 340, 391, 393, 394,
        395
    and China, Communist
        MacArthur on, 396-97
        Truman on, 397
    demilitarized zone, 407-08
    Four Power discussion, 348
    invasion of Korea, South, 340, 365, 370-71
    joint U.S.-Korea, South Statement, 784
    Joint U.S.-U.S.S.R. Commission, 345-47
    military demarcation line, 418
    38th parallel, 339-53, *passim,* 367-418,
        passim
    and U.N., 339, 348-49, 351-53, 354, 356,
        365, 367-69, 372-73, 378-79, 381-83,
        391, 396, 398, 400, 405-13, 414-21,
        passim
Kosygin, Aleksei, 616
Koumintang *see* China, Nationalist (1941-49)
Koun Wick, 639
Kurile Islands, 51, 54, 375
    and U.S.S.R., 112

Ky, Nguyen Cao, 508, 546
Kyushu, 8

L

Laird, Melvin, 562, 645
Lam, 780
Laos, 453, 472, 476, 482, 490
    and China, Communist, 569, 580, 582, 583
    coalition agreement
        Kennedy on, 596-97
        Khrushchev on, 596
    Declaration of Neutrality (1962) and Protocol
        to *see* Geneva Conference on Laos
        (1962)
    and France, 569, 573
    and French Union, 451, 573, 586
    French Union and Associated States, 477
    Geneva Conference (1954), 569, 575-79,
        590
    Geneva Conference (1962), 570, 606
    Geneva Conference (1963), 490
    independence, 477, 573, 581
        Kennedy on, 587, 592
        Khrushchev on, 592
    and Indochina, 569
    Neo Lao Hak Xat Party, 581
    neutrality
        Kennedy on, 570
    and Southeast Asia Treaty Organization,
        587
    Souvanna Phouma, 612-13
    Treaty of Amity with France, 573-74
    U.K.-U.S.S.R. on, 588-90
    and U.S.S.R., 569, 580, 582, 583-84, 608-10
    and U.N., 569, 571, 580-81, 583, 588, 591
    and U.S., 580-81, 585-86, 610-11
        Kennedy on, 586-88, 616
        Rusk on, 590-96
        U.S.S.R. on, 580
    and Viet Minh, 663
    and Vietnam, North, 569, 570-71, 580, 582-
        83, 586, 612
        Harriman on, 613-15
        Nixon on, 617-22
        Rusk on, 606-08
        U.S. on, 782-83
Larsen, Samuel S., 188-89
Lattimore, Owen, 170, 172, 187
    investigation of, 173-81
    see also U.S. State Department Investigation
        of China policy royalty
Lattimore, Vincent, 172
League of Nations, 57
Letourneau, Jean, 450-51
Levine, Isaac Don, 188
Li Chi-shen, 107
Lie, Trygve, 382, 386, 388

Linggadjati Agreement *see* Indonesia
Lodge, Henry Cabot, 449, 485-87, *passim,*
    549, 560
Lon Nol, 625, 645
Lovett, Robert, 347
Luce, Henry, 172

M

MacArthur, Gen. Douglas A., 3-21, *passim,* 42,
    47, 167-73, *passim,* 340-93, *passim*
  on Chinese intervention in Korea, 394-95,
    396-97
  on Derevyanko's letter, 48-49
  on Korea, 399-400
  on meeting with Truman at Wake Island,
    392-93
  recall, 390
    Truman on, 401-03
  on U.S. strategic position in Pacific area,
    383-86
  on supremacy of U.N. forces in Korea, 399
  on surrender of North Korea, 388-89
McCarthy, Joseph, 173-90, *passim*
McCloskey, Robert J., 671
McCoy, Frank R.
  on U.S.-Japanese reparation policy, 42-47
McNamara, Robert S., 485-86, 542
Macapagal, 726
Ma Chan-shan, 135
Madura *see* United Nations
Magsaysay, Ramon, 720
Mainland China *see* China, Communist (1950-
    59), (1960-68), (1971)
Malaysia, 546
Malaysia-Indonesia Dispute,
  Kennedy, R., on, 693
  Philippines, 693
  Stevenson on, 694-97
Malik, Adam, 700
Malik, Jacob, 50, 52, 388
  on Korea, 406
Manchuria, 53, 116-55, *passim,* 361-97, *passim*
  and China, Communist (1941-49)
    Koo on, 122
    Truman on, 132
  Japanese aggression, 120
  and U.S., 120
Manila Agreement *see* Indonesia; U.S.
Manila Conference (1966), 508-09
Manila Pact (1954) *see* Thailand; U.S.
Mao Tse-tung, 116, 184, 223, 261, 546, 771,
    774
Marcos, Ferdinand E., 508, 726, 728
Marianas, 384
Marshall, Gen. George C., 104, 123-32, *passim,*
    153-77, *passim,* 346, 402-03

  on Communist China policy, 123
  on internal problems of China, 124-28
  on Joint Commission on Korea, 345
  on Lattimore, 176
  mission to China
    Koo on, 122-23
    Truman on, 118-19, 121-22, 129-30,
      130-32
  on re-call from China, 123
  on Wedemeyer's report to Truman, 150
Matsu Island, 240-53, *passim*
Matthews, Francis, 371
Mekong River Development Committee, 98
Meo, 571
Meyer, Armin H., 762-65, *passim*
Midway, 383
Mikoyan, Anastas, 583
Minh, Duong Van, 486
Molotov, V.M., 110, 113, 128, 345, 346
  on Korea, 347
Mongolian People's Republic *see* Outer Mongolia
Moorer, Thomas H., 786
Morgenthau, Hans, 309
Morse, Wayne, 191, 526
  on China Lobby, 191-99
Moscow *see* U.S.S.R.
Moscow Agreement *see* U.S.S.R.; U.S.
Mountbatten, Louis, 735
Muccio, John J., 371
Mukden, 134
Mundt, Karl, 528
Murphy, Charles, 392
Mussolini, Benito, 371

N

Nam Il, 424
NATO *see* North Atlantic Treaty Organization
NFLSV *see* National Front for the Liberation of
    South Vietnam; Vietnam War
National Front for the Liberation of South
    Vietnam, 501, 516, 519, 539, 554,
    556
Nehru, Jawarhalal, 588, 735-50, *passim*
Neilsen, Sivert A., 638
Neo Lao Hak Xat Party *see* Laos
Netherlands, 380
  Hague Agreement, 677
  and Indonesia, 677
  West New Guinea Question, Bingham on,
    690-91
New Zealand, 386, 546
Nitze, Paul, 543, 748
Nixon, Richard M., 100, 449, 549, 550-51,
    571, 645, 646, 651, 672, 720, 763,
    774
  and Asia, 98
    Green on, 789-92

on Indochina, 778-81
on Laos, 616-22
on Okinawa, 94-96
on U.S.-U.N. China policy, 770-72
on Vietnam War, 447, 551, 557, 617-22
"Vietnamization," 448, 561-62
on visit to China, Communist, 772-73
Nixon-Sato agreement, 99
Nong, Kimny, 630
North Atlantic Treaty Organization
and France, 454
Norway, 380
Nosavan, 584
nuclear weapons
China, Communist (1960-68), 280-82
Johnson, L.B. on, 282-83
Rusk on, 279
Nutter, B. Warren, 787

O

Ohira, 81
Okazaki, Katsuo, 73
Okinawa, 5, 79, 82-99, *passim,* 376-85, *passim*
762-66, *passim*
Sato on, 94-96
Voice of America facility, 762, 765
Open Door Policy *see* U.S., China
Outer Mongolia, 112, 361, 376

P

Pace, Frank, 371
Pacific Affairs, 174, 177, 178
Packard, David, 788
Pakistan, 357, 360, 380
Central Treaty Organization, 733
and China, Communist (1971), 775
Declaration of Tashkent, 754-56
independence
Truman on, 735
and India
Johnson, L.B. on, 753-54
and India-Kashmir Dispute, 733
Goldberg on, 752
Stevenson on, 751-52
India-Pakistan War
U.S. on, 785-88
Southeast Asia Treaty Organization, 733
and U.S., 740, 775
Eisenhower on, 740-41
Sahrawardy on, 740-41
and U.S. Alliance, 748
and U.S. Mutual Defense Agreement, 736-40

and U.S. Mutual Security Agreement, 741
Panchen Lama, 256
Panmunjom, 420
Paris, 449
Paris Peace Talks *see* Vietnam War
Park Chung Hee, 508
Pathet Lao, 482, 569-71, 578-87, *passim,*
606-18, *passim*
Patterson, John M., 171
Paul VI, Pope, 503
Pauley, Edwin W., 175
P.C.C. *see* Political Consultative Conference, 124
peace corps
Indonesia, 699
Thailand, 665
Peiping *see* China, Communist (1950-59)
Pell, Clairborne, 533
People's Consultative Conference *see* Political
Consultative Conference
Permanent Court of International Justice, 57
Pescadores Islands, 51-54, *passim,* 209-11, 242
Pham Van Dong, 501-02
Philippines, 359-60, 362-93, *passim*
Huk Rebellion, 705
independence, Truman Proclamation, 709
Republic of the Philippines Military
Assistance Act, 707-08
and U.S.,
Amendment on Military Bases
Agreement, 728
Bell Act, 705
Bell Commission, 713-15
Dulles on, 719
Eisenhower on, 723-24
Garcia on, 723-24
Johnson, L.B. on, 726-28, 728-30
Marcos on, 726-28, 728-30
Military Assistance Act, 707-08
Military Defense Board, 721-22
Mutual Defense Treaty, 717-19
Ramos on, 736
Rehabilitation Act, 705
Revised Trade Agreement, 719-20
Rusk on, 736
Treaty Defining Relations, 710-12
war damage claims, 725-26
Southeast Asia Treaty Organization, 705
Subic Bay, 722
"Ping Pong Diplomacy" *see* U.S. and China,
Communist (1971), China, Communist
(1971)
Plain Talk, 188
Political Consultative Conference, 168-69
China, Communist (1941-49)
Marshall on, 124-28
China, Nationalist (1941-49)
Chiang Kai-shek on, 124
Marshall on, 124-28
Portsmouth, Treaty of, 55
Portuguese Territories *see* Goa

Potsdam Proclamation (Declaration) 1945, 7-9,
    17-18, 41-56, *passim,* 119-20, 345
Pramoj M.R. Seni, 662
Protocol to the Declaration on the Neutrality
    of Laos, 610
Pueblo, U.S.S., 341, 429-30, 439-40
    Goldberg, Arthur on, 431-35
    Johnson, L.B. on, 437-39
    Rusk on, 438-39
Pyongyang, 391

Q

Quemoy, 211, 240, 245-53, *passim*

R

Radford, Arthur, 390, 392
Ramos, Narciso, 736
Red China *see* China, Communist (1941-49),
    (1950-59), (1960-68), (1971)
Reischauer, Edwin, 81
Renville Agreement *see* Indonesia, Netherlands
Republican party (U.S.)
    China policy, 375
Rhee, Syngman, 339
    on Korea, South, 416-18
    on United Nations ceasefire in Korea, 416
Richardson, Elliot, 334
Ridgway, Matthew B., 402
Rogers, William, 100, 555, 644
    on China, Communist, U.N. admission
        question, 773-74
    on U.S.-Japanese agreement on Ryukyu and
        Darto Islands, 762-66
Roosevelt, Franklin D., 103, 111-15, *passim,* 650
Ross, Charles, 117, 392
Rostow, Walt, 543
Roth, Andrew, 184
Rowan, Carl T., 697
Royall, Kenneth, 403
Rusk, Dean, 78, 89, 371, 521
    on Bonin Islands, 94
    on Cambodian neutrality, 639
    on China, Communist (1960-68)
        Free Asian Nations, 327-29
        Johnson Administration policy, 315-27
        nuclear weapons test, 279
    on India, 746-47
        China, Communist (1960-68) threat,
            748-49
    on Indonesia, 693, 698, 700
    on Laos, 590-96
    on U.S.S. *Pueblo,* 435, 438-39
    on Ryukyu Islands, 81, 94

on Thailand, 665-67
on Vietnam War, 481-82, 498-99, 606-08
Ryukyu Islands, 5, 51, 53, 79-87, *passim,*
    92-99, *passim,* 362, 376, 762, 763
    Rusk on, 81, 94

S

Sahrawardy, Hussein Shahud, 740
Sakhalin Island, 51
Saigon *see* Vietnam, South
Sato, Eisaku, 762-63, 93-100, *passim*
    joint communiqué with Lyndon B. Johnson,
        85, 90-93
    on Okinawa, 94-96
SCAP *see* Supreme Commander for Allied
        Powers
    see also MacArthur, Douglas A.
SEATO *see* Southeast Asia Treaty Organization
Serrano, Felixberto M., 722
Service, John Stewart, 172-73
    investigation of, 180-89
    see also U.S. State Department Investigations
        of Personnel on China Policy Loyalty
Shen, Sampson C., 202, 206
Sherman, Forrest, 371
Shikoku, 8
Shoup, David M., 525
Shtikov, T.F., 344
Sihanouk, Norodom, 588-92, *passim,* 609,
        633-46, *passim*
    on Cambodia
        neutrality, 631-32
    ouster, 652-53
Sinkiang, 361, 376
Singapore, 384, 546
Sino-Indian Border War *see* India, China
Sino-Soviet bloc
    and Laos, 582
Sino-Soviet Dispute *see* U.S.-Sino-Soviet Dispute
Sino-Soviet Treaty and Agreements, 119
Sino-Soviety Treaty of Friendship and Alliance,
        155
Sisavang Vong, 573
Sisco, Joseph J., 786, 788
Sisowath Sirik Matak, 625
Smith, Walter B., 472
Soebandrio, Raden, 689-90
Soekarno *see* Sukarno, 685
Son Sann, 643
Soong Family, 191
Soong, T.V., 172
Southeast Asia Collective Defense Treaty,
        473-76, 480, 489-91, 520, 666
    U.S. Congress on, 490-91
Southeast Asia Treaty Organization, 520, 669,
        733
    and Cambodia, 630

and India, 741
and Laos, 583, 587
and Pakistan, 733
and Philippines, 705
and Thailand, 659
Rusk on, 592
U.S., 741
Southeast Asian Ministerial Conference on
    Economic Development, 98
Souvanna Phouma, 569-71, 584-96, *passim,*
    607-21, *passim*
Soviet Union *see* Union of Soviet Socialist
    Republics
Sproul, Robert G., 173
Sprouse, Philip D., 632, 634
Stalin, Joseph, 110-12
    interview with Patrick Hurley on China
        problem, 110-11
Stettinius, Edward R., 111, 167
    on U.S.S.R. intervention in China, 111
Stevenson, Adlai E., 488, 641, 743, 751
    on Malaysia dispute, 694-98
    on Vietnam War (U.S.-Vietnam, South-
        Cambodia), 635-38
Stewart, Maxwell, 167
Stilwell, Gen. Joseph, 103, 182-86, *passim*
Stilwell, Richard, 671
Straits Agreement of Montreux, 57
Stuart, John L., 133, 151, 156-57
Sukarno, 546, 677, 685, 693, 699
    ouster of, 700
Sun Yat-sen, 120, 145
Supreme Commander for Allied Powers, 9-20,
    passim, 41-46, *passim*
    see also MacArthur, Douglas
Symington, Stuart, 532

T

Taft, Robert A.
    on U.S.-Korean policy, 373-76
Tai Li, 106
Taiwan, 51̇, 53-54, 104, 129, 138, 191, 200-01,
    209, 215, 219-20, 242, 261, 366,
    372-73, 375-76, 382-85, 388-400,
    passim, 448, 490, 546, 772
    and China, Communist (1971), 776
    and Japan, 385
    Joint Congressional Resolution on Defense,
        213-14
Taiwan Crisis
    Eisenhower on, 210-13
    see also China, Nationalist (1950-59)
Taiwan Straits, 372
Taiwan Straits Crisis, *see* U.S. and China,
    Communist (1950-59)
Taylor, George E., 298
Taylor, Gen. Maxwell D., 485, 542-43, 633

Tet holidays, 515-18, 530, 542
    see also Vietnam War
Thailand, 546, 570
    Declaration of Honolulu, 669
    Free Thai Movement, 662
    and Japan, 662
    Joint Thai-U.S. Committee, 666
    and Laos, 584
    liberation, Byrnes, J.F. on, 662
    Manila Pact (1954), Kennedy on, 667
    Potsdam Proclamation (Declaration), 661
    Southeast Asia Collective Defense Treaty,
        666
    Southeast Asia Treaty Organization, 659, 669
    and U.N., 661
    and U.S., 570, 584, 663-64, 668-70, 673
        Bundy on, 669-70
        Green on, 668
        Kennedy on, 672-73
        Kittikachorn on, 672
        nullification of declaration of war (1942),
            661
        State Department on, 671-72
Thanat Khoman, 665, 670, 673, 693
Thant, U *see* U Thant
Thay Sok, 644
Thieu, Nguyen Van, 508, 546, 552-55,
    passim, 652
Tibet, 262, 448
Tokyo Agreement *see* U.S., Indonesia
Treaty of Amity between France and Laos *see*
    Laos, France
Treaty of Friendship, Alliance and Mutual
    Assistance *see* China, Communist
    (1950-59), U.S.S.R.
Treaty of Friendship and Alliance Between the
    Republic of China and the U.S.S.R.
    see China, Nationalist (1941-49),
    U.S.S.R.
Treaty of Mutual Cooperation and Security
    between the United States and Japan,
    91
Truman, Harry S., 104, 122, 142, 155, 168,
    171, 172, 376, 382, 386, 392, 446,
    451, 709, 735
    on China, Communist (1941-49)
        Marshall mission, 118-19, 121-22, 128,
            129-30, 130-32
    on Hurley resignation, 115-16
    on Japanese acceptance of surrender terms, 9
    on Korean War, 366, 369, 370-72
        Chinese intervention, 395-97
    on MacArthur, meeting at Wake Island,
        389-91
    on MacArthur recall, 401-03
    on Taiwan, 387-88
Tsiang, F.T., 199-200, 203
Tsai Ting-k'ai, 107
Tu Li-ming, 133
Tung Pi-wu, 124

U

U Thant, 503, 509, 640, 753
Unger, Leonard, 611, 673
Union of Soviet Socialist Republics
    and Asia
        Acheson on, 361
    and China, Communist (1941-49), 107-12
        passim
        Acheson, on, 361
        Chiang Kai-shek on, 155
        Molotov on, 110
        Stettinius on, 111-12
    and China, Communist (1950-59)
        admission to U.N., Wadsworth on, 264-66
        Treaty of Friendship and Alliance, 162-64
    and China, Nationalist (1941-49)
        Treaty of Friendship, 113-15
    and Ho Chi Minh, 446
    and India
        Harriman on, 749-50
    and Japan, 49
    and Korean War, 339, 345, 374-75, 391
    and Kurile Islands, 112
    and Laos, 569, 582-83, 590
    Moscow Agreement, 345, 346, 347-48
    and United Kingdom, on Laos, 588
    and U.S., 50-51, 53
        Japanese peace treaty, 50-52
        on Laos, 580, 583-86, 608-10
        U.S.S.R. Joint Commission on Korea, 344
    Yalta Far Eastern Agreement, 112
United Kingdom, 380
    Cairo Declaration, 7-8, 345
    and Laos, 588, 590
    and U.S.S.R., on Laos, 588
    and Vietnam, South, 446
    Yalta Far Eastern Agreement, 112
United Nations, 57, 68, 90, 114, 119, 340,
        453, 471
    Charter, 53, 67-69, 75, 77, 113, 377, 382,
        454, 472-73, 475, 512
    and China, Communist (1971), admission
        question
        U.S. on, 770
    and Indonesia, 677, 679
    and Japan, 56
    and Java, 681
    and Korea, South, 340, 429
    and Korean War, 339, 348-49, 351-52, 354,
        356, 365, 367, 372-73, 378-81, 391,
        396, 398, 400, 405-13
        Neutral Nations Repatriation Commission,
            420, 422-23
        Neutral Nations Supervisory Com-
            mission, 408, 412
        Rhee on, 416
    and Laos, 569, 580-81, 583, 591
    and Madura, 681
    and Sumatra, 681

and Taiwan, 383
and Thailand, 661
and U.S., 582
United Nations Commission for Indonesia,
    680-81
U.S.I.A. *see* United States Information Agency,
    697
United States
    and Asia
        Acheson on, 357-64
        Bundy on, 276
        Johnson, L.B. on, 512-14
        Rusk on, 327
    Baghdad Pact, 741
    and Bonin Islands, 86-87, 92-93
    Cairo Declaration, 7-8, 345
    and Cambodia, 633-35, 641-42
        Bowles on, 643-44
        Dulles on, 630
        Goldberg on, 640-41
        Nixon on, 646-51, 651-56
        Rogers on, 644
        Stevenson on, 635-38
    and Canada, 82
    Central Intelligence Agency, 571
    and China, 64, 109, 121, 128, 131, 383
        Open Door Policy, 103, 360
        Truman on, 119-21, 131
    China Aid Act
        Acheson on, 159
        Marshall on, 154
        Truman on, 156-57
    and China, Communist *see below* United
        States and China, Communist (1941-
        49), (1950-59), (1960-68), (1971)
    China Lobby
        Acheson on, 194-99
        McMahon on, 197
        Morse on, 191-97
    and China, Nationalist *see below* United
        States and China, Nationalist (1941-
        49), (1950-59), (1971)
    and Cuba, passport restrictions, 769
    Declaration of Honolulu, 669
    and Diem, 447
    Far Eastern Advisory Committee, 3
    and France, Indochina War, 446
    and French Union and Associated States,
        450, 453
        Eisenhower on, 477-79
    and India, 736, 756-57, 775
        Dulles on, 741-42, 743
        Goldberg on, 753
        Harriman-Nitze Mission, Kennedy on,
            747-48
        India-Pakistan war, 785-88
        Kennedy on, 749
        Rusk on, 746-47, 748
        U.S.S.R. aid to, Harriman on, 749-50
    and Indonesia, 700-01
        Austin on, 682-85

Bunker on, 699
closing of U.S.I.A. libraries, 697
Dulles on, 687-89
Jones, F.H.P. on, 689
Rusk on, 693-94, 698, 700
State Department on, 694
West Irian, 688
West New Guinea dispute, 688,
    692; Bingham on, 690-91; Dulles
    on, 686
and Japan, 10-12, 41-42, 49, 82, 384
Allied Council, 3
Constitution, 4
Derevyanko on, 47-48
Johnson, U.A. on, 766-68
McCoy on, 42-47
Mutual Cooperation and Security Treaty,
    86, 91-95, *passim,* 100
Mutual Defense Assistance Agreement,
    68-73
Mutual Security Act, 69, 71
Rogers on, 762-66
Security Treaty, 67-68
Joint Thai-U.S. Committee, 666
and Kashmir dispute (India and Pakistan)
Stevenson on, 751-52
and Korea, 64
and Korea, South, 339-40, 355-57, 415,
    775, 784
Hodge on, 351-52
Mutual Defense Treaty, 425-26, 429
and Korean War, Taft on, 373-76
and Laos, 570, 580, 581-82, 595, 610,
    723-83
Dulles on, 663
Kennedy on, 586-88
and Manchuria, 120
Manila Agreement, 699
Manila Pact, (1954), Kennedy on, 667
Moscow Agreement on Korea (1943),
    345-46, 347-48
and Okinawa, 94-95
Voice of America facility, 742, 745
and Pakistan, 775
Eisenhower on, 736, 740-41
Goldberg on, 753
Sahrawardy on, 740-41
Mutual Defense Agreement, 736-40
Mutual Security Agreement, 741
and Pakistan Alliance, 748
Paris Peace talks, 447, 538, 552, 562
Bruce on, 781-82
Lodge on, 549
Nixon on, 779-80
and Philippines, 719-20
Amendment on Military Bases Agree-
    ment, 728
Bell Act, 705
Bell Commission, 713-15
Dulles on, 719
Eisenhower on, 723

Garcia on, 723
Johnson, L.B. on, 726-28, 728-30
Marcos on, 726-28, 728-30
Military Assistance Act, 707-08
Mutual Defense Board, 721-22
Mutual Defense Treaty, 717-19
Ramos on, 736
Rusk on, 736
Rehabilitation Act,705
Subic Bay, Abbott on, 722
Treaty defining relations, 710-12
war damage claims, 725-26
U.S.S. *Pueblo*
Defense Department on, 429
State Department on, 430, 436-37
Republic of Philippines Military Assistance
    Act, 707-08
and Ryukyu Islands, 86-87, 92-93
and Sino-Soviet dispute, 448
Burnett on, 305-08
Fairbank on, 308-09
Green on, 301-04
Hilsman on, 289-93
Hinton on, 294-97
Morgenthau on, 309-15
Taylor on, 298-301
and Southeast Asia Collective Defense
    Treaty, 473-76, 520, 666
State Department Investigations of
    personnel on China policy loyalty
Lattimore, Owen, 173-80
report, 186-90
Service, John Stewart, 180-86
Vincent, John Carter, 165-73
and Taiwan, 382-83, 776
and Thailand, 525, 584, 664-65, 668-69,
    670, 673
Bundy on, 669-70
Dulles on, 663-64
Green on, 668
Kennedy on, 672-73
Kittekachorn, on, 672
Southeast Asia Treaty Organization, 669
State Department on, 671-72
and Tibet, State Department on, 256
Tokyo Agreement, 699
and U.S.S.R., 52-53, 595
on Laos, 580, 585-86, 608-10, 610-11
on United Nations policy in Korea, 396
and Vietnam, North, 571
passport restrictions, 769
and Vietnam, South, 91, 446, 495, 570-71,
    774
Pham Von Dong on, 501-02
and Vietnam war, 447-49, 491-92, 502-03,
    505-06, 538-40
Bruce on, 781-82
Case on, 531
Church on, 529-30
Clark on, 533-34
Clifford on, 540-48

United States (*cont.*)
    "domino theory," 484, 545
    Fulbright on, 524
    Goldberg on, 503, 509-12
    Gore on, 533-34
    Johnson, L.B. on, 447, 486-87, 488-89,
        493-98, 500-01, 505-06, 515, 517,
        519-22, 536-38, 538-40
    Kennedy on, 483-84
    Morse on, 526-28
    Mundt on, 528-29
    Nixon on, 557-65, 778-81
    Paul VI, Pope on, 515-16
    Pell on, 533
    Rusk on, 481, 498-99
    Stevenson on, 635-38, 638-39
    Symington on, 532
    Yalta Far Eastern Agreement, 112
United States and China, Communist (1941-49)
    Acheson on, 106-09
    Hurley on, 105, 110-11
    Marshall on, 123
    Stalin on, 110-11
    Stettinius on, 111-12
    Truman on, 119-21, 128-32
    Political Consultative Conference
        Truman on, 132
United States and China, Communist (1950-59),
        104, 230-35
    admission to U.N., 104
        Wadsworth on, 264-66
    ambassadorial talks, 236-39
    "De Facto" argument
        Dulles on, 225
    Dillon on, 261-64
    Dulles on, 214-16, 220-27
    Engle on, 256-61
    Eisenhower policy, Dulles on, 220-27
    "inevitability" argument
        Dulles on, 225
    mutual exchange of civilians, 216-20
    Taiwan Straits Crisis
        Dulles on, 239-41, 254-55
        Eisenhower on, 245-51, 252
        Green on, 251-52
        Khrushchev on, 241-45
    and Tibet
        Herter on, 255-56
    trade embargo, 227-28
    travel by American citizens
        Herter on, 220-30
United States and China, Communist (1960-68),
        79, 267
    admission to U.N., 104
        Harriman on, 286
    Bundy on, 276-79
    Fulbright on, 275-76
    Green on, 283-86
    Hilsman on, 267-75
    Katzenbach on, 329-33
    relaxation of trade restrictions, 334-35
    Richardson on, 334
    Rusk on, 315-27
    Warsaw Meetings, 336
United States and China, Communist (1971)
    admission to U.N.,
        Rogers on, 773
    Bray on, 769
    exchange of athletic teams, 769-70
    Nixon on, 771-72
    Nixon visit
        Chou En-lai on, Nixon on, 774-77
    "Ping Pong Diplomacy," 769
United States and China, Nationalist (1941-49),
        53, 105-06
    Acheson on, 158-59, 160-61
    Hurley on, 105, 110-11
    Marshall on, 123
    Stalin on, 110-11
    Stuart on, 157-58
    Truman on, 119-21, 122, 128-32, 156-57
    World War II Policy, 105
United States and China, Nationalist (1950-59),
        103
    China Lobby, 199-207
    Eisenhower policy
        Dulles on, 220-27, *passim*
    Joint Congressional Resolution Defense,
        213-14
    Mutual Defense Treaty, 208-10
        Eisenhower on, 211
    Nixon on, 772
United States Information Agency, 697
U.S.-U.S.S.R. Joint Commission on Korea, 344

V

Vandenberg, Arthur, 165, 371
Van Hollen, Christopher, 787
veterans of Foreign Wars, 383, 386, 387, 390
    Korean War
        MacArthur on, 383-86
Vientiane *see* Laos
Viet Cong, 481, 485-86, 491, 625-37, *passim*
Viet Minh, 445-46, 450, 569, 593
Vietnam, 86, 341, 453, 472, 476
    and China, 446
    elections (1956), 446
    and France, 445
    and French Union and Associated States,
        451, 477
    Geneva Conference (1954), 501
    and Indochina
        France on, U.S. on, 477
    New Lunar Year *see* Tet holidays
    reunification, 501
    17th parallel, 446
Vietnam, Free *see* Vietnam, South
Vietnam, North, 91, 447, 481, 486, 491, 495,
        499
    and China, Communist (1950-59), 480

Geneva Conference on Vietnam (1954), 501
   and Laos, 569, 570-71, 580, 582, 583, 586
      Nixon on, 617-22
      Rusk on, 606-08
   Manila Conference (1966), 508-09
   and U.S., 498, 501-02, 571
Vietnam, South, 86, 445, 447, 451, 482, 499*
   and Cambodia, 625, 633
      Stevenson on, 635-38
   Constitution, 479
   Diem Government, 447
   domino theory, 484
   Geneva Conference (1954), 471, 490
   Manila Conference (1966), 508-09
   17th parallel, 482
   and U.S., 91, 478-79, 570-71, 774*
      Eisenhower on, 479-80
      Johnson, L.B. on, 486-87
      Kennedy on, 482, 485
      Pham Von Dong on, 501-02
Vietnam War*
   China, Communist, 499-500
   de Gaulle on, 507
   Demilitarized Zone, 549
   Gulf of Tonkin incident
      Johnson, L.B. on, 488-89
   Ho Chi Minh on, 504-05, 515, 518-19
   Ho Chi Minh Trail see Ho Chi Minh Trail
   International Control Commission, 490,
      571, 607, 618, 637, 643
   and Laos
      U.S.S.R. on, 608-10
      U.S. on, 610-11, 782-83
   National Front for the Liberation of South
      Vietnam, 501, 516, 519, 539, 554,
      556
   Paris peace talks, 447, 538-40, 549, 551, 562
      Bruce on, 781-82
      Lodge on, 549
      Nixon on, 779-80
   Paul VI on, 515-16
   Tet holidays, 515-18, passim, 530, 542
   and U.S. see United States
   U Thant on, 509-11
Vietnamization, 449, 778
   Nixon on, 561-62
Vincent, John Carter, investigation of, 165-73
   see also U.S. State Department Investigation
      of Personnel on China Policy Loyalty,
      165-73
V-J Day, 129
Voice of America, 762, 765

Vyshinsky, Andrei Y., 162, 164

W

Wadsworth, James J., 264
Wake Island, 390
Wallace, Henry, 170
Wang Ping-nan, 216, 261
Wang Shih-chieh, 113
Wang Shi-hsueh, 172
Webb, 371
Wedemeyer, General Albert, 103-05, 107-08,
      116, 183
   on China, Nationalist (1941-49), 136-40
   on mission to China, 140-42
West Irian see Indonesia, United States
Westmoreland, William, 542-43
West New Guinea Question see Indonesia,
      United States, Netherlands
Wheeler, Earle G., 542
White, Theodore, 172
Williams, Maurice, 786-87
Wilson, Harold, 616
Wilson, Woodrow, 650
Wirtz, W. Willard, 89
Woodward, Gilbert H., 436-39
Wright, Hamilton, Jr., 199-204, passim
Wright, Hamilton, Sr., 199, 205

Y

Yahya Khan, 786
Yalta Conference, 18, 51, 53, 104, 143
   Wedemeyer on, 142
Yalta Far Eastern Agreement, 112
   see also U.K.; U.S.S.R.; U.S.
Yeh, George K.C., 210
Yenan, 117
Yost, Charles W., 636, 638
Yugoslavia, 109
Yu Ta Wei, 123

Z

Ziegler, Ronald L., 770
Zumwalt, Elmo R. Jr., 787

*The Jan., 1973 Vietnam Agreement and Protocols, the Henry Kissinger press conferences of Oct. 26, 1972 and Jan. 24, 1973 and President Nixon's statement of Jan. 23, 1973 have been included as Appendix B.